T0338594

Encyclopedia of Data Science and Machine Learning

John Wang
Montclair State University, USA

Volume I

IGI Global
PUBLISHER of TIMELY KNOWLEDGE

Published in the United States of America by
IGI Global
Engineering Science Reference (an imprint of IGI Global)
701 E. Chocolate Avenue
Hershey PA, USA 17033
Tel: 717-533-8845
Fax: 717-533-8661
E-mail: cust@igi-global.com
Web site: http://www.igi-global.com

Copyright © 2023 by IGI Global. All rights reserved. No part of this publication may be reproduced, stored or distributed in
any form or by any means, electronic or mechanical, including photocopying, without written permission from the publisher.
Product or company names used in this set are for identification purposes only. Inclusion of the names of the products or
companies does not indicate a claim of ownership by IGI Global of the trademark or registered trademark.

Library of Congress Cataloging-in-Publication Data

Names: Wang, John, 1955- editor.
Title: Encyclopedia of data science and machine learning / John Wang,
   editor.
Description: Hershey, PA : Engineering Science Reference, an imprint of IGI
   Global, [2023] | Includes bibliographical references and index. |
   Summary: "This book examines current, state-of-the-art research in the
   areas of data science, machine learning, data mining, optimization,
   artificial intelligence, statistics, and the interactions, linkages, and
   applications of knowledge-based business with information systems"--
   Provided by publisher.
Identifiers: LCCN 2021027689 (print) | LCCN 2021027690 (ebook) | ISBN
   9781799892205 (h/c) | ISBN 9781799892212 (ebook)
Subjects: LCSH: Big data. | Data mining. | Machine learning.
Classification: LCC QA76.9.B45 E54 2022 (print) | LCC QA76.9.B45 (ebook)
   | DDC 005.7--dc23
LC record available at https://lccn.loc.gov/2021027689
LC ebook record available at https://lccn.loc.gov/2021027690

British Cataloguing in Publication Data
A Cataloguing in Publication record for this book is available from the British Library.

All work contributed to this book is new, previously-unpublished material. The views expressed in this book are those of the
authors, but not necessarily of the publisher.

For electronic access to this publication, please contact: eresources@igi-global.com.

Editorial Advisory Board

Xueqi Cheng, *Chinese Academy of Science, China*
Verena Kantere, *University of Ottawa, Canada*
Srikanta Patnaik, *SOA University, India*
Hongming Wang, *Harvard University, USA*
Yanchang Zhao, *Commonwealth Scientific and Industrial Research Organisation (CSIRO), Australia*

List of Contributors

Alphabetical Table of Contents

Volume I: 1-618; Volume II: 619-1246; Volume III: 1247-1870; Volume IV: 1871-2498; Volume V: 2499-3143

Table of Contents by Category

Volume I

Section: Accounting Analytics

Wikil Kwak, University of Nebraska at Omaha, USA
Xiaoyan Cheng, University of Nebraska at Omaha, USA
Yong Shi, University of Nebraska at Omaha, USA
Fangyao Liu, Southwest Minzu University, China
Kevin Kwak, University of Nebraska at Omaha, USA

Toshifumi Takada, National Chung Cheng University, Taiwan

Section: Approximation Methods

Jean-Éric Pelet, LARGEPA, Panthéon-Assas University, Paris, France
Santiago Belda, Universidad de Alicante, Spain
Dounia Arezki, Computer Science Faculty, Science and Technology University of Oran, Algeria

Section: Autonomous Learning Systems

Indraneel Dabhade, O Automation, India

Section: Big Data Applications

Section: Big Data as a Service

Section: Big Data Systems and Tools

Section: Business Intelligence

Volume II

Section: Causal Analysis

Section: Chaos Control, Modeling, and Engineering

Section: Cloud Infrastructure

Section: Cognitive Science

Section: Computational Intelligence

Section: Computational Statistics

Section: Computer Vision

Section: Customer Analytics

Section: Data Processing, Data Pipeline, and Data Engineering

Volume III

Section: Data Visualization and Visual Mining

Section: Decision, Support System

Section: Deep Neural Network (DNN) of Deep Learning

Section: E-Learning Technologies and Tools

Section: Emerging Technologies, Applications, and Related Issues

Section: Ensemble Learning

Ahmet Tezcan Tekin, Istanbul Technical University, Turkey
Ferhan Çebi, Istanbul Technical University, Turkey
Tolga Kaya, Istanbul Technical University, Turkey

Section: Feature Engineering

Volume IV

Section: Financial Services Analytics

Section: Fuzzy Logic and Soft Computing

Section: Gradient-Boosting Decision Trees

Section: Graph Learning

Section: High-Throughput Data Analysis

Section: Industry 4.0

Section: Information Extraction

    Fabian N. Murrieta-Rico, Universidad Politécnica de Baja California, Mexico
    Moisés Rivas-López, Universidad Politécnica de Baja California, Mexico
    Oleg Sergiyenko, Universidad Autónoma de Baja California, Mexico
    Vitalii Petranovskii, Universidad Nacional Autónoma de México, Mexico
    Joel Antúnez-García, Universidad Nacional Autónoma de México, Mexico
    Julio C. Rodríguez-Quiñonez, Universidad Autónoma de Baja California, Mexico
    Wendy Flores-Fuentes, Universidad Autónoma de Baja California, Mexico
    Abelardo Mercado Herrera, Universidad Politécnica de Baja California, Mexico
    Araceli Gárate García, Universidad Politécnica de Baja California, Mexico

Section: Internet of Things

    Shivlal Mewada, Government Holkar Science College, India

    Matthew J. Drake, Duquesne University, USA

Section: Malware Analysis

    Thomas Alan Woolman, On Target Technologies, Inc., USA
    Philip Lunsford, East Carolina University, USA

Section: Management Analytics

    Maximiliano Emanuel Korstanje, University of Palermo, Argentina
    Martha Omara Robert Beatón, University of Havana, Cuba
    Maite Echarri Chávez, University of Havana, Cuba
    Massiel Martínez Carballo, University of Havana, Cuba
    Victor Martinez Robert, University of Havana, Cuba

    Jorge Gomes, Universidade Lusófona das Humanidades e Tecnologias, Portugal
    Mário Romão, ISEG, Universidade de Lisboa, Portugal

Section: Marketing Analytics

    Tasnia Fatin, Putra Business School, Universiti Putra Malaysia, Malaysia
    Mahmud Ullah, Department of Marketing, University of Dhaka, Bangladesh
    Nayem Rahman, School of Business and Information Technology, Purdue University Global, USA

Section: Object Detection

Section: Performance Metrics

Section: Predictive Analytics

Section: Reinforcement Learning

Section: Simulation and Modeling

Section: Smart City

Section: Social Media Analytics

Section: Supply Chain Analytics and Management

Section: Symbolic Learning

Section: Time Series Analysis

Section: Transfer Learning

Section: Transport Analytics

Section: Unsupervised and Supervised Learning

Foreword

There has been tremendous progress made in Data Science and Machine Learning over the last 10 – 15 years, leading to the Data Science becoming the major driving force of the Fourth Industrial Revolution and a significant factor in the current cycle of economic expansion. The need for data scientists is growing exponentially and machine learning has become one of the "hottest" professions in the labor market.

The field of Data Science is expanding both in-depth and in-breadth. In particular, we have witnessed widespread adoption of data science methods across a broad class of industries and functional areas, including health sciences and pharmaceuticals, finance, accounting, marketing, human resource management, operations and supply chains. Data-driven approaches have been deployed in such diverse set of applications as drug discovery, analysis of medical data and decision support tools for physicians, financial applications, including robo-advising, predictive maintenance of equipment and defect detection, Internet of Things (IoT), precision agriculture, physics and chemistry, to name a few. All these industries and applications enjoy adoption of a wide range of machine learning methods, the scope of which grew significantly over the last 10 – 15 years. In addition to the evolutionary growth and expansion of classical machine learning techniques, the last decade has witnessed revolutionary breakthroughs in such areas as Deep Learning, scalable machine learning methods capable of handling Big Data, the size of which grows exponentially over time in many applications, and the analysis of unstructured data, such as text using NLP-based methods, images and videos using Computer Vision techniques, and voice using Speech Recognition methods.

Given all this progress in Machine Learning and Data Science, it is high time to aggregate all this new knowledge "under one roof," and this Encyclopedia of Data Science and Machine Learning serves this purpose. It covers 188 different topics across the whole spectrum of the field written by leading academic scholars and industry practitioners describing the progress made in the respective areas over the last 10 – 15 years and reflecting the State-of-the-Art for each topic.

Since data science and machine learning are evolving rapidly, the authors also describe the challenges and present promising future research directions in their respective areas, delineating interesting work that lies ahead for the scholars to address these challenges. Therefore, this Encyclopedia remains what it is – a milestone on a long and exciting road that lies ahead of us in Data Science and Machine Learning.

Alexander Tuzhilin
New York University, USA
May 2022

Preface

Big Data and Machine Learning (BDML) are driving and harnessing the power of the Fourth Industrial Revolution, also referred to as Industry 4.0 or 4IR, which revolutionizes the way companies, organizations, and institutions operate and develop. With the age of Big Data upon us, we risk drowning in a flood of digital data. Big Data has now become a critical part of the business world and daily life, as the synthesis and synergy of Machine Learning (ML) and Big Data (BD) have enormous potential.

BDML not only deals with descriptive and predictive analytics but also focuses on prescriptive analytics through digital technology and interconnectivity. It has continuously explored its "depth" and expanded its "breadth". BDML will remain to maximize the citizens' "wealth" while promoting society's "health".

The *Encyclopedia of Data Science and Machine Learning* examines current, state-of-the-art research in the areas of data science, ML, data mining (DM), optimization, artificial intelligence (AI), statistics, and the interactions, linkages, and applications of knowledge-based business with information systems. It provides an international forum for practitioners, educators, and researchers to advance the knowledge and practice of all facets of BDML, emphasizing emerging theories, principles, models, processes, and applications to inspire and circulate cutting-edge findings into research, business, and communities (Wang, 2022).

How can a manager get out of a data-flooded "mire"? How can a confused decision-maker navigate through a "maze"? How can an over-burdened problem solver clean up a "mess"? How can an exhausted scientist bypass a "myth"? The answer to all of the above is to employ BDML.

As Roy et al. (2022) point out, data has become the center point for almost every organization. For quite a long time, we are familiar with Descriptive Analytics (what happened in the past) and Diagnostic Analytics (why something happened in the past), as well as Predictive Analytics (what is most likely to happen in the future). However, BDML could go much above and beyond them with Prescriptive Analytics (what should be done now), which recommends actions companies, and organizations can take to affect those outcomes. The digital transformation, the horizontal and vertical integration of these production systems, as well as the exploitation via optimization models, can make a gigantic jump with this giant digital leverage.

BDML can turn *Data* into *value*; Transform *information* into *intelligence;* Change *patterns* into *profit;* Convert *relationships* into *resources*. Companies and organizations can make *Faster* (real-time or near real-time), *Frequent*, and *Fact-based* decisions. In an ever-evolving market, 4IR with a set of technologies can stimulate innovations and rapid responses. Knowledge workers can proactively take action before an unfriendly event occurs (Wang, 2008).

Having been penetrated and integrated into almost every aspect of our work and life, as well as our society itself, AI and related cutting-edge technologies will enhance human capacities, improve efficiencies, and optimize people's lives. AI would not replace human intelligence, rather than amplify it. As *AI evolves* and *humans* adapt, AI and humans go forward together in the long run because AI and people both bring different capabilities to society.

According to Klaus Schwab, the World Economic Forum Founder and Executive Chairman, 4IR intellectualizes precipitous change to industrial and societal prototypes and processes in the 21st century due to increasing interconnectivity and smart automation and finally blurs the lines among the physical, digital, and biological worlds. Part of the 4IR is the manner in which all types of machines and devices interact, correspond, and cooperate with each other. Even though there will be obvious job losses due to the replacement of tasks that humans have conducted for years by autonomous machines and/or software. On the contrary, there could be new business opportunities and plenty of new jobs for controlling "the new electricity" (Philbeck & Davis, 2018; Moll, 2022).

There are 207 qualified full chapters among 271 accepted proposals. Finally, the encyclopedia contains a collection of 187 high-quality chapters, which were written by an international team of more than 370 experts representing leading scientists and talented young scholars from more than 45 countries and regions, including Algeria, Argentina, Austria, Bangladesh, Brazil, Canada, Chile, China, Colombia, Cuba, Denmark, Egypt, El Salvador, Finland, France, Germany, Ghana, Greece, Hong Kong, Hungary, Indonesia, Iraq, Japan, Lebanon, Macau, Malaysia, Mexico, Netherland, New Zealand, Poland, Portugal, Saudi Arabia, Serbia, Singapore, South Africa, Sweden, Switzerland, Syria, Taiwan, Tunisia, Turkey, UK, USA, Venezuela, Vietnam, etc.

They have contributed great effort to create a source of solid, practical information, informed by the sound underlying theory that should become a resource for all people involved in this dynamic new field. Let's take a peek at a few of them:

Jaydip Sen has published around 300 articles in reputed international journals and referred conference proceedings (IEEE Xplore, ACM Digital Library, Springer LNCS, etc.), and 18 book chapters in books published by internationally renowned publishing houses. He is a Senior Member of ACM, USA a Member of IEEE, USA. He has been listed among the top 2% scientists in the globe as per studies conducted by Stanford University for the last consecutive three years 2019 - 2021. In his contributed chapter Prof. Sen and his co-author, Dutta have evaluated the performance of two risk-based portfolio design algorithms.

Leung - who has authored more than 300 refereed publications on the topics of data science, ML, BDM and analytics, and visual analytics (including those in ACM TODS, IEEE ICDE, and IEEE ICDM) - presents two encyclopedia articles. One of them presents up-to-date definitions in BDM and analytics in the high-performance computing environment and focuses on mining frequent patterns with the MapReduce programming model. Another one provides the latest comprehensive coverage on key concepts and applications for BD visualization; it focuses on visualizing BD, frequent patterns, and association rules.

Lorenzo Magnani is Editor-in-Chief of the Series Sapere, Springer. Thanks to his logico-epistemological and cognitive studies on the problem of abductive cognition (that regards all kinds of reasoning to hypotheses) explained in this chapter both virtues and limitations of some DL applications, taking advantage of the analysis of the famous AlphaGo/AlphaZero program and the concepts of locked and unlocked strategies. Furthermore, he is the author of many important articles and books on epistemology, logic, cognitive science, and the relationships between ethics, technology, and violence.

The chapter 'AI is transforming insurance with five emerging business models' is the culmination of three years of research into how AI is disrupting insurance. Zarifis has recently won a 'best paper award' at a leading conference and Cheng has recently been published in MIS Quarterly for related work. AI is disrupting many distinct parts of our life, but insurance is particularly interesting as some issues like risk and privacy concerns are more important. After several case studies, this chapter identifies that there are five emerging models in insurance that are optimal for AI.

In "Artificial Intelligence, Consumers, and the Experience Economy," Chang and Mukherjee's excellent synthesis of AI and consumers in the modern economy provides a much-needed knowledge base for stakeholders tasked to deploy AI. In "Using Machine Learning Methods to Extract Behavioral Insights from Consumer Data," they present a comprehensive discussion of new data sources and state-of-the-art techniques for researchers and practitioners in computational social science. The chapters are built on their projects supported by the Ministry of Education, Singapore, under its Academic Research Fund (AcRF) Tier 2 Grant No. MOE2019-T2-1-183 and Grant No. MOE2018-T2-1-181, respectively.

Based on many years of application development by CY Pang and S. Pang's cognitive data analysis of many industrial projects, this chapter proposes a programming paradigm specific to BD processing. Pang was the lead architect of a $1.6 billion enterprise software project and was awarded a special architectural design trophy. He has received awards of $20,000 and $5,000 for outstanding innovation from a company he previously worked for. By the way, CY Pang was awarded a Prestige Scholarship from Peter House, Cambridge to complete his Ph.D. at the University of Cambridge, UK.

Vitor provides an excellent overview of multidimensional search methods for optimization and the potential these methods have to solve optimization problems more quickly. With almost ten years of industry experience, Vitor is an expert in optimization methods and the modeling of complex systems using operations research and data analytics techniques. He is also a recipient of the Nebraska EPSCoR FIRST Award, supported by the National Science Foundation to advance the research of early-career tenure-track faculty.

Lee's chapter on evidence-based data-driven pain management bears multi-facet importance. Nearly 40 million anesthetics are administered each year in the United States. And over 10.7% of Americans use prescription pain medication on a regular basis. The findings highlight the optimal safe dose and delivery mechanism to achieve the best outcome. The study showcases the persistence of overprescription of opioid-type drugs, as it finds that the use of fentanyl has little effect on the outcome and should be avoided.

Auditors must evaluate the volatility and uncertainty of the client company at the initial stage of the audit contract because it directly influences the audit risk. Takada contributes to auditing research and accounting education for 40 years. He has been awarded for his research and contributions to his excellent papers and accounting education by the *Chinese Auditing Association* and by the *Japanese Auditing Association.*

Nguyen and Quinn propose an optimal approach to tackle the well-known issue of the imbalance in bankruptcy prediction. Their approach has been evaluated through a rigorous computation including the most popular current methods in the literature. They have also made other main contributions in the area of imbalanced classification by winning the 2020 Literati Awards for Outstanding Author Contribution.

Rodríguez is the Bioethics of Displacement pioneer, a field that merges futurism, belongingness, and life. He has also published analytic papers and fieldwork on crises and big social changes such as pandemics, Anthropocene, AI takeover, cyborgs, digital securitization and terrorist attacks. As a chair, the author leads the research on the first decolonized corruption index. Torres shares his more than 15 years of wealth of experience in Predictive Maintenance management as a speaker at global summits such as Scalable and PMM Tech Dates. The author leads the first non-taxonomic error mode proponent of AI implementation.

Kurpicz-Briki, Glauser, and Schmid are using unique API technologies to measure the impact of online search behavior using several different online channels. Their method allows the identification of the specific channels, where keywords have been searched, and a restriction of regions, using the domains. Such technologies provide a major benefit for different application domains, including public health. In times such as a pandemic crisis, it is highly relevant for different stakeholders to identify the impact of their communications on the user community as well as the well-being of the population. Using the method proposed by the authors, this can be done while fully respecting the privacy of the users.

Sensors sense the environment and process large sets of data. Monitoring the data to detect malicious content is one of the biggest challenges. The previous work used mean variation to ease the surveillance of information. Ambika's proposal minimizes the effort by classifying the streamed data into three subsets. It uses the k-nearest neighbor procedure to accomplish the same. The work conserves 10.77% of energy and tracks 27.58% of more packets. Map-reduce methodology manages large amounts of data to a certain extent. Ambika's other proposal aims to increase processing speed by 29.6% using a hashing methodology.

In today's world, text-based sentiment analysis brings the attention of all. By looking at the people requirement, Tripathy and Sharaff propose a hybridized Genetic Algorithm (GA)-based feature selection method to achieve a better model performance. In the current study, they have customized the GA by using the SVM to evaluate the fitness value of the solutions. The proposed idea is essential as the technique reduces the computational cost by reducing sufficient features without affecting the performance. The proposed model can be implemented in any field to filter out the sentiment from the user's review.

Alberg and Hadad present the novel Interval Gradient Prediction Tree ML Algorithm that can process incoming mean-variance aggregated multivariate temporal data and make stable interval predictions of a target numerical variable. Empirical evaluations of multi-sensor aircraft datasets have demonstrated that this algorithm provides better readability and similar performance compared to other ML regression tree algorithms.

The environmental, societal, and cultural imperatives press for innovative, prompt, and practical solutions for grave humanitarian problems we face in the 21st century. The climate crisis is felt everywhere; natural disasters are rampant. Can technology provide reasonable means to humanitarian supply chains? What potential uses can AI offer in establishing sustainable humanitarian logistics (SHL)? Ülkü, an award-winning professor and the director of CRSSCA-Centre for Research in Sustainable Supply Chain Analytics, and his research associate Oguntola of Dalhousie University - Canada review the latest research on the applications of AI technology on SHL.

Aguiar-Pérez, the leading author of this chapter, provides the audience an insight into what ML is and its relation with AI or DL. He has an extended experience in the field of ML, DL, BD, and IoT in various sectors (automotive, smart roads, agriculture, livestock, heritage, etc.), including collaboration with companies, EU-funded research projects, publications, and postgraduate teaching experience. The rest of the authors work with him in the Data Engineering Research Unit of the University of Valladolid.

Bagui, a highly accomplished author of several books on databases and Oracle, presents a very timely chapter on the improvements made in Oracle 19c's multitenant container architecture and shows how these improvements aid in the management of Big Data from the perspective of application development. The added functionality that comes with the integration of Big Data platforms, alongside the flexibility and improvement that comes with a container and pluggable databases, has allowed Oracle to be in the forefront in the handling of Big Data.

As an internationally renowned interdisciplinary information and data professional, Koltay's chapter on Research Data Management (RDM) is of interest not only for both professionals of DS and ML but is related to any research activity. He is also a widely published author in these fields. In 2021, his contribution to IGI Global books included an entry on information overload. His book, titled Research Data Management and Data Literacy (Chandos, 2021) contains a more detailed explanation of the subjects, contained in this chapter.

Zhao is a DS professional with experience in industry, teaching, and research. He is a leading BD expert in the IR BD & AI Lab in New Jersey, USA. He provides multiple chapters to the book by covering a broad range of BD applications in vast perspectives of urgent demands in DS research objectives, such as DSS, DL, computer vision, BD architecture designs, and applied BD analytics in Covid-19 research. As such, he did excellent work in those chapters and made significant contributions to the book.

Based on their discovery of action rules and meta-actions from client datasets, Duan and Ras propose a strategy for improving the number of promoters and decreasing the number of detractors among customers. Moreover, the improved/enhanced action rules can be utilized in developing actionable strategies for decision makers to reduce customer churn, which will contribute to the overall customer churn study in the business field. The authors target the domain represented by many clients, each one involved with customers in the same type of business. Clients are heavy equipment repair shops, and customers are owners of such equipment.

The A2E Process Model for Data Analytics is simple without being simplistic and comprehensive without being complicated. It balances technology with humanity and theories with practices. This model reflects Jay Wang's decades-long multi-disciplinary training and experience in STEM, Behavioral Science, and Management Science. While existing process models such as CRISP-DM, SEMMA, and KDD were developed for technical professionals with limitations and low adoption rates, the A2E Model is more approachable to subject matter experts, business analysts, and social scientists. The A2E Model will elevate the analytics profession by fostering interdisciplinary collaborations of all stakeholders and increasing the effectiveness and impacts of analytics efforts.

Turuk explores Audio and video-based Emotion Recognition using the Backpropagation Algorithm, which is the backbone of ML and DL architectures. This chapter analyses everyday human emotions such as Happy, Sad, Neutral, and Angry using audio-visual cues. The audio features such as Energy & MFCC and video features using the Gabor filter are extracted. Mutual information is computed using video features. The readers will benefit and motivated to conduct further research in this domain. The application may be extended to a lie detector using Emotions.

Stojanović and Marković-Petrović focus on continuous cyber security risk assessment in Industrial Internet of Things (IIoT) networks, and particularly on possibilities of DL approaches to achieve the goal. The authors successfully complement their previous work regarding the cyber security of industrial control systems. They concisely review the theoretical background and provide an excellent framework for the continuous risk assessment process in the IIoT environment. DL can be integrated into edge-computing-based systems and used for feature extraction and risk classification from massive raw data. The chapter ends with a list of proposals for further studies.

Climate change is a very important issue and each person on our planet must have a culture of keeping it clean. Pollution increased yearly due to the increased consumption of fossil fuels. Alsultanny has many research papers in climate change and renewable energy. He led a UNDP team for writing reports on energy consumption in Bahrain. Alsultanny did an innovative method in his chapter, by utilizing the pollution gases data, these data currently are BD, because they are registered yearly in every minute, and from many monitoring pollutions stations.

Deliyska and Ivanova conducted timely research and practical work representing an important contribution to data modeling in sustainable science. Applying ontological engineering and a coevolutionary approach, a unique metamodel of sustainable development is created containing structured knowledge and mutual links between environmental, social, and economic dimensions in this interdisciplinary area. Specialists in different fields can use the proposed metamodel as a tool for terminology clarification, knowledge extraction, and interchange and for the structuring of ML models of sustainable development processes.

Hedayati and Schniederjans provide a broad spectrum of issues that come into play when using digital technologies to benefit healthcare. This is even more important where the pandemic has forced healthcare models to rapidly adjust towards compliance with local, regional, and national policy. The dissemination and creation of knowledge become paramount when considering the benefits and drawbacks of the rapid changes in technology applications worldwide. The authors consider several insights from the American Hospital Association Compliance to provide some questions researchers and practitioners may consider when addressing knowledge management via digital technology implementation in healthcare settings.

Pratihar and Kundu apply the theory of fuzzy logic to develop a classification and authentication system for beverages. It emphasizes the versatility of fuzzy logic to deal with the higher dimensional and highly non-linear sensor data obtained from e-tongue for different beverage samples. Commonly used mapping techniques (for dimension reduction of a data set) and clustering techniques (for classification) were also briefly discussed. This study provides a perspective on developing a fuzzy logic-based classifier/authenticator system in the future for beverages, foods, and others and their quality control and monitoring.

Drake discusses the use of IoT technology to improve SCM. As firms look to improve their supply chain resilience in response to the COVID-19 pandemic and other disruptions, IoT data increases visibility, traceability, and can help firms to mitigate risks through added agility and responsiveness. The improved decision-making made possible by IoT data creates a competitive advantage in the market.

Today, high-dimensional data (multi-omics data) are widely used. The high dimensionality of the data creates problems (time, cost, diagnosis, and treatment) in studies. Ipekten et al. introduce the existing solutions to these problems and commonly used methods. Also, the authors present the advantages of the methods over each other and enlighten the researchers that using suitable methods in terms of performance can increase the reliability and accuracy of the studies. Finally, the authors advise on what can be done in the future.

Learning analytics (LA), a promising field of study that started more than a decade ago but has blossomed in recent years, addresses the challenges of LA specifically in education, integrating it as a fundamental element of the Smart Classroom. Ifenthaler and Siemens among others discuss the primary features, the benefits, and some experiences. In addition, the team of authors of the chapter has contributed more than twelve publications on this topic in the last 3 years in leading journals and publishers.

Current advances in AI and ML in particular have raised several concerns regarding the trustworthiness and explainability of deployed AI systems. Knowledge-Based approaches based on symbolic representations and reasoning mechanisms can be used to deploy AI systems that are explainable and compliant with corresponding ethical and legal guidelines, thus complementing purely data-driven approaches.

Batsakis and Matsatsinis, both having vast theoretical backgrounds and experience in this research area, offer an overview of knowledge-based AI methods for the interested AI practitioner.

Noteboom and Zeng provide a comprehensive review of applications of AI and ML and data analytics techniques in clinical decision support systems (CDSSs) and make contributions including, 1) the current status of data-driven CDSSs, 2) identification and quantification of the extent to which theories and frameworks have guided the research, 3) understanding the synergy between AI/ML algorithms and modes of data analytics, 4) directions for advancing data-driven CDSSs to realize their potential in healthcare.

Fisogni investigates the emotional environment which is grounded in any human/machine interaction. Through the lenses of metaphysics and system thinking the author sketches a highly valuable insight, for sure an unprecedented challenge for DSs. In fact, only a philosophical foundation of the big issues of this realm can bring about a change in the quality of understanding an increasingly melted environment humans/machines in the Onlife era.

In "Hedonic Hunger and Obesity", Demirok and Uysal touch upon a remarkable topic and explain ways of identification for people with hedonic nutrition and the conditions that are effective in the states that trigger hunger state in humans. In addition, in this text, the authors ensample hormones that suppress and trigger hunger.

Yen and her coauthors contributed a chapter on how ML creates the virtual singer industry. Virtual singers have great market potential and even advantages over their human counterparts. Despite the bright future of virtual singers, the chapter has discussed difficulties virtual singers face, especially their copyright protection by legislation. Literature on the technical aspects of virtual singers is also reviewed, and a list of additional readings is provided for readers interested in the ML algorithms behind virtual singers.

Rastogi is working on Biofeedback therapy and its effect on Diabetes diseases, a currently very active healthcare domain. He brings back the glory of Indian Ancient Vedic Sciences of Jap, Pranayama, Healing techniques, and the effect of Yajna and Mantra science on Diseases and pollution control. Also, He has developed some interesting mathematical models with algorithms on Swarm Intelligence approaches like PSO, ACO BCO, etc. for better human life via Spiritual Index and higher consciousness.

Isikhan presents a comparison of a new proposal for the modeling of Ceiling and Floor Effect dependent variables and classical methods. It has been noticed that there are very few publications evaluating the regression modeling of ceiling and floor effect observations in recent years. The modeling method with regression-based imputation, which clinicians can use as an alternative to classical models for ceiling and floor effective observations, is explained in detail. The performances of the newly proposed imputation-based regression and other classical methods were validated based on both real clinical data, synthetic data, as well as a 500 replicated cross-validation method.

Drignei has extensive experience with time series modeling and analysis. Prior to this work, he addressed statistical modeling aspects of space-time data, such as temperatures recorded over space and time. His research has been published in leading statistics journals. The current work deals with seasonal times series recorded at a large number of time points. Such data sets will become more common in the future, in areas such as business, industry, and science. Therefore, this chapter is timely and important because it sheds new light on modeling aspects of this type of data sets.

Data visualization plays a key role in the decision-making process. Visualization allows for data to be consumable. If data is not consumable, there is a tendency to ignore the facts and rely more on biases. Researchers have found that cognitive biases do exist within data visualizations and can affect decision-making abilities. Anderson and Hardin provide background on cognitive biases related to data visualizations, with a particular interest in visual analytics in BD environments. A review of recent studies related to mitigating cognitive biases is presented. Recommendations for mitigating biases in visualizations are provided to practitioners.

Puzzanghera explores the impact of AI on administrative law. He combines IT systems with administrative activity and researches the processors that prepare content and the implications that arise. He analyzes the European Commission's proposal in regard to the legislation of AI in Europe and the importance of safeguarding human rights in the introduction of AI in administrative activity.

How ML impacts the catering industry? Liu et al. provide a comprehensive vision to readers with real-life examples and academic research. Researchers at business schools may have their attention drawn to the impact of ML on operations, management, and marketing, while scholars with solid ML backgrounds may become aware of industry issues, identify new research questions, and link their expertise to practical problems through reading the chapter.

Di Wang's research interests include 4D printing technology, robot control, remanufactured industry, and energy schedule in the smart city. Combinatorial optimization is a widely applied field at the forefront of combinatorics and theoretical computer science. With BD challenges, deep reinforcement learning opens new doors to solve complex combinatorial optimization problems with overwhelming advantages over traditional methods.

Firmansyah and Harsanto focus on exploring BD and Islamic finance. The utilization of BD in Islamic financial institutions (IFIs) has been perceived as a source of competitive advantage in today's era. Many IFIs have been more dependent on BD technologies than ever before in order to keep up with the changing customers' demands, lifestyles, and preferences.

With his experience of working in both industry and academic research, Indraneel highlights progress made in integrating AI with industry and helps bridge the reality and challenges faced while summarizing the state of Industry 4.0. The author engages audiences from different sectors without overburdening the reader with incoherent technical details. A practitioner in the fields of DS and cybersecurity, the author brings experience interacting with clients and customers from different fields, including manufacturing, legal, and product developers.

Yang, Wu, & Forrest examine the textual aspects of consumer reviews. As a critical source of information for online shoppers, researchers have spent considerable time examining the potential impact of consumer reviews on purchasing behavior. The authors contribute to the existing body of knowledge by proposing a conceptual framework for capturing the internal relationships between major textual features discovered in prior research.

Kara and Gonce Koçken are researchers studying mathematical programming problems in fuzzy environments. In the study, a novel fuzzy solution approach to multi-objective solid transportation problems is developed by using different membership functions, which can help the studies in transportation systems.

Millham demonstrates the various spheres of the emerging 4IR and how they interrelate with the application, opportunities, expectations, and challenges of a smart city. Because many of these smart city applications are very complex and interact with each other using various technologies, several nature-inspired algorithms are introduced as a way to provide intelligent and coordinated management of these entities.

The development of novel measurement and detection techniques is a rapidly growing area, where the generation of vast amounts of information requires novel methods for analysis. Murrieta-Rico explores a new direction of his research by combing the know-how for generating a big dataset from a digital frequency measurement, with the application of the principal component analysis (PCA). As a result, a powerful methodology for data analysis is presented. In addition, these results can be used for extending the capabilities of ML systems based on sensors.

Coimbra, Chimenti, and Nogueira contribute to the debate related to human-machine interaction in social media. The work helped to understand the mechanisms and motivators of this relationship. In addition, the article presented a historical evolution of the debate on the interaction between machines and men in decision-making, distributing the result of the literature review in three historical cycles. The research was carried out through a survey of YouTube users to understand the interaction mechanism along with its motivators.

As a transformational general-purpose technology, AI is impacting marketing as a function, and marketing managers' activities, capabilities, and performance. Oberoi emphasizes how the job of a marketing manager will be evolving into understanding which kind of AI can and should be applied to which kind of marketing actions for better performance. Marketing managers will have to go through a learning curve and acquire new skills.

Singh and Dev have discussed the concepts of data warehouse and OLAP technology to deal with real-life applications efficiently. The topic is useful in the modern digital era as businesses are dealing with data from heterogeneous sources. The chapter presents the case study of the tourism industry as it deals with multidimensional data like tourist, hospitality, and tourist products. This chapter will be helpful in understanding how to generate multi-dimensional reports that will show the information according to the needs of policymakers.

Ramos has made many contributions to the potential of Business Intelligence tools, combined with DM algorithms methods to produce insights about the tourism business, highlighting an aspect of the investment potential of tourism organizations in this type of system, from those related to accommodation, management of tourist destinations, to tourist transport, restaurants, among other businesses complementary to the tourist activity, with a view to innovation and increasing financial performance, which includes examples ranging from the application of OLAP techniques to the application of ML methods.

Balsam depicts the meaning and role of metamodels in defining the abstract syntax of the language by which developers communicate, design, and implement systems including the selection of the design, implementation methods, and techniques for increasingly complex systems to satisfy customers' needs, particularly if the system has to be delivered in a considerably fleeting time. The author highlights different aspects of meta-models standards, categories, the process of creating the metamodel, and challenges in the research of metamodeling.

Dharmapala contributes a novel method to the field of research in 'Classification of employee categories in allocating a reward, with input features from survey responses.' In the past, researchers conducted qualitative and quantitative analyses on this subject as it is an important topic to any organization that strives to boost the morale of its employees. The author opened a new direction in future research on the subject by using ML algorithms, and the results obtained were promising.

Mudrakola identifies the gap and future scope for Breast cancer applications like the impact of chemical therapy, prognosis analysis among various treatment types and stages, etc. From basic to the latest trends, the author's extensive literature survey will direct the root to aspects needed to analyze work on medical applications specific to Breast cancer.

Rani et al. highlight the venues of user-generated content (UGC) in Industry 4.0. This chapter's contribution is highly interesting for any digital content creator and non-paid professionals. The importance of UGC on consumer behavior in the era of Industry 4.0 will be explained, allowing stakeholders to assess their efficacy in Internet communication and enhancing the digital process required for modern marketing. The chapter aims to link existing ideas and provide a holistic picture of UGC by concentrating on future research.

Ibrahim et al. seek to provide an understanding of the relationship between member support exchange behavior and self-disclosure intention in online health support communities using a data-driven literature review. Seeking or providing support in online communities may be useful but having to disclose personal information publicly online is a critical privacy risk – intention counts.

Rusko introduces the main perspectives of industrial revolutions. He found interesting backgrounding details for the chapter about the disruptions of the industrial revolutions. Kosonen updates the paper with the effects of Covid-19 and contemporary digitizing development.

I would like to highlight a number of authors who have received special stunning honors: Eva K Lee has published over 220 research articles, and fifty government and state reports, and has received patents on innovative medical systems and devices. She is frequently tapped by a variety of health and security policymakers in Washington for her expertise in personalized medicine, chronic diseases, healthcare quality, modeling and decision support, vaccine research and national security, pandemic, and medical preparedness. Lee has received multiple prestigious analytics and practice excellence awards including INFORMS Franz Edelman award, Daniel H Wagner prize, and the Caterpillar and Innovative Applications in Analytics Award for novel cancer therapeutics, bioterrorism emergency response, and mass casualty mitigation, personalized disease management, ML for best practice discovery, transforming clinical workflow and patient care, vaccine immunity prediction, and reducing hospital-acquired infections. She is an INFORMS Fellow. She is also inducted into the American Institute for Medical and Biological Engineering (AIMBE) College of Fellows, the first IE/OR engineer to be nominated and elected for this honor. Her work has been funded by CDC, HHS, NIH, NSF, and DTRA. Lee was an NSF CAREER Young Investigator and Whitaker Foundation Young Investigator recipient.

Petry and Yager are both internationally known for their research in computational intelligence, in the area of fuzzy set theory and applications, and are both IEEE Fellows and have received prestigious awards from the IEEE. They have collaborated here as it represents extensions of their previous research on this topic. Hierarchical concept generalization is one important approach to dealing with the complex issues involving BD. This chapter provides insights on how to extend hierarchical generalization to data with interval and intuitionistic forms of uncertainty.

The globalization of the software development industry continues to experience significant growth. The increasing trend of globalization brings new challenges and increases the scope of the core functions of the software development process. Pal introduces a distributed software development knowledge management architecture. Kamalendu has published research articles in the software development community in the ACM SIGMIS Database, Expert Systems with Applications, DSSs, and conferences. Kamalendu was awarded the best research paper on data analytic work at a recent international conference. He is a member of the British Computer Society, the IET, and the IEEE Computer Society.

Badia's research has been funded by the National Science Foundation (including a prestigious CAREER Award) and has resulted in over 50 publications in scientific journals and conferences. His chapter demonstrates how to use SQL in order to prepare data that resides in database tables for analysis. The reader is guided through steps for Exploratory Data Analysis (EDA), data cleaning (including dealing with missing data, outliers, and duplicates), and other tasks that are an integral part of the Data Scientist day-to-day. The references provide a guide for further study.

Srinivasan explains the three components of graph analytics and provides illustrative examples as well as code for implementation. His chapter is one of the few primers of graph DS/analytics that covers a variety of topics in the discipline. The author does active research in graph analytics methods and applications in healthcare, ML explainability, and DL and regularly publishes in top journals and conferences in information systems, healthcare, and computer science. He received best paper awards in INFORMS Workshop on Data Science (2021) and the 6th International Conference on Digital Health (2016), respectively.

Knowledge explosion pushes BDML, a multidisciplinary subject, to ever-expanding regions. Inclusion, omission, emphasis, evolution, and even revolution are part of our professional life. In spite of our efforts to be careful, should you find any ambiguities of perceived inaccuracies, please contact me at prof.johnwang@gmail.com.

John Wang
Montclair State University, USA

REFERENCES

Moll, I. (2022). The Fourth Industrial Revolution: A new ideology. *tripleC: Communication, Capitalism & Critique*, *20*(1), 45–61.

Philbeck, T., & Davis, N. (2018). The Fourth Industrial Revolution: Shaping a new era. *Journal of International Affairs*, *72*(1), 17–22.

Roy, D., Srivastava, R., Jat, M., & Karaca, M. S. (2022). A complete overview of analytics techniques: Descriptive, predictive, and prescriptive. *Decision Intelligence Analytics and the Implementation of Strategic Business Management*, 15-30.

Wang, J. (Ed.). (2008). *Data Warehousing and Mining: Concepts, Methodologies, Tools, and Applications* (Vols. 1–6). IGI Global. doi:10.4018/978-1-59904-951-9

Wang, J. (Ed.). (2022). *Encyclopedia of Data Science and Machine Learning*. IGI Global. https://www.igi-global.com/book/encyclopedia-data-science-machine-learning/276507

Acknowledgment

The editor would like to thank all authors for their insights and excellent contributions to this major volume. I also want to thank the many anonymous reviewers who assisted me in the peer-reviewing process and provided comprehensive and indispensable inputs that improved our book significantly. In particular, the Editorial Advisory Board members, including Xueqi Cheng (Chinese Academy of Science), Verena Kantere (University of Ottawa, Canada), Srikanta Patnaik (SOA University, India), Hongming Wang (Harvard University), and Yanchang Zhao (CSIRO, Australia), have all made immense contributions in terms of advice and assistance, enhancing the quality of this volume. My sincere appreciation also goes to Prof. Alexander Tuzhilin (New York University). Despite his busy schedule, he has written three forewords for my consecutive encyclopaedias, over an 18-year span, in this expanding and exploring area.

In addition, the editor wishes to acknowledge the help of all involved in the development process of this book, without whose support the project could not have been satisfactorily completed. I owe my thanks to the staff at IGI Global, whose support and contributions have been invaluable throughout the entire process, from inception to final publication. Special thanks go to Gianna Walker, Angelina Olivas, Katelyn McLoughlin, and Melissa Wagner, who continuously prodded me via email to keep the project on schedule, and to Jan Travers and Lindsay Wertman, whose enthusiasm motivated me to accept their invitation to take on this project.

I would also like to extend my thanks to my brothers Zhengxian, Shubert (an artist, https://portraitartist.com/detail/6467), and sister Joyce Mu, who stood solidly behind me and contributed in their own unique ways. We are thankful for the scholarships which we have been provided, without which it would not have been possible for all of us to come and study in the U.S.

Finally, I want to thank my family: my parents for supporting me spiritually throughout my life and providing endless encouragement; my wife Hongyu for taking care of two active and rebellious teenagers, conducting all family chores, and not complaining to me too much.

This book was special due to the stresses and difficulties posed by the Covid-19 pandemic. We thank and salute the authors who had to overcome numerous challenges to help make this volume a reality. Our authors had to persevere through unprecedented circumstances to enable this masterful encyclopedia. Now, it is time to celebrate and reap the fruits of our demanding work! Cheese and cheers!

Section 1
Accounting Analytics

Auditor Change Prediction Using Data Mining and Audit Reports

Wikil Kwak
University of Nebraska at Omaha, USA

Xiaoyan Cheng
University of Nebraska at Omaha, USA

Yong Shi
University of Nebraska at Omaha, USA

Fangyao Liu
Southwest Minzu University, China

Kevin Kwak
University of Nebraska at Omaha, USA

INTRODUCTION

The emergence of big data and the increasing use of analytics has brought both opportunities and challenges to the audit profession (Appelbaum, Kogan, & Vasarhelyi, 2018; Appelbaum, Showalter, Sun, & Vasarhelyi, 2021). Audit reports should convey a firm's financial wellbeing to stakeholders including investors, managers, debtholders, and regulators. Thus, audit reports represent the formal communication between the auditor and the interested parties. Auditors have the option to choose four different types of auditor report opinions: unqualified opinion, qualified opinion, disclaimer of opinion, and adverse opinion. Unlike an unqualified opinion, a qualified opinion signals a lack of conformity with Generally Accepted Accounting Principles (GAAP) and casts doubt on the credibility of financial statements. Chow and Rice (1982) document that the audited firms, after receiving a qualified opinion, tend to switch auditors more often than firms receiving a clean opinion. This switch is motivated by opinion shopping (seeking a new auditor who is willing to provide an improved audit opinion). However, Williams (1988) finds no significant relation between the receipt of a qualified opinion and auditor changes. Considerable research (Krishnan & Stephens, 1995; Krishnan, Krishnan, & Stephens, 1996; Chen, Peng, Xue, Yang, & Ye, 2016) has examined the policy implications regarding firms changing auditors after receiving a qualified opinion. In this chapter, we use data mining approaches to revisit the prediction of auditor changes upon the receipt of a qualified opinion in U.S. firms.

A couple decades ago, the American Institute of Certified Public Accountants (AICPA) and Institutes of Internal Auditors (IIA) endorsed data mining as one of the top ten technologies of tomorrow (Koh, 2004). However, there are not many studies in the U.S. to examine the relation between audit opinions and auditor changes using data mining techniques. Several studies investigated audit opinion issues and their overall prediction rates were qualitatively similar in predicting auditor changes using traditional logit or discriminant analysis (Maggina & Tsakianganos, 2011; Fernández-Gámez, García-Lagos, &

DOI: 10.4018/978-1-7998-9220-5.ch001

Copyright © 2023, IGI Global. Copying or distributing in print or electronic forms without written permission of IGI Global is prohibited.

Sánches-Serrano, 2016). This chapter presents an effort to better understand the application of big data techniques in auditor change decision. A stream of research (Koyuncugil & Ozgulbas, 2012; Zhou, Lu, & Fujita, 2015; Read & Yezegel, 2016) in financial distress modelling uses data mining tools to forecast bankruptcy, and these techniques help auditors improve their judgment when issuing auditor report opinions. Various algorithms and techniques like Support Vector Machine (SVM), decision tree, and k-means are used for our study as they are the most popular in knowledge discovery.

The chapter proceeds as follows: The next section presents relevant prior research. The third section discusses sampling criteria, sources of data, and reports the findings. The last section summarizes and discusses the conclusions of this chapter and provides further research avenues.

BACKGROUND AND PRIOR RESEARCH

Financial distress variables in predicting bankruptcy are useful for auditors to predict going concern evaluation (Gepp, Linnenluecke, O'Neill, & Smith, 2018). A stream of research (Sundgren & Svanstrom, 2014; Fernández-Gámez et al., 2016) in financial distress predicts audit opinion decisions. Sundgren and Svanstrom (2014) find that the phases of auditor careers are related to audit reporting quality, proxied by the auditors' propensity to issue a going-concern opinion prior to bankruptcy filings. Fernández-Gámez et al. (2016) utilized neural networks to predict a qualified audit opinion using corporate governance and financial ratios. Nevertheless, non-Big 4 firms tend to be reluctant to use big data techniques to determine going concern of a firm (Read & Yezegel, 2016).

Another stream of research centers on the prediction of auditor changes. Prior studies reveal that there is a positive association between bankruptcy and auditor changes. Hudaib and Cooke (2005) assume that financial distress may influence a firm's decision to change auditors either directly or indirectly. They found that the probability of switching auditors increases as financial health declines using financial ratio variables or the Z-score variable in their multivariate logistic regression. Dhaliwal, Lamoreaux, Lennox, and Mauler (2015) document that firms with Big-4 auditors have significant influence over auditor selection by management. Moreover, Landsman, Nelson, and Rountree (2009) used client-specific audit and financial risk factors, along with client misalignment, to model auditor switch decisions in pre- and post-Enron periods. In this study, we include Andersen as an audit firm with the Enron scandal. To further examine the accuracy of auditor changes, Sun (2007) suggests that adding industry effect, stock returns, and advanced statistical methods may increase the prediction rate. Bankruptcy is an extreme form of financial distress, with most of the variables used by Altman (1968) and Ohlson (1980) in their bankruptcy prediction studies related to the auditor changes decision. It is assumed that the auditor change decision is made by top management, but the audit committee also participates in the auditor selection and change process.

Classification is the most common data mining method, which uses a set of pre-tagged datasets to train the model for future prediction. Fraud detection and risk analysis are classic examples of applications in this technology. SVM and decision trees are the most well-known algorithms in classification or two category (0, 1) prediction such as auditor change or bankruptcy studies. Support Vector Machine (SVM) was developed by Vladimir Vapnik and is primarily used in the application of classification problems, though it can also be used for regression analysis (Cortes & Vapnik, 1995). The algorithm realizes classifications by finding the most appropriate hyper-planes that can successfully differentiate between classes in a training dataset. The decision of a hyper-plane is to maximize the distances from the closest points in each of the different classes. The algorithm learning process of SVM can be formulated as a problem of optimization. The decision tree summarizes the patterns using the format of the binary tree (Safavian & Landgrebe, 1991). Since the result of the decision tree is understandable, it is commonly used in operation management. The decision tree is built top-down from the root node. The process of constructing a decision tree is all about finding a node that provides the highest information gain. The information gain is based on the decrease in entropy after splitting on a specific node (attribute).

Clustering is the method of identifying similar classes of objects. Clustering differs from classification because the training objects in clustering are not tagged. The k-means algorithm is the most popular algorithm in clustering and is used to partition observations into k clusters by Euclidian distance (Wagstaff, Cardie, Rogers, & Schroedl, 2001). An iterative algorithm is designed to find clusters that minimize the group dispersion and maximize the between-group distance.

Case-based reasoning can solve new problems and provide suggestions by recalling similar experience. It is based on the K-nearest neighbors (KNN) principle that similar input should have the same output (Chen et al., 2016).

Recently, Baranes and Palas (2019) used SVM to predict profit movement to forecast firm performance. They converted XBRL financial data to excel format and used SVM to predict firm performance. They got 84.2 percent of prediction rates using Israeli data. Lahmiri (2016) also proposed that SVM is the best method in bankruptcy prediction studies from his comparative data mining study. They can be categorized as supervised learning and unsupervised learning. Classification and regression analysis are the most common methods in supervised learning, whereas the most common method in unsupervised learning is clustering. SVMs are effective when underlying data is typically non-linear and non-stationary (Chen et al., 2016).

Previously discussed data mining tools have recently become popular in a business applications context, and its techniques are becoming more powerful in terms of overall prediction rates. Audit firms will soon introduce big data analytics into the audit process (Rose, Rose, Sanderson, & Thibodeau, 2017). If we had applied data mining tools to the Fannie Mae Mortgage portfolio, we could have decreased default during the financial crisis (Mamonov & Benbunan-Fich, 2017). We apply the most current data mining tools for several of our studies and try to show data mining applications in the accounting and finance context. Our chapter presents data mining applications for accounting studies.

Using macroeconomic indicators as drivers of distress, Mousavi and Ouenniche (2018) applied statistical models to predict financial distress for a sample of UK-listed companies. Kim, Mun, and Bae (2018) proposed a different approach and employed Support Vector Machine (SVM) methods to predict bankruptcy for a sample of Korean firms. Kim et al. (2018)'s findings show that SVM methods perform better for financial distress prediction than existing methods. Similar work has also been undertaken by Shi (2010). Klepac and Hampel (2018) went one step further and argued that decision tree approaches are better than SVM methods in predicting bankruptcy of 1,000 medium-sized retail business companies in the European Union (EU). Recently, Batena and Asghari (2020) used logit and genetic algorithm (GA) models to predict bankruptcy and found superiority of the GA methods. The use of big data methods represents an opportunity for auditors to avoid the costly error of issuing an unqualified opinion prior to bankruptcy (Read & Yezegel, 2016). If a firm is close to the bankruptcy stage due to financial distress or debt default, then the firm is likely to engage in audit opinion shopping activities by switching auditors. However, most data mining tools do not provide each variable's contribution for the overall prediction model. By contrast, the logit analysis provides incremental information value of a qualified audit opinion. For instance, Cheng and Kwak (2018) demonstrate that the prediction of auditor changes under the logit model performs well using financial and other data from the Form 10-K report and a qualified audit opinion increases the likelihood of auditor changes. The results indicate that a qualified audit opinion, along with financial distress factors, adds significant information value in predicting auditor changes based on the logit analysis. In this chapter, we use data mining approaches to predict auditor changes upon the receipt of a qualified opinion for a sample of U.S. firms.

Multiple studies have applied data mining techniques to predict auditor changes. SVM methods are found to perform well in predicting auditor changes, as SVM methods employ mathematical programming as a base to construct different versions of classifiers (Shi, 2010). Sariannidis, Papadakis, Garefalakis, Melonakos, and Kyriaki-Argyro (2020) used decision tree and other data mining methods to predict credit card default using Taiwanese data. They used the tree model derived from historical data, as it is easier to predict the result for future records. Klepac and Hampel (2018) propose an alternative approach and suggest that decision trees produce more accurate predictions than SVM methods. Li, Zhou, Ren, and Spector (2019) also proposed a financial management information system model prediction based on the decision tree approach of data mining. Based on the financial analysis-related factors, the accuracy of the other datasets is more than 80%. Usually, decision trees extract financial data from subject categories and business processes. The objective of decision trees is to divide observations into mutually exclusive and exhaustive subgroups (Koh, 2004). The k-nearest neighbor's algorithm is a non-parametric classification method. Boskou and Kirkos (2019) use text mining tools to predict whether a Big 4 audit firm audits the Athens Stock Exchange firms. It is proven that a Big 4 audit firm charges higher audit fees and it is expected to have higher Internal Audit Quality. Their KNN data mining tool shows 85% accuracy.

The above review shows that studies have used big data techniques to model auditor changes decisions. Given that previous empirical studies show differential prediction rates under different data mining tools, we compare the prediction rates in auditor changes decisions by employing SVM, decision tree, and K-Nearest Neighbor (KNN) methods in this study.

Since this chapter's focus is the prediction of auditor changes after receiving a qualified audit opinion, traditional logit model variables used by Ohlson (1980), and Altman (1968) will be used. In addition, audit fees, Big-4 auditors, and Andersen are added in our data mining models. Hoitash, Hoitash, and Bedard (2008) find that audit fees are relatively adjusted risk factors. Data mining models may provide similar prediction rates compared with traditional logit or discriminant models, but it cannot be determined which variables contribute to overall prediction rates. Data mining approaches may increase prediction rates, and we want to identify which data mining method is the best in predicting auditor changes decision using U.S. data.

SAMPLE AND EMPIRICAL RESULTS

Sampling Criteria

We collected auditor change firms from 2001 to 2006 from the Audit Analytics database. We use the same data set from Cheng and Kwak's (2018) study for prediction rate comparison purposes. We include the first auditor change data only if there are more than one auditor changes during this test period. The final sample consists of 1,842 firms that possess financial statement data one year before the auditor change is available. We used a matched-pair design, as auditor changes are not random events and previous studies applied the same approaches. The pair-matched control sample firms are with no auditor change within the same industry by two-digit industry codes and comparable size used by total assets. Final control firms are matched with treatment firms in the year with the auditor change. Other financial data are from Compustat and Audit Analytics.

Empirical Results

Table 1 presents the descriptive statistics for firms with auditor changes (Panel A) and without auditor changes (Panel B). All variables except *FU_TL, SIZE, MKT_TD,* and *CHIN* are statistically significant between sample firms and control firms. Funds from Operations divided by Total Liabilities are more negative for auditor change firms, but the differences are not significant (-0.43 vs. -0.37, respectively). The size variable should not be different, as we matched sample and control firms based on firm size. Market Value of Equity divided by Book Value of Total Debt ratios are not significantly different (5.01 vs. 6.69, respectively). Generally, non-auditor change firms' market values are higher than auditor change firms. The means of a qualified auditor opinion (*Qualified*) firms with auditor changes are significantly higher than those of control firms. Liquidity measures such as the means of Total Liabilities divided by Total Assets (*TL_TA*), the OENEG variable equivalent to one if *TL_TA* is greater than one, and Total Current Liabilities divided by Current Assets (*CL_CA*) in auditor change firms are significantly higher than in those of non-auditor change firms. Similarly, the mean Working Capital divided by Total Assets (*WCA_TA*) in auditor change firms is significantly lower than those of non-auditor change firms. These results indicate that firms with auditor changes tend to have worse liquidity.

For profitability, the Means of Retained Earnings divided by Total Assets (*RE_TA*), Net Income divided by Total Assets (*NI_TA*), and Earnings before Income and Taxes divided by Total Assets (*EBIT_TA*) in auditor change firms are significantly lower than those of non-auditor change firms. Interestingly, Altman, Haldeman, and Narayanan's (1977) cumulative profitability variable, *RE/TA* (Retained Earnings/Total Assets), is significantly more negative for the audit change firms than those of control firms. This result may show that auditor change firms are already in bad shape financially. In addition, we found that firms with auditor changes are more likely to be audited by non-Big 4 auditors. The growth opportunity (*Growth*) in auditor change firms is much lower than that in non-auditor change firms as expected. Overall, the results in Table 1 suggest that firms with auditor changes are significantly different from firms without audit changes in terms of a qualified audit opinion, level of financial distress, growth opportunity, and auditor characteristics.

Variable Descriptions:

Size =Total Assets/Gross Domestic Products;

TL/TA=Total Liabilities/Total Assets (Ohlson (1980) ratio);

WCA/TA=Working Capital/Total Assets (Altman (1968) ratio and (Ohlson (1980) ratio));

CL/CA=Total Current Liabilities/Total Current Assets (Ohlson (1980) ratio) ;

NI/TA=Net Income/Total Assets (Ohlson (1980) ratio) ;

FU/TL=Funds from Operations/Total Liabilities (Ohlson (1980) ratio);

INTWO= if Net Income<**0** or lag (Net Income) <**0** then INTWO=**1**; else INTWO=**0** (Ohlson (1980) dummy variable);

OENEG=if TL/TA>**1** then OENEG=**1**; else OENEG=**0** (Ohlson (1980) dummy variable);

CHIN= (Net Income- lag (Net Income))/ [absolute (Net Income) + absolute (lag Net Income)] (Ohlson (1980) ratio);

RE/TA = Retained Earnings/Total Assets (Altman (1968) ratio);

EBIT/TA = Earnings Before Interest and Taxes/Total Assets (Altman (1968) ratio);

MKV/TD = Market Value of Equity/Book Value of Total Debt (Altman (1968) ratio);

SALE/TA = Sales/Total Assets (Altman (1968) ratio);

B4 = if the firm's auditor is from Big 4 audit firms; 0 otherwise;

Andersen = 1 if the firm's auditor is Author Andersen; 0 otherwise;

Table 1. Descriptive statistics

Panel B: Firms Without Auditor Changes						
Variable	**N**	**Mean**	**Median**	**Std Dev**	**Minimum**	**Maximum**
Qualified	1842	0.40	0.00	0.49	0.00	1.00
CL_CA	1842	1.12	0.50	3.59	0.03	71.56
EBIT_TA	1842	-0.26	0.01	1.13	-18.36	0.35
FU_TL	1842	-0.37	0.07	1.80	-23.68	5.51
INTWO	1842	0.54	1.00	0.50	0.00	1.00
NI_TA	1842	-0.37	-0.02	1.34	-21.29	0.40
SIZE	1842	5.10	4.99	2.15	0.03	12.32
RE_TA	1842	-2.27	-0.21	9.00	-142.98	0.74
TL_TA	1842	0.60	0.43	1.23	0.02	31.90
OENEG	1842	0.08	0.00	0.27	0.00	1.00
SALE_TA	1842	0.89	0.67	0.87	-0.03	10.92
MKV_TD	1842	6.69	1.25	117.02	0.00	3637.32
WCA_TA	1842	0.17	0.23	0.88	-19.59	0.93
Growth	1842	0.08	0.07	0.37	-3.30	2.20
CHIN	1842	0.03	0.04	0.57	-1.00	1.00
B4	1842	0.78	1.00	0.41	0.00	1.00
Andersen	1842	0.05	0.00	0.23	0.00	1.00
Audit Fee	1842	0.71	0.77	0.24	0.00	1.00

Panel A: Firms With Auditor Changes							
Variable	**N**	**Mean**	**Median**	**Std Dev**	**Minimum**	**Maximum**	**T-diff**
Qualified	1842	0.48	0.00	0.50	0.00	1.00	4.33***
CL_CA	1842	1.51	0.61	4.06	0.03	52.50	3.08***
EBIT_TA	1842	-0.46	-0.03	1.42	-18.97	0.35	-4.67***
FU_TL	1842	-0.43	0.02	2.00	-38.19	3.40	-0.84
INTWO	1842	0.61	1.00	0.49	0.00	1.00	3.89***
NI_TA	1842	-0.64	-0.07	1.95	-31.26	0.38	-4.92***
SIZE	1842	4.94	4.52	2.28	0.02	12.12	2.01
RE_TA	1842	-5.54	-0.50	16.71	-268.83	0.73	-7.40***
TL_TA	1842	0.86	0.52	1.74	0.02	29.44	5.22***
OENEG	1842	0.15	0.00	0.35	0.00	1.00	6.71***
SALE_TA	1842	1.14	0.93	1.09	0.00	9.65	7.98***
MKV_TD	1842	5.01	1.05	27.72	0.00	604.66	-0.60
WCA_TA	1842	-0.04	0.18	1.35	-20.53	0.93	-5.43***
Growth	1842	0.01	0.03	0.50	-3.51	2.28	-4.66***
CHIN	1842	0.01	0.04	0.59	-1.00	1.00	-1.13
B4	1842	0.35	0.00	0.48	0.00	1.00	-29.47***
Andersen	1842	0.18	0.00	0.39	0.00	1.00	12.11***
Audit Fee	1842	0.76	0.82	0.22	0.00	1.00	6.19***

[1]t-value for testing mean differences between bankrupt and non-bankrupt firms

*: $p < 0.10$; **: $p < 0.05$; ***: $p < 0.001$

Table 2. Auditors change prediction results with total firms

	Predicted Change		
	No Change	Change	Total
Panel A: Prediction based on Decision Tree using Financial Variables (Randomly pick up 80% for training and 20% for testing)			
No Change = 0	286	72	358
Percentage	79.89%	20.11%	100%
Change =1	76	303	379
Percentage	20.05%	79.95%	100%
Overall Prediction Rate	79.92%		
Panel B: Prediction based on SVM using Financial Variables (Randomly pick up 80% for training and 20% for testing)			
No Change = 0	259	99	358
Percentage	72.35%	27.65%	100%
Change =1	135	244	379
Percentage	35.62%	64.38%	100%
Overall Prediction Rate	68.48%		
Panel C: Prediction Based on KNN Using Financial Variables (Randomly pick up 80% for training and 20% for testing)			
No Change = 0	256	102	358
Percentage	71.51%	28.49%	100%
Change =1	115	264	379
Percentage	30.34%	69.66%	100%
Overall Prediction Rate	70.57%		

Audit Fee = Total audit fee divided by total assets.

Table 2 presents auditor change prediction rates with total firms. We use three common data mining tools in accounting and finance prediction studies. We randomly pick up 80 percent for training and use 20 percent for testing. Among the three methods, Decision Tree in Panel A shows a 79.92 percent prediction accuracy rate, SVM in Panel B shows 68.48 percent, and KNN in Panel C shows 70.57 percent. Cheng and Kwak's study (2018) shows 77.87 percent using logit analysis. Therefore, we can conclude that predicting auditor changes with data mining tools is similar to or equivalent to traditional logit or discriminant studies. However, this study's prediction rates are much better than Kwak, Eldridge, Shi, and Kou's (2011) prior study as we added the qualified audit opinion with auditor changes.

Table 3 presents auditor change prediction with or without a qualified audit opinion. We pull the same procedures as before and take 80 percent for training and for 20 percent testing. Panel A and B show decision tree data mining results without and with a qualified opinion, Panel C and D show SVM data mining results without and with a qualified opinion, and Panel E and F show KNN data mining results without and with a qualified opinion. For these analyses, we want to check the incremental effects of a qualified audit opinion for data mining applications, but there is no significant incremental information in these cases. We divided samples into smaller groups, and they show overall lower prediction rates. From these results, the qualified audit opinion is not significant in data mining models.

Table 3. Auditors change prediction with or without a qualified opinion

	Predicted Change		
	Predicted Unqualified Opinion	Predicted Qualified Opinion	Total
Panel A: Prediction Without a Qualified Opinion Based on Decision Tree Using Financial Variables (Randomly pick up 80 percent for training and 20 percent for testing)			
Qualified Opinion =0	156	58	214
Percentage	72.90%	27.10%	
Qualified Opinion =1	90	111	201
Percentage	44.78%	55.22%	
Overall Prediction Rate	65.55%		
Panel B: Prediction With a Qualified Opinion Based on Decision Tree Using Financial Variables (Randomly pick up 80 percent for training and 20 percent for testing)			
Qualified Opinion =0	78	68	146
Percentage	53.42%	46.58%	
Qualified Opinion =1	53	122	175
Percentage	30.29%	69.71%	
Overall Prediction Rate	63.36%		
Panel C: Prediction Without a Qualified Opinion Based on SVM Using Financial Variables (Randomly pick up 80 percent for training and 20 percent for testing)			
Qualified Opinion =0	170	44	214
Percentage	79.44%	20.56%	
Qualified Opinion =1	86	115	201
Percentage	42.79%	57.21%	
Overall Prediction Rate	70.47%		
Panel D: Prediction With a Qualified Opinion Based on SVM Using Financial Variables (Randomly pick up 80 percent for training and 20 percent for testing)			
Qualified Opinion =0	66	80	146
Percentage	45.21%	54.79%	
Qualified Opinion =1	34	141	175
Percentage	19.43%	80.57%	
Overall Prediction Rate	69.30%		
Panel E: Prediction Without a Qualified Opinion Based on KNN Using Financial Variables (Randomly pick up 80 percent for training and 20 percent for testing)			
Qualified Opinion =0	119	95	214
Percentage	55.61%	44.39%	
Qualified Opinion =1	82	119	201
Percentage	40.80%	59.20%	
Overall Prediction Rate	57.41%		
Panel F: Prediction With a Qualified Opinion Based on KNN Using Financial Variables (Randomly pick up 80 percent for training and 20 percent for testing)			
Qualified Opinion =0	80	66	146
Percentage	54.79%	45.21%	
Qualified Opinion =1	74	101	175
Percentage	42.29%	57.71%	
Overall Prediction Rate	57.41%%		

FUTURE RESEARCH DIRECTIONS

Our current study shows that quality audit opinions do not add incremental information value to predict auditor changes. However, previous Cheng and Kwak's (2018) study showed quality audit opinions add incremental information value. Therefore, future research needs to pursue this issue further. In addition, if firm characteristics such as managers' auditor change motivation, audit committee, or market return variables are included, it is promising that our data mining models could be improved. We also need to update our data to see current conclusion is valid.

CONCLUSION

In this study, several data mining methods were used to compare traditional logit studies and revisit the topic of the information value of a qualified audit opinion in predicting auditor changes. Since a qualified audit opinion is designed to give warnings to financial statement users about the audited firm's financial conditions, it is expected that most firms' internal control systems should be better after the implementation of the SOX Act (2002) requirements. Thus, auditor change prediction models are expected to be more accurate when a qualified audit opinion is used as a factor in the prediction model. In addition to the qualified audit opinion, this logit model includes other financial distress variables that prior research has found to be associated with auditor changes. This prediction model has used data mining methods to show that a qualified audit opinion does not have additional information value to predict auditor changes, or the qualified audit opinion has already been reflected in a firm's financial conditions.

REFERENCES

Altman, E. (1968). Financial ratios, discriminant analysis and the prediction of corporate bankruptcy. *The Journal of Finance*, *23*(3), 589–609. doi:10.1111/j.1540-6261.1968.tb00843.x

Altman, E., Haldeman, R. G., & Narayanan, P. (1977). ZETA analysis: A new model to identify bankruptcy risk of corporations. *Journal of Banking & Finance*, *1*(1), 29–54. doi:10.1016/0378-4266(77)90017-6

Appelbaum, D. A., Kogan, A., & Vasarhelyi, M. A. (2018). Analytical procedures in external auditing: A comprehensive literature survey and framework for external audit analytics. *Journal of Accounting Literature*, *40*(1), 83–101. doi:10.1016/j.acclit.2018.01.001

Appelbaum, D. A., Showalter, D. S., Sun, T., & Vasarhelyi, M. A. (2021). A framework for auditor data literacy: A normative position. *Accounting Horizons*, *35*(2), 5–25. doi:10.2308/HORIZONS-19-127

Baranes, A., & Palas, R. (2019). Earning movement prediction using machine learning-Support Vector Machines (SVM). *Journal of Management Information and Decision Sciences*, *22*(2), 36–53.

Batena, L., & Asghari, F. (2020). Bankruptcy prediction using logit and genetic algorithm methods: A comparative analysis. *Computational Economics*, *55*(1), 335–348. doi:10.100710614-016-9590-3

Boskou, G., Kirkos, E., & Spathis, C. (2019). Classifying internal audit quality using textual analysis: The case of auditor selection. *Managerial Auditing Journal*, *34*(8), 924–950. doi:10.1108/MAJ-01-2018-1785

Chen, F., Peng, S., Xue, S., Yang, Z., & Ye, F. (2016). Do audit clients successfully engage in opinion shopping? Partner-level evidence. *Journal of Accounting Research*, *54*(1), 79–112. doi:10.1111/1475-679X.12097

Cheng, X., & Kwak, W. (2018). Predicting audit changes with qualified audit opinions using logit analysis. *Journal of Accounting and Finance*, *17*(8), 29–39.

Chow, C. W., & Rice, S. J. (1982). Qualified audit opinions and auditor switching. *The Accounting Review*, *57*(2), 326–335.

Cortes, C., & Vapnik, V. (1995). Support vector machine. *Machine Learning*, *20*(3), 273–297. doi:10.1007/BF00994018

Dhaliwal, S., Lamoreaux, P. T., Lennox, C. S., & Mauler, L. M. (2015). Management Influence on auditor selection and subsequent impairment of auditor independence during the post-SOX period. *Contemporary Accounting Research*, *32*(2), 575–607. doi:10.1111/1911-3846.12079

Fernández-Gámez, M. A., García-Lagos, F., & Sánches-Serrano, J. R. (2016). Integrating corporate governance and financial variables for the identification of qualified audit opinions with neural networks. *Neural Computing & Applications*, *27*(5), 1427–1444. doi:10.100700521-015-1944-6

Gepp, A., Linnenluecke, M. K., O'Neill, T. J., & Smith, T. (2018). Big data techniques in auditing research and practice: Current trends and future opportunities. *Journal of Accounting Literature*, *40*(1), 102–115. doi:10.1016/j.acclit.2017.05.003

Hoitash, R., Hoitash, U., & Bedard, J. C. (2008). Internal control quality and audit pricing under the Sarbanes-Oxley Act. *Auditing*, *27*(1), 105–126. doi:10.2308/aud.2008.27.1.105

Hudaib, M., & Cooke, T. (2005). The impact of managing director changes and financial distress on audit qualification and auditor switching. *Journal of Business Finance & Accounting*, *32*(9/10), 1703–1739. doi:10.1111/j.0306-686X.2005.00645.x

Kim, S., Mun, B. M., & Bae, S. J. (2018). Data depth-based support vector machines for predicting corporate bankruptcy. *Applied Intelligence*, *48*(3), 791–804. doi:10.100710489-017-1011-3

Klepac, V., & Hampel, D. (2018). Predicting bankruptcy of manufacturing companies in EU. *E+M. Ekonomie a Management*, *21*(1), 159–174. doi:10.15240/tul/001/2018-1-011

Koh, H. C. (2004). Going concern prediction using data mining techniques. *Managerial Auditing Journal*, *19*(3), 462–476. doi:10.1108/02686900410524436

Koyuncugil, A., & Ozgulbas, N. (2012). Financial early warning system model and data mining application for risk detection. *Expert Systems with Applications*, *39*(6), 6238–6253. doi:10.1016/j.eswa.2011.12.021

Krishnan, J., Krishnan, J., & Stephens, R. G. (1996). The Simultaneous Relation Between Auditor Switching and Audit Opinion: An Empirical Analysis. *Accounting and Business Research*, *26*(3), 224–236. doi:10.1080/00014788.1996.9729513

Krishnan, J., & Stephens, R. G. (1995). Evidence on opinion shopping from audit opinion conservatism. *Journal of Accounting and Public Policy*, *14*(3), 179–201. doi:10.1016/0278-4254(95)00020-F

Kwak, W., Eldridge, S., Shi, Y., & Kou, G. (2011). Predicting auditor changes using financial distress variables and the multiple criteria linear programming (MCLP) and other data mining approaches. *Journal of Applied Business Research, 27*(5), 73–84. doi:10.19030/jabr.v27i5.5597

Lahmiri, S. (2016). Features selection, data mining and financial risk classification: A comparative study. *Intelligent Systems in Accounting, Finance & Management, 23*(4), 265–275. doi:10.1002/isaf.1395

Landsman, W., Nelson, K., & Rountree, B. (2009). Auditor switches in the pre- and post-Enron eras: Risk or realignment? *The Accounting Review, 84*(2), 531–558. doi:10.2308/accr.2009.84.2.531

Li, W., Zhou, Q., Ren, J., & Spector, S. (2019). Data mining optimization model for financial management information system based on improved genetic algorithm. *Information Systems and e-Business Management*, 14.

Maggina, A., & Tsakianganos, A. A. (2011). Predicting audit opinions evidence from the Athens stock exchange. *Journal of Applied Business Research, 27*(4), 53–68. doi:10.19030/jabr.v27i4.4656

Mamonov, S., & Benbunan-Fich, R. (2017). What can we learn from past mistakes? Lessons from data mining the Fannie Mae mortgage portfolio. *Journal of Real Estate Research, 39*(2), 235–262. doi:10.1080/10835547.2017.12091471

Mousavi, M. M., & Ouenniche, J. (2018). Multi-criteria ranking of corporate distress prediction models: Empirical evaluation and methodological contributions. *Annals of Operations Research, 271*(2), 853–886. doi:10.100710479-018-2814-2

Ohlson, J. (1980). Financial ratios and the probabilistic prediction of bankruptcy. *Journal of Accounting Research, 18*(1), 109–131. doi:10.2307/2490395

Read, W. J., & Yezegel, A. (2016). Auditor tenure and going concern opinions for bankrupt clients: Additional evidence. *Auditing, 35*(1), 163–179. doi:10.2308/ajpt-51217

Rose, A. M., Rose, J. M., Sanderson, K., & Thibodeau, J. C. (2017). When should audit firms introduce analyses of big data into the audit process? *Journal of Information Systems, 31*(3), 81–99. doi:10.2308/isys-51837

Safavian, S. R., & Landgrebe, D. (1991). A survey of decision tree classifier methodology. *IEEE Transactions on Systems, Man, and Cybernetics, 21*(3), 660–674. doi:10.1109/21.97458

Sariannidis, N., Papadakis, S., Garefalakis, A., Melonakos, C., & Kyriaki-Argyro, T. (2020). Default avoidance on credit card portfolios using accounting, demographical and exploratory factors: Decision making based on machine learning (ML) techniques. *Annals of Operations Research, 294*(1-2), 715–739. doi:10.100710479-019-03188-0

Shi, Y. (2010). Multiple criteria optimization-based data mining methods and applications: A systematic survey. *Knowledge and Information Systems, 24*(3), 369–391. doi:10.100710115-009-0268-1

SOX: Sarbanes-Oxley Act. (2002).

Sun, L. (2007). A re-evaluation of auditors' opinions versus statistical models in bankruptcy prediction. *Review of Quantitative Finance and Accounting, 28*(1), 55–78. doi:10.100711156-006-0003-x

Sundgren, S., & Svanstrom, T. (2014). Auditor-in-charge characteristics and going-concern reporting. *Contemporary Accounting Research, 31*(2), 531–550. doi:10.1111/1911-3846.12035

Wagstaff, K., Cardie, C., Rogers, S., & Schroedl, S. (2001). Constrained k-means clustering with background knowledge. *Proceedings of the 18th International Conference on Machine Learning,* 577–584.

Williams, D. D. (1988). The potential determinants of auditor change. *Journal of Business Finance & Accounting, 15*(2), 243–261. doi:10.1111/j.1468-5957.1988.tb00133.x

Zhou, L. G., Lu, D., & Fujita, H. (2015). The performance of corporate financial distress prediction models with features selection guided by domain knowledge and data mining approaches. *Knowledge-Based Systems, 85,* 52–61. doi:10.1016/j.knosys.2015.04.017

ADDITIONAL READING

Bertrand, C., Fokoue, E., & Zhang, H. (2009). Principles and Theory for Data Mining and Machine Learning. Springer.

Han, J., Pei, J. & Kamber, M. (2011). *Data Mining: Concepts and Techniques.* Morgan Kauffmann.

Kwak, W., & Shi, Y. (2021). Bankruptcy Prediction Studies Across Countries Using Multiple Criteria Linear Programming (MCLP) and Other Data Mining Approaches. In C. F. Lee (Ed.), *Encyclopedia of Finance.* doi:10.1007/978-3-030-73443-5_76-1

Kwak, W., Shi, Y., & Lee, C. F. (2020). Data mining applications in accounting and finance context. Handbook of Financial Econometrics, Mathematics, Statistics, and Machine Learning, 1, 823-857.

Olson, D., & Shi, Y. (2007). *Introduction to Business Data Mining.* McGraw-Hill/Irwin.

Provost, F., & Fawcett, T. (2013). *Data Science for Business: What You Need to Know about Data Mining and Data-Analytic Thinking.* O'Reilly Publishing.

Shi, Y. (2022). *Advances in Big Data Analytics: Theory, Algorithm and Practice.* Springer. doi:10.1007/978-981-16-3607-3

Shi, Y., Tian, Y., Kou, G., Peng, Y., & Li, J. P. (2011). *Optimization based Data Mining: Theory and Applications.* Springer. doi:10.1007/978-0-85729-504-0

Shi, Y., Zhang, L., Tian, Y., & Li, X. (2015). *Intelligent Knowledge: A Study beyond Data Mining.* Springer. doi:10.1007/978-3-662-46193-8

KEY TERMS AND DEFINITIONS

Auditor Changes: Firms may change auditors after receiving a qualified opinion in favor of their favorable audit reports called "opinion shopping."

Data Mining: Classification or prediction is the most common data mining method, which uses a set of pre-tagged datasets to train the model for future prediction. Fraud detection, auditor changes, and risk analysis are classic examples of applications in this technology.

Decision Tree: The decision tree summarizes the patterns using the format of the binary tree and it is commonly used in operation management.

K-Nearest Neighbor: (KNN): The k-Nearest Neighbor algorithm is the most popular algorithm in clustering and is used to partition observations into k clusters by Euclidian distance.

Logit Analysis: Logit analysis is used to model the probability of a certain group such as the auditor change group in statistics.

Qualified Audit Opinion: A qualified opinion signals a lack of conformity with Generally Accepted Accounting Principles (GAAP) and casts doubt on the credibility of financial statements.

Support Vector Machine (SVM): SVM is primarily used in the application of classification problems, though it can also be used for regression analysis.

Volatility of Semiconductor Companies

Toshifumi Takada
https://orcid.org/0000-0003-4606-0909
National Chung Cheng University, Taiwan

INTRODUCTION

The objective of this article is to evaluate the volatility of semiconductor manufacturing companies in Taiwan and Japan. Auditors must evaluate volatility that resides in client companies. The procedure of the evaluation must be done at the beginning of the audit. Volatility is called an inherent risk or risk of material misstatement in auditing practice, and it is also called business risk in the new audit guideline. In this article, we define volatility as equivalent to inherent risk, risk of material misstatement, or business risk.

BACKGROUND

The Statement of Audit Standard #315 (2020) of the Japanese Institute of Certified Public Accountants defines inherent risk as follows: "Inherent risk is the events and environments influencing misrepresentations of financial statements when the necessary internal controls don't exist in the client's company. The factors of inherent risk occur on the side of client companies." Inherent risk is recognized by factors such as rapid change of the market, fluctuated profit and loss of the companies, speed of innovation, bankruptcy of related companies, etc. Volatility can be evaluated by observing and measuring factors in the client companies.

This article is a case study to evaluate volatility of top 10 listed semiconductor companies in Taiwan and Japan using their financial statements and stock prices. The financial statements are disclosed at the stock market and we can get them by Market Observation Post System (MOPS) at Taiwan Stock Exchange and Electronic Disclosure for Investors' Network (EDINET) at Tokyo Stock Exchange. In this article, we use income momentums and fluctuations calculated as the rate of change of sales, ordinal profit, and net profit data from the financial statements. We also use stock price as it represents an objective value of the companies in the stock market.

The reason why we focus on semiconductor companies in Taiwan and Japan is that semiconductor companies in Taiwan show very high performance during the past 10 years, and on the contrary Japanese semiconductor companies' performance fell during the same period. By comparing Taiwanese and Japanese companies' volatility, we can show the significance of evaluating volatility by auditors. This can contribute to improve the audit practice of risk-based procedure.

DOI: 10.4018/978-1-7998-9220-5.ch002

Copyright © 2023, IGI Global. Copying or distributing in print or electronic forms without written permission of IGI Global is prohibited.

FOCUS OF THE ARTICLE

Analysis of Risk-based Audit Procedure

Modern auditing practice is done by a risk-based procedure. The audit practice guideline shows its theoretical framework. First, we analyze the framework by using stochastic probability numbers. Applying Bayes Theorem, we show how to revise the detection risk and we also show that the evaluation of volatility is a starting line of the risk-based auditing procedure.

Case Study of Taiwanese Semiconductor Companies

Semiconductor companies have led the Taiwanese economy for the past 10 years. The Taiwanese government established a science park in Hsinchu in the 1980s. People who studied IT technologies in the US returned to Taiwan and they started IT businesses there. A few universities and the public research organizations have had alliances with them. One of the success factors of Taiwanese semiconductor companies is said to be that some of them focused on the pre-process of semiconductor manufacturing called a foundry business model.

Our case here deals with top 10 Taiwanese semiconductor companies. We use their financial statements disclosed at the Taipei Stock Market's MOPS. As the contents of financial statements are level data, we process them into income momentums (rate of change of sales, ordinal profit, net profit, and total assets) for the most recent 10 years. We also use the rate of change of stock prices in the same period. Volatility as a business risk is evaluated by fluctuations recognized by the negative income momentums.

Case Study of Japanese Semiconductor Companies

Japanese semiconductor companies used to be ranked among the top three in the world in the 1990s and occupied 50% of the global market share. Because of several reasons, they have descended since the end of the 1990s and the market share declined to 6% in 2020. There were big semiconductor manufacturing companies all over Japan in the 1990s but many of them have closed. One of the characteristics of Japanese semiconductor companies is that most of them are not foundries but some of them are computer manufacturing companies, electric appliance manufacturing companies, and so on.

We use the financial statements disclosed at the Tokyo Stock Exchange and we can download them by EDINET. To compare the Japanese companies with Taiwanese companies, we also calculate income momentums and fluctuations, and we evaluate volatility.

Basics of Risk-based Audi Procedure

The theoretical relationship of Audit Risk (AR), Inherent Risk (IR), Control Risk (CR), and Detection Risk (DR) was defined in Audit Standards and its practice guidelines as follows.

$$AR = IR \times CR \times DR \tag{1}$$

Here the risks in the equation above were defined as
Audit Risk: the misstatement probability after the audit
Inherent Risk: the misstatement probability when internal control doesn't exist in a client company

Control Risk: the misstatement probability after internal control
Detection Risk: the misstatement probability tolerable by an auditor
This equation (1) is converted to

$$DR = \frac{AR}{IR \times CR} = \frac{AR}{RMM} = \frac{AR}{BR} \tag{2}$$

Here Risk of Material Misstatement (*RMM*) is considered as combined risks of Inherent Risk and Control Risk. As RMM resides in a client company, it is equivalent to volatility in this article.

Each risk can be evaluated by the interval scale and the probability of occurrence. Consider the case in which today's stock price of a company is $500 and you are asked to forecast the stock price tomorrow. For example, when we are allowed to forecast the price within the interval between 1$ and $1,000. We can easily forecast tomorrow's price with the probability almost 100% between the interval above. Well, forecast the same stock price tomorrow between $490 and $510. Then the probability will become lower such as 10% or even much lower.

Auditors evaluate volatility of a client's company at the first stage of audit procedure. It depends on the factors caused by the economic environment and the financial condition of the client company. Experienced auditors have enough knowledge to evaluate volatility. But in the case of a new client, they need to collect much more evidence and evidential matter because they don't have enough knowledge about volatility. We must note that auditors can't control volatility because it resides in a client company and its surrounding economic condition.

Audit Risk (AR) is considered as a target probability of risk by auditors. Target risk means that auditors have the probability as a given tolerant number. For example, consider the case in which AR is 0.01 (1%). This means that auditors can't detect misstatement of the client company's financial statements by 1%. One time of auditing out of 100 times will not be detected by auditors. AR may be decided by an audit team or by an accounting firm. AR is not an objective probability but a subjective one. As auditors are professional accountants, they are thought to have experience and knowledge to give a reasonable AR.

Equation (2) shows that RMM is evaluated and that the target AR is given, then DR is calculated. DR is also a tolerance probability of auditors. A high DR means that auditors need not use many resources (time and manpower) to such audit propositions to be investigated. On the contrary, a low DR means that auditors need to use much more time and manpower, which is called a detailed audit procedure. We can recognize that DR and RMM is a relationship of inverse proportionality. If RMM is large, then DR becomes small and vice versa.

When the target AR is 0.05 (5%), then DR varies inversely with RMM probabilities. DR varies from $0.5 \rightarrow 0.1 \rightarrow 0.05$ accordingly RMM varies from $0.1 \rightarrow 0.5 \rightarrow 1.0$. RMM 0.1 means both reliable internal control and very low inherent risk. On the contrary, RMM 1.0 means the not reliable nor effective internal control resulted in the high inherent risk. We can understand that when AR= 0.05 and RMM is reliable level at 0.1, then DR is tolerable as high as the level at the probability of 0.5 (50%). This probability means that auditors need not use lots of resources. On the contrary, when AR = 0.05 and RMM is high probability at 1.0, then DR must be very low probability as 0.05. This probability means that auditors are required to do a very detailed audit procedure using lots of time and manpower.

The analysis of risk-based audit procedure above is understood by many professional auditors. This analysis is a theoretical explanation and practitioners don't use the probability numbers in their practice but they execute subjective judgment.

Table 1. Shows DR matrix of AR and RMM

AR \ RMM	0.1	0.2	0.3	0.4	0.5	0.6	0.7	0.8	0.9	1
0.01	0.1	0.05	0.033333	0.025	0.02	0.016667	0.014286	0.0125	0.011111	0.01
0.02	0.2	0.1	0.066667	0.05	0.04	0.033333	0.028571	0.025	0.022222	0.02
0.03	0.3	0.15	0.1	0.075	0.06	0.05	0.042857	0.0375	0.033333	0.03
0.04	0.4	0.2	0.133333	0.1	0.08	0.066667	0.057143	0.05	0.044444	0.04
0.05	0.5	0.25	0.166667	0.125	0.1	0.083333	0.071429	0.0625	0.055556	0.05
0.06	0.6	0.3	0.2	0.15	0.12	0.1	0.085714	0.075	0.066667	0.06
0.07	0.7	0.35	0.233333	0.175	0.14	0.116667	0.1	0.0875	0.077778	0.07
0.08	0.8	0.4	0.266667	0.2	0.16	0.133333	0.114286	0.1	0.088889	0.08
0.09	0.9	0.45	0.3	0.225	0.18	0.15	0.128571	0.1125	0.1	0.09
0.1	1	0.5	0.333333	0.25	0.2	0.166667	0.142857	0.125	0.111111	0.1

Revision of DR by Bayes Theorem

In a case in which material misstatement (window dressing) occurred and the auditor found the incident during the audit, how do they revise the initial DR? In this chapter, we show how to revise initial risks by using Bayes Theorem. As is well known, Bayes Theorem taught us how to revise the initial probability when additional information is added. It defines the prior probability and posterior probability as follows.

Probability of misstatement (AR): $P\{F\}$ (3)

Estimated volatility (RMM): $P\{a\}$ (4)

Prior Probability: Probability of DR under $P\{a\}$

$P\{F|a\}$ (5)

Posterior Probability: Probability of revised DR as

$P\{a|F\}$ (6)

In the table 1, we define $P\{F\}$ = AR (target probability) and $P\{a\}$ = RMM (volatility), $P\{F|a\}$ = DR (tolerable probability). For example, suppose AR = 0.01, RMM = 0.2, then DR = 0.05. According to Bayes Theorem,

$$P\{a\,|\,F\} = \frac{P\{F\,|\,a\} \times P\{F\}}{P\{a\}}$$ (7)

$= (0.5 \times 0.01) \div 0.2 = 0.0025$

In this case, DR is revised from 0.05 to 0.0025 as a posterior probability. This means that when auditors detected a material misstatement during the audit, they needed to do much more detailed audit procedures as the tolerant probability was revised from 5% to 0.25%.

Table 2 shows posterior probabilities $P\{a|F\}$ revised by additional information detected by auditors. Here suppose that a target probability AR $= P\{F\} = 0.01$ and that RMM (volatility) $= P\{a\}$, $P\{F|a\} =$ DR (tolerant prior probability). $P\{a|F\}$ represents revised DR (posterior probability).

Table 2. Revised DR by Bayse Theorem

AR = 0.01

RMM	0.1	0.2	0.3	0.4	0.5	0.6	0.7	0.8	0.9	1
DR	0.1	0.05	0.033	0.025	0.02	0.017	0.014	0.012	0.011	0.01
Revised	0.01	0.0025	0.0011	0.000625	0.0004	0.000283	0.0002	0.00015	0.000122	0.0001

AR=0.05

RMM	0.1	0.2	0.3	0.4	0.5	0.6	0.7	0.8	0.9	1
DR	0.5	0.25	0.17	0.13	0.1	0.08	0.07	0.06	0.055	0.05
Revised	0.25	0.0625	0.028333	0.01625	0.01	0.006667	0.005	0.00375	0.003056	0.0025

AR=0.1

RMM	0.1	0.2	0.3	0.4	0.5	0.6	0.7	0.8	0.9	1
DR	1	0.5	0.33	0.25	0.2	0.17	0.14	0.13	0.11	0.1
Revised	1	0.25	0.11	0.0625	0.04	0.028333	0.02	0.01625	0.012222	0.01

Initial DR varies from 0.1 to 0.01 according to the volatility. Revised DRs have become much lower probability from 0.01 to 0.0001.

Revised DR (Table 2) becomes much lower than initial DR (Table 1) when auditors get additional information of material misstatement. We have evidence about this in practice when auditors detect window dressing during the audit procedure. In the Olympus case the audit firm in charge did a forensic audit. The expense was triple that of an ordinal audit.

Prior Studies

Business risk also resides in the business companies as they are operating in the market economy. There were many cases of misstatement (window dressing) and auditors couldn't detect them. Business risk and thus volatility must be evaluated at the first stage of auditing procedure. Prior studies focusing on risks related to audit started in 1980s and they have continued till now in 2021. Researchers found several factors that indicated misstatement of financial statements.

Colbert (1988) did an experiment on inherent risk. She used 4 independent variables related to the inventory risk: (1) turnover rate, (2) pressure of sales performance, (3) variance of inventory prices, (4) quality of accountants in charge. 65 professional accountants anticipated the experiment; 25 CPAs from Big 8 divided into A group (12) and B group (13); 16 CPAs from international accounting firms other than Big 8 as group C; 14 CPAs from local accounting firms as group D.

Respondents were required to evaluate 4 independent variables above from High to Low 9 levels. She analyzed the responses by using ANOVA and found that

(1) All the 4 independent variables influenced the evaluation of inherent risk. Quality of accountants in charge had the largest effects on the auditor evaluation.

(2) She analyzed the variance of evaluations among the groups from (A) to (D). Coefficient of group (A) was higher than groups (B), (C), and (D). This implied that group (A) auditors had knowledge of risk-based audit procedures.

Houghton and Fogarty (1991) The objective of this paper was to evaluate inherent risk; they test the hypothesis (1) irregularities detected in journal entries more often than other evidential matters, and (2) experienced auditors can recognize the propositions with higher risks. They mailed a questionnaire to the professional accountants in the USA (326) UK (96), and South Africa (58).

They concluded that (a) material irregularities occurred more often in journal entries, (b) experienced accountants could recognize propositions with possible higher risks, (c) Inherent risk is related to the present financial statements errors, (d) Auditors can evaluate inherent risk easily when the client company co-operates with them.

After the 2000s, research focusing on audit risk model has continued. Many research papers can be found in academic journals. The researcher has surveyed the following four papers on the audit risk model.

Curtis and Turley (2007) examined the impact of the business risk audit (BRA). BRA was implemented in the 1990s and it influenced audit practices. This paper was a report by examining a set of audit files over the five years (1996-2000) spanning the implementation of the BRA and the interviews with audit team members. BRA was said to have the potential to enhance audit effectiveness, deep understanding of business, environment, and business process. As a result, auditors could recognize management fraud and business failure risks. The objective of this paper was to understand how the BRA made changes in auditing procedure, difficulties encountered in operationalizing the BRA, and relationships between a program in the introduction of the BRA and practices.

The conclusion was that while the BRA was developed by the administrative sections of the accounting firms, the considerations of practicing auditors who regarded audits as legitimate were not adequate. They also raised a question about the ability of BRA to generate additional revenue through providing added value for the client. The BRA was expected by the practicing auditors to provide value to the client but they could not require the client to pay for it.

Hogan and Wilkins (2008) demonstrated whether internal control deficiencies increased audit fees. As is well known, Sarbanes-Oxley Act (SOX) 2002 required all listed companies in the US to disclose internal control reports. They must ensure that material financial statement misstatements either cannot occur within the function of internal control or will be detected and corrected by management before financial reports are disclosed. The purpose of their paper was to determine whether the audit risk model was descriptive of what occurred in practice; that is, the relationship between audit fees and the internal control deficiencies. Audit fees were thought to be the proxy of audit works.

The conclusion was that audit fees were significantly higher for the internal control deficiency firms. In addition, they got a result that the fee increment was highest for the firms that have the most substantial internal control problems. They also indicated that the internal control deficiency firms have higher levels of inherent risk and information risk than other firms in the same industry.

McKee (2014) did research focusing on financial fraud risk for audit planning. Financial frauds have been one of the big issues in auditing. The Enron scandal of 2001 was typical. Professional auditors have seldom encountered such issues during their careers. As a result, they have not had enough knowledge to detect frauds. Financial and accounting frauds resulting in bankruptcy have been a real headache for professional auditors because the frauds have not been forecasted at the stage of audit planning. McKee and Lensberg (2002) developed a model to forecast bankruptcy in 2002. They used a logistic regression model and a database of 91 financial fraud cases.

In their model, three independent variables were used: (1) company size (base 10 logarithm), (2) auditor tenure (number of years), and (3) McKee-Lensberg bankruptcy probability. They tested 91 cases in the database and the performance of their model was 69.2% detection percentage out of 91 cases. This percentage was much better than a similar model. Financial fraud risk can be used for detection risk in risk-based auditing methods.

Heldiifanny and Tobing (2018) analyzed the implementation of a risk-based internal audit plan. This is a case study of University X (X is a tentative name but it may be a real university). The authors recognize that we are now in the era of digital revolution but university as higher education is far behind (disruption of higher education). They indicated six risks: information system risk, project risk, activity risk, infrastructure risk, entity risk, center of administration risk, and entity risk, and organs in faculty and study program risk.

The research method used is field study by interviews with internal audit division of University X, collecting data from a few reports of University X (Annual Work Plan 2015-2017, Strategic Plan 2015-2018, Self-Assessment Report 2016, and University X statistics 2012-2016. Their major observations are (1) risk in teaching and learning process, (2) risk in the technology capability among the faculty and staff, (3) information technology risk and graduate student development risk. They concluded that the internal audit division should act as a catalyst of change and they made recommendations: University X should begin to consider risks beyond financial, operational, and compliance risks, completing and adjusting internal audit scopes every year, etc.

SOLUTIONS AND RECOMMENDATIONS

Case Study 1: Volatility of Taiwanese Semiconductor Companies

Here in this paper, volatility is defined as unstableness of business. In professional auditing standards, inherent risk and control risk combined is called risk of material misstatement (RMM). Prior to the concept of RMM, it was divided into Inherent Risk (IR) and Control Risk (CR). Business risk is now replaced by RMM. Business Risk is a concept with much wider meaning than RMM. These concepts of risks are considered as volatility of business. Volatility can be evaluated by fluctuations of sales, turnover between profit and loss, income momentum, etc.

The next chapter deals with a case study to evaluate volatility of Taiwanese semiconductor companies. Semiconductor companies in Taiwan have been ascending for the past 10 years and one of the companies is evaluated as top ranked in the world now in 2021.

Descriptive Statistics of Top 10 Semiconductor Companies in Taiwan Since 2010

Table 3 shows the income momentums (rate of change of sales, ordinal profit, net profit, and total assets) of a top semiconductor company T1 in Taiwan since 2010. We collected the data of top 10 semiconductor companies in Taiwan (T1 to T10) but just T1 is shown here. Vertical line between 2013 and 2012 shows the beginning of International Financial Reporting Standards (IFRS) used.

Table 3. Semiconductor companies in Taiwan Top 1

(100 million NT$, %)

T1	2020	2019	2018	2017	2016	2015	2014	2013	2012	2011	2010	2009
Sales Amount		10,699	10,314	9,774	9,479	8,434	7,628	5,970	5,066	4,214	4,186	2,994
Rate of Change		3.73	5.52	3.11	12.39	10.57	27.77	17.84	20.22	0.67	39.81	
Ordinal Profit		3,453	3,511	3,453	3,343	3,065	2,637	1,880	1,768	1,389	1,548	892
Rate of Change		-1.65	1.68	3.29	9.07	16.23	40.27	6.33	27.29	-10.27	73.54	
Net Profit		3,334	3,610	3,143	3,231	2,918	2,757	2,045	1,661	1,342	1,616	892
Rate of Change		-7.65	14.86	-2.72	10.73	5.84	34.82	23.12	23.77	-16.96	81.17	
Total Assets		22,648	20,901	19,919	18,864	16,575	14,950	12,630	9,461	7,614	7,012	5,774
Rate of Change		8.36	4.93	5.59	13.81	10.87	18.37	33.50	24.26	8.59	21.44	
											(NT$, %)	
Stock Price	601	339	232	183	139.5	139.5	104.5	99.6	75	71.1	64.9	44.1
Rate of Ch	77.29	46.12	26.78	31.18	0.00	33.49	4.92	32.80	5.49	9.55	47.17	

After IFRS

From descriptive statistics of top 10 companies, we can get the average rate of change of sales, ordinal profit, net profit, and total assets. Table 4 represents the income momentum of 10 years of Taiwanese semiconductor companies. In addition, we can get the average rate of change of stock price. Stock price represents the value of a company evaluated by the shareholders. The shareholders of a listed companies consist of a variety of organizations and persons and they are scattered globally. Stock price represents their evaluation of a company. Each transaction of selling and buying a stock is subjective judgment but the stock price in the stock market results in an objective evaluation by many shareholders. Note that T3 is a newly established company and as just a year of data was available we excluded T3 from the calculation of averages.

Table 4. Rate of change – Taiwanese semiconductor companies

(%, times)

	Sales	Ordinal Profit	Net Profit	Total Assets	Stock Price	Fluctuations
T1	14.16	16.58	16.7	14.97	28.62	5
T2	16.91	2.99	19.8	14.16	17.18	14
T4	6.62	22.91	23.61	3.1	15.49	17
T5	6.3	81.4	8.55	4.11	8.41	12
T6	53.37	101.84	31.74	36.9	62.83	7
T7	9.83	9.71	10.46	3.95	23.43	16
T8	17.38	31.77	39.64	15.26	39.92	10
T9	8.88	25.82	23.65	7.85	32.62	15
T10	11.15	16.88	16.77	13.6	29.36	9
Average	16.07	34.43	21.21	12.66	28.65	11.67

Negative income momentum is counted and the number of times of negative momentum is recorded in the column of fluctuations in Table 2. For example, T1's fluctuations are 5 times out of 40 (4 income momentums × 10 years). T4's fluctuations are 17 times out of 40. A negative income momentum of sales represents that the sales of a year decreased from the previous year. Fluctuation constitutes one of the factors of volatility as the number of times of negative momentum represents the descending trend of a company.

Evaluation of Volatility by the Standard Deviation

Volatility is the degree of unstableness. Companies are doing business operations and the result of operations is moving upward or downward every day. That is, it is unstable. The degree of unstableness can be measured by the fluctuations of negative rate of changes in sales amount, profit, or stock price, etc. Fluctuation is one of the factors influencing unstableness of the system. Negative rate of change represents fluctuation of a business company.

In addition, it is measured between the expected value and the realized value. We can suppose that each company's rate of change hypothesizes the expected value as an average of 10 years, then the volatility can be measured by the standard deviation of the realized value. Table 5 shows the volatility of top 10 semiconductor companies in Taiwan.

Table 5. Volatility of Taiwanese semiconductor companies

	Sales	Ordinal Profit	Net Profit	Total Assets	Stock Price
T1	12.46	24.8	27.56	9.28	23.13
T2	41.87	40.95	68.04	16.24	55.22
T4	32.67	118.61	112.5	14.59	60.6
T5	13.27	166.57	74.26	6.45	39.42
T6	66.14	183.75	81.87	53.73	124.3
T7	13.81	26.99	25.84	10.66	66.04
T8	14.23	27	26.16	21.13	85.44
T9	7.99	62.9	62.69	20.68	47.73
T10	6.5	25.86	27.34	17.03	57.28
Average	23.22	75.27	56.25	18.87	62.13

Results

Our observation of top 10 semiconductor companies in Taiwan is as follows.

(a)   T1 is the most stable company in the top 10 due to just 5 times of negative income momentum and low volatility.

(b) All the top 10 companies were stable as the average number of negative income momentum was 11.67 times out of 40 (29%).

(c) The stock price in 10 years since 2010 ascended on average 24.65% yearly.

Volatility is considered as business risk by professional auditors. If it is high, auditors evaluate that the business is unstable from our observations above, so we can say that the volatility of semiconductor companies in Taiwan is not so high that they can set the tolerance level of detection risk high. This means that they need not use lots of audit resources.

Case Study 2: Volatility of Japanese Semiconductor Companies and Comparative Study ASE STUDY Between Japan and Taiwan

As mentioned above, Japanese semiconductor manufacturing companies used to occupy 50% of the global market share in the 1990s and some of them were ranked top 3 in the world. But they have been descending rapidly since the end of the 1990s and its market share has declined to 6% in 2020. It is said that one of the reasons why Japanese semiconductor companies decline is their business model. They are electric appliance manufacturing companies (Hitachi, Mitsubishi Electronics, Sony, etc.) or computer manufacturing companies (Fujitsu, NEC, Toshiba, etc.). This descending trend continues now in 2021.

Descriptive Data of Top 10 Semiconductor Companies in Japan Since 2009

Table 6 shows the income momentums (rate of change of sales, ordinal profit, net profit, and total assets) of a top semiconductor companies J1 in Japan since 2010. We collected descriptive statistics of top 10 semiconductor companies (J1 to J10) in Japan but we just show that of J1. Note that over 500% data is replaced to zero as such data can be thought abnormal for a few reasons.

Table 6. Semiconductor company in Japan – Top 1

| | | | | | | | | | | | (100million jpy, %) | |
J1	2020	2019	2018	2017	2016	2015	2014	2013	2012	2011	2010	2009
Sales	9,006	9,149	8,934	8,377	8,135	8,106	7,599	7,457	7,035	6,890	6,912	7,666
Rate of Change	-1.59	2.35	6.23	2.89	0.36	6.25	1.87	5.66	2.06	-0.32	-10.91	
Ordinal Profit	445	634	560	462	456	431	367	257	185	72	-537	-207
Rate of Change	-42.47	11.67	17.50	1.30	5.48	14.85	29.97	28.02	61.08	0.00	-61.45	
Net Profit	268	386	528	722	-497	884	507	353	124	-199	67	-733
Rate of Change	-44.03	-36.79	-36.74	168.84	-277.87	42.65	30.37	64.87	260.48	-133.67	0.00	
Total Assets	9.968	9.526	9.147	8.866	8.453	9.045	8.107	7.655	7.928	8.057	9.089	9.089
Rate of Change	4.43	3.98	3.07	4.66	-7.00	10.37	5.58	-3.57	-1.63	-12.81	0.00	
											(jpy, %)	
Stock Price	2,449	3,140	724	661	389	567	461	274	218	263	255	116
Rate of Change	-28.22	0.00	8.70	41.15	-45.76	18.69	40.56	20.44	-20.64	3.04	54.51	

From descriptive statistics, we can also get the average rate of change of sales, ordinal profit, net profit, and total assets. Table 7 shows the income momentum of 10 years of Japanese semiconductor companies. Note that J10 is a newly established company and as we can't get enough data, we excluded J10 from the calculation of averages.

Table 7. Rate of change – Japanese semiconductor companies and comparison

						(%, times)
	Sales	Ordinal Profit	Net Profit	Total Assets	Stock Price	Fluctuation
J1	1.35	6	3.47	0.64	11.04	14
J2	3.87	-0.53	-8.39	0.31	12.94	18
J3	0.88	119.32	-1.3	6.04	10.77	12
J4	4.17	62.27	103.16	6.03	16.16	19
J5	-5.42	22.56	2.23	-3.48	7.58	24
J6	9.52	11.36	9.92	7.5	9.05	11
J7	1.97	46.45	48.3	2.65	15.75	15
J8	1.11	28.53	33.96	2.76	26.99	15
J9	-0.05	31.52	41.08	0.58	9.39	18
Average	1.93	36.39	25.83	2.56	13.30	16.22
T1-T10	16.07	34.43	21.21	12.66	28.65	11.67

Negative income momentum is counted and the number of times of negative momentum is recorded in the column of fluctuations in Table 5. We found that the Japanese semiconductor companies experienced more times of negative income momentum than the Taiwanese semiconductor companies. For example, J1's fluctuations are 14 times and T1 is just 5 times. Average times of negative income momentum of Japanese companies are 16.22 and Taiwanese companies are 11.67. Fluctuation represents the unstableness of a company. The Japanese semiconductor companies have shown more instability than Taiwanese companies.

Table 8. Volatility of Japanese semiconductor companies and comparison

	Sales	Ordinal Profit	Net Profit	Total Assets	Stock Price
J1	4.99	31.11	149.23	6.78	31.06
J2	23.59	222.98	89.99	30.90	46.15
J3	7.13	165.34	119.55	3	41.51
J4	12.11	142.82	169.55	25.12	46.83
J5	5.86	63.25	89.85	11.61	37.32
J6	17.35	40.85	47.98	5.13	41.89
J7	6.32	111.98	127.01	4.26	34.01
J8	8.52	77.59	85.43	7.99	48.6
J9	8.03	50.18	59.81	14.73	41.17
Average	10.43	100.68	104.27	12.17	40.95
T1-T10	23.22	75.27	56.25	18.87	62.13

Evaluation of Volatility of Japanese Semiconductor Companies

Table 8 shows the volatility of top 10 semiconductor companies in Japan compared with Taiwanese companies.

To compare the companies, Table 8 shows the Taiwanese companies' average number in the last line. As sales amount and stock price of the Taiwanese companies are almost positive, both numbers are much higher than those of the Japanese companies.

Results

Our observation of top 10 semiconductor companies in Japan and the comparison analysis of 2 countries is as follows.

(a)   Japanese semiconductor companies were unstable these years compared with Taiwanese companies as the times of negative income momentum was 16.22 (Taiwan: 11.67).
(b)   The stock price ascended on average 13.30% yearly but the rate was much lower than Taiwan (28.65%).
(c)   Table 9 shows the comparative analysis of each income momentum and the stock price.

Table 9. % Square test

		Sales	Ordinal Profit	Net Profit	Total Assets	Stock Price
Taiwan	Average	16.07	34.43	21.21	12.66	28.65
	sd	23.22	75.27	56.25	18.87	62.13
Japan	Average	4.36	12.19	8.61	3.50	10.09
	sd	4.85	13.54	9.56	3.89	11.31

χSquare Value =	66.71

degree of freedom = 4

Significance Level 0.05 = 9.49;   0.01 = 13.28;   0.001 = 18.47

Average = expected value; sd = observed value

As the χ Square Value is 66.69 and it exceeds the significance level 0.001. This means that semiconductor companies in Taiwan and Japan is independent (= difference exists) at the significance level of 99.9%.

FUTURE RESEARCH DIRECTIONS

We used Earning Per Share (EPS) for the redundancy test. EPS represents a measure for the satisfaction of shareholders. Total Shareholders Return (TSR) is thought to be a better measure for shareholders.

Because the Tokyo Stock Exchange requires listed companies to disclose TSR whereas it is not required for Taiwanese companies at the Taiwan Stock Exchange we decided to use EPS here.

Table 10 shows EPS and its change rate of semiconductor companies in Taiwan and Japan for five years since 2016. We can recognize the following facts.

(1) EPSs of Taiwanese companies are stable. On the contrary, Japanese companies' EPSs are unstable.
(2) The trend of change rate is upward in Taiwanese companies and Japanese companies trend is up and down.
(3) As volatility is defined as unstableness of business, Taiwanese companies are doing much more stable business than Japanese companies.

Table 10. Basic earnings per share for 5 years from 2016 to 2020

Taiwanese Semiconductor Companies					(NT$)
# \ year	2016	2017	2018	2019	2020
T1	12.89	13.23	13.54	13.32	19.97
T2	15.15	15.56	13.26	14.69	26.01
T3	N/A	5.63	5.95	3.96	6.47
T4	8.67	13.92	12.86	3.23	2.51
T5	0.68	0.79	0.58	0.82	2.42
T6	2.54	12.68	31.18	31.35	30.11
T7	8.22	8.26	10.5	13.03	19.42
T8	6.04	9.34	7.39	10.59	15.45
T9	3.38	2.75	3.76	3.58	3.85
T10	6.02	6.71	8.57	13.13	16.93
*T3 started business in 2017.					
Average	7.07	8.89	10.76	10.77	14.31
Change Rate		25.78	21.06	0.1	32.91

Japanese Semiconductor Companies				(jpy -> NTD)	
# \ year	2016	2017	2018	2019	2020
J1	10.73	14.34	66.09	70.47	50.39
J2	N/A	15.3	7.64	-0.93	6.63
J3	29.75	14.52	99.58	180.85	117.91
J4	61.73	62.47	88.04	107.82	61.92
J5	-470.87	35.3	79.68	0.51	16.96
J6	N/A	N/A	N/A	N/A	N/A
J7	N/A	N/A	29.8	26.41	25.85
J8	1.77	17.93	-117.81	40.93	-57.46
J9	116.39	144.5	128.71	74.38	8.77
J10 N/A	N/A	N/A	N/A	N/A	N/A
* J6 and J10 are excluded because they are not listed companies.					
Average	-250.5	43.48	5.44	62.56	28.87
Change Rate		117.36	-87.5	1050.97	-53.85

If we do the research in the future, we may get the new findings in addition to our main part of the research above.

CONCLUSION

Risk-based audit procedure starts from the evaluation of volatility. All the other procedures follow this evaluation. In this article we analyzed the theoretical framework of the relationship of 4 risks in auditing and the revision of detection risk by using Bayes Theorem. After this theoretical analysis we evaluated volatility of the semiconductor companies in Taiwan and Japan as case studies. From the disclosed financial statements and stock price we calculated the income momentum, times of negative momentums, and observed volatility values.

We made the following conclusions.

(1) Detection risk, inherent risk, control risk, risk of material misstatement, and business risk are related theoretically as follows:

$$DR = \frac{AR}{IR \times CR} = \frac{AR}{RMM} = \frac{AR}{BR}$$

(2) Volatility is equivalent to IR × CR, RMM, or BR. It resides in the client company. Auditors can't control it but just evaluate it.

(3) Volatility can be evaluated by the times of negative income momentums and the standard deviation of income momentum. Two case studies of the semiconductor companies of Taiwan and Japan clearly demonstrate the different values of volatility.

REFERENCES

Brockman, P. G., & Lee, H. S. (2022). Implications of CEO succession origin and in-house experience for audit pricing. *Journal of Accounting, Auditing & Finance, 37*(1), 173–204. doi:10.1177/0148558X19832104

Cho, J. S. (2022). The effect of earnings volatility on stock price delay. *Scientific Annals of Economics and Business, 69*(1), 1–12. doi:10.47743aeb-2022-0002

Colbert, J. L. (1988). Inherent risk: An investigation of auditors' judgments. *Accounting, Organizations and Society, 13*(2), 111–121. doi:10.1016/0361-3682(88)90039-6

Curtis, E., & Stuart, T. (2007). The business risk audit - A longitudinal case study of an audit engagement. *Accounting, Organizations and Society, 32*(4-5), 439–461. doi:10.1016/j.aos.2006.09.004

Electronic Disclosure for Investors' Network. (2021). *Web has reached financial statements of the listed companies at Tokyo Stock Exchange.* Retrieved April 17, 2022, from https://disclosure.edinet-fsa.go.jp/

Heldifanny, R. A., & Tobing, R. P. (2018). Evaluation of risk-based Internal audit plan implementation in the era of technology disruption: Case study at university x. *Advances in Social Science. Education and Humanities, 348*, 316–322.

Hogan, C. E., & Wilkins, M. S. (2008). Evidence on the audit risk model: Do auditors increase audit fees in the presence of internal control deficiencies? *Contemporary Accounting Research, 25*(1), 219–242. doi:10.1506/car.25.1.9

Houghton, C. W., & Fogarty, J. A. (1991). Inherent risk. *Auditing, 10*(1), 1–21.

Ijiri, Y. (1986). A framework for triple-entry bookkeeping. *The Accounting Review, 61*(4), 745–759.

Ijiri, Y. (1988). Momentum accounting and managerial goals on impulses. *Management Science, 34*(2), 160–166. doi:10.1287/mnsc.34.2.160

Japanese Institute of Certified Public Association. (2020). Statement of auditing standards: Vol. 315. Japanese Institute of Certified Public Association.

Lennox, C. S., Schmidt, J. J., & Thompson, A. M. (2022). *Why are expanded audit reports not informative to investors? Evidence from the United Kingdom. In Review of Accounting Studies.* Springer.

Market Observation Post System. (2021). *Web has reached the financial statements of the listed companies at Taipei Stock Exchange.* Retrieved January to April 17, 2022, from https://emops.twse.com.tw/server-java/t58query

McKee, T. E. (2014). Evaluating financial fraud risk during audit planning. *The CPA Journal*, 28–32.

McKee, T. E., & Lensberg, T. (2002). Genetic programming and rough sets: A hybrid approach to bankruptcy classification. *European Journal of Operational Research*, *138*(2), 436–451. doi:10.1016/S0377-2217(01)00130-8

Shinnihon Audit Firm, E. Y. (2002). *Report of the committee on audit investigation.* Retrieved April 17, 2022, from https://www.olympus.co.jp/jp/common/pdf/nr20120117.pdf

World Semiconductor Trade Statistics. (2021). *Web has reached statistics of the semiconductor trade in the world.* Retrieved April 17, 2022, from https://www.wsts.org/

ADDITIONAL READING

Ijiri, Y. (1967). *The foundations of accounting measurement.* Prentice-Hall International.

Ijiri, Y. (1975). *Theory of accounting measurement.* American Accounting Association.

Paton, W. A., & Littleton, A. C. (1940). *An introduction to corporate accounting standards.* American Accounting Association.

Shirata, Y. (2003). *Corporate bankruptcy forecasting model.* Chuokeizaisha.

Shirata, Y. (2019). *Bankruptcy forecasting model and corporate ranking by artificial intelligence.* Zeimukeirikyokai.

Takada, T. (2020). Study of CIM and IoT – Simulation for cost performance analysis –. *Computer Audit*, *42*, 4–25.

Takada, T., Sakaki, M., Aoyagi, S., & Kawaguchi, H. (2019). Cybersecurity and AI – Implications for internal auditing –. *Computer Audit*, *40*, 31–48.

Takada, T., & Suga, Y. (2021). School accounting education in Japan– In relation to economic development of the country. *Computer Audit*, *44*, 62–74.

KEY TERMS AND DEFINITIONS

Audit Risk: Audit risk is defined as Inherent Risk x Control Risk x Audit Risk and it is the probability that an auditor fails to detect the material misstatement of the financial statement.

Control Risk: Listed companies are required to install the internal control. Control risk is defined as the probability even when the internal control is installed, it fails to detect the material misstatement of the financial statement.

Detection Risk: Detection risk can be controlled by an auditor by how much audit resources used for a specific audit point. Given the audit risk and the inherent risk, the detection risk is inverse proportional to the control risk; in case the control risk is small, the detection risk can be set high. This means that the audit resource can be saved, and vice versa.

Inherent Risk: Inherent risk is defined as the risk of an object without an audit. A client company are engaged in a business, and it invests its resources for the business. No one can forecast whether the investment is successful or not. The result is variant in some extent. The variance is thought to be inherent risk.

Volatility: Volatility is defined as the fluctuations of the magnitude between the former condition and the present condition. For example, a company's former profit is 100 and its present profit is 110, then the volatility of the profit of this company is (110-100) / 100 = 0.1. External auditor needs to evaluate the volatility of a client company.

Section 2
Approximation Methods

Use of AI in Predicting Trends in Vegetation Dynamics in Africa

Jean-Éric Pelet

https://orcid.org/0000-0001-7069-8131

LARGEPA, Panthéon-Assas University, Paris, France

Santiago Belda

Universidad de Alicante, Spain

Dounia Arezki

Computer Science Faculty, Science and Technology University of Oran, Algeria

INTRODUCTION OF THE START-UP ENVIRONMENT AFRICA

The African continent offers through its dynamic demographic outlook rich promises for investors and entrepreneurs. The growth rate of the African population is exponential. In 1950 the African population was 250 Million inhabitants, 900 million in 2010, and 1,3 m billion today (National Institute of Demographic Studies, INED). Current forecasts point to a population that should reach 2.3 billion (INED) and 4.5 billion at the end of the century according to the United Nations (UN).

In 2050 Nigeria will be the third most populous country of the world with an estimated population of 433 million inhabitants compared with that of the USA, 423 million inhabitants of European Union, 500 Million inhabitants, China, 1,3 billion, and the India 1,6 billion.

Authors estimate that in 2050, Africa's GDP will be close to that of the European Union (Severino and Hadjenberg, 2016). At the same time the population will exceed two billion inhabitants. Two economic sectors seem particularly attractive: agro-business and Telecom. Africa jumped step infrastructure in fixed-line telephony to fully enter the era of mobile phones. The African continent is therefore in mobile telephony today, the second largest market in the world behind Asia. In the field of agro-food and the agro-business market estimated at 313 billion dollars in 2010 will reach 1000 billion in 2030 according to Severino and Hadjenberg (2016).

Such dynamism coupled with the emergence of a middle class and the emergence of a new generation of entrepreneurs, SME owners, of investors, constitute an extremely favorable environment for the development of start-ups in Africa. However, these undeniable assets should not mask the diseases plaguing the continent and that we will discuss.

BACKGROUND: THE EVILS SUFFERED BY AFRICA

Chronic Political Instability

In the fall of the colonial system, peace and stability were two of the main challenges African countries faced because of their political and institutional history. Although the colonial period was short-lived,

DOI: 10.4018/978-1-7998-9220-5.ch003

Copyright © 2023, IGI Global. Copying or distributing in print or electronic forms without written permission of IGI Global is prohibited.

it had strong impacts and participated in the complete remodeling of the continent as it is underlined in many works including « General History of Africa, vol. 7 » (UNESCO). It created new states, redefined the stakes of power, reoriented economic structures crystallized new interests... The risk, under these conditions, was to see the continent sink into interminable border wars after the end of colonial regulation (Shillington, 1995).

A posteriori, Africa does indeed appear to be *"the region of the world most affected by armed struggles or political crises that bear the seeds of war"* (Shillington, 1995). As it can be seen on the map, (Figure 1) a significant number of African countries which is far from exhaustive was affected by some form of conflict between the first independence and the early 1990s. (Tableau Public, 2019). Compared to Europe and the United States, Africa has experienced a higher number of conflicts. Their number also remained high until 2002, a period from which they seem to decrease (Tableau Public, 2022).

Since 2010, West Africa has experienced an intensification of violence and an increase in conflicts (Amnesty International). While the growth prospects seem very encouraging, these difficulties could hamper its future development and fuel the question about the economic and social advances made by the countries of the sub-region (Mali, Burkina Faso, Nigeria, Ghana, Sierra Leone, etc.). West Africa has indeed been destabilized by outbreaks of violence, the resurgence of conflicts and the rise of religious extremism, in particular in Mali and northern Nigeria (RFI, 29.09.2013). Drug trafficking and maritime piracy have also quickly taken root there, contributing to the lasting weakening of countries like Guinea-Bissau. The main challenge for the sub-region will be to overcome violence and fragility in its most vulnerable areas to let continue the impressive progress made over the past decade in strengthening democracy and economic development.

There is dramatic record characterized by an infant mortality rate of 74 per 1000 compared to an average of 44 per 1000 worldwide and 6 per 1000 in the United States and Europe. While life expectancy is 70 years on average globally, it is only 63 years in Africa (INED).

FOCUS OF THE ARTICLE: A CONTINENT RICH IN NATURAL RESOURCES BUT AN ABSENCE AND A LACK OF REDISTRIBUTION OF BENEFITS

African countries have a significant share of the world's reserves of natural resources, which in itself represents a reason of hope for the future of the continent. According to information gathered by the correspondent of the Turkish press agency Anadolu (https://www.aa.com.tr/), a significant volume of minerals (oil, natural gas, diamonds, gold, uranium, cobalt, platinum, copper, tantalum) used in the production of manufactured products are extracted from the subsoil of the African continent. Africa has long been despoiled by foreign hands and even today, new discoveries of deposits are attracting the appetite of large international groups. The largest cobalt resources are utilized in the manufacture of mobile phones and laptops; they are extracted in Rwanda and the Democratic Republic of Congo (DRC). The DRC alone supplies more than half of the world's cobalt ore needs. When it comes to gold and diamonds, some African countries are among the biggest players in the sector. Botswana, South Africa and the DRC are among the largest diamond producers in the world along with Russia and Canada. For gold, it is South Africa and Ghana. Used as fuel in nuclear power plants, uranium is one of the continent's other assets. Niger and Namibia are placed respectively in 4th and 5th position in the list of uranium producers in the world after Kazakhstan, Canada and Australia. In addition, rhodium and platinum, two elements that are the essential components to produce car catalytic converters, come mainly from South Africa.

Figure 1. A security gap that shows African conflicts have occurred over the last 15 years - Source: Tableau Public - Interactive map located on the website: https://public.tableau.com/profile/hamis.b#!/vi zhome/15YearsOfArmedConflictsInAfrica-V2/15YearsOfConflictsInAfrica-v2 - Extracted from Internet on 02/28/2022

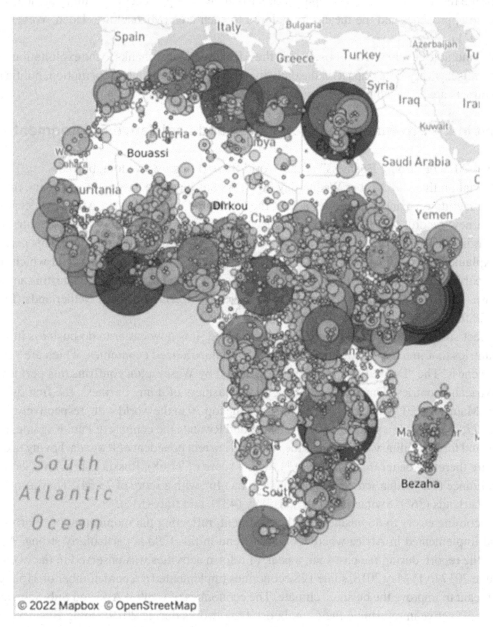

Despite the presence of large reserves of oil and natural gas, some African countries are not yet able to extract them on their own. But according to some estimates, in the near future, Mozambique, Kenya and Ethiopia will be among the important players in the energy sector (TRT, 13.05.2019). In Mozambique, during the last ten years, large reserves of natural gas and coal were discovered. This country should, by 2022, be among the largest exporters of liquefied gas. Nigeria and Angola, are ranking at the top of the list of oil producers in Africa and they are respectively 13th and 14th largest world producers. Regarding natural gas, Algeria, Egypt and Nigeria are at the top of the African table.

Along with the natural resources, African countries are developing access to sustainable energy for both sustainable development and climate change mitigation. They thus mobilize private investors to use their natural resources and develop the infrastructures that are needed. However, the situation of the use of the resources and the development of sustainable energy access is country-scaled. That is to say, that the approaches and the means are tailored to each area (Michaelowa, Hoch, Weber, Kassaye & Hailu, 2021).

Even if a notable development is observed in the African economy thanks to the exploitation of natural resources, this has very little impact on the daily life of the population due to corruption, political crises, secret contracts are arranged for the account of large.

A Deficit in a « Pro-Business » Regulatory and Legislative Environment

The edition 2019 of "Doing Business" of the World Bank (https://www.doingbusiness.org/) was made an advertorial on the 31th October Wednesday 2019. As has been the case in recent years, the race for reforms to facilitate business continues across the world and particularly in Africa, which again this year sets a new record. It is therefore now easier to do business in certain African countries than in other emerging ones and even so-called advanced economies, particularly in Europe. This performance can be explained above all by the all-out reforms implemented in the Continent, and which for many countries paradoxically illustrate the delay they show in terms of attractiveness. Mauritius and Rwanda in this case, thus overtake France, Spain, Italy and even Switzerland and the Netherlands (La tribune Afrique, 28.03.2018).

It is a fact sufficiently rare to deserve being underlined. It is now easier to do business in some African countries that in many European ones and other industrialized economies, which are yet rated in competitiveness. The "Doing Business" report published by Washington confirms this performance of certain African countries. Thus, in the ranking on the easiness of doing business, the first two African countries, Mauritius (20th) and Rwanda (29th), rise to the top 30 in the world with, respectively, a score of 79.58 and 77,88 points on a scale of 100. The island and Rwanda the country of Paul Kagame, Rwandan politician and former military leader. He is the sixth and current president of Rwanda, having taken office in 2000, are therefore better than Spain (30 th), with a score of 77.68), Russia (31th with a score 77,37), and even France (32th with a score of 77.29) and China (46th with a score of 73.64). They also are ahead of the Netherlands (36th), Switzerland (38th), Turkey (43th), and Italy (51th).

It is becoming easier to do business on the continent, reflecting the momentum of reforms that are made and implemented in Africa where the world trend in this field is particularly strong. According to data of the report, during the past year, a peak of reform activities was observed in the world, where from 2 June 2017 to 1st May 2018, some 128 economies implemented a record number of 315 regulatory reforms meant to improve the business climate. The economies of Central Asia and Sub-Saharan Africa were the most active in reforming their regulatory frameworks during 2019. Doing Business coverage period with four in five economies significantly improves business regulation in the two regions.

With a total of 108 reforms compared to 83 in the previous edition, sub-Saharan Africa again recorded a record number of reforms this year. In addition, 2019 was marked by the highest number of reforming economies, with 40 of the region's 48 economies having implemented at least one reform, while the previous record was 37 economies two years ago. The region also has four of the 10 most reforming economies of this year: Togo, Kenya, Ivory Coast and Rwanda. According to the report, *"while the reforms introduced by the countries of this region cover a large number of areas, many relate to the transfer of property and the settlement of insolvency".*

Morocco, which completes the top three African top ranked economies, ranks at 60th place with a jump of 9 places compared to the 2018 edition, like Kenya, ranking at the 61th place, gaining more than 19 places, this year.

Business Practices with Little Regard for Ethical Rules

The Global Compact (https://www.unglobalcompact.org/) is an initiative of the United Nations launched in 2000 to encourage businesses worldwide to adopt a socially responsible attitude. In 2004 the nations have allowed the adoption of the 10th principle on the fight against corruption. For many, corruption primarily concerns the public sector, in fact it concerns both the public and private sectors. Often, both pass the buck. The private sector blames the public sector. It reacts by saying it is the private sector that is the instigator. In truth, because of supply and demand, the two are accomplices. But it is true that more the public authorities intervene in economic activity in general, more there is abuse and corruption. However, corruption is positively correlated to business process digitization, that explains that corruption participates to the development of some sectors by that foreign investments are not sufficient to get rid of corruption (Adomako, Amankwah-Amoah, Tarba & Khand, 2021). In principle, if the rules of the game are clear and enforced, if we distinguish between competition in the private sector, on one hand, and regulations and public entities, on the other hand, the risks of corruption are less.

Corruption, experts say, is a structural problem affecting the whole of society. It concerns both the private and the public sectors. It affects education, the basic economic system, the regulatory system, the management of the economy and, more generally, ethical values. Some analysts of corruption in developing countries, argue that it is the result of too much intervention by the State. For others, this intervention is just not where it should be. In Africa, the state is generally very weak and its powers are limited. Clearer rules and more efficient regulation mean less corruption.

In most countries, since the adoption of the United Nations Convention against Corruption in 2003, corruption has come under criminal law. The problem is how to apply the law effectively. This is true not only for corruption but also for many other issues... The ability of public institutions to uphold and implement the instruments that the highest authorities of the state have ratified is partly based on institutional capacity. But it is also about setting priorities, which is considered important.

What is new today, unlike ten years ago, is that companies are asking for the rules of the game to be clearly defined. Ten years ago, they only defended liberalism, arguing that any form of regulation was bad. Today, this is no longer the case. They say we need technical standards that reward good and effective policies and practices. They say that if cracking down on corruption doesn't work, nothing else will.

During the various Global Compact conferences, the question of payments to be made always comes up. Indeed, African entrepreneurs consider corruption as a priority absolute which must be prevented. They may not say it in public, because they are dependent on the hand that feeds them. But when they speak collectively, they make it very clear that corruption is a serious problem that hurts them. If there was less corruption and had stronger institutional support, they would become more competitive and their businesses would grow faster.

How do you convince a company to stop paying bribes, especially in countries where corruption is rampant and where many other companies pay bribes or kickbacks to get business? This is the fundamental problem. The answer to this question is twofold. Policies must be adopted to improve the situation. Collective action is the only way to go. We need to mobilize a number of like-minded companies who all agree that they would be better off if there were less corruption. None will certainly want to take the first step. But if we manage to encourage them to work together, at the same time, and possibly with public partners, we have a good chance of making a difference. This has already been done in a few countries, including Malawi.

Foreign companies from OECD member countries are often controlled by shareholders, legislators and the media in their own countries. Any violation, even a minor one, can spark an uproar. African companies face material problems, particularly in the areas of regulation, access to energy or transport. The issue may be different, but often the process followed to find solutions may be very similar. African governments want to attract the Foreign Direct Investment (FDI). In doing so, they are sometimes less vivid than they should be.

It was not long ago, members of UNCTAD (United Nations Conference on Trade and Development) argued that there was a risk that countries compete to obtain foreign direct investment playing who will be the highest bidder and thus end up losing their negotiating skills. It is difficult to know to what extent this argument is valid. But given the need to create jobs and improve the living conditions of large numbers of people, one can understand their desire to attract FDI. As the countries of Asia, in particular China, have become important players in this field, the number of potential investors is increased. This is a good thing for African countries, especially since now they have more choices and hopefully their ability to negotiate will be enhanced.

Reports of large-scale corruption in Africa often point to the role of foreign banks, which help corrupt leaders deposit their loot into secret offshore accounts. The recent financial crisis has also drawn attention to the rather opaque practices of many financial institutions. The financial crisis has rung the alarm bell for many. It made it clear that creating long-term value and maximizing short-term profit are not necessarily the same thing. Corruption may undermine the sustainable development perspectives of the African countries if the anti-corruption measures and drives remain slow (Dorasamy & Fagbadebo, 2021). The increased control exercised by the legal bodies, whether in relation to tax evasion, abuse of power or corruption, can only be welcomed. Having a financial sector that is not a vector of abuse of power is of paramount importance. An ecosystem based on technological innovations, allows today in Africa money transfers at acceptable costs (in part thanks to crypto-currencies / blockchain).

How do Investors Structure Finance and Develop Africa?

New approaches: Africa, land of opportunities and potential, soil or finance and funding finally arrive with more transparency and, hopefully, more efficiency. African businesses need capital. African countries adopted and still adopt measures to reduce financial deposits and to increase financial activity hence improving financial efficiency. The quality of institution is partly correlated to private investment (Asongu, Nnanna & Tchamyou, 2021). According to the African Development Bank, sub-Saharan SMEs would need 421 billion dollars to finance their growth. Alongside traditional players, banks and states, we see the emergence in Africa of investment funds that drain capital from around the world to the continent. Funds are fashionable, a sign of the attractiveness of African economies.

Moreover, entrepreneurship and desire to succeed, viscerally has African DNA, they were able to speak with the arrival of funding, education and support by new private structures, but also with PPP (Public Private Partnerships) created for purposes like investment clubs, FabLabs, incubators, new crowdfunding platforms and transaction website.

Who Are its Financial Players? Who are Structuring its New Financing Networks?

Three major families of actors wish to invest more in Africa and are ready to finance FabLabs, incubators, local companies ranging from SMEs to mid- sized companies:

- Traditional financial players: public such as the EIB (European Investment Bank), AFD (French: Agence Française de Développement), BPI France (French: Banque Publique d'Investissement France), regional development banks such as BDEAC (French: Banque de Développement de l'Afrique Centrale)
- The corporates, international groups like Orange, MTN (Mobile Telephone Networks)
- Diasporas via investment clubs and other investment funds, and crowdfunding platforms

In this geographical, economic and technical field, France and the UK perfectly find their place in this ecosystem by their extreme knowledge of business models and "start-up", as they bring in Council, to mentor[6] and structure them. Financing new structures while educating and mentoring these young shoots, here is the project that remains to be carried out.

The FabLabs and Their Financing

The wave of FabLabs began in the United States in 1998, under the leadership of Neil Gershenfeld (http://ng.cba.mit.edu/), professor at MIT. These are workshops designed to be open, shared and collaborative. Their objective is to offer a physical space bringing together digital tools (laser cutouts, 3D printers, etc.) whose use is common in order to allow an individual to create, to invent. Thus, they make it possible to design, prototype, manufacture and test the most diverse objects.

With more than forty places, we can only confirm the vitality of this movement on the African continent. The FabLab is a new place of innovation which, in difficult conditions, often calls for resourcefulness and relies on the creativity and strong will of its promoters. These are places that fit both in a territory, but also in the multiple resources and online communities (free software, OpenStreetMap, social networks).

These structured organizations that are winning over all the countries of the continent seek their funding in crowdfunding platforms, as in private partnerships. The FDA (French Development Agency) as various public Francophone organizations are focused on innovation involved in the financial support case by case. Educational and pooling of expertise and skills, the FabLabs are now seeking their growth through public and / or private funding. In the context of CSR, these FabLabs, also comparable to our « old cooperatives », could easily be financed by large groups who would find there a more than positive return for their images and their territorial conquests...

Africa Investment Clubs

The vocation of a club is to bring together the ecosystems of French and African investment capital in order to promote support for the development of African companies of all sizes through equity, a particularly healthy mode of financing African companies and help companies already supported by French private equity in strengthening their African activities.

Their actions thus aim to support and strengthen African investment capital by all means, to promote its understanding by European actors, in particular institutional investors, to mobilize the expertise available within France Invest (new name of the French association of investors in capital), to strengthen relations between France Invest, which represents the private equity business in France, the leading private equity market in continental Europe, and the private equity players mobilized in favor of the African continent. China also invests in African countries because of their natural resources' wealth, China wants to trade their resources with their infrastructures and their transactions (Gunessee & Hu, 2021).

Through the structuring of funds dedicated to Africa, the « African Clubs » allow the development of human capital and skills while promoting respect for compliance rules (compliance with laws and regulations). Winner of over 15 awards of excellence, EIC Corporation (https://eic-corporation.org/), is committed to build an ecosystem of alternative finance for considerably reduce financial illiteracy, by promoting real financial inclusion of populations. EIC Corporation is currently participating in the ongoing consultations on the bill on alternative and crowdfunding in Ivory Coast and is preparing to deploy its network to the African diaspora in Europe and around the world, through the 50 Vice-Presidents who join the RIDAAF network which is an International Network of Africans Diaspora and Afro Descendants (« Réseau International des Diaspora Africaines et Afro Descendants » in french).

Investments Funds in Africa

Africa has been the scene of an unprecedented investment race in recent years. With billions of dollars, contracts with African countries are multiplying at an impressive speed and investment envelopes keep growing. The potential of Africa is therefore no longer to be proven and arouses all envy. These last 12 months between 2018 and 2019 were marked by a renewed interest of France for Africa in particular with the new policy of President Emmanuel Macron has blown a wind of renewal on the elations French with the mainland. Thus, just a few months after his installation at the Élysée Palace, he organized an initiatory tour in Africa during which he announced a billion euros of investment in African SMEs.

This investment will be distributed as follows:

- 750 million euros for Proparco, AFD subsidiary responsible for the private sector, which will be used to invest in capital in African SMEs over the period 2018-2022
- 120 million euros injected into a second FISEA fund (Investment and Support Fund for Businesses in Africa). FISEA is a fund owned by AFD and advised by PROPARCO which aims to take relatively risky participations in unstable countries and sectors traditionally neglected by investors
- A fourth version of Averroès Finance IV (investment fund), matched with € 60 million by AFD and BPI France. Averroès Finance IV is a fund of funds with a target size of 150 million euros. The objective of Averroès Finance IV is to invest in high-performance funds that operate in separate countries so as to cover the entire African continent
- 33 million euros for the Franco-African fund supplied by AFD and BPI France and managed by AfricInvest
- The great novelty of this investment project is the creation of a financing facility endowed with 15 million euros to be invested exclusively in the field of the digital economy.

Through these major investments, France affirms its confidence in the potential of the African continent and hopes to contribute to its development while generating added value with a multiplier effect of 1 to 10 for these billion investments.

Private Funds

Strategic private investors. Nationals from the African diaspora (physical persons of African descents who are in France) and the "corporate" (companies) that have a direct economic interest, seek to invest in companies wishing to strengthen their core business and develop their presence in their market. By partnering with an investment fund, these investors interested in development possibilities in sub-Saharan Africa can benefit from the presence of a local partner with a regional business network, able to organize the process. identification and facilitate the transaction.

Financial investors look to opportunities that guarantee a considerable return on investment while minimizing their risks.

Funding via Crowdfunding Platforms

Between meso and microfinance and where banks do not invest, growing platform's crowdfunding raise funds to meet the needs as an investment fund raising service in the capital start-ups, such as support for African entrepreneurs who apply the values of a social and solidarity economy as financing for their business or as a crowdfunding platform by donation, dedicated to entrepreneurial projects. The priority areas for action are in most cases higher education, medicine, the environment, renewable energies, agriculture, technology and culture. There is a lack of infrastructures which explains the need of development and investment means in Africa (Iddawela, Lee & Rodríguez-Pose, 2021).

Incubators and Africa

Across French-speaking Africa, incubators are rapidly emerging to support a new generation of young entrepreneurs. Despite their enormous potential, incubators are only one of the many players in a true entrepreneurial. This is why it is increasingly important that incubators - in addition to allocating the necessary resources, services and funding to promising start-ups - provide incubates with a platform to share and transfer knowledge through ecosystem, not only with their peers, but also with investors, research centers, industry experts, on which their businesses will eventually depend.

As in all developing countries, the private sector is the main engine of economic growth. In this context, small and medium-sized enterprises (SMEs) form an essential cog in the creation of jobs and wealth, thus making it possible to improve the quality of life of populations. However, the development of the private sector is faced with many constraints which hinder the establishment of a dense fabric of SMEs: business environment, predominance of the informal sector, poor access to finance. Faced with these structural difficulties, the incubators present in sub-Saharan Africa.are struggling to bring out innovative companies whose dual economic and social objectives induce a higher level of risk and limited or delayed economic profitability. Both incubators and innovative African companies thus experience structural difficulty in accessing funding.

This can be explained by the lack of business incubation institutions, particularly in South Africa to promote an entrepreneurial ecosystem which entails more and more economic growth. African countries do not have employment strategy and platforms to accelerate entrepreneurship in those countries (Lose, 2021). It is within this framework that AFD (French: Agence Française de Développement), BPI (French: Banque Publique d'Investissement), EIB (European Investment Bank) and other international organizations are supporting programs in several sub-Saharan countries to structure and network incubators.

The private sector should join its structures to boost the economic and financial dynamics necessary for the proper development of its incubates. The business incubators creation model and start-up incubators instilled and developed by company Orange is an example to follow.

Funding by Remittances from Diasporas

The blockchains and crypto money become the new financial tools to service these diasporas (Huet, 2021). There is a craze. Indeed, these tools meet the following two needs: the costs of international money transfer and the low percentage of commission on exchange rates. Today, transferring CFA Francs and change in international currencies has a cost of about 15% of the amount transferred. Crypto and fintech space could be a way to disrupt the costly networks that force African transactions through Western institutions, hence African countries could manage their own transaction system without the need of Western institutions (Cirolia, Hall & Nyamnjoh, 2021).

International companies are not mistaken and are investing heavily on the continent in all sectors seeking positions in the rapid regional economic structure. The diasporas play a capital role in the management of financing, management and choice of financial structures as well as in the financial evangelization of local economic actors.

It still remains difficult to approach the continent. But the share's market are to be taken and these virgin lands offer beautiful prospects with admission tickets still low. Among the horizons considered by many entrepreneurs, artificial intelligence (AI) seems to promise many fields of application, allowing financial investors to get back on their feet as this innovation brings hope.

SOLUTIONS AND RECOMMENDATIONS: ARTIFICIAL INTELLIGENCE AS A SOLUTION TO AFRICAN PROBLEMS

Artificial intelligence (AI) consists of using the computer to perform massive amounts of analysis of large volumes of data, whether it be to assess risks, establish diagnoses, or make decisions that are useful to humans. By allowing the machine to learn on its own on the basis of these masses of information, AI dramatically improves logic, offering African countries that have mastered it the opportunity to rise to the rank of developed countries.

One of the first challenges for an AI-oriented strategy on African soil and across the continent concerns the infrastructure needed to work with the Internet, which is not ubiquitous. Only twenty percent of the African population has access to the network. In particular, broadband remains marginal even though it is what allows the use of applications and services requiring AI.

So, for someone in Togo, it is difficult to imagine finding a job in this field or even creating a start-up given the weakness of the Internet network and the possible developments at the entrepreneurial level. This first problem linked to the poverty of the infrastructure causes a brain drain and young Togolese may prefer Tunisia, Morocco, Rwanda or South Africa, countries more connected to the network. The young developers, programmers etc. prefer to finish training or find a job in better equipped countries such as France, Canada, and the United States for example. To remedy this, an opening path is based on AI.

Another problem posed by AI in Africa concerns misconceptions and in particular those which consist in thinking that qualified jobs linked to this field of new technologies are likely to destroy workplaces and thus make jobs scarce in an African demography, which is set to take off in the coming years. Even though AI can be used to monitor the patient's health in more depth, it is difficult, for now at least, to simply get it admitted. AI makes it possible to improve health and to launch early warnings in the event of an epidemic or to offer teleconsultations in areas without doctors. It also helps save forests, build new forms of solidarity and improve the education system.

Through various examples, we will see how Africa can take the turn of AI thanks to start-ups that understand and will understand the challenges of jumping on the train already launched at high speed by Chinese and American station managers. A conclusion showing the difficulties of companies to internationalize from Africa will follow.

At the Origin of the "AI" Project

The AI raises many challenges for Africa. The meetings for digital transformation in Africa (Assises de la Transformation Digitale en Afrique = ADTA) which took place on November 22 and 23, 2018 in Paris indicate that AI should really be implemented in Africa within 1 to 2 years, around 2022-2023.

AI does not require the deployment of special facilities that need significant financial investments. For example, the Internet is a modern marketing choice in Niger according to Akinola and Okunade (2016). Despite its enormous potential, it is still largely underutilized. Yet people between the ages of 18 and 45 form a substantial majority of Internet users in Niger. Although the majority of respondents to the survey conducted by Akinola and Okunade (2016) indicate that they were aware of the availability of marketing and advertising messages, only 4%, the bulk of which are from the working class aged 32 to 45, indicate that they use the Internet in a basic way to search for advertising and marketing messages. Others use the Internet for social media more than for advertising and marketing messages.

Due to the use of the Cloud for online data storage, there is no longer any need to deploy servers for the large volumes of data processed by African companies (La Tribune Afrique, 2018). The notion of « *reach* » must be explained here. It consists in allowing a demographic in full explosion of equitable access to AI, without recourse to installed structures, human or infrastructural. AI must therefore be accessible to as many people as possible. However, the implementation of AI opens up opportunities for the African continent thanks to the emergence of a dynamic and young entrepreneurial structure. Start-ups could thus be created in this direction.

THE PREFERRED FIELDS OF AI

At the Agricultural Level

In the field of agriculture, AI makes it possible to work on soil aridity thanks to sensors measuring aridity which indicate other areas which are in the same case throughout the continent. For example, the structure of a forest is mainly defined by its size and the distribution of its trees per unit. In this context, the diameter is the most important variable, used to model both the measurement of volume and to figure out the understanding of its growth (Miguel et al., 2016). The potential of AI in the context of a Brazilian eucalyptus forest has made it possible. Thanks to the calculation linked to this information, to anticipate the needs due to the highlighting of statistics indicating the precision of the residual distributions and the errors of histograms. The same type of calculation is possible in the African continent regarding trees specific to different countries, threatened by worsening climatic conditions - as it is getting warmer and warmer.

Using earth monitoring techniques, we have been able to retrieve vegetation seasonal trends in an African agricultural region. The data used consists of time-series satellite images, LAI (Leaf Area Index), FAPAR (Fraction of Absorbed Photosynthetically Active Radiation) and chlorophyll collected from the area. For this study, we mainly relied on FAPAR.

The Operating Constraints of This Data Collection Required Several Essential Preprocessing Steps:

First, biophysical retrieval models were generated by means of a trained Machine Learning Regression Algorithm (MLRA) using simulated data coming from radiative transfer models. Among various tested MLRAs, the Variational Heteroscedastic Gaussian Process Regression (VHGPR) was evaluated as the best performing to train the retrieval model. The training and retrieval were conducted in the Automated Radiative Transfer Models Operator (ARTMO) software framework.

A variational heteroscedastic Gaussian process regression (VHGPR) CROSS-VALIDATION training was applied to the model for Leaf area index, fraction of absorbed photosynthetically active Radiation FAPAR retrieval using the automated radiative transfer model's operators MLRAs toolbox (Rivera-Caicedo et al., 2017) cross-validation With K=4, the RTM SCOPE is a soil-vegetation-atmosphere scheme that includes soil-leaf-canopy RTMs along 162 with a micro-meteorological model for simulating turbulent heat exchange, and a plant physiological model for photosynthesis (Van der Tol et al., 2014). This was used to generate a database of reflectance spectra corresponding to a variety of canopy realization that served as input to train the model. The creation of the model was conducted on the ARTMO toolbox. We started by creating a project and chose a machine which could learn the regression algorithm (MLRA) in the retrieval option. At this stage, we introduced the input data and we specified the location of the biophysical parameters that we wanted to retrieve using this model. Secondly, we picked GPRM as the learning algorithm between the large variety available in the ARTMO toolbox, as well as the type of sensor: K-fold (cross validation method) was used for the cross-validation. During the preprocessing stage, we resampled the data, and created the model for nine 'bands' adapted to the images. For model training purposes, we conducted an evaluation for the FAPAR extracting model trained with distinct machine learning algorithms. Namely, the Variational Heteroscedastic Gaussian Process Regression (VHGPR) and the gaussian process regression.

Index Vegetation Product Retrieval Maps (Model Application)

LAI and FAPAR products have been produced from the sentinel-2 imagery obtained from the Copernicus platform (European Union's Earth Observation Program); the retrieval step was conducted on the ARTMO software. We applied the biophysical variables model retrieval directly to the time series, a sample of the LAI and FAPAR product on Figure.2/3.

Subsequently, in view of retrieving the phonological parameters from the obtained vegetation products, a novel times series toolbox as part of the ARTMO framework was used. The framework is called: the "Decomposition and Analysis of Time Series software" (DATimeS) [Figure 4]. DATimeS provides temporal interpolation among other functionalities, with several advanced MLRAs for gap filling, smoothing functions and subsequent calculation of phenology indicators. Various MLRAs were tested for gap filling to reconstruct cloud-free maps of biophysical variables at a step of 10 days.

Figure 2. FAPAR map

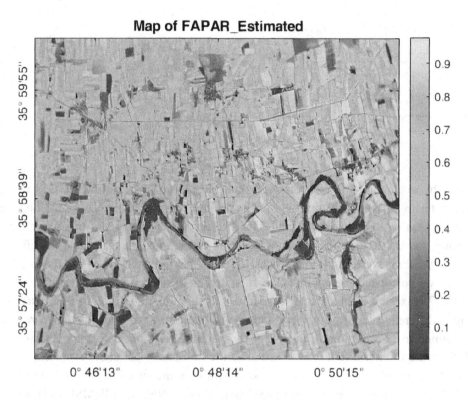

Figure 3. LAI map

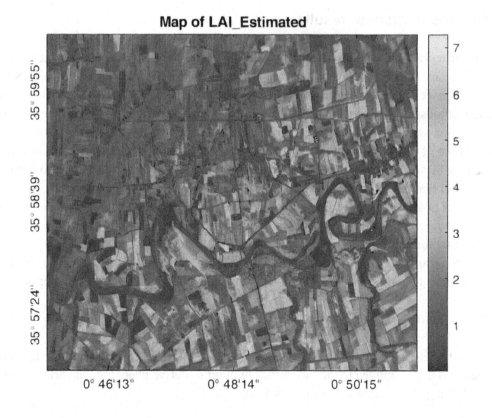

Figure 4. DATimeS interface for Gap filling

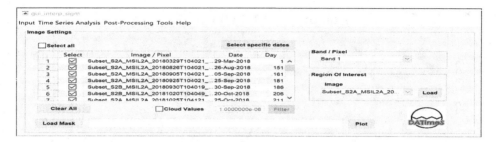

We started by evaluating the efficiency of multiple algorithms (parametric and non-parametric regressions) in terms of reconstruction and performance. The region used was mainly composed of cereal. First, we kept out one map from the FAPAR time series to be used as reference for assessment purposes, being the date 03-01-2019. Next, a selection of the most powerful and therefore, promising interpolation algorithms were run to reconstruct the FAPAR information on the date of the reference image. Finally, we calculated the goodness-of-fit statistics of reference map, versus the reconstructed map for 1,345,075 pixels. It is important to take into consideration that the algorithms used in this evaluation belong to different categories, namely 'parametric' and 'non-parametric', therefore have different modeling assumptions. Consequently, the use of the traditional Akaike Information Criteria (AIC) and Bayesian Information Criteria (BIC) that normalize the number of parameters has not been taken into consideration for the analysis. The statistical assessment measures used in this study are: coefficient of variation R^2, 'root' meaning 'square error RMSE' and 'relative RMSE' (RRMSE [%]). An overview of the validation results and processing time is provided in Table 1.

The Map Reconstruction Results

The error estimates (RMSE, RRMSE) which provide a description of the algorithms' image reconstruction capability. The most accurate reconstruction was obtained with GPR with a relative error of 8.54% and a R^2 of 0.9048. The second-best reconstruction was obtained with the next interpolation. The following top-performing methods are KRR and then BAGTREE; the rest of the methods perform substantially lower.

A flowless reconstruction is nearly impossible due to factors at the different stages of acquisition and manipulation of data (Atkinson, 2012). A remark hereby is that a perfect reconstruction is virtually impossible to achieve, not only due to the sources of noisiness in original data, but also because of the smoothing effect that the fitting methods have on the original series (M. Atkinson, 2012).

The recorded processing time indicates that the Fourier and the conventional interpolation methods are extremely fast; processing the sub-set only took about half a minute. Conversely, the accurate sigmoid took significantly longer, as it is about one thousand times slower.

Taking both accuracy and processing speed into account, GPR and spline interpolations turn out to be the most efficient interpolators, with GPR more accurate but spline faster by a factor of 70.

Phenology Indication

Aiming to study the seasonal pattern in vegetation variation, DATimeS was used. Firstly, a region of interest was created and applied to the time series in order to derive phenological variables such as the start and end of a growing season, see Figures 5-10.

Table 1. Goodness-of-fit statistics and processing time for the reference vs. FAPAR- reconstructed map as produced by the gap-filling methods.1,345,075 pixels

Methods	ME	MEA	RMSE [%]	RELRMSE	R	R2	NSE Time
ARES	-0.1584	0.1819	0.2280	90.2142	0.7419	0.5504	-1.0496
BAGTREE	0.0122	0.1121	0.1444	34.0513	0.8142	0.6630	0.2591
GPR	-0.0413	0.0642	0.0854	23.0634	0.9512	0.9048	0.8634
KNRR	-0.0028	0.1084	0.1500	36.6954	0.7895	0.6233	0.4911
KRR	-0.0362	0.0711	0.1219	32.4620	0.8879	0.7884	0.7595
Whittaker	0.1380	0.3004	0.4540	82.5986	0.6772	0.4585	0.3401
Fourier1	0.2402	0.3750	0.5231	80.2508	0.6005	0.3606	0.1530
Fourier2	0.2419	0.3692	0.5119	78.3240	0.6083	0.3700	0.1523
Fourier3	0.2120	0.3619	0.5162	82.7608	0.6206	0.3852	0.2122
Next	-0.0062	0.0575	0.0824	20.3285	0.9411	0.8856	0.8759
Polyfit	-0.0399	0.1610	0.1966	52.8818	0.6078	0.3694	-0.7288
Previous	-0.0967	0.1939	0.2543	80.7123	0.6110	0.3734	0.1985
Spline	-0.0373	0.0678	0.2019	53.9221	0.7562	0.5719	0.5546

Figure 5. Region of interest

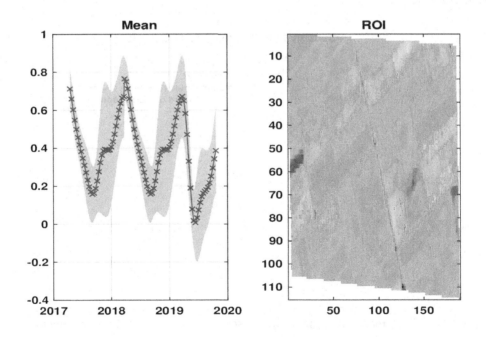

Figure 6. Season amplitude (Season 1)

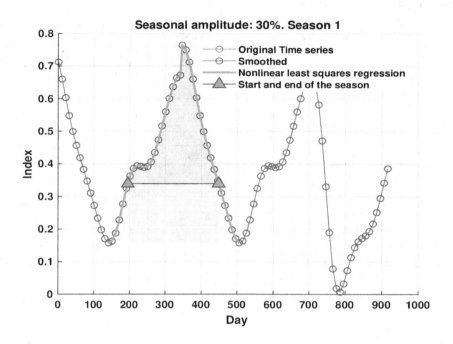

Figure 7. Season amplitude (Season 2)

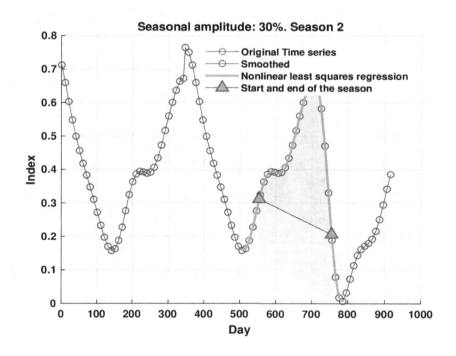

Figure 8. Start of the season

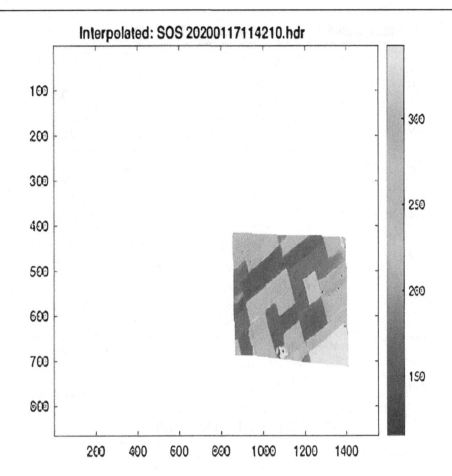

As a final step, we have a preview of the vegetation state at the start of the season, the end of the season and when it is at a maximum value. In the fight against climate change, monitoring the health of ecosystems can be of crucial importance in a context of sustainable development and increasing human pressure on nature (Plamondon Emond, Roulot-Ganzmann and Girouard, 2019). AI makes it possible to develop machine learning algorithms intended to exploit data from the environmental genome of biodiversity and thus to find solutions and develop methods to heal a sick environment. As part of the implementation of the AI environment and of climate change, predictive algorithms used to save time, money and effectiveness by knowing such a chemical composition in real time a technique that can also be used in the water industry or in the use of obsolete equipment for one industry but which can be useful for another.

AI also makes it possible to optimize power grids with multiple energy sources by offering users the answer to whether they are using energy supplied by a diesel power plant, that generated by a wind turbine or that stored in reserves., which would be useful in remote areas... Data analysis algorithms would help in decision making. AI makes it possible to take good decisions in real time on the basis of constraints such as the use of renewable energies which continuously fluctuates according to the weather. AI is also used to protect endangered species.

Figure 9. Maximum value

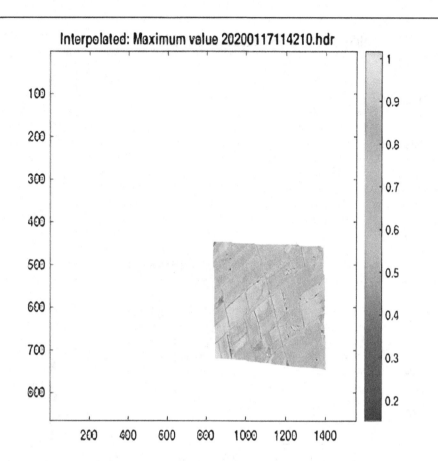

Fight Against Poaching

By inserting an object, the size of a large battery into the rhino horn, players in the world of information technology such as Cisco, Google or Microsoft, follow the movements of these animals and thus help protect them from poaching, knowing that they are on the verge of extinction (Sciences et Avenir, 2019). This tag makes it possible to follow the animal, to know when it is approaching a potentially dangerous area and to warn the guards in charge of its protection. Associated with other sensors, the geolocation of the animal in real time promotes the speed of action of intervention teams. The use of specific radio protocols offers more guarantees in terms of security than GPS collars which are much too heavy and therefore require more energy than the deployment of connected objects linked to AI. The objective is also to put online user guides that are free to access. Promoting access to knowledge is also one of the goals that AI can easily achieve.

The preservation of ecosystems and sustainable development in African states over vast territories requires the use of new technologies. AI and the Internet of Things (IoT) are here at the service of the conservation of African heritage. Whether it is to fight against poaching, to preserve ecosystems and biodiversity or to limit conflicts between humans and wild animals, IoT and AI help to restore the image of the African continent on its diversity.

Figure 10. End of the season

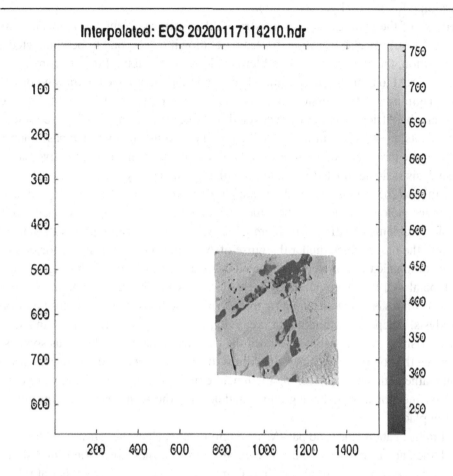

The artificial 3D vision associated to the progress of morphometry and statistics prevents stray dog attacks unfairly attributed to wild predators causing them persecution. On the contrary, this system makes it possible to identify the footprints left by poachers and their dogs to give more room to justice. Side connected objects, cameras serving as a trap operating hours, operating in the trunks of the trees, they are used to detect the passage of animals otherwise difficult to study as wolf packs where other animals especially stealth... Acoustic or infrared sensors, motion detectors, trackers, drones, at the same time help provide the animal protectors with useful information enabling them to make decisions. One of the difficulties of these solutions lies in the fact that the abundance of ideas generated by developers and the constraints in the field, associated with limited resources and poorly or unskilled personnel, represent a major obstacle to the deployment of these technologies. However, the African reserves are for the most part underfunded.

In the Education Sector

In the education and training sector, AI allows better monitoring of students which results in the optimization of classes for potential in countries where the lack of public funding leads to overcrowding.

Recognized by the Moroccan state as the fourth industrial revolution, AI will help increase education and lifelong training for adults (Lyonnel, 2018).

Considered one of the great challenges in Africa, AI is seen as an engine of social transformation and economic growth, provided that the infrastructure allowing everyone to be connected does exist. Along with education, the unemployment problem could also, through AI be overcome. The objective may therefore be for AI to promote more equitable education, to guarantee the training of new forms of profession by imagining what professions are expected in the future and to prevent data security. The use of its own data by Africa when they are coveted by large American and Chinese multinationals in particular, represents an objective in itself for the continent to use its own databases and while *data analysts* are still quite rare. The hope is then based on machine learning and predictive models that can process data analysis in an automated way... to do without a data analyst.

Turok's postulate (2016) is based on the principle that Africa must become a producer and not a consumer of the technologies it needs to become self-reliant and a developed country. To do so, fight against the major problems of Africa which are poverty, disease, corruption or war, mathematics and science constitute the bases which, under the guise of AI, will serve as an engine for this momentum. Computers, telecommunications systems, advanced medical technologies are the engines of commerce, prosperity and social well-being provided they are owned by users. The author explains that from elementary school, mathematics is too often taught by rote learning methods. This promotes memorization, but not critical analysis, independent thinking or creativity, necessary for mathematics and science. However, companies wishing to work using AI recruit the best mathematics graduates as soon as they leave university to create the complex necessary algorithms for this AI. Therefore, to create a bridge between young African mathematicians - by teaching them mathematics perhaps in another way so that they can start their own business or work in large groups - and develop the AI necessary for the continent, plans need to be put in place.

Africa has brains in abundance and pan-African initiatives such as the AIMS which means "African Institute for Mathematical Sciences" (https://www.aims.ac.za/), may allow the establishment of such bridges. Indeed, the heterogeneity of classes in different African countries, whether at the level of languages, ethnicities, religions, offers this diversity necessary for creativity and thus transcends differences, a source of division in the past. An example is provided by the author with Angelina Lutambi born in the Dodoma region of Tanzania where HIV has killed a large share of the population. Passionate about mathematics, Angelina financed her studies by selling cold drinks with her siblings. A scholarship enabled her to study at the University of Dar Es-Salam and then she arrived at AIMS South Africa in 2004. She was able to obtain a doctorate in epidemiology in Switzerland and now heads the Ifakara Health Institute in Tanzania. It was there that she designed mathematical, statistical and computer models to inform and advise on public health decision-making on HIV, tuberculosis and other serious diseases. The young people resulting from this kind of initiative such as AIMS find the conditions allowing them to evolve, to learn to write and to create computational models, necessary to find solutions, whether it is about disease as fight against the Ebola crisis or any other field requiring important mathematical calculations. This is what happened with this other example, in Ethiopia. A young Ethiopian woman has managed to become a renowned scientist through the use of new technologies. Her objective: to help her country in the mapping of rivers to achieve a national irrigation plan. For this, it is important to prevent Africa from the total dependence to the giants of the Internet and a new form of colonization otherwise called "cyber colonization".

These AIMS centers are not just places of training for brilliant young Africans of the continent. They are also used to bring back citizens who have studied abroad. Mathematics, and science in general, remain the main tool that can be used by humanity, helping to solve societal problems and improve everyday life. It is in this sense that the Next Einstein Forum (https://nef.org/) will welcome in its next event in 2020 in Nairobi, Kenya, mathematicians from all backgrounds, in addition to Africa.

Following the forum on AI in Africa organized by UNESCO in Benguerir, Morocco on December 12 and 13, 2018, the newspaper "Le Monde" published an article on the possible drifts between the Internet giants represented by the Americans (GAFAM - Google Amazon Facebook Apple and Microsoft), on the African continent and the Chinese (Baidu Huawei Alibaba Tencent and Xiaomi). The main pitfall to be avoided would consist in a stranglehold by these foreigners on African data and an offer unsuited to the specific needs and responses required in Africa (Baumard Maryline, 2018).

ZOOM on China: What happens there could happen in Africa, as the Chinese are settling there more and more - In his article, Colinet (2019) interviews novelist Bernard Minier and explains to us after going to Hong Kong, that *"China has become a world leader in research and development, it files more patents than the United States: it is the leading supplier of scientific publications, the leading holder of digital data because its huge population is also the most connected in the world and it has given up on its privacy».* In case some Chinese are tempted to escape the system, the Communist Party has planned everything by taking control of the Internet and banning Facebook. In the health field, the deployment of AI, genetic manipulation and the selection of embryos after sequencing are gradually being considered as the norm. In 10 or 20 years, thanks to this selection of embryos, the intellectual average of the Chinese population will be higher than that of Europeans. The Chinese are closely followed by the Russians, the Israelis, and all are far ahead of France. As Minier explains, *" it's mysterious, it's anxiety-provoking, it's a world that has interwoven the digital and the living, which advocates transparency and which works in secrecy, which explodes the notion of privacy ".*

THERE IS AN INTERNATIONALIZATION OF AFRICAN SMES FACTORS

African companies have considerably increased their internationalization activities over the past twenty years. Thanks to Foreign Direct Investment (FDI), African companies are expanding, representing serious competitors to foreign multinationals. Large African companies are not the only economic players in Africa, in fact most of this reality is provided by SMEs. Internationalization is the only promising avenue for growth in sub-Saharan Africa (Fafchamps et al., 2008). The internationalization of companies from emerging countries is the result of several combinations of determinants such as those related to industry or sectoral factors, those linked to the resources and capacities of the company or factors related to the company and finally factors identified institutionally, according to Schmidt and Hansen (2017). The internationalization and establishment patterns of companies in developing countries appear to be linked to institutional and environmental factors in the country of origin and the host market (Omokaro-Romanus et al., 2018). Government and institution are becoming key determinants of the internationalization of African SMEs, hence the important role of favorable regulations as well as infrastructural and institutional similarities between countries of origin and host countries. Government supports are also important factors for the internationalization of SMEs (reduction of export costs, facilitation of business relationships) according to Matenge (2011). A common language with international partners and a common ethnic identity can be useful in overcoming risks in developed markets. The language promotes understanding of the labor laws and business ethics of the host market (Omokaro-Romanus et al., 2018). Trade liberalization and technological development in the field of telecommunications, Internet in particular, are also necessary for the development of networks and business opportunities (Matenge, 2011). This helps to facilitate access to customers, distributors, partners and suppliers internationally.

CONCLUSION

Problems related to political instability, lack of infrastructure, high banking fees and costs, lack of finance and technology, trade restrictions and transportation costs, excessive bureaucracy and corruption including level of customs officers of African countries, which added to each other, do not necessarily help an African SME to internationalize. Sectorial or industrial factors such as local competition limit the internationalization of companies to develop in other markets. The characteristics of the markets and the attractiveness of the location can also be decisive in an African SME internationalization strategy. Internal or resource factors, along with factors linked to the firm (resources and organizational capacities) and factors linked to the managerial resources of the company, must also be considered in an internationalization strategy. Small businesses seem to have more difficulty internationalizing compared to large businesses. Conversely, age, which means "more experience", seems an asset although young companies are more proactive, flexible and aggressive in foreign markets already in place. Inter-company relations or belonging to networks make it possible to increase the internationalization of African companies through more or less formal relations.

The reputation, technological progress, the know-how of the company, the knowledge of the market and distinctive capacities such as the ability to operate in a weak and unstable institutional environment (Matenge, 2011), constitute other points favorable to the process. Internationalization of small businesses on the African continent. Added to this is the profile, the strategic intention and the entrepreneurial culture of the leaders which must also be taken into consideration in order to internationalize an African SME.

The work of Akotch and Munyoki (2018) converges on these results and shows by wanting to establish the determinants of growth in the sector of the banking industry in Kenya, that the size of the company, its profitability, the development of its products, market penetration, but also innovation and technology, significantly increased the banking industry in Kenya. Profitability affects growth in the banking industry sector and contributes significantly to this growth. Market development is a significant determinant of this growth in the banking industry sector. Through the development of its markets, banks create new markets, adopting a diversification favorable to a growth strategy at the same time as the creation of new products for existing markets. Market penetration significantly enhances this growth in the banking industry in Kenya therefore market penetration is a significant determinant of growth for companies that are already entering both local and existing foreign markets. Thus, they increase their existing market shares and easily respond to new market opportunities. But it is the innovation and technology of banks that allows them to gain competitive advantages, just as they can improve results vis-à-vis non-innovative or less innovative companies in terms of growth. However, banks should focus on their needs and use the right technology and the right innovation to achieve their goals rather than investing in innovation and technology because other banks have done so.

FUTURE RESEARCH DIRECTIONS

Too slow market penetration is also proving to be another major problem hindering the successful progress of the banking industry in Kenya. Governments must therefore take the right steps to ensure fair competition in the banking industry in Kenya and thus promote market penetration by respecting banks. Investments in research to understand changing trends in consumer needs are necessary for the development of their products. Banks should also invest in market growth to improve the size of their structure and consequently increase their turnover. Specifically, if efforts are made to get data from the African continent, Africans may use all the resources and potential of the AI which would have this done for them.

Conflict of Interests

The authors have not declared any conflict of interests.

ACKNOWLEDGMENT

The authors deeply thank Bernard Attali and Marc Bittoun from Gouvernance & Valeurs, 27-29 rue Raffet - 75016 Paris, for their great discussion on entrepreneurship during the International Forum organized by the Marketing Maghrebin Association, the 7-8th of March, 2019, in Hammamet, Tunisia.

REFERENCES

Adomako, S., Amankwah-Amoah, J., Tarba, S. Y., & Khan, Z. (2021). Perceived corruption, business process digitization, and SMEs' degree of internationalization in sub-Saharan Africa. *Journal of Business Research, 123*, 196–207. doi:10.1016/j.jbusres.2020.09.065

Africanews. (2018). *Morocco hosts international forum on artificial intelligence in Africa.* https://www.africanews.com/2018/12/19/morocco-hosts-international-forum-on-artificial-intelligence-in-africa/

Akinola, O. O., & Okunade, D. O. (2016). Evaluating the use of internet as a medium for marketing and advertising messages in Nigeria. *African Journal of Marketing Management, 8*(2), 12–19. doi:10.5897/AJMM2015.0459

Akotch, W. F., & Munyoki, J. M. (2018). Determinants of growth in the banking industry in Kenya. *African Journal of Marketing Management, 8*(1), 1–11.

Asongu, S. A., Nnanna, J., & Tchamyou, V. S. (2021). Finance, Institutions, and Private Investment in Africa. *Politics & Policy, 49*(2), 309–351. doi:10.1111/polp.12395

Atkinson, P. M., Jeganathan, C., Dash, J., & Atzberger, C. (2012). Inter-comparison of four models for smoothing satellite sensor time-series data to estimate vegetation phenology. *Remote Sensing of Environment, 123*, 400–417. doi:10.1016/j.rse.2012.04.001

Baumard, M. (2018). Artificial intelligence: Africa facing the giants of the Net. *Le Monde.* https://www.lemonde.fr/afrique/article/2018/12/17/intelligence-artificielle-l-afrique-face-aux-geants-du-net_5398882_3212.html

Cirolia, L. R., Hall, S., & Nyamnjoh, H. (2022). Remittance micro-worlds and migrant infrastructure: Circulations, disruptions, and the movement of money. *Transactions of the Institute of British Geographers, 47*(1), 63–76. doi:10.1111/tran.12467

Colinet, C. (2019). *Artificial intelligence: Bernard Minier reveals what China has in store for us*. https://www.lanouvellerepublique.fr/a-la-une/intelligence-artificielle-bernard-minier-devoile-ce-que-la-chine-nous-reserve

Dorasamy, N., & Fagbadebo, O. (Eds.). (2021). *Public Procurement, Corruption and the Crisis of Governance in Africa*. Palgrave Macmillan. doi:10.1007/978-3-030-63857-3

Fafchamps, M., El Hamine, S., & Zeufack, A. (2008). Learning to export: Evidence from Moroccan manufacturing. *Journal of African Economies*, *17*(2), 305–355. doi:10.1093/jae/ejm008

Gunessee, S., & Hu, S. (2021). Chinese cross-border mergers and acquisitions in the developing world: Is Africa unique? *Thunderbird International Business Review*, *63*(1), 27–41. doi:10.1002/tie.22169

Huet, J. (2021). *Digital in Africa*. Pearson.

Iddawela, Y., Lee, N., & Rodríguez-Pose, A. (2021). Quality of sub-national government and regional development in Africa. *The Journal of Development Studies*, *57*(8), 1282–1302. doi:10.1080/0022038 8.2021.1873286

Lose, T. (2021). Institutionalised business incubation: A frontier for accelerating entrepreneurship in African countries. *Academy of Entrepreneurship Journal*, *27*, 1–10.

Matenge, T. (2011). Small Firm Internationalization-A developing country perspective. *International Journal of Business Administration*, *2*(4), 103. doi:10.5430/ijba.v2n4p103

Michaelowa, A., Hoch, S., Weber, A. K., Kassaye, R., & Hailu, T. (2021). Mobilising private climate finance for sustainable energy access and climate change mitigation in Sub-Saharan Africa. *Climate Policy*, *21*(1), 47–62. doi:10.1080/14693062.2020.1796568

Miguel, E. P., & Concei, Ã. (2016). Artificial intelligence tools in predicting the volume of trees within a forest stand. *African Journal of Agricultural Research*, *11*(21), 1914–1923. doi:10.5897/AJAR2016.11015

Omokaro-Romanus, C., Anchor, J. R., & Konara, P. (2019). The internationalization of Nigerian firms: Motivations and location patterns. *Thunderbird International Business Review*, *61*(1), 75–88. doi:10.1002/tie.21962

Plamondon, E. E., Roulot-Ganzmann, H., & Girouard, C. (2019). L'IA dans la lutte contre les changements climatiques. *Le Devoir*. https://www.ledevoir.com/societe/science/550291/l-ia-dans-la-lutte-contre-les-changements-climatiques

Public Table. (2019). *Data can produce amazing visualizations*. https://public.tableau.com/fr-fr/s/. Interactive map

Rivera-Caicedo, J. P., Verrelst, J., Muñoz-Marí, J., Camps-Valls, G., & Moreno, J. (2017). Hyperspectral dimensionality reduction for biophysical variable statistical retrieval. *ISPRS Journal of Photogrammetry and Remote Sensing*, *132*, 88–101. doi:10.1016/j.isprsjprs.2017.08.012

Schmidt, A., & Hansen, M. W. (2017). Internationalization Strategies of African Firms: A Survey of 210 Food Processing Firms from Tanzania, Kenya and Zambia. Academic Press.

Sciences et Avenir. (2019). When new technologies help fight against poaching. *Sciences et Avenir with Reuters*. https://www.sciencesetavenir.fr/animaux/biodiversite/la-technologies-aide-a-lutter-contre-le-braconnage_130501

Severino, J. M., & Hajdenberg, J. (2016). *Entreprenante Afrique*. Odile Jacob.

Shillington, K. (1995). *History of Africa* (1st ed.). Palgrave.

The Africa Tribune. (2018). *Artificial intelligence: Key to profound changes in Africa, AI creates as many opportunities as challenges*. https://afrique.latribune.fr/africa-tech/2018-12-08/intelligence-artificielle-cle-de-changements-profonds-en-afrique-l-ia-cree-autant-d-opportunites-que-de-defis-800188.html

Turok, N. (2016). Mathematics and science are essential to develop Africa. *The Conversation*. https://theconversation.com/mathematiques-et-sciences-sont-essential-to-develop-africa-55486

Zoubeyda, M. (2019). *The factors of internationalization of African SMEs: case of Ivorian SMEs*. Paper presented at the 9th International Conference ATLAS AFMI (Association Francophone de Management International), Friborg, Switzerland.

ADDITIONAL READING

Batista, T. S., Teodoro, L. P. R., Azevedo, G. B. D., Azevedo, G. T. D. O. S., Poersch, N. L., Borges, M. V. V., & Teodoro, P. E. (2022). Artificial neural networks and non-linear regression for quantifying the wood volume in eucalyptus species. *Southern Forests*, *84*(1), 1–7. doi:10.2989/20702620.2021.1976604

Berhanu, B., Bisrat, E., Gil, Y., Khider, D., Osorio, M., Ratnakar, V., & Vargas, H. (2022). *An AI Approach to Integrating Climate*. Hydrology, and Agriculture Models.

Borges, M. V. V., de Oliveira Garcia, J., Batista, T. S., Silva, A. N. M., Baio, F. H. R., da Silva, C. A. Jr, ... Teodoro, P. E. (2022). High-throughput phenotyping of two plant-size traits of Eucalyptus species using neural networks. *Journal of Forestry Research*, *33*(2), 591–599. doi:10.100711676-021-01360-6

Cedric, L. S., Adoni, W. Y. H., Aworka, R., Zoueu, J. T., Mutombo, F. K., Krichen, M., & Kimpolo, C. L. M. (2022). Crops Yield Prediction Based on Machine Learning Models: Case of West African Countries. *Smart Agricultural Technology*, 100049.

Güner, Ş. T., Diamantopoulou, M. J., Poudel, K. P., Çömez, A., & Özçelik, R. (2022). Employing artificial neural network for effective biomass prediction: An alternative approach. *Computers and Electronics in Agriculture*, *192*, 106596. doi:10.1016/j.compag.2021.106596

Jahani, A., & Saffariha, M. (2022). Tree failure prediction model (TFPM): Machine learning techniques comparison in failure hazard assessment of Platanus orientalis in urban forestry. *Natural Hazards*, *110*(2), 881–898. doi:10.100711069-021-04972-7

Job, I., Essien, E. N., & Ododo, E. (2022). A Review Application of Machine Learning in Agriculture Supply Chain to Improve Food and Agriculture Industry. *Asia-Africa Journal of Agriculture*, *1*, 66–78.

Karwitha, M., Wyche, S., Oslon, J., & Kimurto, P. (2022, April). Addressing the Agricultural Labor Burden in Kenya: Evaluating Using Human-Centered Design to Improve Farmers' Agricultural Tools. *Egerton University International Conference*.

Molinaro, M., & Orzes, G. (2022). From forest to finished products: The contribution of Industry 4.0 technologies to the wood sector. *Computers in Industry*, *138*, 103637. doi:10.1016/j.compind.2022.103637

KEY TERMS AND DEFINITIONS

Blockchains: A blockchain is a growing list of records, called blocks, that are linked together using cryptography. Each block contains a cryptographic hash of the previous block, a timestamp, and transaction data (generally represented as a Merkle tree). The timestamp proves that the transaction data existed when the block was published to get into its hash. As blocks each contain information about the block previous to it, they form a chain, with each additional block reinforcing the ones before it. Therefore, blockchains are resistant to modification of their data because once recorded, the data in any given block cannot be altered retroactively without altering all subsequent blocks.

Crowdfunding: Crowdfunding is the practice of funding a project or venture by raising money from a large number of people, in modern times typically via the Internet. It is a form of crowdsourcing and alternative finance. In 2015, over US$34 billion were raised worldwide by crowdfunding.

Crypto Money (or Cryptocurrency): A cryptocurrency, crypto-currency, or crypto is a digital currency designed to work as a medium of exchange through a computer network that is not reliant on any central authority, such as a government or bank, to uphold or maintain it.

Diaspora: It's the dispersion or spread of any people from their original homeland. African diaspora represent physical persons of African descents who are in France.

Earth Monitoring Techniques: Artificial intelligence (AI) is playing an increasingly important part in our daily lives, whether it is providing our personalized social media feeds, online shopping, or streaming movie suggestions, or even the mapping apps that route us around traffic jams. On a bigger scale, AI is already having a major impact on healthcare, finance, farming and many other sectors and its influence is predicted to expand rapidly in the coming years. One area where there is considerable untapped potential for AI is in the field of Earth observation through Earth Monitoring Techniques that can be used to help manage large datasets, find new insights in data, and generate new products and services.

FabLab: Fabrication laboratory is a small-scale workshop offering (personal) digital fabrication. A fab lab is typically equipped with an array of flexible computer-controlled tools that cover several different length scales and various materials, with the aim to make "almost anything". This includes technology-enabled products generally perceived as limited to mass production.

FAPAR (Fraction of Absorbed Photosynthetically Active Radiation): The fraction of absorbed photosynthetically active radiation (FAPAR, sometimes also noted fAPAR or fPAR) is the fraction of the incoming solar radiation in the photosynthetically active radiation spectral region that is absorbed by a photosynthetic organism, typically describing the light absorption across an integrated plant canopy.

Leaf Area Index (LAI): It is a dimensionless quantity that characterizes plant canopies. It is defined as the one-sided green leaf area per unit ground surface area (LAI = leaf area / ground area, m2 / m2) in broadleaf canopies. In conifers, three definitions for LAI have been used: Half of the total needle surface area per unit ground surface area, projected (or one-sided, in accordance the definition for broadleaf canopies) needle area per unit ground area, total needle surface area per unit ground area.

Section 3
Autonomous Learning Systems

Data Science for Industry 4.0

Indraneel Dabhade

https://orcid.org/0000-0002-2988-890X

O Automation, India

INTRODUCTION

Minsky defines *artificial intelligence* as "the science of making machines do things that would require intelligence if done by [people]" (Minsky, 1969). "...any software with as much as an 'if statement' can be considered a form of narrow Artificial Intelligence" (Yampolskiy & Spellchecker, 2016). The learning systems modeled are a result of our understanding of learning theories. The most prominent of these systems are impressed with an error reduction objective. This chapter tries to highlight the effects of these intelligent systems in commercial applications. The sections included in this article are learning systems, big computing, semantics, supply chain, manufacturing, corporation, information security, quantum computing, and autonomous systems. The chapter also sheds light on the safety, ethics, and limitations of applying advanced learning techniques to self-governed systems.

LEARNING MACHINES

Thinking is a direct product of consciousness levels. Dehaene et al. (2017) distinguish conscious computation into two crucial dimensions. They are C1: global availability of relevant information and C2: a cognitive system that self-monitors. The current state of machine learning algorithms encompasses both these dimensions. The most complex learning challenges lie in modeling systems replicative of human emotions. Fear is one such emotion, difficult to capture holistically with static rules. Machines capable of learning fear display better autonomous behavior (Hutson, 2019). The safest and most reliable systems are those that showcase zero errors.

One of the earliest contributors to experimental machine learning, Arthur Samuel, while devising procedures for a machine to play checkers, introduced the concepts of 'rote learning' and 'learning by generalization' (Samuel, 1959). Donald Michie expounded on this idea with the 'Parable of Self-Improvement,' which states '...rarely occurring problems will gravitate to the bottom and frequently occurring problems to the top' (Michie, 1968). Michie asserts:

- that the apparatus of evaluation associated with any function shall comprise a "rule part" (computational procedure) and a "rote part" (lookup table);
- that evaluation in the computer shall on each given occasion proceed whether by rule, or by rote, or by a blend of the two, solely as dictated by the expediency of the moment;
- that the rule versus rote decisions shall be handled by the machine behind the scenes; and
- that various kinds of interaction be permitted to occur between the rule part and the rote part.

DOI: 10.4018/978-1-7998-9220-5.ch004

Copyright © 2023, IGI Global. Copying or distributing in print or electronic forms without written permission of IGI Global is prohibited.

Today, machine learning algorithms have developed to handle higher statistical complexity. Non-monotonicity (i.e., rejection and reform of prior decisions) and the ability to work on high-dimensional data have added power to the learning models.

BIG COMPUTING

Jim Gray's seminal work on data processing in the '90s laid the foundation for high-speed access to data residing on nodes. In his 2007 lecture to the Computer Science and Technology Board of the National Research Council, he introduced the fourth research paradigm of 'Data-Intensive Science' to the existing three (positivism/postpositivism; interpretivism/constructivism; and critical theory), thus defining 'eScience' as the synthesis of technology and science. 'GrayWulf' set an example for other applications, including CERN's Large Hadron Collider (LHC), Virtual Observatory (VO) for astronomical data, and the National Center for Biotechnology Information (NCBI) in genomics (Szalay A. S., 2009).

Users, capitalizing on the interconnected nature of global information networks, push to scale computational processes and storage resources. Redundancy, fault tolerance, security, and speed are features that add trust and confidence to this adoption. A hurdle in running complex algorithms, including those of nonlinear optimizations, is a time-based constraint. Problems, including getting stuck at a local minimum of a solution landscape, handle suboptimal solutions. Improved cloud computing infrastructure reduces the computation expense for finding better solutions to everyday problems. To measure big data, Laney (2001) introduced the 3Vs.

Volume: Volume of the data.
Velocity: Data transfer speed.
Variety: Type of data handled.

In addition, are

Veracity (added by IBM): Quality of the data.
Variability (added by SAS): Change in data loads.
Value (added by Oracle): Value offered by the data.

While industry standards may exist for data communication, there is a need for a solid standard to exchange the science and information collected from the data. Wirth & Hipp (2000) opened the efforts to establish such a standard by introducing the CRoss Industry Standard Processing for Data Mining (CRISP-DM).

Industry wise, a tradeoff between real-time and batch processing has introduced several big data platforms, including Pentaho (suitable for batch processing) and SQLstream s-Server (suitable for real-time processing) (Philip Chen & Zhang, 2014). They inducted seven principles for designing big data systems.

Principle 1: Good architectures and frameworks are necessary and on the top priority.
Principle 2: Support a variety of analytical methods.
Principle 3: No size fits all.
Principle 4: Bring the analysis to data.
Principle 5: Processing must be distributable for in-memory computation.

Principle 6: Data storage must be distributable for in-memory storage.

Principle 7: Coordination is needed between processing and data units.

SECURITY DATA SCIENCE

The security community benefits from the use of data science tools. Developing strategies based on probabilistic models have primarily been their theme. Intelligence data collected through direct and indirect sources helps locate terrorists and criminals. Bad actors showcase anomalous behavior. Learning systems that detect signs of such behavior alert authorities. These applications range from physical security to intelligent digital firewalls.

The application of Generative Adversarial Networks (GANS) to produce realistic fake images and videos has opened new doors for identity theft. The AI world's race between good and evil has created pathways for budding entrepreneurs to monetize.

Semantics

O. W. Holmes Jr. states, 'A word is not a crystal, transparent and unchanged; it is the skin of a living thought...' The role of semantic learning grows with increased text. A machine to generate rules based on symbols (text characters) needs access to prior knowledge. In a parable, a person with no knowledge of the Chinese language is placed in a room with a basket full of Chinese characters. His task is to follow a rule book and match characters. While he may perform the task, does he understand the rule behind the semantics and thus make sense of the joined characters? The process limits machine understanding to known symbolism (Searle, 1990). Big data with advanced learning systems widens the selection of intelligent responses generated for static symbolic states. Chatbots, voice recognition software and real-time translators are harnessing the power of advances in natural language processing.

Law

Edward H. Levi defines *law* as a 'moving classification system' (Levi, 1948). Law is a 'holistic entity on the verge of evolving into a codified computer system of legal services...that will evolve toward [the] ideal system...' (Gray, 1997). The goal of this system is to protect and promote liberties and rights. An intelligent system interprets the law in a way that observes this goal. Legal reasoning is a relatively unknown area of applying machine learning. A. L. Gardner provides three reasons for applying artificial intelligence in law (Gardner, 1987).

1. The law has a tradition of examining its reasoning process.
2. Legal reasoning is stylized.
3. Much of the legal knowledge is readily accessible and relatively well structured, codified, and indexed.

Learning systems can structure rules with logical symbolism and further implement argument creation backed with nonmonotonic reasoning. *Legal arguments* are essentially logical debates assisted with prior knowledge and reasoning.

TAXMAN is an example of the early adoption of artificial intelligence in legal matters (corporate reorganization law). The model behind the tool relies on Semantic Information Processing, a field introduced by Marvin Minsky, to generate syntactic and sematic structures (McCarty, 1977). Using TAXMAN as a tool, McCarty describes a fictitious case of a New Jersey corporation trying to incorporate in Delaware. The options posed to the decision system include legitimate actions and other 'devious forms of conveyance masquerading as a corporate reorganization.' This example is an illustration of the complexity involved in making financially beneficial yet lawful choices. The challenge of considering law as interpretation in intelligent machines is understanding the context and semantic structures of the argument. More the number of interpretations, the more the learning. Intelligence of a learned machine is the test of identifying the interpretation.

An intelligent legal system collects facts, interprets the law, and, if required, may simulate a debate. IBM® had experimented with an autonomous debating system, code-named 'Project Debater.' The goal was to simulate a debate between a machine, implementing machine learning techniques, and a human. The model included four modules addressing the four challenges posed to a learned system: argument mining (search for data), argument knowledge base (capture commonalities and differences between arguments), argument rebuttal (syntactic modeling of the argument, and generating a rebuttal based on 'mined text evidence' queried from a database), and finally debate construction (rule-based system integrating cluster analysis and content generation) (Slonim et al., 2021). We classify *natural language processing* tasks as 'narrow AI,' Project Debater was classified as 'composite AI,' which replicates broader human cognitive activities. Usage of personal digital assistants and intelligent controls are examples of syntactic learning of big data.

Intellectual Property

The intellectual property industry is another law domain that benefits from advanced semantic learning models. Identifying copyright infringements, plagiarisms, and even patent violations have become accessible with a vast amount of data captured and shared publicly. Learning models assist in deeper text comparison by changing from matching words to match ideas. Such applications filter and improve the quality of public knowledge, embedding trust in the entire process of knowledge discovery.

Supply Chain

Learning algorithms, with their ability to formulate rules and patterns, have found applications in the supply chain industry. Traditionally, forecasts in the supply chain industry rely on age-old techniques comprising moving averages and trend analysis. The quality of forecasts determines the nature of lean operations. Carbonneau et al. (2008) explore the application of machine learning techniques to demand forecasts. Their experimentation with individual tools confers the advantages of Recurrent Neural Networks and Support Vector Machines over other methods when tested for forecast accuracy. A commonly observed bullwhip effect handles wastage through time, resources, and excess inventory. Information asymmetry and lack of open communication are primarily responsible for this effect. Open Communication Channels (OCC) and Electronic Data Interchange (EDI) for inter-organizational systems (IOS) would seem to benefit the entire supply chain financially; yet, studies show that may not always be a popular option. Every link in the chain may have its own incentive to exploit information asymmetry (Premkumar, 2000).

The popularization of blockchains for cryptocurrency has also found beneficial applications in the supply chain industry. Blockchains are forging new directions in supply chain finance; the benefits of transparency and trustworthy ledgers add confidence in the supplier-client relationship. Finding a unique nonce poses challenges to produce better algorithms. They have sped up the information flow in the chain. Creditors are more confident in their investments, while suppliers benefit from the early release of funds. A world bank governed cryptocurrency may soon replace gold as a standard to measure a country's wealth.

Manufacturing

Robots implementing machine learning algorithms fed with big data introduce a hybrid ecosystem, particularly cyber-physical systems. Integration of IoT in the manufacturing field has offset many redundant and labor-intensive tasks. Materials, Machines, Methods, Measurements, and Modeling represent the 5Ms of such a system (Lee et al., 2013). Learning based on the interplay of data embeds machines with 'self-awareness.' Self-Aware machines are better at Prognostics and Health Management (PHM). Watchdog Agent® is an example of a PHM. Self-aware machines with learned states offer better fault tolerance.

Lean manufacturing techniques, including 'Kanban,' rely on order pattern recognition at various stages in the manufacturing process. The results are lower inventory levels. Increased computational capacities and the ability to process extensive data; algorithms can forecast demands at various workstations.

Optimization is at the heart of any machine learning implementation. NP-hard and NP-complete are types of optimization problems that pose challenges in the supply chain and manufacturing industry. Research conducted by Monostori et al. (1998) and Pham & Afify (2005) applying machine learning techniques to such optimization problems have improved utilization and reduced wastage.

Corporation

As most companies turn into data companies, it is common to see corporate leadership educating themselves in scientific fields. Deep market insights with predictive analytics assist companies in implementing strategies responsive to competition. The additional throttle that big data analytics provides assists leaders in implementing game-theoretic strategies to leverage and better negotiate deals. In the past decade, deep learning implementations have taken roots across disciplines and, with their versatile applications, aim to disrupt commerce as we see. From game-changing innovations to lean management, algorithms form a significant part of everyday operations.

Financial institutes benefit from advances in the data science field. Venture capitalism is one such institute. Venture capitalists face difficulties in assessing high-technology companies relying heavily on research and development (Gompers & Lerner, 2001). One critical measure venture capitalist used to access an investment opportunity is the hurdle rate. Hurdle rates are a challenge to quantify. They reflect the challenges the investment will face. With a broader window to past data, coupled with the power of statistical inferencing, investors gain confidence to make better decisions.

Provost & Fawcett (2013) emphasize the importance of investors in data science ventures to be well versed with data science principles 'to assess investment opportunities correctly.' They further emphasize the disadvantage to the firm in the presence of a knowledge gap between the working data scientists and management. A challenge for a company's management is to adapt themselves to technical fields. Pipeline implementations and coherent modules have brought obscure algorithms within reach of non-technical users. Higher-level programming languages with AI-assisted editors have sped up the development and deployment of customizable applications. An open community of users and developers has provided a robust architecture to test software libraries thoroughly and increase trust for their public use. Data-driven companies have proved to be more productive than their competitors (5% more productive and 6% more profitable (McAfee & Brynjolfsson, 2012)).

Pricing

Business analytics plays a vital role for companies as they traverse through the periods of a typical business lifecycle. For instance, companies often choose between scaling and unloading less profitable customers at the product's maturity stage to maintain profitability. The metric used for this decision is the customer's future value. Based on this metric, firms determine the investments to attract new or hold existing customers.

Pricing strategies affect the sales and overall profitability of a firm. Selling low to potentially affluent customers is a common misjudgment of the market. Customers often cannot recognize the actual price of goods they purchase. All these issues are effects of information asymmetry. The Billion Prices Project at the Massachusetts Institute of Technology aims to reduce price arbitrage with product prices across sellers made available publicly.

Digital Footprint

Digital Footprint is a digital trace left behind by a user while traversing digital platforms. These digital footprints carry marketable value. Free usage of digital products often comes at the expense of companies selling personal data. Hiring managers, marketers, and even security professionals gaining access to such information leverage it for their benefit.

Clustering, segregation based on wealth, often considered in 'Redlining,' have found a new medium using digital footprints. *Creditworthiness* is the primary measure used by financial institutions to extend economic benefits to individuals and enterprises. These footprints often reveal information ranging from frequently used search terms to the smart device's operating system (OS). With the aid of data science tools, financial institutions use OS information to predict the income quartile of the user (Bertrand & Kamenica, 2018). Research shows an improvement in the information context of a financial model using digital footprints over ones that rely on credit bureau scores alone. The predictive power of the footprints to forecast a change in credit bureau score supplements its otherwise complementary role. A decrease in the default rate highlights the footprints' economic benefits (Berg et al., 2020). Societal influences impact individual behaviors. Peer-to-peer (P2P) borrowing and lending is also a dimension of credit markets. Lenders in such markets judge borrowers by their social presence, particularly the company of the people. A study conducted on 'Prosper.com,' a P2P lending marketplace, showcases individual credit behavior as a social network function (Lin et al., 2012). Stronger credit quality conveyed by friends referred to as 'soft information,' has substantial economic effects. The role of financial intermediaries relies heavily on understanding the information asymmetry. The transparency and power portrayed by big data analytics can reduce this asymmetry while maintaining confidence in the P2P lending market. Digital foot printing complemented with soft information contributes to solving an adverse selection problem, a vital component of the lending market.

Economics

Economists often debate over the importance of being theoretical versus data-intensive. There was a significant decrease in theoretical economic papers submitted to top economic journals over a three-decade study from 1983 to 2011 (Hamermesh, 2013). Jackson (2019) suggests the need to '...approach data with some direction and hypothesis in hand. Theory suggests which designs to test, and models provide the first steps in testing a design.' Extensive data lead to enormous sets of models. Overfitting is not an attribute of complexity but an attempt to find a model that perfectly fits the training data. Learning models can never be free of biases (Mitchell, 1980). Most machine learning algorithms intend to improve accuracy. Simplicity does not lead to greater accuracy (Domingos, 1999).

Autonomous Motion

Autonomous motion is the sleeping giant of advanced technologies. Autonomous vehicles are an application of artificial intelligence infused into everyday transportation. A vehicle's longitudinal and lateral motion governed by artificial intelligence poses a unique challenge for experts across disciplines. The investment made in developing autonomous systems pays dividends in maintaining safe conscious decision-making across all vehicles on the road. The AIC triad in information security includes Availability, Integrity, and Confidentiality of data at rest, in process, and motion. Considering dilemmas faced in introducing autonomous machines, manufacturers and regulators need to accomplish three objectives: being consistent, not causing public outrage, and not discouraging buyers (Bonnefon et al., 2016).

Autonomous motion is a prime example of machines displacing humans. Improved computing infrastructure and high-speed availability of big data have added trust in artificial intelligence supplemented automation. Bainbridge's four-decade-old prophecy '...automation of industrial processes may expand rather than eliminate problems with the human operator.', still stays validated (Bainbridge, 1983). While automation begets more automation, Bainbridge mentions the 'camouflage' effect: Automatic controls camouflage system failure by controlling variable changes (Ganesh, 2020). Overlearning may work. Overlearning buys time, and artificially induced false alarms force deep learning. Robotics has found a way into surgery as early as 2000 with the da Vinci Surgical System. While courts and agencies debate the introduction procedure of autonomous motion in everyday life, authorities classify autonomy into six levels, including:

Level 0: no autonomy;
Level 1: robot assistance;
Level 2: task autonomy;
Level 3: conditional autonomy;
Level 4: high autonomy; and
Level 5: total autonomy.

LIMITATIONS

Big data, machine learning techniques, and data science tools are susceptible to misguided and uniformed applications. The financial sector is one such area. Predictions in the stock market are a challenge to many. One widespread misstep is to underestimate the stochastic nature of processes. Preliminary checks, including those for normality and identification of data distribution type, are often overlooked.

Having more data is not akin to having more information. Hosni & Vulpiani (2018) demonstrate the regenerative effects of additional data on weather forecasting. They further point that a false positivity rate of even 0.08% to 0.18% (in the SKYNET program to monitor mobile phone networks in Pakistan) resulted in misclassifying 99 thousand Pakistanis as terrorists. Buchanan (2019) supporting this claim argues for a tradeoff between modeling and quantitative analysis. Google Flu Trends (GFT) is another example wherein an algorithmic misrepresented model has not captured ground reality. Two realities that often-offset effective implementation are overfitting and sampling. GFT attempted to match 50 million search terms to fit 1152 data points (Ginsberg et al., 2009). Einav & Levin (2014) argue for a case-by-case evaluation to overcome the deluging impact of big data, as in 'the data deluge makes the scientific methods obsolete' (Anderson, 2008).

There are risks of over-reliance on artificial intelligence. A Byzantine Generals Problem applied to other aspects of governance also applies to machine-controlled systems. The entire ecosystem of block-chains relies on the confidence to resist a byzantine fault. The majority rules the roost, even if they are wrong, and especially for an unattended system.

Ethics

The move into autonomous motion comes attached with liabilities and ethical choices. The dilemma of who takes responsibility for accidents has found many voices. One prominent example is Madeliene Elish, who introduces the Moral Crumple Zone: Humans bear the legal responsibility in human-robot systems with limited control over which they have limited control. A notable case *is Jones vs. W + M Automation* (Jones v W+M Automation Inc., 2006). Here, a robotic gantry installed by General Motors without an interlock system caused an injury to an employee. The courts passed a judgment under the 'component part' doctrine '...the manufacturer of a non-defective component cannot be held liable if this component is installed into another defective product' (Jamjoom et al., 2020).

Problems with the AV misidentifying the object have resulted in crashes (National Transportation Safety Board, 2018; Shepardson, 2018; Tesla, 2016). We are moving from humans crying for help to machines crying for help. We call it 'heteromation' (Ekbia & Nardi, 2014). Machines displacing humans require a human overview. An example of a fatality caused by the weakness in heteromation is a distracted driver not heeding to the AV's alerts handled the Tesla crash in 2017 (National Transport Safety Board, 2017). A popular solution is to quadruplex crucial information flows. Decision-making (DM) is key to autonomous motion. Computational biologists infer that decision-making is a tradeoff between exploring new options versus exploiting the current best option. V2X (Vehicle-to-Everything) communication may encourage decentralized DM models. The two phases of the model are positive feedback with quorum detection to trigger a consensus choice (Golman et al., 2015).

Quantum Computation

The hardware application of the big data science revolution includes a new paradigm in quantum comput-ing. From the 'Universal Quantum Simulator' (Feynman R, 1982) to creating a framework for a Quantum Boltzmann Machine (Amin et al., 2018), a practical machine 'D-Wave' is one of many projects currently in the race to achieve computing superiority. *Appendix A* highlights the advances in developing quantum computers. A quantum speedup readjusts a problem complexity. With specialized processors called quantum annealers, quantum computers improve efficiency for running machine learning programs, including Principal Component Analysis, Least-squares Fitting, Support Vector Machines, Bayesian Inferencing, and Reinforcement Learning (Biamonte et al., 2017).

FUTURE RESEARCH DIRECTIONS

Advances in machine learning techniques with improved hardware support will affect the market through autonomous systems. Research in the fields of epistemology and neuroscience is crucial for advances in machine learning systems. Further understanding the human brain and evolutionary activities in different species will introduce better learning algorithms. Healthcare is another area that will experience the impact of advancements in these fields. Research in autonomous surgical robots begets understanding beyond technical fields into ethics, safety, and liabilities. An autonomous system differs from an automatic system, wherein an autonomous system learns rules and tweaks them when introduced with new information. The case for liability arises where validating the new rules is subject to personal biases. Frameworks and standards for autonomous systems are still in the developmental stage. While the world may benefit from such artificial learning systems, generic adoptions still pose challenges to lawmakers and scientists. From an economic standpoint, one needs to monitor the shift in paradigms as different industries adopt autonomous systems.

CONCLUSION

In the quest to stay relevant, many industries are searching for ways to reduce waste and lean down operations. A practical solution has been to leverage the power of big data and to replace redundant tasks with intelligent systems. Big data has allowed deeper insights and, in cases, exposed true intentions behind actions. When most newcomers to the market intend to attract customers by introducing solutions that force customers to change their behavior, many are leveraging the power of advanced data science tools and machine learning techniques.

REFERENCES

Amin, M. H., Andriyash, E., Rolfe, J., Kulchytskyy, B., & Melko, R. (2018). Quantum Boltzmann Machine. *Physical Review X*, *8*(2), 021050. Advance online publication. doi:10.1103/PhysRevX.8.021050

Anderson, C. (2008, June 23). *The End of Theory: The Data Deluge Makes the Scientific Method Obsolete*. Wired. https://www.wired.com/2008/06/pb-theory/

Bainbridge, L. (1983). Ironies of automation. *Automatica*, *19*(6), 775–779. doi:10.1016/0005-1098(83)90046-8

Berg, T., Burg, V., Gombović, A., & Puri, M. (2020). On the Rise of FinTechs: Credit Scoring Using Digital Footprints. *Review of Financial Studies*, *33*(7), 2845–2897. doi:10.1093/rfs/hhz099

Bertrand, M., & Kamenica, E. (2018). Coming Apart? Cultural Distances in the United States over. *Time*. Advance online publication. doi:10.3386/w24771

Biamonte, J., Wittek, P., Pancotti, N., Rebentrost, P., Wiebe, N., & Lloyd, S. (2017). Quantum machine learning. *Nature*, *549*(7671), 195–202. doi:10.1038/nature23474 PMID:28905917

Bonnefon, J.-F., Shariff, A., & Rahwan, I. (2016). The social dilemma of autonomous vehicles. *Science*, *352*(6293), 1573–1576. doi:10.1126cience.aaf2654 PMID:27339987

Buchanan, M. (2019). The limits of machine prediction. *Nature Physics*, *15*(4), 304–304. doi:10.103841567-019-0489-5

Carbonneau, R., Laframboise, K., & Vahidov, R. (2008). Application of machine learning techniques for supply chain demand forecasting. *European Journal of Operational Research*, *184*(3), 1140–1154. doi:10.1016/j.ejor.2006.12.004

Dehaene, S., Lau, H., & Kouider, S. (2017). What is consciousness, and could machines have it? *Science*, *358*(6362), 486–492. doi:10.1126cience.aan8871 PMID:29074769

Deutsch, D. (1985). Quantum Theory, the Church-Turing Principle and the Universal Quantum Computer. In *Proceedings of the Royal Society of London. Series A, Mathematical and Physical Sciences* (pp. 97–117). Academic Press.

Domingos, P. (1999). The Role of Occam's Razor in Knowledge Discovery. *Data Mining and Knowledge Discovery*, *3*(4), 409–425. doi:10.1023/A:1009868929893

Einav, L., & Levin, J. (2014). Economics in the age of big data. *Science*, *346*(6210), 1243089–1243089. doi:10.1126cience.1243089 PMID:25378629

Ekbia, H., & Nardi, B. (2014). Heteromation and its (dis)contents: The invisible division of labor between humans and machines. *First Monday*. Advance online publication. doi:10.5210/fm.v19i6.5331

Feynman, R. (1982). A Computer-Algebraic Approach to the Simulation of Multi-Qubit Systems. *International Journal of Theoretical Physics*, *21*, 467. doi:10.1007/BF02650179

Fredkin, E., & Toffoli, T. (1982). Conservative logic. *International Journal of Theoretical Physics*, *21*(3-4), 219–253. doi:10.1007/BF01857727

Ganesh, M. I. (2020). The ironies of autonomy. *Humanities and Social Sciences Communications*, *7*(1), 157. doi:10.105741599-020-00646-0

Gardner, A. L. (1987). *An Artificial Intelligence Approach to Legal Reasoning*. The MIT Press.

Ginsberg, J., Mohebbi, M. H., Patel, R. S., Brammer, L., Smolinski, M. S., & Brilliant, L. (2009). Detecting influenza epidemics using search engine query data. *Nature*, *457*(7232), 1012–1014. doi:10.1038/nature07634 PMID:19020500

Golman, R., Hagmann, D., & Miller, J. H. (2015, September 18). Polya's bees: A model of decentralized decision-making. *Science Advances*, *1*(8), e1500253. Advance online publication. doi:10.1126ciadv.1500253 PMID:26601255

Gompers, P., & Lerner, J. (2001). The Venture Capital Revolution. *The Journal of Economic Perspectives*, *15*(2), 145–168. doi:10.1257/jep.15.2.145

Gray, P. N. (1997). *Artificial Legal Intelligence*. Taylor & Francis Ltd.

Hamermesh, D. S. (2013). Six Decades of Top Economics Publishing: Who and How? *Journal of Economic Literature*, *51*(1), 162–172. doi:10.1257/jel.51.1.162

Hosni, H., & Vulpiani, A. (2018). Forecasting in Light of Big Data. *Philosophy & Technology*, *31*(4), 557–569. doi:10.100713347-017-0265-3

Hutson, M. (2019, May 10). Scientists teach computers fear—To make them better drivers. *Science*. Advance online publication. doi:10.1126cience.aay0007

Jackson, M. O. (2019). *The Role of Theory in an Age of Design and Big Data.*, doi:10.1007/978-3-030-18050-8_72

Jamjoom, A. A. B., Jamjoom, A. M. A., & Marcus, H. J. (2020). Exploring public opinion about liability and responsibility in surgical robotics. *Nature Machine Intelligence*, *2*(4), 194–196. Advance online publication. doi:10.103842256-020-0169-2

Laney, D. (2001). 3D Data Management: Controlling Data Volume, Velocity and Variety. META Group Research Note.

Lee, J., Lapira, E., Bagheri, B., & Kao, H. (2013). Recent advances and trends in predictive manufacturing systems in big data environment. *Manufacturing Letters*, *1*(1), 38–41. doi:10.1016/j.mfglet.2013.09.005

Levi, E. H. (1948). *An Introduction to Legal Reasoning* (Vol. 15). University of Chicago Law Review.

Lin, M., Prabhala, N. R., & Viswanathan, S. (2012). Judging Borrowers by the Company They Keep: Friendship Networks and Information Asymmetry in Online Peer-to-Peer Lending. *Management Science*, *59*(1), 17–35. doi:10.1287/mnsc.1120.1560

McAfee, A., & Brynjolfsson, E. (2012). Big Data: The Management Revolution. *Harvard Business Review*, 90. PMID:23074865

McCarty, L. T. (1977). Reflections on "Taxman": An Experiment in Artificial Intelligence and Legal Reasoning. *Harvard Law Review*, *90*(5), 837. doi:10.2307/1340132

Michie, D. (1968). "Memo" Functions and Machine Learning. *Nature*, *218*(5136), 19–22. doi:10.1038/218019a0

Minsky, M. (1969). *Semantic Information Processing* (M. Minsky, Ed.). The MIT Press.

Mitchell, T. (1980). *The Need for Biases in Learning Generalizations*. Academic Press.

Monostori, L., Hornyák, J., Egresits, C., & Viharos, Z. J. (1998). Soft computing and hybrid AI approaches to intelligent manufacturing. Lecture Notes in Computer Science, 765-774. doi:10.1007/3-540-64574-8_463

National Transport Safety Board. (2017). *Highway Investigation - 46 Docket Items - HWY16FH018*. https://data.ntsb.gov/Docket?ProjectID=93548

National Transportation Safety Board. (2018). *Preliminary Report Highway: HWY18MH010*. https://www.ntsb.gov/investigations/AccidentReports/Pages/HWY18MH010-prelim.aspx

Pham, D. T., & Afify, A. A. (2005). Machine-learning techniques and their applications in manufacturing. *Proceedings of the Institution of Mechanical Engineers. Part B, Journal of Engineering Manufacture, 219*(5), 395–412. doi:10.1243/095440505X32274

Philip Chen, C. L., & Zhang, C. Y. (2014). Data-intensive applications, challenges, techniques and technologies: A survey on Big Data. *Information Sciences, 275,* 314–347. doi:10.1016/j.ins.2014.01.015

Premkumar, G. P. (2000). Interorganization Systems and Supply Chain Management: An Information Processing Perspective. *Information Systems Management, 17*(3), 56–69. doi:10.1201/1078/43192.17.3.20000601/31241.8

Provost, F., & Fawcett, T. (2013). Data Science and its Relationship to Big Data and Data-Driven Decision Making. *Big Data, 1*(1), 51–59. doi:10.1089/big.2013.1508 PMID:27447038

Roetteler, M., Naehrig, M., Svore, K. M., & Lauter, K. (2017). *Quantum resource estimates for computing elliptic curve discrete logarithms.* Academic Press.

Samuel, A. L. (1959). Some Studies in Machine Learning Using the Game of Checkers. *IBM Journal of Research and Development, 3*(3), 210–229. doi:10.1147/rd.33.0210

Searle, J. R. (1990). Is the Brain's Mind a Computer Program? *Scientific American, 262*(1), 26–31. doi:10.1038cientificamerican0190-26 PMID:2294583

Shepardson, D. (2018, March). *Tesla says crashed vehicle had been on autopilot prior to accident.* Reuters.

Shor, P. W. (1997). Polynomial-Time Algorithms for Prime Factorization and Discrete Logarithms on a Quantum Computer. *SIAM Journal on Computing, 26*(5), 124–134. doi:10.1137/S0097539795293172

Slonim, N., Bilu, Y., Alzate, C., Bar-Haim, R., Bogin, B., Bonin, F., Choshen, L., Cohen-Karlik, E., Dankin, L., Edelstein, L., Ein-Dor, L., Friedman-Melamed, R., Gavron, A., Gera, A., Gleize, M., Gretz, S., Gutfreund, D., Halfon, A., Hershcovich, D., ... Aharonov, R. (2021). An autonomous debating system. *Nature, 591*(7850), 379–384. doi:10.103841586-021-03215-w PMID:33731946

Szalay, A. S. (2009). GrayWulf: Scalable Clustered Architecture for Data Intensive Computing. *2009 42nd Hawaii International Conference on System Sciences,* 1–10. 10.1109/HICSS.2009.234

Tesla. (2016, June). *A Tragic Loss.* https://www.Tesla.Com/Blog

Toffoli, T. (1980). Reversible computing. In *International Colloquium on Automata, Languages, and Programming* (pp. 632–644). Springer. 10.21236/ADA082021

Wirth, R., & Hipp, J. (2000). CRISP-DM: Towards a Standard Process Model for DataMining. In *Proceedings of the 4th International Conference on the Practical Applications of Knowledge Discovery and Data Mining.* (pp. 526–534). Academic Press.

Yampolskiy, R. v., & Spellchecker, M. S. (2016). Artificial Intelligence Safety and Cybersecurity: A Timeline of AI Failures. https://arxiv.org/abs/1610.07997

ADDITIONAL READING

Amodei, D., Olah, C., Steinhardt, J., Christiano, P., Schulman, J., & Mané, D. (2016). *Concrete Problems in AI Safety*. Academic Press.

Cavallo, A. (2018). Scraped Data and Sticky Prices. *The Review of Economics and Statistics*, *100*(1), 105–119. Advance online publication. doi:10.1162/REST_a_00652

Dworkin, R. (1982). Law as Interpretation. *Critical Inquiry*, *9*(1), 179–200. Advance online publication. doi:10.1086/448194

Fagnant, D. J., & Kockelman, K. (2015). Preparing a nation for autonomous vehicles: Opportunities, barriers and policy recommendations. *Transportation Research Part A, Policy and Practice*, *77*, 167–181. doi:10.1016/j.tra.2015.04.003

Lamport, L., Shostak, R., & Pease, M. (2019). The Byzantine general's problem. In *Concurrency: The Works of Leslie Lamport*. Association for Computing Machinery. doi:10.1145/3335772.3335936

Lasi, H., Fettke, P., Kemper, H.-G., Feld, T., & Hoffmann, M. (2014). Industry 4.0. *Business & Information Systems Engineering*, *6*(4), 239–242. Advance online publication. doi:10.100712599-014-0334-4

McKinsey. (2020, November 17). *The state of AI in 2020*. McKinsey and Company. https://www.mckinsey.com/business-functions/mckinsey-analytics/our-insights/global-survey-the-state-of-ai-in-2020

Shor, P. W., & Preskill, J. (2000). Simple Proof of Security of the BB84 Quantum Key Distribution Protocol. *Physical Review Letters*, *85*(2), 441–444. Advance online publication. doi:10.1103/PhysRevLett.85.441 PMID:10991303

Stilgoe, J. (2019). Self-driving cars will take a while to get right. *Nature Machine Intelligence*, *1*(5), 202–203. Advance online publication. doi:10.103842256-019-0046-z

KEY TERMS AND DEFINITIONS

Autonomous System: A self-learning system capable of using real time information to make goal-based decisions.

Byzantine Generals Problem: A problem faced by decentralized systems to propagate trust when system nodes go rogue.

Digital Footprint: A trail of data left by user using smart devices.

Heteromation: Machines compensating for human effort.

Nonce: A generated pseudo-random number that plays a critical role in blockchain technology.

Quantum Annealing: Solving complex optimization problems using quantum fluctuations.

Redlining: A community based discriminatory practice implemented by financial institutes often considered biased, derogatory, and illegal.

APPENDIX A

A quantum computer following the laws of quantum mechanics will permit a unitary transformation of state vectors (Shor, 1997). He further argues in favor of computational reversibility not being a primary requirement for gates to operate. Alternatives to classical gates, including a Toffoli gate (Toffoli, 1980) and a Fredkin gate (Fredkin & Toffoli, 1982), have emulated reversibility conditions for quantum computers. A significant reason for considering quantum computation is the possibility of speeding up processes. With 'Quantum Parallelism,' specific probabilistic tasks can be performed faster. The physical version of the Church-Turing principle states:

'Every finitely realizable physical system can be perfectly simulated by a universal model computing machine operating by finite mean.'

The quantum theory is compatible with this version of the principle (Deutsch D, 1985). Advancement noted by incrementing the number of qubits a machine can handle has more profound implications in cryptography. Quantum cryptography, a quantum key distribution system with the BB84 protocol, provides higher security with a shorter key size. The most advanced quantum computer can produce 5000 qubits, which is twice what is required to break a NIST standardized curve P-256 (128-bit key size Elliptic Curve Cryptography (Roetteler et al., 2017)).

Section 4
Big Data Applications

A Patient–Centered Data–Driven Analysis of Epidural Anesthesia

A

Eva K. Lee
Georgia Institute of Technology, USA

Haozheng Tian
Georgia Institute of Technology, USA

Xin Wei
Georgia Institute of Technology, USA

Jinha Lee
 https://orcid.org/0000-0002-9018-387X
Bowling Green State University, USA

INTRODUCTION

According to the 2019 Center for Diseases Control and Prevention birth statistics, of the 3.75 million newborns delivered in the United States, about 31.7% were delivered by Cesarean section (C-section).

Epidural anesthesia provides regional anesthesia for C-section. This local anesthetic is injected into an area of the lower back just outside the spinal-fluid sac. It takes about 15 to 20 minutes to work, and the anesthesiologist can leave the catheter in place to allow for top-offs.

The potential consequences of failed or misplaced epidural needles are well known to obstetric anesthesiologists. A well-documented epidural complication, a "wet tap," results in a headache and possible total spinal anesthesia/block, requiring immediate maintenance of the patient's airway and blood pressure. The inadvertent intravenous injection of local anesthetic into a vein in the epidural space leads to seizures and fatal cardiac arrhythmias. Equally worrisome is the inadequate epidural block leading to complications during a C-section. These complications include an emergency general anesthetic, resulting in airway loss, hypoxemia, hypercarbia and death (Cheng et al. 2015; Dunham et al, 2014; Liu et al., 2015). However, to date, limited research has been performed regarding standardization of the epidural analgesia procedure to avoid practice variance and ensure minimal complications.

In this chapter, we report on an in-depth study of epidural process to capture practice variance and quantify the time and dose required to achieve the desired sensory level. Using a data-driven and machine learning approach, we establish a safe and quickly effective epidural dose that can be administered through the epidural needle prior to the insertion of the epidural catheter. Based on clinical results, we quantify complications for a dose as large as 20 ml that is injected through the epidural needle. We contrast the proficiency of physician practice and provide insights on their preference in medication (including use of opioid-type drug) and dosage. Understanding the causes and effects of such variation can help providers avoid practices that negatively impact outcomes. The machine learning analysis reveals practice characteristics that result in the best outcome with the fewest complications. Our findings facilitate the establishment of improved clinical practice guidelines (CPG) for care outcome and delivery improvement.

DOI: 10.4018/978-1-7998-9220-5.ch005

Copyright © 2023, IGI Global. Copying or distributing in print or electronic forms without written permission of IGI Global is prohibited.

BACKGROUND

Traditionally, the epidural catheter is placed, aspirated, and a test dose of medication is given to detect the possibility of an intravascular (IV) or intrathecal (IT) catheter prior to administering additional doses of local anesthetic and opioids. More rapid injection is often possible through the epidural needle given the relatively larger gauge and shorter length compared to a catheter (Omote et al., 1992), which could potentially enhance the spread of medication within the epidural space. However, there have been very few studies in which anesthesia providers have initiated labor analgesia by injecting medications through the epidural needle immediately after loss of resistance to achieve faster onset of pain relief (Gambling et al., 2013). The rationale for potentially improved analgesia onset with epidural needle injection is uncertain. In addition to faster onset of analgesia, it has been reported that dosing through the epidural needle may result in improved quality of epidural anesthesia compared to dosing through the catheter (Cesur et al., 2005). However, other investigations in obstetric (Husain et al., 1997) and non-obstetric (Yun et al., 2004) patients receiving epidural anesthesia have observed a similar onset and quality of surgical anesthesia as well as a similar level of sensory blockade when dosing through the needle versus the catheter. In a small double-blind prospective investigation (n=60), Raster et al. 2017 directly compared needle and catheter injection of epidural medications for the initiation of labor analgesia. Their results showed that epidural needle and catheter injection of medications result in similar onset of analgesia and sensory blockade, quality of labor analgesia, patient satisfaction, and complication rates. To date little is known regarding practice and patient outcome related to large doses of local anesthetic injected through the epidural needle.

MATERIALS AND METHODS

The study design involves five major steps: 1) Develop process maps of patient and epidural service workflow via objective process observations and structured interviews. 2) Perform time-motion studies of epidural processes, record complications and practice variance, and analyze hospital data. 3) Perform statistical analysis of collected data, conduct system analysis on practice variance, and quantify effective dose-sensory level achievement, 4) Develop a machine-learning model to predict patient/outcome characteristics. 5) Develop a computerized simulation-optimization system to simulate current performance, optimize systems, and estimate anticipated global improvement. 6) Report findings and establish practice guideline recommendations for improved quality of care.

Epidural Workflow and Services

Figure 1 summarizes the observed epidural process performed by anesthesiologists. The green denotes the observed practice variance. Anesthesiologists choose one of three basic techniques of loss of resistance (or a combination thereof) to identify the proper epidural space: air, saline, or local anesthetic. Medication dosages vary by provider, with most injecting as much as 20 ml through the epidural needle prior to inserting the epidural catheter.

Figure 1. This figure summarizes the anesthesiologist epidural procedure workflow process. Green highlights those processes with variance among providers.

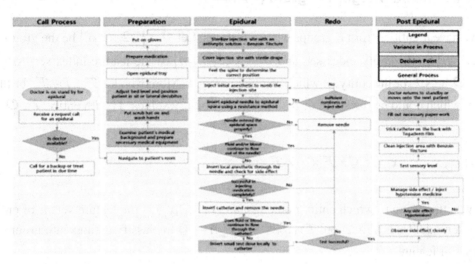

Observations, Time-Motion Studies, and Chart Review

Data collected from January 2014 through December 2014 includes patient demographics, vital signs, medication type and dosage, time to achieve sensory level, outcomes, and response to medication. We conducted time-motion studies, and measured service time for each step of the epidural workflow. Variability of practitioners and processes were also captured. In addition, a random sample of clinical charts was gathered and reviewed to serve as an independent validation set for our machine learning and system simulation-optimization analysis.

Two types of epidural approaches were defined based upon the primary delivery mechanism of the majority dose. If the majority of the dose is delivered through a needle (> 50%), it is defined as a needle-based approach. Likewise, a catheter-based approach delivers the majority dose through a catheter.

Statistical Analysis

Statistical analysis was conducted to quantify variations and their associated outcome. Variations on delivery types and associated complications, time to sensory level, medications and dosage, epidural approaches (needle-based versus catheter-based), and practitioner performance were noted.

Statistical analyses were performed using MATLAB (MATLAB and Statistics Toolbox). Statistical significance was assessed at the 0.05 level. Descriptive statistics were calculated for all variables of interest including median and 25th to 75th percentiles and counts and percentages when appropriate. Two-sample t-tests and Wilcoxon rank-sum tests were used to compare continuous variables between groups and Chi-square tests were used for comparing categorical variables between groups.

Next, a machine learning predictive framework was designed to uncover key factors that influence and predict hypotension. Specifically, we used discriminant analysis via mixed integer program (DAMIP) as our classifier (Lee, 2007; Lee et al., 2012) and contrasted its performance to other popular classifiers.

Machine-Learning Predictive Analytic Framework: Discriminant Analysis via Mixed Integer Program (DAMIP)

Suppose we have n entities from K groups with m features. Let $\mathcal{G} = \{1, 2, \ldots, K\}$ be the group index set, $\mathcal{O} = \{1, 2, \ldots, n\}$ be the entity index set, and $\mathcal{F} = \{1, 2, \ldots, m\}$ be the feature index set. Also, let $\mathcal{O}_k$, $k \in \mathcal{G}$ and $\mathcal{O}_k \subseteq \mathcal{O}$, be the entity set which belong to group k. Moreover, let $\mathcal{F}_j$, $j \in \mathcal{F}$, be the domain of feature j, which could be the space of real, integer, or binary values. The ith entity, $i \in \mathcal{O}$, is represented as

$$(y_i, x_i) = (y_i, x_{i1}, \ldots, x_{im}) \in \mathcal{G} \times \mathcal{F}_1 \times \cdots \times \mathcal{F}_m,$$

where y_i is the group to which entity i belongs, and $(x_{i1}, \ldots, x_{im})$ is the feature vector of entity i. The classification model finds a function $f : (\mathcal{F}_1 \times \cdots \times \mathcal{F}_m) \to \mathcal{G}$ to classify entities into groups based on a selected set of features.

Let πk be the prior probability of group k and $f k_{(} x)$ be the conditional probability density function for the entity $x \in \mathbb{R}^m$ of group k, $k \in \mathcal{G}$. Also let $\alpha h_{kf}(0,1)$, $h, k \in \mathcal{G}, h \neq k$, be the upperbound for the misclassification percentage that group h entities are misclassified into group k. DAMIP seeks a partition $\{P_0, P_1, \ldots, P_K\}$ of $\mathbb{R}^K$, where P_k, $k \in \mathcal{G}$, is the region for group k, and P_0 is the reserved judgement region with entities for which group assignment are reserved (for potential further exploration).

Let u_{ki} be a 0/1 variable to denote if entity i is classified to group k or not. Mathematically, DAMIP (Lee, Gallagher, and Patterson, 2003; Lee 2007; Lee and Wu, 2009; Lee, 2009) can be formulated as

$$\mathbf{Max} \sum_{i \in \mathcal{O}} u_{y_i i} \tag{1}$$

sets

$$L_{ki} = \pi_k f_k(x_i) - \sum_{h \in \mathcal{G}, h \neq k} f_h(x_i) \lambda_{hk} \quad \forall i \in \mathcal{O}, k \in \mathcal{G} \tag{2}$$

$$u_{ki} = \begin{cases} 1 & \text{if } k = \arg\max\{0, L_{hi} : h \in \mathcal{G}\} \\ 0 & otherwise \end{cases} \quad \forall i \in \mathcal{O}, k \in \{0\} \cup \mathcal{G} \tag{3}$$

$$\sum_{k \in \{0\} \cup \mathcal{G}} u_{ki} = 1 \quad \forall i \in \mathcal{O} \tag{4}$$

$$\sum_{i:i \in \mathcal{O}_h} u_{ki} \leq \alpha_{hk} n_h \quad \forall h, k \in \mathcal{G}, h \neq k \tag{5}$$

$u_{ki} \in \{0,1\} \quad \forall i \in \mathcal{O}, k \in \{0\} \cup \mathcal{G}$

L_{ki} *unrestricted in sign* $\forall i \in \mathcal{O}, k \in \mathcal{G}$

$\lambda_{hk} \geq 0 \quad \forall h, k \in \mathcal{G}, h \neq k$

The objective function (1) maximizes the number of entities classified into the correct group. Constraints (2) and (3) govern the placement of an entity into each of the groups in $\mathcal{G}$ or the reserved-judgment region. Thus, the variables L_{ki} and λh_k provide the shape of the partition of the groups in the $\mathcal{G}$ space. Constraint (4) ensures that an entity is assigned to exactly one group. Constraint (5) allows the users to preset the desirable misclassification levels, which can be specified as overall errors for each group, pairwise errors, or overall errors for all groups together. With the reserved-judgment region in place, the system ensures that a solution that satisfies the preset errors always exists.

The entities correspond to the patients. The features are patient demographics, health conditions and clinical history, epidural workflow (processes, medication, and dosage), and provider experience and delivery characteristics. The goal is to undercover discriminatory features that can predict which patients will have a higher likelihood of complications. Ten-fold cross-validation is performed on the training set to obtain an unbiased estimate. To gauge the predictive accuracy, we perform blind prediction on an independent set of subjects.

DAMIP has many appealing characteristics including: 1) the resulting classification rule is strongly universally consistent, given that the Bayes optimal rule for classification is known (Brooks and Lee, 2010; 2014), 2) the misclassification rates are consistently lower than other classification approaches in both simulated data and real-world data; 3) the DAMIP classifiers appear to be insensitive to the choice of prior probabilities, yet capable of reducing misclassification rates; 4) the resulting classifier is robust and perform well on imbalanced data, regardless of the proportions of training entities from each group (Brooks and Lee, 2010; Lee and Wu, 2012; Lee et al., 2012).

We compared the performance of DAMIP against other classifiers: classification tree, logistic regression, Naive Bayes, random forest k-nearest neighbors, and support vector machine.

A Computerized Simulation-Optimization System

A simulation-optimization computational framework was then designed for modeling and optimizing the entire epidural clinical workflow. This allows for the development of improved CPGs. Parameters in the simulation include the entire epidural workflow as shown in Figure 1. The model captures delivery characteristics, service times, types, and probabilities for each provider; response, risk factors, and outcome characteristics (including complication) of each patient; and overall throughput of processes. The model was fitted using the data collected from our time-motion studies and observations to simulate the annual hospital patient visits and treatment performance. It captures practice variations statistically and allows us to investigate improvement strategies. We first fine-tuned the model to reflect the hospital's regular performance. Then using the validation set from chart review, we further fine-tuned and cross-validated the accuracy of our model. The system was then optimized to identify areas for improvement.

FINDINGS AND RECOMMENDATIONS

Northside Hospital delivers the highest number of newborns in the United States (the Centers for Medicare & Medicaid Services). During the study period, 19,651 deliveries were performed with 55.3% vaginal birth and 44.7% C-section. Among these, 75.1% received epidural analgesia. A total of 667 C-section cases under routine epidural analgesia were observed in full detail. Most of them (93.85%) were performed with patients in the sitting position, with 60.42% of the patients receiving the injection of anesthesia at position L23. The observations covered 44 anesthesiologists.

The independent set used for validation consisted of 1,398 patients obtained through chart review, among which 892 cases were C-section. This represented roughly 10% of the newborns delivered from January to September 2015.

Observed Group Versus Independent Chart Review Group

General The average age (32.72 vs. 32.00, p = 0.0007), weight (188.73 lb vs. 183.41 lb, p = 0.0011), and height (163.63 cm vs. 162.38 cm, p = 0.0035) are higher in the observation set then the validation set, but the pregnancy length is similar (38.16 weeks vs. 38.31 weeks, p = 0.5353). Additionally, both systolic (127.19 mmHg vs. 125.41 mmHg, p = 0.0426) and diastolic (77.90 vs. 75.42, p = 0.0004) in the observed group are higher than those in the validation group. 73.02% of the C-section patients in the observed group had a prior delivery and it is 62.27% for the validation set. Hence, there may be more complications in the observed group.

Sensory Level Achievement Sensory level is an important indicator to measure the effect of anesthesia. A higher than desired anesthesia level (high block) can cause motor block, dyspnea, apnea and even loss of consciousness. Both observed and validation groups showed similar achieved sensory level, with T4 (obs.: 61.07%, val.: 74.76%) and T6 (obs.: 22.29%, val.: 7.57%) being the most frequent ones. The average time to achieve sensory level is 15.95 minutes in the observed group.

Needle-Based Versus Catheter-Based Approach

We seek to quantify the effective dose to achieve the desired sensory level and to evaluate the safety and utility of injecting large doses (up to 20 ml) in the epidural space through the epidural needle.

Among the 667 observed cases, 637 cases (95.50%) were needle-based, and 30 cases (4.50%) were catheter-based. In the needle-based approach, in almost all cases, over 90% of the dose was delivered through the needle, whereas for the catheter-based approach, an average of 58.76% of the dose was delivered via the catheter.

Sensory Level Achievement The needle-based approach achieved a higher sensory level (average T4.79) than the catheter-based approach (average T5.23), but the difference is not statistically significant (p = 0.0841).

Figure 2 shows that the most frequent sensory levels were T4 (needle-based: 62.10%, catheter-based 36.67%) and T6 (needle-based: 21.77%, catheter-based: 33.33%). Compared to the catheter-based approach, the needle-based approach that achieved sensory level were more skewed to higher levels.

Time to Achieve The average time to achieve sensory level in the needle-based approach was 15.80 minutes versus 18.97 minutes for catheter-based (p = 0.0391, Figure 3a). *Hence, this study reports that the needle-based approach is faster and more effective in achieving the required sensory result.* Furthermore, the needle-based approach uses a smaller dose than the catheter-based approach (mean 25.81 ml versus

Figure 2. Distribution of sensory levels for needle- and catheter-based approaches

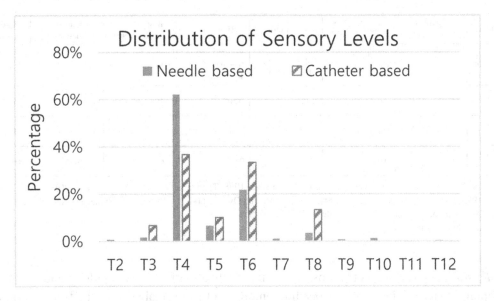

29.13 ml, $p = 0.0029$, Figure 3b). *These findings support the conclusion that the needle-based approach is more dose-effective, achieving better sensory level faster than the traditional catheter-based approach.*

Complications

General Statistics We observed the following incidence percentage: hypertension 55.32%, blood in the catheter/needle 2.10%, epidural replaced 3.60%, wet tap 0.15%, high block 0.30%, fainting 0.15%, and nausea/vomiting 0.45%. Since hypotension was the most common complication, we present detailed analysis on hypotension in a dedicated section. Table 1 contrasts this hospital's complication incidence to published results (Crawford, 1972; Eappen, 1998; Jenkins, 2005; Norris et al., 1994; Pan, Bogard, and Owen, 2004; .Paech et al., 1998; Sadashivaiah et al., 2010; Sprigge and Harper, 2008; Thangamuthu, 2013; Vallejo, et al., 2010; Van de Velde et al., 2008; Verstraete et al., 2014). We note that these published results are all catheter-based since they did not inject the dose via the epidural needles. *In contrast to published results, the complication incidence of the needle-based approach is comparable to the traditional catheter-based approach.*

Figure 3. (a) Distribution of time to sensory level, (b) Distribution of total dosage for needle vs catheter based

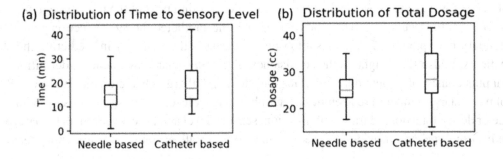

Table 1. This table contrasts Northside Hospital's complications to published results

Complications	Epidural replace	Nausea/Vomit	Wet tap	High block	Blood in the catheter/ needle	Re-do local anesthetic	Re-do loss of resistance
Known literature	4.7%- 17.8% (n=181-10995)[1]	1% (n=388) (Norris et al., 1994)	0.43%-3.2% (n=141-29749)[2]	0.02%-0.07% (n=10995-145550)[3]	N/A	N/A	N/A
Observed cases (n=667)	3.60%	0.45%	0.15%	0.30%	2.10%	4.05%	5.55%
Needle-based (n=637)	3.45%	0.47%	0.00%	0.31%	1.88%	3.77%	5.34%
Catheter-based (n=30)	6.67%	0.0%	3.33%	0.0%	6.67%	10.0%	10.0%

[1]Crawford, 1972; Eappen, 1998; 1994; Pan et al., 2004; .Paech et al., 1998; Thangamuthu, 2013; Vallejo, et al., 2010)

[2]Crawford, 1972; Eappen, 1998; Norris et al., 1994; Pan, Bogard, and Owen, 2004; .Paech et al., 1998; Sadashivaiah et al., 2010; Sprigge and Harper, 2008; Vallejo, et al., 2010; Van de Velde et al., 2008; Verstraete et al., 2014)

[3](Paech ey al., 1998;Jenkins, 2005)

Hypotension Hypotension is the most frequent complication for spinal, epidural and combined spinal and epidural anesthesia (CSE). Depending on different labor analgesia methods and definitions of hypotension, reported hypotension rates can be as high as 70% (Cascio et al., 1997; Rout et al., 1992). In this study, the reported hypotension rate was 55.32% across the two approaches. The average age was 33.04 for the hypotension group and 32.32 for the non-hypotension group ($p < 0.040$).

Table 2 contrasts our hypotension rates to published results. Since all previously reported results except one involved very small sample sizes, the only meaningful comparison is based on the "30% drop of mean arterial pressure (MAP)" definition.

Table 2 reports first the complication statistics for the observed cases. To validate that the observed cases are representative of the overall hospital practice, we also report the complication statistics for the 1,398 charts reviewed, among which we focus on the 892 C-section cases. The results correlate well that the observed group is of higher risk than the chart-review group. We also separate the needle-based versus the catheter-based cases (Table 3).

The study reveals that the needle-based approach requires a smaller dose and results in a faster and more effective epidural analgesia without increasing the incidence of hypotension.

Uncovering Features for Predicting Hypotension

Machine learning is employed to uncover clinical and patient features that can predict hypotension. This allows for potential clinical practice guideline modification and/or early provider intervention to mitigate the effect. Our study consists of three parts. First, we used 533 observations from the first nine months (January – September 2014) and partitioned them randomly into two sets for training and blind prediction. Next, we used the established predictive rules to blind predict the next three months of 134 patients (October to December 2014). And finally, we blind-predicted the 892 C-section patients for the period January to September 2015. This allows us to measure the accuracy in predicting the status of future patients. It also sheds light on the consistency of the physicians' hypotension definition.

The inputs consist of patient demographics, physical and allergy characteristics and overall health, weeks of pregnancy, number of redo epidurals, number of re-boluses and dose, test dose, epidural needle and catheter doses, total dose, duration of injection, sensory level and time achieved, delivery type, position, medication type, and provider. We seek to uncover a small subset of discriminatory features that

Table 2. Comparison of hypotension rates

Hypotension definition	Percentage and sample size from literature, n=107 (KIÖHR et al., 2010)	Percentage and sample size in our study	
		Observed cases (n=667)	Chart review cases (n=892)
<90 mm Hg, systolic	16.3%	31.03%	23.54%
<90 mm Hg or a 20% decrease from baseline, systolic	54.8%	60.87%	48.65%
<100 mm Hg, systolic	41.5%	58.92%	50.56%
<100 mm Hg or >20% reduction from baseline, systolic	59.3%	72.41%	60.65%
<100 mm Hg or >30% reduction from baseline, systolic	46.7%	62.22%	53.14%
30% Drop of MAP	46.5%, n=919(Maayan-Metzger et al., 2010)	38.98%	29.37%

can predict hypotension. DAMIP returns 27 predictive rules each achieving greater than 82% 10-fold cross-validation accuracy and greater than 85% blind prediction accuracy for predicting hypotension and non-hypotension in patients for the period January – September 2014. The discriminatory features selected include weeks of pregnancy, number of redos, epidural needle/catheter dose, number of re-boluses and dosage, and patients' allergy. When blind predicting against new patients from October – December 2014, the predictive accuracy reaches 89%. Further, it reaches > 85% when blind predicting patients from January – September 2015.

Table 4 shows the consistently good predictive accuracy of DAMIP in both hypotension and non-hypotension patients. The better performance of DAMIP over other classifiers may be due to the fact that its resulting classification rule is *strongly universally consistent*, given that the Bayes optimal rule for classification is known. In addition, DAMIP handles imbalanced data very well.

Identified provider practice features offer an opportunity for CPG improvement, whereas patient characteristics allow for targeted/personalized care intervention. In the simulation study below, we used

Table 3. Comparison of hypotension for needle- and catheter-based approaches

Hypotension standards	OverallPercent	Percent in needle-based approach	Percent in catheter-based approach	χ^2 test statistic	P-value
<90 mm Hg, systolic	31.03%	31.55%	20.00%	1.232443	0.2669
<90 mm Hg or a 20% decrease from baseline, systolic	56.97%	61.07%	56.67%	0.091160	0.7627
<100 mm Hg, systolic	58.92%	31.55%	53.33%	4.177185	0.0410
<100 mm Hg or >20% reduction from baseline, systolic	72.41%	72.68%	66.67%	0.143280	0.7050
<100 mm Hg or >30% reduction from baseline, systolic	62.22%	62.48%	56.67%	0.155639	0.6932
30% Drop of MAP	38.98%	39.40%	30.00%	0.649923	0.4201

Table 4. DAMIP classification results for predicting hypotension and comparison against other classifiers

Classifier	10-fold cross validation (416 cases) unbiased estimate		Blind prediction			
			117 cases(Jan – Sept 2014)		134 cases(Oct – Dec 2014)	
	Hypotension	Normal	Hypotension	Normal	Hypotension	Normal
Classification Tree	71.61%	51.76%	73.85%	30.56%	79.05%	35.71%
Logistic Regression	88.24%	43.53%	61.54%	34.72%	67.62%	45.24%
Naive Bayes	87.47%	42.35%	78.46%	11.11%	89.52%	19.05%
Random forest	98.21%	27.65%	96.92%	2.78%	100.00%	1.19%
k-nearest neighbors	86.19%	20.59%	80.00%	15.28%	86.67%	17.86%
SVM	68.29%	42.94%	69.23%	31.94%	72.38%	27.38%
DAMIP	**82.50%**	**82.00%**	**90.70%**	**87.50%**	**89.20%**	**91.40%**

the identified predictive rules and their associated discriminatory features to construct care/delivery redesign experiments to reduce hypotension incidence.

Predictive Model of Sensory Level

Machine learning is further applied to predict the sensory level. Achieving the appropriate level of sensory blockade is critical for the C-section procedure. Dosage wrongly administered into the subarachnoid space will cause the block to extend too high up and can result in a series of side effects, including hypotension, decrease of cardiac output and loss of breath (Ward et al., 1965).

Accurate prediction could assist providers in prognosis with an early determination of outcome, which would give them an adequate amount of time for treatment and patient care. The prediction herein employs 18 continuous and 20 categorical features covering the biometrics of patients, use of medicine, procedures, etc. The predictive algorithms include an optimized random forest, a deep neural network, and a gradient boost regression model. The neural network and gradient boost regression model perform equally well with the lowest mean relative error of 0.15-0.16. Random forest achieves the best mean squared error of 1.59, indicating that it can better handle the diverse range in sensory level (Table 5).

To understand the importance of factors in contributing to the sensory level achievement, we applied SHAP (SHapley Additive exPlanation) value (Lundberg et al., 2018) to infer individual and interactional effects. The random forest model reports that total dosage, duration of injection, weight and physicians' experience are top features that positively impact sensory level. Meanwhile, higher initial blood pressure, being overweight, and operation redo are indications of unsatisfactory sensory level (Figure 4).

The effect of factors on sensory level is not monotonic. For example, initial diastolic blood pressure has zero or slightly positive effect on sensory level when within the range of 55-86 mmhg. However, when the pressure is too high (>90 mmhg) or too low (<50 mmhg), it is significantly harder for the body to achieve the required sensory level (Figure 5). It is also possible to compensate the negative effect of high diastolic blood pressure by increasing the total dosage, indicated by the negative correlation when the pressure is greater than 90 mmhg. Similarly, total dosage is intuitively positive on achieving sensory level until the dosage reaches greater than 35 cc (Figure 6). This phenomenon represents situations where the patient's body is not responding well to the initial anesthetics and multiple re-boluses must be administered. It is worth noting that in the group with high total dosage (>35 cc), the patients

Table 5. Performance comparison of random forest, neural network, and gradient boost regression in predicting sensory level. MSE: mean squared error, MAE: mean average error, MRE: mean relative error.

Dataset		Random forest	Neural network	Gradient boost
Training	MSE	1.2564	2.0033	2.1303
	MAE	0.9042	0.9204	0.8121
	MRE	0.1866	0.1687	0.1362
Test	MSE	1.5878	1.8657	2.1403
	MAE	0.9972	0.9179	0.9128
	MRE	0.1987	0.1643	0.1540

are significantly taller (p=0.0053), further confirming that height is a negative factor on sensory level achieving.

System Simulation and Clinical Practice Improvement

We first ran the computer simulation model using parameters established from the 667 observed cases. The simulation was run for 19,651 patients to reflect the total number of newborns delivered during a calendar year. We focused on highly revealing issues based on our outcome findings: redo epidural procedure, hypotension, and other complications such as blood in catheter/needle, wet tap, high block, and nausea and vomiting. The expected time for completing the entire epidural workflow was 9.26 minutes under current conditions.

Guided by the machine learning results and the identified discriminatory features, we optimized the needle-base epidural dose administration process. Table 6 summarizes briefly the anticipated changes from the current practice on three scenarios. These scenarios focus on physician variations on administering medication, test dosage, and total dosage. Each scenario is characterized by the physician's individual epidural technique. This includes actual physicians' characteristics such as their selection of medications, loss of resistance technique, and injecting durations.

Scenario 1 reflects a moderate needle dose with a tight total needle dose across all practitioners (15-18 ml). Scenario 2 allows for higher needle dose up to 25 ml. Scenario 3 offers broader dose variance reflecting current practice while limiting needle dose to within 20 ml.

Table 7 shows that Scenario 1 results in the lowest redo rate, hypotension rate, and total procedure time, whereas Scenario 3 shows acceptable results for hypotension. Northside Hospital delivers 19,651 newborns annually, with 75.1% receiving epidural analgesia. Hence the reduction in patient complication cases would be substantial. Overall, all three scenarios improve the procedure time. Using a high epidural needle dose, Scenario 2 performs worse than the current practice. For the 892 C-section chart review cases, the hypotension rate is 21% among patients satisfying Scenario 1 criteria.

Practice Variance Among Providers

Forty-four physicians were observed. The years of practice ranged from 6 to 30 years. All physicians reported using the needle-based approach with over 68% acquiring the skill at Northside Hospital.

We categorized them by years of practice: greater than 25 years (long), between 10 to 25 years (medium), and fewer than 10 years (short). Analysis shows that there is no significant difference in

Figure 4. Feature importance (SHAP value) of random forest model

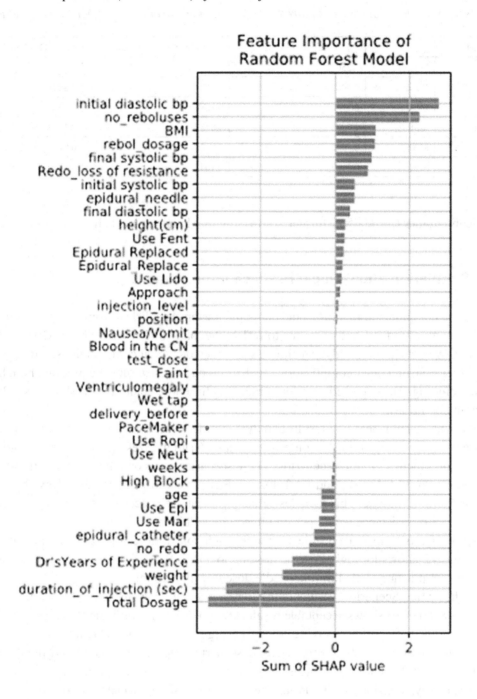

prescribed epidural dosage for C-section (long vs. medium: $p < 0.8590$, short vs. medium: $p < 0.6623$, long vs. short: $p < 0.8245$).

Figure 7 (blue) shows the preference in the loss of resistance techniques with 42.92% of providers favoring the use of air. These choices result in significantly different time to sensory level. When local anesthetics is used, the average time to sensory level is the lowest among all techniques (local anesthetics: 14.79 min, overall: 15.95 min, $p = 0.0304$). And using-only-saline gives the lowest rebolus rate

Figure 5. Interaction of initial diastolic blood pressure and total dosage

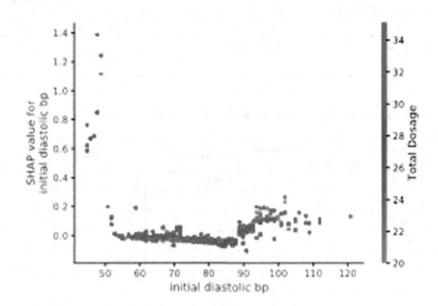

(16.33% compared to overall rate of 41.42%). Table 8 shows that air + saline is an inferior technique: it results in 47.37% rebolus and requires a longer time to sensory level than all other techniques (21.11 min, p = 0.0402).

Figure 6. Interaction of total dosage and height

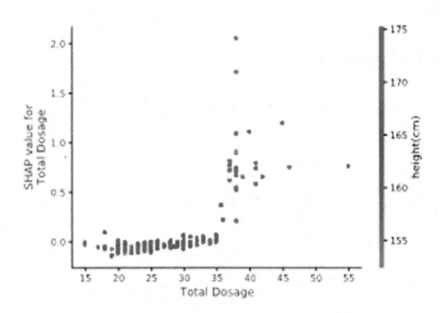

Table 6. Simulation scenarios performed to investigate potential reduction in complications

	Scenario 1: Needle dosage of 15-18 ml	Scenario 2: Needle dosage 20-25 ml	Scenario 3: Diverse dose range
Test dosage	2 ~ 5 ml	0 ~ 5 ml	0 ~ 5 ml
Epidural needle dose	15 ~ 18 ml	20 ~ 25 ml	5 ~ 20 ml
Total dosage	15 ~ 25 ml	20 ~ 30 ml	10 ~ 30 ml

Table 7. Contrast of complication rates using 3 scenarios of the needle-based approach

Complication type	Occurrence rate per year: Current performance		Scenario 1	Scenario 2	Scenario 3
Redo epidural process	Needle	5.14%	**4.18%**	4.75%	4.92%
	Catheter	5.15%			
Replace epidural	2.80%		**2.40%**	2.88%	3.02%
*Hypotension	50.89%		**31.82%**	55.43%	49.47%
Blood in catheter/needle	0.32%		**0.31%**	0.32%	0.33%
Wet tap	0.17%		**0.16%**	0.18%	0.17%
High block	0.33%		**0.33%**	0.33%	0.33%
Nausea/Vomit	0.35%		**0.34%**	0.35%	0.35%
Faint	0.17%		**0.17%**	0.16%	0.17%
Procedure time	9.26 minutes		**5.12 mins**	5.98 mins	5.78 mins

*Based on the definition used by Northside Hospital providers.

While there is a marginal difference in the epidural replaced rate, the overall redo rate appears to be the lowest among physicians with a medium number of years of experience. This may be explained by the fact that they have adequate experience and knowledge and are in prime condition to deliver high quality service. The statistics also show that experienced physicians have the lowest redo rate in loss of resistance (Figure8).

Figure 7. Loss of resistance techniques

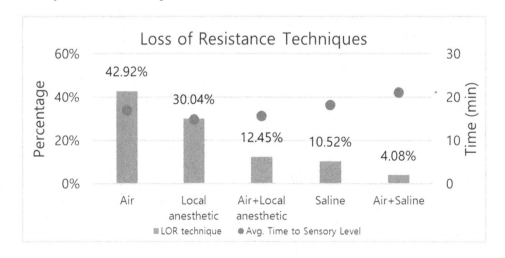

Table 8. Frequency of re-bolus versus loss of resistance techniques

Los of resistance technique	Air	Air+Local anesthetic	Air+Saline	Local anesthetic	Saline
Frequency of re-bolus	30%	16.33%	47.37%	35.00%	25.86%

A

Figure 8. Redo rates with respect to the years of practice of anesthesiologists

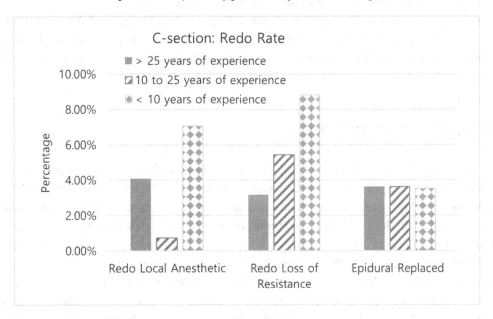

Patients treated by anesthesiologists with either a medium or a long number of years of experience also have a significantly shorter time to sensory level when compared to those administered by less-experienced providers (Table 9). Meanwhile, the contrast of difference of hypotension rate, total dosage prescribed, and sensory level show no significant difference with the number of years of experience.

Drug Types and Use of Opioids

Anesthesiologists have different drug preferences and overall, fifty-one medicine combinations were used. Lidocaine is the most common medicine and is used in 88.79% of all C-section cases. The top five combination drugs are 1) Lidocaine 2%, NaHCO3, Epi, Fentanyl (29.83%), 2) Lidocaine 2%, NaHCO3, Epi (16.05%), 3) Lidocaine 2%, Epi (12.84%), 4) Lidocaine 2% (11.24%), and 5) Lidocaine 2%, Epi, Fentanyl (7.49%); these five combinations are used in over 50% of all patient cases. 49.70% of all cases

Table 9. Years of experience and time to sensory level

Years of experience		Avg. time to sensory level (min)		t test statistics	p-values
Short	Medium	17.31	15.59	2.45842927	0.01462619
Short	Long	17.31	15.40	2.49430328	0.01314172
Medium	Long	15.59	15.40	0.34005402	0.73399864

involved the opioid fentanyl as one of the components. In 39.46% of the cases, fentanyl was combined with epinephrine.

Lidocaine with epinephrine is more acidic compared to standalone lidocaine, and the acidity causes pain during injection (Frank and Lalonde, 2012). To neutralize the acidity, NaHCO3 (neut) is applied. Our findings show that neut has little effect on the time to sensory. We found that "lidocaine + epi" is better in achieving sensory level when compared to Marcaine (15.61 min vs. 17.33 min, p = 0.0649). In 78.4% of the total cases, epinephrine is added to the medicine to prevent hypotension. In the cases where Lidocaine is used as the main medicine, epinephrine is beneficial to achieving higher and faster sensory level (sensory level: 4.77 (1.330) vs. 5.26 (1.77), p = 0.0120; time: 15.61 min vs. 17.67 min, p = 0.0303). More importantly, there is no significant difference in outcome if fentanyl is used or not (with fentanyl: 15.65 min, without fentanyl: 16.37 min, p = 0.2114). *Our study supports a conclusion that fentanyl can be avoided in epidural anesthesia.*

FUTURE RESEARCH DIRECTIONS

This study demonstrates how the use of a broad range of informatics techniques can help to uncover practice characteristics that are critical for care improvement. Of the 3,745,279 documented births in the United States in 2019, 31.7% were delivered via cesarean delivery (Martin et al., 2019); and among women delivering vaginally, as high as 61% received epidural or spinal anesthesia (Osterman and Martin, 2011). The potential consequences of a failed or misplaced epidural needle are well known to anesthesiologists who practice obstetric anesthesia. While much has been analyzed regarding complications, especially hypotension, there has been limited research regarding the dose-sensory response and standardization of the epidural analgesia procedure to reduce practice variance and maintain low rates of complication. Provision of neuraxial labor analgesia in a timely manner has been shown to be important to many parturients on open-ended patient surveys (Attanasio et al., 2015). Thus, it is important to examine the efficacy and safety of epidural dosing techniques that may shorten analgesic onset.

The rationale for potentially improved analgesia onset with epidural needle injection is uncertain. Dosing prior to placement of the catheter, such as with a combined spinal and epidural approach or through the epidural needle, may have the additional benefit of allowing labor analgesia to commence in instances which catheter placement is in an epidural vein and additional procedure time is necessary. In addition to faster onset of analgesia, it has been reported that dosing through the epidural needle may result in improved quality of epidural anesthesia compared to dosing through the catheter (Cesur et al., 2005). Other studies in obstetric (Husain et al., 1997; Ristev et al., 2017) and non-obstetric (Yun et al., 2004) patients receiving epidural anesthesia have observed a similar outcome. Recently, Ristev et al. 2017 performed the first study in comparing needle and catheter injection of epidural medications for the initiation of *labor (natural birth)* analgesia. There remains a serious lack of research examining the potential benefits and risks of initiating labor analgesia with injection of anesthetic medications through the epidural needle, especially among C-section patients. Moreover, little is known regarding practice and patient outcome related to a large dose injected through the epidural needle.

Uncover and Quantify Safe Dosage and Efficacy of Needle-based Epidural Delivery Technique

We hypothesized that needle injection directly into the epidural space would shorten analgesic onset and improve the quality of subsequent labor analgesia compared to catheter injection. With increasing demand on quality of medical service and evidence of outcome, the medical providers seek to work collaboratively with medical informaticians and systems engineers to comprehensively analyze the performance of the epidural anesthesia service. Leveraging the unique clinical practice at Northside Hospital, we evaluate the safety of a needle-based epidural technique for elective caesarian sections and establish evidence of a safe-level of epidural needle dose. We also analyze and quantify the dose-sensory response evidence and the associated complications in the hands of experienced anesthesiologists. For an objective comparison, we contrast our findings to published results. To the best of our knowledge, there is no previous comparative effectiveness study analyzing dosage delivered via needle versus catheter.

Our findings indicate that a needle-based approach is faster and more dose-effective in achieving comparable sensory level than the traditional catheter-based approach. Injecting large doses (up to 20 ml) in the epidural space through the epidural needle is safe, with complication rates similar to those of the traditional catheter-based approach reported in published literature. Further, if the needle dose is kept under 18 ml, the resulting hypotension rate will be significantly lower than current catheter delivery practice.

Uncover Discriminatory Features that Predict Complications and Sensory Level Achievement

We identified a small subset of discriminatory features, including weeks of pregnancy, patient allergies, number of redos, epidural needle/catheter dose, number of re-boluses and dosage that can predict hypotension with an 85% confidence level using our DAMIP machine learning approach. The identified patient characteristics allow for precautionary care intervention for at-risk patients during the epidural procedure. The provider practice features offer an opportunity for clinical practice guideline development and process improvement. Using system simulation and optimization, we investigated scenarios to reduce the hypotension incidence. Our results suggest that the hypotension rates can be driven down to 31% while the needle dose can be as high as 18 ml. A cohort of 1,398 patients obtained via chart review is used to validate our findings to ensure that they are representative of the hospital's clinical practice.

Using machine learning, we quantified the features and their interactive and combination effect to achieving proper sensory level. With accurate predictions of sensory level, our findings can assist anesthesiologists in prognosis with early determination of outcome. Subsequently, the advanced information will allow prompt treatment and patient care.

Our analysis also reveals that total dosage, duration of injection, patient weight, and physicians' experience are the top features that positively impact sensory level. Higher initial blood pressure, being overweight, and operation redo are indications of unsatisfactory sensory level. Additionally, using the SHAP value, we discovered the non-monotonic effect of factors. This again confirms the sophistication in constructing optimum practice guidance in epidural anesthesia. By breaking down the underlying factors, it is possible to advance the knowledge and practice for a better outcome.

Practice Variance and Over-Prescription of Fentanyl

We contrasted the proficiency of physician practice and provided insights on their preference in medication and dosage. Understanding the causes and effects of variation can help providers and healthcare organizations avoid practices that negatively impact outcomes. Our results establish evidence of safe and effective epidural needle dosage. They confirm that needle injection directly into the epidural space shortens analgesic onset, reduces medication dosage, and improves the quality of subsequent labor analgesia when compared to catheter injection. This facilitates evidence-based dose delivery to patients that results in safer and more effective pain control during child delivery. The new CPG results in fewer complications and helps with training of anesthesiologists based on evidence-based best practice. *Our study also supports the conclusion that the use of fentanyl has little effect on the outcome and can be avoided in epidural anesthesia.*

Currently, there are very few reported studies in which anesthesia providers have initiated labor analgesia by injecting medications through the epidural needle immediately after loss of resistance to achieve faster onset of pain relief. Northside Hospital offers a unique opportunity for in-depth study in the efficacy and quality of a needle-based epidural approach due to the large volume of newborns delivered annually. While the design of a direct clinical comparison may be desirable, most of the expertise of the site's physicians is with a needle-based approach. Consequently, comparing the outcome of this site to reported published results offers an unbiased perspective. While this study was performed for obstetric patients, the practice of injecting dose via epidural needles is commonly used for pain relief in childbirth and various types of surgeries. Thus, our analyses are broadly generalizable to epidural practice in various types of surgeries that require localized anesthesia.

CONCLUSION

This chapter investigates practice variance in performing epidural anesthesia for cesarean section. Specifically, we analyze the safety and efficacy of a large-dose, needle-based epidural technique where the anesthetic dose is administered through an epidural needle prior to insertion of the epidural catheter. Using a data-driven informatics and machine learning approach, our findings show that the needle-based technique is faster and more dose-effective in achieving sensory level than the catheter-based approach. We also find that injecting large doses in the epidural space through the epidural needle is safe, with complication rates similar to those catheter-based approach reported in published literature. Further, machine learning reveals that a needle dose of at most 18 ml offers lower hypotension complication. The machine learning framework can predict hypotension incidents with 85% accuracy. Machine learning results also show that total dosage, duration of injection, weight and physicians' experience are top features that positively impact sensory level. Some of these features (e.g., blood pressure, total dosage) have non-monotonic interactive effects on sensory achievement. The findings facilitate pain relief improvement and establish an improved clinical practice guideline for training and the dissemination of safe practices. The successful prediction of hypotension allows for early intervention to minimize the effects of complication. Furthermore, although almost 50% of the drug combinations used involve fentanyl, our findings show that fentanyl has little effect on the outcome and should be avoided in epidural anesthesia. The practice of injecting dose via epidural needles is commonly used for pain relief in childbirth and various types of surgeries. Thus, the data-driven machine learning approach is broadly applicable to advances in quality improvement. The results are generalizable to epidural practice in various types of surgeries that require localized anesthesia.

ACKNOWLEDGMENT

This work is partially supported by grants from the National Science Foundation, IIP-0832390 and IIP-1361532, and the Northside Anesthesiology Consultants, LLC. Findings and conclusions in this paper are those of the authors and do not necessarily reflect the views of the National Science Foundation and the Northside Anesthesiology Consultants, LLC. The authors would like to acknowledge the Georgia Tech students Lavannya Atri, Layla Bouzoubaa, Jamie Lee, Janice Liang, Rodriguez Robert, Raghav Srinath, Patrick Terry, Manik G Vig, Chaz Woodall, Stephanie Zhang for conducting the time-motion study, reviewing manually the scanned patient charts, and developing the initial process maps. The authors would also like to acknowledge the Northside interns Will Lewis, and David Little for assisting in chart reviews and collecting clinical data. The authors specially thank Dr. Alan R Kaplan MD for his guidance and collaboration to make the study a success. The authors also thank Barbara Brown for her tireless effort in guiding the team in all aspects of hospital access and questions, and for Jane Markel, Dr Doug Smith, MD, Dr. John Neeld, Jr. MD, and Dr. Billy Thomas, MD for their leadership support. We also thank Dr. Franklin Dexter for his invaluable comments regarding this work, and Judy Lamana for proofreading the manuscript.

REFERENCES

Attanasio, L., Kozhimannil, K. B., Jou, J., McPherson, M. E., & Camann, W. (2015). Women's experiences with neuraxial labor analgesia in the listening to mothers II survey: A content analysis of open-ended responses. *Anesthesia and Analgesia*, *121*(4), 974–980. doi:10.1213/ANE.0000000000000546 PMID:25412403

Brooks, J. P., & Lee, E. K. (2010). Analysis of the consistency of a mixed integer programming-based multi-category constrained discriminant model. *Annals of Operations Research*, *174*(1), 147–168. doi:10.100710479-008-0424-0

Brooks, J. P., & Lee, E. K. (2014). Solving a multigroup mixed-integer programming-based constrained discrimination model. *INFORMS Journal on Computing*, *26*(3), 567–585. doi:10.1287/ijoc.2013.0584

Cascio, M., Pygon, B., Bernett, C., & Ramanathan, S. (1997). Labour analgesia with intrathecal fentanyl decreases maternal stress. *Canadian Journal of Anaesthesia*, *44*(6), 605–609. doi:10.1007/BF03015443 PMID:9187779

Cesur, M., Alici, H. A., Erdem, A. F., Silbir, F., & Yuksek, M. S. (2005). Administration of local anesthetic through the epidural needle before catheter insertion improves the quality of anesthesia and reduces catheter-related complications. *Anesthesia and Analgesia*, *101*(5), 1501–1505. doi:10.1213/01. ANE.0000181005.50958.1E PMID:16244020

Cheng, Q., Zhang, J., Wang, H., Zhang, R., Yue, Y., & Li, L. (2015). Effect of Acute Hypercapnia on Outcomes and Predictive Risk Factors for Complications among Patients Receiving Bronchoscopic Interventions under General Anesthesia. *PLoS One*, *10*(7), e0130771. doi:10.1371/journal.pone.0130771 PMID:26147645

Crawford, J. S. (1972). The second thousand epidural blocks in an obstetric hospital practice. *British Journal of Anaesthesia*, *44*(12), 1277–1287. doi:10.1093/bja/44.12.1277 PMID:4265424

Dunham, C. M., Hileman, B. M., Hutchinson, A. E., Chance, E. A., & Huang, G. S. (2014). Perioperative hypoxemia is common with horizontal positioning during general anesthesia and is associated with major adverse outcomes: A retrospective study of consecutive patients. *BMC Anesthesiology*, *14*(1), 43. doi:10.1186/1471-2253-14-43 PMID:24940115

Eappen, S., Blinn, A., & Segal, S. (1998). Incidence of epidural catheter replacement in parturients: A retrospective chart review. *International Journal of Obstetric Anesthesia*, *7*(4), 220–225. doi:10.1016/S0959-289X(98)80042-3 PMID:15321183

Frank, S. G., & Lalonde, D. H. (2012). How acidic is the lidocaine we are injecting, and how much bicarbonate should we add? *The Canadian Journal of Plastic Surgery*, *20*(2), 71–73. doi:10.1177/229255031202000207 PMID:23730153

Gambling, D., Berkowitz, J., Farrell, T. R., Pue, A., & Shay, D. (2013). A randomized controlled comparison of epidural analgesia and combined spinal-epidural analgesia in a private practice setting: Pain scores during first and second stages of labor and at delivery. *Anesthesia and Analgesia*, *16*(3), 636–643. doi:10.1213/ANE.0b013e31827e4e29 PMID:23400985

Husain, F., Herman, N., Karuparthy, V., Knape, K., & Downing, J. (1997). A comparison of catheter vs needle injection of local anesthetic for induction of epidural anesthesia for cesarean section. *International Journal of Obstetric Anesthesia*, *6*(2), 101–106. doi:10.1016/S0959-289X(97)80006-4 PMID:15321290

Jenkins, J. G. (2005). Some immediate serious complications of obstetric epidural analgesia and anaesthesia: A prospective study of 145 550 epidurals. *International Journal of Obstetric Anesthesia*, *14*(1), 37–42. doi:10.1016/j.ijoa.2004.07.009 PMID:15627537

Kl, Ö. H. R. S., Roth, R., Hofmann, T., Rossaint, R., & Heesen, M. (2010). Definitions of hypotension after spinal anaesthesia for caesarean section: Literature search and application to parturients. *Acta Anaesthesiologica Scandinavica*, *54*(8), 909–921. doi:10.1111/j.1399-6576.2010.02239.x PMID:20455872

Lee, E. K., Gallagher, R. J., & Patterson, D. A. (2003). A linear programming approach to discriminant analysis with a reserved-judgment region. *INFORMS Journal on Computing*, *5*(1), 23–41. doi:10.1287/ijoc.15.1.23.15158

Lee, E. K., Wu, T. L., Goldstein, F., & Levey, A. (2012). Predictive Model for Early Detection of Mild Cognitive Impairment and Alzheimer's Disease. Optimization and Data Analysis in Biomedical Informatics. *Fields Institute Communications.*, *63*, 83–97. doi:10.1007/978-1-4614-4133-5_4

Lee, E. K., & Wu, T. L. (2009). Classification and disease prediction via mathematical programming. In Handbook of Optimization in Medicine (pp. 381-430). Springer Optimization and Its Applications 26. Springer. doi:10.1007/978-0-387-09770-1_12

Lee, E. K., Yuan, F., Hirsh, D. A., Mallory, M. D., & Simon, H. K. (2012). A clinical decision tool for predicting patient care characteristics: patients returning within 72 hours in the emergency department. In *AMIA Annual Symposium Proceedings*. American Medical Informatics Association.

Lee, E. K. (2007). Large-scale optimization-based classification models in medicine and biology. *Annals of Biomedical Engineering, 35*(6), 1095–1109. doi:10.100710439-007-9317-7 PMID:17503186

Lee, E. K. (2009). *Machine learning framework for classification in medicine and biology. Integration of AI and OR Techniques in Constraint Programming for Combinatorial Optimization Problems.* Lecture Notes in Computer Science, 5547.

Liu, S. S., Strodtbeck, W. M., Richman, J. M., & Wu, C. L. (2005). A comparison of regional versus general anesthesia for ambulatory anesthesia: A meta-analysis of randomized controlled trials. *Anesthesia and Analgesia, 101*(6), 1634–1642. doi:10.1213/01.ANE.0000180829.70036.4F PMID:16301234

Lundberg, S. M., Erion, G. G., & Lee, S. I. (2018). *Consistent individualized feature attribution for tree ensembles.* arXiv preprint arXiv:180203888.

Maayan-Metzger, A., Schushan-Eisen, I., Todris, L., Etchin, A., & Kuint, J. (2010). Maternal hypotension during elective cesarean section and short-term neonatal outcome. *American Journal of Obstetrics and Gynecology, 202*(1), e1-e5.

Martin, J. A., Hamilton, B. E., Osterman, M. J. K., & Driscoll, A. K. (2019). Births; Final Data for 2019. National Center for Health Statistics.: Vol. 70. *Number 2. MATLAB and Statistics Toolbox.* The MathWorks, Inc.

Norris, M. C., Grieco, W. M., Borkowski, M., Leighton, B. L., Arkoosh, V. A., Huffnagle, H. J., & Huffnagle, S. (1994). Complications of labor analgesia: Epidural versus combined spinal epidural techniques. *Anesthesia and Analgesia, 79*(3), 529–537. doi:10.1213/00000539-199409000-00022 PMID:8067559

Omote, K., Namiki, A., & Iwasaki, H. (1992). Epidural administration and analgesic spread: Comparison of injection with catheters and needles. *Journal of Anesthesia, 6*(3), 289–293. doi:10.10070054020060289 PMID:15278539

Osterman, M. J. K., & Martin, J. A. (2011). *Epidural and Spinal Anesthesia Use During Labor: 27-state Reporting Area, 2008.* National Center for Health Statistics.

Paech, M., Godkin, R., & Webster, S. (1998). Complications of obstetric epidural analgesia and anaesthesia: A prospective analysis of 10 995 cases. *International Journal of Obstetric Anesthesia, 7*(1), 5–11. doi:10.1016/S0959-289X(98)80021-6 PMID:15321239

Pan, P., Bogard, T., & Owen, M. (2004). Incidence and characteristics of failures in obstetric neuraxial analgesia and anesthesia: A retrospective analysis of 19,259 deliveries. *International Journal of Obstetric Anesthesia, 13*(4), 227–233. doi:10.1016/j.ijoa.2004.04.008 PMID:15477051

Ristev, G., Sipes, A. C., Mahoney, B., Lipps, J., Chan, G., & Coffman, J. C. (2017). Initiation of labor analgesia with injection of local anesthetic through the epidural needle compared to the catheter. *Journal of Pain Research, 10*, 2789–2796. doi:10.2147/JPR.S145138 PMID:29263693

Rout, C., Akoojee, S., Rocke, D., & Gouws, E. (1992). Rapid administration of crystalloid preload does not decrease the incidence of hypotension after spinal anaesthesia for elective caesarean section. *British Journal of Anaesthesia, 68*(4), 394–397. doi:10.1093/bja/68.4.394 PMID:1642918

Sadashivaiah, J., Wilson, R., McLure, H., & Lyons, G. (2010). Double-space combined spinal-epidural technique for elective caesarean section: A review of 10 years' experience in a UK teaching maternity unit. *International Journal of Obstetric Anesthesia, 19*(2), 183–187. doi:10.1016/j.ijoa.2009.06.005 PMID:19945843

Sprigge, J., & Harper, S. (2008). Accidental dural puncture and post dural puncture headache in obstetric anaesthesia: presentation and management: A 23-year survey in a district general hospital. *Anaesthesia, 63*(1), 36–43. doi:10.1111/j.1365-2044.2007.05285.x PMID:18086069

Thangamuthu, A., Russell, I. F., & Purva, M. (2013). Epidural failure rate using a standardised definition. *International Journal of Obstetric Anesthesia, 22*(4), 310–315. doi:10.1016/j.ijoa.2013.04.013 PMID:23932551

Vallejo, M. C., Phelps, A. L., Singh, S., Orebaugh, S. L., & Sah, N. (2010). Ultrasound decreases the failed labor epidural rate in resident trainees. *International Journal of Obstetric Anesthesia, 9*(4), 373–378. doi:10.1016/j.ijoa.2010.04.002 PMID:20696564

Van de Velde, M., Schepers, R., Berends, N., Vandermeersch, E., & De Buck, F. (2008). Ten years of experience with accidental dural puncture and post-dural puncture headache in a tertiary obstetric anaesthesia department. *International Journal of Obstetric Anesthesia, 17*(4), 329–335. doi:10.1016/j.ijoa.2007.04.009 PMID:18691871

Verstraete, S., Walters, M. A., Devroe, S., Roofthooft, E., & Van De Velde, M. (2014). Lower incidence of post-dural puncture headache with spinal catheterization after accidental dural puncture in obstetric patients. *Acta Anaesthesiologica Scandinavica, 58*(10), 1233–1239. doi:10.1111/aas.12394 PMID:25307708

Ward, R. J., Bonica, J. J., Freund, F. G., Akamatsu, T., Danziger, F., & Englesson, S. (1965). Epidural and subarachnoid anesthesia: Cardiovascular and respiratory effects. *Journal of the American Medical Association, 191*(4), 275–278. doi:10.1001/jama.1965.03080040017003 PMID:5899742

Yun, M., Yong-Chul, K., Lim, Y., & Choi, G. (2004). The differential flow of epidural local anaesthetic via needle or catheter: A prospective randomized double-blind study. *Anaesthesia and Intensive Care, 32*(3), 377–382. doi:10.1177/0310057X0403200313 PMID:15264734

ADDITIONAL READING

Ashaye, T., Hounsome, N., Carnes, D., Taylor, S. J. C., Homer, K., Eldridge, S., Spencer, A., Rahman, A., Foell, J., & Underwood, M. R. (2018). Opioid prescribing for chronic musculoskeletal pain in UK primary care: Results from a cohort analysis of the COPERS trial. *BMJ Open, 8*(6), e019491. Advance online publication. doi:10.1136/bmjopen-2017-019491 PMID:29880563

Keita, H., Deruelle, P., Bouvet, L., Bonnin, M., Chassard, D., Bouthors, A. S., Lopard, E., & Benhamou, D. (2021). Raising awareness to prevent, recognise and manage acute pain during caesarean delivery: The French Practice Bulletin. *Anaesthesia Critical Care & Pain Medicine*, 40(5), 100934. Advance online publication. doi:10.1016/j.accpm.2021.100934 PMID:34400388

Orhun, G., Sungur, Z., Koltka, K., Karadeniz, M. S., Yavru, H. A., Gürvit, H., & Şentürk, M. (2020). Comparison of epidural analgesia combined with general anesthesia and general anesthesia for postoperative cognitive dysfunction in elderly patients. *Ulusal Travma ve Acil Cerrahi Dergisi*, 26(1). Advance online publication. doi:10.14744/tjtes.2019.04135 PMID:31942729

Shibasaki, S., Kawamura, H., Homma, S., Yosida, T., Takahashi, S., Takahashi, M., Takahashi, N., & Taketomi, A. (2016). A comparison between fentanyl plus celecoxib therapy and epidural anesthesia for postoperative pain management following laparoscopic gastrectomy. *Surgery Today*, 46(10), 1209–1216. Advance online publication. doi:10.100700595-015-1290-4 PMID:26695406

Tanaka, H., Kamiya, C., Katsuragi, S., Tanaka, K., Yoshimatsu, J., & Ikeda, T. (2018). Effect of epidural anesthesia in labor; pregnancy with cardiovascular disease. *Taiwanese Journal of Obstetrics & Gynecology*, 57(2), 190–193. Advance online publication. doi:10.1016/j.tjog.2018.02.004 PMID:29673659

Toledano, R. D., & Leffert, L. (2021). What's New in Neuraxial Labor Analgesia. In Current Anesthesiology Reports (Vol. 11, Issue 3). doi:10.100740140-021-00453-6

Wang, Y., & Xu, M. (2020). Comparison of ropivacaine combined with sufentanil for epidural anesthesia and spinal-epidural anesthesia in labor analgesia. *BMC Anesthesiology*, 20(1), 1. Advance online publication. doi:10.118612871-019-0855-y PMID:31898488

Yang, Z., Li, D., Zhang, K., Yang, F., Li, M., & Wang, L. (2019). Comparison of epidural anesthesia with chloroprocaine and lidocaine for outpatient knee arthroscopy. *Journal of Orthopaedic Surgery (Hong Kong)*, 27(3). Advance online publication. doi:10.1177/2309499019865534 PMID:31370751

KEY TERMS AND DEFINITIONS

Cesarean Section: C-section, or Cesarean birth is the surgical delivery of a baby through a cut (incision) made in the mother's abdomen and uterus. Health care providers use it when they believe it is safer for the mother, the baby, or both. The incision made in the skin may be: Up-and-down (vertical).

Clinical Practice Guidelines: "Systematically developed statements to assist practitioner decisions about appropriate health care for specific clinical circumstances" (Field & Lohr, 1990). They can be used to reduce inappropriate variations in practice and to promote the delivery of high quality, evidence-based health care. They may also provide a mechanism by which healthcare professionals can be made accountable for clinical activities. The Institute of Medicine (IOM) (2012) defines clinical practice guidelines as "statements that include recommendations, intended to optimize patient care, which are informed by a systematic review of evidence and an assessment of the benefits and harms of alternative care options."

Epidural Anesthesia: A regional anesthesia that blocks pain in a particular region of the body. It is performed where a medicine is injected into the epidural space around the spinal cord. The goal of an epidural is to provide analgesia, or pain relief, rather than anesthesia, which leads to a total lack of feeling. Epidurals block the nerve impulses from the lower spinal segments. This results in decreased sensation in the lower half of the body.

Hypotension: Also known as low blood pressure, is a blood pressure under 90/60 mm/Hg. In many people, it has no symptoms. When it does cause symptoms, these are usually unpleasant or disruptive, including dizziness, fainting and more.

Machine Learning: A method of data analysis that automates analytical model building. It is a branch of artificial intelligence based on the idea that systems can learn from data, identify patterns, and make decisions with minimal human intervention.

Opioids: A broad group of pain-relieving drugs that work by interacting with opioid receptors in the cells.

Pain Management: An aspect of medicine and health care involving relief of pain in various dimensions, from acute and simple to chronic and challenging.

Practice Variance in Healthcare: A deviation from normal standards of care. Medical practice variation reflects practice differences among health care clinicians and includes overuse and underuse, both of which can have negative consequences for patients.

Simulation: A model that mimics the operation of an existing or proposed system, providing evidence for decision-making by being able to test different scenarios or process changes.

Analysis of Big Data

A

Sabyasachi Pramanik

ⓘ https://orcid.org/0000-0002-9431-8751

Haldia Institute of Technology, India

Samir Kumar Bandyopadhyay

The Bhowanipur Education Society College, India

INTRODUCTION

The intelligent utilization of technology can be through data mining (Sanad, Z. et al. 2021) which draws upon broad work in territories, for e.g. statistics (Bhattacharya, A., et al., 2021), machine learning (Gupta, A., et al., 2021), databases (Oliveira, A. Y., et al., 2021), pattern recognition (Abrams, Z. B., 2021), and high performance computing (Brinkmann, A., et al., 2020) to find interesting and beforehand obscure information in datasets. So how precisely does data mining (Pappalardo, A. et al., 2021) give everyone the information about things that anyone didn't have a clue, couldn't watch or foresee what may occur straightaway? The procedure used to play out these accomplishments is called demonstrating. Despite the fact that demonstrating procedures have been around for a very long time, it is just with the appearance of computing advances that enable us to store enormous measures of data and utilize computerized display systems that one would be able to anticipate and understand the concealed pattern inside data. It can be understood that big data are unquestionable, publications and research journals are full of anecdotes and case reports highlight the importance of such data for organizations. For example, McAfee and Brynjolfsson (McAfee, 2012) discern a physical bookstore that can monitor the books sold and that can connect those purchases with a single client, for e.g. Amazon, whether they have a devotion service. Online stories would document not just what was offered, how and why, but also how people navigated their platform and how innovations and promotional deals affected them, and they will also use this knowledge to anticipate what consumers want next. Instead, they would document internet retailers with almost total exactness what they are offering. Some claim, though, that the importance of big data goes beyond that. McAfee and Brynjolfsson (2012) also ensure that big data is innovative in handling companies and users. They claim that since evidence is small, it makes sense for people with high roles to determine according to their instinct: their experience and their own clinical habits. Big data, they claim, would bring a death to the HiPPOs-the emotions of the highest paying individual until the actions of management are actually guided by data. Others go a further step to say that big data makes a whole part of human intelligence redundant.

BACKGROUND

The abstraction, encoding and chronicling of domestic documents and their distribution using data processing machines was originally published by Luhn (1958) (Luhn, H. P., et al., 2021), who used it to explain the abstraction, encoding, and chronicling of internal documents. After, the paradigm shifted and the need to turn simplistic data into usable decision making information became more stress able in the

DOI: 10.4018/978-1-7998-9220-5.ch006

Copyright © 2023, IGI Global. Copying or distributing in print or electronic forms without written permission of IGI Global is prohibited.

Figure 1. Flow diagram of business intelligence

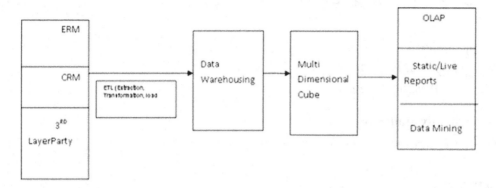

1980s. The term business intelligence (Pramanik, S., et al., 2021) is often used to describe a number of practices like competition intelligence. The Gartner Group therefore currently prefers an umbrella concept that covers software, technology and system, as well as the best practices to enhance and maximize decision making and efficiency access to and analysis of information. The flow diagram for Business Intelligence and big data are shown below.

Business Analytics and Business Intelligence

Market analytics from big data may certainly be of tremendous use, but the present wave of science is unable to cope with the word coined for the web-based study in early days of the internet. We ought

Figure 2. Flow diagram of big data

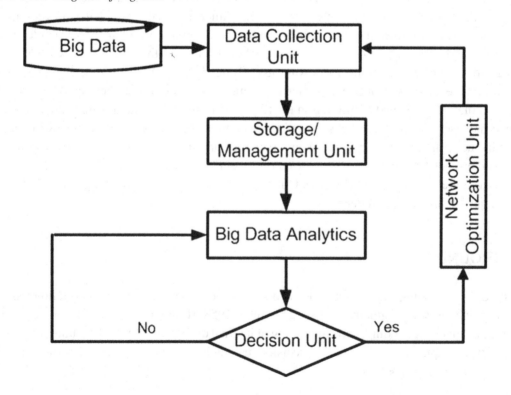

to analyze the massive data phenomenon in more depth to explain why this occurs. In this relation, we will use the terms "Three Vs" volume, veracity and velocity- which is first generated to explain trends in e-commerce development. Let us first describe big data. There is no fixed amount of gigabytes, terabytes or petabytes that distinguish big data (Fan, C., et al. 2021) from normal data. Data storage is still evolving, because what seem to be lots of good data at the moment could seem like a perfectly reasonable volume over a year or two. Moreover, every relationship is different, because a financial services firm does not feel like any of the data metrics that appears to be daunting for a little retail shop. More researchers however, describe massive volumes of data as three Vs. We call it big data if the following properties of the data store are:

1. Volume: Big data is a collection of data that is so large that it is put aside or stored by the organization that appears to address problems. Currently, phenomena such as e-commerce, mobility, web-based life and the IoT produce so much knowledge that virtually every affiliation actually meets those criteria.
2. Velocity: As an individual create new data at a fast rate and need to respond in real time, we are speeding up big data. Many e-commerce applications, online existence or IoT (Tun, S. Y. Y., et al., 2021) connections follow this big data criterion.

Range: If the data exist in a number of organizations, the diversity of big data is related. Big data collection, including data in organized relationships database management systems (RDBMSs) typically contains e-mail addresses, word processing documents and images as well as well as video presentations.

Three features face a range of problems in the big data projects of any organization. Any of those big data issues that are commonly recognized include:

Dealing with Data Growth

The clearest issue with big data is essentially to put that knowledge away and to analyze it. IDC reports that the amount of knowledge accumulated on the IT structures of the earth is compounded by around every two years in its Digital Universe survey. By 2020, the number of a heap of tablets form Earth to Moon would be adequate to fill 6.6 times, and businesses keep approximately 85% of the details responsible. Many of these data are unstructured, which means they are not contained on a database. It is difficult to search and evaluate records, photos, music, videos and other unstructured data. Therefore it is no wondered that the IDG study found that "the collection of unstructured data is a problem-from 31% in 2015 to 45% in 2016. Associations are collaborating on various different technologies in order to tackle data development. Converged and fully converged networks and software-defined computing, when it comes to data, will make the size of the technology simpler for businesses. And technology such as compression reduction and tiring will minimize space estimation and high data storage costs. Management and analysis are used by businesses to figure out what they need from their enterprises by means of equipment such as NoSQL (Gomes, C., et al., 2021) databases, Hadoop (Ashghar, H., et al., 2021), Spark, the big data research tools, business intelligence applications, artificial intelligence thinking and machine learning.

Generating Insights in a Timely Manner

Associations undoubtedly would like not to store their big data either, but to accomplish their corporate goals they have to use the big data. According to the survey by New Vantage Collaborators, the following priorities for big data ventures were:

1. Reduction of operating productivity costs
2. Build a society guided by data
3. Creation and disruption of new avenues
4. Speed up the introduction of new technologies and resources
5. Start new goods and services

Such strategies can make companies more competitive, but they can gain only a limited amount of information from their vast volumes of data and track this knowledge quickly. All of us must have quicker decision-making criteria particularly in finance, insurance and healthcare as found by the 2016 PWC Global Data and Analytics Survey. Any businesses are searching for a newer generation of ETL and analysis instruments to reduce the time it takes to produce reports significantly. They invest in real time investigative tools that allow them to adapt quickly to industry trends.

Recruiting and Retaining Big Data Talent

The market of big data experts has risen and as a result the big data researchers have a considerably higher pay. Also organizations need professionals with big data expertise to create, handle and operate certain applications that produce knowledge. The Robert Half Technology Salary Guide 2017 estimated averages of $135,000 to $ 196,000 for big data technicians and $ 11600 - $16300 for data scientists. Also analysts in business intelligence were paying, earning $ 118,000 to $ 138,750 annually. Associations have a number of alternatives for dealing with talent shortages. In the first place, they increased their budgets with recruiting and retention activities. Second, they gave their newer workers more preparatory training in order to grow the skills they require from within. Thirdly, several organizations search for innovations. They purchase self-service and/or machine-learning inquiry structures. These tools developed for practitioners without a degree in data science will help organizations meet the big data goals even without the prospect of hiring a lot of big data personnel experts.

1. Integrating Big Data Disparate Sources

Data processing is complicated by the complexity associated with large data. Big data comes from different sources-business apps, internet-based life sources, email networks, documentation generated by staff etc. It can be extremely daunting to incorporate all of these details and balance them with the intention of generating reports. Vendors sell a number of ETL and data integration products intended to ease the process but several businesses claim that the data integration issue has not yet been overcome. Many businesses go to new technological frameworks in response. 89% of the respondents said in the IDG study that in the next 12 years their businesses expect to invest in new big data instruments. When asked what kind of products they wanted to buy, integration technology was second behind data processing tools.

2.   Validation of Data

The concept of data acceptance is closely connected to the idea of system incorporation. Comparable data from various systems is also collected through partnerships and data from these different systems usually cannot be recognized. The e-commerce system for e.g. will display regular transactions to a certain degree, whereas the ERP system has a slightly different amount. Or an EHR (Ahmad, F. S., et al. 2021) system can have a single address for the patient, where a joint pharmacy store has another record address. Otherwise, the EHR system may have a single address for the patient. The mechanism on which such documents are decided is called data governance so as the documents are correct, usable and secure. And data governance is the fastest growing area of concern in the At Scale 2016 Large Data Sophistication Survey cited by respondents. The complexities of data processing are very complicated and generally involve a mixture of structure and technology. Associations also create an assembly of persons to supervise data collection and compose policies and procedures. They should also engage in data protection initiatives intended to enhance data security (Pramanik, S and Raja, S. S., 2020) and help ensure the quality and usability of big data stores.

3.   Securing Big Data

Moreover, stability is a huge problem for large data storage organizations. After all, certain Large Data Stores may be enticing to hacker targets or specialized APIs. Most organizations, however, tend to assume that their current data protection approaches are still suitable for their big data needs. In the IDG study, less than half (39%) of these surveyed said that their large data-servers or analyses were focused on additional security measures. Extra measures include identification and access management (59%), protection of data (52%), and the division of data (42%) for those who use extra steps.

4.   Organizational Resistance

It can be daunting to not just the technical dimensions of big data that humans can still be a challenge. 85% of the people surveyed said that their organizations were willing to build a data focused community in the New Vantage Partners study, but only 37.5% indicated that they succeeded. When asked about the barriers to the society, people within their organizations pointed out three main hurdles:

- Insufficient coordination of authority (4.6%)
- Failure to pick and appreciate middle management (42%)
- Aversion to market or lack of awareness (43%)

The main aim for organizations to take advantage of big data resources is to find every other path. Especially for big corporation, this form of transition can be incredibly complicated. PwC advised that one can invest in sound leading figures that appreciate and criticize the data technologies in order to enhance the organization's decision making capability. One path to developing leadership of this sort is to name a Chief Data Officer, a move taken by 55% of Fortune 500 businesses through New Vantage Partners. Nevertheless, in the event that businesses stay competitive in the digital ecosystem, corporation needs directors, administrators and supervisors who work on solving the big data problems with or without a Chief Data Officer.

Issues related to Big Data Handling

Big data analysis is a tool used in the large repositories to expose hidden relationship and abstract relations and allow efficient decision-making through dynamic inspection and representation approaches. In several various processes, vast data is processed including data collection and storage, extraction and cleaning, data processing, representation, query generation, data selection, interpretation and analysis. There are complexities with all these measures. The main challenges with data mining include complexity, scale, distance, reliability and security.

1. Heterogeneity and Incompleteness

Big data exam's difficulties stem from their vast scope as does the inclusion in the gathered and processed data of mixed data dependent on the multiple trends (heterogeneous data). The data has many trends and laws owing to the complex heterogeneous mixture data. The trends fluctuate considerably. Data can be organized as well as unstructured. 80% of organizational data were unstructured. They are very special and have no single organization. There will be email files; photos, pdf notes, medical records, X-beams, voice transmission, pictures (Pramanik, S., et al. 2021), video and sound etc and they cannot be processed as organized data inline/segment form. It is a remarkable task for the big data mining to turn this data into an organized framework for later analysis. Therefore, to manage these details, emerging technology must be embraced. Incomplete data causes confusion and can be handled through data processing. It's also a struggle to do this correctly. The lack of data field values for such sample corresponds to insufficient results. Different conditions can allow missing values to occur, such as a sensor node bug or certain structural policies to purposely circumvent certain values. Whereas most sophisticated data mining analyses include responses on handling missing values to generate enhanced models (compared to the models from initial data). For this reason there are various attribution methods and the effective approaches are to fill out values observed most frequently or to construct learning models to predict future values for each field, based on the values observed in one case.

2. Scale and Complexity

It is difficult to handle huge and rapidly growing data volumes. The handling of growing data volumes is not enough for traditional computing systems. Additional difficulties due to adaptability and sophistication of data that must be processed include data surveys, relationships, processing and simulation.

3. Timeliness

As the data sets are growing in scale, it takes time to evaluate them. Results of the enquiry are expected urgently in such conditions. In the case of alleged credit card theft, for e.g., preferably it can be detected by stopping a transaction from happening by some way before the transaction is done. Obviously, it is not possible in real time to complete the evaluation of a user's buying background. Thus, halfway results need to be generated in advance such that a finite amount of cumulative estimation of new data can be utilized to achieve a snapshot. For a broad dataset, elements that satisfy a stated criterion always have to be found. This form of search is likely to occur frequently during the data review. It is clearly illogical to search the whole collection of data to find relevant components. In such instances, index systems are generated early enough that certification components can be found easily. The problem is that only such groups of parameters are accepted by each index structure.

How Big Data and Business Intelligence Work Together?

1. Analysts and data scientists focus on statistical testing for the longest possible time to assist them in determining business day by day. However, big data will change this whole situation.

2. There is still more information coming online and incorporating it into current business intelligence (BI), CRM, (Chen, C., et al., 2021) ERP and other essential business networks. This puts the customer's clear perspective at the heart. While most customer care and sales reps were not aware of the effect, some businesses want to see if this will be quick.

3. Big data have provided an instrument available to line-level administrators for the most part of complimentary and regression surveys. This helped managers make realistic and long-term business decisions using non-transactional knowledge.

4. Big data, though, would not ignore the normal BI computers. Big data would make BI a reliable and versatile platform for certain companies, despite everything. You will still continue to analyze the past in order to forecast the future, but with the massive data you will have to do more. Business intelligence will never depart in this way, however big data will boost it.

5. How do you decide if the findings in the current exploration arenas will really be visible in the future? Many ladies prefer high-heels, for e.g., rather than traditional heel pumps. In this case, preliminary research studies may reveal that more high-heel shoes are cheaper than the normal heel shoes, which means that high-heel shoes sell more.

6. That's a connection, therefore not a source. If we think closely about the true sales details obtained from your business intelligence tools, you may know that you are, for e.g., pleased with your new marketing activities because retailers are turning to high-heel shoes.

7. Life on the internet is still enjoyable. It allows retailers to know how consumers respond to different goods and which shops sell the most. This encourages retailers to store the shops in compliance with the feedback of the customer. BI and big data allow you to analyze these trends and connect your brand with your area of operation and consumer answers. Without that, you will take a huge chance to market your goods with a fateful window.

8. Many decisions had already been based on verifiable evidence and the pattern could have continued if it occurred. But big data analysis helps with a flash clip.

9. This is done by incorporating open source software, i.e., the origins of big data processes. Today the cloud is able to quickly gather and preserve vast quantities of data that were previously not understood or people have little insight into how to do it.

10. The primary force behind big data is also known as unstructured data. It has no impact on this. This is usually connected to the geographical data, combined with the current customer standardized level files and with streams from new sources. This allows you to learn how consumers respond to your products in a certain online networking level. This produces a new instrument which is very strong.

11. Two things happened to big data. It allows gaining more information from multiple sources that can be integrated on a smaller scale. In the sense of this strategic business judgment, for e.g. one can quickly alter behavior using technologies like advanced cells.

4. Shortening time to answer key to big data analytics

The best benefit of this method of the study is to reduce the response time. Data scientists are currently in search of the fastest possible time to answer questions and models that take months to answer. Big data and AI tools have made it easier to work with information before transforming, streamlining or re-rationalizing it.

How Might Big Data Impact Industry Structure and Enhance Margins?

How will big data impact the farming and nutrition industries? There are various effects on the market structure and the profit margins of individual companies, but two specific effects are: 1) Improvement in distribution in network links to increase outputs and dealers of sustenance and productivity, and 2) improvement in ranch manufacturing practices.

In terms of the features, buyers, particularly in the developing market, are becoming increasingly demanding. Customary characteristics such as wholesome quality, flavor, texture, reasonability and protection of plant or creature protein goods, remain pillars of customer preferences, but predictability and consistent requirements have been improved. With a particular emphasis on hygiene and safety, a whole chain traceability scheme may minimize exposure to hazardous goods and mitigate loss of quality across the supply and customer chain. Quality/security/ traceability structures powered by massive data have the ability to satisfy these elevated customer demands.

Other attributes are becoming more important in the molding of consumer buying behavior much as perceptions of society from the feeding industry attributes those economists refer to as "credential" attributes are typically difficult to quantify. They are also a factor of the way the commodity is produced and handled across the whole supply chain (Ruel, S., et al., 2021), from breeding to retail chains. These include non-chemical or anti-microbial, natural production processes produced locally and/or families, animal protection methods, sustainable manufacturing/processing/distribution systems. Such qualities can include the flowing: Since multiple credentials features and are not the last product characteristics, but procedures or events that occur or do not occur over the value or material network, reporting and validation are also only carried out by whole-chain follow up programs. Data and information systems are also important in each stage of the store network for monitoring and evaluation of processes and activities. Likewise, the actual commodity (cereals), which is streaming through this distribution network (Ghosh, R., et al., 2021) with the purpose of credibly selling the last commodity and being verified as providing the qualities that the customer wants must either tagged or connected to the physical details and knowledge. Some claimed that it may be more important to encourage the use of big data technology than to encourage market efficiencies at the producer levels in the opportunity to enhance hygiene, product efficiency and traceability to ensure that the quantities of reputation and responsiveness to customers' demands and social standards are assured.

How do customers want to pay for reliability characteristics that require diverse and costly manufacturing procedures, as well as specific and exorbitant distribution processes across the procurement network from suppliers to consumers (following segregating, transporting, managing and purchasing). Many experiments show that a meat and creature protein section would in any case compensate for special characteristics. For instance, Olynk, Tonsor and Wolf (2010) report the cost of USDA pork cleaves to be charged by the customers to a $1.74 per pound premium-PVP has reported that the manufacturing process does not accommodate individual boxes and slowdowns. Furthermore Olynk (2012) found that customers are charged for access to hay, for unregulated use and non-use of crates and for slowing down milk production. Wolf, Tonsor and Olynk (2011) found that the customers were typically prepared to pay large premiums on the nearby family farming for milk provided without rBST with a guaranteed increase in sanitation, when cases are checked in America Agricultural Department. In addition, a more comprehensive integration of the shop network from the knowledge provide to the grocery supplier may theoretically lead to greater productivity through increased resource control and product stream preparation of both specific goods and supply chains. Big data technology and information management would promote this convergence. In all processes (from grain and livestock production to manufacturing and distribution) the problems of organization and inventory control for e.g. have the capacity for costly inventory storage and degradation (waste, water, food, quality), if the operation is well-coordinated. Big data explanatory projects and systems will increasingly be powered by information and communication systems which promote coordination and enhance the capacity to cater to current product streams and forecast future scenarios, bottlenecks or unnecessary supply.

Big Data Versus Business Intelligence

For big data versus business intelligence, just scale and time have respectively dilated and accelerated. The million events per month are as yet present but the order of the magnitude is currently 100 million and the time of the order of the second. The 50 million individual records have become 50 million charts oriented. And, once more, this concerns just a few high-traffic players whose needs for real-time data investigation are significant. One thinks about the well-realized informal communication sites but likewise to the online sellers whose recommendation engines fuel to business intelligence in near real-time. The need for those who drive and decide whether they are business leaders, long distance commanders or space mission managers lie not in the data but rather in the information contained therein, and information, it is necessary to have the correct level. Too little is uncertainty. To an extreme and it becomes indecisive. It is additionally necessary to have accurate information just to be aware of it at the appropriate time. The acceleration of trade induced by the increased interconnections and more efficient vehicle technology has further reduced the reasonably delay between the occurrence of an event and its detection and presentation to the decision-maker. This delay is known as the latency of the event detection presentation cycle. In the event that the majority of the verifiable decision chains were satisfied with 24 hour latency, this period is never again acceptable because the characteristic period of numerous business processes of the order of a minute or even a second, millisecond on account of completely automated processes. Once this is done, one can nevertheless say that one remains in a traditional problem of systematic extraction and synthetic presentation of information. What is never again exemplary is the assortment of sources that are often external and the growth of the mass of data to be interpreted. It is this growth characteristic that imposes the need for versatility characterization that is called big data. Big data is a way to deal with business intelligence characterized by

- A level of integration of internal and external data I varied and mutable organization
- A distributed architecture for data storage and processing
- A very weak latency of the event detection presentation cycle

FOCUS OF THE ARTICLE

Taking BI – Busting the Big Data Myths

1. Big data is an IT problem: It is surely not. It influences everyone and can revolutionize the way the whole company operates. Companies who only use big data in their IT programs prefer to see their current deals at poor quality rates. From the beginning, it pays to include everything.

2. We don't have the best potential to fulfill big data requirements: that's BI's elegance. Your peers (whichever degree of experience they are) can quickly grasp and exploit a structured agreement. And streamlined, repetitive procedures allow it simple and convenient for you to view the details you need in your business on big visual dashboards.

3. The data we gather is mess-we will never master it: it is not unusual to mistake data, but an efficient data processing system like Meson-BI makes recording, washing, handling and review of information much simpler-so "awful data" is never an argument anymore.

We also reviewed a range of examples of big data implementations as guidance for the development of skilful urban applications. Various measures have been successful and useful elements have been implemented to strengthen municipal facilities and technologies. The table below reveals the use of big data in various main city areas of the world through actual shrewd city ventures. The table below reveals. An analysis of some of the actual deployments showed that large data represent shrewd town components have advantages.

Table given below summarizes these benefits within the different application domains used in smart cities (Wang, E.K., 2021).

FUTURE RESEARCH DIRECTIONS

India needs to accelerate the role of big data in social innovation. Data is the most daily instrument in the world that affects global economic components. Today, about 25 bytes of data are generated every day. By 2030, four times the digital data will be accessible than all of the world's grains of sand. Via Big Data Analytics, this data is used to propel businesses and the global economy via useful insights and informed decision-making. In order to refine their goods and services the science and industry worlds have integrated Big Data successfully. For example, Flipkart analyses daily for data-driven decision making 25 million columns of inventory data. Likewise, with the help of big data development, Snapdeal and HomeShop18 are projected to produce 30% to 40. Yet social corporations are pursuing the corporate and science sectors by the processing and analysis of immense data initiatives. India has been plagued by at least 29 numbers of social challenges, including pollution. Big data is used to coordinate and provide tailored structure and funding to have full social impact and community growth to address these social problems. Their ability to collect information Public and private sector both aim to leverage the power of Big Data in the social hemisphere in the same way. Aadhaar is the world's biggest biometric initiative collecting a billion Indian citizens' demographic and biometric data. The database will easily expand to as much as 20 petabytes and can be used for the detection and control of major societal network problems. This has also been used to use Jan Dhan-Aadhaar-Mobile (JAM) as a mobile financial inclusion device and to pass direct benefits for LPG. In order to promote the role of the big data in social growth, India needs to take many steps further.

First of all, national databases need to be built on basic and complicated problems including poverty, malnutrition, education and shelter. The data bank should be structured in such a way that it is interoperable and scalable. Companies should focus on developing multi-sector partnerships to facilitate knowledge sharing on issues relating to society. For example, World Bank organizations are actively

Table 1. Big data projects in smart city components

Smart city components	Big Data Projects	Location
Transportation. Mobility, and Logistics	An automated traffic stream simulation based on smart traffic lights and flag as part of a smart city initiative (ATISMART model). Three main components should be taken into account for rapid simulation time for the traffic stream: city man, cars and smart signs. There are some specifications, such as network controls, traffic lights and CAS as the logical centre of the model and the Java framework for the GUI, to incorporate an intelligent traffic stream.	USA
Healthcare	"Ministry of Health and Welfare has established the Social Security Integrated Distribution Network with 385 forms of public information from 35 departments and for the central government to administer social welfare program and program in general, as well as for the near-by states	South Korea
Public Safety	"Age. Agriculture, Forestry and Fisheries and Department of Public Administration and Protection, or MOPAS aim to dispose of a mechanism of prevention of foot and mouth diseases, harnessing the big data creature diseases in other parts of the country, reports of rituals and travel, breeding ranch surveys, relocation of farm animals and livestock workers.".	South Korea
	"In 2004, the Singapore government initiated the Risk Evaluations and Horizon Scanning (RAHS) program under the National Security Coordinating Center. To resolve public protection, infectious diseases and other national issues. The proactive monitoring of global risks such as terrorist acts, contagious illnesses and financial crises through the compilation and dissection of large-scale web centers. A noteworthy requirement for the REC is to examine potential scenarios involving avian influenza imports into Singapore and to analyze the danger of South-East Asian outbreaks.	Singapore
Education	NEdNet is an integrated framework which encompasses network infrastructure services, education 21 and learning services that promote higher-order thinking skills, support self-directed, customized learning based around learners and support decision making activities. NEdNet is a framework of learning.	Thailand
Natural resources & energy	In 2004, in order to strengthen government capacity to resolve cross-ministerial and multidisciplinary issues. 21 the UK administration established the Horizon Scanning Center (HSC). In 2011, Foresight International Aspects of Climate Change by the HSC discussed climate change and its impact on food and water security, regional conflicts, international stability and protection by an in-depth study of various data sources.	UK
Government & agency administration	"A massively scalable distributed architecture evolves to perform a real time analysis of high-volume streaming data. For the recognition and representation, the program architecture and device management focused on Hadoop, stream processing and data storage are used in thousands of real-time sources".	USA
	"As a step towards online disclosure and openness, the US government released data.gov in 2009. It is a repository of 420,894 logistics, infrastructure, wellness, education, public resources and data collection datasets."	USA
	"In 2011, Syracuse, NY, initiated a Smarter City initiative in partnership with IBM, with the goal of using big data in predicting and avoiding empty homes. The Information Technology Department of Michigan developed a data centre to provide a knowledge base".	USA

working towards public access to such databases. In comparison, massive data sets may be applied in the corporate sector to further create social change. Second, social science initiatives can help decision-

Table 2. Benefits of big data projects in smart city components

Smart City Components	Benefits of Big Data Projects in Smart City Components
Smart Healthcare	• Enable the gathering, review and usage of patient records by healthcare professionals (Dutta, S., et al., 2021) and physicians, and can also be used by insurance firms and some government departments. • Endorse the collection of specific events for routine or on demand scanning, reviewing, and barring future health conditions. • Improve the volume and individual character of data obtained on health conditions of some patients using intelligent devices associated with the home or emergency care centers to scan characteristics such as circulatory strain, glucose and sleep habits for precise, immediate health responses and detailed information on patients' history.
Smart Energy	Facilitate decision-making relevant to the energy supply in accordance with citizens' actual demands and in each affected area. • Allow for forecasts to be made in an almost real time manner through effective large-scale analysis. Coordination by clear value strategies for the market, demand and output structures for strategic goals (enhanced resources).
Smart Transportation	• Recognize traffic dynamics by real-time data analysis • Reduce the pollution of urban highways by anticipating weather and adjusting traffic regulations. By building a new lane upgrading the infrastructure based on congestion data and gathering information on vehicular and alternate routes, smart cities would be able to minimize traffic and incidents by big data. • Minimize storage network loss by supplier distribution and ease transportation. • Allow traffic information gathered by sensors, smart light bulbs and on-car computer to drivers using mobile phones or other specialist equipment to be analyzed and shared through data streaming. • Submit suggestions to individual agencies to take steps to ease or fix a traffic challenge using big data.
Smart Environment	• Offer meteorological knowledge to improve the country's livestock, provide better education for potential unsafe situations and better energy use control through more detailed demand forecasts.
Smart Safety	• Provide accurate, spatial and temporal maps of geographical regions which help to assess any changes. • Assistance to predict potential changes in the atmosphere or devastating incidents such as earthquake prediction that will save lives and money.
Smart Education	• Optimize scholarly research; for example, astronomers may now analyze a broad dataset of spatial science, using powerful computers rather than manual evaluations. New developments in the field will occur by breaking up and analyzing high-quality digital photographs from space. This refers to various areas of study as medical processes development, environmental assessments and economic and financial measures. • Comportment and teamwork contribute to new understanding. - Student outputs a specific data trail from the evaluation of learners to online habits. By splitting up these statistics, educational organizations will consider whether their services are used in the right way and whether they achieve the right outcomes.
Smart Governance	• Encourages the alignment and collaboration of multiple government departments and integrates their procedures or streamlines them. This would lead to smoother procedures, improved mutual data management and tighter supervision and compliance. • Support for Big Data Analysis to make business decisions. A more successful judgment can be taken in relation to jobs, development and region policies by studying a company's actions and economic progress in terms of its adversaries and climate conditions. • Publish new data owners (citizens) and development authority (public agencies) policies. Publish new policies. Government organizations are trying to help improve data collection, while people are learning how to use the information in order to maximize the level of public service and move it to new expertise. • Support policymakers concentrate on residents' welfare and social problems, infrastructure, transportation, police and other problems.

makers better solve the challenges. As more open-source technology levels come into being, groups will lead to imaginative research and new concepts and goods.

In 2010, the Greater London Authority permitted people to access and use crude crime, fiscal, transport, etcetera data. Private projects like BBC Lab Great Britain 20 have also been very good for shaping public opinion through studies ranging from The Major Stress Test to The Online Behavior Test.

Thirdly, we need to open up doors for current workers to train and develop skills that are crucial for data examiners to cope with social issues. The majority of data scientists today are notably clustered in the business and academic sectors. The creation of the National Data Science Network as a trainer, advisor and provider to social entrepreneurs with big data resources will help shut down this knowledge void.

Fourthly, open forums and dialogue sessions can be produced and encouraged so that the network can exchange lessons learned and implement advanced creative steps. One example is Crowd ANALYTIX USA, a network on which technology experts work and collaborate with multinational companies to address their market problems. Such data science groups concentrate on social environment and are crucial in order to prevent the risk of pushing the needle and use big data to solve social problems.

Around the planet, companies aim to use open data and big data collective solutions to social challenges. creative and

Data Kind UK, for instance, was designed to help use big data in the light of social issues. Data Kind integrates scientists and researchers with non-profit organizations to help them execute large-scale programs and counter the lack of technical workers. 29 In India, correlations such as Outline India push social impact through data studies and experiments.

We are experiencing a new "company" process, which is DICE or Entrepreneurship driven by Architecture, creativity and architecture. This new-age generation of developers uses Big Data analysis and development-oriented projects' to redefine the forms of multinational firms. Big data analysis will have a more accurate judgment and precise structure. It can also encourage creative solutions to address multiple socio economic problems for societies.

Front-Runner Sectors of Big Data and Analytics in India

Let me shed some light on the quiet revolution in the use of broad data and the review in the Government of India, before focusing on the commercial application of science. One of the government's major challenges is to manage large infrastructure programs in due time and track the allocation of direct benefits for the poor. In the government's way of coping with these burning problems, a quiet revolt takes place on this side. Using big data, the satellite image can be analyzed to predict the truth on project success. The impact of direct value transfer can be determined by measuring mobile telephone use over the local locale. The use of mobile telephones is an unstructured service that is used widely for government agencies.

Returning to the market sector, banks and e-commerce Internet firms are the key participants. After 2008 the banks began to understand the value of their already accumulated degrading consumer records. This ultimately prompted them to do more business with current customers through their commitment to consumer desires and torment focus. The new market model of data gave them an opportunity for innovative company strategies to do more for onboard consumers as banking data is more accurate than, for example, retail data from other vertical companies. Indian giant banks, such as State Bank of India, HDFC and ICICI, are pioneers in the use of analysis to develop services and industry.

E-commerce firms are the next key actors in the Big Data Case, Flipkart, Amazon and so on. They can use unstructured and organized data in general in conjunction. E-commerce firms, for example, will need to establish competitive pitch/ upscale measurement. However, with almost 1.5 lakh products, how can the measurement be produced in real time? In comparison, the fragmented data dilemma when few of any odd products are sold regularly and there is an implicit minimal period of time before a consumer buys the same product again.

Big Data for the Next Green Revolution

Unmistakably, population growth and urbanization patterns are predicted to have emotional impacts on global food security by 2050. The influence is multi-sectoral reaching well beyond agriculture to housing, healthcare and technology. Yet technology will redefine those patterns for society's benefit. All parts of the horticultural value chain are troubled by technology which drives myriad opportunities and challenges to feed the 9.6 billion people on Earth profitably by 2050.

At the same time, the increasing need for food and the changing demands for sustainability are pushing capital space change. At present, worldwide is more integrated, producing vast data that can help to push the decision-making process that can transform the ranch supply chain from source to customer. Agricultural firms are subject in their distribution network to a variety of legislation and customer standards. Every one includes essential knowledge that can help corporations make a significant part of their money, provide enhanced clarity in their operations and protect customers, with many touches in the agri-value chain. Big data may provide value for each contact target starting with the correct agri-input range, the measurement of the soil moisture, market price tracking, water management systems testing and the correct distribution point and the right price.

What Data Can Do?

Big-data firms will evaluate seed varieties in multiple regions, soil types and climates. The way that Google can recognize influenza outbreaks based on site search begins helps to detect diseases that may kill a future harvest by cross-sector analysis of crops on demand. In a country like India, where there are 638 000 communities and 130 million farmers speaking 800 languages with 140 million acres of cultivable land under 127 agro-climate regions, 3000 different yields and 1 million varieties, data challenges and potential are enormous. Self-driven vehicles could now fly through fields using Global Positioning System (GPS) to signal less than an inch of error and enable farmers and prepare more specifically. But the actual probability emerges as data are gathered, aggregated and analyzed in real time on thousands of tractors on thousands of homes.

Precision agriculture allows farmers to control their resources, assist production. Improve economic productivity and reduce waste and environmental effects. The latest advancements in big data and advanced test technologies and autonomy from agriculture will profoundly shift the agri-scape and thus offer exciting growth for global agricultural production over the next few decades: for example, aerial photography, sensors and sophisticated local weather forecasts.

Right Information

Farmers need detailed weather data and reliable knowledge about the types of information they will use. Factors for updating knowledge (for example, nutrients, water and pesticide controls) may lead to the security (Pramanik, S., et al., 2013 and Pramanik, S., et al., 2014) of common resources. The use of granular data and the structural capacity to combine multiple sources of knowledge (such as temperature, land and market prices) would help to improve harvest yield and enhance the usage of capital, minimizing costs, for instance. Big Data can provide the right information to make informed decisions as climate change and extreme weather events call for preventive steps to adapt or improve resilience.

Big technology and advanced analysis optimize food processing value chains by identifying key process output determinants and going to continuously increase output precision, consistency and productivity. Big data has also been used to improve production forecasting focused on the imperatives of manufacturers, consumers, proximity to equipment and prices.

It will make the agri-business more noticeable in terms of supply efficiency and more effective in forecasting supply success over time. 21 million tones, mainly because of frightening cold storage centers and cooled cars, inadequate transport infrastructure and insecure power sources, are lost every year in India. Big data has the ability to reduce such losses by systematizing market forecasting.

Connecting the Dots

An agricultural goods exchange stage that connects the small-scale producers to the retail and mass buyers via mobile messages which help to send up-to-date market prices through an SMS application and link farmers to buyers, offering small and minimum agricultural group bartering opportunities.

In India, a structural process should be established to collect the data that could provide incremental incentive. Specifically, a rapid proliferation of mobile technologies in rural areas can allow farmers to boost productivity in these areas based on decisions supported by better, big data-based knowledge. It can also alter agri-business models (Dayakar, R. et al., 2021) and sales models as companies are given the ability to build a profitable revenue stream with new goods and services along these routes. Data expansion provides unparalleled opportunities to consider farmers' use and desires and to provide tailor-made services and goods that are useful to associations.

In view of that, now is the right time for farmers to identify best practices for data use. A market model must be developed in which the data from various participants in the agri-store network can be collected by value. Companies need to prioritize, develop and standardize big data through a corporate data management approach as Digital Data to accomplish the next and revolution.

CONCLUSION

Big data analytics is a broad term that includes a variety of technologies. Of course, sophisticated analytics may be used with big data, but in fact, various forms of technologies collaborate to help you get the most out of your data. Data scientists with a high-level skill set are required to improve your business analytics using big data. The abilities of big data analytics and business analytics must be combined. Knowledge of R and/or Python, the two most popular data manipulation programming languages, is the most significant distinction between the two. Working with enormous amounts of data necessitates optimizing the code that processes it, and those languages have emerged as the top dogs in the analytics field. This is in addition to the standard coding abilities that professionals require, such as SQL. Industry experience is a significant distinction between big data analytics for business analytics and basic approaches. Analysts can decide which datasets are valuable and which aren't if they have that prior knowledge. Big data implementation needs a set of tools as well. Hadoop and other comparable systems provide data processing and storage without the need for additional hardware, allowing software to scale up their analytical capabilities. Internal data may be better contextualized with access to relational databases and other data sources, resulting in more accurate predictions and models.

REFERENCES

Abrams, Z. B., Tally, D. G., Zhang, L., Coombes, C. E., Payne, P. R. O., Abruzzo, L. V., & Coombes, K. R. (2021). Pattern recognition in lymphoid malignancies using CytoGPS and Mercator. *BMC Bioinformatics*, 22(1), 100–112. doi:10.118612859-021-03992-1 PMID:33648439

Ahmad, F. S., Ali, L., Raza-Ul-Mustafa, Khattak, H. A., Hameed, T., Wajahat, I., Kadry, S., & Bukhari, S. A. C. (2021). A hybrid machine learning framework to predict mortality in paralytic ileus patients using electronic health records (EHRs). *Journal of Ambient Intelligence and Humanized Computing*, 12(3), 3283–3293. doi:10.100712652-020-02456-3

Asghar, H., & Nazir, B. (2021). Analysis and implementation of reactive fault tolerance techniques in Hadoop: A comparative study. *The Journal of Supercomputing*, 77(7), 7184–7210. doi:10.100711227-020-03491-9

Au-Yong-Oliveira, M., Pesqueira, A., Sousa, M. J., Dal Mas, F., & Soliman, M. (2021). The Potential of Big Data Research in HealthCare for Medical Doctors' Learning. *Journal of Medical Systems*, 45(1), 13–26. doi:10.100710916-020-01691-7 PMID:33409620

Bhattacharya, A., Ghosal, A., Obaid, A. J., Krit, S., Shukla, V. K., Mandal, K., & Pramanik, S. (2021). Unsupervised Summarization Approach With Computational Statistics of Microblog Data. In *Methodologies and Applications of Computational Statistics for Machine Intelligence*. IGI Global.

Brinkmann, A., Mohror, K., Yu, W., Carns, P., Cortes, T., Klasky, S. A., Miranda, A., Pfreundt, F.-J., Ross, R. B., & Vef, M.-A. (2020). Ad Hoc File Systems for High-Performance Computing. *J. Comput. Sci. Techno*, 35(1), 4–26. doi:10.100711390-020-9801-1

Chen, C., Geng, L., & Zhou, S. (2021). Design and implementation of bank CRM system based on decision tree algorithm. *Neural Computing & Applications*, 33(14), 8237–8247. doi:10.100700521-020-04959-8

Dayakar Rao, B., & Nune, S. D. (2021). Role of Nutrihub Incubation for the Development of Business Opportunities in Millets: An Indian Scenario. In A. Kumar, M. K. Tripathi, D. Joshi, & V. Kumar (Eds.), *Millets and Millet Technology*. Springer. doi:10.1007/978-981-16-0676-2_21

Dutta, S., Pramanik, S., & Bandyopadhyay, S. (2021). Prediction of Weight Gain during COVID-19 for Avoiding Complication in Health. *International Journal of Medical Science and Current Research*, 4(3), 1042–1052. doi:10.20944/preprints202105.0177.v1

Fan, C., Yan, D., Xiao, F., Li, A., An, J., & Kang, X. (2021). Advanced data analytics for enhancing building performances: From data-driven to big data-driven approaches. *Building Simulation*, 14(1), 3–24. doi:10.100712273-020-0723-1

Ghosh, R., Mohanty, S., & Pramanik, S. (2019). Low Energy Adaptive Clustering Hierarchy (LEACH) Protocol for Extending the Lifetime of the Wireless Sensor Network. *International Journal on Computer Science and Engineering*, 7(6), 1118–1124. doi:10.26438/ijcse/v7i6.11181124

Gomes, C., Tavares, E., & Junior, M. N. O. (2021). Cloud storage availability and performance assessment: A study based on NoSQL DBMS. *The Journal of Supercomputing*. Advance online publication. doi:10.100711227-021-03976-1

Gupta, A., Pramanik, S., Bui, H. T., & Ibenu, N. M. (2021). Machine Learning and Deep Learning in Steganography and Steganalysis. In *Multidisciplinary Approach to Modern Digital Steganography*. IGI Global.

Luhn, H. P. (1958). The Automatic Creation of Literature Abstracts. *IBM Journal of Research and Development*, 2(2), 159–165. doi:10.1147/rd.22.0159

Pappalardo, L., Grossi, V., & Pedreschi, D. (2012). Big data: The management revolution. *Harvard Business Review*.

Pappalardo, L., Grossi, V., & Pedreschi, D. (n.d.). Introduction to the special issue on social mining and big data ecosystem for open, responsible data science. *International Journal of Data Science and Analytics, 11*(4), 261–262. doi:10.1007/s41060-021-00253-5

Pramanik, S., & Bandyopadhyay, S. K. (2013). Application of Steganography in Symmetric Key Cryptography with Genetic Algorithm. *International Journal of Computers and Technology, 10*(7), 1791–1799. doi:10.24297/ijct.v10i7.7027

Pramanik, S., & Bandyopadhyay, S. K. (2014). Hiding secret message in an image. *International Journal of Innovative Science. Engineering & Technology, 1*(3), 553–559.

Pramanik, S., & Bandyopadhyay, S. K. (2014). Image Steganography Using Wavelet Transform And Genetic Algorithm. *International Journal of Innovative Research in Advanced Engineering, 1*.

Pramanik, S., Ghosh, R., Mangesh G., M., Narayan, V., Sinha, M., Pandey, D. & Samanta, D. (2021). A Novel Approach Using Steganography and Cryptography in Business Intelligence. *Integration Challenges for Analytics, Business Intelligence, and Data Mining*, 192-217.

Pramanik, S., & Raja, S. S. (2020). A Secured Image Steganography using Image Steganography. *Advances in Mathematics: Scientific Journal, 9*(7), 4533–4541. doi:10.37418/amsj.9.7.22

Pramanik, S., & Singh, R. P. (2017). Role of Steganography in Security Issues. *International Journal of Advance Research in Science and Engineering, 6*(1), 1119–1124.

Ruel, S., El Baz, J., Ivanov, D., & Das, A. (2021). Supply chain viability: Conceptualization, measurement, and nomological validation. *Annals of Operations Research, 8*. Advance online publication. doi:10.100710479-021-03974-9 PMID:33716370

Sanad, Z., & Al-Sartawi, A. (2021). Financial Statements Fraud and Data Mining: A Review. In A. M. Musleh Al-Sartawi, A. Razzaque, & M. M. Kamal (Eds.), *Artificial Intelligence Systems and the Internet of Things in the Digital Era. EAMMIS 2021. Lecture Notes in Networks and Systems* (Vol. 239). Springer. doi:10.1007/978-3-030-77246-8_38

Tun, S. Y. Y., Madanian, S., & Mirza, F. (2021). Internet of things (IoT) applications for elderly care: A reflective review. *Aging Clinical and Experimental Research, 33*(4), 855–867. doi:10.100740520-020-01545-9 PMID:32277435

Wang, E. K., Wang, F., Kumari, S., Yeh, J.-H., & Chen, C.-M. (2021). Intelligent monitor for typhoon in IoT system of smart city. *The Journal of Supercomputing, 77*(3), 3024–3043. doi:10.100711227-020-03381-0

ADDITIONAL READING

Anderson-Grégoire, I. M. (2021). A Big Data Science Solution for Analytics on Moving Objects. In L. Barolli, I. Woungang, & T. Enokido (Eds.), *Advanced Information Networking and Applications. AINA 2021. Lecture Notes in Networks and Systems* (Vol. 226). Springer. doi:10.1007/978-3-030-75075-6_11

Arooj, A., Farooq, M. S., Akram, A., Iqbal, R., Sharma, A., & Dhiman, G. (2022). Big Data Processing and Analysis in Internet of Vehicles: Architecture, Taxonomy, and Open Research Challenges. *Archives of Computational Methods in Engineering*, *29*(2), 793–829. doi:10.100711831-021-09590-x

Bertello, A., Ferraris, A., Bresciani, S., & De Bernardi, P. (2021). Big data analytics (BDA) and degree of internationalization: The interplay between governance of BDA infrastructure and BDA capabilities. *The Journal of Management and Governance*, *25*(4), 1035–1055. doi:10.100710997-020-09542-w

Corsi, A., de Souza, F. F., Pagani, R. N., & Kovaleski, J. L. (2021). Big data analytics as a tool for fighting pandemics: A systematic review of literature. *Journal of Ambient Intelligence and Humanized Computing*, *12*(10), 9163–9180. doi:10.100712652-020-02617-4 PMID:33144892

De Luca, L. M., Herhausen, D., Troilo, G., & Rossi, A. (2021). How and when do big data investments pay off? The role of marketing affordances and service innovation. *Journal of the Academy of Marketing Science*, *49*(4), 790–810. doi:10.100711747-020-00739-x

Fan, C., Yan, D., Xiao, F., Li, A., An, J., & Kang, X. (2021). Advanced data analytics for enhancing building performances: From data-driven to big data-driven approaches. *Building Simulation*, *14*(1), 3–24. doi:10.100712273-020-0723-1

Fathi, M., Haghi Kashani, M., Jameii, S. M., & Mahdipour, E. (2022). Big Data Analytics in Weather Forecasting: A Systematic Review. *Archives of Computational Methods in Engineering*, *29*(2), 1247–1275. doi:10.100711831-021-09616-4

Gu, V. C., Zhou, B., Cao, Q., & Adams, J. (2021). Exploring the relationship between supplier development, big data analytics capability, and firm performance. *Annals of Operations Research*, *302*(1), 151–172. doi:10.100710479-021-03976-7

Monino, J. L. (2021). Data Value, Big Data Analytics, and Decision-Making. *Journal of the Knowledge Economy*, *12*(1), 256–267. doi:10.100713132-016-0396-2

Naqvi, R., Soomro, T. R., Alzoubi, H. M., Ghazal, T. M., & Alshurideh, M. T. (2021). The Nexus Between Big Data and Decision-Making: A Study of Big Data Techniques and Technologies. In *Proceedings of the International Conference on Artificial Intelligence and Computer Vision (AICV2021). AICV Advances in Intelligent Systems and Computing* (vol. 1377). Springer. 10.1007/978-3-030-76346-6_73

Pasupathi, S., Shanmuganathan, V., Madasamy, K., Yesudhas, H. R., & Kim, M. (2021). Trend analysis using agglomerative hierarchical clustering approach for time series big data. *The Journal of Supercomputing*, *77*(7), 6505–6524. doi:10.100711227-020-03580-9

Silik, A., Noori, M., Altabey, W. A., Ghiasi, R., & Wu, Z. (2021). Analytic Wavelet Selection for Time–Frequency Analysis of Big Data Form Civil Structure Monitoring. In C. Rainieri, G. Fabbrocino, N. Caterino, F. Ceroni, & M. A. Notarangelo (Eds.), *Civil Structural Health Monitoring. CSHM 2021. Lecture Notes in Civil Engineering* (Vol. 156). Springer. doi:10.1007/978-3-030-74258-4_29

Visvizi, A., Lytras, M. D., & Aljohani, N. (2021). Big data research for politics: Human centric big data research for policy making, politics, governance and democracy. *Journal of Ambient Intelligence and Humanized Computing, 12*(4), 4303–4304. doi:10.100712652-021-03171-3

KEY TERMS AND DEFINITIONS

Big Data: Big data is a discipline that deals with methods for analysing, methodically extracting information from, or otherwise dealing with data volumes that are too massive or complicated for typical data-processing application software to handle.

Business Analytics: Company analytics is the set of skills, technology, and processes used to iteratively explore and investigate historical business performance in order to obtain insight and drive business model.

Business Intelligence: The tactics and technology utilized by businesses for data analysis and management of business data are referred to as business intelligence.

CRM: Customer relationship management (CRM) is the process through which a company or other organization manages its contacts with customers, usually by analyzing vast quantities of data.

Data Mining: In large amounts of textual or mixed visual and textual data sets, data mining is a process of searching, extracting, and analyzing (that may include) exploring multiple kinds of text graphic patterns (as calligraphic for example), language and literary figures, stylistics, that also includes techniques at the intersection of machine learning, formal linguistics analyses as textual statistics, and database systems.

E-Commerce: E-commerce refers to the electronic purchase and sale of goods using online services via the Internet.

ERP: Enterprise resource planning (ERP) is the integrated management of key business activities, which is often done in real time and handled by software and technology.

Machine Learning: Machine learning is the science of computer algorithms which can learn and develop on their own with experience and data. It is considered to be a component of artificial intelligence.

Security: By restricting others' freedom to act, security provides protection against, or resistance against, possible damage perpetrated by others. Persons and social groupings, objects and institutions, ecosystems, and any other thing or phenomena exposed to undesirable change may all benefit from security.

SQL: SQL is a domain-specific language used in programming and designed for managing data held in a relational database management system, or for stream processing in a relational data stream management system

Big Data Analytics in E–Governance and Other Aspects of Society

Dishit Duggar
Vellore Institute of Technology, Vellore, India

Sarang Mahesh Bang
Vellore Institute of Technology, Vellore, India

B. K. Tripathy
Vellore Institute of Technology, Vellore, India

INTRODUCTION

The world is moving towards more digitized processes for everything, primarily due to the COVID-19 outbreak. This pandemic has compelled governments to invest in big data analytics technology to make the functioning of the public sector faster, scalable, and reliable. With technology speeding up, IT Services have been generating a large amount of big data, and it is harder to process using the traditional data processing technologies. With data growing at such a significant speed, developers need to analyze and make decisions based on big data for better results and recommendations (Tripathy and Deepthi, 2017), (Tripathy, 2017), (Divya and Tripathy, 2020). Having insight into this data will improve the system's overall efficiency (Srividya and Tripathy, 2021). Big Data's scalable nature can easily correlate data and enhance the overall results. All countries' central governments are pushing hard to get more and more citizens of their country online and further digitize the whole process. Governments are trying to make data readily available to people anywhere through digitization, thus saving their time and resources. Therefore data collected from different government schemes are getting added, and the size of this data is increasing exponentially day after day, there is a steep rise in data-driven projects across several countries. Therefore, Big data and E-governance is becoming a crucial aspect of a country's development.

Through E-governance, government facilities are provided to the citizens conveniently and transparently (Agnihotri and Sharma, 2015), (Salwan and Maan, 2020). E-Governance plays a significant role in uplifting the country's economy and making people use digitized apps and websites to reduce human error.

This paper focuses on the Role of Big Data analytics in E-Governance and Society, mainly describing and improving Government measures to manage such a large amount of data efficiently and securely.

Big Data

Big data refers to data sets that are large and complex derived from various sources. Usually, such data sets are too large to be processed using the database techniques and programming languages that make up the bulk of today's technologies. Big data can be structured, unstructured, or semi-structured. Most of the current methods only allow processing structured data and fail for the other two categories (Tripathy et al, 2017), (Seetha et al, 2017).

DOI: 10.4018/978-1-7998-9220-5.ch007

Copyright © 2023, IGI Global. Copying or distributing in print or electronic forms without written permission of IGI Global is prohibited.

B

Big data can be collected from various sources such as information gathered from public apps and websites, public comments on social media sources, information on government schemes and policies, and many more. It is stored in complex, huge databases that can process this data, which is hard for the traditional databases.

Data stored is then processed and analyzed by Big data Analysts to derive insightful info patterns on how the data is being used and suggest changes in the existing system (Labrinidis and Hosagrahar, 2012), (Rajaraman, 2011). Big data has created many opportunities for all types of people. For example, increasing growth in customer data for a company makes them hire new sales representatives to meet the requirement and smooth functioning. This creates employment opportunities for skilled and semi-skilled youths. Small businesses see big data as an opportunity to expand their services in more regions and make their brand available to people.

Big data improves project operations, provides better services to the public by making data available to different government institutions, and helps make important decisions quickly and wisely. With the increase in data generation in various formats, i.e., text, audio, video, image, etc. It has not been easy to manage and analyze with the existing traditional tools, which only work for structured data (Chandarana et al, 2014).

Characteristics of Big Data

1. **Volume:** The name itself is related to size, which is massive. The value of data generated from different sources such as social media platforms, administrative data, etc., is dependent on the size of the data. Data is classified if it is big data or not on the volume of data.
2. **Variety:** It refers to the diverse source of data collected. Data can be structured, unstructured, and semi-structured. Nowadays, a variety of data is collected from sources such as e-mails, PDFs, images, and videos which is a lot more than in earlier times from databases and spreadsheets. This leads to the development of tools which process such a variety of data from nearly every sector in the country.
3. **Velocity:** Refers to the speed generation of the data. The real future of data is determined by how fast data is pre-processed to give the results in as short a time as possible. Big data velocity refers to how fast data flows from different sources such as mobile, social media platforms, etc., to meet the user requirement.

Advantages of Big Data

1. **Innovation:** Big data helps get insightful information for a company's government schemes that can be used to change it into actionable policies and increase performance. For example, it can analyze the customer satisfaction with the products and services, suggesting new reforms to be implemented to boost the company's performance in the market.
2. **Cost Optimization:** Big data tools such as Hadoop and Spark provide a less expensive solution to small businesses for storing this massive amount of data. It allows companies to reduce their production costs by estimating which products are likely to be sold more in this competitive market.
3. **Pricing:** Big data helps you get a clear picture of your business situation in the market, allowing you to price your product to meet customer needs and requirements. Moreover, it helps evaluate the company's financial position so that they get a clear idea of their finances.

4. **Improve Public facilities:** Big data has played an important role in improving public facilities. Health records can now be viewed by a doctor even if he is not in the hospital, and documents can directly be downloaded from the government's official website saving people time to go and collect.

5. **Fraud Detection:** The privacy of big data is an important concern. Using Machine Learning systems with big data, errors can be easily detected, aberration in the dataset can be detected beforehand to avoid system failure. This has led to more companies adopting big data and analytics to make a better place in the market.

E-Governance

E-Governance is defined as the use of modern technologies by the government to collect information and provide services to the citizens of the country (Rajgopalan and Vellaipandian, 2013). It is an electronic way of delivering the services. This helps the government function fairly and transparently and monitor all sectors efficiently. It aims to facilitate and improve the quality and assurance of governance and make citizens actively participate in this process through electronic sources like SMS, e-mail, etc.

The success of any E-Governance project depends upon the efficiency of delivering the citizens' services transparently (Navdeep et al, 2016). Big Data analytics can process large amounts of unstructured data which can be delivered to the right audience and also provide access to this diverse data which was not available quickly before in a presentable manner for better services to the citizens of the country (Agnihotri and Sharma, 2015), (Heeks, 2001).

It can be of four types based on the services they offer. These are Government to Citizens (G2C), Government to Employees (G2E), Government to Government (G2G), and Government to Business (G2B) (Karimi, 2014).

Types of E-Governance

1. **Government-to-Citizens (G2C):** It refers to the government's variety of services/facilities to its citizens. The primary aim is to provide the benefits of government facilities to each citizen and ensure that it is provided neutrally. A citizen can use this service from anywhere.

2. **Government-to-Business (G2B):** Government-to-business includes the various services exchanged between government and business firms. The services can be in the form of policies, regulations, etc. This increases the efficiency of government projects.

3. **Government-to-Government (G2G):** It refers to the interaction between different government firms and agencies. This increases the government's internal functioning, which leads to the smooth functioning of the government. Building relations inside the government is an essential factor for the country's development.

4. **Government-to-Employee (G2E):** Government to Employee refers to the relationship between government and employees. This bond needs to be stronger to offer various facilities like applying for annual leave and checking their employees' balance.

Advantages of E-Governance (Dawes, 2008)

1. **Efficiency:** E-governance increases the working of the current system making it reliable and scalable for future use. With all data available on smartphones, anything can be accessed from anywhere, increasing the efficiency of government-related tasks for common citizens of the country. As for the government, it can access important information and records easily and review the documents submitted by citizens for approval or rejection.

2. **Transparency:** E-governance allows government transparency because it allows citizens to quickly get information about government programs and how the government functions. All the information is readily available for the citizens for access.

3. **Low Expenses:** For a long period, governments used to buy a plethora of stationery for official purposes. E-governance has helped save crores of money by making every official record available in smartphones, reducing the need for paper for official documents, and reducing the need for people to go to government offices to get these documents physically.

4. **Systematic:** E-governance has made it easy for the citizens to access the documents by maintaining them in a systematic order. This makes the whole process and experience smooth for both the citizens and the government.

5. **Improved Administration:** E-governance has made a significant impact on the functioning of the government. Governments now tend to use these technologies to get insight into people's needs and formulate rules and regulations accordingly, resulting in the betterment of the citizens.

Big Data Analytics and Aspects of Society

Big data and big data analytics play an important role in the development of society; be it a small business, education hubs, all generate a large volume of data that needs to be handled using the proper techniques available. Other people should be available to extract the information from this. Data is circulated between different domains in society, which impacts society's future growth. Some other aspects of society are health care and transport, where big data analytics are being used (Borgi et al, 2017), (Dash et al, 2017).

FRAMEWORKS FOR BIG DATA ANALYTICS

Managing Big Data is a challenging task that is impossible with only skilled developers and technology inputs. It requires structure so that the data is helpful in the longer run. Big Data Frameworks provide structure and a standard reference model that the entire organization can follow, maintaining the streamlined data flow. Using a framework for Big Data analysis also accelerates the whole process of Big Data Analytics and takes into account every aspect of data, thereby utilizing it to its fullest.

Apache is a major leader in Big Data Frameworks. Almost all popular Big Data Frameworks are developed by the Apache Software Foundation. Even the big tech giants like Microsoft, Amazon, and Cloudera use a framework based on popular Apache Frameworks. Apache Frameworks provide the highest stability, reliability, and scalability essential for enterprise production level systems (Kamburugamuve et al, 2013). Another reason for its significant popularity is that all Apache-backed frameworks are Open Source and free to use for everyone, giving it an edge against other counterparts that mostly require premium subscriptions to use.

Some popular frameworks by Apache are listed below.

Apache Hadoop

Hadoop is an open-source, Java-based framework used for storing and processing big data. The data is stored on inexpensive commodity servers that run as clusters. The program for Hadoop runs on clusters of machines using the Message-Passing Interface (MPI). Hadoop's distributed file system enables concurrent processing of a vast amount of data to reduce the load on large machines and increase the application's scalability.

Hadoop has been used by many companies, including Google, Hortonworks, Facebook, and Twitter, among others (Tripathy et al, 2016). Hadoop uses the MapReduce programming model for faster storage and retrieval of data from its nodes based on Google's MapReduce programming language (Tripathy et al, 2014). Hadoop is used widely in large-scale distributed computing. Its distributed file system enables faster processing than more expensive centralized systems (Chen and Chun-Yang, 2014). It is used for running applications on commodity hardware, while more expensive systems are reserved for applications requiring more computational or memory resources.

Apache Spark

Apache Spark is an open-source, distributed processing system used for big data workloads. Spark provides fast, scalable ways to analyze large datasets. It distributes data across the nodes of a cluster and allows for interactive queries via its API. Its features include fault-tolerance, versatility, query optimizer (based on SQL), cleaner schemas (via JSON/XML), Scala API.

Spark comes with Spark Core (with Scala and Java APIs), GraphX (a library for graph-parallel computation), additional functionalities such as SQL with Streaming and Machine Learning libraries. Spark's development is also backed by many companies, including Microsoft and Amazon Web Services.

Apache Flink

Apache Flink is a general-purpose cluster computing tool that can handle batch processing, interactive processing, Stream processing, Iterative processing, in-memory processing, graph processing. It excels at processing unbounded and bounded datasets. Apache Flink can process vast amounts of data without compromising performance. It is used in a wide variety of industries, from media-rich social networks, logistics, and financial analytics to internet security, all the way to healthcare and telecommunications.

Apache Flink was written in Java, Groovy, and Scala at Facebook for their internal use. Facebook uses Apache Flink on BigQuery, one of its petabyte-scale data warehousing services. Flink also has a few built-in operators which help in streaming.

Apache Samza

Apache Samza is a stream processing framework tightly tied to the Apache Kafka messaging system. It is a distributed system designed to be deployed on a cluster of servers, and each server can process data streams from Kafka topics.

Samza was created at LinkedIn to deploy anywhere and scale to support large-scale workloads easily. It is most often used as an Apache Hadoop job running on Apache Mesos or as an application container using Docker. Its design avoided most of the pitfalls that other streaming processing systems have by reimagining how work should be partitioned across a distributed system.

It offers a simple API for stream processing built around a reliable queue for message passing between tasks, called a "flow".

Apache Storm

Storm is a distributed real-time computation system for processing large volumes of high-velocity data. Storm is distributed and fault-tolerant at its core and provides exactly-once semantics. Storm implements a dataflow topology that is very similar to an HPC system. The Storm topology consists of spouts, bolts, and the supervisors that manage the execution of these two parts. A spout is a data source for any number of bolts in the cluster that provides data to bolts. Each bolt in Storm is built from a bolt class, with each bolt being responsible for an operation with its input. The supervisors are the brains in Storm. They are responsible for coordinating all the processes in the cluster and gathering information regarding computation progress.

BIG DATA ANALYTICS IN E-GOVERNANCE (Seshathiri et al., 2018)

Big data analytics and E-governance will go hand in hand as it has different useful tools which have the capabilities of abundant mining data helping in analyzing e-governance projects. These tools compile and analyze the dataset and provide a solution that helps the government take and launch initiatives for different classes of people. Big data analytics have significantly impacted e-governance projects, have made the processing of data fair and transparent to the users, and improved customer services to a great extent. People now get information about different government programs initiatives through SMS, e-mail, etc., anywhere in the world.

E-Governance sectors include but are not limited to Healthcare, Transportation, Important documents, Vaccination Reports, Transaction details of E-payments, Government Employee records including salary and pension details, Census data, Education and Land records which are important for the government.

Many techniques used in Big Data Analysis are Data Mining, i.e., managing data with the help of statistics and machine learning (Salwan and Maan, 2020), Regression Analysis which includes manipulating independent variables to see how to effects the dependent variable, Machine Learning, i.e., the technique which allows the machine to learn based on algorithms and experience.

The challenges which could arise while managing Big Data is the security of the data, i.e., sensitive datasets might get leaked if proper security measures are not taken, Threat to Privacy which includes processing of personal and private information of a user like financial details and documents, Lack of Maintenance and updating to latest security measures can result in massive data leaks.

Healthcare Sector

The Healthcare sector generates a plethora of data such as Electronic health records (EHR), clinical records, etc. Due to its fast exponential growth, data processing and getting results quickly is the primary concern in today's world.

Flink would be the best available framework for processing data generated due to low latency, real entry-by-entry processing, and high throughput. Though it is a stream processing framework, it can also handle batch tasks, providing an advantage. It also supports streaming data which does not hinder system optimization.

The existing framework used in this sector is Hadoop because it can handle huge datasets and run on inexpensive hardware. (Nazari et al, 2019)

Unique Citizen Identification

These identification cards consist of the data of nearly every citizen of the country, and each citizen is assigned a unique number. It is crucial to maintain and process this data efficiently for further usage.

The existing and best available framework for these is Hadoop due to its distribution system can process large amounts of data in less time and fetch results in no time, increasing the efficiency and scalability of the application. It can handle diverse data, making it easier for the administrator to monitor the growth and resolve user queries.

Government Records

One of the main concerns for the government to function smoothly is the security of its employees. Often some people, including hackers, tend to threaten and harm government agency employees for inside information, tenders info, etc., which gives concern about the security of these people.

The existing and best available framework for this is Hadoop. Hadoop is the most secure framework (uses Kerberos application for data security), which makes it the best choice to use to process government data.

Payments

Apache Storm would be the best framework for Payments as it is fast, fault-tolerant, scalable, and reliable. It quickly processes streams of data with the unmatchable speed of one million tuples per second per node and can even be used without a computer programming language, adding more advantages to its side.

It would be helpful in real-time analytics with data of high velocity, making it a perfect fit for payments that are real-time and of high velocity. Payments would need a fast and fault-tolerant framework to work properly without fail.

Existing payment methods use Hadoop as their framework mainly due to its cost-effective nature compromising processing time. With a sudden surge in online payments and it being a 60 billion USD plus industry as of 2021, the researchers think Storm would be a better choice in the current and coming times.

Census

Census usually involves a large amount of data coming from each country household, including their names, addresses, income, living facilities, literacy, fertility, and mortality.

To process such a large amount of data, the best available and existing framework in use would be Apache Hadoop due to its right amount of scalability and flexibility and its ability to process and store large amounts of data.

Criminal/Education/Transport Records

All the records that the government collects involve a large amount of data, including text, images, and multiple subfields of a field.

To process such a large amount of data, the best available and existing framework in use would be Apache Hadoop due to its right amount of scalability and flexibility and its ability to process and store large amounts of data.

Vaccine and Vaccination Reports

In this domain, the researchers consider all aspects such as vaccine tracking, real-time availability in hospitals, reports of vaccinated people, and nearest locations to find and book a vaccine slot. Since we are dealing with real-time information processing and a large number of users, Spark and Hadoop would not be good options.

Apache Samza would be the best available framework in this case due to its features of easily detecting anomalies, combating fraud, monitoring performance, notifications with real-time analytics.

CHALLENGES IN BIG DATA

1. **Insufficient Understanding of Big Data:** Often, governments tend to fail in their big data initiatives due to a lack of understanding of the term 'BIG DATA' as they don't have a clear picture of what big data is, what technology is needed to implement it, benefits, etc. This brings them to square one, where they don't have any new choice but to use traditional technology, making their work more difficult.
2. **Lack of Knowledgeable Employees:** One of the biggest challenges faced by almost every government globally is finding skilled professionals who have the relevant skills. Even after finding these professionals, the next major task is to retain them due to increasing job opportunities in Big Companies. Regular employees don't have the required skills to manipulate and handle such a massive amount of data.
3. **Growth in Data:** With the government investing in more big data projects and updating the current ones with more data, there has been an exponential growth in data stored in databases with time. This has led to more processing time and delay in getting information, affecting the completion time of such projects.
4. **Big Data Tool Selection:** Employees often get confused about which tool to select to process a particular dataset. This occurs due to a lack of knowledge about any big data analytics tool. This eventually affects the company's performance, and many resources are wasted in this process.
5. **Security of Data:** Governments tend to ignore the security aspects of the data, not considering it an essential factor over other processes like learning and managing data. Unprotected data is an open invitation to hackers who use this confidential information to exploit the government's reputation.
6. **Expensive to Set-Up:** Although most of the frameworks are Open Source, they still require hardware, developers, and other expenses that add up to setting and maintaining a big data infrastructure. (Condie et al, 2013)

7. **Finding Meaningful Data:** It is a tedious process to find valuable and meaningful data which will provide valuable insights from the raw data provided. Data needs to be cleaned and analyzed first to use the data in future products accordingly. (Condie et al, 2013)
8. **Data Governance and Validation:** Data Governance deals with making sure that the records are usable, accurate, secure, and in compliance with the policies and procedures of the organization. Managing such a large amount of data according to the policies is a tough job that often requires looking over properly.

BIG DATA ANALYTICS TECHNIQUES (Hurwitz et al., 2018), (Xiaofeng et al., 2013), (Condie et al., 2013)

Analysis of Big Data requires various techniques that can act on diverse types of data such as structured, unstructured, and semi-structured of varying sizes of data. Some of the techniques are listed below.

Data Mining

Data mining is extracting patterns and insights using methods from statistics and machine learning (ML) from large data sets. It is a new technology that takes care of many of the tedious tasks previously done manually, such as updating data or accessing it. Through Data mining, many computer-based tools can be created to retrieve information from large volumes of data to be analyzed and processed to make decisions effectively.

Data mining has helped develop software systems that gain knowledge from huge amounts of data and build models that help make better decisions with respect to change in technology (Tripathy et al, 2018).

Machine Learning

Machine Learning is to produce assumptions that would be impossible for humans to predict. It uses various algorithms to accomplish this task. Data mining tools help collect data, whereas Machine learning algorithms help analyze the obtained data and make predictions for future use. These algorithms offer suggestions for improvement based on the results obtained. Machine Learning algorithms tend to analyze trends by identifying patterns, which helps many companies improve their performance, invest in marketing, and plan strategies to ensure the product meets the customers' requirements. Another area where machine learning algorithms can be used is information security. Companies can use these algorithms for penetration testing, intrusion detection, and intrusion prevention purposes. These algorithms are used in developing strategies for dealing with unstructured data (Zion et al, 2021).

Regression Analysis

The goal of Regression Analysis is to figure out how one or more factors may influence the relying variable to spot patterns and trends. Probable outcomes can be predicted and could help make better business decisions in the future by knowing each variable's relationship and how it developed in the past. It's based on the idea that the behavior of one variable is dependent on one or more factors. And each factor can be classified into two groups: independent and dependent. If a variable is independent, another variable doesn't directly influence it. Another variable may be dependent or affected in some way on another variable because the amount of influence depends on something else.

CONCLUSION

Big Data Analytics has changed the way governments collect and analyze information obtained from various sources to gain insights into the particular sector to make more informed decisions and improve the efficiency of the existing working system. A large amount of data collected is processed and used in different E-governance sectors, which improves the existing services provided to the country's citizens. Big Data Analytics in E-governance can provide services transparently to the citizens and help transform how data is collected, analyzed, and used effectively to make future decisions beneficial to the people and government.

The authors have explained the fundamental definitions of Big data and Big data analytics in E-governance and have also suggested the best available frameworks to use in different sectors to make the system more productive, effective, and efficient. On analyzing, the researchers have concluded that Apache-backed frameworks are the best available frameworks for big data analytics for the majority of government sectors to date.

FUTURE WORKS

Big data and big data analytic applications are integral factors for efficiency increment in e-governance. As data will continue to grow, so will the accuracy of models we have currently, further boosting research. More and more cloud storage providers will move towards managing more and more big data. This may also come with massive data branches and data privacy issues, so big data security will play a significant role.

REFERENCES

Agnihotri, N., & Sharma, A. K. (2015). Big data analysis and its need for effective E-governance. *International Journal of Innovations & Advancement in Computer Science*, 4, 219–224.

Borgi, T., Zoghlami, N., & Abed, A. (2017). Big data for transport and logistics: A review. In *2017 International Conference on Advanced Systems and Electric Technologies (IC_ASET)* (pp. 44-49). IEEE.

Chandarana, P., & Vijayalakshmi, M. (2014). Big data analytics frameworks. In *2014 International Conference on Circuits, Systems, Communication and Information Technology Applications (CSC)* (pp. 430-434). IEEE. 10.1109/CSCITA.2014.6839299

Chen, C. L. (2014). Data-intensive applications, challenges, techniques and technologies: A survey on Big Data. *Information Sciences*, 275, 314–347. doi:10.1016/j.ins.2014.01.015

Condie, T., Mineiro, P., Polyzotis, N., & Weimer, M. (2013, April). Machine learning on big data. In *2013 IEEE 29th International Conference on Data Engineering (ICDE)* (pp. 1242-1244). IEEE.

Dash, S., Shakyawar, S. K., Sharma, M., & Kaushik, S. (2019). Big data in health care: Management, analysis and future prospects. *Journal of Big Data*, *6*(1), 1–25. doi:10.118640537-019-0217-0

Dawes, S. (2008). The evolution and continuing challenges of e-governance. *Public Administration Review, 68*, S86-S102.

Divya Zion, G., & Tripathy, B. K. (2020). Comparative Analysis of Tools for Big Data Visualization and Challenges. In S. Anouncia, H. Gohel, & S. Vairamuthu (Eds.), *Data Visualization* (pp. 33–52). Springer. doi:10.1007/978-981-15-2282-6_3

Heeks, R. (2001). *Understanding e-governance for development.* Academic Press.

Hurwitz, J. (2013). Big Data. Academic Press.

Kamburugamuve, S., Fox, G., Leake, D., & Qiu, J. (2013). *Survey of Apache big data stack.* Indiana University, Tech. Rep.

Karimi, H. A. (2014). *Big Data: techniques and technologies in geo-informatics.* CRC Press. doi:10.1201/b16524

Labrinidis, A., & Hosagrahar, V. J. (2012). Challenges and opportunities with big data. *Proceedings of the VLDB Endowment International Conference on Very Large Data Bases, 5*(12), 2032–2033. doi:10.14778/2367502.2367572

Marx, V. (2013). The big challenges of big data. *Nature, 498*(7453), 255-60.

Navdeep, P., Arora, M., & Sharma, N. (2016). Role of big data analytics in analyzing e-Governance projects. *New trends in business and management: An international perspective.*

Nazari, E., Shahriari, M. H., & Tabesh, H. (2019). Big Data analysis in healthcare: Apache Hadoop, apache-spark and apache flink. *Frontiers in Health Informatics, 8*(1), 14. doi:10.30699/fhi.v8i1.180

Rajagopalan, M. R., & Vellaipandiyan, S. (2013). Big data framework for national e-governance plan. In *2013 Eleventh International Conference on ICT and Knowledge Engineering* (pp. 1-5). IEEE. 10.1109/ICTKE.2013.6756283

Rajaraman, V. (2016). Big data analytics. *Resonance, 21*(8), 695–716. doi:10.100712045-016-0376-7

Salwan, P., & Maan, V. K. (2020). E-Governance using Big Data. *Innovations in Computer Science and Engineering: Proceedings of 8th ICICSE*, 123.

Seetha, H., Tripathy, B. K., & Murthy, M. K. (2017). Modern Technologies for Big Data Classification and Clustering, IGI Global.

Seshathiri, D., Kasi, B., Karunkaran, V., & Seetharaman, A. (2018). Big Data for E-Governance. In *2018 International Conference on Recent Trends in Advanced Computing (ICRC)* (pp. 80-84). IEEE.

Srividya, V., & Tripathy, B. K. (2021). Role of Big data in supply chain management. *SCM-DA2021 Springer book-Innovative Supply Chain Management via Digitalization and Artificial Intelligence.*

Tripathy, B. K., Seetha, H., & Murthy, M. K. (2017). Uncertainty Based Clustering Algorithms for Large Data Sets. In Modern Technologies for Big Data Classification and Clustering. IGI Global.

Tripathy, B. K. (2017). Rough set and neighbourhood systems in Big Data Analysis. In Computational Intelligence Applications in Business Intelligence and Big Data Analytics. CRC Press.

Tripathy, B. K., & Deepthi, P. H. (2017). An Investigation of Fuzzy Techniques in clustering of Big Data. In Computational Intelligence Applications in Business Intelligence and Big Data Analytics. CRC Press.

Tripathy, B. K., Deepthi, P. H., & Mittal, D. (2016). Hadoop with Intuitionistic Fuzzy C-means for clustering in Big Data. *Advances in Intelligent Systems and Computing, 438*, 599–610. doi:10.1007/978-981-10-0767-5_62

Tripathy, B. K., Sooraj, T. R., & Mohanty, R. K. (2018). Data Mining Techniques in Big Data for Social Network. In Big Data Analytics: A social network approach. Taylor and Francis.

Tripathy, B. K., Vishwakarma, H. R., & Kothari, D. P. (2014). Neighbourhood Based Knowledge Acquisition Using MapReduce from Big Data over Cloud Computing. *Proceedings, CSIBIG14*, 183–188.

Xiaofeng, M., & Xiang, C. (2013). Big data management: concepts, techniques, and challenges. *Journal of Computer Research and Development, 50*(1), 146.

Zion, G. D., & Tripathy, B. K. (2021). A Survey on Frequent Pattern Mining, in Uncertain Big Data. *Design Engineering*, (7), 3983-4013.

ADDITIONAL READING

Lv, Z., Song, H., Basanta-Val, P., Steed, A., & Jo, M. (2017). Next-generation big data analytics: State of the art, challenges, and future research topics. *IEEE Transactions on Industrial Informatics, 13*(4), 1891–1899. doi:10.1109/TII.2017.2650204

Nandimath, J., Banerjee, E., Patil, A., Kakade, P., Vaidya, S., & Chaturvedi, D. (2013, August). Big data analysis using Apache Hadoop. In *2013 IEEE 14th International Conference on Information Reuse & Integration (IRI)* (pp. 700-703). IEEE. 10.1109/IRI.2013.6642536

O'Leary, D. E. (2013). Artificial intelligence and big data. *IEEE Intelligent Systems, 28*(2), 96–99. doi:10.1109/MIS.2013.39

Saxena, K. B. C. (2005). Towards excellence in e-governance. *International Journal of Public Sector Management, 18*(6), 498–513. doi:10.1108/09513550510616733

Tankard, C. (2012). Big data security. *Network Security, 2012*(7), 5–8. doi:10.1016/S1353-4858(12)70063-6

Yaqoob, I., Hashem, I. A. T., Gani, A., Mokhtar, S., Ahmed, E., Anuar, N. B., & Vasilakos, A. V. (2016). Big data: From beginning to future. *International Journal of Information Management, 36*(6), 1231–1247. doi:10.1016/j.ijinfomgt.2016.07.009

Zhang, D. (2018, October). Big data security and privacy protection. In *8th International Conference on Management and Computer Science (ICMCS 2018)* (Vol. 77, pp. 275-278). Atlantis Press.

KEY TERMS AND DEFINITIONS

Batch Processing: Batch processing is the process of completing batches of jobs simultaneously in a sequential manner.

Big Data: Big data is a collection of data that is larger in volume, has variety and cannot be processed by traditional tools.

Big Data Analytics: Big data analytics is defined as the use of advanced analytical tools to gain insight into a large volume of diverse data sets. These datasets contain structured, semi-structured, and unstructured data from various sources.

Big Data Frameworks: Big data frameworks are tools that store and process massive datasets intending to benefit the organization from the big data.

E-Governance: E-governance can be defined as the use of information and communication technology (ICTs) by governments to provide public services to people more efficiently and transparently.

Message Passing Interface (MPI): Message passing interface is a process of exchanging messages between various computers across the distributed memory.

Stream Processing: Stream processing is the process of evaluating or computing the data as it is received or created.

Big Data and Islamic Finance

B

Egi Arvian Firmansyah

 https://orcid.org/0000-0001-5296-706X

Universiti Brunei Darussalam, Brunei & Universitas Padjadjaran, Indonesia

Budi Harsanto

Universitas Padjadjaran, Indonesia

INTRODUCTION

This book chapter reviews the studies on big data in relation to Islamic finance available in three academic databases, namely, Web of Science (WoS), Scopus, and Google Scholar. Islamic finance is one of the finance research topics gaining more attention in recent years because of its unique features, differentiating itself from conventional finance. Obtaining an insight on this topic will shed light on the big data application in a sharia setting, in which religious values are embedded.

BACKGROUND

Big data can be defined as the tremendous amount of data that can be analyzed using the advanced computer to produce particular patterns, trends, and relationships (Sagiroglu & Sinanc, 2013). Although it was born from the information and technology domain, the application of big data in the business environment has been the concern of many corporations, and it is deemed one of the sources of competitive advantage in the current era (Chen et al., 2018). Also, the studies on big data have been extensively conducted by scholars across the globe (Gandomi & Haider, 2015), both in business settings and others.

Big data technology has been well studied in various fields, such as marketing (Zhao et al., 2019), human resources (El-Kassar & Singh, 2019), operations (Choi et al., 2018; Lu & Xu, 2019), transportation systems (Ghofrani et al., 2018), Internet of Things (Plageras et al., 2018), healthcare (Batko & Ślęzak, 2022; Dash et al., 2019) and Covid-19 case (Awotunde et al., 2021; Wang et al., 2020) The universal purpose of big data has clearly inspired many people in any field to embrace this technology to improve the effectiveness and efficiency of any organization, either profit oriented or non-profit oriented ones. Furthermore, many previous studies have also been recently conducted using a systematic literature review approach on big data. Those studies relate big data to many other aspects, such as tourism (Li et al., 2018; Mariani et al., 2018), supply chain management (Mishra et al., 2018; Nguyen et al., 2018; Rejeb et al., 2022) manufacturing (Cui et al., 2020; Ren et al., 2019), disaster management (Akter & Wamba, 2019; Yu et al., 2018), healthcare (Mehta & Pandit, 2018; Pashazadeh & Navimipour, 2018), text mining in financial sector (Pejić Bach et al., 2019), firm performance (Maroufkhani et al., 2019), transportation research (Kaffash et al., 2021; Neilson et al., 2019), and organization dynamic capabilities (Rialti et al., 2019).

Very few big data studies have been sufficiently published in various journals focusing on Islamic finance. In fact, the general nature of big data can be used either by Islamic or non-Islamic business entities because big data can be considered a religious-neutral application. Therefore, this study aims to

DOI: 10.4018/978-1-7998-9220-5.ch008

Copyright © 2023, IGI Global. Copying or distributing in print or electronic forms without written permission of IGI Global is prohibited.

review the studies that relate big data and Islamic finance published in the journals indexed in Web of Science, Scopus, and Google Scholar. The two indexes, as mentioned earlier, were selected because they are the most well-known and trusted indexing databases in which many scholars are pursuing to have their papers indexed by them. While the third one, namely, Google Scholar, was selected to enhance the results of the review conducted on Web of Science and Scopus indexes.

One distinguishing feature of this present research is that it focuses on a current and specific topic, namely, the big data and Islamic finance, which is rare among Islamic finance studies. The studies on this topic will provide insight into how big data is related to Islamic finance, such as the implementation in Islamic financial institutions across the world, either Muslim or non-Muslim countries. This paper will produce a framework of big data and Islamic finance that will enrich the research of both Islamic finance and big data.

The structure of this paper is as follows. This section outlines the introduction and purposes of this present study. The following section describes the method undertaken, consisting of the document search and document selection to be included in our review. The following section is results and discussion, followed by future research directions and a conclusion in the final sections. Additional reading and key terms, as well as definitions, are provided to enhance the understanding of the readers about big data and Islamic finance.

METHOD

The studies on big data and Islamic finance were retrieved from the three databases, namely, Web of Science (WoS), Scopus, and Google Scholar. To obtain the literature from Web of Science and Scopus, we directly downloaded the documents from those two websites. However, to obtain data from Google Scholar, we utilized Publish or Perish (PoP) software (Harzing, 2010) commonly used in bibliometric or scientometric studies (for instance, Ardianto & Anridho, 2018; Iqbal et al., 2019; Lee et al., 2014). All obtained papers were downloaded and reviewed in order to gain an understanding of the big data studies focusing on Islamic finance. In those Web of Science and Scopus databases, we conducted the article search on August 17, 2021, using the keywords 'big data' and 'Islamic finance' combined. In a slightly different approach, for Google Scholar, we used the word 'big data Islamic' in the title field of PoP software to produce a richer result supporting the results from Web of Science and Scopus. This mechanism enables us to portray the current state of the topic to provide further direction for researchers, primarily those interested in digital finance topics, such as big data. Figure 1 illustrates the process we conducted in this study.

Our initial search in Web of Science and Scopus results in 34 documents merged from the two databases. These documents consist of several items, i.e., journal articles, conference proceedings, reviews, and book chapters. Since the search results produced many irrelevant documents, we then selected the only documents which discuss the big data in Islamic finance settings. The relevant documents consist of the word 'big data' in either the title or abstract fields. Non-relevant documents, such as those only containing the word 'data' and 'big' in the separate locations, are excluded since they have no relationship or relevance with this research topic. As there are documents indexed by both, we only consider them as a single document and are processed in the next stage, namely document selection.

As the initial search using Web of Science and Scopus produced a relatively small number of documents, we conducted an additional search on Google Scholar indexed and managed to obtain five (5) relevant documents from the obtained 16 documents. These documents are expected to enrich our findings

Figure 1. Document search and selection
Source: Authors' elaboration, 2021

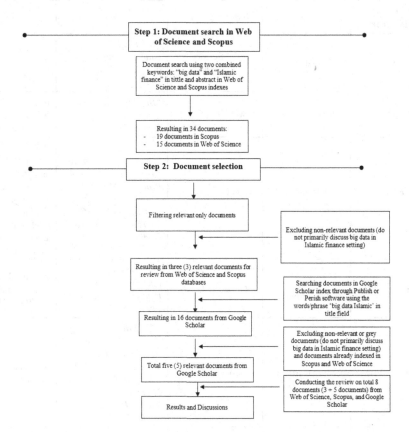

from the two previous databases. Albeit Google Scholar might be considered a less prestigious database as it is not curated based on criteria, we carefully selected the relevant only documents by studying the content in those documents. The non-relevant, grey, and already-included documents in the two previous databases were excluded.

RESULTS AND DISCUSSION

Descriptive Results

As outlined in Figure 1, our research procedure results in eight final relevant articles obtained from three databases or indexes (Web of Science, Scopus, and Google Scholar). The included documents and their data in this study are shown in Table 1 as follows.

Table 1 shows that most of the documents studied in this research (62.5 percent) are categorized as journal articles, followed by conference proceedings (25 percent) and magazine article (12.5 percent). In terms of indexation, most of the documents are indexed by Google Scholar (62.5 percent), followed by Scopus (25 percent) and Web of Science (37.5 percent). This result reveals that the majority of documents focusing on big data and Islamic finance are not indexed by reputable indexes. Therefore, it is highly advisable that researchers in Islamic finance conduct high-quality big data research since the

Table 1. Included documents for review

No	Author(s) and publication year	Type	Indexing source	Title	Slot
1	S. N. Ali (2020)	Journal article	Web of Science and Scopus	*"Big Data, Islamic Finance, and Sustainable Development Goals"*	JKAU: Islamic Econ
2	Mnif et al. (2020)	Journal article	Web of Science	*"Big data tools for Islamic financial analysis"*	Intelligent Systems in Accounting, Finance and Management
3	Majdalawieh et al. (2017)	Conference proceeding	Web of Science and Scopus	*"Developing Adaptive Islamic Law Business Processes Models for Islamic Finance and Banking by Text Mining the Holy Qur'an and Hadith"*	IEEE 15th Intl Conf on Dependable, Autonomic and Secure Computing, 15th Intl Conf on Pervasive Intelligence and Computing, 3rd Intl Conf on Big Data Intelligence and Computing and Cyber Science and Technology Congress
4	Miskam & Eksan (2018)	Conference proceeding	Google Scholar	*"Big Data and FinTech in Islamic Finance: Prospects and Challenges"*	4th Muzakarah Fiqh & International Fiqh Conference (MFIFC 2018)
5	Ridhwan et al. (2014)	Journal article	Google Scholar	*"Big Data Technology in Shari'ah Compliance Risk Management (SCRM): A View of Information Technology in Islamic Finance Risk Management"*	Journal of Islamic Banking & Finance
6	Bakar (2018)	Journal article	Google Scholar	*"Managing economic and Islamic research in big data environment: from computer science perspective"*	Journal of Emerging Economies and Islamic Research
7	Q. Ali et al. (2021)	Journal article	Google Scholar	*"Big data and predictive analytics to optimise social and environmental performance of Islamic banks"*	Environment Systems and Decisions
8	Salim et al. (2019)	Magazine article	Google Scholar	*"Big data analytics and Islamic banking"*	IFHUB

Source: Web of Science, Scopus, Google Scholar, 2021

opportunity is wide open. Furthermore, Table 1 reveals that the slots publishing Islamic finance and big data research are varied. It means none of the slots are more dominant than others quite significantly. Interestingly, we find that those slots do not have to be focused on Islamic topics only. The journals like "Intelligent Systems in Accounting, Finance and Management" and "Environment Systems and Decisions" also accept papers related to Islamic finance topics.

Review Results

B

Having filtered and selected the documents, we subsequently conducted the review, which is the central part of this systematic literature review. This review is conducted to understand the research objective or purposes, methods, primary findings, and suggestions for further research related to big data and Islamic finance. The review results in this study are presented in Table 2 as follows.

As shown in Table 2, research on big data related to Islamic finance has been conducted in previous studies. However, the number of research is negligible. Also, based on data in Table 2, we categorize those studies into four themes as follows.

1. Big data role in Islamic financial institutions
2. Big data and Islamic investment behavior
3. Big data role in Islamic finance research
4. Intertwine of big data, Islamic finance, and SDGs

Big Data Role in Islamic Financial Institutions

Based on data in Table 2, we found that most papers (five papers) discuss big data role in Islamic financial institutions. This theme is relevant because many Islamic financial institutions already have an awareness of big data technology in their operations. Based on our observation, two of the five papers specifically mentioned Islamic banks as the objects of their studies. This research was conducted by Q. Ali et al. (2021) and Salim et al. (2019). The focus of Q. Ali et al. (2021) is on the influence of big data and predictive analytics (BDPA) on social performance and environmental performance of sharia banks. Their study shows that predictive analytics of big data, closely related to artificial intelligence, has been successfully implemented by Islamic bank in improving their social and environmental performances. On the other hand, Salim et al. (2019) focus on the big data utilization for creating more suitable sharia-compliant products offered by Islamic banks. Their studies clearly show that big data in Islamic finance has the similar function in conventional finance, in a sense that it improves company performances.

The third paper included in this theme was authored by Ridhwan et al. (2014), focusing on the topic of risk management in Islamic financial institutions using big data technology. Their idea is that Islamic financial institutions need to utilize big data in mitigating their risks. The nature of Islamic financial institutions (IFIs) is different from their conventional counterparts as they have the sharia non-compliance risk (Elgharbawy, 2020). This type of risk is unique and exclusive to Islamic banks, requiring them to use a particular risk mitigation approach and tools (Tafri et al., 2011). These risk management instruments have been quite challenging for many Islamic finance practitioners as they are not the same as in the conventional one. The Islamic risk management instruments, in addition to being effective in mitigating the risk, they must also be sharia compliant or in line with the sources of rules in Islam, namely, Quran and *hadith*.

The fourth paper included in this theme is a study discussing some cases of big data implementation by Islamic financial institutions (Miskam & Eksan, 2018). These authors present two examples where big data plays a significant role in improving the service provision of IFIs. First, big data was utilized by Wahed corporation to create an Islamic Robo-advisor product. This artificial intelligence technology allows investors to choose sharia-compliant stocks depending on their risk profile and the type of investment portfolio they choose (Belanche et al., 2019; Brenner, 2020; Phoon, 2018). The second example of big data utilization discussed by Miskam & Eksan (2018) is BIMB-Arabesque I Global. This big

Table 2. Review results

No	Author(s) and year	Purpose(s)	Method(s)	Main finding(s)	Suggestions for further studies
			Web of Science & Scopus		
1	S. N. Ali (2020)	This paper observes and portrays big data implementation in attaining SDGs as well as investigating its impact on the Islamic finance sector. The author mainly discusses big data potential in addressing some issues in SDGs, namely, poverty alleviation, climate change, and financial inclusion.	This paper is a qualitative study discussing the relationship between big data, Islamic finance, and SDGs.	The author argues that big data and platforms are essential in attaining SDGs. In addition, big data may contribute to developing the Islamic finance industry, for example, by creating sharia-compliant products tailoring to the needs of the customers. Furthermore, data is considered religiously neutral. Thus, it can be used for good or bad. Islamic values are aligned with SDGs. For instance, Islam forbids excessive water use (and other resources), which may cause climate change.	This paper does not explicitly mention the suggestion for further studies. However, the author of the paper points out that Islamic finance has a bright future, indicated by various innovations, such as in robo-advisory investment.
2	Mnif et al. (2020)	This paper analyzes the behavior of investors in investing in Islamic investment instruments. To do so, the authors utilize three big data tools, namely, social media engagement, search query, and Twitter API with machine learning algorithms.	This paper utilizes a quantitative approach with three measures of investor sentiments. The authors then investigate the results of those three tools whether they affect market sentiment and fluctuation of particular Islamic assets.	Twitter users using the 'Islamic faith' term were found to express positive sentiment. Furthermore, the measures of social media sentiments influence contemporaneous and lagged returns of Islamic assets.	This research is the first empirical paper in the literature of Islamic finance discussing big data. Thus, further empirical research is encouraged based on the findings of this study.
3	Majdalawieh et al. (2017)	This paper has several purposes. First, it aims to develop and confirm Islamic business processes related to some aspects, such as *riba* and Islamic business contracts. Second, it deals with developing and evaluating the Quranic corpus related to sharia finance and business processes.	Statistical analysis and text mining were used on the Holy Quran and hadith related to *Murabaha* contract. Furthermore, the authors validate this finding by performing an interview with Islamic finance experts.	The paper proposes the Islamic financial process model, primarily *Murabaha*, which is considered more appropriate to be adopted by Islamic financial institutions.	There is a need for developing new methods, ways, and controls to improve the system of information owned by Islamic financial institutions.
			Google Scholar		
4	Miskam & Eksan (2018)	The authors primarily discuss how big data is utilized by the Islamic financial sector for the betterment of information sharing, increasing operational efficiency, and increasing customer experiences.	The author uses a qualitative approach by studying previous literature.	The authors emphasize that there must be supportive and appropriate regulations that will safeguard big data implementation by the Islamic financial institutions.	Non-available
5	Ridhwan et al. (2014)	Proposes ideas in implementing big data in sharia-compliant risk management practices conducted by Islamic financial institutions.	This research is qualitative research utilizing an argumentative approach.	The paper proposes the integration of big data and Shari'ah Compliance Risk Management (SCRM), consisting of five elements of the risk level. The authors argued that through big data practices, Islamic financial institutions will be able to mitigate their risks, primarily financial risk, more effectively.	Non-available
6	Bakar (2018)	This paper aims to discuss the up-to-date demand for researchers in Islamic finance to study machine learning algorithms since it is believed to have successfully tackled several issues in the community. In addition, the paper provides some machine learning techniques that can be adapted by Islamic finance researchers to cope with big data.	The author of this paper utilizes a qualitative approach by proposing several techniques that can be used by Islamic finance researchers in dealing with changing research landscape because of big data.	Some examples of machine learning algorithms are provided to be used by Islamic finance researchers.	The author proposes some machine learning algorithms to be conducted by researchers.
7	Q. Ali et al. (2021)	This research focuses on studying the effect of big data and predictive analytics (BDPA) on social performance and environmental performance of sharia banks by utilizing two moderating variables, namely, dynamic capability view as well as organizational culture.	This study is a quantitative study collecting data through the dissemination of a self-administered questionnaire. The sample is 407 employees from 20 sharia banks in Malaysia. The data was analyzed using the PLS technique.	Big data and predictive analytics significantly affect the social and environmental performances of Islamic banks. Furthermore, organizational culture does not moderate the relationship between BDPA and both social and environmental performances.	The primary suggestion of the study is to use a longitudinal study since this research takes one-period data. By conducting a longitudinal study, the relationship between exogenous variables will be understood better.
8	Salim et al. (2019)	This paper discusses some potential big data analytics for improving the financial sector, primarily Islamic financial institutions.	This article uses a qualitative approach by studying previous literature.	The authors suggest that big data analytics can help Islamic banking create better sharia-compliant products suitable to the market.	In creating more suitable and competitive sharia-compliant products, Islamic banks should develop their resources, including human resources, to be more adaptive in utilizing big data tools.

Source: Authors' elaboration, 2021

Figure 2. Big Data and Islamic finance research

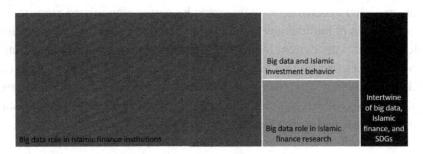

data powered-technology eliminates human biases and intuition in order to build the finest investment portfolio from around 77,000 global listed firms, forming a portfolio of up to 100 stocks every day, using more than a thousand selection criteria, and processing more than a hundred billion data points (TheSunDaily, 2018).

The fifth paper discussing big data role in Islamic financial institutions is authored by Majdalawieh et al. (2017) with the focus of using big data technology to create the most appropriate Islamic financial contract used by Islamic financial institutions. In their research paper, the data mining approach was used on Islamic sources of law, namely, the Holy Quran and hadith. The result of this data mining approach is then compared and verified by conducting a literature study and interview with various parties, primarily the Islamic scholars.

Intertwine of Big Data, Islamic Finance, and SDGs

Our research reveals one paper discussing big data potential for creating appropriate financial services that will tackle various problems in societies, as mentioned by United Nations (UN) in the sustainable development goals (SDGs) (S. N. Ali, 2020). The author argues that big data should be used for improving the quality of our community, and this notion is in line with Islamic teachings. That idea supports the finding of a previous study stating that Islamic financial institutions, primarily, fintech companies have supported the attainment of SDGs (Hudaefi, 2020).

Big Data and Islamic Investment Behavior

The first empirical study on big data related to Islamic finance was conducted by Mnif et al. (2020). Their study utilized a behavioral finance approach to study the determinants of investors in making investment decisions in sharia-compliant assets. Their study is a pioneer in observing big data in Islamic settings in order to provide insight on this technology since many current big data studies related to Islamic finance are only conceptual research using a qualitative approach. It is understandable because, in line with our research findings, big data and Islamic finance research is deemed in an early development stage. It is therefore advisable that Islamic finance researchers perform empirical studies to enrich the literature.

Big Data Role in Islamic Finance Research

A study by Bakar (2018) emphasizes the need for Islamic finance researchers to study big data since it is believed to have changed the Islamic finance research landscape. The author proposed that current-edge technologies brought by big data will undoubtedly augment Islamic finance practices. Therefore, the researchers are expected to catch up with this trend by performing related empirical research.

Based on the discussion of four themes found in our study, we could present the following treemap-style graph, which illustrates the current literature discussing big data in relation to Islamic finance.

In addition to the studies focusing on big data in relation to Islamic finance, our literature searches reveal some big data studies related to Islam - not specifically to Islamic finance. For instance, Menacer et al. (2014) have attempted to collect, organize, and achieve Islamic and Quran-related data and resources on big data. By using a consistent search method, they found a pattern or process for mining the Islamic data mining available in various sources on the Internet. On the other hand, Ahmed & Noordin (2014), in their paper, intend to explore the collection, storage, and protection of big data from the view of the Islamic perspective. By using a qualitative approach by relating the practices of big data and Quran verses, which are the primary source of law in Islam, they argue that storing, backing up, and protecting the privacy of big data are essential to be done by companies to be competitive. These actions are in line with Islamic values, as stated in the Quran.

Kawtharany (2017) attempts to highlight the importance of data science in Quranic studies in order to provide better solutions for society's problems. By utilizing a qualitative study for discussing the possibility of implementing data science in Quranic research, the author proposes that digital newspapers and social data available on the internet can help Quranic researchers solve social issues by creating visualization and patterns. Later, Shaleh (2018) discusses the opportunities as well as challenges of big data in the Islamic perspective by presenting an argumentative point of view regarding big data and its surrounding opportunities and challenges, primarily related to the Islamic view. The author puts forward that reading, as in reading the data or big data, is in line with the first God's (Allah) command in the Quran (chapter Al-Alaq verse 1). The author contents that in today's data-driven era, knowledge must be well disseminated by many people so nobody will be left behind. Thus, education institutions should encourage students to create innovation that is beneficial for humanity. Finally, the author argues that knowledge and education should be shared and maintained for the sake of creating broader benefits. Furthermore, Perdana et al. (2019) propose a model of the knowledge management system (KMS) by utilizing big data technology for improving the knowledge of nurses and doctors in an Islamic hospital in Indonesia. It relates to inpatient services. They suggest further use of the KMS concept for outpatient services, emergency facilities, and health supports.

FUTURE RESEARCH DIRECTIONS

Based on the review results outlined earlier, we found that future studies are certainly needed to be conducted to develop the literature, both the big data and Islamic finance literature. Our study indicates that there has been more research on big data role in Islamic financial institutions than any other themes mentioned in this study, such as the relationship between big data, Islamic finance, and SDGs and the role of big data in Islamic finance research. Therefore, we believe that future research needs to explore other less researched themes because big data keeps developing, and many Islamic financial institutions have started to realize its significance for improving performance and attaining competitive advantage.

CONCLUSION

This literature review is intended to portray the current studies on big data related to Islamic finance. Web of Science and Scopus indexed were first used to search the literature on this topic. However, since the number of studies obtained from these two databases was relatively small, we then extended the search by exploring the Google Scholar database. Finally, we obtained eight relevant documents to be reviewed obtained from those three academic databases.

Our review results indicate that those documents varied in terms of method, purpose, finding, and suggestions for future research. Besides, we could map all those documents into four themes. This thematic approach implies that, in general, future studies on big data in relation to Islamic finance are expected to be conducted by Islamic finance researchers. Since big data itself is closer to the computer science disciple, Islamic finance researchers may collaborate with experts in this field. As a result, the papers of big data related to Islamic finance may also be published in computer science journals, in addition to Islamic finance journals or conference proceedings. By doing so, the literature on big data and Islamic finance will increase, providing more knowledge and insight to the readers.

REFERENCES

Ahmed, I. N. I., & Noordin, M. F. (2014). Big Data Storage, Collection, & Protection with Islamic Perspective. *International Journal of Scientific Research (Ahmedabad, India)*, *3*(12), 2588–2589. https://www.ijsr.net/get_abstract.php?paper_id=SUB141080

Akter, S., & Wamba, S. F. (2019). Big data and disaster management: A systematic review and agenda for future research. *Annals of Operations Research*, *283*(1), 939–959. doi:10.100710479-017-2584-2

Ali, Q., Yaacob, H., Parveen, S., & Zaini, Z. (2021). Big data and predictive analytics to optimise social and environmental performance of Islamic banks. *Environment Systems & Decisions*, *0123456789*(4), 616–632. Advance online publication. doi:10.100710669-021-09823-1

Ali, S. N. (2020). Big Data, Islamic Finance, and Sustainable Development Goals. *JKAU: Islamic Econ*, *33*(1), 83–90. doi:10.4197/Islec

Ardianto, A., & Anridho, N. (2018). Bibliometric analysis of digital accounting research. *International Journal of Digital Accounting Research*, *18*(January), 141–159. doi:10.4192/1577-8517-v18_6

Awotunde, J. B., Adeniyi, E. A., Kolawole, P. O., & Ogundokun, R. O. (2021). Application of big data in COVID-19 epidemic. In *COVID-19 and Islamic Social Finance*. Academic Press. doi:10.1016/B978-0-323-90769-9.00023-2

Bakar, N. A. (2018). Managing economic and Islamic research in big data environment: From computer science perspective. *Journal of Emerging Economies and Islamic Research*, *6*(1), 1. doi:10.24191/jeeir.v6i1.8768

Batko, K., & Ślęzak, A. (2022). The use of Big Data Analytics in healthcare. *Journal of Big Data*, *9*(3), 1–24. 1 doi:0.1186/s40537-021-00553-4

Belanche, D., Casaló, L. V., & Flavián, C. (2019). Artificial Intelligence in FinTech: Understanding robo-advisors adoption among customers. *Industrial Management & Data Systems*, *119*(7), 1411–1430. doi:10.1108/IMDS-08-2018-0368

Brenner, L., & Meyll, T. (2020). Robo-advisors: A substitute for human financial advice? *Journal of Behavioral and Experimental Finance*, *25*, 100275. Advance online publication. doi:10.1016/j. jbef.2020.100275

Chen, H., & Chiang, H. L. R., & Storey, V. (2018). Business Intelligence and Analytics: From Big Data To Big Impact. *MIS Quarterly, 36*(4), 1165–1188.

Choi, T., Wallace, S. W., & Wang, Y. (2018). Big data analytics in operations management. *Production and Operations Management*, *27*(10), 1868–1883. doi:10.1111/poms.12838

Cui, Y., Kara, S., & Chan, K. C. (2020). Manufacturing big data ecosystem: A systematic literature review. *Robotics and Computer-integrated Manufacturing*, *62*, 101861. doi:10.1016/j.rcim.2019.101861

Dash, S., Shakyawar, S. K., Sharma, M., & Kaushik, S. (2019). Big data in healthcare: Management, analysis and future prospects. *Journal of Big Data*, *6*(1), 1–25. doi:10.118640537-019-0217-0

El-Kassar, A.-N., & Singh, S. K. (2019). Green innovation and organizational performance: The influence of big data and the moderating role of management commitment and HR practices. *Technological Forecasting and Social Change*, *144*, 483–498. doi:10.1016/j.techfore.2017.12.016

Elgharbawy, A. (2020). Risk and risk management practices: A comparative study between Islamic and conventional banks in Qatar. *Journal of Islamic Accounting and Business Research*, *11*(8), 1555–1581. doi:10.1108/JIABR-06-2018-0080

Gandomi, A., & Haider, M. (2015). Beyond the hype: Big data concepts, methods, and analytics. *International Journal of Information Management*, *35*(2), 137–144. doi:10.1016/j.ijinfomgt.2014.10.007

Ghofrani, F., He, Q., Goverde, R. M. P., & Liu, X. (2018). Recent applications of big data analytics in railway transportation systems: A survey. *Transportation Research Part C, Emerging Technologies*, *90*, 226–246. doi:10.1016/j.trc.2018.03.010

Harzing, A.-W. (2010). *The publish or perish book*. Tarma Software Research Pty Limited Melbourne.

Hudaefi, F. A. (2020). How does Islamic fintech promote the SDGs? Qualitative evidence from Indonesia. *Qualitative Research in Financial Markets*, *12*(4), 353–366. doi:10.1108/QRFM-05-2019-0058

Iqbal, W., Qadir, J., Tyson, G., Mian, A. N., Hassan, S., & Crowcroft, J. (2019). A bibliometric analysis of publications in computer networking research. *Scientometrics*, *119*(2), 1121–1155. doi:10.100711192-019-03086-z

Kaffash, S., Nguyen, A. T., & Zhu, J. (2021). Big data algorithms and applications in intelligent transportation system: A review and bibliometric analysis. *International Journal of Production Economics*, *231*, 107868. doi:10.1016/j.ijpe.2020.107868

Kawtharany, S. (2017). Big Data: New Development Opportunities in Islamic Studies. *Pure Life, 11*(4). http://p-l.journals.miu.ac.ir/article_341.html

Lee, C. I. S. G., Felps, W., & Baruch, Y. (2014). Toward a taxonomy of career studies through biblio-metric visualization. *Journal of Vocational Behavior*, *85*(3), 339–351. doi:10.1016/j.jvb.2014.08.008

Li, J., Xu, L., Tang, L., Wang, S., & Li, L. (2018). Big data in tourism research: A literature review. *Tourism Management*, *68*, 301–323. doi:10.1016/j.tourman.2018.03.009

Lu, Y., & Xu, X. (2019). Cloud-based manufacturing equipment and big data analytics to enable on-demand manufacturing services. *Robotics and Computer-integrated Manufacturing*, *57*, 92–102. doi:10.1016/j.rcim.2018.11.006

Majdalawieh, M., Marir, F., & Tiemsani, I. (2017). Developing Adaptive Islamic Law Business Processes Models for Islamic Finance and Banking by Text Mining the Holy Qur'an and Hadith. *2017 IEEE 15th Intl Conf on Dependable, Autonomic and Secure Computing, 15th Intl Conf on Pervasive Intelligence and Computing, 3rd Intl Conf on Big Data Intelligence and Computing and Cyber Science and Technology Congress*, 1278–1283. 10.1109/DASC-PICom-DataCom-CyberSciTec.2017.205

Mariani, M., Baggio, R., Fuchs, M., & Höepken, W. (2018). Business intelligence and big data in hospitality and tourism: a systematic literature review. *International Journal of Contemporary Hospitality Management*.

Maroufkhani, P., Wagner, R., Ismail, W. K. W., Baroto, M. B., & Nourani, M. (2019). Big Data Analytics and Firm Performance: A Systematic Review. *Information*, *10*(7), 226. 1 doi:0.3390/INFO10070226

Mehta, N., & Pandit, A. (2018). Concurrence of big data analytics and healthcare: A systematic review. *International Journal of Medical Informatics*, *114*, 57–65. doi:10.1016/j.ijmedinf.2018.03.013 PMID:29673604

Menacer, M., Menacer, A., & Arbaoui, A. (2014). Islamic Resources Big Data mining, Extraction and Archiving. *International Journal of Enhanced Research in Management & Computer Applications*, *3*(12), 20–25.

Mishra, D., Gunasekaran, A., Papadopoulos, T., & Childe, S. J. (2018). Big Data and supply chain management: A review and bibliometric analysis. *Annals of Operations Research*, *270*(1–2), 313–336. doi:10.100710479-016-2236-y

Miskam, S., & Eksan, S. H. R. (2018). Big Data and Fintech in Islamic Finance: Prospects and Challenges. *4th Muzakarah Fiqh & International Fiqh Conference (MFIFC 2018)*, 12–23. https://islamicmarkets.com/publications/big-data-and-fintech-in-islamic-finance-prospects-and-challenges

Mnif, E., Jarboui, A., Hassan, M. K., & Mouakhar, K. (2020). Big data tools for Islamic financial analysis. *Intelligent Systems in Accounting, Finance & Management*, *27*(1), 1–12. doi:10.1002/isaf.1463

Neilson, A., Indratmo, Daniel, B., & Tjandra, S. (2019). Systematic Review of the Literature on Big Data in the Transportation Domain: Concepts and Applications. *Big Data Research*, *17*, 35–44. doi:10.1016/j.bdr.2019.03.001

Nguyen, T., Li, Z., Spiegler, V., Ieromonachou, P., & Lin, Y. (2018). Big data analytics in supply chain management: A state-of-the-art literature review. *Computers & Operations Research*, *98*, 254–264. doi:10.1016/j.cor.2017.07.004

Pashazadeh, A., & Navimipour, N. J. (2018). Big data handling mechanisms in the healthcare applications: A comprehensive and systematic literature review. *Journal of Biomedical Informatics*, *82*, 47–62. doi:10.1016/j.jbi.2018.03.014 PMID:29655946

Pejić Bach, M., Krstić, Ž., Seljan, S., & Turulja, L. (2019). Text Mining for Big Data Analysis in Financial Sector: A Literature Review. *Sustainability*, *11*(5), 1277. Advance online publication. doi:10.3390u11051277

Perdana, T. R., Mujiatun, S., Sfenrianto, S., & Kaburuan, E. R. (2019). Designing knowledge management system with big data for hospital inpatient services: (case study at Islamic Hospital XYZ Pekanbaru). *2019 International Conference on Information and Communications Technology, ICOIACT 2019*, 851–856. 10.1109/ICOIACT46704.2019.8938469

Phoon, K., & Koh, F. (2018). Robo-advisors and wealth management. *Journal of Alternative Investments*, *20*(3), 79–94. doi:10.3905/jai.2018.20.3.079

Plageras, A. P., Psannis, K. E., Stergiou, C., Wang, H., & Gupta, B. B. (2018). Efficient IoT-based sensor BIG Data collection–processing and analysis in smart buildings. *Future Generation Computer Systems*, *82*, 349–357. doi:10.1016/j.future.2017.09.082

Rejeb, A., Keogh, J. G., & Rejeb, K. (2022). Big data in the food supply chain: A literature review. *Journal of Data. Information & Management*, *4*, 33–47. doi:10.100742488-021-00064-0

Ren, S., Zhang, Y., Liu, Y., Sakao, T., Huisingh, D., & Almeida, C. M. V. B. (2019). A comprehensive review of big data analytics throughout product lifecycle to support sustainable smart manufacturing: A framework, challenges and future research directions. *Journal of Cleaner Production*, *210*, 1343–1365. doi:10.1016/j.jclepro.2018.11.025

Rialti, R., Marzi, G., Ciappei, C., & Busso, D. (2019). Big data and dynamic capabilities: A bibliometric analysis and systematic literature review. *Management Decision*, *57*(8), 2052–2068. doi:10.1108/MD-07-2018-0821

Ridhwan, M. S., Khairuddin, N. D., & Suhaimi, M. A. (2014). Big Data Technology in Shari'ah Compliance Risk Management (SCRM): A View of Information Technology in Islamic Finance Risk Management. *Journal of Islamic Banking & Finance*, *31*(3), 84–97. https://www.semanticscholar.org/paper/Big-data-technology-in-shari'ah-compliance-risk-a-Ridhwan-Khairuddin/ad7edeba0676134356462b0c-0c46b61c7c214e51

Sagiroglu, S., & Sinanc, D. (2013). Big data: A Review. *Proceedings of the 2013 International Conference on Collaboration Technologies and Systems, CTS 2013*, 42–47. 10.1109/CTS.2013.6567202

Salim, K., Alchaar, M. O., & Noushad, N. S. (2019). Big Data Analytics and Islamic Banking. *IFHUB*, 9–16. https://ikr.inceif.org/bitstream/INCEIF/3138/1/big_data_analytics_kinan et al.pdf

Shaleh, M. A. (2018). Big Data for the Environment : Opportunities and Challenges from an Islamic Perspective. *Islam and Civilisational Renewal*, *9*(2), 237–240. doi:10.12816/0049469

Tafri, F. H., Rahman, R. A., & Omar, N. (2011). Empirical evidence on the risk management tools practised in Islamic and conventional banks. *Qualitative Research in Financial Markets*, *3*(2), 86–104. doi:10.1108/17554171111155339

TheSunDaily. (2018). *BIMB Invest declares 8% yield for BIMB-Arabesque i Global Dividend Fund 1.* https://www.thesundaily.my/archive/bimb-invest-declares-8-yield-bimb-arabesque-i-global-dividend-fund-1-MUARCH535901

Wang, C. J., Ng, C. Y., & Brook, R. H. (2020). Response to COVID-19 in Taiwan: Big data analytics, new technology, and proactive testing. *Journal of the American Medical Association, 323*(14), 1341–1342. doi:10.1001/jama.2020.3151 PMID:32125371

Yu, M., Yang, C., & Li, Y. (2018). Big data in natural disaster management: A review. *Geosciences, 8*(5), 165. doi:10.3390/geosciences8050165

Zhao, Y., Xu, X., & Wang, M. (2019). Predicting overall customer satisfaction: Big data evidence from hotel online textual reviews. *International Journal of Hospitality Management, 76,* 111–121. doi:10.1016/j.ijhm.2018.03.017

ADDITIONAL READING

Alam, N., & Ali, S. N. (2021). *Fintech, Digital Currency and the Future of Islamic Finance: Strategic, Regulatory and Adoption Issues in the Gulf Cooperation Council.* Palgrave Macmillan. doi:10.1007/978-3-030-49248-9

Askari, H., Iqbal, Z., Krichene, N., & Mirakhor, A. (2010). The Stability of Islamic Finance – Creating a Resilient Financial Environment for a Secure Future. Singapore: John Wiley & Sons (Asia) Pte. Ltd.

Ayub, M. (2007). *Understanding Islamic Finance.* John Wiley & Sons, Ltd.

Hassan, M. K., & Aliyu, S. (2018). A contemporary survey of Islamic banking literature. *Journal of Financial Stability, 34,* 12–43. doi:10.1016/j.jfs.2017.11.006

Millar, R., & Anwar, H. (2008). *Islamic Finance: A Guide for International Business and Investment.* GMB Publishing Ltd.

Mohamed, H., & Ali, H. (2019). *Blockchain, Fintech, and Islamic Finance.* Walter de Gruyter.

Watkins, J. S. (2020). Islamic Finance and Global Capitalism. In Islamic Finance and Global Capitalism: An Alternative to the Market Economy. Palgrave Macmillan. doi:10.1007/978-3-030-59840-2

Zulkhibri, M., Manap, A., & Ali, T. (2019). *Islamic finance, risk-sharing and macroeconomic stability.* Palgrave Macmillan. doi:10.1007/978-3-030-05225-6

KEY TERMS AND DEFINITIONS

Artificial Intelligence (AI): Digital computer or a computer-controlled robot's ability to accomplish tasks typically associated with intelligent beings.

Big Data: A numerous amount of information available on the internet, which can be utilized to figure out the problem in various fields.

Big Data Main Features: Volume, variety, velocity, and veracity.

Hadith: The record consisting of the sayings and traditions of the Prophet Muhammad.

Islamic Big Data: Is a term referring to data storing and disseminating activities that are not against Islamic laws (Sharia).

Islamic Finance: Financial transactions that are compliant with Islamic teachings and law.

Islamic (Sharia) Banks: Banks that operate based on Islamic law.

Murabaha: A contract in Islamic finance which is equivalent to a buying-selling contract.

Quran: The holy book of Muslims and the primary source of law in Islam. The Quran contains history, sciences, and laws that must be adopted by Muslim life.

SDGs: It stands for Sustainable Development Goals, which are a set of 17 interconnected global goals providing a blueprint for a better and more sustainable future for all. The United Nations General Assembly established these goals in 2015, with the goal of achieving them by 2030.

Big Data Helps for Non–Pharmacological Disease Control Measures of COVID–19

B

Peng Zhao

https://orcid.org/0000-0003-1458-8266

INTELLIGENTRABBIT LLC, USA

Yuan Ren

Shanghai Dianji University, China

Xi Chen

Beijing University of Civil Engineering and Architecture, China

INTRODUCTION

During the COVID-19 pandemic, a variety of non-pharmacological disease control measures, including travel restrictions, lockdowns, stay-at-home orders, wearing-a-mask policies, and social distancing regulations, have been implemented by governments and lawmakers. Issuing travel restrictions or lockdown policies can help to mitigate the spread of COVID-19 by reducing human mobility and decreasing the probability of contact (Grépin et al., 2021). It is more important to keep social distancing now claims than ever before, since it is one of the best ways to prevent the spread of the disease except wearing face masks (Milne & Xie, 2020). Wearing masks can significantly reduce the amount of coronavirus transmitted by droplets and aerosols (Eikenberry et al., 2020). Almost all countries now carry out such non-pharmacological disease control policies as mandatory strategies. Based on the proposed requirements by the WHO, the minimum distance between individuals must be kept at least 6 feet to achieve a safe social distancing among the people. The medical researchers have pointed out that individuals with mild or no symptoms may also be carriers of the novel coronavirus (Wang et al., 2020), therefore it is important to require all people to maintain controlled behaviors and to keep social distancing. However, it may be a challenging task to monitor the amount of infection spread and the efficiency of the constraints.

Since the end of 2019, the lives of people all around the world have been drastically affected by the COVID-19 pandemic. The world economy has been in a depression due to a loss of jobs, while face-to-face communication has been restricted to control the infection rate (Feyisa, 2020). Although it has been more than 18 months since the global outbreak, medical researchers are still unable to confirm the end of the pandemic. Despite the effectiveness of the new vaccines by some degrees, the Delta variant leads the significant uncertainty, which makes the situation moving towards the undesired detection. Due to such the circumstance, research communities have pointed out that society may go through a long period of abnormality. Governments have to continue to enforce mask-wearing, social distancing, and quarantines. Many changes for society, including online education, mandatory facial masks, and the vast majority of people working from home, have been made in the new normal, and perhaps continue for a long time (Odusanya et al., 2020).

Cutting-edge technologies, such as machine learning, deep learning, computer vision, and big data analytics, can be applied to implement efficient non-pharmacological disease control measures (Lakhani

DOI: 10.4018/978-1-7998-9220-5.ch009

Copyright © 2023, IGI Global. Copying or distributing in print or electronic forms without written permission of IGI Global is prohibited.

et al., 2020). Motivated by the current demand in disease control for Covid-19, this chapter is designed to investigate how such technologies work to solve a broad range of real-world problems, such as tracking and visualizing stay-at-home measurements, monitoring social distancing regulations, and detecting face-mask-wearing practices. The objectives of this chapter are listed as follows:

- illustrating how big data helps in measuring human mobility to track stay-at-home measures with information retrieval and visual mining.
- investigating how deep learning and computer vision work for implementing a social distancing monitor using a pre-trained detector, i.e. YOLO v3.
- examining how to detect whether individuals wear masks or not using deep learning approaches, along with a real-world testing process.

BACKGROUND

COVID-19 is a highly infectious and crafty virus. In most cases, the infected individuals do not initially exhibit symptoms, while some remain asymptomatic. Thus, a non-negligible fraction of the population can, at any certain time, be a hidden factor of transmissions. In response, governments in many countries have took much effort to develop contact tracing apps for smartphone that help solve the difficult task of tracing all recent contacts of newly confirmed infected individuals (Ahmed et al., 2020). Additionally, it is still challenging to understand the actual human mobility responding to the stay-at-home policies due to the lack of a recorded and large-scale dataset that can describe human mobility during the pandemic (Xiong et al., 2020). Based on the development of big data technologies over the last decade, government departments widely adopt location data of mobile device to analyze human mobility, in order to support policy-making objectives. Researchers also use location data in aggregate shape to further understand general patterns of human movements and behaviors according to the global positioning system (GPS) signals, cell site locations, and bluetooth beacons (Bachir et al., 2019; Song et al., 2010; Stange et al., 2011). Through such analysis, governments and researchers can navigate the spreading of the COVID-19 outbreak and the effectiveness of public health interventions can be measured. COVID-19 mobility tracking programs have been proposed on several platforms which can evaluate human travel distance. Those platforms covers Google's community mobility reports, Apple's mobility trends reports, and Cuebiq's COVID-19 mobility insights. Researchers have applied data extracted from Facebook for Good program to establish the model of mobility patterns in Seattle, in order to quantify its effect on the COVID-19 outbreak (Burstein et al., 2020). However, such studies and reports are restricted to the aggregated level of travel distance due to the lack of individual-level measurements.

With the revolutionary development of the computer hardware capability, based on learning algorithms, the more accurate models and faster monitors can be generated by researchers and scientists, compared to regular machine learning models. Deep learning models, such as convolutional neural networks (CNNs) and deep neural networks (DNNs), have been applied in feature extraction and complex object classification (Gidaris & Komodakis, 2015). These models can also be performed to achieve social distancing monitoring. Punn et al. (2020) developed a DNNs-based monitor for detection of human mobility, which can measure the number of individuals who violated the social distancing. Based on various research objectives, similar studies have been conducted by researchers, which includes detecting the people distancing in a certain manufactory (Khandelwal et al., 2020), monitoring social distancing constrains in crowded scenarios (Sathyamoorthy et al., 2020), and assessing infection risk measurements on the street (Rezaei & Azarmi, 2020). The common types of object detection models were applied in such studies, which contain fast RCNN, Single Shot MultiBox Detector (SSD), and You Only Look Once (YOLO). These detection models are the major methods to establish social distancing monitor systems in the context of COVID-19. However, limitations still exist in the related researches, which includes that inadequate statistical analysis of the result data is provided; accuracy measurements of monitoring system are established based on various datasets without comparable ground truths; no further information at the individual level is exploitable for tracking records and management system.

Several studies are attempting to implement face mask detection using deep learning algorithms into a real-time architecture. A real-time face mask detection system with alarm function has been developed through using deep learning algorithms (Militante & Dionisio, 2020). Yadav (2020) proposed a real-time monitor that can detect safe social distancing and face masks by performing deep learning models on raspberry pi4. Based on edge computing, Kong et al. (2021) applied a deep learning framework, called ECMask, to generate a real-time face mask detection application for COVID-19. Nagrath et al. (2021) created a real-time face mask detection system using single shot multi-box detector. MobileNetV2 (SS-DMNV2) model is utilized, which is based on the deep neural network (DNN). A hybrid mask detection and social distancing monitoring system, proposed by Meivel at al. (2021), can process complex pictures using R-CNN, Fast R-CNN, and Faster R-CNN algorithms. The web-based efficient AI mask recognition application, called WearMask, has been deployed on many common devices that connect to the internet, which is designed based on a server-less edge-computing architecture with the combination of YOLO, NCNN, and WebAssembly (Wang et al., 2021).

FOCUS OF THE ARTICLE

This chapter reveals how artificial intelligence and big data analytics help the non-pharmacological disease control measures. Several cutting-edge technologies, such as contact tracking, mobility measuring, intelligent surveillance video monitoring, are illustrated in terms of the system architecture, the data workflows, and the machine learning/deep learning models. This chapter will also investigate a comprehensive social control system that is designed for disease control measures by integrating above-mentioned technologies. For each component of the system, real-world applications will be represented in the form of examining the capability of the proposed models. The proposed system can detect whether people are keeping social distancing and wearing a face mask in public spaces, along with measuring the mobility assessment, which can be applied to screen the stay-at-home orders using big data and visual mining. A fine-tuned CNN-based network will be applied for monitoring the social distancing, while the face mask detection module is trained by fine-tuning the MobileNet architecture.

SOLUTIONS AND RECOMMENDATIONS

Measuring Human Mobility

Numerous mobility datasets have been collecting from smartphones and social media platforms since the beginning of the pandemic (Kang et al., 2020). Such a data pool can be applied in monitoring human contact and measuring stay-at-home policy measures by analyzing human mobility patterns. Several tech companies have released the mobility index, e.g. Google has collected data from Android users, while Apple users have been tracked via Apple products. However, such mobility datasets have not incorporated individual-level measurements, thereby may not be able to provide the comprehensive vision of the human mobility in the pandemic. Creating a new mobility dataset is essential for analyzing the pandemic-related mobility pattern by combining all available information into one. To do that, this chapter proposes a novel mobility dataset by gathering selected mobility data pools, such as mobility reports, mobility signals collected from mobile phones, and geographical information derived from social media. The new mobile dataset can be applied in analyzing and tracking human mobility patterns through the visual mining approaches.

Mobility reports can be acquired from multiple online reports created by different tech companies, such as Google, Apple, Waze, etc. Human movement features have been detected by region, across different categories of places, such as residential places, workplaces, transit stations, parks, grocery and pharmacy shops, retail and recreation sections. Such information can be download from the Google's COVDI-19 Community Mobility Reports website that contains both state-level and county-level datasets for daily updates in the United States. Similarly, the available mobility information, presented by Apple's COVID-19 Mobility Trends Reports, can be obtained by requests per region, sub-region, and city, which represent data about diving, transportation, and walking trends in the United States. Additional traffic and driving data can be extracted from information acquired from TomTom reports and Waze reports, of which traffic congestions in 80 cities and driving patters in over 40 cities have been provided from coast to coast in the United States. Such datasets can be used in tracking the human mobility in general, however, none of them measures individual-level mobility signals, thereby may not good for monitoring the stay-at-home measures.

To create an individual-level mobility index, several options can be chosen in the form of mobile phone signals and social media information. Two open source datasets can be employed to implement the mobility dataset, e.g. the M50 index (Warren & Skillman, 2020) and the Social Mobility Index (Xu et al., 2020). To generate the M50 index, a bounding box has been used for generating three mobility measures. The first mobility measure is the maximum Haversine distance that is the distance from the starting point of the day. The second mobility measure is a linear measure for the bounding box mobility, which is converted as a linear distance from the area value of the points within the bounding box. The last mobility measure is the convex hull mobility, which is converted as a linear distance from the area value of the convex hull of the points. Furthermore, for each interested location targeted by the reverse geocoding procedure, different statistical parameters, containing the mean, median, and quartiles, are calculated. Among these statistical parameters, the median of the maximum distance mobility is designated as M50. A normalized M50 has been also defined by normalizing the value for each M50 measurement in a location. On the other hand, individual mobility patterns can also be collected from social media. COVID-19-related tweets have been collected based on key information of location through using Twitter streaming API. The dataset contains totally 3,768,959 Twitter users and 469,669,925 tweets posted in the United States. To generate the Twitter Social Mobility index, the weekly location records of users are used as the elements of the coordinate sequence, which can symbolize the statistical number of coordinates in specific time periods. The study has vectorized the home location for certain user through calculating the centroid of all the coordinates. Furthermore, the distance sequence is generated through measuring geodesic distance between two close locations. For the computing of the social mobility index, the standard deviations of these distances are quantified. Each standard deviation has been multiplied with their corresponding operator and then the products of them have been summed up. In general, such an index can reflect the user mobility according to traveling area and routine.

Table 1. The summary of the new human mobility dataset

Geographical level	Original dataset	Dataset type	Frequency of updates
State level	Google reports	Mobility reports	Daily
State level	Apple reports	Mobility reports	Daily
State level	M50 index	Individual mobility	Daily
State level	Social mobility index	Individual mobility	Weekly
County level	Google reports	Mobility reports	Daily
County level	Apple reports	Mobility reports	Daily
County level	M50 index	Individual mobility	Daily
City level	Apple reports	Mobility reports	Daily
City level	TomTom reports	Mobility reports	Daily
City level	Waze reports	Mobility reports	Daily
City level	Social mobility index	Individual mobility	Weekly

Despite accessibilities of open source datasets of the pandemic-mobility information, gathering such mobility data produces a lot of challenges. Different data sources have a variety of geographical and temporal scopes in measuring the mobility. Moreover, mobility reports contain data in the textual format, thereby need to extract useful information using natural language processing. Table 1 summaries the basic meta data of the novel mobility dataset. Such a dataset can be applied to mapping nationwide human mobility patterns, exploring seasonal mobility characteristics per county, and segmenting city-level driving features, as shown in Figure 1. The general mobility pattern in Figure 1A indicates that visiting in parks may lead the failure of the stay-at-home policy in the U.S. due to the difficulty of practicing the social distancing regulation in the outdoor environment. The seasonal mobility patterns, as illustrated in Figure 1B, well describe the relationship between human mobility and Covid-19 spikes. The city-level driving patterns has been captured through Figure 1C using a K-means cluttering, which can segment all major cities in the U.S. into three groups via mean and volatility of the mobility levels throughout the Covid-19 outbreak.

Social Distancing Monitor

Practicing the social distancing regulation has been determined as one of the most effective measures in controlling the spreading of Covid-19. Although the 6-feet physical distancing is mandatory for both indoor and outdoor conditions, such a regulation is difficult to monitor when a large group of population gathering or walking outside in particular (Bouhlel et al., 2021). Cutting-edge technologies, such as big data analytics, machine learning, deep learning, and computer vision, can be applied in automated human detection and screening the social distancing measures between each other using surveillance cameras. A variety of object detection algorithms has been used to implement the social distancing monitor based on pre-trained models, such as R-CNN, SSD, YOLO, etc. Such a deep learning-based monitor can be incorporated in supporting the non-pharmacological disease control measures by detecting social distancing executions in crowd (Yang et al., 2021).

The emergence of deep learning has brought the best application performance for a wide variety of tasks and challenges. Object classification, detection, segmentation, tracking, and recognition are the major tasks that deep learning usually can solve. In recent years, the architectures based on CNN have

Figure 1. Visualizing mobility patterns in the U.S. (A). general human mobility patters; (B). seasonal mobility patterns; (C). Driving pattern segmentations.

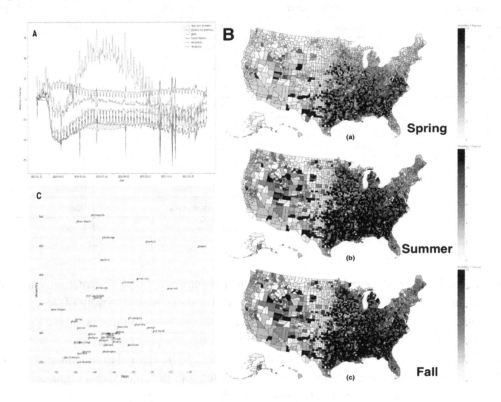

shown remarkable performance improvements, which leads towards the advanced accuracy of object detection. A deep learning based framework is proposed. It utilizes object detection techniques and tracking models to guarantee the social distancing for calming down the rise of COVID-19 cases. In order to maintain the balance of speed and accuracy, YOLO v3 and the Deepsort are utilized as object detection framework and tracking approach. In this process, it usually surrounds each detected object with the bounding boxes. And then, the pairwise L2 norm with computationally efficient vectorized representation is calculated using these bounding boxes, in order to identify the clusters of individuals who do not obey the order of social distancing. Furthermore, to visualize the cluster distribution in the live stream, each bounding box is color-coded according to its relationship with the group where the individuals belonging to the same group are symbolized with the same color. The necessary steps undertaken to compose a framework for monitoring social distancing are as follows:

Step 1. Fine-tune the trained object detection model to recognize and track the person in a footage.

Step 2. The trained model is fed with the surveillance footage. The model generates a set of bounding boxes and an ID for each identified person.

Step 3. Each individual is linked to three-dimensional feature space (x, y, d), where (x, y) represents the centroid coordinates of the bounding box and d defines the depth of the individual as observed from the camera.

Step 4. Pairwise L2 norm is calculated for the set of bounding boxes.

Step 5. The dense matrix of L2 norm is then utilized to assign the neighbors for each individual, which satisfies the closeness sensitivity. With extensive trials the closeness threshold is updated dynamically based on the spatial location of the person in a given frame ranging between (90, 170) pixels.

Step 6. Any individual that meets the closeness property is assigned a neighbor or neighbors to form. Opposite to other people, the group is represented in a different color coding.

To test the reliability of the proposed social distancing monitor, this chapter deploys such an algorithm to perform the real-time detection task using a CCTV surveillance video sample in the VIRAT video dataset (Oh et al., 2011). The visual outputs are shown in Figure 2 that illustrates the model performance via human detection, people tracking and identification, measuring social distancing for single individuals, and monitoring coupled persons on the street. In Figure 2A, each individual has been set up a unique ID, which can be recognized along with the walking trails by the proposed human detector, followed by measuring the social distancing between each other, where red bars indicate that two people are too close, thereby may produce a higher risk, as shown in Figure 2B. Similarly, coupled persons are also detected using the same ideology, of which group identification has been represented in Figure 2C, along with the group social distancing monitor in Figure 2D. To distinguish the risk assessment of the single individual monitor, higher risks for coupled pensions are given a yellow bar.

Figure 2. Social distancing monitor test results. (A). single individuals detection and identification; (B). single individuals social distancing monitor; (C). coupled persons detection and identification; (D). coupled persons social distancing monitor.

Face Mask Detection

During the Covid-19 pandemic, the face-mask policy has becoming more and more important as it can reduce the speed of spreading of the disease (Eikenberry et al., 2020). Individuals are required to wear masks in public areas since the beginning of the pandemic. Wearing a mask is mandatory for everyone who want to get receptions from public and private service providers. However, monitoring whether or not an individual practices such a regulation is still challenging (Nowrin et al., 2021). In the age of artificial intelligence, such a problem can be solved by using deep learning in terms of recognizing features in images and real-time video steams. Both supervised and unsupervised learning can be uses in image recognition and computer vision, whereas most recent studies suggest that common object detection approaches are basically categorized into three major frameworks, such as the CNN-based architecture (i.e. LeNet, VGGNet, ResNet, AlexNet, etc.), the hybrid method incorporating deep learning-based feature extractors and machine learning-based classifiers, and the pre-trained deep transfer learning approach (i.e. MobileNet, VGG-16, YOLO, Inception, Xception, etc).

In the process of application deployment, the most important part in implementing the proposed face mask detector into the real-world applications is to apply the proper algorithm for face mask detection. Even though various methods can be applied to build the image recognition models, it is crucial to consider the model efficiency and complexity by leveraging the factors of model performance. They include the accuracy, overfitting problems, difficulties of the network training process, and the cost efficiency issue. By summarizing the existing studies in this field, an approach based on deep transfer learning by fine-tuning the MobileNetV2 architecture has been used to train face mask detector and applied to the following tasks. A model based on a high-efficient network is proposed, that can be utilized on embedded devices with the limited requirement for computational capacity. The whole network has been implemented through using TensorFlow and Keras, along with the image augmentation process and the transformation of the class vector to the binary class matrix in data processing. Finally, it can be performed through using OpenCV to test and implement the face mask detection for images or real-time video streaming.

To obtain an efficient experimental design, three datasets are employed for training and examining the proposed model given the task in regards of recognizing whether individuals wear masks or not. The first dataset (PRAJNASB), created by Bhandary (2020), consists of over 1300 images for both masked individuals and persons who do not wear masks. The second dataset (LFW) is available from Kaggle, containing over 850 masked face images (Dalkiran, 2020). The Face Detection Data Set and Benchmark (FDDB) has been selected as the third dataset, which contains more than 5100 face images (Jain& Learned-Miller, 2010). Both PRAJNASB and LFW are simulated masked face datasets with pre-labeled images, whereas face images in FDDB are taken from real photos. In this chapter, the proposed model is trained based on a new image set created from those three data sources. Over 100 masked faces and more than 110 face images are randomly selected from LFW and FDDB, respectively, as the extra samples adding to PRAJNASB. Finally, the new image set contains 800 masked faces and 800 no-masked face images. The dataset is divided into a 80% training set and a 20% set for validating. Figure 3 represents the model performance of the proposed face-mask detector by providing a real-world example of the face-covering identification, as shown in Figure 3A, along with the training and testing accuracy matrix and the loss curves of the model in Figure 3B. The proposed detector can achieve a nearly 99% in accuracy on both training and testing sets, indicating that such an algorithm can benefit the current demand in monitoring face-mask regulation significantly. However, such an algorithm relays on a two-stage procedure, i.e. human detection first and face mask detection last, therefore, some problem may appear when the face is not detected.

FUTURE RESEARCH DIRECTIONS

Future research directions should incorporate multiple perspectives throughout tracking human mobility, monitoring social distancing, and detecting face-mask wearing. Firstly, supplementing the human

Figure 3. Test results of the face-mask detector. (A) sample detection output; (B). training and testing epochs v.s. loss and accuracy curves.

B

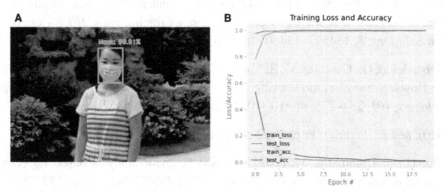

mobility dataset will enlighten the research extension by adding relative mobility indicators based on data collected from multiple data transactions, such as Bluetooth, WiFi, and QR code. Secondly, despite the effectiveness of the social distancing monitor, it cannot track the personal information in regards to violations, thereby more attributes should be involved for measuring the comprehensive feature extractions, such as body temperatures, exposure risks, and other factors related to the disease control measures of Covid-19. Lastly, although the face mask detection can be implemented into the system, real-time detectors are still difficult to deploy in terms of detections in crowd due to the limitation of the model, therefore, alternative methods should be considered for improving the human detection module, e.g. using the tiny face detector.

Besides, as the digital technologies have been widely used to monitoring the social system, the potential violations of ethical values become another significant issues that impact the technical efficiency and adoption. As a result, a broad range of ethical issues, such as security and privacy, data transaction and management, synchronization, over-tracking, over-surveillance, and implementation development and guidelines, should be incorporated to re-think the technological framework of social control measures towards ethical practices. Moreover, the social control system may also be modified by other social factors, such as gender diversities, clothing rules in Sharia-law countries, and social credit systems in totalitarian countries. Such topics can be discussed in the future studies.

CONCLUSION

This chapter investigates how deep learning and big data work to implement the non-pharmacological disease control measures efficiently. State-of-the-art techniques, such as big data analytics, visual mining, deep learning, and computer vision, can be applied in constructing the multi-angle disease control system in terms of human mobility measurement, social distancing monitor, and face mask detection. Experimental results indicate that big data analytics can be applied to track and measure the stay-at-home order using visual mining and cluttering, whereas deep learning can be incorporated in screening social control regulations using computer vision. The proposed system has been examined with real-world problem-solving attempts for each aspect of the non-pharmacological disease control measures of Covid-19, suggesting that such a system can manage the pandemic prevention effectively.

REFERENCES

Ahmed, N., Michelin, R. A., Xue, W., Ruj, S., Malaney, R., Kanhere, S. S., Seneviratne, A., Hu, W., Janicke, H., & Jha, S. K. (2020). A survey of covid-19 contact tracing apps. *IEEE Access: Practical Innovations, Open Solutions*, *8*, 134577–134601. doi:10.1109/ACCESS.2020.3010226

Bachir, D., Khodabandelou, G., Gauthier, V., El Yacoubi, M., & Puchinger, J. (2019). Inferring dynamic origin-destination flows by transport mode using mobile phone data. *Transportation Research Part C, Emerging Technologies*, *101*, 254–275. doi:10.1016/j.trc.2019.02.013

Bhandary, P. (2020). *Mask Classifier*. https://github.com/prajnasb/observations

Bouhlel, F., Mliki, H., & Hammami, M. (2021). Crowd behavior analysis based on convolutional neural network: social distancing control COVID-19. In *VISIGRAPP* (Vol. 5, pp. 273–280). VISAPP. doi:10.5220/0010193002730280

Burstein, R., Hu, H., Thakkar, N., Schroeder, A., Famulare, M., & Klein, D. (2020). *Understanding the impact of COVID-19 policy change in the greater Seattle area using mobility data*. Institute for Disease Modeling.

Dalkiran, M. (2020). *LFW Simulated Masked Face Dataset*. https://www.kaggle.com/muhammeddalkran/lfw-simulated-masked-face-dataset

Eikenberry, S. E., Mancuso, M., Iboi, E., Phan, T., Eikenberry, K., Kuang, Y., Kostelich, E., & Gumel, A. B. (2020). To mask or not to mask: Modeling the potential for face mask use by the general public to curtail the COVID-19 pandemic. *Infectious Disease Modelling*, *5*, 293–308. doi:10.1016/j.idm.2020.04.001 PMID:32355904

Feyisa, H. L. (2020). The world economy at COVID-19 quarantine: contemporary review. *International Journal of Economics, Finance and Management Sciences, 8*(2), 63-74.

Gidaris, S., & Komodakis, N. (2015). Object detection via a multi-region and semantic segmentation-aware cnn model. In *Proceedings of the IEEE international conference on computer vision* (pp. 1134-1142). 10.1109/ICCV.2015.135

Grépin, K. A., Ho, T. L., Liu, Z., Marion, S., Piper, J., Worsnop, C. Z., & Lee, K. (2021). Evidence of the effectiveness of travel-related measures during the early phase of the COVID-19 pandemic: A rapid systematic review. *BMJ Global Health*, *6*(3), e004537. doi:10.1136/bmjgh-2020-004537 PMID:33722793

Kang, Y., Gao, S., Liang, Y., Li, M., Rao, J., & Kruse, J. (2020). Multiscale dynamic human mobility flow dataset in the US during the COVID-19 epidemic. *Scientific Data*, *7*(1), 1–13. doi:10.103841597-020-00734-5 PMID:31896794

Khandelwal, P., Khandelwal, A., & Agarwal, S. (2020). *Using computer vision to enhance safety of workforce in manufacturing in a post covid world*. arXiv preprint arXiv:2005.05287.

Kong, X., Wang, K., Wang, S., Wang, X., Jiang, X., Guo, Y., ... Ni, Q. (2021). Real-time mask identification for COVID-19: an edge computing-based deep learning framework. *IEEE Internet of Things Journal*.

Lakhani, H. V., Pillai, S. S., Zehra, M., Sharma, I., & Sodhi, K. (2020). Systematic review of clinical insights into novel coronavirus (CoVID-19) pandemic: Persisting challenges in US rural population. *International Journal of Environmental Research and Public Health*, *17*(12), 4279. doi:10.3390/ijerph17124279 PMID:32549334

Meivel, S., Devi, K. I., Maheswari, S. U., & Menaka, J. V. (2021). Real time data analysis of face mask detection and social distance measurement using Matlab. *Materials Today: Proceedings*. Advance online publication. doi:10.1016/j.matpr.2020.12.1042 PMID:33643853

Militante, S. V., & Dionisio, N. V. (2020, August). Real-time facemask recognition with alarm system using deep learning. In *2020 11th IEEE Control and System Graduate Research Colloquium (ICSGRC)* (pp. 106-110). IEEE. 10.1109/ICSGRC49013.2020.9232610

Milne, G. J., & Xie, S. (2020). *The effectiveness of social distancing in mitigating COVID-19 spread: a modelling analysis*. MedRxiv., doi:10.1101/2020.03.20.20040055

Nagrath, P., Jain, R., Madan, A., Arora, R., Kataria, P., & Hemanth, J. (2021). SSDMNV2: A real time DNN-based face mask detection system using single shot multibox detector and MobileNetV2. *Sustainable Cities and Society*, *66*, 102692. doi:10.1016/j.scs.2020.102692 PMID:33425664

Nowrin, A., Afroz, S., Rahman, M. S., Mahmud, I., & Cho, Y. Z. (2021). Comprehensive review on facemask detection techniques in the context of covid-19. *IEEE Access*.

Odusanya, O. O., Odugbemi, B. A., Odugbemi, T. O., & Ajisegiri, W. S. (2020). COVID-19: A review of the effectiveness of non-pharmacological interventions. *The Nigerian Postgraduate Medical Journal*, *27*(4), 261. doi:10.4103/npmj.npmj_208_20 PMID:33154276

Oh, S., Hoogs, A., Perera, A., Cuntoor, N., Chen, C. C., Lee, J. T., & Desai, M. (2011, June). A large-scale benchmark dataset for event recognition in surveillance video. In *CVPR 2011* (pp. 3153–3160). IEEE. doi:10.1109/CVPR.2011.5995586

Punn, N. S., Sonbhadra, S. K., & Agarwal, S. (2020). *Monitoring COVID-19 social distancing with person detection and tracking via fine-tuned YOLO v3 and Deepsort techniques*. arXiv preprint arXiv:2005.01385.

Rezaei, M., & Azarmi, M. (2020). Deepsocial: Social distancing monitoring and infection risk assessment in covid-19 pandemic. *Applied Sciences (Basel, Switzerland)*, *10*(21), 7514. doi:10.3390/app10217514

Sathyamoorthy, A. J., Patel, U., Savle, Y. A., Paul, M., & Manocha, D. (2020). *COVID-robot: Monitoring social distancing constraints in crowded scenarios*. arXiv preprint arXiv:2008.06585.

Song, C., Koren, T., Wang, P., & Barabási, A. L. (2010). Modelling the scaling properties of human mobility. *Nature Physics*, *6*(10), 818–823. doi:10.1038/nphys1760

Stange, H., Liebig, T., Hecker, D., Andrienko, G., & Andrienko, N. (2011, November). Analytical workflow of monitoring human mobility in big event settings using bluetooth. In *Proceedings of the 3rd ACM SIGSPATIAL international workshop on indoor spatial awareness* (pp. 51-58). 10.1145/2077357.2077368

Wang, Y., Wang, Y., Chen, Y., & Qin, Q. (2020). Unique epidemiological and clinical features of the emerging 2019 novel coronavirus pneumonia (COVID-19) implicate special control measures. *Journal of Medical Virology*, *92*(6), 568–576. doi:10.1002/jmv.25748 PMID:32134116

Wang, Z., Wang, P., Louis, P. C., Wheless, L. E., & Huo, Y. (2021). *WearMask: Fast in-browser face mask detection with serverless edge computing for COVID-19*. arXiv preprint arXiv:2101.00784.

Warren, M. S., & Skillman, S. W. (2020). *Mobility changes in response to COVID-19*. arXiv preprint arXiv:2003.14228.

Xiong, C., Hu, S., Yang, M., Younes, H., Luo, W., Ghader, S., & Zhang, L. (2020). Mobile device location data reveal human mobility response to state-level stay-at-home orders during the COVID-19 pandemic in the USA. *Journal of the Royal Society, Interface*, *17*(173), 20200344. doi:10.1098/rsif.2020.0344 PMID:33323055

Xu, P., Dredze, M., & Broniatowski, D. A. (2020). The Twitter social mobility index: Measuring social distancing practices with geolocated Tweets. *Journal of Medical Internet Research*, *22*(12), e21499. doi:10.2196/21499 PMID:33048823

Yadav, S. (2020). Deep learning based safe social distancing and face mask detection in public areas for COVID-19 safety guidelines adherence. *International Journal for Research in Applied Science and Engineering Technology*, *8*(7), 1368–1375. doi:10.22214/ijraset.2020.30560

Yang, D., Yurtsever, E., Renganathan, V., Redmill, K. A., & Özgüner, Ü. (2021). A vision-based social distancing and critical density detection system for COVID-19. *Sensors (Basel)*, *21*(13), 4608. doi:10.339021134608 PMID:34283141

ADDITIONAL READING

Abboah-Offei, M., Salifu, Y., Adewale, B., Bayuo, J., Ofosu-Poku, R., & Opare-Lokko, E. B. A. (2021). A rapid review of the use of face mask in preventing the spread of COVID-19. *International Journal of Nursing Studies Advances, 3*, 100013.

Balaji, S., Balamurugan, B., Kumar, T. A., Rajmohan, R., & Kumar, P. P. (2021). *A brief survey on AI based face mask detection system for public places. Irish Interdisciplinary Journal of Science & Research.*

Bonaccorsi, G., Pierri, F., Cinelli, M., Flori, A., Galeazzi, A., Porcelli, F., Schmidt, A. L., Valensise, C. M., Scala, A., Quattrociocchi, W., & Pammolli, F. (2020). Economic and social consequences of human mobility restrictions under COVID-19. *Proceedings of the National Academy of Sciences of the United States of America*, *117*(27), 15530–15535. doi:10.1073/pnas.2007658117 PMID:32554604

Martinho, F. C., & Griffin, I. L. (2021). A cross-sectional survey on the impact of Coronavirus disease 2019 on the clinical practice of endodontists across the United States. *Journal of Endodontics*, *47*(1), 28–38. doi:10.1016/j.joen.2020.10.002 PMID:33058936

Ren, J., Yan, Y., Zhao, H., Ma, P., Zabalza, J., Hussain, Z., Luo, S., Dai, Q., Zhao, S., Sheikh, A., Hussain, A., & Li, H. (2020). A novel intelligent computational approach to model epidemiological trends and assess the impact of non-pharmacological interventions for covid-19. *IEEE Journal of Biomedical and Health Informatics*, *24*(12), 3551–3563. doi:10.1109/JBHI.2020.3027987 PMID:32997638

Tartari, E., Hopman, J., Allegranzi, B., Gao, B., Widmer, A., Cheng, V. C. C., Wong, S. C., Marimuthu, K., Ogunsola, F., & Voss, A. (2020). Perceived challenges of COVID-19 infection prevention and control preparedness: A multinational survey. *Journal of Global Antimicrobial Resistance, 22*, 779–781. doi:10.1016/j.jgar.2020.07.002 PMID:32659504

Tutsoy, O., Polat, A., Çolak, Ş., & Balikci, K. (2020). Development of a multi-dimensional parametric model with non-pharmacological policies for predicting the COVID-19 pandemic casualties. *IEEE Access: Practical Innovations, Open Solutions, 8*, 225272–225283. doi:10.1109/ACCESS.2020.3044929 PMID:34812374

Ulhaq, A., Khan, A., Gomes, D., & Paul, M. (2020). Computer vision for covid-19 control: A survey. arXiv preprint arXiv:2004.09420.

KEY TERMS AND DEFINITIONS

Computer Vision: An automation technology that makes computers to gain high-level understanding from images and videos throughout acquiring, processing, analyzing, and recognizing digital data by transforming visual images into numerical or symbolic information.

Convolutional Neural Network: A typical deep learning model that is commonly used to image classification, object detection, natural language procession, and predictive analysis. Such a network structure is a regularized version of fully connected networks, which belong to the class of artificial neural network.

Deep Learning: A broad family of machine learning models based on neural networks. Typical deep learning models are deep neural networks, convolutional neural networks, recurrent neural networks, deep belief networks, and deep reinforcement learning.

Face Mask Detection: A computer-based monitor that detects whether individuals are wearing a mask or not.

Human Mobility: A measurement that describes how people move within a network or system through tracking and analyzing human behavior patterns demographically and geographically over time.

Non-Pharmacological Disease Control: A set of actions, apart from medicine and vaccination, that communities can slow down the spread of a disease, a.k.a. non-pharmaceutical interventions (NPIs).

Social Distancing Monitor: A technology that is designed to warn individuals when they get too close to each other, particularly relying on communications or contacts in short distances.

Big Data Mining and Analytics With MapReduce

Carson K. Leung

(iD) https://orcid.org/0000-0002-7541-9127

University of Manitoba, Canada

INTRODUCTION

Big Data and *machine learning* are driving Industry 4.0, which is also known as the Fourth Industrial Revolution. Note that the (First) Industrial Revolution transformed manual production to machine production from the late 18th to mid-19th century. The Technological Revolution, which was also known as the Second Industrial Revolution, further industrialized and modernized the industry from the late 19th century to early 20th century through technological advancements and standardization, installations of extensive railroad and telegraph networks, as well as electrification. The Digital Revolution, which was also known as the Third Industrial Revolution, shifted from mechanical and analogue electronic technology to digital electronics, computing and communication technologies in the late 20th century. Now, Big Data have become one of the greatest sources of power in the 21st century, and they have become a critical part of the business world and daily life. In the current era of Big Data, numerous rich data sources are generating huge volumes of a wide variety of valuable data at a high velocity. These Big Data can be of different levels of veracity: They are precise, whereas some others are imprecise and uncertain. Embedded in these Big Data are implicit, previously unknown and potentially useful information and knowledge. This calls for data science, which makes good use of *Big Data mining* and analytics, machine learning, mathematics, statistics and related techniques to manage, mine, analyze and learn from these Big Data to discover hidden gems. This, in turn, may maximize the citizens' wealth and/or promote all society's health. As one of the important Big Data mining and analytics tasks, frequent pattern mining aims to discover interesting knowledge in the forms of frequently occurring sets of merchandise items or events. For example, patterns discovered from business transactions may help reveal shopper trends, which in turn enhances inventory, minimizes customers' cost, and maximizes citizens' wealth. As another example, patterns discovered from health records may help reveal important relationships associated with certain diseases, which in turn leads to improve and promote all society's health. To mine and analyze huge volumes of Big Data in a scalable manner, several algorithms have been proposed that use the MapReduce model—which mines the search space with distributed or parallel computing—for different Big Data mining and analytics tasks. This encyclopedia article covers *Big Data mining and analytics with high performance computing* (*HPC*) and focuses on *frequent pattern mining from Big Data with MapReduce*.

DOI: 10.4018/978-1-7998-9220-5.ch010

Copyright © 2023, IGI Global. Copying or distributing in print or electronic forms without written permission of IGI Global is prohibited.

BACKGROUND

B

Since the introduction of the research problem of *frequent pattern mining* (Agrawal et al., 1993), numerous algorithms have been proposed (Hipp et al., 2000; Ullman, 2000; Ceglar & Roddick, 2006; Aggarwal et al., 2014; Alam et al., 2021, 2022; Chowdhury et al., 2022). Notable ones include the classical Apriori algorithm (Agrawal & Srikant, 1994) and its variants such as the Partition algorithm (Savasere et al., 1995). The Apriori algorithm uses a level-wise breadth-first bottom-up approach with a candidate generate-and-test paradigm to mine frequent patterns from transactional databases of precise data. The Partition algorithm divides the databases into several partitions and applies the Apriori algorithm to each partition to obtain patterns that are locally frequent in the partition. As being locally frequent is a necessary condition for a pattern to be globally frequent, these locally frequent patterns are tested to see if they are globally frequent in the databases. To avoid the candidate generate-and-test paradigm, the tree-based Frequent Pattern-growth (FP-growth) algorithm (Han et al., 2000) was proposed. It uses a depth-first pattern-growth (i.e., divide-and-conquer) approach to mine frequent patterns using a tree structure that captures the contents of the databases. Specifically, the algorithm recursively extracts appropriate tree paths to form projected databases containing relevant transactions and to discover frequent patterns from these projected databases.

For different real-life business, engineering, healthcare, scientific, and social applications and services in modern organizations and society, the available data are not necessarily *precise* but *imprecise or uncertain* (Leung et al., 2014; Cheng et al., 2019; Rahman et al., 2019; Davashi, 2021; Li et al., 2021). Examples include sensor data and privacy-preserving data (Chen et al., 2019; Li & Xu, 2019; Eom et al., 2020; Olawoyin et al., 2021; Jangra & Toshniwal, 2022). Over the past decade, several algorithms have been proposed to mine and analyze these uncertain data. The tree-based UF-growth algorithm (Leung et al., 2008) is an example.

When handling huge volumes of Big Data, it is not unusual for users to have some phenomenon in mind. For example, a manager in an organization is interested in some promotional items. Hence, it would be more desirable if data mining algorithms return only those patterns containing the promotional items rather than returning all frequent patterns, out of which many may be uninteresting to the manager. It leads to *constrained mining*, in which users can express their interests by specifying constraints and the mining algorithm can reduce the computational effort by focusing on mining those patterns that are interesting to the users.

In addition to the aforementioned algorithms that discover frequent patterns *in serial*, there are also *parallel and distributed* frequent pattern mining algorithms (Zaki, 1999). For example, the Count Distribution algorithm (Agrawal & Shafer, 1996) is a parallelization of the Apriori algorithm. It divides transactional databases of precise data and assigns them to parallel processors. Each processor counts the frequency of patterns assigned to it and exchanges this frequency information with other processors. This counting and information exchange process is repeated for each pass/database scan.

As we moves into the new era of Big Data, more efficient mining algorithms are needed because these data are wide varieties of valuable data of different veracities with volumes beyond the ability of commonly-used algorithms for mining and analyzing within a tolerable elapsed time. To handle Big Data, researchers proposed the use of the *MapReduce programming model*.

BIG DATA MINING AND ANALYTICS FOR FREQUENT PATTERNS WITH MAPREDUCE

MapReduce (Dean & Ghemawat, 2004, 2010) is a high-level programming model for processing huge volumes of data. It uses parallel and distributed computing on large clusters or grids of nodes (i.e., commodity machines), which consist of a main node and multiple worker nodes. As implied by its name, MapReduce involves two key functions:

1.   the "map" function, and
2.   the "reduce" function.

To solve a problem using MapReduce, the main node reads and divides input Big Data into several partitions (sub-problems), and then assigns them to different worker nodes. Each worker node executes the *map function* on each partition (sub-problem). The map function takes a pair of ⟨key, value⟩ and returns a list of ⟨key, value⟩ pairs as an intermediate result:

- map: $\langle key_1, value_1 \rangle \mapsto$ list of $\langle key_2, value_2 \rangle$,

where (a) key_1 and key_2 are keys in the same or different domains, and (b) $value_1$ and $value_2$ are the corresponding values in some domains. The pairs in the list of ⟨key, value⟩ pairs for this intermediate result are then shuffled and sorted. Each worker node then executes the *reduce function* on (a) a single key from this intermediate result and (b) the list of all values that appear with this key in the intermediate result. The reduce function "reduces"—by combining, aggregating, summarizing, filtering, and/or transforming—the list of values associated with a given key (for all k keys) in worker nodes and returns a single (aggregated or summarized) value:

- reduce: $\langle key_2,$ list of $value_2 \rangle \mapsto$ a single $value_3$,

where (a) key_2 is a key in some domains, and (b) $value_2$ and $value_3$ are the corresponding values in some domains. Besides a single $value_3$, alternative output could be a list of $\langle key_3, value_3 \rangle$-pairs or a list of $value_3$ (where key_3 is a key in some domains).

With the MapReduce model, users only need to focus on (and specify) the map and reduce functions, without worrying about implementation details for partitioning the input data, scheduling and executing the program across multiple machines, handling machine failures, or managing inter-machine communication.

Earlier works on MapReduce mainly focused on data processing in big databases (Dean & Ghemawat, 2004, 2010) or some Big Data mining tasks other than frequent pattern mining. Examples of Big Data processing with MapReduce include the construction of inverted indexes, the evaluation of queries involving joins or selection, the elimination of duplicates, text processing tasks (Lin & Dyer, 2010) like the word counting of documents, and the processing of data cubes (Lee & Kim, 2016). Examples of Big Data mining with MapReduce include clustering (Li et al., 2019; Dasari & Bhukya, 2022), classification (Mohammed et al., 2021; Hu et al., 2022), and outlier detection (Ceccarello et al., 2019).

Apriori-Based MapReduce Algorithms: SPC, FPC, and DPC

B

To mine frequent patterns from big databases of precise data with MapReduce, Lin et al. (2012) proposed three algorithms—namely, the Single Pass Counting (SPC), Fixed Passes Combined-counting (FPC), and Dynamic Passes Combined-counting (DPC) algorithms—based on both the Apriori and the Count Distribution algorithms. SPC first divides the databases into partitions, and then executes map and reduce functions in each pass k to generate candidate k-itemsets (i.e., candidate patterns each consisting of k items) and count their support/frequency. More specifically, SPC executes the following map and reduce functions in Pass 1:

- map: $\langle$ID of transaction $t_j \in$ partition P_i, contents of $t_j\rangle \mapsto$ list of $\langle$item $x \in t_j$, 1$\rangle$, and
- reduce: $\langle x$, list of 1's$\rangle \mapsto$ list of $\langle$frequent 1-itemset $\{x\}$, $sup(\{x\}) =$ sum of 1's in the list for $x\rangle$.

Here, the worker node corresponding to each partition P_i of the big databases executes the map function by outputting $\langle x, 1\rangle$ (which represents the support of candidate 1-itemset $\{x\}$ in $t_j = 1$) for every item x in transaction $t_j \in P_i$. After grouping all the 1's for each x to form $\langle x$, list of 1's$\rangle$, the reduce function is then executed by summing all the 1's in the list for each x to compute its support $sup(\{x\})$, and outputting $\langle\{x\}, sup(\{x\})\rangle$ (which represents a frequent 1-itemset $\{x\}$ and its frequency) if $sup(\{x\}) \geq$ a user-specific *minsup* threshold.

In each subsequent pass $k \geq 2$, SPC generates candidate k-itemsets from frequent $(k–1)$-itemsets. The worker node corresponding to each partition P_i then outputs $\langle X, 1\rangle$ for every candidate k-itemset X that exists in some transaction $t_j \in P_i$. Afterwards, the reduce function sums all the 1's for each X to compute its support $sup(X)$, and output $\langle X, sup(X)\rangle$ (which represents a frequent k-itemset X and its frequency) if $sup(X) \geq minsup$. In other words, SPC executes the following map and reduce functions in Pass k (for every $k \geq 2$):

- map: $\langle$ID of $t_j \in P_i$, contents of $t_j\rangle \mapsto$ list of $\langle$candidate k-itemset $X \subseteq t_j$, 1$\rangle$, and
- reduce: $\langle X$, list of 1's$\rangle \mapsto$ list of $\langle$frequent k-itemset X, $sup(X) =$ sum of 1's in the list for $X\rangle$.

Figure 1 shows a graphical explanation highlighting key steps in the two sets of map and reduce functions, in which the first set finds frequent 1-itemsets and the second set iteratively finds frequent k-itemsets (for $k \geq 2$). The three algorithms (SPC, FPC and DPC) are similar except that both FPC and DPC apply the *pass bundling* technique to reduce the number of passes/database scans in each P_i when generating candidate itemsets (for Pass $k \geq 3$). For instance, FPC statistically bundles a fixed number of passes (e.g., three passes) to generate all candidate k-, $(k+1)$-, and $(k+2)$-itemsets from frequent $(k–1)$-itemsets. In contrast, DPC dynamically bundles several passes (depending on the number of generated candidates in these bundled passes).

Figure 1. A graphical abstract of key MapReduce functions for Apriori-based frequent pattern mining algorithms

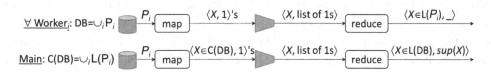

Partition-Based MapReduce Algorithm

The use of the pass bundling technique reduces the number of passes/database scans in each partition P_i. However, the Apriori-based SPC, FPC and DPC algorithms still require multiple passes/database scans when mining frequent patterns from Big Data. In contrast, the MapReduce version of the Partition algorithm—presented by Leskovec et al. (2014)—requires only two passes/database scans. Hence, the Partition-based MapReduce algorithm uses two sets of "map" and "reduce" functions. Specifically, the main node reads and divides big databases of precise data into partitions. The worker node corresponding to each partition P_i then outputs $\langle X, 1 \rangle$ for every candidate pattern X (of any cardinality) that exists in some transaction $t_j \in P_i$. The reduce function then sums all the 1's for each X to find patterns that are locally frequent in P_i. Taking the union of these locally frequent patterns forms global candidate patterns. To summarize, the first set of "map" and "reduce" functions can be expressed as follows:

- map: $\langle$ID of transaction $t_j \in P_i$, contents of $t_j \rangle \mapsto$ list of $\langle$itemset $X \subseteq t_j$, $1 \rangle$, and
- reduce: $\langle X$, list of 1's$\rangle \mapsto$ list of $\langle$locally frequent itemset X, NULL$\rangle$.

Afterwards, the worker node corresponding to each partition P_i outputs $\langle X, 1 \rangle$ for every global candidate pattern X that exists in some transaction $t_j \in P_i$. Then, the reduce function sums all the 1's for each X to compute its support $sup(X)$, and outputs $\langle X, sup(X) \rangle$ (which represents a globally frequent pattern X and its frequency) if $sup(X) \geq minsup$. To summarize, the second set of "map" and "reduce" functions can be expressed as follows:

- map: $\langle$ID of $t_j \in P_i$, contents of $t_j \rangle \mapsto$ list of $\langle$global candidate pattern $X \subseteq t_j$, $1 \rangle$, and
- reduce: $\langle X$, list of 1's$\rangle \mapsto$ list of $\langle$globally frequent pattern X, $sup(X) \rangle$.

Figure 2 shows a graphical explanation highlighting key steps in the two sets of map and reduce functions, in which the first set finds locally frequent patterns from each worker node and the second set finds globally frequent patterns.

Figure 2. A graphical abstract of key MapReduce functions for Partition-based frequent pattern mining algorithms

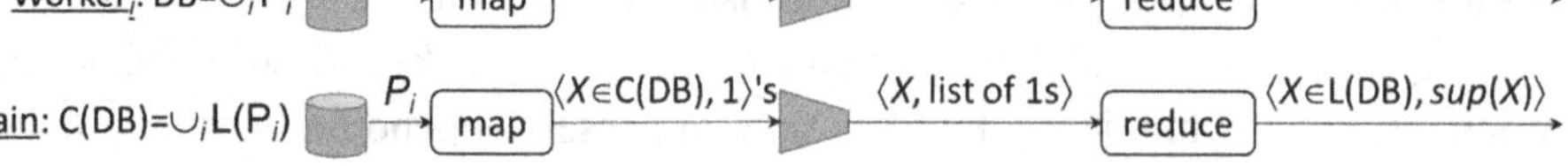

Tree-Based MapReduce Algorithm for Precise Data: PFP

As tree-based algorithms avoid the candidate generate-and-test paradigm of Apriori-based algorithms, Li et al. (2008) proposed the Parallel FP-growth (PFP) algorithm for query recommendation. PFP uses MapReduce to parallelize the tree-based FP-growth algorithm by first reading and dividing big databases of precise data into several partitions. The worker node corresponding to each partition P_i then outputs $\langle \{x\}, 1 \rangle$ for every item x in transaction $t_j \in P_i$. The reduce function then sums all the 1's for each x to compute its support $sup(\{x\})$, and outputs $\langle\{x\}, sup(\{x\})\rangle$ (which represents a frequent 1-itemset $\{x\}$ and its frequency) if $sup(\{x\}) \geq minsup$. In other words, PFP first executes the following set of "map" and "reduce" functions:

- map: $\langle$ID of transaction $t_j \in$ database partition P_i, contents of $t_j\rangle \mapsto$ list of $\langle$item $x \in t_j, 1\rangle$, and
- reduce: $\langle x,$ list of 1's$\rangle \mapsto$ list of $\langle$frequent 1-itemset $\{x\}, sup(\{x\})$ = sum of 1's in the list for $x\rangle$.

Afterwards, PFP reads the big databases a second time to form an $\{x\}$-projected database (i.e., a collection of transactions containing x) for each item x in the list produced from the first reduce function (i.e., for each frequent 1-itemset $\{x\}$). The worker node corresponding to each projected database then executes the following steps:

1. builds appropriate local FP-trees (based on the projected database assigned to the node) to mine frequent k-itemsets (for $k \geq 2$), and
2. outputs $\langle X, sup(X)\rangle$ (which represents a frequent k-itemset X and its frequency) if $sup(X) \geq minsup$.

To summarize, PFP executes the second set of "map" and "reduce" functions as follows:

- map: $\langle$ID of transaction $t_j \in P_i$, contents of $t_j\rangle \mapsto$ list of $\langle\{x\}, \{x\}$-projected database$\rangle$, and
- reduce: $\langle\{x\}, \{x\}$-projected database$\rangle \mapsto$ list of $\langle$frequent itemset $X, sup(X)\rangle$.

Figure 3 shows a graphical explanation highlighting key steps in the two sets of map and reduce functions, in which the first set finds frequent 1-itemsets and the second set finds all frequent k-itemsets (where $k \geq 2$) from the trees representing projected databases. As PFP was designed for query recommendation, it usually takes a third set of "map" and "reduce" functions to aggregate and rank the list of frequent itemsets for the top-K frequent patterns to facilitate recommendations.

Figure 3. A graphical abstract of key MapReduce functions for tree-based frequent pattern mining algorithm

Tree-Based MapReduce Algorithm for Uncertain Data: MR-growth

Big Data can be characterized by at least 5Vs: volume, value, velocity, variety, and veracity. Among the 5Vs, veracity focuses on the quality of data (e.g., precision, uncertainty, messiness, or trustworthiness of data). In many real-life applications, available data can be *uncertain*. Uncertainty of the data may partially be caused by various factors such as imprecision or limitation of measuring instruments, as well as intentional blurring of data for privacy-preserving data. Hence, in these applications, users may be uncertain about the presence or absence of some merchandise items or events. For example, a manager may highly suspect (but cannot guarantee) that a customer is interested in certain products without explicitly asking the customer. The uncertainty of such suspicion can be expressed in terms of existential probability. Hence, to handle uncertain data, each item x in the transaction t_j is associated with an existential probability $P(x, t_j)$ expressing the likelihood of the presence of that item or event. With this notion, each item in a transactional database of precise data can be viewed as an item with a 100% likelihood of being present in the transaction.

When using probabilistic-based mining with the "possible world" interpretation (Leung, 2014), a pattern is considered *frequent* if its expected support is no less than the user-specified *minsup* threshold. When items within a pattern X are independent, the *expected support* of X in the database can be computed by summing (over all transactions) the product (of existential probabilities within X):

- $expSup(X) = \sum t_j (\prod_{x \in X} P(x, t_j))$,

where $P(x, t_j)$ is the existential probability of item x in transaction t_j.

Leung and Hayduk (2013) presented the MapReduce-growth (MR-growth) algorithm, which uses MapReduce to mine frequent patterns from *uncertain* data in a tree-based pattern-growth fashion for Big Data mining. Again, MR-growth uses two sets of the "map" and "reduce" functions. Specifically, the main node reads and divides uncertain data into partitions. The worker node corresponding to each partition P_i then outputs $\langle\{x\}, P(x, t_j)\rangle$ for every item x in transaction $t_j \in P_i$. Note that the map functions for the precise data mining algorithms output $\langle\{x\}, 1\rangle$, which represents the actual support of x in $t_j =$ 1, i.e., x appears 1 time in t_j). In contrast, the map function for MR-growth outputs $\langle\{x\}, P(x, t_j)\rangle$ (where $P(x, t_j)$ indicates the expected support of x in t_j, which means x has a probability of $P(x, t_j)$ to appear in t_j):

- map: $\langle$ID of transaction $t_j \in$ database partition P_i, contents of $t_j\rangle \mapsto$ list of $\langle$item $x \in t_j, P(x, t_j)\rangle$.

Then, the reduce function sums all the $P(x, t_j)$'s for each x to compute its expected support $expSup(\{x\})$, and outputs $\langle\{x\}, expSup(\{x\})\rangle$ (representing a frequent 1-itemset $\{x\}$ and its expected support) if $expSup(\{x\}) \geq minsup$:

- reduce: $\langle x$, list of $P(x, t_j)$'s$\rangle \mapsto$ list of $\langle$frequent 1-itemset $\{x\}, expSup(\{x\})\rangle$,

where $expSup(\{x\}) =$ sum of $P(x, t_j)$ in the list for x. Notice that, when handling precise data, the actual support of $\{x\}$ is its frequency. In contrast, when handling uncertain data, the expected support of $\{x\}$ may not be the same as its frequency. For instance, consider an item b with existential probability of 0.8 that appears only in transaction t_1. Its expected support may be higher than item c that appears six times but with an existential probability of 0.1 in each appearance. Then, $expSup(\{b\}) = 0.8 > 0.6 = expSup(\{c\})$.

Afterwards, MR-growth rereads the big databases to form an $\{x\}$-projected database (i.e., a collection of transactions containing x) for each item x in the list produced from the first reduce function (i.e., for each frequent 1-itemset x). The worker node corresponding to each projected database then executes the following steps:

1. builds appropriate local UF-trees (based on the projected database assigned to the node) to mine frequent k-itemsets (for $k \geq 2$), and
2. outputs $\langle X, expSup(X)\rangle$ (which represents a frequent k-itemset X and its expected support) if $expSup(X) \geq minsup$.

To summarize, MR-growth executes the second set of "map" and "reduce" functions as follows:

- map: $\langle$ID of transaction $t_j \in P_i$, contents of $t_j\rangle \mapsto$ list of $\langle\{x\}, \{x\}$-projected database$\rangle$, and
- reduce: $\langle\{x\}, \{x\}$-projected database$\rangle \mapsto$ list of $\langle$frequent itemset X, $expSup(X)\rangle$.

When compared with PFP, key differences are that MR-growth handles uncertain data and finds frequent itemsets with expected support (instead of actual support) $\geq$ *minsup*.

Constraint-Based MapReduce Algorithm: BigAnt and BigSAM

To mine and analyze huge-volume Big Data, it is not uncommon that users may be interested in only some subsets of these Big Data in many real-life situations. This leads to *constraint-based mining* (Bonchi, 2009; Leung, 2009; Wang et al., 2021), with which users can focus the mining on certain subsets of the Big Data by freely specifying some constraints to express their interest. For example, users can express their interests in finding a collection X of merchandise items having a total price of less than \$220 by specifying a constraint "sum($X.Price$) < \$220". Similarly users can also express their interests in finding a set Y of branches with a minimum GPS coordinate (latitude) of 60°N by specifying a constraint "min($Y.GPSCoordinate$) = 60°N".

To handle these constraints and to focus the mining on those subsets of Big Data that are interesting to users, Leung and Jiang (2014) proposed the BigAnt algorithm to handle the user-specified anti-monotonic constraints by exploring the anti-monotonicity of the constraints, which states that "if a pattern satisfies an anti-monotonic constraint, then so do all its subsets". In other words, if a pattern violates the anti-monotonic constraints, it can be pruned as any of its supersets is guaranteed to violate the constraints. For instance, if sum($Z.Price$) $\geq$ \$220 for some pattern Z, then sum($Z'.Price$) $\geq$ \$220 for any superset Z' of Z. So, the BigAnt algorithm also uses two sets of the "map" and "reduce" functions. The main node reads and divides uncertain data into partitions. The worker node corresponding to each partition P_i then performs constraint checking and outputs $\langle\{x\}, P(x, t_j)\rangle$ for every *valid* item x in transaction $t_j \in P_i$ (when $\{x\}$ satisfies the constraints):

- map: $\langle$ID of transaction $t_j \in$ partition P_i, contents of $t_j\rangle \mapsto$ list of $\langle$valid item $x \in t_j$, $P(x, t_j)\rangle$.

Then, the reduce function sums all the $P(x, t_j)$'s for each valid x to compute its expected support $expSup(\{x\})$, and outputs $\langle\{x\}, expSup(\{x\})\rangle$ (representing a valid frequent 1-itemset $\{x\}$ and its expected support) if $expSup(\{x\}) \geq$ *minsup*:

- reduce: $\langle$valid x, list of $P(x, t_j)$'s$\rangle \mapsto$ list of $\langle$valid frequent 1-itemset $\{x\}$, $expSup(\{x\})\rangle$,

where $expSup(\{x\})$ = sum of $P(x, t_j)$ in the list for x. Afterwards, BigAnt rereads the big databases to form an $\{x\}$-projected database (i.e., a collection of transactions containing x) for each *valid* item x in the list produced from the first reduce function (i.e., for each valid frequent 1-itemset x). The worker node corresponding to each projected database then executes the following steps:

1. builds appropriate local UF-trees (based on the projected database assigned to the node) to mine frequent k-itemsets (for $k \geq 2$),
2. performs constraint checking to find valid ones from these mined frequent k-itemsets, and
3. outputs $\langle$valid X, $expSup(X)\rangle$ (which represents a valid frequent k-itemset X and its expected support) if $expSup(X) \geq$ *minsup* and X is valid with respect to the user-specified constraints.

To summarize, BigAnt executes the second set of "map" and "reduce" functions as follows:

- map: ⟨ID of transaction $t_j \in P_i$, contents of t_j⟩ ↦ list of ⟨valid $\{x\}$, $\{x\}$-projected database⟩, and
- reduce: ⟨valid $\{x\}$, $\{x\}$-projected database⟩ ↦ list of ⟨valid frequent itemset X, $expSup(X)$⟩.

When compared with MR-growth, a key difference is that BigAnt finds frequent itemsets that are valid (i.e., satisfying the user-specified constraints). Note that BigAnt pushes the user-specified anti-monotonic constraints into the Big Data mining process so that it directly discovers frequent patterns that satisfy the constraints.

To a further extent, Jiang et al. (2014) proposed the BigSAM algorithm to explore additional property of some anti-monotonic constraints. Specifically, BigSAM explores the succinctness of the constraints, which reveals that all and only those itemsets satisfying the succinct anti-monotonic (SAM) constraints can be explicitly and precisely generated using only individual items that satisfy the SAM constraints. For instance, any set Y of branches with min($Y.GPSCoordinate$) = 60°N must consist of only branches with GPS coordinate of 60°N. Hence, the BigSAM only needs to perform constraint checking in the first—but not the second—map function.

FUTURE RESEARCH DIRECTIONS

A logical future research direction is to extend the aforementioned MapReduce-based (unconstrained or constrained) frequent pattern mining to the *MapReduce-based* (unconstrained or constrained) *mining of other interesting patterns* from various real-life data science and machine learning applications (e.g., business analytics (Ahn et al., 2019), predictive analytics (Morris et al., 2018; Audu et al., 2019; Souza et al., 2020)). These may include the mining of high-utility patterns, co-location patterns, sequences and graphs (Saleti & Subramanyam, 2020; Yang et al., 2020; Ishita et al., 2022; Lin et al., 2022; Roy et al., 2022).

Interesting patterns also include web and social patterns. To elaborate, due to the popularity of Web-based communities and social networking sites, huge volumes of big social media data (including those Facebook, Instagram and Twitter data about an organization) are available. Embedded in these Big Data are rich sets of meaningful knowledge about the social networks (e.g., social networks within an organization, among different organizations). Hence, a second future research direction is to apply *social media mining and social network analysis* (Xu & Li, 2013; Leung et al., 2013, 2016; Leung, 2018; Abulaish et al., 2020; Hryhoruk & Leung, 2021) to social media data for discovery of rich sets of meaningful knowledge from these Big Data.

Moreover, alternative approaches—besides the MapReduce model in Apache Hadoop—include the use of Apache Spark (Zaharia et al., 2010) (which relies on the concept of resilient distributed dataset), Apache Flink (Carbone et al., 2015) and Apache Storm (Garcia Lopez et al., 2015) (which both process streams of Big Data). They also include the use of edge computing (Yang & Ma, 2015), fog computing (Yi et al., 2015), and dew computing (Ray, 2017). Hence, a third future research direction is to adapt and perform *Big Data mining and analytics* (e.g., constrained or unconstrained frequent patterns about an organization) *in Spark, Flink, Storm, edge, fog, or dew* (Leung et al., 2017b, 2017c; Sarumi et al., 2018; Braun et al., 2019).

Many existing Big Data mining algorithms return the mined results in a textual form—e.g., a textual list of all (constrained or unconstrained) frequent patterns. As "a picture is worth a thousand words", visual representation of the mining results is usually easier to comprehend for users than its equivalent textual representation. Thus, it is desirable to show the mining results interactively by applying the concepts of visual analytics. To enhance user experience in exploring Big Data, a fourth future research direction is to incorporate *visual analytics and interactive technologies* (Zhang et al., 2011; Leung et al., 2011, 2017a; Jentner & Keim, 2019; Leung & Zhang, 2019; Andrienko et al., 2022; Isichei et al., 2022) into Big Data mining. By doing so, the (constrained or unconstrained) frequent patterns mined from Big Data are returned to the users in visual forms.

CONCLUSION

Big Data mining and analytics for data science aims to discover implicit, previously unknown, and potentially useful information and knowledge from huge volumes of a wide variety of veracious but valuable data collected or generated at a high velocity numerous from rich data sources. Among different data science tasks, this encyclopedia article focuses on frequent pattern mining from Big Data with MapReduce. By relying on the MapReduce programming model, researchers only need to specify the "map" and "reduce" functions to discover frequent patterns from:

1. big databases of precise data in a breadth-first manner (e.g., by using the SPC, FPC, and DPC algorithms) or in a depth-first manner (e.g., by using the PFP algorithm), and/or
2. big databases of uncertain data (e.g., by using the MR-growth algorithm).

Such a Big Data mining and analytics process can be sped up (e.g., by using the BigAnt and Big-SAM algorithms, which focus the mining according to the user-specified constraints that express the user interests). The resulting (constrained or unconstrained) frequent patterns mined from Big Data provide users (e.g., executive and management teams of an organization) with new insights and a sound understanding of users' patterns about the organization. Such knowledge is useful is many real-life data science and machine learning applications.

REFERENCES

Abulaish, M., Bhat, I. M., & Bhat, S. Y. (2020). Scaling density-based community detection to large-scale social networks via MapReduce framework. *Journal of Intelligent & Fuzzy Systems*, *38*(2), 1663–1674. doi:10.3233/JIFS-182765

Aggarwal, C. C., Bhuiyan, M. A., & Al Hasan, M. (2014). Frequent pattern mining algorithms: a survey. In C. C. Aggarwal & J. Han (Eds.), *Frequent pattern mining* (pp. 19–64). doi:10.1007/978-3-319-07821-2_2

Agrawal, R., Imieliński, T., & Swami, A. (1993). Mining association rules between sets of items in large databases. *Proceedings of ACM SIGMOD, 1993*, 207-216. 10.1145/170035.170072

Agrawal, R., & Shafer, J. C. (1996). Parallel mining of association rules. *IEEE Transactions on Knowledge and Data Engineering*, *8*(6), 962–969. doi:10.1109/69.553164

Agrawal, R., & Srikant, R. (1994). Fast algorithms for mining association rules in large databases. *Proceedings of VLDB, 1994*, 487–499.

Ahn, S., Couture, S. V., Cuzzocrea, A., Dam, K., Grasso, G. M., Leung, C. K., McCormick, K. L., & Wodi, B. H. (2019). A fuzzy logic based machine learning tool for supporting big data business analytics in complex artificial intelligence environments. *Proceedings of FUZZ-IEEE, 2019*, 1259–1264. doi:10.1109/FUZZ-IEEE.2019.8858791

Alam, M. T., Ahmed, C. F., Samiullah, M., & Leung, C. K. (2021). Mining frequent patterns from hypergraph databases. *Proceedings of PAKDD, 2021*(Part II), 3–15. doi:10.1007/978-3-030-75765-6_1

Alam, M. T., Roy, A., Ahmed, C. F., Islam, M. A., & Leung, C. K. (2022). UGMINE: Utility-based graph mining. *Applied Intelligence*. Advance online publication. doi:10.100710489-022-03385-8

Andrienko, N. V., Andrienko, G. L., Adilova, L., Wrobel, S., & Rhyne, T. (2022). Visual analytics for human-centered machine learning. *IEEE Computer Graphics and Applications, 42*(1), 123–133. doi:10.1109/MCG.2021.3130314 PMID:35077350

Audu, A. A., Cuzzocrea, A., Leung, C. K., MacLeod, K. A., Ohin, N. I., & Pulgar-Vidal, N. C. (2019). An intelligent predictive analytics system for transportation analytics on open data towards the development of a smart city. *Proceedings of CISIS, 2019*, 224–236. doi:10.1007/978-3-030-22354-0_21

Bellatreche, L., Leung, C.K., Xia, Y., & Elbaz, D. (2019). Advances in cloud and big data computing. *Concurrency and Computation: Practice and Experience, 31*(2), e5053:1-e5053:3. . doi:10.1002/cpe.5053

Bonchi, F. (2009). Constraint-based pattern discovery. In J. Wang (Ed.), *Encyclopedia of data warehousing and mining* (2nd ed., pp. 313–319). doi:10.4018/978-1-60566-010-3.ch050

Braun, P., Cuzzocrea, A., Leung, C. K., Pazdor, A. G. M., Souza, J., & Tanbeer, S. K. (2019). Pattern mining from big IoT data with fog computing: models, issues, and research perspectives. *Proceedings of IEEE/ACM CCGrid, 2019*, 854-891. 10.1109/CCGRID.2019.00075

Carbone, P., Katsifodimos, A., Ewen, S., Markl, V., Haridi, S., & Tzoumas, K. (2015). Apache Flink: Stream and batch processing in a single engine. *A Quarterly Bulletin of the Computer Society of the IEEE Technical Committee on Data Engineering, 38*(4), 28–38.

Ceccarello, M., Pietracaprina, A., & Pucci, G. (2019). Solving *k*-center clustering (with outliers) in MapReduce and streaming, almost as accurately as sequentially. *Proceedings of the VLDB Endowment International Conference on Very Large Data Bases, 12*(7), 766–778. doi:10.14778/3317315.3317319

Ceglar, A., & Roddick, J.F. (2006). Association mining. *ACM Computing Surveys, 38*(2), 5:1-5:42. . doi:10.1145/1132956.1132958

Chen, R., Jankovic, F., Marinsek, N., Foschini, L., Kourtis, L., Signorini, A., Pugh, M., Shen, J., Yaari, R., Maljkovic, V., Sunga, M., Song, H. H., Jung, H. J., Tseng, B., & Trister, A. (2019). Developing measures of cognitive impairment in the real world from consumer-grade multimodal sensor streams. *Proceedings of ACM KDD, 2019*, 2145-2155. 10.1145/3292500.3330690

Cheng, J., Yan, D., Hao, X., & Ng, W. (2019). Mining order-preserving submatrices under data uncertainty: A possible-world approach. *Proceedings of IEEE ICDE, 2019*, 1154-1165. 10.1109/ICDE.2019.00106

Chowdhury, M.E.S., Ahmed, C.F., & Leung, C.K. (2022). A new approach for mining correlated frequent subgraphs. *ACM Transactions on Management Information Systems, 13*(1), 9:1-9:28. . doi:10.1145/3473042

Dasari, C.M., & Bhukya, R. (2022). MapReduce paradigm: DNA sequence clustering based on repeats as features. *Expert Systems, 39*(1), e12827:1-e12827:16. . doi:10.1111/exsy.12827

Davashi, R. (2021). UP-tree & UP-Mine: A fast method based on upper bound for frequent pattern mining from uncertain data. *Engineering Applications of Artificial Intelligence, 106*, 104477:1-104477:20. . doi:10.1016/j.engappai.2021.104477

Dean, J., & Ghemawat, S. (2004). MapReduce: simplified data processing on large clusters. *Proceedings of OSDI, 2004*, 137-149.

Dean, J., & Ghemawat, S. (2010). MapReduce: A flexible data processing tool. *Communications of the ACM, 53*(1), 72–77. doi:10.1145/1629175.1629198

Eom, C. S., Lee, C. C., Lee, W., & Leung, C. K. (2020). Effective privacy preserving data publishing by vectorization. *Information Sciences, 527*, 311–328. doi:10.1016/j.ins.2019.09.035

Garcia Lopez, P., Montresor, A., Epema, D., Datta, A., Higashino, T., Iamnitchi, A., Barcellos, M., Felber, P., & Riviere, E. (2015). Edge-centric computing. *Computer Communication Review, 45*(5), 37–42. doi:10.1145/2831347.2831354

Han, J., Pei, J., & Yin, Y. (2000). Mining frequent patterns without candidate generation. *Proceedings of ACM SIGMOD, 2000*, 1-12. 10.1145/342009.335372

Hipp, J., Güntzer, U., & Nakhaeizadeh, G. (2000). Algorithms for association rule mining – a general survey and comparison. *SIGKDD Explorations, 2*(1), 58–64. doi:10.1145/360402.360421

Hryhoruk, C. C. J., & Leung, C. K. (2021). Compressing and mining social network data. *Proceedings of IEEE/ACM ASONAM, 2021*, 545-552. 10.1145/3487351.3489472

Hu, L., Yang, S., Luo, X., Yuan, H., Sedraoui, K., & Zhou, M. (2022). A distributed framework for large-scale protein-protein interaction data analysis and prediction using MapReduce. *IEEE/CAA Journal of Automatica Sinica, 9*(1), 160-172. . doi:10.1109/JAS.2021.1004198

Ishita, S. Z., Ahmed, C. F., & Leung, C. K. (2022). New approaches for mining regular high utility sequential patterns. *Applied Intelligence, 52*(4), 3781–3806. doi:10.100710489-021-02536-7

Isichei, B. C., Leung, C. K., Nguyen, L. T., Morrow, L. B., Ngo, A. T., Pham, T. D., & Cuzzocrea, A. (2022). Sports data management, mining, and visualization. *Proceedings of AINA, 2022*, 141–153. doi:10.1007/978-3-030-99587-4_13

Jangra, S., & Toshniwal, D. (2022). Efficient algorithms for victim item selection in privacy-preserving utility mining. *Future Generation Computer Systems, 128*, 219–234. doi:10.1016/j.future.2021.10.008

Jentner, W., & Keim, D. A. (2019). Visualization and visual analytic techniques for patterns. In P. Fournier-Viger, J. C. Lin, R. Nkambou, B. Vo, & V. S. Tseng (Eds.), *High-utility pattern mining* (pp. 303–337). doi:10.1007/978-3-030-04921-8_12

Jiang, F., Leung, C. K., & MacKinnon, R. K. (2014). BigSAM: Mining interesting patterns from probabilistic databases of uncertain big data. *Proceedings of PAKDD Workshops, 2014*, 780-792. 10.1007/978-3-319-13186-3_70

Lee, S., & Kim, J. (2016). Performance evaluation of MRDataCube for data cube computation algorithm using MapReduce. *Proceedings of BigComp, 2016*, 325-328. 10.1109/BIGCOMP.2016.7425939

Leskovec, J., Rajaraman, A., & Ullman, J. D. (2014). *Mining of massive datasets* (2nd ed.). Cambridge University Press. doi:10.1017/CBO9781139924801

Leung, C. K. (2009). Constraint-based association rule mining. In J. Wang (Ed.), *Encyclopedia of data warehousing and mining* (2nd ed., pp. 307–312). doi:10.4018/978-1-60566-010-3.ch049

Leung, C. K. (2014). Uncertain frequent pattern mining. In C. C. Aggarwal & J. Han (Eds.), *Frequent pattern mining* (pp. 339–367). doi:10.1007/978-3-319-07821-2_14

Leung, C. K. (2015). Big data mining applications and services. *Proceedings of BigDAS, 2015*, 1–8. doi:10.1145/2837060.2837076

Leung, C. K. (2018). Mathematical model for propagation of influence in a social network. In R. Alhajj & J. Rokne (Eds.), *Encyclopedia of social network analysis and mining* (2nd ed., pp. 1261–1269). doi:10.1007/978-1-4939-7131-2_110201

Leung, C. K., Carmichael, C. L., Johnstone, P., Xing, R. R., & Yuen, D. S. H. (2017a). Interactive visual analytics of big data. In J. Lu (Ed.), *Ontologies and big data considerations for effective intelligence* (pp. 1–26). doi:10.4018/978-1-5225-2058-0.ch001

Leung, C. K., Carmichael, C. L., & Teh, E. W. (2011). Visual analytics of social networks: mining and visualizing co-authorship networks. *Proceedings of HCII-FAC, 2011*, 335-345. 10.1007/978-3-642-21852-1_40

Leung, C. K., Deng, D., Hoi, C. S. H., & Lee, W. (2017b). Constrained big data mining in an edge computing environment. In Big Data Applications and Services 2017, (pp. 61-68). doi:10.1007/978-981-13-0695-2_8

Leung, C. K., & Hayduk, Y. (2013). Mining frequent patterns from uncertain data with MapReduce for big data analytics. *Proceedings of DASFAA, 2013*(Part I), 440–455. doi:10.1007/978-3-642-37487-6_33

Leung, C. K., & Jiang, F. (2014). A data science solution for mining interesting patterns from uncertain big data. *Proceedings of IEEE BDCloud, 2014*, 235–242. doi:10.1109/BDCloud.2014.136

Leung, C. K., Jiang, F., Dela Cruz, E. M., & Elango, V. S. (2017c). Association rule mining in collaborative filtering. In V. Bhatnagar (Ed.), *Collaborative filtering using data mining and analysis* (pp. 159–179). doi:10.4018/978-1-5225-0489-4.ch009

Leung, C. K., Jiang, F., Pazdor, A. G. M., & Peddle, A. M. (2016). Parallel social network mining for interesting 'following' patterns. *Concurrency and Computation, 28*(15), 3994–4012. doi:10.1002/cpe.3773

Leung, C. K., MacKinnon, R. K., & Tanbeer, S. K. (2014). Fast algorithms for frequent itemset mining from uncertain data. *Proceedings of IEEE ICDM, 2014*, 893–898. doi:10.1109/ICDM.2014.146

Leung, C. K., Mateo, M. A. F., & Brajczuk, D. A. (2008). A tree-based approach for frequent pattern mining from uncertain data. *Proceedings of PAKDD, 2008*, 653–661. doi:10.1007/978-3-540-68125-0_61

Leung, C. K., Medina, I. J. M., & Tanbeer, S. K. (2013). Analyzing social networks to mine important friends. In G. Xu & L. Li (Eds.), *Social media mining and social network analysis: Emerging research* (pp. 90–104). doi:10.4018/978-1-4666-2806-9.ch006

Leung, C. K., & Zhang, Y. (2019). An HSV-based visual analytic system for data science on music and beyond. *International Journal of Art, Culture and Design Technologies, 8*(1), 68–83. doi:10.4018/IJACDT.2019010105

Li, H., Wang, Y., Zhang, D., Zhang, M., & Chang, E. Y. (2008). PFP: parallel FP-growth for query recommendation. *Proceedings of ACM RecSys, 2008*, 107-114. 10.1145/1454008.1454027

Li, Y., Jiang, H., Lu, J., Li, X., Sun, Z., & Li, M. (2021). MR-BIRCH: A scalable MapReduce-based BIRCH clustering algorithm. *Journal of Intelligent & Fuzzy Systems, 40*(3), 5295–5305. doi:10.3233/JIFS-202079

Li, Y., & Xu, W. (2019). PrivPy: general and scalable privacy-preserving data mining. *Proceedings of ACM KDD, 2019*, 1299-1307. 10.1145/3292500.3330920

Li, Z., Chen, F., Wu, J., Liu, Z., & Liu, W. (2021). Efficient weighted probabilistic frequent itemset mining in uncertain databases. *Expert Systems, 38*(5), e12551:1-e12551:17. . doi:10.1111/exsy.12551

Lin, J., & Dyer, C. (2010). *Data-intensive text processing with MapReduce*. Morgan & Claypool Publishers. doi:10.1007/978-3-031-02136-7

Lin, J.C., Djenouri, Y., Srivastava, G., Li, Y., & Yu, P.S. (2022). Scalable mining of high-utility sequential patterns with three-tier MapReduce model. *ACM Transactions on Knowledge Discovery from Data, 16*(3), 60:1-60:26. doi:10.1145/3487046

Lin, M., Lee, P., & Hsueh, S. (2012). Apriori-based frequent itemset mining algorithms on MapReduce. *Proceedings of ICUIMC, 2012*, 76:1-76:8. 10.1145/2184751.2184842

Madden, S. (2012). From databases to big data. *IEEE Internet Computing, 16*(3), 4–6. doi:10.1109/MIC.2012.50

Mohammed, M. S., Rachapudy, P. S., & Kasa, M. (2021). Big data classification with optimization driven MapReduce framework. *International Journal of Knowledge-based and Intelligent Engineering Systems, 25*(2), 173–183. doi:10.3233/KES-210062

Morris, K. J., Egan, S. D., Linsangan, J. L., Leung, C. K., Cuzzocrea, A., & Hoi, C. S. H. (2018). Token-based adaptive time-series prediction by ensembling linear and non-linear estimators: A machine learning approach for predictive analytics on big stock data. *Proceedings of IEEE ICMLA, 2018*, 1486–1491. doi:10.1109/ICMLA.2018.00242

Olawoyin, A. M., Leung, C. K., & Cuzzocrea, A. (2021). Privacy-preserving publishing and visualization of spatial-temporal information. *Proceedings of IEEE BigData, 2021*, 5420–5429. doi:10.1109/BigData52589.2021.9671564

Rahman, M. M., Ahmed, C. F., & Leung, C. K. (2019). Mining weighted frequent sequences in uncertain databases. *Information Sciences, 479*, 76–100. doi:10.1016/j.ins.2018.11.026

Ray, P. P. (2017). An introduction to dew computing: Definition, concept and implications. *IEEE Access: Practical Innovations, Open Solutions, 6*, 723–737. doi:10.1109/ACCESS.2017.2775042

Roy, K. K., Moon, M. H. H., Rahman, M. M., Ahmed, C. F., & Leung, C. K. (2022). Mining weighted sequential patterns in incremental uncertain databases. *Information Sciences, 582*, 865–896. doi:10.1016/j. ins.2021.10.010

Saleti, S, & Subramanyam, R.B.V. (2020). Distributed mining of high utility time interval sequential patterns using MapReduce approach. *Expert Systems with Applications, 141*, 112967:1-112967:25. . doi:10.1016/j.eswa.2019.112967

Sarumi, O. A., Leung, C. K., & Adetunmbi, A. O. (2018). Spark-based data analytics of sequence motifs in large omics data. *Procedia Computer Science, 126*, 596–605. doi:10.1016/j.procs.2018.07.294

Savasere, A., Omiecinski, E., & Navathe, S. (1995). An efficient algorithm for mining association rules in large databases. *Proceedings of VLDB, 1995*, 432–444.

Shim, K. (2012). MapReduce algorithms for big data analysis. *Proceedings of the VLDB Endowment International Conference on Very Large Data Bases, 5*(12), 2016–2017. doi:10.14778/2367502.2367563

Souza, J., Leung, C. K., & Cuzzocrea, A. (2020). An innovative big data predictive analytics framework over hybrid big data sources with an application for disease analytics. *Proceedings of AINA, 2020*, 669–680. doi:10.1007/978-3-030-44041-1_59

Ullman, J. D. (2000). A survey of association-rule mining. *Proceedings of DS, 2000*, 1–14. doi:10.1007/3-540-44418-1_1

Wang, W., Tian, J., Lv, F., Xin, G., Ma, Y., & Wang, B. (2021). Mining frequent pyramid patterns from time series transaction data with custom constraints. *Computers & Security, 100*, 102088:1-102088:15. . doi:10.1016/j.cose.2020.102088

Xu, G., & Li, L. (Eds.). (2013). *Social media mining and social network analysis: emerging research.*, doi:10.4018/978-1-4666-2806-9

Yang, M., & Ma, R. T. B. (2015). Smooth task migration in Apache Storm. *Proceedings of ACM SIG-MOD, 2015*, 2067-2068. 10.1145/2723372.2764941

Yang, P., Wang, L., & Wang, X. (2020). A MapReduce approach for spatial co-location pattern mining via ordered-clique-growth. *Distributed and Parallel Databases, 38*(2), 531–560. doi:10.100710619-019-07278-7

Yi, S., Hao, Z., Qin, Z., & Li, Q. (2015). Fog computing: Platform and applications. *Proceedings of IEEE HotWeb, 2015*, 73–78. doi:10.1109/HotWeb.2015.22

Zaharia, M., Chowdhury, M., Franklin, M. J., Shenker, S., & Stoica, I. (2010). Spark: cluster computing with working sets. *Proceedings of USENIX HotCloud, 2010*, 10:1-10:7.

Zaki, M. J. (1999). Parallel and distributed association mining: A survey. *IEEE Concurrency, 7*(4), 14–25. doi:10.1109/4434.806975

Zhang, Q., Segall, R. S., & Cao, M. (Eds.). (2011). *Visual analytics and interactive technologies: data, text and web mining applications.* doi:10.4018/978-1-60960-102-7

ADDITIONAL READING

Aggarwal, C. C., & Han, J. (Eds.). (2014). *Frequent pattern mining*. Springer. doi:10.1007/978-3-319-07821-2

Aragon, C., Guha, S., Kogan, M., Muller, M., & Neff, G. (2022). *Human-centered data science: an introduction*. MIT Press.

Bilokon, P. A. (2022). *Python, data science and machine learning - from scratch to productivity*. World Scientific.

Blum, A., Hopcroft, J., & Kannan, R. (2020). *Foundations of data science*. Cambridge University Press. doi:10.1017/9781108755528

Jeyaraj, R., Pugalendhi, G., & Paul, A. (2021). *Big data with Hadoop MapReduce: a classroom approach*. Apple Academic Press.

Li, K., Jiang, H., Yang, L. T., & Cuzzocrea, A. (Eds.). (2015). *Big data: algorithms, analytics, and applications*. Chapman and Hall/CRC. doi:10.1201/b18050

Shi, Y. (2022). *Advances in big data analytics - theory, algorithms and practices*. Springer. doi:10.1007/978-981-16-3607-3

Tan, P., Steinbach, M., Karpatne, A., & Kumar, V. (2019). *Introduction to data mining* (2nd ed.). Pearson.

Wagh, S. J., Bhende, M. S., & Thakare, A. D. (2022). *Fundamentals of data science*. Chapman and Hall/CRC.

Zaki, M. J., & Meira, W. (2020). *Data mining and machine learning: fundamental concepts and algorithms* (2nd ed.). Cambridge University Press. doi:10.1017/9781108564175

KEY TERMS AND DEFINITIONS

Anti-Monotonic Constraint: A constraint C such that, if an itemset S satisfying C, then any subset of S also satisfies C.

Big Data: High-velocity, valuable, and/or multi-variety data with volumes beyond the ability of commonly-used software to capture, manage, and process within a tolerable elapsed time. These Big Data necessitate new forms of processing to deliver high veracity (and low vulnerability) and to enable enhanced decision making, insight, knowledge discovery, and process optimization.

Data Mining: Non-trivial extraction of implicit, previously unknown and potentially useful information from data.

Frequent Pattern (or Frequent Itemset): An itemset or a pattern with its actual support (or expected support) exceeds or equals the user-specified minimum support threshold.

Frequent Pattern Mining: A search and analysis of huge volumes of valuable data for implicit, previously unknown, and potentially useful patterns consisting of frequently co-occurring events or objects. It helps discover frequently co-located trade fairs and frequently purchased bundles of merchandise items.

Itemset: A set of items.

MapReduce: A high-level programming model, which uses the "map" and "reduce" functions, for processing huge volumes of data.

Succinct Constraint: A constraint C such that all itemsets satisfying C can be expressed in terms of powersets of a fixed number of succinct sets using the set union and/or set difference operators. A succinct set is an itemset, in which items are selected from the domain using the usual Structured Query Language (SQL) selection operator. In simple terms, a constraint C is succinct meaning that all and only those itemsets satisfying C can be explicitly and precisely generated using some precise "formula."

Big Data Technologies and Pharmaceutical Manufacturing

B

Joseph E. Kasten

Pennsylvania State University, York, USA

INTRODUCTION

As this article is being prepared, the Covid-19 pandemic continues to be a worldwide problem, although some progress is being made in the world of therapeutics and vaccines. The people of the world have looked to the pharmaceutical researchers, manufacturers, and the logistics organizations that will bring them to the point of use to help us tame this virus and help us all to return to the lives we once lived. The pandemic has brought the pharmaceutical and logistics industries into a focus that they have rarely seen. The focus of this paper is on a very narrow slice of the value chain between the researchers who develop these therapies and those who administer them. This paper examines how the manufacturing of pharmaceuticals benefits from the application of Big Data technologies. More specifically, the paper will describe which pharmaceutical manufacturing processes, as defined in this study, are big data technologies being utilized and how long have the use of these tools to support these processes been studied? Even if the current preoccupation is to get vaccines into the arms of our citizens, an understanding of how these advanced analysis tools promote the efficient and accurate manufacture of drugs is equally important.

The importance of creating a deeper understanding of the role of these technologies in the manufacture of pharmaceuticals is two-fold. First, a better understanding of the analytical tools applied in these operations can provide a platform from which research to identify even better tools and processes might spring. Secondly, an identification of the advanced tools used by pharmaceutical firms in the creation of these amazing compounds will help to broaden the ability of practitioners as well as researchers to identify opportunities to leverage these tools to applications in other related, and possibly unrelated, endeavors. With these benefits in mind, this effort centers on the identification of research that focuses on the technologies in use by the pharmaceutical manufacturers as well as researchers in the field. Using a systematic literature review methodology, the project seeks to identify and categorize the current and future uses of big data technologies in pharmaceutical manufacturing processes.

It is appropriate at this point to define the term "big data technologies." At this point in its development and use, most understand the basic concept of big data: high volume, high velocity, high value, high variability, and often low veracity. These criteria (the five V's) are often used to characterize a big data environment. However, in reality, any dataset with substantial size can fall into a big data category. The issue at hand in this project is not so much the size of the dataset, but rather the functionalities that go along with the concept of big data. These technologies are those that often utilize large datasets to either train the algorithms (such as machine learning and neural networks) or depend on the large dataset to describe a situation that will be used to develop conclusions or evaluate certain patterns (such as in a datamining environment).

The rest of the paper is organized thus: The Background section provides further discussion of the various technologies included in the definition of "big data technologies" as used in this paper. The Methodology section explains how the systematic review process is used in this project. The results

DOI: 10.4018/978-1-7998-9220-5.ch011

Copyright © 2023, IGI Global. Copying or distributing in print or electronic forms without written permission of IGI Global is prohibited.

of the review are presented in the Findings section. These results are put in their proper context in the Solutions and Recommendations section with some closing thoughts and directions for future research being resident in the Conclusion section.

BACKGROUND

This section provides more specific definitions for the concepts under study in this paper. The first is the term "pharmaceutical manufacturing." For the purposes of the current study, this term applies to the processes used to actually create the drugs and compounds in whatever form they might take (tablets, liquids, etc.) as well as the ancillary operations that are necessary to the success of these processes. These might include, but are not limited to, quality control, safety monitoring, material procurement, etc. In short, whatever aspects of pharmaceutical manufacturing that is returned using the search terms detailed in the next section will be considered. It is not the purpose of this study to decide which activities are considered to be part of the manufacturing process, but rather to report on what the researchers and the practitioners in the field consider them to be.

The next term to consider is what has already been designated "big data." As mentioned in the Introduction, most can identify big data when it is presented and likely the technologies associated with it. However, a more specific listing of these technologies is necessary to properly review the literature:

- Deep Learning: A subtype of machine learning that refers to tools such as Artificial Neural Networks (ANN). These tools are trained to make decisions such as classifications or speech recognition. These are considered to be related to big data because the datasets required to train and verify the algorithms commonly fall into the general definition of big data.
- Machine Learning: A broad category of algorithms that can be trained to create the ability to make decisions. There are many different types of training methods and architectures, a full discussion of which is out of the scope of this paper.
- Data Analytics: A broad term covering all of the statistical and mathematical tools and techniques commonly used to analyze and draw meaningful information from big data repositories.
- Datamining: A category of tools that are able to sift through large and sometimes disparate datasets to find trends or categorize the data into subsets that are more descriptive of the concepts buried therein.

This is by no means an exhaustive list of technologies and tools associated with big data, but it provides a representative list of categories of those tools that might be found in a manufacturing environment of this type. In many cases, the tools used to search the databases used in this study have broad enough thesauri that the tools not specified in the search are still returned as part of the search results.

METHODOLOGY

The methodology known as a systematic review of the literature requires that a well-defined, easy to replicate method be in place. Systematic reviews have been used successfully to provide a comprehensive overview of the literature describing a specific area of inquiry. In the case of pharmaceutical manufacturing, this methodology has been used to draw a number of important conclusions about the field from the literature. For instance, Jaberidoost et al (2013) define seven categories of risks to the pharmaceutical supply chain, Ciapponi et al (2021) find significant shortcomings in mobile applications for detecting substandard and counterfeit medicines, and Shaquor and colleagues (2020) find that the manner in which drug-loaded filaments (an important aspect of drug manufacture) are prepared has a significant influence on drug homogeneity and drug loading efficiency. Other examples of important literature reviews in this area are Tetteh and Morris' (2013) work that finds evidence of variation in the way administration costs are measured and how this affects cost effectiveness and a review performed by Almuzaini, Choonara, and Sammons (2013) which demonstrates the quality problems inherent in antimicrobial medicines throughout the lower income countries of Africa and Asia.

In the current study, the approach taken by Briner and Denyers (2012) is used as a framework to address the research questions, which are listed below. The methodology put forth by these authors includes the following:

- Identify the research question(s).
- Locate and select relevant studies
- Critically appraise the studies
- Analyze and synthesize the findings
- Disseminate the findings

There are two research questions being addressed in this study:

1. For which pharmaceutical manufacturing processes are big data technologies, as defined in this study, being utilized?
2. Over what period of time have these tools been used?

In the present study, there are a few ground rules in place that will help to define and streamline the research process. The literature included will be those traditional outlets that are generally used to disseminate research findings such as journal articles, conference papers, and theses/dissertations. This leaves items such as trade journals, white papers, and the like out of the study. This is not to suggest that these documents are of lesser value, only that they will likely not contain significant research results. The purpose of this study is to survey the body of research being performed in this area. Future research should include other types of documents to further define the field and evaluate whether research and practitioner priorities are aligned.

The literature inquiries were carried out in many of the well-known bibliographic databases serving the information technology, business, and healthcare research communities. The databases used were ABI/Inform, Emerald, IEEE Explore, JSTOR, Science Direct, Scopus, Springer, Taylor & Francis, Web of Science, Google Scholar, PubMed, CINAHL, and ACM. The search terms used were "big data," "data analytics," datamining (data mining), "machine learning," "deep learning," combined with pharmaceutical, drug and Pharma 4.0. Initial searches included the search term manufacturing but the returns were inordinately large containing many irrelevant documents. However, it was noted that all of the manufacturing-related articles were returned with only the use of pharmaceutical as a search term, so the remaining searches were completed without the manufacture search term.

The complete set of search term combinations initially returned well over 1000 documents. The vast majority of these were centered on the biological aspects of pharmacology such as predicting the binding properties of peptides or ligands, topics quite far out of the current project's scope. Once these had

Figure 1. Systematic review protocol

been eliminated, the remaining papers were examined to ensure that they were focused on some aspect of pharmaceutical manufacturing. In some cases, the title and and/or abstract made clear that the paper should indeed be included in the study while others required a deeper reading in order to determine the underlying purpose of the work. After these processes were completed, there were 64 papers remaining to be included in the current study. There is no claim made that this is an exhaustive collection of literature regarding the use of big data technologies in the manufacture of pharmaceuticals. However, the increased frequency with which duplicate articles were returned in later databases provides some confidence that the articles included in this study represent a reasonable cross-section of the applicable literature.

Once accepted into the study, papers and other documents were subjected to an open coding process in which the concepts included in the title and abstract were identified and categorized. In cases where the abstract or title did not provide clarity about the main purpose of the document, the analysis was continued into the Introduction and Conclusions of the paper. If those sections proved insufficient to determine the primary thrust of the author, the entire document was analyzed to determine what the primary contribution of the paper is. In some cases, there are a number of points made by the author and it is difficult to determine which is central to the paper. Some papers could be categorized into multiple categories, but great care was taken to select the purpose that best describes the focus of the author. Multiple categorizations is to be expected when working with interdisciplinary research. The entire systematic review protocol used in this study is depicted in Figure 1.

FINDINGS

The Findings are divided into two subsections. The first provides descriptive statistics on the number of papers found of each type as well as within each topic. The second subsection describes the contents of the research themes identified in the analysis.

Descriptive Statistics

The documents included in this study are journal articles, conference proceedings, or book chapters. There were no theses or dissertations returned from the searches. Table 1 presents the breakdown of article types in the findings.

The searches were conducted without temporal boundaries in order to locate those papers that played a seminal role in researching the use of big data technologies in pharmaceutical manufacturing. There were a few very early papers located (the earliest being from 2005) but the main body of papers starts in 2015. Figure 2 presents the time distribution of the papers used in the study. For clarity, the following values were left out of Figure 2: 2005 (1), 2006 (1), 2009 (1), 2010 (1), 2013 (1), 2014 (1), and 2021 (1). The searches were all complete by Jan. 1, 2021, so there will likely be more added to the 2020 total and certainly to the 2021 value.

Table 1. Breakdown of article types in the study

Article Type	Number Returned
journal article	50
conference proceeding	9
book chapter	5

Figure 2. Number of papers published by year

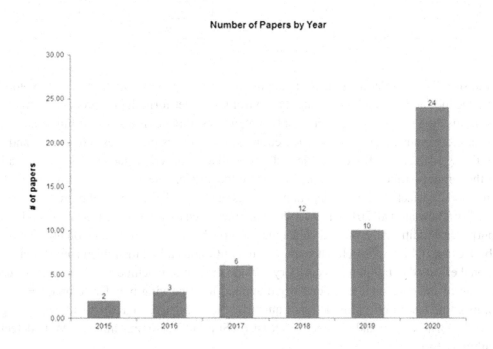

Research Themes

During the course of analyzing the 64 papers in the study, four distinct research themes emerged: manufacturing processes, safety & quality control, factory process control, and manufacturing management. These themes are defined more completely in the following subsections. Moreover, within certain themes there also emerged certain sub-themes, which can be thought of as currents of research within the theme that bunches around certain topics or other common concepts. To assist the reader, Figure 3 provides an overview of the themes and sub-themes evident in the literature.

Manufacturing Processes

The first and largest theme (25 papers) centers on the manufacturing processes that result in the creation of a specific item. In the large majority of cases, the item is a tablet or the components of a tablet, but there are some studies that focus on other products such as crystals and fluid bed granulation.

Figure 3. Themes and Sub-themes in the study

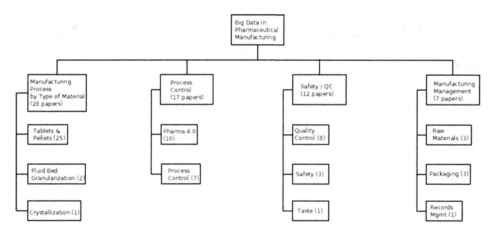

The first sub-theme, tablet manufacturing, consists of those papers that discuss and explore the use of big data technologies to study, evaluate, or control the tablet formulation process. Some examples of papers in this area include Tang et al's study that creates a model rotary die filling system which is used to examine various combinations of turret and paddle speeds on process conditions and material properties (Tang et al, 2020). The data collected is used to develop a machine learning optimization tool. By using the terahertz time – domain spectrographic technique, researchers from Finland and the UK devise a method to detect changes in optical properties of active pharmaceutical ingredients to evaluate product quality (Bawuah et al, 2016). Data collected is then used for quality, optimization, and production control purposes. Additionally, Su and colleagues approach the topic of data reconciliation within the Quality-by-Design (QbD) approach when applied to continuous tablet manufacturing (Su et al, 2019).

Additional efforts that fall into this category include the use of machine learning tools to further the understanding of the core/shell technique when applied to improving powder compactability (Lou et al, 2018), machine learning to provide rapid quantification of active ingredients in Yangwei granules (Zhao et al, 2021), and Doerr and Florence (2020) use a Support Vector machine (SVM) to detect broken pellets within a capsule.

The second sub-theme centers on the big data approach to fluid bed granulation. This process is used to improve powder properties such as flowability and compressability. Though an essential part of the tablet production process, it also feeds other types of products, so it is put in its own sub-theme. Though consisting of only two papers, they are both important contributions. Burggraeve et al (2013) look at the uses of data analytics tools to monitor and improve the fluid bed granulation process by extracting actionable information from the huge amount of data collected at each step. Lourenco et al (2012) describe the use of multivariate data analysis to assure the quality of the results of the process. By applying a QbD approach, they describe how they have reduced the variability in the process by increasing their knowledge of the process.

The last sub-theme, though only containing one paper, centers on the application of machine learning to model an industrial-scale pharmaceutical crystallization process to demonstrate an increased level of control (Nielson et al, 2020) among other applications. Table 2 displays the papers contained in the manufacturing process theme. The table displays these papers by sub-theme, authors, and technology applied.

Table 2. Articles contained in the Manufacturing Process theme

Sub-Theme	Technology	Author(s)
tablet manufacturing	machine learning data analytics/chemometrics artificial neural networks deep learning data mining	Akseli et al, 2017; AlAlaween et al, 2018; Bawuah et al, 2016; Doerr & Florence, 2020; Kachrimanis et al, 2005; Lou et al, 2019; O'Mahony et al, 2018; Elbadawi et al, 2020; Elbadawi et al, 2020; Tang et al, 2020; Zhao et al, 2021 Corredor et al, 2018; Meszaros et al, 2020; Nishii, Matsuzaki & Morita, 2020; Roggo et al, 2020; Shi & Hilden, 2017; Su et al, 2019; Tanaka et al, 2018 Mendyk et al, 2010; O'Mahony et al, 2017; Xu et al, 2020; Zawbaa et al, 2018 Ma et al, 2020; Roggo et al, 2020 Ronowicz et al, 2015
fluid bed granulation	data analytics	Burggraeve et al, 2013; Lourenco et al, 2012
crystallization	machine learning	Nielsen et al, 2020

Factory Processes

This theme differentiates from the previous in that it does not discuss processes that are specific to one product, but rather apply in a factory-wide manner. The general manufacturing industry has adopted the term Industry 4.0 to denote the next iteration of the modern manufacturing environment. This vision includes the use of Internet-of-Things (IoT) to collect data on a wide array of processes that should be monitored during manufacturing as well as the use of distributed manufacturing such that multiple locations and machines can be coordinated by the system to optimize the creation of product. The pharmaceutical version of this is known as Pharma 4.0 and involves a similar set of tools and procedures. In this theme, the two sub-themes noted embody similar concepts. The only difference is that one sub-theme contains those papers labeled specifically as Pharma 4.0.

In the Pharma 4.0 sub-theme, many authors take the time to provide a comprehensive overview of the technologies and overall mindset involved. Peterson et al (2019) discuss the contributions made by these technologies in terms of reducing waste, cost, and cycle time. Morse (2018) discusses the use of information technology and, most importantly, data in the implementation of Pharma 4.0. A survey-based description of the current state of Pharma 4.0

development is provided by Reinhardt, Loiveira and Ring (2020) and a brief discussion of how Pharma 4.0 technologies would manifest in the fluid bed granulation process is provided in McCormack et al (2020).

Many authors discuss the role of specific technologies in the Pharma 4.0 framework, such as robotic process automation (Bhatnagar, 2019), knowledge management (Meneghetti et al, 2016), Internet of Things (Dhingra et al, 2020; Singh et al, 2020), and machine learning (Chi et al, 2009). While knowledge management is not generally considered a big data technology, it was included in this paper because of the reliance on Knowledge Discovery and Datamining (KDD) on large datasets. Likewise, IoT applications are included not because they use big datasets but because they create big datasets, which can then go on to other analysis processes.

Those papers not specifically mentioning Pharma 4.0 but still provide guidance on modern and future manufacturing processes are included in the second sub-theme. These papers provide studies that

Table 3. Articles contained in the Factory Processes theme

Sub-Theme	Author(s)
Pharma 4.0	McCormack et al, 2020; Moree, 2018; Peterson et al, 2019; Reinhardt, Oliveira & Ring, 2020
Advanced Production Processes	Bhatnagar, 2019; Chi et al, 2009; Dhingra et al, 2020; Meneghetti et al, 2016; Singh et al, 2020

center on the use of deep learning to detect interruptions in a process (Carter and Briens, 2018) or to monitor the Vacuum Freeze Drying process (Colucci et al, 2020), the use of chemometric processes to analyze pharmaceutical flow properties (Djuris, Ibric and Djuric, 2013; Megarry et al, 2019), and the role of artificial intelligence tools to characterize silicone oil droplets in protein therapeutics (Probst et al, 2020). Additional examples of the use of big data technologies to enhance manufacturing processes include Su et al's (2020) study using deep learning to screen for certain crystallization patterns in active pharmaceutical ingredients (API), data mining's role in optimizing pharmaceutical manufacturing (Kusiak, 2006), and machine learning in the optimization of multi-step reaction and separation processes (Clayton et al, 2020). Table 3 presents the papers included in the Factory Processes theme.

Safety and Quality Control

The use of big data technologies in creating high quality, safe pharmaceuticals is the focus of the papers in this theme. The majority of these documents are concerned with maintaining the high quality standards that pharmaceutical consumers have grown used to (8 papers). The next two sub-themes deal with making sure drugs are safe (3 papers) and taste as they are intended to (1 paper).

The papers in the quality sub-theme utilize some form of neural network to help determine and predict certain quality factors, such as detecting pharmaceutical injection products (Zhao et al, 2019), predict lifecycle impact of "greener" chemical substitutes in animal feeds (Zhu, Ho and Wang, 2020), and to predict retention of therapeutic proteins after long term storage (Gentiluomo, Roessner and Friess, 2020). Each of these adds directly to the overall quality of the product as well as establishes its fitness for use, in the case of the feed chemical substitutes.

Other work in this sub-theme use other technologies such as data analytics or chemometrics to determine particle shape of active ingredients to ensure that the powders perform properly during the manufacturing process (Yu et al, 2017), to analyze the results of Raman imaging to establish properties of biological materials (Lohumi et al, 2017) or other pharmaceutical nanomaterials (Li and Church, 2014). Lastly, some researchers have turned to deep learning tools to evaluate contamination levels in certain materials (Launey, Perrin and Hirsch, 2019) and support vector machines (SVM), a specific type of machine learning process, to detect defects in glass vials (Liu et al, 2017).

From a safety perspective, researchers have utilized these tools to perform a number of important tasks. Reker et al (2019) use data analytics to characterize the inactive ingredients in various types of medications. Data analytic tools are also used to predict the viability of starting materials to improve the regulatory approval process (Reizman et al, 2019) and to identify safety signals in the manufacturing process (Mahaux et al, 2019)

The final sub-theme has only one paper in it, but represents a fascinating analysis of tools including SVM and neural networks to evaluate the effectiveness of electronic tongues. These tools help pharmaceutical firms evaluate the objective taste of a substance, which has major implications on the consistency

Table 4. Articles contained in the Safety and Quality Control theme

Sub-Theme	Author(s)
Quality	Gentiluomo, Roessner & Friess, 2020; Launey, Perrin & Hirsch, 2019; Li & Church, 2014; Liu et al, 2017; Lohumi et al, 2017; Yu et al, 2017; Zhao et al, 2018; Zhu, Ho & Wang, 2020
Product Safety	Mahaux et al, 2019; Reizman et al, 2019; Reker et al, 2019
Electronic Tongue	Wesoly & Ciosek-Skibinska, 2018

with which patients, especially children, take their medicine on schedule (Wesoly and Ciosek-Skibinska, 2018). Though not exactly a quality or safety issue, this has a major impact on how well a drug is received and exists on the market, similar to the effects of quality or safety characteristics. Table 4 presents the literature contained within the Safety and Quality Control theme.

Manufacturing Management

The final theme contains a group of papers dedicated to the study of the managerial aspects of pharmaceutical manufacturing. Within this theme, like previous themes, there emerged three sub-themes: raw materials/supply chain issues (3 papers), packaging (3 papers), and records management (1 paper).

Data analytics have been used to investigate the role of raw material variability as it applies to process and product quality variability (Stauffer et al, 2018). It has also been used to help qualify providers of pharmaceutical excipient providers (Hertrampf et al, 2015). These materials can influence the manufacturability or performance of a pharmaceutical, thus they are important compounds to understand in terms of quality and accessibility. A deep learning approach is taken to provide an improved method to identify drugs based on infrared spectroscopy as a tool to reduce counterfeiting and supply chain mishaps (Li et al, 2020).

Packaging plays a crucial role in the safety and efficacy of a pharmaceutical. From a big data technology standpoint, the use of deep learning and other machine learning tools are being leveraged to detect irregularities in packaging (Zhang et al, 2018), counterfeit packages (Haase, Arroyo and Trejos, 2020), and to make sure that the proper package is being dispensed in a hospital setting (Chung et al, 2019).

The final sub-theme contains one entry, but represents a very important business function. These authors use a datamining tool to support the Extract, Transform & Load (ETL) processes performed prior to data processing activities (Casola, Siegmund and Sugiyama, 2018). In this case, manufacturing records were pre-processed by this tool and this resulted in significant improvements in the overall data processing process. These types of innovations are critical to the dawning of the Pharma 4.0 environment. Table 5 presents the literature contained in the Manufacturing Management theme.

SOLUTIONS AND RECOMMENDATIONS

A number of other characteristics of the literature studied in this project bear examination. One of these is the breakdown of the body of literature in terms of the type of article, whether theoretical or applied in nature. In this body of literature, 45 papers were classified as applied, in that, they involved the design and testing of a system or tool that performed some task or analysis. An example of this type of work is the study performed by AlAlaween et al (2018) in which machine learning is used to describe various

Table 5. Articles contained in the Manufacturing Management theme

Sub-Theme	Author(s)
Raw materials/Supply chain	Hertrampf et al, 2015; Li et al, 2020; Stauffer et al, 2018
Packaging	Chung et al, 2019; Haase, Arroyo and Trejos, 2020; Zhang et al, 2018
Records Management	Casola, Siegmund & Sugiyama, 2018

aspects of the granulation process. Another is the research performed by Nishii and colleagues (2020) in which they use near-infrared hyperspectral imaging combined with data analytics tools to provide highly accurate quality control measurements on two parameters, active pharmaceutical ingredients and amount of coating, simultaneously. In many of the papers in the study, the researchers made use of publicly available tools and algorithms to perform their analyses. The availability of these tools and the ability to perform these calculations on cloud-based platforms explains the relatively large number of these design-based papers in the sample. Prior to the availability of these cloud-based analysis tools, these studies would have been very expensive to perform and would have slowed down the overall application rate of big data tools to the pharmaceutical manufacturing industry.

The second grouping includes those studies that are more abstract in nature, containing not concrete designs or applications but rather proposals, frameworks, or reviews of a particular topic. Examples of works in this more abstract grouping include a framework of a system that uses machine learning to predict the force needed to disintegrate a tablet made with a specific formulation (Akseli et al, 2017), a framework for a system that uses machine learning for controlling particle processes that are used to provide certain cleansing and purification processes in many pharmaceutical processes (Nielsen et al, 2020), and a description of the basic concepts of machine learning and datamining as applied to various manufacturing processes including pharmaceuticals (Kusiak, 2006).

It is perhaps not surprising that the plurality of the papers in the study coalesce around both the processes of manufacturing specific products such as tablets and the overarching controls evident in the manufacturing process as a whole. Pharma 4.0, as a subset of Industry 4.0 efforts, represents the future of pharmacological manufacturing and deserves at least this level of activity. What is demonstrated, though, is the relatively low level of research activity surrounding issues such as sourcing of materials, sustainability, and the organizational changes necessary to exploit the expanded decision-making capabilities inherent in the use of many big data technologies. There is significant evidence of the importance of these fields to the success of pharmaceutical firms in the longer term. For instance, Shanley (2016) points out the risks involved in not properly qualifying suppliers of important active ingredients and therefore managing the risk of sourcing beyond firm-controlled sources. The rising level of importance of advanced analytical tools in the pharmaceutical industry is discussed broadly by Challener (2020) and research from other industries provides evidence of the importance of aligning organizational processes to evolving decision-making tools and methods (Gürdür et al, 2018). Finally, the sustainability of the pharmaceutical industry, and the supply chain specifically, is also evident in the literature (Low et al, 2016).

FUTURE RESEARCH DIRECTIONS

With these limitations, suggestions for future research center on the topics listed above, and one of the first steps must be to combine the related research from other areas of inquiry into the pharmaceutical industry. There is an extensive body of literature on the use of data analytics in logistics that might be mapped over to the movement of pharmaceutical products, especially those requiring very specialized handling such as two of the Covid-19 vaccines. The same can be said about studies of the alignment of information technology with organizational processes. And, there is a rapidly growing body of research on various aspects of sustainable energy and manufacturing that could provide a valuable starting point for future research in sustainable pharmaceutical manufacturing.

The large amount of similar research in parallel fields might be a reason for the suppressed level of research activity noted above. It might also be that these topics, though of obvious importance, are considered less critical by researchers in the field when compared to those subjects that might appear to contribute more directly to the creation of compounds and the improvement of lives. The third option is that these topics have gotten more attention than it appears in this project but these studies were not returned in the searches. This result is likely due to a lack of connection, in the authors' minds, between these topics and the conceptual field defined in this study as manufacturing and therefore they are likely to be included in studies that are more conceptually "business" in nature. Additional research that centers on this aspect of the pharmaceutical industry should, if this last option is indeed the case, uncover these studies.

CONCLUSION

This article provides a systematic review of the literature surrounding the use of big data technologies in the manufacture of pharmaceutical products. By using a systematic methodology, the scope of the review provides a useful overview of the field of research. A review of this nature benefits two constituencies, researchers and practitioners. Researchers who are well versed in the field are certainly familiar with many of these studies, but a broader perspective is always useful as a tool to widen the scope of an existing research arc. Those researchers new to the field are likely to find this review a good place from which to start a new research project or broaden an existing approach. Many of the papers in this review utilize existing technologies in innovative ways and provide insights into how readily available tools and platforms can be leveraged into insightful and useful research results. Practitioners in fields such as manufacturing management, supply chain management, or any other aspect of pharmaceutical manufacturing management will find this review a useful tool to help them understand the current state of the art in many areas of the business and assist in the formulation of new approaches to managing and improving the processes under their control.

The limitations of a study of this nature center on the choice of search terms and how they affect the results of the search for each database used. While the vocabulary for the topic chosen is relatively stable, enough variation exists that the use of specific search terms in different databases could return different results. Because of this possibility, the same search terms might not reveal the same document in two different databases. Moreover, the wide number of variations in the technologies included in the term "big data" technologies

and the variation in database thesauri make it apparent that the precision of the searches undertaken might pose a limitation to a study of this type. Therefore, this study is meant to provide a guide, not a comprehensive listing, to the body of literature under study. Further research that examines other databases, using different search term combinations, will be useful in further expanding our understanding of the body of literature surrounding the use of big data technologies in the manufacture of pharmaceuticals.

REFERENCES

Akseli, I., Xie, J., Schultz, L., Ladyzhynsky, N., Bramante, T., He, X., Deanne, R., Horspool, K. R., & Schwabe, R. (2017). A practical framework toward prediction of breaking force and disintegration of tablet formulations using machine learning tools. *Journal of Pharmaceutical Sciences*, *106*(1), 234–247. doi:10.1016/j.xphs.2016.08.026 PMID:28340955

AlAlaween, W. H., Khorsheed, B., Mahfouf, M., Gabbott, I., Reynolds, G. K., & Salman, A. D. (2018). Transparent predictive modelling of the twin screw granulation process using a compensated interval type-2 fuzzy system. *European Journal of Pharmaceutics and Biopharmaceutics*, *124*, 138–146. doi:10.1016/j.ejpb.2017.12.015 PMID:29288806

Almuzaini, T., Choonara, I., & Sammons, H. (2013). Substandard and counterfeit medicines: A systematic review of the literature. *BMJ Open*, *3*(8), e002923. Advance online publication. doi:10.1136/bmjopen-2013-002923 PMID:23955188

Bawuah, P., Tan, N., Tweneboah, S. N. A., Ervasti, T., Zeitler, J. A., & Ketolainen, J. (2016). Terahertz study on porosity and mass fraction of active pharmaceutical ingredient of pharmaceutical tablets. *European Journal of Pharmaceutics and Biopharmaceutics*, *105*, 122–133. doi:10.1016/j.ejpb.2016.06.007 PMID:27288937

Bhatnagar N. (2019). Role of robotic process automation in pharmaceutical industries. In *AMLTA 2019*. Springer Nature.

Briner, R. B., & Denyer, D. (2012). Systematic review and evidence synthesis as a practice and scholarship tool. In E. M. Rousseau (Ed.), *The Oxford Handbook of Evidence-Based Management*. Oxford Univ. Press. doi:10.1093/oxfordhb/9780199763986.013.0007

Burggraeve, A., Monteyne, T., Vervaet, C., Remon, J. P., & De Beer, T. (2013). Process analytical tools for monitoring, understanding, and control of pharmaceutical fluidized bed granulation: A review. *European Journal of Pharmaceutics and Biopharmaceutics*, *83*(1), 2–15. doi:10.1016/j.ejpb.2012.09.008 PMID:23041243

Carter, A., & Briens, L. (2018). An application of deep learning to detect process upset during pharmaceutical manufacturing using passive acoustic emissions. *International Journal of Pharmaceutics*, *552*(1-2), 235–240. doi:10.1016/j.ijpharm.2018.08.052 PMID:30253210

Casola, G., Siegmund, M., & Sugiyama, H. (2018). Data mining-based algorithm for pre-processing biopharmaceutical manufacturing records. *Proceedings of the 13th International Symposium on Process Systems Engineering-PSE 2018*. 10.1016/B978-0-444-64241-7.50372-4

Challener CA. (2020). Biopharma analysis benefits from new technology and methods. *Pharamceutical Technology Europe*.

Chi, H.-M., Moskowitz, H., Ersoy, O. K., Altinkemer, K., Gavin, P. F., Huff, B. E., & Olsen, B. A. (2009). Machine learning and genetic algorithms in pharmaceutical development and manufacturing processes. *Decision Support Systems*, *48*(1), 69–80. doi:10.1016/j.dss.2009.06.010

Chung, S.-L., Chen, C.-F., Hsu, G.-S., & Wu, S.-T. (2019). Identification of partially occluded pharmaceutical blister packages. *16th IEEE International Conference on Advanced Video and Signal Based Surveillance* 10.1109/AVSS.2019.8909890

Ciapponi, A., Donato, M., Gülmezoglu, A. M., Alconado, T., & Bardach, A. (2021). Mobile apps for detecting falsified and substandard drugs: A systematic review. *PLoS One, 16*(2), 1–13. doi:10.1371/journal.pone.0246061 PMID:33539433

Clayton, A. D., Schweidtmann, A. M., Clemens, G., Manson, J. A., Taylor, C. J., Nino, C. G., Chamberlain, T. W., Kapur, N., Blacker, A. J., Lapkin, A. A., & Bourne, R. A. (2020). Automated self-optimisation of multi-step reaction and separation processes using machine learning. *Chemical Engineering Journal, 384*, 1–7. doi:10.1016/j.cej.2019.123340

Colucci, D., Morra, L., Zhang, X., Fissore, D., & Lamberti, F. (2020). An automatic computer vision pipeline for the in-line monitoring of freeze-drying processes. *Computers in Industry, 115*, 1–12. doi:10.1016/j.compind.2019.103184

Corredor, C. C., Vikstrom, C., Persson, A., Bu, X., & Both, D. (2018). Development and robustness verification of an at-line transmission Raman method for pharmaceutical tablets using Quality by Design (QbD) Principles. *Journal of Pharmaceutical Innovation, 13*(4), 287–300. doi:10.100712247-018-9334-0

Dhingra, P., Gayathri, N., Kumar, R., & Singanamalla, V. (2020). *Internet of Things-based pharmaceutics data analysis. In Emergence of Pharmaceutical Industry Growth with Industrial IoT Approach.* Elsevier Inc.

Djuris, J., Ibric, S., & Djuric, Z. (2013). *Chemometric methods application in pharmaceutical products and processes analysis and control. In Computer Aided Applications in Pharmaceutical Technology.* Woodhead Publishing Limited. doi:10.1533/9781908818324

Doerr, F. J. S., & Florence, A. J. (2020). A micro-XRT image analysis and machine learning methodology for the characterisation of multi-particulate capsule formulations. *International Journal of Pharmaceutics: X, 2*, 2–10. doi:10.1016/j.ijpx.2020.100041 PMID:32025658

Elbadawi, M., Castro, B. M., Gavins, F. K. H., Ong, J. J., Gaisford, S., Perez, G., & ... . (2020). M3DISEEN: A novel learning approach for predicting the 3D printability of medicines. *International Journal of Pharmaceutics, 590*, 1–12. doi:10.1016/j.ijpharm.2020.119837 PMID:32961295

Elbadawi, M., Gustaffson, T., Gaisford, S., & Basit, A. W. (2020). 3D printing tablets: Predicting printability and drug dissolution from rheological data. *International Journal of Pharmaceutics, 590*, 1–10. doi:10.1016/j.ijpharm.2020.119868 PMID:32950668

Gentiluomo, L., Roessner, D., & Friess, W. (2020). Application of machine learning to predict monomer retention of therapeutic proteins after long term storage. *International Journal of Pharmaceutics, 577*, 1–12. doi:10.1016/j.ijpharm.2020.119039 PMID:31953088

Gürdür, D., El-khoury, J., & Törngren, M. (2018). Digitalizing Swedish industry: What is next? Data analytics readiness assessment of Swedish industry, according to survey results. *Computers in Industry, 105*, 153–163. doi:10.1016/j.compind.2018.12.011

Haase, E., Arroyo, L., & Trejos, T. (2020). Classification of printing inks in pharmaceutical packages by laser-induced breakdown spectroscopy and attenuated total reflectance-Fourier transform infrared spectroscopy. *Spectrochimica Part B, 172*, 1–10. doi:10.1016/j.sab.2020.105963

Hertrampf A, Muller H, Menezes JC, Herdling T. (2015). Advanced qualification of pharmaceutical excipient suppliers by multiple analytics and multivariate analysis combined. *International Journal of Pharmaceutics 495*, 447-58. doi:10.1016/j.ijpharm.2015.08.098

Jaberidoost, M., Nikfar, S., Abdollahiasl, A., & Dinarvand, R. (2013). Pharmaceutical supply chain risks: A systematic review. *Daru: Journal of Faculty of Pharmacy, Tehran University of Medical Sciences, 21*(1), 1–14. PMID:24355166

Kachrimanis, K., Petrides, M., & Malamataris, S. (2005). Flow rate of some pharmaceutical diluents through die-orifices relevant to mini-tableting. *International Journal of Pharmaceutics, 303*(1-2), 72–78. doi:10.1016/j.ijpharm.2005.07.003 PMID:16112532

Kusiak, A. (2006). Data mining: Manufacturing and service applications. *International Journal of Production Research, 44*(18-19), 4175–4191. doi:10.1080/00207540600632216

Launay, A., Perrin, G., & Hirsch, E. (2019). Vision based evaluation of the contamination level in high resolution images for industrial and clinical quality control applications. *Proceedings of the Fourteenth International Conference on Quality Control by Artificial Vision* 10.1117/12.2521442

Li, L., Pan, X., Chen, W., Wei, M., Feng, Y., Yin, L., Hu, C., & Yang, H. (2020). Multi-manufacturer drug identification based on near infrared spectroscopy and deep transfer learning. *Journal of Innovative Optical Health Sciences, 13*(4), 1–13. doi:10.1142/S1793545820500169

Li, Y.-S., & Church, J. S. (2014). Raman spectroscopy in the analysis of food and pharmaceutical nanomaterials. *Yao Wu Shi Pin Fen Xi, 22*(1), 29–48. doi:10.1016/j.jfda.2014.01.003 PMID:24673902

Liu, Y., Chen, S., Tang, T., & Zhao, M. (2017). Defect inspection of medicine vials using LBP features and SVM classifier. *Proceedings of the 2nd International Conference on Image, Vision and Computing*

Lohumi, S., Kim, M. S., Qin, J., & Cho, B.-K. (2017). Raman imaging from microscopy to macroscopy: Quality and safety control of biological materials. *Trends in Analytical Chemistry, 93*, 183–198. doi:10.1016/j.trac.2017.06.002

Lou, H., Chung, J. I., Kiang, Y.-H., Xiao, L.-Y., & Hageman, M. J. (2019). The application of machine learning algorithms in understanding the effect of core/shell technique on improving powder compactability. *International Journal of Pharmaceutics, 555*, 368–379. Advance online publication. doi:10.1016/j.ijpharm.2018.11.039 PMID:30468845

Lourenco, V., Lochmann, D., Reich, G., Menezes, J. C., Herdling, T., & Schewitz, J. (2012). Quality by design study applied to an industrial pharmaceutical fluid bed granulation. *European Journal of Pharmaceutics and Biopharmaceutics, 81*(2), 438–447. doi:10.1016/j.ejpb.2012.03.003 PMID:22446063

Low, Y. S., Halim, I., Adhitya, A., Chew, W., & Sharratt, P. (2016). Systematic framework for design of environmentally sustainable pharmaceutical supply chain network. *Journal of Pharmaceutical Innovation, 11*(3), 250–263. doi:10.100712247-016-9255-8

Ma, X., Kittikunakorn, N., Sorman, B., Xi, H., Chen, A., Marsh, M., Mongeau, A., Piché, N., Williams, R. O. III, & Skomski, D. (2020). Application of deep learning convolutional neural networks for internal tablet defect detection: High accuracy, throughput, and adaptability. *Journal of Pharmaceutical Sciences, 109*(4), 1547–1557. doi:10.1016/j.xphs.2020.01.014 PMID:31982393

Mahaux, O., Bauchau, V., Zeinoun, Z., & Van Holle, L. (2019). Tree-based scan statistic-Application in manufacturing-related safety signal detection. *Vaccine*, *37*(1), 49–55. doi:10.1016/j.vaccine.2018.11.044 PMID:30470642

McCormack, C., O'Callaghan, C., Clarke, G., Jones, I., Kiernan, L., & Walker, G. (2020). Self-guided control of a fluid bed granulation process. *Pharmaceutical Technology Europe*, *32*(1), 32–35.

Megarry, A. J., Swainson, S. M. E., Roberts, R. J., & Reynolds, G. K. (2019). A Big Data approach to pharmaceutical flow properties. *International Journal of Pharmaceutics*, *555*, 337–345. doi:10.1016/j.ijpharm.2018.11.059 PMID:30471375

Mendyk, A., Kleinebudde, P., Thommes, M., Yoo, A., Szlek, J., & Jachowicz, R. (2010). Analysis of pellet properties with use of artificial neural networks. *European Journal of Pharmaceutical Sciences*, *41*(3-4), 421–429. doi:10.1016/j.ejps.2010.07.010 PMID:20659554

Meneghetti, N., Facco, P., Bezzo, F., Himawan, C., Zomer, S., & Barolo, M. (2016). Knowledge management in secondary pharmaceutical manufacturing by mining of data historians-A proof-of-concept study. *International Journal of Pharmaceutics*, *505*(1-2), 394–408. doi:10.1016/j.ijpharm.2016.03.035 PMID:27016500

Meszaros, L. A., Galata, D. L., Madarasz, L., Kote, A., Csorba, K., David, A. Z., Domokos, A., Szabó, E., Nagy, B., Marosi, G., Farkas, A., & Nagy, Z. K. (2020). Digital UV/VIS imaging: A rapid PAT tool for crushing strength, drug content and particle size distribution determination in tablets. *International Journal of Pharmaceutics*, *578*, 1–13. doi:10.1016/j.ijpharm.2020.119174 PMID:32105723

Moree, P. (2018). Implementing pharma 4.0 with OSIsoft PI system. *Pharmaceutical Technology Europe*, *30*(2), 26–27.

Nielsen, R. F., Nazemzadeh, N., Sillesen, L. W., Andersson, M. P., Gernaey, K. V., & Mansouri, S. S. (2020). Hybrid machine learning assisted modelling framework for particle processes. *Computers & Chemical Engineering*, *140*, 1–19. doi:10.1016/j.compchemeng.2020.106916

Nishii, T., Matsuzaki, K., & Morita, S. (2020). Real-time determination and visualization of two independent quantities during a manufacturing process of pharmaceutical tablets by near-infrared hyperspectral imaging combined with multivariate analysis. *International Journal of Pharmaceutics*, *590*, 1–7. doi:10.1016/j.ijpharm.2020.119871 PMID:32980509

O'Mahony, N., Murphy, T., Panduru, K., Riordan, D., & Walsh, J. (2017). Real-time monitoring of powder blend composition using near infrared spectroscopy. *Eleventh International Conference on Sensing Technology* 10.1109/ICSensT.2017.8304431

O'Mahony, N., Murphy, T., Panduru, K., Riordan, D., & Walsh, J. (2018). Machine learning algorithms for estimating powder blend composition using near infrared spectroscopy. *2nd International Symposium on Small-Scale Intelligent Manufacturing Systems*. 10.1109/SIMS.2018.8355297

Peterson, J. J., Kramer, T. T., Hofer, J. D., & Atkins, G. (2019). Opportunities and challenges for statisticians in advanced pharmaceutical manufacturing. *Statistics in Biopharmaceutical Research*, *11*(2), 152–161. doi:10.1080/19466315.2018.1546611

Probst, C., Zayats, A., Venkatachalam, V., & Davidson, B. (2020). Advanced characterization of silicone oil droplets in protein therapeutics using artificial intelligence analysis of imaging flow cytometry data. *Journal of Pharmaceutical Sciences, 109*(10), 2996–3005. doi:10.1016/j.xphs.2020.07.008 PMID:32673625

Reinhardt, I. C., Oliveira, J. C., & Ring, D. T. (2020). Current perspectives on the development of industry 4.0 in the pharmaceutical sector. *Journal of Industrial Information Integration, 18*, 1–11. doi:10.1016/j.jii.2020.100131

Reizman, B. J., Burt, J. L., Frank, S. A., Argentine, M. D., & Garcia-Munoz, S. (2019). Data-driven prediction of risk in drug substance starting materials. *Organic Process Research & Development, 23*(7), 1429–1441. doi:10.1021/acs.oprd.9b00202

Reker, D., Blum, S. M., Steiger, C., Anger, K. E., Sommer, J. M., Fanikos, J., & Traverso, G. (2019). "Inactive" ingredients in oral medications. *Science Translational Medicine, 11*(483), 1–6. doi:10.1126citranslmed.aau6753 PMID:30867323

Roggo, Y., Jelsch, M., Heger, P., Ensslin, S., & Krumme, M. (2020). Deep learning for continuous manufacturing of pharmaceutical solid dosage form. *European Journal of Pharmaceutics and Biopharmaceutics, 153*, 95–105. doi:10.1016/j.ejpb.2020.06.002 PMID:32535045

Roggo, Y., Pauli, V., Jelsch, M., Pellegatti, L., Elbaz, F., Ensslin, S., Kleinebudde, P., & Krumme, M. (2020). Continuous manufacturing process monitoring of pharmaceutical solid dosage form: A case study. *Journal of Pharmaceutical and Biomedical Analysis, 179*, 1–12. doi:10.1016/j.jpba.2019.112971 PMID:31771809

Ronowicz, J., Thommes, M., Kleinebudde, P., & Krysinski, J. (2015). A data mining approach to optimize pellets manufacturing process based on a decision tree algorithm. *European Journal of Pharmaceutical Sciences, 73*, 44–48. doi:10.1016/j.ejps.2015.03.013 PMID:25835791

Shanley A. (2016). Managing risk in raw material sourcing. *Pharmaceutical Technology Europe.*

Shaqour, B., Samaro, A., Verieije, B., Beyers, K., Vervaet, C., & Cos, P. (2020). Production of drug deliver systems using fused filament fabrication: A systematic review. *Pharmaceutics, 12*(6), 517. doi:10.3390/pharmaceutics12060517 PMID:32517052

Shi, Z., & Hilden, J. L. (2017). Small-scale modeling of pharmaceutical powder compression from tap density testers, to roller compactors, and to the tablet press using big data. *Journal of Pharmaceutical Innovation, 12*(1), 41–48. doi:10.100712247-016-9267-4

Singh, M., Sachen, S., Singh, A., & Singh, K. K. (2020). Internet of things in pharma industry: Possibilities and challenges. Emergence of Pharmaceutical Industry Growth with Industrial IoT Approach, 195-216.

Stauffer, F., Vanhoorne, V., Pilcer, G., Chavez, P.-F., Rome, S., Schubert, M. A., Aerts, L., & De Beer, T. (2018). Raw material variability of an active pharmaceutical ingredient and its relevance for processability in secondary continuous pharmaceutical manufacturing. *European Journal of Pharmaceutics and Biopharmaceutics, 127*, 92–103. doi:10.1016/j.ejpb.2018.02.017 PMID:29452241

Su, Q., Bommireddy, Y., Shah, Y., Ganesh, S., Moreno, M., Liu, J., Gonzalez, M., Yazdanpanah, N., O'Connor, T., Reklaitis, G. V., & Nagy, Z. K. (2019). Data reconciliation in the Quality-by-Design (QbD) implementation of pharmaceutical continuous tablet manufacturing. *International Journal of Pharmaceutics, 563,* 259–272. doi:10.1016/j.ijpharm.2019.04.003 PMID:30951859

Su, Z., He, J., Zhou, P., Huang, L., & Zhou, J. (2020). A high-throughput system combining microfluidic hydrogel droplets with deep learning for screening the antisolvent-crystallization conditions of active pharmaceutical ingredients. *Lab on a Chip, 20*(11), 1907–1916. doi:10.1039/D0LC00153H PMID:32420560

Tanaka, R., Kojima, K., Hattori, Y., Ashizawa, K., & Otsuka, M. (2018). Audible acoustic emission data analysis for active pharmaceutical ingredient concentration prediction during tableting processes. *International Journal of Pharmaceutics, 548*(1), 721–727. doi:10.1016/j.ijpharm.2018.07.028 PMID:30003947

Tang, X., Zhang, L., Wu, Z.-F., Sun, P., & Wu, C.-Y. (2020). Data on rotary die filling performance of various pharmaceutical powders. *Data in Brief, 32,* 1–9. doi:10.1016/j.dib.2020.106220 PMID:32923542

Tetteh, E., & Morris, S. (2013). Systematic review of drug administration costs and implications for biopharmaceutical manufacturing. *Applied Health Economics and Health Policy, 11*(5), 445–456. doi:10.100740258-013-0045-x PMID:23846573

Wesoly, M., & Ciosek-Skibinska, P. (2018). Comparison of various data analysis techniques applied for the classification of pharmaceutical samples by electronic tongue. *Sensors and Actuators. B, Chemical, 267,* 570–580. doi:10.1016/j.snb.2018.04.050

Xu, L., Zhu, D., Chen, X., Li, L., Huang, G., & Yuan, L. (2020). Combination of one-dimensional convolutional neural network and negative correlation learning on spectral calibration. *Chemometrics and Intelligent Laboratory Systems, 199,* 1–10. doi:10.1016/j.chemolab.2020.103954

Yu, W., Liao, L., Bharadwaj, R., & Hancock, B. C. (2017). What is the "typical" particle shape of active pharmaceutical ingredients? *Powder Technology, 313,* 1–8. doi:10.1016/j.powtec.2017.02.043

Zawbaa, H. M., Schiano, S., Perez-Gandarillas, L., Grosan, C., Michrafy, A., & Wu, C.-Y. (2018). Computational intelligence modelling of pharmaceutical tabletting processes using bio-inspired optimization algorithms. *Advanced Powder Technology, 29*(12), 2966–2977. doi:10.1016/j.apt.2018.11.008

Zhang, H., Shi, G., Liu, L., Zhao, M., & Liang, Z. (2018). Detection and identification method of medical label barcode based on deep learning. *8th International Conference on Image Processing Theory, Tools and Applications.* 10.1109/IPTA.2018.8608144

Zhao, J., Tian, G., Qui, Y., & Qu, H. (2021). Rapid quantification of active pharmaceutical ingredient for sugar-free *Yangwei* granules in commercial production using FT-NIR spectroscopy based on machine learning techniques. *Spectrochimica Acta. Part A: Molecular and Biomolecular Spectroscopy, 245,* 1–8. doi:10.1016/j.saa.2020.118878 PMID:32919149

Zhao, M., Zhang, H., Liu, L., Liang, Z., & Deng, G. (2018). Joint deep learning and clustering algorithm for liquid particle detection of pharmaceutical injection. *8th International Conference on Image Processing Theory, Tools and Applications.* 10.1109/IPTA.2018.8608158

Zhu, X., Ho, C.-H., & Wang, X. (2020). Application of life cycle assessment and machine learning for high-throughput screening of green chemical substitutes. *ACS Sustainable Chemistry & Engineering, 8*(30), 11141–11151. doi:10.1021/acssuschemeng.0c02211

ADDITIONAL READING

Chi, H.-M., Moskowitz, H., Ersoy, O. K., Altinkemer, K., Gavin, P. F., Huff, B. E., & Olsen, B. A. (2009). Machine learning and genetic algorithms in pharmaceutical development and manufacturing processes. *Decision Support Systems*, *48*(1), 69–80. doi:10.1016/j.dss.2009.06.010

Dhingra, P., Gayathri, N., Kumar, R., & Singanamalla, V. (2020). *Internet of Things-based pharmaceutics data analysis. In Emergence of Pharmaceutical Industry Growth with Industrial IoT Approach.* Elsevier Inc.

Gürdür, D., El-khoury, J., & Törngren, M. (2018). Digitalizing Swedish industry: What is next? Data analytics readiness assessment of Swedish industry, according to survey results. *Computers in Industry*, *105*, 153–163. doi:10.1016/j.compind.2018.12.011

Kusiak, A. (2006). Data mining: Manufacturing and service applications. *International Journal of Production Research*, *44*(18-19), 4175–4191. doi:10.1080/00207540600632216

Li, Y.-S., & Church, J. S. (2014). Raman spectroscopy in the analysis of food and pharmaceutical nanomaterials. *Yao Wu Shi Pin Fen Xi*, *22*(1), 29–48. doi:10.1016/j.jfda.2014.01.003 PMID:24673902

Meneghetti, N., Facco, P., Bezzo, F., Himawan, C., Zomer, S., & Barolo, M. (2016). Knowledge management in secondary pharmaceutical manufacturing by mining of data historians-A proof-of-concept study. *International Journal of Pharmaceutics*, *505*(1-2), 394–408. doi:10.1016/j.ijpharm.2016.03.035 PMID:27016500

KEY TERMS AND DEFINITIONS

Chemometrics: The application of mathematics, statistics, and other data science tools to extract information from data describing chemical properties or interactions.

Data Analytics: A broad term covering all of the statistical and mathematical tools and techniques commonly used to analyze and draw meaningful information from big data repositories.

Datamining: A category of tools that are able to sift through large and sometimes disparate datasets to find trends or categorize the data into subsets that are more descriptive of the concepts buried therein.

Deep Learning: A subtype of machine learning that refers to tools such as Artificial Neural Networks (ANN). These tools are trained to make decisions such as classifications or speech recognition. These are considered to be related to big data because the datasets required to train and verify the algorithms commonly fall into the general definition of big data.

Knowledge Management: The application of technology and organizational processes to promote the capture, classification, storage, and application of organizational knowledge to create value for the organization.

Machine Learning: A broad category of algorithms that can be trained to create the ability to make decisions. There are many different types of training methods and architectures, a full discussion of which is out of the scope of this paper.

Systematic Literature Review: A systematic approach to describing the literature surrounding a well-defined discipline or sub-discipline.

Data Warehouse With OLAP Technology for the Tourism Industry

Preetvanti Singh
Dayalbagh Educational Institute, India

Vijai Dev
Dayalbagh Educational Institute, India

INTRODUCTION

The main objectives of this chapter are to present:

1. Overview of Data Warehouse and OLAP Technologies.
2. Literature review of Data warehousing and OLAP technology.
3. Data warehouse architecture and Integration of Data Warehouse with OLAP technology.
4. Implementation for Tourism Industry.
5. Future research direction in this field.

In the modern digital era, we are living in a data-driven world, where an enormous amount of data is collected and stored on a daily basis. It becomes important to have the ability for accessing and analyzing this data in order to use it effectively. The collection of enormous business data is termed a data warehouse that enables organizations in making decisions. A data warehouse is a central repository of integrated data from one or more than one, unlike data sources. It is a data management system designed to enable and support business intelligence activities.

A large amount of data in data warehouses come from different places such as finance, sales, and marketing. A data warehouse periodically pulls data from these applications and processes it to make it ready for access by the decision-makers. Data warehouse technologies are used by decision-makers to build forecasting models, run logical queries, and identify trends in an organization.

Online Analytical Processing (OLAP)is used to analyze and evaluate data in a warehouse. This technology organizes data in the warehouse using multidimensional models. It breaks down data into dimensions; for example, total sales might be broken into dimensions such as geography and time. Breaking the complex data into multiple dimensions enables analysts to apply OLAP technology for organizing information to easily understand and use business data for efficient decision-making. OLAP plays a vital role in meeting organizations' analytical demands by allowing decision-makers to measure facts across the company.

The tourism industry is closely interconnected with the various global industries/sectors, and contributes towards the complete growth of a country by bringing several economic benefits including building brand value and identity of a country. The benefits of tourism on host destinations include boosting the revenue of the economy, creating a large number of jobs, enriching diversity and culture, and developing the infrastructures of a country.

DOI: 10.4018/978-1-7998-9220-5.ch012

Copyright © 2023, IGI Global. Copying or distributing in print or electronic forms without written permission of IGI Global is prohibited.

BACKGROUND

To enhance the decision-making capabilities using multi-dimensional data, researchers have developed data warehouses for different real-life problems. Al Faris & Nugroho (2018) developed a data warehouse to enable the company in keeping the delivery service time always on target. Analysis was done using OLAP to build a report and dashboard. The operational database was transformed into a data warehouse through the Extract Transform Load (ETL) process. Cuzzocrea, Moussa & Vercelli (2018) applied Lambda architecture to develop an approach for supporting data warehouse maintenance processes in the context of near-real-time OLAP scenarios. Big summary data was utilized and was assessed via an empirical study that focused on the complexity of such OLAP scenarios. Rahutomo, Putri & Pardamean. (2018) built a data warehouse model for education management support. Data was collected through interviews, questionnaires, observations, and literature review. Models were developed using Visual Basic.Net 2008, SQL Server 2005, and Crystal Reports. Schuetz, Schausberger & Schrefl. (2018) developed a semantic data warehouse to support business intelligence in precision dairy farming based on the sensor data. The authors introduced semantic OLAP patterns to automate periodic analysis. Sutedja, Yudha, Khotimah & Vasthi (2018) designed a data warehouse to integrate various operational databases for providing information about students at a university. The design method used 4 stages: selecting the business process, declaring grain, and identifying the dimensions and the facts. A dashboard was developed for providing the relevant and integrated information of students from different angles. Wang (2018) created a multi-dimensional cube of teaching evaluation and extracted knowledge hidden in the data.

Agapito, Zucco & Cannataro (2020) designed a COVID warehouse to model, integrate, and store the COVID-19 data, and pollution and climate data for Italian Regions. Using ETL this data was integrated and organized as a dimensional fact model while considering time and geographical location dimensions. OLAP analysis was performed to provide a heatmap visualizer and extract selected data for further analysis. Dehdouh, Boussaid & Bentayeb (2020) defined a cube operator, MC-CUBE (MapReduce Columnar CUBE) to build columnar NoSQL cubes by considering the non-relational and distributed aspects while storing data warehouses. Khalil & Belaissaoui (2020) implemented big OLAP cubes based on NoSQL key-value stores. Structures for supporting decision-making were presented by responding to OLAP-based analytical operations. Shelest & Holub (2020) discussed the intellectual analysis of outdoor advertising data and suggested a methodology for correct storage of data which is the basis for clear data analysis. Surarso & Gernowo (2020) integrated data warehouse and OLAP with k-medoids clustering for data prediction and control based on the accreditation self-evaluation report matrix of the study program. Data of 3 years was taken for analyzing new students, study periods, their achievements, and lecturers using OLAP technology and the k-medoids cluster. Microsoft data warehouse services and related software architecture were introduced by Wang, Liu & Wu (2020) to solve the problems of slow analysis queries caused by the huge amount of data. Agricultural Science and technology support data was considered for developing the system. Wu, Zhou, Wang & Jiang (2020) developed an urban flood data warehouse with available structured and unstructured urban flood data. Gradient Boosting Decision Tree, regression model, and deep learning model were applied to forecast the depth of the flooded areas. Flood condition maps were produced based on the different rainfall return periods. Yulianto & Kasahara (2020) developed a data warehouse to manage the tuition-fee-level of higher education institutions in Indonesia for providing information of applicants' tuition fees to the administrators. The data warehouse demonstrated four basic dimensions (faculty, year, entrant type, and tuition fee level) regarding applicants, tuition fee level, and payment status.

The architecture of the outpatient healthcare data warehouse was presented by Al Taleb, Hasan & Mahd (2021) as a data repository. Data was collected from two different sources (databases and excel files of outpatient healthcare and hospitals). Different functions like storage and responsiveness to queries were also provided through the developed data warehouse. Chakraborty & Doshi(2021) presented a faster query retrieval method from a data warehouse with reduced storage space and minimal maintenance cost. The executed OLAP queries were stored along with the query results. The input query and stored query were considered synonymous if the functions, relational operators, and criteria used in the input query match with those of the stored query. Kishore & Reddy (2021) proposed ANN (artificial neural network), fuzzy logic, and cat swarm optimization methods for predicting and retrieving the information of land records and security. ANN was used to classify the input data for ordering the information to construct a database of different classes. The mongo database stored a large amount of land record data for facilitating easy maintenance, prompt updating of land records, and security. Kiruthika & Umamaheswari (2021) focused on personalizing data cubes for traders of particular stocks. The system also featured the regular update of the database. Serasinghe, Jayakody, Dayananda & Asanka (2021) discussed the issues that were hindering organizations to make correct decisions by using the warehouse approach. Tremblay & Hevner (2021) investigated approaches to deal with missing data: ignore missing data, show missing data explicitly (e.g., as unknown data values), and design mitigation algorithms for missing data. The authors evaluated the approach with focus groups and controlled experiments. Dahr, Hamoud, Najm & Ahmed (2022) presented a framework to design and implement a sales decision support system. The framework extracts, transforms, and loads from the level of operational data from a data warehouse and building sales cube. Knowledge is extracted using three data mining approaches (decision tree, clustering, and neural network).

The data warehouse approach is also playing a vital role in the tourism sector. A destination management information system was developed by Höpken, Fuchs, Höll, Keil & Lexhagen (2013) for the Swedish ski destination. The authors used business intelligence methods and a data warehousing approach for the same. The destination-wide data warehouse and its underlying multi-dimensional data model were also developed. A data analysis platform was developed by Qiao, Zhang, Li & Zhu (2013) using the data warehouse approach. The framework, key steps of implementation, and application cases were also discussed. Abdul-Aziz, Moawad & Abu-Alam (2015) presented a data warehouse-based decision support system for the tourism sector in Egypt. All the available data sources were integrated into a unified data warehouse to view, retrieve, and analyze the data efficiently. The system enabled the decision-maker in making critical decisions timely. Alfredo, Girsang, Isa & Fajar (2018) developed a data warehouse for flight reservation system to analyze customers' behavior information and was presented using the dashboard or reports. Bourekkadi et al. (2020) presented an analysis strategy of websites, particularly for tourism companies. E-tourism data warehouse was investigated through a website analysis strategy. Multi-axis analysis and statistical analysis were performed to collect the opinions of visitors on the used websites. Chi, Tang & Yin (2021) implemented a hotel big data analysis platform based on Hadoop and Spark technology to provide decision support for user travel and hotel management planning A crawler program was developed to collect basic data including user comment data on city hotels in Qingdao. This was then uploaded to the Hadoop storage platform. Spark was used for big data preprocessing, and Hive to build a big data platform data warehouse. Taufik, Renaldi & Umbara (2021) developed an OLAP-based analytical customer resource management system to analyze customer data and classify it geographically and demographically. Transactional data for hotels of three years was converted into a data warehouse, including the ETL process. Furthermore, OLAP cube operations were performed, and customer reports were generated.

MAIN FOCUS

Seeing the importance of data warehouse and OLAP technologies, this section presents a brief overview of these.

Overview of Data Warehouse

A data warehouse is a subject-oriented, integrated, time-variant, and non-volatile collection of data to support the decision-making process. The construction of a data warehouse reduces the time of acquiring information. It congregates data from multiple sources into a single database to enable fast and accurate analysis.

The data warehouse represents the central repository that stores metadata, summary data, and raw data coming from each source.

- **Metadata** means defining the data about the data. It acts as a directory that helps a decision support system in locating the contents of a data warehouse. These are pieces of information stored in one or more special-purpose metadata repositories that include information of data warehouse contents, their location, and structure, information on the processes in the data warehouse, and refreshing the warehouse with clean, up-to-date, semantically, and structurally reconciled data.
- **Summary data** is generated by the warehouse manager. This data is updated as new data and is loaded into the warehouse. The main role of summary data is to speed up query performance by storing data that is aggregated and/or summarized.
- **Raw data** is the actual data that is loaded into a repository, which has not been processed. This data enables further processing and analysis.

The data warehouse does not produce any data, but it stores the data from various databases. The data warehouse improves data quality so that it delivers excellent query performance, even for complex analytic queries. Data warehousing focuses on business intelligence for decision-making. The data warehouse contains ETL tools, reporting capabilities, numerical analysis, and data mining abilities. Applications of deploying data warehousing technologies are found in many industries like healthcare (Al Taleb, Hasan & Mahd, 2021 and Martin & Davis, 2021); manufacturing (Xie, 2020 and Li, Chen & Liu, 2021), financial services (Arboleda, Guzman-Luna & Torres, 2018 and Kravchenko & Shevgunov, 2021), retail services (Ch, Sai Madhav & Krishna, 2021 and Ying, Sindakis, Aggarwal, Chen & Su, 2021), and telecommunications (Saha, Tripathy & Sahoo, 2021).

Data Warehouse Architecture

The purpose of the Data Warehouse architecture is to provide an integrated environment from the database. Data Warehouse has a three-tier architecture that includes:

1. **The Bottom-tier:** consists of the Data Warehouse server, which may be an RDBMS. It may include several specialized data marts and a metadata repository.
2. **The Middle-tier:** consists of an OLAP server to enable fast query processing. The OLAP server is implemented using either a Relational OLAP model, or a Multidimensional OLAP model.
3. **The Top-tier:** containing Front-end Tools to display the results provided by OLAP.

The components of the architecture include:

1. The Data Sources

The data in the warehouse is consolidated from several operational databases which may include relational databases, analytics databases (developed to manage analytics), data warehouse applications (software for data management), or cloud-based databases. This consolidated data is taken over potentially long periods, and hence is larger than operational databases. Different sources might contain data of varying quality, or use inconsistent representations, codes, and formats, which have to be reconciled.

Data sources also include data from external sources (such as user profile data provided by external consultants). This data is extracted using an API (application program interface) called a *gateway*. A gateway (e.g., ODBC (Open Database Connection) and JDBC (Java Database Connection)) is provided by the underlying database management system and allows the customer programs to generate SQL code to be executed at a server.

2. ETL Process

ETL (Extract, Transform and Load) process collects and refines different types of data coming from different data sources, and then delivers it to a data warehouse. Tools available for the ETL process include Oracle, MarkLogic, and Amazon RedShift. ETL process includes:

a. **Extract:** Before the data is moved to a new destination, it must be extracted from its sources like relational databases, SQL, XML, and, flat files. The extracted data goes to the staging area as the sources may store data in a completely different format.

b. **Transformation:** This second stage, deals with data cleaning and data aggregation to prepare the data for analysis. Rules and regulations are applied to ensure data quality and accessibility. The transformation process consists of the following sub-processes:

   i. **Cleaning:** Resolving inconsistencies, for example filling up NULL values with some default values; or mapping 'M' with 'Male' or 'U.S.A.' and 'America' with 'USA'; removing missing values in data; removing unusable data; or applying formatting rules to the data set, for example, setting the date in 'DD/MM/YYYY' format.

   ii. **Duplication**: Identifying and removing duplicate data.

   iii. **Flagging anomalies**: Removing the inconsistency in the stored data due to updation, deletion, or insertion operations. For example, the name of a student is stored at different locations but is updated only at one location.

   iv. **Key structuring**: Building the keys to establish relationships across tables. Different types of keys are primary keys, foreign keys, alternative keys, composite keys, and surrogate keys.

   v. **Filtering**: Selecting some attributes into the data warehouse.

   vi. **Derivation**: Deriving new calculated values.

   vii. **Joining**: Joining multiple attributes into one attribute.

   viii. **Splitting**: Splitting a single attribute into multiple attributes. For example, splitting Student Name into Student First Name, Student Middle Name, and Student Last Name.

c. **Loading**: In this final phase, extracted, cleaned, and formatted data is loaded into the target data warehouse. Data is aggregated, i.e., summarized and stored in a fact table. This data can now be used for query analysis. Data can be loaded at once (i.e., full load) or at scheduled intervals (incremental loads).

3. Data Warehouse Server

The data warehouse server must have the capability to handle multiple queries at a time and be able to store, manage and secure both new and historical data that can be used for query analysis and business analytics.

4. Data Marts

Data marts allow having multiple groups within the system by segmenting the data in the warehouse into categories. It is a subject-oriented database that is a partitioned portion of a larger data warehouse.

A data mart can be created from an existing data warehouse or from sources like internal operational systems or external data. It is a relational database that stores transactional data in columns and rows for organizing and accessing the data easily. Based on the requirements of the separate business units, businesses can create their own data marts also.

In addition to the main warehouse, there may be several departmental data marts, and data within these may be stored and managed by one or more warehouse servers that present multidimensional views of data to a variety of front-end tools. Finally, the data repository stores and manages metadata and the tools to monitor and administer the warehouse.

5. Front End Tools

The users can analyze the data, gather insights, and create reports by interacting with the gathered information by using various tools:

- **Reporting tools:** These tools enable visualizations in form of graphs and charts to show changes in data over time. These play an important role in understanding the present and analyzing the future performances of the business.
- **OLAP tools:** OLAP tools allow users to analyze multidimensional data from different perspectives. These tools provide fast processing and valuable analysis.
- **Data mining tools:** These tools help in examining data sets to find patterns within the warehouse, determine the correlation between them, and establish relationships in multidimensional data.

Data Dimensional Modeling

The Dimensional Modeling technique is one of the most important techniques of Data warehouse. This technique facilitates complex analyses and visualization. The data in a warehouse is modeled *multidimensionally*. For example, in a hotel management data warehouse, the location of the hotel, rooms in the hotel, hotel services, reservation services, and hotel staff might be some of the dimensions of interest. Usually, these dimensions are hierarchical, for example, the location of the hotel may be organized as a street-city-state-country hierarchy.

The two basic concepts of dimensional modeling are:

- **Fact tables:** Fact tables represent a business process, and contain the measurements, metrics, or facts of business processes. Fact tables contain foreign keys for the dimension tables.
- **Dimension tables:** Dimension tables represent the real-world entities, not the business processes. Columns in a dimension table are the dimension attributes. These tables are generally assigned primary keys. A surrogate primary key may also be added to map the combination of dimension attributes that form the natural key.

Dimensional models are optimized but un-normalized for querying the data. These are scalable and can easily accommodate unexpected new data. Existing tables can be changed by adding new data rows to the table. There is no need to reprogram queries or applications in the data warehouse for accommodating changes. The dimensional model can be built using one of the following schemas:

A. Star Schema

This is the commonly used method to represent a multidimensional data model in a data warehouse. The database consists of a single fact table and a single table (called the dimension table) with corresponding attributes for each dimension. Each tuple in the fact table consists of a pointer (or a foreign key) to each of the dimensions that provide its multidimensional coordinates, and stores the numeric measures for those coordinates.

An example of a star schema is shown in Figure 1(a). This schema shows six-dimension tables (for hotel, visitor, tourist place, booking, bill invoice, and room) and one fact table (*FactInformation*) for the tourism data. The attributes for the dimension table *DimVisitors*, for example, are *VisitorId*, *VisitiPurpose*, *VFirstName*, *VlastName*, *VBirthDate*, *VAddress*, and *VFamIDNum*. The underlined attribute in each dimension table represents the primary key of the table. For example, *VisitorId* is the primary key (PK) for the dimension table *DimVisitors*, and this attribute is of integer type. The fact table *FactInformation* contains the PKs of each dimension table as a foreign key (FK) along with four measures number of *TouristAtPopularDest*, number of *TotalTouristAtDest*, number of *TouristPerYear*, and number of *TouristAtHotels*.

Star schema is easy to understand and provides optimal disk usage, but the dimension tables are not normalized. For example, in the figure, *VFamilyID* does not have Visitor's family lookup table as an OLTP design would have.

B. Snowflake Schema

Star schemas do not explicitly provide support for attribute hierarchies. In *Snowflake schemas*, the centralized fact table is connected to multiple associated dimensions that are related to other dimensions branching out into a snowflake pattern. It provides a refinement of star schemas where the dimensional hierarchy is explicitly represented by normalizing the dimension tables. This enables easily maintaining the dimension tables. As an example, the snowflake schema for tourism data (Figure 1(b)) has a fact table *FactInformation* with seven-dimension tables as in the star schema. The *DimVisitor* dimension table is further split to the *DimVisitorFamily* table to give details of the visitor's family also. This type of information was not included in the star schema. Thus, *VisitorsFamily* is further normalized into an individual table. The main benefit of this is it uses smaller disk space, but because of multiple tables, query performance is reduced.

C. Galaxy Schema

Galaxy Schema or fact constellation means two or more fact tables sharing one or more dimensions. This schema can be implemented between aggregated fact tables or by decomposing a complex Fact table into independent simple Fact tables. The schema is viewed as a collection of stars hence the name galaxy schema. For example, in Figure 1(c), *FactInformation* and *FactInvoice* form a galaxy since they share many dimensions.

This schema defines two fact tables, *FactInformation* and *FactInvoice*. *FactInformation*are treated along four dimensions, hotel, visitors, tourist places, and booking. The schema contains a fact table for getting the information that includes keys to each of the four dimensions, along with four measures: number of*TouristAtPopularDest*, number of *TotalTouristAtDest*, number of *TouristPerYear*, and number of *TouristAtHotels*. The *FactInvoice*table also has four dimensions: Booking, hotel, rooms and bill-invoice, and a measure *NetAmount*. This can have both star and snowflake schemas. This schema is completely normalized. The shared dimensions in the galaxy schema are called conformed dimensions, for example, the *hotel* dimension in the galaxy is a conformed dimension.

Figure 1. Schemas for tourism data warehouse

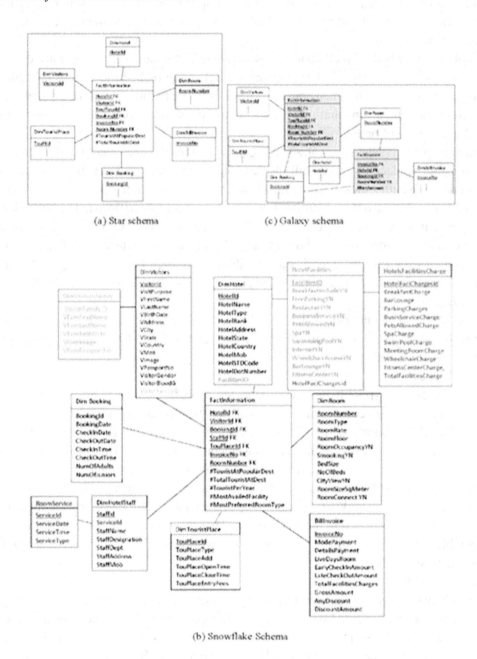

(a) Star schema   (c) Galaxy schema

(b) Snowflake Schema

This schema can be built by splitting the one-star schema into more star schemas. The dimensions are large in this schema based on the level of hierarchy. The schema is useful for aggregating fact tables for better understanding.

Concept of Surrogate Key

The surrogate key is widely used in a data warehouse. The key is a sequentially generated unique number attached with every record in a dimension table of a data warehouse. It is a join between the fact and dimension tables and is used to handle changes in dimension table attributes.

The surrogate key is unique as it is a sequentially generated integer (starting with one and going up to the highest number that is needed) for each record being inserted in the table. However, the key is meaningless because it does not carry any business meaning.

This is an artificial key, used as an alternative to a natural key. The natural keys may be defined in the tables as per the business requirement to uniquely identify a record. A surrogate key is needed when there are very long natural keys, or the data type of the natural key is not appropriate for indexing.

Consider an example where *CustomerId* is defined as a primary key with integer values. Change in this field, from integer to alphanumeric, requires changing all the fact tables. But introducing a surrogate key *KeyCustomer*, *CustomerId* can is updated without updating the fact tables. Thus, one reason to use a surrogate key is to be able to update the natural key easily, without updating all the fact tables that use that dimension.

Another reason is the performance. A natural key may consist of several columns, for example, the primary key of a bank account table is: *branch code + product type code + account number*. Now merging the two banks and their accounts will result in duplication. To avoid duplication, the bank code is prefixed again and now the primary key becomes: *bank code + branch code + product type code + account number*, which is long. Therefore, comes the role of the surrogate key with only one integer column which is much shorter and more performant. It is also quicker to index and quicker to find.

Consider the example of Figure 1(a). Surrogate keys *KeyHotel* (instead of *HotelId*), *KeyVisitor*, *KeyPlace*, *KeyBooking*, *KeyInvoiceNo*, and *KeyRoomNum* are added to each dimension of the star schema.

The Fact tables will now have the fields *KeyHotel*, *KeyVisitor*, *KeyPlace*, *KeyBooking*, *KeyInvoiceNo*, and *KeyRoomNum* as pointers to dimensions and various measures.

OVERVIEW OF ONLINE ANALYTICAL PROCESSING

The data warehouse supports Online Analytical Processing (OLAP) for processing multi-dimensional data models. OLAP is different in terms of the functional and performance requirements from those of the Online Transaction Processing (OLTP) applications because the multidimensional data models and operations of OLAP require special data organization and access methods which are generally not provided by the database management systems targeted for OLTP.

OLAP Server allows analysts to get an insight into the information through fast, consistent, and interactive access to it. These Servers are of three types:

1. **Relational OLAP or ROLAP:** ROLAP servers are placed between the relational back-end server and client front-end tools. It uses relational DBMS for storing and managing the data in a warehouse. ROLAP server is based on a star schema.
2. **Multidimensional OLAP or MOLAP:** MOLAP uses array-based multidimensional storage engines for multidimensional views of data. The server is cube-based. OLAP is performed based on the random-access capability of the arrays.

3. **Hybrid OLAP or HOLAP:** HOLAP is a combination of both ROLAP and MOLAP that deals with higher scalability (a feature of ROLAP) and faster computation (a feature of MOLAP). The HOLAP servers allow storing large data volumes of detailed information.

Some other types of OLAP servers are:

4. **Web OLAP or WOLAP:** It is a web browser-based technology, where OLAP application is accessible by the web browser rather than the client/server as in the traditional OLAP application.
5. **Desktop OLAP or DOLAP:** DOLAP enables desktop analytical processing where the user can download the data from the source and work with the dataset on their desktop. The functionality of DOLAP is limited as compared to other OLAP applications.
6. **Spatial OLAP or SOLAP:** This merges the capabilities of both geographic information systems and OLAP into a single user interface. It provides easy and quick access to the data residing in a spatial database.

OLAP CUBE

OLAP model comprises building a multidimensional database after the process of ETL in a data warehouse. It enables to easily and selectively extract and view data from different angles. The multidimensional database model is also known as a *cube*, as it presents a multidimensional view of data, and where the information is stored in a multidimensional array. The data cube has become a popular model to provide ways for aggregating facts along multiple dimensions. The distinctive feature of the conceptual model for OLAP is focused on:

- *Aggregation* of measures by one or more dimensions as one of the key operations; for example, computing the *total* sales by each year.
- *Comparing* two measures (for example, sales and budget) aggregated by the same dimensions.

An example to present the tourist data as a data cube is shown in Figure 2.

OLAP OPERATIONS

OLAP operations in multi-dimensional data include:

1. **Roll-up:** This operation is used to display summary information. It performs aggregation on a data cube by either climbing up a concept hierarchy for a dimension or by reducing the dimensions. One or more dimensions are removed from the data cube when this operation is performed.
2. **Slice:** The slice operation results in a new sub-cube by selecting a particular dimension from the given cube.
3. **Dice:** Dice selects two or more dimensions from a given cube and provides a new sub-cube.
4. **Pivot:** The pivot or rotation operation rotates the data axes in view for providing an alternative presentation of data.

5. **Drill-down:** Drill-down operation navigates from less detailed data to highly detailed data. It is the reverse of the roll-up operation. The operation is performed by stepping down a concept hierarchy for a dimension or by introducing a new dimension. This operation results in the addition of one or more dimensions to the data cube.

CASE STUDY

This section presents the implementation of data warehouse and OLAP technology for tourism to show its applicability in a real-world situation. Tourism data deals with multidimensional data like tourists, hospitality, and tourism products. This multidimensional data if presented as a Tourism Data Warehouse, can enable fast and efficient decision making.

OLAP data cube was used for storing and analyzing tourism data to enhance the decision-making process as it allows to selectively extract and view data from different viewpoints. Basic analytical operations were performed on the OLAP cube and were implemented using SQL.

Agra was chosen as a case study due to its popularity as a tourist destination all over the world. It is one of the main tourist destinations of India because of its many Mughal-era buildings. These attract various history zealots from archaeology, culture, and literature.

The components of the tourism data warehouse architecture include:

The Data Sources: The tourism data (of the past 5 years) in the warehouse is consolidated from the operational databases as well as literature review and interviewing the experts.

ETL Process: In order to clean data

- Missing values were determined using the moving average method
- Duplicates were identified and removed through observations
- Data was formatted, for example setting the date in the 'DD-Mmm-YYYY' format.
- Data was filtered to reduce the complexity, for example, 25 attributes were identified for the *DimVisitor* table, but only 14 were considered.

This cleaned data was then loaded into the tourism data warehouse.

Front End Tools

SQL was used to implement the tourism data warehouse and the basic OLAP operations.

Snowflake schemas were used to represent the tourism data as shown in Figure 1. There are seven dimension tables for visitors (*DimVisiotor*- to store the details of visitors), hotels (*DimHotel*- to store the details of hotels in the city, particularly Agra), booking (*DimBooking*- to store the booking details of visitors), Staff (*DimStaff*- to store the details of hotel staff), tourist places (*DimTourisPlace*- to store the details of tourist places of Agra), rooms (*DimRoom*- to store the details of hotel rooms) and bill invoice (*BillInvoice*- to store the details visitors' bills) with primary keys underlined in each of the table, and one fact table *FactInformation*. The visitor table *DimVisitor* is further split into *DimVisitorFamily* to give details of the visitor's family. *The hotel* table is split to *HotelFacilities* to give the details of the facilities available at hotels, and is further split to *HotelFacilitiesCharge* to get the charges of each of the facilities mentioned in the *HotelFacilities* table. *DimStaff* is further split into *RoomServices* to give details of staff involved in various room services.

Figure 2. Tourism Data Cube

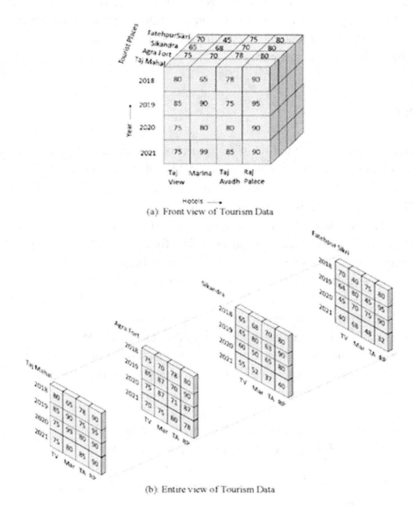

(a) Front view of Tourism Data

(b) Entire view of Tourism Data

Different OLAP cubes could be generated for the data in the tourism data warehouse. Figure 2(a) illustrates a data cube consisting of three dimensions *Hotels*, *Year*, and *Tourist Places*. The time dimension is usually included in the cube as it helps in decision-making. The figure shows the number of visitors in hotels visiting a tourist place at a given time period. Figure 2(a) gives the front view of the cube and Figure 2(b) gives the complete view of the tourism data for each of the dimensions.

This cube can be obtained by implementing the SQL query as shown below

```
SELECT AVG(X) AS AveNumBook FROM
 (SELECT hotelId, COUNT(hotelId) AS X
FROM DimBooking b
 WHERE (b.CheckInDate>=To_date('01-Aug-2018','DD-Mon-YYYY')
AND b. CheckInDate<= To_date('30-Aug-2019','DD-Mon-YYYY'))
GROUP BY CUBE(hotelId));
```

The designed data cubes can be used to perform different OLPA operations (Figure 3) as discussed below:

1. Roll up

The following diagram (Figure 3(a)) illustrates the working of roll-up by reducing the dimensions. Roll-up operation is used to determine *the total number of tourists at famous and non-famous tourist destinations of Agra*. Visitors at Tajmahal and Agra fort are aggregated to get TP1 and Sikandra and Fatehpur Sikri are aggregated to get TP2 for the year 2018.

The SQL query for this operation can be written as

```
SELECT AVG(X) AS AvgTourist FROM
(SELECT hotelId, COUNT(hotelId) AS X
FROM DimBooking b, DimHotel H
WHERE ((b.CheckInDate>=To_date('01-Aug-2018','DD-Mon-YYYY')
AND b. CheckInDate <= To_date('30-Aug-2019','DD-Mon-YYYY'))
AND (H.HotelName = 'Tajmahal' OR H.HotelName= 'AgraFort')
AND (b.hotelId = h.hotelId)) GROUP BY CUBE(hotelId))
SELECT AVG(X) AS AvgTourist FROM
(SELECT hotelId, COUNT(hotelId) AS X
FROM DimBooking b, DimHotel H
WHERE ((b.CheckInDate>=To_date('01-Aug-2020','DD-Mon-YYYY')
AND b. CheckInDate <= To_date('30-Aug-2021','DD-Mon-YYYY'))
AND (H.HotelName = 'Sikandra' OR H.HotelName= 'Fatehpur Sikri')
AND (b.hotelId = h.hotelId)) GROUP BY CUBE(hotelId))
```

2. Slice

A second cube is created with dimensions Room type, Year, and Hotel as shown in Figure 3(b). To determine the *most preferred room type in each of the four hotels for the year 2018*, a slice operation can be performed. Here Slice is performed for the dimension *year by* using the criterion *year= 2018*. This will form a new sub-cube by selecting two dimensions.

SQL implementation is given below:

```
Select Count(*)
from DimRoom R, DimBooking B, DimHotels H
Where R.HotelId = B.HotelId
AND B.HotelId = H.HotelId
AND To_Number(Extract(YEAR from B.BookingDate)  = 2018
Group By R.HotelId, R.RoomNumber, R.RoomType, R.RoomFloor, R.CityViewYN;
SELECT MAX(X) AS MostlyBook
FROM (SELECT H.HotelType, COUNT(H.HotelType) AS X
FROM DimHotels H, DimBooking B
WHERE H.HotelId = B.HotelId AND
To_Number(Extract(YEAR from B.BookingDate)  = 2018
Group by H.HotelType) ;
```

3. Dice

Dice selects two or more dimensions from a given cube and provides a new sub-cube. Considering the cube shown in Figure 3(c), a dice operation will be performed to generate a new sub-cube *showing the number of tourists staying in the two hotels in the year 2018 or 2019 and visiting 2 tourist places.*

The dice operation on the cube based on the following selection criteria involves three dimensions.

(Hotel = "Taj View" or "Marina")

(time = "2018" or "2019")

(Tourist Place =" Taj Mahal" or "Agra Fort")

4. Pivot

The pivot operation is also known as rotation. It rotates the data axes in view to provide an alternative presentation of data. Figure 3(d) illustrates the pivot operation.

5. Drill-down

Figure 3(e) shows a data cube with dimensions Hotel Facilities, Quarter, and Visitor type. The year 2018 is divided into 4 quarters. Now to *determine which type of visitor has availed which facility the most*, drill-down operation can be performed. As can be seen in Figure 3(c) the details are given for every month of the year.

SQL implementation of this operation is as follows:

```
Select Trim(V.VFirstName), trim(V. VLastName)
From DimVisitors V, DimBooking B, FactHotelsFacelitiesYN F, DimHotels H
Where V.VisitorsId= B.VisitorsIdAND
B.HotelId = F.HotelId AND
To_Number(Extract(YEAR from B.BookingDate)  = 2018 AND
(F.Upper(BreakfastIncludeYN) = 'Y'  OR F.Upper(SwimmingPoolYN='Y') OR
F.Upper(MeetingRoomYN='Y') OR  F.Upper(FitnessCenterYN='Y');
Select MAX(X) As MostlyBook
From DimVisitors V, DimBooking B, FactHotelsFacelitiesYN F, DimHotels H
Where V.VisitorsId= B.VisitorsIdAND
B.HotelId = F.HotelId AND
To_Number(Extract(YEAR from B.BookingDate)  = 2018 AND
(F.Upper(BreakfastIncludeYN) = 'Y'  OR F.Upper(SwimmingPoolYN='Y') OR
F.Upper(MeetingRoomYN='Y') OR  F.Upper(FitnessCenterYN='Y');
```

RESULT AND DISCUSSION

The OLAP cubes were used to derive various useful statistics Figure 4. Figure 4(a) shows the tourist arrival at various monuments like Agra Fort, Taj Mahal, Sikandra, and Fathepur Sikri of Agra from 2018 to 2021. Figure 4(b) shows the favoritism of the tourists when they have to choose between the famous monumental places of Agra. Taj Mahal tops the list followed by Agra Fort, Fathepur Sikri and Sikandra. With the Taj Mahal being on top for consecutive years Fatehpur Sikri has seen a downfall. This decision may be influenced by the factors like taxi services, parking, places to eat and enjoy, traffic, and local people's support.

Figure 4(c) shows a comparison between the hotels and the monuments place owing to the factors like distance, restaurants, environment, and cleanliness. It can be seen from Figure 4(d) that hotel Raj

Figure 3. OLAP operations for Tourism Data Cube

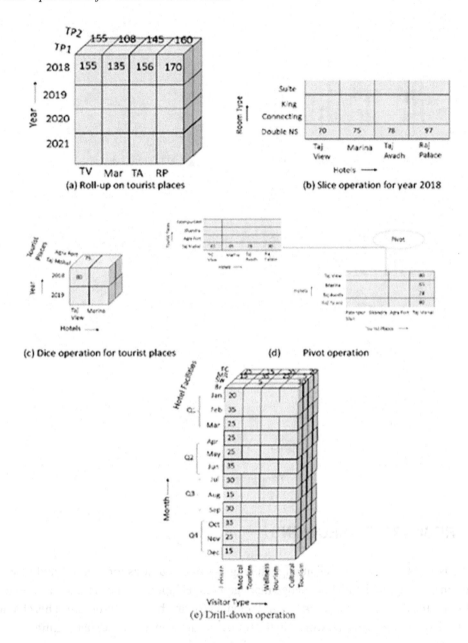

(a) Roll-up on tourist places

(b) Slice operation for year 2018

(c) Dice operation for tourist places

(d) Pivot operation

(e) Drill-down operation

Palace is on top for all the tourists while hotel Taj View and Taj Avadh have been secondary options for them. Hotel Marine has secured an average place for all the monumental places.

Figure 4(e) depicts the trend in the number of tourists arriving at Agra during the last 4 years, i.e., from 2018 to 2021. One of the major reasons for the decrease in the arrival of tourists may be an increase in the covid cases due to which the tourism of the country has received the greatest setback.

Figure 4. Trends of tourists at Agra in the last 4 years

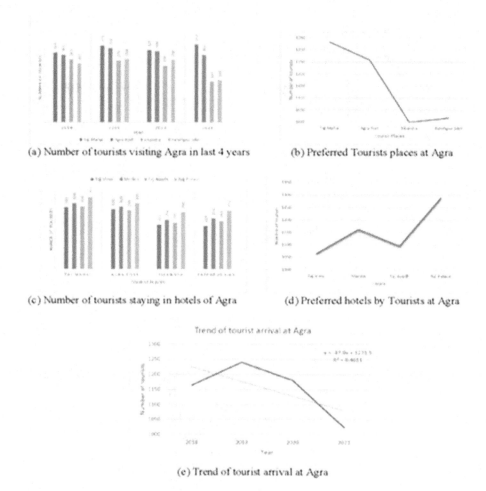

(a) Number of tourists visiting Agra in last 4 years

(b) Preferred Tourists places at Agra

(c) Number of tourists staying in hotels of Agra

(d) Preferred hotels by Tourists at Agra

(e) Trend of tourist arrival at Agra

FUTURE RESEARCH DIRECTIONS

Data warehousing is continuously changing which gives opportunities for practice and research. A data warehouse can be integrated with knowledge management techniques for efficient knowledge discovery.

In the future, the data warehouse can be implemented for any business problem. This chapter presents the basic OLAP operations only. However, in the future, it can be merged with data mining techniques and decision support technologies to provide more efficient real-time decisions to the managers or analysts.

CONCLUSION

This chapter provides an overview of data warehouse and OLAP technologies and presents its implementation for the tourism industry as a case study. First, the overview of Data warehouse and OLAP tools is presented in this chapter. Data warehouse and OLAP tools are based on a multidimensional data model that views data in the form of a data cube. A data cube is defined by dimensions and facts. Dimensions are the entities in an organization. Each dimension has a table associated with it, called a dimension table, to describe the dimension. The fact table contains the names of the facts, or measures, as well as keys to each of the related dimension tables.

The architecture of the data warehouse is discussed next in the chapter. The components of the data warehouse are presented in detail.

To show the real-life application of data warehouse and OLAP technology, the Chapter presents the development of Tourism Data Warehouse. Decision-makers in the tourism sector face challenges in accessing a unified data source that can supply information to meet their inquiries. The developed tourism data warehouse system will support the decision-makers in this aspect. Tourism Data Warehouse deals with multidimensional data like tourist, hospitality, and tourism products. The multidimensional data of the Tourism Data Warehouse was collected at Agra. This data was then used to create Dimension and Fact tables. OLAP data cube was built for tourism data to store and analyze data. This allows the user to easily and selectively extract and view data from different viewpoints. Basic OLAP operations were performed on the OLAP cube and were implemented using SQL.

This chapter will be helpful for the decision-makers to generate multi-dimensional reports that will show the information according to their needs and requirements.

REFERENCES

Abdul-Aziz, T., Moawad, I., & Abu-Alam, W. M. (2015, May). Decision Support System Utilizing Data Warehouse Technique for the Tourism Sector in Egypt. *The 7th International Conference on Information Technology*. 10.15849/icit.2015.0059

Agapito, G., Zucco, C., & Cannataro, M. (2020). COVID-warehouse: A data warehouse of Italian COVID-19, pollution, and climate data. *International Journal of Environmental Research and Public Health*, *17*(15), 5596. doi:10.3390/ijerph17155596 PMID:32756428

Al Faris, F. Z., & Nugroho, A. (2018, September). Development of data warehouse to improve services in IT services company. *2018 International Conference on Information Management and Technology (ICIMTech)*, 483-488. 10.1109/ICIMTech.2018.8528146

Al Taleb, T. M., Hasan, S., & Mahd, Y. Y. (2021). On-line Analytical Processing (OLAP) Operation for Outpatient Healthcare. *Iraqi Journal of Science*, 225-231.

Alfredo, Y. F., Girsang, A. S., Isa, S. M., & Fajar, A. N. (2018, September). Data Warehouse Development For Flight Reservation System. *2018 Indonesian Association for Pattern Recognition International Conference (INAPR)*, 134-140. 10.1109/INAPR.2018.8627015

Arboleda, F. J. M., Guzman-Luna, J. A., & Torres, I. D. (2018). Fraud detection-oriented operators in a data warehouse based on forensic accounting techniques. *Computer Fraud & Security*, *2018*(10), 13–19. doi:10.1016/S1361-3723(18)30098-8

Bourekkadi, S., Slimani, K., Imrani, O. E. L., Ezzaki, M., Babounia, A., & Fakhri, Y. (2020). Toward increasing and investigating e-tourism data warehouse through a websites analysis strategy. *Journal of Theoretical and Applied Information Technology*, *19*, 3222–3232.

Ch, H. R., Sai Madhav, T., & Krishna, C. N. (2021). Building an Effective Data Warehouse for Super Mart. *Design Engineering (London)*, 2347–2353.

Chakraborty, S. A., & Doshi, J. (2021). An Approach for Retrieving Faster Query Results From Data Warehouse Using Synonymous Materialized Queries. *International Journal of Data Warehousing and Mining, 17*(2), 85–105. doi:10.4018/IJDWM.2021040105

Chi, D., Tang, C., & Yin, C. (2021, September). Design and Implementation of Hotel Big Data Analysis Platform Based on Hadoop and Spark. *Journal of Physics: Conference Series, 2010*(1), 012079. doi:10.1088/1742-6596/2010/1/012079

Cuzzocrea, A., Moussa, R., & Vercelli, G. (2018, June). An innovative lambda-architecture-based data warehouse maintenance framework for effective and efficient near-real-time OLAP over big data. *International Conference on Big Data*, 149-165. 10.1007/978-3-319-94301-5_12

Dehdouh, K., Boussaid, O., & Bentayeb, F. (2020). Big data warehouse: Building columnar NoSQL OLAP cubes. *International Journal of Decision Support System Technology, 12*(1), 1–24. doi:10.4018/IJDSST.2020010101

Höpken, W., Fuchs, M., Höll, G., Keil, D., & Lexhagen, M. (2013). Multi-dimensional data modelling for a tourism destination data warehouse. In *Information and communication technologies in tourism 2013*. Springer. doi:10.1007/978-3-642-36309-2_14

Khalil, A., & Belaissaoui, M. (2020, December). Key-value data warehouse: Models and OLAP analysis. *2020 IEEE 2nd International Conference on Electronics, Control, Optimization and Computer Science (ICECOCS)*, 1-6.

Kiruthika, S., & Umamaheswari, E. (2021). Obtaining relevant Data cubes in OLAP for Efficient Online Decision Support Systems. *Annals of the Romanian Society for Cell Biology, 25*(6), 5862–5865.

Kishore, C. D. J., & Reddy, T. B. (2021). An efficient approach for land record classification and information retrieval in data warehouse. *International Journal of Computers and Applications, 43*(1), 80–89. doi:10.1080/1206212X.2018.1514290

Kravchenko, T., & Shevgunov, T. (2021, April). A Brief IT-Project Risk Assessment Procedure for Business Data Warehouse Development. *Computer Science On-line Conference*, 230-240. 10.1007/978-3-030-77448-6_22

Li, B., Chen, R. S., & Liu, C. Y. (2021). Using intelligent technology and real-time feedback algorithm to improve manufacturing process in IoT semiconductor industry. *The Journal of Supercomputing, 77*(5), 4639–4658. doi:10.100711227-020-03457-x

Martin, B., & Davis, K. C. (2021). Multi-Temperate Logical Data Warehouse Design for Large-Scale Healthcare Data. *Big Data Research, 25*, 100255. doi:10.1016/j.bdr.2021.100255

Qiao, X., Zhang, L., Li, N., & Zhu, W. (2013). Constructing a data warehouse based decision support platform for China tourism industry. In *Information and Communication Technologies in Tourism 2014*. Springer. doi:10.1007/978-3-319-03973-2_64

Rahutomo, R., Putri, R. A., & Pardamean, B. (2018, September). Building Datawarehouse for Educational Institutions in 9 Steps. *2018 Indonesian Association for Pattern Recognition International Conference (INAPR)*, 128-133.

Saha, L., Tripathy, H. K., & Sahoo, L. (2021). Business Intelligence Influenced Customer Relationship Management in Telecommunication Industry and Its Security Challenges. *Privacy and Security Issues in Big Data: An Analytical View on Business Intelligence*, 175-188.

Schuetz, C. G., Schausberger, S., & Schrefl, M. (2018). Building an active semantic data warehouse for precision dairy farming. *Journal of Organizational Computing and Electronic Commerce, 28*(2), 122–141. doi:10.1080/10919392.2018.1444344

Serasinghe, C. U., Jayakody, D. C. R., Dayananda, K. T. M. N., & Asanka, D. (2021, April). Design and Implementation of Data Warehouse for a Higher Educational Institute in Sri Lanka. *2021 6th International Conference for Convergence in Technology (I2CT)*, 1-5. 10.1109/I2CT51068.2021.9417820

Shelest, O., & Holub, B. (2020). Olap Systems As The Modern Data Preparation Tools For Outdoor Advertising Data Mining. *Three Seas Economic Journal, 1*(2), 60–66. doi:10.30525/2661-5150/2020-2-10

Surarso, B., & Gernowo, R. (2020, July). Implementation of OLAP and K-Medoids Clustering for Accreditation Data Analysis of Study Programs. *IOP Conference Series. Materials Science and Engineering, 879*(1), 012067. doi:10.1088/1757-899X/879/1/012067

Sutedja, I., Yudha, P., Khotimah, N., & Vasthi, C. (2018, September). Building a Data Warehouse to Support Active Student Management: Analysis and Design. *2018 International Conference on Information Management and Technology (ICIMTech)*, 460-465. 10.1109/ICIMTech.2018.8528196

Taufik, M., Renaldi, F., & Umbara, F. R. (2021, March). Implementing Online Analytical Processing in Hotel Customer Relationship Management. *IOP Conference Series. Materials Science and Engineering, 1115*(1), 012040. doi:10.1088/1757-899X/1115/1/012040

Tremblay, M. C., & Hevner, A. R. (2021). Missing Data in OLAP Cubes: Challenges and Strategies. *Journal of Database Management, 32*(3), 1–28. doi:10.4018/JDM.2021070101

Wang, L., Liu, T., & Wu, D. (2020). Research on display system for agricultural science and technology support data based on Microsoft data warehouse. *MATEC Web of Conferences, 309*, 04014. 10.1051/matecconf/202030904014

Wang, T. (2018, June). Application of Data Warehouse and OLAP Technology in Students' Teaching Evaluation. *2018 IEEE/ACIS 17th International Conference on Computer and Information Science (ICIS)*, 593-598.

Wu, Z., Zhou, Y., Wang, H., & Jiang, Z. (2020). Depth prediction of urban flood under different rainfall return periods based on deep learning and data warehouse. *The Science of the Total Environment, 716*, 137077. doi:10.1016/j.scitotenv.2020.137077 PMID:32036148

Xie, Q. (2020). Machine learning in human resource system of intelligent manufacturing industry. *Enterprise Information Systems*, 1–21.

Ying, S., Sindakis, S., Aggarwal, S., Chen, C., & Su, J. (2021). Managing big data in the retail industry of Singapore: Examining the impact on customer satisfaction and organizational performance. *European Management Journal, 39*(3), 390–400. doi:10.1016/j.emj.2020.04.001

Yulianto, A. A., & Kasahara, Y. (2020). Data warehouse system for multidimensional analysis of tuition fee level in higher education institutions in Indonesia. *International Journal of Advanced Computer Science and Application, 11*(6).

ADDITIONAL READING

Al-Debei, M. M. (2011). Data warehouse as a backbone for business intelligence: Issues and challenges. *European Journal of Economics, Finance and Administrative Sciences, 33*(1), 153–166.

Alhyasat, E. B., & Al-Dalahmeh, M. (2013). *Data warehouse success and strategic oriented business intelligence: a theoretical framework.* arXiv preprint arXiv:1307.7328.

Faisal, S., Sarwar, M., Shahzad, K., Sarwar, S., Jaffry, W., & Yousaf, M. M. (2017). Temporal and evolving data warehouse design. *Scientific Programming*.

Inmon, W. H. (2005). *Building the data warehouse.* John Wiley & Sons.

Jarke, M., Lenzerini, M., Vassiliou, Y., & Vassiliadis, P. (2002). *Fundamentals of data warehouses.* Springer Science & Business Media.

Jukic, N., Vrbsky, S., Nestorov, S., & Sharma, A. (2014). *Database systems: Introduction to databases and data warehouses.* Pearson.

Karami, M., Rahimi, A., & Shahmirzadi, A. H. (2017). Clinical data warehouse: An effective tool to create intelligence in disease management. *The Health Care Manager, 36*(4), 380–384. doi:10.1097/HCM.0000000000000113 PMID:28938242

Kimball, R., & Ross, M. (2011). *The data warehouse toolkit: The complete guide to dimensional modeling.* John Wiley & Sons.

Ponniah, P. (2011). *Data warehousing fundamentals for IT professionals.* John Wiley & Sons.

Prabawa, I. N. A., Arimbawa, D. A. K., & Janardana, I. G. N. (2019). Analysis and Design Data Warehouse For E-Travel Business Optimization. *International Journal of Engineering and Emerging Technology, 4*(1), 25–30.

Prat, N., Akoka, J., & Comyn-Wattiau, I. (2006). A UML-based data warehouse design method. *Decision Support Systems, 42*(3), 1449–1473. doi:10.1016/j.dss.2005.12.001

Vaisman, A., & Zimányi, E. (2014). *Data warehouse systems.* Data-Centric Systems and Applications.

Watson, H. J., & Wixom, B. H. (2007). The current state of business intelligence. *Computer, 40*(9), 96–99. doi:10.1109/MC.2007.331

KEY TERMS AND DEFINITIONS

D

Data Warehouse: Data warehouse is a central repository of integrated data from one or more heterogeneous sources that enables efficient data analysis and reporting. It is considered as a core component of business intelligence.

Multidimensional Database: A multidimensional database is a type of database that is optimized for data warehouses and online analytical processing applications. It allows a user to ask questions related to summarizing a business's operations and trends.

OLAP Cubes: An OLAP (Online analytical processing) cube is a multi-dimensional array of data that helps analyze data for generating insights.

OLPA Solution: An OLAP solution provides business users fast and intuitive access to centralized data and related calculations for analysis and reporting

Schema: Schema refers to the organization of data as a blueprint of how the database is constructed. A database schema represents the logical configuration of all/part of a relational database.

Snowflake Schema: The snowflake schema is represented by centralized fact tables which are connected to multiple dimensions.

SQL: SQL or Structured Query Language is a domain-specific language designed for managing data in a relational database management system.

Tourism: Tourism is travel for pleasure or business. It is also the practice and theory of touring, the business of accommodating, and entertaining tourists, and the business of operating tours.

Defect Detection in Manufacturing via Machine Learning Algorithms

Enes Şanlıtürk
Istanbul Technical University, Turkey

Ahmet Tezcan Tekin
Istanbul Technical University, Turkey

Ferhan Çebi
Istanbul Technical University, Turkey

INTRODUCTION

In our modern world, almost everyone uses a telephone and computer. Besides, there are machines working with computer systems in our houses. Also, computers have become indispensable in public institutions and organizations, factories. With the development of technology, data collection and storage has been simplified. Institutions, governments and individuals collect a large number of data. This data is usually stored in electronic media. The transactions made with devices such as telephones and computers are recorded. It is foreseen in IDC's "Digital Universe Dijital study that digital data will double every two years and the amount of data will be 44 zettabytes (44 trillion gigabytes) by 2020 (Atalay and Çelik, 2017). Although collecting and recording each data seems to be an advantage, extracting meaningful and useful information from such big data has become increasingly difficult. This situation made the big data concept debatable. Therefore, special methods were needed to process and analyze the data. One of these methods is artificial intelligence.

Artificial intelligence studies started with the principle of transferring human intelligence to computers, and the idea of gaining human learning ability to computers has been of great importance. In line with this idea, the desire for machines and computers to learn and make the best decision like human beings has revealed the concept of machine learning.

Computers were initially designed only to perform specific tasks and built to help people in their daily work. Along with the improvements, computers and machines could perform simple tasks and collect and store the desired data about the given assignments. However, these data accumulated on computers did not make sense and did not mean anything. For people, data that can be analyzed and made sense only means meaning and knowledge. This necessitated that computers should reach a certain level by being educated and taught just like humans with the concept of machine learning. Therefore, the "Can the patterns obtained from these observations be discovered and identified by processing the data obtained from the observations with the help of computers?" question is the basis of machine learning (Emir, 2013).

Machine learning and models have been developed because it is impossible to process large amounts of multi-featured data manually. Machine learning is a computer program that optimizes performance criteria using sample data or past experiences (Alpaydın, 2004). With the help of machine learning, more accurate and valid results can be obtained by making forward-looking forecasting and planning

DOI: 10.4018/978-1-7998-9220-5.ch013

Copyright © 2023, IGI Global. Copying or distributing in print or electronic forms without written permission of IGI Global is prohibited.

based on past data. This shows that machine learning is a system that makes it valuable and profitable for companies and individuals from big data stacks.

This study aims to utilize machine learning algorithms to predict and detect product defects in a manufacturing process. In this pursuit, the study was based on a real-life problem of manufacturing companies operating in the white good sector in Turkey. A set of machine learning algorithms were applied to the company's problem dealing with predicting the defects in the painting process. Although there are several algorithms in the literature, the most popular ones are selected for conducting the study: k-nearest neighbour (k-NN), support vector machines (SVM), naive Bayes and random forest. To the best of the authors' knowledge obtained from the literature review on the area, one earlier study applied machine learning algorithms to predict product defects in the painting process. The remaining paper was organized as follows: Section II presents background. Section III introduces briefly the algorithms used in this study. Section IV introduces the methodology and explain the problem the study tried to handle. This part also gives the results obtained from the algorithms. The last part, Section V presents the conclusion of the study and the future research directions.

BACKGROUND

The literature presents several studies using machine learning algorithms to solve problems faced by organizations in various sectors. The authors have employed different algorithms in manufacturing and service sectors such as education, health, finance, and banking.

For example, in their studies conducted in the financial area, Emir (2013), Yapraklı and Erdal (2016), Arsoy and Güreşen (2016) used machine learning algorithms such as SVM and Artificial Neural Networks for the problems. Then they compared the performances of the algorithms. Khandani et al. (2010) applied the techniques to construct nonlinear nonparametric forecasting models of consumer credit risk. Qi (2012), Kartal (2015), Bilgen (2014), Korkem (2013), Ayas and Ekinci (2014), Akman (2010) used different machine learning algorithms such as random forests, decision trees, support vector machines in their biology studies and also for the performance comparison. Bueno et al. (2017), in the field of wind energy using hybrid machine learning techniques, have completed the effectiveness of the wind power ramp. Also, Atasever (2011) made classification studies on satellite imagery in the field of mapping and used the method of boosting, SVM, random forest and regression trees. Priya et al. (2020) used machine learning algorithms to determine fruit quality. Due to the importance of fruit image and colour in marketing, the quality of the fruit has been classified by image processing, so image, colour and Histogram of gradient (HOG) is used on feature extractions.

On the other hand, the authors also used machine learning algorithms for defect prediction. Yildiz and Buldu (2017) used thermal cameras in the quality control unit to detect defects on the fabric and carried out studies to detect fabrics defect by using images from the cameras using the k-NN method. Wu et al. (2019) used computer-aided detection of casting defects in X-ray images with ML algorithms. Gobert et al. implemented in situ defect detection for powder bed fusion (PBF) additive manufacturing using high-resolution imaging via supervised machine learning. Chu and Wang (2014) predicted the number of defective products that may occur in new laptop products by using a robust regression method based on historical data in the computer manufacturing industry. In their studies, they established a reliable development model for error estimation in the new product development process. Zhang et al. (2017) made feature extraction from the existing data primarily in their study called feature extraction in medium plate tension analysis and machine learning approach in defective product estimation. The best sub-selection, heat map, clustering analysis and variable interaction analysis methods were used for feature extraction. Then, using Logistic Regression from Machine Learning Algorithms, they estimated product defects in medium thickness plates. Layouni, Hamdi and Tahar (2017) estimated the length of metal loss defects using pattern-adapted wavelets and machine learning algorithms in oil and gas pipelines. Shi and Chen (2021) use image processing to detect the powder bed defects on the powder spreading process along with laser powder bed fusion. The imaging method is offered to gathering online information about powder beds with different lighting strategies. Then these images are processed by grey histogram. Lastly, defects are classified by implementing different convolution neural networks and their classification results are compared. Li et al. (2021) proffer defect detection algorithm rests on image recognition. Defects and image errors are separated by using the gamma correction algorithm and Sobel edge detection algorithm. Defects in pipelines are effectively decoupled using support vector machines.

Diversely, the authors are many studies related to defective product prediction, mostly to detect errors in software products. Turhan et al. (2009) propose a practical defect prediction approach for companies that do not track defect-related data. Azeem and Usmani (2011) lead to a high-quality study of the detection of software errors and their effects on quality. It is used in software error modelling to reduce the time it takes to detect and repair the error in the software by using the J48 algorithm from Simple Bayesian and Artificial Neural Networks. In their study, Özgür and Erdem (2012) estimated the classification for the Intrusion Detection System using Artificial Neural Networks, Support Vector Machines and AdaBoost methods in the defence industry. Lopes et al. (2020) evaluated using a set of machine learning algorithms to classify software defects automatically.

Bozic, Tabernik and Skocaj (2021) develop deep learning methods, which are frequently used in solving surface defect detection problems through images in quality control processes. A new deep learning architecture is proposed that includes the use of annotations of different details in the task of surface defect detection, from feeble image-level tags to full pixel-level annotations via hash inspection, to eliminate the cost-increasing cumbersome needs of the deep learning method such as high precision tags. Li et al.(2021) designed an automatic subway tunnel surface control system, which includes designing hardware and software parts to detect damages and wear in the subway tunnels. While the hardware part includes the structure that will enable them to capture the surface picture in the tunnel at high speed, they proposed the multi-layer feature fusion network, based on the Faster Region-based Convolutional Neural Network (Faster RCNN) in the software part, which will capture the best defect detection by improving the quality of the images obtained and solving the perception of repetition at the same points in the images. Pham and Liou (2022) developed an online surface defect system for jujubes using Support Vector machines and artificial neural network model over hyperspectral images.

Zhao et al. (2021) studied defect detection in glass bottles using knocking sound signals as the classifier's input. The proposed algorithm combines feature selection with classifier training, employs the wrapper approach to assess the selected features, employs the Shuffled Frog Leaping Algorithm(SFLA) as the search algorithm, and employs the BP Neural Network(BPNN) as the classifier. Hameed, Muralidharan and Ane (2021) compare the classification abilities of a fuzzy classifier and Artificial Neural Network (ANN) using histogram properties on condition monitoring of planetary gearbox. Because planetary gearboxes are essential in power transmission systems, it is possible to forecast machine downtime, production loss, and maintenance plans. Shen et al. (2022) applied Artificial Neural Network (ANN) via voltage waveforms to detect and define the Interface defects of Triboelectric Nanogenerators.

Yang et al. (2020) proposed a deep convolutional neural network-based method for detecting the defect in the cutting wheel since the wear of the cutting wheel significantly reduces the product quality in the production of LCD panels, and it is crucial to follow the cutting wheel. Machine vision is used to create an end-to-end health monitoring system that takes raw pictures as inputs and produces detection results. Since the automation of photovoltaic monitoring methods, which has replaced manual visual inspection, has gained importance in the developing world, Akram et al. (2020) have investigated methods for detecting photovoltaic module defects using isolated deep learning methods and development-model transfer deep learning approaches. Using state-of-the-art deep neural networks, Guo et al. (2020) offer the Faster R-CNN for detecting scratches at nuclear fuel assemblies instead of traditional defect detection algorithms. The main reason is that some conventional defect detection algorithms relying on computer vision instead of manual visual inspection, fuel assembly detection performance is not as good as expected. Also improved Faster R-CNN algorithm was proposed by Liyun et al. (2020) to solve the problem of extraction of some edges that were due to the brightness and contrast of the lighting equipment used in the production inspection process. Unlike faster R-CNN, VGG16 was used, and RoI Pooling was replaced with RoI Align to improve the detection capacity of defects for the detection of sand inclusion defects on the engine surface through images, Zhang et al. (2019) studied an online flaw detection for aluminium alloy in robotic arc welding rely on random forest and arc spectrum. Six spectral features were selected and analyzed by feature extraction and preprocessing the arc spectrum to establish a defect identification model based on random forest and optimal feature subset. This study is one of the examples of the manufacturing monitoring process. In their study, Wang and Cheung (2022) combined heat maps, object size, local offset and density map methods to obtain data in order to more accurately detect surface defects on additive manufacturing using machine learning algorithms.

The literature review on machine learning algorithms shows very few studies related to the usage of these algorithms in detecting physical product defects that are not based on image processing. A comprehensive literature review shows an earlier study conducted to predict product defects on painting using real-life problems data. So, this study is considered to fill the gap in the machine learning applications literature.

PROPOSED METHODOLOGY

Algorithms Used in The Study

In this study, the potential defect products will be estimated by classification resulting from using popular machine learning algorithms. For this purpose, four different algorithms that are Naive Bayes, Support Vector Machines, k-Nearest Neighbour and Random Forest, will be used.

K-Nearest Neighbour (KNN) algorithm is one of the most popular machine learning algorithms was proposed by Cover and Hurt in 1967 (Cover and Hurt, 1967). The KNN algorithm searches the query's k-nearest neighbours in the original dataset based on distance measurements. The most crucial feature of KNN is that no training or learning procedure is needed to produce an effective model. To be precise, given a query and training data set, the KNN algorithm is explicitly used to scan the query's nearest k-nearest neighbours in the dataspace based on distance measurements (Pan et al., 2020).

Support Vector Machine (SVM) is also one of the most popular machine learning algorithms, and it was introduced by Cortes and Vapnik (Cortes and Vapnik, 1995). This algorithm targets to classify via finding a hyperplane with maximum margin to separate the data classes (Costa et al., 2020). SVM is a classifier that searches the maximum margin between classes. The hyperplane which SVM uses is represented with the following equation.

$$w - x + b = 0 \tag{1}$$

In this equation, w represents the weight vector, x represents the input data and b represents the bias in the data.

Naive Bayes classifiers are also used for classification and it has been widely used in many machine learning problems. This algorithm was proposed by Mitchell (Mitchell, 1997). This classifier is based on the simple probabilistic classification which assigns each object to class with their independence level between variables (Zhang et al., 2020). Naive Bayes classifiers are based on the following equation.

$$P(c|F) = P(F|c) * P(c) / P(F) \tag{2}$$

In this equation, P(c) represents the prior probability, P(F) represents what marginal probability, P(c|F) represents the posterior probability and P(F|C) represents the conditional probability.

Random forest (RF) is called an ensemble classifier, consisting of various classification trees (Breiman, 1996). Compared to other supervised machine learning algorithms, the accuracy has been shown to have increased (Wang, 2019). RF is composed of a set of trees for classification. Each tree casts a single unit vote for the most common classification for a new study. RF counts the outcome of each tree and selects classification as the final result, with the most votes (Wang, 2019).

All of these algorithms were applied to the dataset provided by one of the leading manufacturing companies in Turkey. The outcomes of these algorithms are briefly described in the solution to the problem section.

METHODOLOGY

Defect detection is one of the most important processing steps for quality control in the white goods manufacturing industry. Defects in white goods cause substantial economic losses and decreasing customer satisfaction levels. So, detecting defects before the selling process of white goods are significant for white goods producer companies. But detecting the defect in the manufacturing process can prevent economic losses and decrease customer satisfaction.

In Industry 4.0. Era, machine learning technology is used for detecting defects in many industrial areas. In this study, we aim to utilize machine learning algorithms to detect defects in washing machine manufacturing. For this purpose, some of the manufacturing features about washing machines' painting process are prepared for machine learning algorithms and used for classifying defect probabilities. The details of the study are described in the two following subsections: *Introduction of the problem* and *solution to the problem*

Introduction of the Problem

As stated earlier, the study is based on a real-life manufacturing problem of a company that is the leading one surviving their operations in the Turkish white goods sector. In washing machine manufacturing, The powder coating thickness of the parts in the washing machine has to be 20 μ -27 μ. When the parts that are coming out of the furnace are measured, if the paint thickness is outside the tolerance range, the operator manually tries to include the paint thickness in the tolerance range by decreasing or increasing the %. Because thicknesses of more than 27 μ increase the cost and parts that its thickness is less than

D

20 μ can be easily destroyed and abraded against beatings and scratches. At this point, if the paint thickness goes out of the tolerance range, that part is not only out of the tolerance range, but it is out of the tolerance range in 2-3 pieces that are baked in the oven during the measurement. This causes 3-4 pieces to be scraped or reprocessed until the desired tolerance is achieved. Therefore the company has to pay extra cost for 3-4 pieces.

Costs due to the fact that the undesired tolerance in the powder coating unit cannot be intervened immediately and the necessary intervention and adjustment in the subsequent products are delayed further increase the desire to control defect product group. Pre-intervention for the product according to the increases or decreases observed in thickness measurements will significantly reduce these costs. In this respect, it is possible to predict whether the product will be in the desired tolerance range according to the input variables for any product entering the powder coating unit and will provide early intervention.

Literature review shows that machine learning algorithms are one of the most effective methods for making accurate estimations in timely identifying the status of subsequent products by employing existing product data.

The Solution to the Problem

The study aims to uti lize machine learning algorithms to predict and identify timely defect products. For this purpose, predictive performances that are acquired by different learning algorithms will be compared to determine the most suitable machine learning algorithm. Specifically, in this study, learning algorithms are used to predict the defect products in the washing machine production of a business that is operating in the white goods sector. With the proposed algorithm, it is desired to estimate the defected product that may occur during the powder coating stage, which is an essential source of error in the washing machine production stage.

Firstly, by discussing with the experts of the washing machine powder unit of the company on inputs and outputs about analysis, it was identified which factor can affect the quality of the parts in the line while which factors can cause the problems on the parts. After the discussion among the experts, the following factors were agreed to be used in the analysis.

Shift no: the department runs three shifts which each has 8 hours working period of one day. 00:00-08:00 is the first shift, 08:00-16:00 is the second shift and 16: 00-24: 00 is the third shift.
Operator: ID of operator processing the operation corresponding to the measurement.
Experience of operator: Level of operator competence at work. The highest value is 5.
% of colour: It refers to the percentage of the amount of paint that flows to the product per unit time from the paint gun used during powder coating.
Debit: Volumetric flow rate of the paint from the gun per unit time.
Type of part: Refers to the type of product to be painted. There are three types of parts to be painted in the relevant section: Back (A), Front (F) and Body (B)
Teflon: It is the sequence number of the parts that were painted during teflon' lifetime. Teflon, whose lifetime is completed, is replaced by new teflon, and the values in this column continue by giving the value "1" to the first painted part.
Part thickness: The paint thickness of the part comes out of the powder coating process.
Hanger: It is the number of parts brought to the painting unit from the transport system.
Status: Whether the piece coming out of the paint unit is suitable or not according to the measurements.

Once the inputs were identified, necessary data were collected from the line for conducting the analysis. With this data, it was determined whether the washing machine parts were in the desired paint thickness range after leaving the powder painting unit, and the suitable machine learning models were evaluated according to data and purposes of the business. The determined models were run on the data, and a classification result was obtained for each model. Classification successes were measured and compared to four different machine learning algorithms. Thus, it was desired to measure the classification performance of each model.

The parts removed from the powder coating unit are generally measured manually by the operators when the model changes and there is a problem. The value obtained from the measurements is recorded in the control part of that part in the system. As a result of the measurements, 327 observations were reached in 3 months. A section of the data is presented in Table 1.

Table 1. Section of data

Observation number	Shift No	Operator	Experience	% of colour	Debit	Part	Teflon	Thickness	Hanger	Status
...	......	......	......	......	......	......	......	......	......	......
11	3	******	2,5	106	34	A	20	25	1	Correct
12	2	******		102	34	A	21	27	2	Correct
...	......	......	......	......	......	......	......	......	......	......
121	1	******	3	60	53	B	2	26	32	Correct
122	2	******	5	78	53	F	3	29	33	Defect
	......	......	......	......	......	......	......	......	......	......
326	1	******	2,5	59	49	B	1	26	108	Correct
327	1	******	2,5	71	49	B	2	25	109	Correct

Predetermined machine learning algorithms, Random Forest, Naive Bayes, Support Vector Machines and k-Nearest Neighbour, are run on data of the washing machine powder coating unit for defect estimation. 70% of data is used as a training set, and the other is used as a test set. In this direction, four machine learning algorithm performances were compared. These performances are presented in Table 2.

Table 2. General algorithms' performances

Algorithm	k-NN	SVM	Naive Bayes	Random Forest
Accuracy	58.16%	65.31%	90.82%	96.94%

According to comparing of 4 algorithms, Random Forest has the best performance with 96.94%; secondly, Naive Bayes has the good performance with 90.82%, then Support Vector Machines has 65.31% performance and lastly k-Nearest neighbour has the worst estimation performance with 58.16%.

Some features that are a hanger, % of colour, debit, thickness, teflon and experience are normalized with z-transformation and then machine learning algorithms are run on the normalized data. Algorithms' performances on Normalized Data are presented in Table 3.

Table 3. Algorithms' performances on normalized data

Algorithm	k-NN	SVM	Naive Bayes	Random Forest
Accuracy	60.20%	65.31%	90.82%	96.94%

After the data is scaled according to the correlation of features, data is classified with the same algorithms to research the effect of data scalability on defect detection. Thus, the effect of data scalability on algorithm performance is observed. Algorithms' performances on Scabilited Data are presented in Table 4.

Table 4. Algorithms' performances on scabilited data

Algorithm	k-NN	SVM	Naive Bayes	Random Forest
Accuracy	66.33%	65.31%	88.78%	98.98%

CONCLUSION

In this study, it is aimed to estimate possible defect products with machine learning algorithms. Four machine learning algorithms are evaluated on data sets obtained from a real case study. Random Forest, Naive Bayes, Support Vector Machines and k-Nearest Neighbor (k-NN) algorithms which are popular and give good results in the classification, have been used in defect detecting and predictive performance of each algorithm is compared.

Firstly, the general performance of machine learning algorithms for estimating the defected product was measured. Afterwards, the model is developed via data normalization and data scaling that are from feature engineering methods. Thus, the effects of data normalization and scaling on defect detection were observed. The results that obtained from these studies are summarized in Table 5.

Table 5. Comparing of machine learning algorithms performance

Machine Learning Algorithms	General Performance	Performance of Normalized Data	Performance of Scabileted Data
Random Forest	96.94%	96.94%	98.98%
Naive Bayes	90.82%	90.82%	88.78%
Support Vector Machines	65.31%	65.31%	65.31%
K-Nearest Neighbour	58.16%	60.20%	66.33%

Data normalization and data scalability in defect detection show different effects for different algorithms. Data normalization has a positive effect; only the k-nearest neighbour algorithm with %2.04 performance increasing. Data normalization has not had any negative or positive effect on other algorithms performances. This means that normalization does not always affect algorithm performance in defect detection. On the other hand, scaling data shows both positive and negative effects on different algorithms in estimating defect products. The scaling process positively affected the k-nearest neighbour algorithm with an increase of 8.17% and a random forest algorithm with an increase of 2.04%. While no difference was observed in the performance of support vector machines, the scaling process in the simple bayesian algorithm hurt the decrease of 2.04%. Although the same scaling process is performed in the same data set, observing different effects shows that machine learning algorithm type is more important in the data scaling process.

Due to this application, it was estimated whether the product that will be entering the powder coating unit would defect beforehand. According to this estimation, appropriate values should be entered for % of paint or other different inputs. However, a different study can investigate how to determine these values, which will optimize the relations between the inputs and outputs. Considering that 3-4 products will be scrap or recycled with any defect in the current situation, the estimation of Random Forest algorithm and subsequent optimization is expected to produce defected products with the wrong estimation for approximately two products in 100 product production. This shows what the estimation study with an algorithm can provide for the firm.

FUTURE RESEARCH DIRECTIONS

The study has some limitations. One of these limitations is the size of the data. In this study, 327 data were collected for estimating the defected product, so machine learning algorithms were run with a data set of 327 rows. Since machine learning algorithms perform better in a large amount of data, it is thought that more data can be collected and better results can be obtained for machine learning algorithms. Besides, it is suggested for future studies that the algorithms according to the existing data of firms should be supported by improvement studies such as feature engineering. Also, because of our data is an unbalanced dataset, for the measurement accuracy Cohen's kappa coefficient and over-undersampling methods can be used in the future studies. Also in the future, with the increase in data size, in addition to existing algorithms, boosting type ensemble learning algorithms which are XGboost, GBM etc. which have an essential place in the literature, will be added to the current study.

REFERENCES

Akman, M. (2010). *Veri madenciliğine genel bakış ve random forests yönteminin incelenmesi: sağlık alanında bir Uygulama* [An Overview of Data Mining Techniques and Analysis of Random Forests Method: An Application On Medical Field] [Master dissertation, Ankara University Health Sciences Institute]. Turkey council of higher education thesis center database. (No: 247693)

Akram, M. W., Li, G., Jin, Y., Chen, X., Zhu, C., & Ahmad, A. (2020). Automatic detection of photovoltaic module defects in infrared images with isolated and develop-model transfer deep learning. *Solar Energy, 198*, 175–186. doi:10.1016/j.solener.2020.01.055

Alpaydın, E. (2004). *Introduction to Machine Learning*. The MIT Press.

Arsoy, M.F. & Güreşen, E. (2016). Nakit temettü tahmininde makine öğrenmesi yaklaşımı: imalat sektörü üzerine bir araştırma [A Machine Learning Approach for Cash Dividends' Forecasting: A Research on Manufacturing Sector]. *Çankırı Karatekin University Journal of the Faculty of Economics and Administrative Sciences, 6*(1), 307-333.

Atalay, M., & Çelik, E. (2017). Büyük veri analizinde yapay zeka ve makine öğrenmesi uygulamaları (Artificıal Intelligence and Machine Learning Applications in Big Data Analysis). *Mehmet Akif Ersoy University Journal of Social Sciences Institute, 9*(22), 155–172.

Atasever, Ü. H. (2011). *Uydu görüntülerinin sınıflandırılmasında hızlandırma, destek vektör makineleri, rastgele orman ve regresyon ağaçları yöntemlerinin kullanılması* [The Use Of Boosting, Support Vector Machines, Random Forest And Regression Tree Methods in Satellite Images Classification] [Master dissertation, Erciyes University Graduate School of Natural and Applied Science]. Turkey council of higher education thesis center database. (No: 276782)

Ayas, S., & Ekinci, M. (2014). Random forest-based tuberculosis bacteria classification in images of ZN-stained sputum smear samples. *Signal, Image and Video Processing, 8*(S1), 49–61. doi:10.100711760-014-0708-6

Azeem, N., & Usmani, S. (2011). Defect prediction leads to high quality product. *Journal of Software Engineering and Applications, 4*(11), 639–645. doi:10.4236/jsea.2011.411075

Bilgen, İ. (2014). *İnsan ve hiv-1 proteinleri arasındaki etkileşimlerin rastgele orman yöntemi ve birlikte öğrenme yaklaşımı ile tahmin edilmesi* [Predicting Human-HIV1 Protein-Protein Interactions Using Random Forests In A Co-Training Approach] [Master dissertation, Istanbul Technical University Graduate School of Science Engineering and Technology]. Turkey council of higher education thesis center database. (No: 353682)

Bozic, J., Tabernik, D., & Skocaj, D. (2021). Mixed supervision for surface-defect detection: From weakly to fully supervised learning. *Computers in Industry, 129*(103459).

Breiman, L. (1996). Bagging predictors. *Journal of Mach Learn, 40*, 24–123.

Bueno, L. C., Cuadra, L., Fernández, S. J., Rodríguez, J. A., Prieto, L., & Sanz, S. S. (2017). Wind power ramp events prediction with hybrid machine learning regression techniques and reanalysis data. *MDPI Open Access Journal, 10*(11), 1–27.

Chu, T. P., & Wang, F. K. (2014). Defect prediction for new products during the development phase. *Journal of Testing and Evaluation, 42*(4), 989–995. doi:10.1520/JTE20130101

Cortes, C., & Vapnik, V. (1995). Support vector networks. *Machine Learning, 20*(3), 273–297. doi:10.1007/BF00994018

Costa, N. L., Llobodanin, L. A. G., Castro, I. A., & Barbosa, R. (2019). Using Support Vector Machines and neural networks to classify Merlot wines from South America. *Journal of Information Processing in Agriculture, 6*(2), 265–278. doi:10.1016/j.inpa.2018.10.003

Cover, T., & Hart, P. (1967). Nearest Neighbor pattern classification. *IEEE. Inf. Theory, 13*(1), 21–27. doi:10.1109/TIT.1967.1053964

Emir, Ş. (2013). *Yapay sinir ağları ve destek vektör makinelerinin sınıflandırma performanslarının karşılaştırılması: Borsa endeks yönünün tahmini üzerine bir uygulama* [Classification Performance Comparison of Artificial Neural Networks and Support Vector Machines Methods: An Empirical Study on Predicting Stock Market Index Movement Direction] [Doctoral dissertation, Istanbul University Social Science Institute]. Turkey council of higher education thesis center database. (No: 340494)

Gobert, C., Reutzelb, E. W., Petrich, J., Nassar, A. R., & Phoha, S. (2018). Application of supervised machine learning for defect detection during metallic powder bed fusion additive manufacturing using high resolution imaging. *Additive Manufacturing*, *21*, 517–528. doi:10.1016/j.addma.2018.04.005

Guo, Z., Wu, Z., Liu, S., Ma, X., Wang, C., Yan, D., & Niu, F. (2020). Defect detection of nuclear fuel assembly based on deep neural network. *Annals of Nuclear Energy*, *137*(107078). doi:10.1016/j.anucene.2019.107078

Hameed, S. S., Muralidharan, V., & Ane, B. K. (2021). Comparative analysis of fuzzy classifier and ANN with histogram features for defect detection and classification in planetary gearbox. *Applied Soft Computing*, *106*(107306).

Kartal, E. (2015). *Sınıflandırmaya dayalı makine öğrenmesi teknikleri ve kardiyolojik risk değerlendirmesine ilişkin bir uygulama* [Machine Learning Techniques Based On Classification and A Study On Cardiac Risk Assessment] [Doctoral dissertation, Istanbul University Institute of Graduate Studies in Science and Engineering]. Turkey council of higher education thesis center database. (No: 394514)

Khandani, A. E., Kim, A. J., & Lo, A. W. (2010). Consumer credit-risk models via machine-learning algorithms. *Journal of Banking & Finance*, *34*(11), 2767–2787. doi:10.1016/j.jbankfin.2010.06.001

Korkem, E. (2013). *Mikroarray gen ekspresyon veri setlerinde random forest ve naive bayes sınıflama yöntemleri yaklaşımı* [Random Forest and Naive Bayes Approach in Microarray Gene Expressions Data Sets] [Master dissertation, Hacettepe University Institute of Health Sciences]. Turkey council of higher education thesis center database. (No: 329788)

Layouni, M., Hamdi, M. S., & Tahar, S. (2017). Detection and sizing of metal-loss defects in oil and gas pipelines using pattern-adapted wavelets and machine learning. *Applied Soft Computing*, *52*, 247–261. doi:10.1016/j.asoc.2016.10.040

Li, C., Lan, H. Q., Sun, Y. N., & Wang, J. Q. (2021). Detection algorithm of defects on polyethylene gas pipe using image recognition. *International Journal of Pressure Vessels and Piping*, *191*(104381), 104381. doi:10.1016/j.ijpvp.2021.104381

Li, D., Xie, Q., Gong, X., Yu, Z., Xu, J., Sun, Y., & Wang, J. (2021). Automatic defect detection of metro tunnel surfaces using a vision-based inspection system. *Advanced Engineering Informatics*, *47*(101206), 101206. doi:10.1016/j.aei.2020.101206

Liyun, X., Boyu, L., Hong, M., & Xingzhong, L. (2020). Improved Faster R-CNN algorithm for defect detection in powertrain assembly line. *Procedia CIRP*, *93*, 479–484. doi:10.1016/j.procir.2020.04.031

Lopes, F., Agnelo, J., Teixeira, C. A., Laranjeiro, N., & Jorge Bernardino, J. (2020). Automating orthogonal defect classification using machine learning algorithms. *Future Generation Computer Systems*, *102*, 932–947. doi:10.1016/j.future.2019.09.009

Mitchell, T. M. (1997). *Machine Learning*. McGraw-Hill, Inc.

Özgür, A., & Erdem, H. (2012). Saldırı tespit sistemlerinde kullanılan kolay erişilen makine öğrenme algoritmalarının karşılaştırılması [Comparison of Out-of-Box Machine Learning Algorithms used in Intrusion Detection Systems]. *International Journal of Informatics Technologies*, *5*(2), 41–48.

Pan, Y., Pan, Z., Wang, Y., & Wang, W. (2020). A new fast search algorithm for exact k-nearest neighbors based on optimal triangle-inequality-based check strategy. *Journal of Knowledge-Based Systems, 189*(105088), 105088. doi:10.1016/j.knosys.2019.105088

Pham, Q. T., & Liou, N. (2022). The development of on-line surface defect detection system for jujubes based on hyperspectral images. *Computers and Electronics in Agriculture, 194*(106743).

Priya, P. S., Jyoshna, N., Amaraneni, S., & Swamy, J. (2020). Real time fruits quality detection with the help of artificial intelligence. *Materials Today: Proceedings, 33*, 4900–4906. doi:10.1016/j.matpr.2020.08.445

Qi, Y. (2012). *Random forest for bioinformatics.* https://www.cs.cmu.edu/~qyj/papersA08/11-rfbook.pdf

Shen, F., Li, Z., Xin, H., Guo, H., Peng, Y., & Li, K. (2022). Interface Defect Detection and Identification of Triboelectric Nanogenerators via Voltage Waveforms and Artificial Neural Network. *ACS Applied Materials & Interfaces, 14*(2), 3437–3445. doi:10.1021/acsami.1c19718 PMID:35001611

Shi, B., & Chen, Z. (2021). A layer-wise multi-defect detection system for powder bed monitoring: Lighting strategy for imaging, adaptive segmentation and classification. *Materials & Design, 210*(110035), 110035. doi:10.1016/j.matdes.2021.110035

Turhan, B., Menzies, T., Bener, A. B., & Stefano, J. (2009). On the relative value of cross-company and within-company data for defect prediction. *Empirical Software Engineering, 14*(5), 540–578. doi:10.100710664-008-9103-7

Wang, R., & Cheung, C. F. (2022). CenterNet-based defect detection for additive manufacturing. *Expert Systems with Applications, 188*(116000).

Wang, X., Liu, Y., Liang, S., Zhang, W., & Lou, S. (2019). Event identification based on random forest classifier for Φ-OTDR fibre-optic distributed disturbance sensor. *Journal of Infrared Physics and Technology, 97*, 319–325. doi:10.1016/j.infrared.2019.01.003

Wu, B., Zhou, J., Ji, X., Yin, Y., & Shen, X. (2019). Research on Approaches for Computer Aided Detection of Casting Defects in X-ray Images with Feature Engineering and Machine Learning. *Procedia Manufacturing, 37*, 394–401. doi:10.1016/j.promfg.2019.12.065

Yang, S., Li, X., Jia, X., Wang, Y., Zhao, H., & Lee, J. (2020). Deep Learning-Based Intelligent Defect Detection of Cutting Wheels with Industrial Images in Manufacturing. *Procedia Manufacturing, 48*, 902–907. doi:10.1016/j.promfg.2020.05.128

Yapraklı, T. Ş., & Erdal, H. (2016). Firma başarısızlığı tahminlemesi: makine öğrenmesine dayalı bir uygulama [Firm Failure Prediction: A Case Study Based on Machine Learning]. *International Journal of Informatics Technologies, 9*(1), 21–31.

Yıldız, K., & Buldu, A. (2017). Kumaş hata tespiti ve sınıflandırmada dalgacık dönüşümü ve temel bileşen analizi [Wavelet transform and principal component analysis in fabric defect detection and classification]. *Pamukkale University Journal of Engineering Sciences, 23*(5), 622–627. doi:10.5505/pajes.2016.80037

Zhang, H., Zhao, J., Yong, X., Zhang, C., & Ji, Y. (2017). Machine Learning Based Approaches for Medium-thick Plate Stress Analysis Feature Extraction and Product Defect Prediction. *2017 29th Chinese Control and Decision Conference (CCDC)*, 7252-7256, 10.1109/CCDC.2017.7978493

Zhang, H. T., Liu, C. T., Mao, J., Shen, C., Xie, R. L., & Mu, B. (2020). Development of novel in silico prediction model for drug-induced ototoxicity by using naïve Bayes classifier approach. *Journal of Toxicology in Vitro*, *65*(104812), 104812. doi:10.1016/j.tiv.2020.104812 PMID:32109528

Zhang, Z., Yang, Z., Ren, W., & Wen, G. (2019). Random forest-based real-time defect detection of Al alloy in robotic arc welding using optical spectrum. *Journal of Manufacturing Processes*, *42*, 51–59. doi:10.1016/j.jmapro.2019.04.023

Zhao, X., Cao, Y., Zhang, T., & Li, F. (2021). An improve feature selection algorithm for defect detection of glass bottles. *Applied Acoustics*, *174*(107794), 107794. doi:10.1016/j.apacoust.2020.107794

ADDITIONAL READING

Charniak, E., & McDermot, D. (1985). *Introduction to Artificial Intelligence*. Addison-Wesley Longman Publishing Co.

Gobeyn, S., Mouton, A. M., Cord, A. F., Kaim, A., Volk, M., & Goethals, P. L. (2019). Evolutionary algorithms for species distribution modelling: A review in the context of machine learning. *Ecological Modelling*, *392*, 179–195. doi:10.1016/j.ecolmodel.2018.11.013

Hornick, F. M., Marcadé, E., & Venkayala, S. (2007). *Java Data Mining: Strategy, Standard and Practice a Practical Guide for Architecture, Design and Implementation*. Morgan Kaufman. doi:10.1016/B978-012370452-8/50033-5

Li, L., Wu, Y., Ou, Y., Li, Q., Zhou, Y., & Chen, D. (2017, October). Research on machine learning algorithms and feature extraction for time series. In *2017 IEEE 28th annual international symposium on personal, indoor, and mobile radio communications (PIMRC)* (pp. 1-5). IEEE.

Mohammed, M., Khan, M. B., & Bashier, E. B. M. (2016). *Machine Learning: Algorithms and Applications*. CRC Press. doi:10.1201/9781315371658

Mohri, M., Rostamizadeh, A., & Talwalkar, A. (2012). *Foundations of Machine Learning*. The MIT Press.

Shearer, C. (2000). The CRISP-DM model: The new blueprint for data mining. *Journal of Data Warehousing*, *5*(4), 13–22.

Wen, L., Ye, X., & Gao, L. (2020). A new automatic machine learning based hyperparameter optimization for workpiece quality prediction. *Measurement and Control*, *53*(7-8), 1088–1098.

KEY TERMS AND DEFINITIONS

ANN: Artificial neural network.
GBM: Gradient boosting machine.
K-NN: K-nearest neighbour.
ML: Machine learning.
RF: Random forest.
SVM: Support vector machines.

Diving Into the Rabbit Hole:
Understanding Delegation of Decisions

Mateus Coimbra
Universidade Federal do Rio de Janeiro, Brazil

Paula Chimenti
Universidade Federal do Rio de Janeiro, Brazil

Roberto Nogueira
Universidade Federal do Rio de Janeiro, Brazil

INTRODUCTION

Experts have expressed concern about the excessive use of social media, with people systematically declaring to enter social networks for a specific purpose but leaving hours later after diving into the "rabbit hole" (The Guardian, 2020). Rabbit holes can also take on more physical contours, such as when a group of tourists accidentally sunk their car in a lake after following Waze's geolocation recommendations (Mail Online, 2018).

What might have seemed like science fiction a few years ago is now an actual part of our everyday lives. Indeed, Artificial Intelligence is increasingly helping and even replacing human decision-making (Adner & Kapoor, 2016). At the heart of this recent transformation is a technological revolution based on two elements: big data and decision-making algorithms (Chae, 2019). Both constitute strategic pillars of multinational corporations, such as Facebook and Google, which structure their business models based on them. These two elements are key pieces of a new world, in which artificial intelligence is gaining relevance.

Applications like Waze, YouTube and Netflix are fed everyday with huge volumes of data from consumer actions and attitudes. In return, they provide services, convenience, and support for decision-making. This increased participation in our lives raises questions about whether machines will make decisions on our behalf in the future. Although paramount for our future, there is a gap in the literature on decision transfer to machines and its logic. The existing decision-making literature focuses on human to human transfer (Otto et al., 2016; Steffel, M., Williams, E. F., & Perrmann-Graham, J., 2016; Steffel & Williams, 2017; Usta & Häubl, 2010), essentially ignoring the effects of people adopting machine decision-making. Meanwhile, the information technology (IT) literature investigating delegation to machines has focused on the benefits and problems of such delegation, with few articles trying to understand the factors that drive this behavior (Gogoll & Uhl, 2018; Goldbach, C., Kayar, D., Pitz, T., & Sickmann, J., 2019; Schneider & Leyer, 2019; Shrestha, Y. R., Ben-Menahem, S. M., & von Krogh, G., 2019).

Against this backdrop, the present study sought to understand the extent to which people are willing to transfer part of their hedonic decisions to algorithms and what factors motivate that choice. The main questions were as follows: How does this transfer mechanism work? What factors motivate this process? Therefore, this study proposed and tested a model of human delegation of hedonic consumption. The authors tried to understand how human–machine interaction works in a social media environment. The

DOI: 10.4018/978-1-7998-9220-5.ch014

Copyright © 2023, IGI Global. Copying or distributing in print or electronic forms without written permission of IGI Global is prohibited.

authors started with a comprehensive literature review, proposed a theoretical model identifying the mains drivers of the human-machine interaction mechanism, and then tested the model on YouTube users, using structural equation modeling.

The authors chose YouTube because of its relevance as the leading online video-sharing platform and the second-most popular website in the world, behind Google, reaching more than 2 billion users in 100 countries (Alexa Internet, 2020). Its recommendation system is a key feature, created to assist the platform in retaining users on the platform (Kim & Kim, 2018).

BACKGROUND

In this section, the evolution of the interaction between men and machines is discussed, presenting the theories that have emerged. This evolution was constituted from three main cycles: starting the debate about mechanical models on decision making, the aversion to these models and the adoption boom. This literature review was structured based on articles that discussed the interaction between human and machines. The articles were selected from the Scopus database based on the queries "human-machine interaction" and "human-application interaction." Only articles from peer-review journals were considered. The first cycle covers studies that show that machines are more accurate than humans. The second is characterized by studies that point to the emergence of people's aversion to machines in the decision-making process. The latter features articles that show people incorporating algorithms as a part of their decision-making process.

First Cycle: In his seminal book, *Clinical versus Statistical Forecasting*, Meehl (1954) introduced the debate about the possibility of predictions made by formulas. Subsequently, Meehl (1957) analyzed cases of clinical predictions in psychology, showing that human prediction was not better than statistics. Dawes and Corrigan (1974) discussed the effectiveness of applying linear models in decision-making. Dawes (1979) extended the debate to inappropriate linear models, whose variable weights are obtained intuitively. Dawes, R. M., Faust, D., & Meehl, P. E. (1989) confirmed that formulas are superior to the clinical model due to their greater accuracy and ability to understand the predictive capacity of each variable. Wiggins (1981) discussed the necessity of establishing better criteria for measuring variables and developing procedures that assist clinical forecasting. Grove and Meehl (1996) argued that professionals do not adopt mechanical methods for several reasons, such as a fear of unemployment due to technology, the value of their own image, being tied to old methods, the erroneous perception that automatic models would dehumanize patients, a dislike for computers competing against human minds, and a lack of knowledge. Grove, W. M., Zald, D. H., Lebow, B. S., Snitz, B. E., & Nelson, C. (2000) found that, on average, the mechanical method structured by an algorithm performed 10% better than clinical models based on humans.

Second Cycle: Over time, people's concern that their future would be decided by a mathematical method resulted in an aversion to the models. Studies debated that machines did not have the final say, often due to the perception of a human's ability to improve the expected result (Goodwin, 2000). People chose not to follow the decisions made by the machines and were more confident receiving advice from others (Wærn & Ramberg, 1996). Dietvorst, B. J., Simmons, J. P., & Massey, C. (2014) conducted experiments to analyze whether people trusted more the advice from a machine or an expert, revealing a preference for the latter. These findings were corroborated by Prahl and Van Swol (2017), who confirmed a greater aversion to algorithms after they provided bad advice. Regarding recommendation systems, a study concluded that, despite the greater accuracy of the machine's recommendations, people had an

D

aversion to this advice (Yeomans, M., Shah, A., Mullainathan, S., & Kleinberg, J., 2019). The second cycle is marked by studies that confirmed the findings of the first wave in terms of the model's effectiveness, but even with more effective algorithms, people felt that the final decision should be made by humans. Mechanical methods should be used as a source of information to support individuals' decisions.

Third Cycle: In another direction, Dijkstra (1999) showed that 79% of participants trusted the wrong advice presented by the system. Hertz and Wiese (2019) found that individuals tend to rely more on algorithms than on people. They also tend to have greater conformity in their decisions after having contact to virtual avatars, showing agreement with the algorithm's decision (Weger, U. W., Loughnan, S., Sharma, D., & Gonidis, L., 2015). Waytz, A., Heafner, J., & Epley, N. (2014) discovered that the transfer of human elements to machine could increase trust and the adoption of algorithms. Through experiments, Schroeder and Epley (2016) concluded that text voice synthesis produced the effect of anthropomorphism, leading individuals to think that it was a person's text. Longoni and Cian (2020) showed that people tend to prefer a hedonic recommendation when it comes from another human. However, this preference is reversed in situations of utilitarian choice. Currently, applications are a constant part of people's daily lives. Software focused on child learning demonstrates the relationship between machines and people (Martens, M., Rinnert, G. C., & Andersen, C., 2018). A study on the impact of safety applications behind the wheel found that many drivers use the apps along the way (Oviedo-Trespalacios, O., Williamson, A., & King, M., 2019). Researchers found that, through scheduled notifications from an app, they were able to improve people's psychological well-being, reducing stress and improving mood (Fitz, N., Kushlev, K., Jagannathan, R., Lewis, T., Paliwal, D., & Ariely, D., 2019).

The participation of machines in human decision-making has progressively increased. Applications and systems offering recommendations and advice have become a common part of people's everyday lives. In addition, recommendation systems are being improved so that people spend more time consuming products on business platforms (Zhao, Z., Chi, E., Hong, L., Wei, L., Chen, J., Nath, A., Andrews, S., Kumthekar, A., Sathiamoorthy, M., & Yi, X., 2019). This constant improvement of recommendation systems raises the question of whether we are starting a new cycle in which decisions will be made entirely by machines.

The literature on human–machine interaction has focused on the dichotomy of whether it is good or bad to use the machine in the decision-making process. Few studies have examined the factors that would assist in understanding the functioning of this human–machine interaction mechanism. Among the factors found, the authors can highlight the following: Institutional Trust, Value, Delegation, Intention to Use, and Satisfaction. However, several studies dealing with the use of social networks (e.g., YouTube) list factors that lead to this use. Because they deal with the use and choice of media, these factors can help us better understand this phenomenon. Drivers such as Customization, Decision Profile, Dependence, Escapism and Attitude also impact the use of the platform, which may influence the mechanism of human–machine interaction.

At this moment in the evolution of the interaction between human and machines, our research question seeks to understand how this mechanism and its motivations works. To achieve this goal, we conducted a survey with YouTube users. From the literature review were raised ten constructs, their dependency relantionship and the questions for the elaboration of the questionnaire. These constructs will be explained in the following model topic.

THE RESEARCH MODEL

The present work is a comprehensive study of the operation and motivations of the human–machine interaction mechanism on YouTube. Accordingly, the authors integrated different perspectives found in the literature into a comprehensive model in an attempt to explain which factors lead people to transfer their decision-making to algorithms. Before stating the hypotheses presented in this study, it is important to first describe its constructs. All the constructs used in this article were obtained from a review of social media literature and human-machine interaction. For each of these constructs, the dependency relationships between the variables and the questions for the survey were verified.

The model was composed of five independent variables. Customization refers to a greater degree of control over the type of information to which one is exposed when visiting a website (Chakraborty, G., Lala, V., & Warren, D. L., 2003). Escapism means that a person seeks to temporarily avoid, forget about, or escape from real-life stresses and problems (Dindar & Yaman, 2018). Institutional Trust means when individuals generalize their personal trust to large organizations comprised of individuals with whom they have low familiarity, low interdependence, and low continuity of interaction (Lewis & Weigert, 1985). Perceived Value captures how people internalize and become self-regulating with respect to activities that they experience as valuable for themselves (Alexander, V., Blinder, C., & Zak, P. J., 2018). Decision Profile refers to the decision-maker escaping conflict by procrastinating, shifting responsibility to someone else, or constructing wishful rationalizations to bolster the least objectionable alternative (Mann, L., Burnett, P., Radford, M., & Ford, S., 1997).

The model had two mediating variables. Attitude refers to a positive or negative predisposition that a person has towards an object, product, brand, or person (Ajzen & Fishbein, 1980; Davis, 1989). Delegation refers to the transfer of the decision responsibility from people to technology (Schneider & Leyer, 2019). Completing the model, three dependent variables were found in the literature. Dependence refers to a non-chemical and behavioral addiction that involves human–machine interaction (de Bérail, P., Guillon, M., & Bungener, C., 2019). Satisfaction refers to how well a person's expectations are met by a particular product or service (Oliver, 2010). Intention to Use refers to the intention to use YouTube in the future (Davis, 1989).

The research model main theoretical contribution is the integration of different research branches: decision delegation, technology adoption, dependence and social media platforms. In addition, the study proposes the creation of a new construct that evaluates the delegation of decisions to machines, studying its main motivators. The authors intended to analyze whether the delegation process for the machine works as an auxiliary route in the use of the platform, working in parallel with attitude. The model investigates whether these constructs impact the dependence that people may have on the use of the YouTube platform. Finally, the model seeks to understand whether the interaction mechanism leads to different impacts, such as dependence, satisfaction, and intention to use.

METHOD

This study has both descriptive and causal characteristics (Babbie, 2001). Our goal was to describe how the interaction mechanism works on the YouTube platform. The population of this study consists of YouTube users (Khan, 2017), because of its relevance as the leading online video-sharing platform. Its recommendation system is a key feature, created to assist the platform in retaining users on the platform (Kim & Kim, 2018). Through the recommendation system, it would be possible to verify the relationship of consumers with the platform, either through an active or passive posture.

The research was carried out using a survey with non-probabilistic snowball sampling (Morgan, 2008). The temporal approach was cross-sectional, studied in just an instant of time (Churchill & Iacobucci, 2009). The study used scales present in the literature, allowing comparison of the effects in different regions. The study used scales present in the literature, allowing comparison of the effects in different regions. The scales were translated into Portuguese and adapted to the context of this study. After the modifications, they were back-translated into English. The entire process of translation, adaptation, and back-translation was evaluated by experts on the subject. All questionnaire items are measured by a five-point Likert scale. Those scales, of an ordinal nature, can be used as intervals, allowing structural equation model (SEM) analysis (Hair, J. F., Black, W. C., Babin, B. J., & Anderson, R. E., 2010).

With the adapted scales, a questionnaire was prepared, and a pre-test was applied to a sample of 98 people. This step served to verify people's understanding of the stipulated questions as well as the existence of statistical problems, such as two constructs measuring the same effect. The feedback presented by the respondents was analyzed to make adjustments to the questionnaire and scales. The final version of the instrument measures ten constructs through 34 items. The final questionnaire was operationalized using the SurveyMonkey platform. The link to access the questionnaire was sent to respondents. A total of 338 cases were obtained, and after validation processing, there were 297 cases remaining. In the validation process, it was verified whether the respondents had answered all the questions in the questionnaire. In addition, the authors eliminate outliers for a better analysis of the model.

RESULTS

The main age group was 31 to 40 years old, with 73 respondents (25%), followed by 41 to 50 years old, with 61 respondents (21%). Analyzing the data by gender, an almost similar amount is observed among respondents, with women slightly in the majority (51%). In income, the range above R$ 18,000.00 had the highest number of respondents: 68 (23%), followed by R$ 1001 – R$ 4,250.00 and R$ 4,251 – R$ 8,500.00, with 55 (19%) respondents each. All statistics yielded adequate values, indicating that the constructs and the complete structural model were valid and reliable. Analysis was performed using SPSS and Amos 27 software.

In addition to the statistical parameters, the discriminant validities of each construct were assessed. The test compares the averaged extracted variance of each construct to the construct correlation with the other ones. The final model fit was assessed by three fit indices. The χ^2/df found was 1.587, which is below the threshold of 2.0 (Byrne, 2016). The CFI was 0.952, above the threshold of 0.9 (Hair et al., 2010). The last indicator, the RMSEA, was 0.045, falling below the threshold of 0.05 (Hair et al., 2010). The path coefficients were estimated using AMOS 27 maximum likelihood estimation and bootstrapping with 200 sub-samples. All the results of the variables are presented on Table 1 and all relationships can be seen in Figure 1.

DISCUSSION

Delegation in the decision-making literature is predominantly centered on humans (Aggarwal & Mazumdar, 2008; Buehler & Maas, 2018; Ende, J., Kazis, L., Ash, A., & Moskowitz, M. A., 1989; Gogoll & Uhl, 2018; Hollander & Rassuli, 1999; Otto et al., 2016; Steffel et al., 2016; Steffel & Williams, 2017; Usta & Häubl, 2010), with few studies addressing the human–machine relationship (Gogoll &

Figure 1. Model

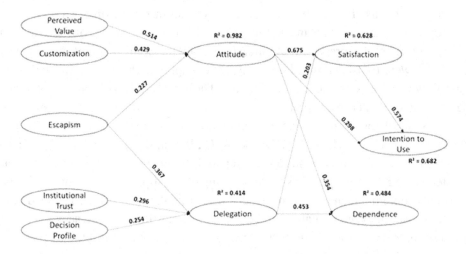

Uhl, 2018; Goldbach et al., 2019; Schneider & Leyer, 2019; Shrestha et al., 2019). In the present study, the authors proposed and tested a model that analyzes the mechanism of human–machine interaction in a social network. The motivators for accepting recommendations in digital platforms were identified and are discussed bellow.

Two Paths With Different Motivators

The results identified two well-defined routes: rational and peripheral. The first focuses on the rational characteristics of the individual and the second on the potential of the algorithm's recommendation. On the rational path, through Attitude, the individual is active in the decision-making process. He is conducting content searches on the platform. On the peripheral path, through delegation, the individual's focus is on using the platform's recommendations without thinking about them in a rational way.

According to the Elaboration Likelihood Model (ELM), the rational and peripheral route differ in the depth of cognitive information processing (Chang, H. H., Lu, Y.-Y., & Lin, S. C., 2020). The peripheral route is associated with a low level of information processing due to individuals investing less time in the analysis of the information, preferring to adhere to the recommendations of the algorithm. The individual makes less effort to analyze the variables involved in the process, choosing not to decide to consume. This phenomenon shows us that the decision profile, related to the lack of interest in deciding, positively impacts delegation. In this scenario where the individual focuses on external recommendations, the credibility of the source is important.

In the main route, there is high information processing, where the individual exerts a high analytical effort. Here, the focus is on the individual's ability to evaluate the information received. In this process, the person enacts an internal mechanism for analyzing the information obtained, being responsible for the decision. This phenomenon of internal analysis of received information demonstrates the impact of Perceived Value on Attitude. This relationship shows that people want to be self-regulating with respect to the activities that they experience. Furthermore, the way information is presented to people is crucial for a more assertive decision, highlighting the positive relationship between Customization and Attitude. A person with more control over the information received will make a consumption decision based on a deeper analysis of the information.

Table 1. Results

Construct	Items	Average Variance Extracted	Composite Reliability	Cronbach's Alpha	Squared Multiple Correlations
Customization	3	0.725	0.888	0.811	-
Escapism	3	0.713	0.881	0.798	-
Institutional Trust	3	0.742	0.896	0.828	-
Value	3	0.766	0.908	0.847	-
Decision Profile	3	0.755	0.902	0.837	-
Attitude	5	0.687	0.917	0.886	0.982
Delegation	3	0.682	0.866	0.768	0.414
Dependence	4	0.706	0.906	0.861	0.484
Satisfaction	4	0.76	0.927	0.894	0.628
Intention to Use	3	0.781	0.915	0.860	0.682
Hi	Path	Standardized Estimate	P		
H1	Customization -> Attitude	0.429	p<0,02		
H2	Escapism -> Attitude	0.227	p<0.03		
H3	Perceived Value -> Attitude	0.514	p<0.01		
H4	Decision Profile -> Delegation	0.254	p<0.02		
H5	Escapism -> Delegation	0.367	p<0.02		
H6	Institutional Trust -> Delegation	0.296	p<0.01		
H7	Attitude -> Dependence	0.354	p<0.02		
H8	Delegation -> Dependence	0.453	p<0.02		
H9	Attitude -> Satisfaction	0.675	p<0.01		
H10	Delegation -> Satisfaction	0.203	p<0.02		
H11	Satisfaction -> Intention to Use	0.574	p<0.02		
H12	Attitude -> Intention to Use	0.298	p<0.02		
Index	Value				
Root Mean Square Error of Approximation (RMSEA)	0.045				
Comparative Fit Index (CFI)	0.952				
χ^2/df	1.587				

According to Rhee and Choi (2020), in the peripheral route there is a low level of involvement with the result. The social recommendation is more impactful than the level of personalization. In contrast, in the main route, there is high motivation to involve with the decision-making. In this scenario, personalization is more important than social recommendation (Rhee & Choi, 2020). This phenomenon offers new insights to explain why customization impacts attitude (main route) and institutional trust impacts delegation (peripheral route).

Escapism: A Motivator in Both Routes

Escapism, which occurs when the individual wishes to escape from daily problems in an online environment, will be present in any interaction with a machine. This was demonstrated by the appearance of the variable in the two routes. Escapism leads people to use social media in search of fun, but this consumption of digital media can occur in a conscious or unconscious way, with the individual behaving actively or passively in the social network. While the active path is more related to experiencing positive experiences such as joy, the passive path may be linked to annoyance, regret, and sadness (Altuwairiqi, M., Jiang, N., & Ali, R., 2019). According to Hagström and Kaldo (2014), there are two types of escapism, positive and negative. This means that people seek to escape because they want to avoid dealing with a stressful situation in their life (negative) or because they want to experience a fantasy mental situation, without necessarily having a negative (positive) motivator. The presence of escapism in both routes could show that there are two types of reasons for escaping to a social network. This result could explain escapism being a motivator of both routes: central and peripheral. The first one has a rational nature, where the individual intentionally searches the content on YouTube in a proactive way (main route). The second is less rational, where the user follows a recommendation (peripheral route).

Same Influence With Different Impacts – Satisfaction And Dependence

According to Jeong, J., Sohn, K., & Kwon, O. (2019), a YouTube recommendation directed to the individual's interests leads to satisfaction. This phenomenon shows the impact of Delegation on Satisfaction. At the same time, both paths can lead to dependence. In the case of attitude, this behavior can be attributed to a negative predisposition for that decision, and in the case of delegation, to a generation of a new habit based on desired responses.

This impact can be better understood through the decision-making literature. According to the theory developed by Bandura (1977), self-efficacy can be defined as people's belief in their own abilities to control the events that occur in their own lives. This variable has been the subject of several studies, which demonstrated the influence of this variable on the degree of dependence developed by a person. Hasan, M. R., Jha, A. K., & Liu, Y (2018) found that a lack of self-efficacy can lead to dependence on online video services. In addition, people will delegate less if they have a greater perception of their ability to control the events that occur in their lives (Buehler & Maas, 2018). Ifinedo (2018) identified that a person's self-efficacy leads to satisfaction in the use of technology. Similarly, Che et al. (2017) found that, while a lack of self-control leads to addiction, the presence of this characteristic prevents this behavior.

FUTURE RESEARCH DIRECTIONS

In addition to verifying the phenomenon on other platforms, future studies could propose new independent constructs for motivators of the interaction mechanism. Options might include guilt, regret of the decision, effort in carrying out the task, personalities, social anxiety, or emotions, such as loneliness, anxiety, and stress. Another possibility would be to expand the concept of decision delegation and its applications. In this study, delegation was observed through the individual's passivity before receiving the platform's recommendations. This effect was measured through automatic YouTube playback. Expanding the concept to scenarios including all of the platform's functionalities instead of focusing only on automatic playback would be a direction for future research.

CONCLUSION

The first cycle was marked by the emergence of a debate on the possibility of decision-making by the machine. The authors realized that, in certain situations, the result achieved by models was consistently better. They realized that the algorithm could handle a greater magnitude of information rather than just relying on certain key variables. This study was carried out using a survey with a sample of 297 YouTube users. Through the realization of a model of structural equations, the authors measured the variables and their relationships. Our proposed model advances the current theory unifying variables from two streams of the literature: human–machine interaction and social networks. This union provides us with a broader view of the phenomenon, helping us to understand human–machine interaction in social networks.

Throughout this work, the authors seek to answer two questions: how the human–machine interaction mechanism works in social media and which factors motivate this process. In the first question, the authors observed the existence of two interaction routes: the main and the peripheral. While the main route is characterized by a greater participation of the individual in decision-making, in the peripheral route the person follows the recommendations of the algorithm. The identification of a peripheral route shows the participation of the algorithm in the decision-making process. The results point to possible full delegation in the future, where the entire decision-making process is done by algorithms.

Regarding the second question, the proposed model showed that five variables influenced the human–machine interaction. Only Escapism proved to be a motivator of both routes, with Perceived Value and Customization being motivators in the main route and Institutional Trust and Decision Profile in the peripheral route. This result shows that, to obtain a better understanding of the interaction mechanism, variables regarding the social network and the individual must be considered.

This work contributes to the academic debate, bringing a new view of the human–machine interaction mechanism. The proposed model applies and shows the operation of this interaction in a social network. In addition, it hints at the possibility of breaking the third cycle, with the emergence of a new paradigm in which decision-making will be carried out entirely by artificial intelligence algorithms. The constant capture of data by machine-learning algorithms could lead to passive participation of individuals in decision-making in digital environments.

In the managerial sphere, the study shows that companies must consider people's trust in the institution. As observed throughout all the cycles of the literature review, and as corroborated by the model, the trust relationship between companies and individuals is fundamental to a good relationship. Examples like Cambridge Analytica/Facebook or Microsoft Twitter chatter bot could contribute to the impact on the company's brand.

In the policymaker sphere, the model showed that the main route leads to greater satisfaction, while the peripheral route tends to be more dependent on the social network. This scenario raises the need for debate, as constant interaction with machines could result in dependence on social networks. This dependence is a concern with the health of individuals. Thus, health protocols must consider emotional aspects and the individual's mental and emotional situation. While using machines has practical advantages, such as easy access to information or less mental effort in the choice process, it also has emotional disadvantages, such as loneliness, low self-esteem, and a way of escaping from daily problems. These elements contribute to a greater isolation of the person.

The results of this work must be analyzed considering its limitations. First, the study used only the YouTube platform to understand the phenomenon of decision delegation for algorithms. A possibility for future study would be to verify if the results are consistent with other digital platforms, such as Facebook and Instagram. In addition, this study could have a sampling bias, as all the data were collected through the snowball method. Finally, the study focused on hedonic consumption, and this topic deserves further studies.

REFERENCES

Adner, R., & Kapoor, R. (2016). Disruption: It's not the tech, it's the timing. *Harvard Business Review*, 1–13.

Aggarwal, P., & Mazumdar, T. (2008). Decision delegation: A conceptualization and empirical investigation. *Psychology and Marketing*, *25*(1), 71–93. doi:10.1002/mar.20201

Ajzen, I., & Fishbein, M. (1980). *Understanding Attitudes and Predicting Social Behavior*. Prentice Hall.

Alexa Internet. (2020). *Youtube para a Imprensa*. https://www.youtube.com/about/press/

Alexander, V., Blinder, C., & Zak, P. J. (2018). Why trust an algorithm? Performance, cognition, and neurophysiology. *Computers in Human Behavior*, *89*, 279–288. doi:10.1016/j.chb.2018.07.026

Altuwairiqi, M., Jiang, N., & Ali, R. (2019). Problematic attachment to social media: Five behavioural archetypes. *International Journal of Environmental Research and Public Health*, *16*(12), 2136. doi:10.3390/ijerph16122136 PMID:31212899

Babbie, E. R. (2001). *The Practice of Social Research*. Wadsworth.

Bandura, A. (1977). Self-efficacy: Toward a unifying theory of behavioral change. *Psychological Review*, *84*(2), 191–215. doi:10.1037/0033-295X.84.2.191 PMID:847061

Buehler, P., & Maas, P. (2018). Consumer empowerment in insurance: Effects on performance risk perceptions in decision making. *International Journal of Bank Marketing*, *36*(6), 1073–1097. doi:10.1108/IJBM-12-2016-0182

Byrne, B. (2016). *Structural Equation Modeling with AMOS: Basic Concepts, Applications, and Programming* (3rd ed.). Routledge. doi:10.4324/9781315757421

Chae, B. (2019). A General framework for studying the evolution of the digital innovation ecosystem: The case of big data. *International Journal of Information Management*, *45*, 83–94. doi:10.1016/j.ijinfomgt.2018.10.023

Chakraborty, G., Lala, V., & Warren, D. L. (2003). What do customers consider important in B2B websites? *Journal of Advertising Research*, *43*(1), 50–61. doi:10.2501/JAR-43-1-50-61

Chang, H. H., Lu, Y.-Y., & Lin, S. C. (2020). An elaboration likelihood model of consumer respond action to facebook second-hand marketplace: Impulsiveness as a moderator. *Information & Management*, *57*(2), 103171. doi:10.1016/j.im.2019.103171

Che, D., Hu, J., Zhen, S., Yu, C., Li, B., Chang, X., & Zhang, W. (2017). Dimensions of emotional intelligence and online gaming addiction in adolescence: The indirect effects of two facets of perceived stress. *Frontiers in Psychology*, *8*, 1206. doi:10.3389/fpsyg.2017.01206 PMID:28751876

Churchill, G. A., & Iacobucci, D. (2009). *Marketing Research: Methodological Foundations*. South-Western College Pub.

Davis, F. D. (1989). Perceived usefulness, perceived ease of use, and user acceptance of information technology. *Management Information Systems Quarterly*, *13*(3), 319. doi:10.2307/249008

Dawes, R. M. (1979). The robust beauty of improper linear models. *The American Psychologist*, *34*(7), 571–582. doi:10.1037/0003-066X.34.7.571

Dawes, R. M., & Corrigan, B. (1974). Linear models in decision making. *Psychological Bulletin*, *81*(2), 95–106. doi:10.1037/h0037613

Dawes, R. M., Faust, D., & Meehl, P. E. (1989). Clinical versus actuarial judgment. *Science*, *243*(4899), 7. doi:10.1126cience.2648573 PMID:2648573

de Bérail, P., Guillon, M., & Bungener, C. (2019). The relations between YouTube addiction, social anxiety and parasocial relationships with YouTubers: A moderated-mediation model based on a cognitive-behavioral framework. *Computers in Human Behavior*, *99*, 190–204. doi:10.1016/j.chb.2019.05.007

Dietvorst, B. J., Simmons, J. P., & Massey, C. (2014). Algorithm aversion: People erroneously avoid algorithms after seeing them err. *Journal of Experimental Psychology. General*, ●●●, 13. PMID:25401381

Dijkstra, J. J. (1999). User agreement with incorrect expert system advice. *Behaviour & Information Technology*, *18*(6), 399–411. doi:10.1080/014492999118832

Dindar, M., & Yaman, N. D. (2018). #IUseTwitterBecause: Content analytic study of a trending topic in Twitter. *Information Technology & People*, *31*(1), 256–277. doi:10.1108/ITP-02-2017-0029

Ende, J., Kazis, L., Ash, A., & Moskowitz, M. A. (1989). Measuring patients' desire for autonomy: Decision making and information-seeking preferences among medical patients. *Journal of General Internal Medicine*, *4*(1), 23–30. doi:10.1007/BF02596485 PMID:2644407

Fitz, N., Kushlev, K., Jagannathan, R., Lewis, T., Paliwal, D., & Ariely, D. (2019). Batching smartphone notifications can improve well-being. *Computers in Human Behavior*, *101*, 84–94. doi:10.1016/j.chb.2019.07.016

Gogoll, J., & Uhl, M. (2018). Rage against the machine: Automation in the moral domain. *Journal of Behavioral and Experimental Economics*, *74*, 97–103. doi:10.1016/j.socec.2018.04.003

Goldbach, C., Kayar, D., Pitz, T., & Sickmann, J. (2019). Transferring decisions to an algorithm: A simple route choice experiment. *Transportation Research Part F: Traffic Psychology and Behaviour*, *65*, 402–417. doi:10.1016/j.trf.2019.08.011

Goodwin, P. (2000). Improving the voluntary integration of statistical forecasts and judgment. *International Journal of Forecasting*, *16*(1), 85–99. doi:10.1016/S0169-2070(99)00026-6

Grove, W. M., & Meehl, P. E. (1996). Comparative Efficiency of Informal (Subjective, Impressionistic) and Formal (Mechanical, Algorithmic) Prediction Procedures: The Clinical-Statistical Controversy. *Psychology, Public Policy, and Law*, *2*(2), 293–323. doi:10.1037/1076-8971.2.2.293

Grove, W. M., Zald, D. H., Lebow, B. S., Snitz, B. E., & Nelson, C. (2000). Clinical versus mechanical prediction: A meta-analysis. *Psychological Assessment*, *12*(1), 19–30. doi:10.1037/1040-3590.12.1.19 PMID:10752360

Hagström, D., & Kaldo, V. (2014). Escapism among players of MMORPGs—Conceptual clarification, its relation to mental health factors, and development of a new measure. *Cyberpsychology, Behavior, and Social Networking, 17*(1), 19–25. doi:10.1089/cyber.2012.0222 PMID:24003967

Hair, J. F., Black, W. C., Babin, B. J., & Anderson, R. E. (2010). *Multivariate Data Analysis*. Prentice-Hall.

Hasan, M. R., Jha, A. K., & Liu, Y. (2018). Excessive use of online video streaming services: Impact of recommender system use, psychological factors, and motives. *Computers in Human Behavior, 80,* 220–228. doi:10.1016/j.chb.2017.11.020

Hertz, N., & Wiese, E. (2019). Good advice is beyond all price, but what if it comes from a machine? *Journal of Experimental Psychology. Applied, 25*(3), 28. doi:10.1037/xap0000205 PMID:30702316

Hollander, S. C., & Rassuli, K. M. (1999). Shopping with other people's money: The marketing management implications of surrogate-mediated consumer decision making. *Journal of Marketing, 63*(2), 102–118. doi:10.1177/002224299906300207

Ifinedo, P. (2018). Determinants of students' continuance intention to use blogs to learn: An empirical investigation. *Behaviour & Information Technology, 37*(4), 381–392. doi:10.1080/0144929X.2018.1436594

Jeong, J., Sohn, K., & Kwon, O. (2019). The effects of content and distribution of recommended items on user satisfaction: Focus on YouTube. *Asia Pacific Journal of Information Systems, 29*(4), 856–874. doi:10.14329/apjis.2019.29.4.856

Khan, M. L. (2017). Social media engagement: What motivates user participation and consumption on YouTube? *Computers in Human Behavior, 66,* 236–247. doi:10.1016/j.chb.2016.09.024

Kim, M. S., & Kim, S. (2018). Factors influencing willingness to provide personal information for personalized recommendations. *Computers in Human Behavior, 88,* 143–152. doi:10.1016/j.chb.2018.06.031

Lewis, J. D., & Weigert, A. (1985). Trust as a social reality. *Social Forces, 63*(4), 967–985. doi:10.2307/2578601

Longoni, C., & Cian, L. (2020). Artificial intelligence in utilitarian vs. hedonic contexts: The "word-of-machine" effect. *Journal of Marketing,* 1–18.

Mail Online. (2018). *Tourists drive into lake champlain after waze directed them down a boat ramp into the freezing waters.* https://www.dailymail.co.uk/news/article-5308303/Waze-directed-tourists-drive-lake.html

Mann, L., Burnett, P., Radford, M., & Ford, S. (1997). The melbourne decision making questionnaire: An instrument for measuring patterns for coping with decisional conflict. *Journal of Behavioral Decision Making, 10*(1), 19. doi:10.1002/(SICI)1099-0771(199703)10:1<1::AID-BDM242>3.0.CO;2-X

Martens, M., Rinnert, G. C., & Andersen, C. (2018). Child-Centered design: Developing an inclusive letter writing app. *Frontiers in Psychology, 9,* 2277. doi:10.3389/fpsyg.2018.02277 PMID:30574104

Meehl, P. E. (1954). *A Theoretical Analysis and a Review of the Evidence.* Univesity of Minnesota Press.

Meehl, P. E. (1957). When shall we use our heads instead of the formula? *Journal of Counseling Psychology, 4*(4), 268–273. doi:10.1037/h0047554

Morgan, D. L. (2008). *The SAGE encyclopedia of qualitative research methods.* SAGE Publications.

Oliver, R. (2010). *Satisfaction: A Behavioral Perspective on the Consumer*. Routledge.

Otto, A. S., Clarkson, J. J., & Kardes, F. R. (2016). Decision sidestepping: How the motivation for closure prompts individuals to bypass decision making. *Journal of Personality and Social Psychology*, *111*(1), 1–16. doi:10.1037/pspa0000057 PMID:27337138

Oviedo-Trespalacios, O., Williamson, A., & King, M. (2019). User preferences and design recommendations for voluntary smartphone applications to prevent distracted driving. *Transportation Research Part F: Traffic Psychology and Behaviour*, *64*, 47–57. doi:10.1016/j.trf.2019.04.018

Prahl, A., & Van Swol, L. (2017). Understanding algorithm aversion: When is advice from automation discounted? *Journal of Forecasting*, *36*(6), 691–702. doi:10.1002/for.2464

Rhee, C. E., & Choi, J. (2020). Effects of personalization and social role in voice shopping: An experimental study on product recommendation by a conversational voice agent. *Computers in Human Behavior*, *109*, 106359. doi:10.1016/j.chb.2020.106359

Schneider, S., & Leyer, M. (2019). Me or information technology? Adoption of artificial intelligence in the delegation of personal strategic decisions. *Managerial and Decision Economics*, *40*(3), 1–9. doi:10.1002/mde.2982

Schroeder, J., & Epley, N. (2016). Mistaking minds and machines: How speech affects dehumanization and anthropomorphism. *Journal of Experimental Psychology. General*, *145*(11), 1427–1437. doi:10.1037/xge0000214 PMID:27513307

Shrestha, Y. R., Ben-Menahem, S. M., & von Krogh, G. (2019). Organizational Decision-Making Structures in the Age of Artificial Intelligence. *California Management Review*, *61*(4), 66–83. doi:10.1177/0008125619862257

Steffel, M., & Williams, E. F. (2017). Delegating decisions: Recruiting others to make choices we might regret. *The Journal of Consumer Research*, *44*(5), 1015–1032. doi:10.1093/jcr/ucx080

Steffel, M., Williams, E. F., & Perrmann-Graham, J. (2016). Passing the buck: Delegating choices to others to avoid responsibility and blame. *Organizational Behavior and Human Decision Processes*, *135*, 32–44. doi:10.1016/j.obhdp.2016.04.006

The Guardian. (2020). *Down the rabbit hole: How QAnon conspiracies thrive on Facebook*. https://www.theguardian.com/technology/2020/jun/25/qanon-facebook-conspiracy-theories-algorithm

Usta, M., & Häubl, G. (2010). Self-regulatory strength and consumers' relinquishment of decision Control: When less effortful decisions are More resource depleting. *JMR, Journal of Marketing Research*, *48*(2), 403–412. doi:10.1509/jmkr.48.2.403

Wærn, Y., & Ramberg, R. (1996). People's perception of human and computer advice. *Computers in Human Behavior*, *12*(1), 17–27. doi:10.1016/0747-5632(95)00016-X

Waytz, A., Heafner, J., & Epley, N. (2014). The mind in the machine: Anthropomorphism increases trust in an autonomous vehicle. *Journal of Experimental Social Psychology*, *52*, 113–117. doi:10.1016/j.jesp.2014.01.005

Weger, U. W., Loughnan, S., Sharma, D., & Gonidis, L. (2015). Virtually compliant: Immersive video gaming increases conformity to false computer judgments. *Psychonomic Bulletin & Review*, *22*(4), 1111–1116. doi:10.375813423-014-0778-z PMID:25585527

Wiggins, J. S. (1981). Clinical and statistical prediction. *Clinical Psychology Review*, *1*(1), 3–18. doi:10.1016/0272-7358(81)90015-5

Yeomans, M., Shah, A., Mullainathan, S., & Kleinberg, J. (2019). Making sense of recommendations. *Journal of Behavioral Decision Making*, *32*(4), 403–414. doi:10.1002/bdm.2118

Zhao, Z., Chi, E., Hong, L., Wei, L., Chen, J., Nath, A., Andrews, S., Kumthekar, A., Sathiamoorthy, M., & Yi, X. (2019). Recommending what video to watch next: A multitask ranking system. *Proceedings of the 13th ACM Conference on Recommender Systems - RecSys '19*, 43–51. 10.1145/3298689.3346997

ADDITIONAL READING

Akter, S., Fosso Wamba, S., Gunasekaran, A., Dubey, R., & Childe, S. J. (2016). How to improve firm performance using big data analytics capability and business strategy alignment? *International Journal of Production Economics*, *182*, 113–131. doi:10.1016/j.ijpe.2016.08.018

André, Q., Carmon, Z., Wertenbroch, K., Crum, A., Frank, D., Goldstein, W., Huber, J., van Boven, L., Weber, B., & Yang, H. (2018). Consumer choice and autonomy in the age of artificial intelligence and big data. *Customer Needs and Solutions*, *5*(1–2), 28–37. doi:10.100740547-017-0085-8

Assunção, M. D., Calheiros, R. N., Bianchi, S., Netto, M. A. S., & Buyya, R. (2015). Big Data computing and clouds: Trends and future directions. *Journal of Parallel and Distributed Computing*, *79–80*, 3–15. doi:10.1016/j.jpdc.2014.08.003

Balakrishnan, J., & Griffiths, M. D. (2017). Social media addiction: What is the role of content in YouTube? *Journal of Behavioral Addictions*, *6*(3), 364–377. doi:10.1556/2006.6.2017.058 PMID:28914072

Bello-Orgaz, G., Jung, J. J., & Camacho, D. (2016). Social big data: Recent achievements and new challenges. *Information Fusion*, *28*, 45–59. doi:10.1016/j.inffus.2015.08.005 PMID:32288689

Blazquez, D., & Domenech, J. (2018). Big data sources and methods for social and economic analyses. *Technological Forecasting and Social Change*, *130*, 99–113. doi:10.1016/j.techfore.2017.07.027

Chen, H., Chiang, R. H. L., & Storey, V. C. (2012). Business intelligence and analytics: From big data to big impact. *Management Information Systems Quarterly*, *36*(4), 25. doi:10.2307/41703503

Sivarajah, U., Kamal, M. M., Irani, Z., & Weerakkody, V. (2017). Critical analysis of big data challenges and analytical methods. *Journal of Business Research*, *70*, 263–286. doi:10.1016/j.jbusres.2016.08.001

KEY TERMS AND DEFINITIONS

D

Attitude: A positive or negative predisposition that a person has towards an object, product, brand, or person (Ajzen & Fishbein, 1980; Davis, 1989).

Delegation: The transfer of the decision responsibility from people to technology (Schneider & Leyer, 2019).

Dependence: A non-chemical and behavioral addiction that involves human–machine interaction (de Bérail, Guillon, &. Bungener, 2019).

Satisfaction: How well a person's expectations are met by a particular product or service (Oliver, 2010).

Importance of AI and ML Towards Smart Sensor Network Utility Enhancement

Sudipta Sahana

iD https://orcid.org/0000-0002-9694-6399

University of Engineering and Management, Kolkata, India

Dharmpal Singh

JIS University, India

Ira Nath

JIS College of Engineering, India

INTRODUCTION

Smart sensor networks are a developing innovation because of late progressions in little scope manufacturability and high-scale mix of different electronic segments in a solitary packaging. A distinctive sensor node (or mote) is an independent bundle of gadgets important to hold various sensors, an inserted microcontroller, a force unit that has restricted limit, which might possibly be sustainable, and a radio transreceiver at its centre. Typical size of a sensor hub is anyplace from a matchbox to a coin, however is relied upon to recoil drastically in the following decade with the energizing guarantee of nanotechnology assembling and creation.

The concept of inclusion of AI & ML are extremely powerful: both of them permits systems to program themselves and advance their performance through a process of unceasing improvement. In regular frameworks, data and codes are essentially run together to deliver the desired output, leaving any issues to be gotten or enhancements to be made by the developer. In divergence, AI & ML systems use the data and the resulting output to develop the code. This program can then be used in conjunction with traditional programming.

Smart Sensor Network

Smart Sensor Networks offers another worldview respect to the way that the customary checking frameworks have been planned, this occurs because of the impact generating by innovation in the public eye. The sending of Data and Transmission strategies or ICT permit us presently depend with little gadgets that can incorporate into the "simple elements" the capability for registering, correspondence and then checking frameworks from here begins to move to those mini devices, capacity of insight that guarantee the arrangement for new frameworks centered in ecological monitoring.

Lately, the most important of the developing innovations that partake a large effect over the arena of exploration for Wireless Smart Sensor Networks assorted variety of highlights and submissions. In its earlier days in Massachusetts Institute of Technology (MIT) were destined as one of the ten revolutions that will astonish the changes in the world (Ayodele, 2010). With a foundation, those systems were equipped and includes components of checking, registering and correspondence and provide for his chief

DOI: 10.4018/978-1-7998-9220-5.ch015

Copyright © 2023, IGI Global. Copying or distributing in print or electronic forms without written permission of IGI Global is prohibited.

that could be the legislature, common, modern and business segments the capacity of instrument, watch, and respond to occasions and wonders in a predetermined domain (Duffy, 1997). Sensor Network will in general extend exponentially as it were with the goal that these little gadgets can be effortlessly sent anyplace and gather any data from the earth. Since this innovation is as yet developing in the social, market infiltration is as yet asking beginning, however there are various examination bunches dynamic in joining the investigation and checking of numerous marvels. In this regard, there are now communities for gathering and preparing information that are being transferred by WSSN, which is the major status of Sensor Signal and Information Processing Center (SENSIP) (Langley & Simon, 1995) drove by the University of Arizona, United States. There are moreover research centers who are simply working here is the circumstance of Center for Embedded Networked Sensing (CENS) (Paradis & Han, 2007) drove for different schools in the United States. Relating for this, the improvement of checking structures subject to downsized smaller than usual solid-state development allows a tremendous noticing structure using Micro-Electro-Mechanical Systems (MEMS) sensors which consolidate for a sort of nano scale electrical, warm, mechanical, optical or stream, among others (Krishnamachari et al., 2002). Then again, for the ecological supervision is one of the principle regions of utilization of this innovation because of its attributes that permit the estimation of boundaries in various natural settings, for example, crop the board, insurance of backwoods fires, horticulture, tremors, dynamic fountain of liquid magma, it is additionally conceivable to utilize large scale instruments for estimating boundaries of enormous scope, for example, avalanches, barometrical meteorology, lastly contamination reads (Al-Karaki & Kamal, 2004) or in any event, for planetary investigation. (Romer & Mattern, 2004)

The essential goal of an intelligent sensor network generally relies on the application; however, the resulting obligations are regular to various organizations.

Choose the assessment of some boundaries for a given territory: In the biological organizations, one might need to know about the temperature, barometrical weights, proportion of the light, and the general dampness in different regions. The model shows that a given sensor center may be related with different kinds of sensors, each with the other reviewing rate and extent and allowed regards.

Distinguish the events manifestation of intrigue and the gauge boundaries for the identified event(s): In the rush hour the gridlock sensor organization, that one might want to recognize for a vehicle traveling through a convergence and will gauge the speed and bearing of the vehicle.

Sensed entity being categorized: It is a vehicle in a rush hour gridlock sensor network a vehicle, a little van, a light truck, a transport, and so on

Entity monitoring: In a military sensor network, track an enemy tank as it moves through the network.

In these four assignments, a huge need of the sensor network is that the vital data be spread to the right end customers. Once in a while, there are really extreme time necessities on this correspondence. For example, the acknowledgment of an intruder in an observation association should be instantly granted to the police with the objective that move can be made.

Type of Sensing

For better communication with ease, short-range radios are showing signs of progress in wireless systems administration, and it's basically that smart sensor networks will turn out to be generally sent. In the following networks, every hub would be outfitted with an assortment of sensors, for example, acoustic, seismic, infrared, actually/movement camcorder, etc.

The hubs might be classified in bunches with the end goal that will be a locally happening occasion that can be distinguished by the greater part of, if not everyone in the hubs. Every hub will be having adequate preparing capacity to decide between several choices, and it will have the option to communicate their choices to different hubs in the groups. One hub might go as the group ace or expert, and it might also contain more extended territory radio, utilizing a convention, for example, IEEE 802.11, Bluetooth, or use Bluestone restrictive steering calculations.

Smart Sensing Technology

A smart sensor is a device that will take input from the physical conditions and uses a built-in compute resources to perform a predefined endless supply of data and information, upon detection of some specific input and then process those data before passing it on. Smart sensors are characterized as sensors furnished with signal molding, implanted calculations, and computerized interfaces. A smart sensor might likewise incorporate various different parts, for example, transducers, speakers, excitation control, simple channels, and remuneration. They have as of late become exceptionally received in versatile and compact gadgets, for example, telephones and tablets.

Smart sensors enable the more accurate and automated collection of conditional data with less erroneous noise amongst the accurately recorded information. These gadgets are commonly used for observing and controlling systems in various situations like smart matrices, combat zone observation, investigation, and an incredible number of uses in science applications.

The smart sensors would also be a crucial and integral element in the Internet of Things (IoT), that increasingly prevalent environment in which almost anything imaginable can be outfitted with a unique identifier (UID) and the ability to transmit data over the Internet or a similar network. One execution of smart sensors is as parts of a Wireless Sensor and actuator of organization (WSAN) and those hubs can be number in thousands, every one of which is associated with at least one different sensors and sensor centers just as individual actuators.

There are many innovative applications in the sensor segment. For instance, Swiss electrical measurement specialists LEM are achieving accomplishment by aiming at measurement excellence for industrial and automotive applications. Mobileye, an Israeli organization that creates progressed vision-based driver emotionally supportive networks using low-power, reasonable registering stages that run a complex article acknowledgment calculation dependent on fake neural networks. Also, Amazon prevailing in the field of smart sensors by creating Echo, which interfaces with the cloud-based Alexa Voice Service to play music, order online, make appointments, pose inquiries, settle on decisions, send messages, and the sky is the limit from there.

A case of smart sensor systems is pocket-type gas detectors prepared to do specifically estimating gases such as hydrogen, hydrogen sulfide, carbon monoxide, and ozone, working on a solitary battery for a year or more. This group of pocket-sized gas finder systems is explicitly intended to be an easy and low force while additionally having a long battery life.

The future of the smart sensor is limitless, some of the ongoing advancement are:

- Encryption libraries – AES/RSA cryptography for sensor networks
- 3G availability to ZigBee, Wi-Fi, and Bluetooth sensors
- Smartphones and Android gadgets recognized by smart sensors
- e-Health Sensor Shield
- Smart lighting sensor answers for smart urban communities

Compared to basic sensors the advantages of smart sensor systems are as follows:

- High reliability and high performance
- Minimum interconnecting cables
- Scalable, flexible system
- Small, rugged packaging
- Minimum cost
- Easy to design, use, and maintain

Smart sensors improve the quality of the following applications:

- Computation
- Cost effectiveness
- Multisensing
- Self-calibration
- Communication

Smart sensors are a crucial and necessary component in the Internet of Things (IoT), and as parts of a remote sensor and actuator organization (WSAN), smart sensors give advanced information and various types of data. Consequently, smart sensors have taken a very important place in the present day of the innovative world. From route frameworks in mobile phones and smart wearable frameworks for wellbeing observing to self-ruling driving, are developing continuously. Smart sensors such as signal molding, inserted capacities, and computerized interfaces, are progressively being received by the cell phone, shopper, and mechanical business sectors, similarly steadily supplanting fundamental sensors.

Signal Processing of Sensor Data

No signal is created without a proper framework set up. The sensors are there just to catch the information. Frameworks can be characteristic systems (Ex. Surface temp. of seas) or man-made systems (Ex. fabricating measures) or essentially inspected data (Ex. Stock costs).

The theory is "The vast majority of the wonder happening in a cycle/framework are caught as various recurrence segments of the sign ".

It's this thought that helps in information mining measure. For instance, Lets state you have a cycle which has temperature sensor which creates a sign. This sign is only temperatures caught at unit time say per second(sampling).

Expect your cycle is fabricating an item. Presently the cycle is redundant; so, in the event that you fabricate 100 such items, at that point you have 100-time arrangement signals.

Presently you need to order which of these items are acceptable and awful. Also, the main you have is time arrangement signals.

At that point from each such time arrangement you can extricate includes and make your own component vector and utilize any off the rack order calculation to group an item as positive or negative.

It's this element extraction where sign preparing fills in as a device.

In light of what are you attempting to accomplish, and the given sign one can utilize any of the beneath signal preparing apparatuses for highlight extraction.

1. Fourier Transforms.

2. Wavelet Transforms.
3. Wigner-Ville conveyances.
4. Experimental Mode disintegration.

The entirety of the above instruments gives frequencies/recurrence groups as yield. Furthermore, every recurrence in a sign compares to a specific wonder happening in a framework.

So fundamentally in the above model we performed time arrangement grouping utilizing signal preparing procedures.

Factual sign preparing has numerous utilizations for instance framework investigation. main driver investigation, determining etc.

Multimodal Smart Sensing

Wireless sensor networks (WSNs) are a generally utilized solution for observing focused applications (e.g., water quality on watersheds, contamination checking in urban areas). These sorts of utilizations are described by the need of two information announcing modes: time-driven and occasion driven. The previous is utilized basically for ceaselessly directing a zone and the last for occasion recognition and following. By exchanging between the two modes, a WSN can improve its vitality effectiveness and occasion detailing dormancy, contrasted with single information announcing plans. We allude to those WSNs, where both information revealing modes are required all the while, as multimodal wireless sensor networks.

Multimodal learning unites a progression of disengaged, heterogenous information from different sensors and information contributions to a solitary model. In contrast to customary unimodal learning frameworks, multimodal frameworks can convey reciprocal data about one another, which will possibly become clear when they are both remembered for the learning cycle. Accordingly, learning-based strategies that join signals from various modalities are fit for producing more hearty induction, or even new bits of knowledge, which would be incomprehensible in a unimodal framework.

Multimodal learning presents two essential advantages:

Different sensors watching a similar information can make more powerful expectations, since recognizing changes in it might possibly be conceivable when the two modalities are available.

The combination of numerous sensors can encourage the catch of corresponding data or patterns that may not be caught by singular modalities.

ARTIFICIAL INTELLIGENCE SENSORS (HODGE & AUSTIN, 2004)

Pressure Sensors

These sensors are nowadays the centre of limelight with their utilities ranging across a diverse range of avenues. The main principle of a pressure sensor is to convert the pressure obtained into a function form, which is usually in a form of an electrical signal. Thus, a pressure sensor usually acts as a transducer. There are several types of sensors, which can be used according to the needs of the user. Different technologies are used in these sensors so that they are capable of providing better and more accurate results. Piezo-resistive pressure sensors, capacitive pressure sensors, and strain gauge-based pressure sensors are some of the widely and commonly user pressure sensors.

Position Sensors

These sensors are one of the integral parts of various industrial processing set-ups and monitoring equipment. As the name suggests they detect the position of a particular object and returns the position of that object as a feedback. There are several working principles based on which these position sensors have a lot of different applications, and thus, it also defines the procedure in which the measurement the position will be performed. Capacitance sensors, linear potentiometers, Eddy current sensors, photoelectric sensors, ultrasonic sensors are some of the most commonly used position sensors.

Temperature Sensors

In today's present scenario temperature sensors are in great demand as they are needed in numerous works. The basic task of a temperature sensor is to detect the temperature of the ambience and modify the obtained data into electronic data which can be used later, for further study and research work. These sensors are also of several types, among these, the sensors can be broadly classified into two parts, the first one requiring direct contact with the object whose temperature is to be monitored and on the other hand there are sensors which do not need any contact with the objects. Negative Temperature Coefficient (NTC) thermistor, Resistance Temperature Detector (RTD), Thermocouple, Semiconductor-based sensors, are some of the widely used temperature sensors.

Optical Sensors

The prime work of an optical sensor is to convert the obtained light rays into electronic signals. The physical quantity of light is firstly measured after which the sensor changes the measured quantity into a form which is understandable by an instrument. These sensors are usually segments of a larger system that integrates a source of light, a measuring device and the optical sensor. These sensors make use of lens and mirror systems to transfer, operate and use the beams of light used in their sensing process, and they make sure that no optical fibers are used. These sensors are used in various fields: contact-less detection, counting are some of the few areas of their application. Broadly these sensors can be classified into two categories: the first one being external sensors which transmit the quantity of light which is required after gathering it, and the other ones are the internal sensors which often measure the change in directions and little bends in the path of light.

Current and Voltage Sensors

Current sensors are also known as current transformers or CTs. These sensors primarily measure the current running through a wire, and this is done using the magnetic field which detects the current and generates a proportional output. These sensors are useful in case of both AC and DC current. These sensors help to compute current passively, without interrupting the circuit. These sensors are used to check sub-metering. This is one of the most common use of current sensors. Hall Effect Current Sensors/DC Current Sensors, Rogowski Coils, Solid core, Open-loop, Closed-loop are some of the widely used current sensors.

The amount of voltage in an object can be calculated and measured with the help of voltage sensors. These sensors are effective in both AC and DC circuits to measure the voltage levels. This sensor takes the voltage as input and the outputs are switches, a current signal, analog voltage signal, or an audible signal.

Flow Sensors

The sensor gadgets which are utilized for estimating the stream rate or amount of a moving fluid or gas, are called stream sensors. By and by, stream detecting innovation turned out to be more precise, sturdy, and financial. It can interface meters with a PC for precise stream readout to distantly control stream or to permit unattended cycle activity. For more mechanical uses new sorts of flowmeters are being presented and more established plans are being improved and refreshed appropriately. Flowmeters can be generally named differential makers and direct flowmeters. Differential flowmeters make a limitation in the stream field. Liquid properties and the suddenness of the withdrawal are two main considerations that assume a significant function in the activity of these meters. There are different sorts of stream sensors. Orifice-plate stream sensors, Turbine flowmeters, Volumetric flowmeters, Vortex-shedding sensors, and so on

Chemical Sensors

A sensor gadget that changes substance data like piece, fixation, synthetic action, halfway weight into any valuable insightful sign is called compound sensors. Substance sensors are touchy which can distinguish any single synthetic or natural particle. They are utilized in numerous fields and progressive enterprises, for example, medication, ecological refining, home security, and numerous others. These sensors normally contain two significant parts associated in arrangement: a compound (atomic) acknowledgment framework which functions as a receptor and a physicochemical transducer. In synthetic sensors the receptor connects with analyte particles and its actual properties are changed in a manner with the end goal that the adding transducer can pick up an electrical sign which gives the yield to the sensors.

Gas Sensors

Gas sensors are devices that detect the presence or concentration of gases in the atmosphere. Based on the concentration of the gas the sensor produces a corresponding potential difference by calibrating the resistance of the material inside the sensor, which can be measured as output voltage. Based on this value of the voltage, the type and concentration of the gas can be determined. Gas sensors are classified based on the sensing elements it is built with. There are various types of gas sensors viz. Metal Oxide based gas Sensor, Optical gas Sensor, Electrochemical gas Sensor, Capacitance-based gas Sensor, Calorimetric gas Sensor and Acoustic based gas Sensor.

Torque, Strain, Gage and Force Sensors

Torque sensors are those sensors that convert torque into an electrical signal. The most common torque sensor is a strain gauge that converts torque into a change in electrical resistance. Most commonly, it is a used device for measuring and recording the torque on a rotating system, such as an engine, gearbox, rotor, etc. Static torque is relatively easy to measure.

Strain gauge sensors are those, whose resistance varies with applied force. These sensors convert force, pressure, tension, weight, etc., to a change in resistance which can then be measured. These sensors can be used to pick up expansion as well as contraction. Membrane Rosette strain gauges, Double linear strain gauges, Linear strain gauges, Full bridge strain gauges, etc.

A gauge sensor is that sensors which should be used when measuring the pressure where the process is influenced by change in atmospheric pressure. Most of these types of sensors contain a single pressure port on the process side and ambient pressure is applied through to the back of the sensing element.

A Force Sensor is a type of sensor that helps in measuring the amount of force applied to an object. By measuring the degree of change in the resistance values of force-sensing resistors, the applied force can be calculated.

Velocity Sensors

Velocity sensors are those which responds to velocity rather than absolute position. For example, dynamic microphones are velocity receivers or alternatively velocity sensors. These microphones cause the coil to move relative to the magnet, which generates a voltage that is proportional to the velocity of that movement. There are various types of velocity sensors, viz. Tachometers, LSV, Accelerometer sensors, Piezoelectric sensors.

DATA PROCESSING USING MACHINE LEARNING

Noise Removal

It has been observed that the occurrences of noisy data significantly impact the prediction of the values in the data set. Many researchers have also opined that noise in data set impact the classification correctness and able to provide the poor prediction of data set results. Therefore, to identify and handling the noise in data for prediction has pinched interest over past many years among the researchers. In the study of literature survey, it has been observed various papers have been published between January 1993 to July 2018 on noise identification and handling. In these study, it has been opined that ensemble-based techniques outperformed the others techniques to identify the noise in term accuracy of identification of noisy detection. Despite the performance of ensemble-based techniques, single based techniques are better in term of efficiency and have shown good performance in noisy data sets. Few authors also opined that, polishing techniques is better in noise handling of data to improve classification accuracy.

Furthermore, ML Algorithms are also used improve accuracy in noisy data by reducing the error. The concept of ML like clustering, adaptive filters like LMS or RLS etc are used to reduce the noise of the data. Removal of noise can be done by Data Collection, Training and Inference. The noise free data help to smart sensors device to make the correct and optimal decision.

Baseline Removal

Removal of baseline wander is a classical problem for long period of time and a new method based on empirical mode decomposition and notch filter are proposed to solve the problem of baseline removal in ECG. Nowadays, researcher have used many different approaches to reduce the baseline drift but they have not received the satisfactory result. Moreover, they have used the artificial neural network (ANN) based approach to remove the baseline drift in electrocardiogram signals. They opined that this system will be optimized based on the both number of hidden layer in ANN and the coefficient matrixes because these matrixes are using perturbation algorithm for optimization and also providing lower computational cost for back propagation algorithm of ANN. Furthermore, they have compared these methods with FIR,

Wavelet-based and Adaptive LMS filtering methods for the optimality and making cross correlation between signal to interference ratio and signal to noise ratio indexes to optimized the baseline problems. Baseline removal is remove by manually, or semi manually taking the help of Photoshop, Power Point "marker" and edge detection etc.. However, it is very hard to reduce 100% baseline error but optimization is possible using aforesaid techniques. This type of removal is very useful to check photo taken by smart sensor network and provide the help to take the clear picture by sensors network devices.

Signal Alignment

Signal alignment is used to analyze the variations or general patterns in individual signals based on the group of time series signal. This process used a pairwise alignment algorithm where two signals are align with time axis. In this time axis, first signal is align with the time axis and second is plot to see the how much the second single is closed to. Most of authors opined that, alignment algorithms mainly focused to extract features like find the locations of significant peaks or peak widths and henceforth used those features to align the signals as an alternative of raw signal. Furthermore, this idea bring quick alignments of signal but it has risks of missing some important features of the signal which leads to inaccurate alignments of the signle. Therefore, researcher has plan to use the some AI/ML techniques to optimized the errors of earlier said technology. They have used the Signal Alignment method based on the idea of Genetic Algorithm . This methods, at the beginning align raw signals by warping function(optimized by using a genetic algorithm.) of first modelling with an ODE model. This proposed methods has been evaluated on synthetic and real world datasets and its performance outperformed other existing algorithm. Signal alignment techniques are helpful to make the signal optimized which is helpful for smart sensors devices to make the correct analysis on the data.

Outlier Detection

Outlier Detection is to used in Data Understanding and Data Pre-processing stages of Predictive Models which is about two-thirds of the effort of predictive models.

An Outlier is an unusual occurrence of elements within a given group of data set. It is like a point/ elements which is placed in the distant from other point/elements. It occurred mainly due to variability in the data set and inference the experimental error.

Outliers are consider generally as acute observations which may happened due sample maximum or sample minimum, or extremely high or low value of the data .Below is the example of an Outlier:

In the Outliers, the attributed are fully explainable and extra care will be required because it will be effect the predictions and the accuracy, if we not detect and handle them well.

Therefore, a concrete decision in continuous manner will be required to take outlier elements and discard it. This decision must be taken at time of building the model with outliers. Outliers are consider as sudden change in the predictions therefore judgement is required to decide whether outliers is necessary and if it is then how to go for it.

Changing the values in outlier/extreme is not a standard procedure because excluded data may be the part of any report.

The outlier detection is also a challenge because sometimes this can effect the statistical analysis of whole data set and, at other times may not be as noticeable. Statisticians have developed many algorithms to detect and treat the outliers and "The Box Plot Rule", Grubbs Test is one of the them. Clustring techniques oh ML can be also used for the outlier detection in the data set . Outlier techniques is useful to

provide the idea to smart sensors device to take the decision on the unusual occurrence data and keep
it for the further analysis. sensors device to take the decision on the unusual occurrence data and keep
it for the further analysis.

Figure 1. Outlier

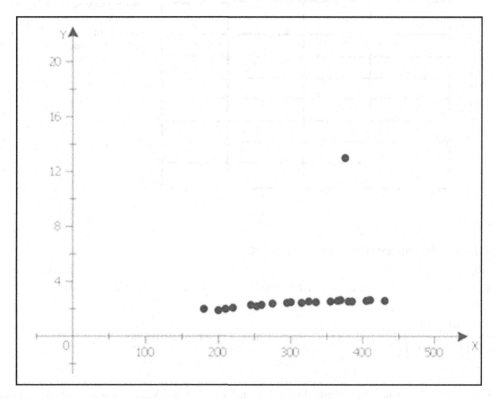

Data Normalization

Data Normalization is the scale value of the attributes into a smaller range using scaling techniques. e.g.
-1.0 to 1.0 or 0.0 to 1.0. otherwise it may lead to a dilution in the result as shown in figure 3.2

There are several methods for Data Normalization as furnished below

- Decimal Scaling
- Min-Max Normalization
- z-Score /zero-mean Normalization)

Decimal Scaling Method For Normalization –

It normalizes the attributes value as formula furnished below where the data value, vi, of data is
normalized to vi' by use of the following formula below –

$$v_i' = \frac{v_i}{10^j}$$

Figure 2. Data normalization

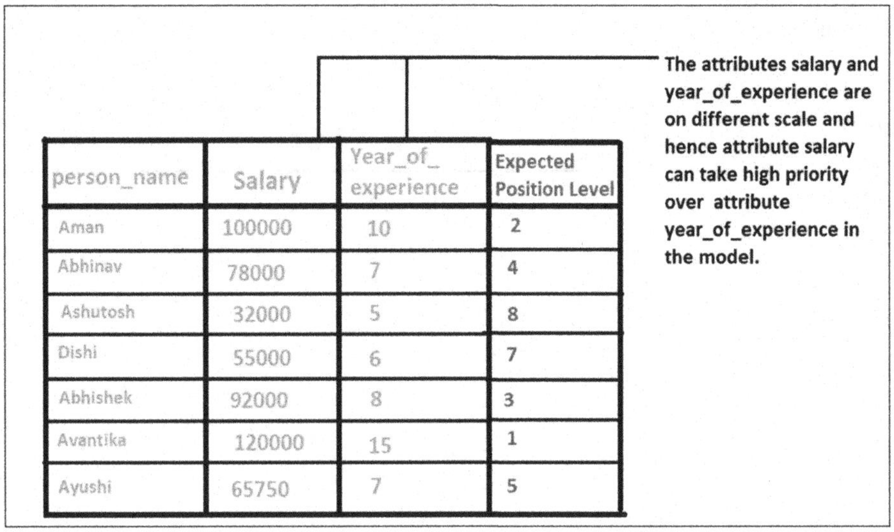

person_name	Salary	Year_of_ experience	Expected Position Level	
Aman	100000	10	2	The attributes salary and year_of_experience are on different scale and hence attribute salary can take high priority over attribute year_of_experience in the model.
Abhinav	78000	7	4	
Ashutosh	32000	5	8	
Dishi	55000	6	7	
Abhishek	92000	8	3	
Avantika	120000	15	1	
Ayushi	65750	7	5	

where j is the smallest integer such that max(|vi'|)<1.

Min-Max Normalization –

In this technique, we can scale the attributes of the data by following the formula

$$v' = \frac{v - \min(A)}{\max(A) - \min(A)} \left(new \max(A) - new \min(A) \right) + new \min(A)$$

Where A is considered as the attribute data value and Min(A) and Max(A) as minimum and maximum of A respectively. Whereas v' is the new value, v is the old value of data. Furthermore, new_max(A) and new_ min(A) represent max and min value of the boundary range respectively.

Z-score normalization –

Here, values of the attributes will normalized using mean and standard deviation of the data A as follow

$$v' = \frac{v - A}{\sigma_A}$$

v' and v are the new and old of data respectively. σA and A represent the standard deviation and the mean of data set respectively. Gradient Descent Based Algorithms, python programming, Normalization using sklearn and many more machine learning algorithm can b used to normalized the data. these normalized data is useful for the analysis because data from different sources have different format . smart sensors will take the data from video, audio, image device and these normalized techniques helpful to provide the analysis on all different formats.

FEATURE EXTRACTION AND DIMENSION REDUCTION

Feature selection is the part of selection of important feature from many existing one. In the feature selection, important features are selected and excluding the less important feature whereas the dimensionality reduction is grouping the features together and transfer features from higher dimension to lower dimension but both are used to reduce the number of features present the data set. Feature selection try to find the missing values, low variance features and highly correlated features and then based on result, remove the less impact feature from the data set whereas in dimension reduction many statistical algorithm like PCA and FA used to reduce the dimension of the data set. how to reduce a dataset dimensionality using Others Feature Extraction Techniques such asICA, LDA, LLE, t-SNE and AE are also used to select the features form the data set. Machine /Ai techniques like convolution neural network discrete cosine transform domain, coherence vector can be used for it. Feature selection in machine learning shown in figure below.

Figure 3. Figure selection processes
Source: https://medium.com/@mehulved1503/feature-selection-and-feature-extraction-in-machine-learning-an-overview-57891c595e96

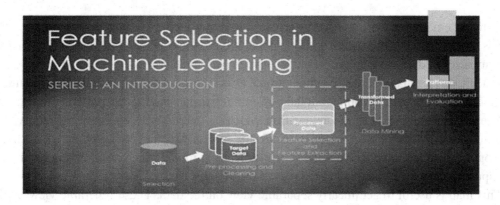

Feature Selection is not the easy task and have different though as furnished below.

When feature selection performed on the real world data the search whole space of possible feature subset is not possible and we have to settle for the approximations of the optimal subset. researchers are trying to find efficient search-heuristics for feature section and reduction .

Feature extraction and dimension reduction can appreciably boost the performance of a learning algorithm in the term of accuracy and computation time which in further easy for the smart sensors device to process the selected feature efficiently and give more weightage on them as compared to the others.

Traditional Multivariate Analysis Methods

Multivariate Analysis: Overview

Multivariate analysis takes the multiple parameters in the experiment and tries to find the relationship among multivariate parameters. But, it is very hard to find the relationship among various parameters because for same question we can get the multiple answers. For instance, the patient's can give multiple

Figure 4. Figure selections
source: https://medium.com/@mehulved1503/feature-selection-and-feature-extraction-in-machine-learning-an-overview-57891c595e96

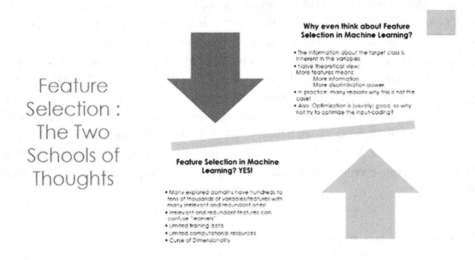

responses to same symptom Therefore, many researcher are suggesting to go for univariate analysis; where hypothesis tests prepared based on the multiple populations. However, classification and discrimination methods are also used to make the distinguish between two populations,

In the Multivariate analysis, much computational effort are required due to complex strcutture of the data therefore due to growth of computational power, multivariate role has increase in the data analysis, and this one also finding value in the application. Machine Learning, Deep Learning, and AI methods enable us to recognize complicated correlations in data sets for which exploratory analysis is not able to do the proper determination of the outline of the underlying model Machine Learning techniques like SVM (Support Vector Machine) and the kernel trick can also used to map the data into higher dimensions . This map is useful to get linearly separable view on the data. These seperable view on the data further helpful to sensors device to select the useful one for the analysis.

Digital Signal Processing-Based Methods

Digital signal are important part for any communication and its processing require good methods to process it for better result. When the data collected by sensors device in form of the digital signal then correct form of the signal is useful for good result . Many Digital signal processing-based methods are existing and few are sated in subsequent section

Wavelet Analysis

Wavelet transform follows the mathematical approach for signal processing where signal can decompose and try to find the special patterns hidden in the signal. It simultaneously display the functions apply to signal and show the local characteristics through time-frequency domain. Wavelet transforms are primarily divided into two groups like continuous wavelet transform (CWT) and discrete wavelet transform (DWT) but CWT will be a very slow in transformation due to extra and useless overlapping feature and duplicity of neighbouring data but DWT is used formula to perform the transformation. This type of analysis is useful to find the special pattern hidden in signal which are collected by smart sensors devices. This techniques help us to analysis the pattern which are usually not seen. 4.2.2 Auto-regressive modelling

Auto-Regressive Modelling

An autoregressive (AR) model is one type of random process to describe positive time-varying processes in economics, nature, etc. It specify specifies how the output variable linearly change with its own previous values. To find the more moving average, the concept of autoregressive–moving-average (ARMA) and autoregressive integrated moving average (ARIMA) models have been proposed based on the of time series, which required more complex stochastic structure. An autoregressive (AR) model have higher correlation, positive or negative in between the variable and this is more likely that the past will predict the future. In machine learning terms, the higher value of these will be weighted in the deep learning algorithm. Autoregression Models can also used the Python programming, tensor flow for the better result.

Feature Subset Selection

Many optimized algorithms can be used to generate the Feature subset selection from the data set and these feature are useful for smart sensors device to make the correct and optimal result. If the optimal feature selection done earlier then it is useful for the sensors device to reject the irrelevant one and select the optimal for the storing and analysis purpose. This process is helpful to save the time for analysis and space of storing the data. Few AI techniques of feature section discussed in subsequent section.

Genetic Algorithm (GA)

Genetic algorithms is a probabilistic search technique based on the of biological evolution It mimics evolution in nature to generate the population from the available knowledge and then using fitness function to find the optimal solution.

At the beginning, a randomly selected initial population will be generated and the selection of the population for the next step is generated based the fitness function. To make the change in the population to reach the optimal solution crossover and mutation will be applied on it. The application leads to a population to a better solutions. The process will be continued until an optimal solution reached and the current generation of population, or some control parameter is exceeded. It has also shown in the figure 4.3.1

Genetic Algorithms explores the possible subsets of features and obtain the features that maximizes the analytical accuracy and minimizes irrelevant attributes. To achieve this, GAs used fitness function on multiple correlation to evaluate the fitness of each feature subset attributes its domain. This process is helpful to reducing the original size of the dataset used,

It has observed that GA performed better than traditional feature selection techniques and n manage data sets with many features. It also not required specific knowledge about the problem under study and can be easily parallelized in computer clusters.

Figure 5. Genetic Algorithm Evolutionary cycle

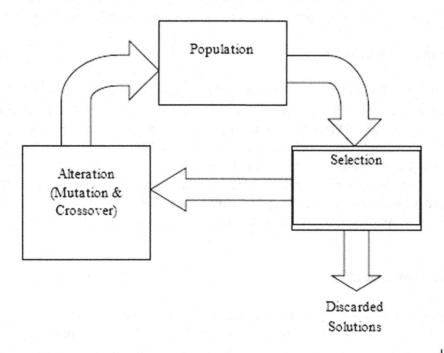

Differential Evolution (DE)

Differential Evolution Algorithm (DEA) is a simple and easy to use algorithm which converge well. This algorithm is close to genetic algorithms but differ in the basic principle of the mutation operator. The flow chart of DEA (Differential Evolution Algorithm) has been shown in figure . At the outset, it generate the initial population from the available data set and thereafter check it with fitness function. The population will be stopped when it satisfy the condition otherwise it will modifies based on the crossover and mutation. Furthermore, the formulation of new populating will be do and again check the fitness criteria. This process is continue until the result reached the optimal solution.

DEA can be used to select the objective function of feature selection and is minimized population vector which is encoded using Binary Encoded Decimal. DEA highly reduces the computational costs as compared to other algorithm.

Simulated Annealing (SA)

Simulated Annealing algorithm has been inspired by cooling of material in a heat bath. In this process, solid is heated over the melting point and then cooled. This algorithm simulates the cooling process by gradually lowering the temperature until to converges to a steady or frozen state.

The idea is applied to data set to find the optimal phase by gradually changing the error for the optimal and when error crossed the threshold, return back to previous stage . This process is use to find the optimal stage in the data set.

It has been observed that many researchers proposed SA as an optimal feature selection algorithm based to determine six denial of service attacks, market analysis, time series prediction etc..

Figure 6. Flowchart of DEA

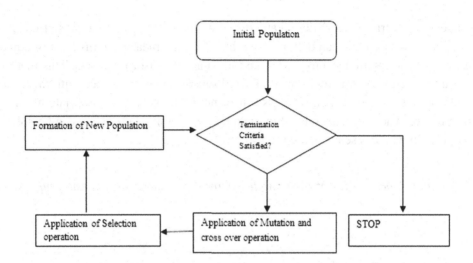

This process is very helpful due to less number of parameters required for the evaluation.

5. TYPES OF ML IN SENSOR NETWORK

The WSN controls a dynamic environment which alters quickly with changing time. This dynamic environment can be created in two ways. One can be created by exterior matters. Other can be originated by the internal developer. The ML can solve the problem of needless reconstruction very easily. ML motivates a large number of real-world implementations that utilize maximum resources. It also extends the lifetime of the utilized network. The predictive models are designed by ML as a lot of tools and heuristics. The ML helps to solve various implementations of wireless sensor networks with marvelous flexibility opportunities. The ML heuristics may be classified into three classes. These are supervised, unsupervised, and reinforcement learning.

In this section, the various types of ML techniques that are utilized to overcome the crucial problems in WSN previously are discussed.

Supervised Learning

The Supervised learning technique is required for plotting function from the input to the output.

The prime goal of this technique is to approximate the plotting function accurately so that the outcome of the newly arrived data can be predicted.

The tags for each data set are provided before this learning technique. These tags are required for the growth of the structure developed for categorization.

The supervised learning heuristics can be used for solving various aspects of wireless sensor networks. The various aspects are aiming for localization, identification of happening, query processing, media access control, security and intrusion detection, and quality of service, data integrity, and identification of a fault.

K-nearest Neighbor (k-NN)

k-NN is a supervised learning heuristic. It categorizes a data set based on the tags of the adjacent data sets. The misplaced sensor node can be forecasted based on the measuring distance of adjacent sensor nodes. Various parameters are used to determine the adjacent sensor node sets. This method does not require maximum energy to compute. The associated sensor nodes are joined with this k value to distinguish k adjacent sensor nodes in a wireless sensor network using an appropriate heuristic which is distributed in nature. The problems related to the query processing subsystem can be solved with this heuristic properly in wireless sensor networks.

Figure 7. Designing of localization of sensor node in wireless sensor networks using supervised learning

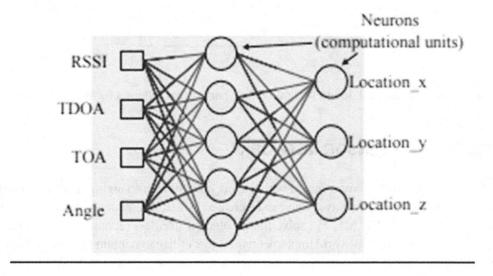

Decision Tree (DT)

DT is a classification technique for forecasting tags of information by repeating the training data set using a tree based on learning. The various construction challenges related to wireless sensor networks can be solved easily using DT. This technique is simple enough. This method is effective to detect the consistency of links in wireless sensor networks by identifying limited important features such as degree of damage and fraud, the average time required for disaster, and reinstate.

Neural Networks (NNs) (Shareef et al., 2008)

The NNs can distinguish the approximate location of missed sensor nodes in a wireless sensor network. Although, the NNs are not so popular in a wireless sensor network for the large computational complexity till now. The computational complexity is large enough due to feeding the weights of the sensor nodes in the network and computational overhead. The NNs can able to resolve various challenges of the wireless sensor network by feeding several outcomes and result margins. Fig.1 shows the identification of the position of a sensor node by NNs in wireless sensor networks.

Support Vector Machines (SVMs)

SVM is a supervised algorithm that acquires to categorize information utilizing labeled data sets. This algorithm can be utilized efficiently for identifying malignant sensor nodes. As shown in Fig.2, this algorithm splits the region into shares in the wireless sensor network. These splits are divided by a thick boundary. The original analysis will be categorized depending upon the portion of the boundary they reside. The vital implementation areas of this algorithm are security aspects and localization in a wireless sensor network.

Figure 8. Illustration of SVM in WSNs with example

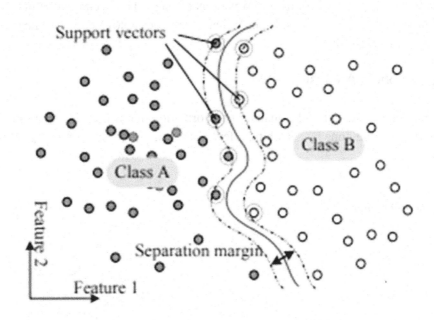

Bayesian Statistics

This algorithm needs comparatively few data set in the count. The major use of this algorithm in wireless sensor networks is measuring the readiness of event consistency utilizing inadequate training data with previous information around surroundings. The necessity of prior information reduces the huge utilization of this algorithm in wireless sensor networks.

Unsupervised Learning

The unsupervised learning is nurtured with the task which has unclassified occurrences. In this learning technique, the classes have to be extracted from the unlabeled dataset. A clustering technique has been used to create a cluster of unclassified samples depending upon some matching measurements.

In the Unsupervised learning technique, it is not required to train the model. Instead of supervising the model, the model has been permitted to execute alone to find out data. This nurtures with unclassified data sets. The heuristics related to unsupervised learning permits you to execute upon more typical jobs related to supervised learning. Unsupervised learning often may be more unpredictable than other learning techniques.

Unsupervised learning discovers all possible new patterns in data. It also assists us to search for characteristics that can be suitable for classification. These are the main reasons for choosing the unsupervised machine learning technique.

Unsupervised learners are not supplied with tags. The main objective of this heuristic is to categorize the training data into various clusters by examining the likeness among them. The problems related to the clustering of sensor nodes and data aggregation in WSN can be solved by this heuristic.

K-means Clustering (Jayaraman et al., 2010; Winter et al., 2005)

This heuristic is utilized to identify data into various clusters. This technique is utilized to solve the problem of class creation in sensor nodes in WSN. This is possible due to the linear complexity and easy execution of this algorithm.

Principal Component Analysis (PCA)

PCA can decrease the overhead of the quantity of information that is transferred among various sensor nodes in WSNs. It can be done by searching a few classes of uncorrelated linear groupings of unique observations.

Figure 9. An example of PCA heuristic

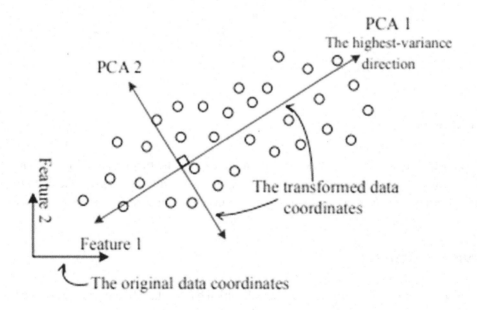

Reinforcement Learning (RL)

This heuristic allows an Agent to accrue knowledge in an interactive environment. Agents use a form of response randomly to acquire knowledge.

The similarity between the supervised learning technique and the RL method is that both take the advantage of plotting and measurement of input and outcome. The main difference between the supervised learning technique and the RL method is that in the supervised learning technique, the Agents are getting an appropriate response for executing a job. The RL technique takes prizes and penalties as indicators for optimistic and adverse behavior.

The main difference between the RL technique and unsupervised learning is in terms of achievement. The main aim of the unsupervised technique is to search for likenesses and variations among training data sets. Whereas, the main aim of the RL technique is to search for the most appropriate structure which will produce an optimal result by accruing collective rewards of the Agents.

RL technique allows the sensor node in a wireless sensor network to know deeply by interrelating with its environment. The Q-learning is the most familiar and useful RL technique. In this technique, the Agent will choose the most appropriate actions which will produce the optimal result in terms of rewards using its skill.

Figure 10. Q-learning technique

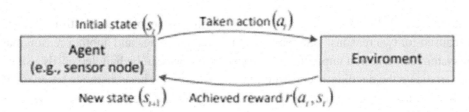

Fig. 4 shows that an Agent changes its achievement on regular basis depending upon the action taken in each particular state. This heuristic is mostly applicable in the system which is distributed in nature such as wireless sensor networks. In a wireless sensor network, every sensor node searches for an appropriate course of action which will produce an optimal result in achieving prizes. This technique is used effectively for solving various problems related to routing in wireless sensor networks.

APPLICATION OF AI & ML IN SMART SENSOR NETWORK (DAS ET AL., 2010; DI & JOO, 2007; FÖRSTER & AMY, 2011; FORSTER, 2007; HODGE & AUSTIN, 2004; HOFFMANN, 1990; KULKARNI ET AL., 2011; OSAMY ET AL., 2022; ZHANG ET AL., 2010)

The emerging technology based on AI and ML can offer an efficient system that can able to solve a huge number of problems related to Smart Sensors Networks. This system based on AI and ML can provide the facility in the formation of innovative products and facilities in various areas. Nowadays, WSN is experiencing boundless enlargement and expansion. AI and WSNs are combined to make our daily life more comfortable and smooth.

Clustering and Data Aggregation

WSN is resource-constrained. Clustering and data aggregations are utilized to decrease the power consumption in the network by reducing the quantity of information broadcast. Various ML heuristics decrease the significant quantity of information transmission and utilize the distributed features of the network. It supplies a relative study of the performance of various techniques to assistance the inventors in scheming suitable ML-based results for the implementation of clustering and data aggregation.

Machine Learning for Routing

The Reinforcement Learning agent attempts to lessen the mean flow latency by estimating multiple routes in a WSN. The mean flow is occurred using more than one route which is controlled by the central hub in WSN. This central hub can accumulate network parameters viz. mean flow latency and reselect the suitable route accordingly.

Localization

The main objective of WSN is the control of ever-changing atmospheres over time. This alteration of behavior is caused for two reasons. One reason is the outsider issues and another reason may be the restriction of system construction unpredictably. These situations can be handled easily using ML. These are useful to eradicate the needless reconstruction of the system. These methods based on ML also can motivate to solve various real-world problems efficiently so that the utilization of available resources will be optimum and the lifetime of the WSN will be boosted.

Smart Grid and Energy Control System

The universal changeover to Smart Grid is acceptable by the requirement to gratify the rising power consumption and assurance the supportable and protected supply of the power system. The most vital methods for evolving Smart Grid are the combination of various sustainable power resources. To meet the upcoming growing requirements in energy, upgraded authority, heuristics, optimal perceptions are required in the customer perspective to build an energy plant.

Smart Buildings

The already present methods in developing Smart Buildings using ML can be divided into two categories- occupant-centric and energy/devices centric. The occupant-centric methods utilize machine learning for inhabitants with assessment and credentials. This method is related to the identification of various activities and assuming likings and performance. The other method that utilizes machine learning is estimating aspects related either to energy or devices.

CONCLUSION

Remote sensor networks are unique in relation to customary network in different perspectives, subsequently requiring conventions what's more, devices that address novel difficulties and restrictions.

As an outcome, remote sensor networks require imaginative answers for energy mindful and ongoing directing, security, planning, limitation, hub bunching, information total, deficiency identification and information integrity. Machine learning & AI gives an assortment of methods to improve the capacity of remote sensor organization to adjust to the dynamic conduct of its general climate.

From the conversation up until now, it turned out to be certain that many plan challenges in remote sensor networks have been resolved using a few machine learning strategies. In outline, receiving machine learning calculations in remote sensor networks needs to consider the restricted assets of the organization, just as the variety of learning topics and examples that will suit the current issue. Also, various issues are as yet open and need further research endeavors, for example, creating lightweight and conveyed message passing strategies, web based learning calculations, various leveled grouping designs and embracing machine learning in asset the executives issue of remote sensor organizations.

REFERENCES

Al-Karaki, J., & Kamal, A. (2004). Routing techniques in wireless sensor networks: A survey. *IEEE Wireless Communications*, *11*(6), 6–28. doi:10.1109/MWC.2004.1368893

Ayodele, T. O. (2010). *Introduction to machine learning. In New Advances in Machine Learning*. InTech.

Das, S., Abraham, A., & Panigrahi, B. K. (2010). *Computational intelligence: Foundations, perspectives, and recent trends*. John Wiley & Sons, Inc.

Di, M., & Joo, E. M. (2007). A survey of machine learning in wireless sensor networks from networking and application perspectives. *6th International Conference on Information, Communications Signal Processing*, 1–5.

Duffy, A. H. (1997). The "what" and "how" of learning in design. *IEEE Expert*, *12*(3), 71–76. doi:10.1109/64.590079

Förster & Amy. (2011). *Machine learning across the WSN layers*. InTech.

Forster, A. (2007). Machine learning techniques applied to wireless ad-hoc networks: Guide and survey. *3rd International Conference on Intelligent Sensors, Sensor Networks and Information*, 365–370. 10.1109/ISSNIP.2007.4496871

Hodge, V. J., & Austin, J. (2004). A survey of outlier detection methodologies. *Artificial Intelligence Review*, *22*(2), 85–126. doi:10.1023/B:AIRE.0000045502.10941.a9

Hoffmann, A. G. (1990). General limitations on machine learning. Academic Press.

Jayaraman, P. P., Zaslavsky, A., & Delsing, J. (2010). *Intelligent processing of k-nearest neighbors queries using mobile data collectors in a location aware 3D wireless sensor network. In Trends in Applied Intelligent Systems*. Springer.

Krishnamachari, B., Estrin, D., & Wicker, S. (2002). The impact of data aggregation in wireless sensor networks. *22nd International Conference on Distributed Computing Systems Workshops*, 575–578. 10.1109/ICDCSW.2002.1030829

Kulkarni, R., Förster, A., & Venayagamoorthy, G. (2011). Computational intelligence in wireless sensor networks: A survey. *IEEE Communications Surveys and Tutorials*, *13*(1), 68–96. doi:10.1109/SURV.2011.040310.00002

Langley, P., & Simon, H. A. (1995). Applications of machine learning and rule induction. *Communications of the ACM*, *38*(11), 54–64. doi:10.1145/219717.219768

Osamy, W., Khedr, A. M., Salim, A., AlAli, A. I., & El-Sawy, A. A. (2022). Recent Studies Utilizing Artificial Intelligence Techniques for Solving Data Collection, Aggregation and Dissemination Challenges in Wireless Sensor Networks: A Review. *Electronics (Basel)*, *11*(3), 313. doi:10.3390/electronics11030313

Paradis, L., & Han, Q. (2007). A survey of fault management in wireless sensor networks. *Journal of Network and Systems Management*, *15*(2), 171–190. doi:10.100710922-007-9062-0

Romer, K., & Mattern, F. (2004). The design space of wireless sensor networks. *IEEE Wireless Communications*, *11*(6), 54–61. doi:10.1109/MWC.2004.1368897

Shareef, A., Zhu, Y., & Musavi, M. (2008). Localization using neural networks in wireless sensor networks. *Proceedings of the 1st International Conference on Mobile Wireless Middleware, Operating Systems, and Applications*, 1–7. 10.4108/ICST.MOBILWARE2008.2901

Winter, J., Xu, Y., & Lee, W.-C. (2005). Energy efficient processing of k nearest neighbor queries in location-aware sensor networks. *2nd International Conference on Mobile and Ubiquitous Systems: Networking and Services*, 281–292. 10.1109/MOBIQUITOUS.2005.28

Zhang, Y., Meratnia, N., & Havinga, P. (2010). Outlier detection techniques for wireless sensor networks: A survey. *IEEE Communications Surveys and Tutorials*, *12*(2), 159–170. doi:10.1109/SURV.2010.021510.00088

Leveraging Wi-Fi Big Data Streams to Support COVID-19 Contact Tracing

Heba Atteya
The American University in Cairo, Egypt

Iman Megahed
ⓘD https://orcid.org/0000-0001-5736-4559
The American University in Cairo, Egypt

Mohamed Abdelmageed El Touhamy
The American University in Cairo, Egypt

INTRODUCTION

The World Health Organization (WHO) announced the discovery of the new coronavirus: SARS-Cov2 or COVID-19, in January 2020. By March 2020, COVID-19 had spread worldwide and was declared a pandemic (Marinoni, van't Land, & Jensen, 2020). By April 2020, more than 3.4 billion people were in lockdown in around 80 countries worldwide. This represented a complete standstill of approximately 43% of the world's population. During the following months, COVID-19 continued to impose a new normal that has disrupted nations, industries, and businesses to an unprecedented level. The World Economic Forum declared that the pandemic had changed education forever (Li & Lalani, 2020). Higher education institutions' characteristics of vibrant campuses, where students experience an engaging, buzzing learning and cultural hub, experienced dramatic challenges (Times Higher Education [THE], n.d.). According to The United Nations Educational, Scientific and Cultural Organization (UNESCO), in April 2020, around 185 schools and higher education institutions closed their doors. The response of higher education institutions at the outset of the pandemic to rapidly adopt technology to maintain academic and operational continuity could be described as heroic, and it most certainly displayed a level of organizational agility that burst traditional stereotypes regarding educational organizations' ability to change. However, this shift to what is now generally recognized as "remote learning," while very impressive, has proven to be no replacement for the campus experience that so many students covet. Many learners had challenges with accessibility, inclusion, and engagement. A vivid reminder that the digital equity gap unfortunately persists—and has continued to widen—during the pandemic (Curtin, 2021).

Founded in 1919, The American University in Cairo (AUC) is an independent, not-for-profit, American-accredited, chartered institution of higher education and center of the intellectual, social, and cultural life of the Arab world. Its community of students, parents, faculty, staff, trustees, and alumni represents more than 60 countries. The University stands as a crossroads for the world's cultures and a vibrant forum for reasoned argument, spirited debate, and understanding across the diversity of languages, facilities, and human experiences (The American University in Cairo [AUC], n.d.).

The COVID-19 pandemic imposed new challenges to AUC's ability to maintain its standards of excellence in delivering on its mission of teaching and learning. Similar to other institutions in higher education worldwide, AUC took this as an opportunity to challenge its functions and work towards opera-

DOI: 10.4018/978-1-7998-9220-5.ch016

Copyright © 2023, IGI Global. Copying or distributing in print or electronic forms without written permission of IGI Global is prohibited.

tional excellence. In March 2020, AUC started preparing its faculty and students for online teaching then shifted its teaching and operations online effectively and efficiently before any higher education institution in Egypt. From the beginning, AUC focused its plans and decisions to overcome the pandemic around two guiding principles, capitalizing on its solid Digital Transformation resources. Those principles are:

1. **Health and Safety**: A commitment to prioritize the health and safety of students, faculty, staff, and the surrounding community in every decision.
2. **Deliver Quality Education**: A commitment to ensuring that the teaching, learning, and research of students, faculty, and postdoctoral fellows will continue at the highest levels of excellence.

In parallel, efforts to ensure the safe and healthy return of the AUC community were necessary. This chapter discusses how AUC leveraged its Wi-Fi infrastructure and Big Data technologies to offer a digital contact tracing solution that respects data privacy and ethics at an insignificant cost.

BACKGROUND

Since COVID-19 is highly transferable in indoor and closed locations, much research focuses on indoor tracking solutions. Indoor tracking systems vary depending on the type of signal used. The most common indoor positioning technologies are based on the radio frequency signals such as Wi-Fi, Bluetooth, and Ultra-Wideband (UWB). These solutions are usually composed of two elements: anchors and location Tags. Anchors are devices placed in the building, while a tag is carried by the person whose location is of interest. All of these technologies have their advantages and disadvantages. The main advantage of the Wi-Fi option is that it can use the pre-existing network infrastructure; Wi-Fi is available in mobile phones and other wearable devices. Thus, the Wi-Fi access point acts as an anchor, and the mobile device acts as a tag. This makes it easy to deploy and cheaper than other solutions requiring special anchors and tags. This advantage also could be applied to the Bluetooth option as Bluetooth is available in mobile phones. Both Wi-Fi and Bluetooth options calculate the distance based on the Received Signal Strength (RSS) principle. The strength of the signal is the main factor to determine the distance, which could lead to inaccuracy of around five meters as the signals vary enormously in the presence of obstacles and moving people. Different materials also affect the signals differently and consequently affect the accuracy of measuring the distance (Niemiller, 2019; Escobar, 2015).

The Singapore Ministry of Health implemented a solution based on the Bluetooth technology, 'TraceTogether'. TraceTogether is a mobile application for tracing and notifying people who came in contact with a Covid-19 case. The user should install the application on his mobile device, keep the app open in the background, and keep Bluetooth on. The other option is a token device for those who do not have a compatible mobile phone or the convenience of having the app on their mobile (Government of Singapore, 2020). The app logs all exchanges with nearby TraceTogether devices. Sometimes the Bluetooth signals could be exchanged through walls. So, when a confirmed case with COVID-19 uploads their Bluetooth proximity data to MOH, it is processed and filtered based on duration and signal strength to identify only the close contacts and notify them (Government of Singapore, 2020). The Bluetooth-based solution is convenient for indoor and outdoor tracing as there is no need for setting up any infrastructure such as Bluetooth beacons or location tags; mobile devices can play both roles. Furthermore, it handles the process of notifying people in contact with a positive case. The main drawback of this solution is that it needs a user-side involvement to download the application, turn on Bluetooth, and keep the application running in the background. Moreover, the calculated distance between devices has a margin of error.

Another solution developed by researchers at the University of Massachusetts Amherst and Singapore Management University is based on Wi-Fi technology. The solution is based on a network-centric approach for contact tracing that relies on passive Wi-Fi sensing. The researchers leveraged the Wi-Fi system logs to analyze the association and dissociation log messages of the connected devices at various access points (APs) on campus. This information helped them reconstruct the infected users' locations (building, room numbers). The solution also analyzes all other users associated with those same access points at those times to determine users who were in contact with the COVID-19 carrier and for how long. The limitation of this solution is that it can exclude true contacts at a close distance from the infected user if they happen to connect to different access points. Alternatively, it can also inaccurately consider distant people connected to the same access point as a contact. (Trived, Zakaria, Balan, & Shenoy, 2020).

The solution presented in this article and implemented at AUC is also based on leveraging Wi-Fi technology. The fundamental difference is that it does not rely on APs connectivity. It uses the Aruba Network Analytics and Location engine installed on top of the network to determine a relative x and y coordinate for each connected device, using a technique called "Triangulation" (Aruba - Hewlette Packard Enterprise Support [HPE], 2018). The triangulation technique allows for overcoming some of the challenges of the solutions that are based solely on APs connectivity.

Solutions based on the Ultra-Wideband (UWB) technology provide the highest accuracy but are not practical to implement. The UWB is a radio-signal-based technology that can accurately measure the Time of Flight (ToF) of the radio signal. ToF determines the start and stop signals and precisely measures the distance between two devices. The accuracy of an indoor tracking system using ultra-wideband is typically within 10cm, which is the most accurate option. The core disadvantage of this technology is that it is not readily available in the buildings or users' mobile phones. It requires an ad-hoc deployment of the anchors across the buildings and a wearable device tag per person (Decawave, n.d.).

Technologies supporting indoor contact tracing solution do share several similarities and slight differences, use cases usually determine the most convenient solution. In the case of AUC in specific, and higher education institutions at large, Wi-Fi based contact tracing was the most suitable solution due to the availability of the infrastructure and implicit utilization of the service.

WI-FI CONTACT TRACING AT THE AMERICAN UNIVERSITY IN CAIRO

Among the critical requirements that would ensure AUC's readiness for a safe campus reopening was the need to deploy measures for COVID case tracking, contact tracing, and testing. These measures had to be in place in a record-breaking time with the available resources. Hence, leveraging all available digital tools and resources was necessary to ensure this mission's timely and effective completion. AUC designed several integrated solutions to address COVID-19 tracking, self-checking, vaccination and testing tracking system, and most importantly, contact tracing.

It was evident that contact tracing of COVID-19 cases was an essential prerequisite for campus safety and the plan to return to campus in hybrid or face-to-face modes for teaching and operations. Manual contact tracing is a challenging process where infected people have to use their recollection of whom they may have come in contact with over multiple days. However, this process can be error-prone due to gaps in memory and panic at the time of diagnosis. It also adds an unprecedented load on the medical team. Hence, the necessity to rely on technology was an expansive transformation opportunity (Hartman, 2020). The Centers for Disease Control and Prevention (CDC) recognized the value behind using digital tools to strengthen contact tracing of COVID-19 cases as a means to complement, not to replace manual contact tracing (World Health Organization [WHO], 2020).

Building on the CDC recommendations, AUC's Business Intelligence team conducted extensive research on possible technologies that would support contact tracing and augment manual contact tracing conducted by the medical team. The research was conducted in collaboration with select members of the Transformation and Infrastructure teams to leverage existing digital tools ensuring financial viability, timely implementation plan, and a high potential for adoption by all community members. Leveraging our existing state-of-the-art Wi-Fi technology would fulfill these three objectives, including easy and smooth adoption. The solution uses the existing AUC Wi-Fi infrastructure and the system logs generated by the Wi-Fi access points to identify contacts of a positive COVID-19 case based on location proximity calculations.

The solution traces a COVID-19 case to all the people they came in four meters proximity with for more than 10 minutes based on the relative location of their mobile devices. This location is calculated and updated every 30 seconds by the Networks Analytics and Location engine installed on top of AUC's WLAN. This wealth of information is streamed into a data-warehouse in a real-time fashion where all the analytics occur. The optimal parameter values for the distance and duration of contact were agreed on during the testing phase through trial and error techniques. In Figure 1. Wi-Fi Mobile Contact Tracing, we provide a brief demonstration of the process of digital contact tracing from a non-technical perspective. The medical team receives the contacts list and uses it during the contact tracing call to help the patient remember whom they came in contact with. The list provides the medical team with the contact information of the contacts to facilitate the process of reaching out to them.

In this chapter, the authors share AUC's experience designing and implementing the solution at no significant additional costs and how it proved to be an effective learning experience for the team on adopting its first Big Data initiative.

SOLUTION ARCHITECTURE

AUC has a robust Wi-Fi network, with around 1000 access points covering the whole campus. Aruba Analytics and Location Engine (ALE) is a virtual context aggregation and location engine that collects and correlates a wealth of information from several network components, including Airwave Server, Access Points, and Wireless Controllers. This generated data is extracted on a real-time basis, loaded to the data storage area, cleansed, and transformed in preparation for analysis and reporting.

The solution architecture has four main tiers, Data Streaming & Ingestion tier, Data Storage tier, Data Preparation & Analytics tier, and Data Reporting & Visualization tier. Figure 2. Represents the detailed solution architecture.

Data Streaming & Ingestion Tier

The data needed to enable the solution comes from two sources with two different loading methods:

1. Wi-Fi Connectivity Data – Wi-Fi Logs

L

The ALE can provide the generated Wi-Fi system logs through two types of APIs: Polling APIs and Publish/Subscribe APIs. The proposed solution depends on the Publish/Subscribe Location API which retrieves the last known location for a specific client's media access control (MAC) address. It processes the upcoming data from the Wi-Fi devices and makes it available to the external analytics and data mining systems via northbound APIs (Aruba - a Hewlett Packard Enterprise Company [HPE], 2019).

These real-time Big Data streams are consumed using the 'ZeroMQ' messaging library by implementing a ZeroMQ to 'BigQuery' Dataflow middleware application to manage streaming data transfer between ALE and BigQuery, the analytical database. AUC has, on average, around 15K devices connected to the Wi-Fi per day. The ALE generates a record of data every 30 seconds for each device to update the latest known location. Also, when users move, their mobile device gets associated with the nearby AP, and the ALE generates a record for the event. The critical requirement of this tier is choosing a solution design that enables reliable real-time Big Data streaming.

2.   Medical Center COVID-19 Case Reporting

The medical center uses an in-house developed application to log the reported COVID-19 cases. The system holds all the medical information related to AUC's confirmed or probable COVID-19 cases, such as symptoms, first symptoms date, last access to campus date, and isolation start and end dates. The data is stored in an operational SQL Server database. The ETL tool, 'DataStage', is used to extract the data and load it into BigQuery in batch-mode every two hours to trigger the digital contact tracing process.

Data Storage Tier

AUC Wi-Fi streams generate around 0.6 GB of data per day. The key requirement for the data storage tier is scalability, robustness, and efficient data processing. Accordingly, we chose BigQuery as the solution's Data warehouse. BigQuery is a cloud server-less, highly scalable data warehouse. Its scalable, distributed analysis engine allows querying terabytes of data in seconds using simple SQL scripts. The solution is mainly depending on two core tables:

1.   The Location table holds the locations of the MAC clients connected to the Wi-Fi. It receives around 5 million records per day with a record size of ~100 Bytes, i.e., roughly 0.5 GB inserted every day into the Location table (Aruba - Hewlette Packard Enterprise Support [HPE], 2018).
2.   The Station table holds the information about the clients associated with the WLAN that send data to the ALE. It receives around 1 million records with a record size of ~80 Bytes, i.e., approximately 80 MB of data inserted every day (Aruba - Hewlette Packard Enterprise Support [HPE], 2018).

In addition to the data fetched from the Wi-Fi system logs, medical COVID-19 reporting data regarding new cases reporting and onset dates of symptoms, increases slowly at a negligible rate of less than 100 records per day.

Table 1. Shows the data dictionary for the location table

Field Name	Data Type	Definition
sta_eth_mac	Varchar	MAC address of the client
sta_location_x	Decimal	X coordinate used to determine client location on a map. This value is based on the number of feet, or meters if configured, the station is from the top left corner of the floor
sta_location_y	Decimal	Y coordinate used to determine client location on a map. This value is based on the number of feet, or meters if configured, the station is from the top left corner of the floor
error_level	Integer	Indicates the radius of horizontal uncertainty,
Associated	Boolean	Indicates whether the client is associated with an AP on the network.
campus_id	Varchar	ID number identifying a specific campus
building_id	Varchar	ID number identifying a specific campus building
floor_id	Varchar	ID number identifying a specific building floor
hashed_sta_eth_mac	Varchar	Anonymized value of the client MAC address
loc_algorithm	Varchar	Indicates how the (X,Y) coordinates are populated:
Altitude	Varchar	Altitude of the floor (defined in VisualRF)
Unit	Varchar	Unit of measurement used for floor specifications

Table 2. Shows the data dictionary for the station table

Field Name	Data Type	Definition
sta_eth_mac	Varchar	MAC address of the client station
username	Varchar	Corresponding username from the user table on the WLAN controller or IAP
role	Varchar	Name of the user role currently assigned to the client. This is only applicable to authenticated users
bssid	Varchar	BSSID of the client
device_type	Varchar	Type of device used by the client
sta_ip_address	Varchar	IP address of the client station
hashed_sta_eth_mac	Varchar	Anonymized value of the client MAC address
hashed_sta_ip_address	Varchar	Anonymized value of the client IP address
ap_name	Varchar	Name of the AP

Data Preparation and Analytics Tier

In this tier, the raw data stored in the staging area on BigQuery needs to undergo some cleansing and transformations to ensure efficient processing and analysis of the data in terms of processing time and cost. BigQuery pricing is highly dependent on the number of bytes processed by each query. Therefore, an efficient data storage design that considers the possible frequent queries is crucial. Data cleansing was necessary to remove data not needed for the use case to guarantee processing time and cost control as the data grows over time. Since the sole purpose of data storage is contact tracing, querying the data for analysis is only triggered when a COVID-19 case is reported, initiating the two-step tracing procedure:

Step 1: Find all co-located people with the confirmed COVID-19 case at any point in time during the infection period.

Step 2: Identify the duration of co-location and filter the contact list for those who were within 4 meters distance from the COVID-19 case for at least ten uninterrupted minutes.

The procedure would scan billions of records daily. Hence, data partitioning and clustering to avoid scanning the whole data table were inevitable. Partitioning divides the large tables into small partitions to limit the scanned bytes per query. If a query filters on the value of the partitioning column, BigQuery will scan only the partitions that match the filter and ignore the other partitions. Clustering sorts the data within a partition based on a specific clustering column. Combining partitioning and clustering can drastically reduce the cost of query processing (Google Cloud Platform, 2022). Accordingly, the researchers chose to partition the Location data by day and cluster it by Floor ID. For example, when a new COVID-19 case is reported, the Station table will be looked up to fetch the MAC Address of the infected user. The algorithm identifies that the user was on campus on a specific day D, time T, building B, floor F, and location L during his infection period. A query that fetches his contacts needs to directly access the partition of day D and will almost scan only the cluster of floor F instead of scanning the whole Location table without partitioning and clustering. This is a considerable saving for the query processing time and cost. It is as simple as performing a SQL query with a join clause on a date, a timestamp that is T +/- 30 sec, building, floor, and location L +/- 4 meters.

After identifying all the co-located users, the contacts list is filtered for those who meet the minimum criteria for consideration as contacts at risk of infection: 10 minutes and 4 meters distance. This step ensures that contacts are excluded from the final list if they were co-located for only a few seconds or distant enough not to get infected. The researchers combined different SQL functionalities, such as Lead and Lag window functions, without using any other programming languages to write efficient scripts to identify all the uninterrupted meeting slots between the contact and the reported case. The SQL scripts calculate contact start time, end time, and the average distance between the case and its contacts during every uninterrupted time slot. Using SQL only helped utilize the power of BigQuery in query execution and speeded up the implementation process drastically.

Other activities conducted to ensure efficient data storage are:

- Filtering out unwanted data received from static devices like PCs, Smart TVs, and other non-mobile devices
- Removing duplicate records and irrelevant observations
- Deleting records of anonymous logins

Data Reporting and Visualization Tier

In this tier, the data is stored in a structure of fact/aggregated tables. It facilitates easy and speedy reporting. The case reporting and digital contact tracing data are aggregated and visualized into dashboards and reports. The AUC COVID-19 dashboard, which is publicly available on the AUC website, helps decision-makers on campus monitor the pandemic situation. The dashboard presents trends of the weekly number of contacts, the number of cases who were on campus during the period of possible infection, and other important KPIs. The dashboard primarily supports informed decision-making concerning opening and closing the campus. Figure 3. shows a screenshot of the AUC Covid-19 Dashboard.

TESTING AND DATA QUALITY ISSUES

Before deployment, the solution underwent testing and iterations of enhancement to pick the most suitable solution parameters. A volunteering sample reported on their contacts on a specific set of days. Their input was compared to the Wi-Fi contact tracing results. The testing exercise revealed some issues; inability to recognize some devices running on the latest version of IOS or Android operating systems, missing usernames of connected devices, and multiple concurrent logins for the same user from different locations. Upon reporting the issues to the networks team, they were resolved with some changes to the ALE configurations. This resulted in enhancing the tracing results.

Through testing, we calculated the margin of error on locating the X and Y coordinates for a connected device and tuned the solution parameters accordingly. ALE locates connected devices depending on the strength of the received signal strength, which could be affected by many factors.

In the second iteration of testing, volunteers received a questionnaire to identify the accuracy of their tracing results. The researchers used the information from the questionnaire to construct a confusion matrix (Markham, 2014). of precision and recall to assess the solution performance. The calculated average recall of the algorithm is 96% which means that the solution successfully recalls 96% of the contacts confirmed by the volunteers. However, the algorithm reached a precision of 57% only, meaning that the Wi-Fi-generated contact list would include 43% of contacts that the volunteers are not sure if they were in contact with. Part of this low precision results from two reasons: memory gaps that hinder the recollection of everyone one would have come in contact with, and the fact that one would visit many public areas on campus where they may not know all the people in their surroundings, such as the food court, library, registrar, students service center, bank, campus plaza. The recall measure is more accurately calculated since people can confirm all people they are sure they were in contact with, once presented with the contact list. Accordingly, the recall will be of higher weight in assessing the solution success.

SOLUTION DEPLOYMENT

Deploying such a tracing solution would have required colossal effort. Thanks to the already existing Wi-Fi infrastructure that is competent enough to serve the solution. We start from the point that the access points already cover the whole campus, and the people already use the Wi-Fi. So, there is no need to add any new access points or request any client-side involvement.

Most of the solution components are SaaS cloud services, such as BigQuery, Data Flow, and Data Studio. So it did not require much effort to deploy the solution. This allowed the speedy deployment of the main solution and allowed the researchers to focus their efforts on solution optimization and reporting. The researchers designed a fully automated sequence of jobs to:

- Extract the new COVID-19 cases from the medical center case reporting system every two hours
- Initiate the tracing procedure
- Send the contacts list to the medical center

The whole process takes on average around 3 minutes, which is very acceptable in such a big data solution and the solution has successfully traced 960 cases since its deployment to production.

CAMPUS AWARENESS AND DATA PRIVACY

The expected benefits and necessity of implementing contact tracing technologies were a clear prerequisite to campus safety. According to an article released by Johns Hopkins Center for Health Security, Contact Tracing Technology was labeled as "A Key to Reopening" (Hartman, 2020). However, contact tracing can infringe on the privacy of sensitive information. A Brookings Institute survey of 2,000 Americans showed that only 30% of respondents were comfortable downloading and using a mobile contact tracing app with increasing privacy protections (Neale, Brooks, Burns, Kelly, & Tryniecki, n.d.).

With a firm conviction on the need to ensure adequate privacy, the implementation team was keen to consider and plan for the extensive safeguard of sensitive information from the beginning. This was essential for many reasons. First, to ensure that AUC continued to abide by all regulatory and compliance guidelines. Second, the ability to reassure AUC constituents that the privacy of this sensitive information was respected and safeguarded. Third, the need to increase constituents' buy-in instead of possible resistance to adoption of this solution which would lead them to turn their Wi-Fi off (Watson, Cicero, Blumenstock, & Fraser, 2020).

To ensure that efforts towards contact tracing will be effective, trusted, and compliant, the solutions proposed had to consider and plan for the extensive safeguard of sensitive information from the design phase of the tools. Among the decisions taken to ensure privacy measures were:

1. Transparency: informing the community that Wi-Fi data was used for COVID contact tracing and giving them the option to opt-out of connecting to Wi-Fi ensured transparency and consent.
2. Data retention: limiting data retention of Wi-Fi data to one month to ensure that this data was only used for COVID contact tracing purposes
3. Contact/Proximity data: basing the solution on detecting data on proximity between community members and refraining from converting this to location tracing
4. Access: access to this data was limited to two members of the Business Intelligence team and the Medical team. Disclosure beyond these teams, even to leaders and supervisors, was on a need to know basis only and aggregate reports where possible.

SOLUTION LIMITATIONS & RECOMMENDATIONS

Although several countries and institutions deployed their digital contact tracing tools in response to COVID-19, there is limited evidence on the effectiveness of the tools (World Health Organization [WHO], 2020). These tools are considered complementary to traditional contact tracing, rather than "single solution" (World Health Organization [WHO], 2020). Among such limitations specific to the AUC use case:

1. Systematic exclusion of some members of the AUC Community who cannot access AUC Wi-Fi but still interact and blend in with the AUC community regularly:
    a. Outsourced blue collars & staff members who do not have authorized AUC Emails to access the AUC Wi-Fi
    b. Campus visitors such as vendors, projects consultants, and staff operating the different food outlets around the campus
    c. The solution is limited to AUC New Cairo premises only. So it can neither support contact tracing on AUC buses nor on gatherings of AUC community members that take place off-campus.

The researchers recommend availing wearable devices that can connect to Wi-Fi for these types of users. This would allow contact tracing them to contacts from the AUC community if they were on campus during their infection period.

2.   Technical limitations of the solution
  a.   The solution is dependent on the AUC Wi-Fi network. If the network is down, the whole solution is down. So, at times of network instability, the digital contact tracing effectiveness is highly compromised.
  b.   The solution is highly dependent on the accuracy of calculating the relative location of each individual by the network analytics and location engine. Aruba ALE calculates the device location using a technique called "Triangulation" based on the Received Signal Strength Indicator (RSSI) from the closest 3 Access points (AP) around each device. This calculation is affected by several factors such as Access points density, client device probing behavior, RSSI variations, device type, and operating system.

The researchers recommend increasing the density of the APs indoors and outdoors, and integrating the solution with other complementary information such as classroom schedules, administrative offices maps to help filter out the improbable contacts.

3.   Cultural challenges
  a.   Adoption: The current adoption/ Wi-Fi connectivity rate is almost 50%. Even though there is room for improvement, this adoption rate is higher than that expected from implementing a mobile app leveraging Bluetooth or some other technology specifically launched for contact tracing. Results from interviewing a sample of individuals who were not connected to the Wi-Fi suggest that individuals either unintentionally forget to connect to the AUC Wi-Fi or intentionally decide to use Mobile Data for better connectivity.
  b.   User credentials sharing: During the data probing and quality phase, the Business Intelligence Team discovered that it is common for AUC members to share their user credentials with other unauthorized users to help them connect to the Wi-Fi.

A lot of general awareness campaigns are continuously ongoing to increase adoption. In addition to intensifying information security awareness efforts to limit the practice of user credentials sharing.

FUTURE RESEARCH DIRECTIONS

The Wi-Fi contact tracing solution at AUC has proved to be an effective tool for complementing and supporting the manual contact tracing process. The researchers recommend enhancing the solution precision by overlaying the Wi-Fi contact tracing output with additional information that would increase the overall precision of the solution, such as class lists and campus maps with classrooms and offices layout. It is also worth analyzing this wealth of information for other use cases to improve:

- Student experience by analyzing their mobility patterns
- Operational efficiencies by determining the different staffing levels through analyzing the traffic at service offices and vendors all around the campus

- Space utilization by analyzing hot zones and lightly utilized spaces to ensure optimal use of the campus resources

CONCLUSION

The COVID-19 pandemic has challenged countries, industries, and sectors shaping our new normal. The higher education industry was among those significantly affected. Teaching and learning, campus culture and student experience, financial health and infrastructure, and faculty and staff operations were all drastically disrupted (Beavens, Bryant, Krishnan, & Law, 2020). To overcome many of these challenges, campuses capitalized on digital transformation like never before and at an unprecedented rate to meet its needs to continue its teaching and learning mission in safe environments. AUC underwent the same transformation speedily and robustly as it was fortunate to have continuously invested in digital systems and platforms. Throughout its journey with COVID, AUC maintained its focus on two pillars: quality education and maintaining a safe environment. While moving teaching and operations online was a hallmark all educational institutions underwent, AUC took its digital mission to support this challenge further, implementing innovative solutions to support COVID-19 tracing, tracking, and testing.

Among the initiatives that stood out the most was AUC's work on contact tracing as a mandatory prerequisite for a safe return to campus. Research on possible financially and technically feasible alternatives revealed the three main options of Bluetooth-based, Wi-Fi-based, and UWB, each having its own merits. Wi-Fi-based contact tracing was the most suitable for AUC as it leverages the existing state-of-the-art Wi-Fi infrastructure without financial burdens or privacy implications. Wi-Fi-based contact tracing solutions are also associated with high adoption rates due to the expanded use of Wi-Fi as a utility. It was also a technologically feasible solution despite its Big Data dimension, which was new to AUC.

This initiative proved successful with 96% recall and 57% precision as a complementary tool for existing manual contact tracing as recommended by CDC. Having such data available in a timely and easy-to-use fashion has supported the Medical team extensively with the sheer magnitude of contacts to safely track upon resuming campus operations. Initial assessment also shows that there is still room for enhancement to improve precision rates.

One apparent gain was the learning experience that has encouraged further exploration of the use of Big Data across various facets of AUC's environment. It has also opened the horizon of senior university leaders to the importance of investing in robust digital landscapes and prospects of moving to smart campuses where endless possibilities loom on the horizon. Whether these enable universities to combat future pandemics or leverage the learning experience, this investment is the only way forward for learning, global players in this industry.

REFERENCES

Aruba - a Hewlett Packard Enterprise Company. (2019). *Aruba analytics and location engine.* Retrieved from Aruba Networks: https://www.arubanetworks.com/assets/ds/DS_ALE.pdf

Aruba - Hewlette Packard Enterprise Support. (2018). *Analytics and location engine 2.0.0.x API guide.* Retrieved from Hewlette Packard Enterprise Support: https://support.hpe.com/hpesc/public/docDisplay?docId=emr_na-a00022647en_us

Beavens, F., Bryant, J., Krishnan, C., & Law, J. (2020, April 3). *Coronavirus: How should US higher education plan for an uncertain future?* Retrieved from McKinsey & Company: https://www.mckinsey.com/industries/public-and-social-sector/our-insights/coronavirus-how-should-us-higher-education-plan-for-an-uncertain-future

Decawave. (n.d.). *What is UWB*. Retrieved from Decawave: https://www.decawave.com/technology1/

Escobar, E. (2015). *How does Wi-Fi work?* Retrieved from Scientific American, a division of Springer Nature America, inc.: https://www.scientificamerican.com/article/how-does-wi-fi-work/#

Google Cloud Platform. (2022). *Introduction to partitioned tables*. Retrieved from BigQuery Documentation: https://cloud.google.com/bigquery/docs/partitioned-tables

Government of Singapore. (2020). *How TraceTogether works?* Retrieved from A Singapore Government Agency: https://www.tracetogether.gov.sg/

Government of Singapore. (2020). *Troubleshooting - why are there bluetooth exchanges with other TraceTogether users?* Retrieved from TraceTogether - A Singapore Government Agency: https://support.tracetogether.gov.sg/hc/en-sg/articles/360050088633-I-m-home-alone-why-are-there-Bluetooth-exchanges-with-other-TraceTogether-users-

Hartman, M. (2020, April 20). *Contact-Tracing technology: A key to reopening*. Retrieved September 30, 2021, from John Hopkins: Bloomberg School of Public Health: https://publichealth.jhu.edu/2020/contact-tracing-technology-a-key-to-reopening

Kreps, S., Zang, B., & McMurry, N. (2020, May 20). *Contact tracing apps face serious adoption obstacles*. Retrieved September 30, 2021, from Brookings: https://www.brookings.edu/techstream/contact-tracing-apps-face-serious-adoption-obstacles/

Li, C., & Lalani, F. (2020, April 29). *The COVID-19 pandemic has changed education forever. This is how.* Retrieved September 30, 2021, from World Economic forum: https://www.weforum.org/agenda/2020/04/coronavirus-education-global-covid19-online-digital-learning/

Marinoni, G., van't Land, H., & Jensen, T. (2020, May). *The impact of COVID-19 on higher education around the world.* International Association of Universities. Retrieved September 30, 2021, from https://www.iau-aiu.net/IMG/pdf/iau_covid19_and_he_survey_report_final_may_2020.pdf

Markham, K. (2014, March 25). *Simple guide to confusion matrix terminology.* Retrieved from Data School: https://www.dataschool.io/simple-guide-to-confusion-matrix-terminology/

Neale, M., Brooks, D., Burns, S., Kelly, B., & Tryniecki, M. (n.d.). *Data Privacy and Gen Z: A Formula for Voluntary Contact Tracing on Campus.* Retrieved September 30, 2021, from Huron Consulting Group: https://www.huronconsultinggroup.com/insights/data-privacy-gen-z-voluntary-contact-tracing

Neale, M., Burns, S., Kelly, B., Tryniecki, M., & Brooks, C. (n.d.). *Data privacy and gen Z: A formula for voluntary contact tracing on campus.* Retrieved from https://www.huronconsultinggroup.com/insights/data-privacy-gen-z-voluntary-contact-tracing

Niemiller, K. (2019). *What is indoor tracking and indoor positioning?* Retrieved from Losant: https://www.losant.com/blog/what-is-indoor-positioning-and-indoor-tracking

The American University in Cairo. (n.d.). *About AUC*. Retrieved September 30, 2021, from The American University in Cairo: https://www.aucegypt.edu/about/about-auc

Times Higher Education. (n.d.). *The impact of coronavirus on higher education*. Retrieved September 30, 2021, from Times Higher Education: https://www.timeshighereducation.com/hub/keystone-academic-solutions/p/impact-coronavirus-higher-education

Trived, A., Zakaria, C., Balan, R., & Shenoy, P. (2020, May). WiFiTrace: Network-based contact tracing for infectious diseases using passive WiFi sensing. *Computing Research Repository*. Retrieved from https://arxiv.org/pdf/2005.12045v2.pdf

Watson, C., Cicero, A., Blumenstock, J., & Fraser, M. (2020, April 10). *A national plan to enable comprehensive COVID-19 case finding and contact tracing in the US*. John Hopkins: Bloomberg School of Public Health. Retrieved September 30, 2021, from Center for Health Security: https://www.centerforhealthsecurity.org/our-work/pubs_archive/pubs-pdfs/2020/200410-national-plan-to-contact-tracing.pdf

World Health Organization. (2020a, June 4). *Digital tools for COVID-19 contact tracing*. World Health Organization. Retrieved September 30, 2021, from https://www.who.int/publications/i/item/WHO-2019-nCoV-Contact_Tracing-Tools_Annex-2020.1

World Health Organization. (2020b, May 28). *Ethical considerations to guide the use of digital proximity tracking technologies for COVID-19 contact tracing*. WHO.

Worldometer. (2021a, September 30). *COVID-19 coronavirus pandemic*. Retrieved September 30, 2021, from Worldometer: https://www.worldometers.info/coronavirus/

Worldometer. (2021b, September 28). *Reported cases and deaths by country or territory*. Retrieved September 28, 2021, from Worldometer: https://www.worldometers.info/coronavirus/#countries

ADDITIONAL READING

Bisio, I., Lavagetto, F., Marchese, M., & Sciarrone, A. (2016). Smart probabilistic fingerprinting for WiFi-based indoor positioning with mobile devices. *Pervasive and Mobile Computing*, *31*, 107–123. doi:10.1016/j.pmcj.2016.02.001

Boeing, P., & Wang, Y. (2021). Decoding China's COVID-19 "virus exceptionalism": Community-based digital contact tracing in Wuhan. *R & D Management*, *51*(4), 339–351. doi:10.1111/radm.12464

Lewis, D. (2020). Why many countries failed at COVID contact-tracing— But some got it right. *Nature*, *588*(7838), 384–387. doi:10.1038/d41586-020-03518-4 PMID:33318682

KEY TERMS AND DEFINITIONS

Clustering: Automatically organizing the content of a table based on the content of one or more columns such that related data is stored on the same block for faster data retrieval.

Confusion Matrix: A table that summarizes the performance of a classification model on a set of labeled data. It compares predictions to actuals and summarizes the model's performance in terms of True Positives, True Negatives, False Positives, and False Negatives.

Contact Tracing: Contact tracing is used by health departments to prevent the spread of infectious disease. In general, contact tracing involves identifying people who have an infectious disease (cases) and people who they came in contact with (contacts) and working with them to interrupt disease spread (Neale et al., n.d.).

Partitioning: Dividing the logical data store (database table) into separate physical data stores to enhance query performance and database manageability.

Precision: The fraction of relevant instances out of the total retrieved instances. It answers the question: "How much of the retrieved instances are correct?" It is the fraction of True positives out of the total positive cases.

Recall: The fraction of relevant instances retrieved. It answers the question: "How many correct instances were retrieved?" It is the fraction of the True positives out of the total True cases.

Received Signal Strength: The strength of the received signal at the receiver's antenna. It is used for measuring the distance between the signal transmitter and receiver.

Time to Flight: A method of calculating the distance between two radio transceivers. It measures the distance by multiplying the time of flight of the signal by the speed of light.

Machine Learning in the Catering Industry

Lanting Yang

(iD) https://orcid.org/0000-0003-3471-0759
City University of Macau, Macao

Haoyu Liu
City University of Macau, Macao

Pi-Ying Yen
Macau University of Science and Technology, Macao

INTRODUCTION

Restaurants provide diverse choices, delicious dishes, and enjoyable environments compared to home cooking. Enjoying foods from restaurants has become a lifestyle, and the catering industry has developed rapidly. In the past, people played the most indispensable roles in the catering industry because of its service nature. Giving customers a satisfying experience is essential in services. However, machine learning, which simulates the human behavior of acquiring knowledge to allow machines to think and act like humans, is now providing a new way to fill these service roles (Jordan & Mitchell, 2015; Wang et al., 2017).

Robots empowered by machine learning can take orders, make recommendations, process foods, collect payments, and even deliver takeaways (Jang & Lee, 2020). Figure 1 shows how machine learning can play a role in various tasks in the catering industry. Customers arriving at a restaurant can place orders with a robot server. After receiving the order, robot cooks can make dishes catering to customers' requests, and when the food is ready, the robot server takes it to the customers' table. When the customers finish, the robot server can process the bill with cash, credit card, or mobile payment. After the customers leave, the customer information and transaction data are recorded to a database and analyzed for recommendations that meet customers' personal preferences the next time.

Figure 1. Machine learning can play a role in various tasks in the catering industry

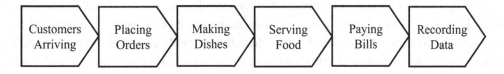

This chapter discusses machine learning in the catering industry in detail. In the next section, the authors describe the background and review relevant research. Then, the authors discuss the opportunities and challenges that machine learning brings to the catering industry, as well as solutions and recommendations to the issues. Finally, the authors conclude the chapter.

DOI: 10.4018/978-1-7998-9220-5.ch017

Copyright © 2023, IGI Global. Copying or distributing in print or electronic forms without written permission of IGI Global is prohibited.

BACKGROUND

The literature on machine learning has surged in recent years. Jordan and Mitchell (2015) introduce machine learning and its applications. They discuss what machine learning is, which areas it relates to, and the value of machine learning in various industries, including healthcare, education, manufacturing, service, finance, and marketing.

Notably, the application of machine learning to the catering industry is widely documented in the literature. In China, prestigious hotpot restaurants like Haidilao use robots with machine learning to replace human staff (Zheng, 2021); in Korea, LG Electronics design robots that can be utilized to carry and deliver foods to customers (Cho, 2020); and in Thailand, five types of restaurant service robots (Order One, Order Two, Serve One, Serve Two, and Slim) work in MK Company's restaurants (Eksiri & Kimura, 2015). With the advances of machine learning, an increasing number of catering companies use this technology to better anticipate the demand from customers (Hess et al., 2021). For example, Yu and Fu (2020) deploy machine learning models to predict the demand for Japanese food based on questionnaires about dietary habits and personal information. Machine learning is also adopted to predict the degree of processing for food (Menichetti et al., 2021) and wine quality (Dahal et al., 2020).

A vast literature presents the advances of machine learning in the catering industry. For example, Jang and Lee (2020) examine attributes of service robots and their impact on restaurant customers. They find that customers' perceived value from interacting with a robot has a significant relationship with likeability (a positive first impression of a robot), intelligence (a robot can complete a task intelligently), and safety (users feel safe when interacting with a robot). Jang and Lee (2020) also affirm the direction of effects between perceived benefits (perceived value) and satisfaction (revisit intention) and give suggestions on how to make restaurants sustainable. Alabdulrahman and Viktor (2021) note that customers with unique tastes are often ignored, suggesting restaurants may lose these customers by not catering to their tastes and following the new trends. They propose a new system using one-class decision tree algorithms to outperform the traditional filtering-based recommendation system in both accuracy and model construction time.

Food delivery is an area of the catering industry to which machine learning already contributes considerably. Liu et al. (2020) find that the actual route that a delivery person take is often different from the route that the system recommends, and the information on roads may be either outdated or incomplete. They invent a novel algorithm that records the preferred routes of delivery people and then recommends their preferred routes in the future. The algorithm also improves the accuracy of navigation and the efficiency of food delivery. Lou et al. (2020) recognize that order allocation in the food delivery industry is complex due to uneven demand and large-scale optimization of human resources. They build a model that considers the deteriorating effect and learning effect, and the model can be utilized in decision-making in order allocation and labor scheduling in food delivery. Moreover, Bertsimas et al. (2021) investigate the prediction of the demand in an area by comparing classical methods and machine learning. They find that machine learning prediction is more accurate than classical methods when with a limited demand history.

OPPORTUNITIES AND CHALLENGES

The adoption of machine learning brings benefits to restaurants. First of all, it saves costs. Restaurants nowadays face the pressure of rising labor costs. The adoption of machine learning allows restaurants to only hire skilled staff while eliminating positions performing routine actions. Compared to traditional restaurants, restaurants with machine learning robots can expect a decrease in labor costs. In 2018, Alibaba, a Chinese multinational technology company, opened a hotpot restaurant with machine learning robots replacing human waiters. Thus, Alibaba considerably lowered the salary costs for their waiters. Haidilao's restaurant in Shanghai also saved nearly 37 percent of kitchen labor costs with the help of machine learning (Zheng, 2021). Alibaba and Haidilao are not the only cases. Creator, a burger restaurant located in San Francisco, has adopted an ordering system that provides options for customers to choose how their burger should be done, as well as allowing them to select cheese, sauce, and toppings (Hambling, 2018). This application saves the labor costs of waiters/waitresses. Beyond replacing human labor, paperless operations are also enabled by machine learning throughout service processes, simplifying communication procedures, shortening communication time, and reducing the chances of mistakes. Robots perform various actions without papers in Haidilao's restaurant, which not only saves time but also avoids losses from errors related to paper operations (Zheng, 2021). In these two aspects, machine learning can significantly save costs for restaurants.

Second, machine learning facilitates better decisions. Philipp Kandal, Head of Engineering at Grab, a Singapore company that provides ridesharing and delivery, believes that machine learning can help restaurants be ten times more productive (Raj, 2021). Let us consider food delivery as an example. In recent years, food delivery has been popular with young people and composes an essential part of the catering industry. However, wasting time and wrong routing are unavoidable in human delivery. For some food delivery platforms, the delivery people arrange delivery routes themselves. When receiving more than one order from a restaurant, they must design routes to all destinations as well as delivery sequences. Machine learning can make these decisions. By having a comprehensive command of real-time data, machine learning delivery can better respond to traffic and weather conditions (Lou et al., 2020; Liu et al., 2020). Zomato, an Indian multinational food delivery company, is now using machine learning to face the challenges in preparation time, delivery time, and delivery people (Vijay & Anup, 2021). Another example is inventory control (Bertsimas et al., 2016; Li & Kuo, 2008). Machine learning controls the supply of raw materials and forecasts future needs (Hess et al., 2021). Consequently, better ordering decisions are enabled so that food is consumed before its expiration date, ensuring safety for customers. In this regard, improvement in decision-making increases customer satisfaction in the catering industry.

Third, machine learning makes personalization possible. Machine learning can extract both population-level and person-level insights from big data (Alabdulrahman & Viktor, 2021). Once customers' personal preferences are learned, restaurants can provide dishes that meet their tastes and provide personalized recommendations. In Haidilao's ordering system, customers need to sign into their accounts every time they order (Zheng, 2021). Then the dishes they order will be recorded by the system so that machine learning can analyze the data to find their personal preferences. The next time the customers come to the restaurant, the machine will recommend the dishes they like. Machine learning can also analyze a population's preferences. Based on the data collected by machine learning, restaurants can update their products or design new dishes. For example, Pizza Hut has systems that can recommend foods to customers depending on the weather (Anna, 2021). McDonald's has also embraced the machine learning technology developed by Dynamic Yield, an Israeli start-up (Keyes, 2019). Dynamic Yield creates technology that can decide what products to promote based on weather, time, or traffic, and McDonald's adopts this technology to help customers choose their ideal meal. For example, using Dynamic Yield's technology, McDonald's can recommend customers McFlurry ice cream on hot days, tell customers which items have been ordered many times at that particular restaurant on that day, or suggest other items according to the customer's primary order. Dynamic Yield's machine learning technology can help McDonald's not only from the customer's perspective but also the staff's. During peak times, the machines recommend to customers items that are easy to make, which highly reduces staff workload.

Fourth, machine learning achieves marketing effects. Since only a few restaurants currently adopt machine learning technology, customers are attracted by this emerging technology, and a promotion effect can be expected. Customers may visit the restaurant not only because of its food but also due to the unique experience. Orion Star, an artificial intelligence startup, launched a new restaurant delivery robot with machine learning and found that the product could increase revenue through customer attraction (Mai, 2021).

Fifth, machine learning also achieves more precise performances than human beings so that customers receive consistent service experiences. For example, it is hard to keep a precise level of spiciness across dishes, and the need to provide low, medium, and high spiciness levels makes quality control even harder. The same logic follows for other ingredients. Robots, on the other hand, allow accuracy so that customers can have consistent experiences each time. In Croatia, a restaurant uses chef robots to make stews, risottos, and pasta for customers accurately and quickly (Chris, 2021). The robots store the ingredients, dispense them into the pot, and stir the food as it cooks. In Haidilao's restaurant in Shanghai, the soup base is also made by machine learning robots (Yu, 2021). Customers can choose their preferred amount of spice, oil, salt, and select over 10000 combinations of ingredients and flavors.

Finally, sustainability is another great bonus of machine learning. Better inventory control and a better understanding of customers' tastes reduce food waste. Specifically, inventories are a particularly significant issue for restaurants and highly related to food waste. Every ingredient has a different expiration date, and inventory management becomes a huge problem. Machine learning can ensure that stocked food is consumed when it is still fresh, which decreases the cost of food waste. Machine learning can also accurately predict customers' present and future tastes and hence the change in demand for different ingredients. For example, Haidilao created a new system to conduct real-time monitoring, management, and maintenance of the entire unmanned back-of-house operations (Zheng, 2021). In its restaurants, machine learning helps manage ingredients to reduce waste and improve sustainability.

Despite its many benefits, there are also challenges behind the utilization of machine learning in the catering industry. Robots are, after all, not humans, and communication between robots and customers may be hindered. Many people are unwilling to talk to a machine rather than a human, or customers unfamiliar with the technology may feel uncomfortable (Luo et al., 2019). At the same time, the pre-programmed service system cannot satisfy every customer's needs: Though machine learning can learn customers' preferences, understanding human feelings and behaviors is too difficult for robots.

Moreover, the initial investment required for machine learning is enormous. Restaurants may be stuck with liquidity problems and unable to break even for a long time. For example, Picnic, a food-automation startup, invented a pizza robot. To order its automated pizza-topping system, restaurants must pay a subscription fee of between $3500 and $5500 per month, depending on the configuration and production volume (Joe, 2021). This is a huge cost for subscribes to Picnic's system, and these restaurants may have a liquidity challenge. Another example is Moley Robotics, a British company, whose robots can perform kitchen tasks like whisking eggs, slicing onions, or frying bacon. However, one Moley costs around 10000 pounds, which may be a big burden for some restaurants (Hambling, 2018). The McDonald's recommender system introduced in the previous section is another example of costly machine learning investment. It costed McDonald's $300 million in 2019 to buy the company that created its recommender system Dynamic Yield, which is a considerable amount even for this fast-food giant.

Finally, managers' opinions may contradict the results from machine learning. For example, machine learning may suggest a product based on historical data, but the manager may believe that another product is more suitable based on his or her past experiences. Balancing data and experience may be a problem for restaurants that utilize machine learning to support decisions.

SOLUTIONS AND RECOMMENDATIONS

This section provides suggestions on how the catering industry may face the challenges mentioned above. To solve the problem that robots may not be able to handle each customer's unique needs, restaurants using machine learning could set aside a few new positions for human staff (Shen, 2021). That is, both machine robots and human staff would be simultaneously present in restaurants and take on different jobs. Robots would be assigned standardized and specialized tasks, while the human staff would be responsible for taking care of duties that machine robots cannot perform well, such as communicating with customers. Another way to tackle the problem is for restaurants to provide a feedback channel after customers finish their meals. If customers feel that their needs were not met by robots, they could complain through this channel. These unique needs would be recorded in a database, which the restaurant would analyze using machine learning. If similar problems were brought up often or recognized as programming defects, the robots embedded with machine learning would be quickly adjusted and improved. In this way, service robots could meet the unique needs of customers.

To solve the problem of the setup costs, restaurants could evaluate investments in technology using capital budgeting techniques (Ko, 2020). Companies should carefully make decisions on investment. Thus, before the companies invest in machine learning technology, they could perform thorough analysis on capital budgeting and rigorously predict whether they could make a profit. Investors could then make decisions according to the results. If the evaluation results did not generate positive expectations, they could deny or decrease the investment, effectively preventing loss. Another tricky choice is the investment timing. It may be a considerable burden for restaurants to bring in machine learning in their early stages. When restaurants' businesses mature, machine learning could serve as a device for market penetration or competing with competitors, and such an investment would be more meaningful.

Regarding the conflicts between managers and machine learning, restaurants could combine their respective advantages. Specifically, restaurants could assign different decisions to managers and machine learning on a case-by-case basis. For example, for a long-term customer who the manager knows well, the manager's recommendation may be preferable, whereas if a new face visits the restaurant, it would be better for machine learning to recommend dishes. Another solution is to have machine learning provide the initial suggestions, and then have the manager refer to the advice to make final decisions. In this way, managers may be presented with novel ideas or recommendations they would not have considered before.

FUTURE RESEARCH DIRECTIONS

To better help restaurants develop their use of machine learning, some future directions deserve investigation. First, as mentioned in the previous section, two possible solutions to solve the problem that machine learning cannot meet customers' unique needs are adding human staff and collecting feedback after customers finish their meals. However, these solutions are associated with further concerns. Though adding human staff could fulfill customer's needs instantly, it might increase costs simultaneously. Collecting customers' feedback for future use may not guarantee that customers come to the restaurant again. Combining these two methods could be possible, but how to synergize them still requires more study. Second, the relationship between machine learning and the environment is worthy of examination. On the one hand, pollution from the catering industry is currently profound, and whether machine learning could improve the environmental friendliness of restaurants is a topic to be explored. On the other hand, an increasing number of restaurants may consider using machine learning in the future, and whether the extensive use of robots will cause excessive power consumption or other negative impact on the environment remains unclear.

CONCLUSION

The use of machine learning is increasingly prevalent nowadays, and its usage has been widely witnessed in drug development and speech synthesis, among other areas. In the catering industry, machine learning can undertake various customer service tasks from customers' arrival to their departure and has made an impact that cannot be ignored. In the current chapter, the authors introduce the application of machine learning in the catering industry. Real-life examples and related literature are provided. Machine learning brings several benefits to the industry, such as saving costs, facilitating better decision-making, supporting personalization, obtaining marketing effects, reaching better performance precision, and enhancing sustainability. Nevertheless, applying machine learning also creates challenges for the industry: (1) Customers may feel uncomfortable when facing nonhumans, and machine learning cannot cater to every need of customers; (2) adopting machine learning is associated with a considerable cost; and (3) there may be conflicts between machine learning and managers in decision making. The authors provide suggestions and recommendations for resolving these challenges and briefly discuss future research directions in this area.

REFERENCES

Alabdulrahman, R., & Viktor, H. (2021). Catering for unique tastes: Targeting grey-sheep users recommender systems through one-class machine learning. *Expert Systems with Applications*, *166*, 114061. doi:10.1016/j.eswa.2020.114061

Anna, C. (2021, August 9). Pizza Hut is building an AI that it says will recommend food to you based on your local weather. *Business Insider*. Retrieved from: https://www.businessinsider.com/pizza-hut-wants-ai-to-recommend-food-based-on-weather-2021-8

Bertsimas, D., Kallus, N., & Hussain, A. (2016). Inventory management in the era of big data. *Production and Operations Management*, *25*(12), 2006–2009. doi:10.1111/poms.2_12637

Cho, M.-H. (2020, February 2). LG deploys service robot in Seoul restaurant. *ZD Net*. Retrieved from: https://www.zdnet.com/article/lg-deploys-service-robot-in-seoul-restaurant/

Chris, A. (2021, August 16). New Croatian restaurant uses five gamma chef robots to make meals. *The Spoon*. Retrieved from: https://thespoon.tech/new-croatian-restaurant-uses-five-gammachef-robots-to-make-meals/

Dahal, K. R., Dahal, J. N., Banjade, H., & Gaire, S. (2020). Prediction of wine quality using machine learning algorithms. *Open Journal of Statistics*, *11*(2), 278–289. doi:10.4236/ojs.2021.112015

Eksiri, A., & Kimura, T. (2015). Restaurant service robots development in Thailand and their real environment evaluation. *Journal of Robotics & Mechatronics*, *27*(1), 91–102. doi:10.20965/jrm.2015.p0091

M

Hambling, D. (2018, December 6). *The chef that can make a gourmet burger every 30 seconds*. BBC. Retrieved from https://www.bbc.com/future/article/20181204-the-chef-making-fast-food-even-faster

Hess, A., Spinler, S., & Winkenbach, M. (2021). Real-time demand forecasting for an urban delivery platform. *Transportation Research Part E, Logistics and Transportation Review*, *145*, 102147. doi:10.1016/j.tre.2020.102147

Jang, H.-W., & Lee, S.-B. (2020). Serving robots: Management and applications for restaurant business sustainability. *Sustainability*, *12*(10), 3998. doi:10.3390u12103998

Joe, G. (2021, August 17). Picnic's Pizzrobot hit the market. *Restaurant Business*. Retrieved from: https://www.restaurantbusinessonline.com/technology/picnics-pizza-robot-hits-market

Jordan, M., & Mitchell, T. (2015). Machine learning: Trends, perspectives, and prospects. *Science*, *349*(6245), 255–260. doi:10.1126cience.aaa8415 PMID:26185243

Keyes, D. (2019, March 28). McDonald's is investing $300 million in AI. *Business Insider*. Retrieved from: https://www.businessinsider.com/mcdonalds-acquires-dynamic-yield-ai-platform-2019-3

Ko, C.-H. (2020). Exploring information technology's adoption in restaurants. *Open Access Library Journal*, *7*(6), 1–17. doi:10.4236/oalib.1106470

Li, S., & Kuo, X. (2008). The inventory management system for automobile spare parts in a central warehouse. *Expert Systems with Applications*, *34*(2), 1144–1153. doi:10.1016/j.eswa.2006.12.003

Liu, S., Jiang, H., Chen, S., Ye, J., He, R., & Sun, Z. (2020). Integrating Dijkstra's algorithm into deep inverse reinforcement learning for food delivery route planning. *Transportation Research Part E, Logistics and Transportation Review*, *142*, 102070. doi:10.1016/j.tre.2020.102070

Lou, Z., Jie, W., & Zhang, S. (2020). Multi-objective optimization for order assignment in food delivery industry with human Factor Considerations. *Sustainability*, *12*(19), 7955. doi:10.3390u12197955

Luo, X., Tong, S., Fang, Z., & Qu, Z. (2019). Frontiers: Machines vs. Humans: The impact of artificial intelligence chatbot disclosure on customer purchases. *Marketing Science*, *38*(6), 937–947. doi:10.1287/mksc.2019.1192

Mai, T. (2021, August 24). Orion Star launches 'Lucki', the robotic waiter. *Robotics & Automation News*. Retrieved from: https://roboticsandautomationnews.com/2021/08/24/orionstar-launches-lucki-the-robotic-waiter/45793/

Menichetti, G., Ravandi, B., Mozaffarian, D., & Barabasi, A.-L. (2021). *Machine learning prediction of food processing*. MedRxiv., doi:10.1101/2021.05.22.21257615

Raj, A. (2021, July 29). Perfecting mapping with AI and machine learning. *Tech Wire Asia*. Retrieved from: https://techwireasia.com/2021/07/perfecting-mapping-with-ai-and-machine-learning/

Shen, N. (2021, August 17). *Meet "Bella," the new robot serving Richmond diners*. Vancouver Is Awesome. Retrieved from: https://www.vancouverisawesome.com/food-and-drink/meet-bella-the-new-robot-serving-richmond-diners-4230541

Vijay, G., & Anup, S. (2021, August 6). What Zomato's $12 billion IPO says about tech companies today. *Harvard Business Review*. Retrieved from: https://hbr.org/2021/08/what-zomatos-12-billion-ipo-says-about-tech-companies-today

Wang, J., Hsu, J., Chen, Q., & Jaume, S. (2017). Machine learning: Magic method vs. massive manpower. *Journal of Management & Engineering Integration*, 10(1), 48–58.

Yu, P., & Fu, M. (2020). Machine learning based intelligent prediction of preference for Japanese food. *2020 4th International Conference on Advances in Image Processing*, 158-163. 10.1145/3441250.3441273

Yu, Z. (2021, April 27). There's a hyper hi-tech Haidilao now open in Lujiazui. *Time Out Shanghai*. Retrieved from: https://www.timeoutshanghai.com/features/Blog-Restaurants/89300/There%E2%80%99s-a-hyper-hi-tech-Haidilao-now-open-in-Lujiazui.html

Zheng, Y. (2021, August 13). Digitalization sweeps catering industry. *China Daily*. Retrieved from: https://www.chinadaily.com.cn/a/202108/13/WS6115cb32a310efa1bd6688f4.html

ADDITIONAL READING

Antons, D., & Breidbach, C. F. (2018). Big data, big insights? Advancing service innovation and design with machine learning. *Journal of Service Research*, 21(1), 17–39. doi:10.1177/1094670517738373

Cukier, K. (2020). Commentary: How AI shapes consumer experiences and expectations. *Journal of Marketing*, 85(1), 152–155. doi:10.1177/0022242920972932

de Vericourt, F., & Perakis, G. (2020). Frontiers in service science: The management of data analytics services: New Challenges and Future Directions. *Service Science*, 12(4), 121–129. doi:10.1287erv.2020.0262

Hoffman, D. L., Moreau, C. P., Stremersch, S., & Wedel, M. (2022). The rise of new technologies in marketing: A framework and outlook. *Journal of Marketing*, 86(1), 1–6. doi:10.1177/00222429211061636

Hollebeek, L., Sprott, D., & Brady, M. (2021). Rise of the machines? customer engagement in Automated Service Interactions. *Journal of Service Research*, 24(1), 3–8. doi:10.1177/1094670520975110

Huang, M.-H., & Rust, R. (2020). Engaged to a robot? the role of AI in Service. *Journal of Service Research*, 24(1), 30–41. doi:10.1177/1094670520902266

Huang, M.-H., & Rust, R. T. (2018). Artificial intelligence in service. *Journal of Service Research*, 21(2), 155–172. doi:10.1177/1094670517752459

Kozinets, R. V., & Gretzel, U. (2020). Commentary: Artificial intelligence: The marketer's dilemma. *Journal of Marketing*, 85(1), 156–159. doi:10.1177/0022242920972933

Misic, V., & Perakis, G. (2020). Data analytics in operations management: A review. *Manufacturing & Service Operations Management*, 22(1), 158–169. doi:10.1287/msom.2019.0805

Olsen, T., & Tomlin, B. (2020). Industry 4.0: Opportunities and challenges for operations management. *Manufacturing & Service Operations Management*, 22(1), 113–122. doi:10.1287/msom.2019.0796

Puntoni, S., Reczek, R. W., Giesler, M., & Botti, S. (2021). Consumers and artificial intelligence: An experiential perspective. *Journal of Marketing*, 85(1), 131–151. doi:10.1177/0022242920953847

KEY TERMS AND DEFINITIONS

M

Artificial Intelligence: Mimicking of human intelligence by machines.

Big Data: Datasets that are large and complex.

Catering Industry: Businesses that provide people food and beverage.

Data Mining: Recognition of patterns in datasets.

Food Delivery: A service that delivers food to customers.

Machine Learning: Algorithms that allow machines to learn automatically.

Robot: A machine that can carry out complex actions automatically.

Speedy Management of Data Using MapReduce Approach

Ambika N.

🆔 https://orcid.org/0000-0003-4452-5514

St. Francis College, India

INTRODUCTION

Data (Coombs, 1960) of large quantities are assembled on daily basis in various kinds of applications like Twitter (Murthy, 2013), Facebook (Miller, 2011) etc. To manage them is very tough task. As they are scalable, they require better algorithms in searching, and sorting the data sets. Big data (Fan, Han, & Liu, 2014) has many challenges including coping with speed in performing the assigned tasks. The huge information arrangements are multithreaded and information access approaches are custom-fitted to huge volumes of semi-organized/unstructured information (Ferrucci & Lally, 2004) (Weiss, Indurkhya, Zhang, & Damerau, 2010).

The MapReduce programming system (Dittrich & Quiané-Ruiz, 2012) utilizes two assignments in practical programming- Map and Reduce. MapReduce (Dean & Ghemawat, 2008) is another preparing structure. Hadoop (Lam, 2010) is its open-source execution on a solitary processing hub or groups. Contrasted and existing preparing ideal models, MapReduce (Sabne, Sakdhnagool, & Eigenmann, 2015) and Hadoop (Shvachko, Kuang, Radia, & Chansler, 2010) enjoy two benefits. The deficiency lenient capacity brings about dependable information handling by reproducing the registering errands and cloning the information lumps on various figuring hubs across the processing bunch. The high-throughput knowledge preparation employs a cluster handling structure and the Hadoop disseminated document framework. Information is put away in the HDFS (Borthakur, 2008) (Karun & Chitharanjan, 2013) and made accessible to the slave hubs for calculation.

The suggested work uses hashing methodology to increase speed in searching the required data. The hashing methodology is used to do so. The attributes used are divided into different categories. The classification is made based on the inclinations. Based on the preference of the classified data, the hashing is applied. The suggestion reduces the mapping using hashing method based on attributes by 29.6% compared to (Dittrich & Quiané-Ruiz, 2012).

The chapter is divided into six divisions. The second section summarizes literature survey. The proposal is explained in third segment. The work is analyzed in section four. Future directions are discussed in section five. The chapter is concluded in segment six.

LITERATURE SURVEY

The following section briefs the various contributions given by different authors. The MapReduce programming system (Dittrich & Quiané-Ruiz, 2012) utilizes two assignments in practical programming- Map and Reduce. MapReduce is another preparing structure. Hadoop is its open-source execution on a solitary processing hub or groups. Contrasted and existing preparing ideal models, MapReduce and

DOI: 10.4018/978-1-7998-9220-5.ch018

Copyright © 2023, IGI Global. Copying or distributing in print or electronic forms without written permission of IGI Global is prohibited.

Hadoop enjoy two benefits. The deficiency lenient capacity brings about dependable information handling by reproducing the registering errands and cloning the information lumps on various figuring hubs across the processing bunch. The high-throughput knowledge preparation employs a cluster handling structure and the Hadoop disseminated document framework. Information is put away in the HDFS and made accessible to the slave hubs for calculation.

It is an engineered pattern (Jiang, Chen, Ooi, Tan, & Wu, 2014) that allows customers to prepare multi-structured data in an individual arrangement. The estimate consists of a collection of systems. Sections are autonomous. Every member employ user-defined reasoning. It prepares the info autonomously and interacts with different parts through information passing. A piece becomes stimulated when it accepts communication from the instructor system. It adaptively arranges to learn from the accommodation arrangement and employs the user-specified purpose to prepare the knowledge. The member corresponds to the returns following the warehouse conformity. The learning of the central conclusions is compiled in communications transmitted to the chief system. The instructor arrangement consists of various synchronized supervisors. It is qualified for three services: identifying assistance, intelligence aid, and agenda-setting. Naming assistance allows a sole namespace to each member. They manage a two-level namespace. The primary level namespace designates a collection of systems working the corresponding customer cipher. The following tier namespace identifies the section from the others. epic allows the client to customize the second-level namespace.

The creative items (Gölzer, Cato, & Amberg, 2015) in stock can interact with every other, evaluate usable data, trigger responses, and collectively have the ability for independent self-control and self-optimization. Smart outcomes can be recognized, positioned at all events, know their past, situation, and alternative approaches to achievement. Smart rendering arrangements are correlated to the company's marketing methods, IT systems, and the complete assessment series in the composition system. It permits real-time administration and optimization of the content succession, commencing with an adaptation to the terminal performance of the stock. The part of the analysis, reservation guidelines is designated. The piece of investigation establishes practices for the quantity of writing which is the foundation for understanding. The specifications are expressed in inevitable reports. It acknowledges agreement and analysis of requirements in the specific circumstances of the article. The choice patterns define determination commands whether a part of the commentary provides to the examination interrogation and aims to summary.

The physical tier (Habib ur Rehman, Jayaraman, Malik, Khan, & Medhat Gaber, 2017) is at the deepest level promotes information gain from portable end machines using onboard and offboard sensing and non-sensory knowledge reservoirs. The information layer at the following level enables connectivity and info substitution from movable boundary designs to fog hosts. The statistics collection course provides functionality to aggregate input streams from joining tools and shows evidence filtration processes to assign beneficial raw knowledge streams in store. The analytics tier guarantees the availability of statistics investigation assistance through store aid providers. The administration panel provides functionalities to communicate with IoT utilization. The portable end machines produce data gathering procedures and assign raw input streams in end hosts. This information acquisition maneuvering improves the price of data transmission among portable end appliances and fog hosts. Secondly, fog hosts are defined by physical neighborhoods. The end arrangements need to be in nearness to serve from store assistance. The data processing and analytic elements are implemented through incorporated co-operations. It is improving the computational load in store. Fourthly, IoT utilization is established on top of the store. The fog computing structures involve high coupling among employment elements at distinctive zones (Ambika 2019; Ambika 2021).

The conceptual frame (Gokalp, Kayabay, Akyol, Eren, & Koçyiğit, 2016) permits arrangement technicians to shape, improve and expand the big data use cases for Industry 4.0 purposes. The structure employs an information course-based visible programming design. It promotes resilient employment advancement. Big Data methodology enables arrangement inventors to grow their big info relationships with an optical director. Relevance are interpreted as addressed designs where points describe data tunneling and motor education procedure and programming methods. They are knowledge streams that communicate to moderate issues. The programming links practice and provides data in a standard to control data from different origins and to be combined with other programming connections. Thus, the purpose reasoning can be organized by combining the programming joints without disturbing their accessories and interfaces. The Consequences of the administrations may be transmitted to engaged participants in various configurations. Each assignment course is described as a programming junction in the visible supervisor.

The system (Shafiee, Barker, & Rasekh, 2018) stocks info. This data pool should be divided and unnecessary to expedite quick questioning and decrease knowledge decline. Hadoop-based technologies with a few elements and relationships provide the essential structure for collecting learning. Hadoop is a dispersed computing ecosystem that promotes the processing and accommodation of facts assortments. A Hadoop-based technology is a customized method that uses the Hadoop conditions to implement an administration. Analytical instruments are correlated to the knowledge pool. The objective of these devices is to cleanse info, load in refraining contents, and separate dangerous information. Added analytics are completed at this step as demographic surveys and forecasting. In combination with the dispersed character of the knowledge pool, the software allows for diffused estimates, such as Apache Spark. It is exercised to make computationally expensive analytics and simulations probable. A middleware element that automatically questions new prepared info and arrangements it to design information offered. The middleware incorporates any conversion.

The proposal (Li & Xiong, 2013) is based on encryption method using signature. The scheme provides the source to transmit PKI to the destination. The security parameters are chosen from two groups of prime order. It uses a generator, bilinear mapping and hash functions. The PKG does the computation. The PKG publishes the system parameters and maintains the master credential. The customer submits the identification to the PKG. The PKG calculates the confidential credential and forwards in the safe way. The client chooses an arbitrary number and computes the confidential data and public credential.

It is an application of the service-oriented design structure method (Xu & Helal, 2015) that automates the rule of detector combination. It uses the Atlas sensing principles and Atlas middleware. The Beneath layer consists of two tiers. The physical course refers to the sensor devices and their descriptions. It has a DDL descriptor file associated with it. The file contains the information required for service registration and discovery. It has a signature and representation of the design and a summary of its functions. It also describes the progress of the sensor. DDL forms a detector from a data-oriented prospect. The procedure of a device is a combination of processing successions. This view is consonant with the service-oriented design. The sensor is represented by assistance that presents an interface to its sections shielded from its interior tool.

It is a hierarchical arrangement (Rani, et al., 2015) where all targets placed are immobile and support the communication based on routing. The below courses consist of sensing devices, group administrators, relay connections, and batch supervisors. The topmost zone is the merging panel. This course is composed of base services that are correlated to the internet. In the lower zones, junctions sense the object or the targets and forward the data to the RN joints. RNs pass the info to the CHS. To support the duty of the CHs and CCOs, CHs transfer the knowledge to the higher tier CCO. The extra guidance is over the data to the topmost of CCO. This process proceeds till the knowledge is transferred to the BS at the highest course. The junctions are not provided to interact with another within the group and with the higher course batch. Learning is conveyed via RNs, and connection with the neighbor batch is through the CHs and CCOs only. This deployment holds energy-efficient and scalable IoT (Nagaraj 2021; Nagaraj 2022).

The study (Hong, et al., 2010) consists of four elements. The DDNS hosts maintain the IP position knowledge. It communicates to a region name to manage the movement of joints. The performance servers assist templates, including multimedia and employment regulations such as Ajax. The principles permit consumers to command the periodical recording of the sensed knowledge. Each performance host is assigned to sensing junctions. The detector has shared servers depending on the production of the link. The hub makes HTTP/TCP/IP header concentration and decompression to include an arrangement with interoperability. The devices function as a Web host and help the sensed info from the surroundings through Web co-operations. In DRESS-WS, when a consumer starts the region name of a particular joint in a standard web browser, the browser correlates to the DDNS host to get a similar IP location. The gateway summarizes the HTTP, TCP, and IP headers and transmits the compressed container to the sensor connection. For the initial admittance, the joint responses with HTTP Redirect moving its performance host. Otherwise, it replies with the inquired knowledge. If the customer accepts HTTP Redirect, the browser automatically demands the template records. The request principles in the templates operate and prepare the sensed learning from the equipment. The layout permits a resource-constrained design to assist its knowledge with a rich client interface.

The design (Kiran, Murphy, Monga, Dugan, & Baveja, 2015) joins clump and stream handling capacities for internet handling and uniformly treats monstrous information volumes, decreasing expenses simultaneously. It caters to three layers. Batch handling for precomputing a lot of informational collections. Speed or genuine-time registering limits idleness by doing continuous computations as the information shows up. The third answers inquiries, communicate to questions and gives the consequences. The design likewise segments datasets to permit different computation contents to be executed.

The proposed framework (Rathore, Ahmad, & Paul, Real time intrusion detection system for ultra-high-speed big data environments., 2016) incorporates a four-layered IDS design- caching layer, filtration, and load-adjusting layer, handling or Hadoop layer, and the dynamic layer. The component determination chooses nine boundaries for characterization utilizing forward choice positioning and reverses end positioning. They use benchmark datasets from three hotspots for investigation, testing, and assessment. The dataset has traffic caught by DARPA, which has different interruptions. Each stream portrays 41 boundaries and marks assault of a particular sort. A preparation dataset of KDD contains 24 explicit interruptions with extra 14 assaults in the testing dataset, which incorporates forswearing of administration assault, client to root assault, remote to nearby assault, and testing assaults.

The work (Fusco, Colombaroni, & Isaenko, 2016) gives steady strategy speed forecasts on enormous organizations. It presents a displaying system that executes some notable organization-organized expectation models. The unwavering quality of traffic measures gathers points of organization. The study considers the appropriateness of various forecast models concerning different traffic conditions, like free-stream, intermittent and non-repetitive blockage. The methodology is the idea of gridlock involves that the computational techniques of brainpower should be transportation-propelled. The review region is out of the essential metropolitan street organization of the EUR locale in the Southern area of Rome, portrayed in 0. The total informational index included one month of crude Floating Car Data got by an armada of around 100,000 GPS-prepared private vehicles, relating to 2.5% of the entire vehicular of the town. Each datum point, distinguished with a recurrence pace of 1 perusing each 2 min, reports the position and speed, the condition of the motor, the voyaged separation from the past estimation, the heading of movement, and the nature of the GPS signal. The creators figure out a half-breed displaying system to coordinate the best-deduced assessment in light of time connection. It is given by a merged Seasonal Autoregressive Integrated Moving Average model, with the spatial relationship assessed through a Bayesian organization.

The emotionally supportive network (Lee, Aydin, Choi, Lekhavat, & Irani, 2018) comprises four significant parts-UI, weather conditions document information parser, weather conditions sway excavator and Practical swarm optimization solver. The UI is an electronic framework for autonomous connection with end clients. Weather conditions need to connect with the source. It changes over unique document information into an information design. It deciphers different parts of the choice emotionally supportive network. Direct administrators can conclude the cruising paces of vessels for every leg. The wellspring of the weather conditions chronicle data of the DSS fixes to Copernicus Maritime Environment Monitoring Service. The weather conditions document information distinctly to this information source.

The work (Rathore, et al., 2018) gathered the information by sending a few remote and wired sensors, observation cameras, and other fixed gadgets. It assembles information from homes, brilliant stopping, climate and water frameworks, vehicular traffic, climate populace, observation framework, and so on. Intelligent City Building uses the framework to settle on a choice in light of the constant information to layout the Smart City. The house sends information created by the sensors. Savvy leaving helps in dealing with the vehicles traveling and leaving zones. The expectation can address the water issue. Public security persistently observes the video of the entire city by reconnaissance cameras. The IDS can be carried out at any organization device, like a switch, switch, and even at ISPs and telecom specialists' entryways and firewalls. The rapid traffic is caught with a fast-catching gadget and drivers. The caught traffic is shipped off the following layer filtration and burdens adjusting server.

PROPOSED WORK

The previous work uses Map and reduce method (Dittrich & Quiané-Ruiz, 2012). The MapReduce programming system utilizes two assignments in practical programming- Map and Reduce. MapReduce is another preparing structure. Hadoop is its open-source execution on a solitary processing hub or groups. Contrasted and existing preparing ideal models, MapReduce and Hadoop enjoy two benefits. The deficiency lenient capacity brings about dependable information handling by reproducing the registering errands and cloning the information lumps on various figuring hubs across the processing bunch. The high-throughput knowledge preparation employing a cluster handling structure and the Hadoop disseminated document framework. Information is put away in the HDFS and made accessible to the slave hubs for calculation.

The suggestion increases speed in searching the required data (Buhl, Röglinger, Moser, & Heidemann, 2013). The hashing methodology (Li, Shrivastava, Moore, & König, 2011) (Pieprzyk & Sadeghiyan, 1993) is used to do so. The attributes used are divided into different categories. The classification is made based on the inclinations. Based on the preference of the classified data, the hashing is applied. Let A_1, A_2.........A_n are the attributes used in the work. Let A_1 be the first preference category. A hash key is derived to this attribute. Let H_1 be the hash key derived. The data belonging to the first classification is put away on the location. It is further bifurcated based on the succeeding attribute. All the data belonging to this is further grouped into another set. Let A_2 be the subsequent attribute considered. The knowledge belonging to this set is assembled together. Figure 1 depicts the implementation of the same. Table 1 is the algorithm used to generate the hash key using the attributes.

Figure 1. Representation of the suggested procedure

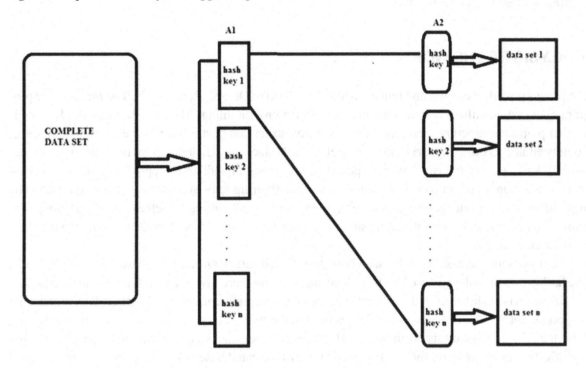

Table 1. generating the hash key using the attribute (24 bits)

Step 1 – Complement the bits in odd position

Step 2 – Group the bits into 3 groups (8 bits each)

Step 3 – Add the bits (group 1 + group 2 + group 3 bits), outcome is 9 bits.

The first outcome bit if not 1, is substituted by 0.

Step 4 – suffix 1 bit to the outcome (10 bits)

Step 5 – XOR extreme bits to generate the final outcome [1 &10 bit, 2 &9 bit, 3&8 bit, 4 & 7 bit, 5&6 bit]

Step 6 – Final outcome is 5 bits

Step 1 – Complement the bits in odd position
Step 2 – Group the bits into 3 groups (8 bits each)
Step 3 – Add the bits (group 1 + group 2 + group 3 bits), outcome is 9 bits.

The first outcome bit if not 1, is substituted by 0.

Step 4 – suffix 1 bit to the outcome (10 bits)

Step 5 – XOR extreme bits to generate the final outcome [1 &10 bit, 2 &9 bit, 3&8 bit, 4 & 7 bit, 5&6 bit]

Step 6 – Final outcome is 5 bits

ANALYSIS OF THE WORK

The previous work uses Map and reduce method (Dittrich & Quiané-Ruiz, 2012). The MapReduce programming system utilizes two assignments in practical programming- Map and Reduce. MapReduce is another preparing structure. Hadoop is its open-source execution on a solitary processing hub or groups. Contrasted and existing preparing ideal models, MapReduce and Hadoop enjoy two benefits. The deficiency lenient capacity brings about dependable information handling by reproducing the registering errands and cloning the information lumps on various figuring hubs across the processing bunch. The high-throughput knowledge preparation employing a cluster handling structure and the Hadoop disseminated document framework. Information is put away in the HDFS and made accessible to the slave hubs for calculation.

The suggestion increases speed in searching the required data (Garofalakis, Gehrke, & Rastogi, 2016). The hashing methodology is used to do so. The attributes used are divided into different categories. The classification is made based on the inclinations. Based on the preference of the classified data, the hashing is applied. Let A_1, A_2.... A_n are the attributes used in the work. Let A_1 be the first preference category. A hash key is derived to this attribute. Let H_1 be the hash key derived. The data belonging to the first classification is put away on the location. It is further bifurcated based on the succeeding attribute. All the data belonging to this is further grouped into another set. Let A_2 be the subsequent attribute considered. The knowledge belonging to this set is assembled together. The suggestion increases speed in searching the required data. The hashing methodology is used to do so. The attributes used are divided into different categories. The classification is made based on the inclinations. Based on the preference of the classified data, the hashing is applied. Table 2 is depiction of the parameters used in Hadoop.

Table 2. parameters used in the work

Parameters used	Description
Minimum data size for group	1024 MB
Maximum data size for a group	50 * 1024 MB
File size	1000 MB
Number of searching request	100
Number of hashes generated based on first attribute	10
Number of hashes generated based on second attribute	5
Number of files used	55
First attribute considered	Creation date
Second attribute considered	Modification date
Simulation time	60ms

- Speed - The previous work uses map-reduce methodology. As the number of files increase, the mapping to the destination also increases. The suggestion reduces the mapping using hashing method based on attributes by 29.6% compared to (Dittrich & Quiané-Ruiz, 2012). The same is represented in the figure 2.

Figure 2. Depiction of speed to search data

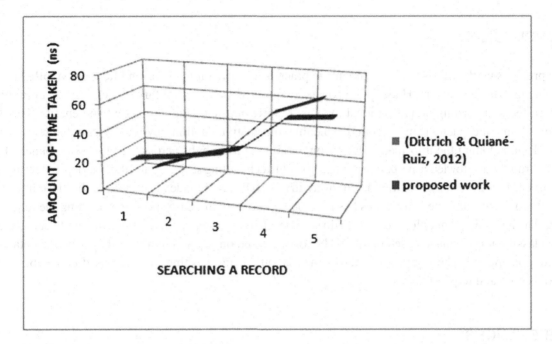

FUTURE RESEARCH DIRECTIONS

The previous work uses Map and reduce method (Dittrich & Quiané-Ruiz, 2012). The MapReduce programming system utilizes two assignments in practical programming- Map and Reduce. MapReduce is another preparing structure. Hadoop is its open-source execution on a solitary processing hub or groups. Contrasted and existing preparing ideal models, MapReduce and Hadoop enjoy two benefits. The deficiency lenient capacity brings about dependable information handling by reproducing the registering errands and cloning the information lumps on various figuring hubs across the processing bunch. The high-throughput knowledge preparation employing a cluster handling structure and the Hadoop disseminated document framework. Information is put away in the HDFS and made accessible to the slave hubs for calculation.

The suggestion increases speed in searching the required data. The hashing methodology is used to do so. The attributes used are divided into different categories. The classification is made based on the inclinations. Based on the preference of the classified data, the hashing is applied. Let A_1, A_2.... A_n are the attributes used in the work. Let A_1 be the first preference category. A hash key is derived to this attribute. Let H_1 be the hash key derived. The data belonging to the first classification is put away on the location. It is further bifurcated based on the succeeding attribute. All the data belonging to this is further grouped into another set. Let A_2 be the subsequent attribute considered. The knowledge belonging to this set is assembled together. The suggestion increases speed in searching the required data. The hashing methodology is used to do so. The attributes used are divided into different categories. The classification is made based on the inclinations. Based on the preference of the classified data, the hashing is applied. The following can be done in future –

- Scalability can be considered. The slave hubs attached has to work in turns to enhance the working of the system.

CONCLUSION

The previous work utilizes two assignments in practical programming- Map and Reduce. MapReduce is another preparing structure. Hadoop is its open-source execution on a solitary processing hub or groups. Contrasted and existing preparing ideal models, MapReduce and Hadoop enjoy two benefits. The deficiency lenient capacity brings about dependable information handling by reproducing the registering errands and cloning the information lumps on various figuring hubs across the processing bunch. The high-throughput knowledge preparation employs a cluster handling structure and the Hadoop disseminated document framework. Information is put away in the HDFS and made accessible to the slave hubs for calculation. The suggested work uses hashing methodology to increase speed in searching the required data. The hashing methodology is used to do so. The attributes used are divided into different categories. The classification is made based on the inclinations. Based on the preference of the classified data, the hashing is applied. The suggestion reduces the mapping using hashing method based on attributes by 29.6% compared to previous work.

REFERENCES

Ambika, N. (2019). Energy-Perceptive Authentication in Virtual Private Networks Using GPS Data. In *Security, privacy and trust in the IoT environment* (pp. 25–38). Springer.

Ambika, N. (2021). A Reliable Blockchain-Based Image Encryption Scheme for IIoT Networks. In *Blockchain and AI Technology in the Industrial Internet of Things* (pp. 81–97). IGI Global.

Borthakur, D. (2008). HDFS architecture guide. *Hadoop Apache Project, 53*(1-13), 2.

Buhl, H. U., Röglinger, M., Moser, F., & Heidemann, J. (2013). Big data. *Business & Information Systems Engineering, 5*(2), 65–69. doi:10.100712599-013-0249-5

Coombs, C. H. (1960). A theory of data. *Psychological Review, 67*(3), 143–159. doi:10.1037/h0047773 PMID:13811748

Dean, J., & Ghemawat, S. (2008). MapReduce: Simplified data processing on large clusters. *Communications of the ACM, 51*(1), 107–113. doi:10.1145/1327452.1327492

Dittrich, J., & Quiané-Ruiz, J. A. (2012). Efficient big data processing in Hadoop MapReduce. *Proceedings of the VLDB Endowment International Conference on Very Large Data Bases, 5*(12), 2014–2015. doi:10.14778/2367502.2367562

Fan, J., Han, F., & Liu, H. (2014). Challenges of big data analysis. *National Science Review, 1*(2), 293–314. doi:10.1093/nsr/nwt032 PMID:25419469

Ferrucci, D., & Lally, A. (2004). UIMA: An architectural approach to unstructured information processing in the corporate research environment. *Natural Language Engineering, 10*(3-4), 327–348. doi:10.1017/S1351324904003523

Fusco, G., Colombaroni, C., & Isaenko, N. (2016). Short-term speed predictions exploiting big data on large urban road networks. *Transportation Research Part C, Emerging Technologies, 73*, 183–201. doi:10.1016/j.trc.2016.10.019

Garofalakis, M., Gehrke, J., & Rastogi, R. (2016). *Data stream management: processing high-speed data streams.* Springer. doi:10.1007/978-3-540-28608-0

Gokalp, M. O., Kayabay, K., Akyol, M. A., Eren, P. E., & Koçyiğit, A. (2016). Big data for industry 4.0: A conceptual framework. *International Conference on Computational Science and Computational Intelligence (CSCI)* (pp. 431-434). IEEE. 10.1109/CSCI.2016.0088

Gölzer, P., Cato, P., & Amberg, M. (2015). Data processing requirements of industry 4.0-use cases for big data applications. European Conference on Information Systems (ECIS).

Habib ur Rehman, M., Jayaraman, P. P., Malik, S. U., Khan, A. U., & Medhat Gaber, M. (2017). Rededge: A novel architecture for big data processing in mobile edge computing environments. *Journal of Sensor and Actuator Networks, 6*(3), 1-22.

Hong, S., Kim, D., Ha, M., Bae, S., Park, S. J., Jung, W., & Kim, J. E. (2010). SNAIL: An IP-based wireless sensor network approach to the internet of things. *IEEE Wireless Communications, 17*(6), 34–42. doi:10.1109/MWC.2010.5675776

Jiang, D., Chen, G., Ooi, B. C., Tan, K. L., & Wu, S. (2014). epiC: An extensible and scalable system for processing big data. *Proceedings of the VLDB Endowment International Conference on Very Large Data Bases, 7*(7), 541–552. doi:10.14778/2732286.2732291

Karun, A. K., & Chitharanjan, K. (2013). *A review on hadoop—HDFS infrastructure extensions. In IEEE conference on information & communication technologies.* IEEE.

Kiran, M., Murphy, P., Monga, I., Dugan, J., & Baveja, S. S. (2015). Lambda architecture for cost-effective batch and speed big data processing. In *IEEE International Conference on Big Data (Big Data)* (pp. 2785-2792). IEEE. 10.1109/BigData.2015.7364082

Lam, C. (2010). *Hadoop in action.* Simon and Schuster.

Lee, H., Aydin, N., Choi, Y., Lekhavat, S., & Irani, Z. (2018). A decision support system for vessel speed decision in maritime logistics using weather archive big data. *Computers & Operations Research, 98*, 330–342. doi:10.1016/j.cor.2017.06.005

Li, F., & Xiong, P. (2013). Practical secure communication for integrating wireless sensor networks into the internet of things. *IEEE Sensors Journal, 13*(10), 3677–3684. doi:10.1109/JSEN.2013.2262271

Li, P., Shrivastava, A., Moore, J., & König, A. (2011). Hashing algorithms for large-scale learning. *Advances in Neural Information Processing Systems, 24*.

Miller, D. (2011). *Tales from facebook.* Polity press.

Murthy, D. (2013). Twitter: Social Communication in the Twitter Age. *International Journal of Interactive Communication Systems and Technologies*, 66–69.

Nagaraj, A. (2021). *Introduction to Sensors in IoT and Cloud Computing Applications*. Bentham Science Publishers.

Nagaraj, A. (2022). Adapting Blockchain for Energy Constrained IoT in Healthcare Environment. In *Sustainable and Advanced Applications of Blockchain in Smart Computational Technologies* (p. 103.) CRC press.

Pieprzyk, J., & Sadeghiyan, B. (1993). *Design of hashing algorithms*. Springer. doi:10.1007/3-540-57500-6

Rani, S., Talwar, R., Malhotra, J., Ahmed, S. H., Sarkar, M., & Song, H. (2015). A novel scheme for an energy efficient Internet of Things based on wireless sensor networks. *Sensors (Basel)*, *15*(11), 28603–28626. doi:10.3390151128603 PMID:26569260

Rathore, M. M., Ahmad, A., & Paul, A. (2016). Real time intrusion detection system for ultra-high-speed big data environments. *The Journal of Supercomputing*, *72*(9), 3489–3510. doi:10.100711227-015-1615-5

Rathore, M. M., Paul, A., Ahmad, A., Chilamkurti, N., Hong, W. H., & Seo, H. (2018). Real-time secure communication for Smart City in high-speed Big Data environment. *Future Generation Computer Systems*, *83*, 638–652. doi:10.1016/j.future.2017.08.006

Sabne, A., Sakdhnagool, P., & Eigenmann, R. (2015). Heterodoop: A mapreduce programming system for accelerator clusters. In *24th International Symposium on High-Performance Parallel and Distributed Computing* (pp. 235-246). ACM. 10.1145/2749246.2749261

Shafiee, M. E., Barker, Z., & Rasekh, A. (2018). Enhancing water system models by integrating big data. *Sustainable Cities and Society*, *37*, 485–491. doi:10.1016/j.scs.2017.11.042

Shvachko, K., Kuang, H., Radia, S., & Chansler, R. (2010). The hadoop distributed file system. In *26th symposium on mass storage systems and technologies (MSST)* (pp. 1-10). IEEE.

Weiss, S. M., Indurkhya, N., Zhang, T., & Damerau, F. (2010). Text mining: predictive methods for analyzing unstructured information. Springer Science & Business Media.

Xu, Y., & Helal, A. (2015). Scalable cloud–sensor architecture for the Internet of Things. *IEEE Internet of Things Journal*, *3*(3), 285–298. doi:10.1109/JIOT.2015.2455555

ADDITIONAL READING

Andoni, A., & Razenshteyn, I. (2015, June). Optimal data-dependent hashing for approximate near neighbors. In *Proceedings of the forty-seventh annual ACM symposium on Theory of computing* (pp. 793-801). 10.1145/2746539.2746553

Buhl, H. U., Röglinger, M., Moser, F., & Heidemann, J. (2013). Big data. *Business & Information Systems Engineering*, *5*(2), 65–69. doi:10.100712599-013-0249-5

Chi, L., & Zhu, X. (2017). Hashing techniques: A survey and taxonomy. *ACM Computing Surveys*, *50*(1), 1–36. doi:10.1145/3047307

S

He, X., Wang, P., & Cheng, J. (2019). K-nearest neighbors hashing. In *Proceedings of the IEEE/CVF Conference on Computer Vision and Pattern Recognition* (pp. 2839-2848). IEEE.

Labrinidis, A., & Jagadish, H. V. (2012). Challenges and opportunities with big data. *Proceedings of the VLDB Endowment International Conference on Very Large Data Bases*, 5(12), 2032–2033. doi:10.14778/2367502.2367572

Leng, C., Wu, J., Cheng, J., Zhang, X., & Lu, H. (2015, June). Hashing for distributed data. In *International Conference on Machine Learning* (pp. 1642-1650). PMLR.

Liu, W., Wang, J., Kumar, S., & Chang, S. F. (2011, January). Hashing with graphs. ICML.

Sagiroglu, S., & Sinanc, D. (2013, May). Big data: A review. In 2013 international conference on collaboration technologies and systems (CTS) (pp. 42-47). IEEE. doi:10.1109/CTS.2013.6567202

Song, J., Yang, Y., Yang, Y., Huang, Z., & Shen, H. T. (2013, June). Inter-media hashing for large-scale retrieval from heterogeneous data sources. In *Proceedings of the 2013 ACM SIGMOD international conference on management of data* (pp. 785-796). 10.1145/2463676.2465274

KEY TERMS AND DEFINITIONS

Attribute: The property of information/input.
Hashing: This is a methodology where the input string is converted to another form.
MapReduce: It is a programming approach used to manage large set of data.

Storage and Query Processing Architectures for RDF Data

Tanvi Chawla

(iD) https://orcid.org/0000-0001-9168-1793

Department of Computer Science and Engineering, Malaviya National Institute of Technology Jaipur, India

INTRODUCTION

Resource Description Framework (RDF) also known as the Semantic Web data model represents data in the form of triples (subject, predicate, object). The RDF data can also be represented in form of a graph where subjects and objects depict the vertices of this graph. A RDF triple is formed by an edge connecting these vertices and the predicate (or property) depicting the edge labels (Peng et al., 2016). RDF is a W3C proposed standard that is used to model objects and represent Semantic Web data. Some of the characteristics of RDF data that are similar to Big data are Velocity, Volume, Veracity and Variety (Özsu, 2016). As the domain of RDF data usage is broadening with its use now not just being limited to Semantic Web, it is becoming quite difficult to handle such large scale RDF data. RDF model is used to represent resources on the web and develop detailed descriptions (also called metadata) for these resources. SPARQL is the W3C proposed query language for querying RDF data. The databases specifically used for storing and querying RDF data are known as triplestores or RDF stores. One of the most popular RDF stores is RDF-3x (Neumann & Weikum, 2008). These triplestores unlike relational databases are optimized to store only RDF data and not any other type of data. The SPARQL query language can be used for querying RDF data from these stores (Banane & Belangour, 2019).

Some of the main challenges in large scale RDF management include storage and query processing. The application of existing SPARQL query optimization techniques on large RDF data is also a huge concern. Many SPARQL queries contain complex joins need to be efficiently executed on this huge RDF data. Some of the popular RDF engines focusing on query performance include RDF-3x (Neumann & Weikum, 2008), Virtuoso (Erling & Mikhailov, 2010), Hexastore (Weiss et al., 2008), TripleBit (Yuan et al., 2013) etc. These engines support RDF storage and SPARQL querying (Yuan et al., 2014). These RDF engines are centralized and thus, store RDF data on a single node. These systems are insufficient for large scale RDF storage and handling complex queries on such huge amount of data. As a result distributed RDF management systems came into existing for improving query performance on large RDF data. These systems partition RDF data among nodes in a cluster and execute SPARQL queries on partitioned RDF data in a distributed manner. One of the main issues faced by distributed RDF systems is the cost of partitioning large RDF data (Harbi et al., 2015). Also, these systems face some bottlenecks while loading or query processing such large RDF data (Cheng & Kotoulas, 2015). Virtuoso Cluster Edition (Erling & Mikhailov, 2010), Clustered TDB (Owens et al., 2009), 4store (Harris et al., 2009) are some of the examples of distributed RDF systems that are built on a specialized computer cluster. The disadvantage with these specialized cluster distributed systems is that they require a dedicated infrastructure. But this limitation can be overcome with distributed RDF systems that use cloud-based solutions.

DOI: 10.4018/978-1-7998-9220-5.ch019

Copyright © 2023, IGI Global. Copying or distributing in print or electronic forms without written permission of IGI Global is prohibited.

The cloud-based RDF systems can be used for multiple purposes and not just for RDF data management. Thus, the existing cloud-based clusters installed with Hadoop MapReduce or Spark framework can be directly used for managing huge RDF data (Schätzle et al., 2011). Some of the advantages of using cloud-based solutions for RDF data management are increased availability and cost reduction. Also, the cloud computing infrastructure can easily store such huge RDF data. The underlying Hadoop Distributed File System (HDFS) of Hadoop can be used for RDF storage and MapReduce or Spark framework can be used for processing SPARQL queries over this stored RDF data in HDFS. The advantage with these cloud-based distributed RDF systems is that the data nodes in a cluster can employ any other storage system (such as a triplestore) instead of the basic file system (i.e. HDFS) for RDF storage (Liu, 2010). Some of the examples of cloud-based distributed RDF systems are SHARD (Rohloff & Schantz, 2010), PigSPARQL (Schätzle et al., 2011), S2RDF (Schätzle et al., 2016), SPARQLGX (Graux et al., 2016) etc. One of the cloud-based distributed RDF systems which does not use HDFS for RDF storage but uses MapReduce for query processing is Huang et al. (Huang et al., 2011). A centralized RDF store (or triple store) such as RDF-3x is installed on each data node in the cluster of these systems. In this chapter, the authors discuss both the types of distributed RDF systems (i) which do not use cloud computing technologies (specialized RDF frameworks) and, (ii) which use cloud computing solutions (cloud-based RDF frameworks).

The rest of the chapter proceeds as follows: Section 3 provides an overview of the different RDF frameworks. In Section 3.1, the centralized RDF frameworks are discussed in detail along with their architecture. Section 3.2 describes the different types of distributed RDF frameworks categorized into specialized and cloud-based along with their architecture. The authors propose a scalable cloud-based RDF framework and describe its architecture in Section 4. Finally, some future research directions are examined in Section 5 and this chapter is concluded in Section 6.

BACKGROUND

Resource Description Framework i.e. RDF is generally used for representing and organizing resources in knowledge graphs owing to its flexible nature . The RDF data is a collection of triples i.e. (s,p,o) where predicate p, represents a relationship between the subject s and object o. The RDF dataset consists of multiple RDF statements which can be represented as a directed graph where edges denote the predicates while the vertices denote the subjects and the objects. Some of the formats used for serializing RDF data are N-Triples (nt), Notation-3 (ns3), RDF/XML, Turtle (ttl) etc. Simple Protocol and RDF Query Language i.e. SPARQL) is a query language used in the Semantic Web. This language is used to fetch data from the RDF data model. A SPARQL query may contain triple patterns, optional patterns, conditions, attributes etc. and the results of the query may yield multiple values (Chawla et al., 2016). SPARQL can be used for querying RDF data, RDFS, and OWL ontologies. The different types of SPARQL queries are star, chain, snowflake, complex etc. A Starshaped query consists of subject-subject joins. Chain-shaped (also known as linear) queries consist of subject-object joins. The snowflake-shaped queries are a combination of multiple star shapes. A complex query is a combination of other query shapes. RDF FRAMEWORKSThe increase in amount of RDF data has led to development of many scalable and efficient schemes for large scale RDF data management. The focus has shifted towards developing scalable RDF frameworks to address this challenge. In this section, different types of RDF frameworks are discussed. These frameworks can be classified as- centralized and distributed. A taxonomy of these frameworks is illustrated in Figure 1.Centralized RDF FrameworksIn these systems, the storage and query processing of RDF data is managed on a single system. The advantage of these systems is that there is no communication cost as SPARQL query processing is done locally. The queries are executed on the single node where RDF data is stored and the results computed are stored in the same machine. But the limitation of these systems is that they have limited memory capacity due to a single node. So, these systems cannot handle large scale RDF data. Also, they are not very suitable for complex queries due to limited computational power of a single machine (Wylot et al., 2018). Chawla et al. (Chawla et al., 2016) and Wylot et al. (Wylot et al., 2018) also discuss some of these frameworks. The centralized frameworks discussed in this section are RDF-3x, gStore, Hexastore, TripleBit and Bitmat.

RDF-3x or RDF Triple eXpress (Neumann & Weikum, 2008) is one of the popular centralized RDF stores. This system stores the index data in a lexicographic order in clustered B+ trees. This system builds indexes over all possible permutations of subject(S), predicate(P) and object(O) i.e. SPO, SOP, PSO, POS, OPS and OSP. Apart, from these 6 indexes RDF-3x also builds projection indexes for each subset of (subject, predicate, object). So, additional 9 indexes i.e. S, P, O, SP, PS, SO, OS, OP, and PO are added to the system.

Figure 1. A categorization of RDF data management systems

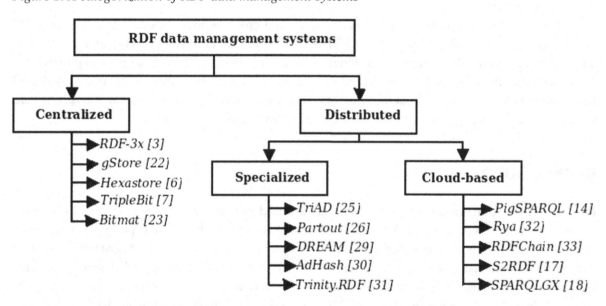

These projection indexes are used for answering some aggregate queries and thus, save overhead of computation of some intermediate results. The statistics provided by these projection indexes are used by cost-based query optimizer of RDF-3x during query optimization. The join cardinalities are estimated by RDF-3x using some refined algorithms to expedite the process of SPARQL query processing. A cost model is used by the query optimizer of RDF-3x for making an optimal choice of best possible join among all possible joins. RDF-3x uses fast merge join and sophisticated bushy join planning for processing SPARQL queries. The drawback of this system is that all indexes need to be scanned even for selective SPARQL queries. Thus, this becomes an overhead for complex SPARQL queries and in case of large scale RDF data.

gStore (Zouet al., 2011) is one RDF system that uses RDF data in the form of a graph. Here, the RDF data is stored as a directed labelled graph where subject and object are encoded as vertices of the graph. The predicate is encoded as a directed edge from subject towards the object that is associated to it. gStore encodes all RDF triples with a given subject and object by maintaining a directed edge (representing predicate or property) from subject to its object. In case, there is more than one property between a subject and object then these properties are represented by multiple edges between these 2 vertices. This system stores the RDF graph over disk in form of an adjacency list table. The system focuses on processing SPARQL queries with wildcards over this disk-based data. Here, each resource in the RDF data is assigned a signature alongwith an integer identifier. Some information about the triples where this resource occurs as the subject is contained in this signature. Some sophisticated indexes built over the signatures are used by this system and these indexes are known as VS-tree i.e. a vertex signature tree. This tree is balanced in such a way that the signature of a resource are represented by each of its leaves. And signatures obtained by performing bitwise OR operation on signature of its children are represented by internal nodes of this tree. This signature is actually a bit-string that is assigned as the signature of each vertex in the RDF graph. The RDF graph is indexed in gStore by mapping it to a data signature graph. The subgraph query matching technique is used for query processing in gStore. Here, a query signature graph is constructed for each SPARQL query where the vertices of a query are encoded into vertex signatures.

Hexastore (Weiss et al., 2008) is a RDF system that supports scalablity of SPARQL queries. In this system, indexing is done by building clustered B+-trees for all permutations of subject(S), predicate(P) and object(O). The six clustered B+-tree indexes that it constructs are SPO, SOP, PSO, POS, OPS and OSP. It eliminates some storage redundancy by sharing some common payload space between these indexes. Like, the SOP and POS indexes share a common materialized set for the associated O values. Thus, Hexastore builds indexes over all these three columns. In this system, many SPARQL queries requiring numerous joins in other RDF systems can easily be answered by using only the index information. The drawback with this system is that it can only support exact SPARQL queries and thus, it cannot handle SPARQL queries contaning wildcards in a scalable way. Hexastore is also not very efficient in handling frequent updates in its stored RDF data as, it needs to modify its six clustered B+-trees for handling these updates.

TripleBit (Yuan et al., 2013) proposed by Yuan et al. is a fast and compact centralized RDF system for storing and querying RDF data. It is based on a compact storage design where a bit matrix storage structure and encoding based compression method is used for efficient storage of RDF data. This kind of storage structure enables this system to extensively use merge joins for query processing. In the proposed triple matrix model, the RDF triples are represented as a 2-dimensional matrix. This matrix is vertically partitioned into multiple disjoint buckets, where each contains triples with the same predicate. This framework uses bitmaps for storing the occurrence or absence of subject-object pairs in a table where the rows represent subject nodes. Here, the data is vertically partitioned in chunks per predicate. This system follows the graph partitioning approach for assigning triples to different machines over a distributed setting (which can be created by installing any centralized system on each node of a cluster) using the METIS graph partitioner. TripleBit comprises of 2 auxiliary indexing structures i.e. ID-Chunk bit matrix and ID-Predicate bit matrix which reduces the number and size of indexes and improves the performance of scan and merge join. In TripleBit, apart from the 2 mentioned indexing structures there are 2 binary aggregate indexes i.e. SP and OP which are compressed using delta compression and stored in chunks. These aggregate indexes are used for selectivity estimation for query optimization during processing. TripleBit employs a dynamic query plan generation algorithm (DQPGA) for executing SPARQL queries with multiple join patterns. The limitation of this system is that although the indexing techniques used here improve query performance but they also result in significant demand for both main memory and disk storage.

Bitmat (Atre& Hendler, 2009) similar to the TripleBit system uses the bit matrix storage structure for storing RDF data. The idea behind this structure is to represent RDF data in a compact manner. This system can be viewed as a three dimensional bit-cube where each unique triple is represented by a bit in a cell and this bit will depict the absence or presence of that triple. This three dimensional bit matrix is flattened into two dimensions for representation of RDF triples in memory. This cube can be flattened in six ways into a Bitmat and each of the resultant structure contributes more efficiently for a particular set of single-join queries. The D-gap compression method is used for compression the data on each row level. The inherent sparsity of Bitmat is handled by maintaining a Bitmat as an array of bit-rows. Each bit-row is a collection of all the RDF triples that have the same subject. The SPARQL join queries are processed using bitwise AND/OR operators on the rows of Bitmat and the query results are returned as another Bitmat. The compact in-memory representation of this system supports management of large RDF data and query execution of multi-join queries in a scalable manner. The advantage of this system is its compact RDF data representation which helps in fast identification of the candidate resultant triples during SPARQL query processing. It also represents intermediate results in a compact format for multi-join SPARQL queries. The drawback of this system is that it does not support dynamic insertion or deletion of RDF triples.

Distributed RDF Frameworks

For tackling the challenge of large scale RDF data, researchers are focusing on development of distributed RDF frameworks (Maet al., 2016). The distributed RDF systems generally, follow a master slave architecture where the master node handles metadata of the slave nodes. The RDF data is actually stored in slave nodes and during SPARQL query processing the slaves exchange data to compute query results. The master handles partitioning of large scale RDF data and stores the data partitions in these slaves. The advantages of these systems are high processing power and large memory space (Wylot et al., 2018). The limitations of these systems include intermediate data shuffling and communication overhead in processing of complex SPARQL queries. The distributed RDF frameworks may or may not use cloud infrastructure for RDF storage and query processing.

Specialized Frameworks

This section describes the distributed RDF frameworks which do not use cloud infrastructure for RDF data management. Some of such frameworks discussed in this section include TriAD, Partout, DREAM, AdHash and Trinity.RDF. The generic architecture of a specialized distributed RDF system is shown in Figure 2.

Figure 2. A general architecture of specialized RDF framework

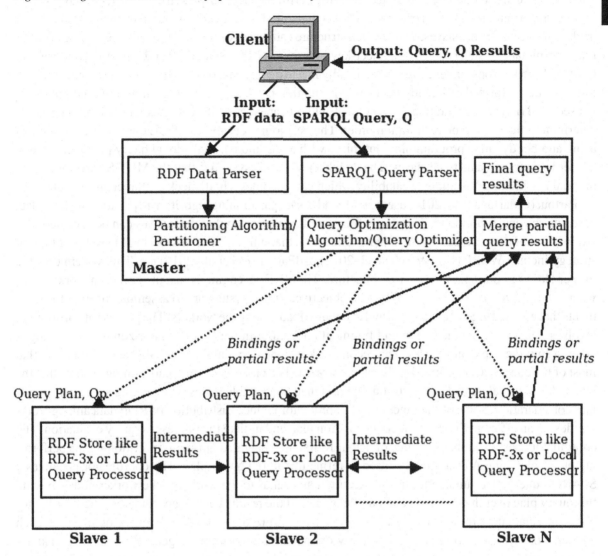

TriAD (Gurajada et al., 2014) stands for Triple-Asynchronous-Distributed system which employs the master-slave architecture for RDF data management. This system uses an asynchronous message passing protocol for communication through messages at the time of query processing. This message passing mechanism is used for parallel evaluation of multiple join operations. TriAD treats the input RDF data as a single large RDF graph and it applies the METIS graph partitioning algorithm on this RDF graph to generate a summary graph. This summary graph is created for maintaining the information of partitioning. It performs indexing over this summary graph at the master node. The indexes for PSO and POS permutations are generated over this summary graph and these indexes are stored as two large in-memory vectors. These indexes are sorted in a lexicographic order. The master node encodes the partitioning information directly into the RDF triples. A horizontal hash-based partitioning scheme is used to partition the encoded RDF triples across slaves. This partitioning method aims at maintaining the locality information obtained by the summary graph and thus, the summary graph partitions are hashed into a grid like distribution pattern. After receiving partitioned RDF triples from master, the slaves create their local permutation indexes over these triples in parallel. As a result, six large in-memory vectors of triples are creates by the slaves. These index structures are used for SPARQL query processing. The six index permutations are arranged as subject-key indexes i.e. SPO, SOP, PSO and object-key indexes i.e. OSP, OPS, POS. These indexes are sorted locally in a lexicographic order so that, the distributed merge-joins can be performed efficiently over these permutations. A dynamic programming based optimizer is used by TriAD for generating a query plan with cheapest cost. It generates an exploratory plan to determining the best graph exploration order. The best join order for SPARQL query is determined by using another dynamic programming optimizer with a cost model. This global query plan generated at master is communicated to all slaves. The drawback with this system is that the METIS partitioner used in intial partitioning has limited scalability which can becomes a bottleneck with increase in data size.

Partout (Galárraga et al., 2014) uses a workload-aware partitioning algorithm to partitioning RDF data based on the query workload. This partitioning method is used so that the queries can be executed on a minimum number of nodes. Some other frameworks that employ similar workload-based partitioning strategy include WARP (Hose& Schenkel, 2013), AdPart (Harbi et al., 2016) etc. This system uses the master-slave or coordinator-worker architecture. The RDF-3x engine is installed on each worker node where data partitions are stored locally. The objectives of this system are to assemble together the fragments that are used together in queries and to balance load among the workers. The process of partitioning involves 2 tasks i.e. fragmentation and fragment allocation. In the first task, horizontal partitioning is done to split the triple into pieces. The second task is done to maintain load balance and to ensure that most of the queries are executed locally at one worker. The process of triple partitioning ensures that the load balance is maintained and partitions are assigned to available nodes while taking space constraints into consideration. Some of the functions of coordinator include distribution of RDF data among workers, design an efficient SPARQL query evaluation plan and initiate the process of query evaluation. The coordinator uses the global statistics of actual RDF data generated at time of partitioning for performing query planning. A cost model is used to refine this initial query plan. The coordinator generates a SPARQL query plan suitable for query execution and sends to the workers. The worker nodes execute this query plan over their local data in parallel and send the results back to coordinator. The coordinator holds the final query results. The local query plan is optimized by the RDF-3x query optimizer at each worker. This system also uses a global query optimization algorithm for generating a query plan according to the selectivity of query predicates. then, some heuristics are used for generating a distributed query execution plan. The drawback of this system is that it takes a lot of time in pre-processing input RDF data and it requires advance knowledge of the typical query workload.

DREAM (Hasan et al., 2016) stands for Distributed RDF Engine with Adaptive Query Planner and Minimal Communication. This system is different from other RDF systems because it partitions SPARQL queries instead of RDF data. In this system, the intermediate data shuffling is avoided completely as here all nodes of the cluster store a copy of the entire dataset. So, it requires exchange of only a small amount of auxiliary data. Thus, DREAM does not use partitioning and instead uses replication where a single database is created to replicate to all workers in cluster. The RDF-3x centralized system is installed on each worker node in the cluster. This RDF-3x engine is responsible for generating statistics and performing query evaluation locally at each worker. A query planner is employed by DREAM for effectively partitioning SPARQL queries. This cost and rule-based query planner uses statistics generated from RDF database to efficiently partition SPARQL queries. This system decomposes or partitions the SPARQL queries into multiple sub-queries. Each worker is responsible for handling a single sub-query. Each worker executes the sub-query in parallel and communicate with each other for returning the final result to the worker. This system exchanges minimum messages during this communication. DREAM is an adaptive distributed system as its query optimizer decides whether to run a SPARQL query in distributed or centralized mode depending on the complexity of a query. The cost model and query planner of this system adaptively selects different number of nodes for different SPARQL queries depending upon the complexity of a query. The drawback is this system is that it suffers from drawback of a centralized RDF engine i.e. RDF-3x installed on each worker node where the entire RDF dataset needs to be loaded. Thus, resulting in an increase in pre-processing overhead.

AdHash (Harbi et al., 2015) is a in-memory RDF system that uses lightweight subject-based hash partitioning strategy to distribute the RDF triples. The lightweight hash partitioning strategy used here helps to minimize the startup cost and it favors processing of subject-based joins in parallel and with no data communication. A locality-aware planner is used for processing of queries that cannot be evaluated in parallel with minimum communication. This system is based on query workload as it keeps monitoring the data access patterns. AdHash dynamically adapts to the workload as it redistributes and replicates frequently accessed data in an incremental manner. A hash based locality scheme is used to maximize the number of joins that can be executed in parallel without any communication. AdHash also uses a locality-aware query optimizer which uses hash-based locality for computing a query evaluation plan that decreases the size of intermediate results that are exchanged between worker nodes in the cluster. The drawbacks of static partitioning schemes are overcome by AdHash by employing an eviction policy for redistributed patterns. Also, it controls replication by operating within a budget. It continuously monitors the executed query workload and updates the created hierarchical heat-map for frequently accessed data patterns incrementally. The hot patterns in this system are replicated and redistributed in a such a manner that the future queries which contain these patterns are executed by the worker nodes in parallel and do not incur any communication. The AdHash system uses master-slave architecture where communication between nodes is done through message passing. The components of a master are: String dictionary, locality-aware query planner, data partitioner, redistribution controller, failure recovery and statistics manager. Storage module, replica index, query processor and local query planner are the components of a worker. AdHash uses two modes for query execution i.e. distributed and parallel mode. The parallel mode is used for queries that do not require any communication and are executed locally by each worker in an independent manner. The distributed mode is used for queries requiring communication. In this mode, the workers concurrently execute the query and intermediate results are exchanged between workers.

Trinity.RDF (Zeng et al., 2013) is a graph-based RDF framework built on top of the Trinity system (a distributed in-memory key-value store). Here, the RDF data is stored in its native graph form and a hash is computed on the values of nodes of this graph to partition it randomly into disjoint parts on the machines in a cluster. Trinity.RDF replaces the query joins with graph exploration for pruning of search space and avoiding generation of useless intermediate results. A SPARQL query is decomposed into a sequence of patterns and an optimized sequence of these patterns is sent to all machines. A sequence of graph explorations are conducted for generating bindings of each of these generated triple patterns. In this sequence, the bindings generated for a previous pattern are used while generating bindings for next triple pattern. The proxy in Trinity.RDF acts as a master and all other nodes that have Trinity engine installed serve as the slaves. A communication protocol based on the Message Passing Interface (MPI) standard is used here for communicating through messages in this system. The SPARQL query is submitted by a user to proxy which generates a corresponding query plan and submits this plan to all slaves (or Trinity machines). Each slave or Trinity machine executes this query plan with coordination of proxy. The bindings or query answers computed by each Trinity machine is sent the proxy. The results are assembled by the proxy and sent back to the user. During query execution the Trinity machines not only coordinate with proxy but also communicate with each other for exchanging the intermediate results. Some of the tasks performed by a proxy (or master) in Trinity.RDF are generating a SPARQL query execution plan based on available indices and statistics; to keep track of each Trinity machine during query processing. The graph exploration strategy used here helps in pruning the invalid triple matchings thereby, avoiding cost of joining large results sets. The drawback of this system is that its graph exploration technique is not very beneficial for non-selective queries.

Cloud-Based Frameworks

The cloud-based distributed RDF systems discussed below use NoSQL stores or HDFS for huge RDF storage and MapReduce or Spark for SPARQL query processing. The distributed RDF frameworks that use cloud computing infrastructure for RDF data management are discussed in this section. Some of such frameworks discussed in this section include S2RDF, SPARQLGX, Sempala, Rya and RDFChain.

PigSPARQL (Schätzle et al., 2011) framework translates the input SPARQL queries into Pig Latin instead of directly implementing these queries on MapReduce. These translated Pig Latin programs are executed as MapReduce jobs. This approach is quite easy as it does not require any changes to the Hadoop framework also, it uses all optimizations that the Apache Pig offers. PigSPARQL uses the popular Jena ARQ engine for generation of syntax and algebra tree. Some of the strategies used here for SPARQL query optimization include selectivity-based rearrangement of triple patterns and early execution of filters. The popular Variable Counting (VC) approach without any pre-computed statistics is used on RDF dataset. Some other strategies used include early projection of redundant data and it also applies multi-joins for reducing the number of joins during optimization. The well known predicate-based vertical partitioning (VP) approach is used here for reducing the number of RDF triples that need to be loaded for executing a SPARQL query. The advantage of this strategy is that it doesn't require more disk space and can be easily done in the beginning using only one MapReduce job. The Pig Latin program is translated into a sequence of MapReduce jobs which are executed in parallel on the Hadoop MapReduce cluster. The Hadoop-MapReduce frameworks like SHARD, PigSPARQL etc. are limited by the batch-oriented nature of MapReduce jobs and using of disk-based operations.

Rya (Punnoose et al., 2015) is built on Accumulo which is a popular key-value store on Hadoop. In Rya, the RDF triples are stored as keys as all information is sorted and indexed by a key in Accumulo. Also, Accumulo does lexicographic sorting on row ID to group and sort the rows. Thus, rows with similar row ID will be grouped and stored together to support faster access. The RDF triples are stored in the row ID part of Accumulo tables. For satisfying all permutations of a triple pattern Rya creates three indexes i.e. SPO, POS and OSP. The row-sorting scheme of Accumulo is used here for efficiently storing and querying of RDF triples across these multiple Accumulo index tables. It uses selectivity-based rearrangement of triple patterns for SPARQL query optimization. The query planner reorders the triple patterns in a query based on the pattern having highest selectivity. This optimization requires pre-computed statistics. Thus, Rya has a built in utility which runs a MapReduce job for counting all distinct subject, predicate and object of a RDF dataset stored in Rya before running a SPARQL query on that dataset. After computation these count statistics are stored in a table for later retrieval. Rya has been used as a plugin for the OpenRDF Sesame framework. This gives it the ability to accept the SPARQL queries and load different RDF formats.

RDFChain (Choi et al., 2013) is a scalable RDF system that provides efficient support for chain SPARQL queries. The number of map jobs are reduced by RDFChain as it processes the maximum number of possible joins in a map job using some statistics (like the number of predicate-object pairs for every subject etc.). This system stores RDF data in a NoSQL database i.e. HBase. By using HBase, the RDFChain avoids the expensive shuffle phase by processing the joins in map phase. The RDF triples are stored in three tables in HBase, these tables are T_{com}, T_{spo} and T_{ops}. The performance of chain queries is improved in this system by using a T_{com} table along with the SPO and OPS index tables. This T_{com} table consist of the RDF triples having terms which co-exist in both the subject and object part of the triples. For e.g. a triple with the term as object is considered as object-predicate-subject (OPS) triple while a triple with term as subject corresponds to subject-predicate-object (SPO) triple. The OPS triples that are not located in T_{com} are stored in T_{ops} and the SPO triples not located in T_{com} are stored in T_{spo}. The chain pattern is a priority of RDFChain for grouping the triples patterns in a SPARQL query. RDFChain is more efficient for processing chain join SPARQL queries as only T_{com} table needs to be scanned for these queries hence, reducing the number of storage accesses. But for processing star pattern SPARQL queries both T_{com} and T_{ops} or T_{spo} need to be accessed. The map jobs are run sequentially in RDFChain.

S2RDF (Schätzle et al., 2016) is a RDF system that is built on top of Apache Spark and uses its proposed partitioning scheme i.e. Extended Vertical Partitioning (ExtVP) to partition stored RDF data. The aim of this partitioning is to reduce the input data during query evaluation. The data skewness is minimized dangling triples not contributing to any join are eliminated by semi-join reductions that are used by ExtVP. The join reductions are pre-computed by ExtVP and the results of this are materialized in tables on the HDFS. These reduced tables are much smaller than the original data tables hence, these reduced tables are used for a join rather than using the base table. The SPARQL queries are translated in S2RDF into SQL jobs which are executed on Spark SQL instead of directly running them on Spark. These generated semi-join reductions are the subset of a vertical-partitioned (VP) table. The reductions represent all the possible join correlations that appear in the SPARQL queries i.e. subject-subject (SS), subject-object (SO), object-subject (OS) and object-object (OO). The main object of S2RDF is efficient execution of SPARQL queries of different shapes. But the drawback of this system is the generation of semi-join reductions at data load time (or at time of data pre-processing) which results in data loading overhead. The computation of these semi-joins is expensive and also generates large network traffic. The possible join relations between the vertical partition tables are pre-computed by ExtVP. For a translated SQL query if the pre-computed semi join tables exist then these are used otherwise, S2RDF only uses the base tables. The RDF data is stored using Parquet columnar storage format on Hadoop Distributed File System (HDFS).

SPARQLGX (Graux et al., 2016) translates the SPARQL queries into the scala code that can be directly executed on Apache Spark. It stores RDF data using the vertical partitioning (VP) strategy where the subject and object (s,o) belonging to the same predicate are stored in a single table. Like other systems such as ProST (Cossu et al., 2018) and S2RDF (Schätzle et al., 2016) that use Spark for query processing which translate SPARQL queries into SQL and use Spark SQL for execution SPARQLGX does not use Spark SQL. It uses its own computations and statistics for optimization. The information about size of intermediate results and data statistics are used by SPARQLGX for optimization. The size of intermediate results during join evaluation is minimized by first evaluating the triple patterns and then joining these subsets according to their common variables. Thus, reducing the size of intermediate results involved in join processing during query evaluation reduces the query execution time as it makes the communication between workers faster. Before translating the query the triple patterns in a query are arranged in ascending order of their selectivity. For computing selectivity to rank the triple patterns the data statistics are computed during pre-processing by counting all distinct subject, predicate and objects. Table 1 lists the storage and query processing platforms used by cloud-based RDF frameworks for storage and query processing.

Table 1. Storage and Query Processing platforms used by cloud-based RDF frameworks

Framework	RDF Data Storage	SPARQL Query Processing
PigSPARQL	HDFS	MapReduce
Rya	Key/value store (Accumulo)	OpenRDF Sesame
RDFChain	NoSQL database (HBase)	MapReduce
S2RDF	HDFS	Spark
SPARQLGX	HDFS	Spark

SCAR- A SCALABLE CLOUD-BASED RDF FRAMEWORK

A scalable RDF framework; ScaR based on the cloud infrastructure as shown in Figure 3 is proposed in this section. This system uses a general purpose Hadoop cluster for storage and processing of large scale RDF data. The purpose behind using cloud-based architecture is that it can be used for storing and processing different types of data and not just RDF data. ScaR is based on adapting existing technologies for large scale RDF data management. Thus, it modifies existing tools for storing RDF data and processing SPARQL queries over stored RDF data. In the first module (module I), the RDF data is given as input by the user to the cloud storage. Firstly, the input RDF data is parsed and stored in N-Triples file format. Then, this data is stored as a single file on HDFS on in tables in a NoSQL database like HBase.

Figure 3. The Architecture of ScaR

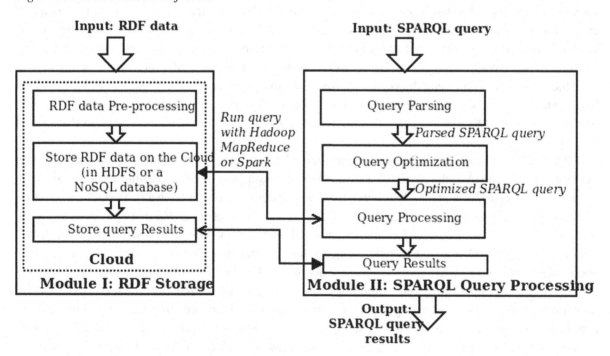

In the second module (module II), the SPARQL query is given as an input by the user. This query is parsed to convert it into a form suitable to be run over the stored RDF data. The query can be translated into MapReduce jobs to be run over Hadoop MapReduce or Spark SQL format to be run with Spark

API. Next, ScaR optimizes the SPARQL query to improve the query performance and for this it uses existing optimization techniques like selectivity-based rearrangement, join reordering etc. The translated and optimized query is run over the RDF data stored on cloud (in module I). The query results returned are stored in the cloud in module I, these results are sent to module II. The second module, gives these query results as output to the user.

FUTURE RESEARCH DIRECTIONS

It is seen that cloud infrastructure is increasingly being used for RDF data management. But there are still several open issues with cloud-based RDF data management. The first issue is SPARQL query optimization on large scale RDF data as the existing query optimization techniques are well suited for small scale data. The second issue is extra storage overhead due to storage of data statistics as part of SPARQL query optimization. Thus, SPARQL query optimization needs more development for distributed RDF architectures.

CONCLUSION

This chapter provides a detailed survey of some of the different type of RDF frameworks. The survey organizes RDF management systems according to the architectures used for handling RDF data i.e. centralized and distributed. The distributed frameworks can further be categorized into:- specialized and cloud-based systems. A proposed cloud-based RDF framework; ScaR used for handling large scale RDF data is described to provide readers a better understanding of the internal components of a distributed RDF framework.

REFERENCES

Atre, M., & Hendler, J. A. (2009). *BitMat: A Main Memory Bit-matrix of RDF Triples.* The 5th International Workshop on Scalable Semantic Web Knowledge Base Systems (SSWS2009), Washington, DC.

Banane, M., & Belangour, A. (2019). An Evaluation and Comparative study of massive RDF Data management approaches based on Big Data Technologies. *International Journal of Emerging Trends in Engineering Research, 7*(7), 48–53. doi:10.30534/ijeter/2019/03772019

Chawla, T., Singh, G., Pilli, E. S., & Govil, M. C. (2016). Research issues in RDF management systems. *International Conference on Emerging Trends in Communication Technologies (ETCT)*, Dehradun, India. 10.1109/ETCT.2016.7882968

Cheng, L., & Kotoulas, S. (2015). Scale-out processing of large RDF datasets. *IEEE Transactions on Big Data, 1*(4), 138–150. doi:10.1109/TBDATA.2015.2505719

Choi, P., Jung, J., & Lee, K.-H. (2013). *RDFChain: Chain Centric Storage for Scalable Join Processing of RDF Graphs using MapReduce and HBase.* International Semantic Web Conference (Posters & Demos), Sydney, Australia.

Cossu, M., Färber, M., & Lausen, G. (2018). PRoST: Distributed Execution of SPARQL Queries Using Mixed Partitioning Strategies. *Proceedings of the 21st International Conference on Extending Database Technology (EDBT)*.

Erling, O., & Mikhailov, I. (2010). Virtuoso: RDF support in a native RDBMS. In Semantic Web Information Management (pp. 501-519). Springer.

Galárraga, L., Hose, K., & Schenkel, R. (2014). Partout: a distributed engine for efficient RDF processing. *Proceedings of the 23rd International Conference on World Wide Web (WWW)*. 10.1145/2567948.2577302

Graux, D., Jachiet, L., Genevès, P., & Layaïda, N. (2016). *Sparqlgx: Efficient distributed evaluation of sparql with apache spark. International Semantic Web Conference*, Kobe, Japan. 10.1007/978-3-319-46547-0_9

Gurajada, S., Seufert, S., Miliaraki, I., & Theobald, M. (2014). TriAD: a distributed shared-nothing RDF engine based on asynchronous message passing. *Proceedings of the SIGMOD international conference on Management of data*. 10.1145/2588555.2610511

Harbi, R., Abdelaziz, I., Kalnis, P., & Mamoulis, N. (2015). Evaluating SPARQL queries on massive RDF datasets. *Proceedings of the VLDB Endowment International Conference on Very Large Data Bases*, 8(12), 1848–1851. doi:10.14778/2824032.2824083

Harbi, R., Abdelaziz, I., Kalnis, P., Mamoulis, N., Ebrahim, Y., & Sahli, M. (2016). Accelerating SPARQL queries by exploiting hash-based locality and adaptive partitioning. *The VLDB Journal*, 25(3), 355–380. doi:10.100700778-016-0420-y

Harris, S., Lamb, N., & Shadbolt, N. (2009). 4store: The design and implementation of a clustered RDF store. *5th International Workshop on Scalable Semantic Web Knowledge Base Systems (SSWS)*, Washington, DC.

Hasan, A., Hammoud, M., Nouri, R., & Sakr, S. (2016). DREAM in action: a distributed and adaptive RDF system on the cloud. *Proceedings of the 25th International Conference Companion on World Wide Web*. 10.1145/2872518.2901923

Hose, K., & Schenkel, R. (2013). *WARP: Workload-aware replication and partitioning for RDF*. IEEE 29th International Conference on Data Engineering Workshops (ICDEW), Brisbane, Australia.

Huang, J., Abadi, D. J., & Ren, K. (2011). Scalable SPARQL querying of large RDF graphs. *Proceedings of the VLDB Endowment International Conference on Very Large Data Bases*, 4(11), 1123–1134. doi:10.14778/3402707.3402747

Liu, J. F. (2010). *Distributed storage and query of large RDF graphs*. Academic Press.

Ma, Z., Capretz, M. A. M., & Yan, L. (2016). Storing massive Resource Description Framework (RDF) data: A survey. *The Knowledge Engineering Review*, 31(4), 391–413. doi:10.1017/S0269888916000217

Neumann, T., & Weikum, G. (2008). RDF-3X: A RISC-style engine for RDF. *Proceedings of the VLDB Endowment International Conference on Very Large Data Bases*, 1(1), 647–659. doi:10.14778/1453856.1453927

Owens, A., Seaborne, A., & Gibbins, N. (2009). Clustered TDB: A clustered triple store for Jena. *Proceedings of the 18th international conference on World Wide Web (WWW)*.

Özsu, M. T. (2016). A survey of RDF data management systems. *Frontiers of Computer Science*, *10*(3), 418–432. doi:10.100711704-016-5554-y

Peng, P., Zou, L., Özsu, M., Chen, L., & Zhao, D. (2016). Processing SPARQL queries over distributed RDF graphs. *The VLDB Journal*, *25*(2), 243–268. doi:10.100700778-015-0415-0

Punnoose, R., Crainiceanu, A., & Rapp, D. (2015). SPARQL in the cloud using Rya. *Information Systems*, *48*, 181–195. doi:10.1016/j.is.2013.07.001

Rohloff, K., & Schantz, R. E. (2010). High-performance, massively scalable distributed systems using the MapReduce software framework: the SHARD triple-store. Programming support innovations for emerging distributed applications (PSI EtA '10), Reno, NV. doi:10.1145/1940747.1940751

Schätzle, A., Przyjaciel-Zablocki, M., & Lausen, G. (2011). PigSPARQL: Mapping SPARQL to pig latin. *Proceedings of the International Workshop on Semantic Web Information Management*. 10.1145/1999299.1999303

Schätzle, A., Przyjaciel-Zablocki, M., Skilevic, S., & Lausen, G. (2016). S2RDF: RDF Querying with SPARQL on Spark. *Proceedings of the VLDB Endowment International Conference on Very Large Data Bases*, *9*(10), 804–815. doi:10.14778/2977797.2977806

Weiss, C., Karras, P., & Bernstein, A. (2008). Hexastore: Sextuple indexing for semantic web data management. *Proceedings of the VLDB Endowment International Conference on Very Large Data Bases*, *1*(1), 1008–1019. doi:10.14778/1453856.1453965

Wylot, M., Hauswirth, M., Cudre-Mauroux, P., & Sakr, S. (2018). RDF data storage and query processing schemes: A survey. *ACM Computing Surveys*, *51*(4), 1–36. doi:10.1145/3177850

Yuan, P., Liu, P., Wu, B., Jin, H., Zhang, W., & Liu, L. (2013). TripleBit: A fast and compact system for large scale RDF data. *Proceedings of the VLDB Endowment International Conference on Very Large Data Bases*, *6*(7), 517–528. doi:10.14778/2536349.2536352

Yuan, P., Xie, C., Jin, H., Liu, L., Yang, G., & Shi, X. (2014). Dynamic and fast processing of queries on large-scale RDF data. *Knowledge and Information Systems*, *41*(2), 311–334. doi:10.100710115-013-0726-7

Zeng, K., Yang, J., Wang, H., Shao, B., & Wang, Z. (2013). A distributed graph engine for web scale RDF data. *Proceedings of the VLDB Endowment International Conference on Very Large Data Bases*, *6*(4), 265–276. doi:10.14778/2535570.2488333

Zou, L., Mo, J., Chen, L., Özsu, M. T., & Zhao, D. (2011). gStore: Answering SPARQL queries via subgraph matching. *Proceedings of the VLDB Endowment International Conference on Very Large Data Bases*, *4*(8), 482–493. doi:10.14778/2002974.2002976

ADDITIONAL READING

Abdelaziz, I., Mansour, E., Ouzzani, M., Aboulnaga, A., & Kalnis, P. (2017). Query Optimizations over Decentralized RDF Graphs. *33rd International Conference on Data Engineering (ICDE)*, San Diego, CA.

Agathangelos, G., Troullinou, G., Kondylakis, H., Stefanidis, K., & Plexousakis, D. (2018). Incremental Data Partitioning of RDF Data in SPARK. *European Semantic Web Conference*, Monterey, CA. 10.1007/978-3-319-98192-5_10

Bahrami, R. A., Gulati, J., & Abulaish, M. (2017). Efficient processing of SPARQL queries over Graph-Frames. *Proc. of the International Conference on Web Intelligence*. 10.1145/3106426.3106534

Chawla, T., Singh, G., & Pilli, E. S. (2017). A shortest path approach to SPARQL chain query optimisation. *International Conference on Advances in Computing, Communications and Informatics (ICACCI)*, Udupi, India. 10.1109/ICACCI.2017.8126102

Chawla, T., Singh, G., & Pilli, E. S. (2018). *JOTR: Join-Optimistic Triple Reordering Approach for SPARQL Query Optimization on Big RDF Data. 9th International Conference on Computing, Communication and Networking Technologies (ICCCNT)*, Bengaluru, India. 10.1109/ICCCNT.2018.8493743

Chawla, T., Singh, G., & Pilli, E. S. (2019). HyPSo: Hybrid Partitioning for Big RDF Storage and Query Processing. *Proceedings of the ACM India Joint International Conference on Data Science and Management of Data (CoDS-COMAD)*. 10.1145/3297001.3297025

Chawla, T., Singh, G., Pilli, E. S., & Govil, M. C. (2020). Storage, partitioning, indexing and retrieval in Big RDF frameworks: A survey. *Computer Science Review*, *38*(1), 1–41. doi:10.1016/j.cosrev.2020.100309

Kalayci, E. G., Kalayci, T. E., & Birant, D. (2015). An ant colony optimisation approach for optimising SPARQL queries by reordering triple patterns. *Information Systems*, *50*, 51–68. doi:10.1016/j.is.2015.01.013

Leng, Y., Zhikui, C., Zhong, F., Li, X., Hu, Y., & Yang, C. (2017). BRGP: A balanced RDF graph partitioning algorithm for cloud storage. *Concurrency and Computation*, *29*(14), e3896. doi:10.1002/cpe.3896

Wylot, M., & Cudre-Mauroux, P. (2016). Diplocloud: Efficient and scalable management of rdf data in the cloud. *IEEE Transactions on Knowledge and Data Engineering*, *28*(3), 659–674. doi:10.1109/TKDE.2015.2499202

KEY TERMS AND DEFINITIONS

Big Data: Big data is any data that is difficult to handle, and cannot be managed by the standard data processing software. The three popular terms associated with Big Data are Volume, Velocity and Variety known as the three V's.

Cloud: A cloud supports storage and management of data on remote servers. It provides these computer system resources mainly computing power and data storage on demand to the users. The cloud services are provided by many companies nowadays to provide convenience to the customers and to save money.

Hadoop: Hadoop is a framework used for processing massive datasets across a cluster of computers in a distributed manner by using a simple programming model.

MapReduce: MapReduce is a programming model used to process large datasets using a parallel and distributed algorithm in a reliable manner.

NOSQL Databases: These are the not only SQL databases that store data different from the relational databases. They support scalable storage and management of large data.

S

RDF: Resource Description Framework (RDF) is a popular model recommended by the World Wide Web Consortium (W3C) to represent resource information on the web.

SPARQL: Simple Protocol and RDF Query Language (SPARQL) is a W3C recommended query language for processing queries over RDF data. A SPARQL query comprises of a Basic Graph Pattern (BGP).

Virtual Singers Empowered by Machine Learning

Siyao Li
City University of Macau, Macao

Haoyu Liu
City University of Macau, Macao

Pi-Ying Yen
Macau University of Science and Technology, Macao

INTRODUCTION

The field of machine learning has been developing over decades, and machine learning techniques are utilized in many areas, such as medicine (Obermeyer & Emanuel, 2016; Rajkomar et al., 2019), natural language processing (Hirschberg & Manning, 2015), and pattern recognition (Fang et al., 2016). With the theory and practice of machine learning becoming more mature, its application areas have also been expanded (Wang et al., 2017).

Empowering virtual singers is one of the newer applications of machine learning. The basis of virtual singers is synthesis software that can create life-like or concert-like voices with computers. Inputting tones and lyrics, producers can synthesize songs through software, and the machine learning technology is used to produce three-dimensional images of virtual singers.

The virtual singer industry was first introduced in the 2000s, when it was a big hit and created history. With the advance of technology during the past twenty years, the industry has been upgraded. Although virtual singers cannot yet overtake traditional singers, they demonstrate a promising and powerful future. According to Chia (2021), China has the biggest potential audience for virtual singers worldwide, and an estimated 390 million people are watching virtual singers. The accompanying animation industry, including TV series and comics, achieved a market value of $35 billion in 2020. Virtual singers have come into people's daily lives. Nescafe and KFC use songs by Luo Tianyi, one of the rising superstars in the virtual singer industry, in advertising campaigns, and Harper's Bazaar put Luo Tianyi's image on the cover of its Chinese edition.

BACKGROUND

One of the most successful virtual singers globally is Hatsune Miku from Japan, who represents a benchmark in the virtual singer area. She won many fans after her debut in 2007 (Liang, 2020), and the song "Tell Your Word", featuring her, ranked first on Japan's iTunes in 2012. Notably, Hatsune Miku is also the first virtual singer to use holographic projection technology to hold concerts: Using a computer-generated voice and 3D graphics, she performs like a real person on the stage. Hatsune Miku performed her first concert in 2009 at Japan's Saitama Super Arena (Corey, 2011). As her influence has increased

DOI: 10.4018/978-1-7998-9220-5.ch020

Copyright © 2023, IGI Global. Copying or distributing in print or electronic forms without written permission of IGI Global is prohibited.

all over the world, she has started to hold concerts overseas. In 2018, she held her first live concert tour in Europe, Hatsune Miku Expo 2018 Euro.

In recent years, more and more virtual singer groups have been emerging in Korea. Aespa, introduced by SM Entertainment and debuting in 2020, is the first girl group to bring the machine learning concept to K-pop (Rowley, 2020). Their latest single song "Next Level" has caught enormous attention. The song was released on 17 May 2021 and entered at Number 33 on the Billboard K-Pop 100 chart, peaking at Number 2 and staying in the top five for weeks (Billboard, 2021). If Hatsune Miku marked the successful emergence of the virtual singer industry, then Aespa has continued this success and is pushing the industry to new heights.

Asia has been the most developed region for the virtual singer industry so far (Chia, 2021). Outside Japan and South Korea, China is also a market of tremendous potential. The latest rising virtual singer is Luo Tianyi, the first virtual singer to make a profit in China. She has attracted hordes of young fans in China, as indicated by her 5 million followers on Weibo. Her songs appear in various advertisements, and the Chinese state-controlled broadcaster has invited her to perform in the New Year's Gala. Luo Tianyi is undoubtedly a great hit in China's virtual singer industry.

Beyond Asia, virtual singers are also gaining popularity in Europe and America. Lil Miquela is a Los Angeles based character who performs rhythm and blues (R&B), electronic music, and popular music. Miquela released her first single song "Not Mine" in August 2017, and one more piece "Over You" in September 2017 (The New York Times, 2019). She released a further 11 songs from 2018 to 2020. By January 2022, Miquela has around three million Instagram followers, and over 80000 streams on Spotify each month. France also has a famous virtual singer named ALYS. ALYS not only sings in French but in Japanese as well. She started her career in March 2014 and was designed as a 21-year-old with a long blue braided ponytail. Her voice was developed by a collaboration between VoxWave and Plogue Art & Technologies. ALYS had her first show, Reve de Machine, at the Trianon in Paris in December 2016 and successfully attracted many fans coming to celebrate Christmas together.

From a technical perspective, the use of machine learning for the music industry has been investigated widely in academia. Readers interested in the technical papers mentioned below may refer to the additional readings.

Nachmani and Wolf (2019) propose an unsupervised method based on a single convolutional neural network (CNN) encoder and a single conditional WaveNet decoder. Their method can create natural voices and high-quality singing from target speakers. Zhang et al. (2020) introduce a singing voice conversion model DurIAN-SC that can produce high-quality voices recognizable as target singers by only adopting their speech data, while Zeng et al. (2021) introduce a large-scale pre-trained model called MusicBERT for music understanding.

Gu et al. (2021) develop the ByteSing system, a Chinese singing voice synthesis (SVS) system that adopts duration-allocated Tacotron-like acoustic models and WaveRNN neural vocoders. They prove by both objective and subjective tests that their proposed SVS method can improve a songs' pitch and spectrogram prediction accuracy, and produce highly natural and high-fidelity songs. In particular, subjective evaluation demonstrates that the system can achieve more than 80 percent of human singing levels, which suggests the effectiveness of their proposed SVS system.

Tae et al. (2021) develop MLP Singer, a parallel Korean singing voice synthesis system, which solves the problem of slow inference speed. MLP Singer consists of multi-layer perceptrons (MLPs). Compared to autoregressive conditional generative adversarial network (GAN) based systems, MLP Singer performs better in terms of audio quality and synthesis speed, especially inference speed.

Lee et al. (2021) concentrate on pronunciation enhancement of voice synthesis. They design a non-autoregressive Korean singing voice system, N-Singer, which can synthesize a Korean singing voice with more accurate pronunciation. N-Singer comprises a transformer based generator, a convolutional neural network (CNN) based postnet, and voicing-aware conditional discriminators. N-Singer is shown by experiments to be more accurate on pronunciation than the baseline model.

Moreover, Huang et al. (2021) present OpenSinger, a large-scale and multi-singer Chinese singing voice dataset, and generate Multi Singer, a fast multi-singer singing voice vocoder with generative adversarial networks.

OPPORTUNITIES AND CHALLENGES

Technology advances constantly connect to content innovation and expansion, and the music industry is no exception. The interaction between machine learning and music generates opportunities for creative users in composition, lyrics writing, and even filmmaking. Creative users can communicate with each other and share innovative ideas inspired by virtual singers, which acts as a spur to the development of the music industry. This phenomenon is called Vocaloid Culture: When one creates a song, someone else can attach a story, design an image, or make a music video. "It is not just music that has been created," said Hiroyuki Ito, the chief executive of Crypton Future Media (Chia, 2021). Innovative users often share their work on the singer's fan site or fan accounts on Twitter, Facebook, and Weibo. For instance, there is a Twitter account called Hourly Hatsune Miku, and it tweets images created by fans every hour.

The unprecedented mixture of machine learning and entertainment can create a remarkable marketing effect. Virtual singers may attract people who are ambivalent about music due to their uniqueness. The number of fans of virtual singers can be huge, and many of them are not only interested in the music itself but are fascinated by the technological aspect of this industry, which contributes a considerable commercial value.

Managing real singers usually requires human resources, time, and money. For instance, in the K-POP industry, applicants who want to become a K-POP star must take training courses for several years after they pass the audition. During the training, agencies will provide them with lessons such as singing, dancing, rapping, and even foreign language (Lee, 2018). This is a tremendous expense. By contrast, since virtual singers do not exist in reality, their management is relatively easy and less costly. Creators can produce songs with synthetic human voices by audio editing software that costs only $225 for a flat fee (Chia, 2021). Hideki Kenmochi, who developed Vocaloid for Yamaha, said that, using Vocaloid, they "do not need a singer" (Corey, 2011).

During the COVID-19 pandemic, online media channels have grown rapidly, and virtual artists have some specific advantages in the current circumstances. Under the pandemic, human singers cannot give performances in person, which significantly restricts the development of the entertainment industry. However, social distancing provides a chance for virtual singers. Virtual singers are products of the information technology times, and their value is maximized through the Internet. Eminent recent evidence shows that virtual singers are able to take advantage of the current hot trend of non-fungible tokens (NFTs) to generate revenue (Cirisano, 2021). For example, FN Meka, a robot rapper who performs music created with machine learning algorithms, managed to sell a "super toilet" NFT for $6400 in March 2021. Another example is Spirit Bomb, a creative studio producing virtual artists with real-life creators. Its character card NFT, featuring the virtual artist XEN, was sold for $4000 in April 2021. Similarly, League of Legends, an online game, sells 'skins' that let players dress like the virtual K-pop girl group K/DA, with the price for 'skins' a few dollars each. Notably, this in-game item generated a revenue of about $50 billion worldwide in 2020, which was even more than the entire music business took in, according to MIDiA Research.

However, one primary concern of virtual singers empowered by machine learning is copyright. In the traditional music industry, works produced by human artists are protected by copyright: A music sample with only two seconds in music composition was considered copyright-protected (Bob et al., 2019). If someone adopts or modifies a musical work produced by human artists without prior permission, he or she may face legal actions. However, the protection of works generated by machine learning is ambiguous. That is, it may be hard to protect the copyright of songs for virtual singers. For example, in the UK, works created by machines are defined as works without human authors. In this situation, there is no specific legislation to enforce copyright, and the development of virtual singers can be considerably affected. In other countries, whether a work is under copyright protection can depend on the extent of human contribution to the final results. According to the Court of Justice of the European Union (CJEU), a work is considered original when it expresses the author's creative choices, personality, or personal touch. Since virtual singers are generated from machine learning that is either operated or accompanied by people, it is hard to determine where the copyright will fall. In sum, though the existing legislation protects works generated by human artists in the traditional music industry, there is a vacuum in the existing legislation for virtual singers to enjoy copyright protection.

Virtual singers also face other complicated challenges. On the one hand, there are concerns regarding the relationship between virtual singers and human singers, as virtual artists may replace actual human artists in the future. On the other hand, it is difficult for virtual singers to relate emotionally to audiences as they are just machine learning algorithms, and human singers are still significantly in demand in the industry.

SOLUTIONS AND RECOMMENDATIONS

Copyright legislation depends largely on human-centered concepts, which denies protection for computer-generated creations (Bob et al., 2019). Thus, it is hard to obtain copyright protection for works generated or performed by machine learning. The existing legislation is principally unfriendly to virtual artists, and the modification of copyright legislation is needed to extend protection to virtual artists. There are also exceptions: Some laws, such as competition law, can effectively protect the outputs of machine learning without human contribution, and these laws can protect virtual artists to a certain degree (Jean-Marc & Frank, 2019). However, when it comes to collaboration between humans and machine learning, it is hard to determine where the copyright will fall. Questions that need to be answered are whether a work is produced by a virtual singer and to what extent. This requires a case-by-case analysis. Therefore, it is necessary to improve the existing legislation to protect virtual artists.

Nowadays, teenagers spend a lot of time online, and what attracts them is the built-in stories and personalities produced by companies that are trying to create a character. According to Ian Simon, co-founder of Spirit Bomb, "what allows people to connect is seeing their story and persona and wanting to follow the next step on their journey" (Cirisano, 2021). Though virtual singers are machine learning algorithms without human feeling, emotional resonance with audiences can also be achieved by a fascinating background story that allows audiences to follow. Moreover, since the interactions between virtual singers and audiences mostly take place on the Internet, these shallow emotional relations are already adequate to win many fans for the industry to develop. According to Trevor McFedries, the creator of virtual singer Miquela, "young people do not differentiate between" virtual singers and human celebrities they follow (Cirisano, 2021). Though the virtual singer industry is still a largely unexplored field, people will have more opportunities to see virtual singers appear in a future stage.

FUTURE RESEARCH DIRECTIONS

Many major entertainment companies have now become investors in virtual artists and have given them a chance for mainstream success. Stephen Cooper, CEO of Warner Music, called virtual artists "not an illogical next step" and said Warner Music is "determined to lead the crossovers of these virtual beings into the music world" (Glenn, 2021). For example, Avex USA, the branch of Japanese music company Avex, invented Spirit Bomb, which Warner Music invests in and treats as one of the most promising brands in the virtual singer industry. This collaboration gives Spirit Bomb an opportunity to create more virtual artists, and more importantly, develop immersive content, such as interactive live streams that allow audiences to influence performances in real-time (Chris, 2021). In this way, the gap between virtual live shows and real experiences is narrowed. With more interactions between virtual artists and audiences, a wider range of fans, who used to have no interest in this industry because of the lack of interactions, will be attached to it. It is around the corner that these creative virtual artists will occupy part of the mainstream market one day. In this context, studying the best way for investors to engage in the virtual artist industry and split the profits with virtual artist producers could be an intriguing issue.

It would also be interesting to study the interaction between virtual singers and live streamers. In the Chinese market, audiences tend to pay great attention to mainstream live streaming, such as Taobao Live. As a result of the COVID-19 pandemic, live streamers have become increasingly popular and profitable. To catch up with this trend, famous idols and actors have started to collaborate with live streamers, and virtual singers are not an exception. The Chinese virtual singer Luo Tianyi hosted alongside top Chinese live streamer Li Jiaqi twice, with their second collaboration almost three million viewers at the peak. During the 618 Shopping Festival, Hatsune Miku joined Taobao live. With her popularity, around ten million page visits and virtual gifts were created (Zhuang, 2020). The combined influence of virtual singers and human live streamers is significant. Many young audiences are attracted by this innovative combination. Humans and virtual images appearing in life at the same time and communicating with audiences provide a fresh experience for viewers, especially young people. Virtual singers are not flat internet images but full characters like a real human. They offer terrific potential to many industries because they are not restricted by location and time. For audiences, virtual singers' advantage in creating fresh experiences benefits the development of both the virtual singer and live streaming industries. In the future, how virtual singers interact with social media and live streamers is worth investigating.

CONCLUSION

Machine learning has shown its power in various industries, and the music industry is one of them. The current chapter briefly introduces virtual singers empowered by machine learning and discusses how machine learning applications affect the music industry in general. Virtual singers have great market potential and even some advantages over their human counterparts: they stimulate creative content; they are able to reach a wider audience; they are easy to manage and save various costs; and physical constraints do not limit them. Nevertheless, virtual singers also face challenges. Concurrent copyright legislation does not cover content from virtual singers, and a lack of ability for virtual singers to communicate with people hinders the further development of the industry. The authors propose possible measures to resolve these challenges, such as expanding legislation to protect the copyright of virtual singers' work and endowing virtual singers with personalities. Moreover, this chapter sheds light on future research directions, including the relationship between investors and creators of virtual singers, and the interaction between virtual singers and live streamers.

REFERENCES

Chia, K. (2021, June 12). Virtual singers headline multibillion-dollar industry in China. *Bloomberg*. Retrieved from: https://www.bloomberg.com/news/articles/2021-06-12/virtual-singers-headline-multi-billion-dollar-industry-in-china

Chris, E. (2021, April 3). The deals: Avex invests in 'virtual artist' label spirit bomb, quality control strikes gaming partnership. *Billboard*. Retrieved from: https://www.billboard.com/amp/articles/business/9534634/spirit-bomb-avex-quality-control-xset-gaming-deals

Cirisano, T. (2021, June 28). Will avatars kill the radio stars? Inside today's virtual artist record labels. *Billboard*. Retrieved from: https://www.billboard.com/articles/business/9593890/virtual-artist-record-labels-avatars/

Corey, T., & Werman, M. (2011, July 4). Digital pop star Hatsune Miku's first live concert. *The World*. Retrieved from: https://theworld.org/stories/2011-07-04/digital-pop-star-hatsune-mikus-first-live-concert

Fang, Y., Yashin, V., Levitan, S., & Balazs, A. (2016). Pattern recognition with "materials that compute". *Science*, *2*(9), 1–10. doi:10.1126ciadv.1601114 PMID:27617290

Glenn, P. (2021). 5 things warner music group's earnings say about the industry's future. *Billboard*. Retrieved from: https://www.billboard.com/amp/articles/business/record-labels/9611135/warner-music-group-earnings-analysis-industry-future

Hirschberg, J., & Manning, C. (2015). Advances in natural language processing. *Science*, *349*(6245), 261–266. doi:10.1126cience.aaa8685 PMID:26185244

Hsu, T. (2019, June 17). These influencers aren't flesh and blood, yet millions follow them. *The New York Times*. Retrieved from: https://www.nytimes.com/2019/06/17/business/media/miquela-virtual-influencer.html

Jean-Marc, D., & Frank, M. (2019). *Authorship in the age of machine learning and artificial intelligence*. The Oxford Handbook of Music Law and Policy.

Korea Staff. (2021, July 29). Aespa ready for the 'next level' with back-to-back k-pop hits & their own 'universe'. *Billboard*. Retrieved from: https://www.billboard.com/articles/news/international/9607462/aespa-next-level-profile

Liang, L.-H. (2020, November 22). *China gives musical talent show a virtual makeover*. BBC. Retrieved from: https://www.bbc.com/news/entertainment-arts-54967096

Obermeyer, Z., & Emanuel, E. (2016). Predicting the future— Big data, machine learning, and clinical medicine. *The New England Journal of Medicine*, *375*(13), 1216–1219. doi:10.1056/NEJMp1606181 PMID:27682033

Rajkomar, A., Dean, J., & Kohane, I. (2019). Machine learning in medicine. *The New England Journal of Medicine*, *380*(14), 1347–1358. doi:10.1056/NEJMra1814259 PMID:30943338

Rowley, G. (2020, November 18). New k-pop girl group Aespa debuts with colorful video for 'Black mamba': Watch. *Billboard*. Retrieved from: https://www.billboard.com/articles/columns/k-town/9485979/aespa-black-mamba-video/

Sturm, B., Iglesias, M., Ben-Tal, O., Miron, M., & Gómez, E. (2019). Artificial intelligence and music: Open questions of copyright law and engineering praxis. *Arts*, *8*(3), 115. doi:10.3390/arts8030115

Wang, J., Hsu, J., Chen, Q., & Jaume, S. (2017). Machine Learning: Magic Method vs. Massive Manpower. *Journal of Management & Engineering Integration*, *10*(1), 48–58.

Zhuang, J. (2020). *Will virtual livestreamers replace humans in China?* Retrieved from: https://jingdaily.com/will-virtual-livestreamers-replace-humans-in-china/

ADDITIONAL READING

Gu, Y., et al. (2021). ByteSing: A Chinese singing voice synthesis system using duration allocated encoder-decoder acoustic models and WaveRNN vocoders. *2021 12th International Symposium on Chinese Spoken Language Processing (ISCSLP)*. 10.1109/ISCSLP49672.2021.9362104

Huang, R., et al.(2021). Multi-singer: Fast multi-singer singing voice vocoder with a large-scale corpus. *Proceedings of the 29th ACM International Conference on Multimedia*. 10.1145/3474085.3475437

Lee, G., Kim, T., Bae, H., Lee, M., Kim, Y., & Cho, H. (2021). N-singer: A non-autoregressive Korean singing voice synthesis system for pronunciation enhancement. *Interspeech*, *2021*, 1589–1593. Advance online publication. doi:10.21437/Interspeech.2021-239

Nachmani, E., & Wolf, L. (2019). Unsupervised singing voice conversion. *Interspeech*, *2019*, 2583–2587. Advance online publication. doi:10.21437/Interspeech.2019-1761

Tae, J., Kim, H., & Lee, Y. (2021). MLP singer: Towards rapid parallel Korean singing voice synthesis. *2021 IEEE 31st International Workshop on Machine Learning for Signal Processing (MLSP)*. 10.1109/MLSP52302.2021.9596184

Zeng, M., Tan, X., Wang, R., Ju, Z., Qin, T., & Liu, T. (2021). MusicBERT: Symbolic music understanding with large-scale pre-training. *Findings of the Association for Computational Linguistics: ACL-IJCNLP*, *2021*, 791–800. Advance online publication. doi:10.18653/v1/2021.findings-acl.70

Zhang, L., Yu, C., Lu, H., Weng, C., Zhang, C., Wu, Y., Xie, X., Li, Z., & Yu, D. (2020). Durian-sc: Duration informed attention network based singing voice conversion system. *Interspeech*, *2020*, 1231–1235. Advance online publication. doi:10.21437/Interspeech.2020-1789

KEY TERMS AND DEFINITIONS

Artificial Intelligence: Simulation of human thinking and actions by machines.

Big Data: Datasets that are in large volume and high variety.

Copyright: Protection of the intellectual property of original works.

Data Mining: Extraction of patterns in datasets.

Entertainment Industry: Businesses that provide people pleasure.

Machine Learning: Artificial intelligence that allows machines to improve automatically.

Virtual Singer: A singer who is not a human being but a virtual character.

Section 5
Big Data as a Service

Analyzing U.S. Maritime Trade and COVID-19 Impact Using Machine Learning

Peter R. Abraldes
Pennsylvania State University, USA

James Rotella
Pennsylvania State University, USA

Partha Mukherjee
Pennsylvania State University, USA

Youakim Badr
Pennsylvania State University, USA

INTRODUCTION

Americans import and export goods in three primary ways: air, land (truck, rail, and pipeline), and sea. Out of the three methods, maritime trade is the primary vessel of international trade. As of 2013, as much as 53% of imports and 38% of exports move through American ports, measured in U.S. dollars. The deepening of the Panama Canal and local passages around U.S. ports has encouraged ocean carriers to realize economies of scale by using larger vessels. The maximum size of a ship increased from about 15,000 twenty-foot equivalent units (TEUs) in 2010 to 23,000 TEUs in 2020 (Manaadiar, 2020).

Although monetary terms are one form of measuring value, its meaning is relative to the current exchange rate and value of the USD. Economists have traditionally focused on monetary measurements such as the product's value and national GDP. Instead, we opt to measure trade in metric tonnage. Over time, general baskets of goods retain relatively constant weights whereas real values vary based on exchange rates, scarcity, and inflation. When measured in metric tonnage, maritime trade accounts for 72.4% of imports and 74.8% of exports to and from the United States. In 2019, the Bureau of U.S. Customs and Border Protection cleared 11,160,342 shipments. Serious importers and exporters overwhelmingly prefer sending their goods by sea.

Goods can be transported by sea in a variety of ways, including liquid bulk, breakbulk, roll-on/roll-off (ro/ro), and containers, with the latter being the preferred method for most shippers (Mittal, Boile, Baveja, & Theofanis, 2013). Liquid bulk can be measured in ISO tanks, ro/ro in units, and breakbulk in cartoons, bags, or boxes. The variety of measurements can make cross-comparison difficult. This is yet another reason to use metric tonnage as the standard unit of comparison. Although valuations in the U.S. dollar may facilitate understanding in broad economic terms, the analysis is only useful for shorter time intervals, when framed in the specific time period studied.

This paper begins by elaborating on literary, industry, and historical support that justifies the chosen attributes and time period. Next, details related to data collection and methodologies are outlined. Data analysis and results are divided into subcategories for each model. Models are developed and evaluated to

DOI: 10.4018/978-1-7998-9220-5.ch021

Copyright © 2023, IGI Global. Copying or distributing in print or electronic forms without written permission of IGI Global is prohibited.

answer the research questions. This is followed by an analytics section to highlight trends. We conclude with a section with recommendations for future research.

Background

Since the end of WWII, the United States has been the standard bearer of neoliberalism and, an advocate of free trade (Chang, 2002; Steger & Roy, 2010). The U.S. entered the 1950s as the primary engine of growth for the world economy. Over the decades its share of imports and exports declined, relative to the rest of the world (Irwin, 2017; Yildrim & Saccomano, 2021). Beginning in the 2010s, some Americans became skeptical that free trade worked for them. This discontent materialized in abrupt trade policy changes in 2016.

Imports gained market share in the 1980s as policy prioritized inflation mitigation and floating exchange rates at the expense of jobs. Proponents of neoliberalism argued that the consumer benefits from the increased quantity and variety of imports. It is estimated that the annual earning power of the average American has increased by over $18,000 per annum between 1950 and 2016 (Hufbauer & Lu, 2019). In 2019, 2.5 trillion dollars of goods were exported while 2.6 trillion dollars of goods were imported. Taken together, the U.S. has benefited from increased trade, in measurable, economic terms.

The changing attitudes toward trade were observed through proxy variables such as unemployment, exchange rates, applied tariff rates, and the size of companies who participate in the international market. Changes among these variables can produce a shock to the global supply chain, influencing the behavior of companies and consumers alike. Wars, famine, and plagues and viruses have had impacts, but these risks have been mostly ignored in recent international trade theory (Irwin, 2017). COVID-19 upended various parts of the supply chain as the pandemic spread throughout the world in 2020 (Baldwin & Di Mauro, 2020). The first effect was a dramatic and rapid reduction in the labor force in affected locations, as workers fell ill or were forced to quarantine (Charlton & Castillo, 2021). International trade was impacted further as borders limited the flow of people and products (Kerr, 2020). These restrictions further exacerbated supply chain disruptions within and among countries, as goods themselves were prioritized differently. However, food and agriculture supply lines were relatively unaffected in the short term, due to narrow time windows between harvest, shipment, and consumption. Even during a pandemic, the global population still needed to eat (Kerr, 2020).

Although the period studied does not include the time period post-global vaccination or data about economic stimulus, enough time has passed to assess the impact of the COVID-19 disruption on international trade, considering this disruption in the context of other possible variables such as unemployment, average applied tariff rates, exchange rates, free trade agreements, and other factors.

The applied tariff rates of countries is one change that may prove transitory or could confound the disruptions caused by the direct or indirect measures of COVID-19. It is still too early to tell if the pandemic will lead to a more decentralized global economic system (Anderson, Rainie, & Vogels., 2021).

There are practical implications of this work for supply chain and logistics professionals. Until the tariff disputes in the late 2010s, the supply chain prioritized "just in time" deliveries, stretched over long distances, that delivered the exact goods, in the right quantities, to the right buyers (Kootanaee, Babu, Nagendra, & Hamid, 2013). Supply chain analytics considered scarcity, strikes, changes in domestic and international policies, and natural disasters, but did not generally anticipate a global pandemic.

This study uses tens of millions of records, aggregating quantitative variables by month and year. Time series, tree-based, and artificial neural network models are used in the attempt to answer some of the research questions, using literature from international trade economists, supply chain professionals, and financial analysts. The study emphasizes the stochastic shocks of pandemics, without confining itself to some standard assumptions about free trade and neoliberalism.

Most businesses will continue to have extensive supply chains across international borders. They will seek to constantly optimize operations and mitigate risk. This uncertainty comes in the form of economic cycles, the labor market, exchange rate fluctuations, tariffs, changes in geopolitical strategies, and local epidemics and global pandemics.

These considerations have led to the development of two research questions:

1. Which variables had the greatest impact on the variation of metric tonnage, between the years 2010 and 2019? Is there a difference when assessing the average shipment or shipments taken together per year?
2. How does the introduction of COVID-19 in 2020 affect the variation of metric tonnage for this time period? Are there differences when considering the average shipment weight versus the aggregate annual metric tonnage?

Data Collection

The questions presented in the analysis are, interconnected and require a variety of data sources to answer sufficiently. Data had to establish historical import and export volumes and composition, as well as account for some potential confounding effects. Examples of these are longitudinal rates for applied tariffs, currency exchange, and unemployment. COVID-19 is measured directly by known case and death counts per state, as well as indirectly by these other metrics.

Data was obtained from various sources, including the U.S. Census Bureau, U.S. Customs and Border Protection via Descartes Datamyne, the New York Times, the Kaiser Family Foundation, the WTO, the Office of the US Trade Representative, Stock Market Quotes & Financial News, and the U.S. Bureau of Labor Statistics. Data feature engineering helped address the sources of metric tonnage variation over the time-frame, including creating categorical bins for some quantitative data.

U.S. states and U.S. ports are consolidated into regional groups. The standardized Harmonized Commodity Description and Coding System (HS) bins all tangible items into 99 chapter codes, ranging from 01 to 99 where the traders define and group products based on common four and six-digit number combinations.

Shipments with multiple HS chapter codes are flagged as having mixed cargoes. Clean HS chapter codes and descriptions are created through clustering techniques, cleaning the original labeling found on the original bills of lading. These consistent category classes are further binned with similar classes into HS groups hypothesized as being the most impacted by the COVID-19 pandemic. 23 HS Classes are categorized into six HS Groups. This includes the HS chapter codes and the general description as listed by the World Customs Organization.

All trading corporations and ocean line carriers were binned by consistent size groups, based on total metric tonnage over 11 years. Foreign countries are also binned by both continent and region. Regions are thought to be separate from continents due to other latent factors relating to history, language, and culture.

Google OpenRefine was instrumental in clustering and cleaning companies, countries, and ports, allowing data dictionaries to be built and used to standardize values (Stephens, 2021). Records are fed into the tool in chunks, using the n-gram fingerprint, metaphone3, and finally the "Soundex" algorithm to standardize variations in nomenclature (Yang & Tsai, 2021).

Table 1. Tonnage ranges for assigning company size

Metric Ton Range	Group Name
100 - 1,000	micro
1,000.01 - 10,000	small
10,000.01 - 100,000	medium
100,000.01 - 1,000,000	large
1,000,000.01 +	huge
NOT AVAILABLE*	unknown
**	missing

The 23 HS classes were grouped in six HS groups as categorized below:

- **Edible (meat, vegetables, fruit)**
  - 02: Meat and edible meat offal.
  - 07: Edible vegetables and certain roots and tubers.
  - 08: Edible fruit and nuts; peel of citrus fruit or melons.
- **Edible with Processing (food that requires additional processing)**
  - 09: Coffee, tea, maté, spices.
  - 10: Cereals.
  - 11: Products of the milling industry; malt; starches; inulin; wheat gluten.
  - 14: Vegetable plaiting materials; vegetable products not elsewhere specified or included.
  - 15: Animal or vegetable fats and oils and their cleavage products prepared edible fats; animal or vegetable waxes.
  - 16: Preparations of meat, of fish or of crustaceans, molluscs or other aquatic invertebrates.
  - 17: Sugars and sugar confectionary.
  - 18: Cocoa and cocoa preparations.
  - 19: Preparations of cereals, flour, starch or milk; bakers' wares.
  - 20: Preparations of vegetables, fruit, nuts or other parts of plants.
- **Vices (alcohol and tobacco)**
  - 22: Beverages, spirits and vinegar.
  - 24: Tobacco and manufactured tobacco substitutes.
- **Pharma**
  - 30: Pharmaceutical products.
- **Raw Input (rubber, forest products, steel)**
  - 40: Rubber and articles thereof.
  - 47: Pulp of wood or of other fibrous cellulosic material; waste and scrap of paper or paperboard
  - 72: Iron and steel.
- **Finished Goods**
  - 73: Articles of iron or steel.
  - 87: Vehicles other than railway or tramway rolling stock, and parts of accessories thereof.
  - 94: Furniture; bedding, mattresses, mattress supports, cushions and similar stuffed furnishings; lamps and lighting fittings, not elsewhere specified or included; illuminated sign illuminated nameplates and the like; prefabricated buildings.

○   95: Toys, games and sports requisites; parts and accessories thereof.

Methodologies

These two research questions rely on the following key assumptions:

- Companies with less than 100 total metric tons over the 11 years are removed from further analysis. Companies are assumed to enter and exit international trade at the same rate. Those that trade less than the minimum are considered insignificant international trade participants.
- Individual transactions with values for metric tonnage, *TEU*s, and *TCVUSD* (U.S. dollar) that had 3.5 standard deviations or more above the mean are dropped. The range was then further reduced from 0 to 2,054 metric tons, to 0 to 250 metric tons, for the final models. This further reduction led to a loss of less than 1% of the remaining records.
- Cargoes via internal ports and airports were not included.
- Countries without tariff and price rates account for <14% of the metric tonnage and <13% of the shipments. These countries play a peripheral role in U.S. trade. Associated records are dropped. The final dataset includes 63 countries and the U.S.
- The U.S. unemployment rate accurately reflects the current labor demand.
- COVID-19 cases and deaths reported by the *New York Times* are representative of actual cases and deaths.
- Data about closures pertains to geographic regions with only one mandated lockdown and may not generalize to locations experiencing multiple lockdowns over time. The period only includes the first year of the pandemic.
- Average applied tariff across an entire harmonized service chapter code is a useful metric. If a country failed to report in a given year, the applied tariff rates remained constant from the year before. Bound tariff rates are not used.

The chosen family of algorithms were:

- ARMA-GARCH (time series model)
- XGBoost (tree-based model)
- MLP Regression (artificial neural network).

ARMA-GARCH Models

The emergence of COVID-19 abruptly impacted volumes across all product categories. Although regular ARIMA models are able to ensure stationarity of the data for the years of 2010 through 2019, they were unable to adequately adapt to data from 2020.

Economic and financial time series data have periods of low variance interrupted by periods of high variance. To create time series models that allow for these heteroskedastic time series, GARCH models were developed (Engle, 2001). To make time series models and forecasts of metric tonnage from the maritime trade shipping data, ARMA-GARCH models were fitted to data to allow for the changing variance observed in the time series (Engle, Rocardi, & Fabozzi., 2012). After the data is aggregated by month and year, the metric tonnage is transformed with a $\log(x)$ transformation to pull in the tail of the distribution enough for the models to fit and converge. Two models will be trained, one trained on

2010-2019 data and one trained on 2010-2020 data with twelve month forecasted. These models try to match the monthly log-difference of metric tonnage. The forecasts will project the average log-difference as well as the metric tonnage and 95% confidence intervals produced from 1,000 simulated paths.

XGBoost Models

Various random forest models are explored, using standard heuristics and a variation of hyperparameter tuning techniques. Models were created for each research question, but ultimately XGBoost was seen as the best performing random forest model.

Hyperparameter tuning is performed on the 2019-2020 datasets to identify the best parameters for models with and without COVID-19 data before building and training XGBoost models to look for confounding effects at the individual transaction level on metric tonnage from tariffs, unemployment, or the dollar value of a shipment. For these models, the transaction year is used instead of the specific individual transaction's date. One set of hyperparameter tuning is conducted with COVID-19 attributes included and the other was performed without the COVID-19 attributes.

The grid search first tunes *max_depth* and *min_child_weight*, then subset size, and finally learning rate with the best values found for each grid search used to tune the next set of hyperparameters (Elith, Leathwick, & Hastie, 2008). The best performing parameters for each of the two models were stored for use in models with COVID-19 and without COVID-19. Tuned models were tested and trained in a 67:33 train: test split against 2019-2020 data both with and without COVID-19 statistics, and a set of four models were trained with the same train: test split on 2010-2019 data to gauge any confounding effects from *US_Unemployment_Rate*, *Average_Tariff*, or *TCVUSD*. The models looking into confounding effects used just one of the three confounding variables with the fourth model using all three for comparison.

MLP Regression Models

A multi-layer perceptron is trained to investigate the impact of COVID-19 data on single transactions' metric tonnage and any potential confounding effects from *TCVUSD*, *Average_Tariff*, and *US_Unemployment_Rate*. Just as with the XGBoost Regressor, hyperparameter tuning is carried out on a MLP regressor with a three-fold cross validation. The transaction year was used in place of transaction date. Data for these models consisted of 2019-2020 data without any missing records or values, with the data min-max scaled, and categorical variables transformed into dummy variables. Layer size, solver, and sampling methods were tested and tuned.

DATA ANALYSIS

Linear Method Exploration

International trade theory and models depend on linear models. Many of these have been formulated in a previous era where they could not harness the computational power of machine learning. This research also began by exploring the possible linear relationships among the attributes. Some of the quantitative variables, such as *TEU*s, are strongly correlated with metric tonnage, with a Pearson coefficient of 0.584. *TEU*s is used as a covariate in ANCOVA models to explore relationships between metric tonnage and third variables, holding *TEU*s constant. All quantitative variables also showed extreme positive skews, requiring transformations in order to explore linear model alternatives. However, the exploration justifies retaining only 18 features for future models.

There are other problems with a linear analysis. The observation residuals are not independent or identically distributed. Past shipment success impacts company behavior, consumer trends, and policy within the trading countries. The success or failure of traders' volumes depends on the initial experience. The binning process of putting companies into size groups helped to mitigate this effect. Since the means and variances increased across the series, a linear model solution is abandoned early in the exploratory process. Time series models were pursued to explain some of the variations of metric tonnage.

Time Series Models

The time series models contend with phenomena during the 11 years. Overall metric tonnage increased rapidly during 2012 and 2013. Once larger volumes are sustained, the implementation of tariffs affected total volumes, but usually affected particular classes of goods at different times, and from different trading partners.

Figure 1. 2010 – 2020 data for ARMA-GARCH Predictions in the upper section whereas the lower section uses data without 2020

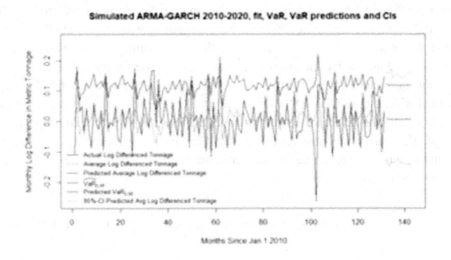

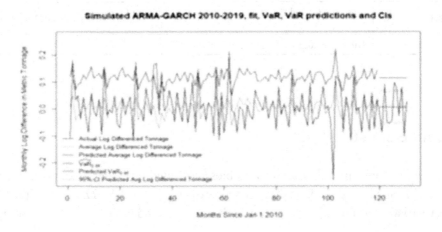

The model trained on 2010-2020 data fit an sGARCH(1,1) ARFIMA(0,0,1) model. The Ljung-Box test on standard residuals and square standard residuals returned a p-value above 0.5 for all lags. The model has an AIC of -2.40.

The upper half of Figure 1 shows the Value at Risk (VaR) for 2021 is estimated to be an average of 1.1 with the forecasted average log-differenced metric tonnage being a modest 0.05 indicating slow average growth amidst a period of high variability. The bottom half of Figure 1 shows the forecasted metric tonnage for 2021 growing slowly from 6.23 million metric tons to 7.15 million metric tons over the course of the year with the final prediction ranging from 5.71 million metric tons to just under 10 million metric tons. The upper bound of the confidence intervals mirrors explosive growth in metric tonnage seen in the third quarter of 2012 through the second quarter of 2013 where the lower bound of the confidence interval predicts a reversion to the slow decline in tonnage seen from 2018 through 2019.

The 2010-2019 model is trained on time up until the onset of the COVID-19 pandemic in the US. Its predictions indicate what tonnage an official might expect for 2020 given they do not know that lockdowns are coming in the following year. The 2010-2019 GARCH model was fitted with ARMA(0,1), garch_order = (1,1), distribution.model = "std", and model = "sGarch". The Ljung-Box test on standard residuals and standard squared residuals both had p values above 0.05 for all lags. The model has an AIC of -2.4.

The model projects metric tonnage ranging from 6 million to 7 million metric tons for 2020 with the average trending upward the whole year– over estimating tonnage in later 2020 without the foresight of the COVID-19 lockdowns. The log-differences for 2020 are predicted to be slightly positive on average, resulting in the near straight-line growth in the tonnage forecast. There are five months for 2020 whose log-differences fall outside of the 95% confidence band beginning with March 2020 as lockdowns and other restrictions begin to take effect in the US. Both the actual Value at Risk (VaR) for 2020 and the predicted VaR for 2020 lie outside the confidence intervals for every month. Table 6 shows the average overprediction in tonnage for each month from the 2010-2019 model is 564,506.5 metric tons. The model trained with just pre-COVID-19 data will have significant errors, frequently overpredicting tonnage for each month and underpredicting variance, evidence of a significant impact on aggregate monthly tonnage. The confidence intervals in lower half of Figure 1 span about half of the range of the intervals seen in the upper half of the figure, further indicating the increase in variability brought on by the pandemic throughout 2020.

Table 2. Monthly tonnage forecast model performance summary for 2010-2019 GARCH model twelve-month forecast

Model	Mean Squared Error (MSE)	Root Mean Squared Error (RMSE)	Mean Absolute Error (MAE)
2010-2019	470,902,720,023	564,506.5	564,506.5

RESULTS

Results from XGBoost

In preliminary random forest models, certain variables accounted for larger amounts of the variation of metric tonnage. This trend continued for the XGBoost regression models. *TEUs* and *TCVUSD* account for the greatest variation in metric tonnage for both research models. In models including these two variables, the *HS_Group* for Finished Goods, *Exchange_Rates,* and *Average_Tariff* also highly influence shipments' metric tonnage. XGBoost's F-score method is used to measure the importance of our attributes and their factor levels. The F-score is a measure of how often an attribute is used to create a split in the forest of XGBoost Regression trees with a higher score indicating more splits and higher importance (Elith et al., 2008).

Random Forest Classifiers were used to future narrow a subset of features from the XGBoost Regression models. These models used the following attributes:

- *Container_LCL/FCL*
- *Metric_Tons*
- *Container_Type_Dry*
- *TCVUSD*
- *Trade_Direction*
- *DateTime*
- *DateTime_YearMonth*
- *Year*
- *DateTime_YearWeek*
- *Foreign_Country_Region*
- *Foreign_Company_Country_Region*
- *Us_company_size*
- *Foreign_company_size*
- *HS_Group_Name*
- *US_Port_State*
- *US_Unemployment_Rate*
- *Average_Tariff*
- *Date Announced*
- *Effective Date*
- *Date_Monthly_COVID*
- *Date_Weekly_COVID*
- *Cases_weekly*
- *Deaths_weekly*

Subsets of the columns were used to see if dependent variable exclusion impacted the remaining variables' performance for predicting the variability in metric tonnage. The top three features for each dataset are listed below.

The three most important attributes from the Random Forest Classifier results are Average_Tariff, US_Unemployment_Rate, and US company size (when huge). The Delta_Case0_Effective is important when we include the data in 2020. Cases prove more important than deaths. The dominance of TCVUSD also cannot be understated. The value and the weight of shipments are highly correlated as discovered in previous iterations of ANCOVA. For this reason, TCVUSD was excluded from the final model.

Exploratory attributes that performed poorly in ANCOVA and XGBoost importance testing are dropped for future models. *HS_Class* is dropped in preference of *HS_Group*. This decision was mostly based on the fact that there are 23 class levels in *HS_Class* versus six class levels for their groupings in *HS_Grou*p. *Trade_Direction* remains in the dataset, but was not used in the models.

Table 3. Summary of most important features for each random forest classifier

Dataset	1st	2nd	3rd
Including COVID-19 statistics and all confounding variables	TCVUSD	Average_Tariff	Delta_Case0_Effective
Excluding COVID-19 statistics, but including all confounding variables	TCVUSD	Average_Tariff	US_Unemployment_Rate
Including only TCVUSD and excluding COVID-19 statistics	TCVUSD	Average_Tariff	US_Employment_Rate
Including only the US_Unemployment_Rate and excluding the COVID-19 statistics	US_Employment_Rate	Year	US_company_size_huge
Including only the Average_Tariff and excluding the COVID-19 statistics	Average_Tariff	Year	US_company_size_huge

XGBoost Result Summary

The models were tuned using the initial values shown in Table 4 with all of the models converging to the tuned values through the hyperparameter tuning process. These tuned values were used for all following models.

Table 4. Hyperparameter tuning for XGBoost models

Parameter	Initial Values	Tuned Value
max_depth	6	8
min_child_weight	1	2
eta	0.3	0.2
subsample	1	0.9
colsample_bytree	1	0.8
objective	reg:squarederror	reg:squarederror

Table 5 shows that XGBoost with the COVID-19 parameters had better mean squared error and root mean squared (RMS) error with just slightly higher mean absolute error (MAE). Including COVID-19 statistics for XGboost will improve on smaller errors, but the aggregate impact of its worse performance on errors greater than one in magnitude outweighs its improvement in performance on the smaller magnitude error transactions as evidenced by the higher mean absolute error.

Table 5. XGBoost regression, model performance without COVID-19 values (2010 - 2019) and with COVID-19 values (2019 - 2020)

Metric	Without COVID-19 Values	With COVID-19 Values
RMSE	343.26	320.43
MAE	22.67	23.08

The model including all three of the confounding attributes performed the best. The performance of each variable mirrors their relative importance with the most important attribute of the three, *TCVUSD*, performing the best alone. *US_Unemployment_Rate* had both the least relative importance of these three attributes and the worst performance in a model alone. All three attributes performed notably worse alone than when they were all present, but the addition of *Average_Tariff* and *US_Unemployment_Rate* to the *TCVUSD* model only yielded modest gains in reduction of both error metrics as shown in Table 6.

Table 6. Model performance for models using XGBoost regression

Metric	TCVUSD	Average_Tariff	Unemployment	All Three
RMSE	380.83	535.35	570.41	368.77
MAE	30.03	42.14	44.02	27.66

MLP Model Result Summary

Table 7 shows the tuned hyperparameters for the MLP models for both the *sgm* and *adam* solvers as well as on datasets with and without COVID-19 data. The *adam* solver model trained with COVID-19 data had lower Mean Absolute Error [MAE] but higher Root Mean Squared Error [RMS] as seen in Table 8. This could be due to the COVID-19 model having more predictions than the COVID-less model with predicted tonnage different from actual tonnage by less than 1 metric ton. The lower MAE for the COVID-19 model indicates that on average the magnitude of its errors are lower than that of the model without COVID-19, but the higher RMSE metrics suggest that when the COVID-19 model errs in predicting tonnage by more than 1 ton, then it is of larger average magnitude than the error for the COVID-less model. The COVID-19 model shows some signs of overfitting in the RMSE metrics, but only a slight increase in the MAE. The COVID-less model does not show signs of overfitting.

Table 7. MLP regression tuned hyperparameters

Parameter	Without COVID-19 #1	Without COVID-19 #2	With COVID-19 #1	With COVID-19 #2
activation	relu	relu	relu	relu
alpha	0.0001	0.0001	0.0001	0.0001
early_stopping	True	True	True	True
hidden_layer_sizes	15	5	22	11
learning_rate	constant	constant	constant	constant
learning_rate_init	0.001	0.001	0.001	0.001
max_iter	1,000	1,000	1,000	1,000
n_iter_no_change	10	10	10	10
power_t	0.5	0.5	0.5	0.5
solver	adam	sgd	adam	sgd
warm_start	False	False	False	False
sampling with replacement	True	False	True	False

There is a notable improvement by changing some of the parameters for the data without the CO-VID-19 data. However, sampling without replacement, with half the hidden layers, and the sgm booster worsens the model results on the test data for the subset of data with years 2019 and 2020 including the COVID-19 factors as seen in Table 9. The interaction between the solver and presence of COVID-19 attributes is also important as evidenced by the adam solver which is performing the best on the CO-VID-19 test data, and the sgm solver performing the best in the absence of COVID-19. The sgm solver performs the best overall but it does show more signs of overfitting than the adam solver.

Table 8. MLP regression model performance, with Adam solver and sampling with replacement

Metric	Without COVID-19 Train	Without COVID-19 Test	With COVID-19 Train	With COVID-19 Test
RMSE	387.32	332.60	413.17	539.29
MAE	66.96	63.96	46.42	47.91

Table 9. MLP regression model performance, with sgm solver and sampling without replacement

Metric	Without COVID-19 Train	Without COVID-19 Test	With COVID-19 Train	With COVID-19 Test
RMSE	75.76	75.58	358.74	650.73
MAE	26.61	26.48	45.04	48.01

Table 10 shows how all the attributes have impacts on the predictive power of the MLP *adam* solver models, but the model that performed the best was the model that included only the average tariff rate. The model including all three of these confounding variables performed the worst. The model tends to overfit on *TCVUSD* and the *US_Unemployment_Rate* data as indicated by the increase in error across the board for these models when moving to the test data. This tendency could contribute to overfitting seen in the COVID-19 data model if these attributes maintain their relatively high predictive power as indicated by the decision tree models.

Table 10. MLP regression model performance summary adam solver

Variables included	Test or Train	Root Mean Squared Error	Mean Absolute Error
All	Train	578.76	72.79
All	Test	506.31	71.22
TCVUSD	Train	545.38	55.74
TCVUSD	Test	685.35	57.92
Average_Tariff	Train	575.71	47.63
Average_Tariff	Test	502.51	46.01
Unemployment	Train	553.47	58.31
Unemployment	Test	689.48	60.35

DISCUSSION OF RESULTS

Discussion of Model Results

XGBoost performed best for predicting the metric tonnage of single transactions, with and without the additional data and attributes from 2020. The inclusion of 2020 data, and COVID-19 related attributes, improved accuracy by reducing the XGBoost tree's root mean square error. However, the MAE increased for all models when they were used to make predictions. There was less metric tonnage traded in the summer months of 2020, with the forecasted aggregate volumes well below the lower confidence level. Annual shipments dropped from 3,797,070 transactions in 2019 to 3,732,462 in 2020, with their average weights falling from 21.4 to 21.3 tons. Over time, these fewer transactions, weighing 1/10 of a ton less, contributed to an aggregate trade volume under the forecast. GARCH models did well for predicting the aggregate trade trends without data for 2020. However, they ended up overestimating tonnage in 2020.

This could indicate that on an individual transaction level, COVID-19 statistics have minimal impact on the tonnage of a single shipment transaction. This could be due to practical business requirements dictating that individual shipments must contain at least a certain threshold of goods to make the entire shipment profitable. COVID-19 statistics, like macroeconomic measures like unemployment, may have a stronger influence on the aggregate levels as there are less workers resulting in shipments moving slower.

Economists typically use linear models to explain international trade based on smaller datasets, with metrics that are aggregated per month or year. The gravity model is used as a bedrock for analysis, focusing on qualitative variables that seek to capture socioeconomic factors such as cultural, linguistic, and political affiliations among trading partners (Chauvin, Lardiane, Morel, Clostermann, & Langard, 2013; Head & Mayer, 2014).

Understanding the limitations of linear regression assumptions and arbitrary weighing of qualitative variables, nonlinear models can be extended to work with high-dimensional fixed effects (Breinlich, Corradi, Rocha, Ruta, Santos Silva, & Sylkin,, 2021; Rahman, Kim, & Laratte., 2021; Xu, Shi, Chen, & Li, 2021). These studies used cross-validation approach to identify the most important variables affecting trade. Financial analysts have long departed the confines of linear regression, using random forest and neural network techniques that are more robust when dealing with stochastic shocks (Tan, Yan, & Zhu, 2019). Finance has also employed boosting methods to further improve upon base models (Qin, Wang, Li, & Ge., 2013).

Discussion of Visual Trends

Total U.S. maritime trade, for the selected 23 *HS_Classes*, increased from 40 million metric tons to 95 million metric tons, from 2010 to 2020. Imports made up most of the tonnage for each year. Export growth proved a predominant trend in 2011 and 2012, though the growth tapered off after 2014. Imports grew rapidly between 2012 and 2013 before growth tapered. The contraction in imports began in 2018 and exports decreased in late 2019 and early 2020 when the pandemic began.

The growth in exports was driven by an expansion in Raw Inputs and to a lesser degree Edibles as a percentage of total tonnage, and the imports were dominated by expansions of Finished Goods as a percentage of total tonnage. All *HS_Group* exports increased when measured in tonnage; Raw Input expanded to account for about 40% of the exports for 23 *HS_Classes*. As a result, its expansion as a percentage of metric tonnage has resulted in a sharp increase in 2011 and 2012. Edibles had a slight expansion as a percentage of exports in 2019 and 2020. The Northeast, Southeast, and Southwest ports increased their market share of exports over the course of these years.

The largest U.S. companies are the biggest winners of international trade. They contributed the most to total volume increase between 2011 and 2014, and dominated market share for the period of study. Medium and large companies also increased market share, although to a lesser degree. The unknown company type is most likely the result of the largest companies masking their identities in the U.S. Customs bills of lading.

There were geographic changes in trade composition over the time shown in Figure 2. Oceania and other North American markets absorbed U.S. exports in 2011 and 2012. The European Union's share of U.S. exports increased only modestly in 2013 before remaining relatively static. However, 2013 saw the growth of other export markets, with U.S. products increasingly destined to China, Other East Asia (not China), South Asia, and Southeast Asia. China's share of U.S. exports peaked in 2016 before beginning to lose market share to other regions of Asia. This may have occurred as companies attempted to find subsidiaries or trading partners outside of China to mitigate the risk of an escalation of the trade war between the United States and China. It is also plausible that some Chinese goods were exported to other Asian countries, relabeled there, and again exported to the U.S.

Figure 2. Change in composition of Finished Goods Imports by the Foreign Country Region

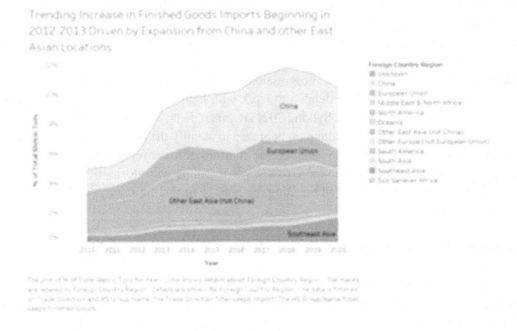

Each of the six HS_Groups played varying roles in the fluctuations of trade volumes over this period. As seen in Figure 2, exports for each category increased in 2012, but the Raw Inputs tonnage increased drastically in June, while the volumes of the other five groups started to increase only after August. The increase in exports is driven by five HS_classes: wood pulp products, iron and steel, vehicles, edible fruits and nuts, and meat. Metric tonnage of pharmaceuticals did not increase much, possibly due to the product, or the method of measurement.

In the same year, import growth was driven primarily by Finished Goods, but with Vices and Edible Goods volume increases in December. During the entire period, Finished Goods, Edibles, and Edibles with processing increased the most, although the Raw Inputs category stagnated and then contracted in volume in the beginning of 2018. In 2020, imports decreased from different geographic regions, during different time periods, and impacted certain *HS_Groups* more than others. Volumes of Finished Goods from China decreased notably in February and March of 2020. The negative trend continued for Finished Goods from China, and then East Asia, in the second quarter of 2020. However, by the end of the year, Finished Goods volumes were increasing again only from China, South Asia, and Southeast Asia. In fact, they increased to such an extent as to surpass their volumes in 2019. Raw Input imports continued to decrease in 2020, a continuation of a longer-term trend, probably exasperated by the pandemic. South American volumes decreased the most. However, this same region exported a relatively larger volume of Edibles in the last quarter of 2019 and first quarter of 2020. In late 2020, South American exports of Processed Edibles increased at the expense of these exports from other North American countries.

The delta in COVID-19 cases and deaths might have impacted trade in states with large labor markets that also happen to have important maritime ports. New York, Texas, and California were among the hardest hit states in 2020, as shown in Figure 3. The number of cases seemed to have a bigger impact than the number of deaths, possibly because lockdowns were instituted as a result of cases versus deaths, and deaths lagged initial cases. It is possible the regional outbreaks delayed the arrival of shipments until labor was able to load or unload vessels.

Figure 3. Analytics for Trade impacted by COVID-19

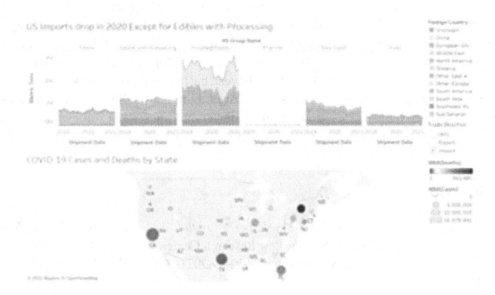

U.S. export volumes also fell for all categories other than Vices and Pharma in March of 2020, as the pandemic was first developing within the U.S. The Edible category exports increased in the last quarter of 2020, while volumes for Edibles with Processing barely increased to pre-2020 levels. U.S. Raw Input exports to China, Oceania, North America, and Europe decreased over 2020. However, South Asia and other East Asia (not China) began importing more Raw Input commodities in this same year.

FUTURE RESEARCH DIRECTIONS

Most of the data is US-centric. Exchange rates are based on foreign currency fluctuations compared to the dollar. Unemployment rates are based on U.S. figures only. Trade data consists of imports or exports with the U.S. as a trading partner. A future study could focus on using foreign unemployment figures, other exchange rate fluctuation combinations, and trade among countries excluding the United States. This type of study would be most useful for a small set of major U.S. trading partners.

Multivariate GARCH models could be used to identify how variance and volatility in specific trade volumes could be correlated with the variance and volatility in unemployment rates, COVID-19 cases, tariff rates, or exchange rates. We could also explore smaller periods to see if the models performed differently given major fluctuations in applied tariff rates, unemployment, or exchange rates. Larger sample sizes could be used for XGBoost and MLP models, to see if this changes the models' performance.

Since this study, there have also been different mutations of the original COVID-19 virus. Countries vaccinated their populations at different rates and used various forms of stimulus to maintain consumption. These variables were not considered, but would have been, if we included data from 2021.

CONCLUSION

This work assessed the driving forces behind trade, as measured in metric tonnage, over an 11-year period, from 2010 through 2020, with U.S. trading partners that account for 87% of shipments or 86% of metric tonnage. The goal was to ultimately determine whether COVID-19 impacted trade volumes. 23 of the 99 HS chapter classes were chosen for analysis, as they were likely impacted by a global pandemic. To understand COVID-19's role on maritime trade, long-term trends and possible confounding variables were identified. Time, the value of a shipment, the average applied tariff, and the U.S. unemployment rate all proved important variables that determined variation in shipment metric tonnage.

COVID-19 affected the rate of trade throughout the year, but the aggregate volumes quickly rebounded. Even during a global pandemic, shipments were delayed, but goods still moved, regardless of which HS Group was assessed. Businesses should plan on slower movements, but still plan to continue trade operations even they encounter these stochastic shocks.

REFERENCES

Anderson, J., Rainie, L., & Vogels, E. (2021). *Experts say the 'new normal' in 2025 will be far more tech-driven, presenting more big challenges.* Pew Research Center. Retrieved 04/25/2022 from: https://www.pewresearch.org/internet/wp-content/uploads/sites/9/2021/02/PI_2021.02.18_New-Normal-2025_FINAL.pdf

Baldwin, R., & Di Mauro, B. (2020). *Economics in the time of COVID-19: A new eBook.* CEPR Press. Retrieved 04/25/2022 from: https://voxeu.org/article/economics-time-covid-19-new-ebook

Breinlich, H., Corradi, V., Rocha, N., Ruta, M., Santos Silva, J., & Zylkin, T. (2021). *Machine Learning in International Trade Research? Evaluating the Impact of Trade Agreements. School of Economics Discussion Papers 0521.* School of Economics, University of Surrey.

Chang, H. (2002). *Kicking away the ladder: Development strategy in historical perspective*. Anthem Press.

Charlton, D., & Castillo, M. (2021). Potential impacts of a pandemic on the US farm labor market. *Applied Economic Perspectives and Policy*, *43*(1), 39–57. doi:10.1002/aepp.13105 PMID:33230406

Chauvin, C., Lardjane, S., Morel, G., Clostermann, J., & Langard, B. (2013). Human and organisational factors in maritime accidents: Analysis of collisions at sea using the HFACS. *Accident; Analysis and Prevention*, *59*, 26–37. doi:10.1016/j.aap.2013.05.006 PMID:23764875

Elith, J., Leathwick, J., & Hastie, T. (2008). A working guide to boosted regression trees. *Journal of Animal Ecology*, *77*(4), 802–813. doi:10.1111/j.1365-2656.2008.01390.x PMID:18397250

Engle, R. (2001). GARCH: The use of ARCH/GARCH models in applied econometrics. *The Journal of Economic Perspectives*, *12*(4), 157–168. doi:10.1257/jep.15.4.157

Engle, R., Focardi, S., & Fabozzi, F. (2012). ARCH/GARCH models in applied financial econometrics. Handbook of Finance. doi:10.1002/9780470404324.hof003060

Head, K., & Mayer, T. (2014). Gravity equations: Workhorse, toolkit, and cookbook. In *Handbook of International Economics 4, 131-95*. Elsevier. doi:10.1016/B978-0-444-54314-1.00003-3

Hufbauer, G., & Lu, Z. (2017). The payoff to America from globalization: A fresh look with a focus on costs to workers. Peterson Institute for International Economics. *Policy Brief*, 17–16.

Irwin, D. (2017). *Clashing over commerce*. University of Chicago Press. doi:10.7208/chicago/9780226399010.001.0001

Kerr, W. (2020). The COVID-19 pandemic and agriculture: Short-and long-run implications for international trade relations. *Canadian Journal of Agricultural Economics/Revue Canadienne D'agroeconomie*, *68*(2), 225-29. doi:10.1111/cjag.12230

Kootanaee, J., Babu, A., Nagendra, K., & Hamid, T. (2013). Just-in-time manufacturing system: From introduction to implement. *International Journal of Economics, Business and Finance.*, *1*(2), 7–25.

Manaadiar, H. (2020). *Shipping and freight review 2020 – the year that was and wasn't*. Retrieved 04/25/2022 from https://www.shippingandfreightresource.com/shipping-and-freight-review-2020/

Mittal, N., Boile, M., Baveja, A., & Theofanis, S. (2013). Determining optimal inland-empty-container depot locations under stochastic demand. *Research in Transportation Economics*, *42*(1), 50–60. doi:10.1016/j.retrec.2012.11.007

Qin, Q., Wang, Q., Li, J., & Ge, S. (2013). Linear and nonlinear trading models with gradient boosted random forests and application to Singapore stock market. *Journal of Intelligent Learning Systems and Applications*, *5*(1), 1–10. doi:10.4236/jilsa.2013.51001

Rahman, S., Kim, J., & Laratte, B. (2021). Disruption in circularity? Impact analysis of COVID-19 on ship recycling using Weibull tonnage estimation and scenario analysis method. *Resources, Conservation and Recycling*, *164*, 105139. doi:10.1016/j.resconrec.2020.105139 PMID:32904429

Steger, M., & Roy, R. (2010). *Neoliberalism: A very short introduction*. Oxford University Press. doi:10.1093/actrade/9780199560516.001.0001

Stephens, O. (2021). *Methods and Theory behind the Clustering Functionality in OpenRefine.* Retrieved 04/25/2022 from https://github.com/OpenRefine/OpenRefine/wiki/Clustering-In-Depth

Tan, Z., Yan, Z., & Zhu, G. (2019). Stock selection with random forest: An exploitation of excess return in the chinese stock market. *Heliyon, 5*(8), e02310. doi:10.1016/j.heliyon.2019.e02310 PMID:31463404

Xu, L., Shi, J., Chen, J., & Li, L. (2021). Estimating the effect of COVID-19 epidemic on shipping trade: An empirical analysis using panel data. *Marine Policy, 133*, 104768. doi:10.1016/j.marpol.2021.104768 PMID:34493890

Yang, D., & Tsai, T. (2021). Piano sheet music identification using dynamic N-gram fingerprinting. *Transactions of the International Society for Music Information Retrieval, 4*(1), 42–51. doi:10.5334/tismir.70

Yildrim, G., & Saccomano, I. (2021). *A year like no other: Overview of U.S. trade in 2020.* International Trade Organization. Retrieved 04/25/2022 from https://blog.trade.gov/2021/03/22/a-year-like-no-other-overview-of-u-s-trade-in-2020/

ADDITIONAL READING

Appelbaum, B. (2019). *The economists' hour: False prophets, free markets, and the fracture of society.* Little, Brown, and Company.

Beider, A., & Morse, S. (2008). *Beider-Morse phonetic matching: An alternative to soundex with fewer false hits.* Retrieved 04/25/2022 from https://stevemorse.org/phonetics/bmpm.htm

Broda, C., & Weinstein, D. (2006). Globalization and the gains from variety. *The Quarterly Journal of Economics, 121*(2), 541–585. doi:10.1162/qjec.2006.121.2.541

Chambers, M., & Liu, M. (2013). *Maritime trade and transportation by the numbers.* Bureau of Transportation Statistics. https://www.bts.gov/archive/publications/by_the_numbers/maritime_trade_and_transportation/index

Feenstra, R. (2015). *Advanced international trade: Theory and evidence.* Princeton University Press.

Gruszczynski, L. (2020). The COVID-19 pandemic and international trade: Temporary turbulence or paradigm shift? *European Journal of Risk Regulation, 11*(2), 337–342. doi:10.1017/err.2020.29

Michael, B. (2021). *LibGuides: OpenRefine: Clustering.* University of Illinois at Urbana-Champaign. Retrieved 04/25/2022 from https://guides.library.illinois.edu/openrefine/clustering

Philips, L. (2012). *Metaphone 3.* Retrieved 04/25/2022 from https://github.com/OpenRefine/OpenRefine/blob/master/main/src/com/google/refine/clustering/binning/Metaphone3.java

KEY TERMS AND DEFINITIONS

A

Descartes Datamyne: Private organization that provides access import-export data of over 50 countries.

HS-6/HS-4: Harmonized System Codes that classifies the traded products in 6 or 4 levels.

ISO Tanks: Tank container unit for transport of liquid bulk cargo.

Ro/Ro: Roll-on/Roll-off units are useful when trading automobiles, tanks, and other farm equipment with wheels.

TCVUSD: Total Calculated Volume in US Dollars.

TEU: Twenty-foot equivalent unit, a widely used metric in containerized shipping.

WTO: World Trade Organization that regulate international trade between nations.

NEW ARP:
Data–Driven Academia Resource Planning for CAS Researchers

Yue Wang

Computer Network Information Center, CAS, China & University of Chinese Academy of Sciences, China

Jianjun Yu

Computer Network Information Center, CAS, China

INTRODUCTION

The CAS (Chinese Academy of Sciences) is the highest academic institution of natural science in China. The ARP (Academia Resource Planning) system is an integrated application system to provide services for the researchers of CAS. With the rapid development of big data technology, the frequently changing of business processes, and the increasing decision-making demands of users, the ARP system meets grand challenges. The NEW ARP reconstructs the original ARP system and builds up an information application ecology covering the main scientific research management business by data-driven concept and big data analysis technology. It's a new-type information system for scientific research management, which also considers the utilization of data resources and data analysis technology. The authors study to provide intelligent data analysis application services through different dimensions, to realize the exploration of scientific research management innovation and intelligent decision making.

The chief contributions of this chapter are as follows. First, it provides a data-driven application framework to adapt the development of new management forms. And it proposes a data-driven workflow engine to meet the dynamically changing needs of approval processes. Further, it implements several data-driven applications and gives some examples of intelligent decision-making based on data analysis and data governance.

The chapter is divided into six parts. First, it is the introduction. The following section describes the background and the challenges that the NEW ARP is facing. Then the authors introduce some main focuses of the chapter, containing data-driven application framework, data-driven workflow engine, and some intelligent applications. The fourth section is the detail of the research. Section five and six look at the future research direction and conclusion.

BACKGROUND

The new generation of information technology is developing in both breadth and depth (Heath, 2019). And deep integration of informatization and multiple business areas is a notable feature of the current development of global informatization. The new generation of information technology, which is represented by cloud computing, big data, and artificial intelligence, is booming and widely used all over the world (Dillon, Wu, & Chang, 2018; Rahm, 2016; Zhu & Zheng, 2018; Newell & Marabelli, 2014).

DOI: 10.4018/978-1-7998-9220-5.ch022

Copyright © 2023, IGI Global. Copying or distributing in print or electronic forms without written permission of IGI Global is prohibited.

The information process characterized by intelligent service is also profoundly affecting and changing the way of human production, life, and cognition (Steininger, 2019). Accelerating the development of information technology has increasingly become a popular choice for most countries in the world. The transformation of the industrial structure is going faster, and the division of the industrial chain is more detailed. As business applications get richer, big data plays a significant role in discovering user needs and guiding product designs (Bechtel & Jayaram, 2020).

Scientific research management is the management of scientific process activities, involving organizations, projects, funds, personnel, assets, and other aspects related (Zhang, Liu, & Song, 2009; Lin, Cen, & Zhou, 2014; You, Li, & Zhao, 2013). Scientific research activities are exploratory and creative, with strong flexibility and uncertainty (Li, 2011). That makes the management work become a complex system engineering. However, innovative and effective management is an essential auxiliary to breakthroughs in science and technology, which can effectively improve the management level of scientific research institutions and promote scientific and technological progress (Yang, 2016; Zhou, 2019; Kang & Liu, 2021). Therefore, the authors hope to improve the efficiency of scientific research management through effective planning and intelligent managing of personnel, projects, scientific research achievements, and so on (Yongtao, 2019).

The ARP refers to ERP and adds the unique element of scientific research management (Ren, Guan, & Pan, 2003; Ji, 2011). It takes the entire life cycle of a scientific research project as the mainline and provides integrated management functions around the scientific research project management, including human resources, scientific research projects, finance, assets, and so on. With constant changes in technology and management, the business processes change frequently, but the data structures and data formats are relatively fixed. In this scenario, the data-driven application framework can solve the problem that the system has poor adaptability to management changes. The traditional information systems are driven by business, which makes it difficult for them to adapt to new forms of management (Hull, Mendling, & Tai, 2003; Romney & Steinbart, 2012; Benbasat, Goldstein, & Mead, 1987). However, data-driven processes can support dynamic changes well, and they simplify business processes. It can also discover the irrationality of business processes by using big data governance, then improve the standardization of management and bring more intelligent applications.

The NEW ARP has reconstructed the entire system to face the challenges of the big data environment (Syed, 2020). By using big-data technologies, it combines the business-driven mode with the data-driven mode and takes smart business applications and intelligent data analysis as the key point to study (Li & Whinston, 2020; Xiao et al., 2021). The NEW ARP solves the problems of the old system and has optimized some aspects, such as improving the adaptability to management changes, reducing the complexity of the business process, getting effective information from the vast amount of data, and so on. So far, the NEW ARP has been used by over one hundred units, receiving about ten million visitors and storing over 1.6 billion business records. It becomes an important foundation for improving the informatization and realizing the capabilities of intelligent management in CAS (Wu, Zhang, F. Liu, C. Liu, & Zhu, 2021).

FOCUS OF THE ARTICLE

Data-Driven Application Framework

Business-driven applications of management information systems are difficult to adapt to the development of new management forms, especially facing constant changes in institutions and norms. With the emergence and application of big data governance concepts, the scientific research management model has developed to a new stage through data-driven promotion (Kandogan, Balakrishnan, Haber, & Pierce, 2014). The NEW ARP makes data-driven concept as its core ideology and takes management functions as the mainline. It connects all the business data effectively to form a data-driven application framework and generates multidimensional and interconnected data sets to improve the efficiency of business flow. Meanwhile, the authors make an in-depth study of data-driven management for the data center to improve the data governance system and resource sharing mechanism. As a result, through data aggregation and governance, the NEW ARP creates high-quality management data sets and gets the data-driven application framework.

Data-Driven Workflow Engine

Lots of businesses in management information systems are related to the approval process. Generally, traditional systems pre-define static business processes by the workflow engine and then perform the transformation of instantiation when a business occurs. In this traditional way, a lot of business knowledge is required when defining deterministic rules through the workflow engine. And the process definition needs to be determined before the system goes live. If there are changes in branch conditions, approval roles, or process links during the execution of the current approval process, it will report an error and interrupt execution. When this happens, the process definition needs to be reset before continuing. In this way, the following problems may arise. For example, the actual business scenario that the pre-defined workflow covered is incomplete, and the system cannot meet the dynamically changing needs, and so on. How to use the data-driven model to get innovation of process management becomes a problem to be studied for the NEW ARP, especially providing data supports for the formation of management rules by data analysis, to innovate the management mode of scientific research management (Chu, 2018).

Data-Driven Applications and Intelligent Decision Making

Scientific research activities show the characteristics of data-intensive under the big data environment (McAfee & Brynjolfsson, 2013). The NEW ARP is not only a simple management system or just used for data storage. It is more about how to use data assets to gain knowledge and make knowledge discovery by big data analysis techniques, and how to produce application results to improve the efficiency of management decisions through data-driven (Li et al., 2012; Ye, Liu, & Zhu, 2020). The authors use digital twin, knowledge graph, and other technologies to research user behavior profiling, intelligent approval prediction, knowledge graph construction of the sci-tech field, and so on (Niu, Liu, & Zhang, 2012; Agrawal, Fischer, & Singh, 2022). They make an in-depth exploration of scientific research management innovation and intelligent decision-making through data analysis and data governance.

SOLUTIONS AND RECOMMENDATIONS

The NEW ARP is a cross-disciplinary effort between computer science and management science, using data-driven as the design concept. It provides six core applications for CAS through the microservices architecture (Francesco, Lago, & Malavolta, 2019), including Human Resource Management, Scientific Research Project Management, Financial Management, Research Condition Management, Electronic Document Management, and International Cooperation Management. The specific functions of each subsystem are as follows.

The human resource management subsystem contains organizational structure management, personnel information management, salary administration, cost accounting, and employee self-service. The scientific research project management subsystem includes project information management, project document management, project funds management, and project approval management. The financial management subsystem consists of income management, reimbursement management, cost-sharing, accounting management, and business audit management. The research condition management subsystem comprises purchasing management, fixed assets management, intangible assets management, consumables management, and assets accounting management. The electronic document management subsystem manages all the documents during the official approval business. The international cooperation management subsystem includes international visit activities management and national cooperation project management.

Each of the subsystems is closely connected with others through data flow, forming the data-driven business system. For example, the human resource management subsystem provides the personnel and department information to all the other subsystems and the positions, pay cards, cost allocation accounting vouchers, and payment accounting vouchers to the financial management subsystem. Meanwhile, the financial management subsystem affords accounting system data, budget control process data, and fund execution information to the scientific research project management subsystem and the research condition management subsystem. The scientific research project management subsystem offers budget control management data and research project accounting account data to others. And the research condition management subsystem supplies purchasing requisition data, warehouse entry information, and asset accounting voucher data.

The NEW ARP realizes data-driven workflow definitions by using big data analysis technology and tries to establish a data-driven-based integrated scientific research management system gradually. The research work of the NEW ARP is committed to serving management decision-making through data governance. The authors have made some attempts in the fusion application of management information systems and managing big data analysis systems. During the research, the business processing systems focus on efficiency and distributed transaction processing, and push historical data or quasi-real-time data to the management big data analysis system. The big data system returns the processing results to the management information system after a batch or quasi-real-time analysis processing, such as prediction of approval results, risk warning, and so on.

Data-Driven Application Framework

During the research process of the ARP data governance system, the authors focus on global data combing. Based on the infrastructure platform and the support platform, the business applications of the NEW ARP are around the business scenarios that occur in the process of scientific research management, and it tries to provide appropriate services for CAS researchers. It condenses source data and index data in

Figure 1. Intelligent architecture of the NEW ARP supported by data driven

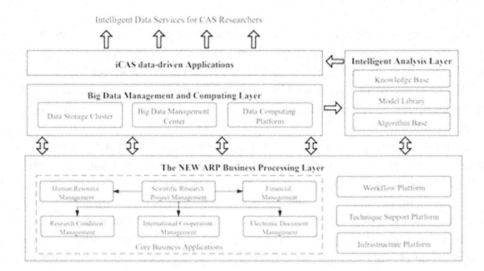

business processes, then forms different data sets to manage the data by classification. There are master data, business data, process data, metadata, state data, etc. Based on all of the data sets, the authors build upper-layer application services through decoupling and micro-service architecture design. The global data, as the most basic data of the system, provides services to all the businesses. Through the inflow and outflow of data between different business applications and the full life cycle operation of business data, the system ensures service efficiency and consistency. The authors use data resources linked to the business itself and decoupled them from business systems to implement the data-driven business framework. Data in each business application is classified and managed according to its characteristics and service attributes. The business data with unique attributes are associated with ids. The system realizes data sharing and efficient business flow within business applications through the association of key IDs.

Based on the efficient flow of business management systems, the authors conduct further research on the framework of managing big data analysis through data aggregation, processing, and fusion analysis. The whole analysis framework is divided into three parts above the business processing layer, the data aggregation layer, the knowledge fusion layer, and the intelligent analysis layer. It takes the data aggregation layer as the hub that connects the entire architecture. The business processing layer corresponds to the management information system. It provides six core applications for CAS researchers through the micro-service architecture (Sirin & Ailamaki, 2020). The knowledge fusion layer and the intelligent analysis layer compose the big data application system. The two parts, the management information system and the big data application system, complement and promote each other through data-driven.

Under the framework of management data analysis, the authors focus on the definition of data-driven process and the applications of data-driven analysis, and they have made some progress in both.

Data-Driven Workflow Engine

The NEW ARP has experimented to innovate from business-driven workflow to data-driven workflow, to shorten the business management process. The authors connect the business itself with data resources, then explore the best path for business management. They try to realize the informationization of scientific research management with the data-driven concept, centering on scientific research

Figure 2. The data-driven application framework of the NEW ARP

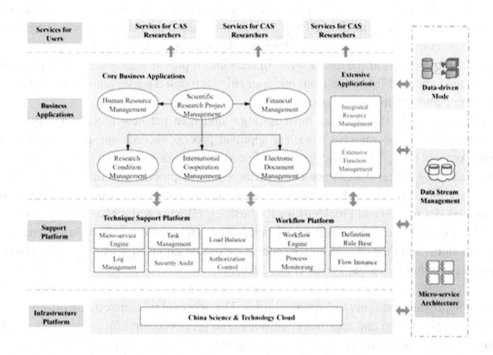

Figure 3. The analysis architecture of the NEW ARP

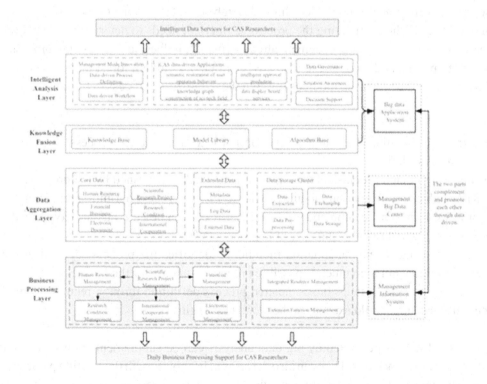

project management. And they attempt to solve the problems of flexible business adaptation through the componentization of basic services, the configuration of extended applications, and the loose coupling mechanism for business modules. They explore conditional data-driven process engines to adapt to rapid business constructions changing on business demands and to support the application of inductive management processes at the micro-level. In addition, it provides a visual configuration interface for business personnel and interprets front-end user rules through a parser automatically to implement process mapping and automatic execution.

The authors decouple the complex business logic and then get new process definitions through machine learning based on massive historical approval process records and deterministic workflow definitions (Agrawal et al., 2019). They use lots of process definitions to form a process definition rule base. After that, they cluster the characteristic attributes of the process definitions using the K-Means clustering algorithm, determine the business type of the current approval process, then recommend possible process definitions and ProcUnits for the business (Bouras & Tsogkas, 2011). After that, they map the final process definitions as process instances that can execute in the workflow engine through regular expressions, and then they build the process definition knowledge to store and retrieve queries for process definitions on this basis (Hao et al., 2020).

A process definition comprises at least one process segment, and each process segment is composed of a series of approval conditions and approval roles. The approval roles determine different examiners under different examination and approval conditions. The process definition is expressed as ((business type), (business scenario), { (process segment), { (approval conditions), (approval roles)}, (next process segment)}}). When estimating the process business type, it needs to determine whether the current business type is one already given in the existing process definition repository firstly. If it belongs to the existing business type, just choose the process definition corresponding to the current business type. Otherwise, try to form a new process definition through the random forest model (Genuer, Poggi, & Tuleau-Malot, 2015). When estimating the process segment, it needs to determine whether the current process segment matches the process segment already given. If it does, just choose the process segment. Otherwise, try to predict and recommend a process segment by random forest model to get a new one.

It mainly involves the following modules through the data-driven process definition implementation process.

§   The extraction module. The primary function is to extract business process definition data and generate process definition.
§   The clustering module. It clusters the characteristic attributes defined by the process.
§   The Knowledge base formation module. It tries to form a process definition repository.
§   The process definition recommendation module. It determines the business type of the current approval process and recommends possible process definitions.
§   The process segment recommendation module. It identifies the process segment in the current process definition and recommends possible process segments for the business.
§   The mapping module. It maps the completed process definition through regular expressions to a process instance that could execute in the workflow engine.

The process definitions generated by big data analysis can be supplemented into the deterministic processes to form static processes. They can also detect conflict points with the existing process instances, predict possible changes and make recommendations of process definitions to adjust processes dynamically. The authors use the data-driven approach and data analysis model to generate data rule conditions and take the conditions as the input, to make the workflow simple and clear during configuration, verification, and execution. This work can reflect the execution status accurately when the workflow executes and lay the groundwork for the process to become self-defined eventually. Experiments show that this attempt is helpful to the application of the data-driven process in the NEW ARP, which makes it more convenient for CAS researchers when dealing with business approval.

Data-Driven Applications and Intelligent Decision Making

The authors use the data-driven concept on the NEW ARP to improve management decision-support efficiency. They have conducted some applications about data-driven scientific research management decision making and have made some progress in four areas of research to provide better service for CAS researchers. The four aspects of the study are user behavior profiling and anomaly detection based on digital twin technology, intelligent approval prediction, knowledge graph construction of the sci-tech field, and data display board services based on data aggregation analysis (Li et al., 2022; Shaoxiong, Shirui, Erik, Pekka, & S., 2021) . Through the secondary use and analysis of the scientific research management data, the authors have improved the management innovation ability of the NEW ARP.

A large-scale information system generates an enormous amount of logs during daily running. For the system operation and security monitoring, it is very important to understand the semantic context of user actions through the logs. The application scope of the NEW ARP is large, and the user group is extensive. How to record user operation behaviors comprehensively and analyze them has become an important problem to be studied urgently. So the authors have made some explorations in user behavior restoration, user behavior analysis, and management behavior portrait modeling, by taking user operations as a sensor to use the log records (Li et al., 2018). They study the machine learning-based method of business semantic restoration from log records and realize the business attribute recognition of the user log sequence through restoring the business semantics of logs and comparing them with actual services. Then they conduct further research on the user business behavior mode mining method based on frequent sequence algorithms and establish the user business behavior model library to build the scientific research management portrait through modeling and visualization. Finally, they restore user behaviors over a long period (Beedkar, Gemulla, & Martens, 2019). They have achieved preliminary results in semantic restoration and patterns discovery of user behavior. Next, they plan to conduct further research on user abnormal behavior detection based on this foundation.

The NEW ARP, as an integrated service application of scientific research management, contains many financial reimbursement business approval receipts and massive historical approval records. The authors combine machine learning algorithms and the business approval receipts, and deeply excavate the historical approval information of the business approval receipts to promote management and service innovation through the big data application (Kantardzic, 2011). They have established an intelligent approval prediction model to research financial reimbursement approval prediction based on the tree model. The researchers forecast the reimbursement results using four classification algorithms, named decision tree, random forest, gradient random tree, and XGBoost (Chen & Guestrin, 2016). The prediction accuracy optimized by the experiments can reach 88.5%. This research could assist the CAS researchers in business approval, hoping to drive intelligent approval through data analysis. Moreover, the authors build a multi-classification model of approval time prediction. They take the k-nearest neighbor algorithm as the standard baseline and use multi-layer perception and tree algorithm models to predict approval times. That could help the managers to optimize the approval structure and facilitate applicants to perceive the approval time to arrange relevant work reasonably.

The NEW ARP has accumulated a great deal of scientific research management data resources when serving the CAS researchers. It shows the power of data by constructing the knowledge graph facing the science and technology domain (Zhou, Wang, Qiao, Xiao, & Du, 2020). Take the intelligent analysis of science and technology cooperation based on the knowledge graph as an example. The researchers study algorithms and models of implicit relationship mining and deep learning to build a knowledge map for Science and Technology, using the data resource of personal information, scientific research projects, and intellectual property in the NEW ARP. They present the analysis results visually about scientific and technology cooperation in multiple terminals through charts, text, colors, icons, and more, serving management decisions through data governance (Wilder, Dilkina, & Tambe, 2019).

The authors also focus on the massive data assets in the NEW ARP. They bring the data together and use aggregation analysis and visual analysis techniques to provide different data-display-board services for different roles of the CAS researchers (Ma, 2007; Ota, Müller, Freire, & Srivastava, 2020). This service supports the display of analysis results and even drilling further to the raw data, which can assist consistency analysis from macro to micro, and gives full play to the application value of big data in assisting management decision-support. Some of the services have been already implemented and in use, such as scientific research project presentation containing project status and change trend, talent analysis theme presentation for personnel composition and mobility, financial analysis presentation on expenditure, etc.

FUTURE RESEARCH DIRECTIONS

The construction of data-driven information service is a long-term process that needs continuous exploration and improvement. With the development of data twinning, the situation analysis of scientific research management, based on big data governance, is the future research direction of the NEW ARP. Along with the management-oriented big data system, the researchers plan to work on how to discover new knowledge and perceive the latest situation through the data assets. They will attempt to construct the domain decision knowledge model to get great implementations of intelligent analysis and decision aids.

CONCLUSION

This chapter expounds on the achievements of the NEW ARP with data governance and data-driven mode as its core design concept. It shows the "service-management-decision support" data ecological environment, which comprises the continuous spiral of expansion around the primary applications and uses the micro-service architecture. On this basis, the researchers of the NEW ARP will continue to explore further about data-driven application mode, to promote scientific and technological innovation through modern scientific research management.

REFERENCES

Agrawal, A., Fischer, M., & Singh, V. (2022). Digital twin: From concept to practice. *Journal of Management Engineering*, *38*(3), 06022001. doi:10.1061/(ASCE)ME.1943-5479.0001034

Agrawal, P., Arya, R., Bindal, A., Bhatia, S., Gagneja, A., Godlewski, J., Low, Y., Muss, T., Paliwal, M., Raman, S., Shah, V., Shen, B., Sugden, L., Zhao, K., & Wu, M. (2019). Data platform for machine learning. *Proceedings of the 2019 International Conference on Management of Data*, 1803-1816. 10.1145/3299869.3314050

Bechtel, C., & Jayaram, J. (2019). Supply chain management: A strategic perspective. *New Zealand Journal of Crop and Horticultural Science, 47*(SP4), 15–34.

Beedkar, K., Gemulla, R., & Martens, W. (2019). A unified framework for frequent sequence mining with subsequence constraints. *ACM Transactions on Database Systems, 44*(3), 11–42. doi:10.1145/3321486

Benbasat, I., Goldstein, D., & Mead, M. (1987). The case research strategy in studies of information systems. *Management Information Systems Quarterly, 11*(3), 369–386. doi:10.2307/248684

Bouras, C., & Tsogkas, V. (2011). Clustering user preferences using w-kmeans. *The 2011 Seventh International Conference on Signal Image Technology & Internet-Based Systems*, 75-82. 10.1109/SITIS.2011.19

Chen, T., & Guestrin, C. (2016). XGBoost: A Scalable Tree boosting system. *The 22nd ACM SIGKDD International Conference on Knowledge Discovery and Data Mining*, 785-794. 10.1145/2939672.2939785

Chu, Y. H. (2018). Research on innovation of enterprise management mode in the Era of Big data. *China Management Informationization, 10*, 62–63.

Dillon, T., Wu, C., & Chang, E. (2018). Cloud computing: Issues and challenges. *Advanced Information Networking and Applications*, 27-33.

Francesco, P., Lago, P., & Malavolta, I. (2019). Architecting with microservices: A systematic mapping study. *Journal of Systems and Software, 150*(4), 77–97. doi:10.1016/j.jss.2019.01.001

Genuer, R., Poggi, J., & Tuleau-Malot, C. (2015). Variable selection using random forests. *Pattern Recognition Letters, 31*(14), 2225–2236. doi:10.1016/j.patrec.2010.03.014

Hao, S., Chai, C., Li, G., Tang, N., Wang, N., & Yu, X. (2020). Outdated fact detection in knowledge bases. *The 2020 IEEE 36th International Conference on Data Engineering*, 1890-1893. 10.1109/ICDE48307.2020.00196

Heath, D. (2019). Prediction machines: the simple economics of artificial intelligence. *Journal of Information Technology Case and Application Research*, 1-4.

Hull, R., Mendling, J., & Tai, S. (2012). Business process management. *Information Systems, 37*(6), 517–517. doi:10.1016/j.is.2011.10.008

Ji, J. C. (2011). Academia resource planning system of Chinese Academy of Sciences. *E-science Technology & Application, 02*, 3–18.

Kandogan, E., Balakrishnan, A., Haber, E., & Pierce, J. (2014). From data to insight: Work practices of analysts in the enterprise. *Computer Graphics and Applications, IEEE, 34*(5), 42–50. doi:10.1109/MCG.2014.62 PMID:25248199

Kang, Y., & Liu, R. (2021). Does the merger of universities promote their scientific research performance? Evidence from China. *Research Policy, 50*(1), 104098. doi:10.1016/j.respol.2020.104098

351

Kantardzic, M. (2011). Data mining: Concepts, models, methods and algorithms. *Journal of Computing and Information Science in Engineering*, *5*(4), 394–395.

Li, J. P., Ji, J. C., Wu, D. S., Lu, J. X., Sun, X. L., & Chen, Y. P. (2012). Study on several problems of decision support models for scientific research management based on ARP. *Science & Technology for Devlopment*, *10*, 18–23.

Li, X. (2011). Scientific development outlook in universities' scientific research management. *Communication Software and Networks*, 605-607.

Li, X., Liu, H., Wang, W., Zheng, Y., Lv, H., & Lv, Z. (2022). Big data analysis of the internet of things in the digital twins of smart city based on deep learning. *Future Generation Computer Systems*, *128*, 167–177. doi:10.1016/j.future.2021.10.006

Li, X., & Whinston, A. (2020). A model of fake data in data-driven analysis. *Journal of Machine Learning Research*, *21*(3), 1–26.

Li, Z., Zhao, H., Liu, Q., Huang, Z., Mei, T., & Chen, E. (2018). Learning from history and present: Next-item recommendation via discriminatively exploiting user behaviors. *KDD: Proceedings / International Conference on Knowledge Discovery & Data Mining. International Conference on Knowledge Discovery & Data Mining*, 1734–1743. doi:10.1145/3219819.3220014

Lin, X., Cen, G., & Zhou, X. (2014). Some key technologies of scientific research management system. *Control and Intelligent Systems*, *42*(1), 1441–1444. doi:10.2316/Journal.201.2014.1.201-2523

Ma, K. (2007). Machine learning to boost the next generation of visualization technology. *IEEE Computer Graphics and Applications*, *27*(5), 6–9. doi:10.1109/MCG.2007.129 PMID:17913018

McAfee, A., & Brynjolfsson, E. (2013). Big data: The management revolution. *Harvard Business Review, 90*(10), 60-6, 68, 128.

Newell, S., & Marabelli, M. (2014). Knowledge management. *Computing Handbook, 42*(1), 1-22.

Niu, L., Lu, J., & Zhang, G. (2012). Cognition-driven decision support for business intelligence: Models, techniques, systems and applications. *Cognition-Driven Decision Support for Business Intelligence*.

Ota, M., Müller, H., Freire, J., & Srivastava, D. (2020). Data-driven domain discovery for structured datasets. *The VLDB Journal*, *13*(7), 953–965.

Rahm, E. (2016). Big data analytics. *IT-Information Technology*, *58*(4), 155–156. doi:10.1515/itit-2016-0024

Ren, Y. P., Guan, R., & Pan, Y. N. (2003). Thoughts on the construction of ARP system. *Bulletin of Chinese Academy of Sciences*, *01*, 54–57.

Romney, M., & Steinbart, P. (2012). *Accounting information systems*. Academic Press.

Shaoxiong, J., Shirui, P., Erik, C., & Pekka, M., & S., Y. (2021). A survey on knowledge graphs: Representation, acquisition and applications. *IEEE Transactions on Neural Networks and Learning Systems*, 494–514. PMID:33900922

Sirin, U., & Ailamaki, A. (2020). Micro-architectural analysis of OLAP: Limitations and opportunities. *The VLDB Journal*, *13*(6), 840–853.

Steininger, D. (2019). Linking information systems and entrepreneurship: A review and agenda for IT-Associated and digital entrepreneurship research. *Information Systems Journal, 29*(2), 363–407. doi:10.1111/isj.12206

Syed, A. (2020). *The challenge of building effective, enterprise-scale data lakes. SIGMOD/PODS '20: International Conference on Management of Data*, Portland. 10.1145/3318464.3393816

Wilder, B., Dilkina, B., & Tambe, M. (2019). Melding the data-decisions pipeline: Decision-focused learning for combinatorial optimization. *Thirty-third AAAI Conference on Artificial Intelligence.*

Wu, J., Zhang, F., Liu, F., Liu, C. X., & Zhu, Y. B. (2021). Research and practice of intelligent macro decision support based on new generation of information technology. *Frontiers of Data and Computing*, 4-15.

Xiao, L., Fanjin, Z., Zhenyu, H., Zhaoyu, W., Li, M., Jing, Z., & Jie, T. (2021). Self-supervised learning: Generative or contrastive. *IEEE Transactions on Knowledge and Data Engineering.*

Yang, D. (2016). The design and implementation of scientific research management system in university. *The 2016 6th International Conference on Mechatronics, Computer and Education Informationization, 130*, 756-759.

Ye, Y. Z., Liu, G. H., & Zhu, Y. Y. (2020). An initial exploration on framework of data assetization. *Big Data Research, 3*, 3–12.

Yongtao, Z. (2019). Research on the application of artificial intelligence technology in scientific research management in colleges and universities. *International Conference on Intelligent Computation Technology and Automation.* 10.1109/ICICTA49267.2019.00100

You, K., Li, J., & Zhao, M. (2013). Research on framework structure for scientific research management system. *Applied Mechanics and Materials, 385-386*, 1776–1779. doi:10.4028/www.scientific.net/AMM.385-386.1776

Zhang, J., Liu, Y., & Song, J. (2009). The scientific research management system of colleges. *Knowledge Acquisition and Modeling, 2009. KAM '09. Second International Symposium, 2*, 289-292.

Zhou, Y. (2019). The network system of scientific research management in local undergraduate colleges and universities based on the web platform. *International Conference on Big Data*, 1632-1638.

Zhou, Y. C., Wang, W. J., Qiao, Z. Y., Xiao, M., & Du, Y. (2020). A survey on the construction methods and applications of sci-tech big data knowledge graph (in Chinese). *Science in China. Information Sciences, 50*, 957–987.

Zhu, L., & Zheng, W. (2018). Informatics, data science, and artificial intelligence. *Journal of the American Medical Association, 320*(11), 1103.0-1104.

ADDITIONAL READING

Chen, G., Wu, G., Gu, Y., Lu, B., & Wei, Q. (2018). The challenges for big data driven research and applications in the context of managerial decision-making: Paradigm shift and research directions. *Journal of Management Sciences in China, 21*(7), 1–10.

Han, J., & Kamber, M. (2006). Data mining: Concepts and techniques. *IBM Journal of Research and Development, 10*(29), 11–18.

Turban, E., Aronson, J., & Liang, T. (2004). Decision support systems and intelligent systems (7th ed.). Academic Press.

Wang, Y., Wang, J., & Cao, R. (2019). Research and Application of A Platform for Artificial Intelligence Computing and Data Services. *Frontiers of Data & Computing, 1*(2), 86–97.

Wiener, M., Saunders, C., & Marabelli, M. (2020). Big-data business models: A critical literature review and multiperspective research framework. *Journal of Information Technology, 35*(1), 66–91. doi:10.1177/0268396219896811

Yang, J., Qiao, P., Li, Y., & Wang, N. (2019). A review of machine-learning classification and algorithms. *Journal of Advances in Information Technology, 35*(6), 36–40.

KEY TERMS AND DEFINITIONS

ARP: Academia Resource Planning. It's a new-type information system for scientific research management used by all researchers of CAS.

CAS: Chinese Academy of Sciences. It's the linchpin of China's drive to explore and harness high technology and the natural sciences for the benefit of China and the world.

Data-Driven: It's a mode that supports business driven by data flow through data aggregation, governance, and analysis technique.

Data-Driven Application Framework: It's a system framework with all the business data connected effectively through data aggregation and governance.

Data-Driven Business Processes: The data-driven business processes are produced by data-driven process engines, and they could adapt to rapid business constructions changing on business demands.

NEW ARP: The NEW ARP reconstructs the original ARP system and builds up an information application ecology covering the main scientific research management business by data-driven concept and big data analysis technology.

Scientific Research Management System: A system for the management of scientific research activities to improve the management level of scientific research institutions and promote scientific and technological progress.

Section 6
Big Data Systems and Tools

A Meta–Analytical Review of Deep Learning Prediction Models for Big Data

Parag Verma

 https://orcid.org/0000-0002-3201-4285

Chitkara University Institute of Engineering and Technology, Chitkara University, India

Vaibhav Chaudhari

 https://orcid.org/0000-0001-5781-2147

Nutanix Technologies India Pvt. Ltd., Bengaluru, India

Ankur Dumka

Women Institute of Technology, Dehradun, India & Graphic Era University (Deemed), Dehradun, India

Raksh Pal Singh Gangwar

Women Institute of Technology, India

INTRODUCTION

In the current mechanistic era, we are faced with daily reality, in which big data produces enormous measures in every part of all fields of science and industry whether, from our own lives, our financial, political, and societal structures also are connected. This presents us with unusual challenges regarding their investigation and interpretation. Examining and interpreting this high volume and hyper-parametric (i.e. big data) is a highly challenging task. This is why there is an important need for strategies for informatics data scientists as machine learning and artificial intelligence, which can help in properly examining and assessing the information that uses this large volume of data. Currently, Deep Learning (DL) is a novel strategy that is pulling in the attention of experts and researchers in understanding and controlling the vast amount of data that cover all areas.

Deep learning delineates a set of learning algorithms of artificial intelligence and machine learning that are used to build learning models that can help to understand and analyze large data and support complex predictions for decision making, for example, a multi-layered neural network originated with several intermediate hidden layers (Yann LeCun, 1989). Deep Learning technology has been applied as the various applications to resolve various existing and forthcoming problems. For the reference point of the way, insufficient coding was the first proposed learning model for basic cells in the visual cortex (Olshausen et al., 1997). This model regularizes sparsely which usually indicates more lexical highlights that play a decent order of cells. It is used over the long run that was increased and a more important learning method set to the trend for orders composed by hand digits/letters of chosen MNSIT data with an error rate of 21.00% (Wan et al., 2013). Further application area includes the acquisition and recognition of the images, discriminate, recognition and acceptability of voice/speech of the user (Krizhevsky et al., 2012; Y LeCun et al., n.d; Graves et al., 2013), through the processing of natural language (Sarikaya et

DOI: 10.4018/978-1-7998-9220-5.ch023

Copyright © 2023, IGI Global. Copying or distributing in print or electronic forms without written permission of IGI Global is prohibited.

al., 2014), acoustic demonstrating (Mohamed et al., 2011), and biological computation modeling (Leung et al., 2014; Zhang et al., 2015; Smolander et al., 2019).

Then again, the targeting point of the review on the intermediate levels that provides as specialized technical subtlety those are commonly disregarded the concepts. Then it provides the interdisciplinary eagerness for profound learning strategies, which supports the technique of data science (Frank Emmert-Streib et al., 2019; F Emmert-Streib et al., 2020), this technique simplifies it for the people who are new to the domain and ready to start The points we chose are intensive around the fundamental system of deep learning techniques that including Convolutional Neural Networks (CNNs), Deep Belief Networks (DBNs) and Auto-Encoders (AEs) systems. Further framework plans that we look at help in understanding these major approaches.

FOCUS OF THE ARTICLE

This chapter focusing on systematic review of the deep learning strategies over various field like agriculture, medical, transportation etc. This review chapter is arranged in the following sections: section 2 covers Convolutional Neural Networks, section 3 discussed about Deep Belief Networks, finally section 4 covers Auto-Encoders. Overall discussion and challenges during preparation of learning model cover under section 5. At last, with conclusion this chapter completes in section 6.

SOLUTIONS AND RECOMMENDATIONS

The solutions and recommendation for the proposed work of the chapter is as follows:

CONVOLUTIONAL NEURAL NETWORKS

CNN is an exclusive from of Feedforward Neural Network using convolution, ReLU function, and pooling layers. A standard CNNs are regularly made out of a few FFNN layers that including pooling convolution and a fully connected layers model.

Normally, in the customary ANNs model, each neuron in a layer is associated with all neurons available in the following layer, while every association defined its parametric boundary in the network model. This can bring about an extremely enormous number of parameters. Rather than utilizing completely associated layers, CNN utilizes neighborhood availability between neuron, i.e., a neuron is just associated with close by neurons in the following layers. This can altogether lessen the complete number of boundaries in the system. Besides, all the associations between neighborhood responsive fields and neurons utilize weights in form of set, and it indicates this arrangement of weights as a kernel of the network. A kernel in the network will be imparted to the various neurons that interface with their nearby responsive fields, and the aftereffects of these figuring between the neighborhood responsive fields and neurons utilizing a similar kernel will be put away in a grid signified as map belongs to the activation. Here the property that has been shared is alluded to as the sharing of weight of CNN models (Yann LeCun et al., 1989). Thus, various portions will bring about various activation functions, and the kernels strength can be balanced through hyper-parameters. In this manner, paying little mind to the absolute number of associations between the network neurons, the overall weight relates just to the size of the nearby open field, i.e., the size of the kernel.

Figure 1. (a) A model for a Convolutional Neural Network. (b) A model for shared weights and neighborhood networks on CNN. The red edges feature the way that hidden layers are associated in a "neighborhood node" way, i.e., few neurons interface the succeeding layers. The marks w_1, w_2, w_3 demonstrate the allowed weight for every association, three shrouded hubs share a similar arrangement of loads w_1, w_2, w_3 when interfacing with three nearby fixes.

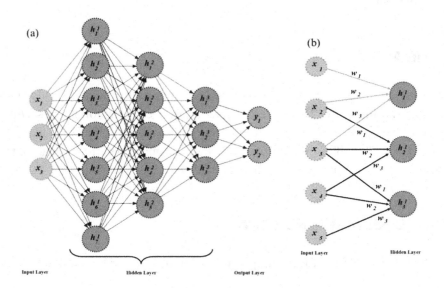

By consolidating the sharing of weight and the nearby network connection property, CNN can deal with information with high measurements. For visualization reference, see figure 1(a) of a CNN including three hidden layers. The figure having, the red edges feature the local area property of network-hidden neurons, i.e., without a doubt, not many neurons interface with the succeeding layers. This local area property of CNN makes the system inadequate contrasted with a FFNN, that is fully connected.

Basic Components of CNN

Convolutional Layer

To build a convolutional neural network a convolutional layer plays a fundamental role. A convolutional layer has a similar objective like an ordinary neural network, which is to change over the contribution to a portrayal of an increasingly conceptual level. Be that as it may, rather than utilizing full connectivity, the convolutional layer utilizes neighborhood network to play out the figuring among input and the neurons in hidden form. A convolutional layer utilizes at any rate one kernel to slide over the input info, playing out a convolution activity between each information area and the network kernel. The outcomes are put away in the activation functions, which can be viewed as the output of the convolutional layer. Critically, the activation functions can cover highlights separated by various network kernels. Every kernel of network can be considered as a component extractor and will impart its weights to all neurons.

It is very important for a convolution process to structure activation functions of a certain size using the characterization of certain spatial components. The fundamental features of which includes:

- **Kernel Size (N):** Every kernel has a fixed size of windows, which is likewise alluded to as a receptive field. The kernel of network will play out a convolution activity with a district coordinating its window size from the information and produce brings about its activation functions.
- **Stride Step (s):** This fundamental parameter represents the amount of pixels that the kernel of network will move to the forwarding position. On the other hand it is set to 1, which means each kernel will serve a determination to move the information volume and 1 pixel thereafter until the information arrives at a predefined outer part. As a result, the stride step can be used to scale back the component of initiation maps as large as the litter activation functions.
- **Zero-padding (P):** This parameter is utilized to indicate what number of zeros one needs to cushion around the fringe of the information. This is exceptionally helpful for safeguarding the component of the information.

The three parameters details above are the most widely recognized hyper-parameters that are used to control the yield volume of a convolutional layer. In particular, the contribution of measurement to the elements of the initiation map of $W_{input} \times H_{input} \times Z$, size of kernel ($N$), Stride Step ($S$), and Zero-padding ($P$), for the hyper-parameters size of $W_{out} \times H_{out} \times D$ can be determined by:

$$W_{out} = \frac{\left(W_{input} - N + 2P\right)}{\left(S+1\right)}, \ H_{out} = \frac{\left(H_{input} - N + 2P\right)}{\left(S+1\right)} \tag{1}$$

A case of how to ascertain the outcome between matrix information provided as input and a kernel of network that can be found in Figure 5. The mutual weights and neighborhood availability help altogether in decreasing the overall parameters qualities of network. Here considering as an example, it is assumed that the information inputted is of 100×100×3 dimensions, in addition to this, it is assumed that the convoluted layer and the volume of the kernel of this model is two, and each kernel is four takes as the size that represents a local receptive field. Thus each kernel becomes of 4×4×3 dimension (where the number 3 represents the depth of the kernel which would equal to the abundance of information volume). If a layer has 100 neurons then, there will be altogether just 4×4×3×2=96 number of parameters in that considered layer since all the 100 neurons will have similar weight for every kernel. This thinks about just the quantity of kernel and the size of the neighborhood network yet doesn't rely upon the quantity of neurons in the layer.

Notwithstanding decreasing the size of the parameters, weights that shared, and neighborhood availability is significant in preparing pictures effectively. The explanation, along these lines, is that neighborhood convolutional activities in a picture bring about qualities that contain certain attributes of the picture on the grounds those in pictures nearby qualities are commonly profoundly corresponded and the measurements framed by the nearby qualities are frequently invariant in the area (LeCun et al., 2015). Thus, utilizing a piece that has similar weights can identify designs from all the nearby areas in the picture, and various bits can extricate various sorts of examples from the picture.

A function from the list of non-linear activities (e.g. ReLu, sigmoid, tanh, etc.) is frequently applied to the qualities from the convolutional activities between the input layer and the kernel of network. These qualities are put away in the activation maps, that will be passed later to the following network layer.

Figure 2. A model for computing the qualities in the activation map. Here, the step is 1 and the zero-padding is 0. The selected kernel slides by 1 pixel at once from left to right beginning from the left top situation, subsequent to arriving at the visitor the bit will begin from the subsequent line and rehash the procedure until the entire information is secured. The red zone demonstrates the neighborhood fix to be tangled with the kernel, and the outcome is put away in the green field in the activation map.

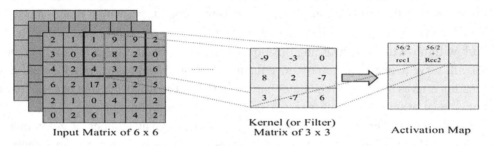

Input Matrix of 6 x 6   Kernel (or Filter) Matrix of 3 x 3   Activation Map

Pooling Layer

Typically in network models, a pooling layer is embedded in the middle of a hard layer and its accompanying lower layers. This pooling layer has to be combined with some pre-defined pooling techniques to reduce input dimensions, which is its most important goal in a network model. At the same time, this layer explains a littler contribution by saving many data as expected. Similarly, a pooling can bring spatial invasiveness to the network (Scherer et al., 2010), which may aid in improving model speculation. Therefore, a pooling layer uses the function of pooling. The pooling layer will check the entire contribution with a predetermined pooling window size such as convolutional layer kernel. For example, using a stride step will be 2, size of window will be 2, and the zero-padding is 0 for the pooling that would be a large part of the size of the input information dimensions.

There are numerous sorts of pooling strategies, for example, averaging pooling, min-pooling, and some progressed pooling techniques. Commonly utilizing pooling technique is max-pooling, as it has been demonstrated to be prevalent in managing images by catching invariances proficiently. (Scherer et al., 2010) Max-pooling extricates the most extreme incentive inside each predetermined sub-window over the activation function. The maximum pooling can be figured as

$$A_{i,j,k} = max\left(R_{i-n:i+n,\, j-n:j+n,k} \right)$$

in which, the value of $A_{i,j,k}$ represents the maximum activation from the network matrix R of size $n{\times}n$ focused at the index value i,j in the kth activation function with a n size of window.

Fully-Connected Network (FNN) Layer

A fully-connected layer works in feed forward neural network (FFNN) as a hidden layer. Curiously, for conventional CNN model, a fully-connected layer is regularly included between the penultimate layer and the yield layer to additionally show a relationship i.e. non-linear among input features (Krizhevsky et al., 2012; Simonyan et al., 2014; Szegedy et al., 2015). Nevertheless, as of current advantage of this has been addressed due to the numerous parameters presented by this, driving conceivably to overfitting. (Simonyan et al., 2014) Accordingly, an ever-increasing number of scientists began to build CNN model without such a fully-connected layer utilizing different procedures like max-after some time pooling to supplant the job of direct layers (Lin et al., 2013; Doshi-Velez et al., 2017).

Important Variants of CNN

Visual Geometric Group Network (VGGNet)

VGGNet is a leading model for investigating the factors that affect the performance of deep CNN network models (Simonyan et al., 2014). Visual Geometry Group and Google DeepMind proposed this model, through this model, researcher investigated the structures with an abundance of 19 (for example, in contrast to 11 for AlexaNet (Krizhevsky et al., 2012).

VGG19 proposes n increased sized model of network by means of increasing the network model with eight weighted layers to 10 weighted layers by combining it with 11 weighted layers. Thus, it expand the boundaries from 61 million to 144 million but still the network take most of the parameters of fully-connected layer. The detailed result shows the rate of error has decreased form 29.60 t0 25.50 on the ILSVRC dataset and with respect to the top-1 error value. Similarly with respect to the top-5 error values it decreased from 10.40 to 8.00 on the ILSVRC dataset in ILSVRC2014. They also piled several 3×3 convolutional layers in absence of a pooling layer to suppress the crusted layer with the size of a huge channel, for example 7×7 or be 11×11 and proposed that this model can be indirectly fit to accept, and reaction fields from those formed with larger channel sizes. Subsequently, two steep 3×3 layers can move from 5×5 open areas to highlights, although not with so much boundaries but with more non-linearity.

Inception Intercepts with GoogleNet

If the performance capabilities of a conventional neural network are to be improved, the simplest way is to stack a lot of its layers and incorporate as many parameters as possible in its layers. (Simonyan et al., 2014) In any case, this would force two important issues. One of which is a large number of limitations would indicate overfitting, and the other is that it is difficult to model.

Google introduced the GoogLeNet (Szegedy et al., 2015). Until the presentation of the beginning, customary best in class CNN designs principally cantered around expanding the size and profundity of the neural system, which likewise expanded the network calculation cost. Interestingly, GoogLeNet acquainted design with accomplishing best in class execution with a lightweight arrange structure.

The thought fundamental an origin arrange design is to keep the network as meagre as could be expected under the circumstances while using the quick framework calculation include gave by a computer system. This thought encourages the primary commencement structure (see Figure 3).

Figure 3 shown a 1×1 convolution and 3×3 max-pooling works at similar level on input information where each passage consists of alternate layer named as 'child later', which include 1×1 convolution layer, 3×3 convolutions and 5×5 convolutions layer. The outcomes from each passage are linked together at output layer. This approach utilizes 1×1 convolution layer to downscale the information picture while holding input data (Lin et al., 2013). They contended that connecting all the highlights extricated by various scales and just the accumulated highlights ought to be sent to the following level. Consequently, the following level can remove highlights from various scales. In addition, this merger structure presented by an initiation square requires less parameter and is more proficient.

Figure 3a. Block structure of competitive and original inception model. Here numerous squares are stacked on head of one another, shaping the info layer for the following block.

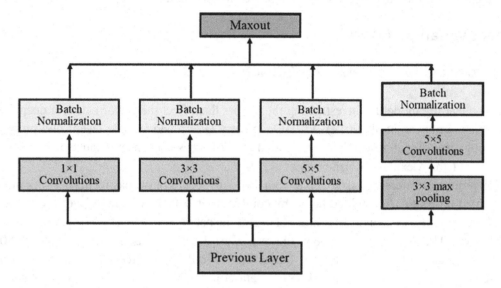

Figure 3b.

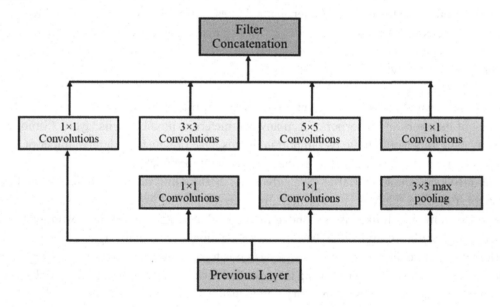

With all the initial structures stacked through this entire system, GoogLeNet displays the front of the pack in the ILSVRC2014 characterization, demonstrating the nature of the infrastructure. This was initially followed by v_1, v_2, v_3, and most recently presented v_4. Each age offered some new highlights, making the system quicker, progressively lighter, and even more remarkable.

ResNet

On a basic level, CNNs model with a more profound structure that perform superior to shallow ones (Simonyan et al., 2014). In principle, more profound systems have a superior capacity to speak to elevated level highlights form the information, hence improving the exactness of expectations. (Donahue et al., 2014) In any case, one can't just stack an ever-increasing number of layers. He and his co-researchers in their research make a conclusion that more layers can hurt the presentation. In their analysis, system A has N layers whereas system B has $N+M$ layers whereas the underlying N layers had a similar structure. While preparing on the CIFAR-10 and ImageNet dataset, organize B demonstrated a higher preparing blunder than arrange B which shows that adding M layers bring better execution, however they got higher blunders, which cannot be clarified by over fitting. The explanation behind this is the misfortune is being enhanced to nearby minima, which is not the same as the disappearing angle marvels. This is eluded to as the performance degrade issue. (He et al., 2016)

ResNet was acquainted with beat the debasement issue of CNNs to push the profundity of a CNN as far as possible (He et al., 2016). In this paper author proposed a novel structure for modeling a CNN network, which is in principle equipped for being reached out to an endless profundity without losing exactness. Authors proposed a Deep Residual Learning structure, which comprises of various leftover squares to address the debasement issue. The structure of the remaining residual blocks appears in fig 4.

Rather than attempting to gain proficiency with the ideal hidden mapping $H(x)$ from each couple of stacked layers, they utilized an identity planning method for input x from contribution to the output layer. Afterword let the system become familiar with the residual mapping $F(x)=H(x)-x$. Subsequent to including personality planning, the first planning can be reformulated as $F(x)=H(x)+x$. The identity planning is acknowledged by making alternate route associations from the information hub straightforwardly to the output node. This can assist with tending to the debasement issue just as the evaporating (detonating) inclination issue of profound systems. In extraordinary cases, further layers can simply become familiar with the identity functions of the contribution to the output layer by essentially computing the residuals as 0. This empowers the capacity for a profound system to perform in any event not more terrible than shallow ones. Likewise, practically speaking, the residuals are rarely 0, which makes it feasible for more profound layers to consistently gain some new useful knowledge from the residuals, in this manner, delivering better outcomes. The usage of ResNet assisted with pushing the layers of CNNs to 152 by stacking supposed leftover squares all through the system. ResNet accomplished the best outcome in the ILSVRC2016 rivalry, with a 3.58% error rate.

DEEP BELIEF NETWORKS

A network model hat interconnects different types of neural systems to form a new neural system model is called the Deep Belief Network (DBN). At a particular point of time, a DBN coordinates RBMs with D-FFNNs. Restricted Boltzmann Machine (RBNs) structure the information unit, although D-FFNNs structure the output unit. As often as possible, RBMs are stacked on each other heads, meaning that more than one RBM is used continuously. This adds to the abundance of DBNs. RBM and D-FFNN are two unique algorithms used for learning for overcoming the diverse idea of systems. RBM algorithm is utilized for introducing a model in unsupervised learning manner. Researcher Glorot with his co-researcher applied supervised learning method for calibration of parameters.

Figure 4. Residual block structure. Inside a block there can be the same number of weight layers as wanted.

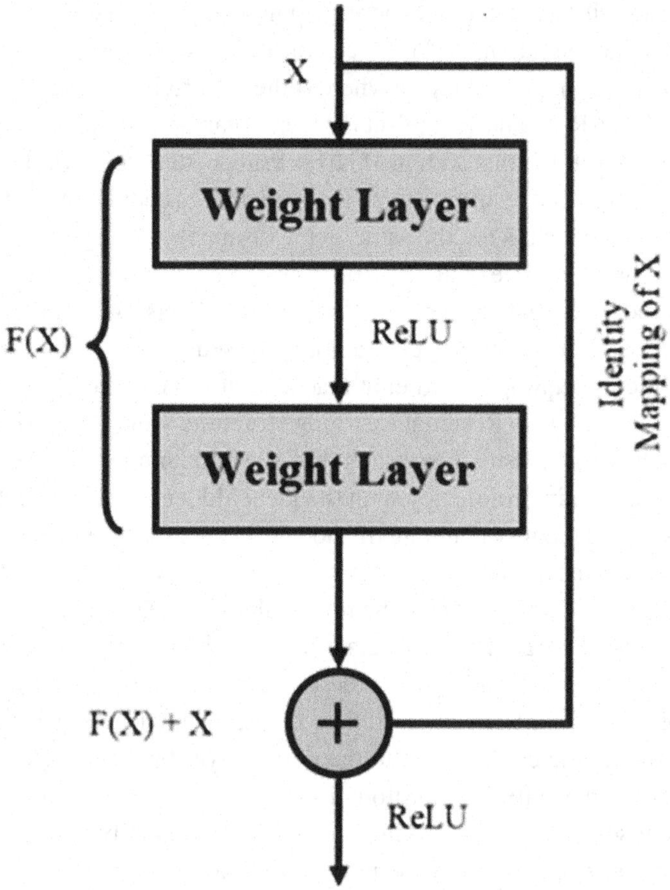

Unsupervised Learning Method: Model Pre-Training Phase

Neural network can be learning by using supervised learning technique and such a learning methodology can be uncommonly moderate. Through unsupervised learning is used to present the model boundaries. The conventional algorithms that are used for learning the neural network like back propagation and so forth were from the start simply prepared to learn shallow design.

Restricted Boltzmann Machine is used for introduction of parameters in unsupervised learning and thus one can acquires an increasingly proficient preparation of the neural system (Hinton et al., 2006).

Boltzmann Machine (BM) differ from Restricted Boltzmann Machine (RBM) in terms of limits in the network structure, BM doesn't carry any predefined limitations whereas RBM have limit in network structure (Fischer et al., 2012).

The estimation of neurons 'v', within the obvious layer is known, yet the neuron esteems 'h' within the concealed layer, are obscure. We can acknowledge the parameters of a system by characterizing energy function 'E' of the model considering limited edition.

Often, and RBM is utilized with binary qualities, i.e. $v_i \in \{0,1\}$ and $h_i \in \{0,1\}$. The energy function is denoted by:

Figure 5. Examples for Boltzmann Machines. (a) The neurons are organized on a circle. (b) The neurons are isolated by their sort. Both Boltzmann Machines are indistinguishable and contrast just in their representation. (c) Transition from a Boltzmann Machine (in left figure) to a Restricted Boltzmann Machine (in right figure).

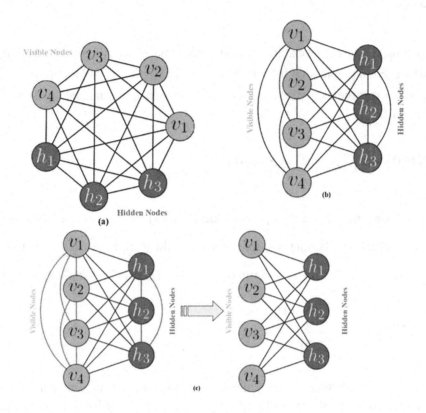

$$E\left(v,h\right) = -\sum_{i}^{m} a_i v_i - \sum_{j}^{n} b_j h_j - \sum_{i}^{m}\sum_{j}^{n} v_i h_j w_{i,j} \tag{2}$$

In which $\Theta = \{a, b, W\}$ is the arrangement of model parameters.

Every design of the framework relates to a likelihood characterized by means of the Boltzmann appropriation in Equation (2):

$$p\left(v,h\right) = \frac{1}{Z} e^{-E\left(v,h\right)} \tag{3}$$

In Equation (3), Z is the parcel work given by:

$$Z = \sum_{\left(v,h\right)} e^{-E\left(v,h\right)} \tag{4}$$

The network probability appointing to an obvious vector v and is given by adding overall conceivable concealed vectors:

$$p(v) = \frac{1}{Z} \sum_h e^{-E(v,h)}$$ (5)

The ideal parameters of the probabilistic model is estimated by utilizing the Maximum-likelihood Estimation (MLE). For a preparation informational index $\mathfrak{D} = \mathfrak{D}_{train} = \{v_1, v_2, ..., v_l\}$ comprising of l patterns, expecting that the examples are iid (indistinguishable and independent) conveyed, the log-likelihood functions:

$$L(\theta) = ln\ \mathcal{L}(\theta|\mathfrak{D}) = ln \prod_{i=1}^{l} p(v_i|\theta) = \sum_{i=1}^{l} ln\ p(v_i|\theta)$$ (6)

For basic cases, one might have the option to locate an explanatory answer for Equation (6) by explaining $\frac{\partial}{\partial\theta} ln\ \mathcal{L}(\theta|\mathfrak{D}) = 0$. Be that as it may, normally, the boundaries should be found numerically. For this, the slope of the log-likelihood is a run of the mill approach for evaluating the ideal parameters:

$$\theta^{(t+1)} = \theta^{(t)} + \Delta\theta^{(t)} = \theta^{(t)} + \eta \frac{\partial L(\theta^{(t)})}{\partial\theta^{(t)}} - \lambda\theta^{(t)} + v" \theta^{(t+1)}$$ (7)

In Equation (7), the consistent, η, before the inclination is the learning rate, and the principal regularization term, $-\lambda\theta^{(t)}$, is value of weight-decay. The weight-decay is utilized to compel the streamlining issue by punishing enormous estimations of θ (Hinton, 2012). The parameters λ is likewise called the weight-cost. The subsequent regularization term in Equation (7) is called energy momentum. The motivation behind the force is to make learning quicker and to lessen potential motions. General, this ought to settle the learning procedure.

For the enhancement, the Stochastic Gradient Ascent (SGA) uses mini-batches. That implies one chooses haphazardly various samples from the training set, 'k' which are very litter than the absolute sample size, and afterward assesses the slope. The parameters θ are then refreshed for smaller than expected mini-batch. This procedure is rehashed iteratively until age in finished. An age is portrayed by utilizing the entire preparation set once. A typical issue is experienced when utilizing smaller than normal groups that are too enormous in light of the fact that this can hinder the learning procedure significantly. Much of the time k is picked somewhere in the range of 10–100 (Hinton, 2012).

Before the slope can be utilized, one needs to surmise the angle of Equation (7). In particular, the subordinates as for the boundaries can be written in the accompanying structure:

$$\begin{cases} \dfrac{\partial \mathcal{L}(\theta|v)}{\partial w_{ij}} = p\big(H_j = 1|v\big)v_i - \sum_v p(v)\,p\big(H_j = 1|v\big)v_i \\[2mm] \quad\quad \dfrac{\partial \mathcal{L}(\theta|v)}{\partial a_i} = v_i - \sum_v p(v)v_i \\[2mm] \dfrac{\partial \mathcal{L}(\theta|v)}{\partial b_j} = p\big(H_j = 1|v\big) - \sum_v p(v)\,p\big(H_j = 1|v\big) \end{cases} \tag{8}$$

In Equation (8), Hi indicates the estimation of the hidden unit i and p(v) is the probability characterized in Equation (5). For the conditional probability, one finds

$$p\big(H_j = 1|v\big) = \sigma\left(\sum_{j=1}^{n} w_{ij} v_i + b_j\right) \tag{9}$$

Furthermore, correspondingly

$$p\big(V_i = 1|h\big) = \sigma\left(\sum_{i=1}^{m} w_{ij} h_j + a_i\right) \tag{10}$$

Utilizing the equation mention above in the introduced structure would be wasteful in light of the fact that these conditions require a summation over every single obvious vector. Therefore, the Contrastive Divergence (CD) strategy is utilized for speeding up for the estimation of the angle. In algorithm, we show the pseudo code of the CD calculation.

Algorithm 1:

Input: RBM (with m visible and n hidden layers) and mini-batch $\bar{\mathcal{D}}$ (sample size k)

Output: Update Δw_{ij}, Δa_i, Δb_j

for $v \in \bar{\mathcal{D}}$ do

$\quad\quad v^{(0)} \leftarrow v$

for $t=0,\dots,k-1$ do

for $j=1,\dots,n$ do sample $h_j^{(t)} \sim p\big(h_j | v^{(t)}\big)$

for $i=1,\dots,n$ do sample $v_j^{(t+1)} \sim p\big(v_j | h^{(t)}\big)$

$\quad\quad$ for $i=1,\dots,m,\ j=1,\dots,n$ do

$\quad\quad\quad\quad \Delta w_{ij} \leftarrow \Delta w_{ij} + p\big(H_j = 1|v^{(0)}\big)v_i^{(0)} - p\big(H_j = 0|v^{(k)}\big)v_i^{(k)}$

$\quad\quad \Delta a_i \leftarrow \Delta a_i + v_i^{(0)} - v_i^{(k)}$

$\quad\quad \Delta b_j \leftarrow \Delta b_j + p\big(H_j = 1|v^{(0)}\big) - p\big(H_j = 1|v^{(k)}\big)$

The CD utilizes Gibbs inspecting for drawing tests from contingent distributions with the goal that the following worth relies just upon the past one. This produces a Markov chain (Hastie et al., 2009). Asymptotically, for $k \to \infty$ the dissemination turns into the genuine fixed circulation. For this situation, the $CD \to ML$. Curiously, as of now $k=1$ can prompt agreeable approximations for the pre-preparing (Carreira-Perpinan et al., 2005).

Figure 6. Visualizing the stacking of RBMs so as to get familiar with the boundaries of a model in an unaided manner

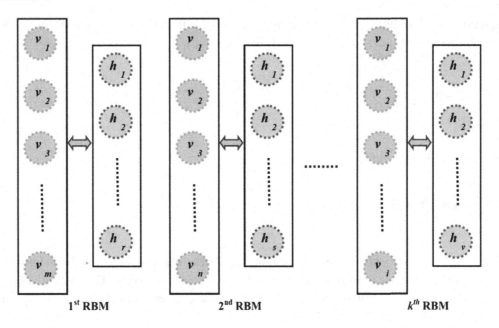

Generally, the pre-tanning of DBNs comprise stacking RBMs. That implies the following RBM is prepared to utilize the concealed layer of the past RBM as an obvious layer. This instates the parameters for each layer. Curiously, the request for this preparation isn't fixed however can change. For example, first and last layer can be prepared, and afterward, the rest of the layers can be prepared Hinton and team (Hinton et al., 2006). A case of stacking of RBMs shown in figure 6.

Supervised Learning Method: Fine-Tuning Phase

Once the parameters of a neural network are initialized, they can be calibrated, as described in the previous advance. For this progression, an approach of supervised learning is applied, that means samples unseen in the pre-training stage, are currently used. For model learning, a mistake limits work (additionally called misfortune work or sometimes target work). One case of this type of error function is the Mean Squared Error (MSE) represented as:

$$E = \frac{1}{2n} \sum_{i-1}^{n} o_i - t_i^2 \qquad (11)$$

Equation (20) have, $o_i = \phi(x_i)$ that represent the ith output of the function from network: $\phi : \mathbb{R}^m \cdot \mathbb{R}^n$ that given the ith input of x_i that comes from the training dataset $\mathfrak{D} = \mathfrak{D}_{train} = \{(x_1, t_1), ..., (x_l, t_l)\}$ and the objective output value represented via t_l.

Essentially, for boosting the function of log-likelihood of a RBM (as from Equation 7), one uses gradient descent to discover the model parameters that lemmatize the function of error.

$$\theta^{(t+1)} = \theta^{(t)} - \text{''} \; \theta^{(t)} = \theta^{(t)} - \eta \frac{\partial E}{\partial \theta^{(t)}} - \lambda \theta^{(t)} + v \cdot \theta^{(t-1)} \tag{12}$$

Parameters (η, λ, and v) in this equation have a similar importance as clarified previously. Once more, the gradient is ordinarily not utilized for the whole training dataset $\mathfrak{D}$, yet rather littler groups are utilized by means of the Stochastic Gradient Descent (SGD).

RBM log-likelihood gradient can be approximated by using CD algorithm 1. For this, the back propagation algorithm has been used to accomplish the task (LeCun et al., 2015).

Let us consider that a_i^l is a activation function of ith unit in l^{th} layer where, $\left(l \in \{2, 3, \cdots, L\}\right)$, b_i^l the relating predisposition and b_{ij}^l the edge weight between the jth unit of the $(l-1)^{th}$ layer and the ith unit of the lth layer. For the function of activation, 'φ' the value of activation of the lth layer with the $(l-1)$ th layer as information is $a^l = \varphi\left(z^{(l)}\right) = \varphi\left(w^{(l)} a^{(l-1)} + b^{(l)}\right)$.

Utilization of the chain rule prompts (Nielsen, 2015):

$$\begin{cases} \delta^{(L)} = \nabla_a E . \varphi'\left(Z^{(L)}\right) \\ \delta^{(L)} = \left(\left(w^{(l+1)}\right)^T \delta^{(l+1)}\right) . \varphi'\left(Z^{(L)}\right) \\ \frac{\partial E}{\partial b_i^{(l)}} = \partial_i^{(l)} \\ \frac{\partial E}{\partial w_{ij}^{(l)}} = x_j^{(l)} \delta_i^{(l)} \end{cases} \tag{13}$$

Equation (13), the vector $\delta^{(L)}$ contains the mistakes of the yield layer (L), though the vector $\delta^{(L)}$ contains the blunders of the lth layer. Here, '$\cdot$' demonstrates the component shrewd result of vectors. From this, the slope of the mistake of the yield layer is given by

$$\nabla_a E = \left\{ \frac{\partial E}{\partial a_1^{(L)}}, ..., \frac{\partial E}{\partial a_k^{(L)}} \right\} \tag{14}$$

Generally, the outcomes of this relies upon the value of E, for example, the value of MSE we computed through $\frac{\partial E}{\partial a_i^{(L)}} = \left(a_j - t_j\right)$. Therefore, the pseudocode for the algorithms of backpropagation can be calculated as appeared in algorithm 2 (Nielsen, 2015). The value of assessed gradients from algorithm

3 then it is used to upgrade the wrights and biases parameters by means of SGD – as formulated in equation (12). More updates are performed utilizing smaller than mini-batches until the entire training data has been utilized (Smolander, Dehmer, et al., 2019).

Algorithm 2:

Input: Mini-batch $\bar{\mathcal{D}}$ (sample size k)
Output: Update Δb, Δw
         for $x \in \bar{\mathcal{D}}$ do
              $a^{(a,1)} \leftarrow x$
         for $l \in \{2,3,\dots, L$ do
              $z^{(x,l)} \leftarrow w^{(l)} a^{(x,l-1)} + b^l$ do
$a^{(x,l)} \leftarrow \varphi\left(z^{(x,l)}\right)$

$$\delta^{(x,l)} \leftarrow \left(\left(w^{(l+1)}\right)^T \delta^{(x,l+1)}\right) * \varphi'\left(z^{(x,l)}\right)$$

for $l \in \{L,\ L-1,\ L-2,\ \dots,\ 2\}$ do
$$\delta^{(x,l)} \leftarrow \left(\left(w^{(l+1)}\right)^T \delta^{(x,l+1)}\right) * \varphi'\left(z^{(x,l)}\right)$$

    for $l \in \{L,\ L-1,\ L-2,\ \dots,\ 2\}$ do
$$\Delta b^{(l)} \leftarrow \Delta b^{(l)} + \frac{1}{k}\sum_x \delta^{(x,l)}$$

$$\Delta w^{(l)} \leftarrow \Delta w^{(l)} + \frac{1}{k}\sum_x \delta^{(x,l)}\left(a^{(x,l-1)}\right)^T$$

Algorithm 3:

Input: Parameters θ, η^+, η^-, D_{max}, D_{min}, $D^{(0)}$ and epoch t
Output: Update $\Delta \theta$
         for θ do
              if $\dfrac{\partial E^{(t-1)}}{\partial \theta} \cdot \dfrac{\partial E^{(t)}}{\partial \theta} > 0$, then
                   $$\Delta^{(t)} \leftarrow min\left(\Delta^{(t-1)}.\eta^+, \Delta_{max}\right)$$
$$\Delta \theta^{(t)} \leftarrow -sgn\left(\frac{\partial E^{(t)}}{\partial \theta}.\Delta^{(t)}\right)$$

         elseif $\dfrac{\partial E^{(t-1)}}{\partial \theta} \cdot \dfrac{\partial E^{(t)}}{\partial \theta} < 0$ then
                   $$\Delta^{(t)} \leftarrow max\left(\Delta^{(t-1)}.\eta^-, \Delta_{min}\right)$$
if $E^{(t)} > E^{(t-1)}$ then
              $$\theta^{(t+1)} \leftarrow \theta^{(t)} - \Delta\theta^{(t+1)}$$
              $$\frac{\partial E^{(t)}}{\partial \theta} \leftarrow 0$$

$$\text{elseif } \frac{\partial E^{(t-1)}}{\partial \theta} \cdot \frac{\partial E^{(t)}}{\partial \theta} = 0 \text{ then}$$

$$\Delta\theta^{(t)} \leftarrow -sgn\left(\frac{\partial E^{(t)}}{\partial \theta} \cdot \Delta^{(t-1)}\right)$$

The algorithm of versatile backpropagation (iRprop⁺) is an alteration of the algorithm of backpropagation that was initially acquainted with accelerating the fundamental of backpropagation algorithms (Bprop) (Riedmiller et al., 1993). There exist minimum four distinct forms of iRprop⁺ (Igel et al., 2000). Algorithm 9 having a pseudocode for algorithm of iIRprop⁺ (which advances the iRprop⁺ with backtracking the weight) is appeared in Smolander, 2019 (Smolander et al., 2019).

As should be obvious in Algorithm 9, iRprop⁺ utilizes data about the indication of the partial subordinate after time step (t − 1) to settle on a choice for updating the parameters. Critically, the resultants of examinations have indicated that the algorithms of iRprop⁺ is quicker than Bprop (Igel et al., 2000)

Demonstration shows the algorithm of backpropagation with SGD that can learn great neural network models even when the pre-training phase is missing or the training data is high volume (LeCun et al., n.d.).

Figure 7. The two phases of DBN learning. (a) The hidden layer (light orange) of one RBM is the contribution of the following RBM. Therefore their measurements are equivalent. (b) The two edges in tweaking indicate the two phases of the backpropagation calculation: the info feedforwarding and the error backpropagation. The orange layer showed the output.

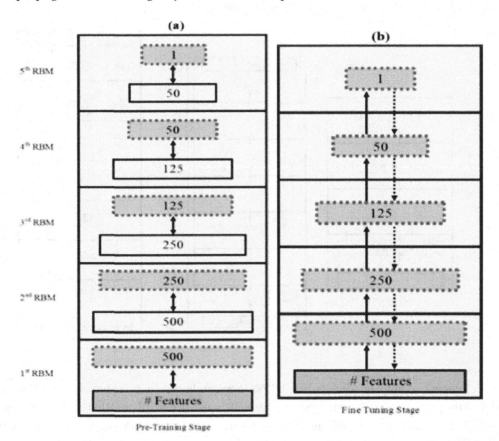

Figure 7, shows a case of the general DBN learning method. Where the left side of the model shows the pre-tanning stage while the right side of the model shows the fine-tuning process.

The DBNs network model have been utilized effectively for some application undertakings, e.g., Natural Language Processing (NLP) (Sarikaya et al., 2014), acoustic modeling technique (Mohamed et al., 2011), automatic image recognition (Hinton et al., 2006) and computational biological science (Zhang et al., 2015).

AUTOENCODER

An Autoencoder is a part of unsupervised learning model that utilized for presenting a learning process that includes selection of features and/or reduction of dimensions. A typical property of autoencoders is the volume of input data and output layer is equivalent with a symmetric architectural approach

(Hinton et al., 2006). The basic thought is to take in planning from an information design x to another encoding c = h(x), which is a perfect world gives as yield design equivalent to the data pattern on input, i.e., x ≈ y = g(c). Henceforth, the encoding of c, which has normally lower measurement than x, permits us to recreate the value of x.

Figure 8. Visualizing the possibility of Autoencoder learning model. The learning of new encoding of the input is spoken to in the code layer (appeared in Green).

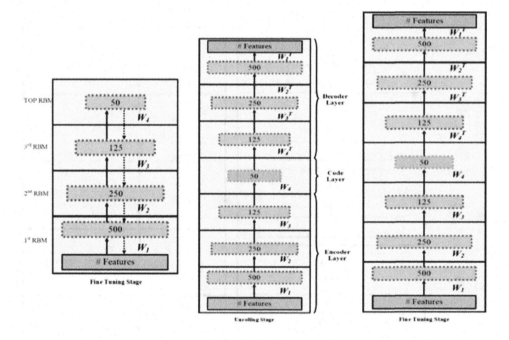

The development of autoencoders is like DBNs. Strikingly the first execution of autoencoder pre-training is just the primary portion of the system with RBMs and afterward unrolled the system. Researcher Hinton & Salakhutdinov used to making along these lines as the network second piece (Hinton et al., 2006). Like DBNs, a stage of pre-training stage I trailed by an adjusting stage. Figure 12, representing the learning procedures that have been appeared. Here, the coding layer relates to the new encoding of c giving, e.g., a diminished element of x.

Labels are not the part of the autoencoder that means this model is an unsupervised learning model. As per the application of the model it has been effectively utilized for reduction of dimensions. Autoencoders can accomplish a vastly improved two-dimensional portrayal of exhibit information when a satisfactory measure of information is accessible (Hinton et al., 2006). Critically, a liner transformation is actualizing by the help of PCAs, while autoencoders support the non-linear paradigm. Typically these outcomes are better execution. We might want to feature that there are numerous expansions of these models, for example, sparse, denoising or variation autoencoder (Vincent et al., 2010; Deng et al., 2013; Pu et al., 2016).

DISCUSSION

General Characteristics of Deep Learning

For all intensive learning models, it is a common property that they perform a structural representation of learning a so-called representation. In some cases, such performances are also called learning features. This means that a network model that able to learns new and improved tasks, as opposed to raw information. Critically, the deep learning model does not achieve proficiency with final representation inside a phase, yet different people compare multilevel delineation changes between hidden layers (LeCun et al., n.d.).

One other regular feature of a deep learning model is that the models are subsequently changes between layers that are non-linear (as see Figure 2). This expands the expressive intensity of the model (Duda et al., 2012). Besides, singular portrayals are not be planned manually, but it can be learned through the training information (Zhang et al., 2015). This property can makes a very flexible deep learning model.

Differences Between Models

As of now, CNNs models are the overwhelming deep learning models for the visionary tasks of a computer (Henaff et al., 2015). These all models are successful when the information comprise of clusters where close by values in an exhibit are connected with one another, e.g., just like the case for the data as pictures, recordings, and sound. Convolutional layers can undoubtedly process high-dimensional contribution by utilizing the neighborhood network and shared weights. In addition, a pooling layer can down the samples of the contributed input without losing basic data. Each convolutional layer is fit for changing over the input image into gatherings of progressively unique highlights utilizing various kernels; accordingly, by stacking numerous convolution layers, the system can change the input image to a portrayal that catches basic and essential pattern from the image that provided as input, in this manner it making exact forecasts.

Nonetheless, additionally, in different regions, CNNs model have demonstrated competitive outcomes that contrasted with other deep learning models, for example in natural language processing (Doshi-Velez et al., 2017; Yang et al., 2020). In particular, CNNs model can be acceptable at extricating neighborhood data from the content and investigating important semantic and syntactic implications among expressions and words. Likewise, the normal synthesis of text information can be handily taken care by an architecture of CNN model. Consequently, CNNs model shows a solid potential in performing arrangement assignments where fruitful expectations vigorously depend on removing key data from input text (Yin et al., 2017).

Classical architecture of the network is to constrict a fully-connected and feedforward relating network to a D-FFNN. This network strikingly, has been demonstrated that a D-FFNN beat different techniques for foreseeing the toxicity of medications (Mayr et al., 2018). Likewise, for sedate objective forecasts, a D-FFNN has been demonstrated to be better analysed than different techniques. This shows that even such an engineering can be effectively utilized in present-day applications.

Ordinarily, RNNs models are utilized for the issues with successive information, for example, discourse and language handling or displaying (Graves et al., 2013; Sundermeyer et al., 2012). While DBNs and CNNs models are feedforward systems, associations in RNNs model that can shape a cycles. This permits to displaying the dynamical changes after some time.

An issue of finding the correct application for deep learning model is that their application areas are not totally unrelated to one another. Rather, as the conversation shows in previous sections that there is impressive cover and as well as can be expected by and large just be found by directing a comparative study.

Interpretable Models vs. Black-Box Models

We can segregate data science model into two models as inferential model and forecast model (Breiman, 2001; Shmueli, 2010). Where inferential model is used with interpretable structure whereas forecast model can be able to forecast the procedure itself example as casual model. An expectation model is only a black-box or a discovery model for making forecasts.

The network models that focus in this review paper works as predicting models. Researcher Hebb proposed Hebbian learning rule which works on model of a systematically motivated learning rule for nervous network model (Hebb, 1949). This is a type of unsupervised learning of neural systems which uses neighboring data from contiguous neurons. Extended version of Hebb's fundamental learning decision rules have been proposed which rely on new natural bits of knowledge.

In present time there is extraordinary enthusiasm for interpretable or logical AI (XAI). Particularly in the biomedical and clinical fields, one might want to have reasonable choices of factual forecast models since patients are influenced (Doshi-Velez et al., 2017; Biran et al., 2017). Still this field is in its early stages, yet in the event that significant understandings of general deep learning models that could be discovered this would unquestionably alter the field.

Thus, the difference between logical AI model and non-explainable models is not much characterized. The difference can be considered using example of inadequate coding model by researcher Olshausen which demonstrate coding of pictures in human visual cortex (Olshausen et al., 1997; Tosic et al., 2011) and utilization of this model is represented by (Charles et al., 2011). In their approach the unsupervised learning model is utilized for getting familiar with ideal meager coding word reference for the grouping of high imagery spectral (HIS) data.

Big Data vs. Small Data Intervened Deep Learning Model

As per the statistics concern, the experimental design area concern is worried about surveying if the accessible example sizes are adequate to lead a specific examination. (for a down to earth model see (Smolander et al., 2019; Srinivas et al., 2020). Interestingly, for all strategies examined in this paper, we expected that the enormous information space suggesting adequate examples. This relates to the perfect case. In any case, we might want to bring up that for specific application, one needs to evaluate this circumstance one case at a time case to guarantee the accessible information (separately the example sizes) are adequate to utilize deep learning models. Shockingly, this issue is not very much spoken to in the flow writing. As a dependable guideline, profound learning models normally perform well for a huge number of tests yet it is to a great extent muddled how they act in a little informational collection. This leaves it to the client to assess the expectations to absorb information of the speculation mistake for an offered model to keep away from deceptive outcomes (Emmert-Streib et al., 2019).

In order to explain the issue above we examine the investigation on the impact of sample size on exactness of grouping of Extended MNIST (EMNIST) information. EMNIST comprises of 280,000 characters in form of handwritten (240,000 training samples and 40, 000 test tests) for 10 adjusted classes (0–9) (Cohen et al., n.d.). A multi-layered Long Short-Term Memory (LSTM) model is used for 10-class transcribed digit characterization task. The network model selected consists of four layers where three are hidden layers and one is fully connected layer and each concealed layer consists of 200 neurons. For our investigations, the cluster size was set to 100 and the preparation tests were haphazardly drawn if the quantity of training tests was < 240, 000 (subsampling).

Figure 9. Classification error of the EMNIST dataset in the dependence on the quantity of preparing tests. The standard blunders are appeared in red and the flat run line compares to a mistake of 5%. The outcomes are arrived at the midpoint of more than 10 free runs.

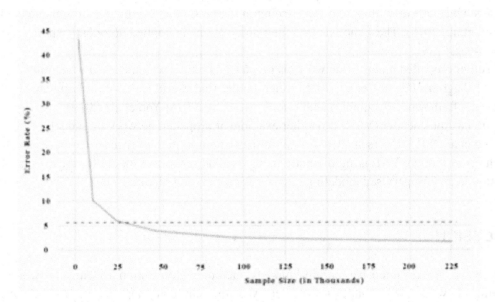

In figure 16, the flat run line compares to a mistake of 5%. The outcomes are arrived at the midpoint of more than 10 free runs. Figure 16 as per the outcomes, one can see that a multiple of thousands training samples that are expected to accomplish in an order of classification error beneath 5% (represented with blue line in dashed form). In particular, more than 25,000 training tests as samples are required. Given the general effortlessness of the issue—order of ten digits, contrasted with arrangement or analysis of malignancy patients—the seriousness of this issue should turn out to be clear. Additionally, these outcomes show that a profound learning model can't do supernatural occurrences. In the event that the quantity of tests is excessively little, the technique separates. Thus, the blend of a model and information is vital for tackling an errand.

Data Types

The example considered in the above sections is the type of problem of data related to the size issue. Models for different information types are text information, picture information, sound information, networks of information, or inference / sensor information (e.g. genomics) to give some examples. Moreover, we can segment the information as per application space from which they begin like text information from clinical delivery, text information from online life, or text information from books. For such classification, the data substance of 'an instance' does not have the same importance for each information type and for each application area. Evaluation of the deep learning models that should be consistently directed by an explicit way in light of the fact that the exchange of information between such models is not straightforward.

FUTURE RESEARCH DIRECTIONS

There are many other advanced networking model in addition to intensive learning model that are outside to these core architectures. Some examples are Reinforcement Learning and Deep Reformation Learning Models which are very important for learning in the present and future (Arulkumaran et al., 2017; Henderson et al., 2018). These models find their applications in applied autonomy, sports, and human services issues.

Some other propelled model of networks is graph CNN model which is used when information having type of diagrams (Henaff et al., 2015). Such model find useful for Natural Language Processing, recommender frameworks, genomics, and science (Li et al., 2018; Yao et al., 2019).

Variational Autoencoder (VAE) is another example of propelled networking model which sets forth plainly (An et al., 2015; Doersch, 2016). VAE utilizes appropriation over inactive spaces as the encoding for the contribution. VAE is significantly being used as generative model for creating comparative information in an unsupervised modeling manner, for generating picture or text.

CONCLUSION

In our research, several intensive learning models, including Conventional Neural Networks (CNN), Deep Billiff Networks (DBN) and Autoencoder (AE) are preliminary audit as they has been conducted looking at current utilities. These models can be seen as center structures that are still the rule of deep learning. Likewise, other section of paper discussed about related ideas which are necessary for understanding of these said models like Restricted Boltzmann machines, and robust/resilient back propagation models. Given the adaptability of system designs that allow "Lego-like" development of fresh innovative models, using the components of classes of center structural we can construct infinite number of neural network models that are discussed in this research. Thus, this research provides to formulate a fundamental understanding of future enhancement in AI.

REFERENCES

An, J., & Cho, S. (2015). Variational autoencoder based anomaly detection using reconstruction probability. *Special Lecture on IE, 2*(1), 1–18.

Arulkumaran, K., Deisenroth, M. P., Brundage, M., & Bharath, A. A. (2017). *A brief survey of deep reinforcement learning.* ArXiv Preprint, ArXiv:1708.05866.

Biran, O., & Cotton, C. (2017). Explanation and justification in machine learning: A survey. *IJCAI-17 Workshop on Explainable AI (XAI), 8*(1), 8–13.

Breiman, L. (2001). Statistical modeling: The two cultures (with comments and a rejoinder by the author). *Statistical Science, 16*(3), 199–231. doi:10.1214s/1009213726

Carreira-Perpinan, M. A., & Hinton, G. E. (2005). On contrastive divergence learning. *Aistats, 10*, 33–40.

Cohen, G., Afshar, S., Tapson, J., & van Schaik, A. E. (n.d.). *An extension of MNIST to handwritten letters.* ArXiv Preprint, ArXiv:1702.05373.

Deng, J., Zhang, Z., Marchi, E., & Schuller, B. (2013). Sparse autoencoder-based feature transfer learning for speech emotion recognition. *Humaine Association Conference on Affective Computing and Intelligent Interaction*, 511–516. 10.1109/ACII.2013.90

Doersch, C. (2016). *Tutorial on variational autoencoders.* ArXiv Preprint, ArXiv:1606.05908.

Donahue, J., Jia, Y., Vinyals, O., Hoffman, J., Zhang, N., Tzeng, E., & Darrell, T. (2014). Decaf: A deep convolutional activation feature for generic visual recognition. *International Conference on Machine Learning*, 647–655.

Doshi-Velez, F., & Kim, B. (2017). *Towards a rigorous science of interpretable machine learning.* ArXiv Preprint ArXiv:1702.08608.

Duda, R. O., Hart, P. E., & Stork, D. G. (2012). *Pattern classification.* John Wiley & Sons.

Emmert-Streib, F. (2006). A heterosynaptic learning rule for neural networks. *International Journal of Modern Physics C, 17*(10), 1501–1520. doi:10.1142/S0129183106009916

Emmert-Streib, F., & Dehmer, M. (2019). Defining data science by a data-driven quantification of the community. *Machine Learning and Knowledge Extraction, 1*(1), 235–251. doi:10.3390/make1010015

Fischer, A., & Igel, C. (2012). An introduction to restricted Boltzmann machines. *Iberoamerican Congress on Pattern Recognition*, 14–36.

Glorot, X., & Bengio, Y. (2010). Understanding the difficulty of training deep feedforward neural networks. *Proceedings of the Thirteenth International Conference on Artificial Intelligence and Statistics*, 249–256.

Graves, A. (2013). *Generating sequences with recurrent neural networks.* ArXiv Preprint, ArXiv:1308.0850.

Graves, A., Mohamed, A., & Hinton, G. (2013). Speech recognition with deep recurrent neural networks. *2013 IEEE International Conference on Acoustics, Speech and Signal Processing*, 6645–6649. 10.1109/ICASSP.2013.6638947

Graves, A., & Schmidhuber, J. (2005). Framewise phoneme classification with bidirectional LSTM and other neural network architectures. *Neural Networks*, *18*(5–6), 602–610. doi:10.1016/j.neunet.2005.06.042 PMID:16112549

Hastie, T., Tibshirani, R., & Friedman, J. (2009). *The elements of statistical learning: data mining, inference, and prediction*. Springer Science & Business Media. doi:10.1007/978-0-387-84858-7

He, K., Zhang, X., Ren, S., & Sun, J. (2016). Deep residual learning for image recognition. *Proceedings of the IEEE Conference on Computer Vision and Pattern Recognition*, 770–778.

Hebb, D. O. (1949). The organization of behavior: a neuropsychological theory. J. Wiley; Chapman & Hall.

Henaff, M., Bruna, J., & LeCun, Y. (2015). *Deep convolutional networks on graph-structured data*. ArXiv Preprint, ArXiv:1506.05163.

Henderson, P., Islam, R., Bachman, P., Pineau, J., Precup, D., & Meger, D. (2018). Deep reinforcement learning that matters. *Thirty-Second AAAI Conference on Artificial Intelligence*.

Hinton, G. E. (2012). A practical guide to training restricted Boltzmann machines. In *Neural networks: Tricks of the trade* (pp. 599–619). Springer. doi:10.1007/978-3-642-35289-8_32

Hinton, G. E., Osindero, S., & Teh, Y.-W. (2006). A fast learning algorithm for deep belief nets. *Neural Computation*, *18*(7), 1527–1554. doi:10.1162/neco.2006.18.7.1527 PMID:16764513

Hinton, G. E., & Salakhutdinov, R. R. (2006). Reducing the dimensionality of data with neural networks. *Science*, *313*(5786), 504–507. doi:10.1126cience.1127647 PMID:16873662

Holzinger, A., Biemann, C., Pattichis, C. S., & Kell, D. B. (2017). *What do we need to build explainable AI systems for the medical domain?* ArXiv Preprint, ArXiv:1712.09923.

Igel, C., & Hüsken, M. (2000). Improving the Rprop learning algorithm. *Proceedings of the Second International ICSC Symposium on Neural Computation (NC 2000)*, 115–121.

Jindal, A., Dua, A., Kumar, N., Das, A. K., Vasilakos, A. V., & Rodrigues, J. J. P. C. (2018). Providing healthcare-as-a-service using fuzzy rule based big data analytics in cloud computing. *IEEE Journal of Biomedical and Health Informatics*, *22*(5), 1605–1618. doi:10.1109/JBHI.2018.2799198 PMID:29994567

Krizhevsky, A., Sutskever, I., & Hinton, G. E. (2012). Imagenet classification with deep convolutional neural networks. *Advances in Neural Information Processing Systems*, 1097–1105.

LeCun, Y. (1989). Generalization and network design strategies. *Connectionism in Perspective*, *19*, 143–155.

LeCun, Y., Bengio, Y., & Hinton, G. (n.d.). *Deep learning. Nature, 521, 436*.

LeCun, Y., Boser, B., Denker, J. S., Henderson, D., Howard, R. E., Hubbard, W., & Jackel, L. D. (1989). Backpropagation applied to handwritten zip code recognition. *Neural Computation*, *1*(4), 541–551. doi:10.1162/neco.1989.1.4.541

Leung, M. K. K., Xiong, H. Y., Lee, L. J., & Frey, B. J. (2014). Deep learning of the tissue-regulated splicing code. *Bioinformatics (Oxford, England)*, *30*(12), i121–i129. doi:10.1093/bioinformatics/btu277 PMID:24931975

Li, R., Wang, S., Zhu, F., & Huang, J. (2018). Adaptive graph convolutional neural networks. *Thirty-Second AAAI Conference on Artificial Intelligence.*

Lin, M., Chen, Q., & Yan, S. (2013). *Network in network.* ArXiv Preprint, ArXiv:1312.4400.

Mayr, A., Klambauer, G., Unterthiner, T., Steijaert, M., Wegner, J. K., Ceulemans, H., Clevert, D.-A., & Hochreiter, S. (2018). Large-scale comparison of machine learning methods for drug target prediction on ChEMBL. *Chemical Science (Cambridge), 9*(24), 5441–5451. doi:10.1039/C8SC00148K PMID:30155234

Mohamed, A., Dahl, G. E., & Hinton, G. (2011). Acoustic modeling using deep belief networks. *IEEE Transactions on Audio, Speech, and Language Processing, 20*(1), 14–22. doi:10.1109/TASL.2011.2109382

Nielsen, M. A. (2015). Neural networks and deep learning (Vol. 2018). Determination Press.

Olshausen, B. A., & Field, D. J. (1997). Sparse coding with an overcomplete basis set: A strategy employed by V1? *Vision Research, 37*(23), 3311–3325. doi:10.1016/S0042-6989(97)00169-7 PMID:9425546

Shmueli, G. (2010). To explain or to predict? *Statistical Science, 25*(3), 289–310. doi:10.1214/10-STS330

Simonyan, K., & Zisserman, A. (2014). *Very deep convolutional networks for large-scale image recognition.* ArXiv Preprint, ArXiv:1409.1556.

Smolander, J., Dehmer, M., & Emmert-Streib, F. (2019). Comparing deep belief networks with support vector machines for classifying gene expression data from complex disorders. *FEBS Open Bio, 9*(7), 1232–1248. doi:10.1002/2211-5463.12652 PMID:31074948

Smolander, J., Stupnikov, A., Glazko, G., Dehmer, M., & Emmert-Streib, F. (2019). Comparing biological information contained in mRNA and non-coding RNAs for classification of lung cancer patients. *BMC Cancer, 19*(1), 1176. doi:10.118612885-019-6338-1 PMID:31796020

Srinivas, J., Das, A. K., & Rodrigues, J. J. P. C. (2020). 2PBDC: Privacy-preserving bigdata collection in cloud environment. *The Journal of Supercomputing, 76*(7), 4772–4801. doi:10.100711227-018-2605-1

Sundermeyer, M., Schlüter, R., & Ney, H. (2012). LSTM neural networks for language modeling. *Thirteenth Annual Conference of the International Speech Communication Association.*

Szegedy, C., Liu, W., Jia, Y., Sermanet, P., Reed, S., Anguelov, D., Erhan, D., Vanhoucke, V., & Rabinovich, A. (2015). Going deeper with convolutions. *Proceedings of the IEEE Conference on Computer Vision and Pattern Recognition,* 1–9.

Tosic, I., & Frossard, P. (2011). Dictionary learning. *IEEE Signal Processing Magazine, 28*(2), 27–38. doi:10.1109/MSP.2010.939537 PMID:20889431

Vincent, P., Larochelle, H., Lajoie, I., Bengio, Y., Manzagol, P.-A., & Bottou, L. (2010). Stacked denoising autoencoders: Learning useful representations in a deep network with a local denoising criterion. *Journal of Machine Learning Research, 11*(12).

Yang, Z., Dehmer, M., Yli-Harja, O., & Emmert-Streib, F. (2020). Combining deep learning with token selection for patient phenotyping from electronic health records. *Scientific Reports, 10*(1), 1–18. doi:10.103841598-020-58178-1 PMID:31996705

Yao, L., Mao, C., & Luo, Y. (2019). Graph convolutional networks for text classification. *Proceedings of the AAAI Conference on Artificial Intelligence, 33,* 7370–7377. doi:10.1609/aaai.v33i01.33017370

Yin, W., Kann, K., Yu, M., & Schütze, H. (2017). *Comparative study of cnn and rnn for natural language processing.* ArXiv Preprint, ArXiv:1702.01923.

ADDITIONAL READING

Charles, A. S., Olshausen, B. A., & Rozell, C. J. (2011). Learning sparse codes for hyperspectral imagery. *IEEE Journal of Selected Topics in Signal Processing, 5*(5), 963–978. doi:10.1109/JSTSP.2011.2149497

Chaudhary, R., Aujla, G. S., Kumar, N., & Rodrigues, J. J. P. C. (2018). Optimized big data management across multi-cloud data centers: Software-defined-network-based analysis. *IEEE Communications Magazine, 56*(2), 118–126. doi:10.1109/MCOM.2018.1700211

Pu, Y., Gan, Z., Henao, R., Yuan, X., Li, C., Stevens, A., & Carin, L. (2016). Variational autoencoder for deep learning of images, labels and captions. *Advances in Neural Information Processing Systems*, 2352–2360.

Riedmiller, M., & Braun, H. (1993). A direct adaptive method for faster backpropagation learning: The RPROP algorithm. *IEEE International Conference on Neural Networks*, 586–591. 10.1109/ICNN.1993.298623

Sarikaya, R., Hinton, G. E., & Deoras, A. (2014). Application of deep belief networks for natural language understanding. *IEEE/ACM Transactions on Audio, Speech, and Language Processing, 22*(4), 778–784. doi:10.1109/TASLP.2014.2303296

Scherer, D., Müller, A., & Behnke, S. (2010). Evaluation of pooling operations in convolutional architectures for object recognition. *International Conference on Artificial Neural Networks*, 92–101.

Wan, L., Zeiler, M., Zhang, S., Le Cun, Y., & Fergus, R. (2013). Regularization of neural networks using dropconnect. *International Conference on Machine Learning*, 1058–1066.

Wazid, M., Das, A. K., Hussain, R., Succi, G., & Rodrigues, J. J. P. C. (2019). Authentication in cloud-driven IoT-based big data environment: Survey and outlook. *Journal of Systems Architecture, 97*, 185–196.

Zhang, X., Zhao, J., & LeCun, Y. (2015). Character-level convolutional networks for text classification. *Advances in Neural Information Processing Systems*, 649–657.

KEY TERMS AND DEFINITIONS

Convolutional Neural Network: Convolutional Neural Network (CNN) is a form of feedforward neural network which make use of convolution, ReLU function, and pooling layers which help in dealing with information with high measurements.

Data Science: Data science is word derived from data and science which include statistics, scientific methods, artificial intelligence, data analysis in order to extract information from data.

Deep Learning (DL): Deep learning is subset of machine learning that is used to build learning models that can help to understand and analyze large data and support complex predictions for decision making.

Machine Learning (ML): Machine learning is a new technology where machine learns from the past data in order to decide and work for future data, thus helps in process of automation.

Neural Networks: It is a set of algorithm that is used for recognizing the relationship between set of data by means of learning process.

Prediction Models: Prediction model predicts the future event or results by means of analyzing the pattern in given set of input data.

Supervised Learning: It is an approach of Artificial Intelligence where computer algorithm is trained on input data that has been labeled for a particular output.

Unsupervised Learning: Unsupervised learning make use of artificial intelligence algorithms for identifying pattern in data sets containing data points that are neither classified nor labeled.

Cluster Analysis as a Decision-Making Tool

Bindu Rani
Sharda University, India

Shri Kant
Sharda University, India

INTRODUCTION

Informative value is a vital factor for the success of any organization's decision making process. Nowadays, evolution of new digital technologies, telecommunication 5G technologies and Internet of Things lead the way towards generation of massive amounts of data exemplified as big data. That data has been characterized by its varying characteristics, few of them are high volume, high dimensionality, diverse formats and rapid velocity. The data can be used to make growth in the financial, marketing and sales and customer services area with all types of competitive advantages. However, merely gathering data does not make a positive impact on organizations. Data must be analyzed and transformed into pieces of beneficial and valuable information (Thirathon *et al.,* 2017).

Data and analytics are playing an essential role to provide support for managers as well as decision makers in functioning their organizations and grasping benefits. As a matter of fact, research studies reveal that data centric organizations accompanied with data analytics make better expedient decisions in terms of high operational productiveness, better customer satisfaction and retention levels. Big data analytics play a key role in an organization to analyze large amounts of data to uncover hidden patterns, correlations and other insights in the data. It helps organizations as a decision driving force towards futuristic solutions (Jeble *et al.,*2018).

The important research questions towards achieving informed decisions are "How can organizations incorporate big data analytics into the decision making process?" and "What data analytics methodologies can be applied to get smarter and informed decisions?"

Clustering, one of the most commonly known data analytical methodology is playing an indispensable role in big data analysis. It has been seen as a precious tool for marketing and business areas providing the capabilities to help in organization's decision making process (Jain, 2010). Hence, improvement and modification in cluster analysis techniques may be considered an effective approach for getting improved decisions. Moreover, important issues of the clustering process lie in assessing the clustering quality and finding optimal cluster numbers in a dataset of various domains. Cluster validation aims for quality assessment and quantitative estimation of true cluster number in datasets.

The implications from these situations highlight the need to consider suitable frameworks to incorporate data analytical techniques in decision making approaches. While considering clustering as a decision making tool, finding appropriate metrics for measuring cluster shape, cluster numbers and cluster quality has always been an exploratory research area across the sphere of data mining.

DOI: 10.4018/978-1-7998-9220-5.ch024

Copyright © 2023, IGI Global. Copying or distributing in print or electronic forms without written permission of IGI Global is prohibited.

BACKGROUD

Big Data-A Term

The extensive use of emerging internet and mobile technologies is the genesis of big data age with huge capacity, complex and rapidly growing data in variety of forms. In 2020, around 2.5 quintillion bytes of data has been generated by internet users and around 1.7 megabytes data by every person in just a second. Google search statistics predicted for year 2021 that Google will get over 1.2 trillion searches per year, and more so 40,000 number of search queries per second.

Besides, big data is omnipresent but its origin is unknown yet. It was stated that in the mid 1990's, John Mashey coined this term at a lunch table conversation at Silicon Graphics Inc.(SGI) (Diebold, 2012). A repeated definition is given by Laney (2001) "Data generated very fast that contains an extensive volume of content". The term became a well-known term till 2011 (Gandomi & Haider, 2015).

Apart from mass of data, big data has been defined by several other characteristics. Doug Laney in 2011 pointed out challenges and opportunities accomplished by growing data into 3 Vs model (Increased Volume, Velocity and Variety). Later in 2011, IDC (International Data Corporation) most significant known name in big data stated that the evolution defines the development of tools and technologies in new form to extract value from big data. This results as the 4th V for big data –Value. The 4 Vs were widely accepted since it drew attention towards the usefulness of big data. It points the most significant problem in big data. If data is not utilized properly, it is only a bunch of data. Another term Veracity has been added as 5th V which means checks the provenance or reliability of the data source and verifies how meaningful the data is i.e truthfulness in data. This is not the end for expansion of Vs, big data is continuously characterizing with more Vs such as Validity, Variability, Vocabulary, Venue and Vague defining new parameters (Sun, 2018).

Role of Big Data Analytics into Decision Making

The big data generation has reformed the perspectives towards the living approach, thinking modes and working styles. The transformation objective is to seize large amounts of data, perceive knowledge and make better decisions.

In an intelligence talk (2017), big data has been termed as fuel for digital world while engine used is analytics. Big data analytics is being exploited as the way to strengthen the effectiveness of the decision making process in each and every field of this revolutionary world. The potentiality to extract value from big data depends on data analytics and it has been considered as the core of the big data transformation age (Jagadish et al., 2014).

Labrinidis & Jagadish (2012) suggested to divide big data process into two main parts: Data management and analytic as shown in Figure 1. Data management concerns with the acquisition and retrieval, storage and preparation of data, although big data analytics is required to involve the techniques for extracting knowledge from big data and converting it into the intelligence.

Practically, big data analytics is concerned with the technologies to transform data gathered from different sources into shaped and smart decisions. These decisions can drive valuable insights and preventing risks and gain an edge over the competitors as a result of enhanced business performance. Few focussing parameters are faster decisions, act and react quickly, decisions making on high quality and complex data. Cluster analysis has been viewed as one of the most significant technique to find groups and patterns in support of managerial decisions.

Figure 1. Big data process

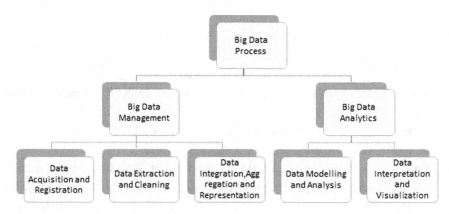

FOCUS OF THE ARTICLE

In this chapter, the authors investigate the role played by big data analytical techniques for improving the decision making process. It will also include different frameworks for effective incorporation of big data analytics into decision making approaches. The main focus is to emphasize cluster analysis as an important tool of data analytics technique to support decision making processes. Hence, the study stress on the critical survey of different clustering methods and algorithms and their associated cluster validity indices.

In further detail, the research introduces the underlying clustering approaches while exploring the universally acceptable clustering algorithms in a comparable way. Furthermore, it focuses on important issues associated with clustering techniques with emphasis on the ways to access the quality of clustering results. It will be correlated with elemental and implied characteristics of the data set under considerations. The study include different types of proximity measures used for calculating similarity and dissimilarity between objects. Finally, this chapter also demonstrates a detailed review on mathematical research to formulate cluster validity indices applied for both crisp and soft clustering methods. As a consequence, the authors will also extend the proposals towards the future in the domain of cluster validation.

SOLUTIONS AND RECOMMENDATIONS

Frameworks for Integrating Big Data Analytics into Decision Making

In organizations, decision makers constantly observe the prospects to make more intelligent decisions. Consequently, they need to take advantage and extract value and knowledge from big data efficiently and effectively in order to enhance decision making process. Therefore, the research trends are moving towards how big data tools and technologies can be integrated into decision process.

Decision support systems (DSS), a type of information system helps the organizations in gathering and analysing massive amount of data and visualize reports that can be used by managers for decision making activities. Simon's research team coined the term DSS in the late 1950's and the early 1960's (Simon, 1960). Simon's theory, included three main phases for decision making process: intelligent, design, choice and named as IDC model. Each phase considers both organizational perspective and technical perspective. Organizational perspective considers gathering information about the members involved in decision making process and technical perspective for storing, accessing, analysing, discovering and sharing knowledge. The author later added the fourth phase as implementation phase and monitoring phase was considered as fifth phase for feedbacks. These phases are widely adopted by decision makers. In consideration of these phases, researchers have attempted to design integrating frameworks to embody big data analytics with decision making process to improve the quality of decisions as outcome.

For instance, a study considered the predictive perspective for structuring the decision problems and suggesting alternatives. An integrated model was proposed which combines big data, business intelligence and decision support system into IDC model with organizational learning. The concept included big data as a provider over which BI tools and techniques can be applied to discover decision opportunities (Turban et al., 2007). An approach has also been suggested for integration of big data analytics into decision making phases with the introduction of challenging issues towards big data (Rani & Kant, 2019).

In support for making improved decisions, a framework: Big Data Analytics and Decision (B-DAD) based on design science methodology was developed and evaluated by applying big data analytics (Elgendy & Elragal, 2016). The framework conceptualize some of the possible approaches for mapping big data tools, technologies and analytics into different phases of decision making process. It followed six stage's design science process (Peffers, 2008). In first two stages, it is assumed that problem identification and objective definition are already known. Next four stages are based on standard rational Simon's theory. The experiment was demonstrated on real data and business problems for relevancy.

The first phase is intelligence phase in which data sources either internal or external needs to be identified. After identifying the data, it is acquired and stored in any big data storage tools. The next phase is design phase to conceptualize path for possible actions to be taken. This phase has been divided into model planning, data analytics and analysing. Model planning is related to appropriate selection of data analytics models and algorithms. It can range from traditional data mining algorithms classification, clustering, regression and association rules to advanced analytics algorithms such as machine learning and AI techniques. In data analytics step, chosen model and algorithm is applied. Here predictive analytics can be applied to analyse current and historical data for making future prediction. In analysing step, analytical outputs are analysed. Next subsequent phase is choice phase in which suggested solutions from design phase are evaluated and decided. Here the decisions are generated actually on the evaluation basis of solutions. Last phase is implementation phase in which previous phase proposed solutions are implemented. Furthermore, it has been extended to have flexibility. In the context of flexibility, new modified framework was also suggested in which moving back and forth between different phases of framework can take place. The framework incorporated important aspects of big data analytics and mapped into different phases of decision-making process. It is applicable not only for research but also in the industries and organizations for enhancing the quality of decision-making process.

CLUSTER ANALYSIS AS DECISION MAKING PROCESS

Cluster analysis is a statistical data mining tools used for grouping objects with the aim to find discrete patterns where objects in one group should have maximum similarity in comparison of objects from other group objects.It is a kind of exploratory data analysis and used as a knowledge discovery process in any organization.

In the view of decision-making process and business applications, it can be considered as a key process to know differentiable attributes on the basis of relationship among data points for large amount of data. Target marketing is one of the best-known objectives of cluster analysis techniques. This can save a lot of time, effort, and money by focussing on group of customers according to their interest and activities rather than entire customers.

Cluster analysis procedure consists of two phases: Model selection phase and cluster validation phase as displayed in Figure 2.

Figure 2. Cluster analysis

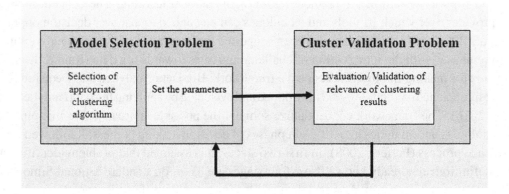

Cluster analysis classify the data according to the intrinsic relationships among data points. No underlying structure of clusters is known in advance. In the model selection phase, an appropriate clustering algorithm is selected according to the data set. Then parameters are set for the selected algorithm. In the second cluster validation phase, clustering results are evaluated or validated. The process from parameter selection to cluster evaluation can be repeated to find optimal results. Finally, it is necessary to inspect the clustering results quantitatively. Cluster validation is the process to deal with the significance of patterns composed by clustering algorithms. Another point of concern is that different clustering algorithms may generate multiple partitions of clusters. Hence, researchers are continuously solving the problems faced by the clustering algorithms to deal with high dimensional data, arbitrary shaped clusters, noisy and interoperable data.

CLUSTERING METHODS AND ALGORITHM

Clustering techniques as unsupervised learning are directed towards finding structures in data by forming clusters. Data points with maximum similarity should form one cluster while data points in different clusters should have maximum dissimilarity. Hence clustering may help to dig more insights from the data. Review of different clustering approaches and algorithms can be explored here (Jain & Dubes 1988; Jain *et al.*, 1999; Xu &Wunsch 2005; Jain 2010). In the direction to remove the effect of initial guess on the performance and convergence of Moving centroid methods, new Automatic and Stable Clustering Algorithm-ASCA has been developed (Kant, 1994). Various clustering algorithms have also been reported for categorical data (Naouali, 2019). In this regard, an approach has been presented to compute initial mode for k-mode clustering algorithm (Khan & Kant, 2006). Practically, selection of appropriate clustering algorithm according to a given data set is a challenging task.

Most commonly known clustering methods are categorized into hard and soft types. In hard clustering, each data item is consigned to precisely one cluster. Hence results are less informative. In soft clustering like fuzzy clustering, the clusters are configured according to fuzzy set theory sharing each data item to each clusters including a membership degree that ranges between 0 and 1. Fuzzy clustering has been based on fuzzy set theory (Zadeh, 1965). Fuzzy set theory introduced the concept of membership function to give the idea of uncertainty of belongings. The first applicability of fuzzy set theory in cluster analysis was reported in a reference paper (Bellman *et al.*, 1966).

In spite of exhaustive research in clustering field, it has been accepted that there is no clustering algorithm that can handle different types of data and different types of clusters. On the basis of distinct data characteristics or clustering objectives, clustering techniques are categorized as shown in Figure. 3 (Han et al., 2011). Various hard and soft clustering algorithms have been developed falling under each category.

Figure 3. Type of clustering methods

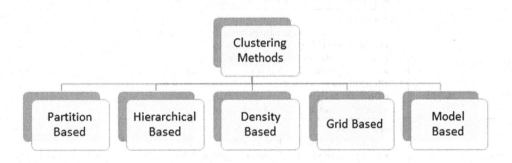

Partition Based clustering: Partitioning clustering partition the data into fixed number of clusters specified in advance. An objective function is minimized by repeating process to optimize the cluster centers. This method is very easy to compute, has low complexity and high computational efficiency. But the drawback is sensitivity for outliers and not suitable for non-convex data. It converges to local minima and requires predetermined cluster numbers.

Hierarchical: In hierarchical clustering, the number of clusters are not specified in prior. This technique finds hierarchical relationship among data points and creates dendogram to cluster. The agglomaration and divisive procedure are used here. The output clusters are formed independently from initial condition. Due to static nature, data points assigned to a cluster cannot be reassigned to another cluster.

Density-based: Density based clustering has the capability to find arbitrary shaped clusters based on their high density regions, connectivity, and boundary. No prior information for number of clusters is required for cluster formation. The clusters are connected dense component which can grow in any dense area.

Grid-based: Grid based clustering partitions the data into form of grid structure. Data points are divided into grids on the basis of statistical values computed by undergoing whole data set. This technique is suitable for parallel processing and has high scalable capacity.

Model-based: Model based clustering selects a particular and best fitted model for each cluster. It has been based on either statistical learning or neural learning methods. In statistical learning, it assumes that the data is generated by a mixture of underlying probability distributions. Automatic determination of cluster numbers is one advantage of model-based clustering.

Clustering Methods with their characteristics and challenging issues have been summarized briefly in Table 1.

Table 1. Clustering methods with their characteristics and challenging issues

Clustering Methods	Characteristics and Challenging issues
Partition Based	**Characteristics** • Finds Spherical based clusters • Uses distance based measures • Effective for small and medium sized dataset. **Challenging issues** • Not able to find arbitrary shaped clusters. • Sensitivity towards noise and outliers • Input parameters required for cluster formation • Specification of number of clusters in advance • Quality of cluster depends on initial centroids selected
Hierarchical methods	**Characteristics** • Cluster formation in the form of hierarchical tree or dendogram. • Dendogram produced is easy to understand. • Two approaches used-Agglomerative and divisive. • Effective approach for small to medium size cluster. **Challenging issues** • Difficulty in correction for wrong merges and splits • Not able to handle missing data and mixed data type
Density-based methods	**Characteristics** • Able to find arbitrarily shaped clusters efficiently • Dense regions of objects in space separated by low density region form clusters • Possibility to remove outliers • Effective approach for small to medium size cluster **Challenging issues** • Require input point features and minimum number of features • Difficulty in facing high dimensional data.
Grid-based methods	**Characteristics** • Based on segmented data space i.e grid data structure rather than original data • Process is dependent on grid size and independent from number of data • Fast processing time • Effective approach for small to medium size cluster **Challenging issues** • Finding suitable size grid • Not able to generate less density cluster with variable density cluster data and arbitrary shaped clusters • Problem of locality of clusters • Problem in handling boundary points. • Low cluster accuracy
Model Based Methods	**Characteristics** • Type of model is specified in prior • Statistical approach • Probability distribution in each component model • Better interoperability • Automatic determination of clusters **Challenging issues** • Dependency on underlying model • Compromise in performance for high dimensional space

Clustering algorithms can be grouped into hard or soft clustering algorithms. But sometimes one algorithms can accumulate the ideas of more than one clustering methods, in this way, it is seemed troublesome to classify a given algorithm subjected to one category. Even comparative studies on clustering algorithms are very difficult due to the lack of universally accepted quantitative evaluation criteria. This study have tried to list few algorithms under each clustering methods for both hard and soft clustering from Table 2 to Table 6. Many more modified clustering algorithms has been reviewed here (Xu & Tian, 2015).

Table 2. Partitional crisp and fuzzy clustering algorithms

Name	Features
Crisp Clustering Algorithms	
k-means (MacQueen J, 1967)	• Simple to implement and Efficient algorithm • Better cluster formation than hierarchical methods • Works on numerical data only and Sensitive for outliers • Time complexity: $O(n)$
k-mode (Huang, 1998)	• Works on categorical data also • Means of clusters replaced by modes of clusters • Time complexity: $O(n)$
Kernel K-means (Schölkopf *et al.*, 1998)	• Able to detect arbitrary shaped cluster • High time complexity
PAM (Partitioning around mediod) (Kaufman & Rousseeuw, 1990)	• First K-mediod algorithm • Median of data is used in place of mean of data • Removal of sensitivity for outliers • More execution time than k-means algorithm • Time Complexity: $O(k(n-k)^2)$
CLARA (Kaufman & Rousseeuw, 2008)	• Consider small portion of data instead of whole data set • Mediods are selected using PAM for each sample • Can deal with large data set than PAM • Time Complexity: $O(k(40+k)^2 + k(n-k))$
Fuzzy Clustering Algorithms	
FCM (Fuzzy C-Means) (Bezdek,1981)	• Obtain fuzzy model from data • An extension of classical crisp k-means • Data points belong to each clusters • Has better performance but computational complexity is higher • Sensitive for noise and outliers • Time complexity: $O(n)$
Kernel FCM (Wu et al.2003)	• Kernel function is used in place of Euclidian distance • Inputs are mapped into high dimensional space • Deal efficiently with fuzzy cluster centers

PROXIMITY MEASURES

Apart from the selection of best clustering algorithm, decision about the appropriate proximity measure (similarity or dissimilarity) has considerable importance for achieving satisfactory clustering results. Calculating the proximity between two data objects is the first and very crucial step in any data analysis process. Comparison studies of varied proximity measures have been reported for different application domains. In spite of a wide range of proximity measures mentioned in literature, a particular measure is usually selected on the basis of characteristics of dataset such as feature format, correlation among data set and data sparsity. The category to which data attribute belong has been considered as the most obvious factor for proximity measures selection. Similarity or dissimilarity measures are building blocks for distance based algorithms such as partition clustering and hierarchical clustering.

There are four basic categories shown in Table 7

Table 3. Hierarchical crisp and fuzzy clustering algorithms

Name	Features
Crisp Clustering Algorithms	
BIRCH (Balance Iterative Reducing Clustering using Hierarchies) (Zhang & Ramakrishnan, 1996)	• First algorithm to handle noisy data • Construct feature tree of clustering and Support only numerical data types • Faster than k-means • Does not perform well in case of non-spherical data. • Cluster output is dependent on the order of input data • Time Complexity: $O(n)$ where n= number of data inputs
CURE (Guha *et al.*, 1998)	• Scalable for large datasets • Uses random sampling to cluster the samples • Time Complexity: $O(n^2 \log n)$
ROCK(Robust Clustering using Links) (Guha *et al.*, 1999)	• Improvement of CURE • Deals with enumeration type data • Time Complexity: $O(n^2 + n\, m_m\, m_a + n^2 \log n)$, m_m and m_a =maximum and average number of neighbour
Fuzzy Clustering Algorithm	
Fuzzy Hierarchical Co-clustering (FHCC) (Zeng & Wu, 2016)	• Used agglomerative hierarchical co- clustering approach with fuzzy set theory • Highly flexible

Table 4. Density based crisp and fuzzy clustering algorithms

Name	Features	
Crisp Clustering Algorithms		
DBSCAN (Density Based Spatial Clustering of Applications with Noise) (Ester *et al.*, 1996)	• No need to define number of clusters in advance • Generate arbitrary shaped clusters • Robust to outliers • Require two input parameters: Eps and Minpts and atleast one point from the respective clusters • Time complexity: $O(n \log n)$ where n= number of points in databse	
DBSCAN-GM Density Based Spatial Clustering of Applications with Noise (Smiti & Elouedi, 2012)	• Exploit the advantage of GM(Gaussian-Means) • Improved algorithm of DBSCAN and Not require input parameters • Good performance on large database • Ability to detect noise in data	
Fuzzy Clustering Algorithms		
Soft DBSCAN-GM(SDG) (Smiti & Elouedi, 2016)	• Improves the cluster quality using fuzzy set theory • Able to generate more dense clusters • Based on objective function • Superior in handling noisy points than FCM(Fuzzy C Means) • Can produce arbitrary shaped clusters	

Table 5. Grid based crisp and fuzzy clustering algorithms

Name	Features
Crisp Clustering Algorithms	
STING (Statistical Information Grid Approach) (Wang *et al.*, 1997)	• Achieve parallelization • Have incremental approach • Can answer multiple queries • Time complexity=$O(K)$,K = number of grid cells at the lowest level
CLIQUE (Clustering In Quest) (Agarwal *et al.*,1998)	• Automatic finding of subspace in high dimensionality • Linearly scalable with number of inputs • Not dependent on number of records in the input • Time complexity=$O(n+k^2)$,
Fuzzy Clustering Algorithms	
Grid base FCM(G-FCM) (Yue & Huang, 2013)	• Grid based partition approach • Faster speed • Higher cluster quality • Can approximate easily the number of clusters
Fuzzy Grid Clustering Algorithm(FGC) (Rao *et al.*, 2011)	• Goal is to reduce the size and borders of the cell • Efficient clustering

Table 6. Model based crisp and fuzzy clustering algorithms

Name	Features
Crisp Clustering Algorithms	
COBWEB (Fisher,1987)	• Based on statistical learning • Assume the probability distribution of each attribute independent • Build classification tree by heuristic approach • Low time complexity
SOM (Kohonen,1990)	• Based on neural network approach and Assume topology in input data • Dimensionality reduction mapping from high dimension input space to low dimension output space • High time complexity
ART (Carpenter & Grossberg, 1987)	• Implemented as incremental type algorithm • Dynamic generation of new neurons • Medium time complexity
Fuzzy Clustering Algorithms	
Autocorrelation-based fuzzy C-means (A-FCM) algorithm (D'Urso & Maharaj, 2009)	• Cluster time series data with fuzzy approach • Dynamic Conditional Score (DCS) model

Table 7. Attribute categories

Type of attribute	Characteristics
Nominal	* Contains name to represent a category(another name: categorical) * No specific order to be followed
Binary	* Nominal values containing two values only.
Ordinal	* Nominal values where specific order exist among names.
Numeric	* Consist of numeric values only

Mehta et al. (2020) provided a comparison on proximity measures that deal with numerical data only. In addition, the authors also defined some text mining specific proximity measures. In a research work, a comparative review on similarity measures for categorical data has been reported and outlier point of view has also been evaluated. Zighed & Abdesselam (2011) compared binary based similarity measures for categorical data. Shirkhorshidi (2015) critically analysed and compared 13 similarity and distance measures against 15 publically available dataset from low to high dimensionality. Few of similarity measures for numerical and categorical data have been defined in this section.

PROXIMITY MEASURES FOR NUMERICAL DATA

(a) Cosine Similarity

It is similarity measure to calculate the normalized inner product between two vectors a and b. Cosine angle is measured between two data points with respect to origin. It works well for sparse datasets where significant number of zeroes are present. Cosine similarity is expressed as by Equation (1)

$$S_c(a,b) = \frac{\sum_{i=1}^{n} a_i b_i}{\sum_{i=1}^{n} (a_i)^2 \sum_{i=1}^{n} (b_i)^2}$$

(1)

And the cosine distance (COS) is calculated as $COS(a,b) = 1 - S_c(a,b)$

(b) Minkowski Distance

It is the most popular dissimilar proximity based on parametric p shown by this Equation (2)

$$d_p(a,b) = \left(\sum_{i=1}^{n} |a_i - b_i|^p \right)^{1/p}$$

(2)

Different values of p lead to different dissimilarity measures. Three different values of p are 1, 2 and infinity.

When p=1 Manhattan distance
    P=2 Euclidean distance
    P=infinity supreme distance

Euclidean distance is commonly used distance metric for proximity evaluation in two or three dimensional space. But it works well when dataset has compact clusters. Another drawback is the tendency of large scaled features for dominating others.

(c)Average Distance

Euclidean distance was improved to overcome its drawbacks. The average distance is characterized by Equation (3)

$$d_{ave} = \left[\frac{1}{n} \sum_{i=1}^{n} \left(a_i - b_i \right)^2 \right]^{1/2} \tag{3}$$

(d) Chord Distance

Chord Distance is another modification form of euclidean distance to overcome the issues. It also solved the problem by scale of measurement successfully. It is the length of chord that joins two normalized points within the hypersphere with radius one. Chord distance is defined as Equation (4)

$$d_{chord} = \left| 2 - 2 \frac{\sum_{i=1}^{n} a_i b_i}{\|a\|_2 \|b\|_2} \right| \tag{4}$$

$$\|x\|_2 = \sqrt{\sum_{i=1}^{n} x_i^2}$$

(e)Pearson Distance

The Pearson distance is calculated by Pearson correlation and is depicted in Equation (5)

$$1 - Corr(a,b) \tag{5}$$

Corr(a,b)= Pearson correlation of two variables a and b

$$Corr\left(a,b\right) = \frac{Cov\left(a,b\right)}{\sigma_a \sigma_b} \tag{6}$$

Where Cov (a,b)= covariance between a and b

σ_a and =Variance of a and variance of b

The range lies in [0, 2]. The Pearson distance experiences the sensitivity towards outliers.

(f) Canberra Distance Metric

This metric is used with the datasets consist of all non-negative numbers. Here p and q are two vectors of n-dimensionality, it is calculated by Equation (7)

$$d\left(p_i, q_i\right) = \sum_{i=1}^{n} \frac{\left|p_i - q_i\right|}{\left|p_i + q_i\right|} \tag{7}$$

(g) Kullback–Leibler Divergence (KLD)

KLD measure is used where dataset follows some probability distribution. Two probability distributions are P_a and P_b. Equation (8) shows the measure

$$D_{KL}\left(P_a \| P_b\right) = \sum_i P_a(i) \log \frac{P_a(i)}{P_b(i)} \tag{8}$$

This measure is considered as non-metric because it is not calculated symmetrically and it does not follow the rule of triangle inequality condition.

(h) Jaccard Similarity Coefficient

Jaccard similarity of two sets (say S1 and S2) is measured by Equation (9)

$$J\left(S_1, S_2\right) = \frac{\left|S_1 \cap S_2\right|}{\left|S_1 \cup S_2\right|} \tag{9}$$

(i) Mahalanobis Distance

Mahalanobis distance is given by Equation (10)

$$d_{mah} = \sqrt{\left(a - b\right) S^{-1} \left(a - b\right)^T} \tag{10}$$

Where S is the Covariance matrix of dataset.

SIMILARITY MEASURES FOR CATEGORICAL DATA

(a) Chi - Squared

Chi-squared statistic was proposed by Karl Pearson in 1900 [15]. It checks any association exist between the categorical variable. The chi square (x^2) is depicted as Equation (11)

$$ch^2 = \sum_{i=1}^{n} \frac{\left(O_i - E_i\right)^2}{E_i} \tag{11}$$

For two variables the range lies between -1 to +1 and for large number of variables, it is from 0 to +1. If the value lies nearest to 1 then there is indication for strong relationship between variables.

(b) Cosine Similarity

Cosine similarity is used to find the similarity of two categorical terms X and Y and is defined as Equation (12)

$$\operatorname{Cos} Sim\left(X,Y\right) = \frac{X \circ Y}{\|X\|\|Y\|} \tag{12}$$

In the context of categorical variables, the Cosine similarity is mostly used in the text mining applications. The range exist between 0 and 1.

(c) Overlap

The overlap measure checks the attributes that are same for two data instances and compute its values. It uses only the diagonal entries of the similarity matrix. The overlap similarity is defined as Equation (13)

$$S_k\left(X_k, Y_k\right) = \begin{cases} 1 \, if \, X_k = Y_k \\ 0 \, otherwise \end{cases} \tag{13}$$

CLUSTER VALIDITY

Clustering algorithms detect hidden patterns by forming clusters which are not known in advance. The clustering algorithms are very sensitive to the number of features in the data set and used input parameters. The number of clusters varies according to these conditions. The main problem in cluster analysis is to find best number of clusters that fit to the data set. Hence, some evaluation methods are required for validating the final cluster partitions of the data sets. The problem of deciding optimal number of clusters in a dataset as well as cluster result evaluation has been subject to cluster validity and the several research efforts has been reported in the literature. (Dave, 1996; Gath and Geva, 1989; Theodoridis & Koutroubas, 1999; Xie and Beni, 1991).

Broadly, three approaches exist for evaluating cluster validity: external, internal and relative (Theodoridis & Koutroubas, 1999). This chapter will focus only on the internal cluster validity criteria. A large number of cluster validity indices have been reviewed here (Milligan and Cooper, 1985; Dimitriadou et al., 2002; Halkidi and Vazirgiannis, 2001; Wang and Zhang, 2007)

Two main criteria for cluster evaluation and selection for optimal clusters (Berry & Linoff, 2011)

1. Compactness: It measures the closeness among data points within each cluster. Two common approaches to calculate the compactness are variance and

2. Separation: It measures the separation distance among clusters. Clusters should be widely separated. Distance between two different clusters can be measured by three approaches: Single Linkage, Complete Linkage and Centroid Distance. Out of these three, the first two approaches are statistical but it requires high computational cost. Third approach is the most widely used that aims to find best clustering pattern.

In accordance with applied algorithm as crisp/soft, two categories of internal validity indices are crisp and fuzzy cluster validity indexes. Crisp clustering might be considered as a unique form of fuzzy clustering. In crisp clustering an object is characterized to one only one cluster with membership value 1 and membership value 0 for all the other clusters. Whereas in fuzzy clustering, object is assigned to all the clusters with membership matrix that specifies the degree of bonding in the form of membership value between 0 to 1 for each cluster. Hence, fuzzy patterns can be transformed into a crisp pattern by substituting the uppermost membership value of an object in fuzzy clustering by 1 and all other membership values by 0. Fuzzy clustering may contribute more insights and deeper information for higher levels of processing than crisp clustering. This section reviews both categories of some well-adapted crisp and fuzzy validity indices.

This chapter reviews both categories of some well-adapted crisp and fuzzy cluster validity indices.

CRISP CLUSTER VALIDITY INDICES

Cluster validity indices have been defined in the form of summation, difference and ratio of compactness and separation measures. The best partition of the data set correspond to either maximum or minimum value. Let a dataset X having a set of N objects in d-dimensional space:

$$X = \left\{ x_1, x_2, \ldots x_N \right\} \subseteq R^P$$

$$C = \{c_1, c_2, \ldots, c_K\}$$

Partitions in a dataset is a set of disjoint clusters into K groups: where

$$\cup_{c_k \in C} c_k = X, c_k \cap c_l = \varnothing \forall k \neq l$$

The centroid of a cluster c_k is the mean vector $\overline{c_k} = 1 / \left| c_k \right| \sum_{x_i \in C_k} x_i$

The centroid of whole dataset $\overline{X} = 1 / N \sum_{x_i \in X} x_i$

(a) Dunn Index (Dunn, 1973)

Dunn index is measured by division of minimum inter-cluster distance from maximum diameter of cluster. It is formulated as Equation (14)

$$D = \min_{1 \le k \le K, i \ne j} \left(\frac{d(C_i, C_j)}{\max\limits_{1 \le k \le K}(\delta(C_k))} \right) \tag{14}$$

Where $\delta(C_k)$ = diameter of cluster C_k

$d(C_i, C_j)$ = minimum distance between C_i and C_j clusters. Maximum value of the index indicates distinctly separated clusters.

(b) Davies-Bouldin Index(DB) (Davies & Bouldin, 1979)

This measure is the ratio of sum of the within cluster scatter to inter-cluster separation. It is expressed as Equation (15)

$$DB = \frac{1}{K} \sum_{i=1}^{k} R_i \tag{15}$$

Minimum value of DB index indicates the optimal partitioning of dataset, where

$$R_i = \max_{j \ne i} \frac{S_i + S_j}{d_{ij}}$$

S_i and S_j =within cluster scatter for i^{th} and j^{th} clusters respectively and it is shown as

$$S_i = \frac{1}{n} \sum_{x \in c_i} \|x - v_i\|$$

Where n_i = number of data points in the cluster C_i

v_i =center of cluster C_n

$d_{ij}\|x - v_i\|$ distance between cluster centers

(c) PBM Index (Pakhira et al., 2004)

Three factors: the number of clusters, the cluster compactness measure and cluster separation measure form PBM index. PBM is maximization index and is expressed as the product of these three factors shown in Equation (16).

$$PBM = \left(\frac{1}{K} \times \frac{E_0}{E} \times D \right)^2 \tag{16}$$

where

$$E = \sum_{i=1}^{K} \sum_{j=1}^{n} \mu_{ij} \left\| x_j - v_k \right\|$$

It is total within cluster scatter

$$E_0 = \sum_{x \in X} \left\| x - v \right\|$$

Where v is the center of clusters $x \in X$

$$D = \max_{i,j=1 \text{ to } K} \left\| v_i - v_j \right\|$$

(d) Silhouette SIL Index (Rousseeuw, 1987)

SIL index is calculated by the mean of all silhouette through all clusters. The maximum value of index indicates the best partitions of the dataset. The index is represented as Equation (17)

$$SIL = \frac{1}{K} \sum_{i=1}^{k} (SIL(C_k)) \tag{17}$$

Where $SIL(C_k)$ = silhouette width of C_k cluster and is represented as

$$SIL(C_k) = \frac{1}{n_k} \sum_{x \in C_k} SIL(x)$$

n_k = number of patterns in C_k

$$SIL(x) = \frac{b(x) - a(x)}{\max(a(x), b(x))} \tag{18}$$

$a(x)$= within cluster mean distance i.e the average distance between x and all other data points belonging to same cluster

$b(x)$= smallest of the mean distances of x to the data points belonging to other clusters.

(e) C-Index (Hubert & Levin, 1976)

It is normalized cohesion measure and presented by Equation (19)

$$CI(C) = \frac{S(C) - S_{\min}(C)}{S_{\max}(C) - S_{\min}(C)} \tag{19}$$

$$S(C) = \sum_{C_k \in C} \sum_{x_i x_j \in C_k} d_e(x_i, x_j)$$

$$S_{\min}(C) = \sum \min(n_w)_{x_i, x_j \in X} \{d_e(x_i, x_j\}$$

$$S_{\max}(C) = \sum \max(n_w)_{x_i, x_j \in X} \{d_e(x_i, x_j\}$$

$d_e(x_i, x_j)$ = Euclidean distance between x_i and x_j

Number of object pairs in a partition that are in same cluster

$$n_w = \sum_{c_k \in C} \binom{|c_k|}{2}$$

(f) S_Dbw Index(SDbw)(Saitta et al., 2007)

This index is formulated into the form of ratio based on Euclidean norm, standard deviation of a set of objects and the standard deviation of a partition. It is defined as Equation (20)

$$SDbw(C) = \frac{1}{K} \sum_{c_k \in C} \frac{\|\sigma(c_k)\|}{\|\sigma(X)\|} + \frac{1}{K(K-1)} \sum_{c_k \in C} \sum_{c_l \in C/c_k} \frac{den(c_k, c_l)}{\max\{den(c_k), den(c_l)\}} \qquad (20)$$

$$den(c_k) = \sum_{x_i \in c_k} f(x_i, \overline{c_k})$$

$$den(c_k, c_l) = \sum_{x_j \in c_k \cup c_l} f\left(x_i, \frac{\overline{c_k} + \overline{c_l}}{2}\right)$$

$$f(x_i, c_k) = \begin{cases} 0 & \text{if } d_e(x_i, \overline{c_k}) > stdev(C), \\ 1 & \text{otherwise} \end{cases}$$

$\|x\| = (x^T x)^{1/2}$

$$\sigma(X) = 1/|X| \sum_{x_j \in X} (x_i, \overline{x})^2$$

$$stdev(C) = 1/K \sqrt{\sum_{c_k \in C} \|\sigma(c_k)\|}$$

FUZZY CLUSTER VALIDITY INDICES

Fuzzy validity indices have been categorized on the basis of membership and data points both. One category takes into account only membership value on the other side second category considers both membership values and data points. Traditional indices such as the partition coefficient, partition entropy and modified version of these indices make use of only partition membership values. However, they have the drawback of monotonic tendency as the cluster number increases. Now, it is widely acknowledged that a good validity index should always incorporate both the parameters.

In this section, few most popular validity indices and their modified versions have been presented. Basic notations used in the indices with their meaning are listed in Table 8.

Table 8. Notation used

Notation	Means
N	No. of data points
C	No. of clusters
m	Fuzzification factor
μ	Membership matrix
μ_{ij}	Membership degree of jth data point into i^{th} cluster
v_i	Cluster center for i^{th} cluster

VALIDITY INDICES COMPRISING ONLY MEMBERSHIP VALUES

(a) Partition Coefficient (PC) (Bezdek, 1974)

PC index was suggested with the concept of minimizing the overall values of pairwise fuzzy intersection in the membership matrix (μ). The index is represented as Equation (21).

$$PC = \frac{\sum_{j=1}^{n}\sum_{i=1}^{c} \mu_{ij}^2}{n} \tag{21}$$

PC is maximization index therefore data points closer to cluster centers will have membership degree nearest to 1. Its value ranges in [1/c, 1].

(b) Partition Entropy (PE)(Bezdek,1975)

PE is a scalar estimation of fuzziness in the membership matrix (μ). It is minimization index and value ranges in [0, $\log_a c$] where a is base of logarithm and range is a ϵ (1, ∞). Index is defined as Equation (22)

$$PE = -\frac{1}{n}\sum_{j=1}^{n}\sum_{i=1}^{c}\left[\mu_{ij}\log_a\left(\mu_{ij}\right)\right] \tag{22}$$

(c) Modified Partition Coefficient (MPC) (Dave, 1996)

Dave proposed a modified index MPC to overcome the drawback of monotonicity in PC function. It is a maximization index Its range lies between [0, 1] and the formula is Equation

$$MPC = 1 - \frac{c}{c-1}(1 - PC) \tag{23}$$

(d) Improved Partition Coefficient(IPC)(Li, 2011)

IPC was designed to overcome drawbacks associated with PC function: monotonic tendency and sensitivity to fuzzification factor m. It is a sort of maximization index as shown in Equation

$$IPC(c) = r(c-1 \to c) - r(c \to c+1)$$
$$= 100 \left[\frac{PC(c-1) - PC(c)}{PC(c-1)} - \frac{PC(c) - PC(c+1)}{PC(c)} \right] \tag{24}$$

The condition for IPC is $2 \leq c \leq c_{max} - 1$ and PC (1) = 1.

(e) Normalized Partition Entropy (NPE)(Dunn,1977)

NPE was defined to eradicate the monotonic tendency of PE function. It is a kind of minimized index and defined as Equation (25)

$$NPE = \frac{nPE}{n-c} \tag{25}$$

(f) P-Index (Chen and Linkens, 2004)

P-index consist of two terms: Compactness within the cluster and separation between clusters. Its objective is to find maximum cohesion and less overlap between pairs of clusters.

$$P - index = \frac{1}{n}\sum_{k=1}^{n}\max_{i}(\mu_{ik}) - \frac{1}{k}\sum_{i=1}^{c-1}\sum_{i=i+1}^{c}\left[\frac{1}{n}\sum_{k=1}^{n}\min(\mu_{ik}, \mu_{jk})\right] \tag{26}$$

Above these indices uses only fuzzy membership degree, so some drawbacks can be experienced:

(i)   Increasing or decreasing monotonic tendency with cluster numbers.
(ii) Sensitivity with the fuzzification factor m.
(iii) No connection with geometrical shape of data points due to no use of data points in function.

VALIDITY INDICES COMPRISING BOTH MEMBERSHIP VALUE AND DATA POINTS

Validity indices based on both membership values and data points are defined in this section:

(a) FS Index (Fukuyama and Sugeno, 1989)

This validity index is in subtraction form of compactness measure $J_m(\mu,v)$ and separation measure $K_m(\mu,v)$. Minimum value of index is considered for better clustering and is shown as Equation (27).

$$FS = J_m(\mu,v) - K_m(\mu,v)$$

$$FS = \sum_{i=1}^{c}\sum_{j=1}^{n} \mu_{ij}^{m}\left(\left\|x_j - v_i\right\|^2 - \left\|v_i - \overline{v}\right\|^2\right) \tag{27}$$

$$\overline{v} = \sum_{i=1}^{c} \frac{v_i}{c}$$

(b) Xie-Beni Index (XB) (Xie-Beni, 1991)

The fuzzy XB validity index was proposed in the division form of compactness measure and separation measure taking into account membership value and data points. Minimum value defines the suitable number of clusters. It is defined as Equation (28).

$$XB = \frac{\sum_{i=1}^{c}\sum_{j=1}^{n} \mu_{ij}^{m}\left\|x_j - v_i\right\|^2}{n\left(\min_{i\neq j}\left\|v_i - v_j\right\|^2\right)} \tag{28}$$

(c) CWB Index (Razaee et al.1998)

This minimization index takes into account both membership matrix and structure of data. It is calculated as Equation (29).

$$CWB = \alpha Scat(c) + Dist(c)$$

$$CWB = \alpha \frac{\sum_{i=1}^{c}\sum_{j=1}^{n} \mu_{ij}\left(x_j - v_i\right)^2}{cn\sigma(x)} + \frac{D_{max}}{D_{min}\sum_{k=1}^{c}\left(\sum_{z=1}^{n} v_k - v_z\right)^{-1}} \tag{29}$$

(d) PBMF Index (Pakhira et al., 2004)

It has three terms. The first term is decremented with the increase of c. The second term measures the compactness. The third part is the maximum distance between classes. The value of first term decreases and the other two parts increase. For optimal clustering, the maximum value of PBMF is considered. It is defined as follows Equation (30)

$$PBMF = \left(\frac{1}{c} \times \frac{\sum_{j=1}^{n} \mu_{1j} \left\| x_j - v_1 \right\|}{\sum_{i=1}^{c} \sum_{j=1}^{n} \mu_{ij} \left\| x_j - v_j \right\|} \times \max_{i,j=1,2,..c} \left\| v_i - v_j \right\| \right)^2 \tag{30}$$

(f) VK Index (Kwon, 1998)

This is the modified form of XB index to reduce the decreasing tendency with number of clusters. Minimum value is considered to find optimal cluster number.

$$VK = \frac{\sum_{i=1}^{c} \sum_{j=1}^{n} \mu_{ij}^{m} \left\| x_j - v_i \right\|^2 + \frac{1}{c} \sum_{i=1}^{c} \left\| v_i - \bar{v} \right\|^2}{\min_{i \neq k} \left\| v_i - v_k \right\|^2} \tag{31}$$

(g) OCVI (Overlap-Compact Validity Index) (Rani & Kant, 2020)

The purpose to formulate this index is to overcome the drawbacks of compactness measure and to find best number of clusters in overlapped cluster datasets.

$$OCVI(c, \mu) = \frac{ovl^N(c, \mu)}{Comp^N(c, \mu)} \tag{32}$$

Where Normalized value of compactness and overlap measure

$$Comp^N(c, \mu) = \frac{Comp(c, \mu)}{Comp_{max}(c, \mu)}$$

$$ovl^N(c, \mu) = \frac{ovl(c, \mu)}{ovl_{max}(c, \mu)}$$

$$overlap(\mu, V; x) = \frac{2}{c(c-1)} \sum_{p \neq q}^{c} \sum_{j=1}^{n} \left[c. \left[\mu_{F_p}(x_j) \wedge \mu_{F_q}(x_j) \right] h(x_j) \right] \tag{33}$$

$$comp = \frac{\sum_{j=1}^{n} 1 - \max_{i} \mu_{ij}}{\sum_{j=1}^{n} \sum_{i=1}^{c} \left\| x_j - v_i \right\|^2 + \frac{1}{c} \sum_{i=1}^{c} \left\| v_i - \bar{v} \right\|^2} \tag{34}$$

It can be remarked that as no single algorithm can be applied for clustering the data, similarly there exist no index that can work well with all clustering algorithms and with all data sets. Hence, the ways for constant research are being directed towards developing more efficient indices which can be exploited with disparate algorithms for various data sets.

FUTURE RESEARCH DIRECTIONS

This research provides a roadmap for data analysis and processing with a decision support system for future exploration. As we have witnessed innumerable successful examples of cluster analysis applications, many inherent problems still exist due to the complexities in data. Researchers are focusing on advanced and innovative techniques and algorithms but needs more in the view of various characteristics of big data. As analysis results greatly depend on the parameters chosen, it is very important to select appropriate parameters also while applying clustering algorithms. Every cluster validity index also depends on clusters obtained from clustering algorithms. Another direction for future work is to practice new cluster validity index with algorithms that can be applied on varied and high dimensional data.

CONCLUSION

Ample amounts of data are generated frequently from various sources such as smartphones, IoT devices, sensors and social media. Understanding and generating information from such vast data is essential for many enterprises, services and even for every domain such as the health care sector, financial sector, telecom sector and transportation sector. Therefore, extensible and efficient algorithms are needed to manage and extract useful information from such a huge amount of data. In the view of this research, the chapter introduced some framework for big data analytics integration for decision support. Cluster analysis has been suggested as most appropriate technique for extracting value from big data. Different clustering techniques and their algorithms are reviewed in this chapter. To validate the clustering results, most well-known cluster validity indices are summarized according to crisp and fuzzy clustering techniques.

REFERENCES

Agrawal, R., Gehrke, J., Gunopulos, D., & Raghavan, P. (1998). Automatic subspace clustering of high dimensional data for data mining applications. *Proceedings 1998 ACM SIGMOD International Conference on Management of Data, 27*, 94–105. 10.1145/276304.276314

Bellman, R. E., Kalaba, R., & Zadeh, L. A. (1966). Abstraction and pattern classification. *Journal of Mathematical Analysis and Applications, 13*(1), 1–7. doi:10.1016/0022-247X(66)90071-0

Berry, M. J. A., & Linoff, G. (2011). Data Mining Techniques: For Marketing, Sales and Customer Relationship Management (3rd ed.). John Wiley & Sons Publishing.

Bezdek, J. C. (1974). Cluster validity with fuzzy sets. *Journal of Cybernetics*, *3*(3), 58–72. doi:10.1080/01969727308546047

Bezdek, J. C. (1975). Mathematical models for systematic and taxonomy. *Eighth International Conference on Numerical Taxonomy*, 143–165.

Bezdek, J. C. (1981). *Pattern Recognition with Fuzzy Objective Function Algorithms*. Plenum Press. doi:10.1007/978-1-4757-0450-1

Carpenter, G., & Grossberg, S. (1987). A massively parallel architecture for a self-organizing neural pattern recognition machine. *Comput Vis Gr Image Process, 37*, 54–115.

Chen, M. Y., & Linkens, D. A. (2004). Rule-base self-generation and simplification for data-driven fuzzy models. *Fuzzy Sets and Systems*, *142*(2), 243–265. doi:10.1016/S0165-0114(03)00160-X

D'Urso, P., & Maharaj, E. A. (2009). Autocorrelation-based fuzzy clustering of time series. *Fuzzy Sets and Systems*, *160*(24), 3565–3589. doi:10.1016/j.fss.2009.04.013

Dave, R. N. (1996). Validating fuzzy partition obtained through c-shells clustering. *Pattern Recognition Letters*, *17*(6), 613–623. doi:10.1016/0167-8655(96)00026-8

Davies, D. L., & Bouldin, D. W. (1979). A Cluster Separation Measure. *IEEE Transactions on Pattern Analysis and Machine Intelligence*, *1*(2), 224–227. doi:10.1109/TPAMI.1979.4766909 PMID:21868852

Diebold, F. X. (2012). *A personal perspective on the origin(s) and development of "big data": The phenomenon, the term, and the discipline*. PIER Working Paper No. 13-003. Available from: doi:10.2139/ssrn.2202843

Dimitriadou, E., Dolnicar, S., & Weingassel, A. (2002). An examination of indexes for determining the number of clusters in binary data sets. *Psychometrika*, *67*(1), 137–160. doi:10.1007/BF02294713

Dunn, J. C. (1973). A fuzzy relative of the ISODATA process and its use in detecting compact well-separated clusters. *Journal of Cybernetics*, *3*(3), 32–57. doi:10.1080/01969727308546046

Dunn, J. C. (1977). Indices of partition fuzziness and the detection of clusters in large data sets. In M. M. Gupta (Ed.), *Fuzzy Automata and decision processes* (pp. 271–284). Elsevier.

Elgendy, N., & Elragal, A. (2016). Big data analytics in support of decision making proces. *Procedia Computer Science*, *100*, 1071–1084. doi:10.1016/j.procs.2016.09.251

Ester, M., Kriegel, H., Sander, J., & Xu, X. (1996). A density-based algorithm for discovering clusters in large spatial databases with noise. *Proceedings of the second ACM SIGKDD international conference on knowledge discovery and data mining*, 226–231.

Fisher, D. (1987). Knowledge acquisition via incremental conceptual clustering. *Machine Learning*, *2*(2), 39–172. doi:10.1007/BF00114265

Fukuyama, Y., & Sugeno, M. (1989). A new method of choosing the number of clusters for the fuzzy c-means method. *Proceedings of the Fifth Fuzzy Systems Symposium*, 247–250.

Gandomi, A., & Haider, M. (2015). Beyond the hype: Big data concepts, methods, and analytics. *International Journal of Information Management, 35*(2), 137–144. doi:10.1016/j.ijinfomgt.2014.10.007

Guha, S., Rastogi, R., & Shim, K. (1998). CURE: An efficient clustering algorithm for large databases. *SIGMOD Record, 27*(2), 73–84. doi:10.1145/276305.276312

Guha, S., Rastogi, R., & Shim, K. (1999). ROCK: a robust clustering algorithm for categorical attributes. *Proceedings of the 15th international conference on data engineering,* 512-521. 10.1109/ICDE.1999.754967

Halkidi, M., & Vazirgiannis, M. (2001). Clustering validity assessment: Finding the optimal partitioning of a data set. *Proc. of the 2001 IEEE Int. Conf. on Data Mining (ICDM'01),* 187-194. 10.1109/ICDM.2001.989517

Han, J., Pei, J., & Kamber, M. (2011). *Data mining: concepts and techniques.* Elsevier.

Huang, Z. (1998). Extensions to the k-means algorithm for clustering large data sets with categorical values. *Data Mining and Knowledge Discovery, 2*(3), 283–304. doi:10.1023/A:1009769707641

Hubert, L. J., & Levin, J. R. (1976). A general statistical framework for assessing categorical clustering in free recall. *Psychological Bulletin, 83*(6), 1072–1080. doi:10.1037/0033-2909.83.6.1072

Jagadish, H. V., Gehrke, J., Labrinidis, A., Papakonstantinou, Y., Patel, J. M., Ramakrishnan, R., & Shahabi, C. (2014). Big Data and Its Technical Challenges. *Communications of the ACM, 57*(7), 86–94. doi:10.1145/2611567

Jain, A. K. (2010). Data clustering: 50 years beyond K means. *Pattern Recognition Letters, 31*(8), 651–666. doi:10.1016/j.patrec.2009.09.011

Jain, A. K., & Dubes, R. C. (1988). Algorithms for Clustering Data. Prentice-Hall Inc.

Jain, A. K., Murty, M. N., & Flynn, P. J. (1999). Data clustering: A Review. *ACM Computing Surveys, 31*(3), 265–323. doi:10.1145/331499.331504

Jeble, S., Kumari, S., & Patil, Y. (2018). Role of Big Data in Decision Making. *Operations and Supply Chain Management: An International Journal, 11*(1), 36–44. doi:10.31387/oscm0300198

Kant, S., Rao, T. L., & Sundaram, P. N. (1994). An Automatic and Stable Clustering Algorithm. *Pattern Recognition Letters, 15*(6), 543–549. doi:10.1016/0167-8655(94)90014-0

Kaufman, L., & Rousseeuw, P. (1990). *Partitioning around medoids (program pam). Finding groups in data: an introduction to cluster analysis.* Wiley. doi:10.1002/9780470316801

Kaufman, L., & Rousseeuw, P. (2008). *Finding groups in data: an introduction to cluster analysis* (Vol. 344). Wiley. doi:10.1002/9780470316801

Khan, S. S., & Kant, S. (2006). Computation of Initial Modes for K-mode Clustering Algorithm Using Evidence Accumulaion. *Proc. AAAI. IJCAI, 7,* 2784–2789.

Kohonen, T. (1990). The self-organizing map. *Proceedings of the IEEE, 78*(9), 1464–1480. doi:10.1109/5.58325

Kwon, S. H. (1998). Cluster validity index for fuzzy clustering. *Electronics Letters*, *34*(22), 2176–2177. doi:10.1049/el:19981523

Labrinidis, A., & Jagadish, V. H. (2012). Challenges and opportunities with big data. *Proceedings of the VLDB Endowment International Conference on Very Large Data Bases*, *5*(12), 2032–2033. doi:10.14778/2367502.2367572

Laney, D. (2001). *3D Data management: Controlling Data volume, velocity, and variety*. META Group, Technical Report. Available from: http://blogs.gartner.com/doug-laney/files/2012/01/ad949-3D-Data-Management-Controlling-Data-Volume-Velocity-and-Variety.pdf

Li, C. S. (2011). The improved partition coefficient. *Procedia Engineering*, *24*, 534–538. doi:10.1016/j.proeng.2011.11.2691

MacQueen, J. (1967). Some methods for classification and analysis of multivariate observations. *Proc Fifth Berkeley Symp Math Stat Probab*, *1*, 281–297.

Mehta, V., Bawa, S., & Singh, S. (2020). Analytical review of clustering techniques and proximity measures. *Artificial Intelligence Review*, *53*(1), 1–29. doi:10.100710462-020-09840-7 PMID:32836651

Milligan, G., & Cooper, M. (1985). An examination of procedures for determining the number of clusters in a data set. *Psychometrika*, *50*(2), 159–179. doi:10.1007/BF02294245

Naouali, S., Salem, S. B., & Chtourou, Z. (2019). Clustering Categorical Data: A Survey. *International Journal of Information Technology & Decision Making*, *19*(1), 49–96. Advance online publication. doi:10.1142/S0219622019300064

Pakhira, K. M., Bandyopadhyay, S., & Maulik, U. (2004). Validity index for crisp and fuzzy clusters. *Pattern Recognition*, *37*(3), 487–501. doi:10.1016/j.patcog.2003.06.005

Peffers, K., Tunnanen, T., Rothenberger, M. A., & Chatterjee, S. (2008). A Design science research methodology for information systems research. *Journal of Management Information Systems*, *24*(3), 45–77. doi:10.2753/MIS0742-1222240302

Rani, B., & Kant, S. (2019). An Approach Toward Integration of Big Data into Decision Making Process. In S. Patnaik, A. Ip, M. Tavana, & V. Jain (Eds.), *New Paradigm in Decision Science and Management. Advances in Intelligent Systems and Computing, 1005* (pp. 207–217). Springer. doi:10.1007/978-981-13-9330-3_19

Rani, B., & Kant, S. (2020). *Estimating Cluster Validity Using Compactness Measure and Overlap Measure for Fuzzy Clustering. International Journal of Business Intelligence and Data Mining*. doi:10.1504/IJBIDM.2022.10036057

Rao, K. Y., Kameswari, C. S., & Phanindra, D. S. (2011). A Fuzzy Grid-Clustering Algorithm. *International Journal of Computer Science and Technology*, *2*(3), 524–526.

Rousseeuw, P. J. (1987). Silhouettes: A graphical aid to the interpretation and validation of cluster analysis. *Journal of Computational and Applied Mathematics*, *20*, 53–65. doi:10.1016/0377-0427(87)90125-7

Saitta, S., Raphael, B., & Smith, I. (2007). A bounded index for cluster validity. In P. Perner (Ed.), Lecture Notes in Computer Science: Vol. 4571. *Machine Learning and Data Mining in Pattern Recognition* (pp. 174–187). Springer. doi:10.1007/978-3-540-73499-4_14

Schölkopf, B., Smola, A., & Müller, K. (1998). Nonlinear component analysis as a kernel eigenvalue problem. *Neural Computation*, *10*(5), 1299–1319. doi:10.1162/089976698300017467

Shirkhorshidi, A. S., Aghabozorgi, S., & Wah, T. Y. (2015). A Comparison Study on Similarity and Dissimilarity Measures in Clustering Continuous Data. *PLoS One*, *10*(12), e0144059. doi:10.1371/journal.pone.0144059 PMID:26658987

Simon, H. A. (1960). *The new science of management decision*. Harper and Row.

Smiti, A., & Elouedi, Z. (2012). DBSCAN-GM: An improved clustering method based on Gaussian Means and DBSCAN techniques. *IEEE 16th International Conference on Intelligent Engineering Systems (INES)*, 573-578.

Smiti, A., & Elouedi, Z. (2016). Fuzzy Density Based Clustering Method: Soft DBSCAN-GM. *IEEE 8th International Conference on Intelligent Systems*, 443-448.

Sun, Z. (2018). 10 Bigs: Big Data and Its Ten Big Characteristics. *PNG Univ. Technol.*, *3*(1), 1–10. doi:10.13140/RG.2.2.31449.62566

Theodoridis, S., & Konstantinos, K. (1999). *Pattern Recognition*. Academic Press.

Thirathon, U., Wieder, B., Matolcsy, Z., & Ossimitz, M.-L. (2017). Big Data, Analytic Culture and Analytic-Based Decision Making Evidence from Australia. *Procedia Computer Science*, *121*, 775–783. doi:10.1016/j.procs.2017.11.100

Turban, E., Aronson, J. E., Liang, T., & Sharda, R. (2007). *Decision support and Business intelligent systems* (8th ed.). Prentice Hall publications.

Wang, W., Yang, J., & Muntz, R. (1997). STING: a statistical information grid approach to spatial data mining. VLDB, 186–195.

Wang, W., & Zhang, Y. (2007). On fuzzy cluster validity indices. *Fuzzy Sets and Systems*, *158*(19), 2095–2117. doi:10.1016/j.fss.2007.03.004

Wu, Z., Xie, W., & Yu, J. (2003). Fuzzy c-means clustering algorithm based on kernel method. *Proceedings of the fifth ICCIMA*, 49–54.

Xie, X. L., & Beni, G. (1991). A validity measure for fuzzy clustering. *IEEE Transactions on Pattern Analysis and Machine Intelligence*, *13*(8), 841–847. doi:10.1109/34.85677

Xu, D., & Tian, Y. (2015). A Comprehensive Survey of Clustering Algorithms. Ann. Data. *Sci.*, *2*(2), 165–193. doi:10.100740745-015-0040-1

Xu, R., & Wunsch, D. II. (2005). Survey of clustering algorithms. *IEEE Transactions on Neural Networks*, *16*(3), 645–678. doi:10.1109/TNN.2005.845141 PMID:15940994

Yue, S., & Huang, X. (2013). A gird-based fuzzy cluster approach. *International Conference on Machine Learning and Cybernetics*, 14-17.

Zadeh, L. A. (1965). Fuzzy sets. *Information and Control*, *8*(3), 338–353. doi:10.1016/S0019-9958(65)90241-X

Zeng, K., & Wu, N. (2016). FHCC: A Soft Hierarchical Clustering Approach for Collaborative Filtering Recommendation. *International Journal of Data Mining & Knowledge Management Process*, *6*(3), 25–36. doi:10.5121/ijdkp.2016.6303

Zhang, T., Ramakrishnan, R., & Livny, M. (1996). BIRCH: An efficient data clustering method for very large databases. *SIGMOD Record*, *25*(2), 103–104. doi:10.1145/235968.233324

Zighed, D., & Abdesselam, R. (2011). Comparing proximity measures for continuous and binary data: topological approach. *International Conference on Machine Learning and Data Mining*.

ADDITIONAL READING

Kitchin, R. (2014). The real-time city? Big data and smart urbanism. *GeoJournal*, *79*(1), 1–14. doi:10.100710708-013-9516-8

Mlitz, K. (2021). *Forecast revenue big data market worldwide 2011-2027*. Statista Inc.

Rawashdeh, M., & Ralescu, A. (2012). Crisp and fuzzy cluster validity: Generalized intra-inter silhouette index. *2012 Annual Meeting of the North American Fuzzy Information Processing Society (NAFIPS)*, 1-6. 10.1109/NAFIPS.2012.6290969

Rodriguez, M. Z., Comin, C. H., Casanova, D., Bruno, O. M., Amancio, D. R., Costa, L. F., & Rodrigues, F. A. (2019). Clustering algorithms: A comparative approach. *PLoS One*, *14*(1), e0210236. doi:10.1371/journal.pone.0210236 PMID:30645617

Sun, Z. (2018). 10 Bigs: Big Data and Its Ten Big Characteristics. *PNG Univ. Technol.*, *3*(1), 1–10. doi:10.13140/RG.2.2.31449.62566

Waller, M. A., & Fawcett, S. E. (2013). Data science, predictive analytics, and big data: A revolution that will transform supply chain design and management. *Journal of Business Logistics*, *34*(2), 77–84. doi:10.1111/jbl.12010

Wang, W., & Zhang, Y. (2007). On fuzzy cluster validity indices. *Fuzzy Sets and Systems*, *158*(19), 2095–2117. doi:10.1016/j.fss.2007.03.004

KEY TERMS AND DEFINITIONS

Big Data: Data generated in the large volume, diverse, complex, longitudinal, and/or distributed form.

Big Data Analytics: An analytics procedure to find knowledgeable value from data.

Cluster Validation: A procedure to measure the quality of clustering output.

Cluster Validation Index: A metric to measure the output of clustering.

Clustering: A technique for grouping the data on the basis of their similarity.

Decision-Making Process: A process to provide intelligent and smart decisions.

Data Lakes

Anjani Kumar
University of Nebraska at Omaha, USA

Parvathi Chundi
University of Nebraska at Omaha, USA

INTRODUCTION

With the advent of the digital world, data gets generated and collected for every action -- while browsing a website, purchasing items on e-commerce websites, watching videos online, etc. These data are generated in real-time and can be in diverse formats structured (relational tables or CSV files), unstructured (text files), & semi-structured (XML or log files). These ever-increasing databases create challenges in an organization where multiple departments may generate a part of the organizational data. For an organization to generate value from the data collected by different departments, these data sources must be accessible across the entire organization, merged, and analyzed in different ways for various purposes. A *Data Lake (DL)* is a centralized, scalable storage location where organizational data can be stored and made available widely across the entire organization for analysis purposes.

There are different requirements for different departments of a company. The Business Intelligence team may need data arranged in a specific format to compute data cubes to create reports and visualizations to answer many business questions. In contrast, the data science team may need data in a raw format to explore future trends or build predictive models.

A **data analysis task** is a process of extracting meaningful information from a massive volume of data. It can be done in various ways, such as creating reports and visualizations to answer business questions and developing a predictive model using machine learning to find patterns. There are mainly two types of data analysis: *quantitative* and *qualitative*. Even though these two tasks are conducted differently, both approaches attempt to *tell a story* from the data. Some commonalities between the two data analyses are data reduction, answering research questions, explaining variation, etc. (Hardy, 2004). A data analysis task is also defined as the accurate evaluation and full exploitation of the data obtained (Brandt & Brandt, 1998).

There are usually four steps for doing any data analysis task (Gorelik, 2019) and they are listed below.

1. **Find & Understand:** An enterprise has vast amounts of data. This massive amount of data is saved in many databases, each containing many tables and each table containing many fields or attributes. A database is the collection of interrelated data that is stored in and managed by a database management system (DBMS) (Silberschatz, Korth, & Sudarshan, 2020). In general, DBMS uses the relational or tabular format to store data and relationships among data. Data are saved in a collection of tables. Each table has multiple *columns*, also known as *attributes*. The attribute names in the table are unique. Each row in the table stores the data as a *record*.

DOI: 10.4018/978-1-7998-9220-5.ch025

Copyright © 2023, IGI Global. Copying or distributing in print or electronic forms without written permission of IGI Global is prohibited.

D

With thousands of tables at an enterprise and each table containing hundreds of fields, it is difficult, if not impossible, to locate the right data sets needed for an analysis task. As a simple example, consider the data analysis task to build sales prediction models for the northeast region of the United States. The analyst should be able to locate the tables where such data are stored among the hundreds of databases in the enterprise. It becomes complicated for an analyst to find and understand the meanings of numerous attributes of these tables. To find the tables with relevant attributes, an analyst may have to manually examine each table or enlist the help of others that might have used or created that table. Therefore, the analyst must first locate the correct fields needed for the data analysis and then understand the data/ attributes in existing databases.

2. **Provision:** Once correct datasets have been located, analysts will need to access this data. Acquiring access to datasets can be tedious in an enterprise. Typically, long-time employees that worked on multiple projects tend to have access to almost all the data in the enterprise, while newer employees may have nearly no access. *Provisioning* is the process of giving the proper right to access the data set so that data can be accessed at the physical (disk) level. A *metadata store* helps provide adequate access to relevant data for analysts. A metadata store contains information about all the datasets. This can be used for finding the right datasets, and then the access request to those datasets can be created. If the data is sensitive, then a de-identified version of the data, where sensitive information is replaced with randomly generated similar information, can be generated prior to granting access.

3. **Prep:** After the provisioning phase, the relevant data is obtained. It is unlikely that the data can be used directly for analysis purposes. Usually, data is not clean and does not come in the proper format. Therefore, the *data preparation* step is applied, which includes cleaning, blending, and shaping the provisioned data. As a part of cleaning, missing and mis-formatted values are fixed, and units are normalized.

As a part of shaping, a subset of relevant fields and rows may be selected. Different tables are joined to present data in a particular format for analysis. This is done by transforming, bucketizing, and aggregating data. Bucketizing is the process of converting continuous values into a discrete set of values. Blending is a technique through which data from different sources create a single, unique dataset for analysis.

4. **Analyze:** After the data preparation step, the provisioned data is in the correct format to carry out the analysis task.

Based on the above four steps, there is a real need to provide users the flexibility to search for and retrieve the data with little overhead and make the required data available in different formats depending on the type of the data analysis task. To support this functionality, the system needs to *ingest* and preserve data in its natural raw format and make the data accessible to the different end-users by converting the raw data into their desired formats. *Data ingestion* is the process of copying data from various sources to a storage platform where DL can access it. Once data is ingested, it generally is transformed and loaded into the DL storage layer for further access. Since all the data use cases are not envisaged at the time of ingestion, the raw data is preserved. For example, a data scientist might be interested in getting data in a *parquet* format, a columnar representation of data stored in an optimized way. At the same time, a business intelligence analyst might be interested in accessing data through a visualization tool such as Tableau. Having raw data gives us the flexibility to run analytics on any time range, which was not planned at the time of ingestion. Further, it helps in the *self-service* paradigm where analysts can explore data through tools like Tableau without needing help from IT.

A DL aims to fulfill the following two requirements: first, ingesting raw data, and second, making it available to various users in their desired formats.

In a DL, there is no need to define a schema in order to ingest data. This means that there is no detailed design of tables, and there is no need to define the inter-relationships (foreign key relationships) among tables at the time of ingestion. *Schema* is defined *on the fly* while reading data from the source into the DL. Since all the data is available in the DL, it is easier to relate data from different departments in an organization. Hence, setting up a DL speeds up the process of analyzing organizational data. Since raw data is available, different kinds of analysis are possible in the future, which may not have been thought of at the time of ingesting the data.

There are mainly three pillars on which a DL is built (Gorelik, 2019), and they are:

1. **The right platform:** Data keeps growing, and it is challenging to plan the volume, variety, and velocity of data in advance. Therefore, DLs should be built on platforms that provide users access to easily extendable storage, such as Amazon Web Services (AWS), Microsoft Azure, Google Cloud Platform (GCP), etc. AWS's S3, GCP's Google cloud storage, or Azure Blob are designed to store an unlimited amount of data in file systems or object-store. This has the advantage that just for saving the file of any format such as XML, JSON, CSV, etc., a schema is not required, whereas to save these data in relational tables, a schema is required.

2. **The right data:** It is difficult to know in advance the right data. Some data that may not seem important enough might become necessary with the changing business and be found during the analysis. If desired data is not available, it might take some months or years to collect it. This is the reason a DL stores almost all kinds of data, even those for which no immediate need is clear. This is possible with a DL since no schema design is required at the time of ingestion. Note that this is in contrast to a *data warehouse* that needs a schema to be set up and tables to be designed prior to storing raw data. Therefore, a data warehouse must change the schema if its purpose changes, whereas a DL is set up with the sole purpose of storing raw data.

3. **The right interfaces:** A DL should have the right interface to extract data suitable for different teams. The Business Intelligence (BI) team may access the DL to build data cubes, whereas the data science team may access the data to construct labeled data. A DL user must be able to use the interfaces to find and access the relevant data independently and efficiently. Otherwise, the enterprise data may become unusable. A DL also has to provide support for all the four steps of a data analysis task, i.e., Find & Understand, Provision, Prep, and Analyze.

Zagan and Danubianu (2020) analyze recent approaches and architectures used in a DL such as CoreDB, Smart Grid Big Data, Ceph, etc. In the survey provided in (Hai, Quix, & Jarke, 2021), authors classify DL systems based on the functions that it provides; for example, Ingestion Layer has two functions, Metadata extraction, and Metadata modeling. GEMMS, DATAMARAN, and Skluma are classified as Metadata extraction of the Ingestion layer. GEMMS extracts metadata from heterogeneous sources. It is useful since the data sources and schemas change over time. Llave (2018) conducted an exploratory study to understand the approaches enterprises take in using the DL. This work finds that there are three important reasons for implementing DL in an enterprise: a DL can be used as staging areas or sources for Data Warehouse; second, a DL can be used as a platform for experimentation for data scientists and analysts; and finally, it can be used for self-service business intelligence which helps in democratizing the data. Sawadogo and Darmont (2021) provide approaches to DL design, especially DL architectures and metadata management. It discusses the various DL architectures such as Zone architectures and Functional architectures. It identifies two types for Metadata categories, Functional Metadata and Structural Metadata. Shepherd, Kesa, Cooper, Onema and Kovacs (2018) explore the DL adoption trends and challenges in implementing DL in enterprises for decision making. Giebler, Groger, Hoos, Schwarz and Mitschang (2019) identify challenges and research gaps in DL architectures, governance, and implementation of DL. Nargesian, Zhu, Miller, Pu and Arocena (2019) review the present data management solutions for DL. It explains how dataset discovery is problematic in DL. It explains the other aspects of DL, such as data extraction, data cleaning, data integration, data versioning, and meta-data management.

This article will explain the history of a DL in the Background section. The following section, Desirable features of a Data Lake system, describes the desirable features of a DL system. The comparison of current data lake systems section compares the three DL systems, i.e., Snowflake, Databricks, and Redshift.

BACKGROUND

This section gives a brief history of the evolution of the DL, starting from Excel sheets, DBMSs, RDBMSs, Data Warehouse (DW) to DL. It provides brief details about tools for creating and maintaining DW and discusses critical differences between DW and DL.

Commercial, government, and other enterprises have always collected and stored data about their citizens, customers, employees, etc. Before the digital revolution, the volume of data generated and collected was not much. Some examples of data generated in that time were old manuscripts, lineage, bills of sale, debt, correspondence between important persons, etc.

In the early days of computerization, programmers created reports based on data by developing specific programs and logic required for the task. But the introduction of spreadsheets empowered analysts by giving them the ability to work with the data directly. However, the spreadsheet can handle only small amounts of data. With the increasing amount of data, there was a need to develop a system that would manage data well and be easy to work with. This led to the development of Relational Database Management Systems (DBMSs). RDBMSs separate data and applications. Users can create a schema that arranged data into a collection of tables and fields. Higher-level Structured Query Language (SQL) is used by users to fetch data using complex query logic.

There are three crucial concepts in RDBMS: *tables* or *relations, primary and foreign keys*, and *normalization*. RDBMS contains tables that have rows and columns. A column is also called an *attribute* or a *field*. Suppose we have a table to store all the information about a student, attributes such *as ID* (called the primary key attribute), *name, address, age, gender*, etc. If we want to add the information about courses taken by the student, we can add the course information such as *course number, name, instructor name, credit hours*, etc., in the same *Student* table. However, this will lead to repetition of information in multiple records in the Student table because each record in the table contains both student and course information. If there is a student in the Student table that has not taken any courses, the course information for that student record will have to be empty. In order to reduce the wastage of storage and provide efficient updates on a table, the *Student* and *Course* information is typically stored in two different tables. The *student* table contains information about students, and the *Course* table contains information about courses. And the *Course* table may include the ID of a student as an attribute (also called foreign key attribute) to record the enrollment of a student in a course. This process of breaking one big table into smaller tables is called *normalization*.

The normalized database design does not work for analytical queries. For example, suppose we want to find the total number of female students enrolled in the Introduction to Computer Science course for the last ten years to find a trend in enrollment. In that case, records from the *Student* and *Course* table must be combined to compute the result, which can be expensive for large databases.

This led to the development of Data Warehouse (DW). A Data Warehouse is a separate database from an operational database. In a DW, data are combined from multiple applications into one system and used for analytics purposes. Walmart created a data warehouse in 1990, which helped it gain an advantage over its competitors significantly (Gorelik, 2019).

Data warehouse uses a relational database that is optimized for aggregation, multi-table joins, and long-running queries where data is not stored in a normalized manner. Ralph Kimball proposed the popular *star schema* data model. This schema consists of a set of dimension and fact tables, and the dimension tables contain details about the entities for which analysis needs to be done.

Different tools are required for creating and maintaining Data Warehouse (DW):

1. **Data Integration Tools**: Data Integration tools help in loading data into DW. Various operation database data is converted into a common dimension table format before loading into the corresponding dimension table. *ETL(Extract, Transform, and Load)* tool takes care of converting data from various sources into dimension table format. If the transform part, which takes care of converting one representation of data into another, is to be done in the database itself, this process is called ELT. ELT stands for Extract, Load, and then Transform.
2. **Data Quality Tools**: These tools ensure the quality of data in DW. For example, the name field cannot have a number, and the invoice amount field should have a number.
3. **Data Modeling Tools**: These tools help in designing schema for DW.
4. **Data Governance Tools**: These tools help in documenting ownership. It manages access control for sensitive data such as Payment Card Industry (PCI), Health Insurance Portability and Accountability Act (HIPAA), and General Data Protection Regulation (GDPR) data.

With the explosion of data, DW is no longer able to support the data needs of the enterprise since it requires conversion of all enterprise data into a suitable dimension table schema for storage and access in a DW. Enterprises could not save data into DW without a suitable and profitable business use case because of DW's high storage and processing cost. This has created a need for a system enterprises can use to store data cheaply without the up-front costs for data modeling. A DL fills this gap. It enables enterprises to save data inexpensively and process it efficiently using distributed scalable computing model. There is no need to do ETL for ingesting data into a DL because a DL does not contain a predefined dimensional data model to transform the raw data into. For this reason, non-tabular data such as JSON, XML, columnar formats, log files can also be easily handled in a DL. **Table 1** shows the main differences between DW and DL.

In October of 2010, James Dixon, CTO of Pentaho, invented the term Data Lake and he described it in his blog: "*If you think of a datamart as a store of bottled water – cleansed and packaged and structured for easy consumption – the data lake is a large body of water in a more natural state. The contents of the data lake stream in from a source to fill the lake, and various users of the lake can come to examine, dive in, or take samples*".

Table 1. Key differences between DW and DL (Hai et al., 2021; Shepherd et al., 2018)

Criteria	Data Warehouse	Data Lake
Data Ingestion	ETL	Load-as-is
Ingested Data format	Structured	Heterogeneous (structured, semi-structured, and unstructured)
Data storage	Relational databases	Hadoop, Relational databases, NoSQL, etc.
Data access	SQL queries (OLTP, OLAP)	Different query languages (e.g., SQL, Cypher) Programming languages(e.g., Java, Python, R, Scala)
Processing	Schema-on-write	Schema-on-read
Agility	Less agile, fixed, and hard to modify the configuration	Highly agile, re-configuration as needed
Security	Mature	Maturing
Users	Business professionals	Data scientists, Data analysts, general users

DESIRABLE FEATURES OF A DATA LAKE SYSTEM

In this section, the authors describe the architecture of a DL and a list of important features of a DL. Authors also describe the different categorizations of a DL such as Lambda and Kappa architecture, Zone and Functional architecture, and data-linked principles.

According to (Mathis, 2017), a DL has five main components. These are *Ingestion, Storage, Processing, Data Governance, and Consumption*. Ingestion takes care of ingesting batch as well as streaming data. There are different kinds of storage such as cloud storage (HDFS, S3, GCP, etc.), On-premises storage (HDFS, NAS), and SQL or NoSQL databases. The consumption component makes data accessible to different users for their analytical needs. The data governance component consists of metadata management, search and lineage of the metadata, life cycle management, data quality, security, audit logging, and authentication & authorization.

Sawadogo and Darmont (2021) defines a DL: "A data lake is a scalable storage and analysis system for data of any type, retained in their native format and used mainly by data specialists (statisticians, data scientists or analysts) for knowledge extraction." It should have the following features:

- It should be able to ingest data in its natural raw format without requiring any designs of the tables in advance.
- It should be able to scale horizontally in terms of storage and processing since the data keeps growing with time.
- It should have a metadata management system that helps users find the correct data set quickly and accurately.
- It should have a Data Governance mechanism to protect sensitive data and for self-service access management.
- It should make the data accessible to the different end-users in their desired formats.

Since DL does not enforce schema at the time of ingestion, it becomes crucial to maintain a metadata management system. The metadata management system should be able to save business metadata such as data field names and their meanings, operational metadata such as data location and file size, and technical metadata such as field names along with the data type, lengths, etc. This will help the DL users in navigating the DL more efficiently. Without the metadata management systems, even though data is present in the DL but may not be visible to the users, this will lead to DL becoming a data swamp.

Figure 1. Data lake architecture

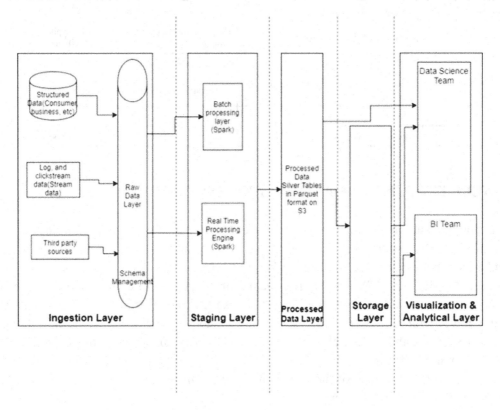

Figure 1 refers to our depiction of DL architecture. It has five layers:

1. **Ingestion Layer**: In this layer, data is ingested from various sources such as transactional databases, log and clickstream data, third-party sources, IoT, etc. Also, the data comes in different formats such as structured data from databases, semi-structured data such as JSON, XML, etc., from social media sources, or even unstructured data. It could batch or stream data. Airflow is a workflow manager for batch data processing. A batch processing job processes a large amount of data scheduled to run periodically, such as daily, weekly, etc. Kafka and Kinesis is good for ingesting stream data. Stream processing systems are near-real-time. It processes data as soon as it arrives in a smaller chunk. This allows the stream processing systems to have lower latency than batch processing systems (Kleppmann, 2017). The data is saved on the cloud storage such as AWS S3, GCP's Google cloud storage, or Azure's Blob in its raw natural format. This is the raw data layer.

2. **Staging Layer**: In this layer, data is processed in a distributed manner in Spark. Several tools are used here, such as AWS Glue, AWS EMR, or Databricks.

3. **Processed Data Layer**: Once data is processed, it is saved in Parquet format on cloud storage. Parquet format is preferred since it is saved in columnar format and compressed. This results in requiring less storage space and faster access to data.

4. **Storage Layer:** It is not convenient to connect BI tools such as Tableau or PowerBI directly with parquet files. These visualization tools need databases and tables to create dashboards and reports. This storage layer is achieved through various Data Warehouse products such as Snowflake and Redshift. Workflow manager such as Airflow is used for moving the batch-processed data to the storage layer. A streaming platform such as Kinesis or Kafka could be used for moving the stream processed data to the storage layer.

5. **Visualization and Analytical Layer:** Data Science team requires data for doing EDA, Deep learning (DL), or Machine Learning (ML). Depending on the requirement, they can get this data from the storage or the processed data layer for doing EDA, Modeling, and visualization for creating dashboards and reports.

There are mainly two DL architectures: Lambda and Kappa architecture. Lambda architecture has two branches, one for batch processing and the other for real-time processing. In Kappa architecture, everything is a stream (Lin, 2017). Reliability, Scalability, and Maintainability are the three most important concerns in software systems and are also important in a DL (Kleppmann, 2017). There are other categorizations of DL architectures, such as Zone architecture and Functional architecture (Sawadogo & Darmont, 2021). Zone architecture assigns data to a zone according to its degree of refinement. Zaloni's DL adopts a six-zone architecture: the transient loading zone, the raw data zone, the trusted zone, the discovery sandbox zone, the consumption zone, and the governance zone (LaPlante, 2016). Lambda architecture is a particular kind of zone architecture. Zone architecture of DL leads to multiple copies of the data, which makes data lineage and data analysis harder.

Functional architectures define DL's components based on the basic functions. There are four basic functions of Data Lake (LaPlante, 2016):

1. a data ingestion function to connect with data sources
2. a data storage function to persist raw as well as refined data
3. a data processing function
4. a data access function to allow raw and refined data querying.

Functional architectures help in matching required technologies since each component has clearly defined functions.

DL provides flexibility and agility in ingesting data in their original source form. Even though the analytics are not designed yet, ingested raw data can be used for any future analytics. This leads to one drawback of DL as well. Knowledge about the ingested data is lost or not recorded at the time of ingestion. It is not possible to infer the proper ways in which different datasets can be used together without this knowledge. The *linked data principles* help in mitigating this drawback (Adamou & d'Aquin, 2020). Different datasets can be associated with a set of one or more graphs, and a query engine can be used to find the meaning and association of different datasets. Linked data principles is not a set of technologies; rather, it is a paradigm that can be implemented by various evolving technology stacks. These principles follow a set of conventions (Adamou & d'Aquin, 2020):

- Use a unique identifier to reference each entity in the data.
- Make it possible for those identifiers to be looked up to by anyone.
- Use standards to represent the information that is returned by looking up those identifiers.
- Ensure that the information references other things by their identifiers wherever applicable.

If the data follow the above four design principles, then such data is called linked data. There are different metadata models such as DCMI (Dublin Core Metadata Initiative) and VoID (Vocabulary of Interlinked Datasets) that are used as a part of the Linked Data approach (Diamantini et al., 2018).

COMPARISON OF CURRENT DATA LAKE SYSTEMS

This section describes a comparative study of three popular DLs -- **Snowflake, Databricks, and Redshift**. It compares these three DLs based on nine features: Cloud object stores, ACID properties, Scale compute separately, Scale storage separately, ETL support, Cluster pool, Machine learning libraries, Open source, and Cloud agnostic.

There are various ways in which DL could be implemented. Generally, the platforms used for a DL are Hadoop, Amazon Web Services (AWS), Microsoft Azure, and Google Cloud Platform (GCP). The cost of these storage methods is generally between one-tenth and one-hundredth of a commercial database (Kachaoui, 2020). These platforms

provide an expandable storage system without degrading the performance, unlike the commercial database wherein the

storage is planned and provisioned in advance. These storage systems do not need the schema to save files, unlike the commercial database.

Snowflake

Dageville et al. (2016) describe the design of Snowflake and its multi-cluster, shared-data architecture and points out the key features of Snowflake, such as high elasticity and availability, working with semi-structured and schema-less data, time travel, and security. Time travel enables fetching changed or deleted data at any point within a configurable period. Snowflake's architecture consists mainly of three important layers: *Data storage layer* such as AWS S3, Azure, and GCP, *Virtual warehouses*, which executes the query; and *the cloud services* which manage all the other parts such as virtual warehouses, queries, and all the metadata related to the database, access control information, encryption keys, etc.

Snowflake has a *VARIANT* type which can save any kind of data without schema to be specified at the time of the ingestion and can handle large amounts of raw data efficiently. There is no need to run a cluster to access the metadata of the data stored in the DL. This helps democratize the metadata information to anyone in the organization, even without access to the actual data corresponding to the metadata. Snowflake provides role-based access control for the database objects so that access to data in the DL can be controlled carefully. It has full end-to-end data encryption capability by encrypting the data while in transfer and before writing to local disk or AWS S3. With all these capabilities, Snowflake is a good candidate for creating DL.

Databricks

Armbrust et al. (2020) describe how *Delta Lake*, Databricks DL, can maintain the integrity and consistency (popularly known as ACID properties) of the data stored in its DL. It saves the files into *Apache Parquet* format and can efficiently handle large amounts of raw data, although acquiring extra computational resources may be slow sometimes. Delta Lake DL provides the metadata for the raw data stored in the cloud. However, in order to access the metadata, one of the Delta Lake clusters must be up and running. Delta Lake uses AWS roles to implement role-based access control to the data. It has the concept of *bronze, silver*, and *gold* tables. The *bronze* table saves the raw data in its natural form, and after the transformation *silver* table is formed. The *gold* table is the aggregated version of the table that the Business Intelligence team can use directly. Delta Lake is capable of making the raw data available in different formats such as JSON, CSV, Parquet, etc.

Table 2. Data Lake comparisons

Sl. No.	Features	Snowflake	Databricks	Redshift
1	Cloud object stores	Yes	Yes	Yes
2	ACID properties	Yes	Yes	Yes
3	Scale compute separately	Yes	Yes	No
4	Scale storage separately	Yes	Yes	No
5	ETL support	Only SQL based	Yes	Only SQL based
6	Cluster pool	Yes	No	No
7	Machine learning libraries	No	Yes	No
8	Open source	No	No	No
9	Cloud agnostic	Yes	Yes	No

Delta Lake features include time travel and rollbacks, streaming ingestion, data layout optimization, caching, audit logging, schema evolution and enforcement, and connectors to query and ETL engines. In case of wrong ingestion, data can be rolled back to an old version. Due to real-time data generation, there is a need to have a streaming data pipeline. Delta Lake enables streaming data ingestion without needing a separate streaming message bus, such as Apache Kafka. Data layout optimization improves query performance significantly. Delta Lake supports data layout optimization by compacting objects, reorganizing records in a table by a given set of attributes. Caching of frequently accessed data improves query performance. This is implemented safely in Delta Lake through immutable objects. Delta Lake keeps a history of schema updates for enabling schema evolution over a period of time. Delta lake tables can be accessed by other query and ETL engines such as Redshift, Snowflake. Delta Lake connectors enable this.

Redshift

Gupta et al. (2015) describe the *Amazon Redshift* as a data warehouse that provides a columnar, scale-out architecture. It, too, has the capability to save the raw data in its natural form in the Super data type without specifying its schema upfront. It can also scale to handle large amounts of data. However, it is done by adding more *nodes,* with each *node* providing fixed compute and storage resources. Redshift is based on the PostgreSQL database and offers many security features.

Redshift has been designed for simplicity. It simplifies the purchase decision process by allowing the customer to resize clusters up or down or to a different instance type. This removes the need for the customer to do advance planning for the capacity and performance estimation. Redshift simplifies the database administration. This reduces maintenance costs for the customer. It simplifies database tuning by making less burden of tuning on customers.

As we can see from the above, all three products can save data in its natural form, easily scale the resources for supporting computation and storage as raw data sizes increase, metadata management, and security. However, their implementation is different. While Databricks uses Apache Spark as the compute engine, Snowflake has the proprietary engine built. All three of them are based on cloud storage and support the ACID properties for the transaction. In the next section, an experiment is done to compare the three tools.

The three DL systems -- *Snowflake, Databricks*, and *Redshift* were compared using various features, and the findings are summarized in **Table 2**. The meaning and importance of the features used for comparison are described below.

A cloud object store is a format for saving unstructured data in the cloud which is durable, available, and scalable. Durability is the measure of data protection from loss or corruption. Availability is the measure of how infrequently the storage system fails. Scalability is the ability of a storage system to grow with the increased storage demand. Durability, availability, and scalability make cloud object store a perfect choice for DL. All three, Snowflake, Databricks, and Redshift, support cloud object-store.

ACID properties ensure the consistency and integrity of the data in the database (or the DL). The data is accessed and possibly updated over time. This property is supported by all three.

Scaling of compute resources is critical for a data lake to handle different kinds of loads. While running analytical queries, DL needs more compute resources in order to perform aggregate and join operations. In addition, a DL should have the capability to scale compute resources to handle compute-intensive analytical queries. Only Snowflake and Databricks can scale compute resources separately from storage resources.

Scaling of storage resources is critical to handle large amounts of raw data, however, while loading data, DL should be able to scale storage resources as per demand without scaling compute resources. Only Snowflake and Databricks can scale storage resources separately.

ETL (Extract, Transform, and Load) **support** is crucial to query, store, shape, and blend the raw data in a DL. ETL can be done through the only SQL in Snowflake and Redshift. However, Databricks supports complex ETL capabilities in various powerful languages such as Pyspark, Scala, SQL, and R.

Cluster pools reduce cluster start and auto-scaling times by maintaining a set of an idle, ready-to-use clusters. Snowflake has the cluster pool capability by default. Databricks can be configured to set up a pool, and cluster can be attached to this pool. Databricks doesn't support a cluster pool by default. Redshift does not support cluster pooling.

Machine learning (ML) **libraries** help in building ML models with the data in the DL. ML libraries are available in Databricks, whereas they are not available in Snowflake or Redshift.

Open source encourages transparency, reliability and generally has a community around them. This is the reason enterprise prefers using an open-source system for which source code is available and fully visible. None of the three DL systems is open source.

A **Cloud agnostic system** is capable of being deployed in any cloud service provider. It helps businesses in choosing the appropriate cloud provider with minimal cost and the best features and be able to change the cloud provider with ease if needed. Snowflake and Databricks are cloud-agnostic, while Redshift is available only in AWS.

FUTURE RESEARCH DIRECTIONS

D

A DL provides many benefits such as the democratization of enterprise data, schema flexibility, and support for storage of data in multiple native formats. However, there is a need for tracking the lineage of data in DL. Data lineage helps in impact analysis, operational intelligence, and business terminology consistency. The current DL technologies provide little or no support for data lineage. Providing support for data lineage will further democratize a DL by making data flow more visible to everyone.

There are many challenges with data lineage. As a part of the data pipeline, data gets processed by many systems and tools. Different tools do the transformation in various programming languages, structured query languages, scripts, or even some visually. It is difficult to represent all the transformations uniformly.

Most BI tools such as Tableau and Qlik and most ETL tools like Informatica and Talend capture lineage information as the data passes through them. Some of the ETL and analysis is done using Python and R scripts. There is no lineage information captured in them. Similarly, data movement is done through FTP and SSH. There is no lineage captured in these. Lineage is useful only when it traces the data flow from source to finish. Some tools aim to fill this gap. Cloudera Navigator finds the lineage information by going through the system logs. Apache Atlas instruments the open-source systems to report lineage, and Apache Falcon lets users provide lineage information manually.

The current solutions for data lineage rely on heuristics (Cui & Widom, 2003), code analysis (Moresmau et al., 2021), and manual annotation of data (Bhagwat et al., 2005). Further research is needed to design generic solutions for data lineage in a DL.

CONCLUSION

The recent exponential growth in enterprise data combined with the need to democratize data access and monetize the data has led to the invention of Data Lake technology. Traditional relational database systems store enterprise data as relations and support massive numbers of transactions daily to retrieve and update the enterprise data. The need to discover temporal and spatial trends and other interesting nuggets of information from data has led to the invention of data warehouses that support time-consuming analytical operations on massive amounts of enterprise data. However, the need for a pre-defined data model (or schema) for a data warehouse has limited its utility as enterprises grew to acquire data in unstructured and semi-structured formats, which proved to be tedious for a DW to handle.

DL technology is popular for its flexibility to handle different raw data formats at the ingestion time as well as at the time of retrieval from the data lake. It typically includes the following five layers data ingestion, staging, processed data, storage, and visualization, and analytics. These five layers together provide access to seemingly infinite computation and storage resources for democratizing data access and for supporting a wide variety of analytics tasks in an enterprise. The three most popular DL technologies, Snowflake, Databricks, and Redshift, all provide the basic operations of a DL.

REFERENCES

Adamou, A., & d'Aquin, M. (2020). Linked data principles for data lakes. *Data Lakes*, 145–169.

Armbrust, M., Das, T., Sun, L., Yavuz, B., Zhu, S., Murthy, M., Torres, J., van Hovell, H., Ionescu, A., Luszczak, A., Świtakowski, M., Szafrański, M., Li, X., Ueshin, T., Mokhtar, M., Boncz, P., Ghodsi, A., Paranjpye, S., Senster, P., ... Zaharia, M. (2020). Delta lake: High-performance ACID table storage over cloud object stores. *Proceedings of the VLDB Endowment International Conference on Very Large Data Bases*, *13*(12), 3411–3424. doi:10.14778/3415478.3415560

Bhagwat, D., Chiticariu, L., Tan, W.-C., & Vijayvargiya, G. (2005). An annotation management system for relational databases. *The VLDB Journal*, *14*(4), 373–396. doi:10.100700778-005-0156-6

Cui, Y., & Widom, J. (2003). Lineage tracing for general data warehouse transformations. *The VLDB Journal*, *12*(1), 41–58. doi:10.100700778-002-0083-8

Dageville, B., Huang, J., Lee, A. W., Motivala, A., Munir, A. Q., Pelley, S., Povinec, P., Rahn, G., Triantafyllis, S., Unterbrunner, P., Cruanes, T., Zukowski, M., Antonov, V., Avanes, A., Bock, J., Claybaugh, J., Engovatov, D., & Hentschel, M. (2016). The snowflake elastic data warehouse. *Proceedings of the 2016 International Conference on Management of Data - SIGMOD '16*, 215–226. 10.1145/2882903.2903741

Diamantini, C., Lo Giudice, P., Musarella, L., Potena, D., Storti, E., & Ursino, D. (2018). A new metadata model to uniformly handle heterogeneous data lake sources. *European Conference on Advances in Databases and Information Systems*, 165-177. 10.1007/978-3-030-00063-9_17

Giebler, C., Gröger, C., Hoos, E., Schwarz, H., & Mitschang, B. (2019). Leveraging the data lake: Current state and challenges. *International Conference on Big Data Analytics and Knowledge Discovery*, 179–188. 10.1007/978-3-030-27520-4_13

Gorelik, A. (2019). *The enterprise big data lake: Delivering the promise of big data and data science.* O'Reilly Media, Inc.

Gupta, A., Agarwal, D., Tan, D., Kulesza, J., Pathak, R., Stefani, S., & Srinivasan, V. (2015). Amazon redshift and the case for simpler data warehouses. *Proceedings of the 2015 ACM SIGMOD International Conference on Management of Data*, 1917–1923. 10.1145/2723372.2742795

Hai, R., Quix, C., & Jarke, M. (2021). Data lake concept and systems. *Survey (London, England)*. ArXiv2106.09592

Hardy, P. M. A. (2004). *Handbook of data analysis.* SAGE. doi:10.4135/9781848608184

Kachaoui, J. (2020). From single architectural design to a reference conceptual meta-model: An intelligent data lake for new data insights. *International Journal of Emerging Trends in Engineering Research*, *8*(4), 1460–1465. doi:10.30534/ijeter/2020/85842020

Kleppmann, M. (2017). *Designing data-intensive applications: The big ideas behind reliable, scalable, and maintainable systems* (1st ed.). O'Reilly Media.

LaPlante, A. (2016). *Architecting data lakes.* O'Reilly Media.

Lin, J. (2017). The lambda and the kappa. *IEEE Internet Computing*, *21*(5), 60–66. doi:10.1109/MIC.2017.3481351

Llave, M. R. (2018). Data lakes in business intelligence: Reporting from the trenches. *Procedia Computer Science*, *138*, 516–524. doi:10.1016/j.procs.2018.10.071

Mathis, C. (2017). Data lakes. *Datenbank-Spektrum: Zeitschrift fur Datenbanktechnologie: Organ der Fachgruppe Datenbanken der Gesellschaft fur Informatik e.V, 17*(3), 289–293. doi:10.100713222-017-0272-7

Moresmau, J. P., Schyns, F., Sommerweiss, U., Grabowsky, L., Richter, J.-U., Gomes, H., Csapo, G., Baensch, K., Wiedemer, G., & Treiber, M. (2021). *Intelligent metadata management and data lineage tracing* (U.S. Patent No. 11,086,751). U.S. Patent and Trademark Office.

Nargesian, F., Zhu, E., Miller, R. J., Pu, K. Q., & Arocena, P. C. (2019). Data lake management: Challenges and opportunities. *Proceedings of the VLDB Endowment International Conference on Very Large Data Bases, 12*(12), 1986–1989. doi:10.14778/3352063.3352116

Sawadogo, P., & Darmont, J. (2021). On data lake architectures and metadata management. *Journal of Intelligent Information Systems, 56*(1), 97–120. doi:10.100710844-020-00608-7

Shepherd, A., Kesa, C., Cooper, J., Onema, J., & Kovacs, P. (2018). Opportunities and challenges associated with implementing data lakes for enterprise decision-making. *Issues in Information Systems, 19*(1).

Silberschatz, A., Korth, H. F., & Sudarshan, S. (2020). *Database system concepts*. McGraw-Hill.

Zagan, E., & Danubianu, M. (2020). Data lake approaches: A survey. *2020 International Conference on Development and Application Systems (DAS)*, 189–193. 10.1109/DAS49615.2020.9108912

ADDITIONAL READING

Couto, J., Borges, O., Ruiz, D., Marczak, S., & Prikladnicki, R. (2019). A mapping study about data lakes: an improved definition and possible architectures. 31st international conference on software engineering and knowledge engineering (SEKE 2019), 453–458. doi:10.18293/SEKE2019-129

Curino, C., Moon, H. J., Deutsch, A., & Zaniolo, C. (2013). Automating the database schema evolution process. *The VLDB Journal, 22*(1), 73–98. doi:10.100700778-012-0302-x

Diamantini, C., Giudice, P. L., Musarella, L., Potena, D., Storti, E., & Ursino, D. (2018). A New Metadata Model to Uniformly Handle Heterogeneous Data Lake Sources. *European Conference on Advances in Databases and Information Systems*, 165– 177. 10.1007/978-3-030-00063-9_17

Giebler, C., Groger, C., Hoos, E., Schwarz, H., & Mitschang, B. (2019). Leveraging the data lake - current state ˙ and challenges. *Proceedings of the 21st international conference on big data analytics and knowledge discovery*, 179-188. 10.1007/978-3-030-27520-4_13

Inmon, B. (2016). *Data Lake architecture: Designing the Data Lake and avoiding the garbage dump*. Technics Publications.

Klettke, M., Awolin, H., St¨orl, U., M¨uller, D., & Scherzinger, S. (2017). Uncovering the evolution history of data lakes. *IEEE International Conference on Big Data*, 2462–2471. 10.1109/BigData.2017.8258204

LaPlante, A., & Sharma, B. (2016). *Architecting data lakes data management architectures for advanced business use cases*. O'Reilly Media Inc.

Mehmood, H., Gilman, E., Cortes, M., Kostakos, P., Byrne, A., Valta, K., Tekes, S., & Riekki, J. (2019). Implementing big data lake for heterogeneous data sources. *2019 IEEE 35Th International Conference on Data Engineering Workshops*, 37–44. 10.1109/ICDEW.2019.00-37

Ravat, F., & Zhao, Y. (2019). Metadata management for data lakes. *23rd European Conference on Advances in Databases and Information Systems*, 37-44. 10.1007/978-3-030-30278-8_5

Wibowo, M., Sulaiman, S., & Shamsuddin, S. M. (2017). Machine Learning in Data Lake for Combining Data Silos. *International Conference on Data Mining and Big Data*, 294–306. 10.1007/978-3-319-61845-6_30

KEY TERMS AND DEFINITIONS

ACID: ACID is an acronym that stands for Atomicity, Consistency, Isolation, and Durability. In case of failures, these properties ensure the accuracy and integrity of the data in the database.

Cloud Agnostic: Cloud agnostic system is capable of being deployed in any cloud service provider. It helps businesses in choosing the appropriate cloud provider with minimal cost and the best features.

Cluster: A cluster is a set of compute nodes that work in sync to process a job. The job could be data engineering, data science, analytics, or any machine learning workload.

Cluster Pool: Cluster pool is a set of idle and ready-to-use instances. This reduces cluster start time as instances are waiting to be used as a part of cluster nodes.

Compute Resources: Compute resources provide processing capabilities. More processing is required for a compute-intensive process such as processing complex analytical queries.

EDA: EDA stands for Exploratory Data Analysis. It is essential to understand data in order to apply various machine learning techniques. The technique is used to analyze data sets by summarizing their main characteristics.

ETL: ETL stands for Extract, Transform, and Load. It is a data integration tool through which various data sources in different formats can be consolidated into a single location, such as Data Warehouse.

Schema: A schema defines data organization such as field order, its type (string, integer, etc.). Also, it describes the relationships between tables in a given database by defining primary and foreign keys.

Storage Resources: Storage resources provide physical storage space capability. Suppose a DL grows in size, but its analytical queries requirement remains same. In this particular case, more physical storage space is required to save increased size of DL however compute resources remain the same.

Streaming: Data generated in real-time continuously.

Datafied Modelling of Self–Disclosure in Online Health Communication

Adamkolo Mohammed Ibrahim
https://orcid.org/0000-0003-1662-7054
University of Maiduguri, Nigeria

Hajara Umar Sanda
Bayero University, Kano, Nigeria

Nassir Abba-Aji
University of Maiduguri, Nigeria

Md Salleh Hassan
Universiti Putra Malaysia, Malaysia

Phuong Thi Vi
https://orcid.org/0000-0002-5914-3626
Thai Nguyen University, Vietnam

INTRODUCTION

People are seeking and sharing health information online in greater numbers as information and communication technologies (ICTs) advance (Oh, & Syn, 2015). Seventy-two per cent of adult internet users in the United States have reported looking for medical information online (Rideout, & Fox, 2018). Online health support communities (OHSCs) have risen to prominence as a valuable resource for doctors, patients, and caregivers (Liu, Liu, & Guo, 2020). The literature shows that online health support communities play a critical role in creating a virtual space that is accessible to people from all over the world for those dealing with potentially fatal diseases (Abiola, Udofia, & Zakari, 2013; Huang, ChengalurSmith, & Pinsonneault, 2019). This is especially important for chronic diseases like diabetes, where patients expect not only to receive ongoing medical treatment but also to receive support and companionship from others who have had similar experiences. In exchange for personalised suggestions and peer support, one user participation mechanism commonly seen in online health support communities is the generation of a large amount of personal information and emotional feelings (Fernandes, & Costa, 2021). According to previous research, online health support community users are willing to share their personal information publicly to take advantage of the convenience of online services (Atanasova, Kamin, & Petrič, 2018; Cavusoglu Phan, Cavusoglu, & Airoldi, 2016; Jozani, Ayaburi, Ko, & Choo, 2020). Online health support community users can gain medical knowledge, emotional comfort, and strengthen both online and offline social connections through active engagement (Wang, Zhao, & Street, 2017). As a result, user-generated content, particularly those involving self-disclosure, are the fundamental building blocks that distinguish online health support communities and contribute to both the provision and the seeking of social support.

DOI: 10.4018/978-1-7998-9220-5.ch026

Copyright © 2023, IGI Global. Copying or distributing in print or electronic forms without written permission of IGI Global is prohibited.

Although online health support community users' information disclosure "may meet their basic needs for obtaining social support and forming social connections, when they give up some degree of privacy and personal control," they risk exposing their personal data (Liu, Miltgen, & Xia, 2022). Meanwhile, disclosed personal information leads to easily retrievable digital traces that can be collected by a variety of parties, resulting in unexpected privacy intrusions (Jain, Sahoo, & Kaubiyal, 2021) such as malicious attacks (e.g., phishing), illegal interests (e.g., doxing), and crimes (e.g., burglary, racketeering, and robbery). According to Walters (2017), most adult internet users are concerned about their personal information being disclosed on the internet, which can be used to identify a user's political inclination, purchasing habits, lifestyles, and so on (Wu, 2019).

As a result, digital footprints can be consolidated to profile a person efficiently and precisely, revealing more information than ever before. Health data, as a type of personal information, is extremely sensitive and valuable, if not the most valuable, to not only the individuals who possess it but also to companies and governments, particularly when the contents are expressed through personal narratives (Ma, Zuo, M., & Liu, 2021). Users' lack of awareness of privacy management during information exchange in online health support communities may result in the disclosure of personal characteristics such as identity, medical records, test results, and insurance details, to name a few. Furthermore, sensitive information like this can accumulate over time, resulting in unintended consequences and biases against users, even if the disclosure is intended for seeking or providing support with fellow online health support community users. For example, a patient's therapeutic trajectory can be determined by analysing many of their online posts over time (Abiola et al., 2013; Taylor, & Pagliari, 2018). Similarly, patients in online health support communities face a dilemma of self-disclosure: while it is associated with negative outcomes, it is unavoidable in obtaining social support from other online health support community users.

While a large body of literature has contributed to a better understanding of online health support community users' disclosure patterns, current research is lacking in the following areas. Firstly, many previous studies relied on surveys or interviews to investigate users' privacy perceptions, which can sometimes fail to accurately reflect users' actual personal information disclosure behaviours in the real world, e.g., privacy paradox (e.g., Atanasova et al., 2018; Cavusoglu et al., 2016; Wu, Vitak, & Zimmer, 2020). Secondly, while user role (Wang, Zuo, & Zhao,, 2015a) is an important concept in online health support communities research, it is rarely considered when researching self-disclosure behaviours. Furthermore, the changing intentions of one's self-disclosure patterns in online health support communities are expected to be revealed by the dynamic nature of user roles. To address these gaps, this study adds a new construct of altruistic user role (AUR) to Fishbein and Ajzen's theory of reasoned action (Fishbein, & Ajzen, 1975; LaCaille, 2020). The chapter presents a conceptual framework developed from a data-driven computationally intensive review of literature for a study using a set of publicly available data from a peertopeer online health support communities designed for diabetic patients, using a mix of methods including manual coding, deep learning-based text mining techniques and econometric analysis. The implications of the proposed modified Theory of Reasoned Action are discussed.

BACKGROUND

TuDiabetes.Org PeertoPeer Online Health Support Community

To address the proposed research questions, this study focuses on TuDiabetes.org, a peertopeer online health support community for diabetic people and their caregivers. The advantages of utilising this online health support community are threefold. First, TuDiabetes.org focuses on interactions between diabetic patients and their caregivers. Unlike platforms where patients consult physicians on a variety of health issues, TuDiabetes.org has a more relaxed vibe for informal communication, intending to facilitate peer support. Second, diabetes is a long-term illness. As a result, people require constant information and encouragement during and after treatments, and ample diagnostic and therapeutic stories must be provided over time. TuDiabetes.org has also been around for over 13 years.

Major technological advancements are influencing the rapid evolution of virtual health communities. This rapid adoption demonstrates the virtual health support forums' ability to assist patients, caregivers, families, and healthcare professionals. TuDiabetes.org is a vibrant, peer-to-peer virtual health support community for people living with diabetes, their families, and caregivers. Because it represents a vibrant, virtual healthy community on the internet, it was chosen for analysis in this study. In a safe and unsupervised environment, members are free to share and express their thoughts. Understanding the communication threads of members within a vibrant, virtual healthy online community can be gained by investigating how they share thoughts within this community (Abiola et al., 2013; Johnson, Islind, Lindroth, Angenete, & Gellerstedt, 2021; Litchman, Walker, Ng, Wawrzynski, 2019; McMahon, 2013).

Furthermore, as an online health support community, TuDiabetes.org is a virtual community of people living with all types of diabetes, had more than 35,000 registered members (50% have type 1 diabetes, 20% have type 2 diabetes, and 30% are labelled others) as of September 2014, and EsTuDiabetes.org, its Spanish-language counterpart, had more than 29,000 registered members (20% had type 1 diabetes, 50% had type 2 diabetes, and 30% were labelled others (Litchman et al., 2019).

Every month, thousands of unique visitors visit popular diabetes blogs. A live, weekly one-hour forum on Twitter using hashtags #dsma (Short for Diabetes Social Media Advocacy), where people with diabetes interact in real-time: in 2010, there was an average of 40-50 participants per week, current rates average 60-100 participants posting 700-1000 comments per week, depending on the topic and time of year. In 2007, the sites TuDiabetes and EsTuDiabetes were launched as the first social networks for people with diabetes and their families. TuDiabetes and EsTuDiabetes both had over 65,000 registered members and more than 200,000 monthly visitors (Litchman et al., 2019; Mukta, Paik, Lu, & Kanhere, 2022).

According to the website, TuDiabetes.org (2011), is a virtual community for people affected by diabetes and it is run by the Diabetes Hands Foundation, which is a non-profit organisation. It is an online community where "members assist one another, educate ourselves, and share the daily steps we take to stay healthy while living with this extremely dangerous condition" (TuDiabetes.org, Tab About Us, 2011). Community support, health and wellness, communication and information, diversity and respect, creative expression, and transparency are all values that members hold dear. It has housed TuDiabetes.org since its inception in 2007 (Litchman et al., 2019). The virtual community currently has over 19,290 members who are diabetics or family members of diabetics. Members can create their own pages, invite friends, and join member groups (Wikipedia.com, 2019).

METHODS

The study conducts a datadriven computationallyintensive theory development using a set of publicly available data from a peertopeer online health support communities designed for diabetic patients, using a mix of methods including manual coding, deep learning-based text mining techniques and econometric analysis. The literature was reviewed considering the data generated. Peer communication is primarily accomplished through user-generated textual content, which reflects user behaviour to a large extent.

The largescale unstructured textual data that results provides an enormous opportunity for datadriven analytic approaches to understanding selfdisclosure behaviour using cuttingedge deep learning techniques. Between October 2008 and September 2019, 3.8 million public posts were retrieved from over 18,300 registered users which were used to answer the research questions. Manually coding each of the 3.8 million posts would be extremely difficult, if not impossible. Machine learning methods were employed to detect selfdisclosure and social support in the posts using a preannotated training set based on a curated guideline as shown in Tables 1and 2. The reviewed literature was sourced based on the curated guidelines (codes and themes) in Tables 1 and 2.

Table 1. Annotation of Social Support

Type of Support	Definition
Informational support	Transmission of information and guidance. The content of the post is related to pieces of advice, referrals, teaching and personal experience with treatment or symptoms, which might include medical information for the patients. Such support can help users get better knowledge on how to handle their conditions.
Emotional support	transmitted through sharing poignant events: the expression of understanding or empathy that the patient is not alone, the post of encouragement that the patient could get better with a particular treatment. Emotional support content contains affection, affirming, validation, sympathy, caring concern etc., which can help the patients reduces their levels of stress.

Table 2. Annotation of Self-Disclosure

Category	Coding Guideline	Example of Posts
Disclosing Identity Information (IDInfo)	This is related to narrative content about a user's identity, such as name, gender, resident location, emails, photos, affiliations, etc. This genre is usually by no means directly relevant to users' knowledge and physical well-being, yet imposing high privacy costs	"You sound like a good trooper! You also must be a great nurse! Both my father and sister are nurses."
Disclosing Personal Health Information (PHI)	Describes clinical information related to diabetes history, symptoms, treatments, and outcomes, such as time of diagnosis, diabetes stage/type, treatment progress, and regimen	"I have had the wound in my leg for 7 weeks and it has gotten a little larger and the needle-like pain isn't getting better."
Multi-categories	A mix of IDInfo and PHI	"Well....saw the specialist at the University Hospital, Diabetes Department. The doctor was very blunt and to the point. ... He thinks I should not have any more surgeries because my innate lymphoid cells (ILC) is everywhere and it would be like having four flat tires and only changing one… I appreciate your friendships. I'm glad that none of you has this crazy combination that I have. Take care, Julie."

REVIEW OF LITERATURE

The Concept of Social Support in Online Health Support Communities

Since the last decade, online health support communities have been useful channels for seeking and sharing health-related information (Oh, & Syn, 2015). The benefits of online health support communities include unhindered, round the clock accessibility to people beyond the restrictions of geographical boundaries, cost savings, lack of embarrassment and diverse support networks (Chen, Baird, & Straub,

2019; Zhang, Liu, Chen, Wang, Gao, & Zhu, 2018a). As a series of virtual discussion groups consisting of members who share collective interests and concerns in health topics (Dulli, Ridgeway, Packer, Plourde, Mumuni, Idaboh et al., 2018; Wang, Zhao, & Street, 2017), social support can help patients and their families cope with daily stress and fight diseases (Sun, Zhang, & Feng, 2022). Collaboration is at the heart of online health support community existence and growth. Members of online health support communities interact online with similar peers to seek, receive, and provide various types of social support (Ibegbulam, Akpom, Enem, & Onyam, 2018; Wang et al., 2017).

The term "social support" usually refers to an exchange of resources between individuals to improve the receiver's well-being (Uchino, Bowen, Kent de Grey, Mikel, & Fisher, 2018). According to the nature of exchanged resources, community psychologists have identified different types of social support, such as informational support, emotional support, companionship, and instrumental support (Farsi, Martinez-Menchaca, Ahmed, & Farsi, 2022; Rueger, Dolfsma, & Aalbers, 2021). Informational and emotional support are the main targets for examining social support in online communities (e.g., Chen et al., 2019; Huang et al., 2019; Moore, 2022), as they are the most common types of social support (Huang et al., 2019). On the other hand, there is no clear guidance on how to seek or provide social support when it comes to companionship. It is, rather, a two-way relationship between users on both ends (Wang et al., 2017). Instrumental support is usually limited by geographical proximity (Dulli et al., 2018; Gilligan, Suitor, Rurka, & Silverstein, 2020). It refers to the assistance received physically or tangibly, such as calling for an mbulance or receiving medicine delivery. As a result, it is rarely the primary mode of social exchange in online health support communities. Following previous research, this study focuses on informational and emotional support seeking or seeking social support (SSS) and providing social support (PSS).

The Concept of Self Disclosure in Online Health Support Communities

In today's information age driven by the digital revolution, various online communities have large amounts of user-generated content, which is frequently accompanied by personal data. Information disclosure is simply defined as "...the personal information individuals intentionally and voluntarily reveal about themselves to others in an interpersonal relationship..." (Lowry, Cao, & Everard, 2011, p. 11), which implies the prevalence of self-disclosure in virtual spaces such as e-banking, ecommerce, social network services and geographical location-based services (Dulli et al., 2018; Lowry et al., 2011).

Personal information must be shared in the context of online health support communities, which differs from other online communities in terms of their unique participation group, motivation and demands (Shannon, Jansen, Williams, Cáceres, Motta, Odhiambo et al., 2019). One distinguishing feature from a health epidemiological standpoint is the complexities and nuances of health issues. For example, eating organic honey may improve cardiovascular health but it also increases the risk of raising blood sugar, which is not advisable for diabetic patients to consume. This suggests that decontextualising health messages for online health support community users may result in ambiguity or even mismatched support (Yan, 2018). Similarly, the extent to which online health support community users disclose their personal situations influences the quality of online health consultation and diagnosis (Abiola et al., 2013; Zhang, Liu, Chen, Wang, Gao, & Zhu, 2018b). As a result, when an online health support community user with diabetes seeks social support online, they must more or less disclose personal information such as age, diabetes type, medication, health records, and so on for fellow users to provide more appropriate and personalised social support. When involving one's own experience, a post attempting to provide social support to others can be perceived as convincing and empathetic. However, online health support community users may be concerned about potential risks associated with selfdisclosure of personal information that could be used for commercial purposes without proper authorization. As a result, selfdisclosure plays a paradoxical role in online health support communities, facilitating social support exchange while also exposing users to the risk of information leakage.

This study, which is based on Le, Hoang, & Pham (2022) and Wu et al. (2020) works, focuses on two types of selfdisclosure:

1. Identity information (IDInfo): This refers to narrative content about a user's identity, such as a user's name, gender, residence, emails, photos, affiliations, and so on. This genre is usually unrelated to users' knowledge or physical well-being, but it imposes high privacy costs that prevent users from disclosing such information; and
2. Personal health information (PHI): This refers to clinical information about cancer history, symptoms, treatments, and outcomes. This category also includes the time of diagnosis, cancer stage, treatment progress and regimen.

The Concept of Altruistic User Roles in Online Health Support Communities

Online health support community users' voluntary contributions may transit into different levels based on their social interactions online, motivated by mechanisms such as reciprocity, peer recognition, and selfimage (Kokkodis et al., 2020). During the various stages of involvement in online health support communities, users may play distinct social roles in seeking and providing social support (Wang, Zuo, & Zhao, 2015b). According to Voss (2021), and Jawad and Al-Khalidi (2021), people have two basic interests – one for themselves and one for others – and they are expected to behave differently and play different roles in their communities (Zhang et al., 2019). Selfcentered users in online health support communities, in particular, are preoccupied with their own health issues, whereas altruistic members are more concerned with the needs of others.

Furthermore, the user role is dynamic and can change over time for two reasons. First, a user's priorities may shift, resulting in a role shift in online health support communities. For example, a newly diagnosed patient may have questions or concerns about their health condition, prompting them to seek support through an online health support community. With more knowledge and experience, they may evolve into information providers who frequently provide social support motivated by altruism, indicating a shift from a selfcentered to a communitycentered user role. Second, peer interactions in online health support communities can have an impact on users' future roles. Receiving informational support, for example, is linked to users' future role as communitycentered contributors. As a result, when analysing online health support community user behaviours, it is both important and necessary to consider the temporal characteristics (Ibegbulam et al., 2018; Wang et al., 2015b).

Modifying the Theory of Reasoned Action in the Context of Online Health Support Communities

Privacy Calculus in the Context of the Theory of Reasoned Action

The Theory of Reasoned Action (Fishbein, & Ajzen, 1975; LaCaille, 2020) is a general account of the determinants of volitional behaviour that aims to explain and predict volitional behaviour by looking at the underlying basic motivation to do something. According to the Theory of Reasoned Action, one's intention to (or not to) performs a given behaviour is determined by two factors, namely one's attitude toward the behaviour and one's subjective norm. In particular, an attitude refers to how people feel about a particular behaviour, whereas subjective norm refers to one's general perception of whether important others want to see the behaviour performed. In other words, both personal attitudinal judgments and social normative considerations influence intentions. The determinant of one's attitudinal component, in particular, is her primary belief about whether or not the associated outcome is positive, as well as her level of confidence in that belief. The normative component's determinants are based on her assessment of specific salient others' normative expectations, i.e., what I believe other online health support community users want me to do. In addition, subjective norm is also dependent on the individual's motivation to comply with those referents, i.e., how much I want to do what other online health support community users think I should do.

Social support represents the users' anticipated positive outcomes, whereas negative outcomes as cost are proportional to the extent of one's selfdisclosure due to potential privacy leakage. People's motivation to conform to their social circle's views and perceptions is considered by the subjective norm, which refers to the perceived social pressure to perform or not perform a behaviour. The extent of selfdisclosure in terms of personal health information and identity information from nonfocal users is conceptualised as subjective norm in the context of this study.

Online health support community users are expected to disclose personal information to obtain social support, which is also required to meet the demand for community benefits. Meanwhile, emotional support takes the form of reciprocally supportive exchanges of providing and receiving similar support. Receiving assistance without offering assistance can result in feelings of guilt, shame and inability to live independently (Zhang et al., 2018b). In emotional communication, open and sincere disclosures of private intimate information, such as sharing feelings and fantasies, have been seen as an important sign of a close relationship (Trepte, 2021). As a result, users are typically willing to share their personal health information and/or identity information in an online health support community in exchange for information and/or emotional support.

Incorporating Altruistic User Role in the Theory of Reasoned Action

Selfcentered interests, communitycentred interests, or both motivate online health support community users to participate in the community. Users with different motivations have different behavioural patterns when it comes to selfdisclosure intentions. The different roles users play help to achieve the balance of online health support communities in terms of seeking and providing social support. By exhibiting health support-seeking behaviours in their early stages in an online health support community, where they are more likely to disclose personal information, users can primarily contribute to social support provision after they gain more experience with a particular chronic disease. In addition to the attitudinal and normative components in the original Theory of Reasoned Action, altruistic user role (AUR), as well as its transition can provide important signals to understand online health support community users' disclosure behaviour.

Given the discourse above, the following research question (RQ) was asked:

RQ1: What is the relationship between one's 'altruistic user role' and his or her follow-up selfdisclosure behaviour in an online health support community?

Furthermore, when confronted with lifethreatening problems, people are more likely to take risks with selfdisclosure than when confronted with other themes such as goods, investment, or public affairs (Peng, Cao, Zhang, Cao, Zhang, Zhu, & Miao, 2021). Indeed, for a newcomer to an online health support community who has recently been diagnosed with a disease, the desire to seek support from others who have gone through similar experiences may intuitively strengthen her intention to disclose personal information with little regard for potential privacy risks (Zhang et al., 2018b). It is also possible that she simply observes and consumes posts from others in similar situations, resulting in low selfdisclosure intentions. Providers, on the other hand, maybe prone to selfdisclosure to demonstrate empathy. In the meantime, one can offer assistance without divulging any personal information. Generic encouragements or facts, on the other hand, can cheer up those who need assistance.

Given the discourse above, the following RQ was asked:

RQ2: Does 'altruistic user role' moderate the relationship between one's attitude and his or her follow-up self-disclosure intention in an online health support community?

Meanwhile, according to the Theory of Reasoned Action, online health support community users are motivated to follow the rules of their peers. However, the intensity of such motivation varies depending on the user's role. Whether a user seeks or provides assistance, his or her behaviour intention can be influenced by other users in the same online health support community. Reciprocity is a prominent feature of online health support communities and refers to a mutual exchange between users. It is a critical predictor of follow-up social support provision (Zhang et al., 2018b). It emphasises users' willingness to repay favours to others, particularly those who have previously aided them (Bauer, & Ariely, 2021). Inaction, on the other hand, will wreak havoc on the online health support community's healthy, functional, and dynamic environments. Given the various motivations of various user roles, the extent to which others' selfdisclosure patterns may have different effects on one's future disclosure intention is unknown. Figure 1 shows the modified Theory of Reasoned Action in online health support communities (OHSCs).

Given the discourse above, the following RQ was asked:

RQ3: Does 'altruistic user role' influence the relationship between one's subjective norm and his or her follow-up self-disclosure intention in an online health support community?

Identifying Health Support Posts with Self Disclosure and Social Support Likelihoods

Online health support community users' posts serve as a conduit for datadriven detection via text mining, which outperforms surveys and questionnaires in terms of reducing subjective biases and handling large amounts of digital trace data. It is worth noting that a post can disclose both identity information and personal health information at the same time, each with its own set of key characteristics. This study could assess the predictive probabilities for each post regarding their likelihoods of disclosing IDInfo, disclosing PHI, PSS and SSS, manifesting posting users' intentions to take the corresponding actions, by applying the bestperforming classification models to the rest of this study's dataset.

Finally, it is worth noting that the proposed theoretical framework applies to user selfdisclosure behaviours in peertopeer online health support communities. The contributors are motivated by mental rewards rather than professional or monetary gains, unlike their physiciandriven counterparts (see Dulli et al., 2018; Liu et al., 2020; Wang, Yan, Zhou, Guo, & Heim, 2020). As a result, such an online health

Figure 1. The modified Theory of Reasoned Action in the context of online health communities with Altruistic User Role (AUR)

Note: *A positive link is directly put from attitude and subjective norm towards behavioural intention (self-disclosure intention) based on the Theory of Reasoned Action.*

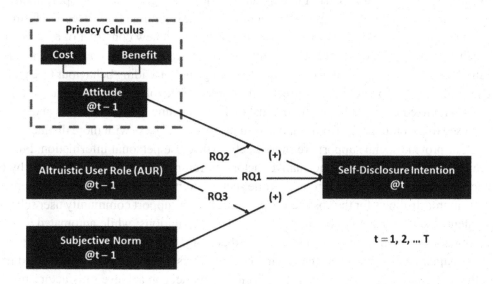

support community must maintain a group of actively engaged users to sustain the community and assist others who require contextrelated assistance.

FUTURE RESEARCH DIRECTIONS

Finally, this chapter suggests some future directions. Firstly, it is recommended that future research should provide the outcomes on the delineation of the relationship between users' support exchange behaviour and selfdisclosure intention as well as the modification of the theory of reasoned action by the incorporation of a new construct, namely altruistic user role (AUR), which captures user inclination toward providing or seeking social support. While the proposed modified version of the Theory of Reasoned Action was developed in the context of online health support communities, it can be adapted to better understand user behaviours in other types of online communities that involve user support exchange. The success and activity of online question and answer (Q&A) communities such as StackExchange and Quora, for example, is largely dependent on user engagement. The modified Theory of Reasoned Action proposed in this paper may reveal a variety of user behaviours in addition to selfdisclosure by adapting the constructs to specific contexts. Furthermore, future research could explore a wider range of online health forums and use direct interaction with users to learn more about their perspectives. It would also be beneficial to compare the benefits and risks of moderated versus unmoderated online health forums, which have the potential to reduce the spread of misinformation (e.g., Moore, & Ayers, 2017). In addition, further research should be conducted to determine whether online health forums promote mistrust of healthcare professionals and, if so, how best to address this issue.

CONCLUSION

Online health support communities play an important role in promoting good health. There are few theoretical frameworks dedicated to better understanding the exchange of social support in the literature on user behaviour in online health support communities. By developing this conceptual framework for incorporation into the modified Theory of Reasoned Action with a new construct of altruistic user role (AUR), which is an important concept in the context of online health support communities, this chapter aims to gain a better understanding of users' support-seeking and -providing behaviour (see Huang et al., 2019; Wang et al., 2017). To uncover the direct and indirect effects of user role on one's future selfdisclosure intention, mixed methods including manual coding, machine learning models and econometric analyses are used to develop theory from a datadriven perspective. Users with more distinct inclinations to either seek or provide social support are more likely to disclose personal information. Furthermore, the positive effects of attitudinal and normative factors on future disclosure are amplified by the relative tendency of support provision. Moreover, while such a computationally intensive theoretical model modification approach allows for the abstraction of online health support community user selfdisclosure behaviour intentions, this chapter is bound by two possible limitations: while automated text analytics could make it easier to label millions of usergenerated content, the applied classifications are far from perfect. This chapter argues, however, that such labelling errors would be minor and would have little impact on the data analysis, given that this study's current model can achieve satisfactory results.

Furthermore, by breaking down the concept of privacy concerns, this chapter contributes to our understanding of patients' privacy preferences. Different types of information trigger different concerns and different users have different concerns. Understanding privacy concerns and sharing behaviour from the patient's perspective is an ongoing process, as the technology and user base of online health communities are constantly changing (e.g., Farnood, Johnston, & Mair, 2021). However, this knowledge is necessary to maximise the positive impact of online health communities on wellbeing.

This research has implications for the creation of online health support communities. Reading and reviewing content from online communities has been shown to have significant benefits for many patient groups (Farnood et al., 2021; Kaufman, & Whitehead, 2018). There are now several types of online health communities, some of which protect identity to the extent that patients can only log in individually to access their medical records so that confidentiality is maintained. Kaiser Permanente's "My Health Manager" and Mayo Clinic's "Patient Online Services" are a few examples of such forums. Whereas others build on existing social networks without the appearance of anonymity. Genentech's "Circle of Support" app for breast cancer patients and the "Cancer Sucks!" community are a few examples. This chapter suggests a middle ground. Systems should protect patient anonymity while facilitating the sharing of clinical information to meet patient preferences.

REFERENCES

Abiola, T., Udofia, O., & Zakari, M. (2013). Psychometric properties of the 3-item Oslo social support scale among clinical students of Bayero University Kano, Nigeria. *Malaysian Journal of Psychiatry*, 22(2), 32–41.

Atanasova, S., Kamin, T., & Petrič, G. (2018). The benefits and challenges of online professional-patient interaction: Comparing views between users and health professional moderators in an online health community. *Computers in Human Behavior*, *83*, 106–118. doi:10.1016/j.chb.2018.01.031

Bauer, P. J., & Ariely, D. (2021). Expression of concern: effort for payment: A tale of two markets. *Psychological Science*, *32*(8), 1338–1339. doi:10.1177/09567976211035782 PMID:34296633

Cavusoglu, H., Phan, T. Q., Cavusoglu, H., & Airoldi, E. M. (2016). Assessing the impact of granular privacy controls on content sharing and disclosure on Facebook. *Information Systems Research*, *27*(4), 848–879. doi:10.1287/isre.2016.0672

Chen, L., Baird, A., & Straub, D. (2019). Fostering participant health knowledge and attitudes: An econometric study of a chronic disease-focused online health community. *Journal of Management Information Systems*, *36*(1), 194–229. doi:10.1080/07421222.2018.1550547

Dulli, L., Ridgeway, K., Packer, C., Plourde, K. F., Mumuni, T., Idaboh, T., Olumide, A., Ojengbede, O., & McCarraher, D. R. (2018). An online support group intervention for adolescents living with HIV in Nigeria: A pre-post test study. *JMIR Public Health and Surveillance*, *4*(4), e12397. doi:10.2196/12397 PMID:30487116

Farnood, A., Johnston, B., & Mair, F. S. (2021). Understanding the use of heart failure online health forums: A qualitative study. *European Journal of Cardiovascular Nursing*. Advance online publication. doi:10.1093/eurjcn/zvab090 PMID:34739058

Farsi, D., Martinez-Menchaca, H. R., Ahmed, M., & Farsi, N. (2022). Social media and health care (Part II): Narrative review of social media use by patients. *Journal of Medical Internet Research*, *24*(1), e30379. doi:10.2196/30379 PMID:34994706

Fernandes, T., & Costa, M. (2021). Privacy concerns with COVID-19 tracking apps: A privacy calculus approach. *Journal of Consumer Marketing*. doi:10.1108/JCM-03-2021-4510

Fishbein, M., & Ajzen, I. (1975). *Intention and behaviour: An introduction to theory and research.* Addison-Wesley. doi:10.4236/tel.2018.813176

Gilligan, M., Suitor, J. J., Rurka, M., & Silverstein, M. (2020). Multigenerational social support in the face of the COVID-19 pandemic. *Journal of Family Theory & Review*, *12*(4), 431–447. doi:10.1111/jftr.12397 PMID:34367339

Huang, K. Y., Chengalur-Smith, I. S., & Pinsonneault, A. (2019). Sharing is caring: Social support provision and companionship activities in healthcare virtual support communities. *Management Information Systems Quarterly*, *43*(2), 395–424. doi:10.25300/MISQ/2019/13225

Ibegbulam, I. J., Akpom, C. C., Enem, F. N., & Onyam, D. I. (2018). Use of the internet as a source for reproductive health information seeking among adolescent girls in secondary schools in Enugu, Nigeria. *Health Information and Libraries Journal*, *35*(4), 298–308. doi:10.1111/hir.12242 PMID:30426642

Jain, A. K., Sahoo, S. R., & Kaubiyal, J. (2021). Online social networks security and privacy: Comprehensive review and analysis. *Complex & Intelligent Systems*, *7*(5), 2157–2177. doi:10.100740747-021-00409-7

Jawad, H. H., & Al-Khalidi, M. A. (2021). Foundations of the social theory of Weber. *Al-Adab Journal*, *1*(138, Supplement 1), 383–396. doi:10.31973/aj.v2i138.1739

Johansson, V., Islind, A. S., Lindroth, T., Angenete, E., & Gellerstedt, M. (2021). Online Communities as a Driver for Patient Empowerment: Systematic Review. *Journal of Medical Internet Research*, *23*(2), e19910. doi:10.2196/19910 PMID:33560233

Jozani, M., Ayaburi, E., Ko, M., & Choo, K. K. R. (2020). Privacy concerns and benefits of engagement with social media-enabled apps: A privacy calculus perspective. *Computers in Human Behavior*, *107*, 106260. doi:10.1016/j.chb.2020.106260

Kaufman, S., & Whitehead, K. A. (2018). Producing, ratifying, and resisting support in an online support forum. *Health*, *22*(3), 223–239. doi:10.1177/1363459315628043 PMID:26851264

Kokkodis, M., Lappas, T., & Ransbotham, S. (2020). From lurkers to workers: Predicting voluntary contribution and community welfare. *Information Systems Research*, *31*(2), 607–626. doi:10.1287/isre.2019.0905

LaCaille, L. (2020). Theory of reasoned action. In M. D. Gellman (Ed.), *Encyclopedia of behavioural medicine* (pp. 2231–2234). Springer. doi:10.1007/978-3-030-39903-0_1619

Le, L. H., Hoang, P. A., & Pham, H. C. (2022). Sharing health information across online platforms: A systematic review. *Health Communication*, 1–13. doi:10.1080/10410236.2021.2019920 PMID:34978235

Litchman, M. L., Walker, H. R., Ng, A. H., Wawrzynski, S. E., Oser, S. M., Greenwood, D. A., Gee, P. M., Lackey, M., & Oser, T. K. (2019). State of the science: A scoping review and gap analysis of diabetes online communities. *Journal of Diabetes Science and Technology*, *13*(3), 466–492. doi:10.1177/1932296819831042 PMID:30854884

Liu, B., Miltgen, C. L., & Xia, H. (2022). Disclosure decisions and the moderating effects of privacy feedback and choice. *Decision Support Systems*, *113717*. Advance online publication. doi:10.1016/j.dss.2021.113717

Liu, Q. B., Liu, X., & Guo, X. (2020). The effects of participating in a physician-driven online health community in managing chronic disease: Evidence from two natural experiments. *Management Information Systems Quarterly*, *44*(1), 391–419. doi:10.25300/MISQ/2020/15102

Lowry, P. B., Cao, J., & Everard, A. (2011). Privacy concerns versus desire for interpersonal awareness in driving the use of self-disclosure technologies: The case of instant messaging in two cultures. *Journal of Management Information Systems*, *27*(4), 163–200. doi:10.2753/MIS0742-1222270406

Ma, D., Zuo, M., & Liu, L. (2021). The information needs of Chinese family members of cancer patients in the online health community: What and why? *Information Processing & Management*, *58*(3), 102517. doi:10.1016/j.ipm.2021.102517

McMahon, K. L. (2013). Power and pitfalls of social media in diabetes care. *Diabetes Spectrum*, *26*(4), 232–235. doi:10.2337/diaspect.26.4.232

Moore, D., & Ayers, S. (2017). Virtual voices: Social support and stigma in postnatal mental illness Internet forums. *Psychology Health and Medicine*, *22*(5), 546–551. doi:10.1080/13548506.2016.1189580 PMID:27218265

Moore, J. L. (2022). Exploring healthy connection: Communication, social networks, and wellbeing. In M. Khosrow-Pour (Ed.), *Research anthology on improving health literacy through patient communication and mass media* (pp. 317–329). IGI Global. doi:10.4018/978-1-6684-2414-8.ch018

Mukta, R., Paik, H. Y., Lu, Q., & Kanhere, S. S. (2022). A survey of data minimisation techniques in blockchain-based healthcare. *Computer Networks*, *108766*. Advance online publication. doi:10.1016/j.comnet.2022.108766

Oh, S., & Syn, S. Y. (2015). Motivations for sharing information and social support in social media: A comparative analysis of Facebook, Twitter, delicious, YouTube, and Flickr. *Journal of the Association for Information Science and Technology*, *66*(10), 2045–2060. doi:10.1002/asi.23320

Peng, J., Cao, F., Zhang, Y., Cao, Y., Zhang, Y., Zhu, X., & Miao, D. (2021). Reflections on motivation: How regulatory focus influences self-framing and risky decision making. *Current Psychology (New Brunswick, N.J.)*, *40*(6), 2927–2937. doi:10.100712144-019-00217-w

Rideout, V., & Fox, S. (2018). Digital health practices, social media use, and mental well-being among teens and young adults in the U.S. *Articles, abstracts and reports*, 1093. https://digitalcommons.psjhealth.org/publications/1093

Rueger, J., Dolfsma, W., & Aalbers, R. (2021). Perception of peer advice in online health communities: Access to lay expertise. *Social Science & Medicine*, *277*, 113117. doi:10.1016/j.socscimed.2020.113117 PMID:33865092

Shannon, G., Jansen, M., Williams, K., Cáceres, C., Motta, A., Odhiambo, A., Eleveld, A., & Mannell, J. (2019). Gender equality in science, medicine, and global health: Where are we at and why does it matter? *Lancet*, *393*(10171), 560–569. doi:10.1016/S0140-6736(18)33135-0 PMID:30739691

Sun, Y., Zhang, F., & Feng, Y. (2022). Do individuals disclose or withhold information following the same logic: A configurational perspective of information disclosure in social media. *Aslib Journal of Information Management*. doi:10.1108/AJIM-06-2021-0180

Taylor, J., & Pagliari, C. (2018). #Deathbedlive: The end-of-life trajectory, reflected in a cancer patient's tweets. *BMC Palliative Care*, *17*(1), 1–10. doi:10.118612904-018-0273-9 PMID:29357865

Trepte, S. (2021). The social media privacy model: Privacy and communication in the light of social media affordances. *Communication Theory*, *31*(4), 549–570. doi:10.1093/ct/qtz035

Uchino, B. N., Bowen, K., Kent de Grey, R., Mikel, J., & Fisher, E. B. (2018). Social support and physical health: Models, mechanisms, and opportunities. In E. B. Fisher, L. D. Cameron, A. J. Christensen, U. Ehlert, Y. Guo, B. Oldenburg, & F. J. Snoek (Eds.), *Principles and concepts of behavioural medicine* (pp. 341–372). Springer. doi:10.1007/978-0-387-93826-4_12

Voss, T. (2021). James S. Coleman: Foundations of Social Theory. In K. Kraemer & F. Brugger (Eds.), *Schlüsselwerke der wirtschaftssoziologie* (pp. 223–234). Springer VS. doi:10.1007/978-3-658-31439-2_19

Walters, N. (2017). *Maintaining privacy and security while connected to the internet*. AARP Public Policy Institute. https://www.aarp.org/content/dam/aarp/ppi/2017/08/maintaining-privacy-and-security-while-connected-to-the-internet.pdf

Wang, L., Yan, L., Zhou, T., Guo, X., & Heim, G. R. (2020). Understanding physicians' online-offline behaviour dynamics: An empirical study. *Information Systems Research*, *31*(2), 537–555. doi:10.1287/isre.2019.0901

Wang, X., Zhao, K., & Street, N. (2017). Analysing and predicting user participation in online health communities: A social support perspective. *Journal of Medical Internet Research*, *19*(4), e130. doi:10.2196/jmir.6834 PMID:28438725

Wang, X., Zuo, Z., & Zhao, K. (2015a). The evolution and diffusion of user roles in online health communities: A social support perspective. In *2015 International Conference on Healthcare Informatics* (pp. 48–56). IEEE. 10.1109/ICHI.2015.12

Wang, X., Zuo, Z., & Zhao, K. (2015b). The evolution and diffusion of user roles in online health communities: A social support perspective. *Healthcare Informatics (ICHI), 2015 International Conference on*, 48–56.

Wu, P. F. (2019). The privacy paradox in the context of online social networking: A self-identity perspective. *Journal of the Association for Information Science and Technology*, *70*(3), 207–217. doi:10.1002/asi.24113

Wu, P. F., Vitak, J., & Zimmer, M. T. (2020). A contextual approach to information privacy research. *Journal of the Association for Information Science and Technology*, *71*(4), 485–490. doi:10.1002/asi.24232

Yan, L. (2018). Good intentions, bad outcomes: The effects of mismatches between social sup port and health outcomes in an online weight loss community. *Production and Operations Management*, *27*(1), 9–27. doi:10.1111/poms.12793

Zhang, X., Fang, Y., He, W., Zhang, Y., & Liu, X. (2019). Epistemic motivation, task reflexivity, and knowledge contribution behaviour on team wikis: A cross-level moderation model. *Journal of the Association for Information Science and Technology*, *70*(5), 448–461. doi:10.1002/asi.24129

Zhang, X., Liu, S., Chen, X., Wang, L., Gao, B., & Zhu, Q. (2018a). Health information privacy concerns, antecedents, and information disclosure intention in online health communities. *Information & Management*, *55*(4), 482–493. doi:10.1016/j.im.2017.11.003

Zhang, X., Liu, S., Chen, X., Wang, L., Gao, B., & Zhu, Q. (2018b). Health information privacy concerns, antecedents, and information disclosure intention in online health communities. *Information & Management*, *55*(4), 482–493. doi:10.1016/j.im.2017.11.003

ADDITIONAL READING

Acquisti, A., Brandimarte, L., & Loewenstein, G. (2015). Privacy and human behaviour in the age of information. *Science*, *347*(6221), 509–514. doi:10.1126cience.aaa1465 PMID:25635091

Chen, W., Wei, X., & Zhu, K. X. (2018). Engaging voluntary contributions in online communities: A hidden Markov model. *Management Information Systems Quarterly*, *42*(1), 83–100. doi:10.25300/MISQ/2018/14196

Henningsen, A., & Henningsen, G. (2019). Analysis of panel data using R. In M. Tsionas (Ed.), *Panel Data Econometrics* (pp. 345–396). Academic Press. doi:10.1016/B978-0-12-814367-4.00012-5

Kartiwi, M., & Munassar, F. H. (2019). Assessment of perceived barriers on online health information seeking activities among university students: Case study of Malaysia. *Journal of Information Systems and Digital Technologies*, *1*(1), 25–30.

Lim, W. M., & Weissmann, M. A. (2021). Toward a theory of behavioural control. *Journal of Strategic Marketing*, 1–27. doi:10.1080/0965254X.2021.1890190

Mmonu, N. A., Aifah, A., Onakomaiya, D., & Ogedegbe, G. (2021). Why the global health community should support the EndSARS movement in Nigeria. *Lancet*, *397*(10275), 666–667. doi:10.1016/S0140-6736(21)00194-X PMID:33610205

Settanni, M., Azucar, D., & Marengo, D. (2018). Predicting individual characteristics from digital traces on social media: A metanalysis. *Cyberpsychology, Behavior, and Social Networking*, *21*(4), 217–228. doi:10.1089/cyber.2017.0384 PMID:29624439

Wright, K. B., Cai, X., Fisher, C., Rising, C. J., Burke-Garcia, A., & Afanaseva, D. (2021). A content analysis of social support messages about environmental breast cancer risk within blogs for mothers. *Health Communication*, *36*(13), 1796–1804. doi:10.1080/10410236.2020.1800241 PMID:32744079

KEY TERMS AND DEFINITIONS

Altruistic User Role: The dynamics of the various roles a user plays while providing and/or seeking social support online are referred to as the altruistic user role. Individual users' intentional contributions in online health support communities may pass through various levels, influenced by mechanisms such as reciprocity, peer recognition, and selfimage. During various stages of involvement, some users may play prominent social roles in seeking and providing social support. Individuals are expected to behave differently and play different roles in online communities based on their two basic interests, one for themselves and the other for others. Self-centred users, in particular, are preoccupied with their own health issues, whereas altruistic users are more concerned with the needs of others.

Data-Driven (Research) Approach: Simply put, this term refers to the exploratory approach that analyses data to extract scientifically interesting insights (such as patterns, e.g.,) by applying analytical techniques and modes of reasoning.

Health Communication: This refers to the multifaceted and multidisciplinary approach to reach different audiences and share health-related information with the goal of influencing, engaging, and supporting individuals, communities, health professionals, special groups, policymakers and the public to champion, introduce, adopt, or sustain a behaviour, practice, or policy that will ultimately improve health outcomes.

Identity Information: This refers to narrative content about a user's identity, such as name, gender, resident location, emails, photos, affiliations, and other narrative content about a user's identity are examples of identity information. Although this genre is rarely directly related to users' knowledge or physical well-being, it does impose high privacy costs that prevent users from disclosing such information.

Machine Learning Algorithms: Pre-programmed algorithms receive and analyse input data to predict output values that are within an acceptable range. These algorithms learn and optimise their operations as new data is added, improving performance, and developing intelligence over time. Algorithms are a set of rules that a computer follows to accomplish a specific goal procedure for solving.

Online Health Support Communities: These are online social platforms or networks where members assist one another in dealing with health-related issues. Caregivers and community members frequently share information with fellow patients and their families to educate them about illnesses, seek and provide social support, and even form networks with others in similar situations.

Online Self-Disclosure (Intention): In a nutshell, this term refers to the voluntary disclosure of personal information to others with whom one is in an interpersonal relationship in certain online environments or spaces. It also refers to individuals in interpersonal relationships voluntarily disclosing vital personal information about themselves to others in online, or virtual environments/spaces such as social media platforms, ecommerce, and geographical location-based services such as GPS.

Online Social Support: Online social support refers to a resource exchange between individuals in online or virtual environments to improve the receiver's wellbeing. Community psychologists, for example, have identified various types of social support based on the nature of exchanged resources, such as informational, emotional, companionship, and instrumental support. Informational and emotional support are the most common types of social support, so they are the focus of research into social support in online communities. In contrast to online information support, instrumental support, which refers to the assistance received physically or tangibly such as calling for an ambulance or receiving medicine delivery, is usually limited by geographical proximity.

Personal Health Information: Personal health information refers to narrative content about a user's identity that is related to their health care status and histories, such as symptoms, treatments, outcomes, diagnosis time, treatment progress, and regimen.

Social Support Exchange: This is the exchange, or give-and-take, of psychological and/or material resources between and among members of a social network of friends, families, and others to assist individual members affected by a health challenge, such as stress, diabetes, or cancer, in coping with the challenges and improving their well-being.

Extending Graph Databases With Relational Concepts

Kornelije Rabuzin
Faculty of Organization and Informatics, University of Zagreb, Croatia

Mirko Čubrilo
University North, Croatia

Martina Šestak
Faculty of Electrical Engineering and Computer Science, University of Maribor, Slovenia

INTRODUCTION

Data science is a topic that uses different scientific methods, techniques, and algorithms for extracting useful information and knowledge from data. There are several reasons to use data science; for explaining what happened in the past, what is happening in the present, and even try to predict what is most likely to happen in the future. Data science is an interdisciplinary field, which includes data analysis, machine learning, business intelligence, quantitative methods, data visualization, data preparation, statistics, etc. Due to the heterogeneity of the subjects inside data science, it is not easy to be an expert in all of them, and it takes a large amount of time to master the different subjects. Because of that, some people predict that educational institutions will not be able to produce enough data scientists in the near future, which was already recognized by some countries, including the EU.

The core component of data science is data, and without it, data scientists would not be able to perform their work. Another important topic is the data source, which can be categorized as un-, semi- and structured sources. As a brief explanation, unstructured data can be for example an email - a collection of words without any structure behind it - while structured data can be found in a database where data is grouped into tables, and each row of some table shares the same structure with the rows that come before or after. Regarding semi-structured sources, a good example are XML documents, since XML nodes in the same document can have different structures. A relational database, which is a type of structured data source, can be a good data source, since people are familiar with them.

During the past decade, computer systems had to store and manage large amounts of data coming from different sources. For example, the Internet is being used on a daily basis by millions of users, and the size of generated text, messages, searches, posts, images, videos, etc. is enormous. Furthermore, many Internet of Things (IoT) devices are connected to the Internet and they also tend to generate large amounts of different types of data. While in the past one would easily talk about gigabytes and terabytes of data, today it is usual to deal with petabytes and exabytes, even though this scale is expected to grow to zettabytes and yottabytes in the future. It is clear that turning to this new field (Big Data), there is a constant need to find scalable solutions for efficient data storage and management. When the frequency and volume of data generation started to increase 15 years ago, the goal was to rethink and find new ways of handling and storing large amounts of data. The solutions that were used in early 2000s were just not suitable anymore for efficiently handling the huge amounts of generated data. Relational databases,

DOI: 10.4018/978-1-7998-9220-5.ch027

Copyright © 2023, IGI Global. Copying or distributing in print or electronic forms without written permission of IGI Global is prohibited.

which were efficient solutions for everyday business transactional applications, are not appropriate for extremely large amounts of data, with possibly different structures and schema. These databases were not capable to store and manage the data in a satisfactory manner, leading to difficulties in real time data processing, as well as ad-hoc data querying.

In order to store and manage the data, NoSQL database systems were introduced. These are used today by many companies for different purposes, and they can be categorized into four main NoSQL database types: document-oriented, column-oriented, key-value and graph databases. In this chapter, the focus is put on graph databases, as they turned out to be an excellent choice to store and query large amounts of interconnected data, often generated by modern information systems. In general, graph databases represent a database solution based on a graph data structure, where data is stored in the form of nodes connected with relationships, where both elements can have properties as attributes, which describe real-world objects. The other NoSQL databases types also have their own advantages. For instance, key-value databases can quickly retrieve the value for the specified key; document-oriented systems can store all the important data for an entity in a single document; column-store systems are similar to relational databases with an increased flexibility to the schema. Thus, it can be concluded that each type is suitable for different application and can be interchangeably used to resolve different challenges.

As graph databases have certain advantages over relational databases, they have been increasingly used as a source of information in data science projects. There are already some datasets with a graph database structure available for data science projects ("Awesome Public Datasets as Neo4j Graph," n.d.). One author of this chapter was included in a previous data science project that used graph databases in the telecommunication industry as well, although the use of graph databases in telecommunication industry is not entirely new (Lehotay-Kéry & Kiss, 2020). The developed solution detected, in real time, potential problems that could significantly reduce the quality of the service. Health data science can also benefit from graph databases. In (Liu et al., 2021) it was proposed a graph database called EpiGraphDB, whose purpose was to store biomedical and epidemiological relationships between data, with the goal of using the solution as a database and data mining platform for health data science.

In this chapter, the idea is to briefly explain and analyse what concepts that characterize relational databases are still missing in graph databases, and how they could be implemented. Some of the reasons to do this are related to data quality, which is an important part of data science. If data quality is low, the conclusions that are drawn from the analysis of the data could be potentially wrong, especially when handling large amounts of data. Data quality in graph databases could be increased, if the missing concepts of relational databases were implemented. NoSQL systems were introduced to tackle the data-related problems in practice and because of that, it is important to understand that NoSQL databases do not have a solid mathematical foundation, as relational databases, nor a standardized query language, as SQL. This fact also applies to graph databases. For example, graph databases use query languages different from SQL, where triggers, node inheritance, advanced integrity constraints, among others, are not supported. Although graph databases have some advantages, as a high speed of reading of interconnected data when compared to relational databases, they still have some weaknesses that are not present in relational databases.

A few years ago, the authors received several university grants to explore what is missing in graph databases and what could be further implemented in order to extend the list of functional characteristics. First, query languages for graph databases were examined, and it was determined that the majority of people used the Cypher Query Language (CQL), or Gremlin. However, there are several languages, each with its own syntax, which implies a certain learning curve for its users. The authors' idea was that a language similar to SQL could help the improvement of this learning process. Further on, the support for integrity constraints was examined (UNIQUE, NOT NULL, etc.), which are used in relational databases to ensure data consistency and integrity. Without integrity constraints specified for a given database, the stored data quality has a high probability to be low. This represents a problem, especially in the data warehousing projects where such data is often a strong basis for business decision making. The obtained research results indicated that there is limited support for data integrity concepts in graph databases. Further analysis revealed that active databases and triggers were also not supported, as well as the possibility to implement node inheritance. The identified drawbacks and possible solutions should increase data quality, adding additional features to existing graph database management systems, while making the use of data easier and more intuitive with a new query interface. Also, an improved data quality and an easier data management should reduce the data pre-processing time in the majority of data science projects.

Data preparation is a key activity that requires a lot of time in data science projects. It is a well-known fact that almost 70 or even 80% of the time in data warehousing and data mining projects has to be invested in data preparation. As it was already described, efficient analysis relies on quality data, which means that data have to be standardized, consistent and error-free. The solutions proposed in this chapter should tackle this, since they increase the quality of data, ensure the consistency, reduce the number of errors, and make data more usable through the developed interface.

Although many different Graph Database Management Systems (GDBMSs) are available on the market, for the implementation purposes the decision was to use Neo4j. The system was popular during the time of development, and it was concluded that it could be extended to support new functionalities. In the next sections the following is described:

1. How to set up a working environment and how to solve technical challenges when extending the selected GDBMS' functionalities - the extension of the system obliges for both a working environment and several components to operate together,
2. How to implement integrity constraints in graph databases – it will be demonstrated how UNIQUE and CHECK constraints were implemented,
3. How to implement triggers in graph databases – it will be explained what steps are necessary to implement different triggers,
4. How to implement the node inheritance concept – it will be discussed how node inheritance can be achieved in graph databases,
5. How to implement a new visual query language for graph databases that resembles SQL– the prototype query language called Gremlin by Example (GBE) will be described. This language looks like Query by Example (QBE), which is used in Microsoft Access, but is based on Gremlin. Database users have been familiar with QBE for years, so the idea was that a similar solution for graph databases would also be useful.

Finally, some open questions will be specified as well as future research directions. Some parts of this research have already been published in (Maleković, Rabuzin, & Šestak, 2016; Rabuzin & Šestak, 2019; Rabuzin, Maleković, & Šestak, 2016; Rabuzin & Šestak, 2018; Rabuzin, Šestak, & Konecki, 2016; Šestak, Rabuzin, & Novak, 2016).

BACKGROUND

When talking about general papers on graph databases, it is not possible to avoid one of the most relevant books on the subject (Robinson, Webber, & Eifrem, 2013). Regarding graph theory, a great book reference can be (Wilson, 1996). When referring to graph and relational databases, as well as advantages of each one, the following could be indicated (Cheng, Ding, Wang, Lu, & Du, 2019), (Chen, Song, Zhao, & Li, 2020), (Kaliyar, 2015) or (de Oliveira, de Souza, Moreira, & Seraphim, 2020).

Looking at state-of-the-art research in the field of graph databases, it is possible to see the focus on graph database different applications. Graph databases have been used in the biomedical domain (Timón-Reina, Rincón, & Martínez-Tomás, 2021), fraud detection (Srivastava & Singh, 2022), social network analysis (Rani, Goyal, & Gadia, 2020), credit card fraud detection (Prusti, Das, & Rath, 2021), e-commerce (Tuteja & Kumar, 2022), transport system modelling (Shibanova, Stroganov, & Rudakov, 2021), network forensics (Cermak & Sramkova, 2021), criminal investigations (Carnaz, Nogueira, & Antunes, 2021), manufacturing industry (Kim, Yahia, Segonds, Véron, & Fau, 2021), healthcare domain to fight diabetes (Dedié et al., 2021), security log events analysis (Lagraa & State, 2021), for construction of knowledge graphs (Hao et al., 2021), etc.

There is a clear lack in research around the exploration, discussion and implementation of new features to existing database management systems. In this section, a few interesting approaches that are used to extend existing graph database features will be described.

When data quality is discussed, only a few papers have identified data quality in graph databases. In (Reddy, 2019) authors deal with the visualization-enabled graph data quality assessment. In (Skavantzos, Zhao, & Link, 2021), the authors also discuss data quality, and they connect it to uniqueness and existence constraints in graph databases. In (Bajaj & Bick, 2020), the authors review NoSQL systems and discuss data quality in that respect.

Regarding integrity constraints, in (Miranda Reina, Huf, Presser, & Siqueira, 2021), the authors identified that some of the constraints are missing, and because of that they proposed and implemented several new integrity constraints: conditions on node attributes, required edges, type of in/out nodes of an edge and edge cardinality. The authors also mention that there is space to improve the consistency of stored data. The importance of key constraints is clear, which is discussed further in (Link, 2020). W3C's validation specification for graph databases called Shapes Constraint Language (SHACL) has been discussed in (Schaffenrath et al., 2020). The importance of integrity constraints has also been identified in (Pokorný, Valenta, & Kovačič, 2017).

Now, looking at existing query languages and new visual interfaces, in (Wu & Nakamoto, 2019), the authors identified the need to implement a mechanism that would be able to query relationships and their properties in graph databases, proposing RelSeeker as a database query language based on Datalog. In (Wang, Zou, Cao, & Xie, 2019), the authors also claim the difficulty to construct Cypher query efficiently, proposing instead a natural language question interface for graph databases. In (Debrouvier, Parodi, Perazzo, Soliani, & Vaisman, 2021), the authors proposed a high-level graph query language called T-GQL, together with a collection of algorithms for computing different kinds of temporal paths in a graph.

So, although there exists some research on graph database management systems' extension like integrity constraints and data quality, in this chapter, some new ideas and research directions are presented, including node inheritance and trigger specification, as well as visual query interfaces that are similar to some existing interfaces used in relational databases. To the best of authors' knowledge, no similar works existed in the literature at the time of writing.

TECHNICAL CHALLENGES

In order to implement the relational database concepts, Neo4j was chosen as basis of implementation, since it was one of the best and most widely used GDBMSs at the time of writing, and it was possible to extend the system as needed.

The first question that needs to be answered is how to extend a database management system, in order to implement new functional characteristics. Generally speaking, there are two possible approaches - (1) the integrated and (2) the layered approach. While the integrated approach means that the system has to be extended by changing its source code, the layered approach implies that a new layer is added on top of the existing system, where new functional characteristics are implemented within that layer. Since the idea was to implement additional elements, the latter approach was chosen, allowing more flexibility in the development. The Neo4j 2.3.5 Community version was used, which offers several Neo4j plugins, different Java APIs and other native Java implementations for system extension. Neo4j plugins are pre-built scripts that are executed on the server. They are often distributed as Java-compiled (JAR) files, which can be deployed in a plug-and-play manner to be used by the server. Nevertheless, they often require an advanced knowledge of the plugin's code syntax, which is quite limited regarding flexibility.

On the other side, the Java API approach implies less manual work by the developer, but it brings more complexity in terms of finding compatible API versions offered by different vendors, which are necessary to implement a certain functionality. Since the goal was to develop a Gremlin query language-based solution for querying the Neo4j graph database, the most suitable options were provided by Tinkerpop. Additionally, Neo4j offered an official Java driver as a dependency, but Gremlin query language was not supported by the driver, since Cypher is the official query language in Neo4j.

In the end, Tinkerpop's Neo4j-Gremlin API was selected, combined with its Gremlin Java implementation. This option best suited the needs of the project, so the implementation of integrity constraints as an extension to the Neo4j GDBMS could be possible.

INTEGRITY CONSTRAINTS

It is known that integrity constraints are crucial in database design, as they represent an implementation of the domain's business rules in the database context. If integrity constraints are not used, data quality problems can emerge, like partial data, data whose value is out of allowed range of values or inconsistent data. Integrity constraints can be used so these problems do not appear in the application. The list of the most often used integrity constraints includes:

1. NOT NULL – it means that the column's value has to be entered;
2. UNIQUE – it means that the value that has been entered has to be unique, i.e., it cannot appear in some other row (for the same column);
3. CHECK – it means that the value has to be, for example, equal, greater, or less, than a given value, or that the value should be in some specific range;
4. PRIMARY KEY – it means that the value has to be entered and it has to be unique as well;
5. FOREIGN KEY – it ensures that the value of a column is the same as the value of some (primary key) column from another, or possibly same, table;
6. Triggers – they are used to specify more complex business rules.

The following example presents how these constraints are used by following the SQL syntax in relational databases:

```
CREATE TABLE users (
ID SERIAL PRIMARY KEY,
firstname VARCHAR(100) NOT NULL,
lastname VARCHAR(200) NOT NULL,
UNIQUE(firstname, lastname)
);
CREATE TABLE books (
ID SERIAL PRIMARY KEY,
title VARCHAR(200) NOT NULL CONSTRAINT c1 UNIQUE,
year_published INT CHECK (year_published > 1990 AND year_published < 2015)
);
CREATE TABLE borrowed (
ID SERIAL PRIMARY KEY,
user INT NOT NULL REFERENCES users ON DELETE RESTRICT ON UPDATE CASCADE,
book INT NOT NULL REFERENCES book ON DELETE RESTRICT ON UPDATE CASCADE,
date_borrowed DATE NOT NULL
);
```

The previous SQL code can be interpreted as follows: for the users table, the value of the ID column needs to be incremented automatically and is used as the primary key, and the firstname and lastname column values have to be entered and their combination has to be unique. For the books table, the ID column specification is the same, whereas the title column value has to be entered and to be unique (there is a named constraint called c1), and the year_published column value must be between 1990 and 2015. Finally, a weak borrowed table (child table) has to be created, where both the user and book column values can only be equal to some value that exists in the ID column of the users or books table (parent table), respectively. If the value in the parent table is deleted, it cannot be deleted if a referencing value exists in the child table. On the other hand, if the values in the parent table should be updated, the same applies for the child table, i.e., the column would be automatically updated in the child table as well.

When the project started and Neo4j was selected, integrity constraints such as UNIQUE or CHECK were not supported, and the goal was to extend the system to include support for these types of constraints.

UNIQUE Integrity Constraint

According to the database theory, the goal of the UNIQUE integrity constraint is to prevent users from entering duplicate values in the database. Once specified, a UNIQUE constraint specifies that a given column value must be unique, i.e., the value cannot appear in more than one table row. In the graph database context, the UNIQUE constraint specifies that a given node or relationship property value must be non-repeating and, as such, is already supported by Neo4j. However, in earlier work, the idea was to extend the UNIQUE constraint concept to entire nodes and relationships being unique, i.e., all node or relationship property values would need to be unique.

In the proposed "Gremlin by Example" language, which is explained later in the chapter, it is possible to create a node or a relationship with a UNIQUE constraint by selecting the node/relationship type, entering its property values, and marking that node/relationship as UNIQUE. In the background, this process will trigger the evaluation of possible violation of the UNIQUE constraints, which includes checking whether there is an existing node or relationship with the same property values in the database. If the result of this evaluation is negative, meaning that the new node/relationship does not violate the UNIQUE constraint, one can proceed with inserting this node/relationship. An example source code for a UNIQUE constraint evaluation and node creation for unique user nodes in the database is shown in Figure 1.

If the user tries to repeat this process and re-insert 'William Shakespeare' as the Author node in the database, the UNIQUE constraint created earlier would be violated and the entire process would result in an error message.

Figure 1. Source code for the UNIQUE integrity constraint

```
if(g.V().has("Label", a.getLabel()).has("Firstname", a.getFirstname())
        .has("Lastname", a.getLastname()).toList().iterator().hasNext())
{
    result = g.V().has("Label", a.getLabel()).has("Firstname", a.getFirstname())
            .has("Lastname", a.getLastname()).toList().iterator().next();
}

try (Transaction tx = db.tx()) {
    vertex = db.addVertex(a.getLabel());

    vertex.property("Label", a.getLabel());
    vertex.property("Firstname", a.getFirstname());
    vertex.property("Lastname", a.getLastname());
    tx.commit();
}
```

CHECK Integrity Constraint

In certain situations, it is necessary that the column values meet the allowed range specified by the domain's business rules (e.g., users of a platform need to be older than 18). For such cases, a CHECK constraint can be specified in a database, which checks if a given column value meets the constraint's parameters when inserting new data. In the graph database context, the proposed CHECK constraint can be specified on a node or relationship property, and it can be used to specify that a given property must be in a range (BETWEEN) or set (IN) of values allowed for that property.

In the sample case depicted in Figure 2, it is demonstrated how to create a CHECK constraint on a Book node type, which limits possible values of the YearPublished property to a range between 1990 and 2015.

Please note that the CHECK constraint is specified up front, i.e., before inserting nodes or relationships in the graph database. Later, when a user tries to insert a new book, the CHECK BookYearConstraint integrity constraint will be evaluated before the INSERT statement, i.e. transaction, is carried out entirely. As a result, inserting a book published before 1990 or after 2015 will produce an error.

Figure 2. Creating an example CHECK constraint for books' YearPublished property

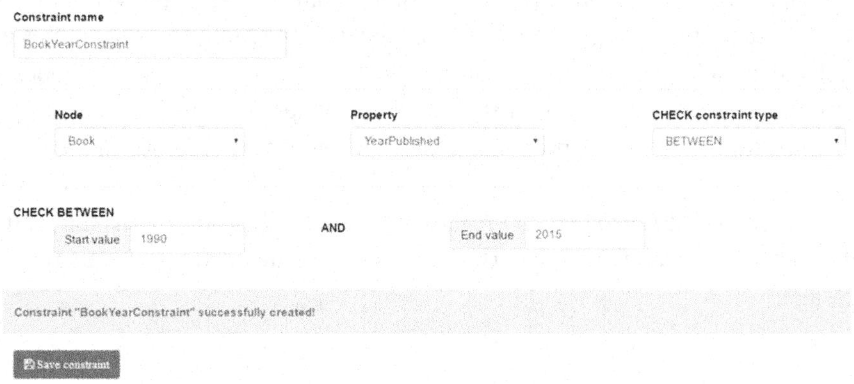

Constraint name

BookYearConstraint

Node	Property	CHECK constraint type
Book	YearPublished	BETWEEN

CHECK BETWEEN

Start value 1990   AND   End value 2015

Constraint "BookYearConstraint" successfully created!

Save constraint

TRIGGERS

Although people are familiar with triggers, they are rarely acquainted with the theory of active databases, which has been developed in the background. Many things that have been done in the active database theory some decades ago, have still not been implemented in existing database systems, including systems like Neo4j.

A trigger is a database object that is activated when some event occurs. The simplest events include INSERT, UPDATE or DELETE statements, but other types of events do exist as well (time events, method events, complex events, special constructs, etc.). When the event occurs, the trigger is activated, although it does not mean that the trigger will be executed. The execution step depends on the condition evaluation of the underlying Event-Condition-Action (ECA) rule. So, when a trigger is activated, its condition has to be evaluated first, and then one can tell whether the trigger, i.e. its action part, is going to be executed or not. The execution usually means that some more complex business logic is going to be performed, some complex values are going to be calculated, some data is going to be written in other tables and/ or databases, etc. The following is a simple statement that is used to create a trigger in PostgreSQL 13:

```
CREATE [ CONSTRAINT ] TRIGGER name { BEFORE | AFTER | INSTEAD OF } { event [
OR ... ] }
    ON table_name
    [ FROM referenced_table_name ]
    [ NOT DEFERRABLE | [ DEFERRABLE ] [ INITIALLY IMMEDIATE | INITIALLY DE-
FERRED] ]
    [ REFERENCING { { OLD | NEW } TABLE [ AS ] transition_relation_name } [
...] ]
    [ FOR [ EACH ] { ROW | STATEMENT } ]
    [ WHEN (condition) ]
    EXECUTE { FUNCTION | PROCEDURE } function_name (arguments)
```

So, a trigger is created on a table, and supported events include statements like INSERT, UPDATE, DELETE and TRUNCATE. It can also be specified on a BEFORE event, AFTER event or INSTEAD OF event related to the trigger, meaning that it can be activated and selected for execution before, after or instead of the event. There is also a possibility to postpone (defer) the execution to a later moment, if needed. A trigger can be executed for each row that is affected by the statement, or for each statement, which means only once. The WHEN condition is used to detail the condition that has to be specified, and the FUNCTION or PROCEDURE options denote the function or procedure, respectively, which is going to be executed. There are other details relevant for trigger executions, but they are heavily dependent on the characteristics of the selected DBMSs, which exceeds the scope of this chapter.

At the moment of this research, Neo4j did not support the trigger mechanism. For that reason, it was decided to add the support for triggers, and it was also decided to enable easier trigger specification through the proposed GBE approach. Specifically, it was decided to extend the so-called Trigger by Example approach, which enabled us to create triggers in a visual manner. It has been demonstrated how users can create AFTER INSERT triggers, which are evaluated after they insert nodes in the database with specific property values. By analogy, a BEFORE INSERT trigger would be used in the case an action is needed before inserting a new node (e.g., to implement referential integrity in graph databases). In the example, an UPDATE operation is performed to the generic Property2 value of all nodes labelled Node1 after a new node of type Node1, with Property1 property value 4 is inserted. In its background, the trigger rule executes the database transaction, followed by the action on data, which falls into the subgraph included in the trigger's action and meets the defined criteria. This kind of triggers is particularly applicable for maintaining aggregate tables in data warehouses.

Later on, after some time, triggers were added and it was possible to use them in Neo4j (apoc.trigger. enabled=true in $NEO4J_HOME/config/neo4j.conf). However, the proposed approach relied on Trigger By Example presented in (Lee, Mao, Chiu, & Chu, 2005), where the main goal was to enable easier, graphical trigger specifications in the graph database.

NODE INHERITANCE

Although object-oriented databases were promising in the past, object-relational databases such as PostgreSQL are more popular today. What is an object-relational database? Basically, it is a relational database that adopted some concepts from the object-oriented paradigm. For instance, PostgreSQL uses object id, and also supports table inheritance. The table inheritance property allows the creation of a new table that inherits the column specification and some constraint specifications from some other table. The new table can be created as a copy, which means that there is no connection between the two tables once they are created, or there is a chance to create the two tables in such a way that any change to the main table is automatically visible in the inherited table as well. This is very convenient in some situations, for example, when there is a need to have two tables with identical structure, one for testing and one for production purposes.

Neo4j did not support the inheritance concept at the time of the project, and because of that, the system was extended in such a way that a new node can be created based on other already created node. For instance, one could use the proposed node inheritance concept to speed up the inserting of new books in the database by automatically retrieving the available node type properties so that the user then only needs to enter the property values. In the background, each node or relationship type is implemented as a class, which is instantiated each time a new node/relationship of that type is created.

In the proposed approach, the node inheritance can be easily achieved through copying and extending an existing class definition together with its attributes and methods. In the selected example, the Book node label can be inherited by specific book types such as Journal or Magazine, which would include additional relevant properties and methods.

GREMLIN BY EXAMPLE

Gremlin by Example (GBE) is a visual query language proposed by the authors, and to be used primarily for Neo4j. Regarding query language in NoSQL systems, one main disadvantage is that there is no universal query language, contrarily to SQL for relational database systems. Generally speaking, each system has its own query language, or languages, and new language(s) must be learned in order to be able to use these new systems.

Although SQL is widely perceived as the universal language used for relational databases, the truth is that this is not the only existing language. For example, Query by Example (QBE) is another language supported in e. g. MS Access. The main idea of QBE is that people can build queries graphically, and do not have to be familiar with SQL syntax to query the database, thus significantly flattening the learning curve for the language syntax. As a result, less experienced users are also able to use databases, as they do not have to be familiar with all statements and clauses that are supported in SQL.

In the QBE language supported by Microsoft Access, first one or more tables must be selected, which will be queried in the formulated query. The next phase is to include one or more columns, or filter data based on some additional formula (Criteria), as well as the selection of how the result should be sorted (Sort). It is possible to switch to SQL view, which makes the query formulation task easier to understand and follow the concepts.

Figure 3. Example query formulation in Gremlin by Example

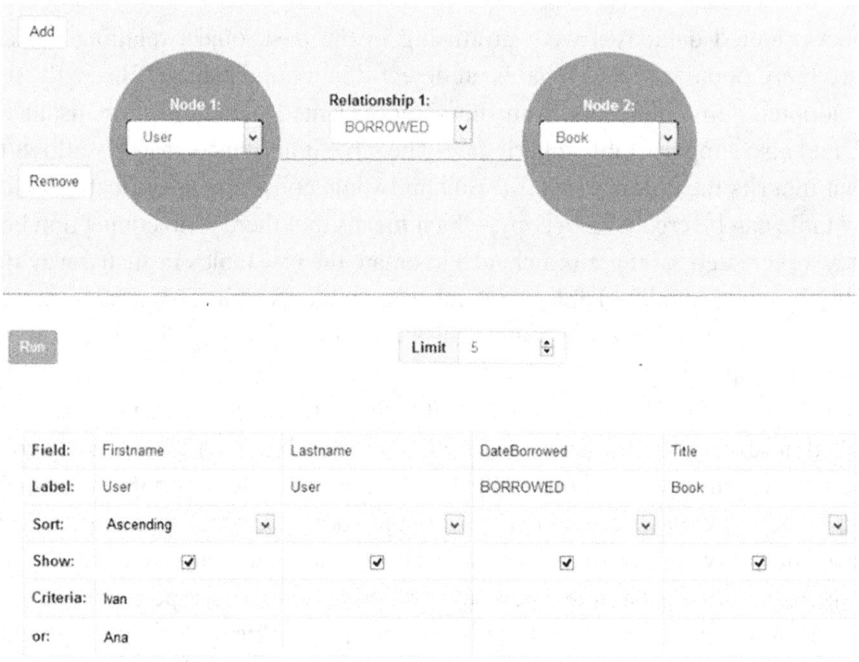

Field:	Firstname		Lastname		DateBorrowed		Title	
Label:	User		User		BORROWED		Book	
Sort:	Ascending	⌄		⌄		⌄		⌄
Show:		✔		✔		✔		✔
Criteria:	Ivan							
or:	Ana							

The idea that was followed when implementing the Gremlin by Example (GBE) visual query language is similar to QBE (Figure 3). The users formulate the query by:

- selecting combinations of different query parameters via the graphical user interface (GUI), such as the node or relationship types that form the target sub-graph,
- node/relationship properties to be queried and (possibly) displayed in the query result,
- sorting option,
- additional criteria on the property values,
- number of entries retrieved from the database.

Therefore, the proposed GBE language enables users to formulate graph database queries in a declarative manner, i.e., by only specifying what needs to be retrieved from the database, while the underlying Gremlin syntax implementation determines the graph traversal steps to be performed to obtain the desired query result.

Another query language that can be used with Neo4j is called the CQL. As Cypher does not support advanced features presented above, the goal is to build a visual version similar to GBE that could support them. The Cypher by Example (CBE) language implementation is currently being developed as a proof-of-concept solution, but the initial testing results are promising and will be presented in the future work.

SOLUTIONS AND RECOMMENDATIONS

As it was already explained, the goal was to extend graph databases and to implement the missing relational concepts so that graph databases would be more suitable for everyday business operations and for data science projects in general. All the work presented in the chapter has been developed within several university grants that were given to the different authors. Although, in the meantime, some systems implemented some of the concepts proposed in this chapter, there are still some ideas, which have never been addressed, like node inheritance, or visual query interface, which would improve the query experience to graph databases users.

For people who deal with data and who conduct data science projects, graph databases are considered to be a tool that can be extremely useful to analyse large amounts of interconnected data. One example is social network analysis, together with graph algorithms that are used for the purpose. Since some concepts from relational databases were not supported in graph databases, this chapter presented how authors tackled the lack of these characteristics and how they implemented them. It is believed that people from the area could benefit from the presented lessons that were learned over the years.

What are the benefits of the proposed extensions/implementations of integrity constraints? The most important benefits are listed below:

- First of all, by using constraints it was ensured that the inserted node / relationship property values are in compliance to the domain's business rules, which serves to prove the goal of integrity constraints;
- The UNIQUE constraint prevents data redundancy in the graph database, which both ensures data integrity and prevents the unnecessary use of system resources for storing duplicated data;

- The Gremlin by Example approach makes the entire integrity constraint specification process clearer and easier to follow for the end users, and flattens the learning curve for unexperienced database users;
- The table inheritance feature brings a simpler long-term database maintenance, encourages the re-use of database schema components, and enables a comprehensive querying approach to both parent and all child tables.

In the beginning of this work, a list of research questions was given, which were answered in the rest of the sections. Data quality should never be jeopardized in any way, since bad data is of no use and any analysis which relies on bad data can be very problematic. Integrity constraint implementation is important to increase data quality and easier data management is also a desirable feature. It is not always easy to learn a new language, and people do require some time to get acquainted, or to become a proficient user. Using a new technology by using an old, well-known interface is definitely a desirable feature.

Finally, there are some open questions and relational database concepts that authors are currently exploring (like CBE), which are still not supported in graph database management systems. The plan is to continue the work and to implement them in the near future.

FUTURE RESEARCH DIRECTIONS

As part of future work, the plan is to continue improving the GBE language and analyse the usability by the users. Also, the plan is to aggregate all research efforts related to graph database integrity (integrity constraints, triggers, etc.) into a comprehensive framework, which includes an overview of formal characteristics of integrity constraints and enables a more straightforward implementation of integrity constraints in graph databases.

At this point of time authors put focus on data types and domains, as current support in the graph databases is still not satisfactory. Also, possible approaches to view implementation are also in the focus, because views have their own advantages, like easier query specification and data protection. Furthermore, it would also be interesting to check how graph databases could be used for data warehousing purposes, as relational data warehouse implementations still exhibit some performance problems.

CONCLUSION

To summarise, data quality, intuitive query language, faster node creation, triggers and other advanced integrity constraints, are of great importance to graph databases, which are becoming the primary source of data for data science projects. All these features are often useful in solving practical problems when working with real data. People who have used relational databases are familiar with the concepts, and they expect such functional characteristics in graph databases as well.

In this chapter, an overview of research attempts to tackle the graph database integrity and querying challenges was presented, which should help to make the graph database technology more accessible to a wider audience, increasing its maturity level. The authors believe that a brief overview of research activities could be useful to readers, students, professors, as well as to developers who implement and maintain Neo4j, or other GDBMSs.

REFERENCES

Awesome public datasets as Neo4j graph. (n.d.). Retrieved April 25, 2022, from https://www.kaggle.com/startupsci/awesome-datasets-graph?select=datasets.csv

Bajaj, A., & Bick, W. (2020). The rise of NoSQL systems: Research and pedagogy. *Journal of Database Management, 31*(3), 67–82. doi:10.4018/JDM.2020070104

Carnaz, G., Nogueira, V. B., & Antunes, M. (2021). A graph database representation of Portuguese criminal-related documents. *Informatics (MDPI), 8*(2), 37. doi:10.3390/informatics8020037

Cermak, M., & Sramkova, D. (2021). GRANEF: Utilization of a graph database for network forensics. In *Proceedings of the 18th International Conference on Security and Cryptography, SECRYPT 2021* (pp. 785–790). SciTePress Digital Library. Available at https://www.scitepress.org/ProceedingsDetails.aspx?ID=KCtjG7Wri7M=&t=1 doi:10.5220/0010581807850790

Chen, J., Song, Q., Zhao, C., & Li, Z. (2020). Graph database and relational database performance comparison on a transportation network. In *Communications in Computer and Information Science* (Vol. 1244, pp. 407–418). Springer., doi:10.1007/978-981-15-6634-9_37

Cheng, Y., Ding, P., Wang, T., Lu, W., & Du, X. (2019). Which category is better: Benchmarking relational and graph database management systems. *Data Science and Engineering, 4*(4), 309–322. doi:10.100741019-019-00110-3

de Oliveira, A. T., de Souza, A. D., Moreira, E. M., & Seraphim, E. (2020). Mapping and conversion between relational and graph databases models: A systematic literature review. In J. Kacprzyk (Ed.), *Advances in Intelligent Systems and Computing* (Vol. 1134, pp. 539–543). Springer. doi:10.1007/978-3-030-43020-7_71

Debrouvier, A., Parodi, E., Perazzo, M., Soliani, V., & Vaisman, A. (2021). A model and query language for temporal graph databases. *The VLDB Journal, 30*(5), 825–858. doi:10.100700778-021-00675-4

Dedié, A., Bleimehl, T., Täger, J., Preusse, M., Hrabě de Angelis, M., & Jarasch, A. (2021). DZD-connect: Using connected data to fight diabetes. *Der Diabetologe (Heidelberg.), 17*(8), 780–787. doi:10.100711428-021-00807-y

Hao, X., Ji, Z., Li, X., Yin, L., Liu, L., Sun, M., Liu, Q., & Yang, R. (2021). Construction and application of a knowledge graph. *Remote Sensing, 13*(13), 2511. doi:10.3390/rs13132511

Kaliyar, R. K. (2015). Graph databases: A survey. In *Proceedings of the 2015 International Conference on Computing, Communication & Automation (ICCCA)*, (pp. 785–790). IEEE. 10.1109/CCAA.2015.7148480

Kim, L., Yahia, E., Segonds, F., Véron, P., & Fau, V. (2021). Key issues for a manufacturing data query system based on graph. *International Journal on Interactive Design and Manufacturing, 15*(4), 397–407. doi:10.100712008-021-00768-y

Lagraa, S., & State, R. (2021). What database do you choose for heterogeneous security log events analysis? In T. Ahmed, O. Festor, Y. Ghamri-Doudane, J. Kang, A. Schaeffer-Filho, A. Lahmadi, & E. Madeira (Eds.), *2021 IFIP/IEEE Internation Symposium on Integrated Network Management (IM 2021)*, (pp. 812–817). Bordeaux, France: IEEE.

Lee, D., Mao, W., Chiu, H., & Chu, W. W. (2005). Designing triggers with trigger-by-example. *Knowledge and Information Systems*, *7*(1), 110–134. doi:10.100710115-003-0126-5

Lehotay-Kéry, P., & Kiss, A. (2020). Process, analyze and visualize telecommunication network configuration data in graph database. *Vietnam Journal of Computer Science*, *7*(1), 65–76. doi:10.1142/S2196888820500037

Link, S. (2020). Neo4j keys. In *Including Subseries Lecture Notes in Artificial Intelligence and Lecture Notes in Bioinformatics), 12400 LNCS* (pp. 19–33). Lecture Notes in Computer Science. Springer. doi:10.1007/978-3-030-62522-1_2

Liu, Y., Elsworth, B., Erola, P., Haberland, V., Hemani, G., Lyon, M., Zheng, J., Lloys, O., Vabistsevits, M., & Gaunt, T. R. (2021). EpiGraphDB: A database and data mining platform for health data science. *Bioinformatics (Oxford, England)*, *37*(9), 1304–1311. doi:10.1093/bioinformatics/btaa961 PMID:33165574

Maleković, M., Rabuzin, K., & Šestak, M. (2016). Graph databases - are they really so new. *International Journal of Advances in Science Engineering and Technology, 4*(4), 8–12.

Miranda Reina, F., Huf, A., Presser, D., & Siqueira, F. (2021). Extending the integrity constraint support in a graph database. *IEEE Latin America Transactions*, *19*(4), 604–611. doi:10.1109/TLA.2021.9448543

Pokorný, J., Valenta, M., & Kovačič, J. (2017). Integrity constraints in graph databases. *Procedia Computer Science*, *109*, 975–981. doi:10.1016/j.procs.2017.05.456

Prusti, D., Das, D., & Rath, S. K. (2021). Credit card fraud detection technique by applying graph database model. *Arabian Journal for Science and Engineering*, *46*(9), 1–20. doi:10.100713369-021-05682-9

Rabuzin, K., Maleković, M., & Šestak, M. (2016). Gremlin by example. In H. R. Arabnia, F. G. Tinetti, & M. Yang (Eds.), *Proceedings of the 2016 International Conference on Advances in Big Data Analytics*, (pp. 144–149). CSREA Press.

Rabuzin, K., & Šestak, M. (2018). Towards inheritance in graph databases. In *2018 International Conference on Information Management and Processing, ICIMP 2018* (pp. 115–119). London, UK: IEEE. 10.1109/ICIMP1.2018.8325851

Rabuzin, K., & Šestak, M. (2019). Creating triggers with trigger-by-example in graph databases. In *DATA 2019 - Proceedings of the 8th International Conference on Data Science, Technology and Applications*, online (pp. 137-145). Prague, Czech Republic: SciTePress Digital Library. doi:10.5220/0007829601370144

Rabuzin, K., Šestak, M., & Konecki, M. (2016). Implementing UNIQUE integrity constraint in graph databases. In *The Eleventh International Multi-Conference on Computing in the Global Information Technology* (pp. 48–53). IARIA.

Rani, A., Goyal, N., & Gadia, S. K. (2020). Provenance framework for Twitter data using zero-information loss graph database. *ACM International Conference Proceeding Series*, 74–82. 10.1145/3430984.3431014

Reddy, K. (2019). Interactive graph data integration system with spatial-oriented visualization and feedback-driven provenance. *IEEE Access: Practical Innovations, Open Solutions*, *7*, 101336–101344. doi:10.1109/ACCESS.2019.2928847

Robinson, I., Webber, J., & Eifrem, E. (2013). *Graph databases: New opportunities for connected data*. O'Reilly Media, Inc.

Schaffenrath, R., Proksch, D., Kopp, M., Albasini, I., Panasiuk, O., & Fensel, A. (2020). Benchmark for performance evaluation of SHACL implementations in graph databases. In *Including Subseries Lecture Notes in Artificial Intelligence and Lecture Notes in Bioinformatics), 12173 LNCS* (pp. 82–96). Lecture Notes in Computer Science. Springer. doi:10.1007/978-3-030-57977-7_6

Šestak, M., Rabuzin, K., & Novak, M. (2016). Integrity constraints in graph databases-implementation challenges. In *Proceedings of Central European Conference on Information and Intelligent Systems*, (pp. 23-30). Varaždin, Croatia: Faculty of Organization and Informatics.

Shibanova, D. A., Stroganov, I. V., & Rudakov, I. V. (2021). Data formalization in transport system modeling using a graph database. In *Proceedings of the 2021 IEEE Conference of Russian Young Researchers in Electrical and Electronic Engineering (ElConRus 2021)* (pp. 2245–2251). St. Petersburg, Russia: IEEE. 10.1109/ElConRus51938.2021.9396137

Skavantzos, P., Zhao, K., & Link, S. (2021). Uniqueness constraints on property graphs. In *Including Subseries Lecture Notes in Artificial Intelligence and Lecture Notes in Bioinformatics), 12751 LNCS* (pp. 280–295). Lecture Notes in Computer Science. Springer. doi:10.1007/978-3-030-79382-1_17

Srivastava, S., & Singh, A. K. (2022). Fraud detection in the distributed graph database. *Cluster Computing*, 1–23. doi:10.100710586-022-03540-3

Timón-Reina, S., Rincón, M., & Martínez-Tomás, R. (2021). An overview of graph databases and their applications in the biomedical domain. *Database: The Journal of Biological Databases and Curation*, 1-22. . doi:10.1093/database/baab026

Tuteja, S., & Kumar, R. (2022). Query-driven graph models in e-commerce. *Innovations in Systems and Software Engineering*, 1–19. doi:10.100711334-021-00421-7

Wang, M., Zou, Y., Cao, Y., & Xie, B. (2019). Searching software knowledge graph with question. In *Including Subseries Lecture Notes in Artificial Intelligence and Lecture Notes in Bioinformatics), 11602 LNCS* (pp. 115–131). Lecture Notes in Computer Science. Springer. doi:10.1007/978-3-030-22888-0_9

Wilson, J. R. (1996). *Graph theory*. Addison Wesley.

Wu, J., & Nakamoto, Y. (2019). RelSeeker: Relationship-based query language in a graph database for social networks. In M. Alsmirat, & Y. Jararweh (Eds.), *Proceedings of the International Conference on Internet of Things: Systems, Management and Security* (pp. 268–273). Granada, Spain: IEEE. 10.1109/SNAMS.2019.8931872

ADDITIONAL READING

Angles, R., Arenas, M., Barceló, P., Hogan, A., Reutter, J., & Vrgoč, D. (2017). Foundations of modern query languages for graph databases. *ACM Computing Surveys*, *50*(5), 1–40. doi:10.1145/3104031

Angles, R., & Gutierrez, C. (2008). Survey of graph database models. *ACM Computing Surveys*, *40*(1), 1–39. doi:10.1145/1322432.1322433

Bonifati, A., Furniss, P., Green, A., Harmer, R., Oshurko, E., & Voigt, H. (2019, November). Schema validation and evolution for graph databases. In *Proceedings of the International Conference on Conceptual Modeling*, (pp. 448-456). Salvador, Brazil: Springer. 10.1007/978-3-030-33223-5_37

Lu, Y., & Hu, F. (2019). Secure dynamic big graph data: Scalable, low-cost remote data integrity checking. *IEEE Access: Practical Innovations, Open Solutions*, 7, 12888–12900. doi:10.1109/ACCESS.2019.2892442

Reina, F., Huf, A., Presser, D., & Siqueira, F. (2020, September). Modeling and enforcing integrity constraints on graph databases. In *Proceedings of the International Conference on Database and Expert Systems Applications*, (pp. 269-284). Bilbao, Spain: Springer. 10.1007/978-3-030-59003-1_18

Reina, F., Luiz, A. F., de Oliveira Rech, L., Netto, H. V., & Siqueira, F. (2019). Providing data integrity in graph databases. In *Proceedings of the 2019 XLV Latin American Computing Conference (CLEI)*, (pp. 1-10). IEEE.

Reina, F. M., Huf, A., Presser, D., & Siqueira, F. (2021). Extending the integrity constraint support in a graph database. *IEEE Latin America Transactions*, 19(4), 604–611. doi:10.1109/TLA.2021.9448543

Wood, P. T. (2012). Query languages for graph databases. *SIGMOD Record*, 41(1), 50–60. doi:10.1145/2206869.2206879

KEY TERMS AND DEFINITIONS

Graph Database Management System: A category of NoSQL Database Management Systems, which stores data in graph-like structures that consist of nodes and relationships.

Integrity Constraints: Rules that are used to maintain the quality of data in a database.

Neo4j: The most widely used Graph Database Management System.

NoSQL: A generation of database systems, which do not use SQL as the primary database query language and tackle the challenges (e.g., scalability, flexibility) attributed to traditional relational databases.

Query by Example (QBE): An alternative visual approach to querying databases through the use of graphical user interface without having to manually write the query in a given query language syntax.

Structured Query Language (SQL): The most important and wide-spread querying language for relational databases.

Triggers: Database objects that are activated when something happens in the database.

Free Text to Standardized Concepts to Clinical Decisions

F

Eva K. Lee
Georgia Institute of Technology, USA

Brent M. Egan
American Medical Association, USA

INTRODUCTION

Clinical decision making is complicated since it requires physicians to infer information from a given case and determine the best treatment based on their knowledge. Data from electronic medical records (EMRs) can reveal critical variables that impact treatment outcomes and inform the allocation of limited time and resources, allowing physicians to practice evidence-based treatment tailored to individual patient conditions. On a larger scale, realistically modifiable social determinants of health that will improve community health can potentially be discovered and addressed.

Although EMR adoption is spreading across the industry, many providers continue to document clinical findings, procedures, and outcomes with "free text" natural language in their EMRs. They have difficulty (manually) mapping concepts to standardized terminologies and struggle with application programs that use structured clinical data. This creates challenges for (multi-site) comparative effectiveness studies. Standardized clinical terminologies (e.g., SNOMED-CT, LOINC, RxNorm, UMLS) are essential to facilitate interoperability among EMR systems. They allow seamless sharing and exchange of healthcare information for quality care delivery and coordination among multiple sites. However, the volume and number of available clinical terminologies are large and expanding. Further, due to the increase in medical knowledge and the continued development of more advanced computerized medical systems, the use of clinical terminologies has extended beyond diagnostic classification.

This chapter summarizes our work in (1) designing an efficient, robust, and customizable information extraction and pre-processing pipeline for electronic medical records; (2) automatic mapping, standardization, and establishing interoperability; (3) uncovering best practices across multiple sites via machine learning; and (4) optimizing access timing and treatment decisions for chronic kidney disease patients Lee et al., 2016, 2019, 2021, 2022; Lee & Uppal 2020).

The work tackles over 800 clinical sites covering 9,000 providers and de-identified data for over 3.0 million patients with health records spanning the last 26 years. To the best of our knowledge, EMR data analysis across hundreds of sites and millions of patients has not been attempted previously. Such analysis requires effective database management, data extraction, preprocessing, and integration. In addition, temporal data mining of longitudinal health data cannot currently be achieved through statistically and computationally efficient methodologies and is still under-explored. This is a particularly important issue when analyzing outcome, health equity, and health conditions for chronic disease patients.

We first extract cohorts of patients from EMRs by disease / symptoms, and treatment features. Content discovery, concept mapping and interoperability are then established among EMRs from the 800+ clinical sites by developing a system that rapidly extracts and accurately maps free text to concise structured

DOI: 10.4018/978-1-7998-9220-5.ch028

Copyright © 2023, IGI Global. Copying or distributing in print or electronic forms without written permission of IGI Global is prohibited.

medical concepts. Multiple concepts and contents are extracted, and mapped, including patient diagnoses, laboratory results, medications, and procedures, which allows shared characterization and hierarchical comparison. A mixed integer programming-based machine learning model (DAMIP) is next applied to establish classification rules with relatively small subsets of discriminatory features that can be used to predict treatment outcomes for cardiovascular and chronic kidney diseases. Based on our results, optimal treatment design and associated new clinical practice guideline for chronic kidney disease pre-dialysis initiation is demonstrated. The results facilitate improved outcome, health quality, and cost-reduction for patients. Our findings can speed dissemination and implementation of *best practice* among all sites. Rapid learning across multiple sites show that improvement can be achieved within 12 months with a better health outcome, enhanced quality, and reduced cost. The next step will involve analyzing 60 million patients across the United States.

BACKGROUND

Data Extraction, Encryption, and Concept Standardization

It is challenging to establish an efficient data extraction schema for EMR due to the complexity of data and lack of data standards. A common task in EMR is case detection – identifying a cohort of patients with a certain condition or symptom. Coded data such as International Classification of Diseases (ICD) are often not sufficient or accurate (Birman-Deych et al., 2005, Sonabend W et al., 2020). Informatics approaches combining structured EMR data with narrative text data achieve better performance (Li et al., 2008; Savova et al., 2010). Key clinical items can be extracted from narrative texts with methods such as pattern matching using regular expressions (Long, 2005; Turchin et al., 2006; Friedlin and McDonald, 2006; Ravikumar & Ramakanth Kumar, 2021), full or partial parsing based on morpho-semantems (Baud et al., 1998; Mamlin et al., 2003), and syntactic and semantic analysis (Friedman et al., 1994; Jain and Friedman, 1997). Increasingly, more complex statistical and rule-based machine learning approaches (Bashyam and Taira, 2005; Taira and Soderland, 1999) have been developed to tackle this challenge. Biomedical Named Entity Recognition (NER) – the "task of identifying words and phrases in free text that belong to certain classes of interest" (Settles, 2004), allows users to identify key clinical concepts such as physician visits, referrals, dietary management, and suspected problems normally not present in structured data tables.

Once patient information is extracted, data security and confidentiality must be ensured through de-identification steps. According to the Health Insurance Portability and Accountability Act (HIPAA), patients' Protected Health Information (PHI) must be de-identified or anonymized for commercial and research use. PHI exists in both structured and unstructured clinical records (Zikopoulos and Eaton, 2011). This includes patient names, addresses, phone numbers, etc. Manual and rule-based or lexicon-based methods have been used to achieve PHI de-identification (Sweeney, 1996; Ruch et al., 2000; Taira et al., 2002), but they are extremely time-consuming and can be inaccurate. Machine learning approaches have also been developed (Sibanda and Uzuner, 2006; Wellner et al., 2007; Szarvas et al., 2007; Phuong & Chau, 2016). However, due to the complexity of data schemas and the heterogeneity of data structures, it is very challenging to detect PHI with high sensitivity.

Because EMR data include various types of records for patients, data standardization is essential prior to analytic investigation. With multiple facilities and providers, the problem is compounded as data heterogeneity becomes a major issue due to the significant practice variation in style of reporting, use of terminologies, and descriptive content.

Tackling the problem of data heterogeneity is essential for conducting predictive analytics using artificial intelligence. Many clinical records in the EMR adhere to different terminology systems and can cause problems such as data redundancy and inconsistency, hindering the performance of automated machine learning models. To establish interoperability among various naming systems, standardization of data is necessary. In our previous work, (Lee et al., 2016), clinical concepts were standardized by a concept mapping system which links concepts describing diagnosis, laboratory, and medications to the standardized SNOMED-CT terminologies.

Standardization of terminologies not only facilitates the analysis of EMR data but can also increase the efficiency of operations and information sharing, thereby facilitating knowledge transfer and reducing practice variance among health care organizations.

Unsupervised Learning

Longitudinal clinical data recorded during care delivery are often incomplete and non-uniform and thus challenging for quantitative analysis. Identifying subgroups of patients who experience symptoms with varying severity (Miaskowski et al., 2006) or respond to treatment procedures differently may reveal critical risks or clinical/treatment factors that impact patient outcome. Laboratory and vitals measurements before, during, and after treatment / procedures may act as markers of disease severity (Wells et al., 2013) and characterize recovery process. Uncovering patient clusters also have prognostic significance – by constructing cluster-based mortality prediction models, one can achieve superior performance when compared to treating all patient episodes as a single group (Marlin et al., 2012). However, time-series laboratory and vital data often exhibit different lengths and frequencies due to varying syndromes and treatment schedules for different patients, or physician practice variance. Thus, conventional clustering algorithms aiming to identify patient subgroups cannot be applied directly. Pre-processing methods such as interpolation (Lee et al., 2000; Kreindler and Lumsden, 2016) and resampling (Carlstein, 1992, (Rama et al., 2019) can normalize time series data, allowing clustering approaches such as K-means (Hartigan & Wong, 1979) to be used. Alternatively, clustering algorithms have been customized for variable-length time series. These algorithms can be characterized into 3 types: (1) time-based (Agrawal et al., 1993; Chan & Fu, 1999; Latecki et al., 2005; Yi, B & Faloutsos, 2000), (2) shape-based (Marteau, 2009; Sakoe & Chiba, 1971; Vlachos et al., 2002), and (3) structural-based (Kalpakis et al., 2001; Smyth, 1997). They utilize a variety of similarity (distance) measures such as Dynamic Time Warping (DTW) (Sakoe, 1971; Lee et al., 2019; Nim et al., 2019), Longest Common Subsequence (LCSS) (Das et al., 1997), Cosine Wavelets (Huhtala et al., 1999), Edit distance with Real Penalty (ERP)(Chen & Ng, 2004), Global Alignment Kernel (GAK) (Cuturi et al., 2007), and Time-Warp Edit Distance (TWED) (Marteau, 2009).

While in some cases disease severity can be characterized by a single type of laboratory measurement — for example, serum cholesterol levels can be used to characterize conditions of patients with hyperlipidemia (Wells et al., 2013), --- in other cases severity can be better defined by multiple laboratory measurement time series. For instance, systolic blood pressure and diastolic blood pressure should both be considered for patients with hypertension. Clustering approaches for such Multivariate Time Series (MTS) (Brockwell et al., 2002; Lee et al., 2019) are limited. Existing PCA-based (Singhal and Seborg, 2005), Hidden Markov Model (HMM)-based, partition-based (Liao, 2007), and model-based approaches (Košmelj and Batagelj, 1990, Ramoni et al., 2002) have been applied to a variety of fields including chemistry and manufacturing but have not been utilized in clinical settings. This is likely due to the irregularity of clinical time series. Clustering approaches have not been developed for MTS with irregular intervals and unequal lengths. The project described in this chapter developed methodologies for these "irregular MTS".

Supervised Learning

The use of predictive modeling for clinical decision making has great value in improving outcomes, enhancing patients' experiences, and reducing health care costs (Amarasingham et al., 2014). The discriminatory features identified, and the criteria developed via a machine learning framework can be used to design and optimize evidence-based treatment plans and to disseminate such knowledge through "rapid learning" across multiple sites (Lee et al., 2016).

To utilize existing machine learning frameworks, one must first transform clinical variables into suitable forms of input features, or potential predictor variables. Continuous variables including laboratory measurements, vital signs, and drug dosages can be flattened into mean, median, or most-recent-value representations (Gultepe et al., 2014; Taylor et al., 2016; Wu et al., 2010). They can also be discretized, clustered, or binarized into "Yes/No" variables (Kawaler et al., 2012; Taylor et al., 2016; Wu et al., 2010; Zhai et al., 2014). Discrete variables including procedure, diagnosis, and prescription can be represented as binary/categorical features (Kawaler et al., 2012; Panahiazar et al., 2015; Taylor et al., 2016; Zhai et al., 2014). In some cases, most recent diagnosis or procedure are isolated as nominal input features (Kawaler et al., 2012; Wu et al., 2010; Zhai et al., 2014).

Many state-of-the-art supervised learning algorithms have been utilized in the clinical setting. Among them, Support Vector Machine (SVM) (Asadi et al., 2014; Banerjee et al., 2019; Fraiwan et al., 2021; Kawaler et al., 2012; Månsson et al., 2015; Panahiazar et al., 2015; Wu et al., 2010), Tree-based and Ensemble methods (Cruz & Wishart, 2006; Kawaler et al., 2012; Khalilia et al., 2011; Panahiazar et al., 2015; Taylor et al., 2016; Wu et al., 2010), Logistic Regression (Månsson et al., 2015; Panahiazar et al., 2015; Sonabend W et al., 2020; Taylor et al., 2016; Wu et al., 2010; Zhai et al., 2014), Naïve Bayes (Cruz & Wishart, 2006; Kawaler et al., 2012), and Artificial Neural Network (Asadi et al., 2014; Fraiwan et al., 2021) are the most commonly used in classification tasks. One crucial problem that often rises in the clinical setting is imbalanced datasets, especially when the goal is to maximize the machine learning model's ability to distinguish the minority class (Cohen et al., 2006). Strategies to address this concern include resampling the dataset (Cohen et al., 2006; Passos et al., 2016; Wall et al., 2012) and modifying the classification algorithm (Cohen et al., 2006). This chapter describes a discrete support vector machine that can handle imbalanced datasets well.

Feature selection algorithms are essential for narrowing down the list of discriminatory factors in supervised learning models (Ruiz-Perez et al., 2020). Reducing the number of predictor variables not only results in faster computations, but also allow for implementation of practical clinical guidelines. The most commonly used methods such as correlation-based feature selection (Kawaler et al., 2012; Zhai et al., 2014), feature importance from tree-based classifiers (Asadi et al., 2014; Taylor et al., 2016; Wu et al., 2010), and Lasso (T. F. Lee, Chao, et al., 2014; T. F. Lee, Liou, et al., 2014; Wu et al., 2010) have all shown successes in the clinical setting. Recently, wrapper-based approaches have also gained interest (Lee et al., 2012; Sun et al., 2015). They use feature selection algorithms to search through the space of attribute subsets with cross-validation accuracy from the classification module as a measure of goodness (Lee et al., 2012).

MATERIALS AND METHODS

Establishing Interoperability: From Free-text Natural Language to Standardized Medical Concepts

Data Extraction and Encryption

Clarity database from EMR system stores patient data in over 7,000 tables with over 60,000 columns with daily update. Structured Query Language (SQL) written in Oracle SQL Developer is the primary programming language used to access the database. We extracted patient cohorts characterized by (1) Disease or Symptoms; and (2) Treatment Features. A novel extraction algorithm was developed that combines ICD-9 / ICD-10 diagnosis codes with billing information, laboratory data or narratives in clinical notes for more accurate case detection (cite). Semantic matching of key terms describing medical conditions was employed. We note that encounter-level data containing physician visits and referrals, dietary management, prognosis, and suspected problems are only revealed in the clinical notes. For treatment features, we must first identify all the possible vocabularies that represent the chosen disease. The targeted patient cohort contains millions of patient records amounting to terabytes of data. Table partitions were created to retrieve data by chunks and reduce local storage loads. Temporary views are used to reduce server loads. The data were encrypted to adhere to the HIPAA guidelines.

Concepts, Clinical and Decision Process Extraction from Narrative Clinical Texts

An end-to-end "pipeline" for extracting key clinical features and decision processes from narrative documents was developed (Lee et al., 2019). Our new interactive content extraction, recognition, and construction tool (CERC) performs content summarization and concept recognition to extract key clinical features including problems, procedures, tests, and decisions ((Lee et al., 2022; Lee & Uppal, 2020). E.g., a glomerular filtration rate (GFR) < 35 in the clinical note highlights disease progression with respect to a certain time point. It also reflects effects over previous clinical action, prescribed medication, or procedure, and resulting downstream decisions/actions. Some of these features can be consolidated and mapped to standard medical ontologies; while new concepts may be established and directly input into machine learning algorithms for knowledge discovery. Here, timeline of events, conditions of health, medication prescriptions, and effects are established.

Dataset Description and Management

A relational database was designed using Postgres 9.2.18 to store the pre-preprocessed EMR data of 3.0 million patients collected from 800 healthcare facilities. Thirteen tables were created containing patient records pertaining to procedures, demographics, diagnosis codes, laboratory measurements, and medications. Indices were developed for each table to enable rapid search and table joins for data querying. The data size for indices is an additional 11 GB, totaling 27 GB for the entire compressed text-only database. We label this the CCI-health database, where CCI stands for Care Coordination Institute. In the CCI-health database, 2.46 million patients are associated with a diagnosis, 1.89 million are associated with procedures, 1.33 million are associated with laboratories, and 955,000 are linked to medications (Lee et al., 2019).

Data Integration and Mapping to Standardized Medical Concepts

Laboratory and medication records are described with free text entries without unique codes for each entry. Since clinicians may describe identical treatments with many possible variations, it is essential to map entries to structured concepts without ambiguity. Overall, 803 unique laboratory phrases and 9,755 medication phrases were extracted from the patient records. We used Metamap to map laboratory and medication terms to UMLS Metathesaurus terms. Laboratory and medication terms were then linked to LOINC and RxNorm terms respectively, using the UMLS MRCONSO and RXNCONSO tables. Finally, LOINC and RxNorm terms established from the CCI-health database were linked to SNOMED-CT ontology using the UMLS MRREL and RXNREL tables. In our implementation, for LOINC, only concepts that have the name "procedure" were returned from the MRREL table. For RxNorm, only concepts that have "has_form", "has_ingredient", and "has_tradename" relationships were returned from the RXNREL table. When medication entries in an EMR and a SNOMED concept were named completely differently, relationships could still be found due to rules such as tradenames and ingredients. Figures 1a and 1b show the workflows for mapping laboratory and medication phrases to SNOMED-CT concepts.

Some of the patient data employs ICD-9 codes for patient diagnoses (Forrey et al., 1996). This makes the mapping procedure to SNOMED-CT concepts slightly different from those designed for laboratories and medications. The ICD9CM_SNOMED_MAP table in UMLS can be used to map ICD-9 directly to SNOMED-CT concepts. However, this does not include all ICD-9 codes that are associated with patients in the CCI-health database. Metamap was then used to analyze the descriptions of the remaining ICD codes that are not found in the ICD9CM_SNOMED_MAP table to map them to UMLS Metathesaurus concepts. The MRCONSO table was then used to map the UMLS concepts to associated SNOMED-CT concepts (Figure 1c).

Procedures in the EMR database are recorded using the Healthcare Common Procedure Coding System (HCPCS), which consists of two levels: the level I common Current Procedural Terminology (CPT) codes and the Level II codes which identify products, supplies, and services not included in CPT (HCPCS, 2003). Mapping procedures to SNOMED-CT requires a more holistic approach than that of the other concepts since HCPCS contains codes for clinical labs, medications, and procedures/interventions (Foley et al., 2007). Although HCPCS is one of the source vocabularies in the UMLS, many codes do not have direct matches to SNOMED-CT concepts. To overcome this, we developed the following mapping process: First, concept strings corresponding to the procedure codes were extracted from the MRCONSO table. Of the 11,374 unique codes, 7,570 had one or more matches in the MRCONSO table. Next, MetaMap was used to identify one or more UMLS candidate concepts that are associated with these extracted concepts. We then selected those candidate concepts that have the highest evaluation score using MetaMap's natural language processing. Some of these UMLS concepts have corresponding Metathesaurus concepts that could be linked to SNOMED-CT concepts directly. Otherwise, LOINC and RxNorm terms were used to link them to SNOMED-CT using MRREL and RXNREL tables (Figure 1d). If a UMLS concept could be linked to both LOINC and RxNorm sources, we selected the source with the higher matching score.

Implementation and Automation of Mapping Process

Although the mapping approaches for labs, medications, diagnoses, and procedures are different, they share similar intermediate steps and can be automated. Herein, we briefly discussed steps to set up the necessary knowledge databases and software, and how the scripts were deployed to establish the mapping tables.

Figure 1. Process map for (a.) laboratory phrases, (b.) medication phrases, (c.) diagnosis ICD-9/ICD-10 codes, and (d.) procedure codes to SNOMED-CT concepts respectively

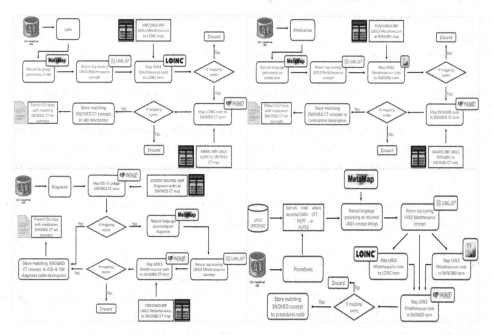

The Postgres 9.2.18 database was set up on a Red Hat Enterprise Linux Server release 7.3 operating system. MetamorphoSys, the UMLS installation tool was downloaded from the NLM website (2016AB release) and used to generate the UMLS data in the Rich Release Format (RRF) files. We used the Postgres table and index creation scripts provided by UMLS (UMLS, 2013) to load the RRF files into the database. Metamap 2016 v2 binaries were downloaded from National Institutes of Health and installed. After setting up the EMR database, the UMLS knowledge databases, and Metamap, a script was developed in Python 3.6.8 to streamline the mapping procedure. It is readily deployable after specifying the input file containing the terms to be mapped, UMLS database access credentials, the path to Metamap binaries, and the mapping output database and output file names. The script reads, analyzes, and stores matching SNOMED-CT concepts to labs, medications, diagnoses, and procedures in the EMR for rapid retrieval and further expert evaluation (Lee et al., 2019).

Runtime Complexity Analysis

Since the pipeline is composed of multiple steps and utilizes multiple algorithms, the running time varies with the number of input parameters. In general, the entire process scales linearly with the number of input vocabularies. We analyzed the scaling behavior of the pipeline empirically by conducting several computational experiments. Let n be the number of input vocabularies / phrases. The most time-consuming step of the mapping pipeline is Metamap's natural language processing step during which the input text undergoes a lexical/syntactic analysis consisting of seven major steps:

1. *Tokenization* uses a regular expression-based approach which runs at $O(n)$ (Aronson, 1996);
2. *Part of speech (POS) tagging* was implemented with the Viterbi Algorithm (Cutting et al., 1992), which uses a bigram Hidden Markov Model with 60 possible states corresponding to the POS

tags (Smith et al., 2004). The asymptotic complexity of the Viterbi Algorithm is $O(n|V|^2)$, where V equals the number of possible POS tags;

3. *Lexical lookup of words in SPECIALIST lexicon* is a simple dictionary lookup process requiring $O(n)$ time;

4. *Identification of phrases and lexical heads by the SPECIALIST parser* (Aronson & Lang, 2010) takes $O(n)$ time;

5. *Variant generation* takes $O(mn)$ time, where m is the number of words in the lexicon (Aronson, 1996);

6. *Candidate retrieval* is dependent on the number of variants generated in step 5. This step consists of (i) tokenization of the variants and (ii) lexical lookup for the first canonical-form token. Both steps use $O(k)$ time, where k is the number of variants generated. Therefore, this step takes a total of $O(nk)$ time;

7. *The mapping construction* evaluates each candidate and generates a Matchmap (Aronson, 1996). This step uses $O(cn)$ time, where c is the number of candidates retrieved in step 6.

Since $V, m, k,$ and c can all be considered as constants, and each step above scales linearly with the number of input vocabularies n, the total running time of Metamap natural language processing uses linear time $O(n)$. The remaining steps of the mapping pipeline involves selecting the concept type filtering, source vocabulary matching, and filtering, each of which also uses linear time $O(n)$. Thus, the entire mapping pipeline has an asymptotic runtime complexity of $O(n)$(Lee et al., 2019).

Refinement and Validation of Mapping Results

SNOMED-CT provides a rich hierarchy enabling semantic distances between concepts to be measured by path distances. We developed a Neo4j Graph Database for the CCI-health data to rapidly compute common ancestor queries between the mapped SNOMED-CT terms. In our Neo4j Graph Database, tab delimited files of all SNOMED concepts and relationships are exported from SNOMED CT Postgres relational database tables. The tab-delimited files were then loaded directly into Neo4j community edition 2.0.0 using their batch inserter (Neo4j).

The root node of the ontological graph corresponds to the Concept Name "SNOMED CT Concept". The resulting graph typically has numerous cycles, which greatly impede graph operations. We addressed this by removing edges from these cycles to construct a directed acyclic graph (DAG). Edges were removed from each cycle based on three different criteria: (1) maximum depth, (2) shortest path, and (3) fan-in count (in-degree). Maximum depth is the maximum number of nodes between the current node and the root node of the ontological graph. In each cycle, we removed the edges whose source node has a smaller maximum depth than its target node. The shortest path is the shortest distance (number of edges) from the current node to the root. In cases where the maximum depth of all the nodes in the cycles are equal, we selected edges whose source node has a shorter shortest path than its target node to remove. Finally, if all the nodes in the cycle have equal maximum depths and shortest paths, we use the Fan-in count criteria. Fan-in count is the number of incoming edges to the current node in the cycle. Nodes with larger degrees of incoming edges are expected to represent more generalized concepts. Therefore, we removed edges whose source node has a larger fan-in count than its target nod. These criteria are selected to reduce the likelihood of a node representing a more specific concept from becoming a parent of a node representing a more generalized concept in the final concept graph.

The resulting acyclic directed SNOMED-CT Graph database facilitates rapid graph computations such as shortest paths and common ancestor queries. This is beneficial since laboratories, diagnoses, medications, and procedures are all mapped to multiple SNOMED-CT concepts that can be too specific for machine learning analysis.

In our implementation, all nodes were assigned a depth level according to the minimum number of edges that must be traversed to reach the root. The root is at depth level 0. All the mapped SNOMED-CT concepts can then be generalized to concepts at a higher depth level (Lee et al., 2016). It is important to choose an appropriate depth level to accurately distinguish patient characteristics from one another. For medications and diagnosis, a depth level of 2 was chosen. A depth level of 3 was chosen for laboratories, since assigning lower depth levels returned concepts that were too general (Lee et al., 2016). Since procedure terms cover a broad spectrum of clinical terminologies and are mapped to SNOMED-CT via multiple source vocabularies, no concept generalization was performed, instead the mapping results were evaluated by clinical experts to ensure coverage and accuracy. For a given SNOMED-CT concept, Neo4j can quickly calculate all the possible paths to the root. With the Cypher query language, Neo4j returns all nodes for a given depth level that are crossed from all paths to the root of the hierarchy. After converting all SNOMED-CT concepts mapped from laboratory, medication, and diagnosis, we removed concepts that are too general and do not provide key information in characterizing patients. Examples include "Disorder of body system (362965005)", "Measurement procedure (122869004)", "Chemical procedure (83762000)", and "Types of drugs (278471000)". Upon cleaning, we arrived at the final integrated dataset that includes additional features for predictive analysis.

Clustering Patients for Multi-Site Outcome Analysis

We developed a novel clustering approach for irregular MTS based on existing distance metrics for variable-length time series. DTW, soft-DTW, and Global GAK (Cuturi et al., 2007) were used to calculate the pairwise distances between variable-length univariate time series. An aggregation function was then applied to the distance between all pairs of corresponding univariate time series composing the MTS. This produces a pairwise distance matrix representing the similarity between each pair of patients.

Clustering based on a pairwise matrix can be done using hierarchical or medoid-based clustering algorithms, because it is difficult to determine the length of the cluster centers when using partition-based clustering algorithms such as K-means (Liao, 2007). In this work, we applied the K-medoids (Park & Jun, 2009) clustering algorithm to the distance matrices. We briefly describe the clustering design below.

Cardiovascular Disease

About 18.2 million adults aged 20 and older have cardiovascular diseases (CVD). According to CDC, CVD is the No. 1 cause of death in the US. The CCI-health database contains 37,742 patients with CVD. Through our mapping, each patient is eventually characterized by 11 raw features including demographics, treatment duration, and co-existing conditions, and 1,757 standardized features in SNOMED-CT terminologies including laboratory tests, diagnosed problems, and medications. These 1,757 standardized features were mapped from 19,800 raw features from the database. For each patient, treatment duration was determined by calculating the elapsed time between diagnosis (indicated by the first prescription of a medication) and the last recorded activity (i.e., procedure, lab, etc.). Measurements of lipids and lipoproteins were processed into time series since these are closely related to cardiovascular conditions and can potentially be used to characterize the severity of CVD. Lack of high-density lipoproteins (HDL) is significantly associated with the development of heart disease (Gordon et al., 1977). In contrast, low-density lipoprotein (LDL) increases the risk of heart disease and is considered a "bad" cholesterol (Gordon et al., 1977). Triglycerides are also associated with incidence of heart disease but has a less significant effect (Gordon et al., 1977).

We used HDL, LDL, and Triglyceride measurements to form an MTS containing three time series for each patient. Each of these time series was resampled to quarterly frequency. Gaps in the data were filled by propagating the non-NaN values forward first, and then backward along a series. For each of the three types of laboratory measurements, we removed patients with fewer than three measurements after resampling from the dataset. This produces a data set containing 450 patients. The GAK distance between each pair of corresponding time series was calculated. The pairwise distance between each pair of MTS was then obtained by averaging the three distances for each pair of corresponding univariate time series. Specifically, given two patients, P^1 and P^2, each with m lab measurement time series, their pairwise distance was calculated using the following equation:

$$\text{Distance } (P^1, P^2) = \frac{1}{m}\left(\sum\nolimits_{t=1}^{m} D_{GAK}\left(P_t^1 P_t^2\right)\right).$$

Chronic Kidney Disease

About 37 million US adults suffer from chronic kidney disease (CKD) (CDC, 2019, 2021). And CKD has been recognized as a leading public health problem worldwide. The global estimated prevalence of CKD is 13.4% (11.7-15.1%), and patients with end-stage kidney disease (ESKD) needing renal replacement therapy is estimated between 4.902 and 7.083 million Shabaka et al., 2021).

CKD can be divided into 5 stages based on estimated glomerular filtration rate (eGFR) measurement. Early diagnosis of CKD prevents patients from regressing into late-stage CKD which causes serious complications. Late-stage CKD can lead to ESKD and CVD, which steeply increase patient pain and economic burden. However, the gradual loss of kidney function is difficult to diagnose due to the absence of direct evidence from clinical trials (Moyer, 2012). Hence frequent and regular measure of serum creatinine—used to calculate eGFR—is essential for evaluating changes in renal functions. Identifying trends in eGFR is more important than one-off readings, as suggested by the Renal Association, "a progressive fall in eGFR across serial measurements is more concerning than stable readings which don't change over time" (2019).

EMR provides a possibility for health care organization to monitor and identify early-stage CKD. Lenart et al. developed clustering techniques to detect progression of CKD (Lenart et al., 2016). K-medoids clustering was applied on patients' routine measurements and lab tests such as blood pressure, body mass index, Hemoglobin A1c (HbA1c), triglycerides and high-density lipid cholesterol (Lenart et al., 2016). The Cluster Progression Score (CPS) was designed to measure patients' relative health status (Lenart et al., 2016). This clustering process can help a health care organization detect early-stage CKD by monitoring recorded lab measurements.

The extracted dataset from EPIC EMR covers 33,303 patients with the ICD-9 code starting with "585" or ICD-10 code starting with "N18", both referring to "Chronic Kidney Disease". This dataset spans the years 1997-2018 and is composed of patient-level data (24Mb), problem lists (288Mb), medications (6.74Gb), billings (1.90Gb), laboratory orders (8.66Gb), and clinical notes (18.55 Gb), totaling 36.16 Gigabytes.

Patient eGFR laboratory test results were used as indications of disease progression. eGFR records were retrieved by the following method. (1) Component IDs for lab records matching the query string "%eGFR%" or "%GLOMERULAR FILTRATION RATE%" were retrieved. (2) Irrelevant lab components were discarded, leaving 16 unique component IDs. eGFR records matching these component IDs are examined it was discovered that only records corresponding to two component IDs "12122727" and "12122728" were well-maintained in the EMR. (3) eGFR lab records were then retrieved by patient IDs and these two component IDs. (4) Missing, erroneous, and duplicated records were removed, and the remaining records were sorted by date and transformed into time series format for each patient.

Optimization-Based Classifier: Discriminant Analysis via Mixed Integer Program (DAMIP)

Suppose we have n entities from K groups with m features. Let $\mathcal{G} = \{1,2,\ldots,K\}$ be the group index set, $\mathcal{O} = \{1,2,\ldots,n\}$ be the entity index set, and $\mathcal{F} = \{1,2,\ldots,m\}$ be the feature index set. Also, let $\mathcal{O}_k$, $k \in \mathcal{G}$ and $\mathcal{O}_k \subseteq \mathcal{O}$, be the entity set which belong to group k. Moreover, let $\mathcal{F}_j$, $j \in \mathcal{F}$, be the domain of feature j, which could be the space of real, integer, or binary values. The ith entity, $i \in \mathcal{O}$, is represented as

$$\left(y_i, \boldsymbol{x}_i\right) = \left(y_i, x_{i1}, \ldots, x_{im}\right) \in \mathcal{G} \times \mathcal{F}_1 \times \cdots \times \mathcal{F}_m,$$

where y_i is the group to which entity i belongs, and $(x_{i1}, \ldots, x_{im})$ is the feature vector of entity i. The classification model finds a function $f : \left(\mathcal{F}_1 \times \cdots \times \mathcal{F}_m\right) \to \mathcal{G}$ to classify entities into groups based on a selected set of features.

Let πk be the prior probability of group k and f$k_{(}$x) be the conditional probability density function for the entity $\boldsymbol{x} \in \mathbb{R}^m$ of group k, $k \in \mathcal{G}$. Also let $\alpha h_{k \in}(0,1)$, $h, k \in \mathcal{G}, h \neq k$, be the upperbound for the misclassification percentage that group h entities are misclassified into group k. DAMIP seeks a partition $\{P_0, P_1, \ldots, P_K\}$ of $\mathbb{R}^K$, where P_k, $k \in \mathcal{G}$, is the region for group k, and P_0 is the reserved judgement region with entities for which group assignment are reserved (for potential further exploration).

Let u_{ki} be the binary variable to denote if entity i is classified to group k or not. Mathematically, DAMIP (Gallagher et al., 1997; Lee, 2007, 2009; Lee et al., 2003, 2012) can be formulated as

$$\text{Max} \sum_{i \in \mathcal{O}} u_{y_i i} \tag{1}$$

$$\text{s.t.} \ L_{ki} = \pi_k f_k\left(\boldsymbol{x}_i\right) - \sum_{h \in \mathcal{G}, h \neq k} f_h\left(\boldsymbol{x}_i\right)\lambda_{hk} \quad \forall i \in \mathcal{O}, k \in \mathcal{G} \tag{2}$$

$$u_{ki} = \begin{cases} 1 & \text{if } k = \arg\max\left\{0, L_{hi} : h \in \mathcal{G}\right\} \\ 0 & \text{otherwise} \end{cases} \quad \forall i \in \mathcal{O}, k \in \{0\} \cup \mathcal{G} \tag{3}$$

$$\sum_{k \in \{0\} \cup \mathcal{G}} u_{ki} = 1 \quad \forall i \in \mathcal{O} \tag{4}$$

$$\sum_{i:i \in \mathcal{O}_h} u_{ki} \leq \alpha_{hk} n_h \quad \forall h,k \in \mathcal{G}, h \neq k \tag{5}$$

$$u_{ki} \in \{0,1\} \quad \forall i \in \mathcal{O}, k \in \{0\} \cup \mathcal{G}$$

L_{ki} *unrestricted in sign* $\forall i \in \mathcal{O}, k \in \mathcal{G}$

$$\lambda_{hk} \geq 0 \quad \forall h,k \in \mathcal{G}, h \neq k$$

The objective function (1) maximizes the number of entities classified correctly. Constraints (2) and (3) govern the placement of an entity into each of the groups in G or the reserved-judgment region. Thus, the variables L_{ki} and λh_k provide the shape of the partition of the groups in the G space. Constraint (4) ensures that an entity is assigned to exactly one group. Constraint (5) allows the users to preset the desirable misclassification levels, which can be specified as overall errors for each group, pairwise errors, or overall errors for all groups together. With the reserved judgment in place, the mathematical system ensures that a solution that satisfies the preset errors always exists.

Mathematically, DAMIP is *NP-hard*. The model has many appealing characteristics including: (i) the resulting DAMIP-classification rule is *strongly universally consistent*, given that the Bayes optimal rule for classification is known (Brooks & Lee, 2010, 2014); (ii) the misclassification rates using the DAMIP method are consistently lower than other classification approaches in both simulated data and real-world data; (iii) the classification rules from DAMIP appear to be insensitive to the specification of prior probabilities, yet capable of reducing misclassification rates when the number of training entities from each group is different; and (iv) the DAMIP model generates stable classification rules on imbalanced data, regardless of the proportions of training entities from each group (Gallagher et al., 1997; Lee, 2007, 2009; Lee et al., 2003, 2012).

Computationally, DAMIP is the first multiple-group classification model that includes a reserved judgment and the ability to constrain the misclassification rates simultaneously within the model. Further, Constraint (2) serves to transform the attributes from their original space to the group space, serving as dimension reduction. In Brooks and Lee (2010) and Brooks and Lee (2014), we have shown that DAMIP is difficult to solve (Brooks & Lee, 2010, 2014). We applied the hypergraphic structures that Lee, Wei, and Maheshwary derived to efficiently solve these instances (Lee et al., 2021).

By maximizing the number of correctly classified entities, the predictive rule is robust and not skewed by errors committed by observed values. The associated optimal decision variable values (L_{ki} and $\lambda h_{k)}$ form the classification rule, which consists of the discriminatory attributes (e.g., demographics, treatment duration, health conditions, laboratory results, medications, decisions, etc.).

The entities in our model correspond to the groups of patients: e.g., "Good Outcome", and "Non-Satisfactory Outcome". The goal was to uncover discriminatory factors that can predict these groups. Identifying patients with "Good Outcome" and care characteristics will establish best practice and evidence for providers.

In the classification analysis, the model was first applied to the training set to identify the discriminatory features and establish the classification rules using a 10-fold cross-validation unbiased estimate. The predictive accuracy of each classifier was further assessed by applying the rule to the blind-prediction set. DAMIP returns classifiers that include as few features as possible.

We contrasted the DAMIP approach with eight classification algorithms implemented with the Python Scikit-learn package (Pedregosa et al., 2011) including Logistic Regression, SVM, K-nearest neighbors, ExtraTrees, Random Forest, Decision Tree, Neural Network, Gradient Boosting, and Bernoulli Naïve Bayes. Randomized Lasso and Recursive Feature Elimination with Random Forest Classifier were coupled with these classifiers for feature selection (Geurts et al., 2006).

RESULTS AND CLINICAL ADVANCES

Data Interoperability Among 800 Clinical Sites

Free text entries from laboratories, medications, procedures, and ICD9/ICD10 diagnosis codes were all successfully mapped to SNOMED-CT concepts. Specifically, 2.35 million of 2.46 million patients contain at least one diagnosis code that can be mapped to SNOMED-CT. Table 1 shows the percentage of successfully linked phrases and the associated patient coverage. We note that a small percentage (4.5%, 121,500) of patients contributes to a large number of unlinked diagnosis codes.

Table 1. Percentage of successfully linked phrases and the associated patient coverage

Terminologies	No of unique phrases	% linked to SNOMED-CT	% of patient covered
Laboratory	803	75.00%	90.20%
Medication	9755	60.40%	84.10%
Diagnosis codes	29371	36.20%	95.50%
Procedure	11374	66.90%	94.70%

Medications can have many brand names and a range of ingredients. Laboratory and procedures may also be described by physicians with a great deal of variation. Variations and ambiguity among phrases are eliminated by our mapping algorithm.

The mapping created tens of thousands of new features for each patient. Specifically, a total of 24,766 entries for laboratories, medications, procedures, and diagnosis codes were mapped to 18,264 SNOMED-CT concepts. For each patient, a feature is created for each mapped medical concept indicating whether a patient received a medication, was given a diagnosis, or given a laboratory test, or underwent a procedure. Furthermore, many of these features were closely related. It is thus beneficial to generalize them to reduce the total number of features per patient. In our implementation, these mapped SNOMED-CT concepts were generalized into level 2 nodes for medications and diagnoses and level 3 nodes for laboratories.

Empirical Experiments on Running Time

To demonstrate the efficiency of the mapping pipeline, empirical experiments were conducted as follows: 15,000 unique phrases were extracted from the database, with 5,000 related to each medication, laboratory, and procedure (corresponding to CPT code). The mapping pipeline for each category of phrases was run using incrementing subsets of 1000, 2000, 3000, 4000, and 5000. Mapping of the diagnosis code was excluded since it can be achieved without the Metamap processing step. Table 2 compares the CPU time of each experiment. The empirical results confirm that the processing time grows linearly with respect to the number of input phrases within each category. Mapping of each input phrase takes on average 1-1.6 seconds. Thus, our mapping pipeline is highly efficient and scales linearly.

Table 2. Runtime of mapping pipeline for medication, laboratory, and procedure phrases in CPU-seconds

Number of input phrases	Time in CPU seconds		
	Medication	**Laboratory**	**Procedure**
1000	1,101.1	1,298.0	1,285.7
2000	2,033.6	2,356.9	2,227.7
3000	3,028.3	3,346.8	3,329.9
4000	4,034.2	4,660.7	4,375.3
5000	5,000.9	5,626.5	5,349.7

Clustering to Establish Treatment Outcome Groups

Cardiovascular Disease

K-medoids clustering performed on the CVD distance matrix partitioned the patients into 3 groups. The clinical experts examined the raw laboratory records for each group and associated the cluster characteristics as "Good", "Medium", and "Poor" outcomes (blue, red, green). Figure 2 show the raw HDL, LDL, and Triglyceride laboratory records by cluster. The "Poor Outcome" group is well-segregated from the two groups, showing high variability in HDL and LDL levels, which is a high-risk factor for myocardial infarction. Although the "Good" and "Medium" outcome groups have similar trajectories of cholesterol levels, the "Good" outcome has slightly higher HDL levels, lower LDL and Triglyceride levels, and shows more consistency in all three types of cholesterol levels.

The goal of machine learning is to uncover discriminatory features that can predict good outcome. For classification, we considered the "Good Outcome" group versus the "Not-Satisfactory Outcome" group, with the latter group consisting of the "Medium" and "Poor" outcome clusters. Table 3 shows the patient partition for machine learning training and blind prediction.

Chronic Kidney Disease

K-medoids clustering performed on the CKD distance matrix partitioned the patients into 3 groups also. Figure 3 illustrates the eGFR trends for a sample of patients from each group over a period of 120 months. We can observe that the eGFR trend is sustaining steadily among the patients in the "Good" cluster, whereas patients in the "Poor" cluster have rapid eGFR drop over the same period.

Table 3. Partition of CVD patients for training and blind prediction

Total Patients	10-fold Cross validation training set			Blind prediction set		
	Total	Non-Satisfactory Outcome	Good Outcome	Total	Non-Satisfactory Outcome	Good Outcome
450	314	218	96	136	94	42

Figure 2. HDL, LDL, and Triglyceride laboratory records for each patient cluster

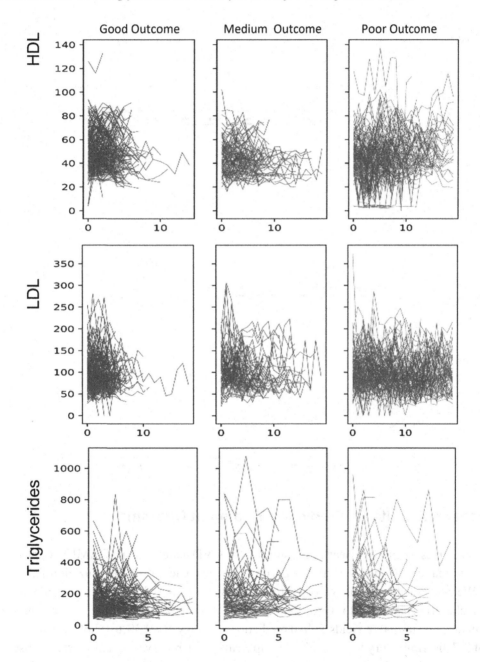

Figure 3. CKD patient clusters for the 3 groups respectively. "Good Outcome" group sustains a steady eGFR trend. These patients remain in Stage 2 or 3 over a period of 120 months. "Medium Outcome" group has a wider fluctuation in eGFR trend. These patients enter Stage 3 and Stage 4 over a period of 120 months. "Poor Outcome" group exhibits a rapid drop in eGFR. These patients fall into Stage 4 and Stage 5 over a period of 120 months

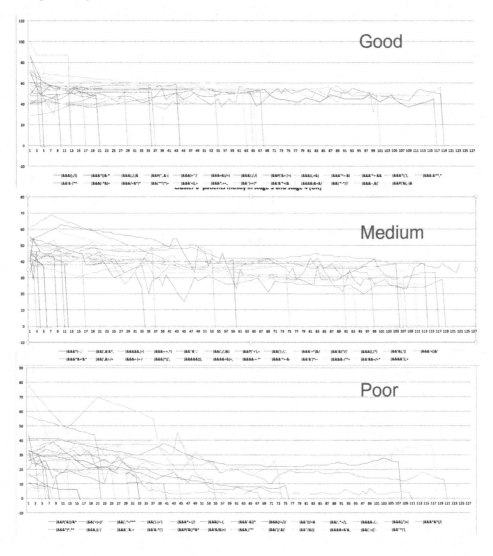

Classification Results on Predicting Treatment Outcome

Table 4 summarizes the machine learning results for the CVD patients using DAMIP, coupled with either an exact combinatorial feature selection algorithm or a particle swarm optimization feature selection heuristic. We contrasted the accuracy of 10-fold cross validation and DAMIP blind prediction.

DAMIP classified patients into "Good Outcome" vs "Non-Satisfactory Outcome" by uncovering a set of discriminatory features that yields a blind prediction accuracy of 89.3% to 97.6%. Each rule (a column) consists of 3-7 discriminatory features. The multiple rules with relatively small subsets of discriminatory features afford flexibility for different sites (and different patient populations) to adopt different policies for implementing the best practice. In contrast, among the eight commonly used classifiers, Random Forest achieves the best results, with 10-fold cross validation unbiased estimates of 75% and 90% for "Good Outcome" and "Not-Satisfactory Outcome" respectively. The blind prediction is slightly worse, about 73% and 89% respectively. All the other methods suffered from imbalanced data and the accuracy for "Good Outcome" was uniformly below 60%. Note that Randomized Lasso selected sixteen discriminatory features. In contrast, the DAMIP results offer higher accuracy with fewer discriminatory features.

The results for CKD patients are similar: DAMIP classified CKD patients into "Good Outcome" vs "Non-Satisfactory Outcome" by uncovering a set of 6-10 discriminatory features that yields a blind prediction accuracy of 91.3% and 96.5% respectively.

Table 4. DAMIP classification rules in predicting CVD Treatment

Discriminatory feature (chosen from 1,768 features)	Exact combinatorial search					Heuristics particle swarm optimization				
Treatment Length	X	X	X	X	X	X	X	X	X	X
Glucose measurement, urine (procedure)	X			X	X	X	X	X	X	X
Synthetic steroid (substance)			X	X	X		X	X	X	
Acute digestive system disorder (disorder)						X		X		
Inflammatory disorder of upper respiratory tract (disorder)				X		X	X	X	X	X
Calcium channel blocking agent (product)	X	X	X							
Neoplasm by body site (disorder)		X	X							
Diabetic - poor control (finding)						X	X			
Implantation (procedure)						X	X			
Investigations (procedure)						X	X			
Acute disorder of ear (disorder)									X	
Disorder of immune system (navigational concept)					X					
Allergen or pseudoallergen (substance)									X	
Oral form naproxen (product)										X
Electrocardiogram finding (finding)									X	X
Disinfectants and cleansers (product)									X	X
Imaging (procedure)									X	X
Accuracy of 10-fold cross validation (%), Good Outcome	85.3	87.6	87.6	89.9	87.6	90.3	90.3	90.3	90.3	89.4
Accuracy of 10-fold cross validation (%), Non-Satisfactory Outcome	91.6	86.4	85.4	86.4	85.4	86.4	86.4	86.4	86.4	86.4
Accuracy of DAMIP blind prediction (%), Good Outcome	89.3	91.4	91.4	93.6	91.4	91.9	93.6	92.5	92.5	92.5
Accuracy of DAMIP blind prediction (%), Non-Satisfactory Outcome	97.6	92.8	92.8	90.4	92.8	92.5	90.4	90.4	95.2	97.6

Generating New Clinical Practice Guidelines for Treatment Decision

The machine learning results offer opportunities for evidence-based patient-centered clinical decision support. We describe herein one such application.

Optimal timing of dialysis initiation in patients with end-stage kidney disease (ESKD) is important for reducing the risk of increased morbimortality due to uraemic complications (Caro Martínez et al., 2019; Heaf et al., 2021). In the absence of a national guideline, the best time to start dialysis remains an open challenge, with 40%-70% of initiations being suboptimal (Brown et al., 2015; Mendelssohn et al., 2009). The timing is often ad-hoc with no consistency nor standard. The difficulty in achieving a common "gold standard" lies partly in the high heterogeneity among patients and available treatment conditions, and partly in the random factors in disease progression and treatment process

Hemodialysis (HD) offers higher dialysis efficacy and better capacity control, though there is a greater impact on hemodynamics and an increased tendency to bleed. Peritoneal dialysis (PD) is done more continuously than HD. It results in less accumulation of potassium, sodium and fluid; and allows a more flexible diet than on HD. It also sustains a longer lasting residual kidney function. The preparation for HD, which includes creating a vascular access (the arteriovenous (AV) fistula or the AV graft), takes about 6-12 months, PD takes only 3-6 months. Emergency dialysis is performed via a central venous catheter (CVC) (Choi et al., 2020; Foley, 2004; Genovesi et al., 2017; Swai et al., 2020; Vonesh et al., 2006).-

The initiation of dialysis can be classified into three types: *optimal start, suboptimal start* and *crash start*. -An optimal start occurs when patients initiate dialysis electively in an outpatient setting using the patient's chosen chronic dialysis modality with a mature AVF or PD catheter, Suboptimal initiation refers to dialysis initiation in an inpatient setting and / or in an unplanned way of dialysis choice. Crash start means patient did not receive any nephrology care before starting dialysis.

The goal of our clinical decision model is to determine an outcome-driven threshold of eGFR for creating dialysis access of various types that maximizes the goodness of the patient's health (measured partly by patient's eGFR value). In addition to modeling clinical criteria, patient preference is also incorporated. To the best of our knowledge, this is the *first-of-its-kind optimal timing model* established.

We applied our novel extraction-mapping algorithm and DAMIP to a separate patient cohort of 10,579 chronic kidney patients with 144,249 eGFR measurements from 2011 to 2018. Using the DAMIP results on the clinical and decision processes and outcome evidence, we developed a stochastic Markov decision model to determine an optimal pre-dialysis care policy. Table 5 shows the optimal timing (policy) for dialysis initiation and optimal dialysis start. The optimal results were incorporated within a clinical practice guideline. The new policy was implemented in October 2018 among the Southeast Permanente Medical Group hospitals. The resulting policy offers a better outcome for the patients, specifically it saves lives, improves patients' quality of life, and reduces 35% of their treatment costs. Table 6 contrasts the prior practice to the new policy. The optimal timing led to an increase in PD enrollment from 0.2% to 9.5%, 35% reduction in HD enrollment, 96% reduction of emergency dialysis (CVC), and 29% increase in pre-dialysis. The results are promising as patients realize the importance to proactively prepare themselves and many chose the PD option. The new practice leads to a reduction of 45% in avoidable deaths. Although cost is not our objective, an optimal access timing reduces the overall cost by 30.5%. Although PD is 22% more costly than HD, the overall positive treatment effects outweigh the cost. Long term analyses and tracking of results and potential refinement may be necessary. The new clinical practice guideline may potentially serve as a national guideline for other chronic kidney disease patients.

Thus, this work has critical health practice implications. Through data-driven interoperability and predictive analytics, using our novel mapping algorithm and DAMIP, we have established and identified practice characteristics that result in good outcome. The extraction-mapping system and DAMIP are scalable and generalizable to different hospital settings. New concepts, and clinical and decision processes extracted prove to be important for our effort in optimizing clinical decisions for improved outcome. Details of the CKD study are reported in a separate manuscript (Lee et al., 2022).

Table 5. Optimal initiation time for dialysis returned from the Markov clinical decision model

Type	Optimal Initiation time	Begin dialysis
HP	GFR < 20	GFR < 12
PD	GFR < 18	GFR < 10
Suboptimal	With uremia	GFR < 7
	Without uremia	GFR < 10

Table 6. Implementation results for chronic kidney disease patients, including a breakout for the patients who died

Treatment Distribution, Cost / Patient	Hemodialysis	Peritoneal dialysis	Central venous catheter (Suboptimal)	Pre-dialysis	Death	All-patient-average
Practice prior July 2018	16.70%	0.20%	8.80%	51.70%	22.60%	$37,363
	$32,187	$41,081	$57,802	$4,718	$107,876	
New Policy	10.90%	9.50%	0.30%	66.70%	12.60% **-45%**	$25,971 **-30.5%**
	$30,542	$41,759	$45,776	$5,042	$120,428	

FUTURE RESEARCH DIRECTIONS

We have successfully developed a systematic analytic pipeline to address the challenges associated with big data in healthcare. This pipeline is composed of technologies and innovations related to information extraction, data pre-processing, terminology standardization, longitudinal data mining, feature selection and supervised learning. The technologies developed fill some of the most important gaps in the current healthcare industry (Lee et al., 2016, 2019, 2021; Lee & Uppal 2020).

The extraction pipeline organizes data into a structured, machine-readable format which can be effectively applied in clinical research studies to generate practical and unbiased insights from a holistic perspective. The automated mapping process establishes interoperability among the heterogeneous data systems from multiple health care sites and providers. It significantly reduces data dimension and redundancy, addressing the issue of the "curse of dimensionality" associated with big data. It also has the potential to facilitate the reimbursement process, improve clinical decision support, and promote the exchange of information among multiple sites.

Longitudinal health data remains under-utilized and challenging for analytic investigation. Given the complexity of irregular multivariate time series and the difficulty involved in labelling clusters, it is necessary to combine effective visualization techniques with quantitative measures to achieve this task. Mining these multivariate longitudinal health data is conducive to understanding patient conditions from an evolving perspective. It opens new doors to improving clinical outcome assessment, prognostic tools, and personalized care.

Besides the results of cardiovascular diseases and chronic kidney diseases reported herein, best practice results were also obtained for diabetes (Lee et al., 2016) and hypertension. The connected interoperable database, consisting of over 800+ clinical sites, includes patients with multiple chronic diseases including cancer, asthma, stroke, respiratory disease, injuries, Alzheimer's disease, influenza and pneumonia, and septicemia.

Future advances will include (1) implementing practical clinical intervention strategies based on uncovered best practices and evidence; (2) applying our knowledge discovery to other diseases; (3) exploring more efficient, comprehensive, and accurate information extraction approaches; (4) improving the efficiency of time series clustering algorithms and developing more rigorous evaluation metrics for clinical time series clustering results; (5) monitoring health status and performing rapid analytics based on existing data to identify the earliest sign of health risk; and (6) developing advanced analytical methods that can support real-time decision making.

CONCLUSION

In this chapter, we discuss the integration of content extraction, knowledge recognition, concept summarization, and terminology mapping into an automatic pipeline to establish data interoperability and concept standardization among EMRs from 800+ clinical sites. The system can be easily extended to achieve rapid integration and standardization of clinical data from other EMR systems. The pipeline scales linearly with input data and is highly efficient for massive, distributed data processing. It provides a unique way to link structured medical concepts despite the extreme variations that can occur during clinical diagnosis and documentation. Most importantly, the novel extraction-mapping algorithm and DAMIP system can be effectively applied to clinical big data analytics. The resulting evidence can be incorporated into clinical models to optimize treatment plans, improve care coordination and site-wide performance (Lee et al., 2018, 2022).

Overall, results from machine learning best-practice discovery for cardiovascular disease and chronic kidney disease yield good blind prediction accuracies of at least 89%. The analyses reveal that for each disease the best practice was only used at fewer than 5% of the clinical sites. This offers an excellent opportunity for knowledge sharing and rapid learning, speeding dissemination and implementation of *best practice* among all sites. Results from the optimal dialysis initiation model for chronic kidney disease and subsequent implementation of a new clinical practice guideline led to improved outcome, better health quality, and cost-reduction for patients (Lee et al., 2022).

The unmapped new concepts offer new knowledge of cognitive thinking and future establishment of new ontologies. Uncovered clinical and decision processes offer opportunities for standardizing and optimizing healthcare delivery for outcome and quality improvement.

ACKNOWLEDGMENT

This project received the first runner-up prize at the 2019 Caterpillar and INFORMS Innovative Applications in Analytics Award. This work is partially supported by grants from the National Science Foundation (IIP-1361532), the Care Coordination Institute, and in-kind support from the Southeast Permanente Medical Group. Findings and conclusions in this paper are those of the authors and do not necessarily reflect the views of the National Science Foundation, the Care Coordination Institute, or the Southeast Permanente Medical Group. The authors would like to acknowledge the participation of Yuanbo Wang, Matthew Hagen, Xin Wei, and Zhuonan Li on this project. The authors would like to thank Dr. Jeffrey Hoffman, Dr. Rahul Nayak and Dr. Nirvan Mukerji from the Southeast Permanente Medical Group for their clinical advice and collaboration. The authors also thank the Georgia Institute of Technology students, Thomas Adams, Chenman Cheng, Scott Eckhaus, Qixuan Hou, Ayush Kayastha,

Chris Kwan, Eunho Kwon, Di Liu, Joe Malecki, Autumn Phillips, and Peijue Zhang, who helped with the initial usage and testing of the anonymized data.

REFERENCES

Agrawal, R., Faloutsos, C., & Swami, A. (1993). Efficient similarity search in sequence databases. Lecture Notes in Computer Science (Including Subseries Lecture Notes in Artificial Intelligence and Lecture Notes in Bioinformatics), 730. doi:10.1007/3-540-57301-1_5

Amarasingham, R., Patzer, R. E., Huesch, M., Nguyen, N. Q., & Xie, B. (2014). Implementing electronic health care predictive analytics: Considerations and challenges. *Health Affairs*, *33*(7), 1148–1154. Advance online publication. doi:10.1377/hlthaff.2014.0352 PMID:25006140

Aronson, A. R. (1996). *MetaMap Technical Notes*. https://lhncbc.nlm.nih.gov/ii/information/Papers/metamap.tech.pdf

Aronson, A. R., & Lang, F. M. (2010). An overview of MetaMap: Historical perspective and recent advances. *Journal of the American Medical Informatics Association: JAMIA*, *17*(3), 229–236. Advance online publication. doi:10.1136/jamia.2009.002733 PMID:20442139

Asadi, H., Dowling, R., Yan, B., & Mitchell, P. (2014). Machine learning for outcome prediction of acute ischemic stroke post intra-arterial therapy. *PLoS One*, *9*(2), e88225. Advance online publication. doi:10.1371/journal.pone.0088225 PMID:24520356

Banerjee, I., Sofela, M., Yang, J., Chen, J. H., Shah, N. H., Ball, R., Mushlin, A. I., Desai, M., Bledsoe, J., Amrhein, T., Rubin, D. L., Zamanian, R., & Lungren, M. P. (2019). Development and Performance of the Pulmonary Embolism Result Forecast Model (PERFORM) for Computed Tomography Clinical Decision Support. *JAMA Network Open*, *2*(8), e198719. Advance online publication. doi:10.1001/jamanetworkopen.2019.8719 PMID:31390040

Bashyam, V., & Taira, R. K. (2005). Indexing anatomical phrases in neuro-radiology reports to the UMLS 2005AA. *AMIA ... Annual Symposium Proceedings / AMIA Symposium. AMIA Symposium.*

Baud, R. H., Lovis, C., Rassinoux, A. M., & Scherrer, J. R. (1998). Morpho-semantic parsing of medical expressions. *Proceedings / AMIA ... Annual Symposium. AMIA Symposium.*

Birman-Deych, E., Waterman, A. D., Yan, Y., Nilasena, D. S., Radford, M. J., & Gage, B. F. (2005). Accuracy of ICD-9-CM codes for identifying cardiovascular and stroke risk factors. In Medical Care (Vol. 43, Issue 5). doi:10.1097/01.mlr.0000160417.39497.a9

Brockwell, P. J., & Davis, R. A. (2002). Introduction to Time Series and Forecasting (2nd ed.). Springer-Verlag. doi:10.1007/b97391

Brooks, J. P., & Lee, E. K. (2010). Analysis of the consistency of a mixed integer programming-based multi-category constrained discriminant model. *Annals of Operations Research*, *174*(1), 147–168. Advance online publication. doi:10.100710479-008-0424-0

Brooks, J. P., & Lee, E. K. (2014). Solving a multigroup mixed-integer programming-based constrained discrimination model. *INFORMS Journal on Computing*, *26*(3), 567–585. Advance online publication. doi:10.1287/ijoc.2013.0584

Brown, P. A., Akbari, A., Molnar, A. O., Taran, S., Bissonnette, J., Sood, M., & Hiremath, S. (2015). Factors associated with unplanned dialysis starts in patients followed by nephrologists: A retropective cohort study. *PLoS One*, *10*(6), e0130080. Advance online publication. doi:10.1371/journal.pone.0130080 PMID:26047510

Caro Martínez, A., Olry de Labry Lima, A., Muñoz Terol, J. M., Mendoza García, Ó. J., Remón Rodríguez, C., García Mochón, L., Castro de la Nuez, P., & Aresté Fosalba, N. (2019). Optimal start in dialysis shows increased survival in patients with chronic kidney disease. *PLoS One*, *14*(7), e0219037. doi:10.1371/journal.pone.0219037 PMID:31361758

CDC. (2019). Chronic Kidney Disease in the United States, 2019. CDC, 1.

Chan, K., & Fu, A. W. (1999). Efficient time series matching by wavelets. *Proceedings - International Conference on Data Engineering*. 10.1109/ICDE.1999.754915

Chen, L., & Ng, R. (2004). On The Marriage of Lp-norms and Edit Distance. *Proceedings 2004 VLDB Conference*. 10.1016/B978-012088469-8/50070-X

Choi, S. J., Obi, Y., Ko, G. J., You, A. S., Eriguchi, R., Wang, M., Rhee, C. M., & Kalantar-Zadeh, K. (2020). Comparing Patient Survival of Home Hemodialysis and Peritoneal Dialysis Patients. *American Journal of Nephrology*, *51*(3), 192–200. Advance online publication. doi:10.1159/000504691 PMID:31991403

Cohen, G., Hilario, M., Sax, H., Hugonnet, S., & Geissbuhler, A. (2006). Learning from imbalanced data in surveillance of nosocomial infection. *Artificial Intelligence in Medicine*, *37*(1), 7–18. Advance online publication. doi:10.1016/j.artmed.2005.03.002 PMID:16233974

Cruz, J. A., & Wishart, D. S. (2006). Applications of machine learning in cancer prediction and prognosis. In Cancer Informatics (Vol. 2). doi:10.1177/117693510600200030

Cutting, D., Kupiec, J., Pedersen, J., & Sibun, P. (1992). *A practical part-of-speech tagger*. doi:10.3115/974499.974523

Cuturi, M., Vert, J. P., Birkenes, Ø., & Matsui, T. (2007). A kernel for time series based on global alignments. *ICASSP, IEEE International Conference on Acoustics, Speech and Signal Processing - Proceedings, 2*. 10.1109/ICASSP.2007.366260

Das, G., Gunopulos, D., & Mannila, H. (1997). Finding similar time series. Lecture Notes in Computer Science (Including Subseries Lecture Notes in Artificial Intelligence and Lecture Notes in Bioinformatics), 1263. doi:10.1007/3-540-63223-9_109

Foley, M., Hall, C., Perron, K., & D'Andrea, R. (2007). Translation, please: Mapping translates clinical data between the many languages that document it. *Journal of American Health Information Management Association*, *78*(2). PMID:17366991

Foley, R. N. (2004). Comparing the incomparable: Hemodialysis versus peritoneal dialysis in observational studies. In Peritoneal Dialysis International (Vol. 24, Issue 3). doi:10.1177/089686080402400303

Forrey, A. W., Mcdonald, C. J., Demoor, G., Huff, S. M., Leavelle, D., Leland, D., Fiers, T., Charles, L., Griffin, B., Stalling, F., Tullis, A., Hutchins, K., & Baenziger, J. (1996). Logical Observation Identifier Names and Codes (LOINC) database: A public use set of codes and names for electronic reporting of clinical laboratory test results. *Clinical Chemistry, 42*(1), 81–90. Advance online publication. doi:10.1093/clinchem/42.1.81 PMID:8565239

Friedlin, J., & McDonald, C. J. (2006). A natural language processing system to extract and code concepts relating to congestive heart failure from chest radiology reports. *AMIA ... Annual Symposium Proceedings / AMIA Symposium. AMIA Symposium.*

Friedman, C., Alderson, P. O., Austin, J. H. M., Cimino, J. J., & Johnson, S. B. (1994). A general natural-language text processor for clinical radiology. *Journal of the American Medical Informatics Association: JAMIA, 1*(2), 161–174. Advance online publication. doi:10.1136/jamia.1994.95236146 PMID:7719797

Gallagher, R. J., Lee, E. K., & Patterson, D. A. (1997). Constrained discriminant analysis via 0/1 mixed integer programming. *Annals of Operations Research, 74*, 65–88. Advance online publication. doi:10.1023/A:1018943025993

Genovesi, S., Porcu, L., Luise, M. C., Riva, H., Nava, E., Contaldo, G., Stella, A., Pozzi, C., Ondei, P., Minoretti, C., Gallieni, M., Pontoriero, G., Conte, F., Torri, V., Bertoli, S., & Vincenti, A. (2017). Sudden Death in End Stage Renal Disease: Comparing Hemodialysis versus Peritoneal Dialysis. *Blood Purification, 44*(1), 77–88. Advance online publication. doi:10.1159/000464347 PMID:28365692

Geurts, P., Ernst, D., & Wehenkel, L. (2006). Extremely randomized trees. *Machine Learning, 63*(1), 3–42. doi:10.100710994-006-6226-1

Gordon, T., Castelli, W. P., Hjortland, M. C., Kannel, W. B., & Dawber, T. R. (1977). High density lipoprotein as a protective factor against coronary heart disease. The Framingham study. *The American Journal of Medicine, 62*(5), 707–714. Advance online publication. doi:10.1016/0002-9343(77)90874-9 PMID:193398

Gultepe, E., Green, J. P., Nguyen, H., Adams, J., Albertson, T., & Tagkopoulos, I. (2014). From vital signs to clinical outcomes for patients with sepsis: A machine learning basis for a clinical decision support system. *Journal of the American Medical Informatics Association: JAMIA, 21*(2), 315–325. Advance online publication. doi:10.1136/amiajnl-2013-001815 PMID:23959843

Hartigan, J. A., & Wong, M. A. (1979). Algorithm AS 136: A K-Means Clustering Algorithm. *Applied Statistics, 28*(1), 100. Advance online publication. doi:10.2307/2346830

HCPCS. (2003). *Medicare Cf, Services M. Healthcare Common Procedure Coding System (HCPCS). Centers for Medicare & Medicaid Services.* ww.cms.gov/Medicare/Fraud-and-Abuse/PhysicianSelfReferral

Heaf, J., Heiro, M., Petersons, A., Vernere, B., Povlsen, J., Sørensen, A. B., Clyne, N., Bumblyte, I., Zilinskiene, A., Randers, E., Løkkegaard, N., Ots-Rosenberg, M., Kjellevold, S., Kampmann, J. D., Rogland, B., Lagreid, I., Heimburger, O., & Lindholm, B. (2021). Suboptimal dialysis initiation is associated with comorbidities and uraemia progression rate but not with estimated glomerular filtration rate. *Clinical Kidney Journal, 14*(3), 933–942. Advance online publication. doi:10.1093/ckjfaa041 PMID:33777377

Huhtala, Y., Karkkainen, J., & Toivonen, H. T. (1999). Mining for similarities in aligned time series using wavelets. *Data Mining and Knowledge Discovery: Theory, Tools, and Technology, 3695*, 150–160. Advance online publication. doi:10.1117/12.339977

Jain, N. L., & Friedman, C. (1997). Identification of Findings Suspicious for Breast Cancer Based on Natural Language Processing of Mammogram Reports. *Journal of the American Medical Informatics Association: JAMIA, 4*. PMID:9357741

Kalpakis, K., Gada, D., & Puttagunta, V. (2001). Distance measures for effective clustering of ARIMA time-series. *Proceedings - IEEE International Conference on Data Mining, ICDM*. 10.1109/ICDM.2001.989529

Kawaler, E., Cobian, A., Peissig, P., Cross, D., Yale, S., & Craven, M. (2012). Learning to predict post-hospitalization VTE risk from EHR data. *Annual Symposium Proceedings / AMIA Symposium. AMIA Symposium, 2012*.

Khalilia, M., Chakraborty, S., & Popescu, M. (2011). Predicting disease risks from highly imbalanced data using random forest. *BMC Medical Informatics and Decision Making, 11*(1), 51. Advance online publication. doi:10.1186/1472-6947-11-51 PMID:21801360

Košmelj, K., & Batagelj, V. (1990). Cross-sectional approach for clustering time varying data. *Journal of Classification, 7*(1), 99–109. Advance online publication. doi:10.1007/BF01889706

Kreindler, D. M., & Lumsden, C. J. (2006). The effects of the irregular sample and missing data in time series analysis. *Nonlinear Dynamics Psychology and Life Sciences, 10*(2), 149–172. Advance online publication. doi:10.1201/9781439820025-9 PMID:16519865

Latecki, L. J., Megalooikonomou, V., Wang, Q., Lakaemper, R., Ratanamahatana, C. A., & Keogh, E. (2005). Elastic partial matching of time series. Lecture Notes in Computer Science (Including Subseries Lecture Notes in Artificial Intelligence and Lecture Notes in Bioinformatics), 3721 LNAI. doi:10.1007/11564126_60

Lee, C. F., Lee, J. C., & Lee, A. C. (2013). *Statistics for business and financial economics* (3rd ed.). doi:10.1007/978-1-4614-5897-5

Lee, E. K., Wei, X., & Maheshwary, S. (2021). Facets of conflict hyper graphs. *Submitted*.

Lee, E. K. (2007). Large-scale optimization-based classification models in medicine and biology. *Annals of Biomedical Engineering, 35*(6), 1095–1109. Advance online publication. doi:10.100710439-007-9317-7 PMID:17503186

Lee, E. K. (2009). Machine learning framework for classification in medicine and biology. Lecture Notes in Computer Science (Including Subseries Lecture Notes in Artificial Intelligence and Lecture Notes in Bioinformatics), 5547. doi:10.1007/978-3-642-01929-6_1

Lee, E. K., Gallagher, R. J., & Patterson, D. A. (2003). A linear programming approach to discriminant analysis with a reserved-judgment region. *INFORMS Journal on Computing, 15*(1), 23–41. Advance online publication. doi:10.1287/ijoc.15.1.23.15158

Lee, E. K., Hoffman, J. X., Mukerji, N. X., & Nayak, R. S. (2022). *A Data-Driven Evidence-Based Patient-Centered Optimal Initiation Time for Dialysis Treatment*. Preprint.

Lee, E. K., Li, Z., Wang, Y., Hagen, M. S., Davis, R., & Egan, B. M. (2021). Multi-Site Best Practice Discovery: From Free Text to Standardized Concepts to Clinical Decisions. *2021 IEEE International Conference on Bioinformatics and Biomedicine (BIBM)*, 2766–2773. 10.1109/BIBM52615.2021.9669414

Lee, E. K., & Uppal, K. (2020). CERC: An interactive content extraction, recognition, and construction tool for clinical and biomedical text. *BMC Medical Informatics and Decision Making*, *20*(S14), 306. Advance online publication. doi:10.118612911-020-01330-8 PMID:33323109

Lee, E. K., Wang, Y., Hagen, M. S., Wei, X., Davis, R. A., & Egan, B. M. (2016). Machine learning: Multi-site evidence-based best practice discovery. Lecture Notes in Computer Science (Including Subseries Lecture Notes in Artificial Intelligence and Lecture Notes in Bioinformatics), 10122. doi:10.1007/978-3-319-51469-7_1

Lee, E. K., Wang, Y., He, Y., & Egan, B. M. (2019). An efficient, robust, and customizable information extraction and pre-processing pipeline for electronic health records. *IC3K 2019 - Proceedings of the 11th International Joint Conference on Knowledge Discovery, Knowledge Engineering and Knowledge Management, 1*. 10.5220/0008071303100321

Lee, E. K., Wei, X., Baker-Witt, F., Wright, M. D., & Quarshie, A. (2018). Outcome-driven personalized treatment design for managing diabetes. *Interfaces*, *48*(5), 422–435. Advance online publication. doi:10.1287/inte.2018.0964

Lee, E. K., Yuan, F., Hirsh, D. A., Mallory, M. D., & Simon, H. K. (2012). A clinical decision tool for predicting patient care characteristics: patients returning within 72 hours in the emergency department. *Annual Symposium Proceedings / AMIA Symposium. AMIA Symposium, 2012*, 495-504.

Lee, T. F., Chao, P. J., Ting, H. M., Chang, L., Huang, Y. J., Wu, J. M., Wang, H. Y., Horng, M. F., Chang, C. M., Lan, J. H., Huang, Y. Y., Fang, F. M., & Leung, S. W. (2014). Using multivariate regression model with least absolute shrinkage and selection operator (LASSO) to predict the incidence of xerostomia after intensity-modulated radiotherapy for head and neck cancer. *PLoS One*, *9*(2), e89700. Advance online publication. doi:10.1371/journal.pone.0089700 PMID:24586971

Lee, T. F., Liou, M. H., Huang, Y. J., Chao, P. J., Ting, H. M., Lee, H. Y., & Fang, F. M. (2014). LASSO NTCP predictors for the incidence of xerostomia in patients with head and neck squamous cell carcinoma and nasopharyngeal carcinoma. *Scientific Reports*, *4*(1), 6217. Advance online publication. doi:10.1038rep06217 PMID:25163814

Lenart, M., Mascarenhas, N., Xiong, R., & Flower, A. (2016). Identifying risk of progression for patients with Chronic Kidney Disease using clustering models. *2016 IEEE Systems and Information Engineering Design Symposium, SIEDS 2016*. 10.1109/SIEDS.2016.7489303

Li, L., Chase, H. S., Patel, C. O., Friedman, C., & Weng, C. (2008). Comparing ICD9-encoded diagnoses and NLP-processed discharge summaries for clinical trials pre-screening: A case study. *Annual Symposium Proceedings / AMIA Symposium. AMIA Symposium.*

Long, W. (2005). Extracting diagnoses from discharge summaries. *Annual Symposium Proceedings / AMIA Symposium. AMIA Symposium.*

Mamlin, B. W., Heinze, D. T., & McDonald, C. J. (2003). Automated extraction and normalization of findings from cancer-related free-text radiology reports. *Annual Symposium Proceedings / AMIA Symposium. AMIA Symposium.*

Månsson, K. N. T., Frick, A., Boraxbekk, C. J., Marquand, A. F., Williams, S. C. R., Carlbring, P., Andersson, G., & Furmark, T. (2015). Predicting long-term outcome of Internet-delivered cognitive behavior therapy for social anxiety disorder using fMRI and support vector machine learning. *Translational Psychiatry*, *5*(3), e530. Advance online publication. doi:10.1038/tp.2015.22 PMID:25781229

Marlin, B. M., Kale, D. C., Khemani, R. G., & Wetzel, R. C. (2012). Unsupervised pattern discovery in electronic health care data using probabilistic clustering models. *IHI'12 - Proceedings of the 2nd ACM SIGHIT International Health Informatics Symposium.* 10.1145/2110363.2110408

Marteau, P. F. (2009). Time warp edit distance with stiffness adjustment for time series matching. *IEEE Transactions on Pattern Analysis and Machine Intelligence*, *31*(2), 306–318. Advance online publication. doi:10.1109/TPAMI.2008.76 PMID:19110495

Mendelssohn, D. C., Malmberg, C., & Hamandi, B. (2009). An integrated review of "unplanned" dialysis initiation: Reframing the terminology to "suboptimal" initiation. *BMC Nephrology*, *10*(1), 22. Advance online publication. doi:10.1186/1471-2369-10-22 PMID:19674452

MetaMap. (n.d.). *A Tool For Recognizing UMLS Concepts in Text.* Retrieved February 21, 2022, from https://metamap.nlm.nih.gov/

Miaskowski, C., Cooper, B. A., Paul, S. M., Dodd, M., Lee, K., Aouizerat, B. E., West, C., Cho, M., & Bank, A. (2006). Subgroups of patients with cancer with different symptom experiences and quality-of-life outcomes: A cluster analysis. *Oncology Nursing Forum*, *33*(5), E79–E89. Advance online publication. doi:10.1188/06.ONF.E79-E89 PMID:16955115

Moyer, V. A. (2012). Screening for Chronic Kidney Disease: U.S. Preventive Services Task Force Recommendation Statement. *Annals of Internal Medicine*, *157*(8), 567. doi:10.7326/0003-4819-157-8-201210160-00533 PMID:22928170

Neo4j. (n.d.). *Neo4j Graph Data Platform.* Retrieved February 21, 2022, from https://neo4j.com/

Nim, H. T., Connelly, K., Vincent, F. B., Petitjean, F., Hoi, A., Koelmeyer, R., Boyd, S. E., & Morand, E. F. (2019). Novel methods of incorporating time in longitudinal multivariate analysis reveals hidden associations with disease activity in systemic lupus erythematosus. *Frontiers in Immunology*, *10*(JULY), 1649. Advance online publication. doi:10.3389/fimmu.2019.01649 PMID:31379847

Panahiazar, M., Taslimitehrani, V., Pereira, N., & Pathak, J. (2015). Using EHRs and Machine Learning for Heart Failure Survival Analysis. *Studies in Health Technology and Informatics*, *216*. Advance online publication. doi:10.3233/978-1-61499-564-7-40 PMID:26262006

Park, H. S., & Jun, C. H. (2009). A simple and fast algorithm for K-medoids clustering. *Expert Systems with Applications*, *36*(2), 3336–3341. Advance online publication. doi:10.1016/j.eswa.2008.01.039

Passos, I. C., Mwangi, B., Cao, B., Hamilton, J. E., Wu, M. J., Zhang, X. Y., Zunta-Soares, G. B., Quevedo, J., Kauer-Sant'Anna, M., Kapczinski, F., & Soares, J. C. (2016). Identifying a clinical signature of suicidality among patients with mood disorders: A pilot study using a machine learning approach. *Journal of Affective Disorders*, *193*, 109–116. Advance online publication. doi:10.1016/j.jad.2015.12.066 PMID:26773901

Pedregosa, F., Varoquaux, G., Gramfort, A., Michel, V., Thirion, B., Grisel, O., Blondel, M., Prettenhofer, P., Weiss, R., Dubourg, V., Vanderplas, J., Passos, A., Cournapeau, D., Brucher, M., Perrot, M., & Duchesnay, É. (2011). Scikit-learn: Machine learning in Python. *Journal of Machine Learning Research*, 12.

Phuong, N. D., & Chau, V. T. N. (2016). Automatic de-identification of medical records with a multilevel hybrid semi-supervised learning approach. *2016 IEEE RIVF International Conference on Computing and Communication Technologies: Research, Innovation, and Vision for the Future, RIVF 2016 - Proceedings*. 10.1109/RIVF.2016.7800267

Rama, K., Canhaõ, H., Carvalho, A. M., & Vinga, S. (2019). AliCluoral sequence alignment for clustering longitudinal clinical data. *BMC Medical Informatics and Decision Making*, *19*(1), 289. Advance online publication. doi:10.118612911-019-1013-7 PMID:31888660

Ramoni, M., Sebastiani, P., & Cohen, P. (2002). Bayesian clustering by dynamics. *Machine Learning*, *47*(1), 91–121. Advance online publication. doi:10.1023/A:1013635829250

Ravikumar, J., & Ramakanth Kumar, P. (2021). Machine learning model for clinical named entity recognition. *Iranian Journal of Electrical and Computer Engineering*, *11*(2), 1689. Advance online publication. doi:10.11591/ijece.v11i2.pp1689-1696

Ruch, P., Baud, R. H., Rassinoux, A. M., Bouillon, P., & Robert, G. (2000). Medical document anonymization with a semantic lexicon. *Proceedings / Annual Symposium. AMIA Symposium.*

Ruiz-Perez, D., Guan, H., Madhivanan, P., Mathee, K., & Narasimhan, G. (2020). So you think you can PLS-DA? *BMC Bioinformatics*, *21*(S1), 2. Advance online publication. doi:10.118612859-019-3310-7 PMID:33297937

Sakoe, H., & Chiba, S. (1971). A dynamic programming approach to continuous speech recognition. *Proceedings of the Seventh International Congress on Acoustics*, 3.

Savova, G. K., Fan, J., Ye, Z., Murphy, S. P., Zheng, J., Chute, C. G., & Kullo, I. J. (2010). Discovering peripheral arterial disease cases from radiology notes using natural language processing. *AMIA ... Annual Symposium Proceedings / AMIA Symposium. AMIA Symposium, 2010.*

Settles, B. (2004). *Biomedical named entity recognition using conditional random fields and rich feature sets*. doi:10.3115/1567594.1567618

Seymour, L., Brockwell, P. J., & Davis, R. A. (1997). Introduction to Time Series and Forecasting. *Journal of the American Statistical Association*, *92*(440), 1647. Advance online publication. doi:10.2307/2965440

Shabaka, A., Cases-Corona, C., & Fernandez-Juarez, G. (2021). Therapeutic Insights in Chronic Kidney Disease Progression. In Frontiers in Medicine (Vol. 8). doi:10.3389/fmed.2021.645187

Sibanda, T., & Uzuner, O. (2006). Role of local context in automatic deidentification of ungrammatical, fragmented text. *HLT-NAACL 2006 - Human Language Technology Conference of the North American Chapter of the Association of Computational Linguistics, Proceedings of the Main Conference.* 10.3115/1220835.1220844

Singhal, A., & Seborg, D. E. (2005). Clustering multivariate time-series data. *Journal of Chemometrics, 19*(8), 427–438. Advance online publication. doi:10.1002/cem.945

Smith, L., Rindflesch, T., & Wilbur, W. J. (2004). MedPost: A part-of-speech tagger for bioMedical text. *Bioinformatics (Oxford, England), 20*(14), 2320–2321. Advance online publication. doi:10.1093/bioinformatics/bth227 PMID:15073016

Smyth, P. (1997). Clustering sequences with hidden Markov models. *Advances in Neural Information Processing Systems.*

Sonabend, W. (2020). Automated ICD coding via unsupervised knowledge integration (UNITE). *International Journal of Medical Informatics, 139*, 104135. Advance online publication. doi:10.1016/j.ijmedinf.2020.104135 PMID:32361145

Sun, Y., Yao, J., & Goodison, S. (2015). Feature selection for nonlinear regression and its application to cancer research. *SIAM International Conference on Data Mining 2015, SDM 2015.* 10.1137/1.9781611974010.9

Swai, J., Zhao, X., Noube, J. R., & Ming, G. (2020). Systematic review and meta-Analysis of clinical outcomes comparison between different initial dialysis modalities in end-stage renal disease patients due to lupus nephritis prior to renal transplantation. In BMC Nephrology (Vol. 21, Issue 1). doi:10.118612882-020-01811-y

Sweeney, L. (1996). Replacing personally-identifying information in medical records, the Scrub system. *Proceedings : A Conference of the American Medical Informatics Association / ... AMIA Annual Fall Symposium. AMIA Fall Symposium.*

Szarvas, G., Farkas, R., & Busa-Fekete, R. (2007). State-of-the-art Anonymization of Medical Records Using an Iterative Machine Learning Framework. *Journal of the American Medical Informatics Association: JAMIA, 14*(5). Advance online publication. doi:10.1197/jamia.M2441 PMID:17823086

Taira, R. K., Bui, A. A. T., & Kangarloo, H. (2002). Identification of patient name references within medical documents using semantic selectional restrictions. *Proceedings / AMIA ... Annual Symposium. AMIA Symposium.*

Taira, R. K., & Soderland, S. G. (1999). A statistical natural language processor for medical reports. *Proceedings / AMIA ... Annual Symposium. AMIA Symposium.*

Taylor, R. A., Pare, J. R., Venkatesh, A. K., Mowafi, H., Melnick, E. R., Fleischman, W., & Hall, M. K. (2016). Prediction of In-hospital Mortality in Emergency Department Patients with Sepsis: A Local Big Data-Driven, Machine Learning Approach. *Academic Emergency Medicine, 23*(3), 269–278. Advance online publication. doi:10.1111/acem.12876 PMID:26679719

Turchin, A., Kolatkar, N. S., Grant, R. W., Makhni, E. C., Pendergrass, M. L., & Einbinder, J. S. (2006). Using Regular Expressions to Abstract Blood Pressure and Treatment Intensification Information from the Text of Physician Notes. *Journal of the American Medical Informatics Association: JAMIA, 13*(6), 691–695. Advance online publication. doi:10.1197/jamia.M2078 PMID:16929043

UMLS. (2013). *PostgreSQL load & index scripts*. https://www.nlm.nih.gov/research/umls/implementation_resources/community/dbloadscripts/pgsql_all_tables_sql.zip

Vlachos, M., Kollios, G., & Gunopulos, D. (2002). Discovering similar multidimensional trajectories. *Proceedings - International Conference on Data Engineering*. 10.1109/ICDE.2002.994784

Vonesh, E. F., Snyder, J. J., Foley, R. N., & Collins, A. J. (2006). Mortality studies comparing peritoneal dialysis and hemodialysis: What do they tell us? *Kidney International*, *70*(SUPPL. 103), S3–S11. Advance online publication. doi:10.1038j.ki.5001910 PMID:17080109

Wall, D. P., Kosmicki, J., Deluca, T. F., Harstad, E., & Fusaro, V. A. (2012). Use of machine learning to shorten observation-based screening and diagnosis of autism. *Translational Psychiatry*, *2*(4), e100. Advance online publication. doi:10.1038/tp.2012.10 PMID:22832900

Warren Liao, T. (2007). A clustering procedure for exploratory mining of vector time series. *Pattern Recognition*, *40*(9), 2550–2562. Advance online publication. doi:10.1016/j.patcog.2007.01.005

Wellner, B., Huyck, M., Mardis, S., Aberdeen, J., Morgan, A., Peshkin, L., Yeh, A., Hitzeman, J., & Hirschman, L. (2007). Rapidly Retargetable Approaches to De-identification in Medical Records. *Journal of the American Medical Informatics Association: JAMIA*, *14*(5), 564–573. Advance online publication. doi:10.1197/jamia.M2435 PMID:17600096

Wells, B. J., Nowacki, A. S., Chagin, K., & Kattan, M. W. (2013). Strategies for Handling Missing Data in Electronic Health Record Derived Data. *EGEMs (Generating Evidence & Methods to Improve Patient Outcomes)*, *1*(3). doi:10.13063/2327-9214.1035

Wu, J., Roy, J., & Stewart, W. F. (2010). Prediction modeling using EHR data: Challenges, strategies, and a comparison of machine learning approaches. *Medical Care*, *48*(6, SUPPL.), S106–S113. Advance online publication. doi:10.1097/MLR.0b013e3181de9e17 PMID:20473190

Yi, B. K., & Faloutsos, C. (2000). Fast Time Sequence Indexing for Arbitrary Lp norms. *Proc. of the 26st Int. Conf. on VLDB'00*.

Zhai, H., Brady, P., Li, Q., Lingren, T., Ni, Y., Wheeler, D. S., & Solti, I. (2014). Developing and evaluating a machine learning based algorithm to predict the need of pediatric intensive care unit transfer for newly hospitalized children. *Resuscitation*, *85*(8), 1065–1071. Advance online publication. doi:10.1016/j.resuscitation.2014.04.009 PMID:24813568

ADDITIONAL READING

Chen, K., Canfield, S., Blackwell, J., Houmes, S., Jones, S., & Lindsley, J. (2020). Optimization of lipid-lowering therapy for high cardiovascular risk patients through electronic medical record reporting and pharmacist evaluation. *Journal of Managed Care & Specialty Pharmacy*, *26*(8), 1010–1016. Advance online publication. doi:10.18553/jmcp.2020.26.8.1010 PMID:32715962

Hamade, N., Terry, A., & Malvankar-Mehta, M. (2019). Interventions to improve the use of EMRs in primary health care: a systematic review and meta-analysis. In BMJ Health and Care Informatics (Vol. 26, Issue 1). doi:10.1136/bmjhci-2019-000023

Haskew, J., Rø, G., Turner, K., Kimanga, D., Sirengo, M., & Sharif, S. (2015). Implementation of a cloud-based electronic medical record to reduce gaps in the HIV treatment continuum in rural Kenya. *PLoS One*, *10*(8), e0135361. Advance online publication. doi:10.1371/journal.pone.0135361 PMID:26252212

Lin, F. P. Y., Pokorny, A., Teng, C., & Epstein, R. J. (2017). TEPAPA: A novel in silico feature learning pipeline for mining prognostic and associative factors from text-based electronic medical records. *Scientific Reports*, *7*(1), 6918. Advance online publication. doi:10.103841598-017-07111-0 PMID:28761061

Maddux, D. M. D., & Toffelmire, T. (2021). Optimal Dialysis Start: Lessons Learned from Canada and the US. Fresenius Medical Care North America. *Nephrology research*. https://fmcna.com/insights/amr/2021/optimal-dialysis-start-lessons-learned-us-canada/

Martín-Merino, E., Calderón-Larrañaga, A., Hawley, S., Poblador-Plou, B., Llorente-García, A., Petersen, I., & Prieto-Alhambra, D. (2018). The impact of different strategies to handle missing data on both precision and bias in a drug safety study: A multidatabase multinational population-based cohort study. *Clinical Epidemiology*, *10*, 643–654. Advance online publication. doi:10.2147/CLEP.S154914 PMID:29892204

Mendelssohn, D. C., Curtis, B., Yeates, K., Langlois, S., MacRae, J. M., Semeniuk, L. M., Camacho, F., & McFarlane, P. (2011). Suboptimal initiation of dialysis with and without early referral to a nephrologist. *Nephrology, Dialysis, Transplantation*, *26*(9), 2959–2965. Advance online publication. doi:10.1093/ndt/gfq843 PMID:21282303

Tunbridge, M., Cho, Y., & Johnson, D. W. (2019). Urgent-start peritoneal dialysis: Is it ready for prime time? *Current Opinion in Nephrology and Hypertension*, *28*(6), 631–640. Advance online publication. doi:10.1097/MNH.0000000000000545 PMID:31436551

Wang, L., Meng, J. Y., Xu, P. P., & Peng, K. X. (2017). Similarity dynamical clustering algorithm based on multidimensional shape features for time series. Gongcheng Kexue Xuebao/Chinese. *Journal of Engineering (Stevenage, England)*, *39*(7). Advance online publication. doi:10.13374/j.issn2095-9389.2017.07.019

KEY TERMS AND DEFINITIONS

Cardiovascular Diseases: Heart conditions that include diseased vessels, structural problems, and blood clots.

Chronic Kidney Disease: CKD, also known as chronic renal disease, is a condition characterized by a gradual loss of kidney function over time.

Clinical Decision Support: An information technology system that provides clinicians, staff, patients, or other individuals with knowledge and person-specific information, intelligently filtered or presented at appropriate times, to enhance health and health care delivery.

Clinical Practice Guidelines: "Systematically developed statements to assist practitioner decisions about appropriate health care for specific clinical circumstances" (Field & Lohr, 1990) They can be used to reduce inappropriate variations in practice and to promote the delivery of high quality, evidence-based health care. They may also provide a mechanism by which healthcare professionals can be made accountable for clinical activities. The Institute of Medicine (IOM) (2012) defines clinical practice guidelines as "statements that include recommendations, intended to optimize patient care, which are informed by a systematic review of evidence and an assessment of the benefits and harms of alternative care options."

Dialysis: In medicine, dialysis is the process of removing excess water, solutes, and toxins from the blood in people whose kidneys can no longer perform these functions naturally. This is referred to as renal replacement therapy. The first successful dialysis was performed in 1943.

Electronic Medical Record: A systematized collection of patient and population electronically stored health and medical information in a digital format. These records can be shared across different health care settings.

Evidence-Based Practice: A practice that has been rigorously evaluated via scientific evidence and shown to make a positive, statistically significant difference in important outcomes.

Glomerular Filtration Rate: The kidney's filtration rate. It measures how well the kidney filters blood.

Health Information Interoperability: The ability of two or more systems to exchange health information and use the information once it is received.

Health Insurance Portability and Accountability Act (HIPAA): A federal law that required the creation of national standards to protect sensitive patient health information from being disclosed without the patient's consent or knowledge.

Machine Learning: A method of data analysis that automates analytical model building. It is a branch of artificial intelligence based on the idea that systems can learn from data, identify patterns, and make decisions with minimal human intervention.

Standardization: The process of implementing and developing technical standards based on the consensus of different parties that include firms, users, interest groups, standards organizations, and governments.

Systematized Nomenclature of Medicine: A systematic, computer-processable collection of medical terms, in human and veterinary medicine, to provide codes, terms, synonyms and definitions which cover anatomy, diseases, findings, procedures, microorganisms, substances, etc.

Unstructured Text: Written content that lacks metadata and cannot readily be indexed or mapped onto standard database fields.

Internet Search Behavior in Times of COVID–19 Lockdown and Opening

Mascha Kurpicz-Briki
Applied Machine Intelligence, Bern University of Applied Sciences, Switzerland

Christoph Glauser
Institute for Applied Argumentation Research (IFAAR), Switzerland

Loris Schmid
https://orcid.org/0000-0003-2244-1109
Institute for Applied Argumentation Research (IFAAR), Switzerland

INTRODUCTION

Data Science is a wide field with many different application domains. For example, different applications exist in the field of business and economics (Madaleno et al., 2021). But even beyond that, other fields such as social sciences or medicine do benefit from the power of *big data*. This chapter illustrates a specific use case on how such approaches have been used in the context of the COVID-19 pandemic. This use case illustrates how data science and big data can be used as a powerful instrument to monitor the crisis.

The Corona crisis is a difficult phase for the population of the several affected countries. In particular, first research in the field suggests that symptoms of anxiety and depression, and self-reported stress are common psychological reactions to the Corona crisis (Rajkumar, 2020). It is therefore crucial to further examine the well-being of the population during such a global pandemic crisis.

In this work the authors analyze the online search behavior of the Swiss online population during the COVID-19 lockdown and in particular during the application of the step-wise exit plan of the Swiss Government during summer 2020 before the second wave of October 2020. The authors monitor keywords of different categories such as social and community topics or specific facilities involved in the exit plan.

BACKGROUND

Previous work has shown that online searches for COVID-19 in different countries in Europe are not correlated with COVID-19 epidemiology (i.e. incidence and mortality) but are strongly correlated with international WHO announcements (Szmuda et al., 2020). Also, the well-being of the population has been studied in different contexts, for example by examining the effects of the isolation on the mood and relationships in pregnant women during the Corona crisis (Milne et al., 2020). In another study data from the largest German helpline service were examined, which contacts increased by 20% in the first week of the lockdown (Armbruster&Klotzbücher, 2020). It has also been shown that the lockdown can have an impact on gambling behavior (Håkansson, 2020) or the consumption of pornography (Mestre-Bach et al., 2020). These studies provide interesting insights; however, they do each only cover a rather

DOI: 10.4018/978-1-7998-9220-5.ch029

Copyright © 2023, IGI Global. Copying or distributing in print or electronic forms without written permission of IGI Global is prohibited.

small part of the population. In this study the authors cover the entire online population of Switzerland in their data, i.e., 6.9 million active internet users of Switzerland (ITU, 2016), by analyzing the search behavior on a large number of online channels in Switzerland.

A recent study has investigated the information and communication behavior of the German speaking Swiss population during the first phase of the Corona crisis (Friemel et al., 2020). Among their findings is a large trust of the population in the public institutions, including the medical institutions, the Federal Office for Public Health, the Federal Council and also the public media services.

In this chapter the authors will first describe the materials and methods used in this study. Then, the results of their monitoring are presented. In the end they discuss the potential consequences and limitations of this study.

MATERIALS AND METHODS

Research Questions

In this study, the following three research questions have been addressed:

- How does the interest in Corona/COVID-19 evolve over time and what wording is used?
- How does online search for social and community topics evolve during the lockdown and during the implementation of the exit plan?
- How do the measures announced by the exit plan influence the online search for specific facilities?

Each research question was identified by specific keywords in German and French which have been monitored continuously while the lockdown was still on, and first exit plans have been announced by the Swiss public administration. The extracted data shows how often these keywords have been searched for and how this number varies over time, without revealing a single user's identity at any point. It therefore allows to draw conclusions about the whole Swiss population's online search behavior during and after COVID-19 lockdown. It also draws the big picture on how the topics of these days have been understood, adapted and even actively taken up by most of the Swiss internet users. Around 65% of the Swiss population have German as their primary language, whereas 23% speak French as first language.

Methodology

Our methods are based on (Maletzke, 1963) presenting a mass media science communication framework. The framework involves a n-to-n communication from communicators (C), statement or message (S), media (M) and recipients (R). In our case, M=social media, search engines and e-shops, and R=active users doing internet search world-wide. Therefore, our work continuously extends the original stimulus-to-response model, in order to adapt it for online communication.

Data Collection

The method relates to comparisons between the digital content that is offered during Corona times and the content, which is searched for in a defined online universe (mostly on the basis of a country, or on different country domains and where these are missing, based on (ITU, 2016) user data) working with comparable data from as many different sources as possible. This approach is unique because it does not include secondary media information, but rather the active searches by the user community itself, measured by API or software interfaces on the respective platforms where any kind of search field is offered to the user. All API data and search data, which is directly provided by the suppliers, is thoroughly parametrized by a number of different parameters like timeframe, currency, keyword frequency, keyword trends, technology, language etc.

The data collected in this way are particularly valuable for early science, but also for market research, e-shops, product trends, relevance checks, advertising and website planning, or for predictive analytics in political campaigns and as digital impact KPI's in general.

The search behavior of the online population is constantly changing. Today, depending on the target group, "special interest" search options are often searched on platforms such as Snapchat, facebook and Instagram. In addition to this, in the authors' experience, on average 30-40% of the universal search today is on social media and e-shops. New search options are also constantly being added while old ones are disappearing. These changes are becoming increasingly important to online research. The power of search data has been proven in several use cases to measure the attitude, the sentiment or the opinion of the broad population, for example to study racial animus during the elections (Stephens-Davidowitz, 2014) or to detect feelings such as low self-esteem (Zaman et al., 2019). It has been shown that such valid and reliable methods improve the results of traditional surveys, since participants tend to lie in surveys (Stephens-Davidowitz&Pabon, 2017). Furthermore, it has been shown that only a specific part of the population participates in surveys which can lead to biases in the results (Wright, 2005). It has been estimated that 87.2% of the Swiss population (ITU, 2016) are using the internet and thus different types of search engines, social media and e-shops.

Most of the contemporary research on search is limited to Google data or social media hashtag, e.g., (Szmuda et al., 2020) or (Rovetta&Bhagavathula, 2020), with the strong limitation that only one part of the active internet population is covered. This study uses a new cross channel approach, extracting data from 14'103 sources worldwide including search engines (e.g., Wikipedia, Google, Bing, Yahoo!, Ask, Lycos, Alexa, Technorati, MetaCrawler, Search.com, local SE's etc.), social network platforms (e.g., facebook, Twitter, Linkedin etc.) and e-shop searches (e.g., Amazon, ebay, Alibaba etc.). The harvested data is analyzed systematically to reveal the queries submitted by internet users and the frequencies of those queries by the domains of 203 countries. The possibility to examine, parametrize and compare numerous search engines and social networks allows to gain valid and reliable aggregated insights into the internet search behavior in terms of content of the digitally active Swiss population, counting approximately 6.9 million users in Switzerland (ITU, 2016) during and after the COVID-19 lockdown. Using this multi-channel approach, some of the challenges in big data (as shown for example by Khan et al. (2019)), such as variability and variety, can be overcome.

The crawl is adjusted to take into account only a predefined geographical country based on the country domain. In this study the focus was put on Switzerland. The scope of this work was defined on current and publicly communicated keywords in German and French language to target the majority of the Swiss population and its active searches. The digital monitoring period started at the end of February and ended mid-June in 2020.

COVID-19 Lockdown and Exit Plan

Due to the Corona crisis, several types of businesses were closed by the government. As opposed to other countries, there was no general lockdown enforced by the law in Switzerland, which was often discussed in the media, e.g., (Schäfer, 2020). However, the government recommended the population to stay at home and groups of more than five persons were forbidden by law.

The original exit plan of the Swiss Government (as announced April 16th 2020 by the Federal Council of Switzerland) considered three steps between April and June 2020 to re-open step by step different facilities, as shown in Figure 1.

The opening for mass events had at this point not been defined yet. The measures from June 8th were then specified in detail and the opening was allowed already from June 6th in order to include an additional weekend. In particular, touristic services such as mountain transport services and campsites were included in the updated measure.

The initial plan did not include gastronomic facilities. However, restaurants were allowed to open on May 11th, with some restrictions regarding the number of persons per table. These measures were reduced on June 6th, to allow even larger groups in restaurants.

RESULTS

In this section the authors describe the results of the monitoring. During the monitoring phase, the search behavior of the online population based on different categories of keywords was analyzed.

Naming the Corona Virus

The authors first studied the naming of COVID-19 that was used during the crisis. The results show that during lockdown the wording used for the virus has significantly evolved. Whereas in February it was also referred to as Corona Virus, later in April mainly the interest into the more scientifically influenced term COVID-19 increases significantly and continues to be an extremely searched topic until the end of the measurements in June. Figure 2 shows the results.

Figure 1. The exit plan as initially announced by the Swiss Government on April 16th, 2020

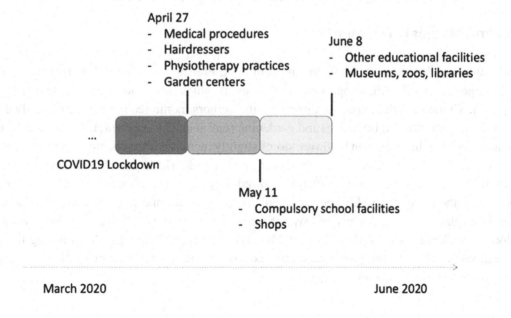

Figure 2. Total number of searches for selected keywords naming the virus

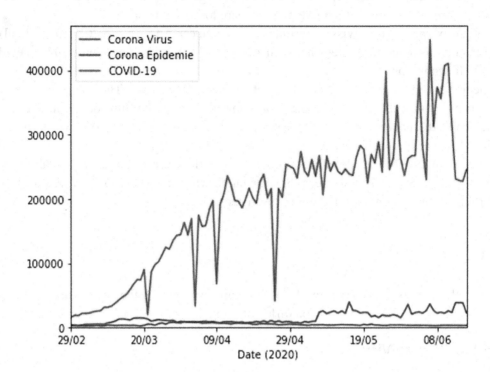

In addition to the search volume per country, the authors also measured how often and on which channels (multi-channel) the words Corona Virus and COVID-19 have been searched for between May 16th and June 16th 2020 (total search volume divided by average search per channel) in Switzerland. It is interesting to see that the Corona Virus search volume was, from the very beginning, very high on Twitter, where probably most of the media journalists have tried to get the latest information on the Corona Virus for their media publications about this topic. The term Corona Virus is more popular on Twitter, whereas COVID-19 is searched more on Google. Figures 3 and 4 show the results.

Shops and Medical Treatments

Garden centers and hardware stores (German: Baumarkt, French: (grande surface de) bricolage) were allowed to open on April 27th, as opposed to other shops which were considered in the exit plan only on May 11th. To measure the impact of this event, the authors monitored the keywords hardware store (German: Baumarkt, French: bricolage) and gardening (German: Gartenarbeit, French: jardinage). The results indicated that the interest in hardware stores slightly increases after opening, and has a peak once all the other shops are opened as well some days after May 11th. The keyword gardening for the search behavior of French speaking Swiss population showed only a minor peak around April 27th and is flat otherwise. For the German speaking Swiss population, a peak around May 23rd could be identified. This can be explained by the Ascension Day, where due to a public holiday on Thursday, many Swiss had a longer weekend between May 21st and 24th. Whereas typically people travel during this period of the year, due to the Corona crisis the authors assume that they dedicated more effort to gardening instead. Figure 5 shows the results.

Figure 3. Channels for the keyword Corona Virus from May 16th to June 16th 2020, total search volume

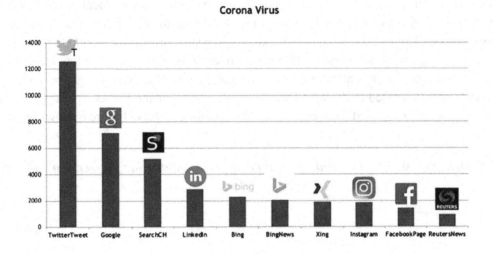

Figure 4. Channels for the keyword COVID-19 from May 16th to June 16th, 2020, total search volume

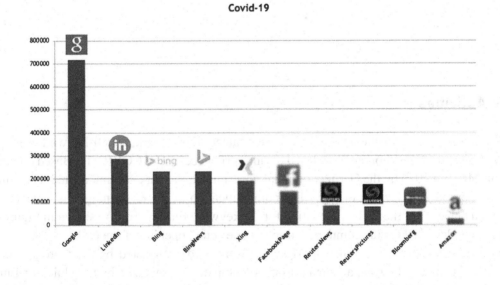

Figure 5. Search interest in the keyword's hardware store and gardening for German and French

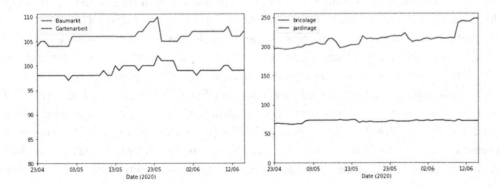

The study identified a slight increase of the search activity for physiotherapy from April 27th, when such services were allowed again to receive patients. At the same date, medical practices such as pediatricians (German: Kinderarzt, French: pédiatre) were allowed to receive patients for not emergency treatments or checks. However, it could only be identified a very small peak around that date. Since for the German speaking Swiss online population the number of searches was very low for this keyword, one can assume that the search behavior might be different between the language regions in Switzerland (this will be further discussed in the next Discussion section). For the French speaking Swiss online population, the authors identified a larger peak in the beginning of June. Figure 6 shows the results.

Figure 6. Search interest in the keyword's physiotherapy and pediatrician for German and French

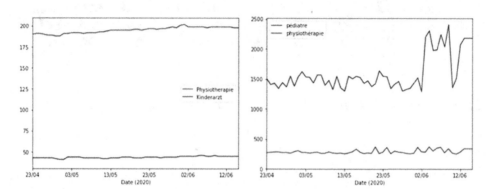

Leisure Activities

During the Corona crisis, leisure possibilities were reduced. Europapark, a well-known leisure park in Germany close to the Swiss border, was closed during spring because of COVID-19. Based on measures decided on May 6th 2020 by the German regional government, the park communicated its opening for the summer season 2020 by end of May. The communication of the re-opening was reflected in the online search behavior of the Swiss population for the keyword Europapark. As shown in Figure 7, two peaks could be identified for the communication and the actual opening of the park.

Not only leisure activities but also sport events were hardly impacted by the Corona crisis. For example, the Champions League, an annual football competition organized by the Union of European Football Associations UEFA, was paused during the crisis. Whereas local football leagues re-started with training and matches earlier (e.g. the Swiss Football League on June 6th (Swiss Football League, 2020)), the Champions League was announced to be continued only in August (SRF, 2020). However, the results shown in Figure 7 of the online search behavior indicate that there is an impatience in the population and therefore there was an increased search for the keyword Champions League starting at the end of May. For words such as Champions League or Europapark that are proper names or for words that are the same in both French and German, no separation of the two groups is possible.

The authors also considered the keyword party (German: Party, French: faire la fête), where for French they considered the verb to party, since the direct translation of party to French has a broader meaning than in German. Whereas for the French speaking Swiss population the interest in online searches for party increased with more and more easing measures being announced by the government, the German speaking Swiss population lost interest in the keyword party in the beginning of June as shown in Figure 8.

Figure 7. Search interest in the keywords Champions League and Europapark (same word for German and French)

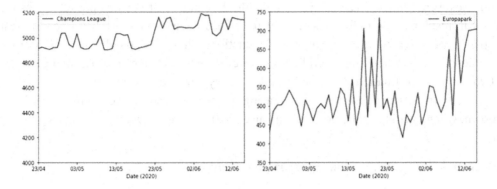

Figure 8. Search interest in the keywords Party in German and to party in French

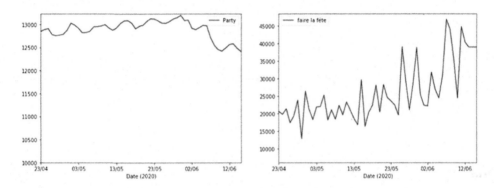

The corona crisis had a devastating impact on the festival season 2020. Well-known summer music festivals such as the Montreux Jazz Festival or Gurtenfestival had to be cancelled due to COVID-19. Figure 9 shows the results from the monitoring for the keyword festival. Even if most festivals were cancelled, the interest in this keyword increased closer to the festival season.

Figure 9. Search interest in the keyword festival (same word for German and French), and the keyword restaurant (for German and French)

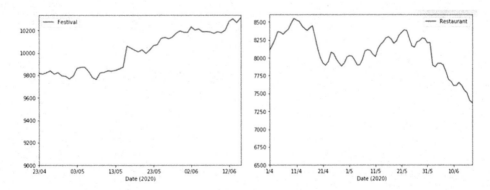

The results for restaurant (German: Restaurant, French: restaurant) were rather surprising. Restaurants and other gastronomic facilities were mainly re-opened on May 11th, along with the shops. However, groups at tables were limited. Starting from June 6th, the number of persons per table was increased. The interest in restaurants in online searches of the Swiss population decreased once the restaurants were re-opened, as shown in Figure 9. Possible explanations will be discussed in the Discussion section.

Next to the local leisure activities, traveling was severely reduced during the crisis. The authors identified the two common destinations Paris and London as keywords to measure the interest of the internet population in city trips. They observed an increasing interest in these two keywords towards the end of the lockdown, when opening of the borders was discussed. Figure 10 shows the results.

Figure 10. Search interest in the keywords Paris and London

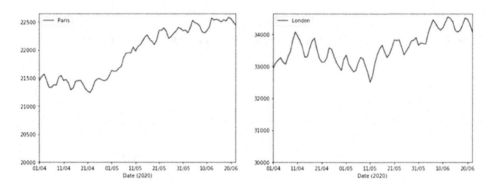

Emotions

The authors selected keywords to capture the mood of the Swiss population during the Corona crisis. They considered the keyword lonely (German: einsam, French: seul/e). In French, they considered the female and the male form respectively. Even though the exit plan started in April and re-opened most of the shops in mid of May, the German speaking Swiss internet population searched for the keyword lonely reaching the peak only in the beginning of June. As shown in Figure 11, the authors could not confirm this result for the French speaking Swiss online population.

Figure 11. Search interest in the keyword lonely for German and French

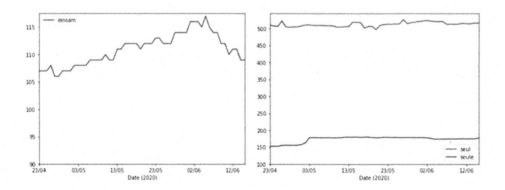

Another keyword the authors considered was happy (German: glücklich, French: heureux/heureuse). Again, they considered both the female and the male version of the word for French, for German the word is the same for both genders. The authors found an indication that the end of the lockdown had a positive impact on the well-being of the German speaking Swiss online population. The keyword happy was more and more searched towards the end of the lockdown. As shown in Figure 12, the corresponding result for the French speaking Swiss online population was less evident.

Figure 12. Search interest in the keyword happy for German and French

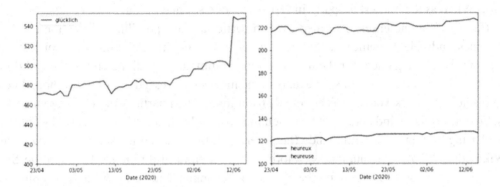

DISCUSSION

In this section the authors discuss the potential consequences and conclusions based on the previously described results and state hypotheses to be verified in future work. They also compare their results to existing work in the field, where possible.

Same Virus – Different Names

The results of this work show that during lockdown the wording used for the virus has significantly evolved, from the keyword Corona Virus in the beginning to the keyword COVID-19 being mainly used during the crisis first by scientists and later taken over by the media. This indicates a maturity transformation of the society during lockdown, by using the more scientific term COVID-19 instead of Corona Virus.

A study in the United States showed that searches for the keyword coronavirus increased by 35% on the day the first case was announced and decreased back to the baseline level in less than a week or two (Bento et al., 2020). The authors cannot confirm or reject these findings for Switzerland, since the monitoring in this work started after the early phase of the Corona crisis in Europe.

Cultural Differences

In previous work it has been shown that cultural differences have an impact on bias in pre-trained word embeddings, a concept from natural language processing (Kurpicz-Briki, 2020). The results from this study indicate that such cultural differences might exist as well in online search behavior. In this work, the authors compared the search behavior of the online population of Switzerland (domain .ch) for both German and French language. These are the two main languages (of four national languages) of

Switzerland, that are spoken in the two largest regions of the country respectively. It was noticed that the results, and thus the impact of the Corona crisis, were different between the two populations, even though the same channels were used for gathering the data.

For example, the authors noticed that pediatrician in French is a common search term, whereas the corresponding word in German is not searched as often. They suspect that in the German speaking part of Switzerland it might be more common to search for the specific name of the treating doctor instead of the generic term. However, this claim will need to be validated in future research. It shows, that the definition of the scope from the very beginning is crucial.

The authors also found a major difference between the French and the German results for the keyword party. Whereas the interest for party in German decreases in early June, the corresponding French keyword (faire la fête) increases. So-called Corona parties are one possible explanation for this result. In such parties, individuals gather during the lockdown to explicitly catch the virus, or just not being worried about the consequences for themselves or the community. With the end of the lockdown, also the existence and thus discussion of such events in the internet decreased. As of the author's knowledge, there is no scientific work yet identifying the distribution of such parties among different countries or cultures. First information indicated that this phenomenon has been noted in Germany, the United States, the United Kingdom and the Netherlands (however, lack of evidence for such parties was discussed later (Wikipedia, 2020)). The authors therefore suspect a cultural difference between the Swiss and French speaking regions of Switzerland (being due to the language more exposed to the cultural impact of Germany and France respectively) that causes this difference in the results of the experiment. In the last part of the results section the authors described how the keywords regarding the mood (happy and lonely) were searched during the lockdown. However, they obtained different results for German and French keywords, even though the data was from Switzerland and measured on the same channels in both cases. It seems that the sentiment of the German speaking online population is more reflected in their search behavior as compared to the French speaking online population. However, this claim needs to be verified by future work. Cultural differences between German and French speaking Switzerland have been previously discussed: A study analyzing the discussions around genetic engineering came to the conclusion, that the communication behavior between the two regions differ (Suter et al., 1998).

Gender Differences

We noticed that there is a difference between the male and the female version of adjectives in French. This is the case for *heureux* (engl. happy, male version of the word) and *heureuse* (engl. happy, female version), as well as *seul* (engl. lonely, male version) and *seule* (engl. lonely, female version). In both cases, the male version is searched more often. One possible explanation is that the male version is used more often in general in the French language, being still often used as the generic form. This will need to be further explored in future research.

Dreaming of the Impossible

The results show that the keyword restaurant was searched more during the time of the lockdown (when restaurants were closed) than afterwards. The authors obtained a similar result for the German speaking internet population for the keyword party. One possible explanation is that online searches reflect things that users would want to do during the lockdown, but cannot (as a kind of *wishful searching* deviated from *wishful thinking*). There is indication in the results that after the lockdown, when people can actually go to the restaurant and to parties again, the interest in online searches for these topics decreases. Therefore, the authors suggest to further explore this phenomenon in future work.

FUTURE RESEARCH DIRECTIONS

One challenge of this study was the selection of the keywords. Since the implementation consists of a live monitoring, the keywords had to be selected before starting the monitoring. In a dynamic context such as a global pandemic crisis, this was challenging and some new keywords that were only identified at a later point in time could not be considered in the monitoring anymore.

For words that are the same in French and German (e.g., restaurant), no distinction between the two language regions was possible. The data collection relies in both cases on the domains .ch and .swiss.

CONCLUSION

In this study the online search behavior of the Swiss population during the lockdown of the Corona crisis was monitored. The authors observed the impact of the exit plan announced by the Swiss government on search behavior and the genuine search interest in social and community topics. They found several indications that cultural differences between the language regions in Switzerland exist also with regards to the online search behavior and examined the naming of the virus used in online search during the crisis.

Some of their hypotheses could be confirmed, other hypotheses could only be confirmed partially for one language region or could not be confirmed at all. It can be assumed that for these hypotheses the wording selected for the keyword monitoring was the cause. Selecting the right keywords for the monitoring in advance in such a dynamic situation was one of the major challenges encountered in this study. It would be interesting to work in further research on the selection of search keywords in disruptive times and to work with more broad word clouds instead of single keywords.

REFERENCES

Armbruster, S., & Klotzbücher, V. (2020). *Lost in lockdown? Covid-19, social distancing, and mental health in Germany (No. 2020-04)*. Diskussionsbeiträge.

Bento, A. I., Nguyen, T., Wing, C., Lozano-Rojas, F., Ahn, Y. Y., & Simon, K. (2020). Evidence from internet search data shows information-seeking responses to news of local COVID-19 cases. *Proceedings of the National Academy of Sciences of the United States of America, 117*(21), 11220–11222. doi:10.1073/pnas.2005335117 PMID:32366658

Friemel, T. N., Geber, S., & Egli, S. (2020). Informations- und kommunikationsverhalten in der corona-krise. Technical report, Institut für Kommunikationswissenschaft und Medienforschung (IKMZ), University of Zurich, 2020.

Håkansson, A. (2020). Impact of COVID-19 on online gambling–a general population survey during the pandemic. *Frontiers in Psychology, 11*, 2588. doi:10.3389/fpsyg.2020.568543 PMID:33101137

International Telecommunication Union (ITU). (2016). Available https://www.internetlivestats.com/internet-users-by-country/

Khan, N., Naim, A., Hussain, M. R., Naveed, Q. N., Ahmad, N., & Qamar, S. (2019, May). The 51 v's of big data: survey, technologies, characteristics, opportunities, issues and challenges. *Proceedings of the International Conference on Omni-Layer Intelligent Systems*, 19-24. 10.1145/3312614.3312623

Kurpicz-Briki, M. (2020). Cultural differences in bias? origin and gender bias in pre-trained German and French word embeddings. *Proceedings of the 5th SwissText & 16th KONVENS Joint Conference 2020*.

Madaleno, M., Marques, J. L., & Tufail, M. (2021). Data Science in Economics and Business: Roots and Applications. In *Handbook of research on applied data science and artificial intelligence in business and industry* (pp. 544–568). IGI Global. doi:10.4018/978-1-7998-6985-6.ch026

Maletzke, G. 1. (1963). Psychologie der Massenkommunikation: Theorie und Systematik. Hamburg: Verlag Hans Bredow-Institut.

Mestre-Bach, G., Blycker, G. R., & Potenza, M. N. (2020). Pornography use in the setting of the CO-VID-19 pandemic. *Journal of Behavioral Addictions*, 9(2), 181–183. doi:10.1556/2006.2020.00015 PMID:32663384

Milne, S. J., Corbett, G. A., Hehir, M. P., Lindow, S. W., Mohan, S., Reagu, S., Farrell, T., & O'Connell, M. P. (2020). Effects of isolation on mood and relationships in pregnant women during the covid-19 pandemic. *European Journal of Obstetrics, Gynecology, and Reproductive Biology*, 252, 610–611. doi:10.1016/j.ejogrb.2020.06.009 PMID:32616415

Rajkumar, R. P. (2020). Covid-19 and mental health: A review of the existing literature. *Asian Journal of Psychiatry*, 52, 102066. doi:10.1016/j.ajp.2020.102066 PMID:32302935

Rovetta, A., & Bhagavathula, A. S. (2020). Global infodemiology of covid-19: Focus on google web searches and instagram hashtags. medRxiv, 2020. doi:10.1101/2020.05.21.20108910

Schäfer, F. (2020). *Coronavirus - eine ausgangssperre ginge zu weit*. Neue Zürcher Zeitung NZZ. Available https://www.nzz.ch/meinung/ coronavirus-eine-ausgangssperre-ginge-zu-weit-ld.1547389/

Schweizer Radio und Fernsehen SRF. (2020). *Uefa hat entschieden: Champions und europa league gehen im august weiter*. Schweizer Radio und Fernsehen SRF. Available https://www.srf.ch/sport/fussball/fussball-allgemein/uefa-hat-entschieden-champions-und-europa-league-gehen-im-august-weiter

Stephens-Davidowitz, S. (2014). The cost of racial animus on a black candidate: Evidence using Google search data. *Journal of Public Economics*, 118, 26–40. doi:10.1016/j.jpubeco.2014.04.010

Stephens-Davidowitz, S., & Pabon, A. (2017). *Everybody lies: Big data, new data, and what the internet can tell us about who we really are*. HarperCollins.

Suter, C., Glauser, C., & Oegerli, T. (1998). Der öffentliche Diskurs zur Genschutz-Inititative. *Expertensicht und Mediendebatte. Bio World*, 5(98), 33–38.

Swiss Football League. (2020). Available https://www.football.ch/sfv/corona-news/covid-19-schutz-konzept-fuer-trainings-und-spielbetrieb-ab-6-6-2020.aspx

Szmuda, T., Ali, S., Hetzger, T. V., Rosvall, P., & Słoniewski, P. (2020). Are online searches for the novel coronavirus (COVID-19) related to media or epidemiology? A cross-sectional study. *International Journal of Infectious Diseases*, *97*, 386–390. doi:10.1016/j.ijid.2020.06.028 PMID:32535297

Wikipedia. (2020). Available https://en.wikipedia.org/wiki/COVID-19_party

Wright, K. B. (2005). Researching Internet-based populations: Advantages and disadvantages of online survey research, online questionnaire authoring software packages, and web survey services. *Journal of Computer-mediated Communication, 10*(3).

Zaman, A., Acharyya, R., Kautz, H., & Silenzio, V. (2019, May). Detecting low self-esteem in youths from web search data. In *The World Wide Web Conference* (pp. 2270-2280). 10.1145/3308558.3313557

ADDITIONAL READING

Deopa, N., & Fortunato, P. (2021). Coronagraben in Switzerland: Culture and social distancing in times of COVID-19. *Journal of Population Economics*, *34*(4), 1355–1383. doi:10.100700148-021-00865-y PMID:34334956

Elmer, T., Mepham, K., & Stadtfeld, C. (2020). Students under lockdown: Comparisons of students' social networks and mental health before and during the COVID-19 crisis in Switzerland. *PLoS One*, *15*(7), e0236337. doi:10.1371/journal.pone.0236337 PMID:32702065

Glauser, C., Schmid, L., & Kurpicz-Briki, M. (2020, September). Identifying the public interest in COVID-19 contact tracing apps in Switzerland based on online search behavior. In *Proceedings of the 13th International Conference on Theory and Practice of Electronic Governance* (pp. 120-123). 10.1145/3428502.3428517

Molloy, J., Schatzmann, T., Schoeman, B., Tchervenkov, C., Hintermann, B., & Axhausen, K. W. (2021). Observed impacts of the Covid-19 first wave on travel behaviour in Switzerland based on a large GPS panel. *Transport Policy*, *104*, 43–51. doi:10.1016/j.tranpol.2021.01.009

Salathé, M., Althaus, C. L., Neher, R., Stringhini, S., Hodcroft, E., Fellay, J., Zwahlen, M., Senti, G., Battegay, M., Wilder-Smith, A., Eckerle, I., Egger, M., & Low, N. (2020). COVID-19 epidemic in Switzerland: On the importance of testing, contact tracing and isolation. *Swiss Medical Weekly*, *150*(1112). Advance online publication. doi:10.4414mw.2020.20225 PMID:32191813

Schmid, L., & Glauser, C. (2021, July). New ecosystem based on big data for more digital impact. In *International Conference on Applied Human Factors and Ergonomics* (pp. 18-26). Springer. 10.1007/978-3-030-80840-2_2

Selby, K., Durand, M. A., Gouveia, A., Bosisio, F., Barazzetti, G., Hostettler, M., D'Acremont, V., Kaufmann, A., & von Plessen, C. (2020). Citizen responses to government restrictions in Switzerland during the COVID-19 pandemic: Cross-sectional survey. *JMIR Formative Research*, *4*(12), e20871. doi:10.2196/20871 PMID:33156809

KEY TERMS AND DEFINITIONS

Application Programming Interface (API): A set of features that allows an automated access of an application or service.

Big Data: The large amount of data that is being generated and needs to be processed by new digital tools and technologies.

Corona Crisis: Worldwide pandemic crisis starting in 2020 with the spread of the COVID-19 disease.

Online Population: Part of a country's population using online services such as e-mail, search, social media, or others.

Search Data: Data about keywords and topics that have been searched in online search engines.

Search Engine: Online service to allow keyword search on the internet to find relevant websites.

World Health Organization (WHO): Specialized agency of the United Nations (UN) dealing with public health.

Interparadigmatic Perspectives Are Supported by Data Structures

Gilbert Ahamer

https://orcid.org/0000-0003-2140-7654

Austrian Academy of Sciences, Austria

BACKGROUND

The *organisations* involved in the following cases include secondary schools, universities, university clusters, transnational university partnerships, international environmental NGOs, and the European Union's external policy. These organisations range from public to private and from idealistic to pragmatic. All of them plan to "change the world" and for that target they undertake to *exchange views and perspectives* among the stakeholders concerned. This paper approaches to find answers to the specific set of questions through cases of international collaborative educational projects.

SETTING THE STAGE – SEVERAL CASE STUDIES

The novelty in this research lies in providing concrete cases with concrete statistical data.

Learning Means "Reflecting while Acting"

The approach to learning named "reflection in action" (Haberman & Suresh, 2021, Nizamis et al., 2021) is especially appropriate for international cooperation.

Here, the object of learning is not regarded as something unchangeable (such as facts in natural sciences), but rather as the result of a constructivist procedure.

In such a procedure, individual perceptions (e.g. of international conflicts such as the complex Nagorny Karabakh conflict between two Caucasian states) are reshaped and reframed, which constitutes the core of "learning" on a societal level.

An early historic example for such *dialogic reframing* might be Galileo Galilei's (1632) strategy of making a discourse out of life's irreconcilable problems: "Dialogue of the two most important systems of the world" that were at odds at his time. As another example, the "greatest American philosopher" according to his students, John Dewey, sees *dialogue as the basis of education* (Wang, 2021) – and art as the most effective communication that exists (Dennis, 1970: 3).

Learning is Facilitated by a "Geography of Opinions and Perspectives"

Geography is the branch of science offering *perspectives onto reality*. Let us use such an unusual definition for the following deliberations.

Consequently, *geography creates spaces* (of understanding) that may be converging in the best case. The main tool for converging spaces of understanding is the dialogue. The circle of argumentation is closed.

DOI: 10.4018/978-1-7998-9220-5.ch030

Copyright © 2023, IGI Global. Copying or distributing in print or electronic forms without written permission of IGI Global is prohibited.

Fundamentally, spaces are "spaces of (common) understanding", i.e. clusters of the same or similar "explanatory software" for the perceptions of the world. In our century, fortunately the path of intercultural understanding is followed more at the expense of thinking in terms of "cultural clashes".

An audacious statement can be made: *Our world is the entirety of perceptions.* (Our world is not the entirety of facts.) In this train of thought, it makes sense to envisage a (spatial) documentation of "perspectives onto realities" that would complement classical mapping by the additional aspect of the individual's opinion (Ahamer 2019).

Figure 1. Our world as the entirety of perceptions of reality. Above far left: one human perception of reality; above left: many perceptions, in disorder; above right: the dimensions represent possible perspectives, e.g. scientific disciplines, values, cultures or religions. Below far left and left: many perceptions, each aligned by the identities of two scientific cultures; below right: the entirety of all viewers' perception, taking all possible standpoints. Far right: to become aware of all possible perspectives onto realities will facilitate the dialogue among viewers (compare Figure 4).

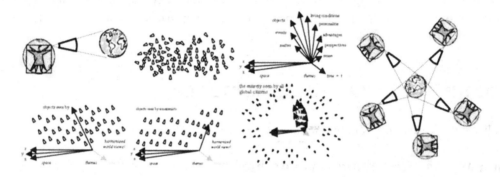

Actually, the approach of "attributing a place to each perspective onto reality" is not as theoretic as it might seem at first glance. Any democracy lives on "mapping all perspectives" into the seats of a parliament – this is state-of-the-art. Not only stable states but also transnational procedures are designed this way: one of the vastest self-responsible and peaceful political restructuring processes is an example, namely the recent European integration process and the ongoing European Neighbourhood Policy with the EU's new neighbour states.

European Integration as Prime Case for a Discursive Building of Structures

As a response to the new geopolitical situation following the events of 1989, the European Union (EU) has seen a round of enlargement in May 2004 based on dialogic procedures, and consequently adopted a new framework for relations with its neighbours, the *European Neighbourhood Policy* (ENP, 2021). The ENP offers neighbouring countries the prospect of an increasingly closer relationship with the EU with the overall goal of fostering the political and economic reform processes including democratization (Berman, 1997), promoting closer economic integration as well as legal and technical approximation and sustainable development. In ENP, the cluster of ex-communist "transition economies" is comprised as ENP-East.

The central element of the ENP is a bilateral Action Plan (AP) which clearly sets out policy targets and benchmarks through which progress with an individual neighbouring country can be assessed over several years. The ENP Action Plan defines a considerable number of priority areas among which environment, aviation and education, which are at the core of the five cases reported in this article. Such deeper integration is based on – if not common – at least approximating human and societal values and constitutes a case of "identity building", as mentioned by Castells above (Castells, 1996-8).

European political genesis, its enlargement and subsequent neighbourhood policy represent "societal learning" in the deeper sense of the word.

In a theoretical approach, Eder (2007: 33) discerns two steps in the process of (European or any large-scale political) integration:

I.   Transcending the utilitarian needs and
II.   Closing the gaps by discourse.

Eder's (2007) paper develops a sociological perspective on the process of social integration that has been initiated in the course of the evolution of European political institutions. An abstract notion of social integration is presented as providing an analytical framework for understanding and explaining the process of socially integrating a culturally heterogeneous Europe. The key concept is that of a *transnational space of communication and its discursive closure* (compare Bourdieu, 1997). The central theoretical idea is to use communicative density (compare Ahamer, 2012a, b, c, 2013a, b, c, 2014, 2015) as the criterion of the emergence of a communicative space in which two different types of experience make possible its discursive closure:

1.   the experience of being *treated in a fair way by the others* inhabiting this space (the *cognitive* capital of a community) and
2.   the *construction of a common memory frame* resulting from the confrontation of differing national (and subnational) memories in this space (the *narrative* capital of a community).

Thus two mechanisms can be identified which explain discursive closure. This model leaves open whether this will happen, but it offers a strategy for identifying the extent and the causes of such processes without recourse to normatively motivated wishful thinking.

The main dimensions of such a creation of a society are increasing density of interaction (or density of communication) in a European social space and its discursive closure by cognitive and narrative construction of mutuality, common ground and common interest (Eder, 2007: 37).

The two factors listed above are seen as forms of accumulation of *symbolic capital* while the two mentioned appearances of symbolic capital are relevant: cognitive capital and narrative capital (p. 39). In Bourdieu's concept of symbolic capital memory and remembrance become a constitutive part of the structure of collective social practice. Cultures of remembrance are a form of symbolic capital that attributes a certain value (or lack of value) to the constituents of the "common" (Eder, 2007: 40, Bourdieu, 1997, MacGregor, 2002).

On the practical level of countries, a well-targeted strategy for the creation and further development of such communality is a series of so-called Twinning projects that have been developed by the European commission for the mutual help of administrations in the member states and the candidate countries. Twinning means "Institution Building" (compare Berman, 1997). A suitable definition of the *"Twinning principles"* applicable to European neighbourhood countries (from Belarus across Azerbaijan to Morocco) can be found on the Twinning web page (EU, 2009):

- "In addition to meeting requirements laid down in the EU's agreements with third countries, Twinning must also aim at developing *structural* reforms.
- At the end of a project, any new or adapted system must be *self-sufficient* and function under the auspices of the beneficiary country.
- Projects must also include some elements relating to the adoption of EU *legislation*. An approximation to the acquis communautaire is called for, rather than full integration of EU legislation as was demanded of the candidate countries.
- The local partner in a Twinning should be represented by a *public body* that is capable of working with a Member State organisation which has a similar structure and function.
- The beneficiary country partner must be able to adapt and take on board *change*: the Twinning project is not about the EU providing one-way technical assistance."

Several cases for Twinnings will be presented in the practical part of this contribution.

Social Spaces and Social Capital

At the end of the above *theoretical section* "setting the stage" we refresh some of the proposed approaches: Apart from the well-known notion of "human capital" also other vocabulary has entered scientific reasoning while denoting *structural stocks of a community* of varying degree of novelty to the reader – such as "*social capital*" (Adler & Kwon, 2000, Bourdieu, 1997). There is evidence for the connection between social networks and social capital (Mohan & Mohan, 2002: 196, Burt, 2000). Entrepreneurship (Chung & Gibbons, 1997), civil society (Hyden, 1997) and civic engagement (Kenworthy, 1997, Larsen et al., 2004, Brownlow, 2005, Purcell, 2001, Kirby, 2007) have been linked to social capital in several studies. Attempts have been made to map social structures (Zheng & Niu, 2007) or to explain their topology by biological arguments (Lemke, 2000). Anyhow, e-learning can be seen as the reconstruction of space along other lines.

Information technologies such as the internet (Arnold, 2003), social network sites (Hargittai, 2008) and other "public electronic spaces" (Crang, 2000) were identified to enhance the making of *social spaces* – a diagnosis that can be corroborated by the authors to the extent that appropriate application of ICT is cared for, best in a stepwise and rhythmised manner.

Before the start of the following *practical chapter* containing the "case descriptions" we link both chapters by stating that all cases implement the above main guiding ideas of dialogue and discourse for societal learning. The network society is implemented by mapping controversial perspective into one interdisciplinary and intercultural synthetic view. New common spaces of understanding are stretched out and new and common identities are synthesised as structural capital.

Case Global Studies (GS)

Over the last decade, initiatives for "Global Studies" have emerged in the Austrian cities of Vienna, Graz, Salzburg and Innsbruck. The idea is to found a sound scientific curriculum that is inspired by developmental ethics. The first of these developmental studies has been established at the University of Vienna and has recently reached an annual throughput of some two hundred students per year.

Formally, this initiative has been led by the Department for African Studies in Vienna, but is still identified as a "project" and is carried out mainly by a group of half a dozen university lecturers. Despite the growing importance of developmental studies on an international level and their longer traditions in the Anglo-Saxon countries, the institution building process at the University of Vienna has been very slow.

At Graz University, a "bundle of electives" has been offered since 2003 (www.uni-graz.at/globalstudies) and is currently merged into a regular curriculum for the master course "Global Study". Whereas the Viennese initiative is mostly rooted in political sciences and sociology, the Graz initiative always maintained a very broad scope encompassing all faculties of this university: economics, political science, international law, languages, theology, global change, and sociological methods. The Graz curriculum is composed of 6 components and ensures a broad understanding. The Graz initiative was founded by a long-standing expert in peace research, Dr. Karl Kumpfmüller, and was implemented by a peer group of active members of Graz University (Ahamer & Kumpfmüller, 2013; Ahamer & Mayer, 2013), the so-called "Steering Committee Global Studies", who have been meeting bimonthly for the last 6 years. This bundle of electives amounts to 24 hours per semester or 36 ECTS, of which the only mandatory lecture is one introductory lecture to Global Studies held by the founder and one of the authors. A strength of the master curriculum is the mandatory three-month practical that might consist in developmental work abroad.

The Salzburg initiative is organised by initiative of the Institute for Geography and has accumulated a budget of eight hours per semester for a just starting curriculum also called "Global Studies". The Innsbruck initiative gained momentum after the biannual Austrian developmental conference 2008 in Innsbruck.

Case ESD

The conviction that only radical reforms of our present economic system can heal the environmental and economic crisis to a sufficient extent, has led to the foundation of the European panel on the promotion of sustainable development ESD. This is a loose but clearly organized group of idealists, who have formed as a vivid and constructive discussion round with illustrious authors of critical books in Austria. In an iterative process of mutual review, a book was authored that immediately after its publication reached the second highest rank of the evaluated books in future science (Ahamer & Jekel, 2010). This structured discussion process is maintained and will soon lead to a second reworked edition of the book "The turn of the Titanic". ESD has its own website (www.esd-eu.org) but is mainly relying on personal contacts and face-to-face debates and structured discussion. In no other case is the orientation to "discursive society" so clearly implemented as in ESD. The special chance and the special risk at the same time of this idealistic corporation might be the strong individualism and the deep ethical motivation that cared for a small but very dedicated group of activists, who managed to disseminate their thoughts in numerous public discussions and debates, especially with high-ranking stakeholders from industry, banking and administration.

Case Environmental Systems Analysis (USW)

A worldwide unique curriculum is "Environmental Systems Analysis" (Umweltsystemwissenschaften, USW) at Graz University, which comprises 5 specialties: economics, business administration, geography, chemistry and physics. Students of USW have to select one of these 5 specialties and additionally complete one quarter of their studies in the field of systems analysis, including a so-called "interdisciplinary practical" (IP). The special identity of USW is to train interdisciplinary dialogue already during the course of studies as a constitutive element. More than a dozen of such IPs have been conducted by one of the authors.

Problems related to Environmental Systems Analysis are the increasing character of this curriculum as a mass course of study. The number of students has reached 200 per year, which is a considerable change compared to the initial years of a dozen students who had to apply for their own curricula to be accepted by the university authorities as "studium irregulare". Initially swept away by a very positive public response, the percentage of highly motivated students has decreased to a normal level. An institution that might have been the hope for a generation may even lose its inner drive after having become part of "the system".

A *web-supported negotiation game "Surfing Global Change"* (SGC) was used as a dramatic foundation for these interdisciplinary practicals. SGC is a discussion-oriented negotiation game that trains consensus building (Ahamer & Schrei, 2004).

Its structure along time is symbolically depicted in Figure 2 that leads through the five levels of SGC. Rhythmisation of social procedures is the key didactic element of this web-supported negotiation game (Ahamer, 2005, 2008).

Figure 2. Symbolic depiction of the communicative setting (left) and the consecutive social processes (right) in which the five phases of Surfing Global Change (SGC) are developing: the evolution from dwelling upon single technical details towards a coherent view.

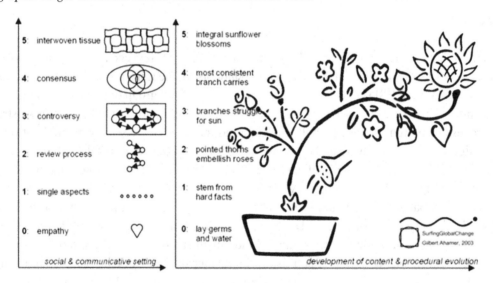

A brief outline of the social processes and the game activities that are used for the design of consensus building can be taken from Figure 3. recently, SGC was in parts applied to secondary schools and learning with virtual globes (Vogler et al., 2010).

The entire set of rules can be retrieved in journals (Ahamer, 2004). Experience has shown that SGC can be applied effectively to "distributed learning processes", especially to intercultural learning processes, because the focus is on viewing others' standpoints and dealing with them.

Lessons learned from the invention of SGC are: how can the rhythmized interplay of different communicative phases (real ó virtual; conflict ó cooperation; etc.) be applied to other learning settings? Two dozens of SGC games have been implemented to date at two Austrian universities and received positive feedback from students. SGC represents the idea of *"learning as gaming"*.

Figure 3. A folder displays the successive levels of gaming in SGC (© G. Ahamer)

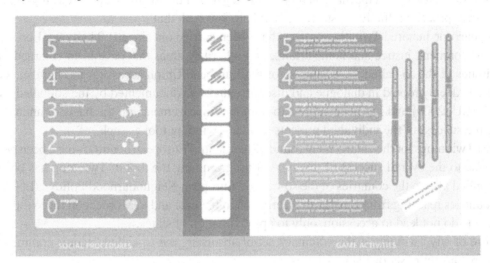

Case Twinning as a Tool

The historic processes of the break-up of the former Eastern-European Bloc in the year 1989 and the subsequent independence of these nation states has led them to pursue,, membership in the European Union. Consequently, a political and administrative tool on a continental scale had to be developed, that would be useful in defining a clear process of these new states towards restructuring into a democratic society. Such societal procedures can only occur on a voluntary basis; or else they would not be successful because of a lack of perceived ownership in the respective administrations. In 1998, the European Commission started the first "Twinning projects" that where designed to train administrative staff in the candidate countries for their future duties as member state administrations.

The main idea of these Twinning projects is to *jointly solve issues* posed by membership. Both physically and symbolically, civil servants of the candidate country and of a new member state sit next to one another and together face their issues and problems of daily work. Training is done on the job, in partnership, on the same height of eyes (symbolically and literally) and in a non-confrontational manner. The experts of the new member states are not standing "in front" of the experts of the candidate countries and giving them "good advice", but the "common enemy" is the task to be mastered. Therefore, the stakeholders are trained for their future roles as colleagues on EU level (Ahamer, 2013d). Additionally, the spirit of work and the democratic culture of self-responsible fulfilment of work duties are implemented in real live, not only theoretically taught. The side effects of gradually adapting to a different work attitude after decades of communism where rules and regulations might have been perceived as unnecessary attack on the individual might have constituted the most important achievement in many cases. Hence, Twinning offered a double achievement: learning new matters and new procedures. Anyhow, learning procedures always necessitates "matters" as a substrate of learning.

According to the philosophy of Twinning, concrete projects had to be formulated and applied for by people in the candidate country's administration. Often the most dedicated individuals have taken the effort to define a Twinning project and thus have contributed to the advancement of their specialties and maybe sometimes also to their personal careers. However, an almost invisible "cultural change" in EU financing took place, namely the shift from "demand driven" to "accession driven" projects. Whereas the first type of projects often meant: "candidate country demands, EU pays", towards "if you fulfil your own tasks in approaching the EU system, we will help you with that".

Every year, one hundred Twinning projects have been carried out since 1998 all over Europe in such areas as environment, justice and home affairs, and other key areas that have been enlarged to practically all issues of the so-called 33 "chapters" of the European Union accession mechanism. Twinning philosophy is deeply rooted in dialogue and discourse and was documented by the so-called Twinning Handbook (EU, 2009) and has been subject to iterative improvements on the basis of annual reviews assessing the success of the individual projects and the Twinning tool as such.

The last Twinnings for the enlargement round of the Central European countries have been performed in 2006. Due to the overall success of this type of programming the tool of Twinning has been subsequently applied also to the countries of the so-called "European Neighbourhood Policy" (ENP). This is a set of countries reaching from Belarus to Azerbaijan in the East and to Morocco in the West; however, these projects do not lead to accession, only to approximation of states.

The core of any Twinning is the voluntary act of absorbing the so-called "acquis communautaire" which means the entire set of EU legislation.

Many Twinning projects have a typical budget of one million Euros. Regarding the project structure, key roles are the "Resident Twinning Advisor" (RTA), who resides in the beneficiary country for one to two years and acts as a link between the European Union member states (MS) and the candidate countries or beneficiary countries (BC). RTAs report to the project leaders, one from the BC and one from the MS. Apart from the long-term expert RTA, typically five to forty short-term experts (STE) come to missions in the beneficiary country for typically one or two weeks. They should cooperate on a daily basis with their local homologues, who are civil servants on the beneficiary side. Twinning experts must come from an administration and are typically civil servants; STEs are not consultants in the usual sense of the word. This leads to the main characteristic of Twinning: *Twinning is institution building*, not technical consultancy. Twinning means "*strengthening of institutions*"; after a Twinning the beneficiary country should be able to perform its administrative tasks relying on its own strengths, its own motivation and its own financial and organisational means.

Twinning is certainly not a theoretical exercise limited to science only. It means changed realities in such concrete fields as taxation, border control, anti-corruption within the police, waste management, vocational education, or aviation safety. In this sense Twinning is institutional learning and societal learning in the sense as described in the first chapters. Twinnings may be seen as *one of the most effective methods for societal learning* as such.

Often considerable obstacles may arise in intercultural understanding. Also very often, the understanding prevails that the "western consultants" come, do the work and leave and thus spare the local consultants from this workload. Such an attitude would not comply with the requested ownership leading to empowerment of the beneficiary.

An overall analysis of the Twinning tool will arrive at seeing as a highly effective program enabling smooth transition processes of a large group of countries towards a democratic system. The latest enlargement of the European Union might even be seen as a third world war without one single victim. It represents possibly the first example in human history of an area one thousand kilometres wide encompassing an entire continent that has deliberately and voluntarily changed its political system, ultimately backed by the will of the majority of the population.

The core of the success of a Twinning lies in its potential to provide new perspectives on the same reality by incorporating the Twinning partner's view. When jointly sitting over a task, the expert colleagues exchange their views in an undramatic manner as part of their daily lives in an atmosphere that does not encourage competition but constitutes a win-win situation where the personal success of each one is the highest when having attained consensus with the partner. However, also cases of less harmonious Twinnings have been experienced where the long-term expert was replaced on the basis of dissatisfaction in the beneficiary country.

Synthesis of all Cases: Participation When Mapping

The common issue of all cases presented is the procedures by which citizens can partake in constructing "realities", be they architectures, buildings, highways, high voltage lines, political agreement or strategic alliances. Each of the above case studies has developed a rhythm of how to combine individual perspectives to arrive at the same desired results: common perspectives. Pushing constructivism into an extreme: reality is defined by consensus; diverging concepts will never come interpersonally "true", they remain individual "consciousness". Figure 4 sketches 360°-like perspectives of the presented case studies – similar to the approach of the fictitious "bird's perspective" that classical geography has adhered to for centuries.

Figure 4. Participation in mapping constitutes the preferable way of constructing realities (compare with Figure 1)

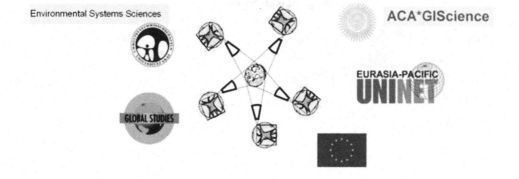

Experimental Data on Dialogic Communicative Behaviour of GS Students

The underlying research study was elaborated more precisely in case study 8 in Ahamer (2019, chapters 9 & 24) and includes statistical analyses of communication behaviour in peer-review-oriented university lectures, but – for reasons of paper space – cannot be reproduced here. These results prove that peer-oriented action does lead to deeper learning and changes in (academic & every-day life's) mentalities.

As mentioned, in all above-mentioned cases (especially in GS and USW) the underlying didactic and pedagogic idea was to use participating students' large dialogic potential within a learning platform in order to strengthen students' understanding of standpoints different from their own (Ahamer & Jekel, 2010). Figure 5 shows that this target was reached quantitatively, both if measured by means of time and hits. Expressed in an aggregated manner, over 128 hours were spent in discussion fora (45% of all sessions) while 101 hours were spent retrieving and reading files (35% of all sessions) by students (first two bars in Figure 6). The insert in Figure 7 stresses again the fact that work on the peer-reviewable "standpoints on developmental theories" has exclusively taken place after the last lecture in the lecture hall. The essence of this assignment was to interparadigmatically compare opposing developmental approaches, of which "neo-colonialism" and dependency theory" might represent extreme views.

Figure 5. Both the measured distribution of web page hits (at left) and of invested time (at right) in a learning platform for GS students shows that dialogic tools in the platform (posting, reviewing) were used more frequently than monologic tools (content conveyed by lecture notes).

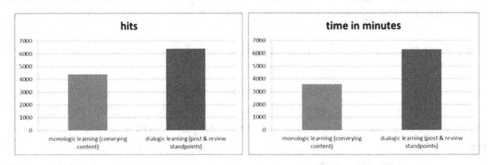

Figure 6 shows that discussion fora (dialogic tools) received more hits than downloadable files or (monologic tools).

Figure 6. Tools: more "fora" (red) than "files" or "folders" (blue)!

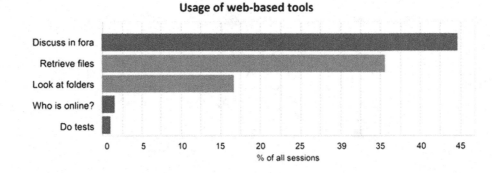

The single one most hit page was the one leading to the "1 page standpoint on diverse developmental theories" that had to be reviewed by all students in order to foster interparadigmatic understanding (top bar in Figure 7 and Figure 8).

Both Figure 7 and Figure 8 show that single web pages regarding *dialogic learning* (red) were used more frequently than for *monologic learning* (blue). The conclusion is that students prefer a communicative structure when studying. Hence, IT-based learning constructed as dialogue is far more accepted by learners than mere "file download" – which is an embryonic style of e-learning.

CONCLUSION

This text has provided an overview of "dialogic learning". For complex interdisciplinary and intercultural issues, "learning" is seen as converging different and divergent world views into a common synthetic perspective on reality. Manuel Castells concept of the "network society" combines easily with such concept.

Figure 7. Hits to single web pages on the web platform (at left). Insert at right: the most important web pages are differentiated into "before" and "after" the last course at the lecture hall in order to quantify the "virtual only" student activities: the peer-reviewable "standpoints" were worked on only after the end of face-to-face courses.

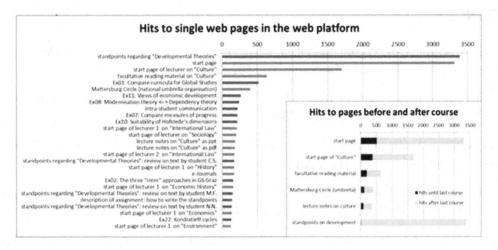

Figure 8. Visiting times for single web pages on the web platform. The page for the reviewable standpoints on developmental theories was by far the most visited of all pages – a clear success for dialogic and discoursive learning.

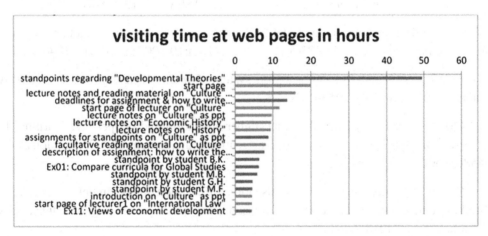

One motto of this entire volume is: how have organizations adapted to the advancement of learning options? Therefore, this contribution illustrates the genesis and evolutive growth of "structural capital and social capital" which consists in common institutions, common procedures and common values of diverse individuals, communities and societies.

The target of this contribution is transcultural learning. Cultures may be delimited spatially, politically, or also mentally such as different scientific disciplines.

Consequently, the described 14 cases in this contribution

- extending on both individual and societal learning
- comprising aspects of interdisciplinary and intercultural learning settings

all attempt to illustrate that a suitable way to "make a change" in our world is to exchange and adapt our world views.

REFERENCES

Adler, P. S., & Kwon, S.-W. (2002). Social capital: Prospects for a new concept. *Academy of Management Review*, *27*(1), 17–40. doi:10.5465/amr.2002.5922314

Ahamer, G. (2004). Negotiate your future: Web based role play. *Campus-Wide Information Systems*, *21*(1), 35–58. doi:10.1108/10650740410512329

Ahamer, G. (2005). 'Surfing Global Change': How didactic visions can be implemented. *Campus-Wide Information Systems*, *22*(5), 298–319. doi:10.1108/10650740510632217

Ahamer, G. (2008). Virtual Structures for mutual review promote understanding of opposed standpoints. *The Turkish Online Journal of Distance Education*, *9*(1), 17-43. https://tojde.anadolu.edu.tr/

Ahamer, G. (2012a). Training to bridge multicultural geographies of perspectives. *Campus-Wide Information Systems*, *29*(1), 21–44. doi:10.1108/10650741211192037

Ahamer, G. (2012b). A four-dimensional Maxwell equation for social processes in web-based learning and teaching – windrose dynamics as GIS: Games' intrinsic spaces. *International Journal of Web-Based Learning and Teaching Technologies*, *7*(3), 1–19. doi:10.4018/jwltt.2012070101

Ahamer, G. (2012c). Geo-referenceable model for the transfer of radioactive fallout from sediments to plants. *Water, Air, and Soil Pollution*, *223*(5), 2511–2524. doi:10.100711270-011-1044-x

Ahamer, G. (2013a). A planet-wide information system. *Campus-Wide Information Systems*, *30*(5), 369–378. doi:10.1108/CWIS-08-2013-0032

Ahamer, G. (2013b). GISS and GISP facilitate higher education and cooperative learning design. In Handbook of Research on Transnational Higher Education Management. IGI Global. doi:10.4018/978-1-4666-4458-8.ch001

Ahamer, G. (2013c). Quality assurance in transnational education management – the developmental "Global Studies" curriculum. In Handbook of Research on Transnational Higher Education Management. IGI Global. doi:10.4018/978-1-4666-4458-8.ch015

Ahamer, G. (2013d). Game, not fight: Change climate change! *Simulation and Gaming –. International Journal (Toronto, Ont.)*, *44*(2-3), 272–301. doi:10.1177/1046878112470541

Ahamer, G. (2014). Kon-Tiki: Spatio-temporal maps for socio-economic sustainability. *Journal for Multicultural Education*, *8*(3), 206–223. doi:10.1108/JME-05-2014-0022

Ahamer, G. (2015). Applying student-generated theories about global change and energy demand. *International Journal of Information and Learning Technology*, *32*(5), 258–271. doi:10.1108/IJILT-01-2015-0002

Ahamer, G. (2019). *Mapping Global Dynamics – Geographic perspectives from local pollution to global evolution*. Springer International Publishing. https://link.springer.com/book/10.1007/978-3-319-51704-9

Ahamer, G. (2022). Converging international cooperation supported by data structures. In Encyclopedia of Data Science and Machine Learning. IGI Global.

Ahamer, G., & Jekel, T. (2010). Make a change by exchanging views. In S. Mukerji & P. Tripathi (Eds.), *Cases on Transnational Learning and Technologically Enabled Environments* (pp. 1–20). doi:10.4018/978-1-61520-749-7.ch001

Ahamer, G., & Kumpfmüller, K. (2013). Education and literature for development in responsibility – Partnership hedges globalization. In Handbook of Research on Transnational Higher Education Management. IGI Global.

Ahamer, G., & Mayer, J. (2013). Forward looking: Structural change and institutions in highest-income countries and globally. *Campus-Wide Information Systems*, *30*(5), 386–403. doi:10.1108/CWIS-08-2013-0034

Ahamer, G., & Schrei, C. (2004). Exercise 'Technology Assessment' through a gaming procedure. *Journal of Desert Research*, *5*(2), 224–252.

Arnold, M. (2003). Intranets, community, and social capital: The case of Williams Bay. *Bulletin of Science, Technology & Society*, *23*(2), 78–87. doi:10.1177/0270467603251297

Berman, S. (1997). Civil society and political institutionalization. *The American Behavioral Scientist*, *5*(5), 562–574. doi:10.1177/0002764297040005003

Bourdieu, P. (1997). In A. H. Halsey, H. Lauder, P. Brown, & A. S. Wells (Eds.), *The forms of capital. education: Culture, Economy, and Society* (pp. 46–58). Oxford University Press.

Brownlow, A. (2005). A Geography of men's fear. *Geoforum*, *36*(5), 581–592. doi:10.1016/j.geoforum.2004.11.005

Burt, R. S. (2000). The network structure of social capital. *Research in Organizational Behavior*, *22*, 345–423. doi:10.1016/S0191-3085(00)22009-1

Castells, M. (1996-8). *The information age: Economy, society and culture*. Cambridge, MA: Blackwell.

Chung, L. H., & Gibbons, P. T. (1997). Corporate Entrepreneurship: The roles of ideology and social capital. *Group & Organization Management*, *22*(1), 10–30. doi:10.1177/1059601197221004

Crang, M. (2000). Public space, urban space and electronic space: Would the real city please stand up? *Urban Studies (Edinburgh, Scotland)*, *37*(2), 301–317. doi:10.1080/0042098002203

Dennis, L. (1970). Dewey's brief for the fine arts. *Studies in Art Education*, *11*(3), 3–8. doi:10.2307/1319771

Derudder, B., Devriendt, L., & Witlox, F. (2007). An empirical analysis of former Soviet cities in transnational airline networks. *Eurasian Geography and Economics*, *48*(1), 95–110. doi:10.2747/1538-7216.48.1.95

Eder, K. (2007). Europe as a particular space of communication. On the question of the social integration of a culturally heterogeneous community. *Berliner Journal fur Soziologie, 17*(1), 33-50+140.

ENP. (2021). *European Neighbourhood Policy*. https://ec.europa.eu/world/enp/

EU. (2009). *Boosting co-operation through Twinning*. European Commission, EuropeAid. Retrieved from https://ec.europa.eu/europeaid/where/neighbourhood/overview/Twinning_en.htm

Galilei, G. (1632). Dialogo dei due massimi sistemi del mondo, tolemaico e copernicano. Academic Press.

Haberman, J., & Suresh, S. (2021). Ensemble size judgments account for size constancy. *Attention, Perception & Psychophysics, 83*(3), 925–933. doi:10.375813414-020-02144-6 PMID:33083990

Hargittai, E. (2008). Whose space? Differences among users and non-users of social network sites. *Journal of Computer-Mediated Communication, 13*(1), 276–297. doi:10.1111/j.1083-6101.2007.00396.x

Hyden, G. (1997). Civil society, social capital, and development: Dissection of a complex discourse. *Studies in Comparative International Development, 32*(1), 3–30. doi:10.1007/BF02696304

Kenworthy, L. (1997). Civic engagement, social capital, and economic cooperation. *The American Behavioral Scientist, 5*(5), 645–656. doi:10.1177/0002764297040005010

Kirby, A. (2007). The production of private space and its implications for urban social relations. *Political Geography, 27*(1), 74–95. doi:10.1016/j.polgeo.2007.06.010

Larsen, L., Harlan, S. L., Bolin, B., Hackett, E. J., Hope, D., Kirby, A., Nelson, A., Rex, T. R., & Wolf, S. (2004). Bonding and bridging. understanding the relationship between social capital and civic action. *Journal of Planning Education and Research, 24*(1), 64–77. doi:10.1177/0739456X04267181

Lemke, J. L. (2000). Across the scales of time: Artifacts, activities, and meanings in ecosocial systems. *Mind, Culture, and Activity, 7*(4), 273–290. doi:10.1207/S15327884MCA0704_03

MacGregor, S. (2002). New perspectives for distributed design support. *Journal of Desert Research, 2*(2).

Mohan, G., & Mohan, J. (2002). Placing social capital. *Progress in Human Geography, 26*(2), 191–210. doi:10.1191/0309132502ph364ra

Nizamis, K., Athanasiou, A., Almpani, S., Dimitrousis, C., & Astaras, A. (2021). Converging robotic technologies in targeted neural rehabilitation: A review of emerging solutions and challenges. *Sensors (Basel), 21*(6), 1–37. doi:10.339021062084 PMID:33809721

Purcell, M. (2001). Neighborhood activism among homeowners as a politics of space. *The Professional Geographer, 53*(2), 178–194. doi:10.1111/0033-0124.00278

Taylor, P. J., Derudder, B., García, C. G., & Witlox, F. (2007). From north-south to 'global' south an investigation of a changing 'south' using airline flows between cities, 1970-2005. *Geography Compass, 3*(2), 836–855. doi:10.1111/j.1749-8198.2009.00216.x

Thöni, C., & Volk, S. (2021). Converging evidence for greater male variability in time, risk, and social preferences. *Proceedings of the National Academy of Sciences of the United States of America, 118*(23), e2026112118. Advance online publication. doi:10.1073/pnas.2026112118 PMID:34088838

Toutain, T. G., Baptista, A. F., Japyassú, H. F., Rosário, R. S., Porto, J. A., Campbell, F. Q., & Miranda, J. G. V. (2020). Does meditation lead to a stable mind? synchronous stability and time-varying graphs in meditators. *Journal of Complex Networks, 8*(6), 1–14. doi:10.1093/comnet/cnaa049

Vogler, R., Ahamer, G., & Jekel, T. (2010). GEOKOM-PEP. Pupil led research into the effects of geovisualization. *AGIT Conference*. http://www.gi-forum.org/index.php?option=com_content&view=article&id=71:learning-with-gi&catid=3:info-for-participants&Itemid=20

Wang, J. (2021). Editor's description and coverage. *Encyclopedia of Data Science and Machine Learning*. Available at https://www.igi-global.com/book/encyclopedia-data-science-machine-learning/276507

Zheng, J., & Niu, J. (2007). Computer and computational sciences - Unified mapping of social networks into 3D space. IMSCCS 2007, Second International Multi-Symposiums on Computer and Computational Sciences.

Oracle 19c's Multitenant Container Architecture and Big Data

Sikha Bagui

https://orcid.org/0000-0002-1886-4582

University of West Florida, USA

Mark Rauch

University of West Florida, USA

INTRODUCTION

The importance of Big Data cannot be understated, and its value will continue to grow alongside it. With the exponential growth in data, developers have had to adjust database architecture in an to attempt to keep pace with Big Data. In late 2016 Oracle introduced a major architectural overhaul to its relational database system that would bring about changes needed to function in a market that supported Big Data. The introduction of multitenant architecture in 12c opened the door for Oracle and Oracle has continued to improve upon it. Recently, Oracle tagged its 19c version as a long-term release candidate for this architecture going forward. Historically Oracle has not been known for its ability to manage Big Data, but with these recent changes, it aims to remedy that. With Oracle 19c comes improvements in Oracle's container architecture.

The container architecture is a logical collection of data or metadata within a multitenant architecture, which allow for applications to be developed quickly and have workload portability. Hussein et al. (2019) discuss the idea of a container as a Service (CaaS) in a cloud environment. Multi-tenant architecture allows multiple users to share a single instance of a software application and its underlying resources. Containers, units within the container architecture, are bundled units of software with all their dependencies, packaged so that applications can run quickly and reliably when transported from one computing environment to another. Container architecture is being used by Google (Sanchez, 2014) and IBM (IBM Cloud, n.d.). Google, who has been using container architecture since 2004, is integrating containers into it's Cloud Platform (Sanchez, 2014). Red Hat-IBM has been named the leader in multi-cloud container development ("Containers on IBM Cloud", n.d.).

Oracle 19c's new multitenant architecture enables an Oracle database to function as a multitenant container database (CDB). A CDB is composed of pluggable databases (PDBs), which are a movable collection of schemas, schema objects and non-schema objects ("Administrator's Guide," n.d.).

In this chapter, the architectural changes that come with 19c multitenant architecture are presented. The architectural features discussed are: automated indexing, the online table move feature, pluggable database relocation, rapid home provisioning, preventing schema-only locks, and auditing. These are presented in the form of case studies, demonstrating the improvements that come with 19c when compared with an environment that is currently running Oracle 11g.

The rest of this chapter is organized as follows. Section two presents the traditional oracle architecture; section three presents the multitenant architecture, including the advantages of the multitenant architecture and shared multitenant architecture; section four presents big data and oracle in the context of big

DOI: 10.4018/978-1-7998-9220-5.ch031

Copyright © 2023, IGI Global. Copying or distributing in print or electronic forms without written permission of IGI Global is prohibited.

data, including how multitenant architecture resolves issues that were a problem in the past; section five describes the experimentation, the grid and database installs; section six demonstrates the improvements of the multitenant architectural features in Oracle 19c; and section seven presents the conclusions.

BACKGROUND: TRADITIONAL ORACLE ARCHITECTURE

Oracle databases traditionally consist of at least one database instance. The database itself is a set of files that store its data, and these files can exist independently of the database instance. The database instance is a set of memory structures called the system global area (SGA) and a set of background processes. The instance can exist independently of the database files. When a user connects to the Oracle database, a client process is created with its own server process. Each server process has its own private session memory known as program global area (PGA) ("Oracle® Database. Database Concepts," 2021). It is through the application that interactions are made across either multiple logical databases within a single physical database, or a single logical database distributed across multiple physical databases ("Oracle® Database. Database Concepts," 2021). Each of these memory structures have far more depth to them inclusive of the many different processes hosted within. This traditional structure has been deprecated in favor of a new one, hence the focus of this chapter.

FOCUS OF ARTICLE: MULTITENANT ARCHITECTURE

Buyya et al. (2018) and Hillman et al. (2021) have looked at multi-tenant architecture. They have discussed multi-tenant architecture from a scheduling perspective. Oracle 19c uses a multitenant architecture, which enables an Oracle database to be a CDB. A container database can contain either zero, one, or many pluggable databases (PDB). A PDB is a portable collection of schemas, schema objects, and non-schema objects that appears to an Oracle Net client as a non-CDB ("Oracle® Database. Database Concepts," 2021). This portable and pluggable database has many benefits and it solves several problems that have plagued the traditional architecture.

Advantages of the Multitenant Architecture

Whether large or small, there are benefits to migrating to this new architecture, though the larger enterprises will see more merit. Large enterprises may use hundreds or thousands of databases, often running on multiple physical servers. Current technology allows for this and can withstand heavy workloads. Historically a database may only use a fraction of that server's hardware capacity, and this would lead to either under provisioning equipment or over provisioning it. Multitenant architecture allows the consolidation of multiple physical databases across different hardware into a single database structure on a single piece of hardware. Broadly speaking, the immediate benefits of using a multitenant architecture include ("Oracle® Database. Database Concepts," 2021):

- Hardware cost reduction
- More efficient movement of code
- Easier management and monitoring of the physical database
- Separation of raw data and code

- Separation of duties between administrators if necessary.

Also considering the benefits of manageability within the architecture, the following benefits can be added to the above list ("Oracle® Database. Database Concepts," 2021):

- Allows for easier upgrades
- Easier testing
- Ability to restore via flashback to specific PDB's
- The ability to set performance limits on memory and input/output at the PDB level.

How the Multitenant Architecture Works

Initially we mentioned that it was through the application where configuration dictated whether interactions were made, and this has not changed as far as the application knows because it sees the PDB as the database it would normally connect to. But PDB's can be rapidly provisioned, and they are portable, which makes it quite easy to move and load balance. A typical CDB will host several PDB's and since most common operations are performed at the CDB level, it allows for greater efficiency and allocation of resources. The CDB will host a single set of background process and a single global memory area which is than shared across all the PDBs. It is this concept that allows the multitenant architecture to see such large operational and technical efficiency gains. Of course, when it comes to the sharing of any resources in technology, steps must be taken to ensure security is considered (Oracle Multitenant with Oracle Database 19c," 2019).

Shared Multitenant Architecture and Dealing with Security Concerns

With shared multitenant architecture comes the idea of comprehensive isolation. This concept is Oracle's response to security concerns when migrating to multitenant and it has four main parts.

The first part is access control mechanism, which includes features such as self-contained PDB's for each tenant or application if desired. This will allow a hard separation of access if you work in a field where data separation or privacy is required, such as healthcare. On top of this you can add lockdown profiles, which is where the administrators can implement access restrictions at a user or schema level to each of the PDB's within the CDB. Lastly in 19c there is the introduction of the PDB Nest which is where a runtime environment hierarchy is created that mirrors the container hierarchy. This allows for multiple PDB's to be linked together via a single virtual environment to allow greater flexibility without compromising security.

The second part of the comprehensive isolation architecture is to prevent unauthorized administrative access. The idea here is to limit access given to administrators of the databases that tend to be given shared access but have different roles. This is referring to a separation of access between infrastructure database administrators and application database administrators. Oracle refers to this as "locking the front door".

The third part of the comprehensive isolation architecture is protecting from direct access to the data files. This implies the use of transparent data encryption across all the PDBs and each PDB has its own separate encryption key. This will protect the data at rest and Oracle refers to it as "locking the back door".

The fourth and last part of the comprehensive isolation architecture is resource isolation. This part covers a separation of the resources once allocated to avoid performance degradation from the shared resource pool. A good example of this is a means of avoiding a denial-of-service attack since that individual resource can be isolated and limited on what it has access to ("Oracle Multitenant with Oracle Database 19c," 2019).

This brief overview shows how Oracle has changed its architecture to allow greater efficiency and management of resources. These benefits can be seen in Big Data applications, which is an area that Oracle has not been well known for prior to Oracle 19c. Before reviewing how the changes in the multitenant architecture have improved Oracle's relationship with Big Data, Big Data is explained and then a discussion of Oracle's stance towards it is presented.

BIG DATA

What is Big Data

In 2001 the definition of Big Data was created by Gartner which described it as data that contained greater variety arriving in increasing volumes and with even higher velocity (Katal et al., 2013). This introduces the three V's which are the initial components of Big Data, volume, velocity, and variety. Volume being the amount of data, velocity being the fast rate at which data is transferred, and variety being the different types of data that are available. Over time two more V's have been added, value and veracity. Value refers to the idea that data has intrinsic value, but it is of no use until that value is discovered. Veracity refers to how truthful the data is and how much can you rely upon it (Katal et al., 2013). That leads to the question of, is all big data the same? Of course not, there are three main types of Big Data. Big Data can be structured, unstructured, or semi-structured. Structured data is any data that can be stored, accessed, or processed in the form of fixed format (Taylor, 2022). Fixed format is when the data format is defined and well known in advance. Unstructured data is any data with an unknown form which poses multiple challenges in terms of processing or deriving value out of it. Since the format is unstructured it is usually unknown, which tends to be data where there is a combination of random formats such as video, text, images, files, etc. Lastly, there is semi-structured data which will contain both the above mentioned structured and unstructured data, but the key difference is that there is not any defined format to the data (Taylor, 2022). Oracle maintains a stance which is centered on the idea that you can evolve your current enterprise data architecture to incorporate big data and deliver business value, leveraging their historical reliability, flexibility, and performance to meet requirements ("Oracle Multitenant with Oracle Database 19c," 2019). How Oracle accomplishes these above goals is presented next.

Oracle and Big Data

Oracle attempts to accomplish this by providing a complete and integrated solution to address the full spectrum of big data requirements. This solution is known as Oracle Big Data Appliance. This all-in-one solution is how Oracle aims to confront the historical issues of a non-optimized RDBMS for big data. The solution is made up of several layers of optimized equipment and software to provide these results. It starts with an Oracle database running on Oracle Linux. This is where we will be focusing on how these multitenant architecture aids with processing Big Data, but we will also briefly cover the other parts of Oracle Big Data Appliance. Oracle Big Data Appliance is the hardware sitting in front of the Oracle Database and within it are several key components required for processing large amounts of data. The first layer is Oracle Linux and Cloudera's Distribution including Apache Hadoop which covers the operating and file systems. The Hadoop distributed file system is a highly scalable file system that provides reliability and replication of the data across multiple servers. The Map Reduce engine provides the platform for massive parallel execution of algorithms written in Java. Cloudera Manager is the administrative tool and the Oracle Enterprise Manager is used for monitoring. Lastly, Apache projects cover a large portion of the quality-of-life support that comes from projects such as Hive, Pig, Oozie, Zookeeper, HBase, Sqoop and Spark ("Oracle® Big Data Appliance Software User's Guide," 2020). Oracle recommends having the storage run on Oracle Exadata since this is optimized to run Oracle products more efficiently. The next question is, what exactly is this optimized hardware and software trying to alleviate, what issues plague Oracle when it comes to Big Data?

Issues with Big Data

Big Data is notoriously known for its size as the name implies. Over the years the amount of data that is produced is staggering to say least. Oracle is not known for its affordability when it comes to its products and licensing. Thus, when you look at Big Data it is easy to see where storage costs would be an issue historically. Granted storage and processing costs have dropped in recent years which has helped alleviate some of this fiscal burden there are still other areas that need to be looked at. Five main concerns with scalability for big data exist and they are (Katal et al., 2013):

- Efficiency of storage systems when it comes to read and write operations.
- Multiple storage spaces and communications given the volume and variety of data collections.
- Data analytics workflows supported by efficient underlying data management infrastructures.
- Parallel programming models to deal with the execution of data analytics tasks that may require large amounts of computing and memory resources.
- Effective and accessible use of cloud resources and transparency.

How Multitenant Resolves Big Data's Issues

Starting with the Oracle multitenant architecture, the process for analyzing transactional data has become well established and the platform leads the data warehouse market by a wide margin[6]. To assist with this in the multitenant platform, Oracle has developed integrated access to the data when using its Big Data Platform product. This integration effectively eliminates the need to move large volumes of data between disparate data stores, and data can be accessed using multiple programming languages where the data is stored in different repositories ("Transforming Data Management with Oracle Database 12c Release 2," 2017). Within the multitenant architecture is also the user of the Oracle Big Data SQL product which allows normal querying and analyzing across Hadoop, NoSQL and Oracle databases. Oracle multitenant architecture also includes support for JSON and broad support of non-relational data such as XML, text, spatial, and graph ("Transforming Data Management with Oracle Database 12c Release 2," 2017). Oracles multitenant architecture also provides the benefits of being designed to take advantage of cloud services more efficiently. This gives access to lower costs and greater productivity as users can move PDB's between CDB's while also having PDB's designed to manage certain types of data. Lastly, the Oracle multitenant architecture provides the agility of PDB clones, refreshes, relocates and elastic scaling as features that can assist with the incorporation of Big Data and data warehousing ("Transforming Data Management with Oracle Database 12c Release 2," 2017). The next section describes how to setup this new multi-tenant architecture in Oracle 19c.

EXPERIMENTATIONAL SETUP

This section presents some highlights on Oracle 19c grid and database installs. First the grid install has to be done and then the database install, as shown in Figure 1.

Figure 1. Oracle 19c grid and database installs

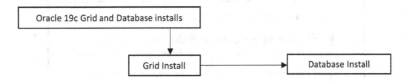

19c Grid Install

The required installation files can be obtained from Oracle's distribution site ("Oracle Database 19c (19.3),"n.d.). A full setup will include the need to install both the grid and the database. Grid will host our automatic storage manager (ASM), as shown in Figure 2.

Figure 2. Installation files

```
-rw-r--r-- 1 oracle oinstall 3059705302 Mar 19 14:59 LINUX.X64_193000_db_home.zip
-rw-r--r-- 1 oracle oinstall 2889184573 Mar 19 15:06 LINUX.X64_193000_grid_home.zip
```

After the required software has been acquired, the 19c staging directory needs to be created, as shown below in Figure 3.

Figure 3. Installation directory

```
drwxr-xr-x  2 oracle oinstall 4096 Mar 20 12:07 19.3.0
```

Next the grid install has to be done. The process for the grid install is presented in Figure 4.

In this work, the ASM storage platform was used instead of the normal file system storage since ASM has several key features that are useful. These key features include the automatic redistribution of storage as the data files grow, the input and output spread to avoid hot spots on the disk, and the ability to use Enterprise Manager to control storage. ASM disk groups were created, one for the grid install and one for the databases. Appropriate linux groups for user accounts were set up and the installer was pointed to the staging directory created as the grid base.

Figure 4. Grid install setup

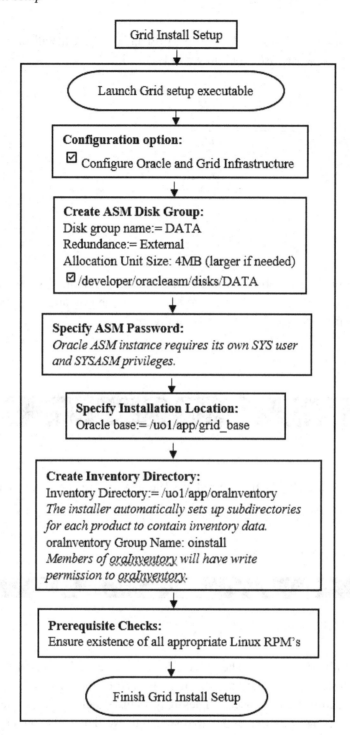

19c Database Install

After the grid install, the next step is to move to the database install that includes the container database and pluggable database. Next, the staging directories are created for the database install and the associated files are moved into that directory. Figure 5 presents the database install setup that will allow us to utilize this new architecture.

The database install should be set up such that a pluggable database structure is configurable for each database for specific purposes. This will allow better tuning for each database. We should be able to move pluggable databases between container databases as a more efficient means of migrating data. In the database install, memory will be allocated and sample schemas added. ASM, configured in the Grid Install, should be utilized.

Figure 5. Database install setup

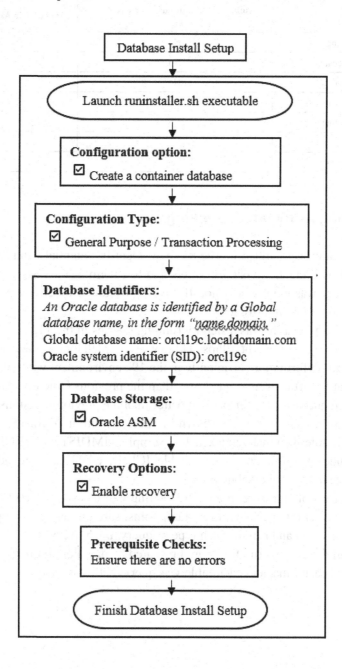

Multitenant Architecture Testing

The following section contains a series of use cases where several new features of Oracle 19c are tested. Some of these features did not exist in the Oracle11g architecture and other features have been improved upon significantly in the multitenant architecture, as shown in Table 1. Oracle maintains a comprehensive list of changes by version in their security guide ("Changes in This Release for Oracle Database Security Guide," n.d.).

Table 1. Features tested

Features Tested	Available in Traditional Arch. (Oracle 11g)	Available in Multi-Tenant (Oracle 19c)
Automated Indexing	No	Yes
Online Table Move Feature	No	Yes
PDB Relocation	No	Yes
Rapid Home Patching	No	Yes
PDB IO Rate Limiting	No	Yes
Prevent Schema-Only Locks	No	Yes
Variations of Auditing	Yes	Yes

Use Case 1: Testing Automated Indexing

Automatic indexing is a process added in 19c that will identify potential candidate indexes based on table column usage. It will create invisible indexes and test them against SQL statements in order to determine if performance was improved or not. If it is improved it will become a new index, if not it is flagged as unusable and will be removed.

The automated indexing feature was tested by running queries in the 11g environment and running the same queries in the 19c environment. Elapsed time was recorded for both sets of runs. The query will automatically index and perform more efficiently in the 19c environment without any additional input. Initial results were that first runs were a bit slower than the previous Oracle version, but by the end of the third day of runs all queries were performing better than the previous versions.

A set of 15 tables from one schema, as shown in Table 2, were used for the runs. As can be seen from the Table 2, some tables had many indexes, for example, MMDIST and REQLINE had 13 indexes, APDISTRIB had 14 indexes, and so on. Only one table, ICICRAUDIT, had one index. The tables in this schema also had a large number of attributes.

To determine the effect of auto indexing and recreating indexes, six different types of queries were run: Single table queries, two table joins, three table joins, sub-queries, grouping and aggregates. 18 different queries were created and run for each type of query. Each query was run four times each over a three-day period, and the average run times are presented by day. For all queries, different tables and attributes were selected each time, and each table was queried at least once.

Table 2. Testing tables

Schema	Tables	Number of Indexes	Num of Attributes	Num of Rows	Size
LAWDEV10	MMDIST	13	17,792,055	17,586,735	5.19 GB
	GLTRANS	3	15,819,825	15,522,910	6.19 GB
	RQAUDIT	2	7,348,283	7,348,283	2.06 GB
	POAUDIT	3	7,179,683	6,718,573	1.75 GB
	ICICRAUDIT	1	5,640,633	5,640,633	1.31 GB
	ICTRANS	4	4,708,112	4,670,679	3.62 GB
	RQTRANS	4	4,963,665	4,600,477	720 MB
	REQLINE	13	4,546,112	4,526,107	5 GB
	EDEVENTDTL	1	4,669,047	4,434,915	496 MB
	APDISTRIB	14	3,961,941	3,879,194	2.21 GB
	POMATCHOBJ	5	3,922,381	3,650,124	1.31 GB
	ICTRANSDTL	5	3,711,301	3,352,321	768 MB
	WHSHIPLINE	7	2,904,065	2,891,867	912 MB
	ICAUDIT	5	2,879,502	2,846,706	2.81 GB
	POLINE	16	2,694,088	2,692,808	3.44 GB
	MAINVDTL	11	2,666,668	2,685,836	1.94 GB

The results are presented in Table 3. The column, Day 3-1, shows the difference between day 3 and day 1. In Oracle 19c, it can be noted that the time went down in day 3 (shown by the negative sign). The highest amount of reduction in time was in the single table queries (52ms), followed by the GROUP BYs (22ms). The least amount of reduction in time was with the aggregations, but overall, there was a greater reduction in time with Oracle 19c than with Oracle 11g.

Use Case 2: Testing the Online Table Move

Traditionally moving a table from one tablespace to another was an offline only process. That is, the table would be unavailable for use until the process had completed. Additionally, it would invalidate the indexes not allowing them to be used until each index was rebuilt. Online table move keeps the table available for use and will automatically maintain the indexes.

The online table move feature of the multitenant architecture was tested by creating a table and indexes, and then changing the default tablespace of the table. This should invalidate the indexes in the 11g environment. In the 19c environment, it should automate the rebuilding of the indexes when the tablespace gets changed.

This case was started by creating a new table, PERSONS, under the lawdev10 user and an index MV_TABLESPACE_EX, as shown in Figure 6.

It can be noted that the table, PERSONS, is under the SYSTEM tablespace and that the index MV_TABLESPACE_EX is valid. The online table move feature is tested by moving the PERSONS table to the LAWSON tablespace. This would invalidate the index in Oracle 11g. Figure 7 shows the successful post tablespace move.

Table 3. Results of testing

	Table Name	11G				19c			
		Elapsed Times in ms							
		Day 1	Day 2	Day 3	Day3-1	Day 1	Day 2	Day 3	Day 3-1
Single Table Query	MMDIST	4.20	4.16	4.21	0.01	4.47	5.12	4.14	-0.33
	GLTRANS	2.48	2.45	2.49	0.01	3.14	3.31	3.06	-0.08
	REQLINE	0.40	0.41	0.39	-0.01	2.08	1.20	0.40	-1.68
	WHSHIPLINE	0.36	0.36	0.37	0.01	0.35	0.39	0.35	0.00
Average difference between Days 1 and 3					0.01				-0.52
Two Table Join	RQAUDIT	1.26	1.27	1.26	0.00	1.52	1.28	1.19	-0.33
	POAUDIT	0.04	0.04	0.04	0.00	0.08	0.11	0.04	-0.04
	APDISTRIB	0.24	0.25	0.24	0.00	0.19	0.13	0.12	-0.07
	POMATCHOBJ	0.24	0.24	0.25	0.01	0.20	0.17	0.15	-0.05
Average difference between Days 1 and 3					0.00				-0.12
Three Table Join	ICICRAUDIT	1.36	1.37	1.37	0.01	1.38	1.42	1.29	-0.09
	ICTRANS	0.21	0.21	0.21	0.00	0.27	0.37	0.21	-0.06
	POLINE	0.12	0.13	0.12	0.00	0.25	0.14	0.13	-0.12
	MAINVDTL	0.10	0.10	0.09	-0.01	0.12	0.11	0.09	-0.03
Average difference between Days 1 and 3					0.00				-0.08
Sub-Query	MMDIST	5.25	5.27	5.26	0.01	4.32	5.03	4.27	-0.05
	APDISTRIB	0.30	0.31	0.30	0.00	0.31	0.26	0.23	-0.08
	ICTRANSDTL	0.49	0.48	0.49	0.00	0.40	0.45	0.40	0.00
	MAINVDTL	0.58	0.59	0.58	0.00	0.44	1.00	0.35	-0.09
Average difference between Days 1 and 3					0.00				-0.06
Group By	RQAUDIT	2.19	2.20	2.20	0.01	2.00	2.19	1.59	-0.41
	ICICRAUDIT	1.38	1.38	1.38	0.00	1.20	1.29	1.20	0.00
	RQTRANS	1.10	1.11	1.10	0.00	1.00	1.06	0.57	-0.43
	ICAUDIT	0.17	0.17	0.17	0.00	0.14	0.21	0.11	-0.03
Average difference between Days 1 and 3					0.00				-0.22
Aggregate	MMDIST	0.03	0.03	0.03	0.00	0.01	0.01	0.01	0.00
	GLTRANS	0.01	0.01	0.01	0.00	0.01	0.01	0.01	0.00
	POAUDIT	0.03	0.03	0.03	0.00	0.01	0.01	0.01	0.00
	REQLINE	0.01	0.01	0.01	0.00	0.03	0.01	0.01	-0.02
Average difference between Days 1 and 3					0.00				-0.01

From the post tablespace move we can see that the PERSONS table is now under the LAWTEST tablespace and that the index MV_TABLESPACE_EX is still valid. This shows that we were able to move the tablespace using the online feature and that it rebuilt the indexes automatically.

Figure 6. Creation of table and index

```
SQL> select table_name, tablespace_name from dba_tables where table_name='PERSONS';

TABLE_NAME
-------------------
TABLESPACE_NAME
-------------------
PERSONS
SYSTEM


SQL> select index_name, status from dba_indexes where table_name='PERSONS';

INDEX_NAME
-------------------
STATUS
--------
MV_TABLESPACE_EX
VALID

SYS_C0073555
VALID
```

Figure 7. Post tablespace move

```
SQL> alter table lawdev10.persons move online tablespace lawtest;

Table altered.

SQL> select table_name, tablespace_name from dba_tables where table_name='PERSONS';

TABLE_NAME
-------------------
TABLESPACE_NAME
-------------------
PERSONS
LAWTEST


SQL> select index_name, status from dba_indexes where table_name='PERSONS';

INDEX_NAME
-------------------
STATUS
--------
MV_TABLESPACE_EX
VALID

SYS_C0073555
VALID
```

Use Case 3: Testing Pluggable Database Relocation Features

In 19c, the pluggable database relocation feature was added. This allows a pluggable database to be relocated seamlessly between container databases once configuration has been set. This improves the availability and mobility of pluggable databases.

To test the pluggable database relocation features of the multitenant architecture, a pluggable database was migrated between two different container databases to validate the high availability infrastructure. A pluggable database should be openable in the new container database without any export or import process.

This scenario is tested by logging into the current container database, "oemsrv". CDB is queried to see what pluggable databases are on it and Figure 8 shows that "oemrep" exists in this container.

Figure 8. PDB's in OEMSRV

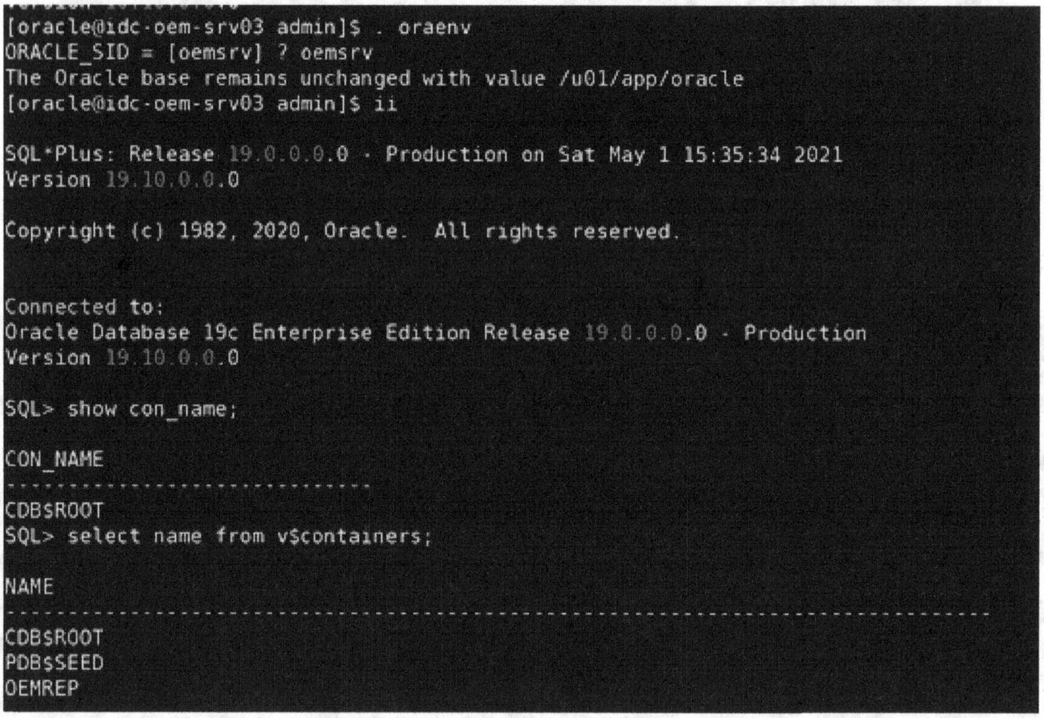

```
[oracle@idc-oem-srv03 admin]$ . oraenv
ORACLE_SID = [oemsrv] ? oemsrv
The Oracle base remains unchanged with value /u01/app/oracle
[oracle@idc-oem-srv03 admin]$ ii

SQL*Plus: Release 19.0.0.0.0 - Production on Sat May 1 15:35:34 2021
Version 19.10.0.0.0

Copyright (c) 1982, 2020, Oracle.  All rights reserved.


Connected to:
Oracle Database 19c Enterprise Edition Release 19.0.0.0.0 - Production
Version 19.10.0.0.0

SQL> show con_name;

CON_NAME
------------------------------
CDB$ROOT
SQL> select name from v$containers;

NAME
--------------------------------------------------------------------------------
CDB$ROOT
PDB$SEED
OEMREP
```

Next, the target container database is queried to see what containers are in it, as shown in figure 9.

Inside the target container, a link between the two containers is created to relocate the pluggable database, as shown in Figure 10.

With the link established, we log back into the original container database "oemsrv" and relocate the pluggable databases over from the "oemtest" container. Figure 11 shows this process. The pluggable database could be relocated between container databases without an issue.

Use Case 4: Testing the Rapid Home Patching Features

The idea behind rapid patching is that when a fresh database is created all you have to do is relocate the database into an existing environment and it is able to acquire patching via data patch without having to go through the entire installation process.

Figure 9. PDB's in OEMTEST

```
[oracle@idc-oem-srv03 admin]$ . oraenv
ORACLE_SID = [oemsrv] ? oemtest
The Oracle base remains unchanged with value /u01/app/oracle
[oracle@idc-oem-srv03 admin]$ ii

SQL*Plus: Release 19.0.0.0.0 - Production on Sat May 1 15:41:45 2021
Version 19.10.0.0.0

Copyright (c) 1982, 2020, Oracle.  All rights reserved.


Connected to:
Oracle Database 19c Enterprise Edition Release 19.0.0.0.0 - Production
Version 19.10.0.0.0

SQL> show con_name;

CON_NAME
-----------------------------
CDB$ROOT
SQL> select name from v$containers;

NAME
--------------------------------------------------------------------------------
CDB$ROOT
PDB$SEED
OEMTEST2
```

Figure 10. A link between two containers created

```
SQL> CREATE PUBLIC DATABASE LINK clone_link
  CONNECT TO c##remote_clone_user IDENTIFIED BY remote_clone_user USING '(DESCRIPTION = (ADDRESS_LIST =(ADDRESS = (PROTOCOL = TCP)
(HOST = <hostip>)(PORT = 1522))
(CONNECT_DATA = (SERVICE_NAME = oemtest)))';  2    3

Database link created.
```

Figure 11. PDB relocated to OEMSRV

```
SQL> CREATE PLUGGABLE DATABASE oemtest2 FROM oemtest2@clone_link RELOCATE AVAILABILITY MAX;

Pluggable database created.

SQL> show pdbs

    CON_ID CON_NAME                       OPEN MODE  RESTRICTED
---------- ------------------------------ ---------- ----------
         2 PDB$SEED                       READ ONLY  NO
         3 OEMREP                         READ WRITE NO
         4 OEMTEST3                       MOUNTED
         5 OEMTEST2                       MOUNTED
SQL> select name from v$database;

NAME
---------
OEMSRV
```

To test the rapid home patching features of the multitenant architecture, automated patching and provisioning of the database software was tested. The container database was patched to a newer version and a non-patched pluggable database was migrated to that container database than data patch was ran. All new pluggable databases should be patchable via data patch when being plugged into an updated container database.

This scenario can be checked by going back to the original upgrade. Once updated, this will put OEMSRV as a 19.3.0 container database. The numbers are slightly different as it is patched, and the container database is currently at 19.10. This can be verified by logging into the database and checking the current version, as shown in Figure 12.

When the upgrade was performed, only the container database was upgraded. Then a pluggable database was added without having to go through the whole upgrade process. The same actions can be performed to validate that OEMREP has been automatically upgraded to the latest version as well, as shown in Figure 13. Hence, the pluggable database was relocated to an updated container database and patched without having to go through the entire process.

Figure 12. Version of container database

```
SQL*Plus: Release 19.0.0.0.0 - Production on Wed May 5 12:56:27 2021
Version 19.10.0.0.0

Copyright (c) 1982, 2020, Oracle.  All rights reserved.


Connected to:
Oracle Database 19c Enterprise Edition Release 19.0.0.0.0 - Production
Version 19.10.0.0.0

SQL> select name from v$database;

NAME
---------
OEMSRV
```

Figure 13. Version of pluggable database

```
[oracle@idc-oem-srv03 bin]$ sqlplus mrauch@oemrep

SQL*Plus: Release 19.0.0.0.0 - Production on Wed May 5 13:00:56 2021
Version 19.10.0.0.0

Copyright (c) 1982, 2020, Oracle.  All rights reserved.

Enter password:
Last Successful login time: Wed May 05 2021 12:59:54 -04:00

Connected to:
Oracle Database 19c Enterprise Edition Release 19.0.0.0.0 - Production
Version 19.10.0.0.0
```

Use Case 5: Testing the Pluggable Database IO Rate Limit Feature

In earlier releases of the multi-tenant architecture, there was no way to control the amount of IO used by an individual pluggable database. This feature allows control over having additional pluggable databases consuming excess disk IO and hindering performance.

The pluggable database IO rate limit feature was tested by setting thresholds on different databases and then benchmarking them against each other. The throttled pluggable databases should see performance impacts sooner than the non-throttled ones but should not have any performance impact on those non-throttled pluggable databases.

We would begin by logging into the container database to ensure that no global thresholds have been set for the max IO rate limit, as shown in Figure 14.

Figure 14. CDB Non-throttled parameter

```
Connected to:
Oracle Database 19c Enterprise Edition Release 19.0.0.0.0 - Production
Version 19.10.0.0.0

SQL> show con_name;

CON_NAME
------------------------------
CDB$ROOT
SQL> show parameter MAX_IOPS;

NAME                                 TYPE        VALUE
------------------------------------ ----------- ------------------------------
max_iops                             integer     0
```

Next, log into the pluggable database to ensure there are no existing threshold holds, as shown in Figure 15.

Figure 15. PDB Non-throttled parameter

```
SQL> alter session set container=oemtest2;

Session altered.

SQL> show parameter MAX_IOPS;

NAME                                 TYPE        VALUE
------------------------------------ ----------- ------------------------------
max_iops                             integer     0
SQL>
```

Then, set the IO limit threshold and query the parameter, as shown in Figure 16.

Figure 16. PDB throttled parameter

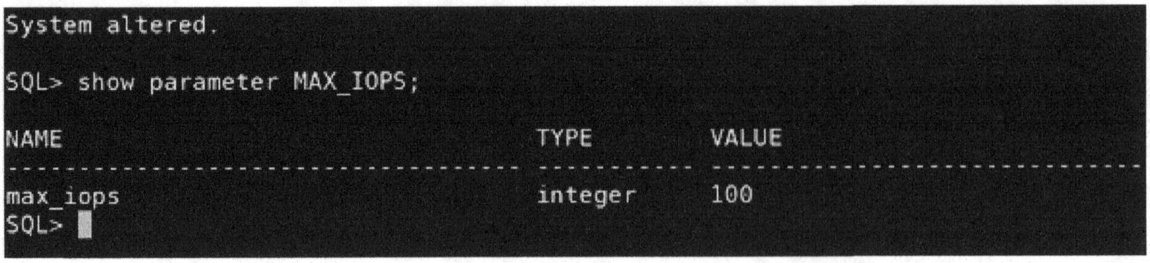

```
System altered.

SQL> show parameter MAX_IOPS;

NAME                                    TYPE       VALUE
-----------------------------------     --------   ---------------------
max_iops                                integer    100
SQL>
```

Returning to the container we can see that the CDB parameter was unaffected by this, as shown in Figure 17. This shows the global thresholds being set for rate limitation in the pluggable database.

Figure 17. CDB parameter post change

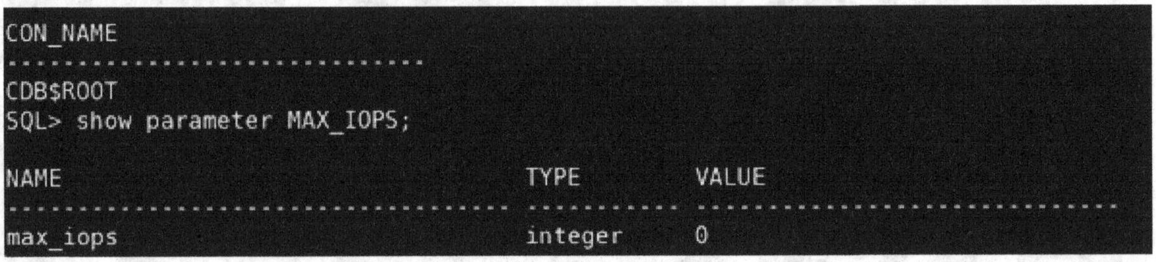

```
CON_NAME
------------------------------
CDB$ROOT
SQL> show parameter MAX_IOPS;

NAME                                    TYPE       VALUE
-----------------------------------     --------   ---------------------
max_iops                                integer    0
```

Use Case 6: Testing the Ability to Limit Default User Accounts

It is not uncommon to allow users to update a schema via a direct connection but it is common to prevent the use of shared credentials. An issue can occur though when users end up locking the default user account via failed login attempts that will cause all proxy connections to also fail.

The objective of this use case is to test the ability to limit default user accounts to schema-only levels and remove the ability to accidently lock schema-only accounts via proxy connection. Schema-only accounts will not be linked via shared credential access and locking one user account will not lock the schema-only account.

Figure 18. Test user created

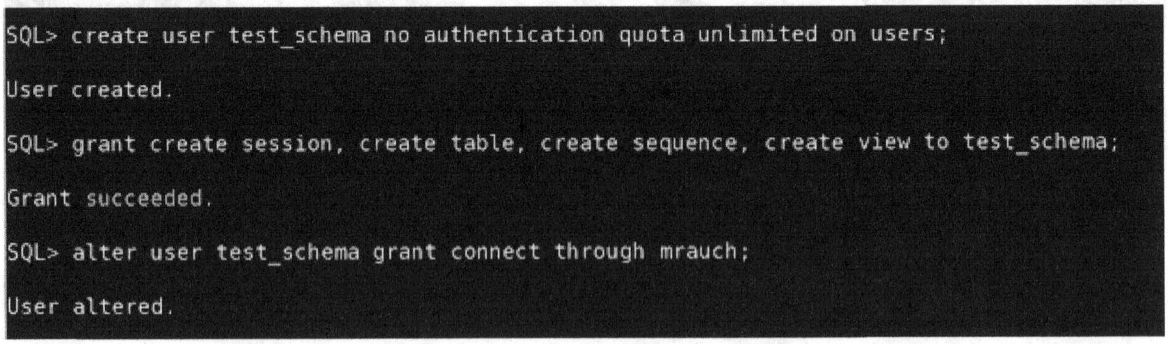

```
SQL> create user test_schema no authentication quota unlimited on users;

User created.

SQL> grant create session, create table, create sequence, create view to test_schema;

Grant succeeded.

SQL> alter user test_schema grant connect through mrauch;

User altered.
```

To test this process, a test user schema is created and connected via proxy to a user account, as shown in Figure 18.

Next, we verify that the test_schema user is set to no authentication, meaning that we should not be able to connect to it via direct proxy. We can connect to the mrauch test user, but when we attempt to connect via direct proxy to test_schema it fails, as shown in Figure 19. The test user account was not able to direct proxy via a null password.

Figure 19. Test user fails to proxy connect

```
SQL> select USERNAME, AUTHENTICATION_TYPE from dba_users where USERNAME='TEST_SCHEMA';

USERNAME                          AUTHENTI
--------------------------------  --------
TEST_SCHEMA                       NONE

SQL> conn mrauch/mrauch@oemtest2;
Connected.
SQL> conn TEST_SCHEMA@oemtest2;
Enter password:
ERROR:
ORA-01005: null password given; logon denied


Warning: You are no longer connected to ORACLE.
SQL>
```

This will prevent user accounts from being susceptible to lock out via proxy, as well as increase the security by denying logins with null passwords.

Use Case 7: Testing the Ability to Audit Changes based on User Privileges

Auditing in databases has always existed but it hasn't been readily available for users to understand. Improvements have been made to simplify it across the board. Changes can now be made based on different privilege levels to allow improved auditing.

Here the ability to audit changes based on user privileges, user actions, and user roles is tested. Oracle 19c allows us to produce an audit of user activities based on privileges, roles, and actions. Query the audsys.aud$unified system table to produce a readable version of user activities.

This is tested by creating three test users. Using the sysdba account, three different types of auditing are created. Each user is tested to a different auditing metric. First, we test privilege auditing against test user one, next we test action auditing against user two and lastly we test role auditing against test user three. As sys, we are able to produce a report for each of the respective audits created.

Privilege Auditing

Privilege auditing is a type of auditing designed around auditing access granted via the use of system privileges. The privilege auditing policy is created for the test user with regards to creating tables, as shown in Figure 20.

Figure 20. Privilege audit policy

```
SQL> CREATE AUDIT POLICY test_audit_policy
  PRIVILEGES CREATE TABLE, CREATE SEQUENCE
  WHEN    'SYS_CONTEXT(''USERENV'', ''SESSION_USER'') = ''TEST'''
  EVALUATE PER SESSION
  CONTAINER = CURRENT;  2    3    4    5

Audit policy created.

SQL> AUDIT POLICY test_audit_policy;

Audit succeeded.
```

Figure 21 shows the details of the policy in a more readable format.

Figure 21. Privilege audit readable

```
AUDIT_OPTION     CONDITION_ AUDIT_CONDITION
---------------- ---------- -----------------------------------------------------------
CREATE SEQUENCE SESSION    SYS_CONTEXT('USERENV', 'SESSION_USER') = 'TEST'
CREATE TABLE    SESSION    SYS_CONTEXT('USERENV', 'SESSION_USER') = 'TEST'
```

As shown in Figure 22, we can log in as the test user and create some objects.

Figure 22. Privilege audit actions

```
[oracle@idc-oem-srv03 u01]$ sqlplus test/test@oemtest3;

SQL*Plus: Release 19.0.0.0.0 - Production on Thu Jul 1 18:32:29 2021
Version 19.10.0.0.0

Copyright (c) 1982, 2020, Oracle.  All rights reserved.


Connected to:
Oracle Database 19c Enterprise Edition Release 19.0.0.0.0 - Production
Version 19.10.0.0.0

SQL> CREATE TABLE tab1 (id NUMBER);

Table created.

SQL> CREATE SEQUENCE tab1_seq;

Sequence created.
```

Returning to the sys user, we can query the audit_trail to see the activity of the test user proving the privilege level auditing works, as shown in Figure 23.

Figure 23. Privilege audit validation

```
EVENT_TIMESTAMP                 DBUSERNAME ACTION_NAME            OBJECT_SCH
- - - - - - - - - - - - - - -   - - - - -  - - - - - - - - - -   - - - - - -
OBJECT_NAME
- - - - - - - - - - - - - -
01-JUL-21 06.32.36.784600 PM    TEST       CREATE TABLE           TEST
TAB1

01-JUL-21 06.32.45.562878 PM    TEST       CREATE SEQUENCE        TEST
TAB1_SEQ
```

Before moving on, we will disable this audit and clean it up to avoid any conflicts with other tests.

Action Auditing

Action auditing is a type of auditing designed to audit actions against objects rather than privileges. The next level of auditing that will be tested is at the action level. Logging in again as the first test user, we will create some tables and sequences, as shown in Figure 24.

Figure 24. Action audit preparation

```
SQL> CREATE TABLE tab1 (
  id NUMBER,
  CONSTRAINT tab1_pk PRIMARY KEY (id)
); 2   3    4

Table created.

SQL> CREATE SEQUENCE tab1_seq;

Sequence created.

SQL> CREATE TABLE tab2 (
  id NUMBER,
  CONSTRAINT tab2_pk PRIMARY KEY (id)
); 2   3    4

Table created.

SQL> CREATE SEQUENCE tab2_seq;

Sequence created.
```

Now we will grant some privileges to the second test user account, as shown in Figure 25.

Figure 25. Action audit grants

```
SQL> GRANT SELECT, INSERT, UPDATE, DELETE ON tab1 TO test2;

Grant succeeded.

SQL> GRANT SELECT ON tab1_seq TO test2;

Grant succeeded.

SQL> GRANT SELECT, INSERT, UPDATE, DELETE ON tab2 TO test2;

Grant succeeded.

SQL> GRANT SELECT ON tab2_seq TO test2;

Grant succeeded.
```

From here, we will connect as sys to create an audit policy that monitors actions against the objects that will perform on the second test user shortly, as shown in Figure 26.

Figure 26. Action audit policy

```
SQL> CREATE AUDIT POLICY test_audit_policy
  ACTIONS DELETE ON test.tab1,
          INSERT ON test.tab1,
          UPDATE ON test.tab1,
          SELECT ON test.tab1_seq,
          ALL ON test.tab2,
          SELECT ON test.tab2_seq
  WHEN    'SYS_CONTEXT(''USERENV'', ''SESSION_USER'') = ''TEST2'''
  EVALUATE PER SESSION
  2    3    4    5    6    7    8    9    10    CONTAINER = CURRENT;

Audit policy created.

SQL> AUDIT POLICY test_audit_policy;

Audit succeeded.
```

Adding in the readable format below, as shown in Figure 27.

Figure 27. Action audit policy readable

```
OBJECT_SCHEMA   OBJECT_NAME   OBJECT_TYPE   AUDIT_OPTION   CONDITION_ AUDIT_CONDITION
---------------------------------------------------------------------------------------
TEST            TAB1          TABLE         DELETE         SESSION    SYS_CONTEXT( USERENV , SESSION_USER ) = TEST2
TEST            TAB1          TABLE         INSERT         SESSION    SYS_CONTEXT( USERENV , SESSION_USER ) = TEST2
TEST            TAB1          TABLE         UPDATE         SESSION    SYS_CONTEXT( USERENV , SESSION_USER ) = TEST2
TEST            TAB1_SEQ      SEQUENCE      SELECT         SESSION    SYS_CONTEXT( USERENV , SESSION_USER ) = TEST2
TEST            TAB2          TABLE         ALL            SESSION    SYS_CONTEXT( USERENV , SESSION_USER ) = TEST2
TEST            TAB2_SEQ      SEQUENCE      SELECT         SESSION    SYS_CONTEXT( USERENV , SESSION_USER ) = TEST2

6 rows selected.
```

All this leaves is testing the audit policy. First, log in as test user one to perform some actions that should not meet the policy condition, as shown in Figure 28.

Figure 28. Action audit policy test 1

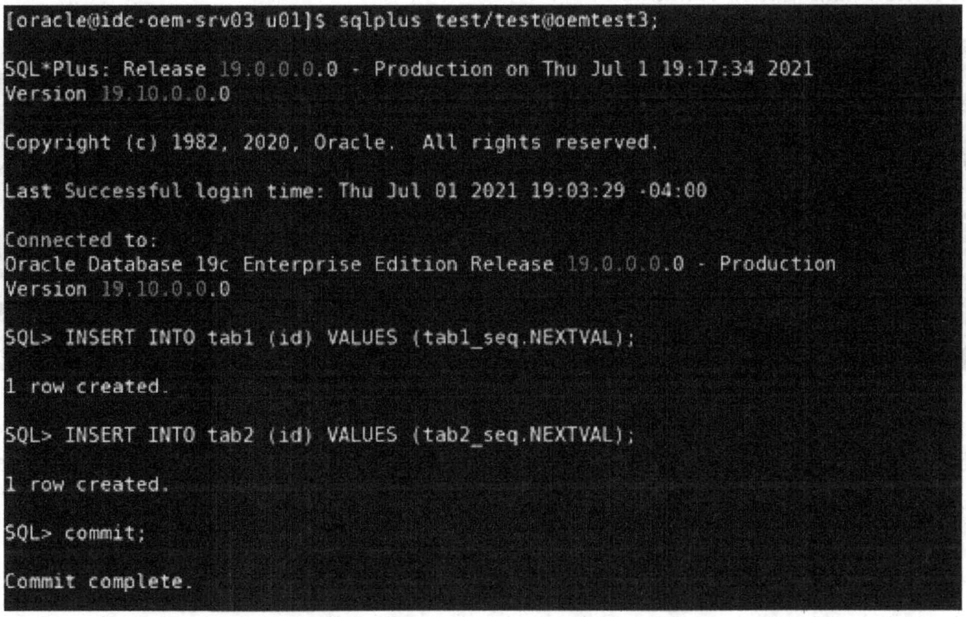

```
[oracle@idc-oem-srv03 u01]$ sqlplus test/test@oemtest3;

SQL*Plus: Release 19.0.0.0.0 - Production on Thu Jul 1 19:17:34 2021
Version 19.10.0.0.0

Copyright (c) 1982, 2020, Oracle.  All rights reserved.

Last Successful login time: Thu Jul 01 2021 19:03:29 -04:00

Connected to:
Oracle Database 19c Enterprise Edition Release 19.0.0.0.0 - Production
Version 19.10.0.0.0

SQL> INSERT INTO tab1 (id) VALUES (tab1_seq.NEXTVAL);

1 row created.

SQL> INSERT INTO tab2 (id) VALUES (tab2_seq.NEXTVAL);

1 row created.

SQL> commit;

Commit complete.
```

Second, log in as test user two and perform some actions that meet the policy condition, as shown in Figure 29.

Figure 29. Action audit policy test 2

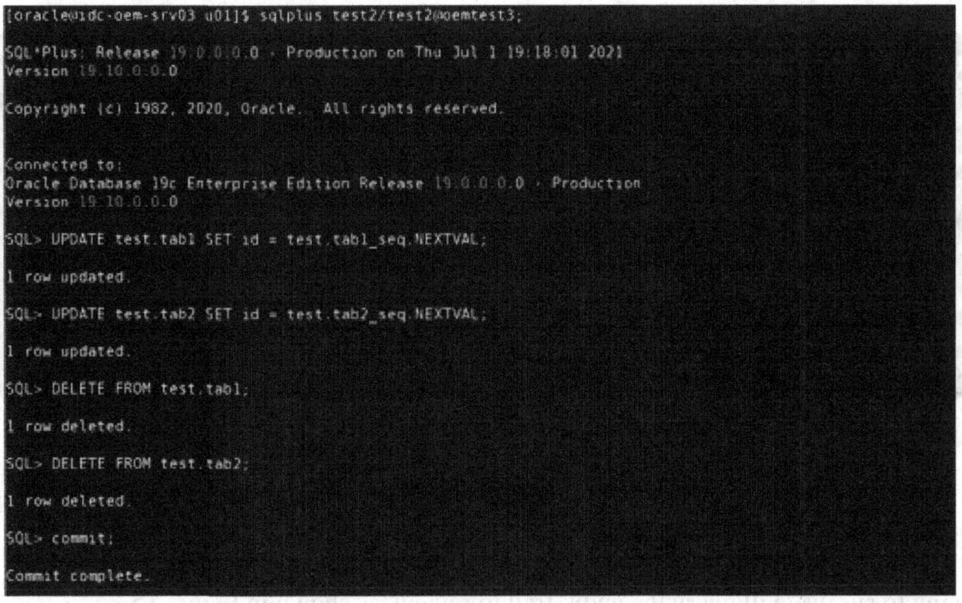

```
[oracle@idc-oem-srv03 u01]$ sqlplus test2/test2@oemtest3;

SQL*Plus: Release 19.0.0.0.0 - Production on Thu Jul 1 19:18:01 2021
Version 19.10.0.0.0

Copyright (c) 1982, 2020, Oracle.  All rights reserved.

Connected to:
Oracle Database 19c Enterprise Edition Release 19.0.0.0.0 - Production
Version 19.10.0.0.0

SQL> UPDATE test.tab1 SET id = test.tab1_seq.NEXTVAL;

1 row updated.

SQL> UPDATE test.tab2 SET id = test.tab2_seq.NEXTVAL;

1 row updated.

SQL> DELETE FROM test.tab1;

1 row deleted.

SQL> DELETE FROM test.tab2;

1 row deleted.

SQL> commit;

Commit complete.
```

Third, log in as sys and query the audit_trail to view the results, shown in Figure 6.25. The first two rows are showing the steps created during the privilege audit testing. Note that the two inserts we did above from the first test user did not show up in Figure 30.

Figure 30. Action audit policy validation

```
EVENT_TIMESTAMP                DBUSERNAME  ACTION_NAME      OBJECT_SCH  OBJECT_NAME
-----------------------------  ----------  ---------------  ----------  -------------------
01-JUL-21 06.32.36.784600 PM   TEST        CREATE TABLE     TEST        TAB1
01-JUL-21 06.32.45.562878 PM   TEST        CREATE SEQUENCE  TEST        TAB1_SEQ
01-JUL-21 07.18.07.957084 PM   TEST2       SELECT           TEST        TAB1_SEQ
01-JUL-21 07.18.07.964344 PM   TEST2       UPDATE           TEST        TAB1
01-JUL-21 07.18.11.287832 PM   TEST2       SELECT           TEST        TAB2_SEQ
01-JUL-21 07.18.11.288248 PM   TEST2       UPDATE           TEST        TAB2
01-JUL-21 07.18.15.500666 PM   TEST2       DELETE           TEST        TAB1
01-JUL-21 07.18.18.814645 PM   TEST2       DELETE           TEST        TAB2

8 rows selected.
```

Like before, we need to clean up this audit policy to ensure it does not conflict with the next set of testing.

Role Auditing

Role based auditing is a type of auditing designed to monitor all actions performed by users that are granted access to a specific role created in the database. The last type of auditing that will be tested is auditing at the role level. We will begin with creating a role and giving it to our third tester, as shown in Figure 31.

Figure 31. Role audit policy preparation

```
SQL> CREATE ROLE create_table_role;

Role created.

SQL> GRANT CREATE TABLE TO create_table_role;

Grant succeeded.

SQL> GRANT create_table_role TO test3;

Grant succeeded.
```

Next, we will create the policy to monitor actions based on role, as shown in Figure 32.
Once again, Figure 33 shows the more readable version.
Next, we can log in as test user three and create a table, as shown in Figure 34.
Returning to sys, we will query the audit_trail to review, as shown in Figure 35.

Figure 32. Role audit policy creation

```
SQL> CREATE AUDIT POLICY create_table_role_policy
  ROLES create_table_role
  WHEN    'SYS_CONTEXT(''USERENV'', ''SESSION_USER'') = ''TEST3'''
  EVALUATE PER SESSION
  CONTAINER = CURRENT;  2    3    4    5

Audit policy created.

SQL> AUDIT POLICY create_table_role_policy;

Audit succeeded.
```

Figure 33. Role audit policy readable

```
AUDIT_OPTION           AUDIT_OPTION_TYPE  CONDITION_  AUDIT_CONDITION
...................    .................  .........   ........................
CREATE_TABLE_ROLE      ROLE PRIVILEGE     SESSION     SYS_CONTEXT('USERENV', 'SESSION_USER') = 'TEST3'
```

Figure 34. Role audit policy test

```
[oracle@idc-oem-srv03 ~]$ sqlplus test3/test3@oemtest3;

SQL*Plus: Release 19.0.0.0.0 - Production on Thu Jul 1 20:09:21 2021
Version 19.10.0.0.0

Copyright (c) 1982, 2020, Oracle.  All rights reserved.


Connected to:
Oracle Database 19c Enterprise Edition Release 19.0.0.0.0 - Production
Version 19.10.0.0.0

SQL> CREATE TABLE tab1 (id NUMBER);

Table created.
```

Figure 35. Role audit policy validation

```
EVENT_TIMESTAMP               DBUSERNAME ACTION_NAME       OBJECT_SCH OBJECT_NAME
............................  .......... ...........       .......... ...........
01-JUL-21 08.09.33.672882 PM  TEST3      CREATE TABLE      TEST3      TAB1
```

One final cleanup of the audit policies will complete these tests. Hence auditing can be configured at different levels.

541

FUTURE RESEARCH DIRECTIONS

The future directions of this work will be along the lines of improving the multi-tenant architecture. Hilman et al. (2021) and Buyya et al. (2018) very comprehensively discuss the extensions of this type of work. These article discusses the scheduling and resource provisioning problems that will have to be addressed in the future.

CONCLUSION

As demonstrated by the use cases, multitenant architecture has drastically improved Oracle's ability to handle Big Data. The added functionality that comes with the integration of Big Data platforms alongside the reduced costs of licensing and storage that comes with 19c, and the multitenant architecture, not only allowed Oracle to stay relevant but has moved it to the forefront of its competitors. There is also the added automation that came with this architectural shift improving functionality and performance. Increases to auditing and security continue to make Oracle appeal to enterprises as technology moves forward. But the field of technology is ever changing and while Big Data continues to evolve so to shall Oracle and it's multitenant architecture.

REFERENCES

Administrator's Guide. (n.d.). https://docs.oracle.com/en/database/oracle/oracle-database/18/multi/introduction-to-the-multitenant-architecture.html#GUID-267F7D12-D33F-4AC9-AA45-E9CD671B6F22

Buyya, R., Rodriguez, M. A., Toosi, A. N., & Park, J. (2018). Cost-Efficient Orchestration of Containers in Clouds: A Vision, Architectural Elements, and Future Directions. *Journal of Physics: Conference Series*, *1108*(1), 012001. doi:10.1088/1742-6596/1108/1/012001

Changes in This Release For Oracle Database Security Guide. (n.d.). Oracle Help Center. https://docs.oracle.com/en/database/oracle/oracle-database/19/dbseg/release-changes.html#GUID-256DEEBF-8FBE-4641-BAE3-D23D53ADFB44

Containers on IBM Cloud. (n.d.). https://www.ibm.com/cloud/containers

Hilman, M. H., Rodrigues, M. A., & Buyya, R. (2021). Multiple Workflows Scheduling in Multi-tenant Distributed Systems: A Taxonomy and Future Directions. *ACM Computing Surveys*, *53*(10), 1–39. doi:10.1145/3368036

Hussein, M. K., Mousa, M. H., Alqarni, M. A. (2019). A Placement Architecture for a Container as a Service (CaaS) in a Cloud Environment. *Journal of Cloud Computing*, *8*.

IBM Cloud. (n.d.). https://www.ibm.com/cloud

Katal, A., Wazid, M., & Goudar, R. (2013). Big data: issues, challenges, tools and good practices. *2013 Sixth International Conference on Contemporary Computing (IC3)*, 404–409. 10.1109/IC3.2013.6612229

Oracle® Big Data Appliance Software User's Guide. (2020). Oracle. https://drive.google.com/file/d/17dkxpMsayafh83h0m_TN9f2q01EvamoX/view?usp=sharing

Oracle Database 19c (19.3). (n.d.). *Oracle database 19c download for Linux x86-64*. Oracle | Integrated Cloud Applications and Platform Services. https://www.oracle.com/database/technologies/oracle19c-linux-downloads.html

Oracle® Database. Database Concepts. (2021). [White Paper]. https://drive.google.com/file/d/1J-6DHVaZIuA_mQD_FWIjJci7utpkXlzh/view?usp=sharing

Oracle Multitenant with Oracle Database 19c. (2019). [White Paper]. https://drive.google.com/file/d/1joSwFplc8LivxBSPuec8GbG4dtcVQtwW/view?usp=sharing

Sanchez, C. (2014). *Everything at Google Runs in Containers*. https://www.infoq.com/news/2014/06/everything-google-containers/

Taylor, D. (2022). *What is Big Data? Introduction, Types, Characteristics, Examples*. https://www.guru99.com/what-is-big-data.html

Transforming Data Management with Oracle Database 12c Release 2. (2017). [White Paper]. https://www.oracle.com/technetwork/database/plug-into-cloud-wp-12c-1896100.pdf

ADDITIONAL READING

Betts, D., Homer, A., & Jez, A. (2013). *Developing Multi-tenant Applications for the Cloud on Windows Azure*. Microsoft Patterns and Practices.

Burns, B. (2018). Designing Distributed Systems. O'Reilly.

Camisso, J., Jetha, H., & Juell, K. (2020). *Kubernetes for Full-Stack Developers*. DigitalOcean.

Juell, K. (2020). *From Containers to Kubernetes with Node.js*. eBook.

Kleppmann, M. (2017). *Designing Data-Intensive Applications: The Big Ideas Behind....* O'Reilly.

Kumar, A. (2019). *Oracle 12c Multi-Tenant Architecture: How Oracle's New Architecture Simplifies Database Consolidation!* Independently published.

Kumar, A. (2021). *Oracle 19c DBA on AWS: Administer Multi-Tenant Database in the Cloud*. Independently published.

Oppenheimer, D. (2021). *Multi-Tenancy in Kubernetes: Best Practices Today, and Future Directions*. Cloud Native Foundation. https://devopsinvent.com/multi-tenancy-in-kubernetes-best-practices-today-and-future-directions-david-oppenheimer/

Pahl, C., Brogi, A., Soldani, J., & Jamshidi, P. (2018). *Cloud Container Technologies: A State-of-the-Art Review*. IEEE Transactions on Cloud Computing. doi:10.1109/TCC.2017.2702586

Varghese, B., & Buyya, R. (2018). Next Generation Cloud Computing: New Trends and Research Directions. *Future Generation Computer Systems*, *79*, 849–861. doi:10.1016/j.future.2017.09.020

KEY TERMS AND DEFINITIONS

Big Data: Data that contains greater variety, arriving in increasing volumes and with high velocity.

Container: Containers are a bundled unit of software with all their dependencies.

Container Architecture: Container architecture is a logical collection of data or metadata within a multitenant architecture.

Container Database: A container database can contain either zero, one, or many pluggable databases.

MapReduce: An engine that provides the platform for massive parallel execution of algorithms written in Java.

Multi-Tenant Architecture: Multi-tenant architecture allows multiple users to share a single instance of a software application and its underlying resources.

Pluggable Databases: These are a movable collection of schemas, schema objects and non-schema objects.

Trending Big Data Tools for Industrial Data Analytics

A. Bazila Banu
Bannari Amman Institute of Technology, India

V. S. Nivedita
Bannari Amman Institute of Technology, India

INTRODUCTION

The Big Data in its natural form is of no usage. Therefore, now let us realize Big Data Analytics. It encapsulates past data into a form that individuals can easily read. This helps in generating reports, such as a company's profits and sales comparison based on quarterly/monthly and annually. It Is further classified into descriptive, predictive, and diagnostic analytics (Chunquan Li et al.,2021). Big data analytics tools are used in various stages of data processing such as Hadoop to collect and evaluate data, MongoDB to handle data that gets updated frequently, Talend for data incorporation and administration, Cassandra to handle aggregates of data, Spark for real-time administering to handle large volume of data in a distributed environment, STORM for time computational approach and Kafka for streaming and handling fault-tolerant storage. It's essential for any organization to find the best way to deal with the varied data sources and still meet the aims of the analytical process (Chunquan Li et al.,2021). This takes a shrewdness approach that integrates hardware, software, and procedures into a wieldy process that delivers results within an adequate time frame Storage is another critical element for Big Data. The data have to be stored in some repositories which can be readily available and secured. This has proved to be an exclusive challenge for many administrations, since network-based storage, such as SANS and NAS are very expensive to purchase and succeed. Storage has evolved to become one of the more unimaginative elements in the typical data center. However, today's enterprises are met with budding needs that can put the strain on storage technologies. But investing in open-source technologies are required to expand the business on a large scale. A case in point is the push for Big Data analytics, a concept that brings BI abilities to large data sets (F. Xu et al., (2019). For the decision maker looking to power Big Data, Hadoop solves the most communal problems linked with Big Data: storing and accessing large amounts of data in an efficient fashion. Big data Analytics is a collection of process that are associated with the industry. Despite of handling various characteristics of Big Data such as volume, velocity, variety, variability, veracity, value, visualization, validity, vulnerability, volatility etc. the Big Data tools are used to generate business outcomes benefitting the organization in various productive means.

DOI: 10.4018/978-1-7998-9220-5.ch032

Copyright © 2023, IGI Global. Copying or distributing in print or electronic forms without written permission of IGI Global is prohibited.

BACKGROUND

Industrial Big Data

In the era of digital economic globalization, intelligent decision making has attracted a lot of attention from the digital industry market. One prime technology in artificial intelligence is big data driven analysis. This enhances the productivity and helps in making wise decisions by mining the hidden knowledge and the potential ability of the Big Data (M. Ghasemaghaei & G. Cali, 2019). Many real-time large-scale data are applied to the industrial process. Mostly the real-time data are streamed from noisy environment Also among the acquired data certain data will be labelled and few may not. Such kind of substantial amount of data with various challenges within are processed and expected to produce an optimized intelligent output without compromising the time and space dimensions. Hence the Big Data processing requires extensible methods to distribute and store real-time data, to suggest and dynamically adapt with the changes made in the process to provide automatic decisions (Ritu Ratra & Preeti Gulia, 2019). Thus, the End-to End Big Data process is expected to integrate, adapt and generalize the data in all stages within to create intelligent decisions with respect to the process.

Therefore, non-traditional techniques and strategies are required to store, organize and process the big data sets. There are several big data tools available, the following are the important big data analytics tools are highly recommended and applied in industry servicing various needs such as data collection, data cleaning, data filtering and extraction, data validation, and data storage.

Hadoop -- To collect and evaluate data.

MongoDB -- To handle data that gets updated frequently.

Talend -- To provide data incorporation and administration.

Cassandra -- To handle aggregates of data.

Spark -- To provide real-time administration while handling large volume of data in the distributed environment.

STORM -- To process high velocity data in distributed real-time computational environment.

The following context discusses the aforementioned tools in detail with working strategies, application possibilities, its merits and exceptions in order to point out how effective the tools are applied in Big Data Analytics.

APACHE HADOOP

Hadoop is an open-source framework developed by Apache Foundation. Apache Hadoop is adopted by various organizations for storing and processing humongous datasets. Hadoop outsmarted supercomputers and turned out to be the fastest system in sorting a terabyte of data in 2008.The journey of Hadoop started from the year 2002 with Apache Nutch Project (see Apache.org,2021). The Nutch's developers got inspired by Google's Google DFS & MapReduce and started implementing the open source framework, the Nutch Distributed File System (NDFS) and map reduce in the middle of 2004. Soon after Doug Cutting and Mike Cafarella developed an independent licensed sub project Hadoop. Hadoop initially contributed only 20 to 40 clusters later in 2006, Yahoo scaled the Hadoop project to more clusters. In 2007, Yahoo started using Hadoop on 1000 node clusters. Later Hadoop confirmed its success and became the most popular. Various releases on Hadoop evolved later. Hadoop 3.1.3 is the latest version of

Hadoop. Apache Hadoop is the most successful and highly demanding next generation platform for big data processing because of its ultimate data processing capabilities

What Hadoop Promises?

Hadoop promises the following features as shown in figure: 01.

Figure 1. Hadoop

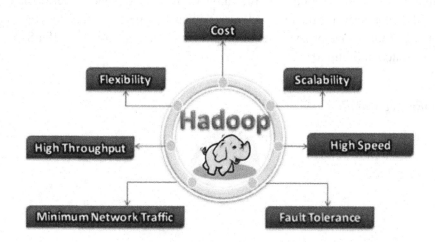

Working of Hadoop

The main components of Hadoop are:

HDFS
Map Reduce
Yarn

HDFS

HDFS is a huge file system designed for storing large files with streaming batch access to data in the file system. HDFS ensures highly fault tolerant and high throughput processing systems. HDFS stores data blocks of size not less than 124 MB and are replicated in different racks with respect to the replication factor set by the developer. HDFS functionalities are based on the Master – Slave paradigm, where the actual data are stored in one or more Data Nodes (Slave Node) and the metadata details are maintained and managed by Namenode(Master Node), Secondary Namenode and Checkpoint node (see Apache. org,2021). The master node and slave nodes are managed by resource manager and Application master.

How is it Different From Traditional DFS?

In Distributed File System the data is moved to the processing part or module where in Hadoop Distributed File System, a simple processing code is sent to the data where it is resided in. Hence network bandwidth payload caused while sending bulk data to the processing module is reduced every time.

Map Reduce

MapReduce is the processing component of Hadoop that enables high scalability across multiple servers in the cluster. A single Hadoop program is performed in two tasks," Map' and "Reduce"(see Apache. org,2021). A Map job takes a set of data and transforms them, where individual data is broken into a key/value pair (tuple) format. A reduce job takes the output of the map job that is intermediately stored in the local system and then it performs the required operation such as partitioning, shuffling, and combining on the data tuples. It forms one or small set of output which is then stored in HDFS. The MapReduce workflow is illustrated in Figure:02

Figure 2. MapReduce Workflow

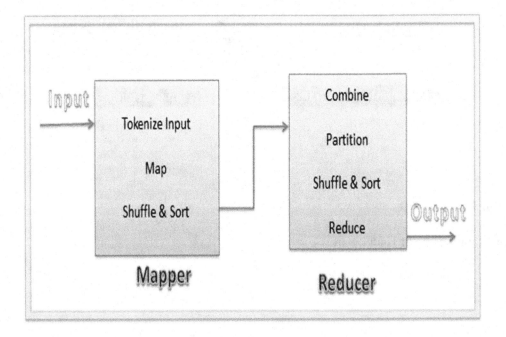

Yet Another Resource Negotiator [YARN]

Apache Hadoop technology YARN stands for Yet Another Resource Negotiator, which is a large-scale distributed operating system for big data applications. Hadoop 2.X versions use YARN for resource management and scheduling capabilities. The main idea of YARN is to run the resource management and job scheduling functionalities in two different software daemons. YARN helps Hadoop in extending its support to various kinds of processing such as interactive processing, graph processing, stream processing etc. to run and process data stored in HDFS (Tom White, 2009).

Hadoop is recommended by business level purposes for the following reasons:

Maintains and manages enormous amounts of data in a file System called HDFS with high levels of availability.

Data Cleaning, processing and wrangling tasks are more efficient in Hadoop.

Extensive Parallel programming helps in processing multiple diverse terabytes of data at high speed.

Replication ensures effective data recovery and fault tolerance towards node failures.

An excellent framework for building distributed, fault tolerant data processing systems which leverage HDFS which is optimized for low latency storage and high throughput performance.

MONGODB

RDBMS is the most preferable storage system over many decades. But the web applications that are built for today's digital trend are expected to model complex data with greater flexibility. These data models may evolve with respect to the development and changes in the applications and hence a flexible model with highly scalability is anticipated for storing and processing such data. NoSQL ("not only SQL") databases were developed to handle the complex data of this internet era by providing a flexible data model / schema that ensures high availability of data at any scale without compromising the speed and performance of the model.

There are four primary types of NoSQL databases: Document database; Key-value stores; Wide Column Stores and Graph Databases (see Apache.org,2021). Among which, document database is the most popular and widely used database model because they support complex data structures and hierarchical relationships within a single document. MongoDB is one of the most efficient open-source document - oriented NoSQL database option for web applications. MongoDB was created by Dwight Merriman and Eliot Horowitz, later Merriman and Horowitz helped form MongoDB Inc. in 2013 and advertised among public in October 2017 under ticker symbol MDB.

MongoDB is an Open Source Nonrelational database management tool that supports various forms of data especially those that doesn't fit well in fixed-schema databases. MongoDB 4.4 is the latest version released in 2020.Document databases generally stores and manipulates its raw data in JSON/BSON format or in any of its equivalent format. MongoDB database stores data dynamically in JSON – like documents. The fundamental unit of processing data in MongoDB is Documents. Set of documents are grouped under Collections. A collection functions similar to relational tables but a data in a collection are not distributed among other different databases. In order to distribute data across multiple systems when data and throughput requirement increase, MongoDB uses the following core features - Horizontal scalability and Automatic Sharding feature. MongoDB can provision any number of storage engines and also provide pluggable storage engine API's for the Third parties to customize their own MongoDB storage Engines (Banker, K et al., 2016). It provides an intelligent platform to locate where to put data.

Working Mechanism

MongoDB processes the documents as records. A record is a data structure that is made up of field and value pairs. The documents that are used for processing is BSON(Binary JSON) which is very similar to JSON (JavaScript Object Notation).The binary representation of JSON-like documents is provided by BSON document storage and data interchange format. Every document has a field-value pair. The field-value pairs in these documents are very similar to column and value in relational databases. Fields resemble the columns and the values can be any type of data including other documents or an array of documents etc. Documents also have a unique identifier called primary key. The document-oriented database structure of MongoDB is shown below in figure:03

Figure 3. Document-Oriented Structure

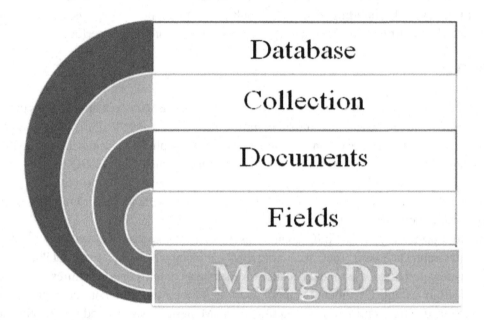

NoSQL databases are the best choice for MongoDB since it is working with large distributed data sets. Because they use a single master architecture that maintains the replicas of all primary databases and hence the operations are automatically replicated to secondary databases during unexpected failovers.

MongoDB management system has a built-in aggregate capability that allows the users to run MapReduce code directly on databases instead of running on Hadoop. MongoDB also has its own file system called GridFS like Hadoop Distributed File System (HDFS). MongoDB can be used in organizations for its ad-hoc queries, indexing, load balancing, aggregation, server-side JavaScript execution and other features (Mithun Satheesh et al., 2015).

MongoDB Application Platforms

MongoDB tool is released in two versions: Community version and commercial version in MongoDB Inc. Community version is open source whereas the Enterprise edition is extended with features like added security, in-memory storage engine, authentication, administration and monitoring capabilities through Ops Manager. Eight application tools are there in MongoDB to perform NoSQL operations in the database with high productivity and performance efficiency.

They are as follows:

MongoDB Compass, MongoDB Connector, MongoDB Charts, MongoDB Studio 3T, NoSQL Booster, Mongo Management Studio, MongoJS Query Analyzer and Nucleon Database Master

MongoDB Compass

MongoDB Compass is the graphical User Interface (GUI) to work with document structure, query data, access index data and more.

MongoDB Connector

MongoDB Connector is exclusively for Business Intelligence users to connect NoSQL databases to their BI tools for visualizing data and generating reports using queries.

MongoDB Charts

MongoDB charts are used to create a variety of visual trends and patterns by exploring MongoDB dataset.

MongoDB Studio 3T

Studio 3T is an open-source tool used for building queries, importing / exporting data, automatic code generation etc. This tool is compatible with all legal releases of MongoDB.

NoSQL Booster

NoSQL Booster is a unique, popular cross-platform GUI tool for MongoDB, this tool provides a significant facility of translating queries directly to languages like C#, Python, JAVA and JavaScript (Node. js). It has Visual Query Builder with which anyone even with no prior knowledge on MongoDB query syntaxes can create statements.

Mongo Management Studio

Mongo Management Studio is an interface that ensures fast manipulation of data and effective execution of MongoDB queries as well. With this tool, development and test processes are made easy.

MongoJS Query Analyzer

MongoJS Query Analyzer provides a rich interactive environment that allows you to execute JavaScript commands and view the results in a tree hierarchy as grid and text results. This tool also provides easy to use features like auto completion and syntax highlighting.

Nucleon Database Master

Nucleon Database Master is a powerful administration and management tool with modern user interface. This tool simplifies all tasks from querying to designing relational and non-relational DBMS. It can import/export any file formats without any limit over size. This tool also provides other features like code parser to check the code, Data package to wrap table data and Database master to manage MongoDB.

Mongodb Atlas

MongoDB Atlas is a Cloud DAAS (Database as a service) launched in 2016 by MongoDB Inc. This service runs on AWA, Microsoft Azure and Google cloud platform. MongoDB has released Stitch, a platform to develop applications on MongoDB Atlas with a plan to extend its work on On-Premise databases.

MONGODB PROS AND CONS

Pros

Highly flexible and scalable.
Ensures high data availability
Renders tremendous performance with Ad-Hoc Querying

Cons

Do not support Joins, Transactions or Indexing.
If the relations are not clearly defined it may lead to duplications of data.
Large In memory consumption.

TALEND

A well governed data is always highly preferred as they reduce risk in your business, especially when making decisions. Talend is an open-source unified platform that renders a wide range of ETL tools for big data integration and management. These tools deliver the features like data quality assessment, data integrity, master data management, enterprise application and API integration, virtual cloud warehouse, and effective processing of data on a big data environment. Talend also extends an excellent support in preparing the data in such a way that they are of good quality and well-governed as well.

Talend Open Studio (TOS) is an effective backend tool that helps Apache Hadoop Big Data users to access, transform, and synchronize the big data (see Talend Open Studio: User Guide, 2011) . TOS can be deployed easily as a stand-alone job or as a service that runs on the Hadoop data clusters. Talend is a download free product which also contains other commercial versions on request, like Talend Administrator Centre (TAC), a GUI based tool that supports scheduling and monitoring and executing Talend jobs. Talend has more than 900 pre-build connectors to cloud-based systems like Amazon S3 and enterprise resources like SQL server, CSV and Excel files. Talend can also be connected to business intelligence tools like Tableau etc.

Talend Open Studio is an excellent IDE for Talend products which reduces development time and offers an easiest way to develop Web services, and connect these services to consume data from diverse sources, like Oracle/SQL databases, ERP, CMS, CRM, etc as shown in figure 04. Majority of the customers implement Talend for data migration and integration because of its pre-build widgets on integration. Talend Open Studio v.7.0.1 is the latest version. With its easy-to-use UI service, Talend is best of its kind. Building data pipelines across various platforms is easier hence this tool is highly opted for data warehousing.

Figure 4. Talend Framework

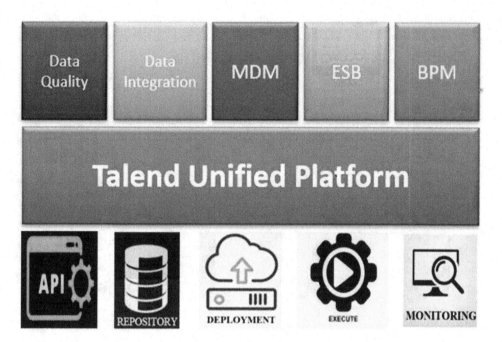

Data Integration

Talend data integration software tool allows easy integration of data between different sources and data warehouses using its thousands of connectors. This tool can easily connect, combine, convert and update data from various sources. It also comes with additional support in providing multi schema log file reports for post data flow. Talend data integration products have several releases and version 7.3 is the latest version with new features and components added for version management and query support.

Architecture

Talend Open Studio Architecture shown in figure 05, contains the following modules:

Clients

Client block may have a web browser and one or more talent studios that performs data integration processes

Talend Server

Talend block contains a web-based application server that maintains and administers all projects.

Database

Database block maintains all databases that are required for administering, auditing, and monitoring. Theyalso manage all access and authorization rights with respect to a project.

Figure 5. Talend Architecture

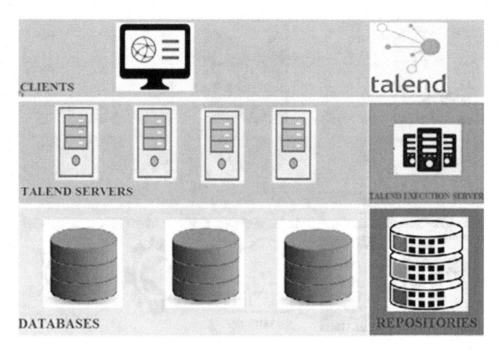

Workspace

Workspace is a directory of all project folders. Every connection to the repository is expected to have at least one directory.

Repository

Repository is a storage space used by all TOS tools to collect data, explain models etc.

Talend Open Studio Extensions

The extensions of TOS are as follows:

Talend Integration suite
Talend on demand
Talend Data quality
Talend ESB
Talend Big Data Integration

TALEND PROS AND CONS

Pros

Highly compatible with data sources

One step for all data integration needs
Simple UI
Ability to build end to end process

Cons

Adding custom component is difficult
Processing and transforming millions of records may be slow.
Lack of proper documentation.

Why is Talend Recommended?

Talend is highly recommended for the following reasons:

Automatic big data integration with graphical interface.
Supports both simple and complex data transformations.
Talend renders various options to create data models, manage metadata, set up permissions and rules
and also it gives excellent support to testing and debugging.
Data governance is achieved with its inexpensive integration with data quality tools and master data
management tools.
Excellent data source connections to Traditional data sources and Big Data and No SQL sources.

APACHE CASSANDRA

Apache Cassandra is a NOSQL distributed database that provides a highly scalable, high – performance access towards a large amount of structured data across many commodity servers with no single point failure. Cassandra was developed at Facebook and open sourced by them in July 2008. Later it as incubated into Apache in March 2009 and made as its top-level project since February 2010.

Cassandra databases are highly scalable because they are distributed (Jeff Carpenter & Eben Hewitt, 2020). Distributed means they can operate on more than one machine while they are viewed in unified manner. The key attribute of Cassandra is the ability of dynamically scaling the databases with no down time using off-the-shelf hardware to any linear extent.

Working

Cassandra follows masterless architecture. Cassandra can have multiple nodes. A single node corresponds to a single Cassandra instance. These nodes are organized as a cluster or in a "ring" fashion and are interacted via peer-to-peer communication using gossip protocol. Each node possesses a set of tokens, based on which the data is distributed among the clusters as shown below in the figure: 06.

Before distributing the data, it is important to determine data locality and mention the partition key to distribute data among nodes. Therefore, whenever data is inserted into the cluster, we have to apply the hash function to the partition key. In between the nodes gossip with one another and communicate which node is responsible for which ranges. The node coordinating the communication is called the coordinator node. The output will be the token that is determined based on the ranges. When it finds

Figure 6. Cassandra Architecture and data distribution

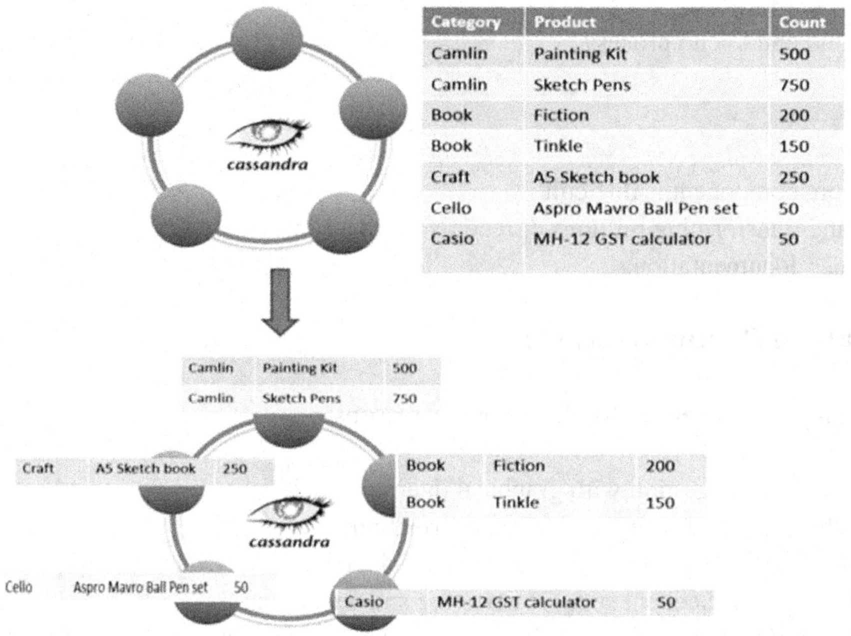

the right node, the data is forwarded to that node. The node that owns the data for that range is called a replica node. Every single data can have more than one replica which is determined by the replication factor. This ensures high reliability and fault tolerance.

Cassandra automatically replicates the data across different data centers. This provides a greater impact on positive performance in such a way that no users suffer from latency due to distance.

Cassandra is by default an AP (Available- Partition Tolerant) database which is depicted in figure: 07. Cassandra's consistency level can be configured on query-basis and is selected based on replication factor.

CASSANDRA PROS AND CONS

Pros

Schema-less Architecture
Eventual and Immediate consistency
Cost effective and low maintenance database platform
Availability and high scalability.

Cons

Better UI is expected
Poor aggregation functions
No JOINS in Cassandra

Figure 7. Consistency model

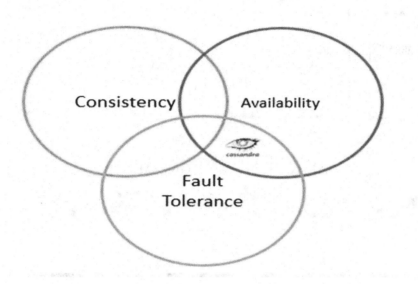

Why is Cassandra Highly Recommended?

Cassandra is highly recommended for the following reasons:

Cassandra provides excellent data availability and partition – tolerant architecture. Also it has no single point failure.

Cassandra is highly suited for applications that require quick read and write abilities.

Cassandra is linearly scalable and hence it maintains a quick response time.

APACHE SPARK

Apache Spark is a unified data analytics processing framework that can quickly perform processing tasks on very large data sets, and also can distribute data processing tasks across multiple computers (see Apache.org,2021). It is designed to deliver computational speed, scalability and programmability required for Big Data, specifically for streaming data, graph data, machine learning and artificial intelligence (AI) applications.

Apache Spark is the only processing framework that combines data and Artificial intelligence (Bill Chambers & Matei Zaharia, 2008) . The Spark ecosystem shown in figure 08, consists of the following modules,

Spark Core
Spark SQL
Spark Streaming and Structures Streaming
MLlib (machine Learning Library)
GraphX
Spark R

Figure 8. Spark Ecosystem

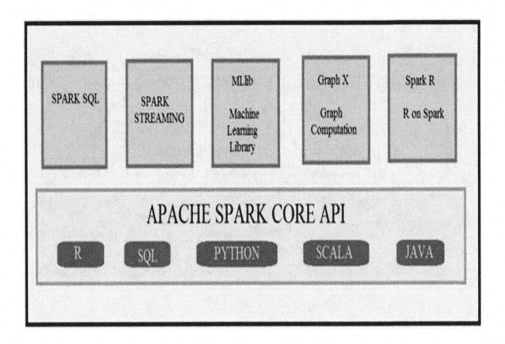

Apache Spark Core

Kernel of the Apache Spark and is responsible for all fundamental functionalities.

Apache Spark SQL

Performs structured as well as semi-structured data analysis.

Apache Spark Streaming

One of the light weight components of Spark ecosystem that performs streaming analytics by ingesting data in mini batches. Apache Streaming work in three phases as shown in figure 09.

Figure 9. Phases of Apache Streaming

Apache MLib

A scalable machine learning library which provides high quality algorithms such as clustering, classification, decomposition, regression and collaborative filtering at high speed.

Apache Spark Graph X

A graph computation engine that enables uses to build, transform, and reason about data at high speed.

Apache Spark R

R language is incorporated into Spark for performing productive statistical analysis.

Spark Analytics engine processes 100X times faster than Hadoop MapReduce. Spark extends the linear scalability and fault tolerance mechanism of MapReduce but in three ways

Spark Analytical Engine can execute more general Directed Acyclic graph (DAG) of operators, so that it can pass the result directly instead of sticking on map then reducing format.
Spark provides a rich set of transformations.
Spark supports in-memory processing across a cluster of machines without relying on storing or recording intermediate data in MapReduce

Spark extends tremendous integration with a variety of tools in the Hadoop Ecosystem. Reading and writing data in all data formats including NoSQL data is also supported.

SPARK PROS AND CONS

Pros

Faster processing
Speed
Ease of use
In-memory data sharing

Cons

No File management system
Memory consumption is high
Higher latency and lower throughput
Intermediate results may be reused

Why is Apache Spark Highly Recommended?

Apache Spark is highly recommended for the following reasons

Spark is well suited for ETL, data integration and other data processing problems for large data sets. Spark has rich APIs for data transformations, ML workloads, or graph workloads.

Spark is really good for machine learning large data sets especially that are processed in split file parallelization.

Spark is also applicable for doing real-time analytics on streaming data.

APACHE STORM

Apache Storm is a free – open-source distributed processing framework for streaming data at extraordinary speed (Jonathan Leibiusky et al.,2012). Apache storm processes over millions of jobs on a node at a fraction of second. This Big data tool is integrated with Hadoop to achieve greater throughputs. Storm is preferred over Spark for the reasons given below in table 1 .

Table 1. Functionality Comparison of Storm and Spark

Functionality	SPARK	STORM
Stream Processing	Batch Processing	Micro-Batch Processing
Latency	Latency of few seconds	Latency of milliseconds
Programming Language	JAVA, SCALA	JAVA, SCALA, Clojure
Reliability	Supports "Exactly once" processing mode	Supports "Exactly once" processing mode but also supports "at least once" and "at most ones" processing modes.

Apache Storm Working

Apache Storm processes real-time data batches very similarly like Hadoop. The components of storm architecture are as shown in figure 10.

Like Hadoop cluster, a storm cluster also uses master slave architecture with Zookeeper coordinating the master and slave components. The storm cluster consists of the following

Nimbus (Master Node)
Supervisor Nodes (Worker Nodes)
Zookeeper cluster (Coordinator Nodes)

Nimbus

Master node responsible for distributing application nodes through multiple worker nodes.

Supervisor Node

Worker node that runs a supervisor daemon that is responsible for starting and stopping the worker process.

Figure 10. Working of Apache Storm

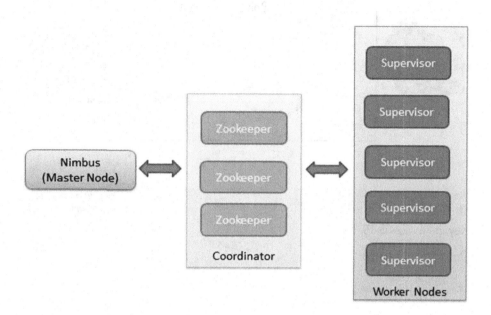

Zookeeper Cluster

Application that organizes different processes as a distributed application. Master node and Worker node communicates through the zookeeper.

Apache Storm Topology

A series of stream transformations in Storm is referred to as a Storm Topology, in which each node represents a bolt or spout. A spout is the source of tuples and bolt is the processing logic unit in Storm. Spout is responsible for listening and reading data from external sources and the bolt is responsible for doing simple transformations of tuples (Sean T. Allen et al., 2015). A tuple is the basic unit of data that is processed by a Storm application. Every tuple contains a predefined list of fields. The value of each field can be a byte, char, integer, float, double, Boolean or byte array. Spout, Bolt and Tuple are the three major components of Apache Storm. The Apache Storm topology is shown below in figure:11

APACHE STORM PROS AND CONS

Pros

Fast and reliable processing system
Horizontally scalable

Figure 11. Apache Storm Topology

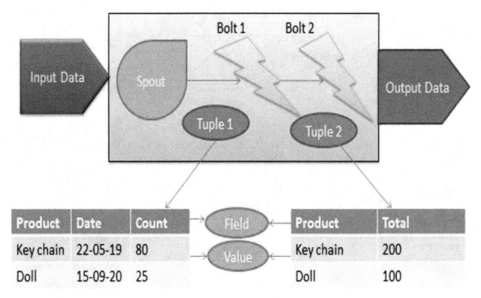

Cons

Initial setup and installation is time consuming
Limited documentation
Lacks in persistency

Why is Apache Storm Highly Recommended?

Apache Storm is highly recommended for the following reasons:

Effective Stream processing across several real time databases
Continuous computations on data streams enables the clients get delivered with the results over a short
period of time
Parallel complex query processing
Highly applied in the scenarios that required making fast decisions.

SOLUTIONS AND RECOMMENDATIONS

The digital era is rapidly transforming as the emergence of Data Analytics and its solution has revolution-
ized the way the Big Data is processed. The impact of this revolution is expected to handle all challenges
and recommends to initiate customer-centric outcomes for the enterprise. A policy for entire enterprise
needs to get cultivated. Always it is wise to initiate with data that is already accessible in the enterprise
rather than new data. Before building the enterprise policy, identify the commercial significances first
and build the policy accordingly. Business case provides decision makers with a management tool hence
every Business case should be developed based on quantifiable outcomes.

FUTURE RESEARCH DIRECTIONS

Association across varied domains and sectors is a challenging task—mostly when distinct sides lack a clear image of their commonly beneficial comforts and the necessary knowledge and skills to realize that dream. Researchers and the industry would benefit from targeted technology development and its efficient transfer to commercial products through Big Data tools. Businesses and governments would benefit from administration that stimulates technology markets while appropriately protecting data and users' confidentiality. Policy makers would benefit from arranging reforms enabling greater adoption of technology. Companies will be benefitted by identifying suitable big data tools for data management, analytics, security and access, like the tools discussed in this chapter.

CONCLUSION

Establishments can use big data tools and software's to make data-driven conclusions that can improve company-related outcomes. The welfare may include more effective advertising, new revenue openings, customer personalization and improved operational proficiency. With an effective policy, these benefits can provide reasonable benefits over opponents. Hence adopting tools like Hadoop, MongoDB, STORM, Cassandra, Spark, and Talend will make the organization to attain data incorporation and administration easily. The data can be distributed and operated with high velocity using real time computational environment through the sufficient usage of Big Data tools.

REFERENCES

Allen, S. T., Jankowski, M., & Peter, P. (2015). *Storm Applied: Strategies for real -time event processing*. Manning Publications.

Carpenter, J., & Hewitt, E. (2020). *Cassandra: The definitive guide - Distributed data at web scale*. O'Reilly Media, Inc.

Ghasemaghaei, M., & Calic, G. (2019), Can big data improve firm decision quality? the role of data quality and data diagnosticity. *Decis. Support. Syst., 120*. DOI: 10.1016/j.dss.2019.03.008

Leibiusky, J., Eisbruch, G., & Simonassi, D. (2012). *Getting Started with STORM*. O'Reilly Media, Inc.

Li, Chen, & Shang. (2021). A review of industrial big data for decision making in intelligent manufacturing. *Engineering Science and Technology, an International Journal, 29*. DOI: doi:10.1016/S2215098621001336

Ratra, R., & Gulia, P. (2019). Big Data Tools and Techniques: A Roadmap for Predictive Analytics. *International Journal of Engineering and Advanced Technology, 9*. Advance online publication. doi:10.35940/ijeat.B2360.129219

Satheesh, M., D'mello, B. J., & Krol, J. (2015). *Web Development with Mongo DB and NodeJS*. Packt Publishing Ltd.

Talend. (2011). *Talend Open Studio: User Guide*. Createspace.

The Apache Foundation. (2021). *Open-Source NoSQL Database*. Apache Cassandra. https://cassandra. apache.org/_/index.html

The Apache Software Foundation. (2021a). *HDFS Architecture*. Apache Hadoop. https://hadoop.apache. org/

The Apache Software Foundation. (2021b). *MapReduce Tutorial*. Apache Hadoop. https://hadoop. apache.org/

White, T. (2009). *Hadoop The Definitive Guide*. O'Reilly Media, Inc.

Xu, F., Li, Y., & Feng, L. (2019). The influence of big data system for used product management on manufacturing-remanufacturing operations. *Journal of Cleaner Production*, *209*. Advance online publication. doi:10.1016/j.jclepro.2018.10.240

ADDITIONAL READING

Banker, K., Hawkins, T., Verch, S., Garrett, D., & Bakkum, P. (2016). *MongoDB in Action: Covers MongoDB Version 3.0*. Manning Publications.

Barton, R. (2013). *Talend Open Studio Cookbook*. Packt Publishing Ltd.

Chambers, B., & Zaharia, M. (2008). *Spark The Definitive Guide*. O'Reilly Media, Inc.

Kane, F. (2017). *Frank Kane's Taming Big Data with Apache Spark and Python*. Packt Publishing Ltd.

Kong, L., Liu, Z., & Wu, J. (2020). A systematic review of big data-based urban sustainability research: State-of-the-science and future directions. *Journal of Cleaner Production*, *273*. Advance online publication. doi:10.1016/j.jclepro.2020.123142

Vidhya, A. (2020). *Introduction to Hadoop Ecosystem for Big Data and Data Engineering*. https://www. analyticsvidhya.com/blog/2020/10/introduction-hadoop-ecosystem/

KEY TERMS AND DEFINITIONS

Batch Processing: Batch data processing is a method of processing large amounts of data at once.

Data Integration: Data integration involves combining data residing in different sources and providing users with a unified view of them.

Database: A database is an organized collection of structured information, or data, typically stored electronically in a computer system.

Dataset: A collection of related sets of information that is composed of separate elements but can be manipulated as a unit by a computer.

Distributed File System (DFS): A Distributed File System (DFS) as the name suggests, is a file system that is distributed on multiple file servers or multiple locations. It allows programs to access or store isolated files as they do with the local ones, allowing programmers to access files from any network or computer. The main purpose of the Distributed File System (DFS) is to allows users of physically distributed systems to share their data and resources by using a Common File System.

Latency: Latency is defined as the delay before a transfer of data begins following an instruction for its transfer.

Non-Relational Databases: A non-relational database stores data in a non-tabular form, and tends to be more flexible than the traditional, SQL-based, relational database structures.

Open-Source: Denoting software for which the original source code is made freely available and may be redistributed and modified.

Stream Processing: Stream processing is a big data technology that focuses on the real-time processing of continuous streams of data in motion.

Web Services: A web service is any piece of software that makes itself available over the internet and uses a standardized XML messaging system.

Section 7
Business Intelligence

Artificial Intelligence, Consumers, and the Experience Economy

Hannah H. Chang
Singapore Management University, Singapore

Anirban Mukherjee
Cornell University, USA

INTRODUCTION

The term Artificial Intelligence (AI) was first used by McCarthy, Minsky, Rochester, and Shannon in a proposal for a summer research project in 1955 (Solomonoff, 1985). It is widely and commonly defined to be "the science and engineering of making intelligent machines" (McCarthy, 2006). Recent technological advances and methodological developments have made AI pervasive in new marketing offerings, ranging from self-driving cars, intelligent voice assistants such as Amazon's Alexa, to burger-making robots at restaurants and rack-moving robots inside warehouses such as Amazon's family of robots (Kiva, Pegasus, Xanthus) and delivery drones. There is optimism, and perhaps even over-optimism, of the potential heralded by AI as a source of greater customizability and personalization and reduced operational costs.

For many businesses planning to develop and deploy AI (and more generally, machine learning algorithms underlying this technology), a promising context is marketing decisions (Davenport, Guha, Grewal, & Bressgott, 2020) in experiential products and services (McKinsey Quarterly, 2021). Experiential products and services are those that are characterized by the sensory experiences they provide to users and consumers (Holbrook & Hirschman, 1982). Common examples include entertainment (e.g., real-life concert performances, movies and shows on Netflix and Disney+), hospitality (e.g., fine-dining restaurants, hotel resorts), and tourism (e.g., amusement parks, travel packages).

Understanding what customers want in experiential products and services is a fundamental challenge for businesses catering to the "experience economy" (Pine & Gilmore, 2011). Given that the primary value of an experiential product lies in the sensory experience that it provided to consumers, experiential products tend to have complex, nuanced, and rich features (Mukherjee & Kadiyali, 2018). There are almost limitless possibilities as businesses aim to develop new experiential products that appeals to the market. For example, Netflix has been reported to hire human coders to develop a proprietary classification system of over 76,000 micro-genres to describe its movies and television shows (Madrigal, 2014), which power both the development of its new entertainment offerings and its recommendation engine that promotes its existing offerings. Examples of such tags include "spy action and adventure movies from the 1930s," "critically-acclaimed emotional underdog movies," and 'British set in Europe Sci-Fi & Fantasy from the 1960s" (Madrigal, 2014). While this process was required for product management and customer experience management, it is likely very expensive and time-consuming to setup and to maintain (to keep up with the fast-changing consumer preferences and wide range of product options in the entertainment industry). Fortunately, recent developments in the AI and machine learning literature present several exciting new possibilities to help businesses better and more effectively cater to the

DOI: 10.4018/978-1-7998-9220-5.ch033

Copyright © 2023, IGI Global. Copying or distributing in print or electronic forms without written permission of IGI Global is prohibited.

experience economy, though exactly how they can manifest in business operations is still largely being discussed and explored (PwC, 2017).

Crucially, the successful development and deployment of AI-based experiential products and services depends on the consumer's willingness to accept and adopt AI technologies and solutions. Current anecdotal evidence, however, suggests that the consumer's receptivity of AI is complex, multiply determined, and hard to anticipate. For example, during the COVID-19 pandemic, Pan Pacific Singapore expanded the functions of its AI digital concierge Mika to handle guest needs (e.g., requests for housekeeping items) (Vouch, 2020), while Henn-na Hotel in Japan drastically reduced its robot services due to escalating guest complaints (Haddad, 2020). Though both hotels deployed AI to provide better lodging experiences, the dramatic difference in AI deployment outcomes is illustrative of the uncertainty that surrounds the acceptance and success of AI products and services in the experiential economy.

The nascent scientific (academic)s evidence corroborates the anecdotal evidence. For example, extant research has found that people place lower trust in dating services that are based on AI algorithms (Castelo, Bos, & Lehmann, 2019), callers to customer service centers end calls early and report lower satisfaction if they realize they are interacting with an AI (Luo, Tong, Fang, & Qu, 2019), and patients are unwilling to utilize health care provided by AI (Longoni, Bonezzi, & Morewedge, 2019), relative to equivalent services offered by human agents. These findings challenge the general assumption (and hope) that customers will adopt AI products and services if these products and services lower search costs and/or increase consumer utility and consumer welfare. In contrast, the anecdotal evidence and emerging empirical findings suggest that consumers may be unwilling to accept and adopt AI solutions—even when such solutions provide superior benefits at a reasonable cost—due to people's fundamental mistrust of, and reticence towards, AI.

Accordingly, the present book chapter discusses the nascent literature on consumers and AI, particularly in the context of experiential products and the experience economy, which are key marketing application contexts (Pine & Gilmore, 2011; McKinsey Quarterly, 2021). The present chapter further draws upon the formal academic literature and leading practitioner press to synthesize current evidence, with suggestions and recommendations for marketing managers and policymakers tasked with driving the deployment and success of AI in the experience economy.

BACKGROUND

Experiential products and services are those that consumers choose, buy, and use solely to experience and enjoy (Holbrook & Hirschman, 1982). The key benefit of an experiential product is "hedonic consumption, that is the feelings, emotions and sensations experienced during product usage" (Cooper-Martin, 1992). Examples of experiential products include going to watch a movie (Mukherjee & Kadiyali, 2011), taking a vacation (Chang & Pham, 2018), and attending a concert (Table 3, Loureiro et al., 2020). As consumers place increasing emphasis on experiences over material possessions (Euromonitor International, 2017), the experience economy is growing in prominence and importance to many nations' overall gross domestic product (Pine & Gilmore, 2011). Recognizing the increasing significance of managing consumer experiences for businesses' long-term success, practitioners are increasingly focusing on customer experiences and experiential marketing—the marketing of a product by emphasizing its experiential benefits. For example, BMW markets its automobiles based on driving experience; the tourism boards of many countries and cities advocate the emotional benefits that visitors derive by experiencing the culture, history, and scenery of specific destinations.

Rapid improvements in AI due to the availability of new data sources and new discoveries in machine learning promise a transformational opportunity for marketing practice, with extensive and diverse applications ranging from product recommendations to digital assistants to dynamic pricing modules to customer relationship management (PwC, 2017; MIT Technology Review Insights, 2020; Mukherjee & Chang, 2022). These improvements are particularly prominent in the context of experiential products and experiential marketing, where AI has helped make the consumer journey frictionless in consumer-facing tasks. For example, Disney uses AI to enhance consumers' visit experiences at Disneyland, Spotify uses AI to enhance listeners' overall music consumption experience, and Amazon uses AI to help make customer ordering process seamless and frictionless.

Moreover, the swift adoption and deployment of AI has been fueled by the increasing widespread accessibility and affordability of developing and deploying AI (see Chang & Mukherjee, 2022 for a discussion on machine learning methods and data sources for publicly available customer data). Concrete examples of tools to facilitate the deployment of AI that are available in today's market include Google's Cloud Platform, Amazon's Web Services, and Microsoft's Azure, among others. These cloud services allow companies to create AI solutions in a cost-effective way, substantially lowering the barrier to entry and shortening the amount of time to implement AI solutions in marketing contexts. To reduce barriers to entry in deploying AI solutions, many large technology companies have also created tools that offer a "code-free" approach to developing machine learning algorithms—the nuts and bolts of AI technologies—allowing those without coding experience to develop and employ AI. These platforms, combined with numerous large publicly available datasets, make it possible for firms to simplify the process of incorporating AI solutions in their market offerings.

This phenomenon, "making it possible for everyone to create AI systems", has been termed the democratization of AI (Riedl, 2021). As more people access the models, data, and computing resources necessary to build an AI application, the more its benefits can be shared by all users to improve work processes resulting in more innovations. Thus, analysts have speculated that AI could level the playing field for small and medium enterprises relative to large corporations, so improving AI tools for development and deployment and making them more accessible to encourage adoption should be at the top of business priorities (Forbes, 2019).

CONSUMERS AND AI IN THE MODERN EXPERIENCE ECONOMY

Despite the novelty and usefulness of an AI innovation, its success is not guaranteed in the real-world, as it requires consumers to accept and adopt the AI as part and parcel of daily living. Consider the following examples: Bank of America's (BoA) chatbot Erica that provides customer service support; Lemonade, an insurtech that utilizes AI-powered interfaces to sell and manage insurance policies; Amazon's Alexa, a digital assistant that uses speech recognition and natural language processing to streamline consumers' digital lives; and Disney's Imagineers who use AI to bring characters to life. In each case, the AI product or service is profoundly creative and innovative and brings to market product solutions that are both novel and useful (Cropley & Cropley, 2010; Mukherjee, Chang, & Chattopadhyay, 2019).

Much of the economic opportunity that AI is expected to bring to the global economy depends on consumers, with 45% (or over US$7 trillion) of total economic gains estimated to come from consumer demand for new AI-enhanced ("smart") products and AI-enabled personalized services (PwC, 2017). In many AI applications in marketing, AI-enabled products and services interact directly with consumers on a wide range of tasks. These tasks include offering support in customer service encounters via chatbots,

569

providing customized product recommendations in ecommerce, and helping customers place orders. For example, Netflix is using AI to better personalize movie recommendations to consumers based on prior viewing habits and on the time, location, and device used. Through conversational AI (e.g., using speech recognition, natural language processing), Amazon's digital assistant Alexa is transforming the customer purchase journey by making purchase seamless and frictionless. During the COVID-19 pandemic, many US universities began to use virtual assistants to answer student queries (NYTimes, 2020). Several hotels in Singapore, including Andaz, Parkroyal Collection Marina Bay, and Pan Pacific, began to utilize AI-powered digital concierge solutions to deliver customer service. Not only can AI improve business productivity, it also holds the promise to augment consumer capacities and enhance consumer experiences, thereby improving overall consumer well-being.

Given these positive benefits, will consumers accept and adopt these innovations? On the one hand, the innovations promise new benefits such as coordinating daily activities (e.g., scheduling a robot to vacuum the house, automatically paying the bills), discovering engaging and interesting content, and reducing the effort and time required for chores such as driving to the grocery store. On the other hand, the products also require an acceptance of the access and control that these solutions require over personal information and personal activities that may not unacceptable to consumers. Crucially, there is insufficient empirically based guidance as to best practices for understanding, designing, and managing consumer experiences that are delivered and augmented using AI technologies (Marketing Science Institute, 2020).

The uncertainty in consumer receptivity toward AI and, relatedly, differences in the success of AI implementations is most likely due to the myriad social, cultural, and psychological factors (e.g., consumer motivations; Pham & Chang, 2008) that influence consumer journeys and customer satisfaction. To drive the successful deployment of AI in marketing, it is therefore crucial to consider consumer psychology—how consumers perceive, feel, and respond toward AI—as germane to the acceptance and success of AI innovations in marketing (Mukherjee & Chang, 2018). Other key stakeholders—computer scientists (AI developers), businesses, and public agencies—in the marketplace appear ready for the AI revolution. However, due to the emergence of AI products and services being a new phenomenon, relatively little is known about individuals' (consumers') receptivity of AI innovations in marketing (Mukherjee, Yang, Xiao, & Chattopadhyay, 2017).

These issues are compounded in the case of experiential products and the experience economy. Experiential products are composed of experiential product attributes—aspects of one's experience when consuming the product or service, such as the ambience in an upscale restaurant (Gilovich & Gallo, 2020)—that are inextricably linked to the personality of the human being who delivers them. For example, a visit to a wine store depends profoundly on to the personality of the salesperson who engages the customer, gauges his/her preferences, and recommends products. The salesperson engages in conceptual education—educating the consumer on "how the wine is produced generally and discussions of wine varietals in general" (Mukherjee & Chang, 2022).

Will a wine store that replaces a human salesperson with an AI salesperson be as successful? The answer to this question is not clear because on the one hand while the adoption of AI and the use of an AI salesperson may lead to a more detailed understanding of the customer's preferences, a more seamless experience, and a more expansive set of recommendations; on the other hand, the absence of the empathy and charm of a human salesperson may detract from the intimate wine purchase experience that the customer is familiar with and enjoys.

Importantly, in addition to the overall appeal of the AI salesperson, the consumer behavior and marketing literatures provide several arguments for why the AI salesperson may not be as effective as may be expected from a purely economic perspective (based on rationality).

First, it is typical for artificial intelligence to play a greater role in facilitating purchases that are made for future consumption (e.g., a chatbot on an e-retailer's website; ordering products using conversational AI). Consumers rely less on their feelings for temporally distant consumption than for temporally closer consumption (Chang & Pham, 2013). Therefore, we would expect that the analytical viewpoint will dominate when purchasing for the future, as is natural when purchasing online using an AI agent (such as a chatbot), thereby shaping what and how much the consumers purchase—a critical factor in determining the financial implications of having an AI salesperson. Some initial empirical evidence, consistent with the view that certain domains and decision contexts promote greater reliance on affective feelings versus analytical thinking—have been found in consumers' reaction toward product recommendations (Longoni & Cian, 2020). Longoni and Cian (2020) found that consumers show lower acceptance (and greater resistance) to AI-based recommendations when hedonic product features (those that provide rich sensory experiences such as tasting notes of wines, scent of fragrances, thrill of rollercoaster rides) are salient for consumer judgment and decision making, compared to human-based recommendations.

Second, the success of the AI agent may be determined by general facets of consumer behavior that do not relate to AI but apply to the AI solution. For example, prior research has found that "consumers' increased self-focused attention promotes their relative reliance on affective feelings when they make decisions" (Chang & Hung, 2018). It would follow that if the AI sales agent was manifested in contexts promoting self-focused attention—such as personalized recommendations, AI agents addressing customers by their first names ("Hello Adriana, what can I help you with today?") or even AI agents with reflective surfaces in their physical designs—we would anticipate that the consumer would behave differently than if the same agent in the same context and environment was manifested in a device with a matte (unreflective) finish.

Third, firms' knowledge of consumers' experiential product preferences is limited due to the limitations of extant marketing research methods (Mukherjee & Chang, 2022), which limits the accuracy of the data that is available to train the machine learning algorithms underlying the AI, and thus likely limits the efficacy of AI-driven sales algorithms and models.

As these examples and arguments demonstrate, the success of AI in the experiential economy is thus difficult, and perhaps even impossible, to understand and predict. This is at least in part due to the extant knowledge base on consumer receptivity and AI—relatively little is known about the consumer psychology of AI consumer-AI interactions are still a recent and new phenomenon (e.g., voice-enabled assistants, digital content curators). It is not clear whether insights from prior scientific studies can be extended to this context, given that AI-enabled products often vastly differ from prior products, in scale, performance, and dynamics. Moreover, extant empirical findings have documented substantial differences in consumer behavior across countries and cultural backgrounds, in aspects that might have downstream consequences for consumers' receptiveness toward AI solutions. For example, consumers across markets and cultures show profound difference in how they respond to social environment (e.g., toward service providers; Shavitt & Cho, 2016; Hong & Chang, 2015), their risk attitudes toward technological innovation (Weber & Morris, 2010), and various aspects of their consumption behavior (e.g., brand perceptions, product attitudes) in marketing contexts (Shavitt, Lee, & Torelli, 2009). These findings on cultural differences in consumer behavior underscore the complexity in predicting consumers' reaction toward various AI solutions. Finally, emerging academic papers in this nascent area typically explore the psychology of automation (e.g., people's reaction toward human job replacement by robots; Granulo et al., 2019) or the use of computer algorithms (e.g., people's trust in tasks performed by an algorithm; Castelo et al., 2019). While automation and computer algorithms are two important features of AI, there is much more to AI, and more richness and nuances in consumers' interactions with AI solutions that are yet to be addressed.

While AI has recently been implemented to help companies in various consumer-facing tasks—improved recommendation engines, digital content curations (e.g., news, music, and movies)—most companies still rely on traditional (survey-based) measurement and data analyses methods to measure the efficacy of their marketing practices and customer experiences (McKinsey Quarterly, 2021). Collectively, these factors describe nontrivial challenges faced by today's businesses when they consider AI and consumers in the experience economy—(1) in consumer-facing tasks, there are substantial uncertainties in consumers' overall receptivity and adoption of AI technologies offered by businesses and at the same time, (2) there is lack of empirical framework and data for a precise measurement of consumer experiences with AI technologies. These create challenges for managers and business practitioners to navigate in today's competitive marketplace for effective managerial decision making.

SOLUTIONS AND RECOMMENDATIONS

The current state of knowledge lacks a keen and detailed understanding of the consumer's decision journey as shaped and determined by the consumer's interactions with AI and manifested in the consumers' purchases (Hermann, 2021; Puntoni, Reczek, Giesler, & Botti, 2021). Suggestions for best practices to manage challenges in AI deployment, as well as recommendations to develop and deploy successful AI products, would provide helpful inputs for businesses in the modern experience economy. Below, solutions and recommendations are presented for businesses keen to kickstart the process for creating successful AI products and deploying them in the experience economy.

As a starting point, manager and practitioners should grasp the range of possible AI solutions and the scope and objectives of their applicability. The umbrella term of "Artificial Intelligence" entails a large set of possibilities. Therefore, understanding what each solution is designed for, what it can and cannot do, and how it has been deployed in the market by other businesses can help practitioners think of ways to apply the technology and integrate it into operations. Being cognizant of the strengths and weaknesses of each technology and how different AI are designed to solve different problems is crucial for deployment. For example, a class of machine learning (ML) techniques known as computer vision is good at classifying visual objects and making predictions given sufficient and diverse past information (Chang, Mukherjee, & Chattopadhyay, 2022). Another class of ML techniques used in computational linguistics, natural language processing, has been applied in a wide variety of areas across AI deployments involving texts-based information (Mukherjee, Xiao, Wang, & Contractor, 2018); they include recommendation engines, chatbots, fraud detection, article writing, and even music creation (Marr, 2019). They are possible marketing use-cases for AI in the experience economy.

Once managers and practitioners have a specific aim in mind, they should consider the data that would be required to train the AI solution (PwC, 2017). AI models require vast amounts of data in model training. Knowing about the data requirement in advance can in turn help managers better plan, collate, and collect relevant data about their customers. Ensuring proper data practices can provide useful insights, through traditional techniques, which sets up a solid basis for AI deployments for the company going forward. On top of the company's internal data, managers can consider accessing publicly available data (see Chang & Mukherjee, 2022 for examples of customer-relevant data) or off-the-shelf, pretrained AI models to expedite the preparation work for eventual AI deployment (Riedl, 2021). There are many such options that are user-friendly, cost effective, and accessible in the market; it may be worthwhile to consider open-sourced AI solutions and other vendor platforms that provide AI-as-a-Service. Well known platforms and service providers include Google, Microsoft, and Amazon, IBM Watson, and SAS (see Chang, Mukherjee, & Chattopadhyay, 2021 for such application in the context of crowdfunding). These options have given small-and-medium-sized enterprises greater access to AI technology (more specifically, the algorithms) without a large initial investment in monetary and manpower resources. These create an accessible starting point to build an AI application for initial testing and deployment; in the process, the additional data generated can also help build a contextual, representative dataset for the company. AI needs customization for businesses to unleash its intended benefits (c.f. Borges, Laurindo, Spínola, Gonçalves, & Mattos, 2020). Therefore, datasets designed to purpose (i.e., data specifically collected for the marketing application at hand for the company in question) can help continually improve the effectiveness of AI as a solution going forward.

When thinking of which AI solutions to deploy, managers and practitioners are sometimes overly optimistic and overambitious. Most successful AI deployments are simple solutions that are easy to implement, bring measurable benefits, and are concrete in the objectives they aim to achieve. Most small and medium sized businesses, such as are common in experiential industries (e.g., restaurants, tourist attractions), cannot afford to go for complicated projects that require large amounts of capital and trained manpower (Columbus, 2017). Instead, it is preferable to start with more modest and achievable goals, which can help the organization feel more comfortable and confident in its AI deployment, familiarize its employees with AI technologies, and can encourage stakeholders to invest more into AI in the future. By running AI pilots to perform specific tasks sequentially; as the ROI of the AI applications manifest, it would likely be easier to get greater buy-in from relevant stakeholders and build a road map for successful AI deployment (Groom, 2019).

FUTURE RESEARCH DIRECTIONS

As AI products and services are a new phenomenon, there is a wealth of possible research directions and ideas, as described by recent calls by business practitioners (e.g., PwC, 2017; Thomas, 2020) and marketing scholars in consumer experiences (e.g., Ameen et al., 2021; Puntoni et al., 2021), service interactions (e.g., Hermann, 2021; Huang & Rust, 2021a), and general marketing practices (e.g., Huang & Rust, 2021b). Many nations around the world have made AI development an integral part of their national policies going forward. For example, the United States—a leader in AI technology and applications in marketing, with the most AI patent filings globally (PwC, 2017)—describe its AI policy outlook in a document published by Select Committee on Artificial Intelligence, White House, USA. China—with tremendous growth in AI systems and another leader in number of AI patent filings globally (PwC, 2017)—has outlined its plan for AI growth in its Next Generation AI Development Plan, as part of the China Institute for Science and Technology Policy. Similarly, Singapore has demonstrated strong government support (with various support schemes and initiatives) in advancing AI technology for deployment by large companies and small-and-medium-sized enterprises, as evident in Singapore's the Smart Nation Initiative and National AI Strategy.

CONCLUSION

Given the ongoing development in AI and the opportunities afforded by this technology, it is imperative for managers, policymakers, and enthusiasts alike to examine the consumer psychology of AI —how consumers perceive, feel, and respond toward AI—which is likely to be germane to the success for AI deployments in the experience economy. Computer scientists have made great stride in the development of algorithm-driven AI systems and machine learning methods. Businesses have begun or are planning to incorporate AI systems in their business and operating models (Thomas, 2020). Public agencies around the world are encouraging digital transformation and inclusiveness. However, less is known about individuals' (consumers') receptivity toward AI-enabled systems in marketing contexts. Therefore, to harness the economic potential that AI brings to the marketplace, research is needed to fathom the psychology of consumer-AI interaction.

ACKNOWLEDGMENT

This research was supported by the Ministry of Education, Singapore, under its Academic Research Fund (AcRF) Tier 2 Grant No. MOE2019-T2-1-183. Any opinions, findings, and conclusions or recommendations expressed in this material are those of the authors and do not necessarily reflect the views of the Singapore Ministry of Education.

REFERENCES

Ameen, N., Tarhini, A., Reppel, A., & Anand, A. (2021). Customer experiences in the age of artificial intelligence. *Computers in Human Behavior*, *114*, 106548. doi:10.1016/j.chb.2020.106548 PMID:32905175

Borges, A. F., Laurindo, F. J., Spínola, M. M., Gonçalves, R. F., & Mattos, C. A. (2020). The strategic use of artificial intelligence in the digital era: Systematic literature review and future research directions. *International Journal of Information Management*, 102225.

Castelo, N., Bos, M. W., & Lehmann, D. R. (2019). Task-dependent algorithm aversion. *JMR, Journal of Marketing Research*, *56*(5), 809–825. doi:10.1177/0022243719851788

Chang, H. H., & Hung, I. W. (2018). Mirror, mirror on the retail wall: Self-focused attention promotes reliance on feelings in consumer decisions. *JMR, Journal of Marketing Research*, *55*(4), 586–599. doi:10.1509/jmr.15.0080

Chang, H. H., & Mukherjee, A. (2022). Using machine learning methods to extract behavioral insights from consumer data. In J. Wang (Ed.), *Encyclopaedia of data science and machine learning*. IGI Global.

Chang, H. H., Mukherjee, A., & Chattopadhyay, A. (2021). The impact of single versus multiple narrating voices in persuasive videos. In T. Bradford, A. Keinan, & M. Thomson (Eds.), Advances in consumer research (pp. 388-389). Association for Consumer Research.

Chang, H. H., Mukherjee, A., & Chattopadhyay, A. (2022). Designing persuasive voiceover narration in crowdfunding videos. In A. Humphreys, G. Packard, & K. Gielens (Eds.), *AMA winter academic conference proceedings* (pp. 217-218). American Marketing Association.

Chang, H. H., & Pham, M. T. (2013). Affect as a decision-making system of the present. *The Journal of Consumer Research*, *40*(1), 42–63. doi:10.1086/668644

Chang, H. H., & Pham, M. T. (2018). Affective boundaries of scope insensitivity. *The Journal of Consumer Research*, *45*(2), 403–428. doi:10.1093/jcr/ucy007

Columbus, L. (2017). McKinsey's State Of Machine Learning And AI, 2017. *Forbes*. Available online: https://www.forbes.com/sites/louiscolumbus/2017/07/09/mckinseys-state-of-machine-learning-and-ai-2017

Cooper-Martin, E. (1992). *Consumers and movies: Information sources for experiential products*. ACR North American Advances.

Cropley, D., & Cropley, A. (2010). Functional creativity. Cambridge Handbook of Creativity, 301-318.

Davenport, T., Guha, A., Grewal, D., & Bressgott, T. (2020). How artificial intelligence will change the future of marketing. *Journal of the Academy of Marketing Science*, *48*(2), 24–42. doi:10.100711747-019-00696-0

Euromonitor International. (2017). *Experience more across the customer journey*. https://www.euromonitor.com/experience-more-across-the-customer-journey/report

Forbes. (2019). *How Artificial Intelligence Can Level The Playing Field For Mid-Market Companies*. Available online: https://www.forbes.com/sites/forbestechcouncil/2019/09/20/how-artificial-intelligence-can-level-the-playing-field-for-mid-market-companies

Gilovich, T., & Gallo, I. (2020). Consumers' pursuit of material and experiential purchases: A review. *Counselling Psychology Review*, *3*(1), 20–33. doi:10.1002/arcp.1053

Granulo, A., Fuchs, C., & Puntoni, S. (2019). Psychological reactions to human versus robotic job replacement. *Nature Human Behaviour*, *3*(10), 1062–1069. doi:10.103841562-019-0670-y PMID:31384025

Groom, F. M. (2019). Introduction to Artificial Intelligence and Machine Learning. *Artificial Intelligence and Machine Learning for Business for Non-Engineers*, 1.

Haddad, S. (2020). *Inside the hotel run by robots*. https://www.raconteur.net/technology/automation/robot-hotel-ai/

Hermann, E. (2021). Anthropomorphized artificial intelligence, attachment, and consumer behavior. *Marketing Letters*, 1–6.

Holbrook, M. B., & Hirschman, E. C. (1982). The experiential aspects of consumption: Consumer fantasies, feelings, and fun. *The Journal of Consumer Research*, *9*(2), 132–140. doi:10.1086/208906

Hong, J., & Chang, H. H. (2015). I follow my heart and we rely on reasons: The impact of self-construal on reliance on feelings versus reasons in decision making. *The Journal of Consumer Research*, *41*(6), 1392–1411. doi:10.1086/680082

Huang, M. H., & Rust, R. T. (2021a). Engaged to a robot? The role of AI in service. *Journal of Service Research*, *24*(1), 30–41. doi:10.1177/1094670520902266

Huang, M. H., & Rust, R. T. (2021b). A strategic framework for artificial intelligence in marketing. *Journal of the Academy of Marketing Science*, *49*(1), 30–50. doi:10.100711747-020-00749-9

Longoni, C., Bonezzi, A., & Morewedge, C. K. (2019). Resistance to medical artificial intelligence. *The Journal of Consumer Research*, *46*(4), 629–650. doi:10.1093/jcr/ucz013

Longoni, C., & Cian, L. (2020). Artificial intelligence in utilitarian vs. hedonic contexts: The "word-of-machine" effect. *Journal of Marketing*, 91–108.

Loureiro, F., Garcia-Marques, T., & Wegener, D. T. (2020). Norms for 150 consumer products: Perceived complexity, quality objectivity, material/experiential nature, perceived price, familiarity and attitude. *PLoS One*, *15*(9), e0238848. doi:10.1371/journal.pone.0238848 PMID:32956402

Luo, X., Tong, S., Fang, Z., & Qu, Z. (2019). Frontiers: Machines versus humans: The impact of artificial intelligence chatbot disclosure on customer purchases. *Marketing Science*, *38*, 937–947. doi:10.1287/mksc.2019.1192

Madrigal, A. (2014). How Netflix reverse engineered Hollywood. *The Atlantic*. Retrieved from: https://www.theatlantic.com/technology/archive/2014/01/how-netflix-reverse-engineered-hollywood/282679/

Marketing Science Institute. (2020). *2020-2022 Research Priorities*. Available online: https://www.msi.org/wp-content/uploads/2020/09/MSI-2020-22-Research-Priorities-final.pdf

Marr, B. (2019). *Artificial Intelligence in Practice: How 50 Successful Companies used AI and Machine Learning to Solve Problems*. John Wiley & Sons.

McCarthy, J. (2006). *What is AI? / Basic Questions*. Available online: http://jmc.stanford.edu/artificial-intelligence/what-is-ai/index.html

McKinsey, Q. (2020). Prediction. *Future*, *CX*. Retrieved September 28, 2021, from https://www.mckinsey.com/business-functions/marketing-and-sales/our-insights/prediction-the-future-of-cx

MIT Technology Review Insights. (2020). *The global AI agenda: Promise, reality, and a future of data sharing*. Available online: https://www.technologyreview.com/2020/03/26/950287/the-global-ai-agenda-promise-reality-and-a-future-of-data-sharing/

Mukherjee, A., & Chang, H. H. (2018). Innovation and small business success. *Tabla*, 14.

Mukherjee, A., & Chang, H. H. (2022). Describing rosé: An embedding-based method for measuring preferences. In A. Humphreys, G. Packard, & K. Gielens (Eds.), *AMA winter academic conference proceedings* (pp. 150-151). American Marketing Association.

Mukherjee, A., Chang, H. H., & Chattopadhyay, A. (2019). Crowdfunding: sharing the entrepreneurial journey. In R. W. Belk, G. M. Eckhardt, & F. Bardhi (Eds.), *Handbook of the sharing economy* (pp. 152–162). Edward Elgar Publishing. doi:10.4337/9781788110549.00019

Mukherjee, A., & Kadiyali, V. (2011). Modeling multichannel home video demand in the U.S. motion picture industry. *JMR, Journal of Marketing Research*, *48*(6), 985–995. doi:10.1509/jmr.07.0359

Mukherjee, A., & Kadiyali, V. (2018). The competitive dynamics of new DVD releases. *Management Science*, *64*(8), 3536–3553. doi:10.1287/mnsc.2017.2795

Mukherjee, A., Xiao, P., Wang, L., & Contractor, N. (2018). Does the opinion of the crowd predict commercial success? Evidence from Threadless. In Academy of Management Proceedings (pp. 12728). Academy of Management. doi:10.5465/AMBPP.2018.12728abstract

Mukherjee, A., Yang, C. L., Xiao, P., & Chattopadhyay, A. (2017). *Does the crowd support innovation? Innovation claims and success on Kickstarter.* HEC Paris Research Paper No. MKG-2017-1220.

NYTimes. (2020). *College chatbots, with names like iggy and pounce, are here to help.* Available online: https://www.nytimes.com/2020/04/08/education/college-ai-chatbots-students.html

Pham, M. T., & Chang, H. (2008). Regulatory focus and regulatory fit in consumer search and consideration of alternatives. ACR North American Advances.

Pine, B. J., & Gilmore, J. H. (2011). *The Experience Economy.* Harvard Business Press.

Puntoni, S., Reczek, R. W., Giesler, M., & Botti, S. (2021). Consumers and Artificial Intelligence: An Experiential Perspective. *Journal of Marketing*, *85*(1), 131–151. doi:10.1177/0022242920953847

PwC. (2017). *Sizing the prize: What's the real value of AI for your business and how can you capitalise?* Available online: https://www.pwc.com/gx/en/issues/analytics/assets/ pwc-ai-analysis-sizing-the-prize-report.pdf

Riedl, M. (2021). *AI democratization in the era of GPT-3.* Available online: https://thegradient.pub/ai-democratization-in-the-era-of-gpt-3/

Shavitt, S., & Cho, H. (2016). Culture and consumer behavior: The role of horizontal and vertical cultural factors. *Current Opinion in Psychology*, *8*, 149–154. doi:10.1016/j.copsyc.2015.11.007 PMID:28083559

Shavitt, S., Lee, A., & Torelli, C. (2009). New directions in cross-cultural consumer psychology. In M. Wanke (Ed.), *The social psychology of consumer behavior* (pp. 227–250). Psychology Press.

Solomonoff, R. J. (1985). The time scale of artificial intelligence: Reflections on social effects. *Human Systems Management*, *5*(2), 149–153. doi:10.3233/HSM-1985-5207

Thomas, R. (2020). *AI in 2020: From experimentation to adoption.* Available online: https://www.ibm.com/blogs/think/2020/01/ai-in-2020-from-experimentation-to-adoption/

Vouch. (2020). *Pan Pacific Singapore X Vouch case study.* Available online: https://www.vouch.sg/pps-x-vouch/

Weber, E. U., & Morris, M. W. (2010). Culture and judgment and decision making: The constructivist turn. *Perspectives on Psychological Science*, *5*(4), 410–419. doi:10.1177/1745691610375556 PMID:26162187

ADDITIONAL READING

Aghion, P., Jones, B. F., & Jones, C. I. (2019). *9. Artificial Intelligence and Economic Growth.* University of Chicago Press.

Fatima, S., Desouza, K. C., & Dawson, G. S. (2020). National strategic artificial intelligence plans: A multi-dimensional analysis. *Economic Analysis and Policy*, *67*, 178–194. doi:10.1016/j.eap.2020.07.008

LaTour, K. A., & Deighton, J. A. (2019). Learning to become a taste expert. *The Journal of Consumer Research*, *46*(1), 1–19. doi:10.1093/jcr/ucy054

McLeay, F., Osburg, V. S., Yoganathan, V., & Patterson, A. (2021). Replaced by a robot: Service implications in the age of the machine. *Journal of Service Research*, *24*(1), 104–121. doi:10.1177/1094670520933354

KEY TERMS AND DEFINITIONS

Artificial Intelligence: Artificial intelligence is the science and engineering of making intelligent machines and the emulation of human intelligence by machines. Examples of artificial intelligence include natural language processing, speech recognition, and computer vision.

Chatbots: A computer program and statistical model that is designed to simulate conversation with human users.

Experience Economy: Experiential marketing, and the experience economy, is the marketing of a product by emphasizing its experiential benefits. Examples including engaging a firm to provide a birthday party, hiring a Konmari consultant for a Marie Kondo makeover, and visiting the Maldives to celebrate a wedding anniversary.

Experiential Products and Services: Products and services that consumers choose, buy, and use solely to experience and enjoy.

Machine Learning: Machine learning is the development and use of computer algorithms that automatically through experience and by training on data.

Voice-Based Assistants: A voice-based assistant is a software agent that can perform tasks or services for an individual based on voice commands and/or questions.

Business Intelligence Applied to Tourism

Célia M. Q. Ramos

iD https://orcid.org/0000-0002-3413-4897

ESGHT, CinTurs, University of Algarve, Portugal

INTRODUCTION

In today's society, ICT is used to support several kinds of activities in general. However, tourism activity is one that must be influenced by the use of innovative technologies. Therefore, ICT is used in all tourism travel phases, from the beginning (before the trip), where the travelers dream, make a decision and purchase tourism products during the trip and to support and contribute to a positive travel experience, until after the trip, where the main activity is sharing personal histories, and contributing to the creation of digital memories.

At the same time, at tourism destinations, with the use of innovative technologies it starts to be possible to develop an environment associated with smart tourism destinations that could gain insights about customers' actual needs and preferences, where suppliers develop smart experiences and smart business ecosystems and regions start to become smart destinations, where it is possible to collect, exchange and process data (Gretzel et al., 2015). This contributes to offering the best tourism experience in accordance with the tourist profile and at the same time to identifying and developing products and services personalized to tourism customers.

In this technological environment, what differentiates a tourism organization from its competitor is, in many cases, the quality and opportunity of its information, which makes it possible to acquire knowledge about the tourists, allows it to make more appropriate decisions in the definition of new products or services, contributes to the adaptability to new markets, increases competitive capacity and can guarantee survival, even in times of crisis. If it is possible to collect, exchange and process data in a smart environment, then knowing the context becomes information. Information, knowing the meaning, becomes knowledge. Knowledge, knowing the vision, becomes wisdom (intelligence). Finally, wisdom, when combined with an effect (decision), results in big decisions and strategic plans for the smart destination and for supporting the DMO (destination management organizations) (Femenia-Serra et al., 2022), as well as the concept of the DIKWM model (data, information, knowledge, wisdom).

The areas for improving the quantity and quality of information available for decision making are knowledge management and business intelligence. Knowledge management should increase an organization's intellectual capital and includes a set of intangible assets or competencies fundamental to obtaining a competitive advantage for the tourist company. Business intelligence systems combine data with analytical tools to provide information relevant to decision making to improve the quality and availability of this information (Castillo-Clavero et al., 2022).

The knowledge management area helps to: improve the decision-making process, increase the organization's ability to solve problems, increase the organization's capacity to innovate, for example, in terms of differentiation, and offer services and products according to customer preferences. In specific reference to tourism, the activity can contribute toward innovations in this economic sector, such as facial recognition at airports, sites that aggregate and monitor prices for accommodation, organize trips

DOI: 10.4018/978-1-7998-9220-5.ch034

Copyright © 2023, IGI Global. Copying or distributing in print or electronic forms without written permission of IGI Global is prohibited.

inspired by Netflix or sponsor those who write about travel, hotel booking via voice assistant on Google, a robot that welcomes the customer to the hotel, check-in by the guest entrance to a hotel (NFC – near field communications) or check-in by smartphone, as long as the passenger enters the airport at the start, and is tracked to the place where it is located.

Business intelligence is a set of tools, technologies, and operations that enable a company to collect and then present valuable data for a tourism organization in dashboards or reports with insightful information, complementing data mining algorithms to produce insights about the business.

In summary, why should the tourism industry invest in business intelligence? To achieve answers to several questions, such as: which destinations are most sought after, how long reservations are made for, which hotels/restaurants/agencies generate the most revenue, and which products/events/dishes/museums provide more profit. In addition, business intelligence can help to compare homologated periods and see if the variation is positive or negative, to achieve knowledge about the customer, to identify consumption patterns and to forecast tourism demand, among other tasks (Choi et al., 2020; Höpken et al., 2015; Li et al., 2021; Mariani et al., 2018; Vajirakachorn & Chongwatpol, 2017; Valeri, 2020; Xiang et al., 2021; Wang, 2022).

BACKGROUND

In the tourism industry, what differentiates an organization from its competitor is, in many cases, the quality and opportunity of its information. This information contributes to the knowledge acquisition about tourists, allowing a business to make more appropriate decisions when defining new products or services, providing the adaptability to new markets, increasing competitive capacity and guaranteeing survival, even in times of economic or pandemic crisis (Yiu et al., 2020).

Information management is important for all levels of an organization related to tourism, as well as for any other belonging to any economic sector, as it supports the decision-making process and provides decision makers with timely, relevant data to reduce uncertainty in the decision process, and at the same time, controls and corrects deviations through a shared vision of the future, which includes the decisions of the decision maker, such as the elaboration of scenarios (Yiu et al., 2020).

To create value for an organization, it is necessary to manage information like any other economic resource through information systems to support the decision process, also called decision support systems (DSS). Every day, companies have to make decisions related to the allocation of their resources based on forecasts about the future. The DSS should have characteristics to support the process of making a decision, which consists of choosing a way of acting, among several possible alternatives, with the intention of reaching a goal (Santos & Ramos, 2009). The environment associated with this kind of IS should allow the processing and visualization of information interactively, be friendly enough to be used by decision makers, present information in a format and terminology appropriate to its users and be selective in the amount of information it presents (Yiu et al., 2020).

The management of tourist information systems is currently going through a maturity process that implies the need to look at organizations in order to capitalize and develop their intellectual capital, through the application of concepts associated with knowledge management (Vasconcelos & Barão, 2017).

Knowledge management and engineering considers the development of the analytical capacity of information systems, which includes the use of business intelligence tools applied to the data warehouse of the tourism company, in order to generate knowledge about the tourism business, which contributes to innovation, creativity, intelligence and learning from the activity (Santos & Ramos, 2009), and meet the strategies defined by the organization, such as: increasing reservations/direct sales, brand awareness, customer involvement, increasing visits to the website for consultation opportunities and promotions, improving customer communication, increasing customer confidence in information security, and monitoring and improving its online reputation (Chaffey & Ellis-Chadwick, 2019).

Knowledge management, in addition to improving the decision-making process and the organization's ability to solve problems, contributes to innovating and increasing the organization's intellectual capital, which includes the intangible assets which are essential for obtaining a competitive advantage (Santos & Ramos, 2009). Intellectual capital is considered an instrument through the definition of metrics associated with the organization's strategy; it helps to assess economic performance with a view to increasing the company's value (Duffy, 2000).

The organization has tangible capital, for example the value of a product or service. Intangible or intellectual capital, which results from informal activities, and which has value for the organization, consisting of human, structural and relational capital, can be considered a fourth dimension of intellectual property capital, associated, for example, with patents or with the number of prototypes (Vasconcelos & Barão, 2017).

The management of intellectual capital is essential for obtaining a competitive advantage for a tourism organization, as it is associated with the set of skills that the members of the organization have. Structural capital refers to the formal aspects of work organization, as well as physical, social, political and cultural spaces. Human capital refers to the competences and motivation of the organization's members, as well as the learning capacity of the entire organization. Finally, relational capital refers to the quantity and quality of relations between members of the organization and between them and external entities relevant to the business, which includes customers, suppliers, partners and distributors, among others relevant in the tourist distribution chain, as represented in Figure 1.

With regard to relational capital, customer capital is explained through the relationship between companies and their customers, and it is the growth engine of a company (Duffy, 2000), which contributes toward innovation in the offering of products and services with a view to meeting the tourist's well-being.

Figure 1. Knowledge management and intellectual capital indicators (Author's elaboration)

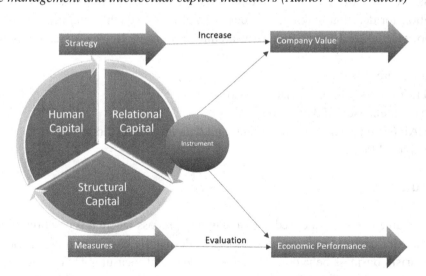

The customer/tourist is one of the pillars of an organization, which leads to the relevance of managing the knowledge associated with customers through metrics, in order to assess customer satisfaction and retention, which are often based on financial indicators, as it is complex to define metrics associated with the (relational) capital of the customer (Gupta & Zeithaml, 2006).

Customer (relational) capital management, also known as customer-associated knowledge management (Liu et al., 2022), has gradually begun to be considered in organizations in general, and consequently in those associated with tourism. The management of knowledge associated with the customer aims to determine their value and to establish long-term relationships with a view to their loyalty. For example, the hotel industry is one of the areas that can benefit the most from customer knowledge management.

Knowledge management contributes to increasing the competitive advantage of a tourist organization, which should be monitored and evaluated by indicators for the measurement of intellectual capital, such as:

§   Capital relational indicators: Online sales (%); Average customer loyalty in years (#); Customer satisfaction index (questionnaire)(%).
§   Structural capital indicators: Investment in new markets (€); Number of ideas suggested spontaneously by employees (#).
§   Human capital indicators: Global innovation capacity (%), i.e., the ratio between the number of new ideas generated and those effectively implemented through a new product or service; Number of new products /services generated by employees (#).

Information systems considered in decision support and knowledge management include business intelligence tools and data mining (DM) methods, which helps to overcome the current digitalization dilemma of an organization, with the aim of enhancing the perspective of learning and strategic management (Mohamad et al., 2022).

BUSINESS INTELLIGENCE

Business intelligence (BI) are systems that combine data with analytical tools in order to provide relevant information for decision making, in order to improve the quality and availability of this information (António et al., 2022). BI systems have an architecture constituted by five steps, as presented in Figure 2:

§   Data sources
§   ETL (extraction, transformation, loading)
§   Data warehouse and data marts
§   OLAP (online analytical processing) and data mining methods
§   Analytical tools.

Data Sources

The data sources step is associated with a planning process where it is essential to identify the data that are relevant for decision support systems and to define the basic key performance indicators for measuring tourism business behavior, among other pertinent measures for monitoring and controlling the organization's results. This BI architecture step is divided into two phases, data identification and data location, which can be internal and external.

Figure 2. Business intelligence architecture (Author's elaboration)

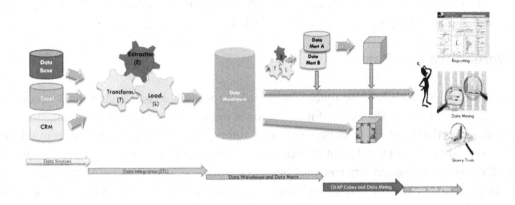

These phases began with determining the sources of data and their characteristics. Due to the "5 Vs" that define big data: data volume, velocity of data collection, data variety, data veracity and data value (Di Tria et al., 2014), selecting a source can be a challenging task once the data is taken from social media, the Internet of Things, open data, and smart cities (Mitch, 2022).

For the location step, it is necessary to search for useful online data using the domain knowledge of the study, intuition, and automatic mechanisms. The data capturing phase is made through known APIs, which will provide the data in different formats (Excel, XML, JSON, etc.) from external and internal sources, or through standard query languages.

ETL (Extraction, Transformation, Loading)

The ETL (extraction, transformation, loading) step, also called the data integrated or data gathered (Ramos et al., 2019), considers three separate functions combined into a single tool. First, the extract function reads data from several data sources and extracts a particular set of data. The transformation function works with the acquired data – it uses rules or search tables or creates combinations with other data – to convert it to a certain state, which is not a direct process, since different sources can have different structures and different meanings for the same organization's features (Martins et al., 2015).

The extracted data is temporarily stored in the data staging area (staging area or DSA), where the process of transformation and data cleansing takes place (Santos & Ramos, 2009). The processing and cleaning of the data consists of the normalization of the data with respect to size and type; the replacement of strange characters; the correction of typos; phonetic comparison to avoid duplication of information, for example, the same name written in different ways, with or without accentuation etc.; the replacement of unfilled data with "Uninformed" (for example); and the standardization of measure units, because in a given system a measurement can have the unit in meters and another in inches, or units with three decimal places in one system and in the other four decimal places. A decision must be made on how to treat the different definitions of information, for example, in one system the definition may be M for men and W for women, and in another system M for male and F for female. In cases such as these one should opt for the most usual definition.

It is also necessary to consolidate the extracted data, to make sure that the information is regular and consistent. For this it is essential to elaborate a set of rules for data conversion and also to include a set of several methods for performing the conversion, that includes the business process management, business process execution language, semantics of intangibles, and business vocabulary rules (Ramos et al., 2019).

Finally, the load function is used to write the resulting data (all the subset) or only changes to a target database, which may or may not have previously existed.

Data Warehouse and Data Marts

After the previous phase (ETL), the upload is carried out to a database created for decision support, called the data warehouse or data mart if it corresponds to the data of the entire organization or only a department, respectively, which is maintained in an autonomous form and separate from the transactional databases that contain the data of the company's operations. A data warehouse is a collection of integrated, non-volatile, subject-oriented data, recorded over time, used to support the decision-making process, as presented in Table 1. All stored information must have associated temporal information and should allow the data to be stored for several years (Santos & Ramos, 2009).

Considering a data warehouse as a repository, it is necessary to follow an appropriate methodology: (i) identification of the architecture, and (ii) use of multidimensional modeling to define the structure of the data warehouse (or data mart) (Santos & Ramos, 2009).

In the first step, the need to choose the most adequate data storage structure for the organization is highlighted: a data warehouse (DW), independent data mart (IDM) or dependent data mart (DDM). In this step, the choice is related to the purpose of the repository, whether it includes organization's global system (DW) or whether it includes an area or department of the organization, and in this case whether it is independent (IDM), meaning it is built with data directly from transaction systems, or dependent (DDM), meaning it works based on the existence of a DW. In the end, the decision is weighed considering several requirements. However, cost is one of the main factors that contributes to the final decision.

Table 1. Characteristics of a Data Warehouse (Santos and Ramos, 2009, p. 80)

Subject-oriented	• Data are organized around the issues of an organization, for example: customers, suppliers and products, among others. • Focused on modeling and analyzing data useful to decision makers rather than on day-to-day operations. • Provides a simple and concise view of a particular subject, excluding useless data for a decision.
Integrated	• The data come from a variety of heterogeneous data source, such as: relational databases, text files or spreadsheets, among others. • Cleaning and integration techniques are necessary to ensure data consistency, such as standardizing the names and meanings of attributes and encodings, among others.
Catalogued temporally	• Operational database: record current values. • Data warehouse: stored in historical terms and relates to a period between five to ten years.
Non-volatile	• Data warehouse is kept physically separate from operational databases. • Data after it is loaded cannot be changed or deleted. • In the data warehouse you can only add more data or see what is already loaded.

To carry out step two, it is necessary to consider an adequate method for modeling, such as multidimensional modeling, which is based on two assumptions (Santos & Ramos, 2009):

- Produce an easy-to-understand and user-made database structure (to facilitate the placement of questions to the system).

- Optimize performance in the processing of issues, as opposed to optimizing the processing of updates as in the relational database model.

The multidimensional model is constituted by several main concepts, including dimensions, which establish the organization of the data, determining possible queries/crossings, for example: region, time, sales channel, etc.; measures, which are the values to be analyzed, such as means, totals and quantities; and facts, which are the data to be grouped, containing the values of each measure for each combination of the existing dimensions.

Multidimensional modeling allows for the development of a data storage structure, which can present one of three schemas (Santos & Ramos, 2009): (i) a star schema, which integrates a single fact table that forms the center of the star and multiple dimension tables linked to the fact table; (ii) a snowflake schema, which is the star scheme whose dimensions are normalized and no longer has a regular structure in each branch and can now have a different extension; and (iii) a constellation schema, which integrates multiple fact tables that share common dimensions and the stars that integrate them can be interconnected by more than one dimension.

The fact tables are the main components of multidimensional models, since they allow for storing or recording the events to be analyzed, where events are numerical values that represent a given metric or measure, a line is associated with a particular event (for example, a sale), and all events must be represented according to the same granularity (detail of the information) (Santos & Ramos, 2009). The dimension tables are part of a diverse set of attributes (columns) by which the business indicators considered in the fact tables can be analyzed, typically integrate descriptions that allow for contextualizing the metrics under analysis (Santos & Ramos, 2009).

OLAP (OnLine Analytical Processing) and Data Mining techniques

Data analysis is another designation to this step, that can be constituted by the application of OLAP (online analytical processing) and data mining techniques. If both are powerful when applied in isolation, they are even more powerful when combined in the same data analysis (Ramos et al., 2019). On one side, OLAP techniques enable the complex analysis of data dynamics and help tourism managers to find new and interesting facts from data they have stored in a data warehouse, and on the other side data mining techniques allow the generation of hypotheses about the data and the discovery of hidden relationships and patterns that are not always obvious, so the ideal is a combination of the two types of techniques in data analysis, also called business analytics (Castillo-Clavero et al., 2022).

OLAP Techniques

OLAP techniques allow for the creation of cubes to analyze information about different perspectives (dimensions), which can be applied in a DW or data marts. The cubes include concepts associated with the different types of exploration of a DW, such as (Santos & Ramos, 2009):

§ A point represents the intersection of values (a fact) with respect to the dimension. Examples: How many double rooms (product 1) are sold on New Year's Day (date D1) to tourists from England (country 1)? Or what are the total sales of the traditional dish (product 1), on New Year's Day (date D1) in the capital (city 1)?

§ A plan shows the plane or slice (slicing). Example: What is the amount of sale of the traditional dish in Faro City, on days D1 to DN (the whole year)?

§ Dicing or dice. Example: What is the amount of sale of product P1 to PN in city C1 to CN, in days from D1 to DN?

In terms of the OLAP potentialities for the tourism industry, these can be related to several areas, such as airlines, accommodation, restaurants and gastronomy, and marketing strategies, among others.

In the airline business, OLAP techniques can be useful for identifying the average airport departure delay, the company with the highest average departure delay for a given airport, the average delay in departures and the average delay in flights by airport (Gioti et al., 2018; Höpken et al., 2014).

The hotel sector is the one that most benefits from OLAP techniques, as it allows for comparative analyses to be made in terms of reputation, or of benchmarking a competitive set, with a hotel image when compared to other hotels of the same segment, such as the average price per district and stars, number of hotels by district and stars or average price in the competitive set, contributing to a innovation that can propel businesses that adopt these techniques to high productivity and efficiency, among others (Höpken et al., 2014; Nyanga et al., 2019).

With regard to gastronomy, restaurants and beverages, OLAP techniques can help to improve the tourist experience, improve the competitiveness of restaurants, and in terms of sustainability can help restaurants monitor and control the quantity prepared, consumed and what is left per person and month, among other issues (Nyanga et al., 2019; Yu et al., 2019).

In regard to the area of tourist marketing, the potential of this technique for customer analysis in terms of behavior, segmentation and loyalty is highlighted (Höpken et al., 2014; Nyanga et al., 2019; Ramos et al., 2019).

Data Mining Techniques

It consists of the search for relationships, patterns or models that are implicit in the data stored in large databases (Santos & Ramos, 2009), with the aim to extract interesting knowledge (nontrivial, previously unknown and useful potentialities) from a large amount of data. The importance and applicability of these techniques emerged due to the enormity of data, high data dimensionality and heterogeneous and to the distributed data where the traditional techniques are inadequate to analyze and discover knowledge. The Data Mining can also be called by alternative names, such as: Knowledge Discovery in Databases (KDD), knowledge extraction, data patterns analysis, business intelligence, etc. The Data Mining process can be divide in six steps, as presented in the figure 3.

Figure 3. Data mining process steps (Author's elaboration)

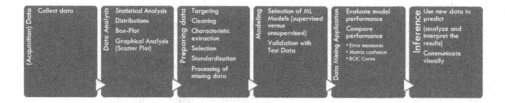

This consists of the search for relationships, patterns or models that are implicit in the data stored in large databases (Santos & Ramos, 2009), with the aim being to extract interesting knowledge (non-trivial, previously unknown and useful potentialities) from a large amount of data. The importance and applicability of these techniques emerged due to the enormity of data, high data dimensionality and heterogeneity, and to the distributed data where the traditional techniques are inadequate for analyzing and discovering knowledge. Data mining is also known by alternative names, such as knowledge discovery in databases (KDD), knowledge extraction, data patterns analysis, business intelligence, etc. The data mining process can be divided into six steps, as presented in Figure 3.

To transform the data into knowledge to support decision making, through the applications of data mining techniques, there is a methodology constituted of a set of steps whose complexity increases or decreases from one business to another, taking into consideration the aim of the analyses, the data dimension, and the nature of the economic activity, which implies a set of relations between the data.

Data mining can help to solve problems with two types of objectives: descriptive (or description) which allows for identifying rules that describe the analyzed data, for example: clustering, association rules, discovery of patterns methods; and predictive (or prediction) that uses some variables that allow the definition of models capable of predicting the future value of a variable, for example: classification and regression methods (António et al., 2022).

In accordance with Han et al. (2011, p. 23), "data mining has incorporated many techniques from other domains such as statistics, machine learning, pattern recognition, database and data warehouse systems, information retrieval, visualization", among others. Statistics investigate, analyze and interpret the data, while machine learning studies how computers can learn or improve their performance based on data (Egger, 2022). A database is a system that creates, manages, stores and processes data to produce new data that belongs to the organization and is associated with its business. Information retrieval is related to the task and concepts for searching for documents or for information in documents, where a typical approach, also called text mining, can be used to discover previously unknown information (Köseoglu et al., 2020), for example, in social media posts, where sentiment analysis has a great potential for tourism as the experience associated with travel involves emotions, helps to create new memories and enhances the discovery of new emotional ties between tourists and destinations, which through sharing and moments in social media contributes to influencing other travelers (Alaei et al., 2019).

Sentiment analysis can help Destination management organizations (DMO) to detect the sentiment associated with a tourism destination, in terms of destination image, gastronomic experience, hospitality quality service, brand monitoring and customer service (Alaei et al., 2019; Jiang et al., 2021; Thelwall, 2019; Yu & Zhang, 2020).

The application of data mining techniques to the tourism industry can contribute toward increasing the competitive intelligence of different types of tourism organizations, that are interlinked and complemented to create the multidimensional tourism product associated with a tourism destination, such as: accommodation, airlines, gastronomy and restaurants and marketing departments.

In hotels and similar areas, data mining techniques can contribute to predicting the expected sale of number of rooms next holiday and human resources management, considering forecasts, increasing customer loyalty, and managing online reputation (Moro et al., 2018).

In the airline industry the data mining techniques can also help to solve problems with objectives like forecasting how many customers will buy a trip to the Algarve, gathering information from the most chosen destinations, forecasting sales of air tickets and the distribution of seats and scheduling crews (Bogicevic et al., 2017; Chakrabarty, 2019), tourism demand forecast with neural networks (Wang, 2022), predict demand for bike-sharing with Machine Learning (Gao & Chen, 2022).

In the gastronomy and restaurant sector, data mining techniques can also help managers in terms of optimizing the meal production capacity, identifying the sentiment for a destination and the customer sentiment about a traditional dish, among others (Jiang et al., 2021; Yu & Zhang, 2020).

For marketing departments, whether belonging to a hotel, to a DMO, or associated with another type of tourism activity, data mining can help with tourist classification in segments to discover the characteristics that allows for grouping segments, what the attributes are that can contribute to a destination return or to increase loyalty, contributing to reputation intelligence (Femenia-Serra et al., 2022; Moro et al., 2019; Ramos et al., 2019; Xia et al., 2019).

Analytical Tools

In terms of analytical tools, also called analytical reports, data exploration and knowledge extraction are performed and used to produce enterprise reports or management reports, dashboards and kpi (Key Performance Indicators). This step considers the regular presentation of information to managers within an organization to support them in the decision-making process. These reports can take the form of graphs, text, and tables, and are usually released through an intranet (or "enterprise portal") as a regularly updated set of web pages, designated by a dashboard, which can show a range of indicators (KPI) on a page and a set of goals for various metrics. Alternatively, they can be sent directly to employees or simply printed and distributed in the traditional way (Ramos et al., 2019).

The reporting types can include results from data mining techniques, presented above; balanced scorecards methods, developed by Kaplan and Norton, that attempt to present an integrated vision of success in an organization; ad hoc analysis, usually performed once to deal with a specific situation and not reused, usually involving building a model in a spreadsheet to allow for the exploration of scenarios; interactive querying and OLAP, which allows for directly manipulating the presentation of the data; and KPI, also called management metrics, that are results-oriented, used to monitor and control business performance in order to quickly identify deviations associated with agreed targets (metrics or measures), which are controlled over a period of time.

SOLUTIONS AND RECOMMENDATIONS

With the abundance of information that is collected by tourism companies, it is necessary to ensure that they use tools with analytical capabilities, which are not limited to analyzing transactions such as relational database systems. In addition to this, it should also be considered that information proliferates on social media on a daily basis, with testimonials from tourists, through sharing their travel experiences, as well as their opinions about a product or service.

This entire panoply of information has to be analyzed, as in addition to guaranteeing the survival of companies, new ones appear every day in the business fabric of countries and the profit margin is increasingly small, so it is necessary to consider all the variables when measuring and evaluating the performance of our company.

Decisions taken by tourism managers cannot be based on intuition, as without analyzing the data they may not detect valuable knowledge about their customers, their suppliers, their competitors, the community or technological changes, that is, the environment in which economic activity develops, thus losing opportunities for differentiation, innovation and growth.

Tourism decision makers need to make efforts to use technology that produces knowledge, such as smart business tools that allow integration with data mining techniques, in addition to considering the acquisition of technology that allows a web search engine to search for information on the Internet, whether be it text, web pages, images, videos, etc.

The impact of Business Intelligence on Innovativeness and consequently on financial performance was investigated and confirmed (Huang et al., 2022), helps to learn and better manage the specifics of the business (Mohamad et al. 2022), as well as allowing the inclusion of queue mechanisms help to manage the complexity of data collection mechanisms from different sources (IoT), which make it possible to obtain quality data in order to use success metrics and improve the economic performance of the organization (Shao et al. ., 2022).

FUTURE RESEARCH DIRECTIONS

Business intelligence is one of the most successful data mining applications, and currently it should be combined with web search applications, which, in addition to the potential in tourism, are also admirable for bioinformatics and health areas. The combination of these two areas would be excellent to apply in health and wellness tourism, which is one of the trends in society today.

In the nineties, it was necessary to guarantee that tourist companies had a similar technological base to guarantee their survival. Since information is the "blood" of this activity, it was necessary to support the conditions for an efficient tourist distribution among all those involved. Currently, with the evolution of information systems and the web, data mining can be considered one of the natural consequences of this evolution (Han et al., 2021), which intensifies the potential of business intelligence for tourist organizations.

Just as business intelligence is linked to data mining, it is also linked to artificial intelligence, social media analytics, the digital economy, privacy protection systems and recommendation systems. Systems integration is increasingly more complete, especially if we take into account all the technologies associated with Industry 4.0 (Lv et al., 2022; Mitch, 2022).

The term "Industry 4.0" represents the technological evolution of integrated information systems in a single local application, to integrated systems in a virtual (cyber-physical) world, which includes the integration of all systems, communication between equipment, the Internet of Things (IoT), integrated into a virtual space (Xu et al., 2018). It is therefore necessary to consider a set of technological resources, such as: mechanisms that guarantee information security in the virtual space; augmented reality; big data; cloud computing; the IoT; autonomous robots; 3D printing; integrated systems; and mobile Internet (Mitch, 2022; Saturno et al., 2017).

The technology associated with Industry 4.0 applied in tourism activity "will boost the development of tourism companies leading to the development of conditions and business models associated with tourism 4.0" (Ramos & Brito, 2020, p. 368). This technological environment could be the main drive for innovation in the tourism activity, which will have an impact on consumers (tourist), producers (product suppliers and services) and government organizations (all infrastructures and the environment where tourism is developed).

Business intelligence tools integrated with the Industry 4.0 technological resources can contribute to accurately predicting customer behaviors and profiles, since the common characteristics of tourists who bought similar products from a tourism company can be found, can predict which tourists have left an organization and had joined the competitor, can help to detect fraudulent transactions/hacking, can help to increase the sales response of tourists, can integrate emotional intelligence and offer products and services that best fit the profile of the tourists, can predict potential tourists' behavior and buying patterns, can identify and recommend products or services purchased together by other tourists, and can also help to analyze trends in or the growth rate of a tourism organization's return of investment.

CONCLUSION

Business intelligence allows tourism organizations to survive, increase their competitiveness and gain access to competitive intelligence. Many decision makers of tourism organizations may still not value this technology or understand why it is important, so, in terms of the conclusion, the question should be asked: "Why should the tourism industry invest in business intelligence?"

To answer the previous question, and in general terms, business intelligence can help identify the destinations that are most sought after, how long the reservations are made for, the hotels/restaurants/agencies that generate the most revenue, and the product/event/dish that produces more profit, as well as compare homologated periods and see if a variation is positive or negative and compare bookings with cancellations.

Travel agencies should invest in business intelligence, as it can help them differentiate themselves, support the configuration of pricing strategies more precisely, discover new trends in the market and define the right promotion to the right customer.

With regard to hotels, an investment in business intelligence helps to analyze the past and to control the present, with the objectives of defining strategies for a better future, using their data to their advantage and generating a vision of the future, providing a holistic view of the entire hotel, including tangible and intangible assets, creating a sustainable business, and acting in accordance with the SDG (sustainable development goals) of the UNWTO (World Tourism Organization).

For airlines, catering, events and other complementary products and services, an investment in business intelligence also brings benefits identical to those mentioned for other activities.

Efforts should be made by tourist organizations so that they have access to real-time business intelligence and data analytics tool applications for big data management and information storage structures to manage a tourist destination and all businesses deployed there, as well as meeting the sustainability objectives of the UNWTO.

ACKNOWLEDGMENT

This paper is financed by National Funds provided by FCT- Foundation for Science and Technology through project UIDB/04020/2020.

REFERENCES

Alaei, A. R., Becken, S., & Stantic, B. (2019). Sentiment analysis in tourism: Capitalizing on big data. *Journal of Travel Research*, 58(2), 175–191. doi:10.1177/0047287517747753

Antonio, N., de Almeida, A., & Nunes, L. (2022). Data mining and predictive analytics for e-tourism. In Z. Xiang, M. Fuchs, U. Gretzel, & W. Höpken (Eds.), *Handbook of e-Tourism* (pp. 1–25). Springer.

B

Bogicevic, V., Yang, W., Bujisic, M., & Bilgihan, A. (2017). Visual data mining: Analysis of airline service quality attributes. *Journal of Quality Assurance in Hospitality & Tourism*, *18*(4), 509–530. doi:10.1080/1528008X.2017.1314799

Castillo-Clavero, A. M., Sánchez-Teba, E. M., & Martínez-Leiva, A. (2022). Big data and artificial intelligence in the touristic sector: Bibliometrics and applications. In *Handbook of Research on Smart Management for Digital Transformation* (pp. 1–26). IGI Global. doi:10.4018/978-1-7998-9008-9.ch001

Chaffey, D., & Ellis-Chadwick, F. (2019). Digital Marketing. Academic Press.

Chakrabarty, N. (2019). A data mining approach to flight arrival delay prediction for American airlines. In *2019 9th Annual Information Technology, Electromechanical Engineering and Microelectronics Conference* (pp. 102-107). IEEE. 10.1109/IEMECONX.2019.8876970

Choi, J., Yoon, J., Chung, J., Coh, B. Y., & Lee, J. M. (2020). Social media analytics and business intelligence research: A systematic review. *Information Processing & Management*, *57*(6), 102279. doi:10.1016/j.ipm.2020.102279

Di Tria, F., Lefons, E., & Tangorra, F. (2014). Big data warehouse automatic design methodology. In *Big Data Management, Technologies, and Applications* (pp. 115–149). IGI Global. doi:10.4018/978-1-4666-4699-5.ch006

Duffy, J. (2000). Measuring customer capital. *Strategy and Leadership*, *28*(5), 10–15. doi:10.1108/10878570010379392

Egger, R. (2022). Machine learning in tourism: A brief overview. In R. Egger (Ed.), *Applied Data Science in Tourism. Tourism on the Verge* (pp. 85–107). Springer. doi:10.1007/978-3-030-88389-8_6

Femenia-Serra, F., Alzua-Sorzabal, A., & Pousa-Unanue, A. (2022). Business intelligence and the public management of destinations: The view of DMOs. In *ENTER22 e-Tourism Conference* (pp. 417–422). Springer. doi:10.1007/978-3-030-94751-4_38

Gao, C., & Chen, Y. (2022). Using machine learning methods to predict demand for bike sharing. In *ENTER22 e-Tourism Conference* (pp. 282–296). Springer. doi:10.1007/978-3-030-94751-4_25

Gioti, H., Ponis, S. T., & Panayiotou, N. (2018). Social business intelligence: Review and research directions. *Journal of Intelligence Studies in Business*, *8*(2), 23–42. doi:10.37380/jisib.v8i2.320

Gretzel, U., Sigala, M., Xiang, Z., & Koo, C. (2015). Smart tourism: Foundations and developments. *Electronic Markets*, *25*(3), 179–188. doi:10.100712525-015-0196-8

Gupta, S., & Zeithaml, V. (2006). Customer metrics and their impact on financial performance. *Marketing Science*, *25*(6), 718–739. doi:10.1287/mksc.1060.0221

Han, J., Pei, J., & Kamber, M. (2011). *Data mining: Concepts and techniques*. Elsevier.

Höpken, W., Fuchs, M., Keil, D., & Lexhagen, M. (2015). Business intelligence for cross-process knowledge extraction at tourism destinations. *Information Technology & Tourism*, *15*(2), 101–130. doi:10.100740558-015-0023-2

Höpken, W., Fuchs, M., & Lexhagen, M. (2014). Tourism knowledge destination. In *Encyclopedia of business analytics and optimization* (pp. 2542–2556). IGI Global. doi:10.4018/978-1-4666-5202-6.ch227

Huang, Z. X., Savita, K. S., & Zhong-jie, J. (2022). The Business Intelligence impact on the financial performance of start-ups. *Information Processing & Management*, *59*(1), 102761. doi:10.1016/j.ipm.2021.102761

Jiang, Q., Chan, C. S., Eichelberger, S., Ma, H., & Pikkemaat, B. (2021). Sentiment analysis of online destination image of Hong Kong held by mainland Chinese tourists. *Current Issues in Tourism*, *24*(17), 2501–2522. doi:10.1080/13683500.2021.1874312

Kim, Y., Huang, J., & Emery, S. (2016). Garbage in, garbage out: Data collection, quality assessment and reporting standards for social media data use in health research, infodemiology and digital disease detection. *Journal of Medical Internet Research*, *18*(2), e41. doi:10.2196/jmir.4738 PMID:26920122

Köseoglu, M. A., Mehraliyev, F., Altin, M., & Okumus, F. (2020). Competitor intelligence and analysis (CIA) model and online reviews: Integrating big data text mining with network analysis for strategic analysis. *Tourism Review*, *76*(3), 529–552. doi:10.1108/TR-10-2019-0406

Li, X., Law, R., Xie, G., & Wang, S. (2021). Review of tourism forecasting research with internet data. *Tourism Management*, *83*, 104245. doi:10.1016/j.tourman.2020.104245

Liu, C., Williams, A. M., & Li, G. (2022). Knowledge management practices of tourism consultants: A project ecology perspective. *Tourism Management*, *91*, 104491. doi:10.1016/j.tourman.2022.104491

Lv, H., Shi, S., & Gursoy, D. (2022). A look back and a leap forward: A review and synthesis of big data and artificial intelligence literature in hospitality and tourism. *Journal of Hospitality Marketing & Management*, *31*(2), 145–175. doi:10.1080/19368623.2021.1937434

Mariani, M., Baggio, R., Fuchs, M., & Höepken, W. (2018). Business intelligence and big data in hospitality and tourism: A systematic literature review. *International Journal of Contemporary Hospitality Management*, *30*(12), 3514–3554. doi:10.1108/IJCHM-07-2017-0461

Martins, D., Ramos, C. M. Q., Rodrigues, J. M. F., Cardoso, P. J. S., Lam, R., & Serra, F. (2015). Challenges in building a big data warehouse applied to the hotel business intelligence. In *Proc. 6th Int. Conf. on Applied Informatics and Computing Theory (AICT'15), in Recent Research in Applied Informatics* (pp. 110-117). WSEAS.

Mitch, L. (2022). AI and big data in tourism. In R. Egger (Ed.), *Applied Data Science in Tourism. Tourism on the Verge* (pp. 3–15). Springer. doi:10.1007/978-3-030-88389-8_1

Mohamad, A. K., Jayakrishnan, M., & Yusof, M. M. (2022). Thriving information system through business intelligence knowledge management excellence framework. *Iranian Journal of Electrical and Computer Engineering*, *12*(1), 506–514. doi:10.11591/ijece.v12i1.pp506-514

Moro, S., Rita, P., & Oliveira, C. (2018). Factors influencing hotels' online prices. *Journal of Hospitality Marketing & Management*, *27*(4), 443–464. doi:10.1080/19368623.2018.1395379

Nyanga, C., Pansiri, J., & Chatibura, D. (2019). Enhancing competitiveness in the tourism industry through the use of business intelligence: A literature review. *Journal of Tourism Futures*, *6*(2), 139–151. doi:10.1108/JTF-11-2018-0069

Ramos, C. M., & Brito, I. S. (2020). The effects of industry 4.0 in tourism and hospitality and future trends in Portugal. In *The Emerald Handbook of ICT in Tourism and Hospitality* (pp. 367–378). Emerald Publishing Limited. doi:10.1108/978-1-83982-688-720201023

Ramos, C. M. Q., Casado-Molina, A. M., & Ignácio-Peláez, J. (2019). An innovative management perspective for organizations through a reputation intelligence management model. *International Journal of Information Systems in the Service Sector*, *11*(4), 1–20. doi:10.4018/IJISSS.2019100101

Santos, M., & Ramos, I. (2009). Business Intelligence (2nd ed.). FCA Editora.

Shao, C., Yang, Y., Juneja, S., & Seetharam, T. (2022). IoT data visualization for business intelligence in corporate finance. *Information Processing & Management*, *59*(1), 102736. doi:10.1016/j.ipm.2021.102736

Thelwall, M. (2019). Sentiment analysis for tourism. In M. Sigala, R. Rahimi, & M. Thelwall (Eds.), *Big Data and Innovation in Tourism, Travel, and Hospitality*. Springer. doi:10.1007/978-981-13-6339-9_6

Vajirakachorn, T., & Chongwatpol, J. (2017). Application of business intelligence in the tourism industry: A case study of a local food festival in Thailand. *Tourism Management Perspectives*, *23*, 75–86. doi:10.1016/j.tmp.2017.05.003

Valeri, M. (2020). Blockchain technology: adoption perspectives in tourism. In *Entrepreneurship and Organizational Change* (pp. 27–35). Springer. doi:10.1007/978-3-030-35415-2_3

Vasconcelos, J. B., & Barão, A. (2017). *Ciência dos dados nas organizações*. FCA Editora.

Wang, L. (2022). Tourism demand forecast based on adaptive neural network technology in business intelligence. *Computational Intelligence and Neuroscience*, *2022*, 1–14. doi:10.1155/2022/1823762 PMID:35087579

Xia, H., Vu, H. Q., Lan, Q., Law, R., & Li, G. (2019). Identifying hotel competitiveness based on hotel feature ratings. *Journal of Hospitality Marketing & Management*, *28*(1), 81–100. doi:10.1080/19368623.2018.1504366

Xiang, Z., Stienmetz, J., & Fesenmaier, D. R. (2021). Smart tourism design: Launching the annals of tourism research curated collection on designing tourism places. *Annals of Tourism Research*, *86*, 103154. doi:10.1016/j.annals.2021.103154

Xu, L. D., Xu, E. L., & Li, L. (2018). Industry 4.0: State of the art and future trends. *International Journal of Production Research*, *56*(8), 2941–2962. doi:10.1080/00207543.2018.1444806

Yiu, L. D., Yeung, A. C., & Cheng, T. E. (2020). The impact of business intelligence systems on profitability and risks of firms. *International Journal of Production Research*, *59*(13), 3951–3974. doi:10.1080/00207543.2020.1756506

Yu, C. E., & Zhang, X. (2020). The embedded feelings in local gastronomy: A sentiment analysis of online reviews. *Journal of Hospitality and Tourism Technology*, *11*(3), 461–478. doi:10.1108/JHTT-02-2019-0028

Yu, D., Xu, D., Wang, D., & Ni, Z. (2019). Hierarchical topic modelling of Twitter data for online analytical processing. *IEEE Access: Practical Innovations, Open Solutions*, *7*, 12373–12385. doi:10.1109/ACCESS.2019.2891902

KEY TERMS AND DEFINITIONS

Business Analytics: Combination of Business Intelligence processes with machine learning algorithms, applied to historical data to obtain new insights that enhance decision-making suited to the company's business.

Business Intelligence: This results from information systems that combine data with analytical tools to provide information relevant to decision making while seeking to improve the quality and availability of this information.

Data Mining: Uses a set of techniques from Statistics, Machine Learning, Pattern Recognition, and Database Management Systems that make it possible to explore a collection of data to detect patterns and discover knowledge in those data.

Decision Support Systems: An interactive data/information processing and visualization system, which supports decision-making, is user-friendly enough to be used by users, presents information in a format and terminology suitable for its decision-makers.

Digital Economy: Designates the new economic relationships that integrate the internet to sell and distribute goods and services.

Knowledge Management: Multidisciplinary approach, expressed through a process that enables the creation, sharing and management of knowledge in an organization to achieve organizational objectives by making the best use of this knowledge.

Machine Learning: Specific aspect of Artificial Intelligence, which considers that systems can learn from data, identify patterns, and make decisions with a minimum of human intervention, gradually improving its accuracy.

Sentiment Analysis: Also known as opinion mining, it is an analysis carried out on textual data to support companies in monitoring customers' opinions about their brand or product to understand their needs and preferences.

Social Media: These aggregates of online communications channels can be considered tools that can be used to define new business models strategically, considering analyses of community user-generated content and information shared with other members of these online communities.

Tourism Experience: This is a set of activities in which individuals engage on their terms, such as pleasant and memorable places, allowing each tourist to build their own travel experiences so that these satisfy a wide range of individual needs, from pleasure to a search for meaning.

Customer Churn Reduction Based on Action Rules and Collaboration

Yuehua Duan

University of North Carolina at Charlotte, USA

Zbigniew W. Ras

iD https://orcid.org/0000-0002-8619-914X

University of North Carolina at Charlotte, USA & Polish-Japanese Academy of Information Technology in Warsaw, Poland

INTRODUCTION

Customer churn, also known as customer attrition, refers to the loss of existing customers who cease the relationship with an organization in a period of time (Renjith, 2017; Jain & Jana, 2021). Customer churn leads to lower volume of service consumption, reduced product purchase, less customer referrals. Furthermore, the cost of acquiring a new customer is much higher than the cost of retaining an existing customer (Siber, 1997). Reducing customer churn can be significantly beneficial (Van den Poel & Lariviere, 2004; Kowalczyk & Slisser, 1997). For example, in financial services, a 5% increase in customer retention produces more than a 25% increase in profit (Reichheld and Detrick, 2003).

It is imperative to build a recommender system that can provide effective recommendations to reduce customer churn. Recommender system is a subclass of information filtering systems that seek to predict the rating or preference a user would give to an item (Ricci, Rokach, & Shapira, 2011). According to the techniques applied, recommender systems are categorized to - collaborative filtering recommender systems, content-based recommender systems, demographic recommender systems, knowledge-based recommender systems, community-based recommender systems, and hybrid recommender systems (Su & Taghi, 2009). The process of building a knowledge-based recommender system is facilitated with the use of knowledge base, which contains data about rules and similarity functions to use during the retrieval process (Jannach, Zanker, Felfernig, & Friedrich, 2011). It relies more on the domain knowledge, by utilizing the expert knowledge to decide which item to recommend, and to what extent this item is meaningful and useful to the user.

Action rule mining is one of the technologies that have been successfully applied in building knowledge-based recommender systems to address the customer churn issue (Tarnowska & Ras, 2019; Tarnowska, Ras, & Daniel, 2020). In a knowledge-based recommender system based on classification rules and action rules, action rule mining is a major step in extracting knowledge in the process of recognizing the recommendations. The quality of action rules determines the effectiveness and coverage of recommender systems. Normally, support and confidence are used to measure the quality of discovered action rules (Ras & Wieczorkowska, 2000; Tzacheva, Sankar, Ramachandran, & Shankar, 2016). In practical applications, action rules are regarded as interesting only if their support and confidence exceed the predefined threshold values. Moreover, if an action rule has a large support and high confidence, it indicates that this action can be applied on a large portion of customers with a high chance (Ras & Tsay, 2003) to be successful. To increase the efficiency of knowledge-based recommender systems which use

DOI: 10.4018/978-1-7998-9220-5.ch035

Copyright © 2023, IGI Global. Copying or distributing in print or electronic forms without written permission of IGI Global is prohibited.

action rule mining for reducing customer churn, it is necessary to improve the quality of discovered action rules. However, there is little research work done which focuses on improving the quality of discovered action rules.

To bridge forementioned gap, the authors propose a guided (by threshold) agglomerative clustering algorithm to improve the confidence and coverage of discovered action rules. Assume that there are many similar businesses called clients and each one is faced with a customer attrition problem. Each client is represented by a decision table describing its customers status (Tarnowska et al., 2020; Duan & Ras, 2021). Customer status, which is a decision attribute, has three values: active, leaving, and lost. In the process of action rule mining, the goal is to discover action patterns which will change customer status from leaving to active. The proposed algorithm aims to improve the quality of action rules extracted from a dataset of a given client by utilizing the knowledge extracted from other semantically similar clients to that given client. The idea is to pick up clients which are not only semantically similar but also which are doing better in business than a given client. By doing that, the given client can follow business recommendations coming from other semantically similar and better performing clients. The algorithm is guided by a threshold value targeting the minimal acceptable improvements in confidence and coverage of discovered action rules. If the improvement is lower than this threshold, algorithm stops.

BACKGROUND

Over the years, there have been many recommender systems proposed to address the customer churn issues. Kim and Yoon (2004) investigated the strategies of businesses in Korean mobile telecommunication services to increase customer loyalty. Their conclusion is that mobile carriers must focus on service quality and offer customer-oriented services to heighten customer satisfaction. Daskalaki, Kopanas, Goudara, and Avouris (2003) built a decision support system to handle customer insolvency for a large telecommunication company. Duan and Ras (2021) designed and implemented a recommender system that can provide actionable recommendations for improving customer churn rate. Wang, Chiang, Hsu, Lin, and Lin (2009) used Decision Tree algorithm to analyze more than 4000 members over three months. The conditional rules produced by Decision Tree algorithm show the characteristics of customer behavior that can lead to customer loss. They use such rules as strategy recommendations to prevent future customer loss.

Action rules are widely applied in building knowledge-based recommender systems. The concept of action rule was proposed by Ras and Wieczorkowska (2000). Action rule is defined as a rule extracted from a decision system that describes a transition of its objects from one decision state to another. Informally, it is defined as a term: $\left[(\omega) \wedge (\alpha \rightarrow \beta) \Rightarrow (\phi \rightarrow \psi)\right]$, where ω denotes a conjunction of fixed stable attributes called the header of the rule, $(\alpha \rightarrow \beta)$ are proposed changes in values of flexible attributes, and $(\phi \rightarrow \psi)$ is a desired change of the decision attribute value. To give an example of an action rule, let's first give the definition of information system. An information system is defined as a pair $S=(U,A)$, where U is a nonempty, finite set of objects called the universe. A is a nonempty, finite set of attributes i.e., $a: U \rightarrow V_a$ for $a \in A$, where V_a is called the domain of a (*Pawlak*, 1981). In an information system S shown in Table 1, there are five objects in X, that is $X=\{x_1, x_2, x_3, x_4, x_5\}$. $A=\{a,c,d\}$ and $V=\{a_1, a_2, c_1, c_2, d_1, d_2\}$. Assume that attribute a is stable and attribute c is flexible. The decision attribute is d. Example of an action rule is $\left[(a,a_2) \wedge (c,c_2 \rightarrow c_1) \Rightarrow (d,d_1 \rightarrow d_2)\right]$. The meaning of this action rule is that for objects having properties (a,a_2), (c,c_2) and (d,d_1) if their flexible attribute value changes from c_2 to c_1, then it is expected that the value d_1 will change to d_2.

Table 1. Information system S

U	a	c	d
x_1	a_1	c_1	d_2
x_2	a_1	c_2	d_2
x_3	a_1	c_2	d_1
x_4	a_2	c_1	d_2
x_5	a_2	c_2	d_1

Support, confidence, and coverage are used to measure the quality of action rules. To give the definition of support, confidence, and coverage of action rule, let's assume that for the action rule $r = \left[(a, a_2) \wedge (c, c_2 \rightarrow c_1) \Rightarrow (d, d_1 \rightarrow d_2) \right]$, Y_1 is the set of objects having description $[(a, a_2) \wedge (c, c_2)]$, and let Y_2 be the set of objects having description $[(a, a_2) \wedge (c, c_1)]$. Z_1 is the set of objects having property (d, d_1) and Z_2 be the set of objects having property (d, d_2).

Then, support of r is defined as

$$Support(r) = card(Y_1 \cap Z_1) \tag{1}$$

Confidence of r is defined as

$$Confidence(r) = \frac{card(Y_1 \cap Z_1)}{card(Y_1)} * \frac{card(Y_2 \cap Z_2)}{card(Y_2)} \tag{2}$$

Coverage of r is defined as the number of objects transferred from Z_1 to Z_2.

There are two approaches for action rule mining: Rule-based approach and Object-based approach. In rule-based approach, prior extraction of classification rules is needed. DEAR (Discovering Extended Action-Rules) (Ras & Tsay, 2003) and DEAR2 (Tsay & Ras, 2005) belong to this category. In object-based approach, action rules are extracted directly from the information system. For instance, ARED (Action Rule Extraction from a Decision Table) is an example of such a system (Im, 2008).

To raise the efficiency of the knowledge-based recommender system that is based on action rules, researchers have explored different solutions to get more profitable action rules. Ras and Tzacheva (2003) proposed the concept of semi-stable attributes. They used a query answering system based on distributed knowledge mining as platform to introduce a non-standard interpretation of semi-stable attributes which allowed them to treat such attributes as flexible. Hence, more action rules can be discovered as the result of decreasing the number of stable attributes in the system. Ras and Tzacheva (2005) proposed the notion of a cost and feasibility of an action rule. They also proposed a heuristic strategy for constructing feasible action rules which have possibly the lowest cost. Tzacheva, Bagavathi, and Suryanarayanaprasad (2018) proposed an algorithm for constructing action graphs and using them to discover actionable patterns of the lowest cost. These research works present different ways that researchers have explored to get more profitable action rules. However, there is little research work conducted to improve the confidence of the discovered action rules.

FOCUS OF THE ARTICLE

To improve the quality of action rules extracted from a dataset representing a given client, we propose a guided (by threshold) agglomerative clustering algorithm which is using knowledge extracted from datasets representing other semantically similar clients to a given client. The algorithm contains five steps:

- Some widely used customer churn classifiers are compared on a client dataset, and then the overall best classifier is chosen.
- The semantic similarity-based distance between any two clients is calculated using the confidence of their best classifiers, and then the semantic similarity-based distance matrix for all clients is built.
- As the result of the agglomerative clustering algorithms, a dendrogram is built based on semantic similarity-based distance matrix. The nearest neighbors of the target client are identified. Such clients are defined as candidate clients.
- The performance scores of the candidate clients and the target client are compared. Candidate clients whose performance scores are higher than performance scores of the target client are the one which datasets are used for extending the dataset of the target client.
- The action rules are extracted from the dataset of a target client as well as from its extended dataset, and then the confidence of the two resulting action rule sets is compared. The algorithm is guided by a threshold value checking how large is the improvement in confidence of discovered action rules by extending the initial dataset of a target client. If the improvement is lower than this threshold, the algorithm stops.

SOLUTIONS AND RECOMMENDATIONS

Guided (by Threshold) Agglomerative Clustering Algorithm

As shown in Figure 1, the guided (by threshold) agglomerative clustering algorithm comprises five synergistic modules - the classification module, the semantic similarity module, the hierarchical clustering module, the client extending module, and the action rule mining module. Assume there are Z similar businesses clients $\{C_1,...,C_z\}$, and each one is faced with a customer attrition problem. Client C_t which is deeply suffering from the customer churn issue, is the target client. The target dataset is defined as D_t. We also define εt as the threshold for a confidence improvement of discovered action rules.

Classification

Two clients are seen as semantically similar if they agree (to a certain level) on the knowledge concerning the classification of active, leaving, and lost customers. To evaluate the semantic similarity between two clients, the precision of the classifier is utilized to calculate the semantic similarity score between two clients. Moreover, the higher accuracy of a classifier leads to higher quality of action rules. Therefore, in classification, we focus on recognizing the best classifier. Some widely used classification algorithms are picked and compared in terms of the classifier precision in customer status which can be active, leaving and lost. Without loss of generality, Random Forest, Artificial Neural Network (ANN), Naive

Figure 1. Design of the algorithm

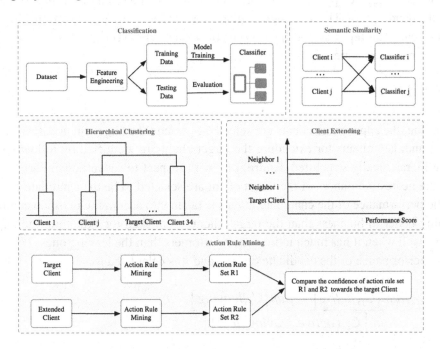

Bayes, Support Vector Machines (SVM) and Extreme Gradient Boosting (XGBoost) have been picked for classification performance comparison.

Semantic Similarity

Kuang, Daniel, Johnston, and Ras (2014) proposed the notion of semantic similarity between two clients by utilizing classification rules discovered from the two corresponding datasets. Inspired by their idea, we utilize the precision of the best classifier to define the semantic similarity between two clients. Assume *Classifier*[i] and *Classifier*[j] are the classifiers for client C_i and client C_j. $Precision_{i\_i}$ is the precision of applying *Classifier*[i] to client C_i. $Precision_{i\_j}$ is the precision of applying *Classifier*[i] to client C_j. $Precision_{j\_j}$ is the precision of applying *Classifier*[j] to client C_j. $Precision_{j\_i}$ is the precision of applying *Classifier*[j] to client C_i. The semantic similarity between clients C_i and C_j is

$$SemSim = \frac{\left|Precision_{i\_i} - Precision_{i\_j}\right| + \left|Precision_{j\_j} - Precision_{j\_i}\right|}{2} \tag{3}$$

Based on the above definition, the semantic similarity score between each pair of the clients is calculated. Then, a semantic similarity-based distance matrix is built based on the semantic similarity scores between all pairs of clients.

Hierarchical Clustering

Agglomerative clustering initializes a cluster system as a set of singleton clusters and proceeds iteratively with merging of the most appropriate cluster(s) until the stopping criterion is achieved (Berkhin, 2006).

In hierarchical clustering, we apply agglomerative clustering on the semantic similarity-based distance matrix to build a dendrogram. The dendrogram gives the semantic similarity relationship among all the clients, in which each leaf represents a client. When the distance between two leaves is smaller, then the two leaves share more semantic similarity.

Client Extending

In client extending, the appropriate clients are selected to extend the target client dataset to an extended dataset. First, candidate clients for extending the target client are identified by following the bottom-up path in the hierarchically structured dendrogram with respect to semantic similarity. Based on the dendrogram, the nearest neighbors of the target client are selected to be the candidate clients. In addition to that, the performance of the candidate clients is taken into account. Only such candidate clients, which are doing better in business than the target client, are picked for extending the target client. A client performs well when it has much more active customers than the leaving ones. *Per_Score* is used to evaluate the performance of the candidate clients, and it is calculated as:

$$Per\_Score_{C_l} = \frac{Num[C_l, active] - Num[C_l, leaving]}{Num[C_l, (active, leaving, lost)]} \tag{4}$$

where C_l refers to a certain client. By $Num[C_l, active]$, we mean the number of active instances in the dataset of client C_l. Similarly, $Num[C_l, leaving]$ means the number of leaving instances in client C_l. Finally, the term $Num[C_l(active, leaving, lost)]$ presents the total number of instances in the dataset of client C_l. The higher is the score, the better performance of the client. Only candidate clients with performance score *Per_Score* that is higher than the target client are used to enlarge the client dataset. We define the extended dataset as D_e.

Action Rule Mining

We extract action rules from the target dataset D_t and extended dataset D_e, respectively. $R_{extended}$ is the set of action rules extracted from this extended dataset. R_{target} stands for action rules extracted from the target client dataset. The confidence of the two action rule sets towards the target dataset is compared. Now, we give the definition of the confidence of an action rule set towards a dataset. Let R be the action rule set extracted from a dataset D There are M action rules in total. Let r_i denotes an action rule in R, while $Conf\_r_i$ denotes its confidence, and N_i denotes the supporting set of r_i (there is no overlapping between sets N_i and N_j). We define the confidence of action rule set R towards dataset D as

$$Confidence_{R\_D} = \frac{\sum_{i=1}^{M}(Conf\_r_i * card(N_i))}{\sum_{i=1}^{M} card(N_i)} \tag{5}$$

Based on this value, the confidence improvement is evaluated. If the improvement is lower than the predefined threshold εt algorithm stops.

Recommendations

When applied in business, the enhanced/improved action rules can be applied in developing actionable strategies for decision-makers to decrease customer churn. Compared with current action rule mining system, the proposed algorithm has two advantages. Firstly, it can generate action rules of higher quality. Such action rules will cover more customers with a better chance to succeed in churn reduction, and the same it will raise the efficiency of the recommender system. Secondly, this algorithm is guided by a threshold value predefined by the managerial personnel. Therefore, when applied the algorithm in building action rule-based recommender system to reduce customer churn, the decision-makers are provided with much more flexibility, and they can optimize their resources in customer churn reduction.

The proposed guided (by threshold) agglomerative clustering algorithm utilizes the hidden knowledge discovered from other semantically similar clients to a given client with a goal to improve the quality of action rules towards the targeted client. It can be a valuable and inspirational reference to other scholars who want to explore the improvement of action rules mining. This algorithm can also be applied to other fields where action rule plays an important role. For instance, the algorithm can be applied to medical diagnosis and treatment (Tarnowska, 2021; Wasyluk, Ras, & Wyrzykowska, 2008), art (Powell, Gelich, & Ras, 2021), and so on.

FUTURE RESEARCH DIRECTIONS

Action rule mining is an important and promising technology that can be applied to build recommender systems for reducing customer churn. To improve the quality of the discovered action rules of the target client, we propose to utilize the knowledge from the other semantically similar but better performing clients. The semantic similarity between two clients is defined by utilizing the precision of the classifier. The dendrogram which is used to reflect the semantic similarity-based relationship among these clients is built. In the future, one of the research directions is to explore other definitions of semantic similarity between two clients. Moreover, other clustering methods should be taken into consideration.

Action rules of higher quality not only mean larger confidence and support, but also require lower cost when applied into practice. Therefore, one future research direction is to add the cost factor into consideration. In this study, the target client is extended with clients that meet two requirements: clients that are its nearest neighbors with respect to the semantic similarity-based dendrogram; clients that are doing better than the target client. In the future, when selecting clients to be used for extending the target client, the cost efficiency should also be considered.

CONCLUSION

Customer churn is a major issue to most of the companies, and recommender system that is utilizing action rule mining technology shows its great value in reducing customer churn. In action rule mining, confidence, support, and coverage are used to measure the quality of the discovered action rules. Action rules with higher confidence and support are more useful to users. However, there is little research work focused on improving the quality of the action rules. In this chapter, we propose a guided (by threshold) agglomerative clustering algorithm to improve the quality of discovered action rules. The algorithm contains five synergistic modules: classification, semantic similarity, hierarchical clustering, client extending, and action rule mining. In the context of customer churn, two clients are seen as semantically similar if they agree on the knowledge concerning active, leaving, and lost customers. To evaluate the semantic similarity between two clients, the precision of the best classifier is utilized to calculate the semantic similarity score between two clients. The semantic similarity scores of each pair of the clients are utilized to build a semantic similarity-based distance matrix. Based on the matrix, a hierarchically structured dendrogram is built. With the help of the dendrogram, the semantically similar clients to a given client are identified. Such clients are defined as candidate clients. Then the performance scores of the candidate clients and the target client are compared. Those clients whose performance scores, are higher than the target client, are selected for dataset extension of a targeted client. Then action rules are extracted from the target dataset and the extended dataset, and we get two action rule sets: the target action rule set and the extended action rule set. Then the confidence of these two action rule sets is calculated and compared. If the confidence improvement is lower than the predefined threshold, algorithm stops.

REFERENCES

Berkhin, P. (2006). A survey of clustering data mining techniques. In *Grouping multidimensional data* (pp. 25–71). Springer. doi:10.1007/3-540-28349-8_2

Burez, J., & den Poel, D. (2007). CRM at a pay-TV company: Using analytical models to reduce customer attrition by targeted marketing for subscription services. *Expert Systems with Applications*, *32*(2), 277–288. doi:10.1016/j.eswa.2005.11.037

Daskalaki, S., Kopanas, I., Goudara, M., & Avouris, N. (2003). Data mining for decision support on customer insolvency in telecommunications business. *European Journal of Operational Research*, *145*(2), 239–255. doi:10.1016/S0377-2217(02)00532-5

Duan, Y., & Ras, Z. (2022). Recommendation System for Improving Churn Rate based on Action Rules and Sentiment Mining. *International Journal of Data Mining. Modelling and Management*, *14*(4), 2. doi:10.1504/IJDMMM.2022.10041468

Im, S., & Raś, Z. W. (2008). Action rule extraction from a decision table: ARED. In *Foundations of Intelligent Systems, Proceedings of ISMIS'08*. Springer. 10.1007/978-3-540-68123-6_18

Jain, N., Tomar, A., & Jana, P. K. (2021). A novel scheme for employee churn problem using multi-attribute decision making approach and machine learning. *Journal of Intelligent Information Systems*, *56*(2), 279–302. doi:10.100710844-020-00614-9

Jannach, D., Zanker, M., Felfernig, A., & Friedrich, G. (2011). An introduction to recommender systems. Cambridge.

Kim, H.-S., & Yoon, C.-H. (2004). Determinants of subscriber churn and customer loyalty in the Korean mobile telephony market. *Telecommunications Policy*, *28*(9–10), 751–765. doi:10.1016/j.telpol.2004.05.013

Kowalczyk, W., & Slisser, F. (1997). Modelling customer retention with rough data models. In *European Symposium on Principles of Data Mining and Knowledge Discovery*. Springer. 10.1007/3-540-63223-9_101

Kuang, J., Daniel, A., Johnston, J., & Raś, Z. W. (2014). Hierarchically structured recommender system for improving NPS of a company. *International Conference on Rough Sets and Current Trends in Computing*, 347–357. 10.1007/978-3-319-08644-6_36

Lee, A. S. H., Claudia, N., Zainol, Z., & Chan, K. W. (2019). Decision Tree: Customer churn analysis for a loyalty program using data mining algorithm. *International Conference on Soft Computing in Data Science*, 14–27. 10.1007/978-981-15-0399-3_2

Pawlak, Z. (1981). Information systems theoretical foundations. *Information Systems, 6*(3), 205–218. doi:10.1016/0306-4379(81)90023-5

Powell, L., Gelich, A., & Ras, Z.W. (2021). How to raise artwork prices using action rules, personalization, and artwork visual features. *Journal of Intelligent Information Systems, 57*(3), 583-599. doi:10.1007/s10844-021-00660-x

Ras, Z. W., Dardzinska, A., Tsay, L. S., & Wasyluk, H. (2008). Association action rules. *IEEE/ICDM Workshop on Mining Complex Data (MCD 2008)*, 283-290. 10.1109/ICDMW.2008.66

Ras, Z. W., & Tsay, L. S. (2003). Discovering extended action-rules (System DEAR). In *Intelligent Information Processing and Web Mining*. Springer. doi:10.1007/978-3-540-36562-4_31

Ras, Z. W., & Tzacheva, A. A. (2003). Discovering semantic inconsistencies to improve action rules mining. In *Intelligent Information Processing and Web Mining*. Springer. doi:10.1007/978-3-540-36562-4_32

Ras, Z. W., & Tzacheva, A. A. (2005). In search for action rules of the lowest cost. In, Security and Rescue Techniques in Multiagent Systems, 261-27. doi:10.1007/3-540-32370-8_19

Ras, Z. W., & Wieczorkowska, A. (2000). Action-Rules: How to increase profit of a company. *Principles of Data Mining and Knowledge Discovery, Proceedings of PKDD'00*, 587-592. 10.1007/3-540-45372-5_70

Reichheld, F., & Detrick, C. (2003). Loyalty: A prescription for cutting costs. *Marketing Management, 12*(5), 24–24.

Renjith, S. (2015). *An integrated framework to recommend personalized retention actions to control B2C E-commerce customer churn.* ArXiv Preprint ArXiv:1511.06975.

Renjith, S. (2017). B2C E-Commerce customer churn management: Churn detection using support vector machine and personalized retention using hybrid recommendations. *International Journal on Future Revolution in Computer Science & Communication Engineering, 3*(11), 34–39.

Ricci, F., Rokach, L., & Shapira, B. (2011). Introduction to recommender systems handbook. In *Recommender systems handbook* (pp. 1–35). Springer. doi:10.1007/978-0-387-85820-3_1

Siber, R. (1997). Combating the Churn Phenomenon-As the problem of customer defection increases, carriers are having to find new strategies for keeping subscribers happy. Telecommunications-International Edition, 31(10), 77-81.

Su, X., & Khoshgoftaar, T. M. (2009). A survey of collaborative filtering techniques. *Advances in Artificial Intelligence, 2009*, 1–19. Advance online publication. doi:10.1155/2009/421425

Tarnowska, K., & Ras, Z.W. (2019). Sentiment Analysis of Customer Data. *Web Intelligence Journal, 17*(4), 343-363. doi:10.3233/WEB-190423

Tarnowska, K., & Ras, Z. W. (2021). NLP-based Customer Loyalty Improvement Recommender System (CLIRS2). Big Data and Cognitive Computing Journal, 5(1), 4. doi:10.3390/bdcc5010004

Tarnowska, K., Ras, Z.W., & Daniel, L. (2020). Recommender system for improving customer loyalty. *Studies in Big Data, 55.*

Tarnowska, K. A. (2021). Emotion-Based Music Recommender System for Tinnitus Patients (EMOTIN). In *Recommender Systems for Medicine and Music. Studies in Computational Intelligence, 946.* Springer. doi:10.1007/978-3-030-66450-3_13

Tsay, L. S., & Ras, Z. W. (2005). Action rules discovery: System DEAR2, method and experiments. *Journal of Experimental & Theoretical Artificial Intelligence, 17*(1-2), 119–128. doi:10.1080/095281 30512331315855

Tzacheva, A. A., Bagavathi, A., & Suryanarayanaprasad, S. C. (2018, September). In Search of Actionable Patterns of Lowest Cost–A Scalable Action Graph Method. *2018 IEEE First International Conference on Artificial Intelligence and Knowledge Engineering (AIKE)*, 119-124. 10.1109/AIKE.2018.00026

Tzacheva, A. A., Sankar, C. C., Ramachandran, S., & Shankar, R. A. (2016, September). Support confidence and utility of action rules triggered by meta-actions. *2016 IEEE International Conference on Knowledge Engineering and Applications (ICKEA)*, 113-120. 10.1109/ICKEA.2016.7803003

Van den Poel, D., & Lariviere, B. (2004). Customer attrition analysis for financial services using proportional hazard models. *European Journal of Operational Research, 157*(1), 196–217. doi:10.1016/S0377-2217(03)00069-9

Wang, Y. F., Chiang, D. A., Hsu, M. H., Lin, C. J., & Lin, I. L. (2009). A recommender system to avoid customer churn: A case study. *Expert Systems with Applications, 36*(4), 8071–8075. doi:10.1016/j.eswa.2008.10.089

Wasyluk, H., Ras, Z. W., & Wyrzykowska, E. (2008). Application of action rules to hepar clinical decision support system. Experimental and Clinical Hepatology, 4(2), 46-48.

ADDITIONAL READING

Clauset, A., Newman, M. E., & Moore, C. (2004). Finding community structure in very large networks. *Physical Review. E, 70*(6), 066111. doi:10.1103/PhysRevE.70.066111 PMID:15697438

Ras, Z. W., & Tzacheva, A. A. (2003). Discovering semantic inconsistencies to improve action rules mining. In *Intelligent Information Processing and Web Mining* (pp. 301–310). Springer. doi:10.1007/978-3-540-36562-4_32

Ras, Z. W., Tzacheva, A. A., Tsay, L. S., & Giirdal, O. (2005, September). Mining for interesting action rules. *IEEE/WIC/ACM International Conference on Intelligent Agent Technology*, 187-193. 10.1109/IAT.2005.98

Rokach, L., & Maimon, O. (2005). Clustering methods. In *Data mining and knowledge discovery handbook* (pp. 321–352). Springer. doi:10.1007/0-387-25465-X_15

Tzacheva, A. A., Sankar, C. C., Ramachandran, S., & Shankar, R. A. (2016, September). Support confidence and utility of action rules triggered by meta-actions. *2016 IEEE International Conference on Knowledge Engineering and Applications (ICKEA)*, 113-120. 10.1109/ICKEA.2016.7803003

Vafeiadis, T., Diamantaras, K. I., Sarigiannidis, G., & Chatzisavvas, K. C. (2015). A comparison of machine learning techniques for customer churn prediction. *Simulation Modelling Practice and Theory*, *55*, 1–9. doi:10.1016/j.simpat.2015.03.003

KEY TERMS AND DEFINITIONS

Accuracy: A measurement that gives the closeness of the measured value to the true value.

Action Rule: A rule that can recommend actions which can lead an object change to a more profitable state based on transformation of flexible attributes.

Classifier: A classifier is an algorithm that can classify data into labeled classes.

Clustering: A task that is grouping objects into clusters by following the rules that objects in the same group share more precisely than those in other groups.

Customer Churn: A phenomenon that customers choose to stop using the product or services of a company.

Dendrogram: A diagram representing a tree structure.

Semantic Similarity: A metric that defines the distance between items based on the likeness of their meaning.

How Artificial Intelligence Is Impacting Marketing?

Poonam Oberoi
Excelia Business School, France

INTRODUCTION

The aim of this chapter is to present the tertiary literature on AI and to discuss the future of AI's impact in the field of marketing. The literature on AI for marketing is growing steadily. This chapter starts by describing some key concepts of the AI literature. It then illustrates a few important consequences of AI on businesses in general. Finally, it unfolds some of the important ways on how AI is already impacting, and will continue to impact, marketing managers' activities, capabilities, and performance. The chapter ends by discussing the future implication for marketing managers.

BACKGROUND

According to the latest study of International Data Corporation (IDC) (accessed on 01/09/2021, source: https://www.idc.com/getdoc.jsp?containerId=US48125621):

The AI software market grew rapidly during 2020, and with accelerated digital disruption, we expect this market to continue to grow over the forecast period [i.e. 2021–2025]. IDC forecasts the overall AI software market will approach $596 billion in revenue in 2025 at a Compound Annual Growth Rate (CAGR) of 17.7%, with the AI-centric part to approach $123.3 billions at a CAGR of 27.8% over the forecast period," says Ritu Jyoti, group vice president of Artificial Intelligence and Automation Research with IDC's software market research and advisory practice. "Today, AI expertise is focused more on developing commercial applications that optimize efficiencies in existing industries. Acceleration of AI adoption and proliferation of smart, intuitive Machine Learning (ML)/Data Learning (DL) algorithms will spawn the creation of new industries and business segments and overall will trigger new opportunities for business monetization.

AI, and Related Concepts:

AI technologies are being used in manufacturing robots, self-driving cars, smart assistants, proactive healthcare management practices and disease mapping, automated financial investing, virtual travel booking agent, social media monitoring, conversational bot, and natural language processing tools. Let us consider certain examples of some companies from different industries and how they are using AI. iRobot is a company from the consumer electronics industry which has developed Roomba 980, a smart robotic vacuum which can use AI to scan room size, and identify obstacles, and decide the most efficient cleaning routes and how much vacuuming is required. Hanson Robotics, a company based in Hong Kong, has developed Sophia, an incredibly advanced social learning humanoid robot. Sophia can communicate using natural language and human-like facial expressions. Such humanoid robots can have vast con-

DOI: 10.4018/978-1-7998-9220-5.ch036

Copyright © 2023, IGI Global. Copying or distributing in print or electronic forms without written permission of IGI Global is prohibited.

sumer and commercial applications, for example in university research and medical training application. Emotech, a company in the Robotics and AI industry based in UK, has created a voice-controlled AI assistant with evolving personality, named Olly. Thanks to evolving machine learning algorithms Olly can study a human's facial expressions, voice inflections, verbal patterns, etc., and can proactively start conversations and is also capable of movement so as to orient itself towards the human user. PathAI, is a Boston-based company in the health diagnostics industry, which created machine learning algorithms to help pathologists analyze tissue samples and to suggest a more accurate diagnostics and propose better treatments. Atomwise is a San Francisco based company in the health industry which uses technology based on Convolutional Neural Networks (CNNs) to create algorithms in order to analyze billions of compounds and fasten the drug discovery processes[1].

It is not a new phenomenon that man has sought to reduce his efforts and to improve his productivity by getting help from machines. However, the distinguishing factor that renders AI unique is that it is making machines intelligent and autonomous. Oberoi (2021) aggregated the works of previous researchers and defined AI as the ability of a system to autonomously learn and interpret from external data and use that knowledge to do specific tasks and achieve goals through rational and flexible adaptation. The Table 1 below provides a few definitions of AI[2].

Table 1. Definitions of AI from academic and non-academic sources

Source	Definition
Non-academic source:	
https://builtin.com/ artificial-intelligence (accessed on 20/06/2020)	"AI is a computer system able to perform tasks that ordinarily require human intelligence... Many of these artificial intelligence systems are powered by machine learning, some of them are powered by deep learning and some of them are powered by very boring things like rules."
Indepth: Artificial Intelligence 2021, Statista Digital Market Outlook, August 2021	Artificial intelligence (AI) essentially refers to computing technologies that are inspired by the ways people use their brains and nervous systems to reason and make decisions, but they typically operate quite differently. There are three main types of AI: machine learning, robotics, artificial neural networks.
Academic source:	
Tegmark (2017), p. 39	AI is the "ability to accomplish any goal, including learning." AI is "non-biological intelligence."
Gibbs et al. (2017), p. 7	AI is "any technique that enables computers to mimic human intelligence using logic, if-then rules, decision trees, and machine learning."
Davenport and Ronanki (2018)	AI depends not on its underlying technology but rather its marketing and business applications, such as automating business processes, gaining insights from data, or engaging customers and employees.
Huang et al. (2019), p. 45	AI is "the ability to learn from various types of data and learn from a massive amount of data (i.e., big data) and update thoughts or actions is what makes us consider a machine to be intelligent."
Haenlein and Kaplan (2019), p. 5	AI as "a system's ability to interpret external data correctly, to learn from such data, and to use those learnings to achieve specific goals and tasks through flexible adaptation."

Huang et al. (2019) explain that there are multiple types of AI systems: mechanically intelligent systems, thinking AI systems, and feeling AI systems. According to Huang et al. (2019) and Huang and Rust (2020, 2021) the mechanically intelligent systems is designed for automating repetitive and routine tasks. For example, remote sensing, machine translation, classification algorithms, clustering algorithms, and dimensionality reduction are some current technologies that can be considered mechanical AI. Thinking AI systems are designed for processing data to arrive at new conclusions or decisions. The data are typically unstructured. Thinking AI is good at recognizing patterns and regularities in data, for example, text mining, speech recognition, and facial recognition. Machine learning, neural networks, and deep learning (neural networks with additional layers) are some of the current methods by which thinking AI processes data. Feeling AI systems are designed for two-way interactions involving humans, and/or for analyzing human feelings and emotions.

Ostrom et al. (2019) categorized AI in another manner as "narrow or weak AI" and "general or strong AI." As explained by Tegmark (2017), when an AI-driven technological product has the ability to accomplish a narrow set of goals, for example, play chess or drive a car it can be categorized as Narrow or Weak AI. Such AI is tailored to a specific problem or task and cannot deal with other challenges unless it is retrained or modified. Wirth (2018) explain that a "strong or general" AI is as powerful and flexible as human intelligence and is not tailored to a specific problem or task. Wirth (2018) also described a third-category hybrid AI, which is a combination of multiple narrow AI technologies

The building blocks of AI are - natural language processing (NLP), image recognition, speech recognition, and machine learning (Kietzmann et al. 2018). Oberoi (2021) summarized these building blocks from previous research as follows. Natural language processing (NLP) allows AI systems to analyze and understand the complex aspects of human language and communication. Conversational agents of chatbots, for example, use NLP softwares. Image recognition is the ability of AI-driven software or machine to recognize and identify objects, living creatures, places, and actions. This has helped marketers and advertisers really grasp the true consumer behavior via their photos and videos. Speech recognition technology allows AI to analyze the meaning of spoken words. Machine learning is a branch of AI that integrates many fields such as mathematics, statistics, computer science, and automation. It has acquired such a fundamental role that it has almost become a synonym of AI. Machine learning's purpose is to develop the capacities of a system to improve by interacting with its environment. There can be supervised learning, semi-supervised or reinforcement learning, and unsupervised learning. In supervised learning, the observations are already labeled, and the goal to be achieved is to assign a preexisting class learned to a new observation. In the case of unsupervised learning, no information is provided on the belonging of the data to a particular class. The recent emergence of big data has made it possible to considerably improve the results of learning models and to invest in areas such as image recognition, automatic translation, etc.

To summarize and conclude this section I provide a quote from Jim Sterns book "Artificial Intelligence for Marketing, Practical Applications":

In brief- AI mimics humans, while machine learning is a system that can figure out how to figure out a specific task. (Stern, 2017, p. 9).

Consequences on Businesses

AI has been categorized as transformational general-purpose technology that will have enormous economic impact across industries (Brynjolfsson and Mcafee, 2017). This implies that companies will have to adopt AI and ML in their core processes and business models to be competitive. AI's importance is emerging due to (1) increasing wealth of digital data available and the physical world in which to apply it, and (2) varying number of domains such as marketing, human resource, finance etc., and varying number of industries such as retail, banking, education, media, health care, etc. are seeing the potential of adopting even the simplest versions of AI tools to improve performance. Currently, AI can be used by managers and organization for (1) automating business processes through robotics and cognitive automation; (2) gaining cognitive insight through data analysis; and (3) cognitive engagement with customers and employees (Davenport and Ronanki 2018). Luca et al. (2016) raise multiple issues with regards to AI implementation. They suggest that managers (1) need to be explicit about their goals, both core and soft, when formulating algorithms; (2) choose wider and diverse data inputs; and (3) consider long-term implications of the query because algorithms tend to be myopic.

Carter (2018) explains that AI is impacting very significantly the informational aspects of organizations and hence impacting information professionals first and foremost. As can be expected information and data quality, and trust and confidence in data, are concerns for information professionals. The ability to ensure data is of highest quality and integrity is a critical skill for information professionals. Information teams are frequently responsible for training and education on Data Protection Regulations and other data governance legislations. They do assist with some aspects of implementation and application, but Legal, Risk and Compliance teams have the absolute responsibility in the organization. According to Carter (2018) information professionals foresee (1) that new technical and AI solutions will mainly require the enhancement of current skills, rather than the acquisition of new ones, however, (2) there will be an increased importance of digital and information literacy within organizations. A 2020 Deloitte study shows results like Carter's 2018 study (see Figure 1).

Figure 1. Expected impact of artificial intelligence (AI) on the number of jobs in their organization in the next three years according to business and HR leaders worldwide as of 2020
Source: Deloitte; ID 1119824

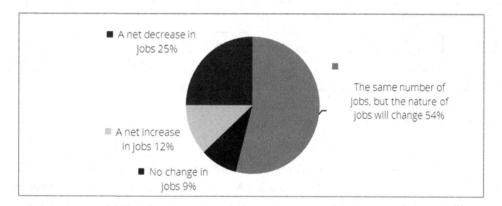

The global AI market in 2021 is 327.5bn USD, and it is projected to reach more than half a trillion U.S. dollars by 2024. The AI market revenue in 2020 was divided into three main segments: software, services, and hardware (see Figure 2). The industries that have become prominent for AI adoption in organizations include high tech and telecommunications, financial services, and healthcare and pharmaceutical (see Table 1).

According to a March 2020 study by data analytics provider IRI, China, the U.S., Japan, Germany, India, South Korea, France, Russia, the UK, and Brazil are the top 10 countries in terms of AI research and development expenditure[3].

Figure 2. Artificial intelligence (AI) market revenue worldwide in 2020, by segment (in billion U.S. dollars)
Source: IDC; Statista; ID 755331

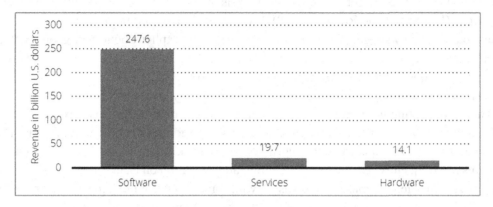

Table 2. AI adoption in organizations worldwide 2020, by industry and function

Artificial intelligence (AI) adoption worldwide 2020, by industry and function (in %)	HR	Manufacturing	Marketing & sales	Product/service development	Risk	Service operations	Strategy & corporate finance	Supply chain management
All industries	8	12	15	21	10	21	7	9
Automotive & Assembly	13	29	10	21	2	16	8	18
Business, legal, and professional services	13	9	16	21	13	20	10	9
Consumer goods/retail	1	19	20	14	3	10	2	10
Financial services	5	5	21	15	32	34	7	2
Healthcare/pharma	3	12	16	15	4	11	2	6
High tech/telecom	14	11	26	37	14	39	9	12

Source: Stanford University; McKinsey; ID 1112982

According to a 2021 report[4], companies from various industries are currently developing AI and related applications. Google, IBM and Microsoft are leading AI innovations in the IT industry, whereas Amazon and eBay are investing in AI to improve their eCommerce platform, and ride-sharing company Uber is using AI for autonomous driving, food deliveries, and mapping research. Collaborative development is on the rise, and leading companies such as Amazon, Apple, Facebook, Google/DeepMind, IBM, and Microsoft are currently working in partnership towards developing AI applications. The acquisition of small-scale AI companies in relevant fields by tech giants like Apple, IBM, and Microsoft is decreasing the learning curve. Table 2 below provides a list of selected leading AI companies.

IMPACT IN THE DOMAIN OF MARKETING

AI is dramatically reshaping and redefining not only the market and what companies can or cannot do with customer experience, but who we are as individuals and groups.

Table 3. List of selected leading AI companies in 2020

Company	Headquarters	Revenue in bnUS$	Key AI areas
Amazon	Washington, U.S.	381.6	Text-to-speech, computer vision, deep learning, NLP
Apple	California, U.S.	274.5	Machine learning
Baidu	Beijing, China	16.4	Machine learning, robotics
eBay	California, U.S.	10.3	Predictive analytics, cloud-based AI, big data
Facebook	California, U.S.	86	Language technology, machine learning, computer vision
Google	California, U.S.	182.5	Machine learning, deep learning, automotive industry
IBM	New York, U.S.	73.6	Machine learning, cognitive architectures
Microsoft	Washington, U.S.	143	Machine vision, machine learning, healthcare
Salesforce	California, U.S.	21.3	Machine learning, analytics
Uber	California, U.S.	11.1	Voice and image recognition, machine learning, automotive industry

Source: Indepth: Artificial Intelligence 2021, Statista Digital Market Outlook, August 2021

(Markus Giesler, chair of the marketing department at York University's Schulich School of Business and director of the Big Design Lab, as cited by Conick (2017)

Huang and Rust (2021) explain AI in marketing is currently gaining importance, due to increasing computing power, lower computing costs, the availability of big data, and the advance of machine learning algorithms and models. Jarek and Mazurek (2019) show that AI influences all aspects of marketing mix impacting both consumer value delivery as well as the marketing organization and management. They provide a long list of examples of application of AI in marketing. For example, virtual assistants (Siri, Google Home, Cortana) are supporting task execution using voice processing technologies, GPS navigation systems provide directions using text processing technologies, face recognition as a way to make payments using face image recognition and processing technology, and developing an individual savings plan thanks to an analysis of the funds available on one's account, receipts, amount of expenses and the way one spends their money using decision making technologies. This means that AI is impacting not only the new products and services that are being developed and proposed to customers, but also how the consumer behavior is evolving.

Ma and Sun (2020) argue that machine learning methods can process large-scale and unstructured data and have flexible model structures that yield strong predictive performance. However, such methods may lack model transparency and interpretability. They further explain that AI-driven trends in the industry, where firms increasingly focus on the entire customer purchase journeys which contain frequent and media-rich interactions and perform large-scale and automated context-dependent personalization and targeting. These trends both are enabled by and drive the continued improvement of the ever more powerful machine learning methods, leading to a positive feedback loop which is transforming all areas of marketing practices.

Stern (2017) explains that AI can be used to solve marketing problems ranging from market research, marketing mix modeling to CRM. For example, in February 2020, Equals 3 announced that the company will begin operating under a new name and will be known as Lucy – their flagship product and now namesake. Lucy, as a product and company, delivers a revolutionary AI-powered enterprise knowledge management solution to address common challenges. Founded in 2015, Lucy helps Fortune 1000 companies and the agencies that serve them make the most of the data-rich environment. Lucy gives organizations an extraordinary competitive advantage by revolutionizing the access, search speed, and answer quality available when they consult their own internal knowledge. The American Marketing Association (AMA) is now working with Lucy to explore how to improve data collection process, analysis, and communication of finding by combining academic data with other data such as client data, purchased secondary data. Lucy would serve as a cognitive companion for marketers. Stern describes AMA's CEO Russ Klien's vision of Lucy becoming the equivalent of Amazon Alexa for marketers. "Someone could say, I am thinking about writing a media plan for detergent, and Lucy will come back and say I have analyzed the social media feeds of everyone who cares about detergent, and here's the best media mix to reach them."

Davenport et al. (2020) explain that AI is likely to influence marketing strategies, including business models, sales process and customer service options, as well as customer behaviors. Such influences can firstly be visible in the form of launch of innovative AI-driven products, for example AI-enabled driverless cars. As per the Indepth: Artificial Intelligence 2021, Statista Digital Market Outlook report (2021) in the automotive sector, AI is primarily used to power autonomous cars, and that these systems expected to become standard in new vehicles in the medium to long term. Even though there are plenty of cars with driver assist features, they still require drivers to take over when an unforeseen event occurs that the car is not programmed to handle. Companies like Drive.ai and Nvidia are using deep learning to give cars full autonomy. Nvidia uses CNNs to learn the entire process of steering a car. According to a report the estimates of the annual sales of self-driving cars is expected to reach approximately 33 million units by 2040, with nearly 76 million vehicles with some level of autonomy sold by 2035. Another study by Bloomberg estimated the Americas region to witness the largest adoption of autonomous vehicles with a penetration rate of 5.4% by 2030, followed by Europe, Middle East and Africa (EMEA) with 3.9% and APAC with 3%. Even though the required hardware, such as sensors, cameras, radars, and ultrasound systems, has contributed a lot to making autonomous cars a reality, it is really the developments in AI that play the most pivotal role. Deep-learning architectures enable cars to learn from their experiences and adapt to real-time situations without human intervention. This is particularly important because it is impossible for software engineers to write programs to cover every variable or driving situation a car may face. In fact, deep-learning is solely responsible for the evolution of cars from driver-assist technologies to fully autonomous vehicles.

Davenport et al. (2020) explain that the second kind of influence would be that AI will affect sales processes. Companies are investing a lot in AI agents to improve telemarketing performance. Luo et al. (2021) explain that as the data-driven capabilities of AI improves companies are using AI coaches to train sales agents. These AI coaches, are softwares that use deep learning algorithms and cognitive speech analytics, can listen to and examine conversations between sales agents and customers. They can then provide sales agents a more data-driven training feedback to improve their performance. AI coaches have high computational power and can be cost-effective. Companies such as MetLife and Zoom use AI coaches Cogito and Chorus, respectively. Luo et al. (2021) find that despite the superior data computational skills of AI coaches their performance is less than that of a human and AI coach team. The lack of soft interpersonal skills of AI coaches can hinder salespeople's learning. Davenport et al. (2020) explain that the downside of this might be that it could trigger unintended negative consequences such as customers not feeling comfortable about AI monitoring their conversations with the salespeople. This discomfort can be augmented if the salespeople are replaced by AI bots which perform sales activities instead of them.

The third kind of marketing practices related impact that Davenport et al. (2020) explain are related with predicting customer needs in online retailing scenario. With the tradition online retailing, companies used to observe the purchasing patterns and propose similar products that customers might find interesting (customers who bought this item also bought). However, with the latest AI technologies applied to online retailing, retailers will use AI to identify customers' preferences and ship items to customers without a formal order, with customers having the option to return what they do not need. This shift would transform retailers' marketing strategies, business models, and customer behaviors (e.g., information search). Businesses like Birchbox, Stitch Fix and Trendy Butler already use AI algorithms to try to predict what their customers want, with varying levels of success.

There are studies which also explain the AI adoption from the customer point of view. If the perception of risk of outcomes increases, then customers are less likely to adopt AI. If the task in question is about choosing a movie or a dress or a more consequential decision like taking certain new treatment the adoption levels will differ (Castelo, 2019). Moreover, if a certain consumption activity is central to a customer's identity, then the customer likes to take credit for consumption outcomes (Leung et al., 2018). Ameen et al. (2021) show the integration of AI in shopping can lead to an improved AI-enabled customer experience. Klaus and Zaichkowsky (2020) propose that AI has taken convenience to a new level for consumers. By using bots, consumers outsource their decisions to algorithms, hence give little attention to traditional consumer decision-making models and brand emphasis. At the moment, this is especially true for low involvement types of decisions, but high involvement decisions are on the cusp of delegating to AI. Therefore, companies need to change how they view consumers' decision-making processes.

Huang and Rust (2020, 2021) studies explain that each of the three type of AI systems (mechanical, thinking and feeling AI systems, described in the section entitled "AI and related concepts" can be related to (a) marketing actions such as standardization, personalization, and relationalization, (b) marketing research actions such as data collection, market analysis and customer understanding, and (c) strategic marketing action of segmentation, targeting and positioning. Using the three-stage framework of marketing activities leveraging the three AI systems, Huang and Rust (2021) explain that for the marketing research activities, AI is used for market intelligence, including mechanical AI for data collection, thinking AI for market analysis, and feeling AI for customer understanding. For the marketing strategy activities, AI is used for the strategic decisions of segmentation, targeting, and positioning. They further explain that the mechanical AI is ideal for discovering novel customer preference patterns in unstructured data, thinking AI is ideal for recommending the best segment(s) to target, and feeling AI is ideal for communicating with the targeted customers about the product. With regards to the marketing mix activities, the AI systems can be used for the benefits of standardization, personalization, and relationalization, individually or synergistically. Hence the Marketers job becomes to decide which AI intelligence(s) to use for which marketing actions.

Table 4 provided below is extracted from Huang and Rust (2021) article. It provides the correspondence between the various marketing activities and the three AI systems.

FUTURE RESEARCH DIRECTIONS

Huang and Rust (2021) provide managerial and research implications of current, emerging and future AI related practices on marketing research, marketing strategy and marketing actions. For conducting data collection for marketing research, the most common tools currently used are surveys, experiments, interviews, panels, and sales data. These tools have their advantages but also their disadvantages. Common disadvantages include points such as the data being out of context, ad hoc, theory driven, collected periodically and not during data generation. In contrast, emerging practices will render data collection

Table 4. Marketing activities in correspondence with AI systems

AI intelligence Strategic decision	Mechanical AI	Thinking AI	Feeling AI
Marketing research	*Data collection* Automate continuous market and customer data sensing, tracking, collecting, and processing	*Market analysis* Use marketing analytics to identify competitors and competitive advantages	*Customer understanding* Use emotional data and customer analytics to understand existing and potential customer needs and wants
Marketing strategy (STP)	*Segmentation* Use mechanical AI to identify novel customer preference patterns	*Targeting* Use thinking AI to recommend the best target segments	*Positioning* Use feeling AI to develop positioning that resonates with customers
Marketing action (4Ps/4Cs)	*Standardization*	*Personalization*	*Relationalization*
Product/Consumer	Automate the process and output of meeting customer needs and wants	Personalize products based on customer preferences	Understand and meet customer emotional needs and wants
Price/Cost	Automate the process of price setting and payment	Personalize prices based on customer willingness to pay	Negotiate price and justify the cost interactively
Place/Convenience	Automate customer access to product	Personalize frontline interactions	Personalize experience for customer engagement
Promotion/Communication	Automate communication with customers	Customize promotional content for personal communication	Tailor communication based on customer emotional preferences and reactions

Note. Product includes tangible goods and intangible services

Source: Extracted from Huang and Rust, 2021.

automated through social network sites, and mobile apps, technological tools such as smart watch, mobile phone etc. These mechanical AI approaches can provide companies real-time data and hence the data are in context, and during the consumption experience. For decision on segmentation the current approach relies on segmentation variables such as demographics, psychographics and behavioral variables and creates an aggregated group of individuals. By contrast, when data mining is used to segment the market, marketers are no longer required to decide on segmentation variables on an a priori basis. Unsupervised machine learning can discover patterns itself based on unlimited number of variables. With regards to the decision on the product factor of the marketing mix, the current practice is to use conjoint analysis to decide what levels of product attributes to include in product development, use test markets to decide whether and to what degree the product will be accepted, and use aggregate sales results after the launch of the product as a proxy for customer feedback. The emerging practice is to use mechanical AI to automate production and service process (e.g., Huang and Rust 2020), use thinking AI, such as cognitive technology, to facilitate product research and development (which is currently more common in drug development), and use feeling AI, such social robots, and conversational bots, to interact with customers, from which they obtain real-time, first-hand customer feedback about the product

Overgoor et al. (2019) explain the following steps which can help distinguish a good application of AI for marketing activities from a poor one. First, marketing managers should have a clear understanding of their marketing objective(s) and how their performance success will be measured while trying to use AI. Second, marketing managers and their team members should have a clear and in-depth understanding of the data that they will feed to AI systems. They should know who collected the data, how they collected it, and how the data has been described. This is important as it will allow them to identify which variables of the data should be associated with the marketing objectives and this will allow them to study such variables better. Third, marketing managers need to work on the crucial task of data preparation. It means selecting the variables of interest and cleaning them. Fourth, marketing managers need to know modeling and decide on how to build the model that will help them decide automatically. This means identifying the technique or techniques that will be used on multiple datasets. A dataset is either split into two datasets, a training and testing set, or into three datasets, a training, validation, and testing set. Finally, marketing managers will have to evaluate the results and decide if they have met the goals that they laid out in the first step of the project, and if yes, then to deploy the Marketing AI solution in a way that will increase business value. As Overgoor et al. (2019) explain one of the things that is very different about Marketing AI, as opposed to traditional data mining, is that when deployed, a Marketing AI system can be set up to continually update itself using new data.

CONCLUSION

In lieu of conclusion I provide the following quote from Mari (2019):

AI-driven marketing activities tries to automatize, optimize, and augment the transformational process of data into actions and interactions with the scope of predicting behaviors, anticipating needs, and personalizing experiences for customers. Designing an AI strategy requires managers to systematically evaluate marketing needs in terms of automation, optimization, and augmentation in relation to the searched benefits of prediction, anticipation, and personalization. Balancing machine-inspired goals with expected benefits forces managers to strategically assess their organization to redesign roles and responsibilities while adequately defining the division of tasks between humans and machines.

REFERENCES

Ameen, N., Tarhini, A., Reppel, A., & Anand, A. (2021). Customer experiences in the age of artificial intelligence. *Computers in Human Behavior*, *114*, 106548. doi:10.1016/j.chb.2020.106548 PMID:32905175

Brynjolfsson, E., & Mcafee, A. (2017). Artificial intelligence, for real. *Harvard Business Review*.

Carter, D. (2018). How real is the impact of artificial intelligence? The business information survey 2018. *Business Information Review*, *35*(3), 99–115. doi:10.1177/0266382118790150

Castelo, N. (2019). *Blurring the line between human and machine: marketing artificial intelligence.* Columbia University.

Conick, H. (2017). The past, present and future of AI in marketing. *Marketing News*, *51*(1), 26–35.

Davenport, T., Guha, A., Grewal, D., & Bressgott, T. (2020). How artificial intelligence will change the future of marketing. *Journal of the Academy of Marketing Science*, *48*(1), 24–42. doi:10.100711747-019-00696-0

Davenport, T. H., & Ronanki, R. (2018). Artificial intelligence for the real world. *Harvard Business Review*, *96*(1), 108–116.

Gibbs, N., Pine, D. W., & Pollack, K. (2017). *Artificial intelligence: The future of humankind.* Academic Press.

Haenlein, M., & Kaplan, A. (2019). A brief history of artificial intelligence: On the past, present, and future of artificial intelligence. *California Management Review*, *61*(4), 5–14. doi:10.1177/0008125619864925

Huang, M. H., Rust, R., & Maksimovic, V. (2019). The feeling economy: Managing in the next generation of artificial intelligence (AI). *California Management Review*, *61*(4), 43–65. doi:10.1177/0008125619863436

Huang, M. H., & Rust, R. T. (2020). Engaged to a robot? The role of AI in service. *Journal of Service Research*. Advance online publication. doi:10.1177/1094670520902266

Huang, M. H., & Rust, R. T. (2021). A strategic framework for artificial intelligence in marketing. *Journal of the Academy of Marketing Science, 49*(1), 30–50. doi:10.100711747-020-00749-9

Jarek, K., & Mazurek, G. (2019). Marketing and Artificial Intelligence. *Central European Business Review, 8*(2).

Kietzmann, J., Paschen, J., & Treen, E. (2018). Artificial intelligence in advertising: How marketers can leverage artificial intelligence along the consumer journey. *Journal of Advertising Research, 58*(3), 263–267. doi:10.2501/JAR-2018-035

Klaus, P., & Zaichkowsky, J. (2020). AI voice bots: A services marketing research agenda. *Journal of Services Marketing, 34*(3), 389–398. doi:10.1108/JSM-01-2019-0043

Leung, E., Paolacci, G., & Puntoni, S. (2018). Man versus machine: Resisting automation in identity-based consumer behavior. *JMR, Journal of Marketing Research, 55*(6), 818–831. doi:10.1177/0022243718818423

Luca, M., Kleinberg, J., & Mullainathan, S. (2016). Algorithms need managers, too. *Harvard Business Review, 94*(1), 20.

Luo, X., Qin, M. S., Fang, Z., & Qu, Z. (2021). Artificial Intelligence Coaches for Sales Agents: Caveats and Solutions. *Journal of Marketing, 85*(2), 14–32. doi:10.1177/0022242920956676

Ma, L., & Sun, B. (2020). Machine learning and AI in marketing–Connecting computing power to human insights. *International Journal of Research in Marketing, 37*(3), 481–504. doi:10.1016/j.ijresmar.2020.04.005

Mari, A. (2019). *The Rise of machine learning in marketing: Goal, process, and benefit of AI-driven marketing*. Academic Press.

Oberoi, P. (2021). Artificial Intelligence and the Future of Businesses. In W. Leal Filho, A. M. Azul, L. Brandli, A. Lange Salvia, & T. Wall (Eds.), *Industry, Innovation and Infrastructure. Encyclopedia of the UN Sustainable Development Goals*. Springer. doi:10.1007/978-3-319-71059-4_145-1

Ostrom, A. L., Fotheringham, D., & Bitner, M. J. (2019). Customer acceptance of AI in service encounters: understanding antecedents and consequences. In *Handbook of Service Science* (Vol. 2, pp. 77–103). Springer.

Overgoor, G., Chica, M., Rand, W., & Weishampel, A. (2019). Letting the computers take over: Using AI to solve marketing problems. *California Management Review, 61*(4), 156–185. doi:10.1177/0008125619859318

Sterne, J. (2017). *Artificial intelligence for marketing: practical applications*. John Wiley & Sons. doi:10.1002/9781119406341

Tegmark, M. (2017). *Life 3.0: Being human in the age of artificial intelligence*. Vintage.

Wirth, N. (2018). Hello marketing, what can artificial intelligence help you with? *International Journal of Market Research, 60*(5), 435–438. doi:10.1177/1470785318776841

ADDITIONAL READING

Agrawal, A., Gans, J., & Goldfarb, A. (2018). *Prediction machines: The simple economics of artificial intelligence*. Harvard Business Press.

Brock, J. K. U., & Von Wangenheim, F. (2019). Demystifying AI: What digital transformation leaders can teach you about realistic artificial intelligence. *California Management Review*, *61*(4), 110–134. doi:10.1177/1536504219865226

Garbuio, M., & Lin, N. (2019). Artificial intelligence as a growth engine for health care startups: Emerging business models. *California Management Review*, *61*(2), 59–83. doi:10.1177/0008125618811931

Kumar, V., Rajan, B., Venkatesan, R., & Lecinski, J. (2019). Understanding the role of artificial intelligence in personalized engagement marketing. *California Management Review*, *61*(4), 135–155. doi:10.1177/0008125619859317

Lawrence, T. (1991). Impacts of artificial intelligence on organizational decision making. *Journal of Behavioral Decision Making*, *4*(3), 195–214. doi:10.1002/bdm.3960040306

Li, H. (2019). Special section introduction: Artificial intelligence and advertising. *Journal of Advertising*, *48*(4), 333–337. doi:10.1080/00913367.2019.1654947

Marcus, G., & Davis, E. (2019). *Rebooting AI: Building artificial intelligence we can trust*. Vintage.

KEY TERMS AND DEFINITIONS

Artificial Intelligence: Artificial intelligence can be defined as the ability of a system to autonomously learn and interpret from external data and use that knowledge to do specific tasks and achieve goals through rational and flexible adaptation.

Augmented Reality: Augmented reality can be defined as an interactive experience of the real-world environment that is enhanced using a technological device and multiple sensory modalities.

Automation: Automation can be defined as the technique of making an apparatus, a process, or a system operate automatically.

Big Data: Big data can be defined as larger, more complex data sets arising from new data sources, and the techniques to analyze and extract meaning from it.

Deep Learning: Deep learning can be defined as a type of machine learning technique that teaches technological software to imitate the way humans learn.

Machine Learning: Machine learning can be defined as making technological software think and act without human intervention.

Robotics: Robotics can be defined as an interdisciplinary branch of computer science and engineering that involves designing and constructing machines to assist humans.

ENDNOTES

[1] Examples extracted from https://builtin.com/artificial-intelligence/examples-ai-in-industry (accessed on 08/10/2021).

2 Davenport et al. (2020) provide various definitions of AI from various domains such as robotics, business and social studies, psychology, etc. They also provide assorted examples of current and future AI applications for diverse industries.

3 Source: Nvidia, International Trade Administration, R&D World, IRI.

4 Indepth: Artificial Intelligence 2021, Statista Digital Market Outlook, August 2021.

About the Contributors

John Wang is a professor in the Department of Information Management and Business Analytics at Montclair State University, USA. Having received a scholarship award, he came to the USA and completed his Ph.D. in operations research at Temple University. Due to his extraordinary contributions beyond a tenured full professor, Dr. Wang has been honored with two special range adjustments in 2006 and 2009, respectively. He has published over 100 refereed papers and seventeen books. He has also developed several computer software programs based on his research findings.

* * *

Nassir Abba-Aji, PhD, is a Senior Lecturer at the Department of Mass Communication, University of Maiduguri, Borno State, Nigeria, and the Sub-Dean, Faculty of Social Sciences of the university. He is a one-time Chairman, Jere Local Government Area, Borno State, as well as Commissioner for Religious Affairs during the Senator Ali Modu Sheriff Administration in Borno State. Dr Nassir has published several articles and book chapters, and has presented papers at several conferences.

Peter Abraldes completed his BA in political science at the University of Pittsburgh. He completed graduate work in statistics and earned his masters in data analytics at the Pennsylvania State University. Peter also spent time studying development economics in Argentina and Brazil, especially how international trade impacts developing countries. His studies include labor economics, trade export policies, and national industrial development policies. He is a maritime trade analyst for the Philadelphia Regional Port Authority, focused on optimizing the organization's cargo development strategy. The strategy includes understanding how the port can differentiate itself and make it more resilient to supply chain disruptions and international policy changes. He has been the scholarship chair for the World Trade Association of Philadelphia since 2018.

Anal Acharya is currently Assistant Professor in Computer Science department in St. Xavier's College, Kolkata. His current research interest is Educational Data Mining.

Prageet Aeron is presently an Assistant Professor at the department of Information Management at MDI Gurgaon. He is a Fellow (FPM) of Computers and Information Systems Group from the Indian Institute of Management Ahmedabad, and a B.Tech from the Indian Institute of Technology-BHU, Varanasi. He has over 10 years of teaching experience across various B-schools in NCR and is actively engaged in teaching and research in the areas of Entrepreneurship, Strategic Information Systems, e-Commerce and Big Data Applications in Management. His research work has been regularly accepted in reputed International Journals and Conferences.

Javier M. Aguiar Pérez is Associate Professor at University of Valladolid, and Head of the Data Engineering Research Unit. His research is focused on Big Data, Artificial Intelligence, and Internet of Things. He has managed international research projects and he has contributed in the standardisation field as expert at the European Telecommunications Standards Institute. He serves as editor, guest editor and reviewer, and author in several international journals, books and conferences. Furthermore, he has been involved as reviewer and rapporteur in several international research initiatives.

Gilbert Ahamer is inclined to analyse fundamentals of philosophy for the target of designing new paradigms driven by foresight when it comes to develop policies for mastering globalisation. As a physicist, environmentalist, economist, technologist, and geographer, he suggests that radically new concepts might beneficially contribute to solving the pressing problems of global change. He co-founded the 'Global Studies' curriculum at Graz University, Austria, studied and established global long-term scenarios when affiliated to the International Institute for Applied Systems Analysis IIASA, and is active in institutionalised dialogue-building for the Environment Agency Austria in Central Asia, Ukraine, and Georgia since his earlier affiliation to the Austrian Academy of Sciences.

Md. Omar Al-Zadid is currently working as a Senior Officer in Bank Asia Limited, Dhaka, Bangladesh. He began his career as a corporate professional in The Daily 'Prothom Alo', one of the top ranking newspapers in Bangladesh. His primary responsibilities in Prothom Alo included key account management and customer relationship management in advertisement department. He achieved 2nd Category Ptak Prize Award in recognition of global supply chain understanding and leadership in the young supply chain community organized by International Supply Chain Education Alliance (ISCEA) in 2013. He obtained Certificate of Achievement for completion of ITES Foundation Skills Training on Digital Marketing under NASSCOM IT-ITES sector Skill Council Certification in 2015. He holds an MBA in Marketing from the University of Dhaka, Bangladesh. His principal research interests include marketing analytics, innovation adoption, digital marketing, online banking, consumer behavior and psychology, Blue Ocean marketing strategy etc.

İnci Albayrak is an Professor in the Department of Mathematical Engineering at Yildiz Technical University (YTU),Turkey, where she has been a faculty member since 1992. She received her BS in 1990, MS in 1993 and PhD in 1997 in Mathematical Engineering from Yildiz Technical University. She had studied spectral theory and operator theory. She has lots of papers in these areas. In recent years, she has collaborated actively with researchers and focused on fuzzy mathematics. She has ongoing research projects about fuzzy linear equation systems and fuzzy linear programming problem.

Dima Alberg is a Researcher in SCE – Shamoon College of Engineering. His areas of specialty are financial data mining, scientific programming, and simulation methods. His current and future research plans focus on developing new models and tools that allow researchers and practitioners to analyze and solve practical problems in data science research areas.

Miguel Alonso Felipe received his M.S. degrees in telecommunication engineering from the University of Valladolid, Spain. In addition, he is PhD Candidate at University of Valladolid and Researcher of the Data Engineering Research Unit. His research is mainly focused on Big Data, Artificial Intelligence, and Internet of Things. Besides, he is co-author of some publications in journals, dealing with topics related to his lines of research.

Yas Alsultanny is the scientist of machine learning, data mining, and quantitative analysis, he is a computer engineering and data analysis PhD holder. He was spent his past 30 years of his life dedicated to the advancement of technological convergence and knowledge transfer to students. He was developed a high standard of research methods for graduate students and MBA through his supervising 100 MSc and PhD theses, and consulting 140 MBA projects, moreover he supervised 40 higher diploma projects and 100 BSc projects. Professor Alsultanny served for a reputed university in Bahrain: Arabian Gulf University (AGU), French Arabian Business School, and University of Bahrain. In Jordan: Applied Science University (ASU), Amman Arab University, Al-Balqa Applied University, and the Arab Academy for Banking and Financial Sciences. In Iraq: University of Baghdad, University of Technology, Al-Mustansiriya University, and Institute of Technology. In Germany: Arab German Academy for Science and Technology (online). Besides these, he was held position director of the AGU University Consultations, Community Services, Training, and Continuous Teaching Centre in Bahrain. And the position of head of the Computer Information Systems department and vice dean College of Information Technology in ASU University in Jordan. Alsultanny was worked a chair of statistical and KPIs committees in AGU University, chair of quality assurance and accreditation committee in Amman Arab University, member of quality assurance and accreditation committee in ASU and AGU Universities, member of establishing PhD Innovation Management programme in AGU University, member of establishing the college of Information Technology, ASU University, member of establishing Graduate College of Computing Studies, Amman Arab University, member of developing MSc Technology Management programme, member council of College of Graduate Studies, AGU University, and member council of College of Information Technology, ASU University. He is a trainer and a consultant for several public and private organizations, he led more than 100 workshops, and main speaker in many symposiums and conferences. He is a main writer of the UN Environment report, as well as member of writing AGU university strategic plans. In addition, he is reviewer and editor for various international journals.

Gerardo Amador Soto is a PhD student in Energy Systems from the National University of Colombia, Researcher in Energy Efficiency for Complex Systems.

Billie Anderson is an Assistant Professor of Applied Statistics at UMKC's Henry W. Bloch School of Management. Billie earned her Ph.D. in Applied Statistics from the University of Alabama, Masters of Mathematics and Statistics from the University of South Alabama, and her Bachelor of Mathematics from Spring Hill College. Before entering academia, Billie was a Research Statistician for SAS. SAS is a statistical software company headquartered in North Carolina. Billie wrote data mining algorithms for the banking and insurance industries. Billie maintained a consultancy relationship with SAS as an analytical trainer from 2012-2020. In this role, she taught analytical-based classes to professionals in organizations to help promote best statistical practices. And, she has consulted with different companies like Ann Taylor, Dunn & Bradstreet, Blue Cross Blue Shield of Michigan, Lowes Home Improvement Store, and Starbucks. She assisted these organizations in applying analytics to solve their business problems. Billie's research focus is in the statistical modeling of credit scoring with a particular interest in reject inference.

Issa Annamoradnejad is a Ph.D. candidate at the Sharif University of Technology, Tehran, Iran.

Rahimberdi Annamoradnejad wrote a chapter on the current and potential application of machine learning for predicting housing prices. He is an Iranian urban planner and an associate professor of geography and urban planning at the University of Mazandaran.

Joel Antúnez-García was born in Ensenada B. C., México, in 1975. He received the B. Sc. degree in Physics from Universidad Autónoma de Baja California (UABC), México, in 1999. The M. Sc. from Centro de Investigación Científica y de Educación Superior de Ensenada (CICESE), México, in 2004. The Ph. D. in Physical-Industrial Engineering from Universidad Autónoma de Nuevo Léon (UANL), Méxio, in 2010. From 2012 to 2013, he did a postdoctoral stay at Centro de Nanociencias y Nanotecnología at UNAM, working on DFT calculations to obtain different zeolites' electronic properties. From 2013-2015 he worked as a professor at Centro de Enseñanza Técnica y Superior (CETYS university). From 2016 to date, he has been involved in the theoretical study of bi-and tri-metallic catalysts based on MoS2 compounds and zeolites.

Dounia Arezki (), after obtaining an MSc in Artificial Intelligence, pursued her Ph.D. program in information technology at the Computer Science faculty of Science and Technology university of Oran (USTO) from 2017 to 2021. January 2022, she started an MSc program in international business. Presently her research interests are focused on spatial data processing, clustering algorithms, data analysis, risk, and project management.

Heba Atteya is the Senior Director of Business Intelligence and Data Analytics unit at The American University in Cairo (AUC). She led the founding team who built AUC's enterprise data-warehouse and business intelligence (BI) platform. In her current role, she manages the full-spectrum of the BI process including: setting AUC's BI roadmap, leading the data architecture and modeling functions, as well as the automated data extraction from the different source systems. Heba completed her MSc in Computer Science at AUC in Spring 2017 in the topic of visualizing large datasets. She earned her bachelor of science in Information Systems with honors in 2010 and joined AUC as a full-time staff member since 2011. She had a successful track record of achievements which qualified her for the position of BI and Data Analytics Director in 2017. Ever since then, she has successfully expanded the BI platform to extract data from the main ERP of the University, the main student information system, and the university CRM, as well as several other source systems providing a 360-degree view of student, faculty, staff and alumni of the University. Recently, she has led the efforts of the AUC's first big data project, analyzing Wi-Fi big data streams to support COVID-19 contact tracing process, as well as AUC's first AI-powered Chat-bot supporting the IT Help Desk function. She has always found inspiration in working with data and finding its underlying hidden patterns. She believes that informed decision-making is what every institution needs to compete in this highly competitive market.

Antonio Badia is an Associate Professor in the Computer Science and Engineering department at the Speed School of Engineering, University of Louisville. His research focuses on database systems and data science; his previous projects have been funded by the National Science Foundation and US Navy. He's the author of over 50 publications and 2 books.

Youakim Badr is an Associate Professor of Data Analytics in the Great Valley campus of the Pennsylvania State University, USA. He earned his Ph.D. in computer science from the National Institute of Applied Sciences (INSA-Lyon), where he worked as an associate professor in the computer science and engineering department. Over the course of his research, Dr. Badr has worked extensively in the area of service computing (distributed systems) and information security. His current research strategy aims at developing a new software engineering approach for designing and deploying "smart connected devices" and building "smart service systems" for the Internet of Things.

Surajit Bag is an Associate Professor at the Institute of Management and Technology, Ghaziabad, India (AACSB accredited). He is also working as a Visiting Associate Professor in the Department of Transport and Supply Chain Management, University of Johannesburg, South Africa. He has 11 years of industry experience. He has teaching experince from India, Morocco, South Africa and U.K. Educationally, Dr. Surajit earned his second Ph.D. in Information Management from the Postgraduate School of Engineering Management, University of Johannesburg, South Africa, and holds his first Ph.D. in Supply Chain Management from the School of Business, University of Petroleum and Energy Studies, India. Prior to getting a Ph.D., he obtained an MBA in Marketing Management (major) from MAKAUT (formerly the West Bengal University of Technology), India. His substantive areas of interest include Industry 4.0, big data, artificial intelligence applications in marketing and supply chain, sustainability. His expertise lies in the areas of Multivariate Data Analysis Techniques, Mediation Analysis, Moderation Analysis, and Structural Equation Modeling. He is familiar with data analysis software such as WarpPLS, PLS-SEM, SPSS, and Python. Surajit has published some of the most cited papers in the Industrial Marketing Management, International Journal of Production Economics, International Journal of Production Research, Technological Forecasting & Social Change, Production, Planning & Control, IEEE Transactions on Engineering Management, Journal of Cleaner Production, Annals of Operations Research, Information Systems Frontiers, Journal of Business Research, and Supply Chain Management: An International Journal. He is the proud recipient of the "AIMS-IRMA Young Management Researcher Award 2016" for his significant contribution to management research. He is the proud recipient of best "Doctoral Research Award 2020" from the Postgraduate School of Engineering Management, University of Johannesburg in recognition of the outstanding academic excellence. Dr. Surajit was listed in World's Top 2% Scientists which was released by Stanford University. He is a professional member of the Association of International Business, (AIB), Chartered Institute of Procurement and Supply (CIPS); Association for Supply Chain Management (ASCM); Institute of Electrical and Electronics Engineers (IEEE); Indian Rubber Institute; Association of Indian Management Scholars (AIMS International); and Operational Research Society of India (ORSI).

Sikha Bagui is Professor and Askew Fellow in the Department of Computer Science, at The University West Florida, Pensacola, Florida. Dr. Bagui is active in publishing peer reviewed journal articles in the areas of database design, data mining, Big Data analytics, machine learning and AI. Dr. Bagui has worked on funded as well unfunded research projects and has 85+ peer reviewed publications, some in highly selected journals and conferences. She has also co-authored several books on database and SQL. Bagui also serves as Associate Editor and is on the editorial board of several journals.

Samir Bandyopadhyay is presently a distinguished professor of The Bhawanipur Education Society College.

Soumya Banerjee is the Chief Technical Advisor & Board member of Must with specialised on ML & Security.

Sarang Bang is currently Studying at Vellore Institute of Technology, Vellore (India) pursuing Btech in Computer Science with Specialization in Data Science. He completed his schooling from Bhavan's Bhagwandas Purohit Vidya Mandir, Nagpur wherein he secured 10 cgpa in 10th grade and few other merit awards . He has been District Level Volleyball player during his schooling year. After choosing PCM and completing his 12th grade with 86.7 percentage he developed a lot of interest in coding and hence chose Computer Science as his career. In VIT, he is core committee member at VIT Mathematical Association Student chapter and also member at Lions Club International Leo Club Victory, Nagpur. He is passionate about Web Development and has worked on many projects as well as contributed to Hackathons as a front end developer. He also has interest in flutter development, machine learning. He wants to focus on a career in research and is currently exploring Machine learning and Artificial Intelligence.

Bazila Banu is a Professor and Head in the Department of Artificial Intelligence and Machine Learning at Bannari Amman Institute of Technology, India. She received her PhD degree in Information and Communication Engineering at Anna University, India in 2015 and guiding PhD Scholars. She holds 16 years of professional experience including academic and software Industry. She published 15 articles in National and International journals . She is an active reviewer and Guest Editor for International journals and technical committee member for International conferences. Her research interest includes Big Data and Data Analytics. She has filed three National level Patents and received grants from AICTE for Margdarshan scheme (19 Lakhs) and National Commission for women.

Isak Barbopoulos, PhD, has worked as a research psychologist studying the situational activation of consumer motives. He is currently working as a data scientist at Insert Coin, where he is developing and implementing a system for adaptive gamification.

Mikel Barrio Conde is a PhD candidate at University of Valladolid, who received his M.S. degrees in telecommunication engineering from the University of Valladolid, Spain. He is researcher of the Data Engineering Research Unit and his research is focused on Artificial Intelligence, and Internet of Things. Also, he is co-author of some publications in journals, dealing with topics related to his lines of his research.

Sotiris Batsakis is a Laboratory Teaching member of the Technical University of Crete, Greece and he has worked as Affiliated Senior Researcher and Senior Lecturer at the University of Huddersfield, UK. He received a diploma in Computer Engineering and Informatics from the University of Patras, Greece with highest distinction, and a Master's degree and a Ph.D. in Electronic and Computer Engineering from the Technical University of Crete Greece. He is an experienced researcher having participated on various research projects and with over 50 research publications in the areas of Knowledge Representation, Artificial Intelligence and Information Retrieval.

Andrew Behrens is an Instructor of business analytics courses at Dakota State University and is pursuing a Ph.D. in Information Systems at Dakota State University. He has worked with Cherie Noteboom for three years and has published in IS Conferences (MWAIS, IACIS, and AMCIS).

Santiago Belda https://orcid.org/0000-0003-3739-6056 (ORCID ID) From 2011 to 2015, he engaged in a PhD in Mathematical Methods and Modeling in Science and Engineering at Universidad de Alicante. He worked in various projects and is currently affiliated to Universidad de Alicante as a Distinguished postdoc researcher Presently his research interests are Astronomy, VLBI, Earth Orientation Parameters, Terrestrial and Celestial Reference Frames. Santiago Belda was partially supported by Generalitat Valenciana SEJIGENT program (SEJIGENT/2021/001), European Union – NextGenerationEU (ZAMBRANO 21-04) and European Research Council (ERC) under the ERC-2017-STG SENTIFLEX project grant number 755617.

Zakaria Bendaoud is an associate professor at the University of Saida. His research focuses on information retrieval, supply chain and transportation.

Mustapha Benramdane is a Ph.D. student in Computer Science at CNAM. His main research domains are matchmaking and Intent-based Contextual Orchestration inside Digital Business Ecosystems and Platforms.

Níssia Bergiante is a Doctor in Transportation Engineering (COPPE UFRJ– Federal University of Rio de Janeiro - Brazil). Production Engineer with a Master in Production Engineering (UFF-Brazil). Background in Production Engineering, focusing on Operational Management and Operational Research, acting on the following subjects: Decision Analysis and Soft Operation Research (Problem Structuring Methods); Operation Management and Process improvement.

Aditi A. Bhoir is a final year undergraduate student, currently pursuing Bachelor of Technology (B. Tech.) in Mechanical Engineering, at Sardar Patel College of Engineering, Mumbai, India. She will be doing Master of Science (MS) in abroad from fall 2022. Her focus research interest is design and robotics.

Trevor J. Bihl is a Senior Research Engineer with the Air Force Research Laboratory, Sensors Directorate where he leads a diverse portfolio in artificial intelligence (AI) and autonomy. Dr. Bihl earned his doctorate in Electrical Engineering from the Air Force Institute of Technology, Wright Patterson AFB, OH, and he also received a bachelor's and master's degree in Electrical Engineering at Ohio University, Athens, OH. Dr. Bihl is a Senior Member of IEEE and he has served as a board member as Vice President of Chapters/Fora for INFORMS (The Institute of Operations Research and the Management Sciences). His research interests include artificial intelligence, autonomous systems, machine learning, and operations research.

Sanjay Krishno Biswas is a faculty of Anthropology at Shahjàlal University of Science and Technology, Bangladesh. He is currently pursuing his Ph.D. His academic interest includes Anthropological Theory, Mobility, and Migration, Diaspora and Transnationality, Ethnicity and Marginality, and Ecology and Climate Change. Mr. Biswas has a number of articles in reputed journals and book chapters from reputed publishers including Routledge.

Karim Bouamrane received the PhD Degree in computer science from the Oran University in 2006. He is full Professor of computer Science at the same university. He is member of computer science laboratory (LIO). He is the head of the team decision and piloting system. His current research interests deal with decision support system, transportation system, risk management, Health system, bio-inspired approach. He participates in several scientific committees' international/national conferences in Algeria and others countries in the same domain and collaborate in Algerian-French scientific projects. He is co-author of more than 60 scientific publications and communications.

Samia Bouzefrane is Professor at the Conservatoire National des Arts et Métiers (Cnam) of Paris. She received her PhD in Computer Science from the University of Poitiers (France) in 1998. After four years at the University of Le Havre (France), she joined in 2002 the CEDRIC Lab of Cnam. She is the co-author of many books (Operating Systems, Smart Cards, and Identity Management Systems). She is a lead expert in the French ministry. She is involved in many scientific workshops and conferences. Her current research areas cover Security and AI Internet of Thing.

Paul Bracewell is Co-Founder of New Zealand-based data science firm, DOT loves data and Adjunct Research Fellow at Victoria University of Wellington. He received his PhD in Statistics from Massey University and has contributed to more than 50 peer reviewed publications.

James Braman is an Associate Professor in the Computer Science/Information Technology Department at the Community College of Baltimore County for the School of Business, Technology and Law. He earned a B.S. and M.S. in Computer Science and D.Sc. in Information Technology from Towson University. He is currently pursuing a M.S. in Thanatology from Marian University. From 2009 to 2017 he was a joint editor-in-chief for the European Alliance for Innovation (EAI) endorsed Transactions on E-Learning with Dr. Giovanni Vincenti. Dr. Braman's research interests include thanatechnology, virtual and augmented reality, e-Learning, affective computing, agent-based technologies, and information retrieval.

Alexis D. Brown is an Assistant Professor in the Computer Science & Information Technology Department at the Community College of Baltimore County. They hold a master's degree in Management Information Systems from the University of Maryland Baltimore County. Their main research interests focus on education and instructional technology but includes varied technology-related topics.

Joseph Budu is an award-winning research scholar within the information systems discipline. He received the University of Ghana Vice Chancellor award for the outstanding doctoral dissertation for the humanities for the 2019/2020 academic year. Prior to this feat, he has undertaken several academic research and consultancies. Dr. Budu has written one mini-book, and one research workbook to guide students in conducting academic research. See https://bit.ly/BuduContentfolio for various contents Joseph has produced (e.g. manuals, blog posts, lead magnets, and presentations).

Rachel Cardarelli graduated from Bryant University with a degree in Actuarial Mathematics and concentration in Applied Statistics. Since graduating, she has been working as an Actuarial Analyst.

Ferhan Çebi is a Professor in Istanbul Technical University Faculty of Management, Management Engineering Department. She holds a B.S. in Chemical Engineering from ITU, a M.S. and a Ph.D. in Management Engineering from ITU. She gives the lectures on Operations Research and Operations Management at the undergraduate level and graduate level. Her main research areas are application of Operations Research techniques to the manufacturing and service problems, production planning and control, fuzziness and mathematical modelling, decision analysis, decision support systems, information technology for competitiveness. She is acting scientific committee member and organization committee member for a number of national & international conferences. Ferhan Cebi is member of editorial boards of International Journal of Information Systems in the Service Sector, International Journal of Information & Decision Sciences, and International Journal of Data Sciences. Her works have been published in several international and national conference proceedings and journals such as Computers and Industrial Engineering, Information Sciences, Information Systems Frontiers, Journal of Enterprise Information Management, Logistics Information Management, International Journal of Information and Decision Sciences.

Shuvro Chakrobartty has made significant contributions to identifying, conceptualizing, and formulating the research objective and methodology, the proposed framework, and the analysis of the findings. With a prior educational background in Computer Science and Business, currently, he is a Ph.D. student of Information Systems at Dakota State University. His research interests lie in responsible AI and data analytics. He has work experience in multiple industries within the software, cloud, and data engineering domain. He is a member of the Association for Information Systems (AIS) professional organizations and serves as a peer-reviewer for multiple conferences, books, and journal publications.

Hannah H. Chang is Associate Professor of Marketing at Lee Kong Chian School of Business, Singapore Management University. She received a PhD in Marketing from Graduate School of Business, Columbia University.

Hsin-Lu Chang is a professor in the Department of Management Information Systems, National Chengchi University. She received a Ph.D. in information systems at the School of Commerce, the University of Illinois at Urbana-Champaign. Her research areas are in E-Commerce, IT value, and technology adoption. She has published in Decision Support Systems, Information Systems Journal, International Journal of Electronic Commerce, Journal of Organizational Computing and Electronic Commerce, and Information Systems and e-Business Management.

D. K. Chaturvedi is Professor in Electrical Engineering at DEI, Agra, India.

Akhilesh Chauhan is a fourth-year Ph.D. (IS) student in the College of Business and Information Systems at the Dakota State University (Madison, S.D., USA). He is received a master's degree in Analytics from Dakota State University. He is currently working as a graduate research assistant at DSU. His current research interest includes association rule mining, machine learning, healthcare informatics, transfer learning, text mining, and data mining.

Tanvi Chawla completed her B.Tech in Information Technology (IT) from MDU, Rohtak in 2012 and received her M.Tech in Software Engineering (SE) from ITM University, Gurgaon in 2014. She has completed her Ph.D. in Computer Science and Engineering (CSE) from Malaviya National Institute of Technology (MNIT), Jaipur in 2022. During her Ph.D. she published articles in premier journals and conferences. Her research interests are Semantic Web, Big Data, Distributed Data Storage, and Processing.

Xi Chen is a lecturer in the College of Humanities at Beijing University of Civil Engineering and Architecture. She is also a research assistant in the Beijing Research Base for Architectural Culture. Her current research interests include English academic writing, settlement evolution, and urbanization in China and the U.S., etc.

Xiaoyan Cheng is a professor at University of Nebraska at Omaha. Dr. Cheng's research has been published in Auditing: A Journal of Practice & Theory, Advances in Accounting, Review of Quantitative Finance and Accounting, Research in Accounting Regulation, Global Finance Journal, Asian Review of Accounting, and Review of Pacific Basin Financial Markets and Policies.

Xusen Cheng is a Professor of Information Systems in the School of Information at Renmin University of China in Beijing. He obtained his PhD degree from the University of Manchester, UK. His research is in the areas of information systems and management particularly focusing on online collaboration, global teams, the sharing economy, e-commerce, and e-learning.

Paula Chimenti is an Associate Professor of Strategy and Innovation at COPPEAD graduate school of business, Federal University of Rio de Janeiro, Brazil. She holds a PhD in Administration from Coppead. She is the coordinator of the Center of Studies in Strategy and Innovation, where she develops research about the impact of disruptive innovations on business ecosystems. She has several works published in journals in Brazil and abroad, such as JGIM and JCR. Her article on Business Ecosystems received the first prize in one of the most important academic conferences in Brazil. She teaches Management Networked Businesses, Digital Marketing and Research Methodology in the Executive MBA, Master's and Doctorate programs at COPPEAD / UFRJ. She coordinated the Master program and Executive MBA programs at COPPEAD. Paula is the cases for teaching Editor for RAC - Revista de Administração Contemporânea, one of the top journals in Brasil.

Jahid Siraz Chowdhuy is a Fellow Ph.D. the program, Department of Social Administration and Justice, Faculty of Arts and Social Sciences, University of Malaya, 50603, Kuala Lumpur, Malaysia and Ex-faculty of Anthropology, Shahjalal University of Science and Technology, Bangladesh.

Parvathi Chundi is a professor of computer science at University of Nebraska at Omaha. Her primary research interests are in the fields of data mining, big data, and computer vision. She is currently focused on developing algorithms for automatic labeling of data for semantic and instance segmentation of biofilm images.

William Chung is an associate professor of Management Sciences at the City University of Hong Kong. He earned his Ph.D. in Management Sciences at the University of Waterloo, Canada. His personal research interests mainly focus on developing mathematical methodologies for energy-environmental policy problems, like large-scale equilibrium models, benchmarking methods for the energy consumption performance of buildings, and decomposition analysis of energy intensity. His papers can be found in the following journals: Operations Research, European Journal of Operational Research (EJOR), Computational Economics, Energy Economics, Energy Policy, Energy, Applied Energy, and Energy and Buildings. In addition, he is the director and founder of the Energy and Environmental Policy Research

Unit at the City University of Hong Kong. He was a visiting professor of the Center for International Energy and Environment Strategy Studies, Renmin University of China.

Mateus Coimbra holds a PhD in Administration from COPPEAD school of business in Federal University of Rio de Janeiro, Brazil.

Mirko Čubrilo is BSc in Mathematics, MSc in Mathematics, PhD in Computer Science (all from Zagreb University, Croatia). Full professor with tenure (Zagreb University, Croatia). Currently engaged at the University of the North (Varaždin, Croatia). Scientific interest includes mathematical logic, theory of algorithms, logic programming, artificial intelligence in a broad context, including neural nets and deep learning. Author of two books on the topics of mathematical logic and programming and more than fifty papers, published in journals and conference proceedings around the world (Germany, Japan, UK, USA, Egypt, Slovakia, Greece, Italy).

Marcin Czajkowski received his Master's degree (2007) and his PhD with honours (2015) in Computer Science from the Bialystok University of Technology, Poland. His research activity mainly concerns bioinformatics, machine learning and data mining, in particular, decision trees, evolutionary algorithms and relative expression analysis.

Jeya Mala D. has a Ph.D. in Software Engineering with Specialization on Software Testing and is currently working as 'Associate Professor Senior' in Vellore Institute of Technology, Chennai, India. She had been in the industry for about 4 years. She has a profound teaching and research experience of more than 24 years. She has published a book on "Object Oriented Analysis and Design using UML" for Tata McGraw Hill Publishers, also she has published 2 edited books for IGI Global, USA. She has published more than 70 papers about her research works at leading international journals and conferences such as IET, ACM, Springer, World Scientific, Computing and Informatics etc. As a researcher, Dr. Jeya Mala had investigated practical aspects of software engineering and object oriented paradigms for effective software development. Her work on Software Testing has fetched grants from UGC under Major Research Project scheme. Her dissertation has been listed as one of the best Ph.D. thesis in the CSIR – Indian Science Abstracts. She has successfully guided numerous Software Development based projects for the IBM- The Great Mind Challenge (TGMC) contest. The project she has mentored during 2007, has received national level Best Top 10 Project Award – 2007, from IBM. Currently she is guiding Ph.D. and M.Phil research scholars under the areas of Software Engineering and optimization techniques. She is a life member of Computer Society of India and an invited member of ACEEE. She forms the reviewer board in Journals like IEEE Transactions on Software Engineering, Elsevier – Information Sciences, Springer, World Scientific, International Journal of Metaheuristics etc. She has organized several sponsored national level conferences and workshops, notably she is one of the organizers of "Research Ideas in Software Engineering and Security (RISES'13) – A run-up event of ICSE 2014 sponsored by Computer Society of India". She has been listed in Marquis Who's Who list in 2011. She has completed certification on Software Testing Fundamentals, Brain bench certification on Java 1.1 programming, IBM certification as Associate Developer Websphere Application Studio. She is a proud recipient of several laurels from industries like Honeywell, IBM and Microsoft for her remarkable contributions in the field of Software Development and Object Orientation.

Karim Dabbabi is currently working as an assistant professor at the Faculty of Sciences of Tunis (FST). He held the postdoctoral position for a year and a half at the same faculty. He obtained his doctorate degree in electronics in July 2019 from the FST in addition to that of a research master's degree in automatic and signal processing from the National School of Engineers of Tunis in 2014. He has worked on various research projects in Automatic Speech Recognition (ASR), speaker diarization, automatic indexing of audio documents, audio segmentation and natural language processing (NLP) in general. In addition, he has worked on the identification of different neurological diseases, including Parkinson's and Alzheimer's using different voice features.

Indraneel Dabhade completed his M.S. in Engineering at Clemson University. He is a CISSP and has studied Cybersecurity from the Massachusetts Institute of Technology Center for Professional Education. He is currently pursuing an advanced certification in information security at the Stanford Center for Professional Development. Indraneel is a published author in Data Science, Human Factors, and Intellectual Property Rights. He has over 7 years of industry experience. Currently, Indraneel heads an automation firm (O Automation) in India.

Debabrata Datta is currently an Assistant Professor In Computer Science at St. Xavier's College (Autonomous), Kolkata. His research interest is Data Analytics and Natural Language Processing.

Magdalene Delighta Angeline D. is currently in the Department of Computer Science and Engineering as Assistant Professor, Joginpally B.R Engineering College, Hyderabad, India. Her research area includes data mining, computer networks. She has a good number of research publications.

Boryana Deliyska is professor retired in Department of Computer Systems and Informatics of University of Forestry, Sofia, Bulgaria. She obtained a PHD Degree in Computer Science from Technical University of Sofia, BG. She has long-standing research and practical experience in Semantic Web technologies, e-learning, computer lexicography, ontology engineering, web design and programming, geographical information systems (GIS), databases and information systems. She teaches information technologies, programming, CAD, computer graphics and computer networks. She is an author of 4 monographies, 7 Elsevier's dictionaries, 18 textbooks, more of 130 journal articles and conference papers.

Javier Del-Pozo-Velázquez received his M.S. degrees in telecommunication engineering from the University of Valladolid, Spain. In addition, he is PhD Candidate at University of Valladolid and Researcher of the Data Engineering Research Unit. His research is mainly focused on Big Data, Artificial Intelligence and Internet of Things. Besides, he is co-author of some publications in journals, dealing with topics related to his lines of research.

Chitra A. Dhawale (Ph.D in Computer Science) is currently working as a Professor Department of Computer Engineering P.R. Pote College of Engineering and Management, Amravati (MS), India. Earlier She worked as a Professor at Symbiosis International University, Pune (MS). To her credit, 06 research scholars have been awarded PhD. so far under her guidance, by S.G.B. Amravati and R.T.M. Nagpur University. Her research interests include Image and Video Processing, Machine Learning, Deep Learning, Multi-Biometric, Big Data Analytics. She has developed many projects for Machine Learning, Deep Learning, Natural Language Processing Algorithms using python. She also has hands on experience in

R-Programming, Hadoop-MapReduce, Apache Spark, Tableau. She has published 02 books, 08 Book Chapters, 26 Research papers in Journals (02- SCI-Indexed,15-Scopus Indexed, 06-UGC Journals and 03 in other research journals) and presented 35 papers in International Conferences (Abroad Conference-08, IEEE-18, ACM-02, Elsevier-01,Springer-04, Others-02) and 19 papers in National Conferences. She has reviewed 09 books for various publishers.

Kritika Dhawale is working as Deep Learning Engineer at SkyLark Drones, Bangalore. She has published 2 book chapters on Deep Learning. Her Research interest is Deep Learning and Cloud Computing.

Harini Dissanayake is a research student at Victoria University of Wellington, New Zealand working on her project 'Data informed decision bias.' The project focuses on identifying discriminatory bias in operational algorithms and remedying sample selection bias in datasets used for informing both commercial and government decisions.

Emmanuel Djaba is an early-stage academic with an avid interest in data science and machine learning. With extensive experience in industry, he is interested in doing innovative research that can be readily applied to interesting problems. He is currently a PhD student at the University of Ghana where he is pursuing a PhD in information systems.

Matt Drake has been a researcher in supply chain management for twenty years, focusing mainly on the areas of supply chain education and ethics. He has published over 30 articles and book chapters during this time. His chapter discusses the use of IoT technology to improve supply chain management. As firms look to improve their supply chain resilience in response to the COVID-19 pandemic and other disruptions, IoT data increases visibility, traceability, and can help firms to mitigate risks through added agility and responsiveness. The improved decision making made possible from IoT data creates a competitive advantage in the market.

Dorin Drignei received his PhD in Statistics from Iowa State University in 2004. Following his graduation, he was a postdoctoral researcher at the National Center for Atmospheric Research for two years. In 2006 he joined Oakland University where he is currently a Professor of Statistics. His current research interests include statistical modeling of big time series data.

Yuehua Duan is a PhD student in Computer Science Department at the University of North Carolina, Charlotte. Her research interests include recommender systems, business analytics, data mining, natural language processing, and machine learning.

Dishit Duggar is currently Studying at Vellore Institute of Technology, Vellore (India) pursuing Btech in Computer Science with Specialization in Information Security. He completed his schooling from Delhi Public School, Jaipur wherein he secured 10 cgpa in 10th grade and was a gold medal recipient for being a scholar for 6 consecutive years. After choosing PCM and completing his 12th grade with 93.8 percentage, He developed a lot of interest in coding and hence chose Computer Science as his career. In VIT, he is the App Lead of VinnovateIT which is a lab setup by Cognizant and also a member at Student Technical Community which is backed by Microsoft. He is passionate about Apps, Blockchain and Machine Learning and has worked on many projects as well as contributed and lead teams in multiple Hackathons. He wants to focus on a career in research and is currently exploring Cyber Security and Artificial Intelligence.

Ankur Dumka is working as Associate Professor and head of department in Women Institute of Technology, Dehradun. He is having more than 10 years of academic and industrial experience. He is having more than 60 research papers in reputed journals and conferences of repute. He contributed 4 books and 12 book chapters with reputed publisher. He is also associated with many reputed journals in the capacity of editorial board members and editor.

Abhishek Dutta has completed BS in Computer Science from Calcutta University and MS in Data Science and Analytics from Maulana Abul Kalam Azad University of Technology, Kolkata, India in 2020. He has authored seven conference papers which are published in IEEE Xplore and Springer Link. His research areas include Machine Learning, Deep Learning and AI applications in Finance.

Santosha Kumar Dwivedy received the Ph.D. in Mechanical Engineering from Indian Institute of Technology Kharagpur (IIT Kharagpur), India in 2000. He is currently Professor in Department of Mechanical Engineering at Indian Institute of Technology Guwahati (IIT Guwahati). He was also a Visiting Professor at Institute of Engineering and Computational Mechanics, University of Stuttgart, Germany under DAAD-IIT faculty exchange scheme. He has over 180 journal and conference publications with a focus on integrating robotics and dynamics in various fields. His research interests include both industrial and medical robotics, biomechanics, nonlinear vibration, and control along with the applications.

Brent M. Egan, MD, is Vice-President, Cardiovascular Disease Prevention in the Improving Health Outcomes group of the American Medical Association. He also serves as Professor of Medicine at the University of South Carolina School of Medicine, Greenville and as Past-President of the South Carolina Upstate affiliate of the American Heart Association. He received his medical degree and training in medicine and hypertension at the University of Michigan. He also served on the Board of Directors and President of the International Society of Hypertension in Blacks for many years. His professional interests center on hypertension, metabolic syndrome and vascular disease, which led to some 350 original papers and reviews. Dr. Egan remains committed to working with colleagues to translate the evidence-base into better cardiovascular health, especially for medically underserved populations.

Amal El Arid has earned a Masters' degree in Electrical and Computer Engineering from the American University of Beirut. She has been an instructor in the Department of Computer Science and Information Technology at the Lebanese International University since 2012. In addition, she specializes in programming and networking fields, earning a trainer certificate from the CISCO organization as a CCNA instructor since 2016. She is now working in the artificial intelligence and machine learning research field.

Houda El Bouhissi graduated with an engineering degree in computer science from Sidi-Bel-Abbes University - Algeria, in 1995. She received her M. Sc. and Ph. D. in computer science from the University of Sidi-Bel-Abbes, Algeria, in 2008 and 2015, respectively. Also, she received an M. Sc. in eLearning from the University of sciences and technologies, Lille1, France. Currently, she is an Assistant Professor at the University of Bejaia, Algeria. Her research interests include recommender systems, sentiments analysis, information systems interoperability, ontology engineering, and machine learning.

Mohamed El Touhamy is a Senior Data Engineer at The American University in Cairo (AUC). He completed his undergraduate studies at the Faculty of Computers and Information, Cairo University, earning a bachelor's degree in Computer Science. Mohamed started his journey in data science in 2017, participating in and leading many mega projects. He has excellent experience in big data engineering, data extraction using different technologies, data quality checks automation, and data warehouse enterprise solution management. He is also a graduate student at The American University in Cairo, seeking his master's degree in Computer Science.

Caner Erden, currently working as Assistant Professor in the Faculty of Applied Sciences, Sakarya University of Applied Sciences, Sakarya, Turkey. He worked as resarch assistant of Industrial Engineering at Sakarya University and researcher at Sakarya University Artificial Intelligence Systems Application and Research between 2012-2020. He holds a PhD degree in Industrial Engineering from Natural Science Institue Industrial Engineering Department, Sakarya University, Turkey with thesis titled "Dynamic Integrated Process Planning, Scheduling and Due Date Assignment". His research interests include scheduling, discrete event simulation, meta-heuristic algorithms, modelling and optimization, decision-making under uncertainty, machine learning and deep learning.

Omar El-Gayar has made a significant contribution to the conceptualization and formulation of the research objective and methodology, the proposed framework, and the interpretation of the findings. He is a Professor of Information Systems at Dakota State University. His research interests include analytics, business intelligence, and decision support. His numerous publications appear in various information technology-related venues. Dr. El-Gayar serves as a peer and program evaluator for accrediting agencies such as the Higher Learning Commission and ABET and as a peer reviewer for numerous journals and conferences. He is a member of the association for Information Systems (AIS).

Gozde Erturk Zararsiz is a faculty member in Biostatistics Department of Erciyes University. Her research mostly focuses on statistical modeling, method comparison, survival analysis and machine learning. Zararsiz completed her M.Sc. from Cukurova University, Institute of Health Sciences, Department of Biostatistics with the thesis entitled as "Evolution of Competing Risks Based on Both Dependent-Independent Real and Simulated Data by Using Self-Developed R Program". In 2015, Zararsiz has started her Ph.D. in Department of Biostatistics of Eskisehir Osmangazi University. During her Ph.D. in 2016, Zararsiz worked as a visiting researcher under the supervision of Prof. Dr. Christoph Klein at the laboratory of the Dr von Hauner Children's Hospital, LMU in Munich. During her research period, Zararsiz has published international papers and received awards. Zararsiz completed her PhD with the thesis entitled as "Bootstrap-Based Regression Approaches in Comparing Laboratory Methods".

Tasnia Fatin is a PhD Candidate in Management at Putra Business School, UPM, Malaysia. She has been a Lecturer of Marketing at Northern University Bangladesh (BBA, MBA) where she has taught Brand Management, Strategic Marketing, Principles of Marketing and Marketing Management. She had also been a Lecturer at Independent University Bangladesh. She takes keen interest in Entrepreneurship and has been running her own Business Solutions Agency and a Skill Training Institute. She holds an

MBA in Marketing from the University of Dhaka. She has also worked as a Strategic Marketing Manager for Prasaad Group of Companies to develop real estate projects home and abroad. She has also separately worked on projects in Urban Waste Management and Sustainable Agriculture that has been presented at George Washington University (USA), MIT (USA), Queens University (Canada) and at KLCC (Malaysia). Her research interests include digital marketing, disruptive innovations and the way they shape the world, IoT (Internet of Things), and sustainable business practices. She participated in several national level, Government level, and International level Youth Conferences and Forums home and abroad mentored by Industry leaders, experts, and professors from Harvard, Oxford, and many other prestigious institutions.

Arafat Febriandirza is a junior researcher at the Research Center for Informatics, The Indonesia Institute of Sciences (LIPI), Indonesia since 2020. He obtained his bachelor degree in Electrical Engineering from University of General Achmad Yani, Indonesia in 2008. He earned a Master's degree in Information Technology from the University of Indonesia in 2011 and a Doctorate in Communication and Transportation Engineering from Wuhan university of Technology in 2018. Arafat Febriandirza's research interests include issues in the field of Machine Learning, Modeling, Simulation, and Social Informatics.

Egi Arvian Firmansyah is a permanent lecturer at the Faculty of Economics and Business Universitas Padjadjaran, Indonesia. He has been published numerous journal articles and conferences proceedings. He is also a finance and managing editor at Jurnal Bisnis dan Manajemen, which is an accredited and reputable journal in Indonesia. Currently, he is a Ph.D student in finance at Universiti Brunei Darussalam.

Robert Leslie Fisher was educated in New York City. He attended Stuyvesant High School, a special science high school, has a bachelors degree (cum laude) in sociology from City College of New York, and a graduate degree in sociology from Columbia University. He is the author of several books including "Invisible Student Scientists (2013)" and the forthcoming Educating Public Interest Professionals and the Student Loan Debt Crisis." He has previously contributed chapters to encyclopedias and handbooks published by IGI Global including John Wang International Handbook of Business Analytics and Optimization as well as the International Encyclopedia of Information Sciences and Technology, and the International Encyclopedia of Modern Educational Technologies, Applications, and Management (both edited by Mehdi Khosrow-Pour). Mr. Fisher resides in the USA. He is an independent contractor.

Wendy Flores-Fuentes received the bachelor's degree in electronic engineering from the Autonomous University of Baja California in 2001, the master's degree in engineering from Technological Institute of Mexicali in 2006, and the Ph.D. degree in science, applied physics, with emphasis on Optoelectronic Scanning Systems for SHM, from Autonomous University of Baja California in June 2014. By now she is the author of 36 journal articles in Elsevier, IEEE, Emerald and Springer, 18 book chapters and 8 books in Springer, Intech, IGI global Lambert Academic and Springer, 46 proceedings articles in IEEE ISIE 2014-2021, IECON 2014, 2018, 2019, the World Congress on Engineering and Computer Science (IAENG 2013), IEEE Section Mexico IEEE ROCC2011, and the VII International Conference on Industrial Engineering ARGOS 2014. Recently, she has organized and participated as Chair of Special Session on ''Machine Vision, Control and Navigation'' at IEEE ISIE 2015-2021 and IECON 2018, 2019. She has participated has Guest Editor at Journal of Sensors with Hindawi, The International Journal of Advanced

Robotic Systems with SAGE, IEEE Sensors, and Elsevier Measurement. She holds 1 patent of Mexico and 1 patent of Ukraine. She has been a reviewer of several articles in Taylor and Francis, IEEE, Elsevier, and EEMJ. Currently, she is a full-time professor at Universidad Autónoma de Baja California, at the Faculty of Engineering. She has been incorporated into CONACYT National Research System in 2015. She did receive the award of "Best session presentation" in WSECS2013 in San-Francisco, USA. She did receive as coauthor the award of "Outstanding Paper in the 2017 Emerald Literati Network Awards for Excellence". Her's interests include optoelectronics, robotics, artificial intelligence, measurement systems, and machine vision systems.

Jeffrey Yi-Lin Forrest is a professor of mathematics and the research coach for the School of Business at Slippery Rock University of Pennsylvania. His research interest covers a wide range of topics, including, but not limited to, economics, finance, mathematics, management, marketing and systems science. As of the end of 2020, he has published over 600 research works, 24 monographs and 27 special topic edited volumes.

Raksh Gangwar is working as Professor and Director in Women Institute of Technology, Dehradun. He is having more than 35 years of experience. He has guided many Ph.D and M.Tech scholars. He is also member of many committee of national/international repute. He has contributed many research papers. He has also contributed many patents under his name.

Ge Gao is a Professor at Zhuhai College of Science and Technology and Management School at Jilin University. Her research focuses on Blockchain application, Supply Chain Management, Big Data application, user interface management in mobile commerce, and Social electronic commerce.

Araceli Gárate-García is a full-time professor at the Universidad Politécnica de Baja California (UPBC) since 2017. She received her PhD in electronics and telecommunications in conjoint between the CICESE research center, Mexico and the IRCCyN research center of the ECN university, France in 2011, the M.Sc. degree in electronics and telecommunications from CICESE research center in 2006 and her bachelor degree in Electronic Engineering in 2003 from the ITM university. Her main research interests are the analysis and control of nonlinear systems with and without time delays and the symbolic computation.

María J. García G. is Bachelor in Chemistry and has a master in Operations Research (OR). Together others authors had increase their investigations, already two hundred and forty, mainly in the areas of Evaluation and Management of Projects, Knowledge Management, Managerial and Social Decision making and OR, especially in multi-criteria decision. They have been presented or published in different countries, having publications and offering their reports, chats or conferences in: Azerbaijan, Finland, Poland, Croatia, Switzerland, Greece, Germany, Italy, Czech Republic, Iceland, Lithuania, Spain, France, Portugal, United States, Panama, Uruguay, Brazil, Mexico, Argentina and Chile besides attending as guest speaker, in lectures to relevant events in Colombia, Peru, Spain and Venezuela. Among other works she is coauthor of: "Inventories control, the Inventory manager and Matrixes Of Weighing with multiplicative factors (MOWwMf)"; "A Methodology of the Decision Support Systems Applied to Other Projects of Investigation"; "Matrixes Of Weighing and catastrophes"; "Multiattribute Model with Multiplicative Factors and Matrixes Of Weighing and the Problem of the Potable Water"

Nuno Geada has a Master's degree in Systems Information Management by Polytechnic Institute of Setúbal - School of Business Sciences and Management -Setúbal, Degree in Industrial Management and Technology by Polytechnic Institute of Setúbal - School of Technology of Setubal. He has written chapters, and papers to journals about topics regarding information technology management and strategic change management. He is from the Editorial Board - Associate Editor from International Journal of Business Strategy and Automation (IJBSA). He is the Editor of the book Reviving Businesses with New Organizational Change Management Strategies. His main research interests in information systems management, strategy, knowledge management, change management, and information technology management adoption in business contexts throw models and frameworks. He works as a Professor and a Researcher.

Natheer K. Gharaibeh is currently Associate Professor at College of Computer Science & Engineering at Yanbu - Taibah University from June 2016. He has more than 17 years of experience: He worked as Assistant Professor at College of Computer Science & Engineering at Yanbu – Taibah University from September. 2013 till June 2016. Before that he worked as an Assistant Professor at Balqa Applied University. He also worked as part-time Lecturer at Jordan University of Science and Technology (JUST) and other Jordanian universities. He published many papers in International Journals and participated in several International Conferences. His current research interests are: Business Intelligence, NLP, IR, Software Engineering, and Knowledge Societies. He got a grant for a joint project from the DFG with Rostock Technical University - Germany. He is editorial board Member, reviewer, and Keynote speaker in many International Journals and Conferences, he also has membership in many International and Technical Societies.

Abichal Ghosh is a final year B.E. student pursuing his degree in Computer Science from BITS Pilani K.K. Birla Goa campus. His field of interest lies in the research areas of Artificial Intelligence, Machine Learning, Deep Learning, Image Processing, Computer Vision and their application in various fields such as Desalination by Membrane technology, Ozonation, and more. Recently, he has been working for the prediction of the optimal conditions of Thin Film Nanocomposite Membranes for efficient desalination. For the topics related to Computer Vision, he has previously worked in the topic of Segmentation and is also currently working on the topic of Learned Image Compression.

Christoph Glauser was born in Berne in 1964. After studying History, Political Science and Media Science in Berne and Law in Geneva, he obtained a doctorate at the University of Berne in 1994. Christoph Glauser then participated in the national research programme, NFP27 at the University of Geneva. As a lecturer in Journalism and Online Research, he worked at various universities. He lectured in the subject, „Organisational Learning" in Social Psychology at the University of Zurich and for six years, he was the leading researcher and lecturer at ETH Zurich. In 1997-1998 he was a Visiting Lecturer at the University of Washington in Seattle, for which he continued to lecture their graduate students in Rome until 2006. During that time, he was Visiting Lecturer for online research at various universities both in Switzerland and abroad. Since 1998, Christoph Glauser has developed a successful career as online expert, CEO and delegate of governing boards, in particular (delete 'of') MMS – Media Monitoring Switzerland AG - and in diverse IT companies. Since 1994, he has been running the Institute for Fundamental Studies in Computer-assisted Content Analyses IFAA in Berne. In 2001, Glauser founded the URL study factory for competition analyses, ArgYou (Arguments for You), in order to study content of websites on the internet and compare these via search engines with the searched-for content (online effect research). In 2006, this company evolved into ArgYou AG in Baar (Switzerland), where he has remained as Chair of the governing board up to the present. For some years, Glauser has been serving on several European committees as an expert in e-governance. Subsequently, in 2007, he was one of the sixteen members of the jury for the European Union e-Government award, which honours the best European e-government projects on behalf of the European Commission. Since 2014 he has been operating the IFAAR find-engine set up directly for purposes of digital evaluation.

Rajesh Godasu is pursuing a Ph.D. in information systems at Dakota State University, his research interest is Deep learning in medical images. He has worked with Dr. Zeng for the past three years on different Machine Learning, Data Science, and Predictive Analytics topics. Conducted research on the Topic "Transfer Learning in Medical Image Classification" and published two papers in Information systems conferences, MWAIS and AMCIS.

Jorge Gomes is a researcher at ADVANCE, ISEG, School of Economics & Management of the Universidade de Lisboa. He holds a PhD in Management from ISEG and a Masters in Management Sciences from ISCTE-IUL, He also have a post-graduation in Project Management from INDEG/ISCTE, and a degree in Geographic Engineering from the Faculty of Sciences of the Universidade de Lisboa. During the past 30 years, he has worked as an engineer, project manager, quality auditor and consultant. Teaches Management at ULHT, Lisboa. His research interests include Benefits Management, Project Management, Project Success, Maturity Models, IS/IT Investments, IS/IT in Healthcare, and IS/IT Management.

Hale Gonce Kocken is an Associate Professor in the Department of Mathematical Engineering at the Yildiz Technical University (YTU), Istanbul, Turkey. She has been a faculty member of YTU since 2004. She completed her Ph.D. entitled "Fuzzy approaches to network analysis" in Applied Mathematics (2011) from the same department. Her current area of research is mathematical programming, supply chain management, and some related Operational Research subjects in multi-criteria and fuzzy environments.

Rick Gorvett is Professor and Chair of the Mathematics Department at Bryant University. He is a Fellow of the Casualty Actuarial Society.

M. Govindarajan is currently an Associate Professor in the Department of Computer Science and Engineering, Annamalai University, Tamil Nadu, India. He received the B.E, M.E and Ph.D Degree in Computer Science and Engineering from Annamalai University, Tamil Nadu, India in 2001, 2005 and 2010 respectively. He did his post-doctoral research in the Department of Computing, Faculty of Engineering and Physical Sciences, University of Surrey, Guildford, Surrey, United Kingdom in 2011 and at CSIR Centre for Mathematical Modelling and Computer Simulation, Bangalore in 2013. He has visited countries like Czech Republic, Austria, Thailand, United Kingdom (twice), Malaysia, U.S.A (twice), and Singapore. He has presented and published more than 140 papers at Conferences and Journals and also received best paper awards. He has delivered invited talks at various national and international conferences. His current research interests include Data Mining and its applications, Web Mining, Text Mining, and Sentiment Mining. He has completed two major projects as principal investigator and has produced four Ph.Ds. He was the recipient of the Achievement Award for the field in the Conference in Bio-Engineering, Computer Science, Knowledge Mining (2006), Prague, Czech Republic. He received

Career Award for Young Teachers (2006), All India Council for Technical Education, New Delhi, India and Young Scientist International Travel Award (2012), Department of Science and Technology, Government of India, New Delhi. He is a Young Scientists awardee under Fast Track Scheme (2013), Department of Science and Technology, Government of India, New Delhi and also granted Young Scientist Fellowship (2013), Tamil Nadu State Council for Science and Technology, Government of Tamil Nadu, Chennai. He also received the Senior Scientist International Travel Award (2016), Department of Science and Technology, Government of India. He has published ten book chapters and also applied patent in the area of data mining. He is an active Member of various professional bodies and Editorial Board Member of various conferences and journals.

Ashwin Gupta has currently completed his BSc with Major in Computer Science from St. Xavier's College, Kolkata. His current research interest is Data Analytics and Machine Learning.

Neha Gupta is currently working as an Professor, Faculty of Computer Applications at Manav Rachna International Institute of Research and Studies, Faridabad campus. She has completed her PhD from Manav Rachna International University and has done R&D Project in CDAC-Noida. She has total of 12+ year of experience in teaching and research. She is a Life Member of ACM CSTA, Tech Republic and Professional Member of IEEE. She has authored and coauthored 30 research papers in SCI/SCOPUS/Peer Reviewed Journals (Scopus indexed) and IEEE/IET Conference proceedings in areas of Web Content Mining, Mobile Computing, and Web Content Adaptation. She is a technical programme committee (TPC) member in various conferences across globe. She is an active reviewer for International Journal of Computer and Information Technology and in various IEEE Conferences around the world. She is one of the Editorial and review board members in International Journal of Research in Engineering and Technology.

Jafar Habibi is an associate professor at the Computer Engineering Department, Sharif University of Technology, Iran. He has been the head of the Computer Society of Iran and the Department of Computer Engineering. His main research interests are Internet of Things, Simulation, System Analysis and Design, and Social Network Analysis.

Christian Haertel studied business informatics at Otto von Guericke University Magdeburg. He joined the VLBA research team in 2021 and accompanies research projects with external partners (e.g., Google Cloud, Accenture Digital). The modelling and development of concepts in the areas of data science and cloud computing are his main areas of research.

J. Michael Hardin is the Provost and Vice President and Professor of Quantitative Analysis at Samford University. Dr. Hardin came to Samford University in July 2015 from the University of Alabama at Tuscaloosa, where he served as the Culverhouse College of Commerce and Business Administration dean. Dr. Hardin had previously served as Culverhouse's senior associate dean, associate dean for research, director of the University of Alabama's NIH Alabama EPSCoR Agency and director of Culverhouse's Institute of Business Intelligence. Dr. Hardin's service as a Culverhouse professor of quantitative analysis, business and statistics was widely credited for establishing the University of Alabama as an internationally-known resource in the field of data analytics. His Culverhouse career followed his numerous administrative and faculty appointments at the University of Alabama in Birmingham in biostatistics, biomathematics, health informatics and computer science. Dr. Hardin holds a Ph.D. in Applied Statistics from the University of Alabama, M.A. in Mathematics from the University of Alabama, M.S. in Research Design and Statistics from Florida State University's College of Education, B.A. in Mathematics from the University of West Florida, B.A. in Philosophy from the University of West Florida and M.Div. from New Orleans Baptist Theological Seminary. He is an ordained Southern Baptist minister. Dr. Hardin has authored or co-authored more than 150 papers in various journals, edited numerous professional journals, authored multiple book chapters, presented more than 250 abstracts at national meetings and given more than 150 invited lectures or talks. For 25 years he served as a National Institutes of Health (NIH) grant reviewer and participated as Investigator or co-Investigator on more than 100 U.S. Department of Health and Human Services/NIH-funded projects. He has served as a consultant for other national healthcare and financial organizations and was among the inventors receiving a U.S. patent licensed to MedMined, a Birmingham-based firm dedicated to controlling hospital infection rates and improving patient care.

Shanmugasundaram Hariharan received his B.E degree specialized in Computer Science and Engineering from Madurai Kammaraj University, Madurai, India in 2002, M.E degree specialized in the field of Computer Science and Engineering from Anna University, Chennai, India in 2004. He holds his Ph.D degree in the area of Information Retrieval from Anna University, Chennai, India. He is a member of IAENG, IACSIT, ISTE, CSTA and has 17 years of experience in teaching. Currently he is working as Professor in Department of Computer Science and Engineering, Vardhaman College of Engineering, India. His research interests include Information Retrieval, Data mining, Opinion Mining, Web mining. He has to his credit several papers in referred journals and conferences. He also serves as editorial board member and as program committee member for several international journals and conferences.

Budi Harsanto is a lecturer at Universitas Padjadjaran, Bandung, Indonesia. His research interests are in sustainability innovation, and operations and supply chain management.

Md Salleh Salleh Hassan, Prof., PhD, is a retired Professor at the Department of Communication, Faculty of Modern Languages and Communication, Universiti Putra Malaysia. He has graduated many PhD, master's and undergraduate students. He was once the Deputy Dean of the Faculty, and has published many research papers, attended many conferences both local and international.

Miralem Helmefalk, PhD, is an assistant senior lecturer at the Department of Marketing in School of Business and Economics at Linnaeus University in Sweden. Miralem's research interests lie in concepts within consumer psychology, digitalization, gamification as well as sensory marketing. He believes that machine learning represents the perfect storm for his research interests.

Gilberto J. Hernández is a Bachelor in Chemistry and have a master in Technology of foods. Together others authors had increase their investigations, mainly in the areas of Food technologies, Playful, in particular in the fantastic sports leagues, Knowledge Management, Managerial and Social Decision making, Logistics, Risk Management and Operations research, especially in multi-criteria decision and making decision under uncertainty and risk. They have been presented or published in different countries, having publications and offering their reports, chats or conferences in: Finland, Poland, Croatia, Switzerland, Greece, Czech Republic, Spain, Portugal and United States besides attending as guest speaker, in lectures to relevant events in Costa Rica and Venezuela. Among other works he is coauthor of: "Enterprise Logistics, Indicators and Physical Distribution Manager"; "Multiattribute Models with Multiplicative factors in the Fantasy Sports"; "The Industrial design manager of LoMoBaP and Knowledge Management"; "Dynamic knowledge: Diagnosis and Customer Service".

José Hernández Ramírez is a Chemical Engineer and have a master in Operations Research. Together others authors had increase their investigations, already above two hundred and forty, mainly in the areas of Knowledge Management, Managerial and Social Decision making, Logistics, Risk Management and Operations research, especially in multi-criteria decision. They have been presented or published in different countries, having publications and offering their reports, chats or conferences in: Azerbaijan, Finland, Croatia, Switzerland, Greece, Germany, Italy, Czech Republic, Iceland, Lithuania, Spain, France, Portugal, United States, Panama, Paraguay, Uruguay, Brazil, Cuba, Mexico, Argentina and Chile besides attending as guest speaker, in reiterated occasions, in lectures to relevant events in Colombia, Peru, Costa Rica, Brazil, Spain and Venezuela. Among other works he is coauthor of: "Teaching Enterprise Logistics through Indicators: Dispatch Manager"; "Enterprise diagnosis and the Environmental manager of LoMoBaP"; "Logistics, Marketing and Knowledge Management in the Community of Consumer".

Thanh Ho received M.S. degree in Computer Science from University of Information Technology, VNU-HCM, Vietnam in 2009 and PhD degree in Computer Science from University of Information Technology, VNU-HCM, Vietnam. He is currently lecturer in Faculty of Information Systems, University of Economics and Law, VNU-HCM, Vietnam in 2018. His research interests are Data mining, Data Analytics, Business Intelligence, Social Network Analysis, and Big Data.

Victoria Hodge is a Research Fellow and Software Developer in the Department of Computer Science at University of York. Her research interests include AI, outlier detection, and data mining. She is currently researching the safety assurance of machine learning for autonomous systems. A focus of this research is assuring robot navigation including localisation. She is on the editorial board of two journals and has authored over 60 refereed publications. She has worked in industry as a software architect for a medical diagnostics company; and as a software developer on condition monitoring in industrial environments, and deep learning for robot navigation.

Essam H. Houssein received his PhD degree in Computer Science in 2012. He is an associate professor at the Faculty of Computers and Information, Minia University, Egypt. He is the founder and chair of the Computing & Artificial Intelligence Research Group (CAIRG) in Egypt. He has more than 100 scientific research papers published in prestigious international journals in the topics for instance meta-heuristics optimization, artificial intelligence, image processing, IoT and its applications. Essam H. Houssein serves as a reviewer of more than 40 journals (Elsevier, Springer, IEEE, etc.). His research interests include WSNs, IoT, AI, Bioinformatics and Biomedical, Image processing, Data mining, and Meta-heuristics Optimization techniques.

Adamkolo Mohammed Ibrahim is a Lecturer at the Department of Mass Communication, University of Maiduguri, Nigeria and a PhD Research Scholar at Bayero University, Kano (BUK), Nigeria. He received his master's degree in Development Communication at Universiti Putra Malaysia (UPM) in 2017. In 2007, he had his first degree (BA Mass Communication) at the Department of Mass Communication, University of Maiduguri, Nigeria. Currently, he teaches mass communication at the University of Maiduguri. He conducts research and writes in ICT adoption for development, social media, cyberbullying, cyber terrorism/conflict, gender and ICT, gender and conflict and online shopping. He has published several journal articles, book chapters and a few books. His most recent work explores the impacts of fake news and hate speech in Nigerian democracy and proposes a theoretical model as a fact-checking tool. More details on his most recent works and all his other publications can be accessed on his website: https://unimaid.academia.edu/AdamkoloMohammedIbrahim. Malam Adamkolo is currently serving as an Editorial Board Member of Jurnal Komunikasi Ikatan Sarjana Komunikasi Indonesia (the Communication Journal of the Indonesian Association of Communication Scholars) and a co-researcher in a research project by The Kukah Centre, Abuja, Nigeria. The proposed title of the research is: "Engaging Local Communities for Peacebuilding, Social Cohesion, Preventing and Countering Violent Extremism in Nigeria's northeast". Adamkolo has received Publons Top Reviewer Award in 2018 (for being among the top 1% global peer reviewers in Psychiatry/Psychology). In 2017, Elsevier had awarded him a certificate of outstanding peer review with one of Elsevier's prestigious journals, Computers in Human Behaviour (CHB) which he reviews for; he also reviews for Emerald's Journal of Systems and Information Technology (JSIT) and several other journals. Much earlier, from 2000 to 2010, he worked as a broadcast journalist in Yobe Broadcasting Corporation (YBC) Damaturu, and from 2008 to 2010 was deployed to Sahel FM (formerly Pride FM, a subsidiary of YBC Damaturu as DJ-cum-producer/presenter/journalist). From 2008 to 2010, he worked as YBC's focal person on UNICEF and Partnership for the Revival of Routine Immunisation in Northern Nigeria-Maternal, newborn and Child Health (PRRINN-MNCH). From September to October 2018, he served as a consultant to ManienDanniels (West Africa Ltd.) and MNCH2 programme.

Funda Ipekten's research focused on a statistical analysis of high-throughput metabolomics data, multi-omics data integration, feature selection for multi-omics.

Adelina Ivanova is Assisted Professor Dr. in Department of Computer Systems and Informatics of University of Forestry, Sofia, Bulgaria. Her research interests are in the areas of ontology engineering, sustainable development, databases, and office information systems.

Sajan T. John is an Associate Professor of Industrial Engineering in the Department of Mechanical Engineering at Viswajyothi College of Engineering and Technology, Vazhakulam, Kerala. He received PhD from the National Institute of Technology Calicut in 2015. His research interests are in the areas of operations research, mathematical modelling, supply chain management and reverse logistics. He has published papers in international journals and proceedings of international and national conferences.

Rachid Kaleche is a PhD student of computer science since 2018. He is member of computer science laboratory (LIO) of Oran 1 university in Algeria. His current research interests deal with artificial intelligence, transportation system, logistic systems, machine learning, and bio-inspired approach. He is co-author of many publications and communications.

Reddi Kamesh received B.Tech in Chemical engineering from Acharya Nagarjuna University, Guntur, India, in 2011, and M.Tech and Ph.D. from Academy of and Innovative Research (AcSIR), CSIR-Indian Institute of Chemical Technology (IICT), Campus, Hyderabad, India, in 2014 and 2019 respectively. Dr. Kamesh has extensive experience in the field of Process Systems Engineering (PSE), Artificial Intelligence (AI) and Machine Learning methods, Integrated Multi-Scale Modelling methods, and Process Intensification. He is working as a scientist in CSIR-IICT since 2016. He has actively engaged in basic research as well as applied research. He has developed process model-based as well as AI-based methodologies to simulate, design, control, and optimize processes, for accelerated product and process design, and to achieve performance improvements to existing processes in terms of improving productivity and selectivity while maintaining their safety and environmental constraints. Dr. Kamesh was a recipient of the Ambuja Young Researchers Award in 2014 from Indian Institute of Chemical Engineers (IIChE).

Shri Kant has received his Ph. D. in applied mathematics from applied mathematics departments of institute of technology, Banaras Hindu University (BHU), Varanasi in 1981. He is working as a Professor and head of "Center of Cyber Security and cryptology", Department of Computer Science and Engineering of Sharda University, India and involved actively in teaching and research mainly in the area of cyber security and Machine learning. His areas of interest are Special Functions, Cryptology, Pattern Recognition, Cluster Analysis, Soft Computing Model, Machine Learning and Data Mining.

Nurdan Kara is an Assistant Prof. in the Department of Mathematics at National Defence University (MSU), Istanbul, Turkey. She has been a faculty member of Ankara University since 1998. She completed her Ph.D. entitled "Fuzzy approaches to multiobjective fractional transportation problem" in Applied Mathematics (2008) from Yildiz Technical University. Her current area of research is mathematical Programming, fractional programming, supply chain management and some related Operational Research subjects in multi criteria and fuzzy environments.

Prasanna Karhade is Associate Professor of IT Management, Shidler College Faculty Fellow and a Faculty Fellow at the Pacific Asian Center for Entrepreneurship [PACE] at the University of Hawai'i at Mānoa. His research interests include digital innovation and digital platforms in growing, rural, eastern, aspirational and transitional [GREAT] economies.

Bouamrane Karim received the PhD Degree in computer science from the Oran University in 2006. He is Professor of computer Science at Oran1 University. He is the head of "Decision and piloting system" team. His current research interests deal with decision support system and logistics in maritime transportation, urban transportation system, production system, health systems and application of bio-inspired based optimization metaheuristic. He participates in several scientific committees' international/national conferences in Algeria and others countries in the same domain and collaborated in Algerian-French scientific projects. He is co-author of more than 40 scientific publications.

Joseph Kasten is an Assistant Professor of Information Science and Technology at the Pennsylvania State University in York, PA. He earned a PhD in Information Science at Long Island University in Brookville, NY, an MBA at Dowling College in Oakdale, NY, and a BS in engineering at Florida Institute of Technology in Melbourne, FL. Before joining academia, Joe was a senior engineer with the Northrop-Grumman Corp. where he worked on various military and commercial projects such as the X-29 and the Boeing 777. His research interests center on the implementation of data analytics within the organization as well as the application of blockchain technology to emerging organizational requirements. Professor Kasten's recent research appears in the International Journal of Business Intelligence Research and International Journal of Healthcare Information Systems and Informatics.

Tolga Kaya is a full-time researcher and lecturer at the department of Management Engineering in Istanbul Technical University. His research areas are consumer modeling, statistical decision making, input-output modeling, multicriteria decision making, machine learning and fuzzy applications in business and management. He has published several papers and presented his research at a number of international conferences in these areas.

Wei Ke, Ph.D., is the Adjunct Associate Professor of Quantitative Revenue and Pricing Analytics at Columbia Business School. Previously, he was Managing Partner and the head of financial services practice in North America at Simon-Kucher & Partners. Wei received a Ph.D. in Decision, Risk, and Operations from Columbia Business School, and a BSc in Electrical Engineering & Applied Mathematics, summa cum laude, from Columbia University.

Vanessa Keppeler is a Senior Associate with PwC Germany's Financial Services Consulting practice. She specializes on the design and implementation of Data and AI Governance. Her research and studies focus on the practical enablement of Explainable AI in Financial Institutions. Vanessa holds a master's degree in Management (Finance).

Mehrnaz Khalaj Hedayati is an Assistant Professor of Management at Georgia College & State University, J. Whitney Bunting College of Business. Mehrnaz received her Ph.D. from the University of Rhode Island in 2020. Mehrnaz has published several academic journal articles. She is a Lean Six Sigma Certified from the URI College of Business. She has taught undergraduate and master's level courses in Business Quantitative Analysis, Business Statistics, and Operations Management. She has also served as ad-hoc reviewer for several academic journals.

Fahima Khanam is a Lecturer in the department of Aviation Operation Management at Bangabandhu Sheikh Mujibur Rahman Aviation and Aerospace University. Prior to joining the BSMRAAU, she served as Lecturer in the Department of Business Administration at Sheikh Burhanuddin Post Graduate College, European University, Victoria University and German University, Bangladesh where she taught Principles of Marketing, Marketing Management, Operations Management, International Business, and Business Communication. She also worked as a corporate professional in The Daily 'Prothom Alo', one of the top daily newspapers in Bangladesh. She holds an MBA in Marketing from University of Dhaka, Bangladesh. Her most recent publication appeared in the International Journal of Big Data and Analytics in Healthcare (IJBDAH). Her principal research interests include e-commerce, online shopping, social media marketing and branding strategy, marketing strategy and technology adoption.

Shardul Khandekar has his BE completed in E&TC and his research area includes machine learning and deep learning.

Mubina Khondkar serves as a Professor in the Department of Marketing at the University of Dhaka. She has interdisciplinary knowledge in the areas of marketing and development economics. She has both industry and research experiences with organizations including ANZ Grindlays Bank, Care Bangladesh, USAID, DFID, Concern, IFPRI, World Bank, SEDF, IFC, JICA, CIDA, UNICEF, BIDS, the University of Manchester, and the University of Cambridge. Her research interests include value chain analysis, marketing, poverty, microfinance, development economics, gender, and women's empowerment. Further details can be found here: https://www.researchgate.net/profile/Mubina-Khondkar.

Soumya Khurana has his BE completed in E&TC and his research area includes machine learning and deep learning.

Necla Koçhan is currently working as a postdoctoral researcher at Izmir Biomedicine and Genome Center, IBG. Her research interests are computational biology, statistical data analysis, fuzzy theory, classification, and biostatistics.

Koharudin is a master student in IPB University, Indonesia. In 2014 he joined the Bureau of Organization and Human Resource, Indonesian Institute of Sciences (LIPI), as IT Engineering. In 2020 He moved to Center for Scientific Data and Documentation, Indonesian Institute of Sciences (LIPI). His current roles include building and maintaining web applications, designing database architecture, integrating data and providing data through service point. He obtained his bachelor degree in Computer Science from the Sepuluh Nopember Institute of Technology in 2011. He has developed some applications such as Human Resources Information System, Mobile applications and API Gateway. His research interests include Bioinformatics, High Performance Computing and Machine Learning.

Tibor Koltay is Professor retired from the Institute of Learning Technologies at Eszterházy Károly Catholic University, in Hungary. He graduated from Eötvös Loránd University (Budapest, Hungary) in 1984 with an MA in Russian. He obtained there his PhD in 2002. In 1992 he was awarded the Certificate of Advanced Studies in Library and Information Science at Kent State University, Kent. OH.

Xiangfen Kong is an Associate Professor from the Civil Aviation University of China. Her research interests include smart airports, system reliability, operational research, and big data.

Elena Kornyshova is an Associate Professor at CNAM, Ph.D. in Economics and Management Sciences and Ph.D. in Computer Science. Her main research domains are method and process engineering, decision-making, enterprise architecture, and digitalization. She is/was involved in organization of multiple international conferences and workshops. She has significant experience in industry and consultancy sector mainly in the fields of IS engineering and enterprise architecture.

Maximiliano E. Korstanje is editor in chief of International Journal of Safety and Security in Tourism (UP Argentina) and Editor in Chief Emeritus of International Journal of Cyber Warfare and Terrorism (IGI-Global US). Korstanje is Senior Researchers in the Department of Economics at University of Palermo, Argentina. In 2015 he was awarded as Visiting Research Fellow at School of Sociology and Social Policy, University of Leeds, UK and the University of La Habana Cuba. In 2017 is elected as Foreign Faculty Member of AMIT, Mexican Academy in the study of Tourism, which is the most prominent institutions dedicated to tourism research in Mexico. He had a vast experience in editorial projects working as advisory member of Elsevier, Routledge, Springer, IGI global and Cambridge Scholar publishing. Korstanje had visited and given seminars in many important universities worldwide. He has also recently been selected to take part of the 2018 Albert Nelson Marquis Lifetime Achievement Award. a great distinction given by Marquis Who´s Who in the world.

Mika Kosonen is a graduate student in University of Lapland. He has bachelor's degree in social sciences and is currently finishing his master's degree. His bachelor's thesis was concerning artificial intelligence and ethics, and master's thesis contributes to morality in human-technology interaction, both with excellent grades. With strong interest in technology and human experience he is always wondering the world where technology mediates the reality, whether in suburbans or the wilderness found in northernmost parts of Europe.

Anjani Kumar is a Ph.D. student of computer science at the University of Nebraska at Omaha. He is working as a Data Scientist at Data Axle Inc. His primary research interests are in the fields of Big Data, Deep Learning, and Machine Learning.

Sameer Kumar is an Associate Professor at Universiti Malaya, Malaysia.

Madhusree Kundu is presently Professor, Department of Chemical Engineering, National Institute of Technology Rourkela, Orissa, India. Currently, HOD, Central Instrument Facility (CIF), NIT Rourkela. Experience: Worked as Process Engineer in Simon Carves India Limited (A Design Consultancy). First Academic Appointment: Assistant Professor, Birla Institute of Technology and Science (BITS) Pilani, Rajasthan, India. PhD: Indian Institute of Technology Kharagpur Research Interest: Fluid Phase equilibrium and its application, Modeling, & Simulation and Control, Chemommetrics/Machine Learning applications, Process Identification monitoring and Control, Biomimetic device development and Digitized Sustainable Agriculture.

Mascha Kurpicz-Briki obtained her PhD in the area of energy-efficient cloud computing at the University of Neuchâtel. After her PhD, she worked a few years in industry, in the area of open-source engineering, cloud computing and analytics. She is now professor for data engineering at the Bern University of Applied Sciences, investigating how to apply digital methods and in particular natural language processing to social and community challenges.

Kevin Kwak is an Information Systems and Accounting student at the University of Nebraska at Omaha. He received a Master's in Accounting and as of this writing is pursuing a Master's in Information Systems. His current interests of study are accounting, data security, and data mining. Currently, he has had five articles published in various journals.

Wikil Kwak is a Professor of Accounting at the University of Nebraska at Omaha. He received Ph.D. in Accounting from the University of Nebraska in Lincoln. Dr. Kwak's research interests include the areas of mathematical programming approaches in bankruptcy prediction, capital budgeting, transfer pricing, performance evaluation and Japanese capital market studies. He has published more than 57 articles in the Engineering Economist, Abacus, Contemporary Accounting Research, Review of Quantitative Finance and Accounting, Management Accountant, Journal of Petroleum Accounting and Financial Management, Business Intelligence and Data Mining, Review of Pacific Basin Financial Markets and Policies, and Multinational Business Review.

Georgios Lampropoulos received his BSc degree with the title of Information Technology Engineer specialized as a Software Engineer from the Department of Information Technology at Alexander

Technological Educational Institute of Thessaloniki (currently named International Hellenic University) in 2017 and he received his MSc in Web Intelligence from the same department in 2019. Currently, he is a PhD candidate and Visiting Lecturer in the Department of Information and Electronic Engineering at International Hellenic University and a MEd student in Education Sciences at Hellenic Open University. He has published his work in several peer reviewed journals and conferences, he has taken part in international research programs and he has also served as a reviewer and a member of the organizing and scientific committees of international conferences and international journals.

Torben Larsen is an MSc Econ from University of Aarhus and an international Degree in Strategic Management from University of Maryland-Tietgenskolen Dk. He has broad experience in regional planning of healthcare with Academic Awards from 1) Association of Hospital Managers in Norway, Lundbeck Fonden Dk and MIE96. He is a former Chief Research Consultant at University of Southern Denmark which included leadership of an EU-sponsored research project in Integrated Homecare. He has been involved with various courses and conferences and has written research papers in Health Economics, Neuroeconomics, Meditation and Biofeedback. 2017 he published "Homo Neuroeconomicus" (IJUDH(1)). 2020 he published "Neuroeconomic Pcyshology. 3 Modules for End-users . . . .", IJPCH Actually, he is giving guest lectures in cybernetic economics.

Matthias Lederer is Full Professor of Information Systems at the Technical University of Applied Sciences Amberg-Weiden. Prior to this, he was a professor at the ISM International School of Management Munich and at the same time Chief Process Officer at the IT Service Center of the Bavarian justice system. His previous positions include research assistant at the University of Erlangen-Nuremberg and strategy consultant at the German industrial company REHAU. His research and studies focus on business process management and IT management. Prof. Lederer holds a doctorate as well as a master's degree in international information systems and is the author of over 70 scientific publications in this field.

Eva Lee applies combinatorial optimization, math programming, game theory, and parallel computation to biological, medical, health systems, and logistics analyses. Her clinical decision-support systems (DSS) assist in disease diagnosis/prediction, treatment design, drug delivery, treatment and healthcare outcome analysis/prediction, and healthcare operations logistics. In logistics, she tackles operations planning and resource allocation, and her DSS addresses inventory control, vehicle dispatching, scheduling, transportation, telecom, portfolio investment, public health emergency treatment response, and facility location/planning. Dr. Lee is Director of the Center for Operations Research in Medicine and HealthCare, a center established through funds from the National Science Foundation and the Whitaker Foundation. The center focuses on biomedicine, public health and defense, translational medical research, medical delivery and preparedness, and the protection of critical infrastructures. She is a subject matter expert in medical systems and public health informatics, logistics and networks, and large-scale connected systems. She previously served as the Senior Health Systems Engineer and Professor for the U.S. Department of Veterans Affairs and was Co-Director for the Center for Health Organization Transformation. Dr. Lee has received numerous practice excellence awards, including the INFORMS Edelman Award on novel cancer therapeutics, the Wagner prize on vaccine immunity prediction, and the Pierskalla award on bioterrorism, emergency response, and mass casualty mitigation She is a fellow at INFORMS and AIMBE. Lee has served on NAE/NAS/IOM, NRC, NBSB, DTRA panel committees related to CBRN and WMD incidents, public health and medical preparedness, and healthcare systems innovation. She holds ten patents on medical systems and devices. Her work has been featured in the New York Times, London Times, disaster documentaries, and in other venues.

Jinha Lee is an Assistant Professor in the Department of Public and Allied Health at Bowling Green State University. His research interests include healthcare operations, data analytics, economic decision analysis, and system modeling in healthcare service. His work has examined practice variance and systems analysis for quality and process improvement and new clinical guidelines establishment. Also, his research has focused on economic analysis on industry networks, resource allocations, and the R&D process in healthcare services. His research primarily utilizes large datasets and clinical observations derived from various healthcare databases and field studies in clinical facilities. He has collaborated actively with hospitals, healthcare research institutes, and healthcare delivery organizations both in the U.S. and in foreign countries.

Ulli Leucht is a Manager in PwC Germany's Financial Services Technology Consulting team. He is an expert in AI and its use in Financial Institutions - which includes how AI use cases are identified, perceived, implemented, operated and surrounding governance, compliance, and legal requirements. Prior to joining PwC Germany, he worked with some of the most innovative FinTechs in the United Kingdom and the United States in the context of AI. Ulli's research and studies focus is the usage of AI in Financial Institutions. He holds a master's degree in Sensors and Cognitive Psychology.

Carson Leung is currently a Professor at the University of Manitoba, Canada. He has contributed more than 300 refereed publications on the topics of big data, computational intelligence, cognitive computing, data analytics, data mining, data science, fuzzy systems, machine learning, social network analysis, and visual analytics. These include eight chapters in IGI Global's books/encyclopedia (e.g., Encyclopedia of Organizational Knowledge, Administration, and Technology (2021)). He has also served on the Organizing Committee of the ACM CIKM, ACM SIGMOD, IEEE DSAA, IEEE ICDM, and other conferences.

Siyao Li is a student at the City University of Macau. She studies in the International Business program.

Gilson B. A. Lima is a Professor in the Industrial Engineering Department at Federal Fluminense University (UFF), Brazil. He received his PhD in the Rio de Janeiro Federal University, Brazil. His current research interests include industrial safety, risk management, industrial maintenance and industrial environmental management.

Yu-Wei Lin is an assistant professor in the Leavey School of Business, Santa Clara University. He received a Ph.D. in information systems at Gies College of Business, the University of Illinois at Urbana-Champaign. His research interests are in User-Generated Content, Healthcare Analytics, Online Review Analysis, Machine Learning, Decision Making, and Decision Support Systems.

Fangyao Liu is an assistant professor in the College of Electronic and Information at the Southwest Minzu University, China. He received Ph.D. in Information Technology from the University of Nebraska at Omaha, USA. Dr. Liu's research interests include the areas of data mining, artificial intelligence, and statistics. He has published more than 20 articles in the International journal of Computers Communications & Control, Journal of Urban Planning and Development, Journal of software, Journal of Asian Development, Journal of Contemporary Management, Procedia Computer Science, and several IEEE conferences.

Haoyu Liu is an assistant professor at the Faculty of Business, City University of Macau. He received an MPhil and a PhD in Operations Management from HKUST Business School in 2017 and 2020, respectively. He serves as a reviewer for Manufacturing & Service Operations Management (MSOM), Naval Research Logistics (NRL), International Journal of Applied Management Science (IJAMS), International Journal of Retail & Distribution Management (IJRDM), International Journal of E-Business Research (IJEBR), International Conference on Information Systems (ICIS), and INFORMS Conference on Service Science (ICSS). He has broad interests in issues related to healthcare, emerging technologies, charitable organizations, and marketing. In solving problems, he employs various techniques, ranging from game-theoretical and stochastic models to typical tools in empirical and experimental studies.

Ran Liu is an Assistant Professor in the Marketing department at Central Connecticut State University. His research focuses on online relationships, user-generated content (UGC), data modeling, and International businesses. He serves as Associate Editor (Asia) for Journal of Eastern European and Central Asian Research (JEECAR) and Faculty Advisor for American Marketing Association Collegiate Chapter.

Cèlia Llurba is currently a PhD student in Educational Technology in the Department of Pedagogy at the URV. Graduate in East Asian Studies from the UOC and a graduate in Mining Engineering from the UPC. She is currently a teacher of Technology in a high school in Cambrils (state employee) and also teaches in the subjects of Vocational Guidance and Citizenship, and Educational Processes and Contexts, within the Master's Degree in Teacher Training at the URV. Her main lines of research are: intellectual learning environments, data analytics and artificial intelligence in intellectual areas.

Manuel Lozano Rodriguez is American University of Sovereign Nations (AUSN) Visiting Prof. in his own discipline that takes bioethics off the medical hegemony to land it on social sciences, futurism, politics and pop culture through metaphysics of displacement. Born in Barcelona in 1978, Ph.D. in Bioethics, Sustainability and Global Public Health, AUSN; Master of Science in Sustainability, Peace and Development, AUSN; Graduate in Fundamentals of Sustainability Organizational, Harvard.

Lorenzo Magnani, philosopher, epistemologist, and cognitive scientist, is a professor of Philosophy of Science at the University of Pavia, Italy, and the director of its Computational Philosophy Laboratory. His previous positions have included: visiting researcher (Carnegie Mellon University, 1992; McGill University, 1992–93; University of Waterloo, 1993; and Georgia Institute of Technology, 1998–99) and visiting professor (visiting professor of Philosophy of Science and Theories of Ethics at Georgia Institute of Technology, 1999–2003; Weissman Distinguished Visiting Professor of Special Studies in Philosophy: Philosophy of Science at Baruch College, City University of New York, 2003). Visiting professor at the Sun Yat-sen University, Canton (Guangzhou), China from 2006 to 2012, in the event of the 50th anniversary of the re-building of the Philosophy Department of Sun Yat-sen University in 2010, an award was given to him to acknowledge his contributions to the areas of philosophy, philosophy of science, logic, and cognitive science. A Doctor Honoris Causa degree was awarded to Lorenzo Magnani by the Senate of the Ştefan cel Mare University, Suceava, Romania. In 2015 Lorenzo Magnani has been appointed member of the International Academy for the Philosophy of the Sciences (AIPS). He currently directs international research programs in the EU, USA, and China. His book Abduction, Reason, and Science (New York, 2001) has become a well-respected work in the field of human cognition. The book Morality in a Technological World (Cambridge, 2007) develops a philosophical and cognitive theory of the relationships between ethics and technology in a naturalistic perspective. The book Abductive Cognition. The Epistemological and Eco-Cognitive Dimensions of Hypothetical Reasoning and the last monograph Understanding Violence. The Intertwining of Morality, Religion, and Violence: A Philosophical Stance have been more recently published by Springer, in 2009 and 2011. A new monograph has been published by Springer in 2017, The Abductive Structure of Scientific Creativity. An Essay on the Ecology of Cognition, together with the Springer Handbook of Model-Based Science (edited with Tommaso Bertolotti). The last book Eco-Cognitive Computationalism. Cognitive Domestication of Ignorant Entities, published by Springer, offers an entirely new dynamic perspective on the nature of computation. He edited books in Chinese, 16 special issues of international academic journals, and 17 collective books, some of them deriving from international conferences. Since 1998, initially in collaboration with Nancy J. Nersessian and Paul Thagard, he created and promoted the MBR Conferences on Model-Based Reasoning. Since 2011 he is the editor of the Book Series Studies in Applied Philosophy, Epistemology and Rational Ethics (SAPERE), Springer, Heidelberg/Berlin.

Mazlina Abdul Majid is an Associate Professor in the Faculty of Computing at University Malaysia Pahang (UMP), Malaysia. She received her PHD in Computer Science from the University of Nottingham, UK. She held various managerial responsibilities as a Deputy Dean of Research and Graduate Studies and currently acts as the head of the Software Engineering Research Group in her Faculty. She also taught courses on the undergraduate and master's levels. She has published 130 research in local and international books, journals and conference proceedings. She is also a member of various committees of international conferences. Her research interests include simulation, software agent, software usability and testing.

Jasna D. Marković-Petrović received her B.Sc. (1992) and M.Sc. (2011) degrees in electrical engineering and her Ph.D. degree (2018) in technical sciences, all from the University of Belgrade, Serbia. She is with the Public Enterprise "Electric Power Industry of Serbia" for more than 25 years. Her activities involve implementation of the technical information system, participation in projects concerning upgrading the remote control system of the hydropower plant, and implementation of the SCADA security system. She is a member of the Serbian National CIGRÉ Study Committee D2. As author or coauthor, she published a number of book chapters, journal articles and conference papers in her field. Her main research interests involve smart grids, SCADA and industrial control systems security, and cyber risk management.

Roberto Marmo received the Laurea (cum laude) in Computer Science from Salerno University (Italy) and Ph.D. in Electronic and Computer Engineering obtained from the University of Pavia (Italy). He is presently contract teacher of computer science at Faculty of Engineering of Pavia University, Italy. His most recent work is concerned with mathematical models and software for social network analysis. He is author of "Social Media Mining", a textbook in Italian language on extraction of information from social media, website http://www.socialmediamining.it.

Nikolaos Matsatsinis is a full Professor of Information and Decision Support Systems in the School of Production Engineering and Management of the Technical University of Crete, Greece. He is President of the Hellenic Operational Research Society (HELORS). He is Director of DSS Lab and Postgraduate Programs. He has contributed as scientific or project coordinator on over of fifty national and international projects. He is chief editor of the Operational Research: An International Journal (Impact Factor 2020: 2.410) and International Journal of Decision Support Systems. He is the author or co-author/editor of 25 books and over of 120 articles in international scientific journals and books. He has organized and participated in the organization of over of ninety scientific conferences, including EURO 2021, and he has over of one hundred and ninety presentations in international and national scientific conferences. His research interests fall into the areas of Intelligent DSS, Multi-Agent Systems, Recommendation Systems, Multicriteria Decision Analysis, Group Decision Making, Operational Research, e-Marketing, Consumer Behaviour Analysis, Data Analysis, Business Intelligence & Business Analytics.

Hubert Maupas is graduated from Ecole Centrale de Lyon (France) and holds a PhD in Integrated Electronics, obtained with several patents and publications. He has spent most of his career in medical device industry and is currently working as COO of MUST, a all-in-one B2B Metaverse platform to manage DBE (Digital Business Ecosystem) embedding advanced matchmaking algorithms.

Iman Megahed is the AVP for Digital Transformation, Chief Strategy and Knowledge Officer at the American University in Cairo (AUC). She is currently responsible for all Information Technology, Information Security, Business Intelligence and institutional effectiveness functions. She co-founded the business intelligence and data governance functions to support informed based decision making. She also founded the office of Online Student Services which applied web services and portal technology to enhance student services. With a successful track record in technology and effectiveness administrative positions in Higher Education since 1992, Iman has accumulated extensive technical expertise, unique project management skills coupled with results-oriented leadership style and passion for informed based decision making. Iman earned her PhD in Organizational Behavior from Cairo University, MBA and BS in Computer Science from The American University in Cairo.

Natarajan Meghanathan is a tenured Full Professor of Computer Science at Jackson State University, Jackson, MS. He graduated with a Ph.D. in Computer Science from The University of Texas at Dallas in May 2005. Dr. Meghanathan has published more than 175 peer-reviewed articles (more than half of them being journal publications). He has also received federal education and research grants from the U. S. National Science Foundation, Army Research Lab and Air Force Research Lab. Dr. Meghanathan has been serving in the editorial board of several international journals and in the Technical Program Committees and Organization Committees of several international conferences. His research interests are Wireless Ad hoc Networks and Sensor Networks, Graph Theory and Network Science, Cyber Security, Machine Learning, Bioinformatics and Computational Biology. For more information, visit https://www.jsums.edu/nmeghanathan.

Abelardo Mercado Herrera has a PhD from the National Institute of Astrophysics, Optics and Electronics (INAOE), specializing in Astrophysics, Postdoctorate in Astrophysics from the Institute of Astronomy from the National Autonomous University of Mexico (UNAM), Electronics Engineer from the Autonomous University of Baja California (UABC). He is a specialist in the mathematical-statistical description of stochastic processes and/or deterministic systems, nonlinear systems, complex systems, chaos theory, among others, as well as its application to physical phenomena such as astronomy, medicine, economics, finance, telecommunications, social sciences etc., in order to determine the dynamics underlying in such processes, and given the case, its connection with real physical variables and possible prediction. He has worked on the development of interfaces and programs to carry out electrical tests in industry, as well as in scientific instrumentation, applied to telemetry, infrared polarimetry, optics and spectroscopy. He has also specialized in image analysis, measurement techniques and noise reduction.

Shivlal Mewada is presently working as an Assistant Professor (contact) in the Dept. of CS, Govt. Holkar (Autonomous, Model) Science College, Indore, India. He shared the responsibility of research activities and coordinator of M.Phil.(CS) at Govt. Holkar Sci. Collage, Indore. He has also received JRF in 2010-11 for M.Phil. Programme under UGC Fellow scheme, New Delhi. He is a member of IEEE since 2013 and editorial member of the ISROSET since 2013. He is a technical committee and editorial member of various reputed journals including Taylor & Francis, Inderscience. He chaired 5 national and international conferences and seminars. He organized 2 special for international conferences. He also contributed to the organization of 2 national and 4 virtual international conferences. Mr. Mewada has published 3 book chapters and over 18 research articles in reputed journals like SCI, Scopus including IEEE conferences. His areas of interest include; cryptography, information security and computational intelligence.

Tanish Ambrishkumar Mishra is an undergraduate student at Sardar Patel College of Engineering, Mumbai, India. Currently pursuing his Bachelor of Technology (B.Tech) in Department of Mechanical Engineering. His research areas of interest are mobile robotics, biomimetic robot design, robotic prosthetic limb design, control systems and AI/ML.

Mayank Modashiya is a Data Scientist 1 at Kenco Group, Chattanooga, TN, USA. He earned is Bachelor's in Engineering in Mechanical Engineering, India. He earned his Masters in Industrial Engineering from the University of Texas at Arlington. Mayank has passion for applying machine learning (ML) and artificial Intelligence (AI) to solve complex supply chain problems. Mayank has more than 2 years' experience in developing and implementing AI/ML for problem solving. His research interest includes supply chain networks, logistics and manufacturing. He is member of INFORMS and IISE.

Jordi Mogas holds a PhD in Educational Technology and a Bachelor's in Information and Documentation with mention in information systems management. Currently, he is a postdoc researcher at GEPS research center (Globalisation, Education and Social Policies), at the Universitat Autònoma de Barcelona, and belongs to ARGET (Applied Research Group in Education and Technology). Dr. Mogas teaches at both the Department of Pedagogy at the Universitat Rovira i Virgili (professor associate) and at the Department of Education at the Universitat Oberta de Catalunya (professor collaborador). His main research lines are: Smart Learning Environments, Virtual Learning Environments and Self-Regulated Learning.

Siddhartha Moulik is working as a Scientist in CSIR-IICT. His field of specialization deals with wastewater treatment, cavitation based advanced oxidation processes, sonochemistry as well as in membrane separation technology along with experiences in practical field applications.

Adam Moyer is an Assistant Professor in the Department of Analytics and Information Systems at Ohio University's College of Business. Moyer received a BBA from Ohio University and has had experience managing information systems for non-profit organizations, has worked as a systems engineer, and has consulted for various companies. While earning an MS in Industrial & Systems Engineering at Ohio University, Adam developed and taught courses related to information systems, programming, system design and deployment, business intelligence, analytics, and cybersecurity at Ohio University. After gaining additional professional experience in the counterintelligence community, Moyer returned to Ohio University and earned a Ph.D. in Mechanical and Systems Engineering.

Anirban Mukherjee is faculty in marketing. He received a PhD in Marketing from The Samuel Curtis Johnson Graduate School of Management, Cornell University.

Anweshan Mukherjee has completed his BSc with Major in Computer Science from St. Xavier's College, Kolkata and is currently pursuing MSc in Computer Science from the same college. His current research interest is Data Analytics and Machine Learning.

Partha Mukherjee, assistant professor of data analytics, received his bachelor's degree in mechanical engineering in 1995 from Jadavpur University in India. He received his Master of Technology in Computer Science from Indian Statistical Institute in 2001. He earned his second graduate degree in computer Science from the University of Tulsa in 2008. He completed his Ph.D. from Penn State in information and technology with a minor in applied statistics in 2016.

Fabian N. Murrieta-Rico received B.Eng. and M.Eng. degrees from Instituto Tecnológico de Mexicali (ITM) in 2004 and 2013 respectively. In 2017, he received his PhD in Materials Physics at Centro de Investigación Científica y Educación Superior de Ensenada (CICESE). He has worked as an automation engineer, systems designer, as a university professor, and as postdoctoral researcher at Facultad de Ingeniería, Arquitectura y Diseño from Universidad Autónoma de Baja California (UABC) and at the Centro de Nanociencias y Nanotecnología from Universidad Nacional Autónoma de México (CNyN-UNAM), currently he works as professor at the Universidad Politécnica de Baja California. His research has been published in different journals and presented at international conferences since 2009. He has served as reviewer for different journals, some of them include IEEE Transactions on Industrial Electronics, IEEE Transactions on Instrumentation, Measurement and Sensor Review. His research interests are focused on the field of time and frequency metrology, the design of wireless sensor networks, automated systems, and highly sensitive chemical detectors.

Balsam A. J. Mustafa holds an MS.c in Information Systems from the UK and earned her Ph.D. in Computer Science (Software Engineering) from Malaysia. Her research interests are in the areas of empirical software engineering, intelligent health care systems, and data mining & analytics. Dr. Balsam has served on more than 25 international conference program committees and journal editorial boards, and has been a keynote and invited speaker at several international conferences. She is a member of IEEE and a professional member of the Association of Computing Machinery (ACM). Dr. Balsam has published 30 technical papers in various refereed journals and conference proceedings.

Ambika N. is an MCA, MPhil, Ph.D. in computer science. She completed her Ph.D. from Bharathiar university in the year 2015. She has 16 years of teaching experience and presently working for St.Francis College, Bangalore. She has guided BCA, MCA and M.Tech students in their projects. Her expertise includes wireless sensor network, Internet of things, cybersecurity. She gives guest lectures in her expertise. She is a reviewer of books, conferences (national/international), encyclopaedia and journals. She is advisory committee member of some conferences. She has many publications in National & international conferences, international books, national and international journals and encyclopaedias. She has some patent publications (National) in computer science division.

Jyotindra Narayan is a regular doctoral fellow at the Department of Mechanical Engineering, Indian Institute of Technology Guwahati, currently practicing and working on "Design, Development and Control Architecture of a Low-cost Lower-Limb Exoskeleton for Mobility Assistance and Gait Rehabilitation". Moreover, he employs the intelligent and soft computing algorithms in his research. He has a substantial experience in kinematics, dynamics and control of robotic devices for medical applications. He has published several journals, book chapters and conference papers on the broad topic of medical and rehabilitation devices.

Ghalia Nasserddine is a Ph.D in information technology and systems. She has been an assistant professor at Lebanese International University since 2010. In addition, she is active research in machine learning, belief function theory, renewable energy and High voltage transmission.

Son Nguyen earned his master's degree in applied mathematics and doctoral degree in mathematics, statistics emphasis, both at Ohio University. He is currently an assistant professor at the department of mathematics at Bryant University. His primary research interests lie in dimensionality reduction, imbalanced learning, and machine learning classification. In addition to the theoretical aspects, he is also interested in applying statistics to other areas such as finance and healthcare.

Van-Ho Nguyen received B.A. degree in Management Information System from Faculty of Information Systems, University of Economics and Law (VNU–HCM), Vietnam in 2015, and Master degree in MIS from School of Business Information Technology from University of Economics Ho Chi Minh City, Vietnam in 2020, respectively. His current research interests include Business Intelligence, Data Analytics, and Machine Learning.

Shivinder Nijjer, currently serving as Assistant Professor in Chitkara University, Punjab, has a doctorate in Business Analytics and Human Resource Management. She has authored books and book chapters in the field of Business Analytics, Information Systems and Strategy for eminent publication groups like Taylor and Francis, Emerald, Pearson and IGI Global. She is currently guiding two PhD candidates and is on reviewer panel of three Scopus indexed journals.

Roberto Nogueira is Grupo Globo Full Professor of Strategy at COPPEAD Graduate School of Business, The Federal University of Rio de Janeiro, where he is also executive director of the Strategy and Innovation Research Center. He joined COPPEAD in 1984 and since that teaches at the MSc, PhD and Executive Education courses. He was visiting professor at the University of San Diego (USA), San Jose State University (USA), Alma Business School (Italy), Audencia (France) and Stellenbosch (South

Africa). He is co-founder and board member of the Executive MBA Consortium for Global Business Innovation, encompassing Business Schools from five continents - Alma Business School (Italy), Cranfield (UK), Coppead (Brazil), ESAN (Peru), FIU (USA), Keio Business School (Japan), Kozminski (Poland), MIR (Russia), Munich Business School (Germany), San Jose State (Silicon Valley - USA) and Stellenbosch (South Africa) promoting the exchange of Executive MBA students. Nogueira wrote two books and has published dozens of scholarly articles on such topics as Corporate Strategy, Business Ecosystems, Innovation and Emerging Technologies and Business Reconfiguration, analyzing sectors such as Health, Energy, Education, Media and Entertainment and Space.

Cherie Noteboom is a Professor of Information Systems in the College of Business and Information Systems, Coordinator of the PhD in Information Systems and Co-Director of the Center of Excellence in Information Systems at Dakota State University. She holds a Ph.D. in Information Technology from the University of Nebraska-Omaha. In addition, she has earned an Education Doctorate in Adult & Higher Education & Administration & MBA from the University of South Dakota. She has a BS degree in computer science from South Dakota State University. She researches in the areas of Information Systems, Healthcare, and Project Management. Her industry experience runs the continuum from technical computer science endeavors to project management and formal management & leadership positions. She has significant experience working with Management Information Systems, Staff Development, Project Management, Application Development, Education, Healthcare, Mentoring, and Leadership.

Zinga Novais is a project manager. She holds a Master's in Project Management from ISEG, School of Economics & Management of the University of Lisbon. She also holds a post-graduation in Project Management and a postgraduation in Management & Business Consulting, both from ISEG - University of Lisbon; and a degree in Public Administration from ISCSP, School of Social and Political Sciences of the University of Lisbon.

Poonam Oberoi is an Associate Professor of Marketing at Excelia Business School. She joined Excelia Group in 2014 after successfully defending her thesis at Grenoble Ecole de Management the same year. On the research front, Dr. Oberoi's primary focus is in the area of innovation and technology management. Her work examines the technology and innovation sourcing decisions that firms make, and the consequences of these decisions. Since her appointment at Excelia Business School, she has published research papers on these topics in well-regarded, peer reviewed, international journals such as M@n@gement and Journal of Business Research. Furthermore, she has published many book chapters and case studies on related topics. For more information, please visit: https://www.excelia-group.com/faculty-research/faculty/oberoi.

Ibrahim Oguntola is a Research Assistant, Industrial Engineering, Dalhousie University, Canada.

Kamalendu Pal is with the Department of Computer Science, School of Science and Technology, City, University of London. Kamalendu received his BSc (Hons) degree in Physics from Calcutta University, India, Postgraduate Diploma in Computer Science from Pune, India, MSc degree in Software Systems Technology from the University of Sheffield, Postgraduate Diploma in Artificial Intelligence from the Kingston University, MPhil degree in Computer Science from the University College London, and MBA degree from the University of Hull, United Kingdom. He has published over seventy-five international research articles (including book chapters) widely in the scientific community with research papers in the ACM SIGMIS Database, Expert Systems with Applications, Decision Support Systems, and conferences. His research interests include knowledge-based systems, decision support systems, blockchain technology, software engineering, service-oriented computing, and ubiquitous computing. He is on the editorial board of an international computer science journal and is a member of the British Computer Society, the Institution of Engineering and Technology, and the IEEE Computer Society.

Ramon Palau is a researcher and lecturer in the Pedagogy Department of the Rovira and Virgili University. As a researcher he did internships in UNESCO París and Leipzig University. His current work as a researcher is in ARGET (Applied Research Group of Education Technology) focused in e-learning, digital technologies, digital competences and educational application of digital technologies. In this group he has participated in several research projects. Currently his research is centered in smart learning environments publishing the first fundings. He has worked as a content developer for several institutions as Universitat Oberta de Catalunya, Fundació URV, Fundació Paco Puerto, Editorial Barcanova and Universitat de Lleida. Previously of the works in academia, he has worked as a primary and secondary teacher as a civil servant. From 2003 until 2007 he had been a principal in a public school. Concerning teaching, in higher education level, he has taught in Master of Educational Technology in Universitat Rovira i Virgili and Universitat Oberta de Catalunya and the Master of Teaching in Secondary School where is the director of the program.

Adam Palmquist is an industrial PhDc at the department of Applied IT at Gothenburg University and works as Chief Scientific Officer (CSO) at the Swedish Gamification company Insert Coin. Palmquist has a background in learning and game design. He is the author of several books addressing the intersection of design, technology, and learning. Adam has worked as a gamification and learning advisor for several international companies in the technology and production industries. His PhD-project is a collaboration between Gothenburg University and Insert Coin concerning Gamified the World Engine (GWEN), a unique system-agnostic API constructed to make gamification designs scalable. The interdisciplinary project transpires at the intersection of Human-Computer Interaction, Design Science in Information Systems and Learning Analytics.

Chung-Yeung Pang received his Ph.D. from Cambridge University, England. He has over 30 years of software development experience in a variety of areas from device drivers, web, and mobile apps to large enterprise IT systems. He has experience in many programming languages, including low-level languages like Assembler and C, high-level languages like COBOL, Java and Ada, AI languages like LISP and Prolog, and mobile app languages like Javascript and Dart. For the past 20 years he has worked as a consultant in various corporate software projects. He worked in the fields of architecture design, development, coaching and management of IT projects. At one time he was a lead architect on a project with a budget of over $ 1 billion. In recent years, despite limited resources and high pressure in some projects, he has led many projects to complete on time and on budget.

Severin Pang completed a combined degree in mathematics, statistics, and economics at the University of Bern. He also received the Swiss federal state diploma for computer engineers. He has more than 10 years of experience in computing engineering in companies such as Swiss Re, Zurich Insurance and IBM. At IBM he implemented AI functionalities for a hovering robot to support ISS astronauts. Severin Pang is currently working as a data scientist at Cognitive Solutions & Innovation AG in Switzerland, where he formulates mathematical models for predictive maintenance of machines, develops an intelligent sensor to detect anomalies in the frequency spectrum, and verifies the effectiveness of fuel-saving measures for Airbus aircraft and optimizes the energy consumption of more than 6000 hotels around the world. He has contributed to a number of publications in the fields of data science, AI, and software engineering.

Renan Payer holds a PhD and a Master's degree in Production Engineering from Fluminense Federal University (Brazil). Graduated in Chemical Engineering (University of the State of Rio de Janeiro UERJ) in Industrial Chemistry (Fluminense Federal University - UFF). He has an MBA in Production and Quality Management. It carries out academic research in the area of sustainability, circular economy and digital transformation.

Jean-Eric Pelet holds a PhD in Marketing, an MBA in Information Systems and a BA (Hns) in Advertising. As an assistant professor in management, he works on problems concerning consumer behaviour when using a website or other information system (e-learning, knowledge management, e-commerce platforms), and how the interface can change that behavior. His main interest lies in the variables that enhance navigation in order to help people to be more efficient with these systems. He works as a visiting professor both in France and abroad (England, Switzerland) teaching e-marketing, ergonomics, usability, and consumer behaviour at Design Schools (Nantes), Business Schools (Paris, Reims), and Universities (Paris Dauphine – Nantes). Dr. Pelet has also actively participated in a number of European Community and National research projects. His current research interests focus on, social networks, interface design, and usability.

María A. Pérez received her M.S. and Ph.D. degrees in telecommunication engineering from the University of Valladolid, Spain, in 1996 and 1999, respectively. She is presently Associate Professor at University of Valladolid, and member of the Data Engineering Research Unit. Her research is focused on Big Data, Artificial Intelligence, Internet of Things, and the application of technology to the learning process. She has managed or participated in numerous international research projects. She is author or co-author of many publications in journals, books, and conferences. In addition, she has been involved as reviewer in several international research initiatives.

Vitalii Petranovskii received the Ph.D. degree in physical chemistry from the Moscow Institute of Crystallography in 1988. From 1993 to 1994, he worked as a Visiting Fellow at the National Institute of Materials Science and Chemical Research, Japan. Since 1995, he has been working with the Center for Nanotechnology and Nanotechnology, National University of Mexico, as the Head of the Department of Nanocatalysis, from 2006 to 2014. He is a member of the Mexican Academy of Sciences, the International Association of Zeolites, and the Russian Chemical Society. He has published over 160 articles in peer-reviewed journals and five invited book chapters. He is also a coauthor of the monograph Clusters and Matrix Isolated Clustered Superstructures (St. Petersburg, 1995). His research interests include the synthesis and properties of nanoparticles deposited on zeolite matrices, and the modification of the zeolite matrices themselves for their high-tech use.

Frederick E. Petry received BS and MS degrees in physics and a PhD in computer and information science from The Ohio State University. He is currently a computer scientist in the Naval Research Laboratory at the Stennis Space Center Mississippi. He has been on the faculty of the University of Alabama in Huntsville, the Ohio State University and Tulane University where he is an Emeritus Professor. His recent research interests include representation of imprecision via soft computing in databases, spatial and environmental and information systems and machine learning. Dr. Petry has over 350 scientific publications including 150 journal articles/book chapters and 9 books written or edited. For his research on the use of fuzzy sets for modeling imprecision in databases and information systems he was elected an IEEE Life Fellow, AAAS Fellow, IFSA Fellow and an ACM Distinguished Scientist. In 2016 he received the IEEE Computational Intelligence Society Pioneer Award.

Birgit Pilch studied Biology and then Technical Protection of Environment at Graz University and Graz University of Technology.

Matthias Pohl is a research associate in the Very Large Business Application Lab at the Otto von Guericke University Magdeburg since 2016. His main research and work interests are data science, statistical modeling and the efficient design of innovative IT solutions. Matthias Pohl studied Mathematics and Informatics and holds a Diplom degree in Mathematics from Otto von Guericke University Magdeburg.

Peter Poschmann, M.Sc., works as a research associate at the Chair of Logistics, Institute of Technology and Management, at the Technical University of Berlin. Within the scope of several research projects, he focuses on the technical application of Machine Learning to logistic problems, in particular the prediction of transport processes. Previously, he worked as a research associate at a Fraunhofer Institute with a focus on Data Science. He graduated in industrial engineering with a specialization in mechanical engineering at the Technical University of Darmstadt.

Brajkishore Prajapati is an associate Data Scientist at Azilen Technologies Pvt. Ltd. He is living in Gwalior, Madhya Pradesh. He is very passionate and loyal to his work and finishes his work on time. His dream is to become one of the great researchers in the field of Artificial Intelligence. He is a very big fan of cricket and reading.

Sabyasachi Pramanik is a Professional IEEE member. He obtained a PhD in Computer Science and Engineering from the Sri Satya Sai University of Technology and Medical Sciences, Bhopal, India. Presently, he is an Assistant Professor, Department of Computer Science and Engineering, Haldia Institute of Technology, India. He has many publications in various reputed international conferences, journals, and online book chapter contributions (Indexed by SCIE, Scopus, ESCI, etc.). He is doing research in the field of Artificial Intelligence, Data Privacy, Cybersecurity, Network Security, and Machine Learning. He is also serving as the editorial board member of many international journals. He is a reviewer of journal articles from IEEE, Springer, Elsevier, Inderscience, IET, and IGI Global. He has reviewed many conference papers, has been a keynote speaker, session chair and has been a technical program committee member in many international conferences. He has authored a book on Wireless Sensor Network. Currently, he is editing 6 books from IGI Global, CRC Press EAI/Springer and Scrivener-Wiley Publications.

Abdurrakhman Prasetyadi is a junior researcher at the Research Center for Data and Information Science, The Indonesia Institute of Sciences (LIPI), Indonesia since 2019. He was a researcher at the Center for Information Technology (UPT BIT LIPI) for 6 years. He obtained his bachelor's degree in

Library and Information Sciences from the University of Padjadjaran, Indonesia in 2008. He earned a Master's degree in Information Technology for Libraries from the IPB University in 2017. Abdurrakhman Prasetyadi's research interests include issues in the field of Library and Information Science, Social Informatics, and Informetrics.

Bitan Pratihar obtained his Bachelor of Technology degree in Chemical Engineering from National Institute of Technology Durgapur, India, in 2017. He completed his Master of Technology degree in Chemical Engineering department of National Institute of Technology Rourkela, India, in 2019. His research interests were the application of Fuzzy Logic in data mining, controller design, and soft sensor design for several chemical engineering applications and others. Currently, he is a doctoral student in Membrane Separation Laboratory of Chemical Engineering Department, Indian Institute of Technology Kharagpur, India.

Alessandro Puzzanghera is a PhD student at the University for foreigners "Dante Alighieri" in Reggio Calabria. He worked many years as legal assistant at the FIDLAW LLP a law firm in London. He successfully completed her studies in the Master of Studies (MSt) postgraduate level degree program of the European Law and Governance School at the European Public Law Organization in Athens. His fields of research include: Artificial Intelligence, Administrative law, Personal Data in particular about GDPR. He published papers for Hart publishing (Oxford), EPLO publication (Athens) and various italian scientific journals.

John Quinn is a Professor of Mathematics at Bryant University and has been teaching there since 1991. Prior to teaching, he was an engineer at the Naval Underwater Systems Center (now the Naval Undersea Warfare Center). He received his Sc.B. degree from Brown University in 1978, and his M.S. and Ph.D. degrees from Harvard University in 1987 and 1991, respectively. Professor Quinn has published in multiple areas. He has done previous research in mathematical programming methods and computable general equilibrium models. He currently does research in probability models and in data mining applications, including the prediction of rare events. He is also doing research in pension modeling, including the effects of health status on retirement payouts.

Parvathi R. is a Professor of School of Computing Science and Engineering at VIT University, Chennai since 2011. She received the Doctoral degree in the field of spatial data mining in the same year. Her teaching experience in the area of computer science includes more than two decades and her research interests include data mining, big data and computational biology.

Sreemathy R. is working as Associate Professor in Pune Institute of Computer Technology, Savitribai Phule Pune University, India. She has her Master's degree in Electronics Engineering from college of Engineering, Pune. Savitribai Phule Pune University and Doctoral degree in Electronics Engineering from Shivaji University, India. Her research areas include signal processing, image processing, Artificial Intelligence, Machine Learning and Deep Learning.

Kornelije Rabuzin is currently a Full Professor at the Faculty of organization and informatics, University of Zagreb, Croatia. He holds Bachelor, Master, and PhD degrees - all in Information Science. He performs research in the area of databases, particularly graph databases, as well as in the field of data warehousing and business intelligence. He has published four books and more than eighty scientific and professional papers.

Kaleche Rachid is a PhD student of computer science since 2018. He is member of computer science laboratory (LIO) of Oran1 university in Algeria. His current research interests deal with artificial intelligence, transportation system, logistic systems, machine learning, bio-inspired approach. He is co-author of many publications and communications.

Rulina Rachmawati earned a bachelor degree in Chemistry from the Sepuluh Nopember Institute of Technology, Indonesia, in 2009. She started her career as a technical librarian at the Library and Archive Agency of the Regional Government of Surabaya city, Indonesia. Her passion for librarianship brought her to pursue a Master of Information Management from RMIT University, Australia, in 2019. Presently, she is a librarian at the Center for Scientific Data and Documentation, the Indonesian Institute of Sciences. Her current roles include providing library services, providing content for the Indonesian Scientific Journal Database (ISJD), and researching data, documentation and information. Her research interests include bibliometrics, library services, information retrieval, and research data management.

Nayem Rahman is an Information Technology (IT) Professional. He has implemented several large projects using data warehousing and big data technologies. He holds a Ph.D. from the Department of Engineering and Technology Management at Portland State University, USA, an M.S. in Systems Science (Modeling & Simulation) from Portland State University, Oregon, USA, and an MBA in Management Information Systems (MIS), Project Management, and Marketing from Wright State University, Ohio, USA. He has authored 40 articles published in various conference proceedings and scholarly journals. He serves on the Editorial Review Board of the International Journal of End-User Computing and Development (IJEUCD). His principal research interests include Big Data Analytics, Big Data Technology Acceptance, Data Mining for Business Intelligence, and Simulation-based Decision Support System (DSS).

Vishnu Rajan is an Assistant Professor in the Production & Operations Management Division at XIME Kochi, Kerala, India. His current research interests include supply chain risk management, operations research, reliability engineering, manufacturing systems management, quantitative techniques and statistics. He has published research articles in reputed peer-reviewed international journals of Taylor & Francis, Emerald, Inderscience, Elsevier, IEEE and IIIE publications. He also has a scientific book chapter to his credit. Besides this, Vishnu serves as an editorial board member of the International Journal of Risk and Contingency Management (IJRCM) of IGI Global.

T. Rajeshwari is freelancer and Yagyopathy researcher. She usually writes up article in science forums related to Hindu Mythology and their scientific proofs. She belongs to Kolkata and travels across globe for social work and spreading the science of Hindu rituals.

P. N. Ram Kumar is Professor in the QM & OM area at the Indian Institute of Management Kozhikode. Prior to this appointment, he had worked as a Post-Doctoral Research Fellow in the School of Mechanical and Aerospace Engineering at the Nanyang Technological University, Singapore. He obtained his Bachelor in Mechanical Engineering from the JNTU Hyderabad in 2003, Master in Industrial Engineering from the PSG College of Technology, Coimbatore in 2005 and PhD from the IIT Madras in 2009.

His primary areas of research include, but not limited to, transportation network optimisation, military logistics, reliability engineering and supply chain management. He has authored several international journal papers and his work has been published in reputed journals such as Journal of the Operational Research Society, Defense and Security Analysis, Strategic Analysis, and Journal of Defense Modeling & Simulation, to name a few.

Perumal Ramasubramanian holds BE, ME from Computer Science and Engineering from Madurai Kamaraj University and PH.D Computer Science from Madurai Kamaraj University in the year 1989, 1996 and 2012. He has 31 years teaching experience in academia. He was published 55 papers in various international journal and conferences. He has authored 14 books and has 135 citations with h-index 5 and i10 index 4. He is also actively involved in various professional societies like Institution of Engineers(I), Computer Science Teachers Association, ISTE, ISRD, etc.

Célia M. Q. Ramos graduated in Computer Engineering from the University of Coimbra, obtained her Master in Electrical and Computers Engineering from the Higher Technical Institute, Lisbon University, and the PhD in Econometrics in the University of the Algarve (UALG), Faculty of Economics, Portugal. She is Associate Professor at School for Management, Hospitality and Tourism, also in the UALG, where she lectures computer science. Areas of research and special interest include the conception and development of business intelligence, information systems, tourism information systems, big data, tourism, machine learning, social media marketing, econometric modelling and panel-data models. Célia Ramos has published in the fields of information systems and tourism, namely, she has authored a book, several book chapters, conference papers and journal articles. At the level of applied research, she has participated in several funded projects.

Anshu Rani has more than 12 years of experience in teaching and learning at various reputed institutes. She is a researcher associated with the online consumer behaviour area.

Bindu Rani is a Ph.D. scholar from Department of Computer Science and Engineering, Sharda University, Greater Noida, India and works as assistant professor in Information Technology Department, Inderprastha Engineering College, Ghaziabad, Dr. A.P.J Abdul Kalam Technical University, India. She received Master in Computer Science and Application degree from Aligarh Muslim University (AMU), India. Her research interests are Data Mining, Big Data and Machine learning techniques.

N. Raghavendra Rao is an Advisor to FINAIT Consultancy Services India. He has a doctorate in the area of Finance. He has a rare distinction of having experience in the combined areas of Information Technology and Finance.

Zbigniew W. Ras is a Professor of Computer Science Department and the Director of the KDD Laboratory at the University of North Carolina, Charlotte. He also holds professorship position in the Institute of Computer Science at the Polish-Japanese Academy of Information Technology in Warsaw, Poland. His areas of specialization include knowledge discovery and data mining, recommender systems, health informatics, business analytics, flexible query answering, music information retrieval, and art.

Rohit Rastogi received his B.E. degree in Computer Science and Engineering from C.C.S.Univ. Meerut in 2003, the M.E. degree in Computer Science from NITTTR-Chandigarh (National Institute of Technical Teachers Training and Research-affiliated to MHRD, Govt. of India), Punjab Univ. Chandigarh in 2010. Currently he is pursuing his Ph.D. In computer science from Dayalbagh Educational Institute, Agra under renowned professor of Electrical Engineering Dr. D.K. Chaturvedi in area of spiritual consciousness. Dr. Santosh Satya of IIT-Delhi and dr. Navneet Arora of IIT-Roorkee have happily consented him to co supervise. He is also working presently with Dr. Piyush Trivedi of DSVV Hardwar, India in center of Scientific spirituality. He is a Associate Professor of CSE Dept. in ABES Engineering. College, Ghaziabad (U.P.-India), affiliated to Dr. A.P. J. Abdul Kalam Technical Univ. Lucknow (earlier Uttar Pradesh Tech. University). Also, he is preparing some interesting algorithms on Swarm Intelligence approaches like PSO, ACO and BCO etc.Rohit Rastogi is involved actively with Vichaar Krnati Abhiyaan and strongly believe that transformation starts within self.

Mark Rauch is a database administrator and a graduate student in the program for Database Management at the University of West Florida. Mark Rauch is actively working in the healthcare industry and has experience working with several Oracle database platforms as well as SQL Server. His experience extends across Oracle 11g, 12c, and 19c. He has also supported several aspects of Oracle Middleware including Oracle Data Integrator, Oracle Enterprise Manager, Web Logic, and Business Publisher.

Yuan Ren is an instructor in Shanghai Dianji University. He was born in 1984. He got his bachelor's degree in mathematics from Jilin University in 2007, and doctor's degree in computer software from Fudan University in 2013. His multidisciplinary research interests include image understanding, artificial intelligence, and data science.

M. Yudhi Rezaldi is a researcher at the Research Center for Informatics, National Research and Innovation Agency (BRIN). His academic qualifications were obtained from Pasundan Universiti Bandung for his bachelor degree, and Mater degree in Magister of Design from Institut Teknologi Bandung (ITB). He completed his PhD in 2020 at Computer Science from Universiti Kebangsaan Malaysia (UKM). And he is also an active member of Himpunan Peneliti Indonesia (Himpenindo). His research interests include visualization, modeling, computer graphics animation, multimedia design, Information Science, particularly disaster. He received an award The best researcher in the 2011 researcher and engineer incentive program in Indonesian Institute of Science (LIPI). and once received the Karya Satya award 10 years in 2018 from the Indonesian government for his services to the country.

Moisés Rivas López was born in June 1, 1960. He received the B.S. and M.S. degrees in Autonomous University of Baja California, México, in 1985, 1991, respectively. He received PhD degree in the same University, on specialty "Optical Scanning for Structural Health Monitoring", in 2010. He has written 5 book chapters and 148 Journal and Proceedings Conference papers. Since 1992 till the present time he has presented different works in several International Congresses of IEEE, ICROS, SICE, AMMAC in USA, England, Japan, turkey and Mexico. Dr. Rivas was Dean of Engineering Institute of Autonomous University Baja California, Since1997 to 2005; also was Rector of Polytechnic University of Baja California, Since2006 to 2010. Since 2012 to 208 was the head of physic engineering department, of Engineering Institute, Autonomous University of Baja California, Mexico. Since 2013 till the present time member of National Researcher System and now is Professor in the Polytechnic University of Baja California.

Julio C. Rodríguez-Quiñonez received the B.S. degree in CETYS, Mexico in 2007. He received the Ph.D. degree from Baja California Autonomous University, México, in 2013. He is currently Full Time Researcher-Professor in the Engineering Faculty of the Autonomous University of Baja California, and member of the National Research System Level 1. Since 2016 is Senior Member of IEEE. He is involved in the development of optical scanning prototype in the Applied Physics Department and research leader in the development of a new stereo vision system prototype. He has been thesis director of 3 Doctor's Degree students and 4 Master's degree students. He holds two patents referred to dynamic triangulation method, has been editor of 4 books, Guest Editor of Measurement, IEEE Sensors Journal, International Journal of Advanced Robotic Systems and Journal of Sensors, written over 70 papers, 8 book chapters and has been a reviewer for IEEE Sensors Journal, Optics and Lasers in Engineering, IEEE Transaction on Mechatronics and Neural Computing and Applications of Springer; he participated as a reviewer and Session Chair of IEEE ISIE conferences in 2014 (Turkey), 2015 (Brazil), 2016 (USA), 2017 (UK), 2019 (Canada), IECON 2018 (USA), IECON 2019 (Portugal), ISIE 2020 (Netherlands), ISIE 2021 (Japan). His current research interests include automated metrology, stereo vision systems, control systems, robot navigation and 3D laser scanners.

Mário José Batista Romão is an Associate Professor of Information Systems, with Aggregation, at ISEG – University of Lisbon. He is Director of the Masters program in Computer Science and Management. He holds a PhD in Management Sciences by ISCTE-IUL and by Computer Integrated Manufacturing at Cranfiel University (UK). He also holds a MsC in Telecommunications and Computer Science, at IST - Instituto Superior Técnico, University of Lisbon. He is Pos-Graduated in Project Management and holds the international certification Project Management Professional (PMP), by PMI – Project Management International. He has a degree in Electrotecnic Engineer by IST.

James Rotella did his BS in physics at Pennsylvania State University and MS in physics at the University of Pittsburgh. While at the University of Pittsburgh he focused on doing epigenetic research in the biophysics department. He went on to work for 4 years as a failure analysis engineer at a Dynamics Inc. working on improving their lines of flexible microelectronics. He focused on improving yield internally in the factory, and designing and carrying out accelerated life and field tests to improve field performance. After working at Dynamics, he moved on to begin work programming at K&L Gates where he maintains analytics pipelines, models, and databases. While at K&L Gates, he completed an Masters in Data Analytics at Pennsylvania State University.

Anirban Roy is the founder of Water-Energy Nexus Laboratory in BITS Pilani Goa Campus Founder and Promoter and CEO of Epione Swajal Solutions India LLP, focussing on Membrane Manufacturing. Experience in membrane synthesis, manufacturing, handling, devices, and prototypes.

Parimal Roy studied in Anthropology. Later he obtained papers on MBA, Project management, and Criminology (paper is better than a certificate) to enhance his knowledge. He is currently working in a state own institution in the field of Training & Development. Decolonizing, Marginal community, subaltern voice, Project management - all are interest arena in academic world. His written book is

Extra-marital love in folk songs. Co-author of Captive minded intellectual; Quantitative Ethnography in Indigenous Research Methodology; and so many book chapters and journals.

Saúl Rozada Raneros is a PhD candidate at University of Valladolid, who received his M.S. degrees in telecommunication engineering from the University of Valladolid, Spain. He is researcher of the Data Engineering Research Unit and his research is focused on Internet of Things, and Virtual Reality. Also, he is co-author of some publications in journals, dealing with topics related to his lines of his research.

Rauno Rusko is University lecturer at the University of Lapland. His research activities focus on cooperation, coopetition, strategic management, supply chain management and entrepreneurship mainly in the branches of information communication technology, forest industry and tourism. His articles appeared in the European Management Journal, Forest Policy and Economics, International Journal of Business Environment, Industrial Marketing Management, International Journal of Innovation in the Digital Economy and International Journal of Tourism Research among others.

Rashid bin Mohd Saad is an educationist and serving as an Assistant professor at the Department of Education at Universiti Malaya. At present, he is working in the Drug Discoveries of Indigenous communities in Bangladesh.

Sheelu Sagar is a research scholar pursuing her PhD in Management from Amity University (AUUP). She graduated with a Bachelor Degree of Science from Delhi University. She received her Post Graduate Degree in Master of Business Administration with distinction from Amity University Uttar Pradesh India in 2019. She is working at a post of Asst. Controller of Examinations, Amity University, Uttar Pradesh. She is associated with various NGOs - in India. She is an Active Member of Gayatri Teerth, ShantiKunj, Haridwar, Trustee - ChaturdhamVed Bhawan Nyas (having various centers all over India), Member Executive Body -Shree JeeGauSadan, Noida. She is a social worker and has been performing Yagya since last 35 years and working for revival of Indian Cultural Heritage through yagna (Hawan), meditation through Gayatri Mantra and pranayama. She is doing her research on Gayatri Mantra.

Rajarshi Saha has currently completed his BSc with Major in Computer Science from St. Xavier's College, Kolkata. His current research interest is Data Analytics and Machine Learning.

Sudipta Sahana is an Associate Professor at a renowned University in West Bengal. For more than 11 years he has worked in this region. He has passed his M.tech degree in Software Engineering and B.Tech Degree in Information Technology from West Bengal University of Technology with a great CGPA/DGPA in 2010 and 2012 respectively. He completed his Ph.D. from the University of Kalyani in 2020. He has published more than 60 papers in referred journals and conferences indexed by Scopus, DBLP, and Google Scholar and working as an editorial team member of many reputed journals. He is a life member of the Computer Society of India (CSI), Computer Science Teachers Association (CSTA), and also a member of the International Association of Computer Science and Information Technology (IACSIT).

Pavithra Salanke has more than a decade of experience in Teaching and she is an active member in the research area of HR using social media.

Hajara U. Sanda, PhD, is an Associate Professor at the Department of Mass Communication, Bayero University, Kano, Kano State, Nigeria. She is also a former Dean, Student Affairs of the university, and has published many research articles, presented many conference papers, and published a couple of books.

Enes Şanlıtürk holds B.S. in Industrial Engineering in Istanbul Technical University and M.S. in Management Engineering in Istanbul Technical University. Also, his Ph.D. education continues in Industrial Engineering in Istanbul Technical University. He has study in Machine Learning. His main contributions is enhancing defect prediction performance in machine learning on production systems. In addition, he works in private sector as an Analyst.

Loris Schmid was born in 1992 in Visp, Switzerland. Studying at the University of Berne he attained a Master of Science in Economics. During the UMUSE2 (User Monitoring of the US Election) project, Loris Schmid was employed by the University of Neuchâtel from August 2020 until February 2021 performing data analysis and processing. He works as an Analyst and Research Assistant at IFAAR since 2019.

Dara Schniederjans is an Associate Professor of Supply Chain Management at the University of Rhode Island, College of Business Administration. Dara received her Ph.D. from Texas Tech University in 2012. Dara has co-authored five books and published over thirty academic journal articles as well as numerous book chapters. Dara has served as a guest co-editor for a special issue on "Business ethics in Social Sciences" in the International Journal of Society Systems Science. She has also served as a website coordinator and new faculty development consortium co-coordinator for Decisions Sciences Institute.

Jaydip Sen obtained his Bachelor of Engineering (B.E) in Electrical Engineering with honors from Jadavpur University, Kolkata, India in 1988, and Master of Technology (M.Tech) in Computer Science with honors from Indian Statistical Institute, Kolkata in 2001. Currently, he is pursuing his PhD on "Security and Privacy in Internet of Things" in Jadavpur University, which is expected to be completed by December 2018. His research areas include security in wired and wireless networks, intrusion detection systems, secure routing protocols in wireless ad hoc and sensor networks, secure multicast and broadcast communication in next generation broadband wireless networks, trust and reputation based systems, sensor networks, and privacy issues in ubiquitous and pervasive communication. He has more than 100 publications in reputed international journals and referred conference proceedings (IEEE Xplore, ACM Digital Library, Springer LNCS etc.), and 6 book chapters in books published by internationally renowned publishing houses e.g. Springer, CRC press, IGI-Global etc. He is a Senior Member of ACM, USA a Member IEEE, USA.

Kishore Kumar Senapati's experiences at BIT, Mesra complement both teaching and research, which brought innovation culture at academia and Industry. He has significant Industry driven research and teaching experience in the leading organizations of the country working nearly two decades, including ≈ 16 years at current place as an Assistant Professor in the Department of Computer Science and Engineering at Birla Institute of Technology, MESRA, Ranchi, INDIA. He has obtained PhD in Engineering from Birla Institute of Technology, MESRA. He has Master of Technology in Computer Science from UTKAL University, ODISHA. He has more than 18 years of teaching and research experience. He has guided more than 41 students of ME & M. Tech and four PhD scholars are currently working under his supervision in Computer Science field. He has capabilities in the area of algorithm design, Image processing, Cyber Security and Machine learning. He has published more than 40 peer reviewed papers on various national and international journals of repute including conference presentations. He has delivered invited talks at various national and international seminars including conferences, symposium, and workshop. He is also professional member of national and international societies. He was also active members in various program committees of international conference and chaired the sessions. He serves as editor of International and National Journal of high repute. He has successfully conducted several workshops in his organization on various topics. He is an honorary computer science expert and serves the nation in multiple areas.

Oleg Yu. Sergiyenko was born in February, 9, 1969. He received the B.S., and M.S., degrees in Kharkiv National University of Automobiles and Highways, Kharkiv, Ukraine, in 1991, 1993, respectively. He received the Ph.D. degree in Kharkiv National Polytechnic University on specialty "Tools and methods of non-destructive control" in 1997. He received the DSc degree in Kharkiv National University of Radio electronics in 2018. He has been an editor of 7 books, written 24 book chapters, 160 papers indexed in Scopus and holds 2 patents of Ukraine and 1 in Mexico. Since 1994 till the present time he was represented by his research works in several International Congresses of IEEE, ICROS, SICE, IMEKO in USA, England, Japan, Canada, Italy, Brazil, Austria, Ukraine, and Mexico. Dr.Sergiyenko in December 2004 was invited by Engineering Institute of Baja California Autonomous University for researcher position. He is currently Head of Applied Physics Department of Engineering Institute of Baja California Autonomous University, Mexico, director of several Masters and Doctorate thesis. He was a member of Program Committees of various international and local conferences. He is member of Academy (Academician) of Applied Radio electronics of Bielorussia, Ukraine and Russia.

Martina Šestak received her Master's degree in Information and Software Engineering from the Faculty of Organization and Informatics, University of Zagreb in 2016. She is currently a Ph.D. student in Computer Science at Faculty of Electrical Engineering and Computer Science in Maribor. She is currently a Teaching Assistant and a member of Laboratory for Information Systems at the Faculty of Electrical Engineering and Computer Science, University of Maribor. Her main research interests include graph databases, data analytics and knowledge graphs.

Rohan Shah is a Director in the Financial Services practice at Simon-Kucher & Partners. Rohan holds a Master's degree in Operations Research, specializing in Financial and Managerial Applications from Columbia University in the City of New York.

Aakanksha Sharaff has completed her graduation in Computer Science and Engineering in 2010 from Government Engineering College, Bilaspur (C.G.). She has completed her post graduation Master of Technology in 2012 in Computer Science & Engineering (Specialization- Software Engineering) from National Institute of Technology, Rourkela and completed Ph.D. degree in Computer Science & Engineering in 2017 from National Institute of Technology Raipur, India. Her area of interest is Software Engineering, Data Mining, Text Mining, and Information Retrieval. She is currently working as an Assistant Professor at NIT Raipur India.

Michael J. Shaw joined the faculty of University of Illinois at Urbana-Champaign in 1984. He has been affiliated with the Gies College of Business, National Center for Supercomputing Applications, and the Information Trust Institute. His research interests include machine learning, digital transformation, and healthcare applications.

Yong Shi is a Professor of University of Nebraska at Omaha. He also serves as the Director, Chinese Academy of Sciences Research Center on Fictitious Economy & Data Science and the Director of the Key Lab of Big Data Mining and Knowledge Management, Chinese Academy of Sciences. He is the counselor of the State Council of PRC (2016), the elected member of the International Eurasian Academy of Science (2017), and elected fellow of the World Academy of Sciences for Advancement of Science in Developing Countries (2015). His research interests include business intelligence, data mining, and multiple criteria decision making. He has published more than 32 books, over 350 papers in various journals and numerous conferences/proceedings papers. He is the Editor-in-Chief of International Journal of Information Technology and Decision Making (SCI), Editor-in-Chief of Annals of Data Science (Springer) and a member of Editorial Board for several academic journals.

Dharmpal Singh received his Bachelor of Computer Science and Engineering and Master of Computer Science and Engineering from West Bengal University of Technology. He has about eight years of experience in teaching and research. At present, he is with JIS College of Engineering, Kalyani, and West Bengal, India as an Associate Professor. Currently, he had done his Ph. D from University of Kalyani. He has about 26 publications in national and international journals and conference proceedings. He is also the editorial board members of many reputed/ referred journal.

Aarushi Siri Agarwal is pursuing an undergraduate degree in Computer Science Engineering at Vellore Institute of Technology Chennai. Her interest is in using Machine Learning algorithms for data analysis, mainly in areas such as Cyber Security and Social Network Analysis.

R. Sridharan is a Professor of Industrial Engineering in the Department of Mechanical Engineering at National Institute of Technology Calicut, India. He received his PhD in 1995 from the Department of Mechanical Engineering at Indian Institute of Technology, Bombay, India. His research interests include modelling and analysis of decision problems in supply chain management, job shop production systems and flexible manufacturing systems. He has published papers in reputed journals such as IJPE, IJPR, JMTM, IJLM, IJAMT, etc. For the outstanding contribution to the field of industrial engineering and the institution, he has been conferred with the Fellowship award by the National Council of the Indian Institution of Industrial Engineering in 2017.

Karthik Srinivasan is an assistant professor of business analytics in the School of Business at University of Kansas (KU). He completed his PhD in Management Information Systems from University of Arizona and his master's in management from Indian Institute of Science. He has also worked as a software developer and a data scientist prior to joining academia. His research focuses on addressing novel and important analytics challenges using statistical machine learning, network science, and natural language processing. His research has been presented in top tier business and healthcare analytics conferences and journals. Karthik teaches database management, data warehousing, big data courses for undergraduates and masters students at KU.

Gautam Srivastava is working as an Assistant Professor with GL Bajaj Institute of Management and Research. He has 15+ years of academic experience. He has completed his Ph.D. from the University of Petroleum and Energy Studies, India. His area of specialization is Marketing. He has published and presented many research papers in national and international journals.

Daniel Staegemann studied computer science at Technical University Berlin (TUB). He received the master's degree in 2017. He is currently pursuing the Ph.D. degree with the Otto von Guericke University Magdeburg. Since 2018, he has been employed as a research associate with OVGU where he has authored numerous papers that have been published in prestigious journals and conferences, for which he is also an active reviewer. His research interest is primarily focused on big data, especially the testing.

Mirjana D. Stojanović received her B.Sc. (1985) and M.Sc. (1993) degrees in electrical engineering and her Ph.D. degree (2005) in technical sciences, all from the University of Belgrade, Serbia. She is currently full professor in Information and Communication Technologies at the Faculty of Transport and Traffic Engineering, University of Belgrade. Previously, she held research position at the Mihailo Pupin Institute, University of Belgrade, and was involved in developing telecommunication equipment and systems for regional power utilities and major Serbian corporate systems. Prof. Stojanović participated in a number of national and international R&D projects, including technical projects of the International Council on Large Electric Systems, CIGRÉ. As author or co-author she published more than 170 book chapters, journal articles, and conference papers in her field. She was lead editor of the book on ICS cyber security in the Future Internet environment. Mirjana Stojanović also published a monograph on teletraffic engineering and two university textbooks (in Serbian). Her research interests include communication protocols, cyber security, service and network management, and Future Internet technologies.

Frank Straube studied Industrial Engineering, received his doctorate in 1987 from the Department of Logistics at the Technical University of Berlin under Prof. Dr.-Ing. H. Baumgarten and subsequently worked in a scientifically oriented practice, including more than 10 years as head of a company with more than 100 employees planning logistics systems. After his habilitation (2004) at the University of St. Gallen, Prof. Straube followed the call to the TU Berlin and since then has been head of the logistics department at the Institute for Technology and Management. He is a member of the editorial boards of international logistics journals. Prof. Straube founded the "International Transfer Center for Logistics (ITCL)" in 2005 to realize innovative planning and training activities for companies. He is a member of different boards at companies and associations to bridge between science and practice.

Hamed Taherdoost is an award-winning leader and R&D professional. He is the founder of Hamta Group and sessional faculty member of University Canada West. He has over 20 years of experience in both industry and academia sectors. Dr. Hamed was lecturer at IAU and PNU universities, a scientific researcher and R&D and Academic Manager at IAU, Research Club, MDTH, NAAS, Pinmo, Tablokar, Requiti, and Hamta Academy. Hamed has authored over 120 scientific articles in peer-reviewed international journals and conference proceedings (h-index = 24; i10-index = 50; February 2021), as well as eight book chapters and seven books in the field of technology and research methodology. He is the author of the Research Skills book and his current papers have been published in Behaviour & Information Technology, Information and Computer Security, Electronics, Annual Data Science, Cogent Business & Management, Procedia Manufacturing, and International Journal of Intelligent Engineering Informatics. He is a Senior Member of the IEEE, IAEEEE, IASED & IEDRC, Working group member of IFIP TC and Member of CSIAC, ACT-IAC, and many other professional bodies. Currently, he is involved in several multidisciplinary research projects among which includes studying innovation in information technology & web development, people's behavior, and technology acceptance.

Toshifumi Takada, Professor of National Chung Cheng University, Taiwan, 2018 to present, and Professor Emeritus of Tohoku University Accounting School, served as a CPA examination commissioner from 2001 to 2003. He has held many important posts, including the special commissioner of the Business Accounting Council of the Financial Service Agency, councilor of the Japan Accounting Association, President of the Japan Audit Association, and Director of the Japan Internal Control Association. Professional Career: 1979-1997 Lecturer, Associate Professor, Professor of Fukushima University, Japan 1997-2018 Professor of Tohoku University, Japan 2018-present Professor of National Chung Cheng University, Taiwan.

Neeti Tandon is Yagypathy researcher, scholar of fundamental physics in Vikram University Ujjain. She is active Volunteer of Gayatri Parivaar and highly involved in philanthropic activities.

Ahmet Tezcan Tekin holds B.S. in Computer Science in Istanbul Technical University and Binghamton University, a M.S. and Ph.D. in Management Engineering in Istanbul Technical University. He has studies in Machine Learning, Fuzzy Clustering etc. He gives lectures on Database Management and Big Data Management in different programs. His main contributions in this research area is improving prediction performance in machine learning with the merging Ensemble Learning approach and fuzzy clustering approach.

Gizem Temelcan obtained her Ph.D. entitled "Optimization of the System Optimum Fuzzy Traffic Assignment Problem" in Mathematical Engineering from Yildiz Technical University in 2020. She is an Assistant Professor in the Department of Computer Engineering at Beykoz University, Istanbul, Turkey. Her research interests are operational research, optimization of linear and nonlinear programming problems in the fuzzy environment.

Ronak Tiwari is a graduate student of Industrial Engineering and Management in the Department of Mechanical Engineering at National Institute of Technology Calicut, India. He worked in the industry for two years after receiving his bachelor's degree. He received his bachelor's degree in Industrial Engineering, in 2018, from Pandit Deendayal Petroleum University, Gujarat, India. He also received a silver medal for his academic performance during his undergraduate studies. He received a Government of India Scholarship under INSPIRE scheme to pursue basic sciences. He is an active researcher, and his research interests are mainly in supply chain risk, supply chain resilience, location theory problems, and humanitarian logistics. He has also acted as a reviewer of some internationally reputed journals.

Carlos Torres is CEO of Power-MI, a cloud platform to manage Predictive Maintenance. Born in San Salvador, 1975. Mechanical Engineer, Universidad Centroamericana "José Simeon Cañas", El Salvador. Master in Science Mechatronics, Universität Siegen, Germany. INSEAD Certificate in Global Management, France. Harvard Business School graduated in Global Management Program, USA.

Cahyo Trianggoro is Junior Researcher at Research Center for Informatics, Indonesia Institute of Science (LIPI). Cahyo is completed study from University of Padjadjaran, where he received a Bachelor degree in Information and Library Science and currently pursue for master degree in graduate school University of Padjadjaran. Cahyo having research interest study in data governance, digital preservation, and social informatics.

B. K. Tripathy is now working as a Professor in SITE, school, VIT, Vellore, India. He has received research/academic fellowships from UGC, DST, SERC and DOE of Govt. of India. Dr. Tripathy has published more than 700 technical papers in international journals, proceedings of international conferences and edited research volumes. He has produced 30 PhDs, 13 MPhils and 5 M.S (By research) under his supervision. Dr. Tripathy has 10 edited volumes, published two text books on Soft Computing and Computer Graphics. He has served as the member of Advisory board or Technical Programme Committee member of more than 125 international conferences inside India and abroad. Also, he has edited 6 research volumes for different publications including IGI and CRC. He is a Fellow of IETE and life/senior member of IEEE, ACM, IRSS, CSI, ACEEE, OMS and IMS. Dr. Tripathy is an editorial board member/reviewer of more than 100 international journals of repute.

Gyananjaya Tripathy has completed his graduation in Information Technology in 2012 from Biju Patnaik University of Technology, Odisha. He has completed his post graduation Master of Technology in 2016 in Computer Science & Engineering (Specialization- Wireless Sensor Network) from Veer Surendra Sai University of Technology, Burla (Odisha) and pursuing his Ph.D. degree in Computer Science & Engineering from National Institute of Technology Raipur, India. His area of interest is Wireless Sensor Network and Sentiment Analysis.

Klaus Turowski (born 1966) studied Business and Engineering at the University of Karlsruhe, achieved his doctorate at the Institute for Business Informatics at the University of Münster and habilitated in Business Informatics at the Faculty of Computer Science at the Otto von Guericke University Magdeburg. In 2000, he deputized the Chair of Business Informatics at the University of the Federal Armed Forces München and, from 2001, he headed the Chair of Business Informatics and Systems Engineering at the University of Augsburg. Since 2011, he is heading the Chair of Business Informatics (AG WI) at the Otto von Guericke University Magdeburg, the Very Large Business Applications Lab (VLBA Lab) and the world's largest SAP University Competence Center (SAP UCC Magdeburg). Additionally, Klaus Turowski worked as a guest lecturer at several universities around the world and was a lecturer at the Universities of Darmstadt and Konstanz. He was a (co-) organizer of a multiplicity of national and international scientific congresses and workshops and acted as a member of several programme commitees, and expert Groups. In the context of his university activities as well as an independent consultant he gained practical experience in industry.

Mousami Turuk is working as Assistant Professor in Pune Institute of Computer Technology, Savitribai Phule Pune University, India. She has her Master's degree in Electronics Engineering from Walchand College of Engineering, Sangli, Shivaji University Kolhapur. She has Doctoral degree in Electronics Engineering from Sant Gadge Baba, Amaravati University India. Her research areas include computer vision, Machine Learning and Deep Learning.

M. Ali Ülkü, Ph.D., M.Sc., is a Full Professor and the Director of the Centre for Research in Sustainable Supply Chain Analytics (CRSSCA), in the Rowe School of Business at Dalhousie University, Canada. Dr. Ülkü's research is on sustainable and circular supply chain and logistics management, and analytical decision models.

Mahmud Ullah is an Associate Professor of Marketing at the Faculty of Business Studies, University of Dhaka, Bangladesh. He teaches Behavioral and Quantitative courses in Business, e.g., Psychology, Organizational Behavior, Consumer Behavior, Business Mathematics, Business Statistics, Quantitative Analyses in Business etc., in addition to the Basic and Specialized Marketing courses like Marketing Management, Non-Profit Marketing, E-Marketing etc. He also taught Basic & Advanced English, and IELTS in a couple of English language Schools in New Zealand during his stay over there between 2002 and 2006. He has conducted a number of research projects sponsored by different international and national organizations like the World Bank (RMB), UNICEF, UNFPA, USAID, JAICA, AUSAID, IPPF, PPD, Die Licht Brucke, Andheri Hilfe, BNSB, FPAB etc. He did most of his research in the field of Health, Education, and Environment. His research interests include ethical aspects of human behavior in all these relevant fields, specifically in the continuously evolving and changing field of Digital Business and Marketing.

Nivedita V. S. is an Assistant Professor in the Department of Computer Science and Technology at Bannari Amman Institute of Technology, India. She is pursuing her doctoral degree in Information and Communication Engineering at Anna University, India. She holds 6 years of professional experience in academic institutions affiliated under Anna University. Her research interests include information filtering and retrieval, explainable intelligence, big data, etc.

Satish Vadlamani is a Director of Data Science and BI at Kenco Group, Chattanooga, TN, USA. He earned B.Tech. in Electronics and Communications Engineering, India. A Masters and Ph.D. in Industrial and Systems Engineering from Mississippi State University, USA. Before joining Kenco, Dr. Vadlamani worked at other global supply chain companies like APLL and XPO. Dr. Vadlamani has passion for applying operations research, machine learning (ML) and artificial (AI) intelligence to solve complex supply chain problems. Dr. Vadlamani has seven years of experience applying ML and AI for problem solving. Dr. Vadlamani has published at multiple journals and conferences and teaches data science and analytics to people around the globe. His research interests include networks, wireless sensor networks, wireless ad-hoc networks, supply chain networks, network interdiction, location problems, transportation, and meta-heuristics. Dr. Vadlamani has been an invited speaker at various colleges, universities, and other professional organizations across the globe. He is a member of IEOM, INFORMS and IISE.

Phuong Vi was born in Thai Nguyen, Vietnam. She is a lecturer at the Faculty of Journalism - Communications, Thai Nguyen University of Science, Vietnam. Her current research focuses on the following: Media culture; Social Media; Journalism History; Online newspaper; Journalism and public opinion; Public Relations. Her research is articles about journalism - modern media; books and book chapters have been published in prestigious international journals. "I am a journalist, researcher, author, writer, and university lecturer that never tires of learning and learning and teaches others for posterity, and for social development."

Takis Vidalis completed his basic legal studies at the University of Athens. In 1995, he received his Ph.D. in law. In 2001 he was elected a senior researcher and legal advisor of the Hellenic National Bioethics Commission (now, Commission for Bioethics and Technoethics). He is the author (or co-author) of 7 books and more than 50 academic papers in topics related to ethics and law of advanced technologies, constitutional law, philosophy of law, and sociology of law. Currently, he teaches "Artificial Intelligence: Ethics and Law", at the Law School of the Univ. of Athens, and "Biolaw and Bioethics," at the International Hellenic University. He is the president of the Research Ethics Committee of the National Centre for Scientific Research "Democritos" (the largest multidisciplinary research centre of Greece), and a member of the European Group on Ethics in Science and New Technologies (European Commission).

Fabio Vitor is an Assistant Professor of operations research in the Department of Mathematical and Statistical Sciences at the University of Nebraska at Omaha. He received a Ph.D. in Industrial Engineering and M.S. in Operations Research from Kansas State University, and a B.S. in Industrial Engineering from Maua Institute of Technology, Brazil. Dr. Vitor has nearly 10 years of industry experience, working for companies such as Monsanto, Kalmar, and Volkswagen. Dr. Vitor's research includes both theoretical and applied topics in operations research. His theoretical research creates algorithms to more quickly solve continuous and discrete optimization problems while some of his applied research has involved the application of optimization models and other operations research tools to reduce inventory costs, improve delivery routings, optimize nursery planting allocation, improve airport operations, and create strategies to overcome human trafficking.

Rogan Vleming is the Head of Data Science & Engineering at Simon-Kucher & Partners. Rogan received an M.B.A. in Finance specializing in financial engineering from McMaster University's DeGroote School of Business, and a B.Sc. in Mechanical Engineering from McMaster University.

Haris Abd Wahab, PhD, is an Associate Professor in the Department of Social Administration and Justice, Faculty of Arts and Social Sciences, University of Malaya, Malaysia. He graduated in the field of human development and community development. He has conducted studies on community work, community development, volunteerism, and disability. He has extensive experience working as a medical social worker at the Ministry of Health, Malaysia.

Chaojie Wang works for The MITRE Corporation, an international thinktank and operator of Federally Funded Research and Development Centers (FFRDC). In his capacity as a principal systems engineer, Dr. Wang advises the federal government on IT Acquisition & Modernization, Data Analytics & Knowledge Management, Health IT and Informatics, and Emerging Technology Evaluation & Adoption. Dr. Wang currently serves as the Editor-in-Chief for the International Journal of Patient-Centered Healthcare (IJPCH) by IGI Global and is on the Editorial Review Board of the Issues in Information System (IIS) by the International Association for Computer Information Systems (IACIS). Dr. Wang teaches Data Science graduate courses at University of Maryland Baltimore County (UMBC) and Healthcare Informatics graduate courses at Harrisburg University of Science and Technology. Dr. Wang holds a Bachelor of Engineering in MIS from Tsinghua University, a Master of Art in Economics and a Master of Science in Statistics both from the University of Toledo, an MBA in Finance from Loyola University Maryland, and a Doctor of Science in Information Systems and Communications from Robert Morris University.

Di Wang received his B.S. and M.S. degree in electrical engineering from Fuzhou University, China and Tianjin University, China. He is currently pursuing his Ph.D. degree in the Industrial Engineering Department, University of Illinois at Chicago, USA. His current research interests include multi-agent systems, distributed control, and energy schedule in the smart city.

Yue Wang is a doctoral candidate at the Computer Network Information Center, Chinese Academy of Sciences. Her research interests cover data mining, machine learning, user behavior analysis, etc. She has been working at the intersection of machine learning and information management for several years. Recently, she is working on NEW ARP technical research. In this paper, she handles the research on the technologies of the NEW ARP.

Manuel Weinke works as a research associate at the Chair of Logistics, Institute of Technology and Management, at the Technical University of Berlin. Within the scope of several research projects, he focuses on the utilization of Machine Learning in logistics management. Previously, he worked as a senior consultant in a management consultancy. He graduated in industrial engineering with a major in logistics, project, and quality management at the Technical University of Berlin.

Thomas A. Woolman is a doctoral student at Indiana State University's Technology Management program, with a concentration in digital communication systems. Mr. Woolman also holds an MBA with a concentration in data analytics from Saint Joseph's University, a Master's degree in Data Analytics from Saint Joseph's University and a Master's degree in Physical Science from Emporia State University. He is the president of On Target Technologies, Inc., a data science and research analytics consulting firm based in Virginia, USA.

Brian G. Wu received his Bachelor of Arts in Mathematics & Piano Music from Albion College in 2014. He pursued his graduate education at Oakland University, where he received his MS in Applied Statistics in 2016 and his PhD in Applied Mathematical Sciences, Applied Statistics Specialization, in 2020. His PhD thesis addressed computational and modeling aspects of big time series data. He will continue his career as a Visiting Assistant Professor at Southwestern University in the 2021-22 academic year.

Tao Wu is an assistant professor of Computer Science at SUNY Oneonta. He has extensive research experience in the fields of data science, information science, wireless communications, wireless networks, and statistical signal processing. He is also an expert in computer hardware and programming.

Mengying Xia's research interests focus on molecular epidemiology and women's health. Her current research involves molecular predictors of ovarian cancer severity, recurrence, and prognosis.

Hang Xiao is a project manager in SSGM at State Street Corporation. He earned a M.S. in Information System from Northeastern University in 2012. His research interests include IoT, AI, Big Data, and Operational Research.

Khadidja Yachba (born in Oran, Algeria) is a Teacher (Assistant Professor) in Computer sciences department of University Centre Relizane and a research assistant at LIO Laboratory, Oran, Algeria. She received her Ph. D. in transport maritime and optimization at University of Oran 1, Ahmed Benbella in 2017. Her research interests are in Decision Support Systems (urban, road, maritime transportation, and health), Optimization, Simulation, Cooperative and Distributed System, Knowledge bases and Multi Criteria Decision Making. Khadidja Yachba has published in journals such as transport and telecommunication, International Journal of Decision Sciences, Risk and Management.

Ronald R. Yager has worked in the area of machine intelligence for over twenty-five years. He has published over 500 papers and more then thirty books in areas related to artificial intelligence, fuzzy sets, decision-making under uncertainty and the fusion of information. He is among the world's top 1% most highly cited researchers with over 85,000 citations. He was the recipient of the IEEE Computational Intelligence Society's highly prestigious Frank Rosenblatt Award in 2016. He was the recipient of the IEEE Systems, Man and Cybernetics Society 2018 Lotfi Zadeh Pioneer Award. He was also the recipient of the IEEE Computational Intelligence Society Pioneer award in Fuzzy Systems. He received honorary doctorates from the Azerbaijan Technical University, the State University of Information Technologies, Sofia Bulgaria and the Rostov on the Don University, Russia. Dr. Yager is a fellow of the IEEE and the Fuzzy Systems Association. He was given a lifetime achievement award by the Polish Academy of Sciences for his contributions. He served at the National Science Foundation as program director in the Information Sciences program. He was a NASA/Stanford visiting fellow and a research associate at the University of California, Berkeley. He has been a lecturer at NATO Advanced Study Institutes. He is a Distinguished Adjunct Professor at King Abdulaziz University, Jeddah, Saudi Arabia. He was a distinguished honorary professor at the Aalborg University Denmark. He was distinguished visiting scientist at King Saud University, Riyadh, Saudi Arabia. He received his undergraduate degree from the City College of New York and his Ph. D. from the Polytechnic University of New York. He was editor and chief of the International Journal of Intelligent Systems. He serves on the editorial board of numerous technology journals. Currently he is an Emeritus Professor at Iona College and is director of the Machine Intelligence.

Jing Yang is an associate professor of management information systems at the State University of New York at Oneonta. She has authored multiple research papers on consumer reviews that have been published in a variety of high-quality peer-reviewed journals, including Decision Support Systems, Nakai Business Review International, Wireless Personal Communications, and the International Journal of Operations Research and Information Systems.

Lanting Yang is a student at the City University of Macau. She studies in the International Business program.

Pi-Ying Yen is an assistant professor at the School of Business, Macau University of Science and Technology. She received her PhD in Industrial Engineering and Decision Analytics from HKUST in 2020. She serves as a reviewer for Manufacturing & Service Operations Management (MSOM) and Naval Research Logistics (NRL). Her research interests include socially responsible operations, supply chain management, and consumer behavior.

Iris Yeung received her B.Soc.Sc. Degree from the University of Hong Kong, M.Sc. degree from Imperial College, University of London, and a Ph.D. degree from University of Kent at Canterbury, UK. Her major research and teaching areas are time series analysis and multivariate data analysis. She has published articles in the Journal of Statistical Computation and Simulations, Statistica Sinica, Journal of Royal Statistical Society: Series C, Journal of Applied Statistical Science, Environmental Monitoring and Assessment, Environmental Science and Pollution Research, Waste Management, Marine Pollution Bulletin, Energy Policy, Applied Energy, Energy and Buildings, and Energy for Sustainable Development. She has participated in a number of consulting projects, including the British Council, Mass Transit Railway Corporation, Hong Kong Ferry (Holdings) Co. Ltd., Greenpeace East Asia, and Environmental Protection Department, The Government of the Hong Kong Special Administrative Region.

Selen Yılmaz Işıkhan carried out an integrated master and doctorate education in biostatistics department of Hacettepe University Faculty of Medicine. She has been working as a lecturer at the same university since 2010. Some examples of her research interests are machine learning, data mining, multivariate statistical analyses, regression analysis, meta analysis, and gut microbiota analysis.

Ambar Yoganingrum is a senior researcher at the Research Center for Informatics, National Research and Innovation Agency (BRIN), Indonesia, since 2019. She was a researcher in Center for Scientific Documentation and Information, Indonesian Institute of Sciences (PDII LIPI) for 18 years. She obtained her bachelor degree in Pharmaceutical Sciences from University of Padjadjaran, Indonesia in 1990. She earned a Master's degree in Health Informatics from the University of Indonesia in 2003 and a Doctorate in Information Systems from the same university in 2015. Ambar Yoganingrum's research interests include issues in the field of Library and Information Sciences, Information processing, Applied Informatics for Social Sciences purposes, and Multimedia.

M. Yossi is an Associate Professor and the Head of the Department of Industrial Engineering and Management at SCE – Shamoon College of Engineering. His areas of specialty are work-study, DEA, and ranking methods. He has published several papers and six books in these areas. He received his BSc, MSc, and Ph.D. (Summa Cum Laude) in Industrial Engineering from the Ben-Gurion University of the Negev, Israel.

William A. Young II is the Director of the Online Masters of Business Administration (OMBA) program, the Director of the Online Masters of Business Analytics (OMBAn), and a Charles G. O'Bleness Associate Professor of Business Analytics in the Department of Analytics and Information Systems. As an Associate Professor, Young received Ohio University's University Professor Award in 2020. Young earned his doctorate in Mechanical and Systems Engineering from Ohio University's Russ College of Engineering and Technology in 2010. William also received a bachelor's and master's degree in Electrical Engineering at Ohio University in 2002 and 2005, respectively. William has collaborated with multidisciplinary teams of faculty, students, and professionals on projects and programs that have been funded by General Electric Aviation, the National Science Foundation, Sogeti Netherlands, and Ohio's Department of Labor. Young's primary research and teaching interests relate to business analytics and operations management.

Jianjun Yu is currently the researcher, doctoral supervisor at the Computer Network Information Center, Chinese Academy of Sciences. His research interests cover big data analysis, collaborative filtering recommendations, and cloud computing. Recently, he is working on New ARP technical research.

Gokmen Zararsiz is a PhD researcher working in Dept. of Biostatistics, Faculty of Medicine, Erciyes University, Turkey.

Alex Zarifis is passionate about researching, teaching and practicing management in its many facets. He has taught in higher education for over ten years at universities including the University of Cambridge, University of Manchester and the University of Mannheim. His research is in the areas of information systems and management. Dr Alex first degree is a BSc in Management with Information Systems from the University of Leeds. His second an MSc in Business Information Technology and a PhD in Business Administration are both from the University of Manchester. The University of Manchester PhD in Business Administration is ranked 1st in the world according to the Financial Times.

David Zeng is a faculty member in College of Business and Information Systems at Dakota State University. David received his PhD at University of California, Irvine specializing in Information Systems. David's Teaching Interests include Predictive Analytics for Decision-making, Programming for Data Analytics (Python), Business Intelligence & Visualization, Deep Learning, AI Applications, Applied AI & applications, and Strategy & Application of AI in Organizations. David's research has been published at top-tier, peer-reviewed journals including MIS Quarterly, and has been funded by both internal and external grants. David received the Merrill D. Hunter Award of Excellence in Research in 2020. David is the Director of Center for Business Analytics Research (CBAR) at DSU.

Jin Zhang is a full professor at the School of Information Studies, University of Wisconsin-Milwaukee, U.S.A. He has published papers in journals such as Journal of the American Society for Information Science and Technology, Information Processing & Management, Journal of Documentation, Journal of Intelligent Information Systems, Online Information Review, etc. His book "Visualization for Information Retrieval" was published in the Information Retrieval Series by Springer in 2008. His research interests include visualization for information retrieval, information retrieval algorithm, metadata, search engine evaluation, consumer health informatics, social media, transaction log analysis, digital libraries, data mining, knowledge system evaluation, and human computer interface design.

Peng Zhao is a data science professional with experience in industry, teaching, and research. He has a broad range of practical data science experience in different industries, including finance, mobile device, consumer intelligence, big data technology, insurance, and biomedical industries. He is a leading machine learning expertise in a Big Data & AI company in New Jersey. He also manages a data scientist team providing a variety of data consulting services to individuals, businesses, and non-profit organizations.

Yuehua Zhao is a research assistant professor at the School of Information Management, Nanjing University, China. Her research interests include consumer health informatics, social network analysis, and social media research.

Index

D

F

M

Recommended Reference Books

IGI Global's reference books are available in three unique pricing formats:
Print Only, E-Book Only, or Print + E-Book.

Shipping fees may apply.

www.igi-global.com

Analyzing Future Applications of AI, Sensors, and Robotics in Society

ISBN: 9781799834991
EISBN: 9781799835011
© 2021; 335 pp.
List Price: US$ 225

Advancements in Model-Driven Architecture in Software Engineering

ISBN: 9781799836612
EISBN: 9781799836636
© 2021; 287 pp.
List Price: US$ 215

Balancing Agile and Disciplined Engineering and Management Approaches for IT Services and Software Products

ISBN: 9781799841654
EISBN: 9781799841661
© 2021; 354 pp.
List Price: US$ 225

Artificial Intelligence Paradigms for Smart Cyber-Physical Systems

ISBN: 9781799851011
EISBN: 9781799851028
© 2021; 392 pp.
List Price: US$ 225

Methodologies and Applications of Supercomputing

ISBN: 9781799871569
EISBN: 9781799871583
© 2021; 393 pp.
List Price: US$ 345

MATLAB® With Applications in Mechanics and Tribology

ISBN: 9781799870784
EISBN: 9781799870807
© 2021; 368 pp.
List Price: US$ 195

Do you want to stay current on the latest research trends, product announcements, news, and special offers?
Join IGI Global's mailing list to receive customized recommendations, exclusive discounts, and more.
Sign up at: **www.igi-global.com/newsletters.**

Publisher of Timely, Peer-Reviewed Inclusive Research Since 1988

www.igi-global.com ✉ Sign up at www.igi-global.com/newsletters f facebook.com/igiglobal t twitter.com/igiglobal in linkedin.com/igiglobal

Ensure Quality Research is Introduced to the Academic Community

Become an Evaluator for IGI Global Authored Book Projects

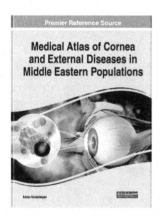
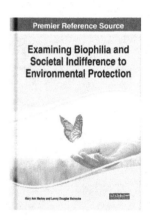
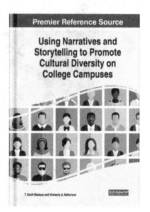

The overall success of an authored book project is dependent on quality and timely manuscript evaluations.

Applications and Inquiries may be sent to:
development@igi-global.com

Applicants must have a doctorate (or equivalent degree) as well as publishing, research, and reviewing experience. Authored Book Evaluators are appointed for one-year terms and are expected to complete at least three evaluations per term. Upon successful completion of this term, evaluators can be considered for an additional term.

If you have a colleague that may be interested in this opportunity, we encourage you to share this information with them.

Easily Identify, Acquire, and Utilize Published
Peer-Reviewed Findings in Support of Your Current Research

IGI Global OnDemand

Purchase Individual IGI Global OnDemand Book Chapters and Journal Articles

For More Information:

www.igi-global.com/e-resources/ondemand/

Browse through 150,000+ Articles and Chapters!

Find specific research related to your current studies and projects that have been contributed
by international researchers from prestigious institutions, including:

- Accurate and Advanced Search

- Affordably Acquire Research

- Instantly Access Your Content

- Benefit from the InfoSci Platform Features

"*It really provides* **an excellent entry into the research literature of the field**. *It presents
a manageable number of* **highly relevant sources** *on topics of interest to a wide range of
researchers. The sources are* **scholarly, but also accessible** *to 'practitioners'.*"

- Ms. Lisa Stimatz, MLS, University of North Carolina at Chapel Hill, USA

Interested in Additional Savings?

Subscribe to

IGI Global OnDemand *Plus*

Learn More

*Acquire content from over 128,000+ research-focused book chapters and 33,000+ scholarly journal
articles for as low as US$ 5 per article/chapter (original retail price for an article/chapter: US$ 37.50).*

6,600+ E-BOOKS.
ADVANCED RESEARCH.
INCLUSIVE & ACCESSIBLE.

IGI Global e-Book Collection

- **Flexible Purchasing Options** (Perpetual, Subscription, EBA, etc.)
- Multi-Year Agreements with **No Price Increases** Guaranteed
- **No Additional Charge** for Multi-User Licensing
- No Maintenance, Hosting, or Archiving Fees
- Transformative **Open Access Options** Available

Request More Information, or Recommend the IGI Global e-Book Collection to Your Institution's Librarian

Among Titles Included in the IGI Global e-Book Collection

Research Anthology on Racial Equity, Identity, and Privilege (3 Vols.)
EISBN: 9781668445082
Price: US$ 895

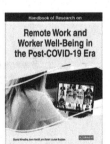

Handbook of Research on Remote Work and Worker Well-Being in the Post-COVID-19 Era
EISBN: 9781799867562
Price: US$ 265

Research Anthology on Big Data Analytics, Architectures, and Applications (4 Vols.)
EISBN: 9781668436639
Price: US$ 1,950

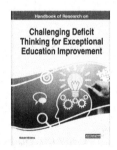

Handbook of Research on Challenging Deficit Thinking for Exceptional Education Improvement
EISBN: 9781799888628
Price: US$ 265

Acquire & Open

When your library acquires an IGI Global e-Book and/or e-Journal Collection, your faculty's published work will be considered for immediate conversion to Open Access *(CC BY License)*, at no additional cost to the library or its faculty *(cost only applies to the e-Collection content being acquired)*, through our popular **Transformative Open Access (Read & Publish) Initiative**.

For More Information or to Request a Free Trial, Contact IGI Global's e-Collections Team: eresources@igi-global.com | 1-866-342-6657 ext. 100 | 717-533-8845 ext. 100

Have Your Work Published and Freely Accessible

Open Access Publishing

With the industry shifting from the more traditional publication models to an open access (OA) publication model, publishers are finding that OA publishing has many benefits that are awarded to authors and editors of published work.

Freely Share Your Research

Higher Discoverability & Citation Impact

Rigorous & Expedited Publishing Process

Increased Advancement & Collaboration

Acquire & Open

When your library acquires an IGI Global e-Book and/or e-Journal Collection, your faculty's published work will be considered for immediate conversion to Open Access *(CC BY License)*, at no additional cost to the library or its faculty *(cost only applies to the e-Collection content being acquired)*, through our popular **Transformative Open Access (Read & Publish) Initiative**.

Provide Up To
100%
OA APC or
CPC Funding

Funding to
Convert or
Start a Journal to
**Platinum
OA**

Support for
Funding an
**OA
Reference
Book**

IGI Global publications are found in a number of prestigious indices, including Web of Science™, Scopus®, Compendex, and PsycINFO®. The selection criteria is very strict and to ensure that journals and books are accepted into the major indexes, IGI Global closely monitors publications against the criteria that the indexes provide to publishers.

WEB OF SCIENCE™   Ⓔ Compendex   **Scopus**®

PsycINFO®   **IET** Inspec

Learn More Here:

For Questions, Contact IGI Global's Open Access Team at openaccessadmin@igi-global.com

IGI Global
PUBLISHER of TIMELY KNOWLEDGE
www.igi-global.com

Printed in the United States
by Baker & Taylor Publisher Services

Printed in the United States
by Baker & Taylor Publisher Services